ENCYCLOP

NEW AGE
BELIEFS

JOHN ANKERBERG, D.MIN.

& JOHN WELDON, PH.D.

HARVEST HOUSE PUBLISHERS
Eugene, Oregon 97402

**ENCYCLOPEDIA OF NEW AGE BELIEFS**

Copyright © 1996 by Harvest House Publishers
Eugene, Oregon 97402

Library of Congress Cataloging-in-Publication Data

Ankerberg, John, 1945-
    Encyclopedia of new age beliefs / John Ankerberg and John Weldon.

       p.    cm. — (in defense of the faith series ; 1)
       Includes bibliographical references and Index.
       ISBN 1-56507-160-3 (alk. paper)
       1. Cults—United States—Controversial literature. 2. Sects—United States—Controversial literature. 3. Cults—United States—Dictionaries. 4. Sects—United States—Dictionaries. 5. New Age movement—United States—Controversial literature. 6. New Age movement —United States—Dictionaries. 7. United States—Religion—1960- 8. Apologetics—Dictionaries. I. Weldon, John. II. Title. III. Series.

BL2525.A57   1996
291—dc20                                 95-34983
                                              CIP

**Printed in the United States of America.**

96 97 98 99 00 01 02 03/DH/10 9 8 7 6 5 4 3

*We make our destinies by our choice of gods.*

—Virgil

*For Ted and Courtney*

John Weldon would especially like to thank Jerry and Traci Johnson; Craig Branch; Phil and Georgia Calhoun; Donald, Jim, and Larry Chadwell; Bill and Beverly Counts; Don Edwards; Tim and Lynn Harris; Bruce and Shari Johnson; Ron and Angel Jolivette; Russell Karaviotis; Gene and Carol Peak; Betty Timson; James Walker; and Victor O. Waters, M.D., for their kind financial assistance on this project.

The authors would like to express their sincere appreciation to Rhonda Spence and Lynda Moore for their excellent job inputting the manuscript.

# CONTENTS

# How to Use This Book

A book of this nature can be intimidating because one may ask, "How do I find the information that I need?" Relax. We have tried to make it easy.

Besides finding your way with the clear chapter titles on the contents page, each chapter begins with an index of main subjects discussed within it. For example, the index for the chapter on New Age Education will immediately help you to find that people such as Jack Canfield and Jean Houston, or issues such as Parent Rights and Church and State, are among the many topics covered. Following each chapter index are the brief "Info at a Glance" sections, which provide pertinent summary information about each chapter's main topic. Then comes the main body, or heart, of each chapter. There is also a helpful index at the back of the book, which will assist the reader in finding topics apart from the chapter titles and chapter indexes.

Single asterisks following certain words mean that these are topics discussed elsewhere in the book. You can find these alphabetically among the topics, or, for more information, consult the back index. Double asterisks refer to notes at the bottoms of the pages. The footnoting system is correlated to the bibliography so that the first number given refers to the book, article, or other item of that number in the bibliography. The second number of a given reference is the page number of that source. For example, 725:77 refers to number 725 in the bibliography and page number 77 in that source.

The material in this book is popularly written and should be considered as introductory and intermediate in nature. Primary or reliable secondary sources are used whenever possible in documenting claims. In providing the reader with a basic critical assessment, we had three goals in mind. One was to document and critique the collective impact of the "new spirituality" in our culture. Another was to document the fundamentally spiritistic nature or potential of these practices and teachings. Finally, we wanted to describe and assess the overall validity or invalidity of the topics from different perspectives, such as scientific, ethical, medical, and biblical. It is our sincere hope that this informative book will prove of value to you as you seek to understand the origins and effects of New Age beliefs.

# Beliefs Behind the "Seens"

You have in your hands a book that is packed with research and able to explain a wide variety of so-called New Age practices and the people associated with them. Behind the "seens," however, is an elaborate, multifaceted way of seeing life that is foreign to most people, Christian or non-Christian. Because the New Age way of seeing life is foreign, people often find its practices unthinkable, or unimaginable ("How could they do *that?*"). Although it is complex, this way of seeing is reducible to a bare minimum of several dominant religious, philosophical, and metaphysical beliefs. It is important to understand these beliefs because they help New Age practices make sense ("Now I see why they do *that*").

These beliefs are like the soil out of which things grow; they give both root and nourishment to New Age practices. They are outlined following so that they may be referred to anytime a reader needs a memory jogger when coming across these terms. Because these beliefs are very different from and at great odds with a biblical Christian way of seeing, we will begin the following sketches with that contrast.

## A Biblical Way of Seeing

A biblical Christian way of seeing life is both monotheistic (*mono*, "one," and *theos*, "god") and trinitarian; that is, a belief in one God in three persons, Father, Son, and Holy Spirit. In Christian monotheism, God is infinite and personal, omniscient, omnipresent, and omnipotent. He is love. He is holy, just, and merciful. He is Yahweh, or Jehovah, in the Old Testament and was incarnated in Jesus Christ who loves mankind, died for our sins, and was resurrected to obtain our salvation.

God is the Creator and is transcendent over all that he has created, including the material world, and is immanent, or active in it. God is not the creation, and the creation is not divine or God or a part of God (pantheism, panentheism). The creation is separate and distinct from God, and it is both finite and real. It is not that God alone is real and that the creation is unreal or illusory. Perhaps we may say that God Himself is "creating reality" and that the creation is "created reality." Both are therefore real, but with certain absolute distinctions between them.

There are also real distinctions among created things. The human body certainly holds a commonness with the dust of the earth, and the lumbering cow is dependent on the grass it eats, but none of these four "things" of creation are "one" in a New Age sense (monism). In a biblical Christian way of seeing, however, besides the clear and real distinctions among the things of creation, there is a oneness, or unity, which is found in Jesus Christ, who, as the agent of God's creation, upholds, or sustains, all things by the word of His mighty power.

In a biblical Christian view, people have been created, and therefore they are finite. They are not divine or a part of God or God (pantheism, panentheism). They are separate and distinct from God, and they are sinful. People are not one with God without the mediator Christ Jesus, the Savior. But they are still utterly unique and special because God made them in His image.

They live once, die, and face judgment to see whether they are in Christ or out of Christ. The direction of their eternal destiny depends on which it is (not karma and reincarnation). And, to finish our purposes here, there is a Christian view about the supernatural. There are the Satan and his demons (evil spirits) and there are God's angels.

Readers interested in a concise statement of biblical Christian beliefs are referred to the Apostle's Creed, which, when placed alongside the following beliefs, shows the radical dissimilarities between the Christian and the New Age ways of seeing.

## A NEW AGE WAY OF SEEING

*Monism (monistic).* Monism (from mono, "one") is a way of seeing in which all reality, both the material and the spiritual, is conceived as a unified whole in which there are ultimately no real distinctions between things. That is, a blade of grass, a rock, a bug, a star, animals, and people are all one reality without ultimate distinctions. This extends to the realm of morals also, where there ultimately are no differences. In answer to a question such as "How many things are there?" monism responds, "Only one."

In the New Age way of seeing there is a strong aversion to harsh dualisms that are common in the West: natural/supernatural; temporal/eternal; material/spiritual; mind/body. Monism gives people a way out of these dualisms. It was the early Greek philosophers who influenced Western thought toward these metaphysical dualisms, by setting body over against soul, matter over against spirit. Several hundred years later under the influence of neoplatonism and gnosticism, the human body and the material world were considered to be evil, while soul and spirit were considered to be good. Very harsh dualisms were imposed on Western thinking from the time of the philosopher and scientist Descartes (1596–1650) and from later scientific thought. Descartes formulated an almost complete dualism between the physical world and the mind. Later scientific thought saw matter as total reality and excluded anything otherworldly from its equations.

Monistic theories differ considerably in the choice of the ultimate principle that "holds all things together," sustains them, and unifies them. For example, in a materialistic monism, substance and energy of a physical nature are regarded as the only reality. Or in what we might call a spiritualistic monism the mind or spirit is taken as the only reality and explains the physical. The latter is prominent by far in the New Age way of seeing. In many schools of thought, this ultimate principle comprises opposites held in counterbalance, such as the complementary polarities *yin* and *yang* that make up the (spiritual) energy *chi* (from the Chinese mystical religion of Taoism).

The pop buzz-phrase for monism is "All is One, One is All." The human problem, according to the New Age way of seeing, is that people just don't see life that way. "Salvation," therefore, is equal to attaining an enlightened state of consciousness wherein a person discovers his or her "oneness" with all things.

*Pantheism, panentheism.* Pantheism (from *pan*, "all," and *theos*, "god") is a way of seeing that identifies everything with God and God with everything. Pantheistic views reach back to great antiquity, to Hinduism and to Brahmanism in particular; and although they are monistic in nature by definition, they vary in the New Age way of seeing according to what is meant by "God." For example, the one great reality—everything—the temporal, the infinite, the seen, the unseen, the animate, the inanimate—may be designated as Nature, or the Cosmos, or the Self, and so on; that is, as "God." Everything is a part of God, or God itself; and thus nothing, not a person nor any other thing, is separate or distinct from God.

Pantheism can be summed up by the pop buzz-phrase "God is All, All is God." In Brahmanism, for example, the one great reality is Brahma(n), who dreams the world and the universe in which people find themselves. The dream is *maya* (illusion), and people find "salvation" by realizing that they are merely part of Brahman's dream state and have been deceived by *maya* into thinking that the world is real.

Panentheism (*en*, "in") puts a slight twist on this; it holds that the world and the universe are included in God but that God is more than these things. Whereas *pantheism* stresses immanence, *panentheism*, though it stresses immanence, maintains that the divine can be both transcendent and immanent. In a way, it is kind of a middle road between pantheism and monotheism. However, both are at great odds with a biblical Christian way of seeing because of their stress on the "divine within." God is intimate rather than alien, indwelling rather than remote; people are not separated from God. The great contrast with the Christian faith, here, is that this kind of immanence encourages people to participate in divine life without the necessity of a mediator between them and God. In a biblical way of seeing, people are separated from God and access to God is through the cross of Jesus Christ.

*Pantheistic monism.* The term "pantheistic monism" is being used more and more frequently to describe what is perhaps the linchpin of the New Age way of seeing. It combines the ideas of pantheism and monism, and it can be summed up in the buzz-phrase "All is One, One is All, All is God."

*Gnosticism.* Gnosticism (from *gnosis*, "knowledge") was a religious and philosophical way of seeing that thrived around the early Christian era and was considered heretical. Its fundamental principle is that salvation comes through knowledge (*gnosis*) rather than through faith (*pistis*) or religious works. The inquiry by the Gnostic (one who knows) is knowledge of an esoteric, or hidden, nature. By this is meant knowledge of special "divine" revelations, not general knowledge acquired through learning or observation.

Such knowledge includes the following ideas. Because the world is seen as hostile and imperfect, then according to the Gnostic view it could not have been made by the Supreme Being, who is considered wholly good and therefore incapable of making anything evil. Thus an evil creator, a kind of lesser disturbed god—usually identified as the God of the Old Testament—made the world of angels, who, usually in concert with this god, made our world. There is a vast gulf between the (evil) material world and the (good) spiritual Godhead. This vast gulf is peopled with many supernatural beings. What that lesser god created disrupted cosmic harmony, which must be restored. The human race, which makes up part of the (evil) material world, is also made up of sparks of the divine fire of the (wholly good) Supreme Being. "Salvation" is about releasing those divine sparks from being enmeshed in (evil) matter. The release occurs as the divine sparks are awakened by *gnosis*. Thus, the esoteric (occult) knowledge sought by the Gnostic is thought to help one transcend evil matter, and so to be "saved." Only the soul, or spirit, is capable of being saved, not the body. (A kind of historical preface to this sort of thinking can be found in Plato's *Dialogues*, in which Socrates suggests to Plato that salvation equates with separating soul from body. In this view, the soul was liberated from evil at death and so "saved" because it was released from the body.)

Many of the early church fathers thought that Simon, the magician mentioned in Acts 8:9–24, was the one primarily responsible for the false teachings of Gnosticism. Ironically, the church's response to Gnosticism in the second century A.D. helped her to clarify a scriptural canon and a creedal theology. In the modern era, Carl Jung did much to popularize Gnostic ideas in psychological terms. And the discovery in the 1940s of the Nag ('Naj') Hammadi Gnostic documents also gave Gnosticism a new life in the West. The New Age conception of life includes much that is Gnostic, especially in its views of Jesus Christ.

*Polytheism.* Polytheism (*poly*, "many," and *theism*, "god") is the belief in many gods, or divine beings, benevolent or malevolent, who have different levels of authority or dominance. People interact with these gods and may enter into deep relationships with them. Early Roman and Greek mythologies (independent traditions which became somewhat fused under Greek influence) are the two most familiar to Westerners. Astrology is a case in point, which in the West has been heavily influenced by a multitude of Greco-Roman heavenly divinities (Mercury, Venus, Mars, Jupiter, etc.) who were assigned a significance with the planets and the stars. Their significance today is largely in terms of the psychological and spiritual significance that has been extrapolated from these ancient mythologies and overlaid on the Zodiac and the planets in contemporary language.

Buddhism and especially Hinduism also come to mind when thinking about polytheism, which sits comfortably with pantheism when "God" (as in Hinduism and Brahmanism) is seen as countless divine aspects, expressions, faces, people, spirit beings. It has been said that the innumerable cultural groups in India becoming absorbed into its systematized social fabric have led to the rise of as many as 33,000,000 gods. Scandinavian (Odin, Thor, Loki, Balder) and Egyptian (Ra/Re, Horus, Nut, Osris) mythologies also have elaborate and complex polytheisms.

In the New Age way of seeing, although there is not a single pattern of polytheistic beliefs, clearly what can rightly be called polytheism appears, as is evident from a dominant New Age theme that people are gods, that is, "christs."

*Animism.* Animism (from *animae*, "spirits") is the belief in myriad spirit beings who are concerned with human affairs and are capable of helping or harming people's interests. Many South American and African tribes were animistic, as are numerous "little religions" and pagan societies around the world. Animism usually includes the belief that trees, rivers, stones, plants, animals, and so on have their own animating force, or spirit. There are a variety of animistic cults associated with the New Age way of seeing, such as the wicca (witchcraft), shamanism, and paganism, all of which are increasingly popular, as is an emphasis on animistic Native American beliefs.

In animism, supernatural beings are attached to particular persons and places or resident in particular creatures, such as (in shamanism) so-called power animals. Animism has a markedly practical dimension. People contact the spirits not so much about what might be called the big questions of life but about urgent mundane matters: securing food, curing illness, averting danger.

It is possible to trace connections between animism and polytheism, which were often regarded as stages of one another during certain periods of history, although the ebb and flow between them is unclear. In the New Age way of seeing, with its reliance on so-called spirit guides, there is a strong neo-animistic dimension.

*Karma and reincarnation.* *Karma* is an old Sanskrit word meaning "deeds, works, actions." Interestingly, the term has evolved in its meaning; a hundred years ago, Karma was understood to simply mean "making." *Reincarnation* means to "come again in the flesh." The two concepts, karma and reincarnation, work together like halves of a pair of scissors: Without one half, you would wonder how the thing worked, or what it was for.

The belief is that people have lived hundreds or thousands of previous lives and that they will live hundreds or thousands of future lifetimes (incarnations). People's karma (actions, deeds) in previous lives determine their physical condition, spiritual state, and practical circumstances in current and succeeding lives. The quality of each lifetime is dependent on their good or bad karma (what they have made for themselves) from previous lives. Good deeds lead to progress and eventual liberation from the round of rebirths. But people regress through bad karma, back to the animal kingdom or even to lower forms of life. Thus every deed, good or bad, has an inevitable consequence, which is why karma and reincarnation are thought of as laws of sowing and reaping. One's current life has been the result of what weighed most heavily from the past, either good or bad.

These laws not only explain one's present condition, they propose a way out of suffering because people who believe this way will want to do their level best of "pay off" all their bad karma by doing good deeds now for their future lives. When a point is reached in which all the bad karma is "paid off," they have evolved spiritually and no longer must reincarnate. They are said to become sheer spirit, having spiritually evolved (a common New Age theme). Or they are thought to have reached nirvana, a state of absolute blessedness attained through the extinction of the self (Buddhism). The laws of karma and reincarnation, therefore, are really a doctrine of self-salvation; that is, the person who offends, pays. There is no need for Jesus Christ's substitutionary death for our sins.

Karma and reincarnation are chief beliefs in Jainism, Buddhism, Hinduism, occultism, and in today's New Age way of seeing. It is a common

New Age theme that the so-called spirit guides are former humans who have evolved spiritually to the point where they no longer need to reincarnate because they have paid all their karmic debts. And this promise to evolve spiritually in like manner is held out to New Age seekers.

*Energy.* In the New Age way of seeing, there is no personal creator God who originally made all things and who is the ultimate cause. As a result of this ontological deficiency, this way of seeing needs its own reason to account for the existence of all things, both seen and unseen. In other words, the New Age view needs to have a kind of creative force that is equivalent to the one true God's creative energies.

The term "energy" is usually used for that creative force. It's an appealing concept because people today think in terms of electricity, solar rays, nuclear power, and so on, which are invisible energies indeed. In fact, New Age literature speaks of electricity, magnetism, and the like as being analogous to the (spiritual) invisible creative force out of which all things exist. The implication is that the ultimate cause of the universe is impersonal, whereas in the Christian view it is personal. It must also be understood that this (New Age) force or energy, is a religious or spiritual *belief* and has nothing to do with the findings of science or the known forces in nature.

This energy goes by countless names. Some of the more popular are: lifeforce, vital force, the Force, animal magnetism, chi (yin/yang), the innate, life energy, universal life energy, cosmic energy, mana, orgone, para-electricity, prana, and vital energy. This energy is said to be that in which all things have their origin and by which all things are sustained. If life is going wrong, or if an evil occurs, or an illness, it is because the life-energy is blocked at some point or out of balance. The solution is to redress that imbalance or unblock the flow. Because the source of the power is impersonal—therefore subject to no will but one's own—anyone who knows the correct "spiritual technologies," such as those found in holistic health care, can tap into and manipulate this invisible force at will. The concept works perfectly within monism, in which matter (including human beings), according to many popular schools of thought, is merely a highly concentrated form of this impersonal or congealed energy. And it also suits pantheism, where people are thought to be gods, or God, having unlimited creative powers to exercise. Hence there is always a lot of talk about balancing, or getting in harmony with, one's life energies, or creating one's own reality. This is the secret of life, health, peace, and well-being—of oneness.

In varying degrees, these views, except for the first, are behind the "seens" of the world's non-monotheistic religions, such as Taoism, Jainism, Buddhism, Hinduism, Persian Zoroastrianism, and much that is today called paganism. The New Age way of seeing incorporates them into itself, with many variations on each theme, which helps to explain why it holds orthodox Christian belief at arm's length. These beliefs also help make sense of New Age practices and the people who use them. For example, the "energy view" explains why New Age people have no need for prayer but are comfortable using crystals mystically in New Age medicine to tap the "cosmic, healing energies" of the universe, or chanting mantras in meditation to attain enlightenment. If there's no one at home in the universe to pray to, you've got to have recourse to some other ultimate source.

All of this is to say that because New Age practices come from a different *way* of seeing life, they are markedly dissimiliar from the religious and spiritual practices that one finds in Christianity. Readers will see many such New Age practices in the following chapters. Whenever the material seems a bit too unbelievable or incredible, it is because New Age people have a "way of seeing" that is different from a biblical Christian one.

*Charles Strohmer*
*Smoky Mountains, Tennessee*

# A COURSE IN MIRACLES/ ATTITUDINAL THERAPY

- Info at a Glance
- Introduction to Attitudinal Therapy
- "Seth"
- *A Course in Miracles*
  - Background
  - Teachings
  - Evaluation
  - Theological Content
  - The Occult

## INFO AT A GLANCE

**Description.** *A Course in Miracles*/Attitudinal Therapy is the alleged regulation or maintenance of physical, mental, and/or spiritual "health" by learning "proper" mental attitudes. For example, *A Course in Miracles* is a daily, one-year New Age occult devotional, allegedly revealed by Jesus Christ Himself who claims He will personally, divinely inspire readers to "complete the atonement." The main purpose here is to help readers live daily "miracles," i.e., to experience daily spiritual growth toward the restructuring of one's perceptions about one's self and the world. This involves revising one's worldview into conformity with a New Age, Hindu belief, and the simultaneous unlearning and undermining of the "evil" beliefs of orthodox Christianity.

**Founder.** The examples cited in the material that follows were received through spiritistic revelations by the late atheistic psychologist Helen Schucman and the late well-known channeler Jane Roberts.

**How does it claim to work?** Because the spirit, mind, and body are interrelated, "proper" mental attitudes may influence the entire person toward desired spiritual, psychological, and/or physical goals.

**Scientific evaluation.** The claims of New Age Attitudinal Therapy have never been demonstrated.

**Examples of occult potential.** Adopting New Age philosophy; altered states of consciousness*; encountering spiritistic revelations and contacts.

**Major problem.** Mental attitudes are gradually restructured to harmonize with a New Age/spiritistic worldview.

**Biblical/Christian evaluation.** The forms of Attitudinal Therapy examined in this chapter are from medium Jane Roberts' *The Nature of Personal Reality,* and the three-volume text, *A Course in Miracles.* These materials comprise occult revelations, and were produced by means that the Bible forbids (Deuteronomy 18:9-12). Cultivating occult or unbiblical attitudes toward life is not in harmony with scriptural purposes but is spiritually dangerous.

For example, the Bible teaches the opposite of what the *Course* teaches on almost every subject. To illustrate, Scripture teaches, "All are not workers of miracles, are they? All do not have gifts of healings, do they?" (1 Corinthians 12:29-30, NASB). But the *Course* teaches that everyone is a worker of miracles and a spiritual healer. However, the basic purpose of these "miracles" is to unlearn

1

orthodox Christianity, especially the belief in Christ's atonement for sin. When *Course* users "participate in the atonement" they learn they are not separate from God, but one essence with Him. The introduction and chapter 1 of the *Course* declare, "This is a course in miracles. It is a required course.... Miracles are everyone's right.... Each day should be devoted to miracles.... Miracles rearrange perception.... Miracles enable you to heal the sick and raise the dead because you made sickness and death yourself, and can therefore abolish both.... This places you under the atonement principle where perception is healed. Until this has occurred, knowledge of the Divine Order is impossible.... When the Atonement has been completed... every member of the family of God [all humanity] must return [into God].... A sense of separation from God is the only lack you really need to correct.... This is a course in mind training" (331:1-13).

**Potential dangers.** The adopting of occult philosophy and practice in the guise of physical, mental, and spiritual enlightenment* or health, leading to physical, psychological, or spiritual problems.

## INTRODUCTION TO ATTITUDINAL THERAPY

Attitudinal "therapy" is an important but often overlooked practice within New Age psychology and medicine. It reminds us such psychology and medicine are concerned with more than mere emotional or physical health; they are also concerned with a particular spiritual worldview and its practices. For example, New Age philosophy teaches that the attainment of genuine health is "holistic"—incorporating complementary spiritual beliefs or practices, mental attitudes, and physical therapies (cf. New Age Medicine).

Attitudinal therapy illustrates what the New Age Movement views as the importance of both mental and spiritual belief to health and wellness.

In one sense, attitudinal therapy encompasses a broad variety of groups and methods, which claim that a particular mental attitude or worldview is important to physical or spiritual health. These would include the Mind Sciences, such as Religious Science (Science of Mind), Unity School of Christianity, Christian Science, and various New Thought religions, which we critiqued in *The Facts on the Mind Sciences* (2639). There are also schools of psychotherapy (especially the transpersonal school) and numerous New Age seminars and fringe psychotherapies or practices, such as Landmark Education's The Forum (formerly est*/The Forum), Silva Mind Control,* yoga,* meditation,* and Buddhist psychology, which teach the connection between attitude and health.

One particular form of attitudinal therapy is common to the New Age Movement. Its basic goal reflects the New Age belief that man is inwardly divine. Therefore, being one essence with God, he powerfully molds and creates his own reality. This is also a fundamental premise of much Western magic, and also Eastern religion and occultism. Man's greatest problem, therefore, is not sin but ignorance. So he must learn how to manipulate his consciousness in order to perceive "true" reality and mold it according to his wishes. Attitudinal therapy or "healing" provides one key approach to this.

Two of the most popular modern texts on attitudinal therapy were both dictated from the spirit world: Jane Roberts' bestselling *The Nature of Personal Reality: A Seth Book* (796) and Helen Schucman's bestselling *A Course in Miracles* (325/330/331). These two books have been read by millions of people, and their concepts have influenced millions more. Our analysis will concentrate on Schucman's text. But because the philosophy of both is related, we will first take a brief look at "Seth."

### "SETH"

The "Seth" books of the late channeler Jane Roberts exert a significant influence in New Age circles. Her publisher, Prentice-Hall, has earned large profits from Roberts' many books, which has sparked the interest of other publishers to do "channeled literature." In fact, Tam Mossman, Roberts' editor at Prentice-Hall, learned to channel an entity called "James," and he edits a quarterly about channeling (1481:185).

"Seth" was Roberts' spirit guide. In Roberts' books, Seth affirms the following fundamental premises of attitudinal therapy: 1) "The real work is done in the mind," 2) "The inner self brings about whatever results the conscious mind desires," and 3) "Basically you create your experience through your beliefs about yourself and the nature of reality" (796:11-12,64,85; cf. pp. 27,75). Seth teaches that each person, as a god, literally creates his entire physical, mental, and spiritual reality. In harmony with the premise of New Age misapplications of quantum physics (see New Age Physics), Seth teaches that the material world is not independent of a person's consciousness. Moment by moment, a person's consciousness actually creates the world and his or her experience in it. Seth explains:

> Your experience in the world of physical matter flows outward from the center of your inner psyche. Then you perceive this experience. Exterior events, circumstances and conditions are meant as a kind of living feedback. Altering the state of the psyche automatically alters the physical circumstances.
>
> There is no other valid way of changing physical events. . . . Your thoughts, feelings and mental pictures can be called incipient exterior events, for in one way or another each of these is materialized into physical reality. . . .
>
> There is nothing in your exterior experience that did not originate within you (796:10).

In other words, this world is not the independent, fixed creation of an infinite personal God. It is not something apart from us, though the Bible teaches that it is (Genesis 1:1-31; John 1:1-3). As Seth emphasizes, we are God, and the world is literally and personally our own creation. He offers specific techniques for attitudinal changes that will allegedly give us the ability to demonstrate our godhood by recreating our reality, according to our personal desires. Cultivating altered states of consciousness* is particularly important to this:

> The methods that I will outline demand concentration and effort. They will also challenge you, and bring into your life expansion and alterations of consciousness of a most rewarding nature.

I am not a physical personality. Basically, however, neither are you. Your experience now is physical. You are a creator translating your expectations into physical form. The world is meant to serve as a reference point. The exterior appearance is a replica of inner desire. You can change your personal world. You do change it without knowing it. You have only to use your ability consciously, to examine the nature of your thoughts and feelings and project those with which you basically agree.

> They coalesce into the events with which you are so intimately familiar. I hope to teach you methods that will allow you to understand the nature of your own reality, and to point a way that will let you change that reality *in whatever way you choose* (796:xxii, emphasis added).

Seth also claims that people must realize that their beliefs about reality "are just that—beliefs *about* reality, not attributes of it." Therefore, "You must then realize that your beliefs are physically materialized. . . . To change the physical effect you must change the original belief—while being quite aware that for a time physical materializations of the old beliefs may still hold" (796:75). Here Seth teaches that we have divine abilities. We are gods who instantly create our reality, and we can mold that reality in any manner we choose. This is a fundamental premise of occult magic.

The relevance of these principles to therapy and healing means that, if we can literally alter physical and mental reality, then this includes the reality of our own minds and bodies. Seth maintains that ". . . all healings are the result of the acceptance of one basic fact: That matter is formed by those inner qualities that give it vitality, that structure follows expectation, that matter at any time can be completely changed by the activation of the creative faculties inherent in all consciousness" (796:xxii-xxiii).

Nevertheless, Seth's theology and moral teachings, not to mention his views on the nature of reality, reveal him to be a lying spirit, an entity the Bible identifies as a demon (280). Not only does Seth lie about God, moral values, and salvation (796:238-42; cf. ref. 280), he also lies about both the nature of humanity and reality itself. If people had the power Seth claims, there would be some evidence for it. Biblically and experientially, however, it is evident that people are not powerful gods who literally create the universe. All history demonstrates that all the "consciousness raising" in the world will not alter our personal reality in the manner Seth argues for.

Seth is a liar, but he teaches what millions of people like to hear: that they are gods who have the potential to control, regulate, and literally create reality. Indeed, to one degree or another, this is a fundamental premise of dozens of New Age groups such as Landmark Education's The Forum (formerly est/The Forum*), Lifespring,* and modern channeling.* Nowhere is this desire for godhood better illustrated than in *A Course in Miracles.*

## A COURSE IN MIRACLES

To date, *A Course in Miracles* has sold over one million sets and has had great impact. It has been or is being translated into French, Spanish, Italian, Portuguese, Hebrew, and many other languages (319a:18). Over a thousand *Course* study groups now exist in the United States and Europe.

The printer for *A Course in Miracles,* Coleman Graphics, Inc., publishes over 50 additional book titles, most of them written by students of the *Course* who have incorporated *Course* philosophy into their writings. One influential example is psychologist Kenneth Wapnick's book, *Christian Psychology in A Course in Miracles.* Wapnick, a Jewish convert to Roman Catholicism, has apparently devoted his life to spreading the good news of the *Course.* His "Foundation for a Course in Miracles" in Roscoe, New York, has published six books on the *Course* that attempt to show its supposed relevance to Christian belief and practice.

According to *New Realities* magazine, even a brief, partial listing of the organizations who recommend the *Course* to their constituents, or who have incorporated it into their curriculum, is impressive: est (The Forum); the Association for Humanistic Psychology; the Center for Attitudinal Healing; the Association for Research and Enlightenment (Edgar Cayce); the Spiritual Frontiers Fellowship (founded by famous trance

medium Arthur Ford); the Association for Transpersonal Psychology; the Institute of Noetic (consciousness) Sciences; Stuart Emery's Actualizations seminar (321:48; cf. ref. 322). From university presidents (such as Glen Olds, former president of Kent State University) to owners of football teams—to "various researchers and authors that read like a 'Who's Who' of the consciousness movement" (321:48), the *Course* continues to expand in popularity. Psychic researcher Willis Harmon, head of the Institute of Noetic Sciences, has called it "the most important book in the English language" (1047:19).

Also, scores of individuals in numerous occupations have incorporated *Course* teachings into their professions. New Age pianist Steven Halpern has set material from the *Course* to music. Michael Stillwater has used its concepts for gardening in his *A Course in Marigolds.* Centerlink, Inc., has even put the *Course* on computer disk.

In light of its sales, the number of its teachers, and its indirect influence through other mediums, a conservative estimate would be that at least five million people have been exposed to the *Course* teachings. For example, prominent New Ager Marianne Williamson is author of the million-copy bestseller, *A Return to Love: Reflections on the Principles of A Course in Miracles* (HarperCollins, 1992), which is heavily based on the *Course.* Her promotions of the *Course* on TV are also numerous. Popular TV host Oprah Winfrey was so enthralled with Williamson's book that she bought a thousand copies for her friends and others, many of noted influence (1047:21).

Influential psychiatrist Gerald Jampolsky also extols *Course* virtues throughout the country, in his lectures and books. He has appeared on the "Phil Donahue Show," "Today," and "60 Minutes." Robert Schuller has hosted Jampolsky at his famous Garden Grove Community Church (320:3). Jampolsky's bestselling books, *There Is a Rainbow Behind Every Cloud, Good-bye to Guilt, Out of Darkness into the Light, Love Is Letting Go of Fear, Teach Only Love,* and *Children as Teachers of Peace* condense basic themes of the *Course.* His Center for Attitudinal Healing was founded in 1975 under the direction of an "inner voice," which instructed him to establish a center where the principles of the *Course* could be taught and demonstrated.

Jampolsky's *Teach Only Love* asserts that the *Course* is "central to attitudinal healing" (323:23). In *Good-Bye to Guilt*, he describes his conversion to the *Course* and its relation to the Center:

> I began to change my way of looking at the world in 1975. Until then I had considered myself a militant atheist, and the last thing I was consciously interested in was being on a spiritual pathway that would lead to God. In that year I was introduced to ... *A Course in Miracles*. ... My resistance was immediate. ... Nevertheless, after reading just one page, I had a sudden and dramatic experience. There was an instantaneous memory of God, a feeling of oneness with everyone in the world, and the belief that my only function on earth was to serve God.
>
> Because of my Jewish background, however, I found that, as I got into the course, I developed a great deal of resistance to its Christian terminology. ...
>
> Because of the profound effect the course had on my life, I decided to apply its principles in working with catastrophically ill children. In 1975, my inner guidance led me to help establish The Center for Attitudinal Healing in Tiburon, California, to fulfill that function (324:4,11).

He explains that the *Course* itself is not used at the Center (the full *Course* program requires a minimum of a year to complete); however, the staff are expected to "adopt and demonstrate the principles of attitudinal healing" taught by the *Course* (324:11).

The Christian church has also been influenced by the *Course*. "Evangelical" Christians, such as author and lesbianism supporter Virginia Mollenkott, in *Speech, Silence, Action*, attest to its alleged benefits in their lives (320:3). Some mainline churches use it as part of their educational programs, because it has received glowing endorsements by numerous Catholic and Protestant clergy.

In fact, the *Course* specifically commends itself toward acceptance within the Christian church. For example, its spirit author claims to be "Jesus Christ" Himself, and distinctively Christian terminology is utilized throughout. SCP [Spiritual Counterfeits Project] researcher Robert Burroughs observes:

> It has also found a ready and expanding audience within the Christian Church, which is not surprising either. Biblical illiteracy is rampant and commitment to orthodoxy often less than vigorous and sometimes consciously absent. Those conditions are aggravated by the very nature of the *Course* writings. Couched in biblical terminology and allegedly dictated by Jesus Christ, they easily confuse and seem designed specifically for that purpose (319:9).

Of course, other non-Christian spiritistic writings have these themes, i.e., 1) the biblical God or Jesus is the alleged author, 2) spiritistic contact in one form or another is encouraged, and 3) a claim to be a message for the Church (e.g., medium Levi M. Arnold's *History of the Origin of All Things* (1852); the occult *Oahspe: A Kosmon Bible* (1882); A.J. Russell's (ed.) *God Calling* (1945; cf. ref. 735). In each case new revelations seek to revise and discredit biblical teachings, usually through sophisticated-sounding spiritual explanations and methods.

Nevertheless, in all such revelations, "God" denies His earlier teachings in Scripture (735).

*Background*

*A Course in Miracles* was channeled through an atheistic psychologist named Helen Schucman. Dr. Schucman, who had an early background in New Thought metaphysics and the occult (1047), would not permit public knowledge of her role as the medium and eight-year channel for the *Course* until after her death in 1981.

As it happens, dream work* played a role in the formation of the *Course* material. Due to job-related stress and a crisis at work, Schucman began to write down and explore her "highly symbolic dreams." This exploration went on for several months. Unexpectedly, one day she heard an inner voice say, "This is a course in miracles. Please take notes." And from this ensued a form of inner dictation. Although it was not a form of automatic writing or trance, the otherworldly nature of the phenomenon made her "very uncomfortable" (1481:23).

The method of transmission was a clear, distinct inner voice that promised "to direct [her] very specifically." The "voice" did just that, and the same spiritistic direction is promised to students of the *Course* (325:477-78). Dr. Schucman described the process as the kind of inner dictation common to many other channeled works. She wrote, "It can't be an hallucination, really, because the Voice does not come from outside. It's all internal. There's no actual sound, and the words come mentally but very clearly. It's a kind of inner dictation you might say" (326:20). Schucman took shorthand dictation from the voice almost daily: "It always resumed dictation precisely where it had left off, no matter how much time had elapsed between sessions" (1526:2).

Dr. Schucman was a most unlikely channel. She was a respected research psychologist, a pragmatic materialist, and a committed atheist before receiving the revelations. Among her prestigious appointments, she had been associate professor at Columbia University's College of Physicians and Surgeons, and associate research scientist and chief psychologist at the Neurological Institute of The Presbyterian Hospital. Her Jewish background and commitment to atheism made her uncomfortable with the "Christian" tone of the messages. Her co-scribe on the project was the late Dr. William Thetford, an agnostic, teacher, and research assistant to the famed psychologist Dr. Carl Rogers (whose humanistic psychology also finally catapulted him into spiritism; 1068:88-92). Thetford held appointments at the Washington School of Psychiatry, Cornell University Medical College, and the College of Physicians and Surgeons of Columbia University. Before his death he was a civilian medical specialist in family medicine at the David Grant USAF Medical Center at Travis Air Force Base, California, and director of the Center for Attitudinal Healing in Tiburon, California (324:214). His prestigious appointments and wide influence gave him many opportunities to publicize the *Course*.

Robert Skutch, publisher of the *Course*, says that the power and tenacity of the "voice" be-

came all the more impressive because of Dr. Schucman's obvious reluctance:

> She did know that the material was coming from an unusually authoritative source—one she did not intellectually believe in.

Thus began the actual transmission of the material which Helen would take down in more than 100 shorthand notebooks over a period of seven-and-a-half years. The situation proved to be tremendously paradoxical. On the one hand, she resented the Voice, objected to taking down the material, was extremely fearful of the content and had to overcome great personal resistance, especially in the beginning stages, in order to continue. On the other hand, it never seriously occurred to her not to do it, even though she frequently was tremendously resentful of the often infuriating interference . . . (326:20).

The *Course* illustrates two characteristics of spiritistic inspiration: 1) when possible, seek a contact that will provide the most impact or credence for the revelation produced (Schucman's scholarly standing provided this credibility), and 2) *force* production of the material, regardless of personal cost to the channeler. (See Shamanism for other illustrations.)

Some might argue that Schucman simply wanted to discredit orthodox Christianity. But nothing in her life or personality suggests she would deliberately go to such lengths merely to undermine Christian belief. Furthermore, the "voice," like the spirits in general, was merciless and unrelenting. This was clearly a force controlling Schucman, not a personally desired writing project to reinvent Christianity:

> The Voice would dictate to Helen almost daily, and sometimes several times a day.... She could, and very often did, refuse to cooperate, at least initially. But she soon discovered she could have no peace until she relented and joined in once again. Despite being aware of this, she still sometimes refused to write for extended periods. When this occurred, it was usually at the urging of her husband that she did return to work, for he knew full well that she could only eliminate her distress by resuming her function as *Course* "scribe," and he was able to convince her that to continue fighting the inevitable could

only have a deleterious effect on their relationship. . . .

The acute terror Helen felt at the beginning did gradually recede, but part of her mind simply never allowed her to get completely used to the idea of being a channel for the Voice. . . . For the most part she was bleakly unbelieving, suspicious and afraid (326:20-23).

Afraid, indeed. Mysterious powers that take control of one's life are something to be feared. Robert Skutch also recorded Schucman's own perception of the phenomenon:

Was the Voice that Helen heard dictating the material really that of Jesus? Both Helen and Bill believed the material must stand on its own, regardless of its alleged authorship. At her deepest level, Helen was certain that the Voice was that of Jesus, and yet she still had ambivalent feelings on the subject. In her own words:

"Having no belief in God, I resented the material I was taking down, and was strongly impelled to attack it and prove it wrong. . . .

But where did the writing come from? Certainly the subject matter itself was the last thing I would have expected to write about, since I knew nothing about the subject. Subsequent to the writing I learned that many of the concepts and even some of the actual terms in the writing are found in both Eastern and Western mystical thought, but I knew nothing of them at the time. Nor did I understand the calm but impressive authority with which the Voice dictated. It was largely because of the strangely compelling nature of this authority that I refer to the Voice with a capital 'V' " (328:78).

Dr. Schucman proceeded to admit her complete bafflement: "I do not understand the [control of] events that led up to the writing. I do not understand the process and I certainly do not understand the authorship. It would be pointless for me to attempt an explanation" (328:78).

Her co-scribe, Dr. Thetford, recorded his own observations in an interview in *New Realities:*

. . . the material was something that transcended anything that either of us could possibly conceive of. And since the content was quite alien to our backgrounds, interests and training,

it was obvious to me that it came from an inspired source. The quality of the material was very compelling, and its poetic beauty added to its impact. . . .

I think that if it had not been for many of the extraordinary experiences that occurred during the summer of 1965, neither Helen nor I would have been willing to accept the material she scribed (328:18).

*Teachings*

*A Course in Miracles* teaches people that for physical and spiritual health, they must accept "proper" attitudes toward themselves, life in general, and the world. What are these proper attitudes? In essence, they are 1) the rejection of biblical understandings about such issues as sin, guilt, and atonement, and 2) the acceptance of New Age occult teachings such as pantheism (All is God; God is All) and psychic development. Specifically, the *Course* offers a form of "Westernized" Hinduism with the distinct goal of changing its readers' perceptions into conformity with the non-dualistic (advaita) school of Vedanta Hinduism. This school maintains that the world is ultimately a dream or illusion, and that all men are inwardly God (see Eastern Gurus). Another chief goal of the *Course* is to encourage the student to accept psychic (spiritistic) guidance.

Volume 1 is the "text" itself, which presents spiritual, metaphysical, and theological teachings, including heretical treatments of Jesus Christ, His death on the cross as a vicarious atonement, the Holy Spirit, and the doctrine of salvation, to name a few (see pages 11-14).

Volume 2 is a "Workbook for Students," which offers 365 spiritual lessons and exercises to help the participant experientially assimilate the new worldview and cultivate an openness to psychic and spiritistic guidance. Volume 2 has two specific goals: 1) learning New Age Hinduism, and 2) unlearning biblical Christianity. Thus, "Part I of Volume 2" is an extensive indoctrination into the religious philosophy of New Age Hinduism, although it is couched in Christian terminology.

"Part II of Volume 2" provides a specific theological "reindoctrination" for unlearning the "errors" taught by the Bible. Some 14 doctrines

7

are covered, including, "What is Forgiveness?"
"What is Salvation?" "What is the World?" "What
is Sin?" "What is the Body?" "What is the Christ?"
"What is the Holy Spirit?" and on through "The
Real World," "The Second Coming," "The Last
Judgment," "Creation," "Miracle," and "Man."

The *Workbook for Students* has specific goals
in mind. For example:

It is the purpose of this workbook to train your
mind to think along the lines the text sets
forth.... The training period is one year. The
exercises are numbered from 1 to 365....

The workbook is divided into two main sections, the first dealing with the undoing of the
way you see now, and the second with acquisition of true perception....

The purpose of the workbook is to train your
mind in a systematic way to a *different perception* of everyone and everything in the world....

...be sure that you do not decide for yourself
that there are some people, situations or things
to which the ideas are inapplicable....

The overall aim of the exercise is to increase
your ability to extend the ideas you will be practicing to include *everything*. This will require no
effort on your part. The exercises themselves
meet the conditions necessary for this kind of
transfer....

Remember only this; you need not believe the
ideas, you need not accept them, and you need
not even welcome them. Some of them you may
actively resist. None of this will matter, or decrease their efficacy. But do not allow yourself to
make exceptions in applying the ideas the
workbook contains, and whatever your reactions to the ideas may be, use them. Nothing
more than that is required (325:1-2, emphasis
added).

Below are some of the titles that describe the
mental exercises offered in the *Course:*

- God is in everything I see.
- I have invented the world I see.
- My mind is part of God's. I am very holy.
- My holiness blesses the world.
- My holiness is my salvation.
- I am the light of the world.

- Forgiveness is my function as the light of the world.
- My salvation comes from me.
- I am entitled to miracles.
- I am among the ministers of God.
- I walk with God in perfect holiness.
- There is no death. The Son of God is free.
- Salvation of the world depends on me.
- I am the holy Son of God Himself.
- God has condemned me not. No more do I.
- The glory of my Father is my own.
- Fear is not justified in any form.
- Let me not see myself as limited.
- The Son of God is my identity.
- My Self is ruler of the universe.
- Let me remember there is no sin.
- My holy vision sees all things as pure.
- The Word of God is given me to speak.
- The Holy Spirit speaks through me today.
- The holy Christ is born in me today.
- I came for the salvation of the world.
- My Father gives all power unto me.
- I choose to see my brother's sinlessness.
- My sinlessness protects me from all harm.
- Peace be to me, the holy Son of God (325:I-IX).

Volume 3 is a "Manual for Teachers" of the
*Course,* and it offers them a sense of "divine destiny" for their spiritual "mission." *Course* teachers
are referred to as "teachers of God":

Except for God's teachers there would be little
hope of salvation, for the world of sin would
seem forever real. The self-deceiving must deceive, for they must teach deception. And what
else is hell? This is a manual for the teachers
of God.

A teacher of God is anyone who chooses to be
one....

They come from all over the world. They come
from all religions and from no religion....

There is a course for every teacher of God. The
form of the course varies greatly. So do the particular teaching aids involved. But the content of
the course never changes. Its central theme is
always, "God's Son is guiltless, and in his innocence is his salvation." It does not matter who
the teacher was before he heard the Call. He has
become a savior by his answer....

Certain pupils have been assigned to each of God's teachers, and they will begin to look for him as soon as he has answered the Call. They were chosen for him because the form of the universal curriculum that he will teach is best for them in view of their level of understanding. His pupils have been waiting for him, for his coming is certain. Again, it is only a matter of time. Once he has chosen to fulfill his role, they are ready to fulfill theirs. . . .

When pupil and teacher come together, a teaching-learning situation begins. . . . The relationship is holy because of that purpose, and God has promised to send His Spirit into any holy relationship (330:2-5).

In addition to the three volumes described previously, an additional manual is suggested: *Psychotherapy: Purpose, Process and Practice,* for integrating *Course* concepts with modern psychotherapy. This is for the professional therapist who wishes to use *Course* teachings in his counseling practice (cf. 2683).

*Course* encouragement toward psychic guidance is also obvious. Brian Van der Horst, writing in *New Realities,* observes that "*Above all,* the *Course* instructs students in the discovery of their own inner guidance, the revelation of a spiritual voice that counsels one in all situations. The Voice or God or Holy Spirit, as it is called . . . gives everything from direction for making decisions on business, career, and life purpose, to advice to the lovelorn" (321:50, emphasis added).

*Evaluation*
All in all, the *Course* is a masterpiece of spiritual strategy. It claims to be a revelation from Jesus Christ Himself, and it is intelligently organized and simply written. It appeals to personal pride and can become almost addicting emotionally. It is carefully designed to radically restructure a person's perception against Christian faith and toward New Age occultism.

We would say the text was designed not only for spiritually searching individuals of a secular or psychic persuasion, but especially for nominal Christians in the church who have recognized the bankruptcy of theological liberalism and desire more spiritual "reality" in their lives.

In essence, the course simultaneously indoctrinates its students in Eastern metaphysics and human potential psychicism, while it specifically insulates them against biblical revelation and true Christianity. In achieving this end, its manipulation of psychological and emotional states is impressive. It offers carefully thought-out spiritual exercises, one for every day of the year.

Publisher Robert Skutch observes, "The concepts of the *Course* are such that anyone who studies the material seriously *must* find that his or her perceptions are changing..." (328:78). (Skutch is the author of *Messages from My Higher Self,* produced through a form of automatic writing.)

*Theological Content*
As noted earlier, Eastern religion, particularly Hinduism (advaita Vedanta), plays an important part in the *Course.* Robert Skutch writes:

What they now had in their possession was a spiritual document that was very closely related to the teachings of the non-dualistic Vedanta of the Hindu religion, and that the profundity of the Vedanta certainly paralleled the obvious profundity of the *Course.* He [Thetford] realized the basic spiritual teachings of both had many striking similarities to each other, and that the main difference between them was that the *Course* was stating the perennial philosophy of eternal truths in Christian terminology with a psychological application that seemed expressly aimed at a contemporary audience (326:24).

In *Course* philosophy, biblical words undergo drastic changes of purpose. Often, the new meanings are the opposite of their biblical meaning. For example, "atonement" no longer refers to Jesus Christ's substitutionary death on the cross for sin. In biblical teaching, the atonement is based on the fact that man's sinfulness separates him from God. Before man can be reconciled to God, there must be a divine judgment of sin. Christ sacrificed His own life on the cross—He was judged in our place—to accomplish this. This is what Christians mean by the word "atonement," or the atoning sacrifice of Christ (John 3:16,18). In 1 John 2:2 and 4:10 we read, "He is the atoning sacrifice for our sins, and not only for ours but also for the sins of the whole world," and, "This is love: not that we loved God, but that he loved us and sent his Son as an atoning sacrifice for our sins." God tells everyone, "Your iniquities have separated you from your God" (Isaiah 59:2), and therefore, because of God's mercy to us, "God presented him [Christ] as a sacrifice of atonement, through faith in his blood [i.e., His death]. He did this to demonstrate his justice . . . at the present time, so as to be just and the one who justifies [those who have] faith in Jesus" (Romans 3:25-26).

But in the *Course*, the word "atonement" means the exact opposite: that one is not, and never has been, separate from God. Therefore, an atoning sacrifice in the biblical sense is meaningless. For the *Course*, the term "atonement" refers to *correcting* the belief that men are separate from God, which is presumed to be a false belief. Hence, because "the atonement" is not yet completed (i.e., some people still think they are separate from God), *Course* students are told they have an important role to play "in the Atonement" (331:7,10). In other words, their job is to help reconcile men to the spiritual truth they are God and therefore cannot be separate from Him.

According to the Bible, God freely pardons, or forgives, a believer's sins on the basis of Jesus Christ's atonement: "Who is a God like you, who pardons sins and forgives the transgression?" (Micah 7:18); and, "[We] are justified freely by his grace through the redemption that came by Christ Jesus" (Romans 3:24). And consider the important words of the apostle John, "If we claim to be without sin, we deceive ourselves and the truth is not in us. If we confess our sins, he is faithful and just and will forgive us our sins and purify us from all unrighteousness. If we claim we have not sinned, we make him out to be a liar and his word has no place in our lives" (1 John 1:8-10, NIV). But the *Course* denies this, just as it rejects the biblical concept of the atonement.

The *Course* also denies the biblical teaching on forgiveness. "Forgiveness" does not pardon sins before God, because sins aren't even real to begin with. Therefore, "forgiveness" merely involves the realization that there never were any sins to pardon. Likewise, "sinners" do not exist,

because "sin" is an illusion. According to an interview with *Course* editor and teacher Kenneth Wapnick:

*Wapnick:* There's a line in the *Course* that says, God does not forgive because he has never condemned. Technically, God doesn't forgive, God simply loves. Forgiveness in the *Course* is the correction for the belief in sin, the belief in separation, the belief in guilt.

*SCP [Spiritual Counterfeits Project]:* Christ did not die for our sins?

*Wapnick:* No. Absolutely not. Because once you see his death in that way, then you make sin real. . . . The whole idea of the *Course* is that sin is an illusion. . . . The crux of the whole thing is that our relationship with God has never been impaired. It's only in our thinking that it was. In other words, for the *Course*, sin never really happened. . . . What Jesus did for us was show us that the separation never really happened (319:13-14).

As a result of this distorted theology, the *Course* approach to "salvation" lies in understanding that no one requires salvation in the biblical sense because all men are already divine. "Salvation" is merely accepting one's "true" identity as being one in essence with God. Each individual is the Son of God; each is already perfect. Therefore we need nothing from God because our true nature *is* God (331:chs. 13,22-23).

Sin, guilt, death, judgment, propitiatory atonement, and other biblical doctrines are viewed as "attack" philosophies by the *Course*. That is, they are concepts which greatly hinder spiritual "progress" and severely damage the realization of our "true" divine nature. Men must become free of these false, enslaving, and evil ideas if they desire true spiritual freedom. Otherwise, they choose to "remain in hell" and to "kill" the God of love (331:chs. 5-6; pp. 374-78).

In the *Course* worldview, orthodox Christian beliefs (biblical teachings given by the one true God) are held to be "evil," "insane," and "antiChrist."

We can see just how unbiblical the instructions of the *Course* are when we contrast them to what the Bible teaches:

• The *Course* explains that men are not separated from God. The Bible teaches, "Your iniquities have separated you from your God; your sins have hidden his face from you, so that he will not hear" (Isaiah 59:1-2, NASB).

• The *Course* explains that there was no atonement for sin and that Jesus Christ did not die on the cross for our sins. The Bible teaches, "He Himself bore our sins in His body on the cross..." (1 Peter 2:24, NASB), and, "Jesus Christ, the Righteous One...is the atoning sacrifice for our sins" (1 John 2:1-2, NASB). Jesus Himself taught, "The Son of man did not come to be served, but to serve, and give His life a ransom for many" (Matthew 20:28, NASB).

• The *Course* explains that no one needs to believe on Jesus Christ for forgiveness of sins. The Bible teaches, "Salvation is found in no one else, for there is no other name under heaven given to men by which we must be saved" (Acts 4:12). Jesus Himself warned, "If you do not believe that I am the one I claim to be, you will indeed die in your sins" (John 8:24). And, "For God so loved the world that he gave his one and only Son that whoever *believes in him* should not perish but have eternal life" (John 3:16, emphasis added).

The following chart gives a representative sampling from *Course* theology to document the antibiblical nature of *A Course in Miracles*. Remember that "Jesus" is supposedly speaking, and every individual is described as "the [or a] Son of God." Obviously, when Jesus described Himself in the Bible as God's "one and *only* son" (John 3:16,18), He was denying *Course* teachings and indicating the most probable source of inspiration for this material. (All quotes except the first three [under "God"] are referenced by volume and page from *A Course in Miracles;* see 325/330/331.)

| | |
|---|---|
| *God* | "The *Course* says that God is impersonal..." (Kenneth Wapnick, in 319:11). |
| | "God Himself is incomplete without me" (324:182). |
| | "God [is] simply...a nonphysical love force that is neither vengeful, judgmental, nor punishing—only loving and forgiving" (324:43-44). |
| *Man* | 1:89   God created you as part of Him. That is both where you are and what you are. It is completely unalterable. It is total inclusion. You cannot change it now or ever. It is forever true. It is not a belief, but a Fact. |
| | 3:67   As God created you, you *have* all power. |
| | 2:353-54   "I am the holy Son of God Himself." Here is your declaration of release from bondage of the world.... You are the holy Son of God Himself.... Be glad today how very easily is hell undone. You need but tell yourself: "I am the holy Son of God Himself. I cannot suffer, cannot be in pain; I cannot suffer loss, nor fail to do/ All that salvation asks."... The Son of God has come in glory to redeem the lost, to save the helpless, and to give the world the gift of his forgiveness.... You who perceive yourself as weak and frail...hear this: All power is given unto you in earth and Heaven. There is nothing that you cannot do.... |
| | Then let the Son of God awaken from his sleep, and opening his holy eyes, return again to bless the world he made. Your glory is the light that saves the world. Do not withhold salvation longer. Look about the world, and see the suffering there. Is not your heart willing to bring your weary brothers rest?... They suffer pain until you have denied its hold on you. They die till you accept your own eternal life. You are the holy Son of God Himself. Remember this, and all the world is free. Remember this, and earth and Heaven are one. |

| | |
|---|---|
| *Sin* | 1:375   Sin is the grand illusion. . . .<br><br>3:81   True perception . . . is the means by which the world is saved from sin, for sin does not exist. And it is this that true perception sees.<br><br>1:377-78   When you are tempted to believe that sin is real, remember this: If sin is real, both God and you are not. . . . Joyously [release] one another from the belief in sin. |
| *Guilt* | 1:243-44   The idea that the guiltless Son of God can attack himself and make himself guilty is insane. In any form, in anyone, *believe this not.* For sin and condemnation are the same, and the belief in one is faith in the other, calling for punishment instead of love. Nothing can justify insanity, and to call for punishment upon yourself must be insane.<br><br>See no one, then, as guilty, and you will affirm the truth of guiltlessness unto yourself. . . . Guilt makes you blind, for while you see one spot of guilt within you, you will not see the light. Do not be afraid to look within. . . . Can you see guilt where God knows there is perfect innocence? |
| *Forgiveness* | 2:475   We are forgiven now. And we are saved from all the wrath we thought belonged to God, and found it was a dream.<br><br>3:79   *Forgiveness* is for God and toward God but not of Him. It is impossible to think of anything He created that could need forgiveness. Forgiveness, then, is an illusion. . . . |
| *Jesus Christ* | 3:83   There is no need for [anyone's] help [in order to] enter Heaven for you have never left. . . . The name of *Jesus* is the name of one who was a man but saw the face of Christ in all his brothers and remembered God. So he became identified with *Christ,* a man no longer, but at one with God. The man was an illusion. . . . Yet who can save [anything] unless he sees illusions and then identifies them as what they are? Jesus remains a Savior because he saw the false without accepting it as true. And Christ needed his form that He might appear to men and save them from their own illusions. In his complete identification with the Christ . . . Jesus became what all of you must be. He led the way for you to follow him. . . . Is he the Christ? O yes, along with you. |
| *The Incarnation and Second Coming* | 1:58   The First Coming of Christ is merely another name for the creation, for Christ is the Son of God. The Second Coming of Christ means nothing more than the end of the ego's rule and the healing of the mind. |
| *Atonement* | 1:32-33,87   If the crucifixion is seen from an upside-down point of view, it does appear as if God permitted and even encouraged one of His Sons to suffer because he was good. This particularly unfortunate interpretation, which arose out of projection, has led many people to be bitterly afraid of God. Such anti-religious concepts enter into many religions. Yet the real Christian should pause and ask, "How could this be?" Is it likely that God Himself would be capable of the kind of thinking which His Own words have clearly stated is unworthy of His Son?<br><br>The best defense, as always, is not to attack another's position, but rather to protect the truth. It is unwise to accept any concept if you have to |

| | |
|---|---|
| *Atonement* (continued) | invert a whole frame of reference in order to justify it. . . . Persecution frequently results in an attempt to "justify" the terrible misperception that God Himself persecuted His Own Son on behalf of salvation. . . . *It is so essential that all such thinking be dispelled that we must be sure that nothing of this kind remains in your mind.* I was not "punished" because *you* were bad. The wholly benign lesson the Atonement teaches is lost if it is tainted with this kind of distortion in any form. . . .<br><br>I have been correctly referred to as "the lamb of God who taketh away the sins of the world," but those who represent the lamb as blood-stained do not understand the meaning of the symbol. . . .<br><br>The message of the crucifixion is perfectly clear: *"Teach only love, for that is what you are."*<br><br>If you interpret the crucifixion in any other way, you are using it as a weapon for assault rather than as the call for peace for which it was intended. The Apostles often misunderstood it, and for the same reason that anyone misunderstands it. Their own imperfect love made them vulnerable to projection, and out of their own fear they spoke of the "wrath of God" as his retaliatory weapon. Nor could they speak of the crucifixion entirely without anger, because their sense of guilt had made them angry (emphasis added). |
| *Salvation* | 2:125   You are one with God. Again, how simple is salvation! It is merely a statement of your true identity.<br><br>1:11,53   A sense of separation from God is the only lack you really need to correct. . . . Salvation is nothing more than "right-mindedness." . . .<br><br>1:47   The journey to the cross should be the last "useless journey. . . ." Do not make the pathetic error of "clinging to the old rugged cross. . . ." This is not the Gospel I intended to offer you. We have another journey to undertake, and if you will read these lessons carefully they will help prepare you to undertake it.<br><br>1:90   The full awareness of the Atonement, then, is the recognition that *the separation [from God] never occurred.* . . . |
| *Death* | 3:63-64   Death is the central dream from which all illusions stem. . . . And no one asks if a benign Creator could will this. . . .<br><br>Death is the symbol of the fear of God. . . . The grimness of the symbol is enough to show it cannot coexist with God. . . . He did not make death because He did not make fear. Both are equally meaningless to Him. . . .<br><br>Teacher of God, your one assignment could be stated thus: Accept no compromise in which death plays a part. . . . And what is the end of death? Nothing but this; the realization that the Son of God is guiltless now and forever. Nothing but this. |
| *Judgment* | 1:29,88,158   The Last Judgment is one of the most threatening ideas in your thinking. This is because you do not understand it. Judgment is not an attribute of God. . . .<br><br>No one is punished for sins, and the Sons of God are not sinners. . . .<br><br>Do not fear the Last Judgment, but welcome it. . . . The Second Coming is merely the return of sense. Can this possibly be fearful? |

| Hell | 3:66   As long as any mind remains possessed of evil dreams, the thought of hell is real. God's teachers have the goal of wakening the minds of those asleep.... |
|---|---|
| The Devil | 1:45   The mind can make the belief in separation very real and very fearful, and this belief *is* the "devil." |
| The Creation | 3:81   The world you see is an illusion of a world. God did not create it. |
| Time | 3:41   The world of time is the world of illusion. |

The above *Course* teachings prove beyond any doubt that the Jesus of the New Testament could not be its source. This means that the entity who dictated the *Course* to Helen Schucman lied when he claimed to be Jesus Christ. Thus, the most logical possibility for the true author of the *Course* is a demon, a spiritual underling of Satan, the one Jesus called a liar and "a murderer from the beginning" (John 8:44).

### The Occult

The spiritistic nature of the *Course* is obvious. Several themes that it has in common with spiritistic revelations are: 1) spirit dictation to a disinterested or hesitant party; 2) forcing production of the revelations; 3) unbiblical content; 4) encouraging psychic guidance. The wholesale denial of God's Word and God's Son is also typical of spiritistic revelations in general (1095).

Again, these spiritistic themes identify the author of the *Course* as a demonic spirit. When the *Course* actively promotes another Jesus, a different spirit, and a false gospel, the Scripture declares that its origin must be demonic (2 Corinthians 11:3-4,13-15). Significantly, even *Course* editor and promoter, psychologist Kenneth Wapnick, commented that "if the Bible were considered literally true, then the Course would have to be viewed as demonically inspired" (319a:23). This is why the Bible itself warns, "Dear friends, do not believe every spirit, but test the spirits to see whether they are from God, because many false prophets have gone out into the world.... Every spirit that does not acknowledge Jesus is not from God. This is the spirit of the antichrist..." (1 John 4:1-3).

Because false christs and false prophets *are* in the world, and lying spirits associated with them, Scripture warns that all who proclaim a false gospel are liable to eternal judgment: "But even if we or an angel from heaven should preach a gospel other than the one we preached to you, let him be eternally condemned" (Galatians 1:8).

That the eventual production of the *Course* was supernaturally arranged behind the scenes by demonic initiative will be obvious to those familiar with the methods of spiritual warfare revealed in Scripture and in the history of occult revelations. The official version of the story is found in *Journey Without Distance: The Story Behind A Course in Miracles* (Celestial Arts, 1984), by Robert Skutch. Apparently, complex human events and encounters were carefully (and miraculously) arranged via otherworldly initiative to ensure its production.

The extent of this occult collaboration, and the power it represents on the part of the spirit world to influence human affairs, is not small; but in light of biblical revelation, neither is it unexpected (2 Corinthians 4:4; 1 John 5:19). Similar manipulations of events and people are found in the lives of innumerable psychics, occultists, and mediums (332). As Dr. Schucman confesses, "The birth of *A Course in Miracles* could not have occurred as it did without every single one of the cast being in the right place at the right time" (326:22).

The *Course* content also promotes occultism and spiritistic guidance, which is another characteristic goal of demonic revelations:

There are, of course, no "unnatural" powers.... Certainly there are many "psychic" powers that are clearly in line with this course. Communication is not limited to the small range of channels the world recognizes.... The seemingly new abilities that may be gathered on the way can be very helpful.... They are valuable teaching aids.... Nothing that is genuine is used to deceive. The Holy Spirit is incapable of deception, and He can use only genuine abilities.... Any ability that anyone develops has the potentiality for good. To this there is no exception. And the more unusual and unexpected the power, the greater its potential usefulness. Salvation has need of all abilities, for what the world would destroy the Holy Spirit would restore.... The Holy Spirit needs these gifts, and those who offer them to Him and Him alone go with Christ's gratitude upon their hearts (330:59-60).

One text comments on the *Course* as follows, "Based largely on the power of affirmation, it provides a way by which some people can find their own 'internal teacher,' to guide them much in the [spiritistic] sense that we have been referring to.... The underlying principle is the same as Seth's central teaching and the findings of modern psychology: Our internal beliefs create what is perceived as reality, and we are imprisoned by the cage of our wrong beliefs" (2394:117; cf. New Age Inner Work).

Not surprisingly, Volume 2 of the *Course* ends with the promise of psychic guidance:

Therefore obey your will, and follow Him Whom you accepted as your voice....

No more specific lessons are assigned, for there is no more need of them. Henceforth, hear but the Voice for God.... He will direct your efforts, telling you exactly what to do, how to direct your mind, and when to come to Him in silence, asking for His sure direction and His certain Word. His is the Word that God has given you. His is the Word you chose to be your own.

And now I place you in His hands, to be his faithful followers, with Him as Guide through every difficulty and all pain that you may think is real.... He has earned your trust by speaking daily to you of your Father and your brother and your Self. He will continue. Now you walk with Him, as certain as is He of where you go; as sure as He [is] of how you should proceed; as confi-

dent as He is of the goal, and of your safe arrival in the end.

The end is certain, and the means as well. To this we say "Amen." You will be told exactly what God wills for you each time there is a choice to make.... You do not walk alone. God's angels hover near and all about. His Love surrounds you, and of this be sure; that I will never leave you comfortless (325:477-78).

As an example of the psychic guidance people have been led to accept through the *Course*, many people have received the author of the *Course* ("Jesus") as their personal spirit guide— in other words, a demon cleverly impersonating Jesus. In his *Good-Bye to Guilt*, Gerald Jampolsky confesses that "Jesus" became his spirit guide and even possesses him, to act and speak through him:

To my complete surprise, I began to develop what I would call a personal relationship with Jesus.... He demonstrated that death was not real, that life is eternal, and that minds can communicate with each other forever, even after the body has been laid aside.

I began to feel his presence in me, and at times I actually felt he was acting through me as an extension of his thoughts, his words, and his actions. I became absorbed by his message that the world could be transformed if all of us would practice forgiveness. At first, I was concerned about what other people might think of me, so I kept my relationship with Jesus a secret.

As my relationship with Jesus has become more comfortable, I am now less concerned about what others might say, and today a prominent picture of Jesus hangs in my living room over the fireplace.... In a way which I cannot fully explain, I have chosen Jesus as my teacher ... (324:62-64).

Jampolsky believes that learning to listen to "the inner voice" is one of three key concepts of the *Course* (324:5):

The voice of love goes by many names, such as the voice of God, Holy spirit, voice of knowing, inner teacher, inner voice, inner guide, and intuition.... It comes from ... the God-self, that is in the center of our being—always there to answer and give us directions in response to any questions that we may ask.

In order to hear this inner guidance, we need to learn to still our minds, have the faith and a little willingness to ask for help—and expect to have our request answered. The voice, or guidance, can come to us as a thought; it can be experienced as inner dictation, or it can be a visualized form. . . (324:52).

Dr. Jampolsky has had such amazing experiences by listening to his inner voice (such as an unexpected meeting with Mrs. Anwar Sadat, apparently also a psychic) that he now follows its guidance "even when it seems irrational" (324:56). Even the dead themselves may be contacted, although the practice is explicitly condemned in Deuteronomy 18:10-12:

Let us know that "communication is never broken, even when the body is destroyed, provided that we do not believe that bodies are essential for communication." Isn't that what Jesus taught the world by the resurrection? (324:136)

No, this is not what Jesus taught. What Jesus taught by His resurrection was that "I am the way and the truth and the life. No one comes to the Father except through me" (John 14:6); and, "I am the resurrection and the life. He who believes in me will live, even though he dies" (John 11:25). Jesus would never promote contact with the dead when the Word of God specifically prohibits it. The Bible warns that no one is to become "a medium or a spiritist, or [a person] who consults the dead. Anyone who does these things is detestable to the LORD" (Deuteronomy 18:11-12).

In summary, *A Course in Miracles* alleges to be the supernatural revelation of a personal, powerful, and controlling psychic "voice" claiming to be Jesus Christ. This "revelation" was given through a skeptical and somewhat fearful atheistic research psychologist over a period of almost eight years. *Course* content, however, promotes psychic guidance and the occult, adamantly denies Jesus Christ, and is intensely antibiblical in its teachings.

# ALTERED STATES OF CONSCIOUSNESS

- Info at a Glance
- Introduction and Influence
- Altered States and Spiritism
- Modern Consciousness Research
- Dangers of Altered States

## INFO AT A GLANCE

**Description.** Altered states of consciousness (ASCs) in a New Age context comprise unusual conditions of perception achieved by the deliberate cultivation of often abnormal mental states, states not normally experienced apart from specific religious techniques and/or occult programs.

**Founder.** Not applicable.

**How does it claim to work?** Most New Age practices or techniques (e.g. yoga,* meditation,* crystal work*), and New Age supernatural experiences (e.g. channeling*) generally claim to trigger or induce ASCs by stilling the mind, regulating psychic energy, or by voluntary spirit possession. Proponents believe these altered states of consciousness produce a "higher" and/or monistic state of consciousness or "being" (e.g. the perception that "all is one") leading to dramatic spiritual revelations and a positive restructuring of the participant's worldview.

**Scientific evaluation.** Science cannot evaluate subjective claims concerning any state of consciousness and ASCs in particular are highly subjective. Research into altered states generally includes a mixture of the scientific investigation of normal, marginally altered consciousness (the sleep-state, dreams) and occult and parapsychological exploration of mystical, occult states.

**Examples of occult potential.** Spirit contact or possession; development of psychic abilities; conversion to occultism; psychic quickening or regeneration.

**Major problems.** Frequent connection to occult practices; dramatic alterations in one's worldview which often insulate a person against biblical truth.

**Biblical/Christian evaluation.** New Age ASCs are prohibited on the basis of their occult alliances.

**Potential dangers.** Mental illness, occult bondage, spirit possession.

*Note:* The sections on Channeling,* Dream Work,* Hypnosis,* Meditation,* Inner Work,* Shamanism,* Visualization,* and Yoga*—practices routinely cultivating altered states—may be read alongside the following material for supporting data.

## INTRODUCTION AND INFLUENCE

By "New Age" altered states of consciousness (ASCs), we mean characteristically pagan and, from our perspective, *abnormal* states of consciousness, where, due to an occult context, spiritistic influence is often present upon the mind and/or outcome of the experience. We do not mean those normal but different states of consciousness such as daydreams, reverie, sleep, imagination, and so on. We also distinguish what we mean by ASCs from similar but not identical conditions found in Scripture, such as divine revelation, vision, and trance (see Ezekiel 1:1; Acts 9:10; 10:10; 11:9-15; 22:7). Occult visions in a New Age context have a different source, involve different experiences and phenomena, and have a different outcome than biblical visions. Our primary purpose in this chapter is to document the relationship between altered states and occultism.

We grant that the cultivation or experience of altered states is not always occult. They may be spontaneous biblical trance or ecstasy, and some mild hypnotic conditions or biofeedback self-regulation. But in many cases, it is difficult to determine where the line can be drawn. The depth and length of consciousness alteration, individual susceptibility to trance, the program involved, purpose and motive, and spiritual context and outcome are all relevant considerations. The problem here is that no one can determine in advance if an ASC will be completely safe. Even mild ASCs aren't necessarily safe, as we later document.

Given the reckless national experimentation with altered states, we believe that developing even mild ASCs should be avoided. It's simply better to stay away from the entire field. As psychotherapist Elsa First illustrates, "There are risks in cultivating altered states of consciousness. One of these risks . . . may be a permanent alienation from ordinary human attachments" (840:165).

We have such concerns for the following reasons. First, we will show that ASCs are notorious for opening the doors to contact the spirit world–something God forbids (Deuteronomy 18:10-12). Because of this, the entire field is fraught with unknown variables and potential dangers. Thus, seeking to develop ASCs is a bit like stepping into a lion's den.

Second, New Age apologists often cite the Bible to justify cultivating ASCs. However, the biblical instances of visions and trances do not support ASC experimentation. In the rare cases where visions or trances happen to believers,

they have a divine origin, as proven by their outcome and associated characteristics. Any study of visions in the Bible will prove this. The visions of Old Testament prophets like Daniel and Ezekiel, or of New Testament apostles Paul and John, were vehicles of divine revelation to fulfill God's purposes to His people. They glorified God, not the spirits, and they supported a biblical worldview and morality, not an occult one. Furthermore, the biblical experiences seem to come unbidden; they are never sought or deliberately cultivated as in New Age methods.

Unfortunately, many people today are now purposely altering their consciousness in spiritual quests that have uncertain parameters. The search for consciousness experimentation through a variety of means has become big business (662), especially in psychology and religion. Noted near-death researcher, psychologist, and New Age consciousness explorer Kenneth Ring of the University of Connecticut observes, "Not since the early days of psychology has there been so much attention devoted to the question of the nature of consciousness and probably no period in Western psychology has exceeded the present one in the interest taken in manipulating states of consciousness" (841:25). Editor John White's *What Is Enlightenment?: Exploring the Goal of the Spiritual Path* is also illustrative. It contains 15 essays by some of the world's leading consciousness pundits, who extol "the new global quest for higher consciousness and transcendence" (843). Included are essays by Zen Buddhist Alan Watts and transpersonal psychologist Ken Wilbur (the alleged "Einstein of consciousness research"), guru-spiritists Da Free John, Meher Baba, and Gopi Krishna, drug experimenter and "perennial philosopher" Aldous Huxley, plus noted professors of religion and psychiatry such as Houston Smith and Buddhist Roger Walsh (see Enlightenment).

Nor is this renewed interest unique. Cultivating ASCs has been part of the spiritual heritage of pagan religion for millennia (500). "Anthropologists have estimated that there are at least four thousand societies in the world today; about 90 percent of them have institutionalized at least one set of procedures for systematic cultivation of specific kinds of altered states" (91:198).

As America has turned to pagan spirituality, it has logically adopted pagan methods. For example, ASCs are now used in certain educational circles (1064) and irresponsibly advocated for children. An article in *Teacher Education* by prominent educator Thomas B. Roberts of Northern Illinois University encourages teachers to use all varieties of altered states in the classroom "at all educational levels" through use of biofeedback, yoga,* meditation,* and other methods (1061:57-58). Noted educator Barbara Clark believes that "guided fantasies and dreams, recognition and use of altered states of consciousness and centering [e.g., meditation] activities will develop more of our intuitive [psychic] abilities" (1063:592). Other leading educators believe that "trances, ASCs, and hypnoid states should prove relaxing and beneficial" for students (708:13; cf. p. 5). Some advocate that forms of *mediumistic* trances should be used in contemporary education (1064: chs. 4-5).

Psychiatrist Annette Hollander writes the following in her *How to Help Your Child Have a Spiritual Life: A Parent's Guide to Inner Development:* "We do not have to be afraid, and we can teach our children not to be afraid, of the very 'altered' states of consciousness that reveal a wider horizon." She encourages the following practices for helping children to develop these altered states of consciousness: hatha yoga,* and the martial arts,* which are said to "develop awareness of the life energy"; training in relaxation; psychic meditation,* working with dreams* and guided fantasy; various body-work methods; and so on (1065:50-60,152).

Altered states are also widely utilized in the growing field of holistic, or New Age, medicine.* In most forms of psychic diagnosis, psychic healing, and psychic surgery, altered states are considered essential. New Age techniques as diverse as Therapeutic Touch, chromotherapy (color healing), auric healing, meditation,* biofeedback, hypnosis,* hypnotic regression* ("past life" therapy), radionics, shamanism,* dream work,* yoga,* crystal healing,* visualization,* medical channeling,* and many others may utilize ASCs either for the practitioner in diagnosis or for the patient in treatment.

In essence, altered states are increasingly seen as a legitimate field of exploration, not only in aspects of modern education and medicine but in schools of psychotherapy—particularly transpersonal psychology—and especially in the multidisciplinary field of what is termed "consciousness research."

Also, for many people, ASCs are perceived as the key to personal and spiritual development. They are viewed as a method for unlocking the secrets of the mind, or even of creation itself. They are seen as the means to secure the higher evolution of individual consciousness and thus offer great potential for human development.

Unfortunately, few experimenters know where this quest takes them. Indeed, one may watch aghast as the committed consciousness explorer is slowly consumed by mystical experience; the addiction increasing as the individual "self" steadily becomes dismantled. As in much paganism (cf. Eastern gurus,* yoga,* shamanism*), the "normal, ordinary" world of reality and the personal self are eventually obliterated, while the seeker of "higher" states of existence is increasingly linked to a shadowy, underground world of spirits, whose control over the experimenter seems to increase with each new "adventure" in consciousness expansion.

Carl was a qualified psychologist with a degree in physics and a personal interest in religion (especially Christianity) and parapsychology, which is the scientific study of the occult (280:40-42). He became a leading parapsychologist, and his personal psychic abilities amazed not only himself but those who knew him. He was enormously excited by Aldous Huxley's *Doors of Perception.* What Huxley achieved by drugs, Carl was certain he could achieve by psychic means; that, and perhaps more. Although fascinated by Christianity, Carl was convinced that the modern churches were corrupting the original teachings of Jesus Christ. Hence he sought "true Christianity" through occult means.

Consumed with a desire to find "original Christianity" (in effect, a Gnostic understanding of Christianity), he immersed himself in cultivating ASCs, reincarnation research, and astral travel. As his studies and involvement in the psychic world continued, he explored realm after realm. He was bright and enthusiastic, not to mention careful. Most of all he was *certain* he was on the road to vast personal discoveries. He had, in his view, all the right motives, as well as the talent, abilities, and opportunities to complement them.

Eventually a Midwestern university offered Carl a professorship and allowed him to teach and continue his experiments, which provided numerous psychic and mystical experiences. Gradually, however, Carl admitted to himself that a deep alteration was taking place within (718:419; cf. pp. 385-488). He had, earlier, some gnawing doubts about the fundamental nature of his spiritual path, but he suppressed them because of their uncomfortable implications. Any doubt about what kind of spirit was leading him could mean a total revision of his work; it could even mean resigning his professorship and renouncing his parapsychological research (718:418).

Giving up his research would have been costly, but after years of painstaking effort, benevolent motives, and great enthusiasm, Carl became consumed by forces so evil he ended up an incoherent shell of a man. He required exorcism and 11 months of hospitalization for recovery.

His eventual renouncement of all study and research in parapsychology was deplored by fellow colleagues, who never learned the real reason for his strange disappearance from that community. He finally concluded:

Solemnly and of my own free will I wish to acknowledge that knowingly and freely I entered into possession by an evil spirit. And, although that spirit came to me under the guise of saving me, perfecting me, helping me to help others, I knew all along it was evil (718:485).

Pursuing altered states may not only result in a wholly unexpected, radical occult transformation of one's worldview and personality; it may also result in demonization (278/904/249/280/291).

## ALTERED STATES AND SPIRITISM

The strong historical linkage between pagan cultures and consciousness manipulation for occult purposes—e.g., spirit possession in shamanism*—indicates that the spirit world has always had a vested interest in encouraging the exploration of ASCs along specific lines, especially those devoted to spirit contact and possession (cf. channeling*).

To show that this vested interest remains true today, we will document several examples. The research of sociologist Erika Bourguignon indicated that of 488 contemporary societies observed, over 90 percent had made trance and spirit-possession states socially acceptable (297:16-17). Obviously, in the West today, trance and possession states are becoming more acceptable. One only need consider promoters like Shirley MacLaine and J. Z. Knight, or the vast influence of the modern channeling* phenomenon (refs. 574-77), or the millions of followers of Eastern gurus.* In all of this, if there is one topic consistently associated with ASCs, it is the spirit world.

Bourguignon observes, "In traditional societies—and to a considerable extent in modern societies as well . . . altered states tend to be spoken of in connection with supernatural entities such as 'spirits' . . . " (297:3; cf. p. 5). According to Bourguignon, "the vast majority of societies" have socially institutionalized the phenomenon of altered states that are typically those associated with spirit contact and spirit possession (297:3-5).

Indeed, numerous texts about consciousness exploration reveal that the modern exploration of altered states is frequently a euphemism for psychic development, occult exploration, and/or spirit contact in general. Among these volumes are Ken Wilbur's *The Atman Project* (1543); Stan and Christina Grof's (eds.) *Spiritual Emergency* (274); Benjamin B. Wolman's and Montague Ullman's (eds.) *Handbook of States of Consciousness* (844); John White's *Frontiers of Consciousness* (760) and *What Is Enlightenment?* (2637); and Jeffrey Mishlove's *The Roots of Consciousness* (500).

More than one text exploring altered or mystical states has stated that the mystical state of consciousness and the state of spirit possession can be one and the same. For example, Cambridge-educated John Ferguson observes in his *Illustrated Encyclopedia of Mysticism* that spirit "possession . . . is the core of mystical experience" (264:148).

In essence, the history of Eastern religion, Western occultism, and modern parapsychology persistently reveals the importance of developing altered states of consciousness for contacting occult dimensions, and that these dimensions are linked to the spirit world.

Nobel scientist Sir John Eccles once commented that the human brain was "a machine that a ghost can operate" (759:19). His statement illustrates the truth that, given the proper conditions, the human mind can become an open door permitting the influence of spirits. If the mind can be so affected that spirits gain some measure of control over it, how do they do so? It would appear that ASCs are the principal method for offering the proper conditions (cf. Hypnosis). And there are an almost unlimited number of methods for inducing ASCs.

Revelations from the spirits themselves often stress the importance of ASCs as essential for contacting them (refs. 574-77). The spirit guides "Orin" and "DaBen," who channel through Sanaya Roman and Dr. Duane Packer respectively, assert, "A trance state is a state of consciousness that allows you to connect with a guide.... Achieving a channeling state is easier ... than [most people] thought it would be.... The trance state creates very subtle changes in your perception of reality" (575:25).

The trance condition itself may involve only a relatively mild altered state. Even channelers comment that "channeling involves the achievement of a slightly relaxed state where you can turn your attention inward and upward to receive messages from higher realms.... Most people who mediate have already begun to access the channeling space" (575:25,28).

In *Adventures in Consciousness*, the late medium Jane Roberts described how her spirit guide "Seth" lead classes in altered states of consciousness exercises in order to facilitate students' occult development and their capacity to contact the spirit world (1066:4). In Dr. Kathryn Ridall's *Channeling: How to Reach Out to Your Spirit Guides*, ASCs are described as the means to begin channeling, that "wonderful adventure in consciousness" (577:1).

Altered states are associated with a large variety of subjects, everything from hypnosis* and other trance states, to possession states (as in channeling* or mediumism and shamanism*), to altered states that are pathological, as in kundalini arousal (see yoga* and shamanism*), to directed visualization* and imagery, lucid dreaming,* drug-induced states of consciousness, meditation,* and biofeedback-induced consciousness, as well as many others.

Why do all these different practices have the potential to induce spirit contact? Because nearly all altered states share some degree of common ground (see ref. 2801), and it is this common ground which is apparently conducive to spirit influence. In essence, almost any continually cultivated altered state is at least potentially capable of producing spirit encounters.

This is the reason altered states have undergirded virtually all of Eastern and Western occultism (500): They are typically prerequisites for the spirit contact necessary for success along the occult path. In other words, the needed spirit contact and/or manifestation of power (e.g., the development of psychic abilities) typically do not occur apart from the altered state. Thus, again, nearly all methods that attempt to induce ASCs have the potential to lead to spirit contact and spirit possession (249; cf. 759:107). The technique is virtually irrelevant; it is the altered state itself that is instrumental in permitting spiritistic influence.

Tal Brooke, in *Riders of the Cosmic Circuit*, offers a detailed examination and critique of Eastern metaphysics, including ASCs developed by the meditative disciplines of Eastern gurus. Brooke, too, reveals that ASCs are typically the means to spirit contact and possession (249:39-50,107-39,165-208).

Consider the late Bhagwan Shree Rajneesh, the influential Indian guru. His early experiences on the road to enlightenment* produced temporary insanity, possession, and almost killed him. Through intense absorption into various altered states, Rajneesh's previous personality disappeared and was replaced by a new consciousness that was entirely alien. The new personality recalled of the encounter, "The one who died, died totally; nothing of him has remained ... not even a shadow. It died totally, utterly.... Another being, absolutely new, not connected at all with the old, started to exist." Rajneesh had become possessed by a "new consciousness," a living personality that directed his mind and body from that day forward (1067:313-14).

It is sobering to realize that, in many quarters, what was once termed "spirit possession" is now often simply termed "altered consciousness." Raymond Prince's *Trance and Possession States* (2638), Erika Bourguignon's *Religion, Altered States of Consciousness and Social Change* (297), and Stan and Christina Grof's *Spiritual Emergency* (759) are three examples of research studies revealing such connections (cf. R. Allison, *Mind in Many Pieces*, 2753).

The reason New Age literature often fails to make any final distinction between occult ASCs and spirit possession is because they are so difficult to separate. Spirit possession is, finally, just the manifestation of another altered state.

Consider the following illustrations that also connect spiritism and altered states:

- When modern parapsychology began in the late nineteenth century, the subjects examined were typically spirit mediums. And most of them had become mediums and contacted the spirit world by experimentation with various forms of hypnosis* and meditation,* or other induced altered states of consciousness. In our chapter on hypnosis, we cite several researchers who failed to see much distinction between a mediumistic trance and a hypnotic one.
- What some researchers term the "shamanistic state of consciousness" (SSC) is considered essential for the shaman to contact his "power animals" or spirit guides (see Shamanism*).
- Spirit mediums routinely enter a light to moderate trance that permits the spirits to take them over and speak messages through them (see Channeling).
- Occult meditation* is generally acknowledged as an excellent method to contact the spirit world.
- Spirits can be contacted through the light trances of dowsing* or a supervised program of dream work.*
- Many New Age disciplines offer various techniques of visualization* as a help to contacting the spirit world.

- Even drugs, such as psychedelics and marijuana, are known to foster contact with the spirit world (841:149/835; cf. 838:72; and Shamanism).

Clearly, modern experimentation with ASCs in general can open a door to the spirit world. What is disconcerting is that modern scientific researchers themselves are increasingly turning to altered states.

## MODERN CONSCIOUSNESS RESEARCH

Modern consciousness research provides the opportunity to blend traditional science (measuring the physical correlates of states of consciousness) and subjective experience (the personal cultivation of altered states for religious purposes). Because these states are so powerful and fascinating, many academic researchers are blending their scientific expertise with their personal exploration of altered states. The end result is what could be termed the "New Age scientist": a person academically trained in the field of science, who attempts to integrate revelations from altered states and personal occult development into his respective discipline.

One example is the eminent scientist Dr. John Lilly, perhaps best known for his research with dolphins. Lilly's autobiography, *The Scientist*, and his *The Deep Self* reveal the typical connection between ASC exploration, spirit contact and guidance, the potential consequences of these practices, and the blending of scientific discipline with occult practices and philosophy (836:109,134-35,180-98,207-08). Since Lilly first published his book in 1978, hundreds and even thousands of scientists have followed in his footsteps (837).

Nevertheless, consider what Dr. Lilly endured as a result of his excursions into altered consciousness. By use of drugs and sensory deprivation, while resting in a water-filled isolation tank, Lilly induced a variety of ASCs and contacted spirit entities who for several years began to subject him to what they termed "ruthless education":

Something begins to approach me. I see new domains, new spaces. I leave my body totally and join some Beings far away. The Beings give me instructions. I am to continue using this chemical agent for educational purposes. . . . The Beings continue teaching me in the luminous space. I am to use this chemical agent to change my current belief systems. . . . Thus began a thirteen-month period of investigation of new spaces, of new domains. . . . The cost of this year was to be several close brushes with death and various disqualifications by professional colleagues. . . . During that year [my] inner reality became projected upon the outer reality (836:144-146). [In other words, Lilly could not distinguish fantasy from reality.]

Consciousness research links to spiritism in other ways. For example, the supposedly scientific process of "mapping" different levels of consciousness is typically drawn from Eastern and occult traditions, which are notoriously dependent upon spiritistic influences (refs. 500/841/758/759).

## DANGERS OF ALTERED STATES

There are clearly risks to cultivating altered states. First, ASCs may induce mental illness in unstable individuals, or they may naturally progress into mental illness, even among the sound of mind. Because no one can know if this will occur, the risk is similar to that of taking powerful, experimental drugs, or like rushing down to the beach to watch a tidal wave. You may or may not be engulfed, but if you are it will be too late to change your mind.

Arnold M. Ludwig, writing in Charles Tart's (ed.) *Altered States of Consciousness*, observes, "As a person enters or is in an ASC, he often experiences fear of losing his grip on reality and losing his self-control" (839:16). For example, in one of her altered states, modern shaman and best-selling author Lynn Andrews could not distinguish reality and believed she was going insane. "I was terrified. I began to inhale great breaths of air, gasping. I sobbed uncontrollably. I had finally done it—I had lost my mind" (842:183).

Those New Agers who successfully "integrate" pathological experiences may, with the proper instruction, come to interpret them positively as an experience of "spiritual emergence" (759) (i.e.

their emergence into a higher state of being). More and more psychologists who personally explore states of consciousness are now blurring the distinction between sanity and insanity and reinterpreting psychopathological conditions as a form of "higher consciousness." Some actually view insanity as a spiritual blessing (259:77/841:149-50). Unfortunately, they rarely seem to ask the right questions concerning the personal, social, and spiritual implications of their interpretations or experiences (see Shamanism*).

Second, as we have seen, altered states can open a person to the supernatural realm and contact with spirits who are really demons (refs. 278/280/291). No one can logically deny that a legitimate connection exists between altered states of consciousness and spirit influence or spirit possession. Psychologist Kenneth Ring is correct when he observes that Western materialism has done society a disservice by not interpreting this consequence properly:

Another common occurrence when functioning at this [particular] level of consciousness is encountering "entities." Though sometimes benevolent, they are more often threatening and are intent on gaining control over the individual's body or consciousness. There are many cases of such instances of attempted or successful possession to be found in the literature on spiritualism, magic, witchcraft and madness, but in the West we have typically dismissed these symptoms of possession as hallucinations. . . .

Such visitations are by no means restricted to those who have ingested a psychedelic agent—they are potentially available to anyone who has entered this region of consciousness by whatever means. . . .

In my own view, many of the claims made by "mental patients" that they are possessed by alien entities are best understood as representing a perfectly accurate assessment of what has happened to them. It is time that we began taking the concept of possession seriously instead of dismissing it as a superstition or an hallucination (841:142-43,150).

A third problem with altered states is their ability to profoundly affect one's perception. For example, the ultimate goal of most ASC programs is the destruction of the "limited" personal self to "uncover" the alleged "true" Self, which is said to be divine and one in essence with God (see Eastern Gurus).

Leading consciousness researcher John White explains:

> But the critical point to be understood is this: the value of mystical and transformative states is not in producing some new experience but in *getting rid of the experiencer.* Getting rid, that is, of the egocentric consciousness which experiences life from a contracted, self-centered point of view rather than the free, unbound perspective of a sage who knows he or she is infinity operating through a finite form. . . .
>
> The perennial wisdom is unchanging; truth is one. That is agreed on by the sages of all major religions and sacred traditions, all hermetic philosophies, genuine mystery schools and higher occult paths. Enlightenment is the core truth of them all. Even more broadly, it is the essence of life the goal of all growth, development, evolution. It is the discovery of what we ultimately are, the answer to the questions: Who am I? Why am I here? Where am I going? What is life all about? . . .
>
> *Enlightenment is realization of the truth of Being.* Our native condition, our true self is Being, traditionally called God (843:xiii).

Unfortunately, this internal experience of oneself as "God" usually seems to be accomplished through possession by a spirit entity who manipulates the states of consciousness toward such false perceptions (e.g., 249).

Of course, we should emphasize again that not all altered states are the result of spiritualistic influence, and one must be careful not to label certain mental states as demonic when they result only from normal or abnormal brain physiology. In other words, many ASCs have no spiritistic influence at all. For example, this would be true for individuals practicing biofeedback or meditation-induced ASCs where the methodology *itself* (and not spiritistic influence) is the cause of the ASCs or of components of them. Indeed, as physiological psychology professor Dr. Elizabeth Hillstrom points out:

Many are due to mundane causes. Many of the unusual visual events in altered states are undoubtedly illusions or hallucinations caused by disruptions in the normal cognitive and perceptual operations of the brain. Others may be due to an abnormal activation of brain mechanisms that are responsible for dreaming. . . . Sensory deprivation and Eastern meditation can also affect the operation of neurons to a certain extent, because both states can apparently alter the electrical patterns (EEGs) that emanate from the brain. There are several phenomena that might be created through interference with the neuronal operations that underlie perception (2659:71-72).

In addition, the fact that everyone can dream indicates that everyone has the capacity to normally experience complex fantasies and vivid imagery in their own consciousness:

Another mind-brain mechanism that may be artificially activated during altered states is the system that creates our dreams. Although human beings vary in their ability to produce fantasy and mental imagery while they are awake, research indicates that virtually everyone experiences vivid complex fantasies while dreaming. This plus other observable characteristics of the dream state suggests that we must have some type of built-in brain mechanism that can create new images, or pull up and modify old ones from memory, and then shape these into incidents or stories without our conscious instruction. Since this mechanism can operate in one altered state (while we are asleep), perhaps it can also operate in others, particularly at deeper levels of those states, when conscious awareness is greatly diminished. This hypothesis is supported by studies of hypnogogic hallucinations brief episodes of dreaming (usually less that 3 minutes) that some people experience when they are fully conscious (2659:75).

Nevertheless, this same author also warns about the development of altered states. She points out that biblical accounts of trances and visions that were used to communicate God's will have particular attributes that distinguish them from New Age varieties. For example, in Acts 10:9-16 where Peter fell into a trance, the

Holy Spirit waited until *after* the vision and trance had passed in order to help the apostle comprehend the vision and then instruct him in what to do. In other words, in distinction to New Age visions and trances, where the spirits work *within* these parameters to give revelations, God works *outside* of them to give His messages:

> In a few biblical cases, contact with spiritual beings [here, godly angels] had such a profound impact that it apparently *induced* an altered state. In one of Daniel's visions (Dan. 10:9) he saw an angel, and the experience was so powerful that he fell into a "deep sleep, [his] face to the ground." Interestingly, the angel did not try to communicate with Daniel when he was in that state. He awakened him and told him to stand up and listen carefully to the message so he could record it accurately (2659:78).

Dr. Hillstrom concludes that there are no indications in Scripture that people should enter altered states or trances in order to draw closer to God, a common theme in New Age circles. She points out that, according to 1 Peter 4:7 (and other Scriptures), Christians are to be "clear minded and self-controlled" so that they may pray or study Scripture. Thus, the biblical means of spiritual growth and sanctification, e.g. meditation on Scripture, prayer, fasting, "are surely not meant to put us into altered states of consciousness" (2659:79). Further, as we have argued all along, these states are clearly open doors to the intrusion of demonic spirits:

> However, it is obvious that such states could certainly magnify any influence that these [demonic] spirits might exert on the human mind. In fact, Satan and his forces could hardly find a more opportune situation in which to deceive or mislead people. If this seems like too strong a statement, stop and review the various characteristics of altered states. In altered states, people are subject to vivid imagery, unconstrained imaginative processes that resist conscious control, and intense emotions. Having largely set aside their ability to think rationally and critically or to exercise their will, they have become hypersuggestible, which means that they are likely to accept any "spiritual truth" that enters their minds. Even more remarkably,

they seem to be primed for mystical experiences and may attach great spiritual significance to virtually any event or thought, no matter how mundane or outlandish. Seeking mystical experiences through altered states, as defined here, looks like an open invitation for deception (2659:79).

Finally, Hillstrom points out some of the further problems with altered states of consciousness besides that of assisting demonic intrusion or deception. Of concern is the fact that the key characteristics of altered states are generally similar:

> Altered states also have important commonalities. They can all impair one's ability to test reality, to think critically and logically or to remember. They create a passive state in which mental events seem to develop on their own and are simply experienced rather that being controlled. Many also weaken emotional restraints, allowing moods to swing from wild jubilation to deep fear and depression. In addition, they can all create perceptual distortions and hallucinations and precipitate unusual bodily sensations like numbness, dizziness, tingling or rushes of energy.... They can make people hypersuggestible, so they are open to many strange beliefs and are easily influenced by the suggestions of other people. Altered states have the singular ability to make all kinds of improbable events seem exceptionally real and significant.... One final effect of altered states is their apparent ability to facilitate or enhance mystical experience ... (2659:69-70).

In conclusion, to develop ASCs is not to participate in a form of higher consciousness or true spirituality, as New Age proponents would have us believe. Rather, it often involves abnormal, regressive states of consciousness—ones particularly conducive to demonic contact and manipulation. The radical change in worldview is characteristically toward the occult, encouraging both occult practices and occult philosophy.

The growing acceptance of altered states by millions of people, their use in psychotherapy, medicine, education, and many other fields is a reflection of the growing influence of paganism in our society.

# Angel Contact, Angel Consciousness, Angel Work

- Info at a Glance
- Introduction and Influence
- Nature and Classifications
- Unfallen Angels in the Bible
- Good Angels Today
- Angels and the Roman Catholic Faith
- Evil Angels Today
- Evil Angels, Biblical Teaching, the Cults
- Evil Angels in the Church
- Evil Angels and the Occult
- Evil Angels, the Environment, Near-Death Experiences, UFO's
- Evil Angels and the New Morality
- Evil Angels, Self-Esteem, Christian Positive Confession Movement
- Evil Angels, Spiritual Deception, Demon Possession

## INFO AT A GLANCE

**Description.** Angel contact, angel consciousness, and angel work refer to New Age forms of communication with alleged heavenly angels for purposes of spiritual assistance, developing altered states of consciousness, psychic powers, or fostering New Age goals in general.**

---

** *Note:* This section constitutes a revised and expanded version of the authors' *The Facts on Angels.*

**Origin.** New Age angel contact began as a logical extension of the modern channeling movement.

**How does it claim to work?** Angel contact works through direct, personal contact with and/or instructions from supposed godly messengers. Contact with alleged heavenly angels is said to be part of an emerging planetary transformation of spirituality that will reveal man's true divine nature and unite him with the cosmos.

**Scientific evaluation.** Not applicable.

**Examples of occult potential.** Almost every occult practice, in some manner, is now associated with "angels."

**Major problem.** It redefines the biblically prohibited spiritism as communication with godly angels (see Deuteronomy 18:10-12).

**Biblical/Christian evaluation.** Good angels are not being contacted in the popular angel revival; instead, demons or fallen angels, who masquerade as godly angels, are deceiving people by confusing the nature of the contacts.

**Potential dangers.** The practice is associated with all forms of occult activity (see 278).

## INTRODUCTION AND INFLUENCE

*Time* magazine recently noted, "If there is such a thing as a universal idea, common across cultures and through the centuries, the belief in angels comes close to it" (2441:58).

Angels do indeed make one of the most intriguing subjects one could study. We agree with leading philosopher Mortimer J. Adler, editor of the *Encyclopedia Britannica* and architect of *The Great Books of the Western World* series, who stated that angels were more fascinating than either science fiction or the concept of extraterrestrial beings (2500:19). Why is this?

According to the Bible, angels have helped to shape the course of human history and continue to do so today. Consider the fallen angel in the Garden of Eden who slyly engineered the moral fall of the entire human race (Genesis 3). Angels mediated the Law of Moses, which altered the course of the Western world (Acts 7:53; Hebrews 2:2). And there have been thousands of angelic encounters throughout history—good and evil—in the lives of ordinary and famous individuals, including Abraham Lincoln, boxer Evander Holyfield, and rock stars George Harrison and Carlos Santana, who invokes the presence of angels before each concert (2501). Noted mystic William Blake said he was under the guidance of angels night and day (2501).

Terrifying angels fill the book of Revelation. Their power over nature and humanity is so awesome that it is difficult to comprehend (Revelation 8:6-12; 9:15). Angels helped Jesus Christ in His wilderness and Gethsemane temptations, and they assisted the early church (Matthew 4:6,11; Luke 22:43; Acts 10:22; 12:7). Clearly, the world is quite literally alive with angels. Directly or indirectly, angels have appeared in nearly every civilization and culture. They have played a role in almost every world religion and are more active in human affairs than people may at first suspect. The "Angel Gabriel" for example, gave Muhammad the anti-Christian revelations in *The Koran*, which now influence over a billion Muslims (2503). So who can ignore the subject of angels?

Until recently, however, angels have been ignored in most quarters, even by the church, in whose Scripture angels play a vital role. When Billy Graham wrote his bestselling book *Angels: God's Secret Agents*, he was surprised at how few books existed on the subject. He said that he had never once heard a sermon preached about them (2504:17).

Even when the *Syntopicon* was published (a topical volume on 102 great ideas or themes cov-

ered in *The Great Books of the Western World*), the subject of angels came close to being omitted. Despite the influence of angels throughout history, and though angels are a recurring theme in the writings of world religions and history, the publisher of the *Encyclopaedia Britannica*, Senator William Benton, and Robert Hutchens, president of the University of Chicago, along with other members of the advisory board, were either incredulous that such an idea should be considered, or they voted it down. Only the insistence and perseverance of one of the great philosophical minds of our own century, Mortimer Adler, prevented the idea from being omitted. As a result, angels became the first subject discussed in the *Syntopicon* (2500:9-10).

Adler's lecture on "Angels and Angelology," which was given at the Aspen Institute of Humanistic Studies, drew a larger audience than any he had experienced in 30 years. That lecture became the impetus for his 1982 book, *The Angels and Us*.

Today, angels are no longer ignored. In theater, television, literature, film, art, and music, angels are back in the popular mind, even among skeptics, who sometimes can't seem to help themselves (2502)!

We think this is to the good for at least three reasons. First, angels inherently remind people of God and of their responsibility to Him. Second, the very subject of a race of spiritual beings brings to mind some of the deepest personal questions man has asked throughout history. If angels exist, then there certainly are higher forms of life in the universe; and perhaps people may think we didn't evolve naturalistically from primordial interstellar gases (cf. 2641). If angels exist, then a spiritual universe exists, which logically carries us back to profound questions about God as Creator and related questions such as "Who am I? Where did I come from? What is the purpose of my life? Where am I going when I die?"

A third reason why angels should not be ignored is because not all angels are good. People need to know this today more than ever before. The Bible reveals the number of evil angels is very large (Revelation 12:3-4,7-9); one out of every three may be malicious (Revelation 12:4).

The Bible tells us there were rebellious angels in heaven. They chose to follow Satan and were cast from heaven with him. In the future, they will once more wage "war in heaven" against the good angels. But once again, "they [will not be] strong enough," and "Satan . . . [will be] thrown down to the earth, and his angels . . . with him" (Revelation 12:7-9 NASB).

For most people, however, the idea of an *evil* angel is a self-contradiction, like dry water or cold heat. Aren't all angels good just because they're angels? But what if all aren't good? Given their numbers and influence, if we don't take time to consider at least the possibility of evil angels, any of us may suffer for it.

When human history is over, and all is said and done, the influence of angels in this world—despite their invisibility—will probably be more obvious and certainly more profound than we suspect. As noted theologian J. I. Packer recently commented, "Both as communicators and as guardians their work is ordinarily unnoticeable, and not until we get to heaven shall we know how much we owe to it" (2505:xii).

Today, however, polls indicate a rising popularity of angels. Almost three out of four adult Americans, including teenagers, believe in angels. That's about 200 million people (2441:56/2506). Worldwide, the figure is estimated to be at least three billion—half of all people on earth. Every year the "American Conference on Angels" holds meetings to discuss the subject; and there are angel seminars, angel newsletters, college courses on angels, and angel sections in bookstores. Besides the Hells Angels, "Charlie's Angels," and Guardian Angels, there is the Angel Watch Network, Angel Collectors Club of America, the National Association of Angel Lovers, and dozens of angel enterprises, such as the "Angels for All Seasons" store in Denver, "Angels in Heaven" Day Nursery in Cleveland, and "Angel Threads," a children's boutique in Tucson. Angel jewelry even made national media attention in the Los Angeles courtroom during the O.J. Simpson trial.

A December 27, 1993, *Time* magazine cover story on angels pointed out the difficulty traditional mainline churches have in dealing with the phenomenon. The article chided that people commune with "angels" as if they were cute little puppy dogs. "In the eyes of traditional church leaders, the popular authors who render angels into household pets, who invite readers to get in touch with their inner angel, or summon their own 'angel psychotherapist,' or view themselves as angels in training are trafficking in discount spirituality. And the churches are at a loss for a response" (2441).

The article rightly argues that "angels" in the New Age Movement have been reduced from their grand biblical stature of magnificent proportions—mighty messengers/soldiers who inspire fear and awe—to Kewpie-doll cherubs, bite-size beings easily digested. "For those who choke too easily on God and his rules, theologians observe, angels are the handy compromise, all fluff and meringue, kind, nonjudgmental. And they are available to everyone, like aspirin. 'Each of us has a guardian angel,' declares Eileen Freeman, who publishes a bimonthly newsletter called *AngelWatch* from her home in Mountainside, New Jersey. 'They're nonthreatening, wise and loving beings. They offer help whether we ask for it or not.' . . . Only in the New Age would it be possible to invent an angel so mellow that it can be ignored. According to the rest of history, anyone who invites an encounter with an angel should be prepared to be changed by it."

The article, noting that five of the ten books on the religious bestseller list for *Publisher's Weekly* were about angels, commented, "This rising fascination is more popular than theological, a grass-roots revolution of the spirit in which all sorts of people are finding all sorts of reasons to seek answers about angels for the first time in their lives" (2441:58). A year later, in December 1994, the NBC evening news ran a special segment about this national fascination.

Thus angels have almost universal good press today, from "Clarence" in the popular Jimmy Stewart movie, *It's a Wonderful Life*, to Michael Landon's angel role in "Highway to Heaven," and the recent "Touched by an Angel" TV series. Angels today always seem to be engaged in good and wonderful deeds.

Perusing titles of recent angel books is also illuminating. Consider what the following titles suggest: *Devotion to the Holy Angels; 100 Ways to Attract the Angels; Send Me Your Guardian Angel; Know Your Angels; Ask Your Angels; Angels for Your Children; Commune with the Angels; Creating with the Angels; Messengers of Light: The Angel's Guide to Spiritual Growth; Angel Wisdom; Answers from the Angels; Angel Voices; The Angels Within Us; Angel Messenger Cards; A Treatise on Angel Magic; Meetings with Angels; Angels and Mortals: Their Co-Creative Power.* These are only several of the hundreds of titles published in the early to mid 1990s, and a large number of them suggest that people are seeking to commune with angels in intimate ways. Today's popular angels play roles from personal friends to guidance counselors to spiritual advisers, and much more.

There are several reasons for this popularity. First, this generation has witnessed a dramatic spiritual awakening, which includes everything from Christianity to the New Age Movement to the darker forms of the occult. This has undoubtedly increased interest in the subject of angels and spirits in general.

Second, there is an associated fascination with the subject because of its larger implications, such as through the questions we raised previously. Third, a preexisting belief system for angels is already in place from Christian, pagan, and almost every other religious tradition. For example, most Roman Catholics are brought up to pray to their guardian angels, and holidays like Christmas and Easter recall angel stories year after year.

Fourth, as people are searching for answers and meaning to life, angels are thought to play a vital role in providing those answers. There is even a growing movement which teaches that angels reside within us and are waiting for us to use them to tap our human potential, enhance creativity, provide psychological fulfillment, and spiritual self-enlightenment. Thus promoters of angel contact offer people what they want and need in troubled times: assurance, love, and guidance. For example, "The angels hold the answers to many of our questions," and "spiritual help is always available

from the angels." Or, "The angels want us to become enlightened . . ." and they "are the caretakers of our souls. . . . Their wonderful love [is] everywhere" (2507).

Fifth, angels by definition can interact with us. The purpose of the good angels is to help us, and the goal of the evil angels is to deceive us. Sixth, in many people's minds, there exists a prior assumption that angels are only good, and therefore, contacting them is also only good and without risk. If angels really can be contacted, why not? Could there be a greater spiritual adventure?

## NATURE AND CLASSIFICATIONS

The Hebrew word *mal'akh* and the Greek word *aggelos* both mean "messenger." This indicates the term "angel" can be used of either men *or* spirits. For example, in Mark 1:2 *aggelos* is applied directly to John the Baptist, "Behold, I send My messenger (*aggelos*) before Your face," and the Hebrew word *mal'akh* is used in the corresponding prophecy of Malachi 3:1.

Because the meaning of the word "angel" is simply that of a "messenger," the context determines if it is a human or an angelic messenger, although in rare cases it is difficult to determine which is meant. By far, the most common biblical use of the term is of a godly spirit messenger, what we normally think of as a good angel.

When Scripture uses the term "holy angel" or "angel," it refers to the godly and unfallen spirits created directly by God (Mark 8:38; Luke 9:26; Acts 10:22; Revelation 14:10). When it refers to "Satan's angels," "evil spirits," "unclean spirits," and so on, it refers to fallen angels who serve Satan (Matthew 12:24; 25:41).

The word "angel" appears some 300 times in 24 books of the Bible. But this does not include synonyms used for angels, such as "sons of God," "holy ones," "morning stars," "cherubim," "seraphs," "ministering spirits," "watchers," and such. In all, the term "angel" or its equivalent is found in 35 books of the Bible.

Angels are spirit beings created directly by God prior to the creation of the universe (Job 38:7). They were created as servants of God, Jesus Christ, and the church in order to perform the will of God in the earth (Hebrews 1:6,14). Apparently innumerable in number, they are of various ranks and abilities, and they have numerous duties (Revelation 5:11; 8:2; 9:15; 12:7; Ephesians 1:21; Colossians 1:16).

Angels are clearly *personal* spirits. They have personal wills (Hebrews 1:6), and they expressed joy at the creation of the world (Job 38:7). They rejoice over a sinner's repentance (Luke 15:10), and they convey concern and consternation, as when the apostle John wrongly attempted to worship an angel (Revelation 22:9). They are curious (1 Peter 1:10-12); they talk to each other (Revelation 14:18); and they worship and praise God (Revelation 7:11). And when in human form, they can communicate directly with men (Genesis 19). Angels command other angels (Revelation 7:3; 14:17-18) or battle demons (Daniel 10:13; Revelation 12:7-8). They appear in dreams (Matthew 1:20) or visibly as mere men (Genesis 18:1-8). They are described as beings of incredible brightness or clothed in shining garments (Luke 24:4). When they appear directly to men, the result is usually one of emotional shock or fear, hence the common biblical refrain of the angels, "Fear not" (Luke 1:12-13; 2:9). In the Bible, only three angels are named: Michael, Gabriel, and Lucifer.

Angels are immortal and can never die (Luke 20:36). As we will see, they are incredibly powerful, and they have great intelligence and wisdom. They may use the same measurements as men (Revelation 21:17) and may eat either human or angelic food (Genesis 19:3; Psalm 78:23-25).

Although they never marry (Luke 20:35-36), this does not necessarily mean they are without gender. Angels apparently have spiritual bodies (2508:29-35). That they can assume human form implies that they have spiritual bodies first. God Himself has a spiritual form (John 5:37) and took on corporeal form in the Person of Jesus Christ. Scripture also tells us that in the resurrection the redeemed in their glorified bodies will be "like" the angels (Philippians 3:21; Matthew 22:30).

In their natural (spiritual) state, angels move at tremendous speeds and are not bound by space and time, at least not in the manner we are. They can be present in great numbers in limited space, as is evidenced by the seven demons simultaneously inhabiting Mary Magdalene. And it seems that thousands of demons inhabited at least one man (Mark 16:9; Luke 8:30). Angels may also be aware of things like men's prayers and future events (Luke 1:13-16). However, despite their abilities, they are not omniscient or omnipotent (Daniel 10:13; Matthew 24:36; 1 Peter 1:11-12; Revelation 12:7).

Morally, there are two kinds of angels: the holy or the elect (1 Timothy 5:21) and the fallen, who are described in the Bible as evil spirits or demons. These rebellious angels will not be redeemed (Hebrews 2:11-17), and their final end is the lake of fire (Matthew 25:41). However, while some of these fallen angels are now free to roam, others are currently kept in eternal bonds (Jude 6; 2 Peter 2:4).

Different classifications among the angels include the cherubim, seraphim, and archangels. Apparently the cherubim are the highest class of angels, having indescribable beauty and power. Cherubim were placed at the east of the Garden of Eden to guard the way to the tree of life after man was expelled (Genesis 3:24). They appear in connection with the dwelling place of God in the Old Testament (Exodus 25:17-22; cf. Hebrews 9:5) and are primarily concerned with the glory and worship of God. For example, the four living creatures of Ezekiel are cherubim (Ezekiel 10:4,18-22). The cherubim are never termed angels, probably because they are not specifically messengers. Their chief purpose is to proclaim and protect God's glory, sovereignty, and holiness. Satan was apparently part of the cherubim class, making his rebellion and fall all the more significant.

Another class comprises the seraphim, who are consumed with personal devotion to God (Isaiah 6:2-3). There are also archangels, such as Michael, angels of yet lower rank, and special groups of angels (Revelation 1:1; 8:2; 15:1,7).

Perhaps we should mention here that the specific term "the angel of the Lord" (*Malach–YHWH*), which is used throughout the Old Testament (e.g. Genesis 22:11-12; Exodus 3:2; 2 Kings 19:35), does not refer to a created angel. It refers to the Old Testament theophanies of Jesus Christ, who appeared to people before His incarnation as "the angel of the Lord." The angel's identity as Jesus Christ is indicated not only by the attributes of deity He possesses, but also because the Jews themselves held this angel to be the divine Messiah (2509).

Although the godly angels are thought to reside in heaven (Revelation 10:1), we are not told about the nature of their specific dwelling places, if any. Of course, if angels do have spiritual bodies, this might indicate they have dwelling places (Jude 6).

In addition, angels have incredible supernatural power. Peter is putting it mildly when he says that they are "greater in might and power" (2 Peter 2:11 NASB). For example, only one angel was sent to destroy the entire city of Jerusalem (1 Chronicles 21:15), and only two angels were sent to destroy Sodom and Gomorrah and all the surrounding cities (Genesis 19:13,24-25). One lone angel is even able to bind Satan himself for ten centuries (Revelation 20:1-3). Destroying angels produced the ten plagues on Egypt, including the death of all Egypt's firstborn (Exodus 12:12-13,23,29-30; Psalm 78:43,49; Hebrews 11:28). The four angels of Revelation have power over the winds of the whole earth (Revelation 7:2-3).

Other angels are indirectly associated with the destruction of one-third of the entire heavens and earth, and one-third of the seas, the rivers, the vegetation, the sun, moon, and stars (Revelation 8–9). In Revelation 9:14-15, four angels destroy one-third of the earth's population.

At the end of the world, angels will gather all the spirits of the saved and unsaved. They gather believers at Jesus Christ's return to earth (Matthew 24:30-31), and they gather the unbelievers for eternal judgment (Matthew 13:39-43). Truly, angels excel in strength (Psalm 103:20). But what is most amazing is that God tells believers in Christ that they will one day judge, and perhaps rule, angels (1 Corinthians 6:2-3).

Nevertheless, many false concepts about angels abound today. Among these erroneous beliefs are that: 1) angels are the human dead, i.e. that we become angels at death; 2) angels perform God's work through occult activities and practices; 3) the devil is not a fallen angel; 4) Jesus Christ was only an angel; 5) simply because they are angels, they can be trusted to be good. These false beliefs indicate how important

it is to discern what Scripture does and does not teach about both the good and the evil angels. If people have no biblical idea of what a good angel really is and does, then any angel claiming to be good can seem credible.

## UNFALLEN ANGELS IN THE BIBLE

The angels who were created by God and Christ exist primarily for them, and have their lives centered around them (Nehemiah 9:6; Colossians 1:16). They worship and serve God and Christ (Philippians 2:9-11; Hebrews 1:6). They glorify and celebrate the praises of God and Christ (Job 38:7; Psalm 148:2; Isaiah 6:3; Luke 2:13-14; Revelation 5:11-12; 7:11-12). They delight to communicate the will of God and Christ, and they delight in obeying God and Christ. In all that they do, they honor God and Christ (Daniel 8:16-17; 9:21-23; 10:11; 12:6,7; Psalm 103:20; Matthew 2:13,20; 6:10; Luke 1:19,28; Acts 5:20; 8:26; 10:5; 27:23; Revelation 1:1).

They execute the purposes of God and Christ, including the governing and judging of the earth (Numbers 22:22; Psalm 103:19-21; Matthew 13:39-42; 28:2; John 5:4; Revelation 5:2; 2 Samuel 24:16; 2 Kings 19:35; Psalm 35:5-6; Acts 12:23; Revelation 16:1). They were active in establishing the Mosaic law of God in the Old Testament (Psalm 68:17; Acts 7:38,53; Galatians 3:19; Hebrews 2:2), and they execute Christ's judgments in the New Testament (2 Thessalonians 1:7-8; Revelation 7–9).

They are also ministering spirits, to believer and unbeliever, especially the former (1 Kings 19:5; 104:4; Luke 16:22; Acts 12:7-11; 27:23; Hebrews 1:14). They guide, provide, encourage, and deliver God's people (Matthew 1:20; 28:5-7; Genesis 21:17-20; 1 Kings 19:5-7; 2 Kings 6:15-17; Daniel 6:20-23; 10:10-12; Acts 5:17-20; 12:5-10). They are sent to answer prayers and to attend to the righteous dead (Daniel 9:20-24; Acts 12:1-17; Revelation 8:4; Luke 16:22; Jude 9). They protect God's people (Psalm 34:7; 35:4-5; Isaiah 63:9), and they may preach to and warn the unbeliever (Revelation 14:6-7). They interpret divine visions (Zechariah 4:1; 5:5; 6:5; Daniel 7:15-27; 8:13-26) and prophesy about the future (Daniel 9:20–10:21; Revelation 1:1; 22:6,8). They can control the forces of nature (Revelation 7:1; 16:3,8-9) and influence nations (Daniel 12:1; Revelation 12:7-9; 13:1-7; 16:13-14).

Biblically, angels are most conspicuous in association with the Person and work of Jesus Christ. They announced His conception, birth, resurrection, ascension, and second coming. They protected and strengthened Jesus Christ during His temptations. They know and delight in the gospel and execute the purposes of Christ. They will accompany Him at His return, and they will gather all people, good and evil, for the final judgment (Matthew 1:20-21; 2:13-15; 4:11; 13:39-43; 16:17; 24:31; 25:31; 28:5-7; Luke 2:10-12; 22:43; John 1:51; 5:22-29; Acts 1:11; Ephesians 3:9-10; 2 Thessalonians 1:7; 1 Timothy 3:6; 1 Peter 1:12).

What is perhaps most relevant for us is that what the good angels do biblically is the opposite of what we find the popular New Age angels doing today. ("Popular angel" is a term we may use for those beings who are in reality evil angels or demons.) Biblically, the good angels do their work for God and then disappear. But the popular angels act like modern spirit guides. They do not worship Christ, and they deny Him and distort His teachings. They reject God's will and rebel against it by seeking to prevent people's salvation.

When we examine the godly angels, we see that their proclamations support God's purposes, their miracles support God's interests, and their preaching communicates God's will. Their love of Christ is proven throughout Scripture and history. In ministering to God's children, they remind them of God's love and care (Matthew 18:10; Psalm 34:7; 91:11-12; Daniel 6:22). Also, their character is proven to be wise and holy by their refusal to be worshiped by men (Colossians 2:18; Revelation 19:10; 22:9) and because their worship and devotion is given solely to God and Christ.

## GOOD ANGELS TODAY

A number of contemporary books recount encouraging and inspiring stories of the holy angels at work in the lives of people throughout history and even today. These angels have saved the lives of Christians, provided encouragement during persecution, and helped in the conversion of non-Christians (2505:3-16,54-61).

In *A Rustle of Angels*, evangelical Christian Marilynn Webber relates her story, which was first published in the *Ladies Home Journal*. One day, despondent over circumstances, she was walking home near some railroad tracks. Slowly crossing over them, she suddenly realized that an oncoming train was so close that "I could see the blue eyes and the terrified face of the engineer." Paralyzed with fear, she was unable to move. Instead of being struck, however, she was miraculously pushed from the tracks as if by a giant hand, even though "no one was there! There was not a person in sight!" (2500:16). She survived, to say the least, with a renewed interest in angels.

In *Celebration of Angels*, we find many stories of deliverance. For example, Walt Shepard was a very depressed non-Christian who had decided to take his own life. He rammed his Sunbeam sports car (at 120 miles an hour) into what he thought was an abandoned car parked on the side of the road. But the car was neither abandoned nor out of gas. It exploded and both vehicles caught on fire. What saved the car's driver and passenger was that they were outside the vehicle resting.

Walt was catapulted through the windshield and landed on the car's engine with fire surrounding him. Pinned and trapped, he passed out. Though the heat was so intense no one could get close enough to help, the police watched in amazement as two men suddenly appeared, pulled Walt out of the fire, held him, and helped place him in the ambulance. The police and a hotel manager "confirmed that two figures walked up to the car as though there were no fire at all. People said the searing heat kept everybody else 50 to 100 feet back. The attending police were dumbstruck by the peculiar rescue" (2505:3-4). Walt nearly died and endured many painful months of hospitalization in a body cast, but he realized he had been saved by angels. He now *knew* God wanted him to live. As a result, he accepted Jesus Christ as his personal Lord and Savior.

Then there is the story of David Moore and his friend Henry Gardner, who were trapped in severe fog in a small plane with only a few minutes of fuel remaining. They radioed the Asheville, North Carolina, airport for emergency instructions but were told the field was closed due to fog and that the airport had no instrument capability for an emergency landing. The pilots were instructed to return to Greenville.

Henry notified the tower that there wasn't enough fuel to return to Greenville and that they needed to land immediately. After a period of silence, a voice said that they could land and that emergency preparations would be undertaken. They were then given specific and detailed instructions, which allowed the plane to land safely. Once on the ground, in a shaky voice, Henry thanked the air traffic controller for saving their lives. After a moment of silence, the controller responded, "What are you talking about? We lost all radio contact with you when we told you to return to Greenville." "You *what?*" Henry asked, incredulous. "We never heard from you again," the controller said. "And we never heard you talking to us or to anyone else. We were stunned when we saw you break through the clouds" (2510:23-27).

Many stories like these are recounted in modern angel literature. Although lives are saved, many more, obviously, are not. As to why this is, that must be left to God's will and wisdom. But clearly, angels are more active in our world than many people would suspect. Like Elisha's servant, if the veil were removed, the average modern would be stunned (2 Kings 6:15-17).

Although Scripture does not explicitly teach that everyone has a guardian angel, many biblical commentators believe that this could be true, at least for believers. Certainly, given the great number of angels and God's love for His own people, it would be a logical conclusion. Scripturally, it appears that children, at least, do have guardian angels (Matthew 18:10).

Certainly there are "guardian angels," those angels whom God sends at specific times to guard, encourage, and protect both His own people and unbelievers, whenever He so chooses.

## ANGELS AND THE ROMAN CATHOLIC FAITH

Like most religions (2529), Roman Catholicism has a long tradition of accepting angelic visitations. A common Catholic "prayer to your guardian angel," which all devout Catholics learn, reads as follows: "Angel of God, my guardian dear, to whom his love commits me here, ever this day (night) be at my side, to light and guard, to rule and guide. Amen" (2530:59).

Officially, the Catholic church teaches that every person has a guardian angel, and that "the angel assigned to the person represents him before God, watches over him, defends, helps in prayer and in thought, and presents the soul of the just person to God after death. Devotion to one's guardian angel is encouraged" (2531:37).

And, the Catholic church is becoming more interested in angels. The *Opus Sanctorum Angelorum* (Work of the Holy Angels) of the Catholic Order of the Holy Cross is now accepted as an "institute recognized by the Church," and Pope John Paul II has expressed a personal interest in angels (2429:28).

Many of the current books on angels are written by Catholics. In *Where Angels Walk*, a *New York Times* bestseller, Catholic Joan Anderson encourages a form of angel contact and prayers to angels. She writes, "Most Catholics believe that everyone receives a guardian angel at birth, a life companion especially suited to one's unique personality. Catholic children learn a comforting little prayer to initiate 'conversation' with their angel and the feast day of guardian angels is celebrated on October 2" (2510:10).

Books such as W. Doyle Gulligan's (ed.) *Devotion to the Holy Angels* (*Lumen Christi*, 1990), and Catholic organizations such as the OSA cited earlier, explain and encourage devotion to angels along the lines of the popular angel phenomenon. For example, when two spiritists describe how to work with spirit guides in *Companions in Spirit*, they assert the following as justification for Catholics to contact spirits: "It should be noted, however, that the Catholic Church has long held to the propriety of praying for help from discarnates who have been elevated to sainthood. . . . Many saints and biblical figures have sought and received the advice of angels, who are master [spirit] guides of a high order. The Holy Spirit disseminates a multitude of emissaries, myriad varieties and degrees of 'angel' [sic]. They all come from the same source and lead back to the same destination. Their ultimate purpose is to help you grow toward God" (349:99–100).

Nevertheless, revelations given by dead Catholic saints, by Mary, and by the angels frequently associated with her, support Catholic theology and teachings that are antibiblical (2434). For example, the occult Marian apparitions at Medjugorje, Yugoslavia, include the appearances of "putti" or child angels, whose messages deny the teachings of Jesus Christ (2532).

Spiritist and popular angel author Terry Lynn Taylor also argues that Catholic Marian devotion is connected with the resurgence of angels. "Mary, the Mother of Christ, is often referred to as the Queen of angels. Mary is touching the lives of those involved in angel consciousness in a deep way . . . that is why . . . the angels are so prevalent now" (2507:Aug. 15).

## EVIL ANGELS TODAY

The issue here is not whether Christians or unbelievers accept angels; it is whether the angels' teachings are biblical. If their teachings are not biblical, then emphasizing the idea that everyone has guardian angels may lead to contact with evil angels who seek to imitate good angels to deceive people spiritually. The emphasis in modern angel and channeled literature is that all people *do* have guardian angels whom they are to contact regularly for instruction and guidance. As Terry Lynn Taylor and Mary Beth Crain state in their daily devotional, which was inspired by the "angels," "Everyone has a guardian angel." And, "When God looks at you, God sees two beings: you and your guardian angel. Your guardian angel is your spiritual traveling companion through life. . . . Your guardian angel knows what you came here to do. . . . Getting to know your guardian angel will help you to get to know yourself" (2507:Intro., Feb. 14). In a similar fashion, two modern spirit guides stress that, "Everyone has a personal guide who

is with them for a lifetime, often referred to as a guardian angel" (575:43).

And all these guardian "angels" have a consistent message: "We seek to enlighten humanity to move more completely into a course of wise actions stemming from a creative involvement with us and with all inspired teachers of love and compassion. . . . We are in your dreams by night and your meditations by day. . . . [Our] guidance is everywhere around you. . . . [We give you] our assurance of your eternal life" (2512:209–10).

In *Answers from the Angels*, Terry Lynn Taylor points out, "Establishing a personal connection with the angels is a simple process. You don't even have to say you believe in angels. Just begin by allowing yourself to be open. . . . After you have become 'angel conscious,' you will want to communicate with the angels in your own special way" (2513:3). Thus, "Angels are ready to help us. All we have to do is acknowledge them" (2514:xv).

The biblical truth that some angels are now evil means that spiritual discernment is a necessity. In an era of worldwide occult revival, no one should attempt the phenomenon of "contacting angels," "channeling angels," developing "angel consciousness," and so on. These are ruses by the fallen evil angels (demons) to hide their spiritual deception.

How do we know the popular angels are not who they claim to be? Because the angels who remained faithful to God are holy and godly in their behavior, and the entities behind the popular angelic revelations are neither. As we saw, biblical angels glorify Jesus Christ and do not give revelations contrary to Scripture. Biblical angels characteristically operate "behind the scenes." The popular angels are more than willing to operate in the open and to communicate in spiritistic fashion.

Even Christians need to exercise discernment. For example, in *A Rustle of Angels*, Marilynn and William Webber cite one illustration of a Christian man who had apparently been deeply hurt by a friend. In a dream one night he had a revelation from an angel who instructed him as follows, "Don't forgive. Get even." In the dream, a nefarious plot then unfolded, something the person had never thought of. It would not only allow him to get even with his friend without anyone knowing he was responsible, it would injure his friend deeply. Here, that the entity seemed like a good angel was belied by the fact that its message was unbiblical (2500:180). The Bible never encourages revenge.

Evil angels are morally corrupt spirits in rebellion against God (Psalm 106:37; Matthew 12:34; Mark 1:36; John 8:44; 2 Peter 2:4; James 2:19; Jude 6). Their rebellion was led by Satan (Jude 6; 1 John 3:8; Matthew 12:24-25, 25:41; Ezekiel 28:12-17) and resulted in their fall and expulsion from heaven (Luke 10:18, Revelation 12:7-9). As a result they became destructive, self-centered creatures who seek to thwart the purposes of God and Christ (Deuteronomy 32:17; Psalm 106:37; Revelation 2:10; 1 Peter 5:8; Ephesians 6:11; Matthew 13:39; Luke 22:31; 1 Thessalonians 2:18; 1 Timothy 4:1; Mark 3:11; 4:15).

One of the demons' principal ploys is to deceive people through false religion or deceptive miracles and thereby to blind pepole to spiritual truth (2 Corinthians 4:4; Acts 26:18; 2 Corinthians 11:14; 2 Thessalonians 2:9,10; Revelation 16:14; 20:10).

Demons are forever set in their ways and have no opportunity for redemption. Thus, they will eventually be cast forever into the lake of fire (Revelation 20:2,3,7-10). This may explain why they responded to Jesus with fear and derision; for example, "What do I have to do with You, Jesus, Son of the Most High God?" (Mark 5:7 NASB; Luke 4:41). And, "Have you come here to torture us before the appointed time?" (Matthew 8:29).

Demons are not the spirits of dead men, or of some pre-Adamite race, as some argue, for the spirits of the human dead are not free to roam (Luke 16:19-31; 2 Peter 2:9). Nor are they merely personifications of evil, or of natural forces, such as the "gods" of nature, as skeptics assume. Nor are demons the superstitious designation for particular natural diseases such as epilepsy or mental illness, because Scripture clearly distinguishes these disorders from demon possession, although it is possible that both can be present or that demon possession could induce mental illness (2515).

However, it must never be forgotten that demons are only creatures who are ultimately constrained by the sovereign power and purpose of God. When needed, the Christian has power over them (1 John 4:4; James 4:7) because Christ Himself was victorious over Satan at the cross (Hebrews 2:14; Colossians 2:15; John 12:31). Jesus proved His complete power over demons (Matthew 12:28; Mark 1:34), often casting them out of people (Matthew 8:31; 15:22-28), and He commanded His disciples to do the same (Matthew 10:1; Mark 6:13; Luke 10:17).

Using the Bible to catalog the powers and abilities of angels in general would give us a glimpse into their capacities which would help us discern the abilities of demons (as corrupted angels). The following list indicates the capacities or methods of fallen angels in general. Some listings refer to the good angels in order to indicate that fallen angels would also have these abilities.

1. Power to torment (Revelation 9:1-11; Luke 8:27-31).
2. Immense power; four angels are released to kill one-third of mankind (Revelation 9:14,15).
3. Considerable influence; the world is said to be greatly affected by Satan's power (2 Corinthians 4:4; 1 John 5:19; in Matthew 4, Jesus did not question Satan's right to grant Him the world's kingdoms).
4. Purposeful deception (Genesis 3:1-5,13).
5. Disguised as good spirits (2 Corinthians 11:14-15).
6. A particular number of rebellious angels are now confined (2 Peter 2:4-5, Jude 6-7); the result of apparent sexual involvement and cohabitation (the exact term "Sons of God," *bene elohim*, is only used of angels, 2516; Genesis 6:1-4).
7. Producing insanity; great physical strength (Luke 8:26-35).

8. Inducing sickness for 18 years; producing suffering and deformities (Luke 13:10-17).

9. Power over nature: Satan produces whirlwinds, fire from heaven, and great miracles in the presence of people (Job 1:16-18; Revelation 13:13, Hebrews 1:7, Psalm 104:4).

10. Power over the human body: Satan produces painful boils or welts (Job 2:7).

11. Dumbness, blindness, and epilepsy; attempted murder (Genesis 19:11; Matthew 9:32,33; 12:22; 17:15,18).

12. Multiple possession; apparently seeking "rest" by possessing humans (Luke 8:30; 11:24-26; Matthew 12:43-45).

13. Convulsions, child possession, mauling (Luke 9:38-39).

14. Animal possession (Matthew 8:30-32).

15. A limited prevision of the future; fortune-telling (Acts 16:16). Despite this apparent ability, demons are not omniscient; any such powers they may have are still subject to God's controlling and intervening providence (Isaiah 44:25-26).

16. Anger, great strength, and power (2 Thessalonians 2:7; 2 Peter 2:11; Acts 19:16).

17. Treacherous natures, scheme wickedly, attack humans (Ephesians 6:10-16; Judges 9:23).

18. Provide supernatural revelations (Hebrews 2:2; Acts 7:53; Galatians 3:19).

19. Animals may recognize them (Numbers 22:23-27).

20. Ability to speak through an animal (a "serpent") (Genesis 3:1-5).

21. Supernatural power to travel (Job 1:7).

22. Instantaneous projection of a false reality (Matthew 4:8).

23. Apparent ability to remove thoughts, to implant thoughts, and to manipulate the mind (John 13:2; Matthew 13:19,38-39).

24. Moral corruption, deception, and murder (John 8:44).

25. Possession of humans (Matthew 8:28; John 13:27).

26. Great wrath (Revelation 12:12).

27. Ability to incite betrayal (Luke 22:3-4).

28. Physical ailments (2 Corinthians 12:7).

29. Deception, blinding minds (2 Corinthians 4:4).

30. Deceive the nations (Revelation 12:9; 20:7-8).

31. Invisibility, but an awareness of their presence (Job 4:15).

32. Ability to terrorize (1 Samuel 16:14-15).

33. Can assume human form (Genesis 19:1-10; John 20:12; Acts 12:8-9; Hebrews 13:2).

34. To a degree, duplicating God's miracles, changing sticks to snakes, water to blood (control over matter/energy), control over animals (Exodus 7:10-12,20-22; 8:6-7; 2 Thessalonians 2:9).

35. Defilement through occult practices and human sacrifice (Deuteronomy 18:9-13).

36. Transport human beings (Matthew 24:31; Luke 16:22).

37. Limited ability over events and human actions (1 Chronicles 21:1; Daniel 10:13; 1 Thessalonians 2:18).

38. Destroying the flesh; power of death (2 Samuel 24:15-17; 1 Corinthians 5:5; Hebrews 2:14; Acts 12:23).

39. Tempt with evil (1 Corinthians 7:5).

40. Objects of pagan worship (Deuteronomy 32:17; 1 Corinthians 10:20; Colossians 2:18).

41. Child sacrifice and murder (Psalm 106:37).

42. Oppression (Acts 10:38).

43. Control humans for their own goals (Revelation 2:10).

44. Pervert the ways of God (Acts 13:10).

45. Fire and brimstone rained down upon a city (destruction of Sodom and Gomorrah; Genesis 19:13,24).

46. Influence dream states (Genesis 31:11),

47. Send pestilence, power to destroy a city (2 Samuel 24:15-16).

48. Communicate by speech to humans (1 Kings 13:18; Acts 23:9).

49. Materialize and dematerialize at will (Luke 2:9,13,15).

50. Vast in number (Hebrews 12:22; Matthew 26:53).

51. Speak to men, control of vocal cords, paralysis and possession (Luke 1:19-20).

52. Different languages (1 Corinthians 13:1).

53. Preach a false gospel and deception about God (1 Kings 22:19-23; Galatians 1:8; 1 Timothy 4:1; 1 John 4:1).

54. False visions and experiences (Jeremiah 23:16; Colossians 2:18).

55. Miracles (Revelation 16:14).

This partial list indicates that demons have more power and influence than people may realize. And the above list is surprisingly relevant for today. In the 1990s almost everything in the list is duplicated somewhere in the world of the occult. For example, as we documented in other sections, evil angels (demons) imitate good angels and express great concern for people's welfare. They also give false visions and revelations in dreams or through channeling,* automatic writing, and so on. They can possess people, perform various miracles, cause insanity, or commit murder. They can produce physical ailments, sicknesses, or mental torments. They can predict the future (albeit in a limited capacity subject to God's sovereignty), encourage occult practices, manipulate the human mind by impressing thoughts, ideas, or images, and they can influence nature. They seek worship, to pervert God's ways, and they can assume physical form at will, from human to child, animal to mythological creature. In the end, in general, they destroy people's lives (278).

The methods of contact are typically those found in the world of the occult—through altered states of consciousness,* meditation,* visualization,* developing psychic abilities, divination,* drug use, magic ritual, and so on. Frequently, the desire and commitment to contact angels or spirits by inviting them into one's life is all that is needed. For example, "Sometimes all it takes to establish communication is the thought of an angel or the desire to connect with one.... Pick an angel to attune to. Have some writing paper nearby in case a message comes through that you want to record" (2507:Jan. 4). Or, "Call a prayer meeting with the angels. Invite your guardian angel, or any angels you like, to join with you. Pray in any way you like, and be aware of any images, words, and ideas that come to you" (2507:Feb. 6).

The most recommended method for establishing contact is through meditation.* Here, one seeks to enter a unitive or a noncognitive, "empty" state of consciousness (2507:Oct.7/2511:27). "There are a variety of approaches to meditation, such as focusing on a mantra, on imagery, or on physical objects, or simply paying attention to one's breathing ... you may want to use the word *angel* as a form of mantra.... The messages may not come to you in words; often angels speak to you with feelings and images.... Centering [e.g., focused attention; occult "alignment"] is a way of synchronizing our energy.... [which connects] with our higher self and with the angels who guide us" (2511:107-09).

Prayer and the creation of an "angel altar" are two additional popular methods for establishing contact (2511:110-12). "Angels love candlelight. Candlelight illuminates and purifies the atmosphere and attracts angels. After you have created your altar or shrine, light the candle and sit quietly in front of it. Draw in the beauty and ask the angels to join you" (2511:111).

Because they are relatively easy to contact for those determined to do so, evil angels can influence people's lives today in almost innumerable ways.

## EVIL ANGELS, BIBLICAL TEACHING, THE CULTS

The godly angels never deny the teachings of Jesus Christ or the Bible. Yet the popular angels do this routinely. Some examples are: "God is the totality of your living experience" (2512:58); "God is life. You and God share the same bed, the same car, the same glass of water. You and God are one" (2512:118).

The popular angels teach basic pagan, New Age beliefs, including Hinduism, occult practice, pantheism (all is God, God is all), universalism, and that Christ dwells within all people, irrespective of faith in Him (2512:63,139).

These "angels" make simple errors of fact in both theological and nontheological areas (2517). Consider the following from *Angel Wisdom:* "The angels do not judge"; "our true selves are angelic"; "all religions . . . worship the same God"; "our souls remain in a pure state of innocence"; "consider the possibility that ultimately everything is true" (cf. 1 John 2:21; 2518).

Besides denying biblical teaching, the popular angels also distort the Bible. If these were godly angels, especially ones who took part in giving the law of God to Moses, they would not distort His Word. In *The Angels Within Us*, Scripture is universally misinterpreted to support the occult, which violates biblical prohibitions against the occult (Deuteronomy 18:9-12). For example; 1) the angel's interpretation of Matthew 5:14 is twisted to teach pantheism and that we are "the creative power of the universe"; 2) 2 Chronicles 20:17 is a "coded message" that "describes what happens when you take on the energy of [the] angel"; 3) Psalm 91:11 is reinterpreted to encour-

age spiritism; 4) John 15:1-11 is distorted to mean that we are to abide within the God-self within us, the occult "I AM Presence" (2537). These angels also direct their contacts to read these passages *in the Bible* (2525:60,122).

Angel channeler and New Age leader John Randolph Price comments, "The angels are extremely practical in showing us our false beliefs" (2525:62), which happens to include traditional Christian interpretation of biblical passages. Concerning the greatest commandment given by Jesus to love God above all else (Matthew 22:37-38), we are told it really means: "Start with the first and greatest commandment, which is to love the Lord Self with every particle of feeling you have . . ." (2525:63).

Sadly, the Bible is being twisted by these so-called angels in order to deceive people into their own demonization. Consider how three popular passages are interpreted: "If we are totally sincere and willing to surrender the lesser in exchange for the greater, the Holy Self will *gently ease the old personality out and will replace that lower energy with Itself.* . . . An entirely new wine skin must be made ready for the new inpouring. Paul said, 'I die daily' (1 Corinthians 15:31)— and this is what we must do to secure the final victory. Remember, 'unless one is born anew, he cannot see the kingdom of God' (John 3:3). And 'whoever loses his life for [the sake of the Christ within] will find it' (Matthew 16:25)." In this citation, "dying daily" to the flesh, spiritual regeneration, or being "born again," and forsaking one's own desires for those of Christ, are all reinterpreted to teach angel possession as "the final victory." Ultimately, to "accept Christ" is to accept the "angel" inside and to allow it to possess you (2525:189-91, emphasis added).

Of course, most people assume that since these beings are angels, it is natural for them to quote Scripture. Isn't this what we expect of angels? As the author of the above citation wrote, "Could an angel possibly be associated with Satan?" (2525:206). Of course not; who would ever expect such a thing?

Here are several revelations from the angels and related biblical texts to look up to see other ways in which these beings could not possibly be the holy angels:

- "You may think that there is only one truth; yet we, your angels, suggest that all of you have your own truth, your own interpretation of divine law. No one way is right or wrong" (2512:113; cf. John 14:6; 1 John 2:21).
- "[It is wrong] to feel that only one way is the authentic path to God" (2512:135; cf. John 10:1-12; Acts 4:12; 1 Timothy 2:5-6).
- "Love. . . . is 'the capacity to allow all other living things to grow into their fullest expression of self' " (2512:138; cf. 1 Corinthians 13:3-8).
- "In Truth I am the Spirit of God . . . for God is all, and all is God" (2525:145; cf. Ezekiel 28:2-4).

Now consider the following meditation provided by the angels, which they wish people to assimilate. Ask yourself if this could possibly come from a godly angel: "All that God is, I AM. . . . I AM divine purity. . . . I AM perfect love, . . . I AM the peace that goes beyond understanding, . . . I AM omnipotent. . . . I AM perfect judgment. . . . I AM the only supply, . . . the I AM THAT I AM . . . for I AM the joy of the world" (2525:276). This clearly denies the teachings of Jesus Christ, who taught that people were evil, not good, and certainly not divine: "If you, then, though you are evil, know how to give good gifts to your children, how much more will your Father in heaven give good gifts to those who ask him!" (Matthew 7:11). And, "For out of the heart come evil thoughts, murder, adultery, sexual immorality, theft, false testimony, slander" (Matthew 15:19).

People may also be surprised to know that scores of modern cults and false religions were instituted or nurtured by "angelic" contact. As we documented thoroughly in *The Mask of Mormonism*, few religions are as anti-Christian as the Mormon faith. Nevertheless, Mormon founder Joseph Smith was led to the alleged "gold plates," from which the *Book of Mormon* was occultly translated, by the "angel Moroni" (2519). Since then, Mormon history has been replete with angelic guidance, direction, and revelation.

In *The Facts on the Jehovah's Witnesses* we documented how "angels" have played a large role in the Jehovah's Witness religion, and even in their terribly biased translation of the Bible, *The New World Translation.*

The noted seventeenth-century medium, Emanuel Swedenborg, also routinely contacted angels and eventually formed another pervasively anti-Christian sect, The Church of the New Jerusalem, sometimes termed the New Church or Swedenborgian faith. Swedenborg's angels were with him continually, whispering, teaching, impressing thoughts and ideas into his mind (1115:749).

Rudolph Steiner, the founder of Anthroposophy (a combination of theosophy and gnostic Christianity), is another illustration of an extremely anti-Christian sect begun with the help of angels. Steiner, heavily influenced by Swedenborg, contacted the dead and other spirits, including angels, whom he described in detail in his writings and lectures. He taught that every person has a guardian angel throughout many incarnations on earth (2520).

Jose Silva, the founder of the eight-million-member occult Silva Mind Control* technique, teaches people to contact "inner advisors" for information and guidance. In part, SMC was started when, during astral projection, Silva contacted what could be termed an "angel" who helped him develop the principles that became Silva Mind Control (2521).

Other examples could be given, including the Self Realization Fellowship founded by Paramahansa Yogananda and the Unity School of Christianity founded by Charles and Myrtle Fillmore (2501). But obviously, the angels who helped begin or who influenced such anti-Christian religious systems could not have been the good angels, since their revelations are antibiblical. Yet these religions either claim to be Christian or to be harmonious with the Christian faith. As a result, they are confusing many people, Christians included.

## EVIL ANGELS IN THE CHURCH

There are other ways in which deceiving spirits have infiltrated the church. The dramatic increase in the number of books advocating angel contact began many years ago with the late Rev. Roland Buck's *Angels on Assignment*. The book, however, has little to do with the holy angels. The content of the book involves spiritistic deception. For example, an examination of its history revealed that some of the "angels'" original statements were changed to make them consistent with biblical teaching. Regardless of Rev. Buck's and publishers Charles and Francis Hunter's sincerity in publishing the book, the "angels'" teachings reveal their true nature (1165).

One issue of *The Christian Parapsychologist*, a magazine devoted to merging Christianity and the occult, was devoted entirely to angels. It included five articles, one each by a psychic, a Swedenborgian, a nature mystic, an anthroposophist, and a Jungian. In "Some Thoughts About Angels," J. Dover Wellman, vicar of Emmanuel Church and author of *A Priest's Psychic Diary*, includes virtually all spirits into the category of deceased humans and encourages various occult methods to contact them:

I believe spiritual entities are all around us. ...In this matter of our realizing the presence of the angels, the initiative always lies with them as superior beings....Jesus Christ was, I believe, one of these pre-existent angelic beings. ...His purpose in dwelling on earth was to inform us of our own potentiality as beings who could be restored to "angelhood."...

When the state of trance frees our spirit-soul from our body-soul, we act as pure spirit. Our extra-sensory perceptions function more efficiently, making known to us that which is otherwise hidden....We are ourselves then approaching the level of the life of the angels....In this condition...our communion with them would be enhanced and their influence upon us much increased (1163:220-21).

Brian Kingslake is a minister of the New Church, which is based on the spiritistic revelations given to Emanuel Swedenborg. He is the author of *Swedenborg Explores the Spiritual Dimension*. In his article "A Heaven of Angels from the Human Race," he accepts the common mediumistic and Swedenborgian teaching that "all the millions of spirits inhabiting the spiritual world—angels and devils alike—are *human*

*beings* who once inhabited this earth, or some other earth in the material universe." He argues that God's alleged purpose is to "form a heaven of angels from the human race" (1163:225).

Dorothy Maclean is a New Age leader and one of several cofounders of the spiritistic Findhorn Community in Scotland. She is the author of several books on how to contact angels and other spirits. In "Angels Today," she discusses her personal experience with angels. "I found that I could not make contact with these angels until I myself was in a state of consciousness similar to theirs....To them we had magnificent divine potentials....We were gods in the making....They await our choice to let our lives be guided by our intuitions, by our angelic awareness, that we may cooperate with them..." (1163:229-32).

In "The Hierarchies Regained," anthroposophical student Evelyn Capel, a minister in Rudolph Steiner's so-called "Christian Community" and author of *The Tenth Hierarchy*, also encourages the interaction of "angels" and humanity along occult lines (1163:232-36). In "Angels and Archetypes," Christopher Bryant, a priest in the Society of St. John the Evangelist and longtime student of occult psychologist Carl Jung, observes, "It is probable that all unknowingly we benefit by the ministry of angels who do their work in the unconscious levels of the mind which are in touch with the psychic world" (1163:240).

The popular late Christian preacher William Branham claimed to speak for God, but throughout his life he was at times guided by lying spirits (his "angels") who would whisper to him and, apparently, occultly "heal" many people each year. Despite his wide influence in Pentecostalism, he denied the true nature of God. He once said, "Trinitarianism [belief in the Trinity] is of the devil! I say that [with the authority of] 'THUS SAITH THE LORD'" (1176:606).

The Rev. Edward W. Oldring, author of *I Work with Angels* and *I Walk and Talk with Angels*, supposedly had "angels" appear to him to assist him in "preparing many [Christian] people... to work with God's angels...and to...cooperate with...the angels" (1177:14-15). He teaches,

"There is a spiritualism [contact with spirits] that is ordained of God.... It is part of God's plan..." (1177:126-27). However, the angels that speak to him give blatantly false interpretations of the Bible (1177:65,68).

One striking example is worthy of a more in-depth analysis. G. Don Gilmore is the minister of Plymouth Congregational Church in Spokane, Washington, and host of the daily radio program "Perspective on Living." He has authored *Angels, Angels Everywhere*, a book on alleged angelic contact. We have selected this book because Gilmore is an educated clergyman who speaks to Christians, and because his book illustrates how spiritism may be disguised through internalizing or psychologizing spiritistic experiences. Gilmore rejects biblical authority and accepts religious things in general to be reflective of true spirituality or godliness. To him, many ancient and modern traditions of "angelic" contact are received as a "viable and acceptable way of experiencing the diversity of God's communication with us" (1166:back cover).

For Gilmore, "angel contact" encompasses a wide range of phenomena. This includes the occult concept of "thought forms," or spiritual manifestations allegedly constructed mentally from psychic energy:

I believe that angels are forms, images, and expressions through which the essences and energy forces of God can be transmitted and that, since there are an infinite number of these forms, the greatest service anyone can pay the angelic host is never consciously to limit the ways angels might appear to us (1166:xi; cf. 164-82).

Here the doors have swung open to virtually all forms of supernatural occult phenomena. Every religious and spiritistic manifestation today claims to be associated with "divine" energy, or the "energy forces of God." Gilmore claims that "God's energy" is not only behind the traditional angelic manifestations in various world religions, but behind much more as well.

One of Gilmore's principal concerns is to develop what he terms "angel consciousness." This is basically a euphemism for psychic devel-

opment, "higher consciousness," or spirit possession. For example, the book *Angel Wisdom* tells us that the book itself "is designed to help you tune in to your 'angel consciousness'... the consciousness that we are divine.... By accepting angel consciousness, you are accepting the responsibility of being a healer.... Regardless of your situation, the angels are present to help you initiate healing" (2507:Intro.,Oct. 20). In other words, "angel consciousness" allows one to become a psychic healer, which, by definition, requires demonic influence (2522).

Thus, one aspect of developing angel consciousness includes a closer association with the spirit world. Terry Lynn Taylor writes: "You will meet angel guides on the [angel-guided spirit] journeys.... These guides are available if you want to make up your own self-love and soul-evolvement council, for the advancement and expression of your purpose for being here on earth. This counsel will be on hand, at all times, to guide you in decisions and creative choices and will always be sending you messages of love.... The angel guides are guardians of a particular universal energy system to tap into. Positive energy systems in the universe are guarded by the angels" (2523:153-54).

"Angel consciousness," therefore, involves an altered state of consciousness* or openness to the psychic realm, which is then interpreted to be involvement with divine energies and powers. A person may develop "angel consciousness" through creative visualization,* which supposedly opens the doors to "the moving streams of unlimited energy" (1166:165). In Pastor Gilmore's words:

The angel-consciousness is something that can be developed. The question is, how to do it. How does one make an angel contact? More comprehensively, how do you develop an angel-consciousness?... It is the process of stretching the muscles of the creative imagination to facilitate a flow of power. It requires time and attention. Most of all, it requires a thorough-going preparation. Angel forms of the past were not produced out of haphazard sloppy thought. They were developed gradually in the creative consciousness.... [William] Blake made a powerful point on this score: "If the doors of perception

41

were cleansed, everything would appear to man as it is, infinite." So let the doors represent the total apparatus for developing angel consciousness (1166:171-72).

Because God's essential "energy forms" are allegedly everywhere, we are told that it is the Christian's responsibility to establish contact with them for spiritual growth. As in occult magic, this may even involve the manipulation of "divine" energies for a variety of purposes. Gilmore argues that the modern "angel phenomenon" is continually changing and "subject to an evolving human consciousness" (1166:164). In other words, as man's spiritual consciousness expands, the manifestations of divine consciousness via angelic forms accommodate themselves accordingly.

Referring to Evelyn Underhill, an authority on mysticism, Gilmore observes, "Evelyn Underhill often speaks about journeying toward the center—which is God—on the conviction that 'angels and archangels are with us.' Their energies are certainly with us, but they are not recognized until people give them a symbol, or image body, through which they might operate" (1166:173).

In common with much occultism, Gilmore suggests that we can actually "raise" angels through the powers of our own consciousness, just as the occult magician attempts to raise spirits or demons through the circle of power in his ritual. Gilmore cites popular occultist Dion Fortune, who interprets angelic contact as communion with our "higher self." Here again, "angel contact" is simply another term for psychic development:

> Could it be that the highest and best angel form is not external to us but one's own best and truest self? Dion Fortune once wrote ... "The Holy Guardian Angel, be it remembered, is really our own high self." ... Add to the Outer Self, Self One, the inner body—intuition, genius, sixth sense, ESP, psychic power, inner knowing—and you might have more angel forms to use in your creative work. The angel-consciousness is a product of careful preparation. Generally speaking, one must develop in this area quietly and purposefully for a long period of time. One needs a slow, integrated discipline of trial and error in

order to create adequate forms through which divine energy can move (1166:173,175-76).

In utilizing one particular form of "angel energy," Gilmore writes that contacting angels is easy. "You will be amazed at how often you will make contact with the energy essence of the angel form ..." (1166:182). He also encourages positive mental affirmations to facilitate the process of angel consciousness and contact. "God and God's helpers are never far away.... The Light of God surrounds me.... The Power of God protects me.... Wherever I am, God is!" (1166:182).

Clearly, Gilmore's "angel" contact encompasses many forms of psychic development, spiritism, and occult manifestations, which is in violation of biblical prohibitions (Deuteronomy 18:9-12). (For an illustration of other "angel" influences in the church, see "Evil Angels, Self-Esteem, Christian Positive Confession Moment" on page 47.)

## EVIL ANGELS AND THE OCCULT

Surveying the different ways in which the popular angels promote occultism would take more space than we have, so we have chosen several pertinent illustrations. In *Angel Wisdom*, people are encouraged to use mantras,* mandalas,* shamanistic vision quests,* contacting one's power animal (a spirit guide who appears in the form of an animal), manipulation of chakras, and psychic healing (2524). In *Angelic Messenger Cards*, people learn to accept contacting the dead (2512:31). In *Creating with the Angels*, people are told, "Dream time is spirit time and offers a great opportunity to play with the angels.... Allow the angels to help you interpret your dreams" (2523:39,41). In *The Angels Within Us*, angels are said to take people deep into altered states of consciousness* in order to establish contact with them (2525:16). The angels also support New Age medicine* and occult holistic health practices (2501).

The books of theosophist and spiritist Geoffrey Hodson are also popular in angel circles. In 1924, Hodson was contacted by an "angel" calling itself "Bethelda," who gave him material for half a dozen books, including the popular *The Brotherhood of Angels and Men* and *The Kingdom of the Gods*. In his *Clairvoyant Investigations* he writes, "I have myself confirmed that these superphysical domains contain innumerable nonphysical beings, such as angels and nature spirits . . ." (1527:2). The teachings of these "angels" encourage theosophical occultism, not biblical truth. The popular angels also promote necromancy, or contacting the dead for divination,* and occult magic (2526).

In one case, where the angels assume a function similar to the demons contacted in magic ritual, people are told, "You can also use this technique to avoid people you fear and loathe. When you use this [magic] satchel, repeat the affirmation, 'There is no such personality in the universe.' Then put the name of the person who owns that personality in the satchel" (2511:81).

Many popular angels also encourage automatic writing, dictation, or speaking in order to get their messages published and in circulation (2512:14,25/2527:122). For example, Karen Goldman, author of *Angel Voices* and *The Angel Book*, believes that "the angels are directing and guiding her writing" (*Angel Voices*, back cover flap). She used the "Sedona Method RELEASE Technique," from the Sedona Institute in Sedona, Arizona, to contact an "inner angel" that now guides her writing (2528). Sally Sharp, author of *100 Ways to Attract the Angels*, was also led into automatic writing by her angels (2501). Meredith L. Young-Sowers writes, "For well over a decade, I've been taught by an angelic presence that describes himself/herself simply as Mentor, meaning 'teacher.' "—many of Mentor's verbatim teachings are given in her books (2512:18).

Rosemary Ellen Guiley, author of *Angels of Mercy* and many books on the occult and mysticism, such as *The Encyclopedia of Witches and Witchcraft*, and *Harper's Encyclopedia of Mystical and Paranormal Experiences*, recalls that her life has been directed by unseen presences, which she interprets as angels, who have guided her into her career:

For many years, I have felt the presence of guiding beings in my life. . . . My initial intuitive sense was that these helping beings were "angels," and that is what I have always called them. . . . My strongest sense of the presence of angels concerns my work as a writer. . . . I feel that angels facilitate my work in numerous ways. . . . I am assisted and influenced by angels. I am grateful for their help, and I acknowledge them daily in my meditation. I sense a small group of angels who are around me all the time, connected to my personal and professional lives. They are joined by other angels who come and go depending on circumstances. . . . When I began work on *Angels of Mercy* the angels came out in force. It seemed I had a small army looking over my shoulder to weigh in with their various influences. . . . In addition to my writing, I lecture a great deal, and I feel the guiding presence of a "speaking angel." . . . I sense his presence. He is a facilitator who helps me organize and deliver talks (2514:xi-xiv, cf. 90).

The name of Guiley's "speaking angel" is "Plato," and he does indeed speak through her, which is similar to many prominent New Age leaders today:

As I began my talk, I felt a distinct shift in my consciousness, as though part of me were displaced to one side. In addition, I could feel the weight of an invisible presence on my shoulders, as though a being perched there. . . . I talked for two hours without looking at a single note, and got rave comments from the audience. "You don't know it, but you're a born teacher!" . . . As time has gone on, I have been increasingly aware of this shift in consciousness when I deliver a talk. Occasionally, someone who is clairvoyant will come up to me afterward and ask me if I know I have an angel or a being standing off to one side of me. "Yes," I say, "that's my speaking angel!" (2514:97-98).

This suggests that a good deal, or perhaps a majority, of the popular angel literature is actually from the "angels" themselves. But then, what field of the occult is *not* infiltrated by fallen angels? Astrology* and other forms of divination,* ceremonial magic, mediumship, seances, witchcraft, satanism, psychic development, and shamanism* are all overrun with fallen angels and their deceptions. As *Harper's Encyclopedia of Mystical and Paranormal Experiences* observes, "In New Age occult and religious beliefs, angels have made a comeback in popularity. They are portrayed in karmic aspects of astrology, channeled, meditated upon, and said to exist in spirit realms. Angelic forces are invoked in magic rituals and various magical systems and witchcraft" (2514:21).

This text also states, "The popular view holds that angels are benevolent beings and are different from demons . . ." (2514:21). Indeed, the primary goal of demons is to confuse people as to who they are and as to their sphere of operation. When people are convinced that the occult is actually angelic, they will be much more willing to experiment. As a result, large numbers of people who contact angels are slowly but surely being led into the occult (cf. 2525/2507/2514).

Perhaps the most troubling aspect of all this is that the "angels" specifically hope to reach children. For example, the author of *The Circle of Angels* was taken over by a spirit who told her through automatic writing, "I am the archangel Michael and together we will save the children" (2501). The end result was the series of *Little Angel Books*, which attempts to help children personally call upon angels through occult meditation.*

The popular angels are also active through various divination* practices. These are as old as mankind and include ancient oracles like the one at Delphi (through whom the spirits or "gods" spoke), the I Ching,* tarot cards,* runes,* and the Ouija board.* Divination can be practiced through everything from bird behavior and animal entrails to skull contours (phrenology), palms (palmistry*), simple dots (geomancy), and sticks (dowsing*).

Today, the angels have entered the business of divination on a large scale. In Alma Daniel's, Timothy Wyllie's, and Andrew Ramer's *Ask Your Angels*, we find a five-step method called the GRACE Process, using the divination method termed the "Angel Oracle," which is essentially a three-part deck of cards. The first set of cards are four archangels, and the random selection of a card is said to connect you with the creative dreaming or problem-solving aspects of that specific angel. The second set of cards has 16 angels. When one of these is selected, it "activates" that angel to help the per-

son select from the third set of cards, which has 24 activities or situations. Once one of these is chosen, the person is to pursue the card's instructions, knowing that the angel from the second set of cards will guide and direct him to fulfill third-card requirements.

Another system of divination is the "Angel Cards," which includes a board game called "The Game of Transformation." It was created while the originators were living at the New Age Findhorn community in Scotland. This game is also intended to establish contact with angels, predict the future, and to develop "higher" consciousness (2511:ch. 14).

Divination lessons are also found in the book *Angelic Messengers Cards: A Divination System for Spiritual Discovery*, which was developed in association with a spirit guide called "Mentor." With this system, one uses cards with pictures of flowers, which angels will then use for the person's spiritual growth. "The cards act as a 'living prayer' to help us resolve problems, develop inner trust, affirm ourselves, and renew and awaken the spiritual energy of love. . . . The *angelic messenger cards* are a divinely-inspired tool for self-discovery and . . . carry the seeds of both personal and planetary transformation" (2512:24-25).

Using any kind of divination method is, in the words of occult authority W. B. Crow, "nearly always dangerous" (2087:29). To our way of thinking, the basis for this conclusion is, because divination links one to demons, the derived information is frequently bad advice, and because it encourages people to make harmful decisions that they otherwise might not.

The popular angels are also greatly influential in the field of channeling.* Channeling "spirit guides" is now a billion-dollar U.S. industry. But channeling angels is no different than channeling spirit guides. In both cases one is possessed by a control spirit, just as if one were a medium at a seance. This is why the messages and phenomena found in angel channeling and in mediumism are essentially the same. Yet most promoters of angel channeling claim that there is a distinction in terms of the *entity* that is being channeled. Mediums are said to channel the discarnate dead, which is different from the channeled angels, who are thought to be a more spiritually advanced life form. Spiritist Meredith L. Young-Sowers (mentioned previously) claims, "Talking to angels is the natural *extension* of the channeling phenomenon of the late 1970s and '80s . . ." (2512:22, emphasis added). But whether one terms them angels, spirit guides, or discarnates, it is essentially the same phenomenon—demonic possession in order to accomplish the demons' purposes.

Spirit guides and angels have been easily linked in the literature. "We all have spiritual guides, *angels* who take us to higher levels of consciousness and knowledge. . . . Our guides may take on physical presence in a dream, during meditation, or in the form of a spiritual advisor or teacher whom we may unexpectedly encounter. . . . [reader affirmation] 'I am open to my spiritual guides, and I greet then with excitement, respect, wonder, and love' " (2507:Dec. 9).

Catholic Roseann Cervelli claims to have been channeling *angels* for over a decade from her home in Martinsville, New Jersey, and some of her channeled revelations were published in *Voices of Love.* How did this begin? After being raised a Catholic and developing a "strong sense of spirituality," she studied the trance revelations of medium and psychic Edgar Cayce. She also learned methods of psychic healing\* and pursued "Christ consciousness." Eventually she received the laying on of hands from a Catholic priest who became her spiritual mentor. When he laid his hands upon Cervelli, she experienced a kind of psychic opening. "After that, for the next year or so, I studied with the priest and other likeminded people. I would have a kind of mystical experience. I would be pulled into a oneness and meditative state. . . . These were my first experiences with the spiritual energies—very loving and very embracing" (2514:98-99).

Eventually she met a medium who channeled a spirit named "Matthew." After taking "Matthew's" occult advice, Cervelli progressed to a form of psychic revelation in which she would receive "energy" coming through her head. Through automatic writing she eventually produced *Voices of Love.* After "Matthew," she met a spirit named "Elliott" and later an entity who introduced itself by saying, "My name is

John, and I have come to teach you about self-love." When "Matthew," "Elliott," and "John" decided to leave, they told Cervelli that she would now be indwelt by a group of angels. And she has been channeling "angels" ever since (2514:98-102). One wonders how she could tell the difference.

Thus, among the standard messages these "angels" want to give people is to inform them that, "We are not separate from God. We *are* God. . . . Not only is God inside of us, but he *is* us" (2514:105).

## EVIL ANGELS, THE ENVIRONMENT, NEAR-DEATH EXPERIENCES, UFO'S

Environmental radicalism has now become a national concern, the result of overzealous activists and politicians whose sometimes misguided ways have done considerably more harm to people than they have provided assistance to the environment (2533). One also finds a deep concern with the environment in most spiritist writings, including among Native Americans, UFO contactees, New Age channeling, and modern angel revelations. The spirits' interest, however, is to promote pantheism and nature worship, not a cleaner environment.

Environmental revelations from the "angels" teach the sacred importance of the environment and how people must be more concerned with the earth as their spiritual parent. People must learn to view the earth as divine and realize that worship of the creation is crucial to a renewed spirituality. This reflects an increasing return to pagan nature worship (the earth itself is revered as a goddess), and to animism (trees, rivers, plants, rocks, and so on are believed to contain living spirits). Even some ideas in Al Gore's book on the environment encourage a pagan approach (2534).

The angels who speak through one angel channeler emphasize, "The larger level of healing we speak of involves healing the relationship between your spirit and the spirit of the Earth. . . . Planet Earth has a life purpose, as you do. . . . Your desire to seek a deeper exchange

45

with Nature encourages her spirit and further balances all levels of life . . ." (2512:162).

The popular angels also endorse the New Age "Gaia" concept: "Your spirit's purpose is to facilitate cooperation between you and Gaia, the Earth. . . . As you awaken your love as a planetary being . . . it will ultimately be the means of healing Earth" (2512:198,206).

Examples of animism are found in the following angelic revelations: "Trees have guardian spirits, and we can learn many things from sitting quietly near a tree and communicating with its energy" (2507:Apr. 30). And, "The Water Spirits are the guardian angels of natural sources of water. . . . All Water Spirits can teach us about our inner feelings. In learning to connect with them, we can gain many benefits" (2535).

The spiritistic Findhorn community in Scotland, with its worship of nature spirits (devas) and angels, is one example of how the popular angels' emphasis on the environment leads to contact with demons under the guise of harmony with Mother Earth. In return for their prayers and for worship to the spirits inside trees, plants, and rivers, the angels promise people physical, emotional, and spiritual healing. They also promise that the earth itself will evolve into perfection (2536).

Near-death research also reveals the modern penchant for "angels." Millions of people have had what is called a near-death experience (NDE). This is where clinically dead individuals have the perception of being out of the body, going through a tunnel, seeing a light, being enveloped by the light, and having some form of contact with a being of light, the dead, or angels. One of the most common elements is the appearance of a "being of light" (often interpreted as an angel) who guides the dying across the threshold of death. Many nurses who are psychic claim to see angels appear to their patients at the moment of death, supposedly to guide their spirits into the afterlife (2538).

Angels may be a frequent occurrence, or at least perception, in NDEs, but many of their messages are no different from those given in the spiritistic tradition. Unfortunately, as we documented in *The Facts on Life After Death* (2642), the deep NDE is characteristically an initiation

into the world of the occult, and so it has far-reaching consequences. (Another good text is Douglas Groothuis' *Deceived by the Light*.)

The popular angels are also associated with UFO's. Modern fascination with UFO's has grown by leaps and bounds since the first modern sighting by Kenneth Arnold in 1947. Today, the field known as ufology is a massive industry having scores of organizations around the world. At least a dozen government investigations and literally millions of sightings, including thousands of alleged UFO entity contacts or abductions, have been reported. Today, people think that UFO's are either hoaxes, misinterpretations, hallucinations, or actual visits from advanced extraterrestrial civilizations.

Probably the last conclusion people arrive at is that UFO's are angelic phenomena, or the product of fallen angels. But this is what they are. Off and on for 20 years coauthor John Weldon has researched this field and has written three books of convincing evidence that UFO's can only be explained by recourse to demonology. Some of this evidence is given in *The Facts on UFOs and Other Supernatural Phenomena* (2643).

## EVIL ANGELS AND THE NEW MORALITY

Several books on angels portray Satan as the good guy. Here is a warped sense of values, which does not make the resulting ethical views surprising. For example, "*Satan* comes from a Hebrew word meaning 'adversary'— and [New Age] teachers may well assume that role to jog the student's memory. And *Lucifer* comes from a Latin word signifying a *light bearer*, which certainly represents the illuminating power of a master tutor" (2525:212). Thus, "The Angel of Materiality and Temptation [i.e., "the Devil"] works with us. . . . It is the energy that enables us to say with understanding, 'I live, yet not I, but Christ liveth in me' " (2525:215). Another book teaches that "Lucifer was really doing God's work . . ." (2539). Elsewhere, we are encouraged to welcome the Angel of Death:

To the average person the Angel of Death is most feared, but to the aspirants, disciples, and initiates he is "the one who is welcomed as the sunrise." Make contact now and ask him to assist you in preparing for the final step of release and acceptance.... Remember there is no such thing as death, only a change of energy.... In Truth that which we call death is but an entrance into a more glorious life of joy, fulfillment, peace, and freedom..." (2525:212, 190-91,185).

"Angel" morality is consistent with that found in the occult in general, a self-generated morality achieved through "higher" consciousness which allows one to justify any kind of lifestyle. The popular "angels" endorse illicit sex (e.g., homosexuality, lesbianism, adultery), abortion, divorce, and virtually any moral lapse one might think of. The popular "Emmanuel" books illustrate this (1119/2451). Some angels endorse these behaviors in the name of a "proper" understanding of certain spiritual truths: that one must move *beyond* good and evil to comprehend the underlying unity of creation or that God encompasses both good and evil within His own being (2512:54,82). We see, then, that confusion about the nature of the devil leads to confusion about God's nature.

Obviously, if "higher" consciousness lies beyond good and evil, and if God Himself encompasses both, then it's not possible to say with certainty what is right or wrong ethically. In the end, plain old selfishness, hedonism, and sensuality win: "Morality ... involves making choices that are best for you ..." (2507:Sept. 8). And, "Most of all, the angels want to encourage you to have fun, be wild, laugh, frolic, play, be courageous, and create spontaneity.... The angels are attracted to free spirits who aren't afraid of being themselves, even if the bulk of society can't seem to understand them.... Personal freedom gives us the chance to be who we really want to be.... Change your mind whenever you please.... Make an ass out of yourself once and a while.... our imperfections makes us interesting.... it is okay to make mistakes or to be 'wrong.'... Know you deserve the best the angels have to offer" (2523:4-6).

We are also told to abandon our preexisting religious beliefs and the rules that come with them because they are far too restricting. "We need to let go of our strict beliefs and accept new information without fear" (2507:July 28). "Creating your own religion is a good way to free your spirit and 'know God on your own terms.'... One of the guiding impulses of the archangel Michael is free thinking" (2523:37). Even deliberately practiced evil in some cases is recommended as a means to spiritual "enlightenment"* (2540).

In other words, if these evil angels are actually messengers from God, the righteous character of God Himself is subverted. Thus, the implications for all of us are hardly insignificant.

## EVIL ANGELS, SELF-ESTEEM, CHRISTIAN POSITIVE CONFESSION MOVEMENT

Given that the devil's sin was pride and self-aggrandizement, it is not surprising that he would find it difficult to relinquish the self-love that produced his notoriety. Unfortunately, people rarely comprehend where a self-love philosophy that mimics the devil's may lead them. Those angel authors who define the devil as "ego-dominated personality," or similar euphemisms, need to rethink the implications (2525:165).

One of the most popular angel teachings is that people must learn to esteem and love themselves above all else, even above God Himself. But since they are God, it's really one and the same thing. Consider a few examples:

- "Our Being is a wonder that has no name ..." (2507:143).

- "We are not separate from God. We are God ... " (2514:105).

- "Self-love will nurture and nourish you.... Forge ahead into the everlasting wonderful effects of true self-love.... Simply allow feelings of love for yourself to emerge. Here they come. Now bask in the light of self-love.... Eventually, you find yourself fully in the golden light as you step forward on the path

47

of self-love with your angelic guide from the energy system of divine love. . . . Regardless of what you think is good or bad, right or wrong, . . . you must accept life as perfect in being just what it is. You are perfect in being who you are right now. . . human life is basically good. . . . You belong to heaven. Love your frailty and your humanity. It connects you to the creative force in the universe. . . . As you love the weakness of being human, you will grow strong inside. . . . Your [angel] teacher speaks. . . . 'You do love yourself, and this is okay. You are beautiful. . . . You are life divine—you are love itself. '. . . The more you generate this heavenly love for yourself the more magnificent life will be. . . . You are transformed by self-love. You thank your angel guide and then thank yourself" (2523:152,156-61).

- "You do not need to ask permission to love yourself, . . . nothing less is sufficient to you or God" (2512:98).
- "[Claiming] your own goodness . . . [will] further goodness on the earth" (2512:102).
- "You have a Buddha nature. . . . Here for your use in meditation is a powerful mantra. . . . 'I am love, I give love, I accept love . . .' " (2512:134).

The problem here is that this kind of self-esteem is based on the false concept that man in his true nature is divine (2541). And once the creation and the creature become God, then everything is reduced to the lowest common denominator and everything in the creation ends up with the same value. As the popular angels teach, "Nature has no favorites; it loves the frog and the fish equally; it supports the bird and the dog in the same ways. . . . You and we, your angelic teachers, are each essential parts of the system, neither more nor less" (2512:174).

If the tree and the rock and the dog and the frog are just as much God as everything else, then there is no fundamental difference between things. The irony is that this does not elevate man, it degrades him to the lowest element of nature.

Regardless, this kind of self-love and self-esteem teaching provides an entrance into the church through modern psychology and the positive confession movement (1970/2491). As noted earlier, many modern angel books use terminology directed toward Christians. One particularly potent occult text encourages readers to "endow each angel with the Will of God, the Love of Christ, and the Action of the Holy Spirit" (2525:31).

As we documented in *The Facts on the Faith Movement* (1970) and *The Facts on False Teachings in the Church* (339), the modern faith/positive confession leaders usually claim that they have received their unique teachings by direct divine revelation, occasionally through the mediation of angels. In these booklets, we have shown that such teachings are not biblical and could not have come from God or the good angels.

If the proponents' claims to supernatural inspiration are legitimate, then only one source of revelation remains. Perhaps it is significant that many spirit guides today have positive confession tapes on sale by their mediums. (The tapes by "DaBen" and "Orin" include such titles as, "Creating Money: The Spiritual Law of Prosperity and Abundance" and "Awakening Your Prosperity Self"; 575:231-32).

The popular angels also support and endorse positive confession teachings. Terry Lynn Taylor remarks, "Angels are the missing link in the chain of . . . self-help, self-development, and self-reliance programs. . . . Angels are heaven-sent agents who are always available to help you create heaven in your life" (2511:xvi).

The entire purpose of the book *Creating with the Angels: An Angel-Guided Journey into Creativity* is to use angels as a means to create success in every area of life (2523:vii-xi). One angel says, "Abundance is a state of mind that leads to physical manifestation of physical resources. But, more important, abundance is a state of spirit that initially awakens the minds to its creative possibilities. You are being led toward abundant thinking, feeling, loving, and participating in life so that you will be in a position to encourage wholism in every form wherever you find it" (2512:214).

The popular angels often speak in the same words and cite the same biblical passages as the modern Christian prosperity teachers. In *The Angels Within Us* we read, "The Bible also says, 'By your words you will be justified, and by your words you will be condemned' (Matt. 12:37); 'Death and life are in the power of the tongue' (Prov. 18:21); and, 'Thou shall also decree a thing, and it shall be established unto thee' (Job 22:28). Charles Fillmore, cofounder of Unity, wrote, 'The spoken word carries vibrations through the universal ether.... And Ernest Holmes, founder of the Church of Religious Science has written, 'The word gives form to the unformed...'" (2525:268).

Other teachings from this same occult book also reflect basic Christian prosperity beliefs: "We should meditate for an understanding of what produced the original condition of lack in our minds, speak the word for a healing of that mental-emotional condition, and then work consciously with the Angel of Abundance to reveal a divinely prosperous life" (2525:58). Or, "Abundance is the true nature of God.... And when you identify this Spirit of God within as your abundance, your consciousness becomes the principle of prosperity. The energy flows into manifestation *through* you, forever reproducing the vibration of your consciousness in the world of form" (2525:56-57). And, "When you contemplate the God Self I Am as infinite supply . . . you are deepening your awareness of the truth of your Reality" (2525:88,96).

One popular angel reveals, "I have promised you unlimited prosperity. . . . I am the Lord your healer, I heal all your diseases, restore health to you, and heal your wounds. This is not to come. It is. In truth, you are healed now; you are whole" (2525:263-64). The author tells his readers, "Make contact with the angel and ask how you are limiting your own success. Let him show you any false beliefs that may be blocking the flow from his perspective" (2525:286).

Other popular angel books advise:

- "True abundance is the ability to see the abundance that is already ours" (2507:Feb. 8).
- "I harness the power that enables me to realize all of my desires and objectives. . . . I have the power to know what is best" (2507:Jan. 11,21).
- "If we believe that we can have something . . . our higher selves—the parts of

our psyches that are in communication with the angels—will begin to create it for us" (2507:May 7).

- "I create my own miracles" (2507:Sept. 14).

That the modern Christian prosperity movement has aligned itself with the *same* teachings has given Christian leadership, across denominational lines, great concern that "faith teaching" is an avenue for the acceptance of doctrines of demons masquerading as angels. Consider the following statements made by several popular faith teachers.

Kenneth Copeland teaches, "When you use the Word in the name of Jesus they [angels] are obligated to follow your command" (1167:104). Gloria Copeland thinks that there may be at least 40,000 angels assigned to each believer; thus, "there is no shortage of angel power" (2545), and, "how long do you think it would take them to make you wealthy?" (1168:86). Unfortunately, "for the most part, the heirs of the promise have not been using the angel power available to them" (1168:65). Thus, "Your words put the angels to work on your behalf to bring to pass whatever you say . . . the words of your mouth bind them or loose them to work for you" (1168:88).

Charles Capps says that God supernaturally revealed the same truths to him. In *Angels* he says, "You need the supernatural beings of God working for you here on earth" (1170:80). In *Releasing the Ability of God* he states, "The Spirit of God spoke this into my spirit just as plainly as if I heard it with my ears. . . . He said: *'The Word says the angels are ministering spirits. These ministering spirits stand beside you daily and listen to the words that you speak. . . . But you are the one who tells them what to do"* (1169:100-01,105). Thus, "Angels will work for you. They will become involved in every area of your life—your home, your business, everything—but only to the extent that you allow them to operate" (1170:173).

Kenneth Hagin claims that in 1958 "the Lord Jesus suddenly appeared" before him, with an angel standing three feet behind Him. In *I Believe in Visions* he reveals, "He [Jesus] said, 'This is your angel.' 'My angel?' I asked. 'Yes, your angel, and if you will respond to him, he will appear to you as I will at times; and he will give you guidance and direction concerning the things of life . . ." (1179:93).

Jerry Savelle says that when we apply the principles of the Faith Movement, "the angels come on the scene to see that what you say comes to pass" (1171:45). John Osteen teaches that, "When you become a covenant-person, God assigns angels to watch you and your family . . ." (1172:45). Robert Tilton says, "When you talk positively about your dream, you not only release its substance, but you release the angels to work for you, causing your dream to come to pass" (1173:54). Benny Hinn also accepts the supposed ministry of the "faith" angels (1175:13).

Our concern is that Christians are being conditioned to have a particular expectation about angels that is not biblical, and that the angelic characteristics and promises are similar to what channelers with spirit guides claim about the spirits they contact.

In 1987, Kenneth Copeland gave a prophecy "from Jesus Christ" in which "Jesus" promised that new and dramatic angel manifestations were going to increase in the church and that many "will have visitations from the spirit realm." Concerning the angels, "Jesus" allegedly told Copeland:

A very outstanding time is on the way. A time is coming when there will be manifestation of angels more than usual, more than there has been in the past. Many of you are going to witness for yourselves the angel that has been put in charge and in command of your ministry and your life. Many of you are going to have visitations from the spirit realm. Many of you will have divinely appointed visions and dreams. . . . Oh, there's no time nor distance in the spirit realm. You'll be connected together at times like you've never witnessed before. Suddenly, you will be standing in that [spiritual] country, and suddenly you'll deliver a message and then suddenly you'll be brought back in your kitchen again. Oh, I have some outstanding things, sayeth the Lord (1178:9).

But this "Jesus" also denied his own deity when he said: "Don't be disturbed when people accuse you of thinking you are God. . . . They crucified me for claiming that I was God. But I didn't claim I was God; I just claimed I walked with Him and that He was in me. Hallelujah. That's what you are doing" (1178: see 2 Timothy 2:13). But in the Bible Jesus did claim to be God when He said, "He who has seen Me has seen the Father" (John 14:9 NASB), and "I and the Father are one" (John 10:30), and "Before Abraham was born, I am" (John 8:58; cf. John 1:1,14; Philippians 2:9; Hebrews 1:3,8-10; Titus 2:13; 2 Peter 1:1).

## EVIL ANGELS, SPIRITUAL DECEPTION, DEMON POSSESSION

We think that the reason demons are impersonating good angels today is not only for purposes of spiritual deception, theologically and philosophically, but also so that they can easily oppress and possess people through the guise of "higher consciousness" and "profound" angelic contact and "union with God." In order to do this, the angels must establish trust with their human contacts, and this may be accomplished when they appear as ghosts, poltergeist phenomena, good angels, or spirits of the dead. In other words, as different in nature than the evil spirits that they are. *A Book of Angels* tells us, "When a spirit enters a room, you feel a chill. . . . When it touches you or when its body passes through you, you feel an arctic cold. . . . *But angels are different, and no one who has seen an angel ever mistakes it for a ghost. Angels are remarkable for their warmth and light.* . . . You are flooded with laughter, happiness. . . . Angels give aid, or bring messages of hope, but what they do *not* do is wander, earth bound, like the lonely spirits who are dead" (2532:17-18).

Obviously, the popular angels camouflage themselves for hidden purposes. Sophy Burnham observes, "Why is it that angels like disguise? It seems they take whatever form the visited person is willing to accept; and sometimes no form at all—a dream, a thought, a surge of power, a sense of guidance" (2532:110).

Another ruse is when the angels discredit the Christian interpretation beforehand. Here, Christians are agents of the "devil," falling prey to false ideas and the consequences of their own misinterpretation of angels as demons. Guiley emphasizes, "If we start mistrusting the agents of light, fearing that they are demons in disguise, then we paralyze ourselves—which is precisely what the dark side wants. They would like us to trust nothing and encase ourselves trembling in fear. Fear is the best weapon the darkness has. Fear is the fertile breeding ground for all evil. . . . The engines of darkness have terrible power, but nonetheless, they cannot stand up to the greater, more awesome power of light and love" (2514:217).

Another deception is when demons seem as kind, loving, and protective as possible. "The angels love us always. . . . Think about how important trust is in your relationship to the angels. . . . I know that I can rely on the angels to teach me more about the true value of trust. . . . I know that the angels are taking good care of my soul. . . . Angels are truly everywhere—kind beings who only want to help and to love us. . . . We, your angelic teachers, . . . [promise] you are held eternally in divine love. . . . We, your angelic teachers, ask you to accept that . . . your long-term best interests are always being considered" (2542).

Besides sounding warm and sincere, the popular angels also appeal to people's egos, to what they want to hear, to their use of intuition alone rather than linked to rational thinking:

> Vulnerability isn't weakness; it is spiritual strength. . . . Living in the moment is one of the most significant universal teachings for improving the quality of your life. . . . Truth is the acceptance of your spirit's voice and a willingness . . . to honor the Force that brings you life. . . . Prayers . . . are met with immediate and direct angelic attention and intervention. . . . Life is confusing when you listen only to your rational thinking. . . . Your heart, your inner mind or spirit, is the great conveyor of wisdom and truth. . . . We, your angelic teachers, expect nothing of you save that you listen to your heart . . ." (2543).

By appealing to human naïveté and the baser instincts in the guise of heavenly spiritual guidance, demons are able to get people exactly where they want them: to possess them. Spirit possession is a universal phenomenon in pagan cultures throughout history. And with the modern revival of the New Age movement, the occult, Eastern religions, channeling, and now the popular angel phenomena, spirit possession is increasing in the West.

In *The Little Book of Angels,* by Peter L. Wilson, we are told that not only can we worship angels, but "there is another sort of angelic rite: one in which they are specifically evoked and called down, either to give and receive messages, or to enter into the body of the ritualist. In its simplest manifestation this results in the phenomenon of possession" (2544:50).

Some angel books even assume that angels already exist within people; it is hardly surprising therefore if advocates one day discover angels unexpectedly speaking out of them. *The Angels Within Us* is a book that teaches people how to become spirit possessed under the theme of enlightenment.* In typical euphemistic jargon, it claims, "Within your individualized energy field, in the microcosm called *you* are twenty-two Causal Powers, or angels, that control your conscious behavior and govern the manifestation of all forms and experiences in your personal life" (2525:9). At this point, possession is assumed whether or not anyone even believes in angels.

In some books, angelic meditations precondition the meditator to accept the concept of possession: "I will unite my spirit with the angels. . . ." Or, "We have the glorious opportunity to learn about the miraculous power of prayer and surrendering to a higher power" (2507:Jan. 23; Feb. 19).

As in the occult, various "energy" concepts are emphasized in popular angel literature to rationalize possession as merely contact with the "forces of nature." One book uses the theme of "nature" to mask possession: "You are *merging* with those on and off the Earth who are guiding your *energy* because you accept a different future for humanity. . . . So when you feel let down . . . talk to Nature. Nature is all around you no matter where on the Earth you live. Nature is all about *merger*, because it functions as one entirely interwoven system. You, like Nature, are becoming more and more *connected* with other light-workers in physical and non-physical reality" (2512:178, emphasis added). In other words, merger with "Nature" becomes the basis for spirit possession, rationalized conceptually as a merging or uniting with Nature's divine energies.

Another book tells people that "love is energy" (2546), and by so doing implies that possession by "angels," or their energy, is a form of *love.* "Many cultures initiate their own spiritual students, and we, your angelic teachers, also initiate our own. Initiation requires you to release preconceived ideas about the period of training you are entering and to accept the higher good and spiritual guidance that places you under the protection [love] and inspiration of the Universe . . . " (2512:142).

Here are several statements by angels or angel authors concerning the "merger" with divine energies:

- Inner authority is spiritual energy born from union with the Divine (2512:97).
- The spiritual energy of your life is welling up deep inside you from the core of your being and circling your spine to renew your life. You are in the process of managing this intense emerging energy so that you will direct it toward awakening the God within (2512:110).
- Each time you allow this flow of creative energy—angel energy—to stream through your being, you expand this energy . . . (2523:xv).
- And the more that you are *aware* of this divine consciousness, the more its dynamic energies can fill the physical-plane person you thought you were. And when the infusion is complete, you awaken and understand that you embody all the Powers of God. . . . You feel the energy building in consciousness . . . your decisions will seem to be made independent of your conscious mind . . ." (2525:50).
- It is the giving up of the personality, a replacing of the human consciousness with divine

consciousness. . . . There is a fading out of one consciousness and a fading in of another . . . (2525:187).

Consider also the words of someone who "tapped into the energy" of an angel. "I felt a tremendous surge of energy move into my back and heard the words, 'I am the strength of Jehovah, mighty in battle to slay those who would defile' " (2525:163). Yet in the same book, the student is encouraged to be possessed by the angel of death and rebirth: "This angel represents the force of metamorphosis, and its function is to . . . condition our consciousness for the final infusion of the God-self energy. . . . This divine agent [is] . . . the Master of Death" (2525:183).

In most occult traditions the theme of death is synonymous with possession because the old person "dies" in the process of transformation to possession. They become a "new" entity in which their old consciousness is now "enlightened." The possessing spirit has complete control—sometimes permanent, lifelong control—of the person's consciousness. This theme is touched on briefly in the section on Eastern Gurus* and in more depth in Tal Brooke's *Riders of the Cosmic Circuit* (249).

Biblical, or godly, angels possess no one. There is no biblical record or historical account of a good angel possessing any person anywhere. Demons, of course, have a long history of possessing people.

In conclusion, we live in an age when people need a more critical attitude toward spiritual phenomena than they usually possess, and this includes having greater discernment toward many practices and beliefs that claim to be Christian. While no one denies the vital and godly ministry of the good angels, the one who ignores the multifaceted activities of the evil angels is the person whose soul may be at risk.

# ASTROLOGY

## INFO AT A GLANCE

**Description.** Astrology is based on the assumption that the stars and planets mysteriously influence people's lives. It teaches that this influence begins at birth and continues throughout a person's life. The *Shorter Oxford English Dictionary* defines astrology as "the art of judging the occult influence of the stars upon human affairs."

**Founder.** Unknown.

**How does it claim to work?** Because the heavens allegedly influence or determine our future, astrology claims to be able to "read" how the heavenly bodies affect people's lives, and so offer helpful counsel about the present and the future.

**Scientific evaluation.** Discredited.

**Examples of occult potential.** Spiritism, in particular. However, a large number of occult practices are associated with astrology including cabalism, numerology,* magic, and witchcraft.

**Major problem.** As an ancient pagan system of divination, astrology easily traps people in occult practices and philosophy.

**Biblical/Christian evaluation.** Astrology is prohibited by name (Isaiah 47:13) and function (divination,* idolatry—Deuteronomy 4:19; 18:9-12; Jeremiah 19:13; Acts 7:42).

**Potential dangers.** The consequences of false predictions in all areas of life (finance, relationships, health, and so on), spiritistic influence, spirit-possession, or even death.

*Note:* Most of this chapter is condensed from the authors' *Astrology* (83), which provides additional documentation.

53

## INTRODUCTION AND INFLUENCE

Approximately a billion people worldwide have some degree of faith in astrology. Science writer, engineer, and astrology critic Lawrence Jerome has written, "The twentieth century has seen a tremendous upswing in the fortunes of astrologers. Easily one quarter of the nearly four billion people living on the earth believe in and follow astrology to some extent" (1193:1).

In America, polls variously estimate the acceptance of astrology at between 20 million to 40 million people. A Gallup poll cited by the *National and International Religion Report* for July 4, 1988, estimated that ten percent of evangelical Christians believe in astrology. Clearly, astrology is not just a passing fad. In the United States alone, it grosses billions of dollars each year.

Not even many religions can claim to have the influence that astrology has. The *Encyclopedia Britannica* observes that astrology has "a sometimes extensive... influence in many civilizations both ancient and modern" (1200:219). Professor Franz Cumont, a leading authority on ancient astrology and curator of the Royal Museum of Antiquities at Brussels (1201:IX), has stated that "up to modern times [astrology] has exercised over Asia and Europe a wider dominion than any religion has ever achieved... [and it has] exercised an endless influence on the creeds and ideas of the most diverse peoples..." (1201:XI,XIII).

In the United States, back in 1933, there was a revival of interest in astrology. At that time well-known occultist and philosopher Manly P. Hall bragged, "Astrology today has probably a greater number of advocates than ever before in its long and illustrious history.... Astrology and all its branches is sweeping over America in a wave of enthusiasm" (1203:9). In our own day, astrologers West and Toonder have concluded that astrology currently "enjoys a popularity unmatched since the decline of Rome" (1204:1). Astronomers Culver and Ianna refer to this modern interest as "the greatest resurgence in astrology" since the Renaissance (1205:IX).

Bernard Gittelson, former public relations consultant representing the West German government, the European Common Market, and the U.S. Department of Commerce, is now a New Age human behavior researcher. Gittelson has calculated that the circulation of newspapers and magazines carrying astrological columns in the United States, Europe, Japan, and South America is over 700 million (1213:338). Concerning France and Germany he states: "In both... it is common for companies to have an astrologer and graphologist on staff, to be consulted in matters of hiring, firing, and promotions. I learned this first hand..." (1213:63-64). A Cable News Network (CNN) report cited astrologers who made the incredible claim that "at least 300 of the Fortune 500 [companies] use astrologers in one way or another" (1219:5).

Even our days of the week are reminders of the influence of astrology:

Monday = moon day

Tuesday = Mars' day (day of Tiw—the Norse "Tyr"—the Martian god of war)

Wednesday = Mercury's day (Woden's day, the Norse Odin, god of the runes*)

Thursday = Jupiter's day (Thor's day, the Nordic Jupiter, god of Thunder)

Friday = Venus' day (Frigg's day, wife of Odin, goddess of marriage)

Saturday = Saturn's day

Sunday = sun day

An examination of the books in print on astrology reveals that this occult art of divination has been applied to literally hundreds of subjects, including pets, babies and children, gambling, cooking, medicine, criminology, dating and marriage, biochemistry, meditation, sex, politics, economics, psychology, feminism, and the Bible (83:19-20). No wonder astrologers confidently assert "there is no area of human experience to which astrology cannot be applied" (1214:60). Many occult practices (e.g., numerology* and tarot cards*) have logical connections to astrology; many world religions and religious cults have their own brands of astrology (e.g., Hinduism and theosophy). Astrologers have also attempted to integrate many of the sciences (e.g., medicine and psychology) with their practice (75-82; 1215:209).

In the field of education, astrology is offered for credit on some high school and college campuses (1216:130). In 1972, the spiritist, Rosicrucian, and astrologer Mae Wilson-Ludlam taught the first accredited high school astrology course (1217:198). But now astrology's influence extends to classes taught at Emory University in Atlanta (1217:175), Stanford University (1216:133), the University of California Extension (1216:125), and to the granting of Ph.D.s in astrology from some universities, such as the University of Pittsburgh (1215).

In 1988, astrology made headlines when it was exposed as influencing the highest level of U.S. national government, the White House. According to Chief of Staff Donald Regan in *For the Record: From Wall Street to Washington*, "Virtually every major move and decision the Reagans made" was based upon the astrological advice of Joan Quigley, Mrs. Reagan's astrologer" (1206:3; refs. 1207-10). The effect this had on people was mixed. But as noted astronomers Culver and Ianna in their text *Astrology: True or False—a Scientific Evaluation* observed: "Astrologers . . . have hailed the acceptance of astrology at the highest levels of government in one of the most powerful nations on earth as a confirmation of its legitimacy" (1195:IX).

What is clear from all of this is that around the world astrology is widely influential today. It has had, and continues to have, a powerful impact in the lives and thinking of hundreds of millions of people.

## BASIC TERMS AND CONCEPTS

Despite its popularity, astrology is confusing to the average person because of its complexity and many unfamiliar words.

The *zodiac* is an imaginary "belt" of sky comprising the 12 astrological signs that the ancients illustrated by mythological figures, both human and animal. In other words, the mythological "signs" of the zodiac are overlayed upon the actual clusters, or constellations, of stars. And importantly, the "signs" exist irrespective of the actual positions of the constellations to which they are said to refer.

The *signs* are the 12 "signs of the zodiac," also known as "sun signs." Everyone is said to be born under one of these 12 signs (Pisces the fish, Leo the lion, Gemini the twins, Taurus the bull, and so on.). Astrologers often group the signs according to psychological aspects or types.

The *houses* are the 12 divisions of the zodiac that are said to correspond symbolically to every area of life. The houses are also imaginary, and the planets are said to travel through the houses, influencing each area of life as they do.

The *horoscope* is a "map" of the heavens for the time of birth, or for any time thereafter. On the horoscope, or chart, an astrologer plots the positions of the planets, signs, and houses, and then from this "map," after interpreting numerous complex rules, many of which vary greatly from one astrologer to another, the astrologer gives a "reading."

Technically, a *delineation* is the name given to an astrological "reading." This is an interpretation resulting from the combination of two or more astrological principles. *Analysis* or *synthesis* is the "complete" interpretation of the whole chart.

There is also the concept of *rulership*. Astrologers believe that each planet "rules" a sign of the Zodiac. For example, Mercury rules, or influences, Gemini and Virgo; Venus is said to rule Taurus and Libra; Saturn Capricorn; Neptune Pisces; and so on. In addition, the signs and their ruling planets are related to certain houses.

Another important term is *aspect*, which refers to the angles between the planets as plotted on a horoscope chart. Certain angles are interpreted as "good" and other angles are "bad," while still others are "neutral" and acquire their "goodness" or "badness" from other astrological indicators. For example, two planets angled at 90 degrees to each other (called a "square") is considered a bad influence. However, two planets angled at 120 degrees to each other (called a "trine") is considered a good influence.

In addition to "good" or "bad" angles, astrological delineations must also take into consideration whether or not the planets are "good" or "bad." Saturn and Mars, for example, are considered "bad"; Venus and Jupiter, "good." But what is the basis for these angles and planets being defined as "good" or "bad"? The astrologers don't know; they simply accept these definitions as they have been handed down. Some astrologers say that these definitions result from thousands of years of observing human experience. Others no longer use the "good" or "bad" designations. They have substituted milder descriptions, such as "externalization" and "internalization," "active" and "passive," "hard" and "soft," "difficult" and "easy." Still, there is no one final, authoritative tradition that has come down through history that all astrologers follow. This is why there are many conflicting astrological theories (83:56-60).

*Transits* are another essential concept. By determining when a planet crosses, or transits, a specific point on the horoscope chart, the astrologer feels he can advise a client as to "favorable" or "unfavorable" conditions. Just as there are good and bad planets and angles, there are good and bad times for undertaking activities. This was why Hitler planned his war strategy by the stars and why other world leaders throughout history have leaned on advice of the stars.

It is evident from all of this that astrological interpretations are not only complicated but highly subjective. How does the astrologer know that Venus or a trine is good, that Mars or a square is bad? How does he know that the first house represents personality, the second house money, the third house communication, the eighth house death, the tenth house occupation? On what factual basis do astrologers make their assertions?

Some astrologers claim their definitions are derived from numerology,* from the meanings allegedly inherent in numbers, which are then related to astrological theory. But if so, where is a factual basis for the numerological meanings? Why don't all astrologers agree on this? There is also disagreement concerning how to divide the 12 houses. A given house for one astrologer may be a different house for another; therefore, entirely different influences would be suggested (1205:62-64).

Astrological interpretations also rest on other questionable foundations. An astrologer can choose from up to 30 different zodiacs (1235:25), 28 different signs (1205:87), and ten different house systems (1236:64).

Even after wading through all this, the astrologer's headache has still not ended. He must choose whether to use the concepts of *nodes, triplicities,* and *quadruplicities.* The moon's nodes relate to the intersection of the moon's orbit with the apparent path of the sun among the stars (the ecliptic). These supposed "intersections" are said to exert certain influences. And there are also the influences from the nodes of the planets, the points at which the orbits of the planets intersect the ecliptic. *Triplicities* refer to how the four astrological elements of fire, earth, air, and water each relate to three signs. For example, Libra, Gemini, and Aquarius are "air" signs. *Quadruplicities* refer to how the three astrological characteristics called "cardinal," "fixed," and "mutable" each relate to four signs. For example, Leo, Scorpio, Aquarius, and Taurus are "fixed" signs. And, as you may suspect by now, the concepts of nodes, triplicities, and quadruplicities, like all other astrological principles, have many diverse meanings and interpretations.

If all this is not enough mental gymnastics, the astrologer can also consider *dignities* and *debilities;* that is, how the influence of a planet is increased (dignity) or decreased (debility) by its placement on the chart. There are dozens of such conditions (1205:8). He also determines whether the signs are positive (active) or negative (passive). And each astrologer must pay special attention to a client's moon sign, and to the rising, or ascending, sign (1192:17,338).

And after all this, the astrologer still must choose which method of prediction he will use. There are three common methods: 1) the previously mentioned transits, 2) primary directions, and 3) secondary progressions (1192:315). And, "No phase of astrology is subject to such differences of opinion" as the means of prediction (1192:121).

Even with all of this, consider that Noel Tyl wrote a 12-volume series, *The Principles and Practices of Astrology*, which is considered introductory material! No wonder there is no one final astrological tradition that all astrologers follow. It is understandable why there are so many conflicting astrological theories. Yet, millions of people still commit their lives to following these unproven assumptions.

## DIFFICULTIES IN CHART INTERPRETATION

Interpreting the horoscope chart is like interpreting Rorschach "inkblots." Not only are there all manner of inkblots, but different interpretations for the same inkblot. In the same way there are any number of factors or variables by which to interpret a horoscope chart, and astrologers disagree on many principles of interpretation. The reason for this is that their interpretations spring from their astrological schooling, their personalities, goals, and purposes, as well as many other factors. Joanne Sanders, an astrologer and coordinator of the Washington, D.C., Astrology Forum, believes that astrologers' "readings vary with the differences in their philosophical outlooks" (1233:14).

There are several basic reasons why such wide disagreement over interpretations exists. A horoscope comprises 30 to 40 major factors, and the astrologer must also interpret another 60 to 70 minor indicators. As a result, there are almost an infinite number of possible combinations, permutations, and meanings.

Doris Chase Doane, president of the American Federation of Astrologers, has admitted that the chief cause that up-and-coming astrologers fail their entrance examination is their inability to properly erect, or construct, a chart (to accurately list and plot all of the indicators). She confesses, *This is the most common reason—the pitfall—for students failing in this and higher examinations.* They do not know how to erect a chart accurately" (1265:38). She has further calculated the *least* possible number of different combinations resulting from the most basic or simple chart. Given 12 signs, 10 planets (8 plus the sun and moon), 12 houses, and 10 aspects, she arrives at the figure of 5.4 times $10^{68}$ possible minimum combinations. This number is roughly equivalent to the estimated number of atoms in the known universe (1237:1)!

Romanian astrologer Sir John Manolesco has also illustrated the complexity an astrologer

faces. He has concluded that of the tens of thousands of astrologers in the Western world there are less than a hundred who can claim to have mastered the subject. "There are at least 43 factors—planets, houses, aspects, strengths and weaknesses, ascendent, critical degrees, sun and moon polarities, constellations, etc.—which combine and influence one another in a thousand different ways. In this labyrinth of complexities, the average (still worse, the untrained) astrologer is as puzzled as his client" (1218:130).

Keep in mind that each astrologer must also obey the cardinal rule of chart interpretation: No indicator can be judged in isolation from any other factor. But it is virtually impossible for any astrologer to know all the indicators, to synthesize the chart "in context," for he knows only a fraction of the total astrological "reality" before him. And how may any reading be truly accurate when one is faced with contradictory interpretations of the data (1241:3)?

Perhaps an analogy will be helpful. Think of a huge, detailed map of the United States. The facts to be remembered on the map may include 50 states, 3000 counties, and at least 6000 chief cities and towns. Then there are highways, rivers, mountains, lakes, parks, and points of interest. In addition, the map's key contains many symbols for interpreting the map properly (e.g., symbols for boundaries, distances, city sizes, types of road).

If this map were an astrologer's chart, how would a person interpret it if he discovered that other maps contradicted this map? What if he discovered no agreement as to the number of states, counties, cities, or their boundaries? What if each map defined the symbols differently? What could he conclude about using any of the maps? Wouldn't he conclude this to be a hopeless situation?

Many astrologers recognize the problems, and to get around them they turn to another source of information. "Before interpreting a chart, it is very good to do one thing: either silently, or aloud, ask for clear guidance from the powers that you choose to create . . . from your higher self, from the divine . . . ask, and you shall receive . . ." (1199:104). The astrologer's only option, then, is either to guess or to trust in a supposed "higher" power, or psychic revelations, to sort things out. We will see below that this often means spiritistic guidance.

To further complicate matters of interpretation, astrologers have different kinds of charts to choose from, all with varying indicators and rules. One authority lists 14 different charts, such as the "solar return," "lunar return," "solar equilibrium," "ingress," and "johndro." (1242:118). Theoretically, there are as many different charts as there are individual schools or systems of astrology, and since each system or school can develop its own chart, the number of different charts must number in the hundreds (refs. 1243-1260/1222/1209/1196). And then there are different types of astrology, such as horary, natal, mundane, electional, medical, and so on. This is why leading authorities advise the following: "As authorities vary in approach to, and rules for delineating the horary chart, you can best prepare yourself by studying one authority in depth" (1265:49). And, "If it works for you, use it" (1264:121).

Viewed worldwide, astrological contradictions are even more apparent. James Braha observes that in India "a seemingly infinite number of rules and astrological techniques have been developed by the Indians" (1246:X). Over and over again he states that they contradict Western methods. In ancient Babylon, the practice of "draconic astrology" (still used today) presents entirely different beliefs, practices and sets of rules (1250:1-58,95-123,143-89). In China there are entirely different astrologies (1248/1266/1246). In Mexico, "Aztec astrology" is different from the above, and so it goes (1249:1-90). Within each of these schools, or systems, subsystems also contradict each other.

Furthermore, every chart indicator, potentially, has not only an exoteric (outer) but also an esoteric (inner) reality, which supposedly unveils "the hidden meaning" (1242:34). Astrologers believe that "each planet in a sign holds a multitude of implications. Besides each sign having an exoteric ruler, considered to be the pure outer expression of the sign's characteristics, a sign has an esoteric ruler" (1242:34).

How did such a hopeless situation originate? Astrologer Richard Nolle describes the educa-

tional "evolution" of an astrologer, which we summarize as: a) begin by learning the "traditional" meanings as they are given (but these are contradictory and the student soon realizes this); therefore, b) assimilate the meanings into "our own frame of reference" to "develop our own particular and unique astrological perspective." In other words, there are no objective standards. Believe whatever you wish. Use the standard text interpretations (which vary), but then feel free to reject the standard interpretations and discover "the answer is within yourselves," and you will be able to "make your own discoveries" (1236:1-2). This is why Nolle acknowledges there are as many different astrologies as there are astrologers (1263:22), and that chart interpretation does not utilize "objective laws" but "intuitive selections" (1236:84).

Someone has satirically said that the process of becoming an astrologer is one of beginning with a state of initial confusion, leading to a state of greater confusion, which is finally rationalized by "intuitive insight." Clearly, the theories of astrology, the symbols, the indicators, and so on carry no ultimate definitive meaning. They are merely vehicles to stimulate the thinking of the astrologer. From that point on it is cosmic roulette as to astrological interpretation.

## ASTROLOGY AND SCIENCE

No one has ever been known to make a serious study of astrology and then reject it, . . . (Nicholas DeVore, The Encyclopedia of Astrology; 1192:VIII).

If astrology were valid, some hard evidence should have accumulated after thousands of years. Instead, astrology has failed every scientific analysis or test to which it has been subjected (science writer Kurt Butler; 1143:106).

Astrologers everywhere adamantly proclaim that astrology is a true science and rationally consistent. Astrologer June Wakefield emphasizes, "Astrology is a science. It is not a pseudoscience . . ." (1196:11). Some astrologers, like Carroll Righter, even go so far as to refer to themselves as scientists (1267:1).

So how can astrology be called a science? Astronomers Culver and Ianna point out there is "nothing more infuriating to the scientist, particularly the astronomer, than the continuing claim . . . of astrologers that astrology is a science . . ." (1195:ix-xi).

Astrologers cannot dispute the fact that there is not one legitimate scientific body anywhere in the entire world that accepts astrology as a science. The reason is simple. Astrology rejects the scientific method and does not qualify as being scientific. Purdue University astronomer Dr. Sherman Kanagy, after three years of investigating astrology, concluded: "Generally what is being said is that the basic claims of astrologers as they [the scientists] understand them are completely inconsistent with what they believe they already know from their own fields of expertise" (87:22). For example, scientific data from astronomy, meteorology, psychology, biology, physics, chemistry, medicine, and physiology contradict astrological theories.

*Arguments For*

Many arguments are routinely set forth by astrologers as evidence that astrology is true. However, not a single one of these arguments cites valid reasons to believe in astrology. Here are some of their main arguments with a brief response (modified from 1101:175).

1. Astrology is true because it is found in many cultures. (So are racism and totalitarianism.)

2. Many great scholars have believed in astrology. (Scholars can be biased or wrong; also, far more scholars have not believed in astrology than have believed in it.)

3. Astrology is true because it has great antiquity and durability. (So has bigotry and murder.)

4. Some kinds of extraterrestrial, or "cosmobiological," influences do exist. (Scientists agree that extraterrestrial influences exist, such as the moon's influence on the tides, but the same scientists also agree such influences have nothing to do with astrology.)

5. Astrology is true because it is based on observation. (If it has been observed to be consistent, then why do astrologers disagree so widely?)

6. Astrology is true because it is an art or philosophy but not a science. (Art does not make truth claims, and disciplines like art and philosophy have factual reasons that judge and support the disciplines. Astrology does not. To argue that astrology is a "scientific art" seems to place astrology in the realm of the unfalsifiable; 87:100.)

7. Elements of modern science and psychology, such as quantum physics and synchronicity, have proven astrology to be true. (Nowhere can quantum physics be applied to proving the theories of astrology; 1205:36-37. Furthermore, synchronicity (meaningful coincidences) is a meaningless concept scientifically. In relation to astrology the supposed correspondences do not in fact exist; 87:116-18.)

8. Astrology is true because it works. (Much of the time it does not work. When astrology does work, we shall see that it works for reasons unrelated to astrological theories.)

Having briefly stated these common arguments for astrology, we will now examine three scientific studies that are claimed by astrologers as proof for astrology. It must first be said that parts of astrology are simply not scientifically testable because of their very nature. For example, the claim to ascertain occult influences lies outside the boundaries of science ("intuition,"* mystical planetary "vibrations," symbolic correspondences, etc.). Nevertheless, both astrologers and scientific investigators of astrology agree that there are definite astrological principles which merit scientific testing (1270:1; 1235:24;1236:82;1263:23).

*Statistical Tests*

*The Mayo-White-Eysenck Study.* This study attempted to determine if astrology could predict in advance whether the personality of adults would be introverted or extroverted. It was done with 2324 adults who had their extroversion and introversion scores tabulated on the Eysenck Personality Inventory (EPI). These scores were then correlated with astrological predictions. The conclusion: *marginal* (astrologers read: favorable) results were obtained that could not be accounted for by chance alone. Five additional studies were done in the same area, and three of these studies did not support the Mayo-White-Eysenck findings.

Eysenck himself, in later research (confirmed by other researchers), came to believe that "the entire astrological effect [of the original study] was due to the subjects' expectations and familiarity with the characteristics associated with their Zodiac sign" (1271:35). The Mayo-White-Eysenck study therefore cannot be used as evidence for validating astrology (1271:36).

*The Guardian-Smithers Study.* This massive study used official census records to test 2.3 million people and compare their occupations with their sun signs. Education professional Alan Smithers used and compared the predictions of 15 of the "most expert and well-qualified astrologers" in Britain. Although a mild correlation was noted, Smithers himself remained unconvinced. He decided that most of the data "can be explained in other ways" (for example, seasonal factors, social habits, belief in astrology). After a later reevaluation, the group of research scientists and psychologists who reexamined the study concluded: "Smither's results...can be explained by statistical fluctuations and self-attribution effects.... The study has limitations ... nevertheless, we suggest that if there were underlying truths [to astrology] they would shine through despite these limitations. They certainly do not support sun-sign astrology" (1272:336).

*Gauquelin's "Neo-Astrology."* Few individuals have done as much research into astrology and possible related cosmic effects as the late French scientist Michel Gauquelin. Yet astrologers who cite Gauquelin as a "big gun" in support of astrology shoot down their own beliefs in the process. The most Gauquelin claimed to discover was minor statistical aberrations that might indicate a cosmo-biological effect. He never claimed to validate traditional astrology in any sense.

For example, Gauquelin's "Mars effect" involved a study that attempted to test whether or not the birth dates of 2088 sports champions were "statistically significant" according to the position of Mars. Gauquelin claimed to have found some slight evidence for this, although he did not consider it an astrological effect (2686:33-46; cf. pp. 55-60). The problem for astrologers is that the "Mars effect" has never

been confirmed in 30 years of subsequent studies. The most that could be concluded was that "the success of replication is a matter of some debate" (1205:216; the controversy may be traced in 1271-75). In 1995, the results of an exhaustive 12-year study by a committee of French scientists was published. Their attempt to independently replicate Gauquelin's findings failed; it offered "no evidence for the Mars effect" (2685:62).

However, Gauquelin's studies on traditional astrology were entirely negative. In one study he tested the alleged influence of the zodiac in relationship to professional success and discovered that: "The results were entirely negative" (1276:57). When astrologers objected that "professional success" was "far too crude a criterion to reveal the astral subtlety of Zodiacal influences," Gauquelin established further elaborate testing to satisfy their complaints. In these tests he reported the same negative conclusions as before.

Gauquelin also tested astrologers' claims concerning personality traits and zodiacal predictions. For this test, 52,188 personality traits were systematically collected from 2000 subjects. What did Gauquelin find? Only that astrological predictions received "a fatal blow" (1276:64).

Again, Gauquelin himself never claimed to have proved astrology, despite the claims of many astrologers that he did. This is evident from the books he authored, including *The Scientific Basis of Astrology: Myth or Reality?* (1277), and his 1979 text, *Dreams and Illusions of Astrology.* In the former, he concluded, "Every attempt, whether of astrologers or scientists, to produce evidence of the validity of astrological laws has been in vain" (1277:139; cf. 1205:64/1269:117-19/1278:7-10).

In his overall research on "astrobiology," Gauquelin wavered back and forth from excitement over possible findings to discouragement and uncertainty over the end results and problems of interpretation. Unfortunately, his life ended, in his words, still being "tormented by [these] two feuding demons" (1269:180-81). At the time of his suicide, he apparently gave instructions that all his data be destroyed (2685). His results have never been subjected to conclusive testing and evaluation by others. As with the "Mars effect," his other results are largely *his* results.

Gauquelin's research is at best interesting, but it cannot be cited as evidence for astrology. There can be no doubt that real scientific support in favor of astrology is nonexistent.

*Arguments Against*

*Sun-sign research.* No other single factor in the astrology chart is given more weight than the sun sign under which people are supposedly born. This is why newspaper and magazine horoscope columns single this out.

In the study entitled "An Empirical Test of Popular Astrology," researcher Ralph Bastedo carefully analyzed the content of astrological literature. He found that it revealed 2375 specific adjectives for the 12 sun signs. Each sign was described by about 200 adjectives. For example, a person who is a "Leo" is strong, domineering, tough—a born leader; a person who is a "Taurus" is indecisive, timid, insecure—not a leader. Also in Bastedo's test, 1000 people were examined for 33 variables, including physical attractiveness, leadership ability, personality traits, and social and religious belief. Bastedo concluded that this test failed to prove any astrological prediction. He said, "*All* of our results can be attributed to random chance" (1279:34, emphasis added).

Tests have also been conducted to determine if the planets influence compatibility in marriage. The results of one test, which involved 2978 couples who married and 478 couples who divorced, proved that people's astrological signs did not significantly alter the divorce rate among those born under "compatible" or "incompatible" signs (1280:211).

Astrologers also claim that scientists and politicians are favored by one sun sign or another. But John McGervy, in doing research on this topic, compared birth dates of 16,634 scientists and 6475 politicians and found *no* correlation to substantiate the astrologers' claims. He concluded beyond doubt that the distribution of signs among these two professions was as random as for the general public (1281:53).

In addition, Dean and Mather have "searched over a thousand books and hundreds of journals and . . . written to hundreds of astrologers around the world, but were unable to find anybody anywhere who could provide a demonstration that the traditional signs actually work the way they are supposed to work" (1195:217).

In conclusion, current scientific evidence shows there is no validity to the astrologers' assertion that your sun sign influences your life. But what about the influence of the moon sign?

*Moon-sign research.* Second in importance to the sun, the moon is one of the most vital considerations in astrology. In the popular press, one often hears about the alleged "influence" of the moon in one or another context. Astrologers speak about the "extensive research" proving that the moon influences human behavior in a variety of ways. But nothing has been proven.

In "The Moon Was Full and Nothing Happened," three researchers discuss the results of their 1985 meta-analysis of 37 specific studies examining the relationship between the four phases of the moon and abnormal, criminal, or deviant behavior. They concluded there was no causal relationship (1282:139). This analysis was first reported in volume 97 of the *Psychological Bulletin*.

Meta-analysis is an important statistical procedure because:

> It allows reviewers to do three things: 1) estimate the overall or combined probability of results from different studies; 2) assess the size of relationships when results are averaged; and 3) identify factors that might help to explain why some studies have obtained apparently reliable results while others have not. This meta-analysis differed in one important respect from those that have been undertaken to resolve controversies in other areas: It included a re-analysis of results from previously published studies (1282:130).

The above conclusions are supported by the eminent astrologer George O. Abell, who confirms in his *Exploration of the Universe* (1982, p. 138) that careful studies that use much larger samples and better controls "*fail* to confirm evidence for such lunar effects" (87:157, emphasis added). In response, astrologers complain that the scientific tests of *individual* astrological factors, such as sun and moon signs, are invalid because astrology only works when *all* the relevant factors in a chart are observed and properly correlated. But adding additional chart factors, including the planets, houses, and aspects, changed nothing. As reported in the *Journal of Clinical Psychology*, volume 33, "*There was no support* for any relationship between personality and astrological parameters in 632 comparative tests" (1195:215, emphasis added).

*Horoscope research.* Numerous independent studies have all concluded that even if one consults the world's best astrologers, there is little agreement among them as to the meaning of a chart. Geoffrey Dean, who has investigated astrology for over 15 years, concludes:

> . . . studies have found mean [average] correlations that are . . . poor. Vernon Clark (1961), in a famous blind trial involving some of the world's best astrologers (for example, Charles Carter and Marc Edmund Jones), obtained results that on inspection reveal 0.13 for 20 astrologers matching ten pairs of charts to case histories, and 0.12 for 30 astrologers judging ten pairs of charts for intelligence. Marcharg (1975) found 0.17 for ten astrologers judging 30 charts for alcoholism. Ross (1975) found only 0.23 for two astrologers rating 102 charts on 5–point scales of the Psychological Screening Inventory, even though both had received a similar training, both taught astrology at the same college in Miami, and both followed Rudhyar's person-centered approach. Vidmar (1979) obtained results that on inspection reveal 0.10 for 28 astrologers matching five pairs of charts to case histories. Fourie et. al. (1980) found 0.16 for two astrologers rating 48 charts on 18 9–point scales of the 16 PF Inventory. Steffert (1983) obtained results that on inspection reveal 0.03 for 27 astrologers judging the charts of 20 married couples for marital happiness. In other words, *in none of these studies was the agreement between astrologers better than useless* (1234:267, emphasis added).

It is not only astrologers who are in the dark concerning the meaning of their charts; their clients are also. Independent studies conducted concerning the clients of astrologers reveal that people who have horoscopes interpreted cannot tell the difference between a "right" chart and a "wrong" chart. That is, an astrologer's client is just as likely to identify someone else's horoscope, rather than their own, as being the one that best describes them.

The tests showed surprising results. They revealed people were as happy with wrong charts (someone else's) as they were with right charts (their own). Researchers also found that astrologers' interpretations "fit" people even when the interpretations were from the wrong chart. These results could not be explained away by astrologers blaming poor chart interpretation or by astrologers claiming the people lacked knowledge of themselves (1283:30/1101:179-80).

In a survey of several other scientific studies determing whether people could tell right charts from wrong charts, Dean reported the studies showed the answer to be: "Unanimously no. The overall trend is not even in the right direction" (1101:180; cf. 1283:30).

*Reversed charts.* Other tests have revealed that people cannot tell authentic charts from charts that have been deliberately reversed. Studies show people rated reverse charts just as highly as authentic charts. Obviously, reverse charts are diametrically the opposite of authentic charts, and people should not be happy with the interpretations. Therefore, the conclusions people drew from the deliberately reversed charts were very wrong, which shows they were completely deceived.

For example, Dean conducted a carefully controlled test which left no room for ambiguity as far as the results were concerned. In his study he concluded:

> The "reversed" charts were derived from the subject's correct one, keeping the same sun sign, but with the planetary aspects changed to indicate the *opposite* personality trait. . . . Whether the horoscope was accurate (correct) or not had no bearing on whether the predictions were perceived to be accurate. These results are most easily understood as indicating that (1) persons are not affected in any way

whatsoever by astrological influences, and (2) the symbols in the chart bear no relationship to the personality traits of the individual they are supposed to represent (1195:219).

Should we be surprised that some astrologers use reversed charts and find them just as useful as regular charts? Clinical psychologist, parapsychologist, and astrologer Ford Hunter, founder of the Chthonian Society, "uses a reversed-horoscope method in reading a person's natal chart." He says, "I . . . reverse the chart to find where the energy flow is going" (1216:118).

Ultimately, these tests show that people tend to accept charts as valid, for a variety of reasons, and wholly unrelated to astrological theory. These reasons include gullibility, expectation, insecurity, attraction to the astrologer, selective memory (remembering only the "hits"), positive thinking, the paying of fees, body language, manipulation by the astrologer, emotional need, and so on. Dean lists 20 different ways in which astrologers can make their practice *seem* to work and make their clients satisfied, and none of them require astrology to be true (1234:263). Yet every astrologer claims that astrological effects are at work.

Researchers have also found that astrologers who used charts were no better in their judgments than those astrologers who did *not* use charts, who were just guessing. In fact, astrologers who used charts actually made slightly *worse* judgments. In 1985, Dean conducted a study reported in *Correlation*, the astrological communities' statistical journal. Using 90 astrologers and 240 subjects, he tested astrology's assumption that astrologers who use charts *must* perform better than astrologers who do not use charts, but are merely guessing. One particular statement recorded by Dean stands out: "If anything, the astrologers' judgments were made worse by looking at birth charts" (1234:266).

*Testing astrological predictions.* Another way to test astrology is to examine the success rate for specific (or even general) predictions of future events. Astrologers say that the proof of astrology can be seen in its high rate of successful, or accurate, predictions. But objective testing by outside researchers has conclusively shown that most forms of astrological predictions have an extremely high failure rate. This does not mean legitimate predictions and divination never occur; outside the conditions of scientific testing, they occur often enough to retain the interest of practioners and clients (cf. pp 71, 122, 132-33, 163-64, 178-79). Published predictions, however, seem to have a worse record than client self-disclosures.

One ambitious study examined over 3000 predictions by leading astrologers (e.g., Jeane Dixon, Sybil Leek, Carroll Righter) and leading astrology publications (e.g., *American Astrology Magazine, Horoscope Magazine, Astrology Magazine*) from 1974 to 1979. The total number of failures was 2673. This is almost a 90 percent failure rate. The astrologers, however, were given the benefit of the doubt for any prediction that could have been attributed to shrewd guessing, vague wording, or inside information. Remove those possibilities, and the failure rate was closer to 100 percent. No astrologer was listed unless the research team could document 100 or more predictions they had made. Culver and Ianna put it very succinctly when they concluded from their study: "The results . . . paint a dismal picture indeed for the traditional astrological claim that 'astrology works'" (1205:169-70).

Not only have astrologers repeatedly failed in specific predictions (or even general predictions), but they have completely failed in predicting events of major importance. The following data listed by Playfair and Hill is typical:

The overall record of astrologers in predicting earthquakes, or anything else, is terrible. Roger Hunter, a geophysicist with the U.S. National Ocean Survey, . . . found that although seventeen major earthquakes took place between January and August 1970, the forecasters in *American Astrology* missed every single one. Of the sixteen quakes they did predict, naming only the month and the country, they were right for only three minor events. They also missed the 31 May disaster in Peru, one of the worst in this century in which 30,000 people died (1284:168).

U.S. Geological Survey scientists Derr and Hunter analyzed 240 earthquake predictions made by 27 different astrologers and found their accuracy was worse than just guessing (1101:169).

Most financiers can well remember the "Black Monday" of October 19, 1987, when the New York stock market fell over 500 points. But few people know that a major astrological publication, *Llewellyn's 1987 Moon-sign Book and Gardening Guide* (1986) predicted this optimistic bit of information for the very week that the market crashed (October 18-24): "Look for a *strong rally* that could take us into December . . ." (in 1195:213, emphasis added).

What do you think happened to all the investors who banked on this piece of astrological advice? If astrology has any predictive value at all, how can it miss such major events (cf. 84:21; 1285:13-14)?

Astrologers have responded to such negative findings in vain. For example, the two most touted books recently attempting to defend astrology are the British text by Robert Parry, *Astrology's Complete Book of Self-Defense* and John Anthony West's *The Case for Astrology,* an expanded version of his earlier work by the same title. Critical reviews (2690) show that such books utterly fail to answer the scientific evidence against astrology (only a very small portion of which we have presented). This evidence is now tantamount to a disproof. Even the British *Astrological Journal* recently noted that a meeting of U.K. research astrologers reported that there were no new areas in which to test astrology (2690:47). Since every area in which astrology has been independently tested has not only failed to confirm astrological claims but has actually disproved them, the issue is settled. Of course, not for the astrologers, who rationalize the evidence away.

Perhaps the astrologers' response to the scientific disproof of their pratice underscores a more fundamental problem, what astronomers Culver and Ianna have labelled "The Gemini Syndrome." This is the tendency for astrologers to mimic the characteristics said to be typical of the Gemini personality: the propensity to speak out of both sides of the mouth. Here is astrological self-deception, the "confident use of glaring inconsistencies," the refusal to face the facts, and the justification of astrology by any means (1234:265). As an example, note the comments of the chairman of the United Kingdom Astrological Association, who is critical of the astrologer's inclination for excuses. He is describing what an astrologer can do to "harmonize" astrological predictions with a person who does not match them. In this following case, he is describing a person who is very meek, but who astrology predicts should be aggressive:

> If I found a very meek and unaggressive person with five planets in Aries, this does not cause me to doubt that Aries means aggression. I may be able to point to his Aries Ascendant, or to his Sun conjunct Saturn, or to his ruler in the twelfth house; and, if none of these alibis are available, I can simply say that he has not yet fulfilled his Aries potential. Or, I can argue (as I have heard argued) that, if a person has an *excess* of planets in a particular sign, he will tend to suppress the characteristics of that sign, because he is scared that, if he reveals them, he will carry them to excess. But if on the next day I meet a very aggressive person who also has five planets in Aries, I will change my tune: I will say that he *had* to be like that because of his planets in Aries (1217:173).

## ALLEGED BIBLICAL EVIDENCE FOR ASTROLOGY

We now turn to another area which astrologers claim supports their views: the Bible.

Joseph Goodavage, author of *Astrology: the Space Age Science* and *Write Your Own Horoscope,* says, "The Bible is full of the philosophy of astrology" (1287:XI). Jeff Mayo, founder of the British "Mayo School of Astrology," remarks, "The Bible is full of astrological references" (1197:7). This view is shared by many other astrologers as well (87:197/1192:VII).

The following are views of the Bible commonly held by astrologers. We have supplied a brief comment after each.

1. The Bible is not the Word of God but the words of great men of history. (What is forgotten is that the Bible claims to be the divinely inspired Word of God; 2 Timothy 3:16,17; cf. 330.)

2. The Bible has been corrupted over the years; thus, many of its alleged astrological and reincarnation teachings have been deleted. (Where is the slightest bit of evidence that shows such material was once in the Bible?)

3. Parts of the Bible were written plainly "in code" and only astrologers understand that code. (Most scholars believe the Bible was written plainly in Hebrew and Greek, since the nation of Israel and the early Christians would have had a hard time deciphering a foreign "code.")

4. Because the Bible was written by great men and because it has been so influential throughout history, some of these men must have been astrologers. Astrology itself is so important and influential, it is difficult to believe none of the biblical authors practiced this great art. (This is still an argument from thin air. Not only that, it completely ignores the fact that Moses, Isaiah, and other Old Testament prophets condemned astrology.)

Now let us take some examples from the Bible itself. In the material below, we will quote the Bible passage alleged to teach astrology; second, we will examine the astrologers' claim about the passage; third, we will give the Christian response to that claim. (Note: all references in this section are from the NIV.)**

*Genesis 1:14.* "God said, 'Let there be lights in the expanse of the sky to separate the day from the night, and let them serve as signs to mark seasons and days and years.' "

By teaching that the word "signs" here indicates heavenly bodies (planets), given by God as astrological signs, astrologers claim the Bible is affirming astrology. Some astrologers assert that the "signs" here refer to Aries, Taurus, Gemini, etc. However, the word "signs" here cannot refer to the astrological signs. In Genesis 1:14-15, the word "signs" is described and defined: "To separate the day from the night, . . . [and] to mark seasons and days and years, and let them be lights in the expanse of the sky to give light on the earth." (See also Genesis 1:16.)

*Genesis 37:9-11.* " 'I [Joseph] had another dream, and this time the sun and moon and 11 stars were bowing down to me.' "

**The authors would like to thank Dr. Sherman Kanagy of Purdue University for some helpful comments in this section.

Astrologers believe the reference to the sun, moon, and 11 stars proves that Joseph and his brothers believed in astrology. However, there is not the slightest indication that they have anything to do with astrology, or even with astronomy. The sun, moon, and 11 stars are used symbolically to refer to Joseph's parents and his brothers. This is the clear statement of the text itself. (See also Genesis 49:3-27.)

*Numbers 24:17.* "A star will come out of Jacob; a scepter will rise out of Israel."

Astrologers claim that the star coming out of Jacob proves there was astrological belief in the days of Moses. But the reference has nothing to do with astrology. The word "star" is metaphorical for a person, the Messiah, who will be a descendant of Jacob. Additional proof of this interpretation is that the text refers not only to a star but to a scepter (a ruler), who will rise out of Israel. In other words, the same person who comes from the line of Jacob will also be a ruler.

*Judges 5:20.* "From the heavens the stars fought, from their courses they fought against Sisera."

Astrologers claim this is a reference to the influence of the stars on Sisera, the commander of Jabin's army. But to do this, they must interpret a poetic or figurative passage literally. These words occur in the "Song of Deborah," which is a poetic victory song describing Israel's victory over her enemies. (See Judges 4:7; 5:20-21; Joshua 10:11-14.)

*Job 9:9-10; 38:31-33.* "He is the Maker of the Bear and Orion, the Pleiades and the constellations of the south. He performs wonders that cannot be fathomed, miracles that cannot be numbered."

" 'Can you bind the beautiful Pleiades? Can you loose the cords of Orion? Can you bring forth the constellations in their seasons or lead out the Bear with its cubs? Do you know the laws of the heavens? Can you set up God's dominion over the earth?' "

Astrologers claim that the mere mention of the constellations here is evidence that the Bible supports astrology. But this is nonsense. Job 9:9-10 refers to God as the Maker of various constellations. The ancient Israelites had limited astronomical knowledge, but they were nonetheless aware that it was God who had created the constellations and who was in charge of the universe.

*Isaiah 13:10; cf. Joel 2:31; Luke 21:25.* "The stars of heaven and their constellations will not show their light. The rising sun will be darkened and the moon will not give its light."

Astrologers believe that these references to the sun and moon being darkened, not giving their light (turning to blood), prove the Bible supports astrology. But all of these references refer to the day of the Lord, the second coming of Jesus Christ. These events have nothing to do with astrology. If astrologers claim them for today, it is obvious that the sun and the moon are not darkened and have not turned to blood. Also, Isaiah 13:7 points out that in that day of the Lord the stars and constellations will not show their light. Would any astrologer claim this occurs today?

*Jeremiah 10:2.* "Do not learn the ways of the nations or be terrified by signs in the sky, though the nations are terrified by them."

Astrologers claim the reference to "signs in the sky" is an astrological reference. We agree that this passage is speaking about astrology; the problem for astrologers is that the passage rebukes trust in astrology. The Bible condemns "the ways of the nations," which refers to their astrological practices. The text also says the nations were terrified by *literal* signs in the sky, not *symbolic* signs in astrological charts. The ancients were terrified by eclipses, since they thought the moon was being "eaten" by demons. Meteors and comets were also seen as portents of evil. In the Bible God tells His people not to be terrified by literal events in the sky, because they are merely things that He has made. He is in control over all things. The context of Jeremiah 10 is to exalt the true God over the idols and the superstitious fears (such as astrology) that control their lives.

*Daniel 4:26.* "Your kingdom will be restored to you when you [Nebuchadnezzar] acknowledge that Heaven rules."

Astrologers claim that this passage reveals that "Heaven" (the stars and planets) "rules" (in-

fluences) over the affairs of men. But it teaches no such thing. Daniel was no astrologer (see the following). The word "heaven" here is used as a symbol for God. Thus, in Daniel 2:37-38, Daniel tells Nebuchadnezzar that it was the God of heaven, not the stars, who gave him dominion over the Babylonian empire.

*Matthew 2:1-11.* "After Jesus was born in Bethlehem in Judea, during the time of King Herod, Magi from the east came to Jerusalem and asked, 'Where is the one who has been born king of the Jews? We saw his star in the east and have come to worship him.' ... After they had heard the king, they went on their way, and the star they had seen in the east went ahead of them until it stopped over the place where the child was. When they saw the star, they were overjoyed. On coming to the house, they saw the child with his mother Mary, and they bowed down and worshiped him."

Astrologers claim that this means the Bible supports astrology. But a careful examination of this passage reveals:

- The star actually moved because it preceded the Magi.
- In some unknown manner the star was able to indicate the exact place Jesus and His parents were staying.
- The star apparently was lost from sight for a period of time, and then became visible again.
- The star seems to have been visible only to the Magi.

This was not a normal star but a miracle from God to guide and direct the Magi to Jesus. This was a temporary phenomenon and had no other purpose than stated. Certainly it had no astrological meaning. If the only purpose for the star was to lead the Magi to Christ, this would also explain why they alone appeared to have seen it.

Astrologers have claimed these Magi were astrologers, but their conclusion is not proven. That these men are mentioned favorably, and that God deals with them especially in relationship to His Son, indicates that they were probably not astrologers. The term "magi" primarily means "wise men," and astrology was part of the practice and interest of some "wise men," but certainly not of all. Nothing in this passage condones or approves the practice of astrology.

*The Book of Daniel.* Astrologers cite the book of Daniel as proof of God's acceptance of astrology because God made Daniel the head of the astrologers and magicians in Babylon (Daniel 2:48). If Daniel was the head of all the Babylonian wise men, it is assumed that he was proficient in astrology. After all, Babylon was widely known for its astrological practices.

There are several astrological misconceptions here. First, the biblical account of Daniel explicitly attributes all of Daniel's success to God alone, not to his alleged practice of astrology or devotion to the stars (Daniel 1:17; 2:27-28; 4:17-18). Second, Daniel was a godly man who, according to his own testimony, abhorred the idolatrous and evil practices of Babylon (Daniel 1:8; 4:27). Third, it is unthinkable that God would have permitted Daniel to engage in the very practices He condemned, and for which the nation itself was now under judgment. Fourth, that Daniel did not embrace astrology is seen in the fact that he exposed the failures of the Babylonian astrologers with the true knowledge given by God.

Far from endorsing astrology, Daniel rejected it and pointed men to the counsel of God. The entire book of Daniel reveals the uselessness of astrology and stands against it. In Daniel, astrologers have a 100 percent failure rate when compared with the words of the one true God (Daniel 2:27-28; 4:7; 5:7-9,12-13,15).

Here is a list of biblical passages that strongly condemn astrology. (Note: In several of the passages, the pagan gods Molech, Astarte (the Asherah pole), and Baal were associated with worship of the heavens as well as human sacrifice.)

| | |
|---|---|
| Leviticus 18:21 | Jeremiah 7:18 |
| Leviticus 20:1-6 | Jeremiah 8:1,2 |
| Deuteronomy 4:19 | Jeremiah 19:13 |
| Deuteronomy 17:2-5 | Ezekiel 8:10-11,16 |
| Deuteronomy 18:9-11 | Amos 5:25-26 |
| 2 Kings 17:16 | Zephaniah 1:4-6 |
| 2 Kings 21:3-6 | Acts 7:42 |
| 2 Kings 23:4,11 | 1 Corinthians 10:20 |
| 2 Kings 23:24 | Galatians 5:19-21 |
| Isaiah 47:13-14 | Colossians 2:8,20 |

Astrology is rejected in the Bible because it is futile and worthless, because it includes involvement with occult powers, and because, as we will see, it is a form of idolatry (worshiping the creation rather than the Creator). Thus, astrology is seen to have no power to save men from their sins; it opens people to demonic deception, and it robs God of the glory that is due Him alone.

The assessment of Drs. Bjornstad and Johnson are correct: "Absolutely NO scriptural passage supports astrology, although several indicate awareness of its existence and that of the accompanying astral worship. Moreover, not a single reference even indicates tolerance of this art" (1453:43).

*The Astrologers' Responses*

Many modern (especially "Christian") astrologers agree that God condemns *worshiping* the stars, as that would be idolatry, but they claim that they are not advocating worship of the stars; rather, they are simply taking advantage of the help and information God has made available through the stars. Let's examine this view.

In Exodus 20, the Ten Commandments are listed. Astrology violates the first two commandments: "You shall have no other gods before me," and, "You shall not bow down to them or worship them." Throughout history, astrologers have actually bowed down to the stars and worshiped them, and even today this occurs in various non-Western nations. But those astrologers who do not literally bow down before the stars nevertheless serve them, which violates the second commandment.

By definition, worship includes the idea of religious devotion and reverence for an object, whether living (a god) or dead (an idol). Many astrologers are pantheists, people who believe the universe is living and that it is divine. The stars and planets are reverenced as part of the larger divine universe. The alleged power of the stars and planets over their lives evokes feelings of religious awe and devotion. To serve means "to perform duties for, to give obedience and reverent honor to, to wait upon." All astrologers serve the heavens in this manner. That is, the positions of the stars are dutifully recorded and the information derived from them is carefully analyzed and religiously obeyed. The heavens are honored for their power as the obedient astrologer trustingly waits upon their "advice." And as the apostle Paul tells us, we become a slave to the thing we obey (Romans 6:16).

## ASTROLOGY AND THE OCCULT

Astrology is related to the occult in four main ways. First, dictionaries often define astrology as an occult art because the practice employs occult divination.* Second, astrology appears to work best when the astrologer himself is psychically or mediumistically sensitive, what most astrologers term "intuitive." (See New Age Intuition.) Third, prolonged use of astrology leads to the development of psychic abilities and the contact of spirit guides. This was admitted by the majority of astrologers we interviewed at the July 4-8, 1988, fiftieth anniversary Las Vegas convention of the American Federation of Astrologers, the oldest and most influential of U.S. astrological societies. Almost all those we interviewed admitted they had spirit guides (1320/1289). Fourth, due to its history and nature, astrology often becomes the introductory course to a wider spectrum of occult practices. In spite of these connections, astrologers often claim that astrology has nothing to do with the occult (1267/1290:14/1213:350). Nevertheless, many occultists today use astrology, and many astrologers practice other occult arts (1292:3/ 1255:21, 23/1294:21/ 1295:77).

Historian, philosopher, and occult authority Dr. John Warwick Montgomery points out what everyone who has studied astrology knows: that astrology is "found virtually everywhere occultism is to be found" (295:96). Examples are everywhere. Astrologer Daniel Logan admits he is involved with mediums and spirits (1291:63-66,169-70). Astrologer Marcus Allen is involved with a spirit guide and studies such esoteric disciplines as yoga,* Zen, Tibetan Buddhism, and the Western magical traditions (1199:2-6). As-

trologers have admitted that astrology is "the key to all the occult sciences" (1292:3), and that "almost all occultists use astrological timing in their work" (1295:77).

Without question, astrology is the most publicly acceptable occult practice. Perhaps no other activity today provides an introduction to occultism so easily. For astrologers to claim that their craft has no associations to the occult is either the result of ignorance or deliberate deception.

## PSYCHOLOGICAL FACTORS

Astrologers claim that their practice really works, which convinces them of the truth of astrology. Indeed, this is the case for all forms of divination.* They seem to work enough of the time to be credible, and thus both practitioners and clients may become convinced of their validity. But as we saw earlier, scientific testing absolutely undermines any legitimacy to the astrological craft. So how can astrology work, or seem to work?

Many times in life we discover that things which seem to be true really aren't. This is why astrology has to be carefully evaluated, to see if it functions according to its stated principles. Since it does not, we must look to other reasons for its success, or seeming success. The reasons are many, but they can be categorized under two broad headings: psychological factors and spiritistic power. In the former, astrology only appears to work; it really does not work. In the latter, astrology provides supernatural information to a client. Yet even astrology's "success" at this point has nothing to do with the truth of astrology, only with the power of spiritism that the astrologer has tapped into. We will begin our evaluation of these topics with a look at some of the psychological reasons why astrology seems to work.

### Client Needs

Astrology seems to work because clients want it to work. True believers in astrology do not wish their faith in astrology to be shaken because they may have emotional, financial, or other investments in astrology already in place.

As a result, they look for ways to confirm astrology. Even common coincidences may become astrological "confirmations" for such persons. Chance events may become imbued with cosmic "meanings." Thus clients often "read in" relevance and meaning to a chart when it is not there. People may accept general or vague statements as applying uniquely to them when they would apply equally to other people. In essence, those who wish to believe in astrology tend to consciously and unconsciously assist the astrologer to counsel them effectively. Astrologer Richard Nolle concedes that astrologers can take advantage of most clients' faith in astrology: "Most people who come to an astrologer want the astrologer to succeed in reading their charts. They are therefore generally sympathetic and cooperative" (1236:83).

People who believe astrology may also fall into the trap of self-fulfilling prophecy. This takes place when seeds of hope or despair are planted in the person's mind by the astrologer. As a result, the client eventually "arranges" or permits the events to be fulfilled. If the astrologer's words are positive, as they usually are, this provides all the more incentive to fulfill the prophecy. Given a poor self-image, pessimism, or a fatalistic outlook on life, even the negative prophecies of the astrologer can become positive when they are self-fulfilling. But whether the astrologer's words are positive or negative, in neither case is it the astrologer who has been successful. It is the client, who has self-fulfilled the astrological predictions.

But what do astrologers and their clients do when the astrological information does not come true, or worse, when it is clearly contradicted? Then they tend to remember the things that are supportive of astrology and ignore or rationalize away the rest. For the most part, those who desire to believe in astrology will not listen to criticism because of the emotional tie or investment which has developed between the person and the practice.

### Theoretical Self-Justification

Astrology seems to work because it satisfies the human need for friendship, personal security, or dependence on others. Given various psychological needs or insecurities, astrology can prey upon anyone's need for certainty about the future or control over life. Astrology warns about the future and advises about problems that may be encountered. People also go to astrologers so that someone else (the astrologer) or something else (the stars) will make the important or painful decisions for them. Other people are lonely or insecure and desire the friendship of someone who seems to be privy to "cosmic" or "divine" wisdom. They feel important by being associated with someone of importance. Others are simply attracted to the astrologer more than to astrology itself.

### Persuasive Power

People want astrology to work because it fits their lifestyle. Astrology per se is without moral values; the impersonal heavens offer no advice on ethics or how to live one's life morally. Thus, any person seeking to justify selfish or sinful behavior can find a logical reason for doing so in astrology. Astrologers themselves seem willing to tolerate, rationalize, or even encourage any behavior, sexuality, or morality the client deems personally important. Their desire is to please the client's wishes, and it is amazing how often the "stars" agree. Whether people convince themselves that the stars have either "compelled" or "inclined" their wrong actions, they feel they can dismiss their guilt, or were not fully responsible for their behavior.

### Astrologer Skill

Astrology seems to work because it is increasingly a New Age psychology. Astrologers who become good counselors, but who attribute their success to astrology, are wrongly accrediting astrology, not good counseling procedure, with their success. Many astrologers encourage other astrologers to take courses in counseling. One astrologer has confided: "Any astrology student planning to use astrology directly with people is advised to enroll in one or more counseling courses, to read books on the counseling process itself, and to gain experiential supervised practice with counseling skills" (1306:143).

Some astrologers argue that it makes sense first to understand a person's background—

heredity, upbringing, marital status, interests, occupation, and so on—rather than to begin with a chart. One reason for this, as we saw, is because the chart itself is so complex and subjective it is extremely difficult, if not impossible, to interpret it accurately (1306:87/1226:20-21). So, first gathering information on a client is certainly helpful. Of course, this is opening the doors more to psychological counseling than to astrological revelations. And to attribute one's success in psychology to astrological theory is deceptive.

There are many other reasons people grant validity to astrology. When this occult pratice is called a science, it is granted credibility by association with science. Astrology is also universally applicable; that is, it can offer advice for virtually any situation, and sooner or later the astrologer will hit on something in the chart that a person feels is personally relevant. And astrologers always have seemingly reasonable explanations for failures. Finally, astrology may seem to work because of the astrologer's attentiveness or seductiveness. In other words, good astrologers are able to "read" a client through physical or verbal clues and can feed back this information to the client as "revelations" from the stars. Other astrologers are adept at psychological manipulation, so that an otherwise meaningless session can seem amazingly relevant.

But what about those times astrology really does work, when it predicts the future or reveals secret knowledge about the client and known only to him? If a form of intelligence beyond the astrologer really is at work here, what is it? (83:185-200). It's certainly not the stars.

## ASTROLOGY AND SPIRITISM

Former astrologer Charles Strohmer remarks that "for most adherents of astrology, it is enough that it 'works.' There is a fascination with the power, without a suspicion as to the nature of that power" (1286:42).

We will now show that astrology works through spiritistic power. The importance of this issue is obvious. If spirits are the real power behind legitimate astrological disclosures, then the acceptance of astrology in society is opening the

doors for millions of people to be influenced by the spirit world. According to the Word of God, this means people are contacting the world of demons, lying spirits whose primary goal is spiritual deception and destruction (277).

What evidence supports the claim that astrology and spiritism are closely linked? In addition to evidence we have already supplied, we offer the following four points which were greatly expanded upon in our book *Astrology: Do the Heavens Rule Our Destiny?* (83:201-55).

### Pagan Religion

Historically, astrology is tied to pagan gods and the spirit world. Astrology has always been connected to spirits through its acceptance of and contact with supernatural spirit beings who were held to be "gods" (1201/1249/1309/1310). In every civilization, the acceptance of polytheism and the contacting and worship of the "gods" has been a fundamentally spiritistic phenomenon (1311; cf. 1 Corinthians 10:20).

### Spiritistic Endorsement

The spirit world actively promotes astrology. That the spirits are interested in promoting astrology can be seen by the following three facts. First, many spirits have channeled* books on astrology through their human mediums. Edgar Cayce's occult "readings" were saturated with astrology (1251). Channeled astrological literature includes Alice Bailey's *Esoteric Astrology* (1258); Cynthia Bohannon's *The North and South Nodes* (1315); Roman Catholic Irene Diamond's works, e.g., *A New Look at the Twelve Houses,* and *Astrology in the Holy Bible;* Ted George and Barbara Parkers' *Sinister Ladies of Mystery: The Dark Astroids of Earth,* and many others (83:210-12). (A related fact is that a large number of professional astrologers actively promote spiritism; we gave several examples in our book on astrology (83:219-20).

Second, many spiritistic societies actively promote astrology, e.g., The White Eagle Lodge, Rosicrucian Fellowship, Theosophical Society, Sabian Assembly, The Church of Light (83:212-19/1318/1342). Virtually none forbid it. Third, some people who first come in contact with the spirit world testify that they were told by the spirits to pursue the study of astrology (e.g., astrologer Irene Diamond [1242]).

*Astrologers' Confessions*

Former astrologers also concede their power was spiritistic. We think it is significant that many former astrologers have now concluded that the power behind astrology did not come from the stars, but from the power of demons.

Karen Winterburn was a professional astrologer for 12 years, schooled in humanistic astrology. In 1988, she took part in the debate with two professional astrologers on "The John Ankerberg Show." But even as an astrologer she admitted, "I was convinced it [the astrological information] wasn't coming from me . . ." (1322). In a prepared statement (signed October 11, 1988) for our book she stated:

The twelve years I spent in the occult involved a logical progression from humanistic astrology to spirit channeling to occult involvement. Astrology as a divination tool was the perfect entrance. It appeared to be secular, technical, and humanistic, a "neutral" tool. In addition, its occult presuppositions were not immediately apparent. When it began to "work" for me, I became hooked. I became driven to find out the "hows" and the "whys."

This led me right into channeling, a sanitized term for spirit mediumship. In 12 years of serious astrological study and professional practice, I never met a really successful astrologer—even the most "scientific" ones—who did not admit among their professional peers *that spiritism was the power behind the craft.* "Spirit guide," "higher self," "ancient god," "cosmic archetype," whatever name is used—the definition points to the same reality: a discarnate, personal intelligence claiming to be a god-in-progress. Such intelligences have access to information and power that many people covet and they have a desire to be trusted and to influence human beings.

Once the astrologer becomes dependent upon one or more of them, these spirit intelligences (the biblical demons) lead the astrologer into forms of spiritual commitment and worship. This is the worst kind of bondage. Seasoned astrologers who have experienced fairly consistent and dramatic successes in character reading

and prognostication invariably become involved in some form of worship of these demons.

I have seen this occur in myriad forms—from the full-blown revival of ancient religions (Egyptian and Chaldean) to the ritualization of Jungian psychotherapy. The bottomline reality is always the worship of the spirits (demons) the astrologer has come to rely on (1100, emphasis added).

Another former professional astrologer (seven years) is Charles Strohmer. In his critique of astrology, *What Your Horoscope Doesn't Tell You,* he also discusses the fundamentally spiritistic nature and power of astrology. "As we look honestly at astrology, we begin to see that adherents of this system—without knowing it—are banging on the door through which communication is established with knowledgeable but yet deceptive spirit beings. . . . In much the same way that the palm of the hand or the crystal [ball] is 'contact material' for the fortune-teller—the horoscopic *chart* is used by the astrologer. . . . It is the mediumistic point of interaction. . . . Without contact with spirit beings, there would be no astrological self-disclosures" (1286:51,54).

Dr. Atlas Laster received his Ph.D. from the University of Pittsburgh for his work on astrology. He was an active astrologer for 13 years. He observed that as an astrologer, "I did not feel that astrology was an occult art" (1215:4). Yet after he renounced astrology, he came to realize "there are certain rituals and knowledge associated with astrology which may attract spirits of divination" (1324:4).

*Spirit Interpretation*

Chart interpretation is often accomplished through spiritistic inspiration. The spirit world can often be the source of astrologers' interpretations of their charts. Some openly admit that they are assisted in their chart interpretations by spirit guides. By this they mean that their spirit guides speak to them directly in their minds and help them interpret a chart. But usually the influence is indirect and less obvious. For example, astrologers may report feeling somehow "directed" to certain chart symbols or factors, or that something in a chart will suddenly "jump out" at them

(1286:53/1306:86-87). In New Age practice, distinguishing spiritistic assistance from normal human intuition is not always easy (see intuition*). That these two sources can be blurred presents a dilemma for the astrologer. How is it possible for them to know that their "intuition" is truly human, and not from the spiritistic source?

In *Astrology: Do the Heavens Rule Our Destiny?* we presented four interrelated lines of evidence showing that the spirit world can indeed be active in helping astrologers to interpret their charts (83:225-55).

1. Like a kind of mandala,* the chart can become a means to altered states of consciousness,* the allegedly "higher" consciousness that is so often promoted by the occult for spirit contact.

2. The chart can become a "living" power (a focusing agent) for spirits to work through. Like a living being, the chart "speaks" to the astrologer through images in the mind, being directed to certain aspects of the chart, and other psychic impressions.

3. Psychic or spiritistic inspiration is often necessary for "proper" chart interpretation (in our book this was documented with five subpoints) and is admitted by many astrologers, e.g., American Federation of Astrologers president Doris Chase Doane agrees that "it is almost impossible" to accurately read a chart without psychic guidance and, as noted, many astrologers of past and present have declared their belief that astrology works by the power of spirits (83:211-20/237-42).

4. Because all forms of divination* sooner or later contact spirits, it is logical to assume divination by means of astrology charts is also spiritistic.

The above information reveals *why* astrology can sometimes work. However, astrologers and their clients must also ask the question, "At what cost"?

## THE DANGERS OF ASTROLOGY

There are dangers from astrology besides those associated with spiritism and other occult practices (278). Science writer Lawrence E. Jerome states, "How much physical and psychological damage such false astrological practices and advice cause cannot even be estimated" (1193:212). Bart Bok, a former president of the prestigious American Astronomical Society, has observed that, "The study and ready availability of astrological predictions can exert an insidious influence on a person's personal judgment" (1327:1). Indeed, if a billion people trust in the false advice of astrology in some degree, one can hardly hazard a guess at the overall personal cost around the world. Even some astrologers confess that practitioners are liable to the characteristic hazards of the trade. These kinds of hazards do not make for a trusting relationship between astrologer and client but further complicate an already potentially dangerous situation.

Leading astrologer Tracy Marks discusses the following potential problems between the astrologer and his client. A little imagination here will reveal how each one can produce harm to the client:

- the astrologer may experience himself as superior to the client.
- the astrologer may encourage the dependency of his clients.
- the astrologer may give clients what they appear to want rather than what they really need.
- astrologers may pass their own values and ideas under the cloak of astrological authority.
- the astrologers' "own sense of powerlessness" may lead them to "disempower [their] clients, imparting deterministic [fatalistic] attitudes."
- the astrologers' own fears concerning certain planets and signs may influence their interpretation and "result in [their] imparting pronouncements which could become destructively self-fulfilling prophecies."
- astrologers may speak in astrological jargon the client cannot understand and use mystical language authoritatively to create "the illusion that [they] are imparting high truths, when indeed [they] may be saying little of significance."
- astrologers may "speak in vague, ungrounded generalities" (1306:151-53).

Marks observes that even "most professional astrologers are guilty on occasion of at least several of the above inadequacies . . ." (1306:151-53). In addition, she admits that astrologers may react more to the chart than to the client; may become egotistical; may devalue the client; and can draw hasty conclusions (1306:155-61).

Astrological predictions or advice can cause people to do things they would otherwise never have done, and sometimes this has led to tragedy. Given the right circumstances, a particular chart interpretation and its potentially powerful influence upon a person could even lead to criminal acts in order to help fulfill or forestall what a person believes is the cosmic influence or destiny upon himself or another. For example, a chart reveals that a company will fail, so the president embezzles funds for his own security; or that a child may be born mentally retarded, so there is an abortion.

German theologian and occult expert Dr. Kurt Koch observes that, "Astrology has been responsible for a number of suicides and murders" (1328:20). He cites examples in his books concerning the effects of the suggestive nature of astrology. For example, a woman murdered her own son because an astrologer predicted he would lead a life of mental illness. The shattered mother went to jail, but the astrologer went free (272:11-12). Dr. Sherman Kanagy, a physics professor at Purdue University observes, "In ancient times women whose babies were born under the sign of Scorpio would often kill their babies by drowning because of the evil significance" (87:108).

Remember that astrologers are: 1) unlicensed and unregulated, 2) require little or no education, 3) can become a "professional" astrologer overnight, 4) are occultists who characteristically reject absolute moral values, and 5) often use their powers over others in a manipulative and authoritarian manner. If the practices of such people force them into demonic collaboration, what kind of answers are clients getting from astrological counseling? In considering the clients of astrologers, we will see additional reasons for concern.

### The Clients of Astrologers

What kind of person seeks out an astrologer? We can determine from the statements of as-

trologers themselves that some and perhaps many clients are those for whom astrology will be most destructive.

*Clients lack values.* For example, astrological counselor Stephen Arroyo observes, "Many people who request astrological assistance are suffering from a lack of values . . ." (1329:246).

*Clients are easily duped or deceived.* Astrologer Jane Evans observes, "I have known too many people to whom self-deception was second nature" (1253:200).

*Clients are looking for the astrologer to make their decisions for them.* This is a problem that is almost universally admitted among astrologers. Some attempt to help such clients become more independent, but others willingly become their "gurus" and enjoy the fact that their client will make no decision without first consulting their "wisdom" (1330:47/1220:XI).

It is the ability of astrologers to justify a person's selfish tendencies that caused Dr. John Warwick Montgomery to give the following warning: "The very elasticity of astrological interpretation is its most dangerous characteristic where people desperately desire a shortcut to self knowledge and solutions to their problems, and where the answers are ambiguous, they inevitably choose according to self-interest. Thus the floodgates are opened to the reinforcement of evil tendencies. . . . It should not be regarded as strange that astrology has so frequently been used to guide evil farther along the path it has already taken" (1332:118).

Because astrologers reject any absolute standard of morality, they prefer a "situation ethics" approach where moral decisions are determined largely by the whim and preference of the astrologer or client. Astrologer Alan Oken observes, "No Path is the Truth Path, for in the Absolute there is not Truthfulness or Falsehood, no right and no wrong, no yes and no no" (1331:85). Even the Alexandrian astronomer and "father" of astrology, Ptolemy (2nd c.A.D.) confessed, "Many of its practitioners are in it for gain rather than truth or wisdom, and pretend to know more than the facts permit" (87:85). Another astrologer testifies,

"The preoccupation with self is really in the interest of evolution. . . . In modern astrology we seek confirmation of our personal importance" (1242:5-6).

*Evil Uses*

Astrologers admit astrology can be used for either "good" or evil purposes. Leading astrologer Sydney Omarr states, "Astrology is there, to be used for the good—or the evil (Hitler!)" (1333:23). Just as there is both black and white witchcraft, one astrology text observes, "There is white and black astrology . . ." (1258:638). Leading astrologer Nicholas deVore confesses that "astrology has often been used to unworthy ends" (1192:VIII).

Adolph Hitler, the ancient Aztecs and their human sacrifices, the modern serial killer known as the Zodiac killer, modern witches and Satanists, have used astrology for evil purposes. All realized that astrology's power may be used malevolently. For whatever reasons, these people decided to choose evil. This is the point. The astrologer is free to choose. Perhaps the most cunning deception here is when, like Hitler, the astrologer uses his craft for evil while *thinking* he is using it for the good.

*Morality and Sex*

In the astrologer's view, morality is often determined by one's subjective or "higher" state of consciousness, not by what one believes or does. Obedience to God would be (perhaps) moral for one person and immoral for another. As one guru who endorses astrology states, "I would like to say to you: obedience [to God] is the greatest sin," and "I teach you disobedience. . . . The devil did a tremendous service to humanity" (1334:368,372,376). But most astrologers are not very concerned with morality in the first place. In fact, many of them believe that moral judgments themselves are the real evil (1264:53,70). Their job, as astrologers, is simply to validate the client's own views, whatever they are (1238:3/1306:145).

One reason astrology is popular is because it permits us to explain our own failures and evils, or whatever we do not like in ourselves, as the fault of the stars. Here is an attractive escape from personal responsibility (84:127/1202:329-30). Astrologers may say that "Saturn did it," or that "the stars weren't auspicious." Virtually anything can be rationalized, any sin or evil, because "What happens to us is what needs to happen to us" (1294:99).

But if there is any place in which astrology promotes sin, it is the area of sexual behavior (1253:170). In an era of AIDS and dozens of other sexually transmitted diseases, this is of no small concern (2649). Astrologer Jeff Green provides an illustration. Here is the case of a woman who was deeply troubled by her sexual immorality. What did she discover through astrological counseling? She realized that she was free to enjoy sexual affairs without guilt by making them "spiritual," even a divine activity. On what basis? Simply because Pluto was in the eighth house in Leo, the south node was in the seventh house in opposition to Mars, and Pisces was in the second house (1238:146-47).

Astrologers also observe chart indicators for bisexuality, homosexuality, lesbianism, sexual sadism, and transexualism (1331:64-75/1336). Since such activities are "indicated," perhaps the one who desires to pursue them will have them justified in his own mind. And the one who does not desire them may live in worry or fear over the possibility, perhaps until he gives in to his astrological "destiny." We can only wonder what an impressionable teenager would think if he went to an astrologer and discovered such "indicators" in his chart. What if he or she were confused about sexuality, especially in an age of gross experimentation and so-called sexual enlightenment?

Consider the advice to a client by Maxine Bell, a famous astrologer to Hollywood's homosexual community: "He didn't come to me for help, he came to me to find out when his next affair was due. He was just finishing up one [affair] and after two nights of being alone he was desperate, so he wondered what his prospects were for a new affair. I gave him the rundown on when the next affair would be likely. Whenever transiting Mars goes over the fifth house that starts things going" (1337:213-14).

Many astrologers believe that homosexuality is as much a part of a person's "destiny pattern" as their birth or death. Maxine Bell states, "If they were homosexuals as they closed their last life and had no desire to quit or reform, then they come back as a homosexual and they have their own karma they bring with them" (1337:210). "I have no wish to change, only to help," says Edith Randall, a celebrated Hollywood astrologer. Her 60,000 astrological readings over the years include "a sizable slice of the homosexual community" (1337:215).

*Fear and Bondage*

One astrologer emphasizes that "an astrological chart is not something to be feared" (1264:3). But thousands of clients of astrologers will disagree. For many people, astrology produces a fear of the future. Although the goal of astrology is allegedly to give the client "power" over the future, in practice it doesn't work this way. This is because astrology teaches people to acknowledge the impersonal whim of the power that stars and planets exert over them. The stars and planets are not persons; they cannot be reasoned with, nor can their influence easily be escaped. Compared to the power and influence of the planets, men are like insects. What can one person do in the face of the power of the universe?

Astrologers acknowledge that astrology can bring ruin to people by the fears it produces (1192:310). Astrologers complain that other astrologers who predict personal disaster, illness, or death are being insensitive or callous. But they are powerless to do anything about it because the astrologers who make such predictions are, after all, only engaging in astrology.

Astrologer-psychiatrist Bernard Rosenblum points out that, "The bad reputation astrology must contend with is partly due to those astrologers who make definite predictions about people's death, divorce, or illness, and other statements that suggest the client must suffer the rest of his life with a difficult psychological problem in order to correct a karmic imbalance. Such astrologers are exhibiting arrogance and insensitivity in the extreme" (1223:121). Other astrologers respond by saying that, after all, these astrologers "see" such events in the chart, so is it not their "moral" duty to warn the client? How is this being "insensitive" to the client?

Jungian analyst and astrologer Alice O. Howell complains, "I am appalled sometimes at the damage that can be done by astrologers who have no understanding of psychology and who are free with 'predictions' and sow seeds of doubt and fear in their clients" (1225:7). Other astrologers respond with, "Why be appalled at astrology?" The very purpose of the chart is to make predictions. If such predictions sow seeds of doubt and fear, that is not the fault of astrology, but the client's own failure to trust the wisdom of the stars. Astrology is a divine art; we only give the client God's will. And why should astrologers be expected to become PhD.s in psychology? So what if some astrologers admit that it is too easy for astrology students to set themselves up as experts and "make devastating prognostications which can seriously undermine the hope and confidence" of the client (1257:7)? It is an astrologer's *duty* to read the chart, and again, a *divine* responsibility. If it is God who is "speaking" through the chart (1216:111), the astrologer must speak God's truth regardless of the consequences (1216:128/1301:1). As one astrologer stated, "I feel I do not have the right to block information. . . . That would be like saying, 'Hey, God, you're wrong! You shouldn't be telling me this now' " (1216:128).

If a severely afflicted Mercury or moon denote the client may or will experience insanity, who can blame the astrologer for expressing this to the client (1237:154)? Perhaps lifelong psychotherapy will prevent it! And what if the birth chart with "Mars afflicted and Saturn and Neptune prominent [but] afflicted" denotes a child will have leukemia (1237:155)? Clearly the stars have revealed it! If the parents are concerned and worried, at least they have been forewarned.

Dane Rudhyar discusses a common occurrence:

The person came disturbed, confused and sensing difficulties ahead; he leaves the astrologer's office with a crystallized expectation of tragedy. "Saturn" is about to hurt him; his wife *may* die, or his kidney *may* need an operation. Saturn. What is there one can do about Saturn, or to Saturn? Nothing apparently. Fear has taken shape and name. The anticipation of disaster torments the mind. . . . It will not help the situation to say

the "influence" of Saturn is of the nature of electromagnetic waves; or that it can be expressed
in a statistical average. It may be much worse to
know one's husband has seventy-five percent
chances of dying or becoming insane, than to
know he *will* die or become insane. Uncertainty
breeds devastating fear far more than the confrontation with the inevitable. And let us not say
"forewarned, forearmed!" It does *not* apply
where Mars, Saturn, squares, oppositions are
present as objective, *evil entities* which are actually and concretely doing something to men. It
does not apply where there is fear (1294:24).

### A Special Case: Death

To predict crippling illness, disease, and insanity is bad enough, but when astrologers see
death in a chart and predict it, as they often do
(83:275-79), one wonders how they can justify
the possible consequences in people's lives. The
questions of "When will I die?" or "When will my
spouse die?" seem to be among the most common questions asked of astrologers (1218:127).

And if, as even astrologers admit, up to 90 percent of astrologers are simple frauds (1234:265),
this is no safegaurd against their using our greatest fears against us for their personal profit. "As
often as not these star-mongers will resort to the
criminal expedient of frightening [a] credulous
client by threatening him or her or [the] next relatives with death or serious disease in a certain
year of life, suggesting at the same time that a
more thoroughgoing and, of course, more expensive analysis of the position of the planets, etc., on
that day and at the particular hour and minutes
might enable them to rectify or 'correct' his terrifying prophecy" (84:111).

Nor should we think that predictions of death
can never be self-fulfilling. There are cases of
people apparently "willing" themselves to death.
These people lose virtually all interest in life and
expect to die, and some do. Whether they believe
in black magic (a "death hex"), or that the stars
have fated it, they do die (1434; cf. 1193:32,212/
1193:104). In their defense, many astrologers
claim that it is no longer "proper" for astrologers
to predict death (1192:224-25). But the damage that has already been done over the years
and continues to be done cannot be so easily
discarded.

### Self-Fulfilling Prophecies

When clients accept an astrologer's invitation
to have their chart read, there are at least three
things working against them: 1) numerous astrological factors can result in harmful or
"malefic" combinations. The odds are that sooner
or later the chart itself will inform clients of something they don't want to hear; 2) the odds are that
the astrologer has a spirit guide directing chart interpretation, and spirit guides are not known for
their love of humanity; 3) the problem of self-fulfilling prophecies. Prominent astrologer Dane
Rudhyar observes the problems associated with
specific predictions, or "definite forecasts," based
on progressions and transits:

> ... the individual has no recourse against the
> impact of such revelations. He is almost totally
> unprotected against their possible negative
> effect. Even if he reasons himself out of being
> consciously affected by the forecast, his *subcon-
> scious memory* does not let go. This is worse ob-
> viously if the event or trend prophesied is
> unfortunate and if fear of its results is aroused—
> *which is the case in nine cases out of ten!*—but it
> can even have psychologically disintegrating ef-
> fects *when the thing expected is very fortunate*,
> for it may lead to a self-satisfied expectancy
> blurring the edges of the individual's efforts
> (1294:95-96, emphasis added).

Rudhyar reveals, "I have received many letters from people telling me how fearful or psychologically confused they have become after
consulting even a well-known astrologer and
being given a biased character analysis and/or
predictions of illness, catastrophe, or even death"
(1101:174; cf. 1222:12/1218:27).

Just a single astrological prediction can have
tragic results because of the power and authority
the clients grant to the astrologer. The magazine
*Astrology Now* interviewed a woman named
Lore Wallace who went to a famous astrologer at
age 17 only to encounter predictions of a difficult
birth and the death of a child. Although this
never occurred, she said that the predictions
"damaged me probably for the rest of my life"
(1101:184).

As a final example of the dangers of astrology,
consider the two following true incidents from

astrological marriage counseling (cf. 1341:223-27). A young man consults an astrologer who informs him that he will marry young, but that his first wife will not be the one "destined" for him. Only his second wife will bring him "true happiness." The man deliberately marries young in order to get his first wife, that is to fulfill the prophecy, so that he will not miss finding his second wife who alone will make him happy. His first wife is very good and devoted and bears him three children. After the third child is born, the husband abandons his wife and family and obtains a divorce. He marries a second wife whom he believes is the one the stars have destined to make him truly happy. Yet within a few months, she joins a cult and makes his life utterly miserable. Soon he divorces her as well (1342:17-18).

Here is just a single prediction and subsequent tragedy. If we multiply this by the millions of astrological predictions given each year, it gives us a look at the true potential of astrology.

Far too many tragedies are "arranged" by astrological predictions. Clients become amazed by accurate self-disclosures; these self-disclosures generate *trust*; trust leads to deception; deception produces unwise or immoral decisions and actions; bad actions bring ruin or destruction (1286:47).

A second illustration reveals not only how easily astrology becomes a vehicle for tragedy but also the spiritual deception hidden beneath the surface. A certain woman was engaged to be married and felt that the advice of an astrologer might be useful. After drawing the horoscope, the astrologer predicted the following: "Your engagement will break up. This man will not marry you. You will not marry at all, but remain single." The woman was devastated. She was so in love with her fiance that she could not bear the thought of losing him. She became depressed and paralyzed with fear. She continually worried that the engagement would break up and that she would never marry. She finally resolved to put an end to her life, but on the day she intended to kill herself, a friend of her fiance was able to stop her. Upon the advice of that friend, she went for pastoral counseling, revealed her plight, repented of her sins and gave her life to Jesus Christ. Soon after that day, her fiance also gave his life to Christ. Today they are contentedly married and have several children. But had it not been for Christ, the disaster which was set afoot by the astrologer could have happened (1328:20-21).

## ASTROLOGY AND CHRISTIANITY: CONTRASTS

The following chart is provided for those who would like to see, at a glance, important topical contrasts between astrology and Christianity and the astrologer and the Christian.

| TOPIC | ASTROLOGY | CHRISTIANITY |
|---|---|---|
| 1. God | Impersonal; Nature | Personal; Triune |
| 2. Jesus | Astrologer; Psychic | Savior-God |
| 3. Personal Means of Salvation | By Personal Merit Through Self-perfection | By God's Grace Through Faith in Christ |
| 4. Redemption Accomplished by | Inevitable Evolutionary Process | Propitiatory Atonement |
| 5. Death | Reincarnation | Glorification |
| 6. The Final State | Cosmic Absorption | Personal Immortality |
| 7. Source of Authority | Astrological Doctrine and Practice | The Bible |
| 8. Mediator | Professional Astrologer | Jesus Christ |

| TOPIC | ASTROLOGY | CHRISTIANITY |
|---|---|---|
| 9. Sin | Ignorance or Karma | Disobedience to God |
| 10. Philosophy | Pantheism, Gnosticism, Polytheism | Theism |
| 11. Nature of Faith | Subjective, Mystical, Blind | Objective, Historic, Factual |
| 12. Morality | Relative, Amoral | Absolute |
| 13. Man | One in Nature with the Divine Cosmos | Created (in God's Image) |
| 14. Relation to the Occult | Accepts | Rejects |

| TOPIC | ASTROLOGER | CHRISTIAN |
|---|---|---|
| 1. Source of Information | Horoscope Chart | Bible |
| 2. Object of Consultation | The Stars' Influence | God |
| 3. Emphasis | Divination | Salvation, Sanctification |
| 4. Object of Faith | Self/Planets and Stars | Jesus Christ |
| 5. Object of Worship and Trust | Creation | Creator |
| 6. Interpreter and Revealer of Ultimate Reality | Horoscope Chart | Holy Spirit/Scriptures |
| 7. Responsible to | Stars | God (83:141-56) |

# Channeling

## INFO AT A GLANCE

**Description.** Channeling occurs when someone permits a spirit entity to possess him or her usually for some form of psychic knowledge or power, e.g., psychic diagnosis or healing, or to use the person's vocal cords to speak in order to give spiritual teachings or practical advice. Various forms of spirit communication by channeling exist, such as automatic writing, narrated visions, and inner voice dictation. In addition, many people say they channel entities who claim to be angels, even though these "angels" are indistinguishable in their methods and teachings from the spirits channeled by occultists in general (see Angels).

**Founder.** The first recorded incident of channeling per se is found in Genesis 3:1 (cf. 2 Corinthians 11:3,13-15).

**How does it claim to work?** Channeling claims to work through a variety of means. For example, through meditation,* relaxation, visualization,* hypnosis,* altered states of consciousness,* and other methods, channelers claim the spirits are able to enter, possess, and control them much in the same manner as a puppeteer controls a puppet. Channelers claim that by permitting spirits to possess and speak through them, mankind can attain a wealth of spiritual and practical wisdom directly from spirits, who have "passed on" and are highly evolved. The spirits claim they can assist people toward true individual, social, and spiritual enlightenment.*

**Scientific evaluation.** Certain aspects of the practice can be scientifically examined, as in parapsychological research, but science cannot evaluate the specific claims made by channelers concerning the spirits existence, nature, or purpose.

**Examples of occult potential.** Channeling is chiefly used for an endless number of occult purposes, from realizing so-called "higher" states of consciousness, to developing psychic powers, to attaining new revelations.

**Major problem.** Channeled spirits who claim to be wise and loving entities, or angels sent from God, are lying spirits which the Bible identifies as demons. Despite their seeming charm and benevolence, this is only a ruse to establish trust. As one channeler points out, "Guides have a vested interest in being friendly" (349:42).

**Biblical/Christian evaluation.** Channeling is part of what the Bible calls Christians to stand against in spiritual warfare (Ephesians 6:10-18). And under the name "mediumship," it is a practice specifically forbidden (Deuteronomy 18:9-12). The hidden purpose of the spirits is to gain the confidence of men so they can influence and control them to bring their eventual spiritual ruin (2 Corinthians 4:4).

**Potential dangers.** Spiritual deception, occult bondage, demon possession, mental breakdown, physical harm, shortened life, financial and other risks perpetrated by fraudulent channelers, and other consequences (refs. 291/270-274/1069).

*Note:* The New Age Movement as a whole is largely undergirded by channeled revelations and activities. Some of this material is excerpted from the authors' *The Facts on Spirit Guides* (Harvest House, 1988). The chapters on *A Course in Miracles,* Crystal Work, Dream Work, Hypnosis, Shamanism, and Visualization offer additional illustrations of how channeling is used in modern New Age occultism. For an analysis of how the popular angel phenomenon relates to channeling and the occult see Angels.

## INTRODUCTION AND INFLUENCE

Channeling is a New Age euphemism for mediumship or spirit possession. When men and women willingly give over their minds and bodies to spirit entities, and these spirits enter and control them, using them to "heal," or to give occult teachings and other information, this is called "channeling." Recent books that promote channeling include Sanaya Roman's and Duane Packer's *Opening to Channel: How to Connect with Your Guide* (575), Kathryn Ridall's *Channeling: How to Reach Out to Your Spirit Guides* (577), and Laeh Garfield's and Jack Grant's *Companions in Spirit: A Guide to Working with Your Spirit Helpers* (349).

Throughout the world, channeling is a multi-billion-dollar business. Famous movie stars, corporate executives, scholars, artists, and businessmen are turning to channeling. Various retreat centers and workshops are springing up around the country which teach people how to open themselves so that the spirits can possess them and they can become channels themselves (280:7-10).

From a historical perspective, we may understand the influencing potential of channeling. For example, in 1851, just three years after the spiritualist revival of 1848, there were an estimated 1200 mediums in Cincinnati, Ohio, as well as hundreds of mediums in other major cities (463:159-60). By 1855, America boasted several thousand mediums and some 2 million followers, which eventually grew to an estimated 8 to 11 million (389:362/1097:318). These channelers (then called mediums) and their followers undergirded an entire century of parapsychological research (the scientific study of the occult) in our country (1098). This research helped to pave the way for the modern occult and New Age revival (1099:161, 174; ref. 1069:51-60).

Today, Los Angeles is estimated to have over a thousand channelers (1102). There are also hundreds of practitioners in other major cities, indicating that we are experiencing another occult revival. But the spirits today are turning to highly sophisticated marketing techniques through books, radio, television, video, and cassette (1103/ 574:49/662:6-7,13-15).

Today, thousands of channeled audio and video cassettes are sold to the public. For example, numerous titles are being marketed by LuminEssence Productions, a New Age business begun by channelers Sanaya Roman (who channels an entity called "Orin") and Duane Packer (who channels "DaBen"). Some of "Orin's" tapes include the following titles (note "Orin's" emphasis on the "laws" of prosperity and abundance, a teaching popular in the "Christian" "faith" movement):

- Discovering Life Purpose—What Am I Here to Do?
- Manifesting Your Destiny
- Radiating Unconditional Love—Becoming the Source
- Self-Love—Learning to Respect and Honor the Self
- Being Your Higher Self
- Opening Up All Your Psychic Abilities
- Lucid Dreaming—Interpreting, Remembering Dreams
- Getting in Touch with Your Power
- Opening the Chakras
- Clearing Blockages
- Taking a Quantum Leap
- Losing Weight, Looking Younger
- Attracting Your Soul Mate
- Having What You Want in a Relationship
- Public Recognition—Getting Your Work Out to the World
- For Self-Employed People: Attracting Business
- Flowing with the Universe
- Living with Joy
- Personal Power Through Awareness
- Creating Money: The Spiritual Law of Prosperity and Abundance.
- Creating Money: Magnetizing Yourself
- Creating Money: Clearing Beliefs and Old Programs
- Creating Money: Releasing Doubts and Fears
- Creating Money: Linking with Your Soul and the Guides
- Creating Money: Aura Clearing, Energy and Lightwork
- Subpersonality Journey: Awakening Your Prosperity Self
- Success: Releasing Fear of Success, Failure, Going for It!
- Abundance: Creating Plenty in EVERY Area of Your Life (575:231-32).

A single channeler can easily channel 50 to 100 audio/video cassettes each year. In addition, the endorsement of channeling by famous television and movie stars is making the practice much more socially acceptable. Shirley MacLaine, Linda Evans (of "Dynasty"), Michael York (of "Romeo and Juliet"), and several others have been quite influential in this (574:4-6,62-68/1096:22).

Actress Sharon Gless, who played "Cagney" on the hit TV series "Cagney and Lacey," won a 1987 "Emmy" for her role on the series. In her acceptance speech, she said that her success was due to "Lazaris," a spirit entity who speaks through medium Jach Pursel. Other famous "friends of Lazaris" have included Lesley Ann Warren, Ted Danson, Barry Manilow, and noted New Age promoter Marilyn Ferguson (1526:490).

The popularity of channeling can also be seen through new retreat centers and workshops around the country where people are taught how to open their minds and bodies to the spirits to become channels themselves. In these gatherings live teaching sessions are conducted by the spirits themselves, speaking through the channelers and motivating people to start study groups, research centers, and magazines devoted to the study and development of channeling (574:4-6,62-68/1103:10). A few of these magazines include *Spirit Speaks, The Channel Sourceletter,* and *Metapsychology: The Journal of Discarnate Intelligence.*

Another area of popularity is the growing influence of channeling in the social sciences, medicine, and other disciplines. We have provided an example in the area of medicine that follows. The spirits are speaking through their human hosts about theories in psychology, medical diagnosis and treatment, the investigation of parapsychology, the study of physics, the application of sociology, and the development of new ideas in theology, archaeology, and other disciplines (1104). In New York, spiritism has been used for several years as an adjunct to psychotherapy in some community mental health centers (1105), and the practice is spreading to other cities.

Not only in America is channeling popular; there is an increasingly visible channeling movement emerging throughout the Western world, including Canada, England, and West Germany (574:61-67/98:13-70). Brazil boasts over a million channelers, or spiritists, with tens of millions of followers (1106:227).

## INDUCTION METHODS

What are the most common methods recommended by channelers and their spirit guides for those seeking to learn how to channel? Various combinations of relaxation techniques, meditation,* visualization,* and self-hypnosis* are usually encouraged. For example, Dr. Kathryn Ridall, a channeler and psychotherapist, offers the following endorsement of meditation: "Meditation transports us to a state which is receptive to spiritual or nonphysical realities. . . . [B]ecause meditation is a tool for expanding consciousness, we can also use it to help us open to our spirit guides. . . . [A]ll willful techniques of meditation share this common thread: they still the mind, the working of the personality, by focusing on an object of meditation" (577:84-86).

In Dr. Ridall's *Channeling: How to Reach Out to Your Spirit Guides* (which Bantam Publishers also offers on audiotape) she discusses the importance of relaxation. If anything hinders the aspirant's ability to relax, "You will need to address this difficulty before you channel." (577:83). Breathing exercises, color work, use of visualization and mantras* are also cited as important components in learning how to relax for channeling (577:84-87).

*Opening to Channel: How to Connect with Your Guide* is a book specifically produced by two spirit entities calling themselves "Orin" and "DaBen." Its purpose is to help readers through a step-by-step process for meeting their own spirit guides. As these spirits tell readers, "We have designed this book for you to show you how to contact your guide" (575:53). The two channelers for these spirits state that "several hundred people have used these procedures to effectively open to channel" (575:65).

In their chapter on achieving a trance state they recommend relaxation techniques and meditation as prerequisites for successful channeling. "Spend a few days becoming familiar with relaxation techniques and learn to concen-

trate as shown in the exercise on concentration. One way to condition yourself to the trance state is through guided meditation tapes" (575:66). In the spirits' exercises for "attuning with life-force energy," they recommend using crystals (cf. Crystal Work; 575:73).

The specific exercises recommended by "Orin" and "DaBen" include deep, slow, rhythmic breathing, various visualization exercises, progressive relaxation techniques, meditation, and so on. They write that while their stated regimes are not absolutely necessary for learning to channel, they are intended to help people "become accustomed to the state of mind that is best for a guide's entry" (575:69). Below we will supply several illustrations; all quoted material comes from the spirits themselves.

After one becomes familiar with the preliminary exercises, "Orin" and "DaBen" comment, "This is it! The time to Open to Channel is now. You've dreamed of it, read about it, thought about it, and now you will do it! In the first process, you'll be welcomed by the guides, call for your special guide, and carry on a 'mental' conversation with him or her. You will be able to determine if this is the guide you will verbally channel; if it is you will proceed to the next process, Verbally Channeling Your Guide" (575:79).

Eleven specific points are cited for the initiate. Visualization* procedures are crucial (e.g., "imagine that many beings of light are coming closer to join you"; "imagine that there is a doorway in front of you. On the other side of this doorway is a world of light. . . . When you are ready, *walk through this doorway*"). Their point 7 also underscores the importance of the imagination: "Ask for the highest guide and teacher who is aligned with you to come forward. Imagine that your guide, a special guide, is coming forward. Sense this guide, feel his or her love for you. Be open to receive. Feel your heart welcoming this guide. Feel the response. Believe that it is really happening! Your imagination is the closest ability you have to channeling, and it is the easiest connection your guide has to you at first" (575:81). Their point 10 encourages the reader to ask for and submit to the spirit's influence: "Ask your guide to begin doing all that he or she can to open the channel, now that you are committed and ready to verbally channel" (575:82).

For actual possession and trance channeling, the spirits recommend the following:

Preparation: have completed all prior exercises and processes. Read through this entire process before you begin, so that you are familiar with its overall direction. Whenever you verbally channel, use a tape recorder. You will gain invaluable insights from listening again to your channeling.... Test the recorder and the microphones.... When you are in a trance state you may find that mechanical things can give you difficulties.... Be sure you have read the earlier sections about a guide's first entry and getting your guide's name. Have the Questions to Ask Your Guide ready, including the Personal Questions.... We suggest that you remain in trance no longer than about 40 minutes the first time ... (575:51).

After the first session is over: "You have made the first connection, there will be many more. Wait an hour or so before going into trance again.... if you wish, put on some special music that will assist you.... Your guide is going to come through your personality and your voice.... As you grow and understand more, we can convey more complex messages to you or messages of a broader scope. We give you the advice you can use and understand in the present" (575:51-52).

The spirits also seek to comfort the novice channeler by assuring him or her that they, the guides, are able to assume literally any form or nationality, and that they will do their best to make the experience of channeling as easy and comforting as possible:

Guides can appear to your inner eye as particular nationalities with clothing that is appropriate. I, Orin, appear to Sanaya as a radiant shimmer of light that slides around her body when she channels. She is aware that I am about eight or nine feet tall. All that she can see whenever she tries to see my face is brilliant white light. I often appear in robes such as your ancient monks wore.

Some report seeing their guides as color. Some perceive their guides as sounds, others feel their

guides are openings in their hearts.... Some people picture their guides as familiar figures they have known.... Guides can appear as American Indians, Chinese sages, East Indian masters.... Guides may appear as either male or female.... Guides will choose an identity that will best accomplish what they are here to do, or one that you can most relate to.... There are as many identities for guides are there are for people, so be open to whatever form or appearance your guide presents him or herself to you in (575:36-37).

## DESCRIPTIONS, TYPES, AND FORMS

What happens during channeling? When a channeler goes into a full trance, it is as if he is falling backwards into a deep sleep. Both his facial muscles and lips twitch as the invading spirit begins to gain control over the person. Once the spirit is in possession of the body, changes in breathing occur and the person's facial features and expressions are different, sometimes greatly different (for example, the late Jane Roberts). What can be most noticeable is when the voice changes, as when a feminine voice becomes deep and masculine (1107). Differences in brainwave patterns (2426:311), various body mannerisms, and individual preferences also occur. For example, a channeler who does not smoke or drink may engage in such activities while possessed.

The person who is possessed by a spirit may describe it as similar to an alcohol blackout or to what occurs during hypnosis.* The person loses consciousness. Later he awakens. He is told he has said and done things he would not normally have done, yet he remembers nothing about it. He is told there was a total takeover of his individual personality. Again, he became like a puppet.

For others, what is first experienced as a powerful impersonal energy outside them transforms itself into a personal entity within them. New Age channeler Shakti Gawain writes, "... as I surrender and trust more, I find my relationship with this higher power becoming more personal. I can literally feel a presence within

me, guiding me, loving me, teaching me...."
(1481:277).

Full trance channeling may involve anything that is normally done in the body, from writing, typing, and painting, to singing, dancing, and composing music, to counseling and teaching others (1108).

Below we present two firsthand reports of what channelers typically experience:

I experience Orin as a very loving, wise, gentle being with a distinct presence. He has wisdom and perspective, as well as a breadth of knowledge, that exceed anything I consciously know. There is a richness of impressions that goes beyond any of the words that he is saying. While I am conscious, I am not able to affect the words as they come through me. I can stop them, but I can't add my own words or change the message. A week before he gives me dictation on a book, I can feel him organizing the ideas and I become aware of bits and pieces of them floating into my consciousness. Once Orin has decided to teach a class on a topic, I'll receive information on the topic at unexpected times, usually when I run or meditate or when I happen to be thinking about the topic or class.

When I channel, I receive many pictures, feelings, and images, and I can hear my own thoughts and comments alongside Orin's. When Orin leaves, my memory of what he said fades like a dream. I can remember the general ideas to some degree, particularly if they have an impact on me personally, but I cannot remember the details of the information unless I read it afterward.... Unless the information is discussed afterwards I remember little of what Orin said. However, when I bring Orin through again he can remember exactly what he told people—even years later.

My experience of trance varies, depending on the information I am bringing through. I go into a very deep trance when channeling information for books and relaying esoteric information of universal knowledge. When I am channeling for other people, my trance is lighter, for it does not take the same amount of Orin's energy to transmit this kind of information (575:31-32).

The above description is fairly typical. The medium is unaware of what goes on while the spirit is possessing her and speaking through her. Unless she is later told the contents, she is unable to remember them. On the other hand, it is also characteristic for the spirits to remember specific details and to be able to pick up at exactly the place they left off, whether days, weeks, months, or years later. They are also able to refer back to technical subjects they spoke on years ago and reference the exact spot at which it was produced on paper. Exactly how they do this is anybody's guess, but perhaps it gives us some gauge of their intelligence.

Now consider our second example of a channeler's experience:

I experience DaBen as a very radiant energy, loving and exacting, who has great caring. His knowledge is very detailed and extensive. Some of the information is so complex that he has been assisting me in developing new words to transmit it. He does not want me to gloss over his concepts or simplify them, even when people cannot immediately understand them. Sometimes I understand them myself only later, after I have put several scientific channelings together and seen the interactions between them. Often I have to consult my physics books to understand what he might be explaining.

I experience fairly light trances when I am working with touch on people's energy systems, particularly because I need to move around and retain awareness of my physical surroundings. My trances are much deeper when I am channeling general information and when DaBen leads people into various experiences of expanded consciousness.

Although DaBen will search for specific information about a person's life in response to questions, it is clear that he prefers to work directly with their energy. Through my touch or by transmitting energy to them, he helps people achieve higher energy states where they can answer their questions themselves.

When I finish channeling I can remember the concepts that were gone over as though my mind is working in a new way. The specifics, however, fade very quickly. When I read the transcripts of the channelings I am amazed at how much more information is contained in them than I remember channeling. It's as if I remember only a few of the hundreds of ideas that are compressed into the words used (575:32-33).

In the previous instance note that the spirit is not only able to induce altered states of consciousness* but that they are achieved by affecting people "energetically." The goal, presumably, is to allow people to experience occult energy in an altered state, which then allows them to access information not normally available. But who can prove this is not really the experience of an indwelling demon? At the least, such an energy phenomenon would involve some form of spiritistic influence or infusion of energy (cf. Eastern Gurus).

Besides the typical experiences, there are two basic types of channeling: intentional and spontaneous. In "intentional" channeling a person actively seeks to be possessed by the spirits. In such cases, the spirits usually wait for the individual's permission to enter the body. In "spontaneous" channeling, the spirits take control when they please. The channeler is at their mercy. Yet even intentional channels may suddenly be taken over without warning and find themselves at the mercy of their formerly polite spirit guides (574:185-86/242:83,87).

Channeling also includes different forms. For example, one form brings complete loss of consciousness, while another involves partial loss of consciousness. Thus, there is full trance possession with total loss of consciousness, and light-to-moderate trance possession, in which the channeler retains partial or even full awareness.

In addition there is "sleep" channeling, where the spirits teach or influence mediums during sleep or in dreams (see Dream Work). Another form is known as "automatism," where the spirit seems only to control part of the body, such as the hands in automatic writing or painting. The Eastern guru Sri Chinmoy, a spiritual adviser at the United Nations, claims to have produced thousands of such paintings (1108).

There is also "clairaudient" channeling, where the medium only hears the words dictated by the spirits, as was true for Helen Schucman, the human amanuensis behind the popular *A Course in Miracles*.* Then there is "clairvoyant" channeling, where the spirits put certain images, pictures, or symbols into the mind of the person for a variety of purposes. This has occurred in some types of Jungian counseling.

There is also what is termed "physical" channeling, where the spirit uses the medium to affect or alter the environment. For example, the spirits, either through a medium or on their own, may materialize images of dead people (called "ectoplasmic manifestations"). They may also move or levitate objects, or imprint them with messages or pictures, or transfer objects from one location to another (known as teleportation; 574:ch. 6).

Whatever form channeling takes, it is clear that the power the medium uses comes only as a result of contact with the possessing spirit. It is universally recognized that apart from these spirits (however they may be defined) the channelers have no power.

## NEW AGE CONNECTION

Channeling is important to the New Age Movement because many of the spirits impart information on a wide variety of New Age philosophies and practices. In fact, channeling as a whole is one of the pillars of the New Age Movement. In our chapter on New Age medicine we cite over 20 examples of how spiritism or the occult influenced the originators of specific New Age therapies plus a large number of New Age health practitioners who have spirit guides, who instruct them in the use of New Age health methods or related areas. Consider the following typical description of a healing and channeling session with a patient: "I will usually both see and hear the guides....I usually have about three teachers that guide me.... The guide also visually appears to fit over me like a glove. The guide begins to move my arms and hands.... My personality self seems to be floating off and above....I feel merged with the guide" (95A:171-72).

In our discussion of acupressure elsewhere (1:89-92) we mentioned Iona Teeguarden, a leading teacher of Jin Shin Do acupressure and cofounder of The Acupressure Workshop in Santa Monica, California. In the preface to her book, *Acupressure Way of Health: Jin Shin Do*, she expresses gratitude to her spirit guide, "Iajai," for its help in her New Age medical practice (11:6).

Edgar Cayce is another example; his spirit guides produced thousands of pages of information on New Age medicine* over the years.

Another spirit entity, "Seth," dictated various texts through medium Jane Roberts on both attitudinal healing* and another popular New Age technique, dream work.* In the book *Seth: Dreams and Projection of Consciousness,* "Seth" cites information showing how dream work can be used to secure a wide variety of New Age goals. In particular, this spirit reveals how dreams can be used to develop spiritistic out-of-body excursions and altered states of consciousness* (63:6-13,39-41,63-64,193-207,350). Consider Roberts' comments about the influence of Seth:

> Seth spoke through me for over two hours, so quickly that the students had trouble taking notes. . . . The personality was not mine. Seth's dry sardonic humor shone from my eyes. The muscles of my face rearranged themselves into different patterns. My normally feminine gestures were replaced by his. Seth was enjoying himself in the guise of an old man, shrewd, lively, quite human. . . . [B]y following his instructions my husband and I are learning to develop our own psychic potentials. . . . Seth does insist that reincarnation is a fact. . . . I began to have out-of-body experiences (astral projections) as I sat in the living room speaking for Seth (1123:3-5).

## INFLUENCE WITH MEDICAL DOCTORS

Another example of channeling's influence can be seen in how medical doctors and psychiatrists are cooperating with spirits in diagnosis and treatment. This would seem to be a concerted effort on the part of the spirit world to lend credibility and prestige to the phenomena of channeling.

Consider the medical practice of neurosurgeon and former Harvard professor C. Norman Shealy, M.D., Ph.D., founder of the 700-member American Holistic Medicine Association. He is the author of *Occult Medicine Can Save Your Life* (103), and coauthor, with spiritist Caroline Myss, of *The Creation of Health: Merging Traditional Medicine with Intuitive Diagnosis* (108). Dr. Shealy has a working relationship with Myss (108:xx-xxiv), who is also copublisher of Stillpoint Publishing Company. This publisher has produced a large number of books for adults and children that have been received through channeling. They are designed to convey the importance of New Age channeling methods (732:1-15).

According to the Stillpoint catalog, Myss provides psychic diagnosis for Dr. Shealy's patients through the help of "Genesis," her spirit guide, even when the patients are hundreds or thousands of miles away (732:5-6,9). (This is reminiscent of the psychic diagnosis channeled through medium Edgar Cayce and hundreds of other psychics who use similar methods. Indeed, scores of doctors, such as William McGarey, M.D., have spent several decades integrating the spiritistic revelations of Cayce and other psychics into their modern medical professions.)

Bernard Siegel, M.D., professor at the Yale University Medical School, is another prominent physician who uses a channeler in his medical practice. "One of my patients is a medium. She regularly gives me information about the living and messages from the dead . . ." (108:xviii). Robert Leichtman, M.D., also uses spirit guides for medical diagnosis (578). He has cowritten some 40 books describing his discussions with spirits of the alleged dead through the mediumship of D. Kendrick Johnson (518).

W. Brugh Joy, M.D., has worked at Johns Hopkins Hospital and the Mayo Clinic in Rochester, MN. In *Joy's Way* (646), he details his conversion to occultism and its supposed value to his medical practice. His experimentation in mysticism and mystical energies resulted one day in his being "commanded" by a voice to reform his medical practice:

> It was a Saturday morning. I had finished rounds at the hospital and was working on some patients' charts in my office when I felt an incredibly strong urge to enter into meditation. It was so strong that I did not understand what was happening to me. I completed the patients' charts and gave in to the impress. A vortex of energy, of a magnitude I had never before experienced, reverberated through my body and threw my awareness into a superheightened state. Then a loud voice—not that of the Inner Teacher—said, in essence: "Your experience and training as an orthodox physician is completed. It's over. The time has come for you to

embark on a rededication of your Beingness to a deeper commitment and action...."

The voice didn't care about my many personal concerns and commitments. It next presented to my awareness that I would soon begin a journey into the world, going first to Findhorn [a spiritistic community in Scotland] and to England, Egypt, India, Nepal near the Tibetan border and perhaps to Japan.... The voice explained clearly that my vision of being a physician had been distorted by boyhood ideals and by the current concepts of science and medicine, which overemphasized the body and external causes and ignored the journey of the soul. I was to begin the study of alternative healing practices and reach insights Western medicine had not yet dared to dream, insights that would unify exoteric and esoteric traditions and thus form the basis of an integrated approach to the art of healing. The last instruction the voice gave me was simply to detach from everything (646:206-07).

Dr. Joy did indeed "detach," and today his commitment is given equally to New Age medical care and the radical spiritual (occult) transformation of his patients' worldviews (646:1-15).

Perhaps an illustration of how one medical doctor became converted to spiritism would be instructive. The pattern for such contacts is fairly typical. It involves careful preparation of the spirits behind the scene, psychic development, contact with spirits, rejection of Christianity, and the spirits assuming of influence or control in the doctor's life. We have selected a portion from psychiatrist Arthur Guirdham's autobiography (557) as an illustration. Here he recounts his conversion from Christian orthodoxy as a child to the ancient heresy of the Cathar faith. Catharism, or Albegensianism, teaches that the creation, the material world, is evil, a manifestation of the devil, who is Jehovah of the Old Testament (557:66-70). The true world is pure spirit and created by the one true God. Man's purpose is to ascend to knowledge of the true world and the true God in the realm of spirit. Man's materially contaminated psyche is eventually purified through reincarnation and by evolving to "higher" levels of consciousness.

Catharism, like all occult beliefs, provides a logical philosophical basis for spirit contact. The true realm of "goodness" is the spiritual world, i.e., the spirit realm; the devil is found only in the material realm. (This doesn't credit much to the practice of conventional medicine!) Regardless, once the spirit world is predefined as the true realm of God, then all contact with the spirit realm is acceptable and divine by definition. Contacting the spirit world is exclusively an encounter with the divine sphere, even a form of "fellowship" with God.

Sooner or later, however, the spirits' teachings reveal that their true nature is demonic. Through Cathar philosophy, therefore, the activity of evil spirits is camouflaged. What is ultimately demonic is wrongly interpreted as contact with the "forces of God." The spirits Dr. Guirdham contacts claim to be people who lived as Cathars in the thirteenth century, who now demand he revive their beliefs as true Christianity (557:202-19). Thus, Dr. Guirdham's spiritism not only dramatically altered his own medical practice but his life's philosophy as well. His books powerfully reveal this (557:124; cf. ref. 120). Consider the following:

I verify the evidence presented to me by different and often discarnate sources. I do this soberly and patiently. It is something which my demon demands. I cannot deny what Braida [his spirit guide] asks of me because to do so would be a mutilation of my psyche.... To me it is an inexpressible relief to find that what I had been brought up to worship was the Satanic God of the Old Testament. It is always a comfort to switch over to God from the Devil... (557:202).

The Dualist [i.e., Cathar] attitude towards nature and the universe was certainly positive and a great help to me as a doctor.... Because I was a Dualist I was enabled to accept [astrological doctrines] easily that the stars and the moon influenced the patients' medical history, and how in those susceptible to the earth's vibrations the pattern of illness was related to the seasons. This was of special importance to me as a psychiatrist.... All I can say is that the more I became saturated with Dualism the greater was my usefulness as a doctor (557:205).

Most important of all Dualism has given me a greater understanding of the nature of death....

I know that, in the next life as in this, there are guides waiting to direct us. . . .

It is clear to me that I am the modest instrument of a cosmic design. I see now that the purpose of my life and its chief happiness is to be passively manipulated. . . . I know that the dead are not dead but are living in a state of altered consciousness. I know that they are around us, that they speak to us and guide us. I know, what I would never have imagined, that they guide us not only by vague exhortations but sometimes with a precision adapted to the unbelieving rationalism of our natures. In my case they have set me a specific task to perform. When my pen moves across the paper I am doing what is asked of me . . . (557:202,205,210-12).

Dr. Guirdham is not alone. A conservative estimate is that hundreds or thousnds of qualified medical doctors, psychiatrists, and nurses around the country are either channelers themselves or currently engaged in using channelers to help them diagnose their patients. Tens of thousands of nurses currently employ a form of psychic healing known as therapeutic touch (1590:391-406). During its heyday, physicians formed a significant portion of the 2000-member Academy of Parapsychology and Medicine (APM), which devoted a good deal of time to research in psychic healing. Partly due to the influence of the APM, the spiritistic phenomenon of psychic healing is currently practiced by hundreds of physicians.

The first APM president was Robert A. Bradley, M.D., a medium and inventor of the Bradley method of natural childbirth. In his article, "The Need for the Academy of Parapsychology and Medicine," he stated that this particular method of childbirth was given to him by his spirit guides, either in dream states or by direct conscious communication. "I'm a great believer in spirit guidance. I think it is the only logical explanation for some of the things that have happened to me. . . . I personally think spirit communication is going on constantly, that we are never alone. The talks I give, the ideas I have on natural childbirth came to me either in sleep or from direct spirit communication" (517:100-01). In this article, and elsewhere, he underscores the importance of spiritism for modern medicine. He says that much important information "comes from altered states of consciousness which are spirit controlled" (517:100-01,106).

In Great Britain, the World Federation of Healers has about 10,000 members, composed largely of professed channelers or mediums. With government approval, these mediums actually treat patients in some 1500 hospitals in Great Britain. The organization has even been given corporate membership in the United Nations Association (98:50).

In America, thousands of physicians have been trained in sophrology and other New Age methods utilizing Eastern and Western mind and body disciplines such as yoga,* autogenics, Zen, Tibetan Buddhism, visualization,* and various somatic (body work) therapies (549:1-3). (See New Age Medicine for additional examples.)

Because of all of this, an increasing number of physicians are being persuaded to incorporate New Age techniques into their medical practices. As in the past, spiritism today is playing a significant role in health care. This is another example of the power of modern channeling.

## MODERN CHANNELERS

Who are the channelers? Channelers come from all walks of life. They include clerks and scholars, artists and businessmen, truck drivers and Ph.D.s, scientists and grade school dropouts, business executives and housewives. They come from all races, nationalities, cultures, and creeds. Some are atheists (initially); others are religious. Except when in a trance and possessed, they look and act normally.

Channelers often channel more than one spirit. Well-known channelers and their main spirit guides include the late Jane Roberts and "Seth." "Seth," through Roberts, produced some 25 different books, which together have sold millions of copies. Another channeler was the late Helen Schucman. Schucman and her spirit guide "Jesus" are the authors of the bestselling *A Course in Miracles,** which boasts over a thousand study groups around the country. Although an atheist at the time of her channeling, she "was brought up mystically inclined" (her father owned an occult bookstore) and was influenced by various mind science groups (574:41-42).

Another channeler is Ruth Montgomery, author of *A Gift of Prophecy*. Her spirit guide is "Lilly." They have written over a dozen bestsellers on New Age and spiritistic topics, including *Here and Hereafter, Aliens Among Us, Threshold to Tomorrow, Companions Along the Way, The Walk-Ins* and *A World Beyond*. Another is Kevin Ryerson and his spirit guide "John," one of Shirley MacLaine's favorite channelers (1109:27). Ryerson is one of the more articulate channelers and has appeared on dozens of radio and TV shows. On these shows he offers live interviews with his spirit guides (574:45). Another channeler is J. Z. Knight, who channels "Ramtha." Knight, who claims to be a former fundamentalist Christian, has sold over a thousand hours of "Ramtha's" videos and audiotapes. Like many channelers, she is now a multimillionaire (574:43-44), although she has also been the focus of much criticism. One more popular channeler is Jack Pursel, who channels "Lazaris." He runs a multimillion-dollar corporation entitled "Concept-Synergy." This corporation is dedicated to making Lazaris' teachings available to the public (574:48-49). Lazaris' teachings have been especially popular among Hollywood movie stars (1110) but are not restricted to Hollywood. Such diverse groups as Mennonites, Mormons, and Catholic nuns also testify to following Lazaris' teachings (574:49).

Elwood Babbitt was greatly influenced by the medium Edgar Cayce and today, according to his biographer Charles H. Hapgood, channels between 100 and 150 individual spirits (576:114). "Occupied throughout his childhood with the spirit world, he often played with spirit children rather than with his peers. While serving in the military, his psychic gifts were often manifested. ... [Babbitt] reports that his own spirit leaves his body and another one then takes possession.... Babbitt's voice and facial expressions change. At the end of the trance, Babbitt has absolutely no recall of what has transpired" (576:115).

Alexander Murray channels a variety of guides: American Indian, Hindu, ancient Greek, Oriental, and others. During 20 years, he has conducted over 4000 trance channeling sessions and been the subject of a large number of research projects. He is also one of television's most frequently taped channelers. Once as a guest of the Parapsychology Society he gave 20 trance demonstrations at the United Nations. He was also taped in trance for ABC's morning show and also for ABC's "Eyewitness News." NBC was sufficiently impressed, and they hired him as a consultant for their daytime soap opera "Search for Tomorrow" (576:123-24).

Mark Venaglia channels an entity called "Benjamin." He offers monthly group sessions in his New York City apartment, which draw hundreds of people. According to Venaglia, "we have thousands of New Yorkers turning to channeling" (576:140). Venaglia's spirit guide, who seems to have a special affection for homosexuals, channeled one transcript that purports to be a cure for AIDS. Indeed, several of those who have allegedly been cured were scheduled to appear on ABC's "20/20" to talk of their recovery (576:141). His spirit guide also speaks of the AIDS-infected homosexual population in glowing terms. "Those with AIDS must come to be thought of as healers.... Those that manifest AIDS are a blessed race, descended from the island of Crete and Gettys,...southwest of the Atlantian continent; an entire civilization of healers and nobles" (576:141).

When Sanaya Roman was still a teenager she visited a psychic who told her she would one day be a channeler. After graduating with highest honors from University of California Berkeley and then entering the business world, she one day decided to study the Seth books of Jane Roberts and as a result, began to experiment with the Ouija board.* Eventually, she became a channel for an entity called "Orin" and has published the bestselling text discussed earlier, *Opening to Channel: How to Connect with Your Guide*. This book is coauthored with channeler Duane Packer, a scientist with a Ph.D. in geology-geophysics. Both channelers have formed a company, LuminEssence Productions, which is in the vanguard of the channeling movement. Together they have taught several thousand people to channel through their weekend channeling courses, which cost $350 per person (576:145-47).

Tam Mossman channels an entity named "James." As an assistant editor at Prentice Hall Publishers, he became involved in channeling through editorial work done on Jane Roberts' "Seth" books. One day while making an appeal to a salesman for Roberts' *The Nature of Personal Reality*, he decided to give a mock portrayal of Seth taking over the body. Instead, Mossman himself was taken over; what he intended as humor became reality: "When I began to do the Seth bit, I felt this great rush of energy—different from anything I had ever experienced before in my life" (576:153).

Within three months Mossman was channeling "James," which he describes as an experience similar to the dream state, although he characteristically has no memory of what happens in trance. Mossman has also graduated to prominence with the channeling community, founding the journal *Metapsychology*, which focuses on the best and latest in trance material, commentary on the entities, and other areas of occult interest.

Ron Scolastico has a Ph.D. in humanistic psychology and has been channeling a number of spirit guides for well over a decade, giving more than 10,000 readings. Darryl Anka channels an entity called "Bashar," who claims to be an extraterrestrial from the constellation Orion. Anka first became interested in UFO's and occult subjects from a UFO close encounter. He then developed a keen interest in mediumship, seeking out the advice of channelers, which eventually resulted in his being contacted by "Bashar" (576:170-71). Paul Norris McClain offers channeling advice to thousands of clients out of his Miami, Florida, home. He channels literally hundreds of guides, spending most of the day in a deep trance.

Shawn Randall channels an entity named "Torah." As a writer suffering writer's block, she joined a class in mediumship taught by Los Angeles channel Thomas Jacobson in order to work through the problem. While meditating near the end of the course, she began to experience extraordinary sensations of energy in her heart and head. She engaged the process of automatic writing to discover what was happening. The answer was given that she was being prepared by the spirits to become a channel. The first entity to contact her was "Martha," followed by "Charles," and then two weeks later "Torah," who became

her principal spirit guide. As an articulate spokesperson for channeling, Randall has channeled on radio shows, appeared on numerous cable television reports, and network news broadcasts, including CBS's "West 57th Street" (576:177-79).

Kathy Reardon became a channeler through the influence of yoga,* Jane Roberts' and Shirley MacLaine's books, and by attending a lecture by a psychic, who invited the class to witness her (the psychic's) own trance channeling. During the session Reardon was spontaneously taken over. "Something strange happened to me while she was trance channeling. I felt different. I suddenly became unable to follow what she was saying. She looked far away and fuzzy.... " (2426:188). She now channels "Moira" and "Arkon," who hail from the Pleiades (2426:193), as well as others. She thinks "channeling and possession are *nothing* alike," and she describes her voluntary possession as "a healthy relationship based on trust" (2426:204).

The above is only a brief list of the several thousand channelers now operating throughout America. Various New Age directories list hundreds of organizations devoted to channeling, many of which offer courses and workshops designed to teach others to channel (576:185-219).

## EVIDENCE FOR CHANNELING

What would lead thinking people to conclude that channeling isn't all fraud and fantasy? Numerous converging lines of evidence suggest the reality of a dimension of spirits who may be contacted by occult methods. First, the belief in the possibility of spirit contact is universal. It has occurred in all countries of the world throughout human history. This is documented by a great body of research. One study of nearly 500 modern societies revealed that 74 percent accepted the reality of not just spirit contact but of actual spirit possession (297:16-17; Table Two). Something must account for so universal a belief. The skeptic who claims that such spirits do not exist holds his view in spite of this evidence.

Second, all major world religions have taught the reality of a spirit world. For example,

Hinduism, Buddhism, Christianity, Judaism, Islam, Taoism, and others all believe in a world of angels and spirits that may interact with people (1111).

Third, possessed people during channeling are able to describe events taking place in another room or on the other side of the world; they exhibit knowledge, power, and abilities which they do not have when they are not possessed (1112).

Fourth, exorcism cannot be adequately explained without assuming the reality of possessing spirits. Jesus Christ Himself believed in the reality of demonic spirits and personally cast them out of individuals (291).

The real issue here is, Who are these particular spirits of ancient and modern channeling? Are they good or evil, and how can we be certain of our answer?

Those most directly involved often say that it is the *information* that comes through the channel, not the *identity* of the entity, which is most important. Channeling promoter and leading parapsychologist Loyd Auerbach argues, "I believe channelers can provide valuable information, as long as we don't get sidetracked in looking more closely at the entity's identity, than at what is communicated" (2426:313; cf. 319). Not surprisingly, he also says, "I just don't buy the actual existence of a Supreme Evil [Satan] or of demonic entities" (2426:314).

In his introduction to channeler Pat Rodegast's text, *Emmanuel's Book*, Ram Dass, the famous Western guru, says of the spirit guide "Emmanuel" that he merely treasures the spiritual friendship and wisdom Emmanuel gives and, "Beyond this, his identity doesn't really matter" (1119:xvii).

But of course it really does matter, as we will see.

## SPIRIT IDENTITIES

Who do the spirits of modern channeling claim they are? The spirits claim to be many things, but always that they are good. Their most common assertion is that they are highly evolved spirits of the human dead. Further, a recent prestigious poll revealed that over 40 percent of all American adults—well over a third of the nation—claim to have been in contact with someone who has died. Of these, 78 percent claimed they saw, 50 percent heard, and 18 percent talked with the dead (574:3).

As noted, the spirits most often claim that they are human spirits who have survived physical death. They claim to be more evolved than we are because they have lived through many lifetimes and discovered the secrets of life and death. Thus, they also claim to reveal important information to people that will hasten their spiritual growth. And the spirits also teach that if enough people will listen to them, they can help to bring a worldwide spiritual awakening. This will produce a universal New Age of peace and harmony (574:1/622:15-16).

We should also keep in mind that because the spirits are polymorphs, they are able to appear in the form most desirable or interesting to the one they are seeking to contact. (We provide examples below.) Thus, for those interested in UFO's and life in outer space, the spirits may appear alien-looking and claim to be extraterrestrials who desire to help humanity. An example is the well-known novelist and contactee Whitley Strieber, whose story was documented in his frightening book *Communion* and in the movie by the same name (see 2764).

The spirits may also imitate the exact image of a deceased loved one or claim to help the deceased evolve more spiritually toward God. They may claim to be the various deities of ancient or modern cultures (or God Himself), Jesus Christ, ascended masters, "group beings," angels, and nature spirits. By doing all this, they spark the interest of the people they are contacting.

They may also claim to be various aspects of the "collective" mind of humanity. (Some of the terms used here include Creative Unconscious, Higher Self, Oversoul, Super-conscious Mind, "Super ESP," Universal Mind, Collective Unconscious.) They may claim to be the Holy Spirit, troubled ghosts, the spirits of animals or plants (dolphins, trees, flowers), multiple human personalities, the inhabitants of mythical cultures (Atlanteans, Lemurians), and more bizarre things, such as an alien computer that exists in the future (574:15,18,168-84/1113:14).

## THE SPIRITS AND NECROMANCY

Critics, realizing that some people claim to channel dolphins, vegetables, and computers, simply look on in disbelief. But again, one of the common claims is to channel the dead. What reason would spirits have for imitating the dead? Why do the spirits want men and women to trust them? Put simply—to deceive them.

The Bible reveals that there are evil and deceiving spirits or demons. These spirits are so corrupted they will never be redeemed; they know they will one day be consigned forever to a place Jesus called hell (Matthew 8:29). Thus, the Bible leads us to conclude the primary motive of these spirits is based upon animosity toward God and hatred of people, both saved and unsaved. They hope to take as many to hell with them as they can by seeking to prevent people's salvation through faith in Jesus Christ (John 8:44; 2 Corinthians 11:3,4,13,14; Hebrews 2:14; 1 Peter 5:8).

One of the easiest ways to fool people is to appeal to their emotional needs. Con artists do this routinely. Just as routinely, at some point in their lives, people have suffered the loss of a loved one, a friend, or an associate. By claiming to be these deceased persons and imitating them, the spirits successfully play on people's emotional needs. It will be easier for people to trust the spirits when people think the spirits are a welcome friend rather than a stranger.

Furthermore, if these spirits can be trusted as the human dead, then people will eventually conclude that the Bible is wrong about God judging unredeemed men and women at the moment of death, confining them to a place of eternal punishment (see Luke 16:19-31; Hebrews 9:27; 2 Peter 2:9). And if the Bible is wrong on such an important point, then how can it be trusted at any point? Furthermore, if, as the spirits say, the dead are not judged, then human sin is not an offense to God requiring separation from Him (Isaiah 59:2). And if sin does not separate man from God, then Christ had no reason to die for man's sin (1 Peter 2:24; 1 John 2:2). According to the spirits' views, man's faith in Christ as Savior from sin is entirely unnecessary (John 3:16).

On the other hand, if what the Bible teaches is true, then men must trust Jesus Christ and receive Him as their personal Lord and Savior. If they do not, then at death they go to judgment, and the spirits have achieved their goal (2 Thessalonians 1:8-10).

In other words, to deceive people, the spirits imply there is no judgment and that Jesus Christ did not die for the world's sin (1 John 2:2). In fact, these demons claim that people are divine and as such do not need salvation. What they recommend are "adjustments" in human thinking to conform to the spirits' teachings. In all this, the spirits have tricked men into rejecting what the Bible teaches about its own authority, God, Jesus Christ, His death, our sinful condition, the necessity of salvation, and final judgment in heaven or hell.

## THE SPIRITS UNMASKED

So the primary issue in channeling is, Who are these spirits that are influencing our culture? And is there any convincing evidence outside the Bible that these spirits, no matter how good they may initially appear, are really evil? In our book *The Coming Darkness* (1095), we documented that the spirits who speak through channelers are not the benign entities they claim to be. The entire history of the influence of these beings upon humanity suggests this. That these spirits are evil has been documented from history, religion, psychology, and from the experiences of channelers themselves.

Indeed, many occultists, such as channelers, shamans, psychics, mediums, and gurus, have testified that the spirits at times have deceived them. These occultists say the spirits first imitate good spirits but actually proceed to trick, lie to, or injure their hosts. As mentioned before, to aid in their deception, the spirits can imitate virtually anyone or anything. Satprem, a disciple of occultist and Hindu guru Sri Aurobindo, confesses what all occultists know, that the spirits "can take all the forms they wish" (1114:199).

The harrowing experience of astral traveler Robert Monroe is typical. In one of his many out-of-body experiences, he relates that he was repeatedly and viciously attacked by evil spirits. At one point in the fray, two of them instantly turned into exact images of his two daughters, emotionally throwing him off balance in his fight against them (1025:138-39). If occultists testify that the spirits have deceived them, it seems reasonable that the spirits should not be trusted.

Another example is the eighteenth-century medium Emanuel Swedenborg. He spent an entire lifetime associating with spirits. In the Western world perhaps no one had more experience with the spirit world than he did. Yet Swedenborg warned that the spirits were so cunning and deceitful that it was almost impossible to determine their true nature. As an occult authority, Swedenborg told people that demonic spirits are gifted actors who routinely imitate the dead. Thus, in a frightening way, Swedenborg still speaks to us today by saying: "When spirits begin to speak with a man, he ought to beware that he believes nothing whatever from them; for they say almost anything. Things are fabricated by them, and they lie.... They would tell so many lies and indeed with solemn affirmation that a man would be astonished.... If a man listens and believes they press on, and deceive, and seduce in [many] ways.... Let men beware therefore [and not believe them]" (1115).

Unfortunately, despite all his cautions, Swedenborg himself fell prey to deceiving spirits by thinking that God had given him special permission to contact the spirit world. Swedenborg ignored the Bible's warning against all forms of spirit contact (Deuteronomy 18:9-12). The reason Swedenborg ignored the Bible was because he believed that "good" spirits had taught him the truth. Yet the "Church of the New Jerusalem" Swedenborg founded as a result of these "good" spirits' teachings has always promoted spiritistic revelation that ranks among the most unbiblical material ever printed (1116).

So, can spirits speaking through channelers be trusted? If evil spirits do exist, and since occultists say that the spirits are deceivers, who can possibly know the real motive and nature of any channeled spirit? Obviously, if these spirits are demons, they could mask their evil intent for years and no one would be the wiser. Some objective standard must be found by which to test them. Unfortunately, channelers themselves admit they do not have any such objective standard; therefore, their trust in the spirits is blind. What can we say to channelers to help them reconsider their commitment to channeling?

The Bible teaches that channeling is spiritual deception (2 Corinthians 11:14; 1 Timothy 4:1). The spirits' goal is false teaching, the consequences of which are learned too late, or fearfully realized after death (Proverbs 16:25; Matthew 24:24; John 8:24,44; Galatians 1:6-8; 1 John 4:1; Revelation 16:14).

Deception and fraud are facts of life. Even bad men succeed in masking their true intentions to deceive others. Jim Jones may be cited as an illustration. Reverend Jones made many claims to being a minister of God. He was engaged in numerous "good works" through his church. But all along many signs were present that something was seriously wrong with Mr. Jones. Authoritarianism, intimidation of others, physical abuse of children, and irrational acts existed side by side with the "good."

But Jones had power and appeal. He had an "explanation" for the evils and the failures. As a result, many ignored the warning signs and believed he was godly. The end result was the tragedy of a mass suicide for over 900 people. A similar example can be seen in the life of David Koresh and the 1993 tragedy in Waco, Texas, where 80 people lost their lives. The same type of situation exists with the spirits who seek to contact men. They claim to be good. They claim to be sent from God. They claim to enlighten us. But sooner or later, all the warning signs are evident.

Unfortunately, people who would never trust a stranger are trusting strange spirits by the thousands. Yet there are dozens of points of similarity between spiritism (or channeling) on the one hand and the classical phenomena of demonism on the other. This includes the demonism of China, India, Japan, and other countries, as well as the demonism described in the Bible (1164:322). Thus, those who trust the spirits do so even though the history of spiritism is littered with evidence that these beings are really demons.

Anyone reading the life stories of occultists will conclude that the spirits bring as much pain and suffering into their hosts' lives as they may safely rationalize. The spirits know what they can get away with and how to cover their tracks; they are master psychologists with long experience in dealing with human nature. Perhaps this is why the channelers themselves sometimes doubt the motives of their spirit helpers.

## CHANNELERS' CONFESSIONS AND SPIRIT MOTIVES

Do many channelers sense that the spirits are not who they claim to be? Yes, and the channelers' doubts are carefully handled by the entities. For example, one of Elisabeth Kubler-Ross' spirit guides, "Salem," "proved" he wasn't a demon to a skeptical priest by allowing himself to be soaked with "holy water" while in fully materialized form. He was supposed to disappear but didn't, thus "proving" he was not a demon (1134:26-27). Mohammad, the prophet of Islam, was not certain if he was possessed by a jinn (an Islamic demon) when receiving the revelations of the Koran, but he was eventually persuaded otherwise (1135).

When unbiblical revelations started coming from Edgar Cayce's trance sessions, the famous medium openly wondered if "the devil might be tempting me to do his work by operating through me when I was conceited enough to think God had given me special power" (403:210). After his first unbiblical reading on reincarnation, he replied, "If ever the devil was going to play a trick on me, this would be it" (403:210). J. Z. Knight went through a period where she felt "Ramtha" might be a demon, but she was eventually persuaded to trust him (1136).

Laeh Garfield, author of *Companions in Spirit,* "was infuriated" at one spirit guide who "had tried to fool me in order to gain my trust" (349:78). She confesses that bad or evil entities can and do "approach you in the *guise* of a guide" (349:97), and that "some spirits are tricksters" (349:92).

Initially, several individuals associated with "The Michael Group," a company of persons involved with spirit messages given to Jessica Lansing, all had their doubts. Lansing herself confessed, "To tell you the truth, we were all pretty scared." Emily, a participant, adds, "I kept thinking about all the warnings in the Bible about various malicious spirits, and I didn't know what to think. The more I considered it the more worried I got" (2393:29).

Another example is Uri Geller, famous for UFO contacts and various psychic powers. Both Geller and his teacher, parapsychologist Andrija Puharich, M.D., had an uneasy feeling that there was something "funny" or "wrong" about their spirit contacts. They suspected they were being "played with" and wondered if the entities were unstable (281:173,188-89).

Gurdjieffian J. G. Bennett discusses the *latihan* experience in the religion of Subud. This personal experience of a supposed mystical "life force" has a number of similarities to spirit possession, and some people seem to sense something evil:

> In the latihan, we are gradually pervaded and permeated with the life force that flows into us from our own awakened soul.... The latihan itself lasts for half an hour or more.... Some trainees are convinced that there is indeed a force, but an evil one. Others are simply afraid. ... Indeed, the sense of being alone in the presence of a great Power is the strongest and clearest element of the whole experience. It is that Power that gives new life to the soul, and not ourselves, not anything that we do (1137:95,103-07).

There are many other cases where channelers have been uneasy or apprehensive over the exact nature of their encounters (349:77,92-93,96,148). Yet in the end, channelers tend to trust their spirit guides implicitly because they have been conditioned by the spirits to do this. For example, Laeh Garfield believes that "the majority of our celestial friends have worked out their human negativity and have no plans to abuse us in any way" (349:96). In response to a question about spiritual duplicity, her faith remains. One person asked her, "How can you be absolutely sure whether or not an entity is a true guide? Couldn't a malevolent spirit strike a friendly pose?" In response she said, "... as long as you approach the prospect of working with spirit guides in a positive fashion, the capricious or invidious entities will keep their distance" (349:92). But how does she know? Given the history of spiritism, one would expect just the opposite—that evil spirits would naturally take advantage of people's good motives, trust, or naïveté, for the specific purpose of deceiving them.

Modern channelers also know what spiritists throughout history have known, that the spirits are indeed interested in contact with men and women. "Spirit beings are as interested in us as we are in them, if not more so. They're interested in our physical world and in us as individuals" (349:1). But spiritists also recognize that the guides have their own agenda. "Guides can do favors for you, but you must return the favor. They're drawn to you and cooperate with you because you're capable of doing what *they* want to have happen in this world" (349:63).

The spirits also become substitutes for the help people ought to be receiving from God. Books on channeling encourage people to ask for spirit guidance, to depend on spirits for protection, to pray to spirits and receive feelings of love, joy, and great peace from them. People learn to trust in their words and advice, and in the end they develop the same kind of personal relationship with their spirit guides that God intends us to have with Him through Jesus Christ. In many cases the relationship seems to be one of trust, care, and love; yet it is one that is always includes the spirits' ulterior motives.

Consider the case of Kevin Kiper, a radio operator from Cocoa Beach, Florida. According to Kevin his spirit guide saved his life, and as a result, Kevin now listens carefully to his guide's advice. On September 25, 1978, a 727 jet from Sacramento collided with a Cessna over San Diego. The Cessna was flying in improper air space. It flew straight into the wing of the jet, tearing out a large section of the wing. The pilots did their best, but it was hopeless, and the passengers knew it. Each of them had 90 seconds to contemplate their fate as the crippled airliner plunged toward earth. Everyone died, and the last comment heard on the flight recorder was, "I love you, Mom." Incidentally, the plane crashed less than a mile from where John Weldon was teaching at a Bible school. It was one of the worst air disasters in American history, and John has said that he will never forget the train of fire trucks and ambulances that rushed past the church toward the three-block area of devastation.

Kevin Kiper was to have been on that flight. As a matter of fact, he was. His spirit guide, a female spirit he calls "Azibeth," has been with him since the age of ten. In September, 1978, while in Sacramento, he made plane reservations to fly to Chicago to see his father, but to go first to San Diego to have breakfast with his aunt. In Sacramento, he boarded the plane for San Diego—the plane on which every passenger less than an hour later was to die. Suddenly Kevin was warned: "A flight attendant spoke to me about my seat, but I didn't really hear her. I was listening instead to what Azibeth was suddenly starting to tell me. She said, 'Get off this plane right now!' So I did" (349:57). "I may have missed breakfast with my aunt, but I also escaped a certain death" (349:57). "After this incident I fully realized that Azibeth does exist. She watches over and protects me. When she talks to me, *I listen*" (349:58). In exchange for key advice at the right time, "Azibeth" has a convert for life. The moral? Save a life, own a life.

Those who learn to trust, love, and obey their spirit guides rarely understand the real nature of their guides. Sure, they provide enough care in order to establish trust, but the relationship is carefully monitored so that any upcoming maliciousness on the spirit's part can be rationalized with various explanations: the spiritual necessity of suffering, the unexpected intrusion of an "evil" ("confused") spirit, karmic rebalancing, and so on. When a person trusts a spirit in all situations, the spirit has, in essence, replaced God.

The spirits also work to keep their contacts from personal faith in Jesus Christ. In this, their hatred for their contacts becomes most evident. The spirits will pull every ruse in the book, feign every kind of love, give every conceivable pleasure, protect from any disaster necessary, to keep people trusting in *them* instead of the one true God and Jesus Christ.

This is to use "love" in the most despicable manner—in the service of evil; it is not love at all, but a pretense and a play on emotion. Jesus Himself taught, "This is eternal life, that they may know Thee, the only true God, and Jesus Christ whom Thou hast sent" (John 17:3 NASB). Why then would "good" spirits disagree with

Jesus Christ Himself, unless they were really something else?

Should a channeler begin to think seriously about Jesus Christ or consider receiving Jesus as personal Savior, the spirit will provide "true" insight. Jesus Christ will be redefined, biblical "errors" will be corrected, "Christ" himself may appear and confirm the lies. The person may be told that receiving Christ as Savior is an error of "primitive" Christianity, perpetrated by "unenlightened" Jews who mistakenly thought Jesus Christ was their Messiah. People may be told that Christianity is a spiritually unevolved religion that will bring great suffering, not only in this life, but especially in the next. And a spirit's response will be carefully tailored to the knowledge, background, and emotional makeup of their contact. Whatever is necessary to keep that person from personal faith in the biblical Christ, this is what is done.

Of course, many people disagree that the spirits are evil. One example is channeling advocate and psychologist Dr. Jon Klimo. He argues those who say that the spirits are demons and evil beings are harming the welfare of humanity. Klimo proposes that occult practices are good and something that mankind needs. In his view, a renaissance of the occult is to be achieved "with less guidance than ever before . . . from the churches of organized religion" (574:297). Klimo writes, "To the extent to which they [the churches] brand and prohibit channeling as demon worship and consorting with 'unfamiliar spirits,' they will be abdicating what should be their role: to help us reconnect ourselves in our own way with our common Source as underlying Reality" (574:297). In other words, "to return to the truth of truths . . . that we are God" (574:296).

But if these spirits are demons, and if the logical, historical, and biblical evidence points to this conclusion, then seeking them will harm mankind, not help it. What if it is a lie that we are God? What if, trusting the spirits' teachings, millions of people believe this lie, not knowing that God says that such a belief is false? What if this results in their eternal judgment? What if those who say the spirits are our helpers do so merely because that is what they want to believe, and that they are unwilling to fact the facts (2426:295,314)?

Unfortunately, people often ignore obvious facts for personal preferences. The need for meaning in life or love can cloud judgment and result in beliefs or decisions that have no basis in reality. To illustrate, consider the reluctance of many today who refuse to believe that spirits even exist. Occult writer Colin Wilson has questioned this reluctance of many to accept the spirits for what they are—real spirits:

> Why do we try so hard to find a theory that rules out living forces? It is as if a doctor tried to find a theory of disease that made no use of the concept of germs. Why do we experience a certain unwillingness to entertain this hypothesis of "discarnate entities?" . . . [It is because] there is an unwillingness to introduce a frightening unknown factor into our picture of the universe (700:460,484).

In a similar fashion, the concept of demons is often rejected because people simply refuse to believe in the reality of a spiritual evil directed personally at them. Yet this is what the Bible teaches, and why we are warned to "be on the alert" (2 Corinthians 4:4; 1 Peter 5:8).

## SPIRIT TEACHINGS

Evidence that evil spirits do have a clearly defined plan of deception, directed specifically at individuals who seek them out, can be seen in their own teachings.

The spirits will teach on almost anything. In *Reincarnation, Channeling and Possession,* parapsychologist Loyd Auerbach discusses the work of Arthur Hastings:

> Dr. Arthur Hastings, a transpersonal psychologist and parapsychologist, provides an overview of channeled information in his excellent book on channeling, *With The Tongues Of Men and Angels: A Study of Channeling.* . . . Hastings also points out certain characteristics of the messages. I've already mentioned that channelers may come through with fictional and technical information, with music and art, with philosophical and spiritual perspectives on the universe and on human experience, as well as information directed at individuals. In a brief

overview, Hastings also lists some of the following: "Social commentary, utopian models . . . Community organization and development . . . Psychological theories, personality typologies, therapies, and consciousness-expanding practices . . . Advice on daily life decisions . . . personal guidance and advice, self-knowledge . . . Diagnosis and treatment of illness and medical needs . . . Information on karma, past lives, life purpose." . . .

The messages themselves often have common characteristics. Hastings and others discuss these commonalities, and I refer you especially to his book and Klimo's for very in-depth discussions of the specifics (2426:171).

One common characteristic of the messages is their antibiblical content, regardless of the overall subject being discussed.

In essence, the spirits' consistent *religious* (and often ethical) teachings, throughout human history, reveals their true identity. At their core, such teachings are amoral, unbiblical, divisive, and opposed to human welfare. Consider a few of the popular teachings of the spirit entity "Emmanuel" in the text by Pat Rodegast titled *Emmanuel's Book*. Morally, Emmanuel teaches the permissibility and desirability of divorce (in "incompatible" marriages); the possibility of "open marriage" (adultery); the permissibility of abortion ("a useful act" when done "with willingness to learn" for "nothing in your human world is absolutely wrong"); homosexuality and bisexuality as normal behavior, even in full recognition of the AIDS plague (1119).

Emmanuel demeans political leaders as ignorant and sick and teaches that the six million Jews who perished in the Holocaust really chose to be murdered in order to grow spiritually. Predictably, Emmanuel says that Hitler and Stalin should not be condemned too severely, for they were part of God and His plan (1120).

Are these the kinds of moral codes men should live by? Are they good ethical teachings in any sense? Can they be considered socially constructive? Are these ideas what we would expect from morally pure, divine, or highly evolved spirit beings? Or are they what we would expect from evil spirit beings? Emmanuel's theological teachings deny and oppose biblical teachings. He

teaches that God and man are one (see Genesis 1–3); that faith in God is unnecessary (see Hebrews 11:1); that Jesus Christ is man's "higher self" (see John 3:16,18; Philippians 2:1-9); that death is "absolutely safe," merely a change without judgment (see John 3:36; Hebrews 9:27; Revelation 20:10-15; 1121).

Other typical New Age beliefs that Emmanuel teaches include: the monistic concept that "all is one," there is no good or evil, cosmic evolution through reincarnation, one-worldism, contact with alleged extraterrestrials, the importance of spirit contact, and so on. (1122).

The thing to remember is that Emmanuel's teachings are not the exception. They represent hundreds of other spirits' teachings.

## RELIGIOUS PHILOSOPHY

Most people consider the teachings of Jesus Christ and the Bible to be exemplary in wisdom, ethical content, and in the positive impact they have had throughout history. It would be difficult to argue that teachings which deny and oppose them should be considered good. If the spirits' teachings reject biblical instruction, on what logical basis can they be considered as the advice of good spirits? It makes more sense that the origin of anti-Christ teachings is from something evil.

So, what are the religious views of the spirits? In general, the spirits agree theologically, which is very interesting. Channeling authority Jon Klimo observes, "Time after time, through different kinds of channels and channelings, similar messages are given" (574:183). First we will present a brief summary to compare the spirits' views from channeled literature with biblical teaching. Then we will quote individual spirits in more detail to further document their unbiblical beliefs.

*God.* The spirits teach that God is ultimately an impersonal force (an "it"), like electricity, or a universal life-energy that constitutes everything. God is "infinite power," "all life," "universal consciousness," and so on. The consensus of "most channeled material" is that "God is all that is," and that "the universe is a multi-dimensional living Being," i.e., God (574:151,173). Thus, "Seth" teaches, "There is no personal God . . . in Christian terms" (1123:270). But the Bible teaches that God is a personal, holy, and loving Being who created the universe distinct from Himself (Genesis 1:1; John 3:16).

*Jesus Christ.* The spirits teach that Jesus is an evolved spirit or a man just like us. Jesus was the person who highly emulated the "Christ spirit," which is said to be part of us all. The spirits say that Jesus died and evolved to a higher state of existence. One spirit confesses that Jesus was only a representative of the impersonal divine force living in all men (the Christ spirit), and that Christians who believe in the biblical Jesus "worship a dead Christ" (1124:137-38,146-53). But the Bible teaches that Christians worship a living Christ, that Jesus *is* the Christ, and that He is fully man and fully God in one Person. He is the unique Son of God (Luke 2:11; John 1:1; Romans 1:4; Philippians 2:1-9; Titus 2:13).

*Man's Nature.* The spirits teach that human nature is perfect and one in essence with God. "White Eagle" says to all people, "You too are part of God" (1125:26). Another spirit teaches it is a "vicious abomination" to teach men that they are evil or sinful (1124:83-84). On the other hand, the Bible teaches that man is a created being and not part of God. Man was created good and innocent, but he sinned by disobeying God, resulting in his being separated from God's fellowship (Genesis 1:27; 3:3-8).

*Sin.* The spirits teach that sin is merely "mistakes," "an illusion," or ignorance of one's own deity. Sin (in a biblical sense) is nothing God is concerned with. One spirit teaches that "talk of sin and guilt" is the true evil, even though it "may be camouflaged by the use of religious buzz words such as 'Jesus loves you' or 'praise the Lord.' . . . If the minister or priest happens to be one who loves to rant and rave about sin and guilt, the forces he draws in will be dark and ugly" (1124:138,141). But the Bible teaches that sin and guilt are real. Sin is disobedience to God's law (1 John 3:4; 5:17), which apart from repentance and faith in Christ will result in God's judgment (John 3:16,36; Matthew 25:46).

*Salvation.* The spirits teach that "salvation" involves realizing that one is already part of God. Each man must accomplish this for himself by practicing various occult techniques. According to the spirits, salvation does not occur by the atoning death of Christ, which one spirit characteristically claims is "a tragic distortion of the real nature of God's love . . . " (1124:149). Spirits speaking through medium Carl Japikse teach that the Christian view of the atonement is a great social and spiritual evil. Being "born again" for salvation is a "hysterical belief," an "escape from responsibility" (1124:149). Believing in Jesus "does not serve the plan of God" (1124:83-87). Accepting Christ as one's Savior at a religious gathering is like "a circus sideshow" (1126:43). Thus, man's "struggle is not between salvation and damnation," and Christians who believe so are "ignorant fanatics" who prefer "spiritual darkness" (1126:41-42,67-69).

But Jesus and the Bible both teach that salvation means receiving the gift of forgiveness of sins from a loving God. "For God so loved the world that he gave his one and only Son, that whoever believes in him shall not perish but have eternal life" (John 3:16). Salvation has been provided for people by God's grace and is received by man through faith in Christ's death (Ephesians 1:7; 2:8,9), because "He [Jesus] is the propitiation for our sins; and not for ours only, but also for those of the whole world" (1 John 2:2 NASB).

*Death.* The spirits teach that at death there is no final judgment because death is merely transition into the amazing spirit world. "All 'spirit teaching' [agrees] . . . there is no hell, no punishment" (1118:523). But Jesus Christ and the Bible both emphasize repeatedly that death brings judgment and entrance either into an eternal heaven or hell (Matthew 25:46; Hebrews 9:27).

*Satan.* The spirits teach there is no devil. As one spirit argues, "There is no devil. . . . It is utterly absurd to believe [in] a 'prince of darkness'" (1124:67). But the Bible teaches that Satan and his demons are real, as Jesus Himself taught (Matthew 4:1-10; 8:16; 17:18).

## INDIVIDUAL SPIRITS' TEACHINGS

Now we will cite the words of some of the most popular spirits in America, because millions of people believe that what *these* spirits teach is consistent with the Bible and Christian faith. As you read the spirits words, ask yourself some questions. Are these teachings true or false? Are they good or evil? Are they what we would expect from good spirits or from deceiving spirits?

1. "Ramtha"—the spirit speaking through medium J. Z. Knight in Douglas Mahr's *Ramtha, Voyage to the New World*, Ballentine, 1987 (citations are listed by pages):

*"Ramtha's" teaching on God.* "The Christian God is an "idiotic deity" (p. 219). "God, the principle, is all things . . ." (p. 250).

*"Ramtha's" teaching on man.* "You are God" (p. 61). "God the Father is you" (p. 136). "Everyone is what you call a psychic . . ." (p. 139); "Love yourself . . . live in the moment, to exalt all that you are" (p. 149).

*"Ramtha's" teaching on sin.* "There is no such thing as evil" (p. 60). "For 2,000 years we have been called sinful creatures . . . [but] we are equal with God or Christ" (pp. 180-81).

*"Ramtha's" teaching on salvation.* "Do not preach to this world . . . the world doesn't need saving—leave it alone" (p. 130). "Relinquish guilt . . . do not live by rules, live by feelings. . . . You are the Lord of Hosts, you are the Prince of Peace" (p. 149). "Now to become enlightened is to make the priority of enlightenment first—the priority of love of Self first" (p. 227).

*"Ramtha's" teaching on death.* "God has never judged you or anyone" (p. 62). "No, there is no Hell and there is no devil" (p. 252).

*"Ramtha's" teaching on Satan and demons.* "Devil? I looked far and wide for the creature. . . . I found him nowhere, [but] I found him thriving in the hearts of frenzied entities in a fervor of madness to save the world from its sins. . . . That is where he is. [Do] you understand?" (pp. 252-53). "The devil is not really evil . . . because he's really God. . . . Who else would he be?" (p. 251).

2. "Jesus"—The spirit who worked through medium Helen Schucman in *A Course in Miracles*,* 1977 (citations are listed by volume and page):

*"Jesus' " teaching on God.* "The recognition of God is the recognition of yourself. There is no separation of God and His creation" (1:136).

*"Jesus' " teaching on Jesus.* "There is nothing about me [Jesus] that you cannot attain" (1:5). "Christ waits for your acceptance of Him as yourself" (1:187). "Is [Jesus] the Christ? O yes, along with you" (1:83).

*"Jesus' " teaching on man.* "God's Name is holy, but no holier than yours. To call upon His Name is but to call upon your own" (2:334). "You are the Holy Son of God Himself" (2:353-54).

*"Jesus' " teaching on sin.* "Sin does not exist" (3:81). "Sin is the grand illusion . . . joyously [release] one another from the belief in sin" (1:375,377-78). "See no one, then, as guilty . . . [within all men] there is perfect innocence." "No one is punished for sins, [and you] are not sinners" (1:88).

*"Jesus' " teaching on salvation.* "[Divine] forgiveness, then, is an illusion . . ." (3:79). "[It is] a terrible misconception that God Himself [judged] His own Son on behalf of salvation. . . . It is so essential that all such thinking be dispelled that we must be sure that nothing of this kind remains in your mind. I was not 'punished' because you were bad" (1:32-33,87). "A sense of separation from God is the only lack you really need to correct." "Salvation is nothing more than 'right-mindedness.'. . . "[Y]ou are one with God" (1:11,53; 2:125). "Do not make the pathetic error of 'clinging to the old rugged cross.'. . . This is not the gospel I . . . intended to offer you" (1:47).

*"Jesus' " teaching on death.* "There is no death, but there is a belief in death" (1:46). "Death is the central dream from which all illusions stem" (3:63).

3. "Seth"—the spirit that spoke through Jane Roberts, written down by her husband in *Seth Speaks*, Prentice Hall, 1972 (citations are listed by pages):

*"Seth's" teaching on God.* God is "All That Is" (p. 405).

*"Seth's" teaching on Jesus.* "He [Jesus] will not come to reward the righteous and send evildoers to eternal doom" (p. 389).

*"Seth's" teaching on sin.* "A strong belief in such [concepts of good and evil] is highly detrimental . . ." (p. 191).

*"Seth's" teaching on salvation.* "The soul . . . is not something you must save or redeem, and it is also something you cannot lose" (p. 89).

*"Seth's" teaching on Satan and demons.* "The devil is a projection of your own psyche . . ." (p. 7). "There are no devils or demons . . ." (p. 405).

4. "Lilly" and other spirits—channeled through medium Ruth Montgomery. (Note: Some of Montgomery's following statements reflect the teachings of spirits which she adopted as her own beliefs.):

*The spirits' teaching on God.* "God is the name of What Is" (2645:74).

*The spirits' teaching on man.* "God wishes that it [psychic ability] be utilized and developed to the fullest potential" (2646:160). "We are God . . ." (453:12).

*The spirits' teaching on death.* "There is no such thing as death" (453:66). "God punishes no man" (2645:174).

*The spirits' teaching on Satan and demons.* "I have seen no signs of a devil on this side of the veil ['veil' here means death]" (453:64). "The devil was not a person ever . . ." (453:65).

5. Various spirits who allegedly knew Jesus on earth, as written through medium Kahlil Gibran in *Jesus, the Son of Man*, New York: A. A. Knopf, 1959 (citations are listed by pages):

*The spirits' views on God.* "Israel should have another God . . ." (p. 32).

*The spirits' views on Jesus.* "Jesus the Nazarene was born and reared like ourselves. . . . He was [only] a man." "Jesus was a man and not a god. . . . It's a pity his followers seek to make a god of such a sage" (pp. 43,109,113).

6. "The Christ"—dozens of spirits call themselves by this name. For example: One claims to

be the biblical Jesus who, after 2000 years in the spirit world, has "acquired new ideas and experiences." He endorses occultism, teaches all men will become God, and encourages his listeners to reject Christian teachings and accept spirit contact (1127).

Another explains how the biblical doctrine of an atoning sacrifice was invented through the early Christians' spiritual neuroses and immaturity. The "Jesus" channeled through Mark Thomas recalls: "Young and baby souls tend to learn through pain. Because of their lack of ability to look inside themselves for the 'redemption' they were seeking, they had to have a 'savior' who would give it to them. . . . I tried to make it clear that I indeed did not come to 'save the world'" (2231:85). This "Jesus" says of heaven ". . . no such place . . . exists" (2231:86).

Consider what you have just read. Do the spirits endorse the occult when God forbids it (Deuteronomy 18:9-12)? Do the spirits deny that there is a devil when Jesus taught the Satan was a real, personal being (Matthew 4:1-10)? Why do you think the spirits claim people are not sinners when all people know in their hearts they are? Why do the spirits teach that God is impersonal when God has revealed Himself in the Bible as a personal Being? Why do the spirits teach people to be selfish when such behavior is universally condemned? Why do the spirits deny that Christ died to forgive sins when Christ Himself taught that this was the reason He came (Matthew 20:28)? Why do the spirits claim that Jesus was simply a man when all the evidence proves He was God incarnate, the only begotten Son of God, as He Himself taught (John 3:16; 5:18; 10:30; 14:6)? Why do the spirits say that people are God, when people know they are not? Why do the spirits deny the existence of evil when its reality is obvious to all?

The point is this: The spirits' religious teachings are exactly what one might expect from evil spirits. The problem is that the very theory that is true, that Satan and demons do exist, is the one most rarely considered by those involved in the very practices. One reason for this is the spirits' ingenious ways by which they hide themselves. We offer examples below under the general themes of "impersonation" and "creative psychology."

## IMPERSONATIONS AND DENIALS OF CHRISTIANITY

If we travel through representative illustrations of spiritistic literature in the last 150 years, we discover a universal denial of biblical Christianity. The following cases illustrate both the subtlety and influence of spiritistic literature in the last century and a half.

1. (1852) Levi M. Arnold, *History of the Origin of All Things* (Kentfield, CA: W–M Publishing Trust, 1961).

Soon after the spiritualist revival of 1848, medium Levi M. Arnold received this revelation, claiming, among other things, to offer the "true" interpretation of Christian faith. The 1852 title page alleged that the text was "written by God's Holy Spirit, through an earthly medium, published by direction of the spirits...." Because it claimed divine inspiration and to offer the true Christian faith, it naturally found appeal among nominal or uninstructed Christians. (The title page of the 1936 edition even read "Revised by Jesus Christ.")

Yet this book denies biblical doctrine, especially the deity of Jesus Christ and His atonement. It says of Jesus Christ, "He is not God.... We ought not to call him God" (p. 105). Concerning the doctrine of atonement, the spirits say, "It is a doctrine born in sin, in pride and in priestcraft. It is a doctrine of devils ... [and] the greatest of abominations" (p. 403).

2. (1886) Phylos, *A Dweller on Two Planets* (Los Angeles: Borden, 1952).

*A Dweller on Two Planets* was written through a teenage medium in 1886, by the control spirit calling itself "Phylos the Thibetan" [sic]. One purpose of Phylos (who claimed to be a "Christian adept") was to promote what has become an essential teaching of liberal and Masonic theology, i.e., that all people are the spiritual children of God. Thus, "All men or women, in churches or out, ... bear witness of the Fatherhood of God, the Sonship of Man, and the Brotherhood of Jesus with all souls, irrespective of creeds or ecclesiastical forms" (p. xvi).

3. (1870) *Oahspe: A Kosmon Bible*, and (1930) *The Urantia Book*.

These massive volumes are still popular in New Age circles today. Together they comprise over 3000 pages of detailed occult philosophy and esotericism whose anti-Christian emphasis is clearly evident. Although frequently abstruse, both volumes have impressed New Agers and other occultists with the profound "wisdom" that may be achieved through contact with the spirit world.

4. (1889) Alexander Smyth, *The Occult Life of Jesus of Nazareth* (El Cajon, CA: Unarius, nd), reprint of 1899 edition.

The title page of the 1899 edition reveals that the medium Alexander Smyth received the content of this book "from spirits who were [allegedly] contemporary mortals with Jesus while on the earth, given through the mediumship of Alexander Smyth." In this book the biblical God is portrayed as "an emotional, vindictive even murderous god...." (preface). The text also illustrates a somewhat common spiritistic theme, that of demons impersonating the spirits of the dead who knew Jesus (like some apostles) and, having found "salvation and truth" in the afterlife, now confess or repent of the falsehoods that they once taught about Jesus or wrote in the Bible.

This is illustrated in one modern version of Smyth's *The Occult Life of Jesus of Nazareth*, which is titled *The True Life of Jesus of Nazareth, The Confessions of Saint Paul*. This book claims that the spirit of the apostle Paul possessed Alexander Smyth in order to tell the world the "truth" about Paul's "false" teachings in the New Testament. For example, "Paul" confesses the following about how he deceived the world with his epistles and their "damning," "wicked," and absurd doctrines:

> Indeed, with a little well performed imposture, I pretended that the spirit of Jesus had appeared to me.... My imposture was generally believed by the disciples and [I went about] ... preaching certain doctrines of my own invention, which I gave to the world as being the doctrines of ... Jesus.... My own fictions and lies I passed off as being the Gospels of truth.... Oh! What a terrible monstrosity! What a mountain of vile imposition I have imposed upon the

world! My deeds while on earth were black and heinous enough; but the wickedness of my doctrines, which I left to after ages of blind, credulous man, were ten thousand times more damning.... The ridiculous and absurd doctrines I preached concerning Jesus—all the nonsense of faith, grace and salvation by the redemption of sins through the blood of Jesus the Christ. [Also] look at the books called the Gospels. ... Examine these books, and see the mass of confused and contradictory nonsense delivered as the teachings of Jesus. See the absurd and ridiculous light in which his character is represented ... (p. 23).

5. (1927) Walter Franklin Pierce, *The Case of Patience Worth* (NewHyde Park, NY: University Books, 1964), reprint.

In capital letters the cover jacket of this book challenges readers with the following: "This book differs from every book hitherto issued on a psychic subject. It consists primarily of literature. The problem is how this literature, displaying such knowledge, genius, and versatility of literary expression, philosophic depth, and piercing art could have originated, beginning suddenly one day, in the mind of a thirty-one-year-old housewife with an eighth grade education."

Here is a brief recap of the story. During her lifetime, Pearl Lenore (Mrs. John Curran) received some three million words, or approximately 10,000 pages of information from the spirit world. The pattern of hereditary transmission of psychic ability was evident; e.g., Mrs. Curran's uncle had been a medium (p. 11). The first communications came through Mrs. Curran's experimentation with a Ouija board* on July 8, 1913. The spirit announced itself as "Patience Worth," a spirit who supposedly lived in seventeenth-century England.

Given its literary style, great debate ensued over how Mrs. Curran could ever have produced and articulated the materials she did, let alone through a Ouija board or spontaneous evocation. Her detailed knowledge of seventeenth-century England, ancient Rome, and other cultures startled even skeptics. In general, the display of knowledge was entirely beyond the conscious capabilities of Mrs. Curran. For example, old French, Anglo-Saxon, and Scandinavian words

were incorporated into different stories without ever confusing them. E. H. Garnett, a Chicago lawyer, commented, "There is, so far as I know, no other person in the world who can, under such circumstances, even remotely approach this work, either in spontaneity, beauty, perfection of form, or in content" (p. 30). Even the *New York Times* (July 8, 1917) marveled at the "remarkable" nature of Mrs. Curran's first two novels.

Mrs. Curran's method fit the pattern of many modern channelers. After extensive work with the Ouija board, she progressed to clairaudient inspiration, where she could hear the words without having laboriously to spell them out through the board. Occult visions also conveyed messages. For example, "when the stories come, the scenes become panoramic with the characters moving and acting their parts, even speaking in converse. The picture is not confined to the point narrated, but takes in everything else within the circle of vision at the time.... If the people talk a foreign language, ... I hear the talk, but over and above is the voice of Patience, either interpreting or giving me the parts she wishes to use as a story.... It is like traveling in new and unknown regions" (cited in D. O. Roberts, C. E. Woodcock, *Elizabethan Episode*, 1961, p. 15).

The philosophy of Patience Worth is as spiritualistic as her theology is heretical. From the beginning, the spirit claimed that its purpose was, through various forms of literary speech, to convince others of the truth of the spiritualist worldview (p. 294). For example, the spirit taught that the dead are close to us, hovering over us, and that efforts should be made on behalf of the living to communicate with them (pp. 295-96). Patience Worth also took pains to caricature Christian belief and Christian ministers and denied and opposed the biblical nature of God and salvation (pp. 35,156,168).

Psychical researcher and noted authority on apparitions, G. N. M. Tyrrell, observed, "Patience was a strongly marked character with a caustic tongue and an emphatic will of her own and bore no discernible resemblance to Mrs. Curran" (*The Personality of Man*, pp. 135,138).

6. (1928) Ida Ekert, ed., *Aubrey Messages* (Los Angeles: Lawrence Austin, 1928).

As a child, Aubrey never liked to go to Sunday school; in fact, he hated the God of the Bible (p. 17). After he died he supposedly began communicating messages about the truth of the afterlife, e.g., "that the blood of Christ does not wipe out our sins is [certain]" (p. 27). Thus, after death there is "no God to judge, no recording angel to read out my sins or to give me praise for anything I had done" (p. 29).

7. (1928) Kahlil Gibran, *Jesus, the Son of Man: His Words and Deeds as Told and Recorded by Those Who Knew Him* (New York: Alfred A. Knopf, 1978).

Kahlil Gibran was a celebrated poet and the author of the well-loved classic *The Prophet*. But he was also a medium who received this and other books by means of psychic impressions. In *Jesus, the Son of Man*, the spirits of those who allegedly knew Jesus revealed the "truth" about Jesus Christ and His teaching through Gibran. In Gibran, one finds a systematic dismantling of New Testament teaching. Gibran's spiritistic revelations accept reincarnation, deny the atonement, alter Scripture and, in general, distort Christianity (pp. 120-35,170,190). Readers are told, "Israel should have another God" (p. 31); and, "this man, Jesus, this Nazarene, he has spoken of a God too vast to be unlike the soul of any man, too knowing to punish, too loving to remember the sins of his creatures" (p. 32).

The apostle "John" reveals that Jesus was merely a man. The "Christ" is the God part of Jesus and also of all people. Thus, "many times the Christ has come into the world and he has walked many lands" (p. 42). "Jotham" of Nazareth states of Jesus, "He was not a God, he was a man like unto ourselves..." (p. 109). Barca, a merchant of Tyre, comments, "I believe that neither the Romans nor the Jews understood Jesus of Nazareth, nor did his disciples who now preach his name" (p. 112). "The Galileans would make a god of him and that is a mistake" (p. 113).

In contrast to a biblical account, the rich man of Matthew 19:16-22 now argues that it was *more* moral for him to stay rich than to give his money to the poor (p. 148)! The spirit of Philip argues on behalf of a pagan concept of reincarnation (p. 170). "Saba of Antioch," who supposedly knew the apostle Paul, tells us of Paul's errors, spiritual bondages and delusions, and that, "He speaks not of Jesus" but of his own falsehoods (pp. 61-62).

In light of all this, Kahlil Gibran concludes by stating that churches today are not built upon the teachings of Jesus and that Jesus' joy does not comfort any Christian (p. 211). In the end, then, Jesus is "a man too weak and infirm to be God" and "a god too much man to call forth adoration" (p. 211).

8. (1934) A. J. Russel (ed.), *God Calling* (New York: Dodd, Mead & Co., 1945).

*God Calling*, which is, incredibly, now published by Revell Publishers as "The Classic Christian Devotional," actually made the evangelical bestseller list twice (1986 and 1988). It also claims to have been inspired by Jesus Christ, and it has been read by millions of Christians.

The two English ladies who received this spiritistic inspiration in 1932-33 describe themselves as the "two listeners." Like the modern New Age channeled text, *A Course in Miracles,** God Calling* claims that its messages were given "by the Living Christ Himself" (p. 3). Thus, "...*we* were being taught... day by day by Him personally, when millions of souls... had to be content with guidance from the Bible..." (p. 10).

Characteristically, however, the text is replete with denials of biblical teaching. For example, "Jesus" affirms the following, verbatim in the text:

- So only I, being God, can recognize the God in Man (p. 103).
- All true love... is God (p. 96).
- [Certain others] can never know the ecstasy ... of spirit communication as you know it (p. 55).
- Trust in the Spirit Forces of the Unseen... (p. 203).
- Power is just God in action (p. 211).
- Looking to Me all your thoughts are God inspired. Act on them and you will be led on. They are not your own impulses but the movement of My spirit... (p. 124).
- I and My Father are One. One in the desire to do good (1981 ed., p. 152).
- I need you more than you need Me (1981 ed., p. 60).

- I await the commands of my children (1981 ed., p. 63).
- I am actually at the center of every man's being . . . (1981 ed., p. 55).
- Love is God. Give them love and you give them God (1982 ed., p. 72).

This text also denies the atonement (pp. 157, 216), subtly encourages psychic development and spiritistic inspiration under the guise of Christ's personal guidance (pp. 44-45,55-56, 117-18,203,207-08,214), and often misinterprets Scripture (p. 56).

9. (1939) Frederick H. Wood, *This Egyptian Miracle* (Philadelphia: David McKay, 1939).

If the goal of the spirits in the case of Patience Worth was to intrigue through literary style, the goal here was to do the same thing through an allegedly lost Egyptian language. In this case the principal spirit guides, "Nona" and "Vola," spoke through the medium "Rosemary" (a pseudonym) in a language that the girl could not possibly have known. By the time the book was published in 1939, Dr. Frederick Wood had collected over 30 volumes of xenoglossic material. The spirit guides said that their purpose was to communicate information about ancient Egypt, occult philosophy (especially reincarnation), and the facts concerning spirit guidance (p. 112).

Rosemary's method of psychic inspiration is similar to modern channeling. After complete relaxation of mind, will, and body, the spirit enters the medium and possesses it, and this is followed by automatic dictation or writing (p. 32). The medium clairaudiently hears Nona say the Egyptian words first, the dictation being sufficiently clear and gradual for her to record them; afterward, no conscious recollection exists. Rosemary explains, "When Nona speaks through me, there is no thinking first. My lips move, and the words come but I cannot tell you how. . . . What Nona has said is not retained at all. I could not repeat what was said, nor could I give the substance of it, after it has been spoken" (pp. 32-33).

The purpose of the spirits was not primarily to give information on ancient Egyptian beliefs and language, lost or otherwise. It was primarily to promote occult philosophy and spirit contact by means of a seemingly credible, or at least inex-

plicable, revelation from the dead who supposedly lived in ancient Egypt. Dr. Wood comments, "The most valuable and important communications made by her [the spirit] through Rosemary are not, in my opinion, the words, phrases and sentences of Egyptian xenoglossy. These are evidential to a remarkable degree, and they have raised the case to its present high standing among students of psychic research in many parts of the world. But far more important, I suggest, are the explanations given of psychic contact in its various aspects . . . " (pp. 29-30).

10. (1950) Wilfred Brandon, *Open the Door* (New York: G & R Anthony, 1950).

The goal of the spirits is twofold: 1) to discredit Christianity, and 2) to promote occultism. In this case, Edith Ellis is the medium through whom the deceased spirit of Wilfred Brandon conveys the "truth" about the afterlife and the importance of occultism. The spirit strongly encourages the "good work done by the societies for psychic research, in the phenomena and investigation of mediumistic powers . . ." (pp. 178-79). To no one's surprise, whereas some of the most spiritually advanced souls in the next life are atheists, the most pitiful and regressive are the Christians (p. 98), who always seem to have the most trouble or the most difficulty adjusting in the next life. For example, "The most difficult class of men are those who are wedded to the ideal of a personal God" (p. 115). Among the "unfortunate souls" who suffer in the next life are those who "come here with the idea of finding 'heaven.' . . . They believe that they are chosen to 'sit on his right hand and to dwell on the actual presence of a personal God.' . . . [W]e are seldom able to convince them that they have been too literal in their acceptance of the statements in the Bible. . . . So we have to carry on a never-ending battle with these poor souls who block their own progress and are of no help whatever in our work" (171-72).

Christians are also "ignoramuses" and "poor bigots" whose personal beliefs prevent them from following the path of spiritual evolution and reincarnation. "We are beginning to wonder how, in this age, there can be so many of these backward mentalities. When you mortals realize the danger of unscientific religious dogma, you will be eager to spread [occult] knowledge by every possible means" (ibid.). Christians who teach biblical falsehoods are "liars," and they are "more dangerous than thieves or even murderers. They are the poisoners of all" and should be condemned as those who have "wrecked the world" (pp. 181-82).

Not unexpectedly, the spirits have absolutely "no condemnation for sinners" because "sin" is merely "the result of ignorance." On the other hand, Christians who hold fast to their "errors" will receive no mercy at all. "There is no mercy for any sinner who holds wrong ideas, and in this we include these who have a fixed idea of deity, of their personal relationship to it, and of their specially favored position in this relationship" (182).

11. (1961) Daisy O. Roberts, Collin E. Woolcock, *Elizabethian Episode* (1961).

"Patience Worth" used literary prose and poetry; "Nona" and other spirits employed ancient Egyptian. With this book we have the alleged spirits of Shakespeare, Hamlet, and others who claim to have dictated a set of Shakespearean plays through medium Daisy O. Roberts. Five years after her husband's death, Mrs. Roberts, who disliked "orthodox church religion," began to experiment with automatic writing (pp. 8-9). But the Shakespearean plays were only the means to the larger goal of promoting occult philosophy. "It will be obvious from even the most casual reading of the scripts to follow that the principle of the reincarnation of souls is one of the fundamental ideas contained therein. So much so that their literal acceptance is impossible without subscribing to this belief" (p. 21).

12. (1971) Rosemary Brown, *Unfinished Symphonies* (New York: Morrow & Company,1971).

From the time she was a young girl Rosemary Brown saw the spirits of the dead. "The first time I saw Franz Liszt, I was about 7 years old and already accustomed to seeing the spirits of the so-called dead" (p. 13).

Rosemary Brown, who learned to play the piano moderately well, nevertheless claimed that, in trance, the spirits of a half dozen great composers dictated compositions through her in their own unique style. Hundreds of pieces of music and a number of albums based on the compositions have been published. "My words and the music are constantly analyzed. The music has been put through countless tests. I have voluntarily taken musical tests, intelligence tests, psychological tests, psychic tests—every kind of test imaginable . . . "(p. 19). Music authorities have investigated Brown's compositions and found them to be similar in style to the deceased composers, but no one has been able to explain exactly how an unaccomplished musician could perform such a feat.

Nevertheless, again we see the common themes: An unexpected phenomenon becomes the vehicle for expanding spiritist philosophy. And the individual revelations by these alleged spirits of the dead composers reject biblical teaching. For example, "I remarked that because of the usual Christian beliefs, there are people who believe that one has to be 'saved' here on earth. 'That is not true,' he [Liszt] said. 'Life on your earth is rather like a nursery school. When people die . . . they still have the chance to go on and to catch up'" to the more advanced spirits (pp. 111-12). Liszt also said that God is "not as those on earth think of Him. God is Spirit, a life-force which permeates everything and is everywhere," personal and impersonal simultaneously (p. 110).

13. (1972) Estelle Roberts, *Fifty Years a Medium* (New York: Avon, 1972).

The spirit guide of Estelle Roberts, "Red Cloud," has also "toiled unceasingly to demonstrate eternal spiritual truth" (p. 210). But again we find the same old spiritistic philosophy. Red Cloud teaches that "God is not a being but a force of good which permeates the universe and is infinite. Evil is not a force, but an error in thought. . . . " "Every individual is part of the whole which is God. And because we are all part of the Infinite Spirit of God, we cannot die." "The gradual unfolding of the consciousness of the Mind of God within us is the process of the evolution of our souls" (pp. 211-12).

14. (1968–1995) The books of Ruth Montgomery.

Medium Ruth Montgomery has written over a dozen books in conjunction with her spirit guides, usually through the method of automatic typing. From the first book they dictated through her, the spirit guides have demeaned Christianity and promoted occultism. In *A Search for the Truth* (1968), her guides emphasized that occult development and spiritistic contacts are positive spiritual methods blessed by God. "The Guides were quick to emphasize that such contact between the two planes is good, not evil." And, "This [ability] could not exist, were it not that God wishes it to be used for the advantage of us all, His children." Thus, "Those who mistakenly call it the work of the devil are shortsighted indeed, for this power would not be suffered to continue through the ages unless God the Father wanted it used" (Bantam, 1968, pp. 159-60).

In *A World Beyond*, Montgomery records the messages of the famous trance medium Arthur Ford, who returned to inform the world of the glories of occultism and the errors of Christianity. Note Ford's description of God: "For if each of us is God, then taken together we are God" (p. 7). "God is the core of the universe from which all else flows forth. He is truth and energy . . . " (p. 30). "I have seen no signs of a devil on this side of the veil" (p. 70). "The devil was not a person ever. . . . Man, not God, created Satan . . . " (p. 71).

The above are examples of only a few of the more obvious cases of spiritistic inspiration. There are also the more subtle but equally large number where such inspiration is unconfessed, and yet the religious and moral implications are just as unbiblical.

For example, few realize how famous novelist Henry Miller's extensive interest in the occult, including theosophy, anthroposophy, magic, Eastern metaphysics, and astrology,* beginning in the mid-1930s (1481:57-58), influenced his pornographic novels. Another famous novelist, Taylor Caldwell, author of such books as *I Judas* and *Great Lion of God* about the apostle Paul, was also influenced by the occult, beginning in 1938 at a spiritualist meeting with Dr. Charles Nicholson of England. At this meeting Caldwell allegedly received a message from her dead father through the medium (Nicholson), encouraging her literary efforts. Subsequent visionary experiences and dreams convinced her concerning the truth of reincarnation and the development of psychic abilities (1966:179-84/2647/2648).

Caldwell's eventual conversion to the occult interested many in that realm. Some have suggested that the meticulous detail of her novels came not from primary research but from a form of spiritistic inspiration, especially since she confessed that her own 1967 text, *Dialogues with the Devil*, came as the result of such a method. In the foreword, she wrote that the devil and his "brother" Michael the archangel are the real authors: ". . . Two personalities took over the book in mid-passage, but what they are I do not know. Certainly the thoughts of the book are not my thoughts."

## "CREATIVE" PSYCHOLOGY

Many channelers claim their spirit guides are only a part of their subconscious minds, their intuition,* or their "creative unconscious." The spirits themselves may claim this (574:304-07). Channelers may say this because they are uncomfortable with the idea that real spirits are actually possessing them. These channelers find it easier to believe that the spirits are merely part of the newfound powers of their own mind or of human genius.

Consider the following comments by one of the leading British mediums, Eileen Garrett: "A further word about the controls may here be in order. I long ago accepted them as working symbols of the subconscious. . . . For myself, I have never been able wholly to accept them as the spiritual dwellers on the threshold, which they seem to believe they are. I rather leaned away from accepting them as such, a fact which is known to them and troubles them not at all" (2425:86-88). The spirits are not at all concerned by Garrett's classification of them as aspects of her own subconscious because it still permits them free rein. (See New Age Intuition and New Age Inner Work for more examples.)

Interestingly enough, modern parapsychology (the scientific study of the occult) has provided much support in the area of relabelling the activity of these spirits. People who would never permit themselves to be possessed by spirits might welcome the "scientific-sounding" idea that they are really only developing natural psychic abilities, or contacting the collective unconscious or their own "archetypes," or the alleged "higher consciousness," or the "divine mind." Once the spirits' activity is masked under the disguise of neutral mind powers, their activity becomes unrecognizable for what it really is: true spirit contact. What is frightening is that many people in the psychological and scientific community and in the psychic community are redefining something supernatural and demonic as something natural and human. Professor Jon Klimo's text, *Channeling: Investigations on Receiving Information from Paranormal Sources,* illustrates this profusely (574:14,20, 39,131,205-320).

In his classic book *The Screwtape Letters,* Oxford scholar C. S. Lewis astutely portrays two devils talking to one another and planning their strategy for deceiving men:

> Our policy, for the moment, is to conceal ourselves. Of course, this has not always been so. We are really faced with a cruel dilemma. When the humans disbelieve in our existence, we lose all the pleasing results of direct terrorism, and we make no magicians. On the other hand, when they believe in us, we cannot make them materialists and skeptics. At least, not yet. I have great hopes that we shall learn in due time how to emotionalize and mythologize their science to such an extent that what is, in effect, a belief in us (though not under that name) will creep in while the human mind remains closed to belief in the Enemy. The "Life Force," the worship of sex and some aspects of Psychoanalysis may here prove useful. If once we can produce our perfect work—the Materialist Magician, the man, not using, but veritably worshipping, what he vaguely calls "Forces" while denying the existence of "spirits"—then the end of the war will be in sight (1128:32-33).

Today, psychology is promoting the activity of spirits under a nonthreatening psychological language. For example, we now have past-life therapy,* inner-counselor therapy, transpersonal psychology, transcultural psychiatry, metapsychiatry, and shamanistic counseling, all of which may verge on or involve spiritism.

Certain concepts in modern psychology, therefore, are becoming a tool for camouflaging

the demonic and expanding its influence in society under another name. Proof of this is seen in that virtually every occult power or spirit manifestation has been "explained" psychologically or parapsychologically, or endorsed humanistically, as the "new powers of the mind." And when psychology redefines these spirits as the hidden potential of the human mind, then one goal of therapy is to tap into these new powers (574:39, 131-32,184,237-53). This approach agrees with the stated purposes of many of the spirits themselves, who say their goal is to "empower" people to get in touch with their own "intuition," "higher self," "creative sub-personality," or "divine potential," so that in the future *everyone* will become a "channel" for something (574:183-84). Desiring invisibility, the spirits want people to view their activity as nothing more than the normal workings of the human mind.

## MULTIPLE PERSONALITIES AND CHANNELING

Although not all cases of multiple personality disorder (MPD) are spiritistic, some clearly are. This illustrates yet another ruse whereby spirits can operate invisibly under the guise of a neutral concept in order to secure their goals.

This area can be quite difficult to sort out. For example, on a recent news magazine television program they interviewed a woman with over 50 multiples. It clearly seemed like a genuine case of MPD. But even where spiritism is not a probable cause, it seems that at least *one* of the personalities often acts like an evil spirit or a demon. In this case, one of the personalities mutilated the woman's body, carving out of the flesh on her arm the words "you must die" and carving an upside-down cross on her forehead. This could simply have been a form of pathological self-mutilation, but we are suspicious when one of the personalities seems to act like a demon, e.g., employing self-mutilation and satanic elements like upside-down crosses. Even if all the other multiples are in fact reflections of a legitimate psychodynamic, how do we know an evil spirit hasn't joined in to mask its own activity?

Also of concern is the fact that multiple personalities usually emerge from altered states of consciousness,* especially hypnosis.* Associate professor of psychology Elizabeth L. Hillstrom, specializing in physiological psychology at Wheaton College, comments: "In most cases, however, new 'personalities' apparently do not manifest themselves in normal consciousness unless they have first made an appearance in the hypnotic state, while the therapist is actively searching for them. This, along with the fact that people with multiple personality disorder are often deeply hypnotizable and suggestible, raises the disturbing possibility that therapists are unwittingly creating many of these personalities with their own suggestions" (2659:67) (cf., Hypnosis)

Other psychological and parapsychological researchers have made similar notations. And, as we will discuss in a moment, they also note that a clearer connection to spiritism is beginning to emerge even in the minds of some secular researchers.

Consider the following comments by transpersonal psychologist Alberto Villoldo and distinguished parapsychological researcher Stanley Krippner in their *Healing States: A Journey into the World of Spiritual Healing and Shamanism:*

> Many psychotherapists have observed the emergence of "subpersonalities" in their work with clients during hypnosis, guided imagery, or emotional catharsis.... In cases of multipersonality, subpersonalities assume identities of their own and will often engage in outrageous experiences of which the person has no knowledge.... Subpersonalities often emerge in hypnosis. In one study, 78 students were hypnotized, after it had been determined that they could enter altered states of consciousness quite easily and go into deep hypnotic states. They were requested to go back to an age preceding their births and be somebody else. This was an easy task for 32 of the students.... [So what really happened here?] Did the hypnotized students manifest subpersonalities? Past lives? Spirit entities? Any or all of these possibilities might be valid and further investigations are needed to produce more data (91:184-85).

In the meantime, some psychotherapists who deal with cases of multipersonality have taken interest in spiritism. Ralph Allison, an American psychiatrist who has worked with many clients demonstrating this problem, has described the "alter personality" as serving a definite and practical purpose. "Repeatedly," he observes, "I encountered aspects of entities of the personality which were *not true alter personalities.* . . . I have come to believe in the possibility of spirit possession." [Allison is the author of *Minds in Many Pieces* (New York: Rawson, Wade, 1980).] There is always a reason for an "alter personality," usually due to abuse or trauma in childhood. Thus, according to Allison, "The discovery of an entity who doesn't serve any recognizable purpose presents a diagnostic problem. Interestingly enough, such entities often refer to themselves as spirits. Over the years, I've encountered too many such cases to dismiss the possibility of spirit possession completely" (91:20-21, emphasis added).

Thus, what is significant about MPD is that a number of psychological researchers and therapists who investigate this phenomenon are *not* always sure if they are dealing with actual spirits or internal alternative personalities. The implications of this are disturbing, to say the least.

The New Age text *Higher Creativity* argues that the phenomenon of multiple personalities may actually help promote the social and scientific acceptance of channeling:

> Recent research on the phenomenon of so-called "multiple personalities" suggests that this term may prove to be an extremely useful metaphor that reduces the scientific aversion to the channeling phenomenon.... The alternate personality—or personalities, since there are often a number of these part-time residents—is typically very dissimilar in such characteristics as speech and thought patterns, mood and temperament, etc.; these differences may show up in physiological changes such as: voice, gender, brain wave patterns, chemical balance in body fluids, and so forth . . .

> The establishment of the reality of alternate personalities may open the door to a scientific dialogue about channeling, a dialogue which has thus far been largely conspicuous by its absence. . . . [I]t is already the case in the literature on multiple personalities that some of these

alternates have rather remarkable capabilities. Using the scientifically accepted metaphor of multiple personalities, it is possible to begin to explore the channeling phenomenon in a scientific way without getting hung-up on the usual metaphysical questions. The existence and apparent wisdom of the channeling source can be noted and explored while leaving open questions about the nature of that source as whether the alternate personality is "really" a person who once lived on the earth, or a being that exists in some trans-terrestrial space or dimensions or merely a phychological off-shoot of the channeler's psyche. Such questions may never fall within the domain of science other than as alternate hypotheses, and yet the fruits of the channeling phenomenon can come to be appreciated and used to the benefit of humankind—leaving open the issue of the ultimate nature of the channeling source, as scientists in fact leave open the issue of the ultimate nature of consciousness and of "ordinary" human personality (2394:119–120).

In a standard text, *Channeling,* Professor Jon Klimo gives examples of the similiarities between MPD and channeling and the difficulty of separating them. But the differences must also be noted; for example, 75 percent of MPD patients apparently report personalities under the age of twelve, a rarity among channelers, and most multiples have several or many personalities, while most channelers have only one or two (574:237–239). Still, there are remarkable parallels in the phenomenon itself, so much so that "a growing number of clinicians and researchers ... are beginning to believe that at least some of the alter personalities are actually impinging from outside the multiple's psyche, as in the case of unwanted possession" (547:237).

When the phenomenon per se is indistinguishable from channeling, and while the personalities give similar or identical messages to those given by the spirits of channeling, one has to be suspicious.

Further illustration of the confusion can be seen in the fact that many times those who are mediums are possessed by spirits, such as Louis Gasparetto, are *conceptualized* as having multipersonality disorder. Consider the following discussion about Gasparetto: "Each subpersonality

when dominant, determines that person's attitudes, showing relatively distinct behavioral patterns. In some subpersonalities, amnesia exists for the thoughts and actions of the other subpersonalities. Some 'alter personalities' may try to sabotage, dominate, or destroy the 'host personality'" (91:38).

If researchers think that some of the personalities in MPD are actual spirits, while other researchers interpret actual spirit possession as MPD, it is easy to see the potential for confusion in sorting out what is actually occurring. Consider the following discussion of the famous trance medium Eileen Garrett, whose main spirit guide was "Uvani," but who also channeled other spirits by the names of "Abduhl Latif," "Tehotah," and "Rama":

> Ira Progoff, a psychiatrist, extensively interviewed Garrett and each of her spirit guides. He observed that Tehotah and Rama emerge from a deeper level of consciousness than did the other two spirits, and that they resembled the "archetypes" or universal symbols written about by Carl Jung. Progoff felt that Garrett was a highly complex person who used her mediumship and spirits in an ingenious way to obtain personality integration (91:184).

> Garrett herself wavered between regarding her voices as her own subpersonalities and as guides from the spirit world. *From a psychological point of view it makes little difference, because they serve the purpose of personality integration.* Furthermore, they provided her with information with which she was unfamiliar in her ordinary state of consciousness—information found to be useful by her clients. Larry Peters and Douglass Price-Williams find the shaman's "astro flight" and the medium's "spirit incorporation or possession" to be highly psychotherapeutic (91:197, emphasis added).

To the contrary, from a psychological point of view it makes all the difference in the world whether we were dealing with real spirits. If spirits serve the purpose of personality integration, or provide "useful information," they are simply using these as a ruse to gain influence or control over a person. The basic problem with modern psychology is that it has no categories to deal effectively with spiritistic intrusion or imitation of MPD. Unfortunately, even those characteristics that *distinguish* MPD from spirit possession *could* be engineered on the part of the spirits. We are not saying this is the case; only that it cannot entirely be ruled out.

## BIBLICAL PERSPECTIVE

All of this harmonizes with what the Bible reveals. Demons are personal evil beings who camouflage themselves for hidden purposes. Their disguises range from promoting themselves as myth to the opposite extreme of promoting themselves as the ultimate reality, God Himself. And, indeed, the majority of people either believe that Satan does not exist or that psychic powers* and contacts with spirits through channeling are actually divine practices and represent contact with God.

In the world today most people believe in the existence of evil, but few recognize the existence of the devil who accounts for great evil. To believe in endless lesser evils, but not in the evil one (Satan), who is responsible for far greater evil, is to not recognize a potentially great threat. If the devil can misdirect our attention through various forms of channeling and get us to think about our own self-interests so that we are not concerned with the state of our soul, the end result is the greatest threat any man or woman can face (Matthew 16:26; Luke 12:20).

The Bible warns us of the devil's deceptions beginning in the Garden (2 Corinthians 2:11; 11:3; Ephesians 6:11). It reports that the devil lied to man in two ways. First, he told Adam and Eve, "You shall be as God." Second, he promised them, "You shall not die." Isn't it interesting that the spirits have never deviated from their master's first lies? The consistency and persistence of these themes throughout history are amazing. And ask yourself some additional questions. Why is it that channeled spirits who are usually considered "good," promote what the Bible teaches is false? Why would good spirits identify themselves with the lies of the devil? Could it be that the reason these spirits have never changed their message is because they don't have another message? And why is it that many former occultists

reveal that the only way to escape from those spirits is through the Jesus Christ of the Bible?

Those who say the Bible has nothing to say about channeling may have never considered the following. The first historical incidence of channeling recorded in the Bible is in Genesis, chapter 3. In the Garden of Eden, the devil used the serpent as a "channel" to trick Eve (Genesis 3:1-5; 2 Corinthians 11:3; Revelation 12:9). Through channeling, the devil deceived Eve into doubting God, with serious consequences. Channeling is thus condemned in the Bible as an evil practice before God (Deuteronomy 18:9-12).

The Bible also warns that "in later times some will fall away from the faith, paying attention to deceitful spirits and doctrines of demons" (1 Timothy 4:1). No one can deny that spiritistic teachings pervert the nature of God, lie about Christ, and distort the way of salvation. This explains why those who trust in spiritistic teachings to the end will face judgment at death. On the authority of Jesus Christ Himself, we discover that hell is real (Matthew 25:46; Luke 16:19-31). The demons who promise that sin is not real and that hell does not exist are bringing eternal ruin to those who trust them. Channeling is thus a form of spiritual warfare, with the souls of men at stake (2 Corinthians 4:4).

This explains why both channeling and its teachings are condemned in Scripture as rebellion against God and as courting His judgment. An example of this is King Manasseh of Judah in ancient Israel. "He practiced witchcraft, used divination, practiced sorcery, and dealt with mediums, and spiritists. He did much evil in the sight of the LORD, provoking Him to anger" (2 Chronicles 33:6 NASB). Likewise in Deuteronomy 18:10-12, God warns His people, "There shall not be found among you anyone . . . who uses divination, one who practices witchcraft . . . or a spiritist, or one who calls up the dead. For whoever does these things is detestable to LORD." The phrase "or spiritist" condemns all aspects of channeling.

## DESTRUCTIVE NATURE

What additional evidence would lead a person to conclude that the channeling spirits are evil? Because channeling contacts demons, it is an evil practice by itself, but it also leads to other evils. Among these are immorality, crime, fraud, and emotional, physical, or spiritual destruction (1069).

It is not just that there are a few cases which illustrate this. There are hundreds of thousands of them littered throughout the history of religion, occultism, spiritism, and parapsychology—mental illness, suicide, physical crippling, blindness, death. People who would never think of playing Russian roulette even once, or who would never carelessly take a dangerous drug, have good reasons for their decisions. The odds of tragedy are too high. Yet the odds of harming oneself from occult practices are at least as high (1069). What is regrettable is that people ignore the evidence. In *The Coming Darkness* we have documented this evidence in detail (1069), and here are several examples.

Professor Edmond Gruss mentions several cases of murder committed on the advice of the spirits. In one case a 15-year-old daughter murdered her father. In another case a 77-year-old man killed his wife in self-defense because she believed the lies the spirits told her about his unfaithfulness (1129:83-94). John Weldon once talked with a self-proclaimed serial killer, whose "religious commission" was to travel the countryside murdering people his spirit guide told him "deserved to die." He claimed the spirits always provided a way for him to dispose of the body safely so they could not be discovered. Historically, the spirits have influenced the murder of tens of thousands of children and adults through human sacrifice, including, in all probability, the Atlanta child murders (1095/1130). The spirits have helped start political revolutions, including the Mexican Revolution of 1910 (1131), and their teachings have sapped the moral strength of countless numbers. They have done this by leading people to commit evil acts which they otherwise would not have committed.

Jesus Himself called the devil a liar and a murderer from the beginning (John 8:44). Those who play into his hands will receive great promises and excitement to begin with, but only deceit and destruction in the long run.

Suicide is a case in point. Channeling teaches that this life is not the end (annihilation), and that there is no final judgment. If this life is sim-

ply too difficult or unpleasant, why not take a way out? Why not enter a world you have been promised is far more glorious? Death, after all, is claimed to be a friend. In fact, the spirits may encourage this. We have read many cases where allegedly "loving" spirits have deliberately induced emotional dependence upon their advice and then at a moment of weakness encouraged their contact to commit suicide (1069/1132). In *The Menace of Spiritualism,* case after case of tragedy is listed. The foreword by Bernard Vaughan, S. J., states, "This very morning I heard of a girl, who being told in a seance by her deceased lover that he would not live on the other side without her, drowned herself to join him, not, I fancy, in heaven" (1133:XII).

Bill Slater, former head of British Broadcasting Corporation (BBC) television drama, after attending an impromptu seance with a Ouija board,* went home and in the early hours of the morning:

> I found myself half-awake, knowing there was some kind of presence massing itself on my chest; it was, to my certain knowledge, making every effort to take over my mind and body. It cost me considerable will-power to concentrate all my faculties to push the thing away, and for what seemed like twenty minutes this spiritual tussle went on between this awful presence and myself. Needless to say, although before going to bed I had felt perfectly happy and at ease with a very good friend, in a flat I knew well, I was now absolutely terrified—I have never known such fear since. I was finally able to call my friend's name; he woke up, put on the light, and was astonished to find me well-nigh a gibbering idiot. I have never since had any psychic experience (849:451).

Nor are such examples surprising. In the Bible, demons are presented as inflicting numerous physical and psychological ailments upon their victims. Many of these parallel today's cases of channeling. While it must be stressed that most illness is not demonically produced, the array of symptoms suggest the possibility of a virtual monopoly over the workings of the human mind and body: skin disease (Job 2:7), destructive and irrational acts (Matthew 8:28; Luke 8:27), deafness and inability to speak (Mark 9:25; Luke 11:17), epileptic-like seizures (Matthew 17:15; Mark 9:17-18, Luke 9:39), blindness (Matthew 12:22), tormenting pain (Revelation 9:1-11), insanity (Luke 8:26-35), severe physical deformity (Luke 13:11-17). Demons can also give a person supernatural strength (Luke 8:29) or attempt to murder them (Matthew 17:15,18). There are numerous accounts of mediums, channelers, and occultists, or those who frequent them, suffering physically in a variety of ways from their practice (ill health, alcoholism, spirit attacks, early deaths, and so on).

Most people do not know that the famous medium Arthur Ford became a morphine addict and alcoholic, which caused him no end of grief (850:16-17). Dr. Nandor Fodor observes: "After prolonged exercise of mediumship intemperance often sets in. The reason is a craving for stimulants following the exhaustion and depletion felt after the seance. Many mediums have been known who succumbed to the craving and died of delirium tremens" (389:234). British Occultist Aleister Crowley and "guru" Jiddhu Krishnamurti endured incessant torment and suffering (1138/1139:347). Bishop Pike died a tragic death from his involvement in spiritism (851). The biography on Edgar Cayce by Joseph Millard reveals the extent of Cayce's suffering, from psychic attacks, to mysterious fires, the periodic loss of his voice, erratic personality changes, emotional torments, constant "bad luck," personal setbacks, and guilt induced by psychic readings that ruined others' lives (400: 98-116,198-201).

Many channelers and other occultists seem to succumb to various vices later in life, from sexual immorality (852:133,140/389:234), to numbing their consciences, to alcoholism and drug addiction (852:135,142/389:234), to crime and worse (853:17,95,116,185; cf. ref. 385).

M. Lamar Keene spent 13 years among professional mediums as a famous (although fraudulent) medium. He observes, "Cheating, lying, stealing, conning—these are sanctified in the ethics of mediumship as I knew it" (852:141). In his public confession, *The Psychic Mafia*, he confesses,

All the mediums I've known or known about have had tragic endings. The Fox sisters, who started it all, wound up as alcoholic derelicts. William Slade, famed for his slate-writing tricks, died insane in a Michigan sanitarium. Margery, the medium, lay on her deathbed a hopeless drunk. The celebrated Arthur Ford fought the battle of the bottle till the very end and lost. ...Wherever I looked it was the same: mediums, at the end of a tawdry life, dying a tawdry death.... I was sick and tired of the whole business—the fraud bit, the drug bit, the drinking bit, the entire thing... (852:147-48).

Spiritist and guru Sri Chinmoy, a spiritual adviser at the United Nations, observes, "Many, many black magicians and people who deal with spirits have been strangled or killed. I know because I've been near quite a few of these cases" (810:62).

Dr. Kurt Koch, after 45 years of counseling the occultly oppressed, said that from his own experience numerous cases of suicides, fatal accidents, strokes, and insanity are found among occult practitioners. "Anyone who has had to observe for 45 years the effects of spiritism can only warn people with all the strength at his disposal" (642:238).

In addition, over many years, the very act of channeling itself appears to have a destructive effect upon the human body. It is as if there is a type of, for lack of a better word, "psychic vampirism" at work, which slowly eats away at a person's physical constitution (854:62/389:235). Edgar Cayce died in misery weighing a mere 60 pounds, apparently physiologically "burned out" from giving too many psychic readings.

Time and again in the lives of psychics, mediums, and spiritists, we have observed the power of the spirits in holding their captives to do their will (2 Timothy 2:24-26). When people attempt to suppress their channeling or mediumship, the result will frequently turn up symptoms of disease or other serious problems, forcing a return to the practice. (See Shamanism for examples.) What is doubly tragic is that for these people it started out so good and promising (280:38-40/1069), and yet it led to such misery and evil. (See refs. 241-45/270-73/291.)

# CRYSTAL WORK

- Info at a Glance
- Introduction and Influence
- Historical Antecedents
- Source of Power

## INFO AT A GLANCE

**Description.** Crystal work is the use of a supposed power inherent within crystals for psychic healing,* divination,* visualization,* developing psychic abilities, channeling,* and other kinds of spirit contact and occult pursuits.

**Founder.** Unknown; but similar practices have been employed for millennia, such as the use of amulets, magical stones, and gems.

**How does it claim to work?** Crystals supposedly contain the shape-induced vibrational frequencies that mystically interconnect with the earth's and the individual's "energy field." They are allegedly used to amplify, or re-align, human "psychic" or cosmic energy for various purposes. For example, when focused and directed, these mystical energies are employed for psychic healing, entering altered states of consciousness,* or various forms of mind training.

**Scientific evaluation.** Discredited.

**Examples of occult potential.** Psychic development, spiritism.

**Major problem.** Crystals per se have no magical powers, and in an occult context they easily become an implement behind which spirits can work.

**Biblical/Christian evaluation.** Prohibited on the basis of its occult use.

**Potential dangers.** The hazards normally associated with occult practice (278).

## INTRODUCTION AND INFLUENCE

*Time* magazine has observed that "crystal power" and "crystal healing" are among the most favored of New Age techniques for expanding consciousness or curing what ails you. Indeed, hundreds of thousands of people are seeking the alleged power within crystals, which are so prized today that "beautiful formations in ancient caves are being ravaged for their quartz" (1143:174). One critical text on alternative medicine goes so far as to claim, "Crystals are fast becoming an accepted part of our mainstream society" (1093:155). If so, it will be because the books and lectures of New Age superstars such as Shirley MacLaine, which actively endorse the use of crystals, have reached millions of people. MacLaine, for example, tells of using crystal power for psychic "centering," or spiritual alignment, which she often employs while in the bathtub:

I checked the positions of my four quartz crystals sitting on each corner of the tub. I had been learning to work with the power of crystals and that discipline had become part of my daily life.

As I chanted my Hindu mantras I visualized white light flowing through my bloodstream. It made me feel centered and balanced. I had learned to draw in white light that I visualized coming from some source above me, and with the sound vibrating through my body, the light traveled through me causing a sensation of calm alignment (347:8-9).

Crystals are used for a variety of psychic pursuits. "According to the nature of the illness, the crystal will become hot or cold as it is passed over the person's aura. The crystal is absorbing the bad energy out of the body, according to these teachings. It is important to remember that the crystals are your teachers. Hold one in your hand. Be open to its power. It will teach you" (997:67).

Despite the novelty for modern Americans, crystal work is a variation upon the old occult belief that gems, stones, rocks, and minerals contain great power which can be magically directed for various uses, such as psychic diagnosis and healing, developing psychic abilities, astral projection, spirit contact, and channeling.*

One of the leading New Age promoters of crystal work is DaEl Walker, a spiritist who founded "The Crystal Awareness Institute." This organization claims to be recognized by the state of California to offer continuing education credit for registered nurses who take crystal classes (203:cover). The institute stresses "research," development and training in crystal work, psychic healing, and expanding human consciousness along New Age lines. Nationwide, over 10,000 people have attended Walker's lectures, workshops, and seminars. Yet he is only one of dozens of popular teachers in the field (203:265).

As in most New Age practices, crystal work is viewed as a technique for manipulating mystical energies. For example, "Crystal Healing is *only* concerned with energy. We believe the physical body is the end result of energy. If the energies of the body can be stimulated and balanced, the physical body *must* repair itself. Crystal Healing is non-intrusive and non-invasive. It only adjusts energy fields" (203:24).

The supposed ability to regulate mystical energies explains why crystal work is employed in a wide variety of occult practices. For example, it may involve manipulating the body's alleged "life energy," (e.g., prana), for healing. It may be used in psychically "examining" the aura, or

"awakening" the chakras (alleged psychic centers in the body), or arousing kundalini energy (see Yoga). Crystals are also employed in such diverse practices as shamanism* (759:84-85), astral projection, dream work,* visualization,* divination,* spirit channeling,* muscle testing,* dowsing,* astrology,* the use of mind-expanding drugs, and even in psychic surgery (202:28, 34,53,73,84,94,101,168,180,183).

## HISTORICAL ANTECEDENTS

As noted, New Age crystal work is a variation upon an ancient occult theme: that of working with objects called amulets and talismans having supposed supernatural powers. This is why many metaphysical traditions, East and West, use these "magical" stones in their occult work. Throughout history, these objects have been associated with the spirit world, and because of this they are believed to possess magical abilities. Consider the following historic and contemporary examples of how crystals and amulets have been associated with spiritism.

- Crystal work is found in both ancient and modern forms of shamanism* (1082:84-85). In native American healing, the shaman will utilize the crystal as a method of diagnosis and treatment. The crystal is believed to be a vehicle through which the healing spirits work (142:138-43).

- The medieval occultist Paracelsus, in many ways the "father" of modern New Age medicine,* owned a talismanic jewel which he believed to be the dwelling place of a powerful spirit named "Azoth" (205:6).

- In many Eastern religions, living spirits are believed to dwell within particular stones. For example, concerning the star sapphire, the cat's eye, and the moonstone, "It is supposed in the East that a living spirit dwells within these stones" (205:8).

- In a variety of ancient and modern religious traditions, gems and stones which are intended for use as amulets are fashioned as beautifully as possible "that they might become fitting abodes for the benevolent spirits believed to animate them and render them efficacious" (205:23).

Because spirits were believed to indwell or to work through these stones, healing and other magical properties were assigned to them. And, ". . . it was believed that certain spiritual or planetary influences had aided in their production and were latent in them" (205:369-70). Thus the talismanic nature of precious stones has been associated historically with astrology.* For example, ". . . the influence over human fortunes ascribed by astrology to the heavenly bodies is conceived to be strengthened by wearing the gem appropriate to certain planets or signs, for a subtle emanation has passed into the stone and radiates from it" (205:339). Furthermore, the color and appearance of the stone was magically associated with particular spirits or "angels": ". . . the color and appearance of the stone was not merely emblematic of the angel, but, by its sympathetic quality [magical power] it was supposed to attract his [the spirit's] influence and to provide a medium for the transmission of his benevolent force to the wearer" (205:339).

## SOURCE OF POWER

What then is the real source of power behind New Age crystal work? As was true in the past, that source today is the spirit world. Although most crystal healers believe that the crystals themselves contain magical powers, the truth is that the crystals have no power and are merely implements behind which spirits may choose to work.

Below we will cite several examples in documentation.

The medium Edgar Cayce encouraged the use of gems as amulets, or containers of occult power in *Scientific Properties and Occult Aspects of 22 Gems, Stones and Metals*. Texts such as Crow's *Precious Stones, Their Occult Power* (538), Fernie's *Occult and Curative Power of Stones*, or Julia Lorusso's *Healing Stones: The Therapeutic Use of Gems and Minerals* (204), all underscore the spiritistic reality underlying crystal use. In the latter book, "[Medium] Julia Lorusso, like Edgar Cayce, found herself constantly channeling references to gemstones in the due process of her current and past-life [reincarnation] readings. Her application of mineral crystals serve many purposes in healing" (204:V).

Not unexpectedly, even many crystal suppliers have turned to spiritism. Consider the case of leading entrepreneur Gary Fleck, who was unexpectedly taken over by a feminine angel claiming to be "a spirit of the inner earth." This spirit wished to inform everyone that crystals were vehicles of supernatural revelation and healing; that they were alive and would provide spiritual guidance and psychic power to those who would ask them for it. The story is told in Drs. David and Sharon Sneed's *The Hidden Agenda: A Critical View of Alternative Medical Therapies*:

> Crystal therapy has a close relationship with the occult. If you doubt it, consider the words of Gary Fleck, one of the country's leading crystal suppliers. A miner by trade, Fleck was drawn into the New Age movement through his love of crystals, an affection he developed as a child growing up in Arizona. Fleck says that one day he led an expedition of crystal lovers into a mine in Arizona so everyone could offer special prayers with their crystals. Upon arriving in the cavern, each pilgrim lit a candle. Suddenly, an "angel" appeared to him.
>
> Almost everyone in the group saw the angel, Fleck insists. She identified herself as Sabatina, a spirit of the inner earth. Then she put her hands on Fleck's head and began to pronounce the role of crystals in human destiny. Fleck tells us he felt as if he were a conduit for a being. He translated the angel's words to an awestruck prayer circle.
>
> What Sabatina supposedly had to say was that crystals and gems "are here to teach and heal. If you want to learn what they can teach and how they can heal, then ask the crystals themselves. They are alive. They should be treated as friends." She went on to say that crystals were only one path to a higher consciousness (1093:156-57).

Incidents like this are fairly common in New Age literature. In fact, no matter where we look in modern New Age crystal work, we discover that the real power in crystals comes from the spirit world, not the crystal itself. Almost every seasoned crystal worker we have talked with, and every book on crystal healing we have read, underscores this.

Several examples of popular texts on crystal healing are illustrative. The late Randall N. Baer had a background in naturopathy, psychedelic drugs, dream work,* mysticism, Hinduism, and other Eastern religions. He was a codirector of the New Age Starcrest Academy of Interdimensional Law and Science in New Mexico and taught classes in yoga,* "dynamic relaxation," holistic health, and related subjects. However, it was by means of crystal work that Baer finally became a New Age channeler.* Through him the spirits produced *Windows of Light: Quartz Crystals and Self-Transformation*, which catapulted him into international prominence as a New Age teacher. His story of "innocently" receiving crystals is multiplied time and again in our culture today:

> Later Baer met Vicky, the woman who has become his wife. Vicky had received a small, perfect quartz crystal from an American Indian medicine man. One of her spirit guides instructed her to give Baer the crystal and ask him to meditate upon it. At first Baer thought this was ridiculous. But his meditation convinced him that the crystal really did have power. Thus began his journey into the world of crystal healing.
>
> Baer and his wife became more and more deeply involved in meditation and in contact with the spirit world. He talked with spirits who identified themselves as Mozart, Moses, White Eagle, White Cloud, Ascended Master Kuthumi, Mary, and a host of others. To him the power emanating from these spirits was overwhelming and utterly intoxicating . . . (1093:157-58).

In his book *Inside the New Age Nightmare*, Baer describes how the spirits instructed him in entering altered states of consciousness* for purposes of channeling* their teachings:

> Approximately three months after moving to the northern New Mexico area, my "spirit guides" gave me instructions to write a book on the subject of crystals. . . .
>
> The spirit guides told me to take 12 quartz crystals and lay them out in a circle, to tape another one to the occult "third eye" and to suspend a large pyramid overhead. I was to sit in the very center of the crystals with my head underneath the pyramid. This was supposed to create a "crystal energy field" having amplified "higher

vibrations" for receiving channeled thoughts from the spirit guides.

> To my amazement, as I would enter a kind of semi-conscious trance, discernible thoughts, inspirations, and pictures would appear in my mind. All this was not my own doing—the spirit guides were transmitting their thoughts and influences to me. My job, effectively, was to take notes and then shape up the material into book form.
>
> Over a period of three months I would take a position in the crystal circle for 10–12 hours per day and receive and transcribe this information (2400:35-36).

The result was the publication of *Windows of Light: Quartz Crystals and Self-Transformation*, which became one of the authoritative texts on crystal work, along with his *The Crystal Connection: A Guidebook for Personal and Planetary Ascension*. Yet Baer's story was not quite finished. A profoundly disturbing event led to his eventual renunciation of New Age work and to his becoming a Christian. In *Inside the New Age Nightmare* he recalls the unexpected revelation he experienced while in a trance state enveloped by a blissful luminosity:

> Rays of bliss radiated through my spirit. I was totally captivated by the power. Suddenly another force stepped in. It took me by complete surprise. In the twinkling of an eye, it was like a supernatural hand had taken me behind the scenes of the experience that I was having. I was taken behind the outer covering of the dazzling luminosity and there saw something that left me literally shaking for a full week. What I saw was the face of devouring darkness! Behind the glittering outer facade of beauty lay a massively powerful, wildly churning face of absolute hatred and unspeakable abominations—the face of demons filled with the power of Satan. (2400:55)

Baer's story illustrates what many crystal workers stress: the ease with which one may contact spirits and become a channeler through using crystals. Uma Silbey's *The Complete Crystal Guidebook* reveals that through crystal work, "You can meet [spirit] guides and beings from different dimensions and uncover ESP abilities.

... A curious thing starts to happen as you work with crystals. You start becoming aware of an energy or force or a "potential" higher than yourself. You start becoming aware of and can begin to interact with something very powerful and wonderful" (202:1).

She observes that those who work with crystals become "channels" for this energy, and she specifically links this with the dangerous occult kundalini energy whose manifestations usually signify spiritistic influence or possession (see Yoga):

Kundalini energy is often awakened when you start working with crystals. You will need to know how to channel this in yourself, to utilize the unleashed energies and powers and learn how to create this in others. There are chakra systems or energy matrixes in the body that become activated as you work, and these can be activated in those you work with. Because the work you will be doing is on the subtle planes, you will need to know about the astral and mental planes, and how to work with them. . . . Because you begin drawing tremendous forces of energy through your body as you work . . . you will need to expand your consciousness beyond your physical body, beyond the environment and into other [spirit] realms.

To work effectively [as a crystal healer] you must be in a state of surrender, becoming a channel through which the creative force or spirit can do its work. You are merely the vehicle. You become like a hollow tube through which this spirit can flow without impediments. . . . To become this channel, you need to learn to become centered, to learn what this state [of altered consciousness] is (202:2-3).

Silbey also explains that those who work with crystals typically develop psychic powers. Thus:

. . . both obvious and subtle changes will happen as you continue work with the exercises and practice with your crystals. . . . You may experience a separation of the physical and psychic selves and the abilities to use one or the other. . . . Psychic energy will become deeply integrated and used in your everyday life. . . . An unlimited flow of creative energy will open up for you that you can direct in any way (202:4).

Various states of higher (and different) . . . consciousness begin to be perceived, experienced and intertwined with "normal" consciousness. Sometimes when this happens you may feel as if you are "going crazy."

As the kundalini rises, different powers tend to develop. These can help you in your crystal work. . . . These powers tend to be those of clairvoyance, clairaudience, psychic healing abilities, astral projection . . . (202:74).

Another aspect of crystal work is the dramatic change in worldview it can bring to the practitioner:

You might be able to sense into the past or the future, see subtle colors and auras, hear subtle sound, astral travel and experience various forms of extra-sensory perception. . . . After experiencing these exercises and doing your crystal work [you discover] that the crystal in other metaphysical work is not an end in itself. Something else is happening with you that is much more important. You seem to be developing a new consciousness and way of being. . . . You seem to experience a state of infinite expansion (202:225).

But again, that the real power for psychic revelations and transformations comes from the spirit world and not the crystal itself is indicated by the fact that after spirit contact is made, the crystals are no longer needed. Many crystal healers told us that crystals are merely devices for *attracting* the spirits who supply the real power. In other words, even when the crystals are dispensed with, the occult power remains because the spirits who are working with the person remain (cf. Divination). Silbey herself confesses that "after some time of working with the crystals, you may find that you can do without them just as effectively. Don't be afraid to let go" (202:5).

She describes a process by which the crystal practitioner can become involved with channeling* (i.e., become a medium) and receive information from the spirit world. The method described is similar to that given for learning Therapeutic Touch and similar forms of psychic healing and related New Age therapies. "What does it feel like to channel? . . . The feeling you have when channeling is as if the information or impressions flow through you" (202:116). She observes that "some people feel as if they must be 'taken over' by another being who proceeds to use their body," and that this "is one possible technique, but it is unnecessary" because channeled information can be received from a spirit source *outside* the body as well (202:115).

In addition, crystal workers have told us that whether the crystals themselves are used or not, they are always treated with the respect and devotion associated to a holy power or a living god; to do otherwise may invite serious consequences and even disaster. This demand for reverence to the implements behind which spirits work (cf. Idol Worship) is characteristic of occult practice (cf. Divination).

DaEl Walker also writes about the spiritistic nature of crystal work. His main text on the subject is dedicated to the spirit "Michael" and other spirits whom he calls "The Masters of the Crystal Brotherhood" (202:V). The book, and most of the information in it about crystals, was channeled through Walker, who can only be described as a spirit medium (203:2,22).

How did Walker become involved in crystal channeling? It began with a popular New Age seminar called Silva Mind Control.* This course has some eight million graduates worldwide and seeks to develop psychic abilities and help participants establish contact with psychic "guides." Walker confesses that after taking the course, "Later explorations introduced me to my spiritual guides who began my internal training" (203:19). For example, during a seance, "The voice offered, in the name of a group called the Hierarchy, to channel this information to us. We were told to come together each week and sit in the same formation with crystals. We sat and channeled once a week for over two years. We recorded and transcribed all the material" (203:20).

Not surprisingly, Walker comments that it was his spirit channeling which "was the real beginning of my crystal training" (203:20). Thus, "The amount and degree of knowledge channel-ing through me deepens and widens. It is a veritable flood which flows unabated.... My internal Master Teacher and Guide is [the spirit entity calling itself] Lord Michael.... I am a messenger for the Crystal Brotherhood, whose purpose is to open the powers of the mind for all who will be part of the coming Aquarian Age" (203:22).

Walker freely admits that in crystal work, "We can receive assistance from the healing masters from the nonphysical world. They can help understand problems of the client, even in past lives, and add their energy in making corrections" (203:251).

In his practice, Walker uses Chinese acupuncture points and meridians as well as the Hindu chakras (203:7-9,31). Like other crystal users, he observes that working with crystals tends to develop psychic abilities (203:18-19). He shows how crystal work can be used in conjunction with any number of "healing" methods and that practitioners of those methods will discover great benefits from using crystals. Some of these methods include dowsing* (203:25), applied kinesiology (muscle testing)* (203:28), visualization* (203:34), balancing "chakras" (203:87), using amulets (203:39), "auric scans" (psychically examining the alleged aura; 203:108), acupuncture (203:113), chiropractic (203:113), absent or psychic healing (203:168-70), color therapy (203:225), and meditation* (203:39). For example, as in Therapeutic Touch, dowsing rods are one tool used to measure alleged mystical energies. "Our favorite tool is the dowsing rod. By measuring the [psychic] energy field before and after any change, we can get an idea of the principles and proprieties of those changes" (203:25).

In conclusion, despite the fact that hundreds of thousands of people currently use crystals, crystals themselves possess no intrinsic power, spiritual or otherwise. As has been true for millennia, they are only a clever disguise behind which the spirit world seeks to operate and influence human beings.

# DIVINATION PRACTICES AND OCCULT "GAMES"

## INFO AT A GLANCE

**Description.** Divination is the attempt to predict or control one's future, or to gain access to hidden information (e.g., psychically) by the assessment of various "indicators" (such as the occult meaning of numbers), or use of particular implements (such as the Ouija board). Examples of divinatory methods include interpreting the positions of the heavenly bodies (astrology)* or the symbols on cards (tarot), analyzing dreams (dream work)* or the flight of birds or liver markings, casting stones or coins or other objects (I Ching), interpreting hand markings (palmistry), and seeking information from dowsing* rods, idols, or oracles (Ezekiel 21:21). Occult games are not necessarily divinatory; however, they

119

attempt to introduce players to occult philosophy or practice in a fun and exciting manner through playing a "game."

**Founder.** Varies; some are unknown.

**Scientific evaluation.** Science cannot evaluate claims to see into the future, although it can test the predictions of diviners (see Astrology for examples). This often reveals fraud or a poor record of divining, or that psychic powers fluctuate greatly under stringent conditions of scientific assessment (see Dowsing.) This is not to say that these methods are never accurate; to the contrary, their persuasiveness is often found in their divinatory power.

**Examples of occult potential.** Psychic development, spiritism.

**Major problem.** Despite their frequent use as forms of social entertainment, divination practices involve serious occult pursuits that carry the same consequences as occult practices in general (278).

**Biblical/Christian evaluation.** Divination is rejected by name (Deuteronomy 18:9-12) as an involvement with spiritistic powers (Hosea 4:12; Acts 16:16-19). (See Dowsing.*) In certain ways, pagan divination is the occult counterpart to biblical divination or prophecy.

**Potential dangers.** Physical, emotional, or financial problems resulting from failed predictions, incorrect medical diagnoses, abuse in psychotherapy, occult bondage. (See Astrology, "Dangers," for examples.) Practitioners are characteristically warned to treat these implements with great respect and deference, lest the powers operating behind them be offended and the practitioner be harmed or perhaps even killed.

*Note:* See Astrology and Dowsing for more in-depth illustrations of divination and for additional examples of personal hazards surrounding divination methods. The material on "Dungeons and Dragons" (p. 154) is excerpted with changes from John Weldon and James Bjornstad, *Playing with Fire* (Moody, 1984).

## INTRODUCTION AND INFLUENCE

While America exits the twentieth and enters the twenty-first century, divination practices are expected to increase significantly as more people seek to discover what the new millennium holds for them individually or for the nation as a whole. Secular and religious predictions of impending disasters or even Armageddon have greatly fueled the renewed interest in divination. Although divination is a popular technique among New Age practitioners, millions of ordinary Americans seem fascinated and hopeful that it may be able to predict their futures. They hope this will benefit them greatly, failing to comprehend the logical consequences of divination practices, as revealed historically.

Divination has existed in all cultures throughout history. Its basic idea involves foretelling the future or accessing occult information by various means. Traditionally, the person who practiced divination was regarded as having supernatural powers.

Despite its frequent modern reformulation in psychological or parapsychological terms (e.g., receiving information from "the unconscious" or "higher" mind, cf. dowsing*), historically, divination has always been an attempt to communicate with the supernatural or "divine" realm in order to secure information from the "gods." Its fundamentally pagan and spiritistic nature has never changed, regardless of how "modern" its practices have become today.

In *Divination: Ancient and Modern*, occultist Dr. John H. Manas argues that the long history of divination forms an inseparable connection to spiritism and the occult (1070:211). For example, he describes divination as an "ancient mysterious art of the gods," i.e., spirits (1070:203). He also explains that the method of spirit contact used in occult divination today was the same one used in ancient times:

The same process [of spirit contact] was followed by the ancient diviners. This can be seen in the meaning of the words used by the ancient Greeks for divination . . . which signify impulse, force, paroxysm, an unnatural condition of the individual concerned, which is under the influence and control of a psychic force, an invisible entity, of a god. This procedure and method of communication with the spirit world was then, as it is today, the most popular (1070:205).

Thus, the ancients interpreted divination as instituting contact with the "gods," while modern practitioners often refer to divination as instituting contact with the spirits. Or, as we noted, the more naturalistically minded believe it to be contact with the untapped powers of the mind. Regardless, ancient diviners "were trance mediums through whom the spirit entity, the god, or as we say today, the control [spirit], or the [spirit] guide, spoke" (1070:212). In other words, "the same methods that were used in ancient times by the Oracles, are used today by the most advanced of our mediums. In ancient times, the discarnate entity . . . was called [a] god. . . . Today these discarnate entities are called spirit controls or guides" (1070:235).

Dr. Manas argues that all forms of successful divination require both psychic development and contact with the spirit world:

Divination is an art and, as such, it has to be mastered through patient effort and spiritual illumination. Certain brain, etheric and mental centers have to be opened and certain dormant faculties developed. It takes a long time according to the aptitude and the development of the candidate. A good diviner must also be a good philosopher and occultist. . . . Only a pure and unselfish diviner will send out high spiritual vibrations, which in turn will attract and make possible his communication with a correspondingly high discarnate entity . . . (1070:261).

With the contemporary occult revival, many ancient methods of divination have reappeared in the last quarter century, and many new forms have also appeared—usually, it seems, through the assistance of the spirit world. Although some of these divination practices are marketed as "games," many declare to be dealing with serious magic.

The methods we discuss are either traditional practices, modern variations, or resurrections of ancient forms of divination, and they may incorporate other occult arts as well. Thus, in one form or another, most of these techniques have been popular occult practices throughout history. But today they can also be found outside occult circles, even in unexpected places such as psychotherapy, education, and the church. For example, of the eight major forms we discuss, we have found at least seven that are used in modern psychotherapy.

One of the subjects we discuss does not deal with divination and the occult directly. "Dungeons and Dragons" is included because of its potential to spark interest in the occult. Unfortunately, its nature as a game of creativity has resulted in many otherwise bright teenagers and adults being led into the tangled labyrinth of occultism.

The following list includes several popular methods, their possible or probable origins, and examples of their use:

- Runes: Viking/European (magic and divination)
- Palmistry: possibly India (divination, character analysis)
- I Ching: Chinese (divination)
- Numerology: unknown (divination, character analysis)
- Tarot: Middle East (divination)
- Cartouche: Egyptian (magic and divination)
- Leela: Hindu (divination)
- Ouija Board, Phoenix Cards: American (divination or spiritism)
- Dungeons and Dragons: American (game of skill with potential occult involvement)
- Star+Gate Symbolic System: American (divination)

With one exception, Dungeons and Dragons, the goal of these practices is either divination or some form of occult self-knowledge or spiritual "enlightenment."* This is not unusual in that such methods are typically tied to a worldview based on ancient pagan magic or Eastern or Western occultism. Thus, those who author books on these subjects typically have a prior interest in the occult. For example, Murray Hope, the author of *The Way of the Cartouche: An Oracle of Ancient Egyptian Magic* (New York: St. Martin's Press, 1985), is also the author of *Practical Egyptian Magic, Practical Greek Magic,* and *The Runes and Crystal Gazing.*

The appeal of these methods is their ability to allegedly divine the future, or the psychological self-insight they claim to offer, which explains their presence in modern psychotherapy. Virtually all the "how-to" books speak of the uncanny knack for accuracy that these practices are purported to have. As David and Julia Line observe in *Fortune Telling by Runes*, "[T]he uncanny knack they have of being right, for the greater part of the time, cannot be explained in purely factual terms. Rational theories can and are applied—but they still remain only theories. At the end of the day, you will either believe in runes or not" (1484:8).

Because of their alleged accuracy and power for self-transformation, certain segments of modern psychology show an increasing interest in these ancient forms of divination, particularly where they help achieve what can be interpreted as psychological insight or "growth." This occurs principally through their ability to act as "counselor" or "guide" in psychological self-evaluation and by their ability to uncover relevant "unconscious dynamics" (e.g., archetypes or dream symbolism), which allegedly promote a more successful experience in psychotherapeutic treatment or in personal and spiritual "growth" (cf. Dream Work).

As a result, their alleged "therapeutic" potential has attracted the interest of at least some segments of modern psychology. This is especially true in those schools most open to such an encounter: Jungian, transpersonal, humanistic, and now hundreds of fringe psychotherapies.

The famous psychoanalyst Carl Jung was a believer in the runes, I Ching, and the tarot, and his theories are often cited in support of the alleged psychological dynamics involved in these forms of divination. And articles in many psychology magazines also explore the psychotherapeutic "potential" of these or related methods.

In essence, modern methods of divination constitute one small portion of the contemporary American occult revival and, given our culture's fascination with the supernatural (not to mention the national penchant for novel psychotherapy), their success seems ensured.

But a fundamental question remains. If these methods work, especially supernaturally, what is their true source of power? Books on these topics often speak in terms of some kind of genuine, even supernatural, power behind these methods. And we will argue that by engaging in these divinatory arts, one can indeed tap a personal source of occult power that has access to hidden information, as well as an ability to manipulate events. In other words, we will show why we believe people are ultimately dealing with contacting spirit entities, and that this is where the genuine source of power is encountered. To our way of thinking, it is more logical to conclude that a supernatural personal intelligence outside space (and, pehaps, to some degree, time) is the source of information and volition, rather than to argue that sticks, dice, cards, and numbers can predict the future or reveal secret information about individuals.

Modern explanations for such uncanny powers often discard or downplay the supernatural in preference for natural, psychological, or parapsychological theories. As occult writer Michael Howard writes in *The Magic of the Runes: Their Origins and Occult Power*:

Today we have invented a brand new technical terminology to describe these powers which our ancestors took for granted. We call them extrasensory perception, parapsychology, precognition, out-of-the-body experiences and telekinesis. Even our feeble attempts to rationalize these powers by giving them pseudo-scientific names cannot disguise how little we really know about them. Nowadays a scientifically educated psychic researcher or "parapsychologist" would laugh at you if you insisted on describing his field of study as "magic" or "magical," but it was so regarded by our forebears—and who is to say they were wrong to do so? (530:53-54)

Many of the millions of people utilizing these systems have indeed discovered that they are powerful. Yet such people are often informed that they are merely utilizing a principle of nature, or a "higher" aspect of their own mind, or nebulous "universal forces." Of course, if the true origin of the power behind these methods is spiritistic, merely assigning the source of power to "natural" causes cannot change their reality.

Thus, historically, those who used these forms of divination viewed their source of power far differently than most modern psychologists and parapsychologists. The real power was attributed to magic and spiritism. When people sought out and obeyed the spirits through these methods, they often achieved their goals; the spirits also achieved theirs.

## CONTACT MATERIAL

All divinatory methods utilize some principal object, which becomes the "focus" or vehicle through which spirits serve the client and produce the needed answers to questions, character analysis, prognostication, and so on. The following lists the "contact object" for a number of common forms of divination:

- Astrology: the horoscope chart
- Tarot: a deck of cards with pictorial symbols
- I Ching: sticks, printed hexagrams
- Runes: dice
- Numerology: numbers
- Ouija board: an alphabet board
- Radionics/psychometry: the divining rod, pendulum, "black box"
- Palmistry: the hand
- Crystal gazing or crystal work: the crystal ball or rock
- Metoscopy/physiognomy/phrenology: the forehead/face/skull
- Geomancy: combinations of dots or points
- Water-dowsing: the forked stick or other object

Considering the above items, is it logical to conclude that mere pieces of paper (horoscope charts) or simple forked sticks, or cards, numbers, hands, dice, letters of the alphabet, rocks, facial lines, head bumps, and dots by themselves never could reveal miraculous information about a person or the future? Perhaps this explains why even many of the practitioners refer to "supernatural influences" operating through such implements.

Just as the pagans of the past and present consult their wooden idols for divination and super-natural assistance, so have these implements been consulted. In many ways, these items are merely portable idols, taking the rightful place of God in people's lives. Rather than turning to "the only true God" (John 17:3) for answers and assistance, diviners rely upon dice and sticks and numbers. As the apostle Paul stated, "The things which the Gentiles sacrifice [to idols], they sacrifice to demons...and I do not want you to become sharers in demons" (1 Corinthians 10:20, NASB; cf. Psalm 106:34-39). The spirits themselves seem to relish the exchange, as well as the consequences (see Romans 1:18-27).

Space does not permit documenting the spiritistic nature of all the systems we will discuss. But we will cite sufficient illustrations to show that practitioners acknowledge or suspect spirit influence in these methods. And the spiritistic nature of these systems can be seen in the following:

1. In origin and source of power these methods are historically tied to idolatry, spiritism, and paganism, which the Bible consistently prohibits as an affront to God and as participation with demons (Deuteronomy 18:9-12; 1 Corinthians 10:20).

2. These practices are supernatural in that they function apart from any known natural mechanism and yet provide access to information unavailable to the five senses. These methods do not work on the basis of any known natural laws. The source of power appears to be both personal and capable of manipulating people and events. And, in harmony with ancient methods, a price is usually exacted for the favors granted.

3. These techniques promote occultism in a variety of forms, remove trust in God, and replace it with faith in pagan magic. In other words, they secure the goals of the demons.

4. These systems carry all the subtle traps and consequences of divinatory practices in general. As occult authority W. B. Crow warns in *A History of Magic, Witchcraft and Occultism*, any type of divination "is nearly always dangerous" (2087:29).

5. These practices: 1) develop a person psychically and 2) may lead to direct spirit contact.

The relationship between the practitioner and the implement is reminiscent of the relationship of the medium to the spirit guide, although in the former the power is mediated through inanimate objects or symbolism. Indeed, if the operation of spirits through such things as amulets (see Crystal Work), charms, diviner's rod, idols, astrology charts, and other inanimate objects are well known, who can be certain this is not also true for the other practices under consideration?

From a biblical view, then, divination suggests demonism. We are not saying that the divinatory paraphernalia themselves (rune dice or stones, tarot cards, I Ching sticks, and suchlike) have supernatural power, only that personal spirits can work through them for hidden (occult) purposes.

## BIBLICAL DIVINATION?

Some allegedly "Christian" diviners have pointed to biblical examples of divination in order to justify their practices. Such examples, however, are either irrelevant or misinterpreted (cf. Dowsing*), or they confuse the source or purpose underlying the prognostication. As we will shortly see, God's people were strictly prohibited from using divination. But there were also times when God had to communicate His will for specific reasons, and He chose particular methods for this. Before Scripture existed or was widely available, there had to be a way to communicate the divine will in necessary circumstances.

Thus, in the Bible, certain exceptional methods were used to discover God's specific will, such as the Urim and Thummim, dreams, through the Old Testament prophetic ministry, and casting lots (Exodus 28:30; Acts 1:24-26).

These methods are replaced today by other means (cf. Hebrews 1:1-2). One reason for this is because God's divine power and Scripture itself supply "everything we need for life and godliness through our knowledge of him" (2 Peter 1:3), and, "All Scripture is God-breathed and is useful for teaching, rebuking, correcting and training in righteousness, so that the man of God may be thoroughly equipped for every good work" (2 Timothy 3:16-17). In cases where Scripture does not supply the specific information God needs to

convey in order to fulfill His will, He uses other methods. The ministry of angels may be used or gifts of the Holy Spirit (Hebrews 2:4; 13:2), or an individual prophecy may be given. Thus, we are told, "Do not put out the Spirit's fire; do not treat prophecies with contempt" (1 Thessalonians 5:19; see 1 Corinthians 12:10; 13:2; 14:1,6,22; 2 Peter 1:20).

Regardless, methods as the Urim and Thummim, casting lots, and so on, were never intended as a general means for people to divine the particulars of their own future, e.g., the Urim and Thummim were used only by the priests of Israel. Further, divination for personal knowledge of the future is both unnecessary and dangerous. In Scripture, God has already told us the broad outlines of future history as it relates to biblical eschatology. His people are to trust in His Word and in His sovereignty over future events, both in their own lives and in the final outcome of human affairs. For very good reasons, God has not and does not reveal our specific, individual futures. For example, no one likes pain, and if we knew the future most of us would try to avoid unpleasant situations, suffering, and tragedy, which may, in fact, be God's will for us; thus avoiding what God has wisely determined is best for us from the eternal perspective.

People grow in their faith and in their ability to endure things. God's will that cannot be endured at one point in life may be able to be endured or accepted at another. And no one but God knows the final cost for not enduring His will (cf. Matthew 19:11-12; John 16:12). Had Jesus not accepted the suffering that was God's purpose for His life, what would have been the outcome? But how many of us would willingly face something like that were divination to reveal it? Only God knows what will finally be accomplished through the sacrifices and sufferings of His saints. This is why Scripture tells us, "Let those also who suffer according to the will of God entrust their souls to a faithful Creator in doing what is right" (1 Peter 4:19 NASB).

Occult divination adopts an entirely different view, one that does not trust God for the future. By seeking to know future events, divination promises to allow the individual to control his future. In this sense, it represents a fundamental rejection of God's infinite, wise, and perfect will, replacing it with the limited and self-serving perspective of the human will. Because it represents a conscious abdication of divine sovereignty for human "control," it is ultimately a confrontation with God. This is why the Bible strictly opposes divination. While it acknowledges that people use divination (e.g., Genesis 4:4-5), it condemns and never endorses such practices:

"Do not practice divination or sorcery" (Leviticus 19:26).

"Let no one be found among you who sacrifices his son or daughter in the fire, who practices divination or sorcery, interprets omens, engages in witchcraft. . . . The nations you will dispossess listen to those who practice sorcery or divination. But as for you, the LORD your God has not permitted you to do so" (Deuteronomy 18:10,14).

"For rebellion is like the sin of divination, and arrogance like the evil of idolatry . . ." (1 Samuel 15:23).

"They sacrificed their sons and daughters in the fire. They practiced divination and sorcery and sold themselves to do evil in the eyes of the LORD, provoking him to anger" (2 Kings 17:17).

"He sacrificed his sons in the fire in the Valley of Ben Hinnom, practiced sorcery, divination and witchcraft, and consulted mediums and spiritists. He did much evil in the eyes of the LORD, provoking him to anger" (2 Chronicles 33:6).

"Then the LORD said to me, 'The prophets are prophesying lies in my name. I have not sent them or appointed them or spoken to them. They are prophesying to you false visions, divinations, idolatries and the delusions of their own minds' " (Jeremiah 14:14).

"Once when we were going to the place of prayer, we were met by a slave girl who had a spirit by which she predicted the future. She earned a great deal of money for her owners by fortune-telling. This girl followed Paul and the rest of us, shouting, 'These men are servants of the Most High God, who are telling you the way [Greek: "a way"] to be saved.' She kept this up for many days. Finally Paul became so troubled that he turned around and said to the spirit, 'In the name of Jesus Christ I command you to come out of her!' At that moment the spirit left her. . . . the owners of the slave girl realized their hope of making money was gone" (Acts 16:16-19).

This last passage (where the diviner attempted to justify her own practice by linking it to the apostles' ministry) reveals the true source of power behind divination: the spirit world. We will document this below.

In conclusion, the difference between the biblical approach and occult approach to the future can be seen in the areas of the source of information (God or Satan), phenomena (Scripture, prophecy, divinely ordained implements or occult, pagan methods), and outcome (glory to God through trust in His will or individual confusion and perhaps destruction from trusting in the devil's will). In the following material we will examine various popular methods to see some of the consequences of rejecting God's will in this matter.

## RUNES

*Introduction*

Runes are ancient Teutonic and Norse alphabet sigils (signs or images) placed upon tiles that are given magical and divinatory properties. The word "rune" derives from the Indo-European root "rw," meaning "secret" or "mystery" (1526:522). Promoters of rune magic often lament that Americans and Europeans are neglecting this powerful form of divination, which has ancient ties with old Western roots. Why use the Chinese I Ching or the Middle Eastern tarot cards when Americans can tap their own unique spiritual heritage? As one rune worker states:

Runes are an alternative to I Ching, Tarot and even tea-leaves and, in many respects, offer significant advantages over their oriental, middle eastern and home-brewed counterparts.

Runes are basically a practical method of fortune-telling and reflect, to some degree, their northern European origins. They are easier to interpret than I Ching and compared with Tarot cards require less intuitive application by the reader (1484:9).

Rune magic, healing, and divination are enjoying a resurgence of popularity. In *The Runic Workbook: Understanding and Using the Power of Runes*, Tony Willis observes:

Runic wisdom is more easily available in the world today in the form of books, articles, lectures and study groups than it has been for the previous nine centuries. Read, study, practise runic divination and magic, and the next... piece of information, the next step along the Path will be revealed to you at the right time and in the right way. The most important lesson you will ever learn is that the Universal Forces are to be trusted (1486:180).

A few of the titles now available include: R. W. Elliott, *Runes*; R. L. Page, *An Introduction to English Runes*; Ralph Blum, *The Book of Runes;* Michael Howard, *The Wisdom of the Runes;* Edred Thorson, *Futhark: A Handbook of Rune Magic;* and David and Julia Line, *Fortune Telling by Runes.*

Like the I Ching, tarot, Ouija board, and other forms of divination, the runes give access to power, but not a power explainable by natural law or conventional science (1484:8). It is a power that reflects our modern return to paganism.

*Recent History*

The remnants of ancient paganism can be seen in widely diverse ways in our culture. For example, the names of our days of the week are astrologically influenced (Sunday = sun day, Monday = moon day, Wednesday = Woden's day, Thursday = Thor's day, etc.), and some of our holidays, such as Christmas and Easter, were once pagan. Something as common as a deck of playing cards is apparently a derivation of an earlier form of the tarot pack.** Thus, it is not surprising to discover that pagan runes have also influenced our history. The British currency called pounds, shillings, and pence was derived in part from the Roman solidus (coin) which bore a runic inscription (1484:21). Some texts on runes mention that Hitler's troops used the runic form of "S" as symbols on their collar badges (530:6f).

Like occult practices in general, runes were once suppressed by the church as a work of the

devil, but rune revivals have occurred periodically. For example, in the late 1800s:

By going underground, the runic system survived as an unpublished and unpublicized magico-mystical tradition in all the Anglo-Saxon, Germanic and Scandinavian countries—and this includes the United States which took in immigrants in large numbers from all those areas. At the end of the nineteenth century, the teaching first began to be written down in a formulated and coherent fashion. The bulk of this work was done by German and Austrian occultists, sometimes using material that had been transmitted orally, but more usually working via the method of analeptic recall (1486:19).

The Germans in particular seem to have been fascinated by the runes, and Naziism not only made use of them but of much other occultism as well (1062). Practitioners David and Julia Line observe:

Although the Church actively tried to stamp out runic divination, it continued to be practised in secret and became inevitably linked with witches, warlocks and their arts.

Runes, both esoteric and practical, continued to be studied throughout history until this century and nowhere else were they held in such high esteem as Germany. Runes became a vital component of the Third Reich's belief in Aryan superiority (1484:18-19).

In fact, the Nazis employed two runes extensively: the swastika (originally a Norse magical symbol known as Thor's hammer) and the " ⟨ " sigil used by the SS troops, originally a symbol of the Earth Mother and the sun (1526:523). The runic connection to German politics and pagan beliefs seems clear:

It was not until the late nineteenth century that runes once more appeared in public consciousness and this was the result of research by German occultists who were trying to revive Teutonic and Norse paganism.

Many of these occultists identified themselves with various extreme forms of German nationalism. One of these was Dr. Bernard Koerner, ... a disciple of the famous German occultist Guido

---

**The major manufacturer of playing cards in the U.S., the United States Playing Card Company of Cincinnati, Ohio, also sells the tarot; its standard order form offers three different varieties.

Von List whose book *The Secrets of Runes* was a best-seller in European occult circles. Another associate of Koerner was Baron von Sebbotten-dorf who edited a magazine called *Runen* or *The Rune* devoted to Aryan paganism, rune lore and anti-Jewish propaganda. . . . It is certain that Hitler and his cronies were fascinated by the runes and their secret occult powers. He even adopted the rune as the symbol of the feared SS elite troops who effectively ruled occupied Europe.

Today, the worship of the old Norse gods still continues. There are Odinist movements in Germany, Britain, Canada, the United States and Australia. Some advocate extreme right wing politics which suggest a link with the German nationalists and many still practise the ancient art of rune magic (530:86-87).

Not surprisingly, the association with Hitlerism drove rune magic underground:

The appropriation of the Runes by the higher echelons of the Nazi party did the advancement of runic lore no good at all in the years following the Second World War. . . . [A]fter the collapse of the Nazi war machine the Allies very naturally wanted nothing at all to do with Runes: neither did the German nation itself, busily repudiating the Nazis and all their works and anxious to avoid guilt by association in any form. The Runes were consequently consigned to the occult wilderness. Only one article on Runes was published in the United Kingdom between the middle forties and the early seventies (1486:20).

In recent decades, runes have experienced another revival, perhaps, at least in part, from the great popularity of J.R.R. Tolkien's *Lord of the Rings*, which deals with Teutonic and Norse mythology. In *The Runic Workbook*, Willis writes of the postwar era:

During this period, the Runes and runic philosophy were being impressed upon the consciousness of the post-war world, particularly among the English-speaking peoples, through the surprising agency of J.R.R. Tolkien. In *The Lord of the Rings*, the Dwarves are said to use the Runes for communications, and this runic alphabet is explained in that part of the Appendix to *The*

*Lord of the Rings* which deals with writing in Middle Earth. Tolkien was a professor of Anglo-Saxon, and the whole work [*The Hobbit* and the three books of *The Lord of the Rings*] is shot through with glimpses of Teutonic Mythology (1486:20).

Willis argues that "the guardians of the runic traditions" (i.e., the spirit world, particularly the ancient pagan gods associated with runes) have now instituted a PR program on behalf of rune magic:

In occult circles, however, it was not until the early eighties, when interest in the Runes had reached a high pitch, that the guardians of the runic tradition gave the order for a further release of information—this time of a deeper and more esoteric nature. This is where we stand today, on the brink of a new dawn of runic instruction. . . . For those who prefer group workings, there are *Odinic Lodges*, as the runic Mystery Schools are called, operating all over Northern Europe, North America, and even Australia (1486:20).

In theory or practice, runes, like other divination, may be combined with additional forms of the occult—astrology,* geomancy, numerology, alchemy, cabalism, the I Ching, tarot, etc. (1488). Rune tiles can be drawn at random and meditated on, cast in lots like the I Ching, or laid out in wheels or crosses like the tarot. One author refers to the runes as "a later and more sophisticated version of the I Ching . . ." (530:74).

*Shamanism*

A survey of the literature will also reveal the connection between runes and ancient shamanism.* Indeed, the modern rune caster is, in part, engaging in a practice that will enable him to develop shamanic skills. For example, Michael Howard's text, *The Magic of the Runes: Their Origins and Occult Power*, is a preliminary introduction to shamanism. He discusses the relationship between the rune masters (priests) and shamans, their common employment of spiritism, and some of the similarities in philosophy and practice. For Howard, the rune master *was* a kind of shaman (530:9-13,29-35,54-59):

The wizards who used the runes for magical purposes regarded themselves as blood kin to Odin, the Nordic god who was popularly accredited with inventing the runic alphabet. As we have seen, they were basically followers of the shamanistic tradition which is one of the oldest, if not the oldest, religious belief systems known to humanity.... Shamanistic spirit drums had occult symbols or demon faces painted on their surfaces and runic characters etched around the rim ... (530:29-31).

Not surprisingly, Howard concludes by noting that through rune work and the related practice of dream work,* "We can indeed become our own shamans" (530:29-31).

Willis, whose text is a standard work on runes in occult circles, also observes the shamanistic orientation of rune magic:

With the purchase of this book, you are on your way to becoming a runic shaman. Resolve to be worthy of this ancient and noble calling. ... Runes are the sacred symbols of the Teutonic races, and in the far past, a complete system of philosophy and magic was erected upon them. This system was handed down from shaman to pupil with word of mouth using the Runes themselves as mnemonies.... The Germanic/Norse tradition is essentially shamanistic.... The clearest description we have of a runic practitioner is of a female shaman. It comes from the *Saga of Erik the Red*, and was written in the thirteenth century (1486:13,17-18).

*Spiritism*

We have noted in several other chapters that occult techniques usually seem to originate from spiritistic revelation; this may be true for runes as well, if we are to believe the mythology. Howard points out that the origin of the runes may indeed be spiritistic, but he prefers the view that the Norse god Odin might have been a prehistoric shaman who discovered the rune system and was later deified. Regardless, given the dependence of shamans on the spirit world for occult power and knowledge, it would remain possible that runic divination originated from contact with the spirit world:

Mythologically, the invention of the runes is credited to the Nordic god Odin. His name is said to be derived from the Old Norse word *Od*, meaning wind or spirit.... The physical description of Odin indicates his sinister reputation.... The gaping eye socket is hidden by a brimmed hat and he leans on a blackthorn staff, accompanied by a raven and a wolf. Odin has the power to raise the dead and divine the future or, like the spirits, to change shape at will; he is also known by the name *Grim*. Travellers would allegedly often "meet the god ... in human form" (530:8).

Howard also describes methods used by shamans for attaining occult knowledge; in one case, the supernatural revelation of the magical rune alphabet and the opening of the chakras or alleged psychic centers of the body (530:12-13). Nevertheless, it is the spirits who are held to be the true source of the runes' power. Thus, "... the elemental spirits associated with the runes ... were regarded as the major source of their mysterious power. In some cases these entities are the gods and goddesses of the Old Norse religion" (530:37). "In pagan Europe people visited the local rune magician who by casting the runes divined the future.... It is also an integral part of the shamanistic tradition which we have examined throughout this book as a thread running through runecraft. As we have seen the ability to look into the future was regarded as a gift from the gods to the shaman who passes it on to the tribe" (530:71).

Not unexpectedly, runework, like the tarot, I Ching, and others, also helps develop people's alleged psychic abilities:

In my experience, the Runes are excellent developers and intensifiers of intuition. They have the power to free the psychic faculties from the restrictive bondage of temporal thought patterns.... Generally, students developing intuition experience either clairvoyance, clairaudience or clairsentience—the psychic or astral equivalents of the physical senses of sight, hearing and touch (1486:34-35; cf. Intuition).

Because rune work constitutes a magical system, it is not surprising to discover the actual invocation of gods or spirits prior to beginning rune divination. And the use of ritual magic may also play a role, as in the following account:

> In occult workings the runes can be used, as any magical alphabets are, to add extra power to the ritual or spell. Before using the runes you should invoke Odin who represents the power inherent in the runic characters. A suggested invocation is given below[:]
>
> Ruler of the Underworld and the crossroads
> I [insert your name] invoke and call upon thee to aid me in the Great Work. At the time I seek [state your intention] with your help and through the wisdom of the magical runes which are under thy protection.
>
> During this invocation visualize the god standing in front of you.... As the paper burns the magician may visualize a ray of blue light emanating from the forehead just above the bridge of the nose, which is the site of the psychic Third Eye and the physical peneal gland, towards the magical image of Odin which has been materialized earlier in the ritual. When this has been achieved, the magician thanks Odin and Baldur for their help. Again a suggested wording is given below:
>
> I [insert own name] thank thee Odin grim lord of the dead and guardian of the runes (530:62, 64; cf. 1486:30).

Other rune practitioners discuss the occult mechanics involved in rune work. Willis mentions the importance of consecration to the spirits, noting their ability to manipulate the mystical energy that is utilized in rune work. In the extended citation following, we see significant parallels to the Kabalistic Master Ritual discussed in David Conway's *Magic: An Occult Primer* (see p. 345,584-85). This indicates the magical nature of rune work, its dependence on the spirits, and the likely spirit possession of the serious rune worker:

> Occult philosophy maintains that energy in its most subtle form can be passed from one object to another.... [I]t is also possible to pass energy from an animate object to inanimate object. In the case of consecration, the animate object

would be the runic magician and the inanimate object the slip of paper or piece of wood or metal bearing the runescript or bindrune petition.... Consecration also implies a "setting apart." ... If you assume this stance, after a few minutes you will begin to feel a tingling sensation building up in the palms of your hands which will then move slowly down your arms and accumulate in the area of your solar plexus. This is the old Teutonic way of drawing energy from the atmosphere, which is itself impregnated with the Life Force. This Life Force is in the safe-keeping of the gods.... Allow this energy to build up for two or three minutes. ... Now, the energy that has built up around your solar plexus will be felt to pass down your arms and out through the palms of your hands into the runescript or bindrune talisman. You may not in the initial stages feel the energy passing out through your palms but you will certainly feel it disperse from the chest area and move down your arms.... [S]ince these subtle energies are manipulated by mind-power, or *intention*, what is more natural than that the energy has relocated itself as the place where you intended it to go? It is a good idea, when standing in the invoking posture, to state your reasons for wanting to accumulate the energy, and to call upon the appropriate god-force, either from the Nordic/Teutonic pantheon or from some other pantheon with which you are familiar, as this helps to ensure that the energies built up are of a sympathetic vibration to the type of talisman you are working on. When the energy has dissipated, thank the gods (or Universal Forces) for their cooperation. Though the gods are not human beings, they are sentient and in many ways respond just like humans to appeals, slights, praise, or being taken for granted (1486:154-56; cf. p. 130).

Indeed, an entire host of gods and goddesses can be invoked in rune magic, with each god helping the occultist to obtain different goals, e.g., "Freyja" for psychic powers, "Thor" for wealth, "Baldur" for psychic healing (530:65).

Runes also have a variety of other purposes, e.g., they may be "engraved on amulets or talismans" (530:67). Willis shows how runes may be integrated with other magical systems, such as kabalism. Combining rune work, visualization,* and kabalism, he shows how to enter "imaginary" astral realms and encounter personal spirit guides (1486:169), or what may be termed "Norns." These spirits may be male, female, or as in shamanism, power animals.

Two final illustrations of the spiritistic aspect of rune work include spirit guides and psychological dynamics. First, spirit guides are important, and, characteristically, they have a far different set of ethics than Christians do: "Where possible, allow yourself to be shown around by a Guide. This is not always an option open to you, but where it is, I urge you to take it. However, not all figures who present themselves as Guides are friendly. . . . The denizens of the Astral Light constitute another order of being with a different set of ethics, values and priorities from those that humankind are used to" (1486:169).

The psychological dynamics involved in the encounter with spirits are also important: "The first Pathworking, The Way to the Norns [i.e., spirit guides], is intended to reawaken any Teutonic, Norse or early Anglo-Saxon memories lying dormant in the personal unconscious and should be performed by any serious runic shaman *before* moving on to the more Qabalistic type of Pathworking" (1486:170).

Finally, after more warnings, the rune worker is given details of the spirits who will contact him or her:

> Once you have made this journey . . . you will usually find one or other of the Three Norns waiting for you. Sometimes all three will be present though generally only one of them will assume the role of Guide at any one time. If none of the sisters are waiting, DO NOT GO ON until one of them comes for you. If they do not appear, go back. . . . Some of the animals, too, will act as Guides if you can induce them to take human form. In animal form they are not to be trusted . . . (1486:173-74).

Not surprisingly, in rune work personal historical research into pagan gods and cultures is encouraged as a means to improve one's knowledge of the gods and spirits (cf. Dungeons and Dragons, following). In conclusion, the neophyte rune-shaman is encouraged to accept the companionship of the gods and spirits as their blessing (1486:179-80).

*Dangers*

Rune work, like all occultism, is not without serious risks (see 278). This is one reason Howard warns against the marketing techniques employed by those who sell runes as a form of popular entertainment: "Rune magic like all practical occult techniques, can be dangerous. Great caution is required and the runes should *never* be treated as an amusing parlour game, an entertainment or a means of making quick money" (530:61).

The attendant ritualistic hazards found in other forms of magic are also warned of in rune work:

> Incorrect use of a rune could spell deadly danger for the magician or witch. The old Rune Masters believed that every rune was associated with an elemental spirit or force which had to be carefully evoked and once conjured into physical form had to be very carefully controlled. . . . Some of the spirits evoked by the shamans were believed by them to be succubi and incubi. These were lustful earth spirits who delighted in sexual relations with humans in the shape of beautiful women or handsome young boys. Their carnal appetites were insatiable and any person who became possessed by them could be literally fornicated to death (530:61; cf. 1069:196-99,336).

> There was also the real danger that people who had not received the proper occult training in runecraft could dabble with them and both hurt themselves and others. For instance, the use of a cursing rune when a healing one was required would have dire results for both the patient and the would-be rune master who would have to face the vengeance of the victim's relatives (530:35).

Finally, the many problems associated with spirit possession in shamanism* may also be relevant to rune work: "Sometimes the shaman spoke in strange languages or unknown dialects. Often he would become possessed by spirits and some of these would try to bring harm to the shaman and those gathered around his entranced body" (530:32).

If rune work is finally related to shamanism*, as the evidence suggests, then rune work magic is dangerous indeed.

## I CHING

*Introduction*

The *I Ching*, or "Book of Changes," is one of the five principal texts of Confucianism and an ancient method of Chinese divination and self-knowledge. It has been practiced for three or four millennia, and to varying degrees it has impacted China, Japan, Korea, and Vietnam (2468:122-23/1491:15). "In China and the countries much influenced by Chinese civilization, Japan, Korea and Vietnam, the book has continued to play an influential role to the present day. In Japan until very recently, military tactics were based on the oracle, and the book was required reading for the higher ranks of Japanese officers" (2468:123).

The I Ching is more than merely a method of divination; as we will see, it is also a philosophy of life linked to the concepts of Taoism (cf. Tai Chi). It has recently been popularized in the West by translators and prominent individuals who are also practitioners. Occult psychoanalyst Carl Jung expressed his faith in the oracle in his autobiography, *Memories, Dreams, Reflections,* and in his foreword to the English translation of the *I Ching* by Richard Wilhelm. As we will see, some modern psychologists also utilize it as an adjunct to psychotherapy, reflecting Jung's belief that one of its functions is to draw information from the unconscious mind. Catering to the modern American desire for "instant" everything, there is even a set of I Ching "playing cards," which permit more rapid "divination."

The I Ching is composed of 64 hexagrams of broken and solid lines. A hexagram is determined by an elaborate method (2468:125) of tossing 50 yarrow sticks in a particular, complex procedure, or by the simpler and allegedly less accurate method of using a toss of three coins three times. Every hexagram has a meaning described by the I Ching, which is to be self-interpreted using intuition* and awareness of the flow and flux of cosmic energy.

*Philosophy*

The I Ching is based upon the precepts of the classical Chinese pagan religious philosophy known as Taoism (1491:38), which involves the cosmic dualism of yin and yang (complementary polarities threaded throughout life, such as male and female). The I Ching claims to be able to give a person an understanding of the "implications" of any given moment, and, allegedly, the best or "wisest" action to then take. Because all life is said to be governed by an "immutable" Law of Change, which is related to the yin and yang polarities, the I Ching is believed to sort out the "life patterns" produced by this law and the best way to respond to them. This is supposedly revealed through an intuitive interpretation of the "meaning" of 64 hexagrams, each having two groups of three lines variously arranged.

Since the cosmic order is in constant change, and since human life and destiny are irreversibly intertwined with this cosmic order, all human situations need corresponding constant revision to "harmonize" with the changes in nature. The purpose of the I Ching is to provide insight into the future so that people may live in harmony with the mercurial cosmic order (1490:LVIII-IX). Thus, the originators:

> ... believed that they had succeeded in analysing Change itself into sixty-four constituent processes, each subdivided into six stages and all interacting upon one another. They invented a method for relating individual affairs to the stages and processes most closely affecting them, thus fashioning a key whereby future generations could unlock the secrets of the future and determine the surest way to live in harmony with the circumstances prevailing. For more than two thousand years, those who have learned to use it have testified to the marvellous results obtained (1490:Foreword).

As noted, the *I Ching* "Book of Changes" has 64 hexagrams; it also uses eight "trigrams," with both solid and broken lines. The possible combinations represent the cosmic symbols illustrating

131

the patterns of change in people, nature, society, and so on. The unbroken lines represent the yang (male) principle, the broken ones represent the yin (female) principle. "According to ancient Chinese belief, every event and thing in the universe arises from the interaction of these two principles. Differences between things results from the varying proportions in them of Yin and Yang" (2468:122). Furthermore:

> Changes are viewed in terms of cycles which consist of opposite movements (e.g., expansion and contraction, rise and fall). When one pole is reached, the movement invariably reverts to the opposite pole. This principle was used to explain the ebb and flow in nature, society, and individuals. One's basic attitude should be to accept this cosmic order and to harmonize or become part of it. Under this conception of change the opposite poles are complementary and the ideal way is to accept both the high and the low poles (302:335).

Although the serious divinatory nature of the oracle is stressed, it is often viewed like runes, as a game of entertainment. As Samuel Reifler writes in *I Ching: A New Interpretation for Modern Times*, "Like its Western counterparts, such as astrology and tarot reading, the *I Ching* is most often used as a parlor game" (1492:1). But the serious nature of the practice is indicated by the power it invokes and the need for ritual. "Facing the table and with his back to the South, the enquirer prostrates himself thrice, lights a stick of incense and—with his mind fully concentrated on the question—mentally or verbally propounds it in the form previously decided upon. While doing so, he takes the divining sticks in his right hand and passes them three times through the incense smoke by describing clockwise circles with his wrist" (1491:79).

Since the I Ching is allegedly a method of self-knowledge, applications are also made to contemporary psychotherapy, especially through the Jungian concept of archetypes:

> The hexagrams embody the universal patterns of situations that lie beneath the collective consciousness of man, and correspond to the arche-

types of present-day thought. The different strata of explanations and commentaries are various attempts to interpret the meanings of these archetypes. Because archetypes lie in the unconscious, their interpretation generally requires the use of a symbolic and esoteric language in order to express what the ordinary language cannot (302:335).

Jungian analyst Joseph L. Henderson, M.D., has said this about the oracle:

> It embodies the kind of reasonableness we associate with modern psychological insight. As a practitioner of analytical psychology I find the wisdom of this book is not only ancient but perennial, and therefore, contemporary, and so I understand that when people use it practically to clarify their lives they are, for the most part, not indulging in wayward superstition but have found an authentic guide to a deeper knowledge of their motives. When, therefore, my patients, as they occasionally do, bring me reports of the things the I Ching has told them I take the communication seriously and feel honored to become at least an amateur interpreter of this old wisdom (1493:52-53).

*Spiritism*

The I Ching, like most forms of divination, is lauded for its uncanny ability to predict the future accurately. Consider the following comments of scholar and practitioner John Blofeld, who assigns the oracle infallibility. In his translation of the I Ching, he refers to its alleged ability to control the future, and he marvels over its "terrifying precision":

> ... it enables any reasonably unselfish person who is capable of fulfilling a few simple conditions both to foresee and to control the course of future events! By rightly interpreting and strictly following the *I Ching*'s interpretation of universal laws, we can make ourselves as farsighted as the lesser Gods! ... It can be used to explain the present and predict the future with almost terrifying precision! ... My aim in making a new translation of this work is to produce a version in the simplest possible language containing clear instructions for its use in divination, so that any

English-speaking person who approaches it sincerely and intelligently can use it as an infallible means of choosing good and avoiding evil. . . . My version is almost wholly concentrated on the aspect of divination (1491:14-16).

. . . What does interest me enormously is that the *Book of Change*, when properly put to the test, responds in such a way as to remove all doubts about its value as to a book of divination. . . . A really skilled interpreter who consults the *Book of Change* correctly will find that the answers given are *never wrong!* (1491:23,33, emphasis added).

Although we deny the *I Ching*'s omniscience, or that it is accurate to the degree Blofeld alleges, testimonies of accuracy can be found easily. Clearly it does work enough of the time to ensure peoples' interest. And no satisfactory, rational explanation for this process can be offered. Indeed, we cannot be dealing with some impersonal manifestation of cosmic law. Rather, it would seem we are encountering an intelligent power and source of information that knows us personally; one that can interact with us so as to arrange particular events and has a limited prevision of the future.

Blofeld confesses that when using the I Ching, he senses he is dealing with a personal, living being, not merely simple sticks forming symbolic hexagrams (Jung also felt as if he were dealing with a living entity; 2468:124). His response to this awareness is common to that of many pagans, who know only too well the reality of a living spirit behind a sacred object or an idol. Consider Blofeld's own amazement:

Like Jung, I have been struck by the extraordinary sensation aroused by my consultations of the book, the feeling that my question has been dealt with *exactly as by a living being* in full possession of even the unspoken facts involved in both the question and its answer. At first this sensation comes near to being terrifying and, even now, I find myself inclined to handle and transport the book rather as if it had feelings capable of being outraged by disrespectful treatment (1491:25, emphasis added).

Blofeld expresses his complete bafflement at the process. Yet what matters to him, and to all

who use these methods, are the results, not the explanation. Whatever the explanation for the power of I Ching, it must incorporate some kind of extremely powerful, living intelligence:

As to how the book succeeds in giving answers which produce this uncanny effect, I do not know. . . . If you say that the oracle owes its effectiveness to the subconscious of the one who asks the questions, or to the unconscious (which is probably universal and therefore common to all men), or to the One Mind (in the Zen sense), or to God or a god or the gods, or to the philosopher's Absolute, I shall be inclined to agree with every one of these suggestions, for I believe that most of all of these terms are imperfect descriptions of a single unknown and unknowable but omnipotent reality. . . . In other words, I am entirely satisfied with the results produced by the *I Ching*, but do not presume to explain the lofty process by which they are achieved (1491:25-26).

Blofeld is very impressed about a living personality that must underlie the information given. He recounts his first attempt to use the oracle for divination. As he did so, he was not at all certain the text did not house, or at least bring him into contact with, a personal, living spiritual being:

The very first time I did this, I was overawed to a degree that amounted to fright, so strong was the impression of having received an answer to my question *from a living, breathing person.* I have scarcely ever used it since without recovering something of that awe, though it soon came to be characterized by a pleasurable excitement rather than by fear. Of course I do not mean to assert that the white pages covered with black printer's ink do in fact house a living spiritual being. I have dwelt at some length on the astonishing effect they produce chiefly as a means of emphasizing how extraordinarily accurate and, so to speak, personal, are its answers in most cases. Yet, if I were asked to assert that the printed pages do not form the dwelling of a spiritual being or at least bring us into contact with one by some mysterious process, I think I should be about as hesitant as I am to assert the contrary (1491:26-27, emphasis added).

133

He also says that "to obtain and interpret responses so accurate and to the point [is] to suggest almost supernatural powers" (1491:35). Not surprisingly, a common feature of pagan spiritism—reverence or worship to the spirits in order to secure their assistance—is also seen as indispensable for correct interpretation of the *I Ching*: "An attitude of reverence—though indispensable—is not the sole condition for correct interpretation of the *Book of Change*" (1491:32). Of course, such reverence is also required in rune work, tarot interpretation, the Ouija board, and other divination methods.

The notorious occultist Aleister Crowley once commented that "other systems of divination are often manipulated by demons who delight in misleading the inquirer," and he felt that the I Ching was somehow above such duplicity. But he still conceded that the oracle was manipulated by personal intelligence: "The intelligences which direct it show no inclination to evade the question or to mislead the querant" (2468:124). Of course, this was only Crowley's personal experience to this point and, certainly, there are many others who have been misled by the oracle. We have no reason to suspect that its duplicity is any less than in other forms of divination. After all, subjectivism is a key component in the divination of the *I Ching* as in other forms of divination. "It is a characteristic of the *I Ching* that it rarely gives a cut-and-dried answer, and the inquirer must usually think hard to apply the interpretation to his own situation" (2468:125).

Nevertheless, our response to all this is to ask, Why do so many practitioners have this particular animistic sense of things? Why this intuition of personal spiritual beings interacting with a book and its hexagrams? Why would truly impersonal forces "care" about our respect? The most logical explanation is because personal spiritual beings do operate through divinatory methods, and they do seek our allegiance.

*Interpretation*

Like all forms of divination, the I Ching has the problem of interpretation. Both the text and the many commentaries written "explaining" the

hexagrams contradict one another. In producing his own translation, Blofeld correctly observes of the original Chinese text:

Its exceedingly terse style in many places justifies a number of widely varying translations; nor it is unlikely that in some passages several simultaneous meanings were deliberately implied. Moreover, the Chinese text includes hardly any pronouns at all, so that my arbitrary inclusion of them for the sake of reasonably good English puts a quite artificial limitation on the meaning.... I cannot always guarantee the accuracy of my translation. Judging from several Chinese versions of the *Book of Change* in my possession, even expert Chinese commentators have widely varying and even contradictory explanations of the more difficult passages (1491:17-18).

Elsewhere Blofeld discusses two additional difficulties for proper interpretation:

There are two insuperable obstacles to providing a reliable guide to interpreting the *I Ching's* responses. The first is that so much depends on the various circumstances leading to the enquiry and upon numerous related facts, some of which may already be present in the enquirer's mind, while others are not recognized as having any connection until either the response itself or subsequent events demonstrate their importance. An elementary example is provided by the fifth line of Hexagram 3, Chun, Difficulty. If that happens to be a moving line, the response will include the words; "Fertility cannot easily be brought about," which will obviously have different meanings for, say, somebody longing to bear a son or daughter, a man considering whether to buy a certain piece of land, a teacher hoping to enlighten a backward child, an administrator about to take charge of a new territory, a person expecting to benefit from a particular friendship or a business man mulling over a new policy (1491:72).

The second difficulty is to interpret the *I Ching* apart from the faculty of intuition* or an altered state of consciousness*:

The second obstacle is that the *Book of Change* can seldom be accurately interpreted in accordance with a particular situation unless the faculty of intuition is allowed to play a decisive role. . . . I wish to warn the enquirer against mistaking his desires or expectations for intuition. . . . True intuition occurs only when the mind has been temporarily withdrawn from all conceptual and intellectual processes by means of Zen-like concentration, during which time our consciousness is cleansed of hopes, fears, expectations and so forth (1491:73).

Correct interpretation of the oracles requires a particular state of mind—here again, students of Zen possess a special advantage—in which respect based on belief is a vital factor (1491:24).

. . . As with oracles the world over, the meaning is so esoteric as to baffle the mind until intuition, careful thought or some unforeseen experience provide a sudden illumination (1491:32-33).

Thus, as Ch'u Chai observes in the introduction to James Legge's translation:

The *I Ching* is like a good poem; the number of words is limited, but the ideas it suggests are limitless. . . . A good reader of the *I Ching* reads "what is between the lines." This means that those latent ideas form an essential, often a principal, part of the *I Ching,* so that in an appreciative, generally reflective approach to its material the reader himself often supplies all the "links" that are necessary to turn these "aphorisms" into a form of reasoning and arguments (1490:XXXVIII).

In other words, *I Ching* interpretation is so elastic it offers a wide range of potential personal applications. This situation makes its genuine power all the more impressive, and spiritistic manipulation all the more easy.

In conclusion, like other forms of divination, the I Ching works, which is precisely the problem. (See "The Power of Spiritistic Insights" on p. 163.) By leading people to regulate their lives and decisions in accordance with harmful occult principles or spiritistic powers, people are subject to forces beyond their control. Thus, as we illustrated in the chapter on astrology, divination methods are fraught with personal risks that few practitioners suspect are present.

## TAROT

*Introduction*

Tarot and other magical cards are also used for divination. The 56 cards of the "minor arcana" and the 21 cards of the "major arcana," plus "the fool," constitute the tarot deck, a method commonly employed by fortune-tellers of all stripes. The influence of these cards extends back into antiquity.

Like runes and the I Ching, tarot cards are often used for personal amusement. One author suggests the cards may be used to "liven up" a party. "One way to break the ice at a party is to bring up the subject of Tarot predictions or Tarot symbolism. Soon almost every guest will have a tale to tell or an opinion to express, . . . and of course there will always be a doubting Thomas or two who will try to explain very rationally why such things cannot possibly work to any truly 'scientific' person's satisfaction. Meanwhile most of the other guests will find themselves thoroughly fascinated and amazed by an antique Tarot set" (1494:1).

Tarot cards have engrossed the elite in Hollywood, politicians, psychologists, and noteworthy members of the fine arts communities. Surrealist Salvador Dali's wife, Gala, was interested in the occult and piqued her husband's interest so that he painted a new set of tarot cards for his wife, illustrated in the 1985 version of *Salvador Dali's Tarot* by Rachael Pollack. Dali is only one of hundreds of famous individuals throughout history who have been interested in the tarot and similar forms of card divination. In the fourteenth and fifteenth centuries, special sets of tarot cards were hand-painted for the royal families of France (the Gringonneur Tarot) and Italy (the Vicont-Sforza Tarot; 1494:9).

*Occult Influence*

A large variety of tarot decks exists, many developed within specific religious or occult traditions, e.g., Egyptian, wiccan, magical, Mayan, Gypsy. Like the I Ching and runes, tarot cards are quite old and no one is certain of their exact origin. Although the earliest decks are traceable to fourteenth-century Europe, the associations go much further back. In *Forbidden Images: The Secrets of the Tarot*, David Le Mieux theorizes, "It also appears that the Tarot was not originally invented as a fortune-telling tool; instead, it was a masterly designed theological and philosophical teaching device that was based on ancient Egyptian pictorial magic" (1494:2).

The possibility of an Egyptian origin is lent a certain credence because the 22 major cards of the tarot "have a remarkable correlation with the most important deities of the mystery religions" spreading throughout the Mediterranean basin around 330 B.C. For example:

I   the Magician—Hermes
II  the High Priestess—Kore-Persephone
III the Empress—Demeter, Isis
IV  the Emperor—Hades, Osiris
XIII Death—Kronos
XV  the Devil—Pan, Hades
XIX the Sun—Helios
XXI the World—Phanes and Ophion
(1525:130-31).

Just as the runes were allegedly an invention of the Norse god Odin, so one theory recounts that tarot originates from the Egyptian god Thoth, called Hermes Trismegistus by the Greeks. "This book was claimed to have been written by the lord of writing, justice, and magic himself, the ancient Egyptian god Thoth; and for that reason it was called *The Book of Thoth. The Book of Thoth* contained the essence of all that was magical, mysterious, and forbidden; and it contained the foundation of the ancient pagan religions" (1492:4-5). Aleister Crowley referred to his version of the tarot deck by the title *The Book of Thoth.* Allegedly, the tarot evolved (in disguised form) from the *Book of Thoth* as a means to protect its occult wisdom (1492:5-7).

No one denies that the tarot has been associated with occultism throughout history, with divination, magic, astrology, kabalism, numerology, and alchemy (1494:1-2,140-41; cf. ref. 1495). Also, some individuals have an innate psychic sensitivity to the cards, which also underscores their occult potential. Le Mieux observes that "a gifted reader builds up a kind of rapport with

the energies in his or her Tarot set" (1492:142). It is not unusual for tarot card readers to speak of having "conversations" with the cards, just as if a second party were present. Theologian Dr. John Warwick Montgomery recalls, in his analysis of the occult, "It is most interesting to observe the reactions of a sensitive person when he first examines these cards. Instead of the indifference which accompanies contact with ordinary playing cards (not due just to their familiarity, but to their banality), there is generally a deep absorption and hushed interest. The cards seem to 'grab' their user" (295:129).

Not surprisingly, for a tarot deck to work the same respect and reverence necessary to the I Ching and runes is recommended (1494:142; cf. Crystal Work). Again, we may be dealing with a living being, not a mere deck of cards.

In his bestseller *Joy's Way*, spiritist and physician W. Brugh Joy describes his own fascination with the tarot and its occult potential:

The Tarot is an excellent teacher, because as the user advances in expanded awareness it reflects this expansion.... The Tarot is one of the best tools I know both for rapid insight into personal motives, time and space relationships ... for reconditioning emotional responses, augmenting the intuitive faculty, restructuring personal belief systems and beginning access to more universal levels of awareness.... I have used the Tarot at the close of personal consultations, asking it to reveal to my outer mind any dynamics, overlooked in the session, that might be important. To my amazement, it often turns up a critical dynamic that has been totally unseen till then (1495:84-87).

The occult nature of the tarot is also the reason for its power. David Le Mieux discusses this potency, including the "card's" ability to develop psychic powers in their user. Like the I Ching and runes, tarot cards work:

Reading with Tarot cards does indeed work. Few people with any real experience or knowledge of the subject will deny that.... I have found that Tarot readings are much more accurate and powerful than those based on astrology or other forms of occult prediction. But one of the big questions is, How? How do Tarot symbols help us reexamine the past and predict the future? Why do the cards seem to increase psychic powers? . . . Many occultists have speculated on the power of the Tarot. Tarots were created to be powerful. . . . Tarots work like magic because they are, by their very nature, magical. They are part of primitive "picture magic," or iconography. Later, these magic pictures were raised up and placed in the sky in the form of astrological symbols. Tarot cards also contain astrological symbolism in its perfect ancient order—a whole realm of man's unconscious experience and memory. . . . The Tarot is a tour de force in ancient numerology—probably the most perfect numerological system ever devised. And still later, the Hebrew cabalists claimed that the sacred alphabet contained the secrets of the universe (1494:1-2).

Writing in *Astral Doorways*, occultist J. H. Brennan points out that the trumps (the 22 cards with symbolic pictures) "can have a very stimulating effect on the intuition" by nature of their symbolism (386:44; cf. Intuition). He also observes that the trumps, in connection with visualization* and imagination, may actually be used as a method for entering the "astral" domain. "In itself, the Tarot is a remarkable system for esoteric study. And in themselves the cards can be used as Astral Doorways. The technique to use is even more simple than that of the Elemental Doorways" (386:48; cf. 1496:121).

The occult nature of the tarot is the principal reason why the church has consistently opposed its use, as even tarot promoters admit:

They represent the outcome of a much more profound doctrine—a secret and forbidden doctrine—a doctrine that was condemned from almost every pulpit in Christian Europe of the fourteenth and fifteenth centuries. . . . The cards were condemned from just about every church pulpit in the land as some sort of evil influence. Priests dubbed the set of Tarot cards "The Devil's Picture Book" and forbade their use for any purpose in most towns and villages (1494:2,9).

*Tarot Psychotherapy*

The tarot cards can also be used with meditation* and psychotherapy. When occultist Alfred Douglas describes some of the cards' esoteric principles in *The Tarot: The Origins, Meaning and Uses of the Cards*, we see how they may be used in psychology, and also the risks of tarot meditation. The potential for the tarot deck to incorporate spiritistic contacts can also be seen via the tarot characters "coming alive," for example, through the personification of the "inner self" as a guardian angel or in the ritual of "dismissing" occult powers (cf. New Age Inner Work*):

The Tarot cards display a powerful array of psychic images, and it can be surmised that they were used not only as teaching aids but as focal points of consciousness during individual meditation. . . . The twenty-two cards of the Tarot major arcana have been used extensively by Western occultists during the past century as an important part of their Qabalistic "Tree of Life" meditation system. . . . The aim of Tarot meditation is to project oneself in the imagination into each card in turn, exploring its imagery, getting the "feel" of its symbolism, uncovering its meaning in terms of one's own psychic structure. . . . Step in your imagination over the threshold of the card as if through an open door, and stand with the characters in their own world. . . . But gradually you will find that new ideas regarding the significance of the images appear in your mind. These may take the form of abstract thoughts which suggest fresh lines of enquiry . . . or the characters might move and perform various actions or even speak, in which case you should listen and try to catch what is being said. Visualise the characters as strongly as you can. . . . It is important when you have finished your meditation that you "close down" properly. The powers which can be invoked during the visualisation process *must be dismissed thoroughly* before you return to everyday consciousness. . . . By building up a detailed account of your progress and discoveries over a period of weeks, months or even years you will gain a true and valuable insight into the inner significance of the mystical quest and its relevance to the realities of your personal psyche. Such a program of meditation not only has a harmonising and therapeutic effect, but can lead in time to what some mystics have called the Knowledge and Companionship of the Holy Guardian Angel, which is the living presence of the inner self (1496:204-08).

Some writers view the tarot as a form of "esoteric psychology," and so it is not surprising that many psychologists have turned to the cards as a method to trigger client self-insight. Angeles Arrien, assistant professor of anthropology at the New Age-oriented California Institute of Integral Studies, asserts, "Basically the tarot is an esoteric psychology, a science that symbolically represents through visual symbols a record of known possibilities of experience. . . . Currently, there is a resurgence of interest to use the tarot as a therapeutic and transformative tool. An effective therapeutic model utilizing the tarot could be devised by looking at esoteric-exoteric systems that have been developed by Eastern cultures" (1497:56,58).

The use of the tarot in psychotherapy is also illustrated by Dr. Genie Z. Laborde, an authority on "Neuro Linguistic Programming" (NLP). Laborde is in charge of John Grinder's "Executive Excellence" program, and she is an educator who received her Ph.D. in the controversial "confluent education" program from the University of California at Santa Barbara (see New Age Education). She points out how easily "psychological processes can be taught and illustrated using the images of the tarot deck. The tarot is used to elicit and dramatize the psychological process of projection, as evidence of a long tradition of archetypes and symbols which can evoke affect, and as visual examples of potential images available from the 'undiscovered self,' Carl Jung's phrase denoting the unconscious of the human psyche" (1498:50).

For example, she incorporates insights from the Aleister Crowley tarot deck, Freud's superego theory, Jung's archetypes, Fritz Perls' introjects, and occultist Roberto Assagiolo's system of psychosynthesis (1498:53).

Dr. Laborde has taught this tarot "therapy" to numerous groups of individuals, including corporation presidents, school and university teachers, psychologists, stockbrokers, editors, and housewives, all of whom say they have personally benefited from the sessions. She states, "The

more I worked with the Tarot the more convinced I became of its rich potential for evoking responses in my own unconscious and in the unconscious of my students" (1498:53-54).

In conclusion, when people freely dabble in tarot magic and divination, or in other forms of the occult, they are asking for the problems characteristically associated with these methods (see 278). Introducing unsuspecting clients to the occult in the form of tarot psychotherapy only complicates matters. Unfortunately, fringe psychotherapy today is utilizing the methods of dozens of occult traditions, many with their own brands of esoteric occult psychology (e.g., 860).

Regardless, the cards are obviously not something to be played with at parties or utilized in divination or for so-called "self-actualization." "Because the cards are so potent symbolically, they are also most dangerous when misused or perverted. Attempts to use them to predict the future are definitely to be discouraged. Tarot symbolism strikes to the recesses of the unconscious, where the archetypes reside. To try to harness this energy for prognostication and the control of one's destiny is simply to ask for trouble" (295:131-32).

*Tarot Progeny: Cartouche and Phoenix Cards*

The popularity of tarot cards has produced a number of related systems, among them Cartouche and the Phoenix cards. In *The Way of Cartouche: An Oracle of Ancient Egyptian Magic,* author Murray Hope describes their history and function. The cards are similar to the tarot in arrangement spread, and they are used for a broad variety of occult activity. The cover jacket describes the cards as a "system of self understanding and awareness that taps into the wisdom of the ancient Egyptians." Thus it is supposedly "an exciting new system of divination because it encapsulates the archetypal and powerful energies known and understood by the ancients and embodies them in identities recognizable in today's world." The Cartouche cards are said to "provide startlingly accurate answers to dreams, family or emotional problems, financial or business matters, protection, spiritual seeking, or any of life's enigmas." And the user is told to "try the Cartouche—you will be astounded by their accuracy."

The Phoenix cards stress divination and self-insight, but they also concentrate on personal growth through understanding one's alleged "past lives" (see Hypnosis). The following promotional description of a standard text, *The Phoenix Cards* (Destiny, 1990), by astrologer and psychic Susan Sheppard, reveals the occult focus of this particular method. (Sheppard is a descendant of the Swedenborgian mystic John Chapman, better known as "Johnny Appleseed.")

This book and deck of 28 Phoenix cards provide the first divination tool especially created for delving into past lives to better understand our experiences in the here and now. Each of the 28 images is a symbolic, visual representation of a particular world culture that will help you recall and bring into sharp focus the times and places of your previous incarnations.

The author explains how our present personalities are psychically programmed to remember who we were in previous existences, where we have been, and what cultures we have played a part in the shaping. The symbols of the Phoenix Deck are at once specific and universal, triggering these unconscious memories to help you discover your latent talents, identify the lessons you most need to learn, and come to terms with unexplained fears, attractions, and other perplexing emotions and impulses.

Several configurations are given for laying out the cards to determine which past lifetimes are the primary keys to your present personality and life experience. This knowledge eliminates confusion about present circumstances, enables you to see yourself more clearly—your habits, values and goals—and facilitates your ability to develop in the directions you choose. With practice, you can also learn to read the Phoenix cards easily and effectively for others (1483:2).

In conclusion, the various forms of divination just examined—runes, I Ching, tarot, Cartouche, and Phoenix—are utilized today by millions of people throughout the world. Those who seek out such methods do so for a variety of reasons, rarely suspecting the demonic nature underlying the power of these systems.

## PALMISTRY

*Introduction*

Palmistry is the occult practice of predicting the future by the details of the hand, including size, shape, lines, nails, and other features. As one standard text asserts, "It is the purpose of Palmistry to teach you how to conquer the ancient art of divination. . . ." (2460:18). It is also commonly used in character analysis. Although its origins are uncertain, it has been practiced in most cultures throughout history. In earlier eras it was often known as chiromancy and contained certain subdivisions, such as onychomancy or divination by the fingernails.

Like many other forms of divination, palmistry has popular entertainment value, which often becomes the means of fostering further interest. "Palmistry has always had an unfailing amusement value" (2459:7), and "palmistry can be used as a pleasant party pastime—a way to get yourself stage center and also to contribute to others' enjoyment. . . . Perhaps the easiest way to establish intimacy with another—and to find out if you really want to know him (her) better—is to say: 'let me look at your hand' " (2457:9).

A number of claims are made for palmistry, almost all of which are false. For example, palmistry claims to be 1) a true science, 2) highly accurate in its psychological diagnosis or prediction of the future, 3) not an occult practice or superstitious, and 4) that "responsible" palmistry is not fatalistic and does not unequivocally predict such things as serious illness, accident, or death. Consider the following illustrations.

In *Medical Palmistry* we read that palmistry deals with science, not occultism: "Unlike those occult arts, modern palmistry is predicated upon a set of criteria as rigid as any in physics. It's claims can be verified or disproved by any unbiased person who cares to investigate them upon an empirical basis" (2461:IX). As far back as 1897, one of the leading texts claimed that palmistry "is fast leaving the ranks of *Occult Sciences* to enter the honored family of *Sciences . . .*" (2460:10; cf. p. 379). We are also told that palmistry is not fatalistic: "Even amateur palmists often discover signs of pending changes, good or bad, in their health, fortunes or careers"

(2461:X), but "there is no absolute fatality shown in the hands" (2461:19).

Despite these claims, we will show that palmistry is not a science but an occult practice. Its overall accuracy is no better than for other forms of divination, and many proponents do continue to predict "inevitable" disease or death for their clients. Of course, they also tell clients how to *avoid* their "fate,"—usually for a price commensurate to the gravity of the problem.

The closest conceivable relationship palmistry bears to science is the discipline of dermatoglyphics, which is "the study of the patterns of parallel ridges and furrows on the epidermis of the hands and feet," e.g., fingerprints. Besides fingerprinting, this field of study has discovered genetic correlations between certain dermatoglyphic features and particular human diseases, such as Turner's Syndrome, Ellis-van Creveld Syndrome, and Rubenstein-Taybi Syndrome, dealing with anomalies of the hands, dwarfism/polydactyly, and broad thumbs and great toes. Down's syndrome may also be included (2469:29-30). "Only with some semantic effort can any of these recognized correlations be construed as resembling those of the palmist," and "the scientifically established connections between palmar and digital features and other aspects of individual biology offer no positive evidence in support of the relationships advocated by the palmist" (2469:29,31).

Of course, in some cases human hands can give evidence of one's occupation (e.g., as a laborer) or habits (e.g., smoking), and thus reveal possible clues to the owner's interests and perhaps even temperament or personality. But such information is limited and far removed from the amount of information palmists allege they can give through their method.

Like all divination, the success of palmistry is due more to the *perception* that it addresses client's needs, rather than to an actual ability to predict the future or analyze a person's character consistently. In other words, practitioners claim to be able to successfully regulate people's present and future life to their benefit. They tell people what they want to hear about themselves or their future. This is a talent especially true of popular and charlatan palmists. As one text advises,

"Always end on an encouraging note, everyone has something to develop and some good fortune coming their way—stress this" (2459:12). Another text states, "Most people today are interested in love, money, success, travel—and care less about health and life expectancy than they used to when life was more precarious. As a beginner, it is wise to confine your reading to the four high-interest areas rather than to foretell disasters, which take some experience to define" (2457:17).

Indeed, palmistry has become part of modern culture because most palmists have become adept at flattering their clients by stressing positive virtues and speaking of sadness or tragedy as being experienced only in the past. Who wouldn't like to have their future revealed as successful and happy (182:2118)? Palmistry claims that it can help people with choices in vocation, decisions regarding a marriage partner or dating, raising children, medical diagnosis, business opportunities, and virtually any area in need advice or counsel. But, as noted, palmists will also reveal the unspoken dangers facing a client in the future, even disasters, which the client can discover how to avoid for a fee.

*Nature*

Palmistry is at least 3000 years old and may have originated in India. The basic theory is that every detail of the hand (not just the palms) has information about the individual's present or future. Included are the hand shape and size, palm configurations and topography, finger shape, size, and configurations, and even features of the fingernails. There are at least a hundred signs, marks, or relationships through which supposed influences, events, or qualities can be "recognized" by the palmist. Depending on the part of the hand studied, palmistry may be divided into three lesser occult methods: 1) chirognomy (the outward shape of the hand), 2) chirosophy (manual formations), and 3) chiromancy (the form of the hand and fingers and its lines and markings; 377:685/2460:379). A related category, solistry, involves reading the foot (cf. Reflexology).

There are also different emphases in palmistry. A palmist may stress one or more of the following: 1) "medical" palmistry, in which a correlation is sought between the hands and physical (or emotional) states; 2) psychotherapeutic palmistry in which a correlation is sought between the hands, character, and personality, pointing out positive and negative aspects, and 3) the attempted correlation between the hands and the client's past, present, and future. This last category is sometimes termed divinatory palmistry, although the label "divination" properly applies to all categories.

As we will see, palmistry has much in common with other forms of divination, especially astrology.* As in astrology, the amount of information that can be "read" from the hand is vast. In terms of major and minor features, the hand has as many or more determinants as the astrologer's chart.

According to palmistry, the left hand allegedly reveals one's destiny and inherited disposition, while the right hand reflects how one's will and environment have modified the person's destiny or fate. (Left-handed persons reverse this rule.) Because the palm is believed to paint a miniature picture of the person and her future (or even her supposed past lives), the hand must be examined in minute detail (cf. 182:2119/2459:17-48).

Thus the hand as a whole is evaluated for the features of the handshake, color, skin texture, flexibility, shape, size, and "type." There are five or six major "types" of hands (square, conic, pointed, spatulate, mixed), although some systems have as many as 14 (2460:56). The fingers and thumb are evaluated for relative spread and size to one another (and to the palm), length, flexibility, smoothness, curvature, shape, and coloration. The fingernails are also evaluated for length, shape, moons, and so on.

The lines of the palms are divided into major and minor categories. There are at least 14 major lines including the lifeline and those of the head, heart, health, fortune, fate, intuition, spirituality, marriage, and children. The lines are also evaluated according to size, shape, relationships between them, and other factors. (Certain lines are found only in some people.) For example, the lifeline deals with one's overall constitution, length of life, or the destiny and dates of outstanding events; the headline deals with intellectual capacities, and the heart line deals with the emotions. Among the minor lines, the Girdle of Venus deals with the passions, the Martian line deals with military glory or personal triumph, and the Mercury line deals with the person's overall well-being.

Just below the fingers on the palms are the "mounts," the fleshly area where the fingers join the palm. These are correlated to astrological planets, e.g., Venus, Jupiter, Saturn, sun (or Uranus), Mercury, moon. There are also tiny line configurations of the palm often found at the top, base, or along the palm lines. These are called series, grills, circles, points, islands, crosses, stars, squares, and triangles. Each of these features is said to represent certain personal characteristics of one's past or future.

The manner in which a person holds his fingers is also thought to be relevant. For example, a space between the first and second finger means the person thinks for himself. If the little finger curves slightly inward toward the sun or ring finger, one supposedly has a shrewd business brain. The larger the thumb, the stronger the self-control and moral force. Small thumbs indicate a weak, impressionable nature. A well-developed Saturn mount indicates a serious, introspective, brooding, reserved type. A grill (like the pound sign on your telephone) on the mount of Mercury (the small finger) reveals cunning or dishonesty. The thumb bent out and backward is "the killer's thumb" and indicates the danger of brutality (cf. 2459:17-48). That all this is nonsense for any credible determination of character or future events is proven by the history of palmistry itself, not to mention that of divination in general.

As in all divination, some predictions will be found to be true but this only indicates a number of random hits. But when spiritism enters the picture, amazing predictions sometimes occur. Anyone who examines their own characteristics based on what palmistry claims will discover its lack of credibility. For example, John Weldon has a grill on the mount of Mercury, which indicates

**141**

he is cunning or dishonest, yet he has always placed a high value on honesty. He also has a thumb bent out and backward, supposedly indicating he has a brutal nature, but people know that just the opposite is true of him.

*Critique*

In the following we will briefly discuss two chief reasons for our distrust of palmistry.

*Conflicting theories.* First, as noted, palmistry is not a science but a dubious method based on conflicting data. Different theories conflict with one another (e.g., ancient versus modern; modern versus more modern), and different schools of interpretation also conflict with one another (2458:98,101,104/2459:38,29,35). That a general agreement exists among *some* palmists is hardly sufficient criteria for the practice to be classified as a legitimate science. This is not enough to sift out highly complex variables that supposedly reveal not only a person's true character but his future as well. If the charts found in palmistry texts (indicating the different features of the hand) don't always agree, how can the prognostications be considered reliable? If the delineation of the mounts don't always agree, and a "minor" line in one book may be designated a "major" line in another book, how can their influence be accurate? Even the number of hand "types" varies (2461:38/2460:30,56/2457:19,75/2459:42).

After reading a dozen books and articles on palmistry, we agree with associate professor of anthropology Michael Alan Park: "There appear to be a number of different versions of the art that claim to be the 'real' palmistry. The versions differ in the number of characteristics observed, in the kinds of characteristics observed, in details concerning the classification, nomenclature, and nature of those characteristics, and in the meaning attributed to different expressions of the characteristics" (2469:22-23).

Of course, one finds the same situation in astrology and other forms of divination, which is why palmists, like astrologers, insist that a novice adhere to one system only. In a leading text we find the following admonition:

Finally, when you will have decided to take this book as your Guide to Palmistry, *attach yourself to it with a will,* until you have mastered its contents from cover to cover. While performing this task *do not open any other work on the subject;* listen to no other teacher. This safeguard against a 'confusion of tongues' applies just as truly to any book and any teacher you may choose instead of the present ones. There can be *but one* commander, when a fortress is to be stormed; *but one* initiator at a time into the realms of such a delicate science as Modern Orthodox Palmistry (2460:11).

Or, put more delicately, "all palmistry, and medical palmistry in particular is still in a transitional state. New insights and data are daily being added to the main body of experimental knowledge already compiled" (2461:XI). Another standard text states that besides the 14 main lines, "there are, in the majority of hands, a certain number of minor lines, almost infinite in their variety and seeming to *defy all orderly classification and logical reading*" (2460:172, emphasis added). This is one obvious explanation for the different theories and interpretations found in palmistry.

Palmists disagree among themselves so much that one leading proponent has thrown out the vast majority of palmist authorities throughout history, retaining only two authorities as credible (2460:12). Another argues that divination by the lines in the hands is itself fraudulent because the success in palmistry is not based upon occult intuition but biological fact (2469:24)!

*Subjectivism.* Palmistry also endures the Achilles' heel of all forms of divination: an entrenched subjectivism. As one practitioner confesses, "Undeniably ... the palmist makes value judgments based in part upon subjective reactions ..." (2461:IX). For example, the palmist, like the astrologer, must not evaluate just any single indicator of the hand; *all* indicators must be carefully assessed and balanced to provide a "general picture." But what if over 100 "indicators" exist? The problem is that this undermines any semblance of credibility because no two palmists will ever agree on even 20 indicators, let alone 100. This means the same person will receive different readings from different palmists. As one text explains:

> Accurate readings depend upon carefully correlating a number of diverse and often contradictory indications to provide an integrated picture. Such a task is far from simple; to do it well and with dependable expertise will require considerable experience. Viewed superficially, for example, signs found in the right hand may present testimony that is just the opposite of that found in the left hand. There may even be markings which negate each other in the same hand (2461:20).

To illustrate the problem further, the above citation from a text on medical palmistry includes this disclaimer: "Even when analysis and the balancing of all factors point *overwhelmingly* to the presence of some pathology, it is unwise, and it is legally foolhardy, to tell a subject unequivocally that he has or is likely to have in the future a certain disease" (2461:21).

Can we imagine this being true in the medical profession? Would a medical doctor reject "overwhelming evidence" and fail to inform his patient of the disease he almost certainly knows is present? Of course not. And so we are told, "The art of medical palmistry itself is enormously complex and requires years of study and experience before the analyst can claim any degree of expertise" (2461:19).

Such disclaimers in palmistry are due to more than mere legal repercussions; most practitioners know they cannot *ultimately* trust their own "science" when it comes to vital issues. Thus in the more "responsible" texts, we may find statements like: "Despite the claims of many palmists that they can virtually pinpoint the date of a given [future] event or pathological episode by consulting this "palmary clock" [certain palm indications], it has been my own observation that dead-center precision is not possible. Even close approximation requires a considerable period of study and experience" (2461:94). And, "In traditional palmistry, certain areas of the palm have been singled out as the sites where signs indicating accidents of a specific kind are likely to be found.... A great deal of research remains before we have sufficient trustworthy evidence upon which to base firm conclusions regarding accidents as shown by special marks in the hand" (2461:159).

The subjective nature of palmistry leads to the general and ambiguous characteristics of many of its prognostications. For example, "A certain amount of agreement exists among palmists that, generally, a clearly marked cross on the mount of Mars beneath that of Jupiter denotes a person who is likely to become involved in acts of violence and, if there are supporting signs, to be seriously injured or killed during impetuous clash [sic] with opposing forces" (2461:162). Such predictions are as useless as the failures are rationalized. Thus only "a certain amount of agreement" exists concerning this prediction, and it is only "generally" true after all. Therefore, lack of corroboration is not, finally, damaging o palmistry. The person was only "likely" to become involved in violence. Furthermore, only if certain "supporting" signs are present is the person who is *involved* in "acts of violence" likely to be seriously injured or killed.

In the end, if palmists disagree because their charts, classifications, theories, and methods of interpretation disagree, then it would seem that palmistry has no more credibility than phrenology, the nineteenth-century study of character traits by the contours of the skull. In fact, when phrenology was in vogue, we find many palmists of the era declaring that the credibility of palmistry was equal to that of phrenology! "Phrenology needs no defender.... [It's success is a] reassuring omen as to what awaits, within a few short years, orthodox, honest, accurate Palmistry.... The scientific world has finally given a verdict ... in favor of the verity of Phrenology, both in theory and in practice.... We are glad to assist in its triumph by demonstrating how accurately Palmistic markings 'dovetail' ... with Phrenological revelations" (2460:357).

The errors one discovers in modern palmistry know no limit. For example, "The Lifeline will be found on all hands" (2459:42). But this is not true, for it is not found on John Weldon's hands. In addition, palmistry "indicators" refer to theories that we can know are false from biblical revelation, such as the concepts of karma and past lives (2457:134). Biblically speaking, just as alleged karmic "indications" are false, other imagined "signs" in the hand must also be false, such as the one allegedly showing "the union of the person with the higher self" (2458:270).

Another falsehood is the notion that "palmar creases" supposedly "break down" at the moment of death because the brain signals, which allegedly maintain them, have now ceased. But a check with a local medical examiner's office will prove this to be false (2469:31). The so-called "murderer's hand" is another falsehood, which is the idea that a particular kind of hand indicates a brutal murderer (2460:68-69). The alleged medical correspondences seen in palmistry are also false (2461:162/2456:98-100).

And all palmists sooner or later run into hands that they simply cannot read, as illustrated in the following illuminating advice given to novice practitioners: "If you run into a confusing hand, it is wise to ask what questions the person wants answered.... Then concentrate on answering the questions. A storehouse of tactful remarks is part of your preparation for palmreading" (2457:17).

### The Occult

Palmistry is conceded by knowledgeable practitioners to be a form of occult divination and not the scientific practice many adherents say it is. Palmistry not only has strong associations to the occult, it is also believed to develop psychic abilities, and it has a relationship to spiritism. For example, if space permitted, a large number of parallels could be made to astrology* (cf. 83). We could also show how, in each case, the parallel disproves its validity (2461:20).

The correlation to astrology is conceded by all. In fact, "palmistry was a logical outgrowth of astrology.... [T]he palm reflects the same celestial influences as those shown in the astrological chart" (2461:6,8). As one encyclopedia points out, "As the palmist approaches the fingers individually, he keeps one eye carefully on the

zodiac, for here is one of the points at which palmistry is correlated to astrology" (2468:175).

Not surprisingly then, many books on palmistry contain sections or chapters on astrology or numerology:

> If you have a working knowledge of astrology, it helps in understanding the palm. And some knowledge is needed simply because certain areas of the palm and the adjacent fingers are named for planets and carry with them the connotations and qualities these planets are concerned with.... It is also helpful to know the astrological sun sign of the person whose hand is being read.... Each planet is also related to a specific area of the palm and various lines that accompany it.... The more you learn about the rulership of the planets and the signs ... the easier it is to evaluate the hand and to assign the proper meaning to the signs you find there (2457:118,120,124).

In addition, palmistry is related to cabalism and other occult practices (2460:10/2457:125). As one book asserts, "Palmistry, along with astrology, forms an integral part of the Cabalistic knowledge system" (2461:12).

In discussing the occult nature of palmistry, several texts reveal its mediumistic potential. "Palmistry ... is one of the esoteric, or occult, sciences, ... [and] to become a professional palm-reader ... would take many years of devoted application to the occult arts.... Professional palmists are somewhat mediumistic and 'see' events this way. As you pursue palmistry, you will find your own ESP sharpened—and will begin to 'read between the lines' so to speak, perhaps even to see future events (clairvoyance) or to hear (clairaudience) things happen" (2457:7, 10,16). An illustration of the spiritistic potential can be seen in the practice of Gopi Aria, a minister of the Morningland sect who, through her work in palmistry, "demonstrates the clarity and perceptive awareness of a telepathic channel for the Ascended Masters of the Spiritual Hierarchy" (2458:15).

Also, as is common for divination in general, palmistry develops psychic abilities. One text observes, it will "help you to develop not only insight, but also your E.S.P. faculties and sensitivity" (2459:9). While modern proponents may argue palmistry is a "rational science," others concede the truth "that clairvoyance *must* be brought to bear when an interpretation is made" (182:2118, emphasis added).

*Dangers*

The dangers of palmistry include those commonly associated with occult practice, including physical, psychological, and spiritual damage (278). Other risks include false medical diagnosis and predictions of disaster or death based on what the palmist supposedly sees in the hands. Although many practitioners confess it is "dangerous for a palmist ever to predict serious illness, and especially death, from a hand" (because "even palmists can make mistakes"; 2468:177), this has not stopped many from making those predictions. This is especially true when considered historically. Although many modern palmists may attempt to avoid the fatalistic aspects, the tide of divinatory history is against them. Divination systems characteristically *reject* chance, otherwise accurate predictions would never be possible. So if palmists reject fatalism they must accept the final irrelevancy of their own art, for mere "indicators" subject to the qualifications of a thousand whims can never boast the accuracy necessary for credibility or trust. Thus, even those who downplay the certainty of a foreseen catastrophic event must nevertheless confess the minute odds that such an event will not come true (2461:151). Consider the following forecast of death. "When the thumb remains turned in under the balance of the fingers during the period of illness, I have found it to be a sure sign of death in the near future" (2456:105).

Palmists themselves are well aware of the destruction their occult craft has caused to many people. One book warns about the consequences of negative predictions. "More harm has been done . . . than can be truly assessed; often the professional palmist sees the sad results years later" (2459:12). And, "Another false reading which has resulted in a great deal of needless anxiety is that concerning a broken life line.

Palmists of the 19th century, who seem to have looked mostly on the dark side in their interpretations, upon finding a break in this line, were prone to make a flat prediction of serious illness or major accident" (2461:90).

Palmistry today may be as popular as ever, but its lack of credibility and damaging consequences precede it. *Caveat emptor.*

## NUMEROLOGY

*Introduction*

Numerology is another modern method of divination, one that attempts to discern the occult significance of numbers. It too is a popular form of entertainment. Like palmistry, numerology is thousands of years old and strongly associated with the occult. The practice of using tarot cards and the cabala are rooted in numerology, and astrology also bears a relationship. As with other forms of divination, there are two principal aspects: 1) character assessment, and 2) divining or predicting the future.

Numerologists claim they cannot only help people to understand themselves better, but that they must also help them to make important decisions in all areas of life. Numerologists claim to offer the following information or advice: choosing the correct marriage partner, vocation, city, or house in which to live; individual "compatibility" with the products one uses; understanding one's mate and friends better; when to buy property or invest in a business; the best days to take a trip, apply for a new job, start a new venture, have surgery, and so on (2464:183-90). Practitioners also allege that numerology can advise clients about what to do or not to do in any given year. It even claims to be able to evaluate the condition of future of nations by their birthdates, as well as many other things. "Numerology is applicable to the most minute personal problems of human life or to gigantic moves in the theatre of international politics" (2465:20). For example:

The day you were born certain powers were bestowed upon you that will be with you your whole life long, since this date is unalterable, its personal vibrations shape every event or incident in your life span.... From the first day of your life to your last, you are governed by the destiny bestowed upon you according to the date of your birth. The numerological value of this birthdate will reveal to you the path of your destiny and suggest the line of personal development to help you attain all you wish from life (2462:24-25).

*False Claims*

Like practitioners in other divinatory fields, numerologists may claim that their profession does not involve the occult. Many advocates insist that numerology is merely "a science of the numbers of life." One leading practitioner states, "Numerology is not fortune-telling, it is instead, a way to understanding through knowledge of numbers" (2463:201). Another encourages readers "not [to] fall into the trap of looking at Numerology as a fortune-telling device. It is not" (2467:46). And, "This is not a matter of fortune-telling, it's plain mathematics revealed in the correlation of human factors to their cosmic pulse-beat as pictured in numbers" (2465:21).

Despite such claims, most numerologists will admit, when pressed, they are engaging in fortune-telling and divination. A fortune-teller is defined in the *Oxford American Dictionary* as "a person who claims to foretell future events in people's lives." Thus, as one practitioner writes, "My system of foretelling the future is based on the esoteric meaning behind numbers, and not on speculation. There is no element of good or bad luck involved, for my calculations are derived from your entire birthpath which, like nature, is immutable and unchangeable. The key to these predictions is found in the ancient Tarot pack of cards" (2464:162). Another advocate states that numerology can bring clients "fame and fortune" (2462:14), and that numerology in general routinely attempts to determine "the path each year will take" (2462:52). And if numerology isn't fortune-telling and divination, why do numerologists boast about their record of accurate predictions? "I can honestly state that

an overwhelming percentage of forecasts I've made have come true. That applies not only to cases in which I have analyzed the number-scopes of individuals but also to predictions on current events which have found their way into print" (2465:10). Or consider the following statement by a professional numerologist who is also a member of several occult societies and has written newspaper columns on numerology: "I have dedicated my life via numerology to discovering the destiny of man. There is no great secret to this destiny. It is revealed in Astrology, Numerology, the Palm of the Hand, the Tarot Deck.... Over the years I personally have worked on over 10,000 charts of living people.... In all cases the lives of the individuals whose charts I worked on went exactly as plotted by the numbers" (2463:287).

In essence, numerologists realize they are engaging in fortune-telling and divination, but often they don't admit it because of the bad reputation of such practices.

However, numerology, like other forms of divination, sometimes provides accurate predictions, but such success does not arise from numerology itself but from spiritistic influences. We documented how this may occur in *Astrology: Do the Heavens Rule Our Destiny?* (83:201-55; cf. Astrology). Despite claims to the contrary, no practitioner has ever demonstrated 100 percent accuracy. To be generous, like diviners in general, numerologists usually fall into the lower quadrant of successes.

*Nature*

How does numerology claim to work? Theories differ considerably, but in one form or another, it claims that our nature and future can be symbolically "reduced" to numbers, and that a proper interpretation of those numbers will reveal almost anything that needs to be known. Two basic principles include the idea that numbers are clues to the underlying structure and nature of the universe and that the name of a thing contains the essence of its being, so that once a person's name is reduced to its number, the truth about that person can supposedly be revealed:

At its popular level numerology is an entertaining and comparatively simple of method of analysing character and predicting the future, in broad and vague terms at least. At a deeper level it is claimed to be one of the major keys to an understanding of the true nature of the universe and it plays an important part in magic and occultism. Like other systems of divination, it finds order and regularity behind the bewildering multiplicity of phenomena and the confusing muddle of events and influences that confront us in the world outside us and in ourselves (2468:158).

There are two basic systems for reducing a person's name to numbers, so that character and destiny can be "read" and foretold. One system is where the numbers from 1 to 9 are written down with the letters of the alphabet written underneath in their normal order: A is 1, B is 2, C is 3, and so on through I is 9, and then J becomes 1, K becomes 2, L becomes 3, etc. A different system uses only the numbers from 1 to 8 but does not list the letters in their usual order because it uses the Hebrew alphabet. This often gives a different letter-number equivalent. Thus H is 5, I is 1, F is 8. There are also lesser systems that differ from these two primary systems. And in any system, the zero is always discarded.

Four key numbers used by numerologists are termed "heart," "personality," "birth," and "personal year." The "heart" number supposedly reveals the inner self or "heart," the person as she really is. The "personality" number reveals a person's outer self, the self she projects. The "birth" number supposedly indicates destiny, and the "personal year" number tells what a specific year will be like.

In all of this, practitioners claim that numerology can be 100 percent accurate, and that there is nothing "false or misleading" about the practice (2463:XII/2462:192). Numerology, however, is extremely complex, and since differing systems give differing results, the problems of subjectivism found in all forms of divination are applicable to numerology as well.

*Critique*

In the material that follows, we will cite seven reasons why we think numerology is a waste of time. First, each of the basic numbers, 1-9, has been assigned a list of key personality characteristics, much like the astrological houses. But do such lists, as supplied in different numerological texts, always agree? No, they don't agree (2468:159-60/2462:18-23/2464:27-35). This means, for example, that the number 2 may be given different characteristics in different texts. Thus, since the "meaning" of the numbers is not uniform, the client may receive conflicting readings from different numerologists.

Second, critical tests of numerology have failed to confirm its predictive ability. For example, in numerology the name a person is given at birth and the name by which a person may now be known, or prefers to be called, may have different meanings. The "birth name" in numerology supposedly describes one's destiny, and the name one chooses to use expresses current personality characteristics. But one study of preferred names indicated that the numerological description given was *not* equivalent to individual's personal self-assessment: "Overall, the results do not leave one with the impression that numerological descriptions for preferred names compare well with the self-perceptions we hold for our personalities" (2470:56). Dr. Weldon tested his own birth number, personal year number, name expression number, individual day number, and other indicators. After reading numerological descriptions of his character, the descriptions failed to fit him approximately 90 percent of the time (2462:31-32,48,90,134).

Third, there are a host of different interpretations and approaches, revealing that numerology is ruled by subjectivism. As in astrology, ancient, medieval, and modern numerology promoters do not have consistent systems, nor do they interpret every indicator in the same manner (182:2026). We have already seen that different numbers may be used for different letters, and this gives different results. Thus the key number for a given name may be either 1 or 4, with each carrying vastly different interpretations. People with the number 1 are said to be powerful individuals having dominating personalities leading to success, while people with the number of 4

147

are likely to encounter "failure, poverty and general gloom" (2468:159):

> One of the problems about analysing yourself numerologically is the fact that your name and birthdate may yield so many different numbers. It is difficult to know how to weigh and combine the varying results and how to exclude the elements of wishful thinking or, with historical figures, of hindsight. And the language of numerologists, like that of astrologers . . . is generally vague and woolly, so that with ingenuity almost anyone's character can be fitted into any given number (182:2023).

In addition, some numerologists use "master numbers" that go beyond 9, such as 11, 22, and 33 rather than the common practice of reducing them to their single digits of 2 (1+1), 4 (2+2), and 6 (3+3)(2462:17). Others reject this approach.

Because of the complexity, frank practitioners will confess the confusion, although the particular method *they* choose always seems to be claimed as the best or most accurate. Not surprisingly, matters deteriorate rapidly when one incorporates additional systems of divination into numerology practice, such as cabalism or astrology. One numerologist refers to:

> . . . the blatant discrepancies that are constantly cropping up in astro-numerology when assigning number influences to planetary rays and vice-versa. Disconcerting contradictions appear in textbooks which necessarily lead the sincere student along the path of confusion. . . . [N]umerology experts know their numbers but are either completely ignorant of astrological fundamentals or know little about them. . . . Then, too, numbers have many meanings. Take their symbolical interpretation when evaluating human character and human destiny. This differs from their religious significance or their ritualistic one as in the light of Cabalistic teachings and the hermetic schools of transcendental magic. One cannot expect these versions to agree with the numerical influences as expounded in this volume. . . . In order to bring system into this confused state of learning, we have exchanged our findings with top professional astrologers, and have succeeded in coming up with a theory we feel is both logical and practical (2465:131-32).

In other words, after agreeing that "astro-numerology" is a mess, the author merely adds one more contradictory system to the picture: his own personal invention. Thus, this same author assigns the following "planets" the following numbers:

Sun = 1
Moon = 2
Mercury = 3
Earth = 4
Mars = 5
Venus = 6
Saturn = 7
Jupiter = 8
Vulcan = 9
Uranus = 11
Neptune = 22
Pluto = 13

It does seem to bother him that no planet "Vulcan" exists. He explains that no one can see Vulcan because "it is invisible even through a telescope, even when it passes over the disk of the sun. But humans can nevertheless *feel* its influence, for it races around the sun in about 6 weeks. Therefore if you *feel* out of sorts one Blue Monday, and you don't know what accounts for it, blame it all on Vulcan" (2465:139, emphasis added).

Another noted numerologist contradicts the preceding by giving the following contrary correspondences between planets and numbers:

Sun = 1
Moon = 2
Jupiter = 3
Earth = 4
Mercury = 5
Venus = 6
Neptune = 7
Saturn = 8
Mars = 9
Pluto = 11
Uranus = 22

In this second list, no less than seven of the planets have completely different numbers assigned to them when compared to the previous list. The author of this list confesses, "There are some professionals who will take exception to a few of the above planetary assignments, but that is neither here nor there. In the last several books I have read, no two have agreed. It is my considered opinion that the above is the most correct interpretation possible" (2463:100). Again, the individual numerologist only assumes his particular system is the best. Like divination in general, numerology is filled with arbitrariness and subjectivism (2464:149,163/82:2026/2466:33-36).

The subjective aspects inherent in interpreting numerological charts are little different from those found in the astrological charts that we detailed in *Astrology: Do the Heavens Rule Our Destiny?* (83). In one instance, exhaustive instructions are given for gaining a "complete interpretation on any individual chart," and these details take up an entire chapter of instructions. For example, "In the short range forecast, the letters pertaining that period from the excursion should be used. The Personal Year, Universal Year, Year Pinnacles, Year Challenge, Periodicity, Monthly Cycles, Personal Month, Universal Month, Month Pinnacles, Month Challenges, must all be considered. If the forecast is to be tightened up even further, the day vibrations must be studied" (2463:283). Leaving aside the delicate issue of studying and interpreting the "day vibrations," would numerologists in general agree with the above citation, let alone all the detailed instructions in the entire chapter? Not at all. Although this author refers to taking the reader "deep into the *exact* science of numerology," he also confesses that "many of these interpretations are the author's own, developed through much hard work and long periods of studying many charts. A few of the charts employed in this book concerning forecasting are the author's creation" (2463:XVII).

This numerologist of more than 25 years also confesses, "Volumes concerning numbers are usually full of misinformation, the majority basing their study upon superstition," and the "science of numerology must now be freed from the chicanery that has surrounded it for *centuries*" (2463:X, XVI, emphasis added). Yet this same writer claims that without the unique knowledge *he* supplies in his book, "the understanding of

numerology is incomplete." Of course, *with* such knowledge a person "will have at their disposal the knowledge of all life, past, present and future. The knowledge of the destinies of empires, corporations, individuals" (2463:246). Another numerologist says, "To my knowledge, no one has ever presented this scientific system of predictions to the public. It represents over 25 years of experience and hard work on my part, gained through observation, trial and error, and research" (2464:162). But her "scientific system of predictions" not only fails, it is also contrary to other systems.

The fourth reason we think numerology is a waste of time is because numerologists make the astonishing claim that one can actually change one's destiny merely by changing one's name! By doing this the person can allegedly find a happy marriage, economic security, vocational success, and so on (2465:114). But if this were true, then everyone in the world should be able to easily mold their destiny into the most fulfilling and positive future imaginable. Since all numerologists who know this secret have presumably already done this, one need only study the lives of numerologists to see whether this claim is true. Numerologists everywhere should live lives far different from the majority of the human race. But obviously there is no evidence at all for such a conclusion.

Indeed, if numerologists can't even get their own numbers aligned or their predictions right, how do we have any assurance they can help us get our lives right? To illustrate only one example of a false prediction, Vincent Lopez, the author of a 1961 text reprinted in 1969, stated, "Regarding [the 1968] Russian aggression: Russia will not stop with the Czechoslovak situation. Her next move will be into West Germany" (2465:12-13).

Fifth, numerologists also have serious philosophical problems. They claim that one's destiny is *determined* by numbers, but also that one's destiny can be *altered*. And numerology, like other forms of divination, does not finally believe in chance. Again, if it did, it could not logically claim to predict the future with great accuracy. Upon what basis is one's name likely to be a

149

reliable index to one's character or future if it was acquired entirely by chance? Numerologists cite various reasons alleging why one's name is not a "chance" event (determined solely by one's parents), but such arguments are not convincing. To claim the universe is intelligent and ordains one's name in harmony with the "cosmic plan" says nothing, since numerologists have never told us what the cosmic plan is.

In addition, who decided that such and such a number means this or that? Why is the number 4 unlucky and "earthly"? What does it mean to be "earthly"? Who assigned this meaning or the range of its implications? Why does number 7 refer to withdrawal from the world, or why should it be considered particularly powerful in magical practice? On what logical basis should anyone accept the number interpretations?

Also, what does one do with the differences in one's own name? For example, the number of the name William F. Meredith is 3, but the number of William *Francis* Meredith is 9, and the number of Bill Meredith is 4; yet all these names refer to the same person (2468:159). So is his name number 3, 4, or 9? Why should it be one number rather than another when their meaning is the same? What about nicknames? Who infallibly determined their significance? What about a woman's maiden name? If her maiden name shows her character before she is married, and if her married name reveals how her marriage has affected her and changed her character and destiny after she is married, what happens at divorce and how do we know? And what happened to the cosmic plan that infallibly assigned her birth name as a reliable interpreter? How does it take into account divorce or a voluntary change of name? Does a divorce and returning to one's maiden name cause one to revert to previous personality and destiny? The answers numerologists give to such queries are not convincing.

Sixth, numerological literature is replete with inaccuracies and absurdities. For example, "Jesus Christ utilized numerology in his teachings, even changing the original names of his disciples to match the numerical vibrations of the mission he

wished them to undertake" (2462:12). Even the numbers of cities and one's address may affect destiny: "Cities and states have their own desires or demands.... Does the city or locality to which I am moving have any of my numbers—destiny, birthpath, soul's urge, or power number? It will be much easier to make a change if you understand it's [the city's] desires and needs.... New York [city] wants inspirational people [the number 11] with ideas [11], who can face the public or limelight and be superior" (2464:187).

Even one's home address is said to be important, its numerical significance dictating the "kind" of home it will be. When John Weldon added up the number of his own home address where he has lived for 4 years, its numerological significance was 3. The prediction for his home was: "If you move into any house with a 3 house number or vibration, you can expect it to be lively and full of company" (2464:189). Since Dr. Weldon is single and rarely entertains, the house is rarely "lively and full of company."

### The Occult and Other Hazards

A last objection to numerology is its strong association to other occult practices. Indeed, most forms of divination are cross-pollinated by other forms. In numerology we especially find astrology,* the cabala, and the tarot to be influential. In almost every book on numerology we read, astrology, cabalism, and the tarot were included as important elements (e.g., 2463:ix,287 2464:6,153,204/2462:12-13,24-25).

Numerologists are often engaged in other occult practices. Helen Hitchcock, author of *Helping Yourself with Numerology,* is a member of two spiritistic religions, Theosophy and Astara. Kevin Avery, author of *The Numbers of Life,* uses astrology, cabalism, and "astronumerology."

The more involved one becomes in the world of the occult, the greater the risk to one's overall health (278). Like all forms of occult divination, numerology leads to bondage to present circumstances and a fear of the future. Numerologists are known to "hurl dire judgment at the 4-afflicted person by proclaiming want, failure, death in a poor house, or a sanitarium for him" (2465:118). Whereas, "if your number is 6, you should try to deal with important matters or decisions only on days which add to 6. You should also live in a house whose number is 6 and a street whose name adds to 6" (182:2023).

Here, of course, we may encounter self-fulfilling prophecies, something found in occult divination in general (see Astrology, "Dangers"). In one example, "Every single element on this chart called for finish, destruction, ruin" (2463:285; cf. pp. xvii, 201-04). What then is the hapless individual who trusts in the cosmic power and wisdom of numbers to do? And what about the predictions of death? In numerology, "Death can be picked out of the [cabalistic] triangles and lines. This does not [necessarily] mean the death of the person involved but could be the death of a person close to the subject. . . . There is no major occurrence that will happen in any life that is not shown on a Kabala" (2463:254).

In fact, whether numerologists seek to reveal only the good indicators in a chart or to supply both good and bad indicators, practitioners fail them regardless. Since all forms of divination, by definition, must predict both the good and the bad, numerologists who fail to read the negative elements of a chart and only read the positive elements are not being true to numerology as a whole. After all, the numbers are supposed to reveal the clients' whole future, so he may employ all available knowledge to his advantage. On the other hand, those who do read the negative elements in their client's lives produce a variety of problems, which we documented in our book on astrology. These include fear and bondage to various predictions and fate, self-fulfilling prophecies, and unwise decisions based solely on information "forecast" by the numbers (83; see Astrology, "Dangers").

In conclusion, numerologists may claim that "all of life is controlled by numbers" (2462:12), but no numerologist can deny that numbers extracted from one's name (or other sources) can produce great confusion or contradiction. Even in the best scenario, this leaves the practitioner at the mercy of subjectivism; in the worst scenario, at the mercy of demonic powers.

## THE OUIJA BOARD

*Introduction*

The December 1994 *Consumer Reports* published the results of a survey among 17,000 young people ages 10 to 14. They answered a query concerning what games they played with and which ones they enjoyed the most. Out of 83 games listed, Monopoly was number one and the Ouija board was number two!

The Ouija board is an alphabet board with a pointer used for various forms of divination or spirit contact. Like the other methods discussed, its usage is ancient:

> Precursors to the Ouija date back to ancient times. In China before the birth of Confucius (c. 551 B.C.), similar instruments were used to communicate with the dead. In Greece during the time of Pythagoras (c. 540 B.C.) divination was done with a table that moved on wheels to point to signs, which were interpreted as revelations from the "unseen world." The rolling table was used through the nineteenth century. Other such devices were used by the ancient Romans as early as the third century A.D., and in the thirteenth century by the Mongols. Some Native Americans used "squdilatc boards" to find missing objects and persons, and obtain spiritual information. In 1853 the planchette came into use in Europe. . . . The Ouija enjoyed enormous popularity during and after World War I, when many people were desperate to communicate with loved ones killed in the war and Spiritualism was in a revival (1526:40).

Many people have documented the occult origin of this "parlor game," which was specifically designed to contact the spirit world. Its nineteenth century development began with prominent French spiritualist, M. Planchette, in 1853, and in 1899, its patent was bought from Elijah J. Bond by William Fuld, an inventor interested in spiritism (1129:24-25). Bond, an American, invented the Ouija board's current form in 1892. In 1966 Fuld, often considered the modern "father" of the Ouija board, sold his patent to Parker Brothers.

Although Parker Brothers keeps sales figures confidential, the board has sold perhaps 20-25 million sets (1129:25-26, 1994 ed.). And in spite of its vast influence, few critical books have been written exposing its dangers. We could find only two. Professor Edmond Gruss' *The Ouija Board: Doorway to the Occult* (1129) is the best; it documents the ancestry of related forms, its modern history and variations, its consequences and hazards, including numerous cases of Ouija-board-related tragedies. Another text is Stoker Hunt's *Ouija: The Most Dangerous Game* (2684), which contains two chapters instructing people in use of the board.

Not surprisingly, the board is often associated with mediumism, spiritism, and spirit possession; as a result, it should be considered anything but a game. Nevertheless, it continues to be marketed as as game, no doubt because of lucrative profits.

Many famous mediums began their trade by experimentation with the Ouija board, such as Mrs. Pearl Lenore Curran, who became the recipient through the board (and later via automatic writing) of the famous "Patience Worth" material (see Channeling chapter, "Impersonations and Denials of Christianity"). In 1919, Stewart Edward White and his wife, Betty, were introduced to entities called "Invisibles," who inspired several books including *The Betty Book*, and *The Unobstructed Universe*. Jane Roberts, famous for her two dozen "Seth" books, is another example (see *A Course in Miracles*). In all three cases, the spiritistic contacts were begun casually and were unexpected.

### Dangers of Spirit Possession and Other Consequences

Even seasoned occultists and psychic researchers warn against using the Ouija board. Medium Edgar Cayce himself called it "dangerous" (1526:419). Edmund Gruss refers to medium Donald Page, an "exorcist" of the "Christian" Spiritualist Church, who asserts that "the majority of possession cases" result from involvement with the Ouija board. Page believes it is one of the quickest and easiest ways to become possessed (1129:52; cf. 1994 ed., p. 84).

Discussing the relation of Ouija boards to automatic writing, psychic researcher Martin

Ebon also alleges that possession is a frequent occurence:

It is common that people who get into this sort of game think of themselves as having been "chosen" for a special task. The ouija board will often say so, either directly or by implication. It may speak of "tests" that the sitters must undergo to show that they are "worthy" of this otherworldly attention. I have not been able to figure out why this is so, but quite often the ouija turns vulgar, abusive or threatening. It grows demanding and hostile, and sitters may find themselves using the board or automatic writing compulsively, as if "possessed" by a spirit, or hearing voices that control and command them. This is no longer rare. I'd say it is now so frequent as to be common (148:IX).

The Association for Research and Enlightenment in Virginia Beach, founded by medium Edgar Cayce, receives "countless letters from a great many who are having serious difficulties as a result of trying Ouija boards and automatic writing" (1129:73). Professor Gruss reveals that, "Reading several dozen letters in the A.R.E. files made it obvious that the patterns of development and entrapment were very similar. Hugh Lynn Cayce wrote that in 1956 there were 274 people who wrote to him that were in trouble because of automatic writing or ouija board use" (1129:67).

Psychic Alan Vaughan also points out the following: "It is significant, however, that the greatest outcry against the use of Ouijas has come from the Spiritualists not the parapsychologists. In England, Spiritualist groups are petitioning to ban the sale of Ouijas as toys for children—not because of vague dangers of 'unhealthy effects on naive, suggestible persons'—but because they fear that the children will become possessed" (1500:164).

Psychic and spiritist Harold Sherman, president of ESP Research Associates Foundation in Little Rock, Arkansas, agrees: "The majority who have become involved with possessive and other entities came by this experience through the ouija board" (1501).

Despite the warnings, most people continue to view the Ouija board as a harmless pastime:

Spiritualists, psychologists, psychiatrists, medical doctors, theologians, and other informed persons have all given warnings on the hazards of using the ouija board and similar devices. In spite of all they have said, it is evident that many persons are still ignorant that dangers exist.

Those who know little or nothing about the occult and ouija board experiences do not understand these warnings concerning the "innocent" use of the board. One who speaks of physical, mental, spiritual, or other problems which might relate to ouija use is often viewed as an extremist, obsessed with groundless fears. How could the use of so simple a device result in anything detrimental to the user? This is often the attitude until, through personal involvement, the reality of the dangers is experienced, and the warnings are then remembered. Often by this time permanent damage has occurred (1129:72-73).

Indeed, the dangers of the Ouija board have been noted long before our modern revival of the occult. Almost 70 years ago, the medium Carl Wickland, M.D., referred to his own encounters when he wrote of "the cases of several persons whose seemingly harmless experiences with automatic writing and the ouija board resulted in such wild insanity that commitment to asylums was necessitated.... Many other disastrous results which followed the use of the supposedly innocent ouija board came to my notice" (1502:28-29).

Edmond Gruss refers to a clipping from the files of the famous magician Houdini, concerning a Dr. Curry, a medical director of the State Insane Asylum of New Jersey, who stated the Ouija board was a "dangerous factor" in unbalancing the mind and predicted that insane asylums would be flooded with patients if interest in them did not wane (1129:75).

Noted psychic researchers Ed and Lorraine Warren refer to one instance where the Ouija board was used "as little more than a joke," and yet it led to the house becoming "infested" with evil spirits (2407:1). Noted occultist Manly P. Hall is founder of the Philosophical Research Society and considered one of the leading authorities on the occult in this century. In *Horizon* magazine for October-December 1944,

pages 76-77, he recalls, "During the last 20-25 years I have had considerable personal experience with persons who have complicated their lives through dabbling with the Ouija board. Out of every hundred such cases, at least 95 are worse off for the experience.... I know of broken homes, estranged families, and even suicides that can be traced directly to this source" (2424:78-79).

Other authorities on the Ouija board, Ed and Lorrain Warren, cited above, state in their book *Graveyard* (1992, pp. 137-38): "Ouija boards are just as dangerous as drugs. They're not to be played with.... [J]ust as parents are responsible for other aspects of the children's lives, they should take equal care to keep the tools of the devil from their children ... especially in an era when satanic cults are on the rise. Remember: Seances and Ouija boards and other occult paraphernalia are dangerous because evil spirits often disguise themselves as your loved ones—and take over your life" (2424:79).

Dr. Thelma Moss, a parapsychologist on the staff of UCLA's Neuropsychiatric Institute, prefaced her discussion of the Ouija board in *The Probability of the Impossible* with: "Warning! For certain persons, the Ouija board is *no game* and can cause serious dissociations of personality" (2628:237).

Some incidents of Ouija board use are bizarre, but they have been documented; for example, Ouija-board-related vampirism. Vampirism is not total fiction; there are many accounts of it in the psychiatric literature. Skeptic William Seabrooke, in his *Witchcraft*, refers to one female "vampire" he actually let suck his own blood in a moment of perverse fascination. Psychic researcher Raymond VanOver refers to a man who was quite serious about his need to drink human blood, particularly that of young girls (148:108).

Blood, of course, has long been used in occultism for any number of purposes. Blood may be drunk in ritual (sometimes at the spirits' request; 583:307-08), offered on altars, used in pacts with the devil, or as a means to materialize spirits. In *Occult Science in India and Among the Ancients*, Chief Justice Louis Jacolliot refers to one formula of magical incantation: "The flowers that he offers to the spirits evoked by him should be colored with the blood of a young virgin, or a child, in case he proposes to cause death" (1485:141). Given the use of blood and the perverted nature of occult practice, it is hardly surprising some people might become "vampires" or feel the need for blood.

In some cases, use of the Ouija board—like astrology**—leads to actual involvement with witchcraft and Satanism. On more than one occasion, the spirits themselves—claiming the participants are now "ready" for more serious occult work—have suggested the players "graduate" to such practices. Carl Johnson, who started dabbling with the Ouija board after occasional earlier brushes with occultism states:

> The "voices" and other eerie stuff began when he and his sister started playing around with a Ouija board a few years ago, he recalls. This led to nightmares, creeping depression, and a suicide attempt—which Carl says left him revitalized and thirsty for blood. So he delicately pricked the leg of his sleeping sister and slaked his thirst. Then, compulsively, he took to sucking blood from slices he made in the arm of a pliant homosexual pal—a practice shared by other young friends when he organized a satanic coven. . . .
>
> Lilith, too, became a vampiric Devil worshipper. She describes ceremonies under full moons in which her teenaged coven would get zonked out on dope and drink blood mixed with wine. Ultimately, she knew things were getting out of hand when one of the cultists proposed kidnapping her own father and offering him up as a ritual sacrifice (1504; cf. 1503:21).

Thankfully, it appears that some, perhaps many, people do not seem to be harmed by the Ouija board; they may have innocently played with it as a child or for fun at a party and suffered no discernible ill effects. The problem is that no one can tell the outcome in advance. There are

also hundreds of cases of innocent or naive occult involvement leading to spirit possession, insanity, financial ruin, adultery, divorce, criminal acts (even murder), and other tragedies, as the books by Edmond Gruss, Stoker Hunt and the literature of occultism and parapsychology proves (1069).

Ouija boards should never be played with, especially for entertainment. Parents should never give the board to their children. Perhaps one day Parker Brothers will no longer deny the ruin that this "game" has brought to thousands of people. Perhaps it will own up to its corporate responsibility and, retaining the copyright, refuse to market this "game" again.

If the Ouija board is an example of a method that is intended to foster occult contacts, there are many others which serve as more subtle introductions. Dungeons and Dragons and other fantasy role playing (FRP) games are among them.

## DUNGEONS AND DRAGONS AND FANTASY ROLE PLAYING GAMES

*Introduction*

In the 1980s, "Dungeons & Dragons" (D & D) and other elaborate fantasy role playing (FRP) games became one of the hottest national pastimes, especially for teenagers and college students. Estimated overall sales increased a thousandfold from 150 thousand dollars in 1975 to 150 million dollars in 1982. And sales have risen even higher since.

Dungeons and Dragons began as an offshoot of the war games of the late 1950s and 1960s, such as Bismarck and Gettysburg. These games involved the use of strategy and the playing out of historical battles with miniature soldiers and landscapes. Thus, war-gaming of the recent past was extended into the ancient past along a "swords and sorcery" theme, where the life and battles of various heroes or wizards could be played out.

D & D is an elaborate fantasy game played out primarily in one's mind using creative imagination. There are dice, although no cards or boards;

---

**Sociologist Edward J. Moody observes, "Those who eventually become Satanists usually have begun with astrology" (533:363).

there are no strict rules, only guidelines. There are also no absolutes, no boundaries, and no time limitations, since FRP games are not single experience contests but ongoing adventures or campaigns traversing from one episode to another. In theory, a single game could last a lifetime.

The "dungeon master," or referee, is someone who is very experienced in D & D. He shapes the fantasy milieu with the aid of maps, monster lists, combat tables, and the psychological and geographical terrain the players will travel. This may involve multilevel dungeons, various occult planes of existence, towns, and other worlds or time periods. All of this is mapped out on graph paper, complete with wizards, treasures, monsters, magical objects, traps, potions, demons, and the gods who reside throughout the various regions.

Each player selects a character whose role he assumes, such as a fighter, assassin, monk, druid, magic user, or thief. The thief, apparently, is one of the best characters to emulate (433:31). Characters are assigned strengths or weaknesses on a scale of 3 to 18 and six principle attributes, including intelligence, strength, and wisdom—all determined by a toss of the dice. A racial stock is also selected from among gnomes, humans, dwarfs, and elves. Each player must decide his or her character's alignment, whether good, neutral, or evil.

*Major Problems*

While the underlying principle of D & D and other FRP games is sound—creative use of the imagination in order to play a game—from a Christian perspective there are several problems with such games.

One problem is that the worldview in which most of these games are conducted is either not Christian or anti-Christian, and although played out in fantasy, it can still have an impact on young or impressionable minds. In the past, similar games at least had a concrete historical setting, often with a moral basis underlying the conflict. Today the games comprise a mixture of fantasy, mythology, and often the occult. Most players participate without ever considering the worldview in which they are role playing. This

means that they do not consider how this might be contrary to their own philosophy and beliefs. Because of the excitement involved and the ease in which players may get "hooked" on FRP, players usually may not notice subtle negative changes that may be occurring in their lives as a result of playing the game. And if they do notice, they may not attribute the changes to the games. If we briefly contrast the general perspective of D & D and related FRP games with a biblical worldview, we can see the possible impact such games may have. The issue is to what extent a "crossover" effect may occur, such that aspects of the role being played in an extended fantasy game are gradually adopted in real life.

For example, most FRP games present no system of absolute morality; morality is for the individual to choose or reject as the player sees fit. Thieves, assassins, sorcerers, and witches may all be role-played and even developed into a kind of "alter ego." In general, FRP games perceive the universe as amoral. Good and evil are presented as equal, opposite poles, and both the characters and the gods are expected to align themselves with one pole or the other.

Although each player brings his own innate moral standards, the game itself provides the player with the potential for laying aside those standards. As one player told us, "In D & D it's better to be evil because you get more advantages—it's easier not to have to worry about doing something wrong." Thus, in many of these games, an immoral use of power, sex, or violence is acceptable. Even activities such as stealing, mutilation, human sacrifice, murder, and rape can be incorporated into the games. Only the pragmatism of the overriding situation and the good or evil characters involved determine the best course of action, or what is "right" or "wrong." Obviously, this contrasts with the biblical worldview, in which morality is absolute and grounded in the character and nature of a holy God.

The theology of most FRP games is not Christian. Probably because of the diversity they offer, FRP games generally present a polytheistic rather than monotheistic worldview; that is, they present the belief in many gods rather than one God. As the D & D manual, *Deities and Demigods,* asserts, "No fantasy world would be complete without the gods, mighty deities who influence the fate of men and move mortals about like chess pieces . . ." (1516:37). This contrasts with the biblical teaching that there is only one true God and that this God is moral, not amoral. Most FRP games also have unbiblical views of the creation, man, and life after death (cf. 433:ch. 3).

It can no longer be denied that children, teenagers, or adults are morally influenced by what they see on TV, for example, through sex and violence. When kids watch six hours of TV a day, this should concern parents because its "values" are being communicated. But many kids play D & D six hours a day; and for some kids, potentially, it may be an even more powerful medium for communicating values than TV because of the active rather than passive participation required.

Another problem is that FRP games are essentially escape fantasy. While everyone needs to escape from the pressures of modern life in some way, for certain people the escape offered in FRP games can become dangerous. There are three issues here: 1) when excessive time is devoted to the game, taking away from more important activities; 2) when excessive identification with a character exists, so that less control remains over one's emotional state; and 3) when role playing and real life are not fully distinguished, so that fantasy and reality become blurred. As one player said, "I am dungeon master 98% of the time. I am the God of my world, the creator who manipulates the gods and humans. . . . When I'm in my world, I control my own world order. . . . The more I play D & D, the more I want to get away from this world. The whole thing is getting very bad" (2629:38).

There is certainly nothing wrong with fantasy per se, which is merely an imaginative departure from the world and from the created order as we know it. But fantasy is not necessarily justified in all cases. A person needs discernment with fantasy just as with any other created thing.

For example, although the fantasy works by J.R.R. Tolkein, C. S. Lewis, and others involve

good and evil characters, they are generally considered a positive use of fantasy because they offer the reflection of an essentially Christian worldview. But when one compares the Christian fantasy of Tolkein and Lewis with modern FRP games, significant differences in theological and moral perspectives, and in context and motive, are apparent. In FRP games, good does not triumph over evil; both coexist as equal and opposite impersonal poles, together in such a manner that good is finally no better than evil, just another tool to use in one's adventure and conquest. Because power and pragmatism are necessary for victory, the end justifies the means.

Thus, FRP games present a number of concerns—for example, how their combination of violence, fantasy, and escapism may influence certain persons, or the blurring of fantasy and reality. In a special two-part segment, "Games That Can Kill," Geraldo Rivera on "Entertainment Tonight" (October 12-13, 1987), cited a figure of over 90 deaths that had been linked to FRP games, particularly Dungeons and Dragons. By the mid-1990s, the figure had risen to several hundred, although apparently no direct link could be established.

*Evaluation*

In *Playing with Fire,* Weldon and Bjornstad pointed out that the alleged benefits of fantasy role playing were questionable in light of other concerns, such as the worldview and the anti-Christian theology underlying these games (433:37-45,83-85). The fun and excitement, the educational approaches to creativity and learning, and the fostering of cooperation and logical skills may all come with a high price tag for some or many participants. If, as fantasy role playing game advocates claim, such games as D & D are harmless and a positive contribution to the players, it seems that the burden of proof lies with them, especially if there appears to be evidence to the contrary.

Although no assessment of FRP games would be complete without at least some consideration of the positive claims, it should also be noted that no assessment should be limited only to a consideration of those claims. A careful examination and evaluation of FRP games in the areas we discuss here, i.e., the role of fantasy, morality, escapism, and the occult, is absolutely necessary if one is going to honestly and objectively assess whether to participate in the games.

*Fantasy.* We have already noted that the ability to fantasize is God-given. There is a good use of fantasy but also an evil use. Fantasy role playing games in general seem to promote the wrong use of fantasy by presenting character roles that assume an amoral use of power, violence, immorality, and sorcery—all things God hates. This runs contrary to the divine instruction given in Philippians 4:8: "Finally, brothers, whatever is true, whatever is noble, whatever is right, whatever is pure, whatever is lovely, whatever is admirable—if anything is excellent or praiseworthy—think about such things."

Furthermore, such role playing could affect the lives of players, especially preadolescent and adolescent players, who are still in the formative stages of developing their personal philosophy, worldview, moral system, and self-image.

*Morality.* FRP games in general promote an amoral universe. In fact, the games contain many activities and practices that God forbids and condemns in the Bible. Thus FRP games have the potential to undermine or negate the influence of Christian morality in a player's life.

*Escape.* Escape, like fantasy, can be used in a wholesome and healthy way or it can be misused. The complexity and ego-involvement in fantasy role playing games in general appears to provide the potential for an unhealthy use of escape, or at the least a wasting of valuable time.

*Occult Influence*

Perhaps our greatest concern is that Dungeons and Dragons and similar FRP games usually introduce players to the occult. Although these games do not offer a direct attempt at occult involvement, as does the Ouija board or similar forms of divination, nevertheless, there is reason for concern.

Dr. Gary North is the scholar and author of an excellent critique on the occult, *Unholy Spirits: Occultism and New Age Humanism.* In unmistakable terms, he warns:

> Without any doubt in my own mind, after years of study of the history of occultism, after having researched a book on the topic, and often having consulted with scholars in the field of historical research, I can say with confidence: these games are the most effective, most magnificently packaged, most profitably marketed, most thoroughly researched introduction to the occult in man's recorded history. Period (1505:8).

Jack Roper, writing in *Moody Monthly* states: "Dungeons and Dragons is a forerunner of a greater acceptance of sorcery in America. It is a socially accepted means of dwelling on mystical, mythological and medieval spiritual forces" (1506:19).

It seems that the authors of the D & D manuals, which discuss the occult, had to have been familiar with occult practices (1515:36-37). The occult powers, practices, and magical spells in the manuals reflect occult practice accurately. Not surprisingly, people have been led into the occult as a result of a newly sparked interest resulting from playing D & D. Even some occultists have utilized these games, either as a means to introduce occult ideas through entertainment, or as a way to encourage people to accept genuine sorcery. In 1980, Philip Bonewitz published *Authentic Thaumaturgy: A Professional Occultist on Improving the Realism of Magic Systems in Fantasy Simulating Games* for just this purpose.

D & D, of course, is not the only FRP game to utilize occultism. Dr. Ronald Enroth, of the Department of Sociology at Westmont College, observes: "The occult connection is even more obvious in the game Chivalry and Sorcery.... The game details the mechanics of spell casting, enchantment and mediumship" (1507:36-37).

The problem is that this is not merely an "innocent" introduction to the occult, but that what is played out in the imagination as a game can also be pursued in a serious manner in real

**157**

life. And the individual player has no guarantee that just because he is "merely" engaged in use of the imagination, the spirit world will not respond when beckoned. In fact, many psychics and mediums recommend the use of the fantasy imagination to help foster psychic development and actual spirit contact (see Visualization, Intuition, New Age Inner Work.)

We cannot discuss all the issues involved, but the following is taken from *Playing with Fire*, ("The Occult Connection"; 433: ch. 5), which supplies an overview of the occult potential in these games.

First, occult *magic and the casting of spells* can be found as an integral part of most games. In Dungeons and Dragons, magic is prevalent and can be used in a variety of ways. For example, witch magic can be used for white or black witchcraft (1512:58-59), a delineation that is true in witchcraft today. There is also a preponderance of spells for different characters, levels, categories, and expectations. Some spells are bestowed by the gods; others are not. Most spells have a verbal component, which means they must be spoken to be effective (1513:40). Much of what is presented is similar to what one would find in sorcery or witchcraft. In Chivalry and Sorcery, the game manual contains instructions on how to cast spells.

Second, occult forms of protective inscriptions can be found in certain games. The "magic circle, pentagram, and thaumaturgic triangle" have all been incorporated into Dungeons and Dragons (1514:112). Players are taught how to use these symbols as forms of protective inscriptions in a fashion similar to the way they are actually used in witchcraft and Satanism. In one account, for example, a spell caster, who has just summoned a demon, is warned that he "must be within a circle of protection (or a thaumaturgic triangle with protection from evil) and the demon confined with a pentagram (circle pentacle) if he or she is to avoid being slain or carried off by the summoned cacodemon" (1513:86-87).

Third, the occult practice of "astral projection," or "soul travel," can be found in a few games. In astral projection, it is believed that the soul can depart from the body and travel to other dimensions and planes. According to Dungeons and Dragons, this practice is possible by various means, including specific magic spells and "psionic" disciplines. Thus, a cleric can, by "casting a seventh level astral spell, project his or her astral body into the Astral Plane, leaving his or her physical body and material possession behind on the Prime Material Plane, (the plane on which the entire universe and all of its parallels have existence). . . . The cleric then leaves the Astral Plane, forming a body on the plane of existence he or she has chosen to enter" (1513:52).

Fourth, the occult practice of necromancy, e.g., communication with the dead, can be found in many games. In Dungeons and Dragons, necromantic spells not only heal wounds, restore strength, limbs, and life, and resurrect the dead, but they also bring forth the dead for divinational and other purposes, in a manner similar to that in spiritism. If a cleric, for example, needs information, he knows that he may summon the dead with a spell. "Upon casting a *speak with the dead* spell the cleric is able to ask several questions of a dead creature in a set period of time and receive answers according to the knowledge of the creature" (1513:48).

In Chivalry and Sorcery, an entire section of the game manual is devoted to necromancy. Here, as in spiritism, the necromancer is actually instructed to seek after a "spirit guide." "A Necromancer will acquire a Shadow Guide, a Spirit of the dead who was once a powerful Necromancer and acts as his Mentor. . . . To summon the Shadow Guide for advice and to be taught new spells, the Necromancer must perform a solemn ceremony . . ." (1515:36).

Fifth, the occult practice of conjuration and summoning of demons and devils can also be found in many games. The *D & D Monster Manual* has a detailed section devoted solely to demons. They are named, described (complete with an artist's sketch), and categorized according to their varying abilities and powers. Players are encouraged to use this information in conjunction with certain spells to summon these beings. Thus, a cleric, for example, using a seventh level gate spell, knows that he "must name the demon, devil, demi-god, god, or similar being he or she desires to make use of the gate and come to the cleric's aid." He is also told that there is "a 100% certainty that something will step through the gate" (1513:53).

Dungeons and Dragons mentions demon possession as a possibility. However, if a player, for example, possesses a "mind bar," it will prevent him "from suffering telepathic influence or possession" by such creatures as demons or devils (1513:115).

Sixth, occult alignment with supernatural powers or deities can be found in some of the games. This is an essential part of such games, as it has been in sorcery and witchcraft throughout the years. In Dungeons and Dragons, the alignment of each character with good (chaotic, lawful, or neutral), neutral (chaotic, lawful, or true), or evil (chaotic, lawful, or neutral), must be determined. The character's class will help in determining this. But beyond this alignment is an alignment with some deity that the character can serve and even worship. Both dungeon masters and players are told, "No fantasy world is complete without the gods, mighty deities who influence the fates of men and move mortals about like chesspieces in their obscure games of power.... They [the gods] are one of the Dungeon Master's most important tools in his or her shaping of events. The gods serve an important purpose for the players as well. Serving a deity is a significant part of AD & D [Advanced Dungeons & Dragons], and all player characters should have a patron god. Alignment assumes its full importance when tied to the worship of a deity" (1516:37).

Seventh, the names of occult, or magic, orders can be found in at least one game. Chivalry and Sorcery mentions such "Magical Orders" as "The Ancient Ones" (druids), "The Kingdom of Wicca" (witchcraft), "The Company of the Dark Brotherhood," and others. Some of these names are reminiscent of real occult groups. The game manual also includes detailed instructions on how players can form their own magic, or occult, order.

In addition to the above, one can find such occult practices as abjuration (the neutralization or negation of magic, spells, and curses), clair-

audience and clairvoyance (the ability to hear or see what is happening at a distance), divination (the knowledge of the future by the aid of the "gods"), summoning of elements (earth, air, water, and fire) and arcane powers, and others. Dungeons and Dragons even includes the primitive occult idea (and practice) of trapping the soul (1513:92).

However, the occult connection does not end with the manuals and materials of these games. In Dungeons and Dragons, for example, frequent reference is made to the importance of actual investigation (i.e., library research) of the pagan, Eastern, occult cultures from which the mythologies and deities are drawn. In fact, some games are "often accompanied by long hours of research into the cultures to be used in the dungeons" (1517).

We are told in *Deities and Demigods*, "The books listed below constitute some of the references used in compiling this work. They, as well as numerous other works, contain much more detailed accounts of the gods and their divine characteristics than can be included herein. Further research is recommended to the DM [Dungeon Master] who wishes to augment the given information" (1516:143).

Two of the books suggested are E. A. Wallis Budge's *The Egyptian Book of the Dead* and Sr. James Frazier's *The Golden Bough*. The former is a potent occult volume chronicling ritualistic preparations and instructions for the dead in their postmortem state; the latter, an anthropological compendium on occult practices in primitive societies.

Similarly, *Gods, Demi-Gods, and Heroes* states: "Further research and reading is recommended into all the myths presented herein. This is the merest of outlines, presented in D & D terms" (1518:Foreword). If "further research and reading is recommended" in the area of mythology, and mythology is defined as "dealing with the gods, demi-gods, and heroes of a particular people, usually involving the supernatural" (1518:Foreword), then is this game not, in effect, encouraging its participants to concentrate their investigation on the supernatural and even occult aspects of pagan cultures?

One might raise the question here as to how such research differs from that of a student in an anthropology course. Does he not research the same cultures? Obviously he does, but there are some important differences. First, the scope of research is somewhat different. In Dungeons and Dragons the primary focus of research appears to be narrow, dealing mostly with the area of the religious or supernatural, even though other aspects of culture may also be included. In an anthropology course, excluding those rare anthropology courses that specifically investigate the occult aspects of various cultures (1519:39-46), the focus is generally much broader and involves several components, one of which is the religious.

Second, the purpose of research is quite different. In Dungeons and Dragons the main purpose is to obtain information that may be useful in the researcher's fantasy role playing. As one player explained, "You try to think like your characters. . . . I'm running Inca characters now so I'm studying Inca culture" (1517). In most anthropology courses the purpose is primarily for the researcher's understanding of the past and demonstration of his skills. (For some students, such research may be done purely to fulfill course requirements.) Despite these differences, it should also be noted that researching occult activities in pagan societies has led at least some scholarly investigators to personal involvement in the occult (cf. Shamanism).

The world of the occult is by its own definition that which is immaterial, hidden, and esoteric. Webster defines "occult" as "hidden from the eye or understanding; invisible and mysterious . . ." or ". . . not revealed, secret; not easily apprehended or understood; not able to be seen or detected." Since the occult is by nature hidden from the eye and not able to be seen or detected, it would seem necessary for those who want to participate in the occult to use their imagination. Imagination, again according to Webster, is "the faculty by which we can bring absent objects and perceptions forcibly before the mind." It is "the act or power of forming a mental image of something not present to the senses or never before wholly perceived in reality." Imagination is the faculty by which one perceives and interacts

with any reality not directly available through the five senses.

It is this potential relationship between the occult and the imagination that is of concern to many, especially in light of the obvious occult content in FRP games. As one researcher has noted:

The very nature of D & D, and FRP in general, is such that the imagination is being guided into encounters with nonmaterial entities, forces, or spirits. Those entities, we are told, are mere fantasies with no basis in reality. If, however, those entities do actually exist in some form in the spirit world, then the line of demarcation between what is pure fantasy and what is actual contact with spiritual, demonic forces becomes extremely abstruse if not entirely nonexistent (1520:3-4).

This is hardly to infer that there is no difference between actual participation in occult activities and imagining the same, or that every time someone participates in imaginative occult activity one will come in contact with occult forces. We simply point out that relegating "occult contact" to mere imagination does not guarantee one freedom from demonic influence.

Today, classes in psychic and spiritual development use imagination and visualization* techniques in their methodology to achieve out-of-body experiences, develop occult powers, and foster contact with spirits. Many of the most popular books on various occult themes allude to these same techniques. Whether one accepts it or not, simple imagination has been used to establish spirit contact (e.g., when an imaginary "inner adviser" suddenly becomes a real being). There are numerous cases in occult literature where demons have actively sought out human contacts under the guise of an "imagined" patron god, ascended master, inner counselor, or spirit helper (cf. New Age Inner Work, Intuition, Dream Work, Visualization).

Regardless of the difference between reality and imagination, a word of caution, such as the following by Elliot Miller, is to the point:

However real this distinction may be in the minds of the players, though, I feel no assurance that the spirit world will not respond when it is beckoned.

When I was of high-school age I was extremely skeptical about anything reputedly supernatural. I recall engaging in a mock seance with a group of friends. Our lightheartedness was turned to fear when suddenly the "medium," my best friend, began to convulse, his eyes rolled back in his head, and a strange voice emerged from his throat. For the following two years this young Jew was tormented by spirits. Withdrawing from all social contacts, he haunted graveyards until he was delivered through the power of Jesus Christ (1521:10).

Furthermore, there is always the possibility that a player may, in everyday life, pursue those occult activities role-played in fantasy. After all, the hope of every dreamer is to live the fantasy.

That some have pursued the occult as a result of their involvement in FRP games is a matter of record. On a major network radio talk show a few years ago, one prominent dungeon master admitted to James Bjornstad that he personally knew of several who had gone on to become involved in witchcraft and spiritism as a result of playing D & D, but he was quick to point out that he saw no harm or danger in this. Subsequent dialogue revealed that his worldview did not allow for anything supernatural. Thus, from his perspective, if there is no supernatural activity, then all occult activity must be understood in terms of functions of the natural realm, psychological powers of the mind. Participation in the occult, to him, cannot be (supernaturally) dangerous. To the contrary, we believe the world of demons is real, and that participation in the occult can be very dangerous (278).

One could argue that FRP is permitted because one is dealing purely in fantasy. We know that God forbids involvement in the occult in reality (Deuteronomy 18:10-12), but what about in fantasy? How does God view someone's imaginative involvement in such a realm? If Jesus considered one's lusting after a woman in his heart (i.e., fantasy) tantamount to adultery, what would He say about someone's pursuing the occult in his mind (i.e., fantasy)? Would He approve, or would He say it was wrong? If one's

mind is centered upon the "imaginative" use of occult power, is he not at least tolerating the *idea* of its use? And again, who can guarantee that the demonic will not respond? Some players have reported actual paranormal or supernatural experiences (the movement of objects and other phenomena) while playing these games.

In conclusion, we are admonished in the Bible to "be on the alert. Your adversary, the devil, prowls about like a roaring lion, seeking someone to devour" (1 Peter 5:8 NASB). We are also told that Satan and his demons are master deceivers: "Satan disguises himself as an angel of light," and "his servants also disguise themselves as servants of righteousness (2 Corinthians 11:14-15 NASB). Satan can make something look desirable and provide fun and excitement—he can use a game that encourages fantasy role playing—if it will attract someone to become involved with him. We need to practice discernment continually "in order that no advantage be taken of us by Satan; for we are not ignorant of his schemes" (2 Corinthians 2:11 NASB).

## STAR+GATE:
## THE DECISION MAKER

*Introduction: Spiritistic Origin*

Star+Gate is a newer "game" developed in 1968 through a kind of psychic intuition (1508:215-45). Although it was not mass-marketed until the early 1980s, it had something of a small cult following in prior years. The game has also had an odd sort of evolution, with twists and turns and, similar to the production of *A Course in Miracles,*\* various synchronistic events.

The inventor of the game is a psychic named Richard H. Geer (not the actor), who claims that the origin of the game is found in an "agreement" he made with the spirit world before he was born, presumably in his last incarnation. In the words of spiritist Caroline Myss, coauthor (with neurosurgeon Norman Shealy) of *The Creation of Health*, and the vice president and editor of the spiritistically oriented Stillpoint Publishing, who wrote the Introduction to Geer's book, "He was able to remember a form of an 'agreement' made with the nonphysical world before his physical birth. The early years of his life gradually activated the memory of this purpose and the result culminated in the development and perfection of STAR+GATE" (1508:III).

Geer himself describes the initial "encounter" and a later mercurial "entity-presence" which "has come and gone nightly for years" (1508:219). Around 1974 Geer had become personally involved with the psychic world. "It wasn't sudden, but I definitely started attracting those kinds of people to my life." As a result of interest in the psychic potential in Star+Gate, "The game blossomed" (1508:232), becoming the catalyst for its eventual success.

The name "Star+Gate" is derived from the individual "star" and "gate" cards in the 96-card deck. They are two of the most significant cards and are intended to symbolize the "energy of life channelled through the postures of the mind" (1508:238).

The game includes a game board and is described and played as follows:

STAR+GATE may well help you to direct the course of your life. Or it may provide a level of assistance for you in understanding a personal relationship or in moving through a professional crisis. . . .

Simply put, the board (the Circle Pattern) is a map of consciousness—orderly, patterned and yet unlimited in its possibilities. And the designs on the cards represent the symbols most commonly recognized by the human subconscious. Formally, these symbols are called archetypes— or original patterns from which all things of the same nature are represented.

A player forms a question in his mind, shuffles the cards and then lays them down according to the STAR+GATE Sky Spread. Three cards represent the energy of the past or literally, the background of a given circumstance. Three other cards represent the energy forming around future events, and four cards are used to represent the present moment.

Once the cards have been laid in place, the player is directed through a process of interpretation— one which involves both sides of these unique cards. The picture side of the cards evokes

hunches and impressions from the player, and the word side triggers rational associations and certain levels experienced in personal situations. . . . At this point, the object is to use the map as a guide which directs the player to the elements or energy a situation lacks and/or requires in order to bring it to completion (1508:I).

Geer gives Star+Gate a kind of cosmic significance. For example:

Where did STAR+GATE come from? What is its purpose? I know that STAR+GATE is not new, not something I invented. . . . I know that the system was not thought up, by me or anyone beyond me. STAR+GATE is, I believe, timeless or beyond time as we know it. . . . The system or "game"—there isn't an adequate word to express STAR+GATE—is a gift, and I know now that, in part I came to deliver the gift. . . . As the system is used and explored by more people, it may well become a standard for understanding the interplay in life between the physical and non-physical, between consciousness and matter, spirit and form (1508:242,244).

*Mystical Parallels*

Star+Gate has some intriguing parallels to other occult and mystical literature and phenomena. Hermann Hesse, the brilliant promoter of Eastern metaphysics (e.g., *Siddhartha*), whom religion professor Dr. Carl A. Raschke refers to as "in a fashion, the literary ambassador for Jung's depth psychology" 1510:156), wrote *Magister Ludi: The Glass Bead Game*. Geer believes Star+Gate "presents the same potential" for humanity as does the glass bead game portrayed in Hesse's novel (1508:242-43).

Geer further observes that the personal mandala* Jung would meditate on daily "was the Star+Gate pattern almost line for line" (1508:243-44). In addition, he shows coincidences to science-fiction writer Roger Zelazney's series of books on Amber, a mystical realm that was the source for the creation of the universe. He also shows coincidences to M. A. Foster's *The Game Players of Zan* (1508:243). The game also allegedly corresponds to scientist-parapsychologist Arthur M. Young's occult theory of consciousness (1508:244). And the underlying theme of behind-the-scenes alien intervention and manipulation of humans that was portrayed in Steven Speilberg's film *Close Encounters of the Third Kind* was also noted for its uncanny resemblances to Geer's life. "Such parallels and coincidences have occurred increasingly over the years. This is all the more reason why the *Close Encounters* story of a subconscious message moved me so deeply. Whether the movie is seen as a metaphor or taken literally, it seems that something is emerging from within us and that STAR+GATE is a part of it" (1508:244).

*Astrology and Psychotherapy*

In his book, Geer discusses his own spiritual background with other forms of divination and how Star+Gate evolved from astrology:

I was aware of Tarot and had tried it a few times. I was fascinated by it, but after a few experiences with it I decided it wasn't for me. I had similar feelings about *I Ching*. I knew it was a good system, but it didn't satisfy me. And so it was with other systems I encountered. . . .

It was only a few days later that I found my model in a full-page ad for a book on astrology. . . . Ideas and plans swam around in my head and became a part of my dreams that night. In the morning I bought art supplies to fashion a game board. . . . I translated the sketch onto the game board by what was becoming standard operating procedure, working by intuition. . . . [G]radually the terminology and geography of STAR+GATE came together, like pieces of a puzzle. . . . From a book on astrology I chose the names of twelve Houses on the circle based on the signs of the zodiac. And from a distillation of several astrological facets, I named the Star points. The former group divided the circle into areas that related to the development of personality and self. The latter described essential energies or types of activity which beings exhibit (1508:222-28; cf. Intuition).

Astrology* remains a significant part of the game; Stargate Enterprises offers a "Personal Portrait" that includes "blending astrology and Star+Gate symbolism" (1508:250).

Like the divinatory methods discussed earlier, Star+Gate further combines the fascination of psychological self-discovery with an alleged glimpse into the future all wrapped up in a complex scheme of symbolism and imagery. And like the other systems, it is claimed to be "incredibly accurate" (1508:jacket).

The *Llewellyn New Times*, a wicca publication, calls Star+Gate ". . . the greatest leap forward in psychological technology since the development of the Tarot." Psychologist Glen Williston states that "as a psychologist I experience great benefit using Star+Gate with my clients. It gives validity to their own answers and solutions" (1508:jacket). Combining as it does Jung's principle of synchronicity, symbolism, visualization* and the use of archetypes, the interests of psychologists is hardly surprising.

In conclusion, millions of people today find the divinatory methods that we have discussed both fascinating and self-illuminating. Unfortunately, these methods open the doors to the occult, and in the long run they will prove more damaging than illuminating (278).

## THE POWER OF SPIRITISTIC INSIGHTS

We began this section by noting the spiritistic association to divination historically. But even today, as we have documented, those practiced in the divinatory arts frequently concede their power is or may be spiritistic. For example, former astrologer Charles Strohmer knows that it is impossible for astrology* and similar forms of divination to work on the basis of their stated principles because they are comprised largely from mythology. But they still work, underscoring their amazing appeal to draw people in:

It has absolutely, and I mean *absolutely*, no way of knowing about real events. According to the intelligence report on astrology so far, self-disclosures are impossible.

A seasoned astrologer, however, knows better. He will tell you that self-disclosures do occur. Experienced numerologists or fortune-tellers will concur regarding their crafts; their clients will tell you the same. In this way, a large amount of trust develops on the part of the client, trust in the craft and in the spokesperson, as a few quarters of the client's life are laid open and recognized by someone who knows only the client's time, place, and date of birth (1286:40-41).

Strohmer continues by noting two personal experiences that confirm the power of divination:

I knew little about Phyllis. After discussing some generalizations with her, I began to "notice" (in a progression of her birth chart) that she currently faced severe adversity on her job, and that this ordeal was being perpetrated by a fellow employee. *Perhaps a supervisor*, I thought. When I could not shake off this impression that was coming to me as I was looking over her chart, I spoke to Phyllis about it, suddenly adding that the ordeal had begun about a year and a half earlier. Phyllis confirmed my discovery.

There was also a curious slant to this delineation. When Phyllis confirmed the self-disclosure, I, for some reason, forecasted that within one year the ordeal would end. I did not know it, but this forecast fit Phyllis' desire. . . . In this way astrology [began] to govern Phyllis. . . .

I also remember Tom. Tom taught occult mind development classes. . . . I wanted to know the astrological *whys* of Tom's supposed powers of astral projection. Eventually, I erected Tom's chart and we discussed it. What sticks out in my mind about this discussion is Tom saying he was uninterested in astrology *before* I delineated his chart. . . . In Tom's chart I saw strong indicators (influences) specifically for the supposed capability of astral travel as opposed to other forms of psychic manifestations. And I told him so. . . . For the astrologer, a confirmation of a self-disclosure is an impressive moment. It is as though he had been attempting the impossible, say, to walk on water, when suddenly—a confirmation! Of course, confirmations also affect the clients. Besides getting them more interested in astrology, confirmations satisfy, at least temporarily, the thirst for an explanation to whatever is occurring in one's life. . . . If astrology can know one unknown thing about me, people think, perhaps it knows other things—things I don't even know about myself. Perhaps it *can* interpret human nature, and spiritual things as well.

And thus, through astrological confirmations, the convinced clients transform a hobby into a way of life (1286:41-42).

In discussing these detailed and specific astrological self-disclosures, Strohmer believes that only the influence of the spirit world can logically explain them. After pointing out how astrologers seem to be mysteriously "directed" to certain elements in a chart, he asks:

What is occurring? The spokesperson's mind is becoming focused upon a portion of the chart that pertains to a detail in a client's life. This is a detail that a familiar spirit is privy to. It is the spirit that is somehow doing the "focusing." The focusing is influenced not by a planet or a mythological relativism but by a deceptive and invisible being who knows both the spokesperson and the client. . . . I was not aware of the defiance Phyllis faced at work. I had no idea that Tom's horoscope would indicate clear and strong "influences" for astral travel. But the spirits knew these details. And because I was the spokesperson, having had the astrological training necessary to recognize the particular [ingredients] that would indicate these specific hot spots in the client's life, while I was studying the charts the spirits made the psychic connection and tied it all together (1286:53-54).

Strohmer is not alone in his convictions that spiritism is the real source of knowledge and power behind astrology and other forms of divination. From the ancient past until modern times, many diviners have claimed spiritistic guidance in their arts. Thus, it is the spirits, not the symbols, who are said to be the authors of the knowledge and information given to a client. For example, the ancient Egyptian god "Thoth" had, as one of his purposes, the revealing of "the wisdom of the astrologers" (1310:54, cf. 1306:147).

The history of astrology is filled with examples of this. Claudius Ptolemy, considered the "father" of ancient astrology and the "Prince of Astrologers," frankly confessed that it was impossible for men on their own power to predict the future. Thus he admitted, "They only who are inspired by the deity can predict particulars" (1509:153).

In the 1650s, the famous astrologer William Lilly and others accepted that the spirits gave astrological knowledge. "Lilly himself conceded the possibility of knowledge by direct angelic revelation; 'many now living' had been so helped, he thought; alchemy indeed could be learned no other way. According to Reginald Scot some held that even knowledge of astrology could be thus acquired: there was a spirit named Bifrons who could make men 'wonderful cunning' in the subject" (1202:634).

In the late nineteenth century, astrologer, medium, and Mason Thomas Burgoyne claimed that a certain class of spirits worked directly with astrologers. He says this group of spirits, whom he believes are too intelligent "to be guilty of fraud," work closely with all astrologers:

> They are the attendant familiars [spirits] of certain classes of mystical students, especially those devoted to alchemy and astrology. It is these beings that usually produce the visions.... They are indeed planetary in nature.... They ... can give much information regarding the orb under whose dominion they act (1260:84).

Many twentieth-century astrologers also teach that the astrologer's task is to become a vehicle for spirit powers (1222:40-47,76; cf. 1250:57/1257:102).

From all of this, it is evident that many diviners confess that spirits can work through their methods. But is it also possible for spirits to work through divination without the practitioner's knowledge? The tradition of the occult leaves no doubt that spirits can work inconspicuously through a person. They do not need to be felt in order to be present (cf. Inner Work, Intuition). For example, as occurs in hypnosis,* the spirits can implant entire sequences of events into the mind, events that never even happened. These are not perceived as dream-like events but are perceived as real as any waking reality.

Consider the experiences of noted scientist and parapsychologist Dr. Andrija Puharich and medium Uri Geller, who discuss their contact with alleged UFO entities. These invisible beings act in a manner similar to the spirit guides of mediums (393:167-223). Dr. Puharich describes the personal impact that this power to manipulate made upon his mind. He refers to a series of events of two entire days' duration that was totally controlled and directed by the spirits, which he names the intelligences from space, or "IS":

> These two days' events numbed me. Sara and Uri experienced one sequence and Ila and I experienced another, in the same time frame. I had discovered the truth about Uri's deepest secret, had had a gun in my hand that felt real, and had had a phone call experience that is real in my mind to this day. But most of all I realized that the four of us had had an experience imprinted on our minds by what could only be the agency of IS. I finally learned that, given the existence of IS, I could never again know which of my experiences were directly imposed upon me by IS and which were not. I have never been so deeply shaken in my life as when I realized the full implication of this power of IS (394:112).

If invisible spirits can implant whole experiences in the mind, surely they can implant and direct simple thoughts, such as in an astrologer's interpretation of the chart, or in reading the symbolism of the tarot, I Ching, or Star+Gate.

Some diviners freely admit that their spirit guides may influence and direct their lives quite unbeknownst to them (1262:119). Astrologer Philip Sedgwick confesses that information can be received by the astrologer from the spirit world; yet because the spirits may choose to remain inconspicuous, the astrologer may never know the true source of such information: "However, this type of channeling does not require losing consciousness, trancing or altering one's state of mind; it just happens. The beauty of this method is that it remains completely inconspicuous" (1264:176).

In the world of mediumism and other forms of spiritism, it is widely conceded that such "spirit-feeding" occurs. Again, this is where one's spirit guides inconspicuously affect the practitioner's or the client's thought processes, to help guide and direct the life. This is, after all, the reason for a spirit *guide*—to guide, direct, and influence.

But the spirits are under no obligation to announce their presence or influence. This is why diviners and spiritists share such similar experiences. For example, Robert Leightman, a spiritist and M.D., acknowledges that the spirits had been giving him important ideas for some time, yet he was completely unaware of the fact. He believed the ideas originated from his own mind. Thus he states of his spirit guides, "What they did was to give me a whole bunch of ideas. And of course I thought, well, my mind has suddenly become brilliant. It was already great before, but now it is absolutely brilliant. I was getting all kinds of ideas from time to time and of course, the spooks [spirits] said they were giving them to me, [but at first I didn't believe it]" (587:40).

We have already documented the fact of sudden, unexpected insights or revelations being given to the diviner. What is significant is that the person may have no idea where the information comes from, or that it could be derived from the spirit world. As Strohmer writes:

This hookup between spirit and spokesperson is subtle. It is not like a phone connection. It is not obvious that information is trickling in from the outside. The certainty of recognizing that there is a voice on the other end is strangely unapparent. The knowledgeable, familiar spirit infiltrates the thinking activity in such a covert way that the astrologer assimilates the data and has no inkling that anything other than his own thoughtlife is responsible for the self-disclosures. I cannot say how this cover-up works, but it is possible to discover *when* it occurs (1286:53).

This is why one must be careful to test the claims of diviners in general; many deliberately hide their spiritism, but others are entirely unaware of it. Still others only appear to avoid occult methods. For example, famous astrologer and occultist Marc Edmund Jones "felt intuition should never be used in delineating astrological charts" (1244:1). From this, one could assume he avoided subjective or psychic methods of chart interpretation. But, in fact, most of his astrological information was derived from the spirit world (1244:11/1342:83-87). Again, caveat emptor.

# DOWSING AND WATER DOWSING

## INFO AT A GLANCE

**Description.** Dowsing is a practice employing divinatory implements and methods in order to search out information, such as a site of water, the nature or location of disease and its proper treatment, lost objects, or missing persons.**

**Founder.** Unknown; the practice is ancient.

**How does it claim to work?** Dowsing claims to work through a practitioner's supposedly natural sensitivity to nature's geomagnetic phenomena, "water radiations," or by some allegedly unconscious "motor ability" operating in an unknown manner.

**Scientific evaluation.** Controlled testing has not confirmed dowsing powers scientifically.

**Examples of occult potential.** The development of altered states of consciousness, psychic powers, or spirit contact are almost always possible.

**Major problem.** Dowsing is not the natural human ability many assume; it is a spiritistic power.

**Biblical/Christian evaluation.** Dowsing is rejected by description (Hosea 4:12) and by nature, i.e., divination (Deuteronomy 18:9-12).

**Potential dangers.** Financial loss and other deception through dowsing failures; health risks through improper medical diagnosis or treatment; occult influences.

## INTRODUCTION AND INFLUENCE

Dowsing and water dowsing are ancient pagan practices that are essentially forms of divination.** The early Greeks called it rhabdomancy, "rod divination." Since ancient times it

---

**Technically, dowsing is a type of radiaesthesia and, by extension, a form of psychometry.

has been associated with pagan gods, the spirit world and occultists (refs. 1071/623/626; cf. Divination). Only in modern times has there been an attempt to place dowsing into the category of a natural human power that functions by currently unknown scientific laws.

Dowsing per se comprises a large category of phenomena encompassing many different forms; its most recognizable aspect today being water dowsing. As Francis Hitching, a member of the British Society of Dowsers, remarks in *Dowsing: The Psi Connection*, dowsing for water is only the tip of the iceberg. In the past, "as now, there were two ways in which the art was practiced: in the narrow sense of water finding, and perhaps mineral finding too, and in the much broader sense of divination in general, in which the rod could be used to gain unlimited knowledge" (623:39-40).

Dowsing is related to New Age Movement in two basic ways. First, the energy said to be employed in dowsing is frequently claimed to be the same energy many New Age practitioners allege that they manipulate: prana, chi, ectoplasm, orgone, mana, and suchlike. This is illustrated in books like Erwin Stark's *A History of Dowsing and Energy Relationships*, which assigns the source of dowsing power to the occult energy concepts found in dozens of cultures (626; see "Occult Aspects," p. 180).

Second, many New Age practitioners employ rod and pendulum dowsing in their work. For example, because they have developed psychic abilities, they often discover they can also dowse or use pendulums. New Age psychics in general may use "map dowsing" to locate a missing object or person. New Age healers may dowse with a rod and pendulum to diagnose a patient and to prescribe homeopathic or other remedies. Dowsing is also used in the popular practices of crystal work* and Therapeutic Touch (1590:396). In addition, dowsing is frequently employed in New Age or transpersonal education*—one reason being the emphasis modern dowsers place upon instructing children in their occult art (1352). And dowsing is fundamentally related to the occult practices of psychometry, radionics, and radiaesthesia, which enjoy widespread support in the New Age Movement (632:3-38/631:53-55).

Dowsing societies exist throughout the world—in Britain (The British Society of Dowsers), Kenya, Sweden, New Zealand, Austria, Argentina, Vietnam, Germany, India, Spain, Israel, Mexico, and other countries. In France, dowsers have a national union, and many countries' memberships run as high as several thousand, such as in the United States and Germany. In the United States, the American Society of Dowsers, founded in 1961, has many M.D.s, lawyers, engineers, scientists, and even ministers among its ranks. Past president Gordon MacLean was a member of the American Institute of Chemical Engineers and a fellow of the American Association for the Advancement of Science.

The modern impact of dowsing is unmistakable. Although dowsing literature often contains claims that are not documented or suspect, dowser Erwin E. Stark is correct when he argues that the influence of dowsing is greater than most people realize. The following account by Stark, at least illustrates the influence of dowsing:

... Nearly 50% of all practicing doctors in France, I have been told, use some form of dowsing in their treatment. ...

Also significant is that virtually every major water pipeline and public utility here and abroad has a "diviner" on its payroll. ... UNESCO has engaged a Dutch dowser and geologist to conduct official investigations. Noted dowser Evelyn Penrose was retained by British Columbia to locate oil and water resources. ...

One authority reports that 150 Soviet geologists are using dowsing in their work. ... Both Moscow State University and the University of Leningrad have established training schools in dowsing in cooperation with the Russian Army. ...

Similarly, articles published in *The New York Times* (1967) confirm the use of dowsing by the First and Third Divisions of the U.S. Marine Corps in both Korea and Vietnam. ...

The Czechoslovakian Army maintains a permanent corps of dowsers. The Canadian Army Engineers also rely on dowsing. At U.S.M.C. Camp Pendleton in Southern California, young enlistees have been screened for their dowsing ability (626:14-16).

*Psychic* magazine is correct in asserting that there is also some influence of dowsing among electrical engineers:

> Power company engineers are the most likely to be found carrying dowsing rods searching for underground lines. Steel plant maintenance engineers in Bethlehem, Pennsylvania, have been known to use the rod for similar reasons. Though publicity shy, these busy engineers do not stop to question this particular ability; they use it, and use it effectively (643:13).

The name "Culligan" is a household word in California and other states due to the Culligan "water softening" service. Founder Emmett Culligan was a proponent of dowsing, and in his *Emmett Culligan on Water* (812), he has a chapter "Water Dowsing Explained."

Dowsing has also made inroads into some high schools and colleges. An issue of *The American Dowser* reports on the first Boulder Free School course in dowsing. Some of the topics included: visualization,* psychic states of mind, map dowsing, dowsing "charts and the Ouija board," psychic healing,* meditation,* higher states of consciousness, shamanism* (Carlos Castaneda and the "huna philosophy"), hypnosis,* and yoga* (1073:15-16).

The following report on Goddard College in Plainfield, Vermont, was also given in the *The American Dowser.* Note how the instructor uses dowsing as a vehicle for introducing students to other forms of psychic activity:

> At Goddard College in Plainfield, Vermont, only twenty miles from the ASD [American Society of Dowsers] headquarters in Danville, faculty and students have for years been free to engage in a variety of psychic studies. Many of these have followed the major tasks pursued by the great psychologist Carl Jung, particularly his investigations of dreams, mandalas and alchemy. Recently faculty and students have been studying dowsing as a technique for tapping intuitive/unconscious resources and knowledge.... Psychic studies are seen as natural areas of inquiry. I find dowsing a convenient tool for enabling students to enter into new experiences and to talk about previous experiences. Many students

cross a threshold in their work once dowsing has been introduced. By dowsing with them I demonstrate that it's acceptable to have and to discuss psychic experiences.... Dowsing is an enlivening tool in numerous kinds of courses. This is especially so in courses geared to study "lateral" or alternative, non-lineal ways of thinking.... [D]owsing belongs in courses set up specifically to uncover the history of psychic research or the characteristics of psychic events. ... It is particularly relevant in courses where psychic material is under consideration, that all students in the class have at least some limited shared experience of a psychic phenomenon. ... The pendulum is by far the most easily accessible dowsing instrument for students (1074:150).

The general literature on dowsing also reveals its influence. For example, a bibliography of the 1920s listed over 600 references, which at that time were said to comprise only a fourth of the total (623:7-8). Today that number has increased significantly. However, even today the literature on dowsing remains poor in quality, e.g., "[T]o read the dowsing literature is an exercise in futility. Even if all the writing were narrowed to the last fifty years, it would still be a collection of contradictions, omissions, and personal opinions.... The frustrating problem in examining dowsing literature is the subjective view taken by every writer" (514:2,32).

## NATURE

How does dowsing claim to work? Dowsers often allege that they possess a natural sensitivity to earth magnetism, water "radiations," or some other geophysical phenomena. They believe their dowsing stick or other device (often an occult pendulum) somehow "focuses" or otherwise "identifies" this energy and through it provides access to an unknown source of information, so that one is able to find water or other things, such as oil, treasure, or lost persons and objects. Virtually all dowsers agree that dowsing is somehow connected to a mysterious form of higher intelligence. As architect Ben Hester, a seasoned researcher of dowsing, comments:

... it is agreed upon by all, that it is the tapping of a superior intelligence. That this intelligence is far superior ... must be admitted. It is frightening to find it is also deceptive, contradictory, undependable, and often harmful. ... It must be remembered; *there is supernormal intelligence involved in every type of dowsing.* Dowsers explain this in a variety of ways:

1. From a throwback to ancestral knowledge or ability.

2. From a breakthrough to that great unused portion of the human brain.

3. From the Universal Mind.

4. As a gift from God.

5. As a gift from Satan (witchcraft, etc.) (514:90, 98-99).

The fact that dowsing "works" is clearly the major defense put forth on behalf of this practice. Dowsers think that if it works it must therefore be both a helpful and legitimate method. Thus, whether dowsing is employed within the New Age Movement or outside of it, the practice is justified on the basis of pragmatic concerns; it works, therefore it is to be employed whenever relevant. As one dowser comments, "What interests us about all dowsers is not the theories they develop but the results they obtain. It is these results which will attract more and more adepts as well as less and less convinced adversaries" (682:116).

On the basis of such pragmatism, Hoffman-La Roche, the huge multinational pharmaceutical company headquartered in Basel, Switzerland, has had dowsers on its payroll since 1944. These dowsers seek water for the company's operations. When interviewed as to the unscientific nature of dowsing, a company spokesman replied as follows: "Roche uses methods that are profitable, whether they are scientific or not. The dowsing method pays ..." (648:106). But so does the racetrack and casino. The deeper question is, Should dowsing be used if it is really a method of occult divination? Before we address this, we will now look at some common dowsing terms and instruments.

## TERMS AND INSTRUMENTS

*Terms for dowsing.* Divining, witching, pendulum dowsing, motorscopy, psychoscopy, rhabdomancy, scanning, radionics, radiaesthesia, geomancy, psychometry, psychogenic water locators, biophysical method, teleradiaesthesia, water forking, map dowsing, water witching, superpendulism, and, of course, water dowsing.

*Terms for the dowser's instruments.* Medicine sticks, index, doodlebug, transcendent rods, L-wires, Y-rods, pendulum, wizard rod, stick, angle wires, rudder, motorscopes, gudgeon, wand, staff, superior rods, shining rods, leaping rods, rotating rods, dipping rods, and, of course, dowsing rods.

*Terms for the dowsing power.* Higher self, unconscious muscular activity, neutral energy, life force, force, universal or cosmic mind, psychic power, fifth force field, sixth or seventh sense, bioplasmic energy, cosmic energy, God, and the Holy Spirit.

*Types of instruments.* Pencils, scissors, pliers, welding rods, jewelry, candles, seashells, needles, bent coat hangers, crowbars, guns, whale or shark bones, barbed wire, clothes, water "bobbers," feathers, "aura" meters—even thumbs, fingers, hands, or feet (i.e., no instruments at all)—and, of course, cut tree or shrub branches.

The instruments of dowsing are nearly endless, as are their uses. As we will see, this underscores the psychic nature of dowsing, in that the dowsing power does not reside in the implement; rather, it operates through the dowser from a source outside him, and it depends upon a particular mental state in order to function effectively. As Hitching observes in his book on dowsing and the occult, "Some of the best dowsers manage to dispense with tools altogether. For fundamentally, dowsing is not in the hands of the equipment; it is a process that happens via the mind" (623:77).

Leading dowser Raymond Willey refers to the dowser who employs merely feet or thumbs, or "uses just his hands, his arms, or ... in some other way, gets a dowsing response without any devices at all" (624:50-51). Gordon MacLean, another dowser, also admits this "natural" use of dowsing: "The ability to dowse with the hands alone is more common than anyone suspected before proper training methods were developed. Even some for whom the rods won't respond at first can quickly be taught how to locate water veins with the bare hands. We've had pupils who could not use the implements at all but could hand dowse with no trouble" (634:25). The famous psychic Uri Geller dowses this way. In his second autobiography, *The Geller Effect*, Geller states that he can both land and map dowse using only his hands.

Obviously, the kind of equipment used is irrelevant. The real question, then, is, What is the true source of the dowser's power? Surprisingly, most dowsers are unconcerned about this; they only care that their practice works (1083:31). But dowsers should be attentive to this issue most of all, because no dowser anywhere can prove that his source of power is really something neutral. In our section on dowsing and the occult that follows, we will show why we are convinced that the real source of dowsing power is lying spirits, which the Bible identifies as demons.

Nevertheless, every effort is made today to remove dowsing practice from the halls of occultism. As dowsing critic Ben Hester remarks:

... The dowsing world has developed its own vocabulary. It changes from generation to generation, and from country to country.... Practical use of dowsing has made modern man desperate to haul it up out of the occult to our scientific way of thinking and speaking....

The modern explanations may be couched in the language of physics, psychology, the psychic, parapsychology, parascience, or even our easy way of presenting paganism in the different popular religions, but they only add up to a collection of personal opinions! The supernatural or occult color of dowsing has not changed down through the centuries (514:xvii,33-34).

## CATEGORIES

One leading authority on dowsing is Raymond C. Willey, author of *Modern Dowsing: The Dowser's Handbook* (624). Willey has dowsed for over 50 years and was instrumental in organizing the American Society of Dowsers (ASD). He served as its secretary and was editor of its periodical, *The American Dowser*, for over a decade. Willey accepts four basic methods of dowsing:

a) *Field Dowsing*—the "traditional" use, e.g., locating water, minerals, objects, etc., on a given terrain, called "witching the area."

b) *Remote Dowsing*—"witching the area" is not required. Here the dowser supernaturally locates the target from a distance of up to several miles.

c) *Map Dowsing*—using a map or sketch, the dowser locates the target, often by use of a pendulum. There are no distance limits here since the dowser claims to locate his target even 10,000 miles away.

d) *Information Dowsing*—using dowsing to obtain needed information on any subject, with neither space nor time limits (624:57-63). Willey confesses, "Information dowsing not only saves time, but can aid greatly to increase the scope of the dowsing process" (624:59).

These four categories of dowsing underscore an important point. When people think of dowsing they often assume the process is confined to the first category: field dowsing. But in fact, all four categories constitute the phenomena of dowsing. Willey concedes that although all four areas logically involve the practice of dowsing, many people only accept the possibility of field dowsing. "Even today, many people, including those well educated and informed on other matters besides dowsing, refuse categorically to accept the facts of Remote Dowsing, Map Dowsing, and Information Dowsing, while grudgingly admitting the possibility of Field Dowsing" (624:59). Why the bias against these other forms of dowsing?

The reason is simple. These other forms of dowsing clearly involve supernatural abilities that have no rational or natural explanation. And this makes some people, even some dowsers, uncomfortable because they prefer to see dowsing as a natural, "scientific" process, a practice that will someday be found to have a rational explanation based on natural laws. Field dowsing appears to offer the greatest opportunity for a natural explanation. The public is therefore presented with a bewildering variety of "naturalistic" or "scientific" theories to supposedly explain the field dowsing, from an innate sensitivity to "radiations" to currently unexplored alleged geophysical phenomena (e.g., "ley lines"; 514:59-71).

Indeed, were the supernatural element not so apparent in *all* forms of dowsing, one might think that simple water dowsing could have a natural explanation. But, as we will see, this is not a credible option. Consider Hester's fourfold classification of dowsing, more precise and relevant than that given by Willey above: 1) terrestrial (field dowsing); 2) dowsing of inanimate objects (psychometry); 3) dowsing the animate world or living things (e.g., medical radionics for diagnosis); 4) information dowsing (remote, map, and all other dowsing; 514:58-94).

In each category, Hester carefully shows why the process cannot be accounted for on the basis of any known laws of science. He reveals that every form of dowsing must be considered a supernatural ability, not a physical one (514:58-94). If we examine the uses of dowsing, we begin to see why. As one scientist observed, "If you tell me that a man can sit on the other side of the Atlantic and look at a map and receive information about something not shown on the map . . . it is impossible. . . . If your dowser can really pinpoint something on a map . . . well, it is supernatural" (623:175).

## USES

Following we list a sampling of dowsing uses taken from *The American Dowser*. These are the uses that dowsers themselves claim to employ. Can anyone read this list and still logically believe dowsing is a natural, scientific practice rather than a supernatural, psychic ability? We don't think so. Dowsers claim their practice has been used:

- to instruct children in developing psychic abilities.
- to find accident-prone highway sections.
- to determine the conditions of the "aura" field.
- in veterinary diagnosis.
- for automobile diagnosis ("car dowsing").
- for "basic information in a pending malpractice suit."
- in narcotics detection.
- to find fish in the lake, and whether or not they are biting!
- for compass directions.
- to find archaeological sites and artifacts ("psychic archaeology").
- to discover blocked water or oil pipes.
- for tracking ships (e.g., predicting the time of their arrival before they appear on the horizon and even their contents and port of origin).
- in building and construction.
- to check an area for snakes.
- to find downed planes, lost ships, or submarines.
- in sport hunting (e.g., dowsing for deer).
- to find unmarked graves.
- to find lost objects, valuables, or murder weapons.
- to find missing persons (e.g., determining whether or not a person is dead by their photograph, and if alive, locating them).
- by students for checking the accuracy of their homework (one person commented, "It works faster than a computer").
- to determine if letters, wills, paintings, and signatures are genuine or forged.
- to find property lines.
- to track storms.
- for treasure hunting (buried treasure, wrecked ships).
- for use in astrology* and other forms of the occult.

- for career choices.

- to hire employees.

- in food and vitamin selection (e.g., determining contaminants or vitamin content in food).

- in color therapy.

- for "noxious ray detection."

- to detect multiple personalities or spirit possession (558).

- to find "subconscious blocks."

- to determine the soil composition and fertilizer needs of your house or garden plants.

- to sort eggs to determine the sex of the chick (645).

If these are not enough, Stark (626:17-24), Willey (624:45), and MacLean (634:18-20) state that dowsing can:

- track down criminals.

- reveal your mate's infidelity.

- locate "subluxations" or cavities (for chiropractors and dentists).

- find answers to any personal problem.

- forecast the weather, detect earthquakes.

- measure intelligence.

- detect pregnancy.

- find the right medical specialist for rare diseases by dowsing the phone book.

- find ghosts or poltergeists.

- detect acupuncture points.

- determine the heights, weights, and ages of wanted kidnappers and rapists.

- determine edible plants in the wilderness.

- find avalanche victims.

- locate the "energy" openings of trees.

- chart an unmapped region of Rhodesia.

- locate concealed termite eggs and fleas on your dog.

- locate bad employees and stolen checks; predict attendance figures.

- select the freshest flowers in a florist shop.

- determine if store items are overpriced.

- teach members of your scout troop.

- determine the composition of moon rocks and whether a planet is inhabited; and diagnose the physical condition of the astronauts before they land!

Now, did we leave anything out? How about returning from the twilight zone?

All of this indicates why the most logical explanation for dowsing is found in the realm of the supernatural. But if we are really dealing with something supernatural, which supernatural realm are we entering—the good or the evil—and how do we tell? Our answer to this question ought to determine the church's response to dowsing.

## DOWSING IN THE CHURCH

The research of architect Ben Hester (514:118,157) and of theologian and occult authority Dr. Kurt Koch reveals that dowsing is considered an acceptable, or at least innocent, practice in the minds of many Christians. While most evangelical Christians are suspicious of dowsing, many others are unsure what to think, and some endorse the practice.

Apparently, the Roman Catholic Church accepts dowsing as a natural ability while simultaneously condemning any supernatural manifestations it may bring (514:15). And it seems as if some popes and priests have employed dowsers (626:12):

Sometime during the sixteenth or seventeenth centuries the [German] Church claimed the dowsing rod as holy Church property. Theodore Besterman in *Water Divining*, pages 188 and 189, tells of the Holy Mass instituted to be read over the rod before allowing it to be used by an outsider. After the Mass, the rod was to be held in the hands and these words intoned, "Dowsing Rod, I adjure you in the name of God the Father, the Son, and the Holy Ghost." Then the rod will work. Francis Hitching, on page 49 of *Pendulum*, remarks that it was common during this time in Germany for the rod to be

173

"Christianized" by placing it in the bed of a newly baptized child, after which the rod was addressed first in the names of the Father, the Son and the Holy Ghost, then in the child's name. . . . Hitching goes on to say that one of the problems of the Church at that time was that so many of their priests were natural born dowsers (514:18-20).

As unpleasant as it may be, the history of dowsing includes a strange association with Christianity, most of it with the early and medieval Church. . . . The Church equated dowsing with sorcery, yet it occasionally condoned it and used it (514:41).

Martin Luther branded dowsing as a form of black magic and a violation of the sixth commandment (623:41; 626:12). Dr. Koch observes:

Even believing Christians are divided on the question of what they should think of rod and pendulum [dowsers]. I have met doctors, pastors, missionaries, and even evangelists who use the rod or pendulum and believe they have received this gift from God. Satan's cunning is very evident here, when even believing Christians are deceived by him (642:185-86).

Ben Hester has had wide experience concerning the practice of dowsing in the church, and he has conducted extensive discussions with Christian dowsers. He observes, "Most Christian dowsers state unequivocally, 'Dowsing for water (or minerals) is *not* divination! It has *nothing* to do with the biblically condemned "wizardry' " . . . (514:198). But Hester himself remarks, ". . . There is no way to avoid the conclusion that the moment the dowser picks up the dowsing device he has accepted one of the oldest witchcraft and sorcery methods known to man" (514:199).

Hester, whose text on the subject is one of the few critical treatments available (514), told us how dowsing was often practiced among one church denomination's leadership. In a letter to us, he also noted a common pattern of denial concerning anything questionable in the practice, especially among Christian dowsers who maintain their "gift is from God." After more than a decade of discussion with Christian and

non-Christian dowsers, Hester regretfully concluded that "those already into it often want nothing to do with the facts" (674:1).

Thankfully, this is not always the case. For example, Hester cited a man who had contacted him concerning his minister, a dowser, who was influencing the congregation to accept dowsing as a divine gift. This individual attempted to have his pastor talk with Mr. Hester, or to at least read his book. But "the minister said he wanted nothing to do with the book or hear of anything I said" (674:1). Still, he accepted the book and the next day this concerned individual phoned Mr. Hester to report that "the minister called him and told him that once he started reading it [Hester's book] he couldn't lay it down and on finishing it he destroyed all of his dowsing equipment and repented of his actions" (674:1).

Hester also states that although many Christian dowsers are innocently deceived in this manner, this does not necessarily excuse personal responsibility:

Is such activity then, innocent sinning? We have found many ways this may happen in dowsing. Childhood innocence and inexperience, faith in a dowser-teacher, ignorance of the complete picture of dowsing, ignorance of the biblical condemnation, and perhaps the worst of all, following the example of the "godly" Christian dowser, being only a few (674:2).

Monty Kline, who is an evangelical Christian promoter of many New Age health methods, argues that the practice of dowsing is a natural ability and therefore acceptable on the following basis:

After some study and considerable experience in dowsing myself, as well as training others, I am quite certain this is merely a natural, explainable phenomenon, just another form of bioenergetic testing.

The dowsing rods basically act as an antenna amplifying the earth's geomagnetic field. . . . My training in dowsing came from a committed, doctrinally-sound, Spirit-filled Christian, and I have trained two other above reproach Christian men (one of them a pastor) in dowsing. An associate recently shared with me that a relative of his, a well-known former evangelical Bible college president, has dowsed for water all his life. Satanically-energized? Give me a break! . . . I see dowsing as demonstrable, repeatable and without any clear scriptural conflict. That passes my test, and hopefully yours (827:6).

Of course, the mere fact that Christians practice dowsing is no guarantee it is either a natural or a godly practice. Even the innocent use of divination* may have consequences. And "there are also the *results* of innocent involvement, unavoidable because of the law of cause and effect [e.g., Galatians 6:7]. All of the disastrous results, physical, mental, and spiritual, are recounted in Dr. Kurt Koch's case histories. These may be suffered by the innocent as well as the informed" (674:2).

If dowsing is a form of spiritistic divination* and forbidden in the Bible, then to practice it is certainly a sin requiring repentance (see "Biblical Prohibitions" later in this section). Christian dowsers need to remember that there are consequences to sin. While some may have innocent flirtations with the occult and never be harmed because of God's protection or other reasons, we should also expect that any genuine Christian involved in dowsing will, sooner or later, come under divine conviction. Biblical history, personal experience, and the previous illustration of the pastor who repudiated dowsing, all show that God will actively work to remove His people from sinful activities. Unfortunately, our citation of Mr. Kline reveals the deceptive nature of the practice and how some Christians remain confused over the issue. We believe that Christians who endorse dowsing and teach it to other Christians should seriously weigh the consequences if it can be demonstrated that dowsing is biblically prohibited. We also think that Christians concerned about dowsing should be able to answer the arguments of its Christian promoters. In the material that follows we will show why the biblical arguments for dowsing are spurious and that dowsing is an occult practice which the Bible forbids. For Christians who believe their Bibles, this should settle the issue of participation in dowsing once and for all.

## CLAIMS FOR BIBLICAL DOWSING

Christian dowsers often attempt to justify dowsing by appealing to the Bible. For example, we are told that Moses was a dowser. He carried a "dowsing rod" (his staff) which he used to seek out water when he struck the rock (Exodus 17:6-7). Jacob's well in John 4:6, and the well at Beer, which "the nobles of the people dug, with the scepter and with their staffs" (Numbers 21:16-18 NASB) are also said to illustrate that dowsing is a biblical practice.

Such claims are false because there is not a single biblical incident where a godly person engages in dowsing on God's command. Any alleged references to dowsing being promoted in Scripture result from faulty interpretation. In Exodus 17:6-7, Moses' action had nothing to do with dowsing. In Hebrew, the word for "staff" reveals that it was a normal walking staff, not an implement for magical purposes like a dowser's rod (cf. Hosea 4:12). And when he struck the rock with his staff, he did not dowse for water over land. Perhaps it goes without saying, but a large rock seems a particularly poor place to dowse for water. Furthermore, this was not a dowser haphazardly seeking out water; it was a prophet obeying God's command, and the result was a miracle far beyond any dowser's power.

Incidents where the Hebrew people dug wells are also misinterpreted by dowsers. John 4:6 doesn't mention dowsing. Dowsers assume that merely because a well is mentioned in Scripture it was probably discovered by dowsing. In Numbers 21:16-18, the text implies that the people dug their well in a normal fashion. It never says they dowsed for water. The mention of their staffs and scepters is only to emphasize that the authority of the princes was present when the well was dug.

Unfortunately, Christian dowsers who think that the Bible teaches dowsing treat Scripture in the same manner as religious cultists who distort it to justify their own particular beliefs and practices (1522). For example, Mormonism teaches that the Bible is the Word of God "in so far as it is translated correctly." Biblical passages that reject Mormon doctrines are said to be "mistranslated," even though in 160 years the

Mormon Church has never supplied evidence of a single alleged mistranslation in favor of Mormon theology (891).

Dowsers employ the same ruse. Passages that refer to digging wells or searching for water—but never mention dowsing—are said to be "mistranslated." If they were "properly" translated, they would have employed the term "dowsing": "We believe that Moses was a dowser because of the Old Testament [record] of his striking the rock and getting water for the Children of Israel, once . . . he had led them out of Egypt and into the Promised Land. We believe that there was a mis-translation, that Moses was a dowser, found a spot and said 'Dig'" (647:58).

## BIBLICAL PROHIBITIONS

There is only one direct reference to dowsing by name in the entire Bible, and in that reference the practice is condemned by God: "My people consult their wooden idol, and their diviner's wand informs them; for a spirit of harlotry has led them astray, and they have played the harlot, departing from their God" (Hosea 4:12 NASB). This passage teaches that those who practice dowsing are being led astray by "a spirit of prostitution," and that they have "departed from their God." And, as we are noting throughout this book, the Bible condemns divination* by name on numerous occasions. Because dowsing is clearly a form of divination, it is also rejected by God on this basis. God tells His people, "There shall not be found among you anyone who . . . uses divination . . ." (Deuteronomy 18:10 NASB).

In Leviticus and other books, God's people are warned: "Do not practice divination or sorcery" (Leviticus 19:26), or to not listen to the occultists in the land: "Do not listen to . . . your diviners, your interpreters of dreams, your mediums or your sorcerers. . . . They prophesy lies" (Jeremiah 27:9-10). Thus, "Do not let the prophets and diviners among you deceive you" (Jeremiah 29:8). Nevertheless, the rebellious Israelites "forsook all the commands of the LORD their God. . . . They practiced divination and sorcery and sold themselves to do evil in the eyes of the LORD, provoking him to anger" (2 Kings 17:16-

17). In the New Testament, when a slave girl was "possessed with a spirit of divination" (Acts 16:16 KJV), the apostle Paul cast out the evil spirit and her power was lost.

The reason for our concern here should be obvious. Christians who practice dowsing are clearly endorsing a form of divination, and, as such, are causing division and deception within the church. According to the Bible, such individuals are to be avoided on two counts: 1) the command to avoid those who cause dissension (2 Timothy 3:5), and 2) the command to avoid those who practice divination (Deuteronomy 18:9-12).

Also note how divination is related to sorcery. Consider the definition and verbatim references supplied under the term "sorcery" listed in *Nave's Topical Bible:*

SORCERY, divination by an alleged assistance of evil spirits. Forbidden, Lev. 19:26-28, 31; 20:5; Deut. 18:9-14. Denounced, Isa. 8:19; Mal. 3:5.

Practiced: By the Egyptians, Isa. 19:3, 11, 12; by the magicians, Ex. 7:11, 22; 8:7, 18; by Balaam, Num. 22:6; 23:23 with chapters 22; 23; by Jezebel, 2 Kin. 9:22; by the Ninevites, Nah. 3:4, 5; by the Babylonians, Isa. 47:9-13; Ezek. 21:21, 22; Dan. 2:2, 10, 27; by Belshazzar, Dan. 5:7, 15; by Simon Magus, Acts 8:9, 11; by Elymans, Acts 13:8; by vagabond Jews, Acts 19:13; by sons of Sceva, Acts 19:14-15; by astrologers, Jer. 10:2; Mic. 3:6, 7; by false prophets, Jr. 14:14; 27:9; 29:8-9; Ezek. 11:6-9; 22-28; Matt. 24:24.

Messages of, false, Ezek. 21:29; Zech. 10:2; Mic. 3:7. Belongs to the works of the flesh, Gal. 5:20. Wickedness of, 1 Sam. 15-22. Vainness of, Isa. 44:25. Punishment for, Ex. 22:18; Lev. 20:27; Deut. 13:4. Divining by familiar spirits, Lev. 20:27; 1 Chr. 10:13; 2 Chr. 33:6; Isa. 8:19; 19:3; 29:4; by entrails, Ezek. 21:21; by images, 2 Kin. 23:24; Ezek. 21:21; by rods, Hos. 4:12.

Saul consulted the Witch of Endor, 1 Sam. 28:7-25. Books of, destroyed, Acts 19:19 (p. 1294).

In light of this clear biblical rejection of dowsing, let us give one final example of how Christian dowsers seek to justify their practice. We will cite minister Norman Evans' article "Dowsing:

Its Biblical Background" from *The American Dowser.*

Reverend Evans finds it difficult to admit that dowsing is not encouraged and taught in Scripture. Rather, he attempts to show that it *is* taught, although "hidden in Biblical references" and "not plainly evident at the first reading" (619:70). He quotes Hosea 4:12 in *defense* of his view: "My people ask counsel at their stocks, and their staff declareth unto them. . ." (619:75). But, somehow, he fails to quote the remainder of the verse: "a spirit of harlotry has led them astray, and they have played the harlot, departing from their God."

Undaunted, he argues that "Abraham, Isaac and Jacob were undoubtedly dowsers" (619:73). He also classifies dowsing as one of the gifts of the Holy Spirit. "I would be very happy if Paul had listed 'dowsing.' But he did not. . . . However, Paul mentions 'knowledge.' I shall classify dowsing within the gift of knowledge" (619:77). He concludes: "As a Christian my gifts are a part of my offering when I yield myself to my Savior. Love is the way in which gifts are to be used. . . . The fact remains that these are gifts of the Spirit, they are still given, and they are relevant to this scientific, materialistic age. Let no one say that a gift that is not understood is inherently evil; only the wrong use of any gift is evil" (619:78).

Reverend Evans, however, never comes even remotely close to showing that dowsing can be considered as the biblical gift of knowledge. His entire argument is spurious. Activities that are clearly condemned biblically can never be used "in love." Would God ever accept those other activities condemned along with divination in Deuteronomy 18:9-12—witchcraft, necromancy, and human sacrifice—merely because the one using them claimed he did so "in love"? Isn't love clearly defined in Scripture (e.g., 1 Corinthians 13:1-8)? For example, "Love does not delight in evil but rejoices with the truth" (v. 6). And isn't the first duty of man to love God above all else and then one's fellowman? Can we say we love God when we disobey His commandments? "This is love for God: to obey his commands" (1 John 5:3). Can we say we love others when we assist them to adopt practices that God condemns as sinful? And why did Evans appeal to the Bible as an authority in one phrase of the verse and reject the next phrase?

Unfortunately, most Christian and even many non-Christian dowsers maintain that their "gift" is from God. One says, "Dowsing is a special talent given by God to all mankind" (620:102). Another states that whether it is used by Christians or witchdoctors, it is a practice requiring faith in a controlling power: "Not that I believe dowsing is reserved exclusively to Christians. There are good [skilled] dowsers in the persons of witchdoctors in Africa, but, it is my belief that anyone not believing in a controlling Spirit, call him God or what you will—can never be a dowser" (621:34).

Even the official "Dowser's Prayer," which hangs on the wall of the American Society of Dowsers in Danville, Vermont, accepts that dowsing is "a gift of God." "The Dowser's Prayer" reads: "Lord, guide my hands, enhance my sensitivity, and bless my purpose that I may be an instrument of Your power and glory in locating what is searched for" (622:169).

In conclusion, those who practice dowsing and are members of evangelical churches should repent and forsake their sin; if they do not, church elders should discipline them. This should be true for any Christian who is living in disobedience to God by engaging in psychic practices. The devil has long sought to confuse spiritual gifts and psychic abilities within the church in order to gain a foothold. The many "Christian" parapsychology societies, which define psychic powers as the "gifts of the Spirit," are a case in point.

If we accept dowsing as a gift from God, there is no logical basis on which to reject other psychic abilities—they too, then, must be given similar approval by the church.

But before we show that dowsing is an occult practice, we must first indicate that dowsing is neither a scientific practice nor a natural human ability (such as the ability anyone has to learn how to drive a car or to cook a meal). If it were either a scientific practice or a normal human ability, anyone with proper training and skill could dowse successfully. Because even experienced dowsers cannot do this, the technique cannot be considered a natural human ability.

## SCIENTIFIC TESTING

Former American Society of Dowsers president Gordon MacLean is correct when he points out, "The precise cause of the dowsing reaction is no better understood today than it was in ancient times" (634:6). Yet dowsers often claim that their practice is scientific. They do so despite many other dowsers who correctly affirm, "Dowsing is witchery," and that it "violates every principle of known science" (635:103).

In fact, universal scientific testing of dowsing disproves claims that dowsing merely represents a natural or learned sensitivity to radiations or other physical phenomena. For example, controlled tests conducted by famous magician and psychic debunker James Randi failed to provide any evidence that dowsers have a special ability to find water. Like other people claiming psychic powers, when their dowsing abilities are tested scientifically, they fail the tests (636:16-20/640: 329-33/641:34-37).

No one can deny that dowsing abilities have been examined in many countries around the world, or that the results debunk the scientific claims of dowsers. Tests in Australia (641), the Netherlands, New Zealand, and elsewhere prove that dowsing does not work on the basis of its stated scientific claims:

Although dowsers have compiled an impressive record of pseudo-scientific data, the mechanism of their art is not clear to themselves.... In 1954, a test in the Netherlands exposed dowsers to magnetic fields which were all stronger than the natural magnetic field of the earth. None of the test persons was able to indicate when a magnetic field was switched on or when it was off.

Here is the result of a controlled experiment with 75 dowsers in New Zealand: "No agreement, [and the] same results could be obtained with guessing."

Equally disappointing are the results of a study conducted by Professor Gassmann at the renowned *Federal Technical Institute* of Zurich, Switzerland. . . . Sixteen well-known and experienced dowsers volunteered for the test. Among them were 11 engineers and technicians, one of them even a university professor. To find a strong radiation source, Professor Gassmann sent the 16 dowsers to 7 fields and asked them to localize the underground water-pipe running under each of them. The largest pipe carried as much as 4000 gallons per minute.

When the drawings of the 16 dowsers were compared, the results were shattering:

Despite intensive research we did not find any criteria that would allow us to accept the findings of any of the dowsers as accurate or even as more reliable than the others. The large pipe was not found by any of them, several dowsers reported water pipes in places where there were none (2:99-100).

In 1984, Michael Martin, professor of philosophy at Boston University, tested Paul Sevigny, then president of the American Society of Dowsers. He reports that even after 40 trials, Sevigny performed at levels worse than chance (637:139). After Martin reviewed his results, as well as those of James Randi, plus a scholarly overview of the evidence for dowsing provided by Evon Vogt and Ray Hyman (638), he concluded, "The available evidence can be succinctly summarized: When dowsers perform under controlled conditions, they do not do better than one would expect by chance" (637:140).

The negative scientific results have caused some materialistic proponents of dowsing to attempt to explain its actual successes by natural means. In this case, dowsers would not be engaging in any kind of miraculous ability, and there would be some kind of rational explanation. For example, a common "natural" explanation involves the concept of "ideomotor action," or the influence of the subconscious mind on muscle activities. Allegedly, this will lead to the manipulation of the dowser's stick. However, the theory of muscular action is untenable, as one dowser points out: "Many people, not dowsers, insist that the dowsing rod moves because of 'unconscious muscular action,' on the part of the dowser. The dowser says that he feels the pull on the stick and cannot understand how his muscles can be working both ways at one time" (1072:101).

We would agree that in some cases natural explanations may account for some of the more mundane phenomena of dowsing, but this is also true for most categories of occult practice. When, for whatever reason, supernatural agencies are not present, supernatural phenomena are not produced, and the practitioner can only be left to his own abilities. This may lead to attempts at "cold reading," fraud, or wish fulfillment, especially if the practitioner has a financial or other personal stake in the outcome, such as his reputation.

But the critics who argue that nothing supernatural is ever involved in dowsing are wrong. Scientific or rationalistic explanations for dowsing phenomena simply do not do justice to the facts, nor are the arguments against dowsing in books such as Korem and Meier's *The Fakers* entirely convincing. When supernatural phenomena are present, spiritistic activity is the most logical explanation for the results of dowsing. And when dowsing is practiced, such an influence may be present whether dowsing attempts are successful or not.

Given the historical and contemporary evidence linking spiritism to divination,* all forms of successful divination that cannot be explained by natural causes, such as fraud, guessing, or coincidence, are most logically functions of spiritistic powers. As a form of divination, dowsing can be no different.

Ben Hester observes that in 500 years no one has been able to offer any physical explanation for dowsing (514:49). "A careful examination of the claims of dowsing as a truly physical phenomenon has shown no basis in fact. This same examination has also shown inconsistencies, contradictions and gross undependability in whatever [proposed] new classification it might fall" (514:159).

In other words, dowsing carries the same dilemma faced by the parapsychologist and his study of persons with psychic abilities: There is a genuine power, but the source of the power and its method of operation are uncontrollable and scientifically undemonstrable. Dowsing abilities are like psychic abilities in their unreliability and in the repeated failure of experimental testing to confirm that they operate on any known physical basis. Rationalists conclude that because dowsing cannot pass the standards of controlled scientific testing that dowsing powers do

not exist. But this fails to account for the nature of dowsing itself:

> Dowsing is an entirely subjective act depending on such things as the dowser's will, frame of mind, emotional reaction to such external stimuli as public expectancy of failure, ridicule, condescension and even the factor of time. Skeptical testers have consistently refused to allow these factors to be considered in controlled testing. Yet, personal contact with dowsers reveals the fact that this sort of human experience cannot be forced into the objective, scientific framework. . . . [T]he expert dowser's personal record (not the public test record) shows their successes beating the odds of chance. Further, dowsing cannot be scientifically tested without dowser participation—a mechanical device or setup is useless. . . .

> In addition, the dowsing fraternity is comprised of a majority of unexperienced learners or the inept, with only a few experts. It is evident that a true picture of dowsing can be found only by reliance on these experts. . . .

> Finally, unshakable belief in the act is an absolute necessity. . . . If this belief is shaken, the dowser *cannot* dowse. The device will not react (1511:1-3).

The reason dowsing powers operate like psychic abilities is because they *are* psychic (i.e., spiritistic) abilities. They are not natural, latent human capacities. Nevertheless, a genuine occult power that operates in dowsing may lead scientific investigators to inadvertently find themselves converts to occult practice:

> This is a perfect illustration of the curious dilemma in which the scientist is caught. . . . Once he makes the step of observing that dowsing, for instance, does work, he is faced with an irresistible need to find out why. At that moment he is in deep trouble, for every bit of his scientific training demands that this "why" must be logically and physically explained. To do this, he has to break one of the most important commandments of science, that of objectivity. He cannot consider all of the observable facts and make them fit in a physical picture. He has crossed over into the emotional. Then if he has learned to dowse, himself, as most investigators

do, he has entered the world of all-out subjectivity. He is lost to his peers. This is exactly the condition of the physicists writing in scientific journals on the subject of dowsing. A perfect example is Dr. Zaboj V. Harvalik, perhaps the foremost scientific investigator of dowsing in the western world. Quoting Christopher Bird again, on page 263 of *The Divining Hand* in an entire chapter devoted to Harvalik, Bird states, "During the ongoing process of his research, Harvalik himself has become so expert in remote, map, and information dowsing, the physics of which he cannot begin to explain. . . ." Two paragraphs later Bird, adds, "The persisting question of whether dowsing is a physical or psychic art continues to trouble Harvalik." However, one would never guess from the positive public statements made by Harvalik, that he has this reservation (514:93-94).

## OCCULT ASPECTS

From ancient times, dowsing has been considered an occult practice and often defined as a form of witchcraft. The common descriptive terms "witching" and "water witching" reveal how closely the taint of witchcraft has remained. Occultist and dowser Christopher Bird, the author of a number of standard New Age texts on dowsing, such as *The Divining Hand*, calls it "one of the world's oldest occult arts" (1071:56). Referring to the ancient mystery traditions, dowser Erwin states, in *A History of Dowsing and Energy Relationship*, "The teaching of mysteries, or psychic functions, which predates the dawn of Christianity, is significant in that it taught dowsing as a psychic technique. The dowser was regarded as a highly intuitive or illuminated being, who achieved this level of awareness through dedicated study and practice of the mysteries" (626:12). Historically, the connection of dowsing to the occult is one reason the church has labeled dowsing as a work of the devil (514:41), as even many dowsers will concede (623:41/626:12; cf. 813:187).

Presidents of dowsing societies, and other dowsing practitioners, freely confess that dowsing is a psychic or occult ability, not a scientific practice (1076). Not surprisingly, book reviews in dowsing magazines, and booktables at dowsing

conventions, are replete with occult topics. In *Dowsing: The Psi Connection*, Hitching provides an extended discussion about the "natural kinship" that dowsers claim "with their ancient predecessors," such as shamans* or witch doctors—those who contact the spirit world and are taken over by them to secure supernatural information and power. A number of illustrations are given from pagan tribal life, noting the connections to dowsing (623:237-42).

Dowsers also have certain characteristics in common with mediums (1075:132-40). For example, they may suffer something similar to the exhaustion that mediums experience from their seances (623:169). Other dowsers have stated that "the first two stages of yoga training [sensory withdrawal, absence of consciousness] . . . could equally as well have been taken from any dowsing manual" (623:243-44).

Because the issue of the true nature of dowsing is so important for the church, we will supply 11 reasons why we are convinced dowsing should be classified as an occult, spiritistic power, and not as a normal human ability. First, the following common characteristics of dowsing practice reveal its true nature.

*Altered Consciousness*

Most dowsers enter an altered state of consciousness or a trance when dowsing. Dowsers admit that a particular "mood" is vital in order for dowsing to work. As in occult practice generally, the trance state does not need to be deep; a light altered state of consciousness is usually all that is necessary. The purpose of these states is always the same: to remove the "hindrance" of the conscious mind. As one dowser points out, "Dowsers, like psychics, must get the conscious [mind] out of the way" (626:83). Because this aspect of dowsing is often not recognized by those outside the practice, we will cite several descriptions as illustrations:

Any person can be trained to program himself or herself into an altered state of consciousness. In other words, any person can achieve the level of consciousness needed to use a dowsing instrument—and to use it successfully! . . . The sensitivity of the dowser, whether a field dowser or a psychic dowser, seems to be achieved by the trance state of the induction process used by dowsers, that is, the dowser must focus his or her mind on one thought only, which automatically cuts off contact with all other sensory input (626:26).

When he starts to dowse, he goes through a marked change in his state of consciousness. A detached air of concentration comes over him (623:182-83).

The secret of good dowsing . . . is a curious state of mind. . . . Dowsing has been compared to a mild state of hypnosis, or trance, or meditation (623:79).

It [the altered state] can become the most critical part of the dowsing process. . . . How does one know that he is "in the mood"? There is no simple way to describe this condition. As the dowser grasps his device he wipes everything out of his mind but the dowsing question. He gives himself over to the mystery of dowsing with confidence. He comes to recognize this state of mind, this attitude toward dowsing. While an experienced dowser cannot always bring himself into this condition, he can recognize when he cannot. If he cannot get "in the mood" he should not start to dowse (630:178).

. . . The dowser enters into a light trance as he or she becomes more involved with the person, place or thing being sought, and less involved with his or her own thoughts. I was once startled by someone when I was map dowsing and was quite surprised to discover how deeply I had become involved in a state of trance. It was almost as though I had left the place where I was sitting and was at the location I was dowsing. Upon being drawn back abruptly to my regular conscious state I was visibly shaken. I was trembling inside (628:70).

Some of our best practitioners go into a state of high concentration when they dowse. . . . Others state the object, then blank out their minds and let the rods take over (634:27).

In other words, anyone can go through the motions, but to be successful at dowsing an altered state of consciousness* is something "every dowser finds necessary" (623:107). This may be either a light trance or something very profound, depending on the individual dowser, his years of experience, and his submission to the process—common facts relevant to psychics and mediums

as well. True dowsers, then, do not just dowse; they must be in a respectful and receptive state, they must request information, and they must be in a type of trance.

There are exceptions, of course, as there are in other psychic activities. The spirits, if they desire, can choose to operate outside a person's altered state, as when they dictate words while the medium is in a normal state of consciousness. Nevertheless, the altered state is clearly a common method for receiving information.

*Psychic Ablilities*

Dowsing develops psychic abilities. As dowsers progress in the practice, many of them discover that they are gradually developing psychic powers. That dowsing can develop psychic abilities, such as telepathy and clairvoyance, is mentioned both by critics (514:106) and by many practicing dowsers (651). Some dowsers say that dowsing practice should be considered an actual program of psychic development. Thus, "recognition of dowsing as the easiest way for most people to discover and demonstrate ESP in themselves is gradually being accepted" (634:5). A member of the British and American Society of Dowsers comments:

> Over many years I find the [dowsing] methods used by me have, in the course of their progress, transferred to Psychometry and now Astral projection, the latter two methods projecting me to all parts of the World, no matter how remote (652:8-9).

Hitching observes:

> There is a shadowy, almost nonexistent barrier between the results of map dowsing as practiced by Bill Lewis and the kind of out-of-body experiences that occur so often in the literature of parapsychology. . . . [T]here is no doubt that many dowsers, consciously or unconsciously, make use of the experience, now generally known as an OBE. The Maine dowser Bob Ater, at the beginning of this book, imagined that he was "hovering like a bird" while he mapdowsed for the two reporters from *The Saturday Evening Post*. John Shelley, formerly president

**181**

of the American Society of Dowsers, became so sensitive that he was able to discard his pendulum and pick up information directly from a site; he reached the point where he could answer telephone requests for help in finding water by visualizing the place to be dowsed and then giving a detailed description to the caller as to where the well should be sunk. There is a noteworthy account in a 1960 issue of the *Journal of the British Society of Dowsers,* in which map dowsing, an OBE and site dowsing all combine in one incident (623:204-5).

Dowsing today ... is uniquely able to link us into this other dimension of energy to provide practical and personal proof of the existence of the paranormal.... Dowsing may also be important in helping to overcome the widespread nervous skepticism about the occult.... [I]n its own way, it is less dramatic a method of gaining access to another world and a new understanding of the mysteries of consciousness: The world of Psi, you might say, at your fingertips (623:264-66).

The fact that dowsing can develop psychic abilities associates dowsing with the world of the occult and spiritism, not science (904:11-22; cf. ref. 278).

*Faith, Respect, and Interaction*

Dowsing requires faith, respect, and a personal interaction and response with the rod. Raymond Willey observes that "you must be prepared to treat this faculty of dowsing with respect" (624:6). Hester remarks:

Anything that causes the dowser to question the act, or to lose "faith" in it, immediately renders him incapable of performing. He can get no answers from his device, or method. We witnessed such a circumstance. An expert dowser was in great demand, and was doing an important job of water witching when we appeared on the scene to interview him. He was curious about our interest in dowsing and about the psychic aspects, of which he seemed to be entirely ignorant. He called us the next day to tell us he had become perturbed about the sorcery aspect of the act, and when he had returned to his day's dowsing, he found that his ability had left him. We have found repeatedly that a mental "set" or faith is an absolute necessity to successful dowsing (514:57-58).

Many additional illustrations of the need for respect and reverence of the implements could be cited from those who use other forms of divination,* such as Ouija boards,* the *I Ching,*\* rune dice,* tarot cards,* ceremonial magic, and other forms of the occult. But if faith and respect are required in dowsing, some people may wonder how dowsing can work for skeptics. The truth is that many occult practices have worked for skeptics, and the result has often been their conversion to occultism. The spirits who operate behind these methods may seek to influence the skeptic. And after "conversion," the spirits demand faith and respect in the implements they work through. If these implements are not given proper reverence, the practitioner may suffer the spirit's discipline or wrath. Contemporary occult practice and the history of idolatry are replete with examples. At a national astrology convention that Weldon attended, a practitioner of crystal work told him the disturbing manner in which the "spirit of the crystal" reacted to his "disrespect" for the crystal. He claimed that the spirit attempted to choke the life from him and almost succeeded. Missiologist G. W. Peters states, "It has been experienced that the transportation of an idol has actually brought serious physical disturbances, destruction and death to the new locality and community" (817:200; cf. 242:141-42).

Nevertheless, many indications exist that a *personal* entity operates through the dowsing implement. For example, the dowser must ask specific questions of his rod or pendulum, which is why all the "how-to" books tell the dowser, "[T]alk to your stick." In reading the accounts of dowsers' personal communications with the supposedly impersonal "force" of dowsing, one is immediately struck by the similarity to Ouija boards* and other forms of psychic oracles that require "yes" or "no" answers. The Ouija board itself, of course, is merely wood, just like the dowser's stick. Yet there is often a living power behind it, an independent, personal entity that demands you to *inquire of it* if you wish success.

Significantly, Willey states of dowsing: "One of its most dramatic features is its 'selectivity.' This means dowsing supplies an answer to a *specific* question.... (You have learned how a *yes* and *no* answer is obtained from dowsing devices, often obtaining answers to questions which cannot be answered from other sources)" (624:67, 111). Another dowser makes the following a universal necessity: "Always decide precisely what you seek and ask for it in unmistakable terms" (634:7; cf. 814:108).

Here is an illustration showing just how dependent people can become on communicating with the stick:

A world wide method of getting answers from the forked stick is to choose a pattern of nods. Holding the stick firmly as possible, questions are asked that can be answered in "yes," "no," "how far," "how deep," etc. [questions], as long as questions can be made this simple. The stick nods in answer. Worldwide witness to this phenomenon is that the stick moves so strongly it cannot be controlled. The historic dowser, Aymar traced four criminals from Lyon to Toulon and to the quay from which three of them had escaped by ship—all by answers from his stick. We watched a water witcher who located a spot over an underground stream. Then by habit he stood quietly over the spot while his stick began to nod. It stopped at 83 and he announced that we would find the stream at that depth (he was right). . . .

Twenty years later when we decided we must drill for a water well, we hired another witcher, not telling him about the earlier witching. He spent some time going over our acreage hunting, finally zeroing in on the exact spot located so long before. We knew because we had marked that original spot with a large rock. This dowser used a heavy curved stick he held firmly at the ends. Over the water it twisted downward in his hands which did not move. He then stood quietly, his eyes closed and holding the stick out over the spot. After several seconds he turned and told us we would find a large stream at 83 feet. The two dowsers could not have known each other. Our man was an official of the Southern California Gas Company, while the old man, now dead many years, was a well driller. Both of them were right. We hit a large stream (40 gallons per minute) at exactly 83 feet in a country where no water was available except as found in a stream (1511:10-11).

Dowsers are thus taught to talk to the power, but one can only ask why, and wonder to whom are they talking. Why would a truly impersonal force need to be conversed with? Why does it require reverence? How can it "demand" this? Unless, of course, one is really dealing with something personal like a spirit entity. Note the following statement by a dowser who attempts to give the practice Jesus' endorsement:

"ASK AND YE SHALL RECEIVE." Be very specific about what you ask for. Include names and times in your questions if you know them. . . .

Whom do you ask? *No one knows that for sure.* Ask God if you wish. Ask your hand or your dowsing instrument or your map. The classic statement of Jesus concerning asking and receiving, with which we are all familiar simply says "ASK" (628:70, emphasis added).

No dowser living knows who or what they are really asking help from. One would think this might make the average dowser, especially the Christian dowser, rather cautious.

So far we have seen indications that the force behind this practice is personal, intelligent, and desirous of human interaction. Perhaps this is one reason Martin Luther referred to dowsing as a form of idolatry (514:15-16; 623:41). If men were only dealing with an impersonal force, it would never require *respect*, or *faith*, or *personal* communication. But aren't these responses exactly what spirit guides require and demand of their human mediums? In the remaining eight items, we will show even more clearly how dowsing is linked to the world of spiritism and the occult.

*Linkage to Occult Practices*

Dowsing is often linked with other forms of occult practice. For example, dowsers frequently employ occult pendulums and radionic devices (815). This is why dowsing societies routinely sell a wide variety of pendulums and other occult implements, such as "aura indicators" (815). In addition, dowsers have made connections between dowsing and many other occult practices, such as astral projection, remote viewing, and, as noted earlier, shamanism* and yoga* (623:130, 204-05,243-44).

Below we will document the dowser's dependence on one particular occult instrument, the pendulum. In fact, rod dowsing is so often linked to pendulum work that the term "rod and pendulum" is standard dowsing nomenclature.

For the American Society of Dowsers (ASD) and other dowsing societies, the rod and pendulum are joined like bread and butter. Occult pendulums are routinely sold by the ASD. The standard "supply list" cites: "pendulum power kits," the "Alden Titanium Pendulum," a bullet-shaped chrome pendulum, a "puget Magnetic Pendulum," a chrome pendulum with a radionic "witness" chamber, as well as marbleized, clear, and black ball pendulums. The ASD also sells "PSI sponders," "energy wheels," and the "Alden Super Sensitive Diviner," which combines the L-Rod pendulum and an "aura indicator" (683). All such implements, however, are useless radionics devices: The psychic power comes from the spirit who works through the operator, not through the device. This explains why the device can eventually be dispensed with (1071).**

Dowsing also makes use of "the witness." A "witness" is a piece of hair, clothing, blood, or other personal belonging or object from which psychic information is desired. *The American Dowser* states:

> Dowsers use witnesses and samples mostly when looking for things in nature, water, ore, oil or gas. A dowser may have a number of small glass tubes or vials that he fastens on the tip of his fork. Others hold such a tube in one of the hands that grasps the fork or holds the pendulum . . . Pendulums are sometimes made hollow, so samples may be placed inside them. . . . A sample is a small amount of the material, liquid or solid, for which the dowser is searching. A witness can be some article used by a person who is missing. . . . Witnesses and samples can be used with any dowsing method, Field Dowsing, Remote Dowsing, Map Dowsing and Information Dowsing (1077:118-19).*

Nevertheless, observe how easily the dowsing rod and pendulum are joined together. *The American Dowser* states: "You can talk to your friends about dowsing and our Society now with the confidence that every one that you discover that has the dowsing faculty will be able to get his dowsing rods and pendulums quickly and get instruction books to tell him or her more about using them"

(653:3). The Society also maintains contact with other organizations that specialize in radionics and psychometry, e.g., the ASD is the American sister organization of the German Society of Dowsers and Pendulum Practitioners (650:68).

Finally, almost all water dowsers are "sensitive" to the pendulum, which is why a majority of dowsers actually use them (1079). "About ten years ago, an enthusiastic friend got me interested in dowsing and, many times since then, my pendulum has helped me make up an undecided mind. Sometimes I have gone contrary to the pendulum's advice and have been sorry" (655:191).

*Hereditary Transfer*

Dowsing abilities may be hereditarily transmitted. Psychic abilities are received either by a process of training and instruction (i.e., by psychic development), by direct transfer from a person with occult powers, or inherited from their forebears, apparently as part of God's judgment on the practice of sorcery (1069).

During his life, Dr. Kurt Koch had counseled over ten thousand people involved in the occult

---

**One article on dowsing points out that, like the dowsing implement itself, the witness is also "entirely dispensable" and therefore "scientific" explanations linking the witness to alleged "radiations" are unconvincing: "With the worthy intention of attempting to place radiesthesia on a scientific basis and of proving that it has no link with so-called occult science, radiesthesists have attempted to explain their practice in a purely physical way: by holding that everything radiates, everything vibrates, and that these radiations or waves cause the dowsing rod to react or the pendulum to oscillate. This point of view has led radiesthesists to bestow great meaning upon exactly what kind of pendulum they use and to develop many different types, some of which are very complex in design. It has led to the use of myriad "witnesses" or samples of the material sought. It has resulted in the fabrication of instruments incorporating all kinds of electrical components, whether condensers, resistors, radio tubes, or others, in the hope of amplifying the radiations themselves or compensating for insufficient sensitivity in individual operators. . . . None of these specific pendulums, none of these complex instruments is deemed indispensable. . . . Nor has any consensus about the application of a method confirmed the vibratory theory. . . . Witnesses are entirely dispensable and have no utility other than a psychological one, that of materializing the thought of the dowser-operator" (1078:13).

(642:188). He reports: "In the field of heredity, a coherence persisting into the third and fourth generations is seen in the case of active occultists. These effects are thus no less persistent in their hold on succeeding generations than those of alcoholism, syphilis, and psychoses" (273:186). Koch also reveals:

> Psychic powers are mostly found in proximity to sins of sorcery. If the forefathers up to the third or even fourth generation were spiritists or if they practiced magic and other forms of occult activity, the descendants are usually psychic. ... Sensitivity to the rod and ability to make a pendulum react are psychic powers. I have investigated the family histories of many people who have a psychic disposition. The gift of using the rod or discovering secret things by means of the pendulum can be acquired in three ways: by heredity, by transference from a powerful worker with the occult or by experimenting with magic formulas as described in occult books. ... The idea of some theologians that psychic powers can be purified and then used in the service of God's kingdom is unscriptural. This is shown by the story of the fortune-teller of Philippi in Acts 16:16-18. If a Christian uses psychic powers, he is committing sin and is in need of forgiveness (642:188).

In other words, the dowsing ability is received in the same three ways that psychic powers in general are received: 1) by months and even years of instruction and practice; 2) by direct transfer; 3) by inheritance. The first way of receiving dowsing power—by instruction and practice—is widely acknowledged by dowsers. Raymond Willey states concerning the second way—inheritance: "Those of you who have the faculty may be able to learn that you have inherited it. It is known to often pass from grandfather to grandson, from mother to son, from father to daughter" (624:6). Another dowser mentions his belief that "one has to be born" a dowser: "Either one can dowse or one cannot" (648:104). The third manner of receiving dowsing powers is from direct transference from teacher to student. This may occur in a similar manner to which Eastern gurus* and spiritistic channelers can transmit "psychic energies" into their students,

making them psychic (see Yoga, Eastern Gurus, Meditation).

All of this continues to reveal that dowsing is an occult ability, not a natural one, let alone a scientific practice.

*Christian Hindrances to Dowsing*

Christian responses to dowsing, such as conversion and prayer, hinder dowsing powers. Conversion to Christ may mean loss of the dowsing ability altogether, and prayer may interrupt or prevent the dowsing process. Hester refers to "case histories of where prayer stopped the dowsing rod cold" (514:118). Hester and Koch both refer to cases where conversion to Christ or prayer ended or hindered the ability to dowse (514:58,188/642:188-91):

> Another case of loss of ability seemed to be traced to an acceptance of Christian belief. We wrote to a doctor whom we had known here as an accomplished dowser. He had moved out of state and we had not heard from him for about three years. He seemed surprised at our inquiry, and he stated that he had lost his ability to dowse when he had been converted to Christianity and had become a "born-again-Christian." This puzzled him until one day as he was reading his Bible, he ran across the biblical proscription against divination (514:58).

Of course, conversion to Christ may not always remove the ability. As is true with other psychic powers, sometimes they are removed totally, sometimes they linger. A number of variables seem responsible for the outcome, including extent of involvement, family history in the occult, sincerity of conversion, the degree of repudiation of the dowsing art, the extent of informed discipleship, and prayer for the person after conversion (1069). And all of this reveals an additional link to spiritism. Regeneration (John 3:3-8; 6:63; 2 Corinthians 5:17) and answers to prayer (Proverbs 15:8,29; 1 John 5:14) deal with the activity of God; when these activities counteract certain practices, then these other practices cannot be activities of God, or else God would be working against Himself.

We would expect the activity of demons to be hindered by conversion or prayer. Jesus, after all, came "to destroy the devil's work" (1 John 3:8). Christian actions may hinder other psychic activity as well, but to think a neutral or natural power would operate so selectively is simply not credible.

Christian dowsers often reply that they have "prayed" about using the device and so feel that it is okay. But does one ever pray about committing the sin of divination? If dowsing is condemned in Scripture (Hosea 4:12; Deuteronomy 18:9-12), there is no need to pray about using the practice. If one is ignorant of the biblical prohibition, that is one thing. But if a person knows that God has warned against divination and then prays about whether it is permissible, this reflects doubt about God's Word and is an insult to Him (James 1:5-8). This is the real problem of much Christian dowsing: unbelief or rebellion. One rationalizes or rejects God's Word and engages in the practice anyway. Is it surprising that Christians can be led astray when they do not believe and trust what God has said in the Bible?

About Christian dowsers, Hester writes:

We know of Christian dowsers who have used it as a tool for their own use and to help others for almost a lifetime. It is impossible to accuse them of being occultists, yet they have been using an occult method in ignorance and innocence....

Then there are Christian dowsers who do know, but they find the desire, or necessity, great enough to take the chance. They may never experience any inkling of occult involvement unless they become conscience stricken and desire to stop. They often confess to having prayed for protection, or they tell themselves that this must be a gift from God, suspecting all the while that it just may be something else. Not once have we ever heard one of them admit to having tested the spirits, or that they prayed for enlightenment. We *have* heard the dowser's smiling prayer, "If this is not from You, do not let it happen!" to show us how wrong we were in our opinion. The rod always worked perfectly after such a prayer....

It is pure presumption to suspect or know and yet to try to pray for protection (514:118,157).

*Uncontrollable and Supernatural*

Dowsing power is uncontrollable and supernatural. If dowsing were really a learned human

ability, then it could be controlled at will, just like any other learned human ability, from bike riding to typing. What proves dowsing is not a human ability is its uncontrollable nature, independent will, and supernatural power. We will look at these important issues in some detail, beginning with a personal illustration.

John Weldon has a friend "Sam," who owns a farm in California. Needing more water, Sam called a local drilling company, only to discover that they employed a dowser to locate water.

Although a committed skeptic, Sam agreed to let the dowser try to find the best spot to drill. The dowser cut a forked branch from a tree and walked the property. Everyone present noticed the forceful thrust of the stick downward. When Sam became more skeptical than ever, the dowser offered to prove the power was real. He challenged Sam to use the stick himself. When Sam walked the property and got to the same spot as before, the stick was powerfully thrust downward as if by an invisible hand. Sam was shaken; he couldn't believe it. He knew he had done nothing to move the stick, but it had still reacted powerfully to the same location. When the rest of Sam's family tried, it worked for two others, but not for three additional members who also tried it.

The next day, Sam explained this incident to Dr. Weldon, who was visiting him at his farm. Weldon told him that it was a spiritistic ability and something to be avoided. Sam, unbelieving of such things, challenged Weldon: "Look, I'll show you it works." As he cut a branch from a tree, Weldon told him that there would be no power manifested. Try as he would, Sam could not get the stick to react, and he kept cutting branches from different trees and bushes, thinking the power resided in the "proper" kind of branch.

Dr. Weldon explained that no power was evident this time because: 1) the dowser was not there, therefore his spirit guide was probably not present, and 2) even if it were present, Weldon explained that he had prayed that God would prohibit any spiritistic activity from being encountered. Yet Sam still did not understand why the power wasn't there. It was obviously present on one day and entirely absent the next day. In the end, Sam employed the dowser, who successfully located water at the spot indicated by the dowsing rod. Today Sam believes in dowsing.

This incident illustrates that dowsing cannot work on the basis of a natural sensitivity to water "radiations," which many dowsers claim. If the theory were true, the experiment should have worked the second time because the water was still there and it had powerfully worked for both Sam and the dowser the day before. And if dowsing were a natural human ability, why did it only work for certain members of Sam's family? The fact that it worked for some but not for others indicates selectivity and shows that some other explanation is necessary.

A former *ASD* editor reveals a conclusion arrived at by many practitioners: that the dowsing power operates independently of the dowser:

There is easily demonstrated evidence that the force which moves the dowsing device is independent of the *searching-out ability* of the dowser. I won't go into any discussion of theories, but will take time to briefly acquaint you with some facts about the behavior of dowsing devices, facts which are not well known to the casual dowser or to the public. These facts, so far as I have been able to find out, have been given little weight by most students of dowsing....

I was also told that many who could create this movement were reluctant to do so in public because there were supernatural implications in the demonstration....

I feel the behavior of dowsing devices under these two conditions calls for serious consideration of the idea there is an unknown force acting as part of the dowsing phenomenon (624:23-24).

Another leader in dowsing reports: "Students of dowsing know that the force can be activated to move devices when no dowsing search is involved, demonstrating that this unknown force has an independent existence, that it is not tied to the information gathering process" (656:75). Clearly, the power of dowsing is too great to be explained by anything natural or human.

An examination of dowsing phenomena itself reveals that a supernatural power is at work. Following are some illustrations:

One day he demonstrated his ability to me and then suggested I try. I was no skeptic; even so, amazement was total as I felt the rough bark

twist in my hands. Hard as I gripped, I couldn't keep that rod vertical, although I persisted until my hands were on the verge of blisters (657:116).

Shafica Karagulla, a neuropsychiatrist and member of the prestigious Royal College of Physicians in Edinburgh, states that ". . . the rod began to bend downward with such force that although I have strong wrists, I could not prevent it" (711:95). Ben Hester cites the book by Dr. Bruce Copen of Sussex, England, *Dowsing For You* (Academic Publications, p. 5):

Strong men have tried all kinds of gadgets to retard the movement of the dowsing rod without avail—the best one can describe the movement of the rod is that the movement, being very sudden, is like a mysterious hand which grasps the end of the rod and either moves it up or down, even at times when one is practicing on something that is *known* to be present, the shock of the movement is so sudden that one wonders where the power comes from.

Based on years of study and conversations with leading dowsers, Hester supplies his own conclusion and then offers a personal anecdote which underscores the power of the force operating behind dowsing:

It can be stated no more clearly, *it is an outside force that moves the rod*, not the slight muscle twitch of the dowser's arms.

We watched and interviewed an internationally known dowser who, at our request used two pairs of pliers to hold his forked stick. The pull downward by some external force was so great it stripped the bark off the stick held in the pliers. We tried to pull the stick up from its downward position and found it necessary to exert what we estimated to be more than a ten pound pull. How could a physicist ignore such a fact? (514:70).

Even dowsers confess that the dowsing power has an independent *will* of its own:

The first time you get a dowsing reaction, it is likely to be a very odd feeling. The rod or the pendulum seems to take off spontaneously, moved by some force which you can't understand or control, and like anything supposedly inanimate which seems to have a will of its own, it can be unnerving (623:68).

It may even be best to pretend that the pendulum or the rod has an independent existence, its movements willed from outside in spite of your rational brain saying that this is impossible. The British dowsing instructor, Tom Graves puts it this way: "Treat the instrument as if it has a life and mind of its own, which in most senses it hasn't but that's beside the point. I sometimes think of instruments as being like cantankerous children: they won't work unless you ask them to, and certainly won't work if you try and force them to; they occasionally lie and sometimes sulk and refuse to work at all; so you have to use a little guile, a little ingenuity, and a little wit to get the results you need." . . .

I like the way Steve Bosback, the Arizona dowser, puts himself in the right frame of mind for dowsing. He settles himself with his rod comfortably poised in the neutral position and asks quietly: "Please indicate when I am ready to receive positive answers to dowsing questions. . . . "

Then he waits, contemplating.

After maybe ten or twenty seconds, the rod stirs faintly to life and then flicks quickly up into his chest. Now, he is ready to work (623:79-80).

And, just as clearly, the dowsing power is not subject to human control:

Looking at the history of tests of dowsing ability held under controlled experimental conditions, it is clear that none of them have unambiguously proved dowsing to be a repeatable faculty to be summoned at will (623:103).

. . . . Dowsers have always been aware of a physical force they could not control (514:6).

This completely ignored the force of the dowsing rod, forked stick, or whatever, that once started in its movement *cannot* be controlled or stopped by the dowser. This is the witness of every experienced dowser. They describe it in such terms as "almost frightening," "challenging," "exciting," and "my greatest experience." Dr. Bruce Copen of Sussex, England, in the introduction to his book *Dowsing For You* describes this vividly. . . . "One thing is very

certain, that once the rod decides to move—it *moves* and nothing can stop it!" (514:69-70).

It is evident, as it is true for the spirits themselves, that dowsing lends access to supernatural information—information a person could not possibly know. The impersonal dowsing rod is supposedly able:

(1) to have total recall of past events, (2) to foretell future events, (3) to project itself through anything, (4) to project itself anywhere instantaneously, (5) to contain infinitely more information than it had ever been taught or heard of, and (6) to advise its present possessor on all things in a manner that can be classed as no less than superhuman. Some dowsers attribute these six characteristics to "the God within you" (514:104-05).

And because dowsing is practiced worldwide, the dowsing power can respond to literally hundreds of languages. The dowser must ask the specific questions to receive specific answers. But how did an impersonal force learn every language under the sun? Actually, how did it learn any language at all?

*Amoral, Yet Personal Energy*

Dowsing utilizes an amoral yet "personal" spiritual energy. This amoral yet personal nature of the power behind dowsing provides another important key for determining its source. Significantly, a demon can also be described as an intelligent, amoral, personal energy residing in the spiritual realm. It too can interact with the physical world, particularly in the realm of "energy" manifestations. And, as we are noting throughout this book, demons are capable of deliberate deception. Sooner or later demons will deceive their contacts (278).

This same kind of deception is found in dowsing. One dowser confessed what many others have experienced: "All of us were mystified. The dowsing reaction was strong—but also wrong" (623:108). Another acknowledged, "In seeking to locate reported hidden treasure, I have dowsed and received 'yes' answers with regard to as many as four different places at a single time. Is it any wonder that there is so much confusion about the value and performance of a dowser?" (626:18).

Hester, too, mentions this deceptive characteristic of dowsing and discusses the extent of the problem. Once again, we can see why Luther classified dowsing as a form of idolatry (623:41): Dowsing subordinates a person to another power, a power to whom he pledges his allegiance, his trust, his loyalty, yet a power of the most dangerous type—an amoral power:

> If dowsing were no more than a physical reaction of the device or the human body, as some modern investigators claim, there would be no particular need to discuss the problem of right and wrong. However, since the device *will* answer questions ... the question of right and wrong becomes a critical issue. In using the information, ... the most frightening conclusion one can draw from this is its danger in the hands of an evil man, and much worse, that this intelligent power source will lend itself to do evil (514:45-47).

*Dangers of Dowsing Practice*

It is the amoral nature of the dowsing power that brings up the subject of the dangers of dowsing practice.

We have documented elsewhere that numerous psychological, spiritual, and physical ailments may be associated with psychic and occult activities (ref. 1069). If dowsing is truly an occult activity, we could expect to encounter similar types of hazards.

T. E. Coalson refers to the characteristic minor ailments, the "large number of the physical discomforts in dowsing: malaise, headaches, tension, and irritability" (643:15). Hester observes: "That it is detrimental to the health of the dowser is matter of record" (514:155), and he supplies a number of illustrations.

Dr. Kurt Koch warns of more serious spiritual consequences when he reveals, "I have several hundred examples concerning pendulum and rod dowsers, and all are negative in character. I cannot understand those theologians and Christian workers who regard dowsing as harmless" (642:273). Thus, dowsers not infrequently have mental and physical problems, as well as psychic and spiritual disturbances, related to their prac-

tice. T. C. Lethbridge's wife, Mina, said of her husband, "Excessive work with the pendulum depleted his vitality and contributed to his death of a heart attack" (1526:440).

Other hazards are more obvious, such as being deceived by the device (e.g., leading to financial loss) or receiving incorrect medical diagnosis with a serious illness, leading to further complications or death. "We found many well drillers reluctant to discuss dowsing, but after friendly conversation their reluctance changed to bitter denunciation of the dowsers and the financial havoc they create by their failures" (514:6). Hitching quotes research chemist P.A. Orgley: "The nuisance value and the menace of dowsing is not sufficiently realized. A water or mineral witcher can cause an awful waste of private and public money. The medical witcher can cause a waste of public life" (623:104).

Not unexpectedly the potential danger in dowsing has been recognized in other ages, as Coalson reports: "Georgius Agricola, in his medieval work *De Re Metallica*, exercised great caution when speaking of dowsers. Claiming that they were led by evil forces, he advised that all those interested in the subject drop it before it became fatal" (643:13). In the fifteenth century no less an occult authority than Paracelsus warned, "Therefore care is to be sedulously taken that ye suffer not yourselves to be seduced by the divination of uncertain arts. For they are vain and frivolous, especially the Divinatory Rods, which have deceived many miners. For if they show anything rightly, they on the contrary deceive ten times" (514:5-6).

As a final warning, Hester discusses his response to a Christian dowser who claimed the technique was harmless:

> ... The record is there for the reading. ... nausea, dizziness, convulsive pains, muscle spasms, loss of memory, fainting and headaches during and after the simplest type of dowsing—water witching. Some dowsers do not recover their sense of well being for hours or many days after witching. This does not include the physical discomfort of some types of dowsing: bleeding hands, burning feet, the rod flying back to slap the dowser in the face as the water is located (we know of one dowser who wears a

crash helmet to take the force of the blow). Even the metal or wood rod forced into an arc at waist level, slaps back against the belly of the witcher with a stinging and resounding whack.

Dr. Kurt Koch has told us of dowsers who, although apparently suffering none of the above effects, have fallen prey to severe psychic disturbances at a later date. Dr. Koch has also recorded case histories of severe psychological and psychic trauma by recipients of medical dowsing. We have written of the harm a dowser can cause a "victim" at will, but it is obvious that if this occult power is used to cause harm, it will seldom, if ever, be confessed (514:199-200).

*Conversion to the Occult*

Dowsing can precipitate psychic involvement or conversion to the occult. This should be obvious by now; however, we will cite one striking illustration of how this "innocent" practice can lead people into occultism. Indeed, part of the problem is just that: its innocent reputation. After all, how could walking around with a shrub branch be dangerous?

We believe it is as dangerous as a child playing with a Ouija board.* *The American Dowser* reports on Werner Nobel, M.D., who had an international reputation in orthopedics and neurology. The following is from his obituary column:

Werner became interested in dowsing about 8 years ago, when a local dowser showed him how to use a forked stick, and he experienced for the first time the powerful mysterious force pulling the stick down against the determined resistance of his tightly clenched fists. His scientific mind, intrigued by this experience, at once opened itself to the possibility that other esoteric phenomena, pooh-poohed by the scientific establishment, might also be real, though wrapped still in mystery. So, with customary initiative and energy, Werner began to collect and master a large library of esoterica, communicated with and travelled widely to meet with leading practitioners of and researchers into the phenomena of dowsing, energy fields, etc., and began research projects in Kirlian photography, animal acupuncture, and psychic healing at the University. He and his wife took a course in psychic healing and both became healers, singly and as a team, Werner especially displaying unusual gifts in this area. He

also learned from a Swiss healer-dowser, Frau Felicitas Ruder, an interesting method of psychic diagnosis by automatic drawing in a meditative state, which he supplemented with information dowsing with the pendulum. His accuracy was very high. And in 1975 he was made a Trustee of the American Society of Dowsers, a role that was one of his greatest pleasures and interest in his last years (1080:5-6).

In his description of the logical steps following a first encounter with a form of divination, Hester goes into more detail:

The certainty of it is that the next step *will* be presented sooner or later. . . . Generally there is a logical order, one building on the last. At least these are the steps that have actually been experienced:

1. Dowsing, using a Ouija board, going to a "reader," etc.

2. An opportunity that can be seized only through further occult means. For instance, if one happens to be in need of further information that cannot be gotten in the yes and no answers of the dowsing device, it may be suggested that a visit to a medium will provide an answer. By this time, that extra bit of information has become so necessary, this step is almost impossible to refuse.

3. After having experienced steps one and two, this important and most attractive new possibility to get information and advice is almost impossible to turn away from. This results in more active participation in mediumism, psychometry, or other exciting psi activities.

4. Some occult ability will suddenly be received. It may be telepathy, retrocognition or precognition, and one is suddenly an active participant in occult manifestations.

5. The final step will be the preparation or indoctrination to receive a "control" or "guide" or "familiar spirit." This may start through vivid and unusual dreams, unexpected and alien (important) ideas, a distinct mental impression (astonishingly different from the usual), and finally, the awareness of something or someone (a presence) nearby—generally at the right hand side. Eventually, after a time of introduction, the guide will

establish an acceptable and recognizable method of communication.

6. Then, although the recipient is not only unaware of the danger, and will not turn back even if warned, the trouble starts. The guide starts giving advice. This advice is valuable, resulting in all sorts of advantages and good things. Then, if the advice is not taken, the guide pushes a little for compliance. Then the advice changes to demands—all for the "good" of the recipient. The demands become stronger and instructions are given as though they *must* be followed. . . . It ends by demanding control of every decision, action, thought and wish. The person who has had no brush with spiritism will find these details impossible to accept as reality. . . . The rest of the picture we have witnessed personally. The person so afflicted begins to lose his own personality, and the change is noticeable to the horror of his relatives and friends. The person withdraws more and more from old associations because he or she recognizes what is happening and cannot control it. A different personality emerges and fear lives with him day and night (514:136-38).

*Dowsing and Spiritism*

Evidence like the above leads Hester to observe that "the staff historically was a tool of witchcraft, magic and sorcery . . ." (514:12), and, ". . . everything we have presented here shows that the forked stick or any other dowsing device has *nothing but* occult associations" (514:156).

Because these associations are so prevalent, even dowsers will confess to the occult nature of the practice. The former president of the British Society of Dowsers, Major General Jedyll Scott Elliot, made the following comment to George Crite at an annual convention of the American Society of Dowsers. This was reported in the article, "Water Witching" by George Crite himself in *New Times* magazine: "What all of us are doing at this convention is witchcraft; in another age we could have been burned for it" (514:7).

But dowsers also admit direct connections to spiritism and the spirit world. A report on one dowsing seminar admitted "that dowsers, that is to say, any class of sensitives, are always surrounded by discarnate entities eager to express

themselves. . . . They most easily accomplish this by breaking in and influencing the movement of whatever dowsing instruments are being used . . ." (627:151). Even well-seasoned practitioners agree:

Verne L. Cameron, the grand old man of dowsing, known all over the world for his ability, and completely generous in sharing his "know-how" tells in *Aquavideo* that his decision to dowse (he was primarily a water dowser) is nothing more than getting in touch with a spirit entity. He makes it sound like the most beneficial experience saying that the entity will tell you things you never dreamed of (514:44).

Dr. Reginald Allen, in *The American Dowser*, comments that "it is some invisible power that helps members of the American Society of Dowsers in their efforts" (1081:68). And some dowsers claim that they contact the dead:

However, many dowsers are convinced that the power source *is* an entity, in fact a spirit of a dead person. One such case, of which we have personal knowledge, is that of a dowser-teacher who held a dowsing seminar in an adjoining city. He allowed us to tape record his classes, and we have those tapes. He stated flatly that several well known historical figures were his "spirit guides." This man was a sincere, humble and able dowser. He expressed his surprise to the class that he should have been singled out for the attention of these spirits (514:114).

One former dowser who became a Christian concluded that dowsing was "nothing more than an *instrument of divination*. The spirit that takes over the mind of the passive dowser is a divining spirit as described in the Bible" (2:104). In fact, nearly every book written by world-famous expert dowsers either accepts the occult aspect of dowsing "or specifically identifies and promotes spirit contact as the means of success" (1511:5).

Even Hitching, a dowser, confesses, "The use of the pendulum in dowsing seems to have grown naturally out of its ancient use, worldwide, among priests and seers to divine the future and receive messages from the world of the spirits" (623:60).

Perhaps this is why occultist P.M.H. Atwater can say, "Dowsing is the most constructive way I know to explore and expand intuitive/psychic abilities" (2815:229).

After lengthy research, including discussions with leading American dowsers, Hester concludes:

> We can be no more positive than to state that dowsing is making contact with the spirit world just as certainly as using the Ouija Board. The spirit world contacted is the world of evil spirits or angels under the leadership of Satan (514:157).

Indeed, as noted earlier, the similarity between dowsing and the Ouija board* is obvious to anyone who is familiar with dowsing:

> Every move, question or word in the dowsing act speaks of supernormal intelligence—greater

intelligence than can be credited to any phenomenon of human intellect. The hallmark of *every* occult experience is undependability. This is the exact trait of dowsing, from simple witching to the claimed sophisticated radionics instrument, and it has been so since ancient times. Every book or pamphlet on dowsing instruction stresses the necessity to ask the device questions from the very first try. They urge the learner to keep trying until the thing suddenly does answer.... Is there any basic difference in this and the use of the Ouija Board? (514:41-42).

Dowsing is neither a scientific technique nor a natural human ability. It is a spiritistic power used by dowsers who may think that they are using a natural or a divine gift. Unfortunately, they are practicing what is biblically forbidden.

# DREAM WORK

## INFO AT A GLANCE

**Description.** Dream work is the attempt to explore and interact with dreams for psychological insight in psychotherapy; for spiritual insight in "Christian" dream work; or in manipulating dreams for occult revelations or "spiritual growth" in New Age practices. Dream work may also be used as an adjunct to physical healing.

**Founder.** Unknown; dream work practices and techniques extend into antiquity.

**How does it claim to work?** Dream work claims that our dreams powerfully reflect or influence spiritual, psychological, and even physical realities. In New Age practice, dreams can be explored and even manipulated (as in lucid dream work) for occult revelations, spirit contact, astral travel, and to induce altered states of consciousness.* In psychotherapy, exploring dreams may open doors to the "unconscious mind" to reveal and help resolve hidden emotional conflicts or other problems. In "Christian" dream work, dreams are seen as signs or even personal messages or revelations from God; therefore, exploring dreams may be seen as the equivalent to "studying" God's Word. In physical healing, dreams may be seen as a means to reveal hindrances to the healing process and assist in the proper treatment.

**Scientific evaluation.** Considerable research has been done on the nature, purpose, and meaning of dreams; however, much still remains tentative or uncertain. There is a legitimate science of clinically investigating dreams and the influence they have. Nevertheless, scientific research into dreams must not be confused with New Age dream work.

**Examples of occult potential:** Dream work can be used to foster many New Age goals, from altering consciousness and developing psychic powers to spirit contact. It is used in many occult disciplines, such as astrology,* and in shamanism* and other forms of sorcery.

**Major problems.** The value of dream work to healing is unsubstantiated. In psychotherapy, dream work interpretation is often subjective and contradictory. In psychotherapeutic and Christian dream work, or in New Age occult manipulation of dreams, the practice may have unexpected or unforeseen negative consequences.

**Biblical/Christian evaluation.** Divinely inspired dreams are relatively rare and are given by God for His purposes to accomplish His will; they cannot be induced or manipulated by men. Normal dreams are not to be given a spiritual significance they do not possess. God's use of dreams in the Bible stands in contrast to their use in psychotherapy, Christian dream work, and occult dream work.

**Potential dangers.** Unintended occult influences. Some researchers have speculated as to possible harmful psychological consequences from personal dream exploration.

## INTRODUCTION

## AND INFLUENCE

*Newsweek* magazine has observed that a "New Age" of revived interest in dreams and dream work has arrived. The article noted, "What was [once] a fad is now mainstream. Even executives are asking their dreams to solve business dilemmas" (333:41).

Like crystal work* and channeling,* dream work is one of the more popular New Age practices. Since 1970, dozens of books on New Age dream work have total sales in the millions. For example, Dr. Ann Faraday's *Dream Power* has sold 600,000 copies (337).

The highly popular *Jungian-Senoi Dreamwork Manual* tells us that its "purpose is to convey to readers everywhere that dreamwork is now an extremely practical tool for a creative self-discovery and even the transformation of one's life" (739:5). In *Dreams and Healing: Expanding the Inner Eye*, Joan Windsor, who presents workshops throughout the country on parapsycholgy and creativity topics, states, "*Dreams and Healing* is the most important book you will ever read if you are at all interested in a practical program of self-help in relation to attuning your mind-body connection to total wellness. Within its pages lies the formula for the realization and maintenance of

a harmonious and joyful balance between physical, mental, and spiritual states of being. ... This is the natural birthright of each soul" (335:XV-XVI).

If one reads through the library of modern dream work books, one finds many such claims like these. Of course, everyone dreams, so everyone has some degree of interest in their dreams. It is not surprising that the things that affect our daily lives may influence the content of our nightly dreams. Dreams can also be fascinating experiences. But does this prove the validity of the dream work as it is commonly practiced today? Does dream work have genuine therapeutic and spiritual value? Are there occult associations to the use of dreams?

Today, many people have questions surrounding their dreams. For example, what about troubling dreams? At one time or another, most of us have had troubling dreams or nightmares. What do they mean? Should nightmares concern us? Probably not, unless they persist. If needed, these may be effectively dealt with in counseling. But legitimate dream *therapy* for persistent, troubling nightmares should not be confused with New Age dream *work*, which attempts to use the dream state for occult applications.

Another question is, "Can God speak through dreams today?" Yes, but it appears to be a relatively rare experience. Can dreams predict the future? Again, in rare cases, it seems that they can. In some cases recurring dreams about tragedy may need to be considered as possible portents, or divine warnings to be prepared for future events.

Dreams can also reflect the condition of our lives. Can dreams provide useful information in some cases? Yes, but one should be circumspect with the information and what is done with it. In the sense that common dreams can reflect common human themes and experiences, dreams may sometimes be significant. But in the sense that they have a consistently profound religious application to our lives, we don't think they merit this approbation. In the following pages we explain why we believe this, and we critically evaluate modern dream work, its practices, and its implications.

## CATEGORIES AND VARIETIES

What is dream work? In general, dream work attempts to remember, explore, evaluate or manipulate normal dreams for psychological, physical, spiritual, or occult purposes. These purposes include physical healing, greater self-understanding in secular counseling, discerning "God's will" in so-called Christian dream work, and a variety of occult goals in New Age dream work.

At the risk of oversimplifying, dream work may be divided into three basic categories: 1) "secular" dream work, as in Freudian, Gestalt, Jungian, humanistic, and other conventional psychotherapy; 2) so-called Christian dream work, popularized by Morton Kelsey, John A. Sanford, and others, which often relies on Jungian psychology; 3) New Age dream work, which incorporates diverse elements from, for example, ancient pagan (e.g., shamanistic*) dream methods, modern spiritistic revelations (e.g., Edgar Cayce, "Seth"), Jungian techniques, and transpersonal ("Eastern") and fringe psychologies. It must be noted that the lines separating these categories are not rigid. Elements of Jungian, humanistic, Christian, and New Age dream work are often mixed together.

Dream work may be utilized in conjunction with a dream work counselor (a conventional therapist or someone who specializes in dreams), with dream work partners in a variety of programs offering dream "workshops" or seminars, or individually by oneself using texts on self-help dream work. New Agers often report that their spirit guides assist them in dream work.

Dream work is employed differently in different disciplines, although most forms share one basic element: the belief that, potentially, dreams are psychic vessels containing a wealth of hidden knowledge, wisdom, and power. It is this fundamental perspective on dreams that has made them so popular in New Age occultism, education, psychology, and healing.

Teacher Patricia Pirmantgen observes, "Educators who have tried dream work in the classroom know that there is no quicker way to capture the interest of a group of students" (1523:49). Transpersonal educators Gay Hendricks and James Fadiman report, "Dreaming is an altered state that is being used successfully by teachers both as a technique and as content. From a transpersonal point of view, dreams are important because they give us messages from the unconscious, and they afford easy access to a different reality. Dreaming is one door to our inner selves" (1524:10).

Psychic researcher Dr. Harmon Bro makes an interesting point in *Edgar Cayce on Dreams*: "The century of the rediscovery of dreams has also been the century of scientific investigation of psychic phenomena" (64:154). The relationship is more than incidental. Since the dawn of time, dreams have brought fascination, fear, and perplexity to men, and their use in the world of the occult is pervasive:

> The interpretation of dreams has always been regarded as an occult science, with a popularity that waxed and waned with fashion and politics. Sigmund Freud's introduction of the concept of using dreams to understand the deeper workings of the mind, although highly controversial at the turn of the century, lifted dream analysis to a new plateau of respectability. Every school of psychology that derives from Freud's theories uses dream analysis as a standard therapeutic tool.

> Even so, there is little agreement about what dreams mean or even why we dream.... Dreaming ... seems to be essential for the restorative function of sleep, but beyond that, its purpose is debated....

> New Age philosophy commonly portrays dreams as a medium for receiving clairvoyant or spiritual information. Various traditional occult systems of dream interpretation are being revived and reinterpreted to be used for this purpose. Such reinterpretation is usually similar to that used in humanistic astrology, which assumes that dream information indicates probabilities of personality patterns and indicates strengths and weaknesses that may be acted upon (1525:55).

Dreams have also been used by God to reveal His will, as indicated many times in the Bible. God used prophetic dreams in the life of the pagan Babylonian King Nebuchadnezzar, and the prophet Daniel interpreted them. God used a dream to instruct Mary's husband, Joseph, to take her as his wife in spite of the unusual circumstances surrounding her pregnancy. God also used a dream to warn Joseph and Mary to flee to Egypt to escape King Herod's attempt to destroy the child, Jesus, the Messiah (Daniel chs. 2,4,7; Matthew 1:20; 2:13).

Scripture also reveals that dreams are used by false prophets and teachers who speak the "delusions of their own minds" to lead people to follow false gods (Jeremiah 23:25-32; Deuteronomy 13:1-5). God warns His people, "Do not listen to . . . your interpreters of dreams" who "prophesy lies" and who counsel against what He has spoken (Jeremiah 27:9-10). Dreams, then, have been used by God to reveal His will and accomplish His purposes, and they have also been used by the self-deceived.

Dreams have also been used by the devil to reveal his will and accomplish his purposes, including new occult revelations, psychic development, spiritistic contacts and guidance, and even spiritual intimidation and spirit possession. That the spirit world is interested in the promotion of dream work for its own purposes can be proven by the many books written on dreams through the agency of spirit-possessed mediums. Two examples are *Edgar Cayce on Dreams* (64) and *Seth: Dreams and Projection of Consciousness* (63).

That dreams are used by both God and the devil shows that dreams can be used for either good or evil. But this should not blind us to the normalcy of dreams; their divine or demonic use is the exception, not the rule. Most of us dream in some form regularly, and we accept our dreams as ordinary components of life. In fact, some people who are experimentally deprived of their dreams for long periods may suffer mild to severe psychological problems. Our point, however, is that dreaming and dream work are worlds apart. Because the latter is becoming increasingly common within our culture, and also in the church, an evaluation of dream work is necessary.

## BASIC CONCERNS

In the following pages, we will briefly address the following issues: 1) Is dream work in secular psychotherapy proven to be effective? 2) Is

Christian dream work really necessary? 3) What are the spiritual dangers of New Age dream work? 4) Can scientific dream research support New Age goals?

In examining these concerns, we should remember that the categories of secular, psychotherapeutic, Christian, and New Age dream work may cross-pollinate in actual practice. Thus, dream work methods in secular psychotherapy may be influenced by New Age methods through humanistic, transpersonal, or Jungian psychology; Christian dream work often incorporates Jungian psychology and sometimes New Age techniques, and even New Age dream work may employ secular psychologies or nominally "Christian" methods.

## DREAM WORK IN PSYCHOTHERAPY

The study of dreams has a legitimate application in pure research, in some schools of psychology, and perhaps in a few forms of psychotherapy. But even here, doors can open to psychic exploration or spiritism (see "Dream Research and New Age Goals" following). Due to space limitations, our concern will be simply to point out that an increasing number of secular researchers are questioning the validity of dream work in modern psychotherapy. Because Christian psychotherapy often depends on secular therapies (2683/855), this would include many forms of dream work common to Christian psychotherapy as well.

Dream work in psychotherapy assumes that by gaining insight into our dreams we may understand the forces in our unconscious mind that cause anxiety or even neuroses and possibly psychoses. Dream work may either be part of a given psychotherapy, or the actual psychotherapy itself. However, therapists in general disagree over the validity of dream interpretation in therapy and over the nature of the problems concerning dream work and the proper interpretation of dreams. Even though modern dream therapy assumes that the insight afforded by understanding dreams is therapeutic and psychologically healthful, this has yet to be demonstrated to the satisfaction of critics.

In addition, dream work itself is questionable to the degree that modern dream work is based upon the dubious or unproven theories of modern psychotherapy. Indeed, modern psychotherapy has run into serious difficulties presented by recent criticisms of many of its methods and underlying theories, not to mention the question of its overall effectiveness (2683/756).

One secular critic of dream work is Dr. Edward Erwin, professor in the Department of Philosophy at the University of Miami and author of several books, plus an article, "Is Psychotherapy More Effective Than a Placebo?" (473:37-51). In his "Holistic Psychotherapies: What Works?" (3:245-72), he questions the effectiveness of the modern therapeutic use of dream work.

Dr. Erwin discusses four assumptions of dream analysis. He states that one problem is whether dreams are what the therapists say they are: internal symbolic pictures representing how we view ourselves, others, and our place in the world. Given recent neurological theories, he suggests this assumption is not yet substantiated. To say that some dreams may reflect certain experiences or concerns in our lives is not to prove that dreams in general have important symbolic meanings for our lives in general.

He then discusses a second premise of dream therapists, which is that "dreams *generally* have a *correct* interpretation, so that when we decode them properly we gain useful insights into ourselves." Given the conflicting nature of dream interpretations, this is an enormous leap of faith by dream therapists. Thus: "The warrant for these two assumptions, however, is challenged by recent neurological theories of dreaming that appear to provide better explanations of all the known facts about dreaming than do purely psychological theories. If the plausibility of these neurological theories is conceded one cannot just assume without argument that dreams *generally* are symbolic pictures that represent how we view ourselves or that dreams generally have a correct interpretation" (995:266).

Erwin argues that even if the above two premises are granted, there remain two further assumptions that must be proven in order to establish the legitimacy of dream analysis based

on its standard arguments. The first is *how to determine* an objective standard for interpreting dreams:

First, we need to assume that there is some way to establish that a certain interpretation is correct; otherwise, neither patient or therapist will be able to distinguish between dream insights and pseudoinsights. Therapists holding different theories—Freudians, Adlerians, Jungians, and others—will often disagree about how to interpret the same sort of dream. How are we to tell which theorist is correct? . . . [For example] the key difficulty with [Christian-Jungian psychotherapist John] Sanford's suggestion is that the patient's so-called "free associations" are often influenced by covert or overt suggestions of the therapists. . . . Sanford [believes that] the unconscious, which has produced the dream in the first place, knows when it is correctly understood. However, he gives no evidence that this theory about the unconscious is correct. If we do not assume Sanford's theory about what the unconscious "knows," then why believe that the reaction of the client is crucial? (995:266-67).

Finally, Dr. Erwin questions a fourth assumption of dream therapists: that the insights afforded through dream analysis have legitimate therapeutic value. He suggests that the evidence cited for such a conclusion is also not yet established.

In other words, there are at least four major premises of modern therapeutic dream work that have yet to be proven: 1) dreams are symbolic representations of our internal and external experience; 2) dreams generally have a correct interpretation; 3) some objective basis exists for determining that correct interpretation; 4) the insights uncovered in dream therapy have legitimate therapeutic value.

In light of this, Erwin thinks that dream analysis may not only be clinically irrelevant but also potentially harmful:

Finally, it might turn out that dream analysis is not only of little clinical value, but is actually harmful, although at present this is speculative. What I have in mind is the fate of the Crick and Mitchison theory that postulates a reverse learning mechanism in which dreaming modifies certain undesirable modes of interaction of network cells in the cerebral cortex. In effect, we dream in order to forget and forgetting is necessary to prevent an overloading of stored associations. Crick and Mitchison point out that on their model, remembering one's dreams should not be encouraged, because such remembering helps to retain patterns of thought best forgotten (995:267).

It could be possible, therefore, that people who participate in dream analysis, rather than gaining insights on how to resolve their problems, are, at least some of the time, aggravating those problems. Dr. Erwin summarizes and concludes his critique of dream analysis with the following:

In sum, for some therapists, the cogency of their rationale for doing dream analysis is dependent on the arguments for Freud's dream theory and these arguments have recently been severely criticized. Even those therapists who do not rely on the Freudian theory often use a rationale that includes the following assumptions: (1) dreams are generally symbolic pictures that represent how we view ourselves and others; (2) dreams generally have a correct interpretation; (3) there is a reliable procedure for determining the correct interpretation; and (4) the insights gained by dream analysis have therapeutic value. Unless some other argument is offered, all four of these assumptions need to be justified; subject to the caveats already expressed, there is some reason to question the evidence for (1) and (2), and even more reason to reject the warrant for (3) and (4) (995:267).

Of course, if the relevance of secular dream work is unestablished, this logically holds true for most all Christian dream work, since this is based on secular methods.

## DREAM WORK IN THE CHURCH

The assumed rationale for Christian dream work is found in four areas: 1) in the claims of secular psychology; 2) in the divine use of dreams in Scripture; 3) in the interest in dreams in church history; 4) in the current use of dreams by some Christian therapists and psy-

chologists, largely dependent on the findings of secular psychotherapy. We question if any of these areas necessarily justify Christian dream work. To explain why, we will give a brief summary evaluation covering the four points mentioned above. Then we will cite six reasons why we believe Christian dream work should be questioned.

*The claims of secular psychology.* Neither secular nor Christian psychology has established a legitimate case for the value of dream analysis, or even a credible defense for secular psychotherapy in general (756).** We supplied some of the documentation for this in *The Facts on Self-Esteem, Psychology and the Recovery Movement* (2683).

*Dreams in the Bible.* The use of dreams in Scripture is distinct from the use of dreams in psychotherapy. It is true that dreams may come from the hand of God; but scripturally they appear to come at His bidding, not ours. And, when they come from God they are revelation events, not normal dreams. And nowhere in the Bible are we told to attempt to manipulate dreams for our own purposes or even our own self-insight. Granted, we are never told not to,

---

**Among the critiques of modern psychology showing problems in its theoretical base, effectiveness, and its potential dangers are: Martin L. Gross, *The Psychological Society* (Random House), Paul Vitz, *Psychology As Religion: The Cult of Self-Worship* (Eerdmans), William Kurt Kilpatrick, *Psychological Seduction: The Failure of Modern Psychology* (Nelson), Thomas Szasz, *The Myth of Mental Illness* (Doubleday) and *Ideology and Insanity* (Anchor), E. Fuller Torrey, *The Mind Game: Witch Doctors and Psychiatrists* (Emerson Hall), Morris N. Eagle, *Recent Developments in Psychoanalysis: A Critical Evaluation* (McGraw Hill), Richard W. Ollheim, *Philosophers on Freud: New Evaluations* (Jason Aronson), R. M. Jurjevich, *The Hoax of Freudism* (Dorrance & Co.), Dorothy Tennov, *Psychotherapy: The Hazardous Cure* (Abelard-Schuman), Mark Cosgrove, *Psychology Gone Awry* (Zondervan), Garth Wood, *The Myth of Neuroses: Overcoming the Illness Excuse* (Harper & Row), and Bernie Zilbergeld, *The Shrinking of America: Myths of Psychological Change* (Little, Brown). These are only a few of the scores of texts that are critical of modern psychotherapy—in addition to literally hundreds of articles.

but whether we do dream work or not should be based on valid reasons for pursuing the practice.

*Dreams in church history.* We do not believe the appeal to practices in church history are relevant because we think that the practices of dream exploration in church history are more questionable than convincing. No one denies that dream exploration can be both innocent and interesting, but in many ways it is simply unimportant. If God wishes to speak to us in a dream, He will, without our help. But both biblical data and church history reveal that this is relatively rare. If "problem" dreams are thrusting themselves upon us, then we may wish to pray for guidance as to the reason, or to see a qualified Christian counselor who respects biblical authority and whose practice is not contaminated by the anti-Christian premises of secular psychotherapy (2683). If dream work or dream therapy were truly important to our spiritual well-being, we would expect God to have commanded it in Scripture.

*Christian dream therapy.* Christian psychotherapy and dream work reveal a sometimes appalling lack of discernment when it comes to secular and even New Age thinking. Christians who are interested in exploring their dreams need to realize that even secular dream work can be tied to psychic exploration, and that it can become a means to spiritistic intrusion or contact. New Age dream work is almost exclusively the psychic use of dreams, which is more common than most assume, as we will later illustrate. We should also remember that merely because a practice is labeled Christian, as in "Christian" dream work, does not mean that it is either biblically wholesome, safe, or genuinely Christian. A large number of churches, groups, and individuals call themselves "Christian," yet reject clear biblical teachings and standards, and they may even experiment with the psychic realm.

Some Christians who are involved in dream workshops perhaps do not realize that the sources of interpretation derive from the dream work materials of liberal theologians, secular psychologists, and even spiritists. Such information taints the dream program with unbiblical premises, philosophies, or practices. Some evangelicals are influenced by Carl Jung, whose extensive personal involvement in the occult (340:170-223) colors many of his theories (339:10-13) and makes such dream work suspect from the start (see 2816).

In general, we think that the importance of dreams is often exaggerated and that time spent in exploring them is often more profitably spent elsewhere. Throughout human history, most people have lived well without attending local dream workshops or having their dreams analyzed in therapy.

## SIX CONCERNS

Below we list six general concerns with so-called "Christian" dream work.

1. Christian dream work often overemphasizes the value of dreams in proportion to their significance. If the legitimacy of dream analysis is unsubstantiated, of what value is the therapy? And some Christian dream work gives dreams a spiritual task they carry only rarely. That is, it makes a rare event (God communicating through dreams) a normal or universal event (dreams per se are communications from God).

This belief that God communicates to us regularly, directly, and personally by dreams makes dreams become normal vehicles for supernatural activity (allegedly divine communication), rather than normal by-products of consciousness that most are. One unfortunate result of this belief is when dreams become divinatory* or vehicles for occult revelations. They can supposedly warn of future events, bring spiritual enlightenment,* assist physical and mental healing, function as an adjunct to inner work,* or guide in making daily decisions. In this role, they can become an actual replacement for the guidance of the Bible. Because they can allegedly function as a form of divine revelation, some Christian dream promoters even advocate dreams as a new means for interpreting Scripture (65:6-7,220-22).

2. Christian dream work manuals may endorse communication with "dream figures" or psychic exploration through dreams, both of

which can lead to outright spiritism (65:41-63/206-18; cf. Inner Work, Visualization).

3. There are a host of problems inherent to the nature of dreams and Christian dream work. We already mentioned the seemingly unresolvable problem of how one accurately interprets dreams. Furthermore, when placed into a secular or New Age context, dreams often become a means to justify personal New Age beliefs and lifestyle. There is also the problem of unjustified suppositions; for example, that dreams are incomplete without dream work, that dream work fosters personal holiness, that dreams deepen our relationship with God.

4. Christian dream work may assume that dreams per se can be the means toward a relationship with God *apart* from Jesus Christ. In this regard they obviously assume too much: that everyone merely by virtue of dream work can establish a personal relationship with God, irrespective of their faith in Christ. The premise here is that a preexisting relationship of human and divine consciousness is *already* present, and that dreams merely amplify, expand, or otherwise help sanctify that already-existing relationship (65:4-8,13-34). Such a premise, however, leads to false assumptions about the nature of our relationship with God apart from regeneration (Ephesians 2:1-3), and about salvation (John 3:16,36; Ephesians 2:4-10), and true spirituality (John 17:3).

5. Christian dream work may allege the relationship of dreams to "divine energies," which are defined far too loosely and may in fact be occult energies. People may therefore fall prey to occult practices under the disguise of "divine" activity. For example, dream work "can take us on a spiritual journey and put us directly in touch with the energies of God" (65:9). However, how do we know that these are really the energies of God?

6. In Christian dream work, both secular and so-called Jungian-Christian ideas are too often accepted without critique on the part of those who employ them. One only need read the reviews of Jungian texts in Christian psychology periodicals to see this. Indeed, a number of periodicals attempting the integration of secular psychology and Christian theology have carried positive articles on Jungian interpretation of dreams and modern dream work (e.g., 501:59-60/502:95,106/503:92).

Some of the major Jungian dream work positions within the church include: Morton Kelsey's *God, Dreams and Revelations* (537); John Sanford's *Dreams and Healing* (474), and *Dreams: God's Forgotten Language* (475); Savary, Berne and Williams' *Dreams and Spiritual Growth: A Christian Approach to Dreamwork* (65). All these have received positive reviews in Christian psychology publications. But consider what these different authors believe and teach.

Morton Kelsey is an Episcopal priest and Jungian analyst who supports various occult practices, accepts the "Christian" parapsychologists' premise that psychic abilities are gifts from God, and views Jesus and His disciples as shamans (342:16-17,69,95). He writes:

Jesus was a man of power. He was greater than all shamans. (A shaman is one in whom the power of God is concentrated and can thus flow out to others.) My students begin to see the role Jesus was fulfilling when they read Mircea Eliade's *Shamanism* and Carlos Castaneda's *Journey to Ixtlan*. . . .

Jesus not only used these powers himself, but he passed the same powers of superhuman knowledge, healing, and exorcism on to his followers. . . . Jesus did not come just to win some kind of spiritual victory in heaven. He came to endow his followers with a new power that would enable them to spread the gospel effectively by using capacities that are out of the ordinary. This is the same kind of psi [psychic] power Jesus himself had. . . .

It appears that almost all Christians who were true disciples were something like shamans in the style of their master, sharing various gifts of power (342:92-95).

Here, Kelsey has confused the spiritistic, occult power of the shaman (see Shamanism) with the power of God, again reflecting the fundamental confusion among "Christian" parapsychologists who wrongly maintain that biblical miracles are equivalent to miracles found in the world of mediumism, spiritism, the occult, and Eastern religion (5:391-453).

John A. Sanford is the son of controversial Christian author Agnes Sanford (see 339:17 and ref. 161 for documentation of some of her unbiblical views and practices). John Sanford is a Jungian therapist who promotes such Jungian methods as the potentially dangerous practice of active imagination (799:140). Again, given Jung's endorsement of occultism (340:170-222) and the many ways in which his theories support occult philosophy and practice (339:10-13), one has to be concerned about the uncritical acceptance of his methods (2816).

Sanford also endorses shamanism. He thinks that its motifs were common among the Old Testament prophets, that Jesus was a shaman, and that the practice offers a legitimate form of spiritual healing:

Biblical scholars are skeptical of the historicity of most of the Book of Daniel, but this story is typically shamanic, and illustrates the shamanistic capacity to enter into special states of consciousness. . . .

A study of shamanism gives us information about the personality of the healer. . . .

The Old Testament prophets were shamanistic in character. . . . Jesus was distinctly shamanistic. He, too, talked with his spirits. . . . Like the shamans, Jesus healed the sick and was on familiar terms with the denizens of the spiritual world . . . (799:75).

That shamanism is a legitimate healing method, Sanford writes:

But perhaps most important of all is the fact that many people today have a shamanistic type of calling. Certain people who fall ill in our time, as well as in times past, are being called to a special life of consciousness and spiritual development, and may even be summoned via their illness to function as healers. . . .

In our day, we speak of the unconscious rather than of the spirit world, but it is the same reality that lies behind both shamanism and contemporary healing of the psyche. To have a direct experience with the unconscious is to begin to step into a shamanistic type of consciousness. Just as the shaman possessed a firsthand

knowledge of his celestial world, so today some people are called upon to explore the geography of the inner world of the unconscious.

Today's healer, . . . will find much in the shamanic tradition that will throw light upon his development and function (799:75,80-81).

Despite Sanford's views, we have shown in our discussion of shamanism* that this practice is always a demonic activity, never a divine one.

Another influential work is called *Dreams and Spiritual Growth*, whose authors are a Catholic theologian, a clinical psychologist, and the founder of the Jungian-Senoi Institute and author of the *Jungian-Senoi Dreamwork Manual*. "Senoi" dream work is increasingly popular in secular as well as some Christian dream work, but, as we shall see, it is a dream work method common to a pagan shamanistic tribe and used for occult purposes, including spirit contact.

All in all, Jung's influence within liberal and even within some conservative Christian theology is significant; however, few, if any, are making serious attempts to sift the issues involved biblically (504:20-27/505:329-32,614-618). In *Inner Healing*, Pastor Don Matzat has cited many concerns about Christian therapists who use Jungian methods, and we refer the reader to his text for details (761:61-75, see also 2816).

When Jung psychologizes and normalizes occult theories and internalizes spiritistic phenomena, how can the therapists who trust his theories sift the normal functions of human consciousness from spiritual deception, where spirits deliberately seek to mask their own activities under psychological constructs? How does the therapist who endorses lively inner conversations with one's alleged "archetypes" or "dream figures" know that their patient is not really conversing with a spirit guide, who is using the idea of archetypes or dream figures to enter a person's life? The Jungian therapists we have talked with, such as Karen Hamaker-Zondag, a European Jungian therapist specializing in astrology, confess they cannot always, or ultimately, distinguish archetypes from spirit guides. How then does a Christian therapist? And are Christian therapists who use Jung's technique of active imagination familiar with the attendant dangers of the process that even lifelong Jungian therapists warn about (687:3-25)?

To the degree that such cautionary sifting is neglected, Christian promoters of Jungian dream work and related methods may be responsible not only for encouraging spiritual confusion, but for potentially opening the doors to occultism in the lives of believers. Regardless of the label "Christian," if biblical authority is rejected and biblical concerns discarded, a variety of pagan influences can easily creep into dream work, with the attendant spiritual consequences we will now discuss.

## NEW AGE DREAM WORK
## AND SPIRITUAL DANGERS

In this section we will cite illustrations from a number of modern texts on dreaming and dream work to show how readily dreams can become the means to hazardous spiritual practices, such as inducing altered states of consciousness,* developing psychic abilities, or channeling* (see 278). These phenomena may occur even when they are not the intended goals of a particular program of dream work.

The extent to which the spirit world is capable of using the dream state is revealed in many books, such as Garfield's *Companions in Spirit*, where the spirits actively employ dreams as a method of contacting people (349:46-47; cf. 152-53): "... ask your guide to bring you a relevant dream. In many cases, the dream will come to you the first night" (349:73).

Another important book is *Dreamwork: Techniques for Discovering the Creative Powers in Dreams* by Unitarian Universalist minister Jeremy Taylor. Taylor states:

It is my experience that as a dream group continues over any substantial period of time, there almost invariably begins to occur events that seem "spooky" and even "supernatural...." Often people will have dream experiences which invite the interpretation of "past life recall" [reincarnation] and "encounters with spirits...." Don't be frightened if and when

such things seem to happen to you or others in your group. These things happen so often that they are clearly natural ... (62:91,93,96).

As to the kinds of psychic experiences encountered in dream work, Taylor explains: "There is a long global tradition of such experiences being associated with the acquisition of power and self-knowledge through yoga, meditation, alchemy, shamanism, and ritual magic" (62:94). Psychologist James H. Donahue, author of *Enigma: Psychology, the Paranormal and Self-Transformation* (60) and *Dream Reality: The Conscious Creation of Dream and Paranormal Experience*, writes that "paranormal perception is, if anything, more common in dreams than in trance" (60:71).

Throughout recorded history, dreams were often used in sacred temples and ritual for divination,* psychic healing, or establishing spirit contact (334:26-83). That ancient dream work was directly connected to the gods and spirits is evident from any number of ancient dream practices, e.g. the Asclepian dream therapy. In this method, "At night, the patients went to the temple [Asclepia] or outlying buildings to await the gods" in order to "absorb the divine communication." Healing was performed "in the presence of the earthly representatives of healing deities." Furthermore, "within the Asclepia, dream therapy or divine sleep, later to be called incubation sleep by Christian practitioners, reached perfection as a healing tool" (143:55).

Various techniques for utilizing or manipulating the dream state in an occult manner are found in many ancient religious traditions and modern practices. Sociologist Norman MacKenzie of the University of Sussex at Brighton, England, states, "The alliance between dreams and divination is an ancient one; wherever magic, superstition and the occult flourish, this link will be found" (334:74). This occult use of dreams, historically, appears to be a result of both the occult receptivity and the expectations of pagan cultures. There is no reason to think that such a relationship between dreams and the occult will not continue to expand in the United States as our culture continues its demise into the labyrinth of the occult.

In shamanism,* the spirits often direct, guide, and influence the shaman through dreams (755:59-117). For example, the Senoi dream methods are fundamentally shamanistic in nature and utilize the dream methods of the Senoi tribe of Malaysia. Spirit contact and revelations occur regularly through the dream state (62:107-114/755:112-15). According to New Age healer Dr. Jeane Achterberg, "An ability to dream in this way [lucid dreams] has been well described by Castaneda and others as being important to shamanic 'seeing' " (143:28).

Lucid dreaming is the ability to recognize a dream consciously as it is occurring and even to consciously participate in the dream and influence its outcome. Lucid dreams come naturally to only about five percent of the population. But developing lucid dreams is routinely utilized in spiritistic dream work as an effective means of inducing astral projection, psychic development, and spirit contact (143:38/336:336-44/338:228-73).

Certified hypnotherapists Richard Dobson and Natasha Frazier, authors of "Trance, Dreams and Shamanism," discuss the importance of dreams and hypnosis* for entering the state of trance conducive to contacting the spirit world shamanistically. "Dream time" is referred to as a *waking* altered state of consciousness,* which is most useful for accomplishing shamanistic goals and also most easily accessed through lucid dreaming. They note that self-hypnosis* can also trigger lucid dreams (2486:38-40).

In Hinduism and Buddhism, so-called "dream yoga" (755:151-170) is employed to help the yogi realize that the world itself is a dream, that death is unreal, and that in his true nature the yogi is one essence with God (see pp. 211-13). And the use of dream states by psychics and mediums for a variety of purposes, often to receive instruction from the spirits, is legion.

## SPIRITISM AND DREAMS

It should be evident that the deliberate cultivation of dream states in some contexts opens people to direct or indirect spiritistic influence. This spiritistic influence occurs in a certain amount of dream work currently done in therapy and a great amount done in popularized dream work. The context in which the program of dream exploration occurs, and the methods used, are a good indication of the spiritual orientation. Following are seven examples from modern dream literature that show how dreams are used by spirits to deceive people into adopting New Age philosophies and practices, and even sorcery. In such examples, the spirits state that they want humans to actively utilize and manipulate the dream state for all kinds of purposes: health, self-insight, intuition,* developing psychically, out-of-body experiences, and so on.

### Jane Roberts and Seth

The book by medium Jane Roberts and her spirit guide "Seth," *Seth, Dreams and Projections of Consciousness*, reveals Seth detailing how he employs a person's dream state. Interestingly, the techniques suggested by Seth and other spirits are virtually the same as those endorsed by many dream-work manuals and dream-work methods. Jane Roberts records: "Following Seth's instructions, my husband and I first learned to recall and record our dreams. Through later experiments, we discovered we could bring our normal waking consciousness into the dream state and 'come awake' while dreaming. Later we began to take bolder steps into these inner areas, learning to manipulate consciousness" (63:6; cf. 337:295-302).

We are told that dream work can lead to a more "flexible" state of consciousness, permitting altered states, astral travel, and spirit contact. "Seth" claims to initiate occult out-of-body experiences in his human contacts. We also discover that dreams can play an important role in the demonization of individuals who experiment with dream work (63:6-13,193-207,189,297,301-04,350). And it is significant that dream work played a key role in the entire phenomenon of Jane Roberts' work with Seth, which has now influenced millions of people (63:39-41,63-64). Roberts describes how important dreams were to her own mediumistic work:

> Though Seth told us that the experiments in dream recall would automatically make our consciousness more flexible, his real meaning

didn't come through to me until I found myself manipulating dreams and later having out-of-body experiences from the dream state.

Before our experiments began, I used to think that dreams were relatively chaotic productions ... a nightly retreat into idiocy for the tired brain.... So I wasn't prepared for Seth's emphasis on the importance of dreams.

If we follow certain "rules" given to us by Seth, we will get more or less predictable results in the dream state.... Seth has always emphasized that all true knowledge must be directly experienced; therefore, I will include throughout this book his instructions and suggestions for dream recall, investigation, and manipulation.

If we ever hope to "map" the dream state, we need a million trained dreamers: a million individuals trained to use dreams as vehicles ... (63:194-95).

Again, some of the processes of dream work that Seth encourages are common to many dream-work methods. He says, "With the method I have just given you, ... you will ... be gaining excellent discipline and training over your own states of consciousness.... We [Seth and other spirits] shall also use them [dream states] to give you training in the utilization of various stages of consciousness" (63:200).

Although Seth has claimed that he can induce out-of-body experiences, parts of the book also discuss how Seth utilizes dreams for helping to induce them. Since Seth teaches that the dream world is as real as the waking world, both lucid dream work and out-of-body experiences are legitimized as "true" reality. (See *A Course in Miracles*.)

It is significant that the view of reality and its relation to dreams espoused by spirit entities like "Seth," in such texts as *The Nature of Personal Reality* (507) and *Seth Dreams and Projection of Consciousness* (63), is either the same or similar to that taught by some cognitive psychologists and secular researchers of lucid dreaming (cf. 338:234,274-75). That Seth views lucid dreams as a stepping-stone to occult out-of-body experiences, and that much current dream work attempts to foster and manipulate lucid dreams, is reason for concern. In addition, that some sec-

ular psychologists and dream researchers both agree with the spirits underscores the fact that the church may get more than it bargained for when it looks to secular dream work as a spiritual discipline.

### Edgar Cayce

Hugh Lynn Cayce, the son of the famous trance medium Edgar Cayce, is coauthor of the text *Dreams: The Language of the Unconscious* (348). In part, this book is based on the spiritistic revelations of Edgar Cayce which are called "Readings." In other words, it represents the teachings of the spirit world concerning dream work.

In the book, the spirits claim that dreams are really an introduction to the psychic world. For Edgar Cayce and the spirits who inspired him, the unconscious realm (or the realm of the "subconscious soul") was one and the same with the psychic realm. To Cayce, psychic events were really internal unconscious phenomena, not supernatural, spiritistic phenomena. Dreams are a doorway to and of the same nature as psychic events in general. This means that both dreams and psychic events are more or less the same thing. Thus, the goal of the spirits is to show us that the conscious *development* of psychic abilities during the day is really no different than the subconscious *experience* of dreams during the night.

These spiritistic revelations teach that giving "proper" attention to one's dreams at night during sleep will help induce the same "events" (that is, psychic ones) during conscious periods in the daytime, or at least it will heighten one's awareness of them. This is why Hugh Lynn Cayce observes, "The dream world appears to be one of the safest and quickest approaches to the psychic world of man" (348:12; cf. p. 50). The readings also claim that both God and "the gods" speak to man through the dream state, and that it is man's responsibility to grow spiritually "through his individual receiving of messages from the higher forces themselves" through dreams (348:10; Reading No. 3744-4).

Another book on Cayce's dream work, *Edgar Cayce on Dreams*, by well-known psychic Harmon H. Bro, states that dreams may be used for the biblically forbidden practice of contacting the dead (Deuteronomy 18:9-12). "According to Cayce, not a few of the dreams where the living meet the dead are for the sake of the dead. Sometimes the dead simply want to be known and recognized as still existent" (64:180). Thus the spirits of the dead, what Cayce often called "discarnates," "are in a position to bring to the dreamer guidance on many things: health, financial affairs, social causes, social service, relationships with the living.... Cayce himself had sometimes received aid from discarnates ... [and] his dead mother spoke through Cayce at the start of a reading for someone else. Cayce remembered the contact later as a dream, but the others in the room heard the words spoken aloud" (64:183).

*The Jungian-Senoi Method*

As noted earlier, Strephon Kaplan-Williams is the founder and director of the Jungian-Senoi Institute in Berkeley, California. He is a practicing Jungian therapist-analyst whose specialty is "transpersonal and holistic healing." He is also an instructor in transpersonal dream work and Jungian psychology at the New Age-oriented John F. Kennedy University. In the *Jungian-Senoi Dreamwork Manual* he discloses the basic premises of much modern dream work: active participation with dreams and dream characters as part of "objective" reality. He writes: "The golden rule of dream work might be stated as follows: *To get to the meaning of dreams, actualize dreams rather than interpret them.*" He also teaches: "*A basic principle is to start with the dream and objectify it,*" and in "the Jungian-Senoi approach we try and start always with the dream, objectify it, and then move out into levels of manifestation" (739:28,80,88).

Kaplan-Williams reveals that "dialoguing" with dream figures is a key part of the Jungian-Senoi method:

The dialogue with dream figures and situations is one of the major techniques of Jungian-Senoi dreamwork.... Discovering the issues [of your dream] can be based in part on using the following *central questions* as the focus for beginning your dialogue.

—What, or who are you?

—Why are you in my dream?
—Why are you acting the way you are in my dream?
—What do you have to tell me?
—Why is such-and-such happening in my dream?
—What do you think/feel about such-and-such?
—What do you want from me? What do you want me to do?
—What is your gift to me?
—What questions would you ask of me?
—What do you think/feel about this dialogue?

At some point a flow may happen and the dialogue becomes almost automatic. . . .

Always bring up your problems about dialogue with the dream figures involved. They are best equipped to help you. They will tell you quite honestly what you may need to do to open up the flow. . . . If the flow gets going for you, if the information coming your way contrasts with your own consciously chosen point of view, then most likely you are not "making up" the dialogue (739:114-15).

But Kaplan-Williams also admits that dream work can lead to spiritistic and necromantic contacts. In his discussion of choosing which "dream being" to dialogue with, he explains that one should:

Also choose, if possible, an entity which has a lot of specificity. We may choose also to dialogue with more than one entity. . . . To develop more than one point of view we can have separate dialogues with opposite entities in the same dream. . . . Dialogue is a major feature of [dream] journalwork. Some of the "life dialogues," which may also appear in dreams, are as follows.

—Dialoguing with one's birth. Why was I born?
—With one's death . . .
—With some person who has died to re-establish or complete the relationship.
—With one's own spirit guide, that presence which may know our essential life direction better than we ourselves do (737:116-118).

He also asserts that in practicing dream work we are also permitting the spirit world, or even the dead, to speak to us:

In doing dialogue ... are we not establishing more harmonious relations between different parts of our psyches? ... Are we not, even, letting the spirit world speak to us? ...

Is there perhaps a psychic connection established in a dialogue with the essence of other persons, living or dead? Several Institute participants have had dialogues with parents, spouses, etc., who have died, and they have been deeply moved. Something besides an exclusively inner spirit seems to be present. Who knows ultimately all that is going on? ...

In many, many dreamwork classes and groups, people have become deeply involved in their dialogues. ... Who can say where such an experience comes from, or even what its meaning is? From my own experience as well as others' experiences, I can say that dream work is soul-work ... [and] what could be more natural than knowing oneself? And this means using the known self to learn and relate to the unknown selves. To know ourselves we must know the various parts of ourselves. ... A dialogue is a relationship between a known and an unknown (739:118-19).

Finally, in his discussion of the dream work application to ritual, magic, and the like, he argues that occult ritual work can play an important part in evoking key dream archetypes:

The practice of ritual can be one of the healing arts. Ritual is potentially the most powerful art form for evoking and transforming the archetypes. ...

We find this same process occurring within so-called primitive or pre-literate cultures which are often rife with ritual practices. ...

Simple rituals are used at the Institute as part of the natural process of working with the unconscious and seeking renewal from its source energies. ...

We also work with relating to symbolic objects, usually from nature, which might embody "spirit in substance" energies. The effect of such a process is to create a deeper more meaningful level of dream-sharing and to evoke the central archetype, inner and outer (739:130).

*Carlos Castaneda's* The Art of Dreaming

"Following don Juan's suggestion, I have refrained from using shamanism, a category proper to anthropology, to classify his knowledge. I have called it all along what he himself called it: sorcery" (2733:VII).

—*Carlos Castaneda*

"Sorcerer ... a magician, especially one supposedly aided by evil spirits." (Oxford American Dictionary)

*The Los Angeles Times* referred to Carlos Castaneda as "one of the godfathers of the New Age movement," and indeed, no other single individual has been more responsible for introducing millions of Americans to sorcery than Castaneda (see Shamanism). After writing his eighth book, *The Power of Silence*, Castaneda spent six years in study, meditation, and dream work and then wrote what is possibly his most significant work, *The Art of Dreaming*.

Castaneda classifies "the art of dreaming" as "the most important" of all the sorcery arts that his Yaqui Indian sorcerer instructor, don Juan Matus, made him practice (2733:VIII). Indeed, for reasons that soon become clear, dream work is the most vital method of the sorcerer's occult armory, and the most dangerous. Yet books of this nature, which powerfully travel into the dark world of the occult, and which instruct others how to do the same through dream-induced out-of-the body experiences, are better left alone by the curious. Reasons in abundance are supplied in the book.

For Castaneda, don Juan, and all sorcery, dream work is the quintessential technique permitting contact not only with the world of spirits and demons but with incredibly bizarre and all-too-frightening realities—realities entirely unknown to the mind of noninitiates. Regardless, whatever the perceived occult benefits of entering of such realms, the end result is that explorers become victims of its seductions and manipulated by demons.

Don Juan himself has to warn Castaneda continually of the risks and dangers. He refers to "the trickery of the inorganic beings [i.e., spirits]," and he declares, "It is absurd to trust the inorganic beings.... [S]orcerer's maneuvers are deadly." Don Juan went on:

> I beseech you to be extraordinarily aware. ... You must be extremely careful, for you are about to fall prey to the inorganic beings. ... The inorganic beings are plotting.... You must seriously consider that the inorganic beings have astounding means at their disposal. ... Their awareness is superb. In comparison, we are children, children with a lot of energy, which the inorganic beings covet.... The inorganic beings don't let anyone go, not without a real fight.... [You may encounter] circumstances that are more dreadful than death. Everything in the sorcerer's path is a matter of life or death, but in the path of dreaming, this matter is enhanced a hundred fold.... That's why you have to go into their realm exactly as if you were venturing into a war zone (2733:103-10).

Once someone enters the world of the sorcerer's dreams, distinguishing reality from fantasy becomes problematic. As Castaneda recalls, "Dreaming of that world, I became aware of what don Juan had said to me many times: that under the influence of dreaming, reality suffers a metamorphosis.... [R]eality becomes fluid.... [W]e are left with very few tools for sensory interpretation and, thus, a sense of an infinite realness that is unreal or an infinite unrealness that could very well be real but is not" (2733:97). For example, attempting to merge the consciousness of everyday life with the consciousness of sorcerer's dreams and other realities was treacherous. Castaneda recalls, "[I]n my daily state I was nearly an idiot, and in the second attention [state of consciousness] I was a lunatic" (2733:125).

According to Castaneda, the more one experiences dreaming in an occult context, the greater one's chances that the spirit world will respond and somehow "enliven" the dreams to a highly dramatic and captivating new level, which permits the kinds of bizarre and horrible things recounted in the book. Castaneda writes:

> Some strange force, which I had never before encountered in my dreaming, had me riveted down.... [I]t was a blob of sheer energy. I was

able to see its energetic sizzling. It seemed to be conscious of me. Suddenly, it lurched onto me and tugged me or prodded me.... [R]ipples of energy went through it, one after another. From that moment on, everything in my dreaming became much more real. I had a very difficult time keeping the idea that I was dreaming a dream. To this difficulty, I had to add the certainty I had that with its touch the scout [spirit] had made an energetic connection with me. I knew what it wanted me to do the instant it seemed to tug me or shove me (2733:88-89).

As Don Juan later told Castaneda:

> [The] awareness of sorcerers grows when they do dreaming. And the moment it grows, something out there acknowledges its growth, recognizes it and makes a bid for it. The inorganic beings are the bidders for that new, enhanced awareness. Dreamers have to be forever on their toes. They are prey the moment they venture out in that predatorial universe. "What do you suggest I do to be safe, don Juan?" "Be on your toes every second!" (2733:101).

Of course, once one enters the realm of demons, no one can be on their toes *every* second. Sooner or later one becomes the victim. In the middle of the book, don Juan sharply warns Castaneda:

"You've gone beyond the point where you could simply quit. Besides, you had the misfortune of being singled out by a [specific entity]. ... They are dependent and possessive, and once they sink their hooks, they never give up." "And what does that mean in my case, don Juan?" "It means real trouble. The specific inorganic being who's running the show is the one you grabbed that fatal day. Over the years, it has grown familiar with you. It knows you intimately.... I am thinking that they are going to trick you," he said. "Like they tricked nagual [sorcerer] Rosendo. They are going to set you up, and you won't see the trap or even suspect it" (2733:123).

Clearly, this is the final lot of all those who use dreams or other methods to assimilate sorcery: in the end they are "set up" for destruction and they don't even know it. Indeed, this has sadly been the lot of Castaneda for over two decades. Manipulated by spirits at their whim, enthralled or tormented as they see fit, Castaneda had become, in the worst sense, someone *used*. Castaneda may think he has some degree of control over his visionary excursions, or that he has attained a state of excellence along the path of sorcery (2733:122), but he is just a pawn of forces that could crush him at will. He knows this, yet he continues.

What Castaneda and others have found—what they encourage us to find by "the art of dreaming"—is far better left alone.

### Dream Work and Inner Teachers

Another text is *Dreams: Discovering Your Inner Teacher* by Clyde Reid; it is typical of the many books which utilize dreams to contact an "inner teacher" (cf. Inner Work). The inner teacher, however, is often indistinguishable from a modern spirit guide. As Clyde observes, "There is much discussion these days about *spirit guides*. This term was once the private property of strange, esoteric people or spiritualists. However, as we increasingly explore the unconscious through dream analysis and meditation, we find that many people are in touch with their spirit guides and are conscious of their help" (61:85).

He says he is often asked, "Are spirit guides the same as the inner teacher?" He responds that because they act in similar ways, they may indeed be one and the same. Clyde also notes, "In the workshops I offer around North America on the subject of dreams and the inner teacher, I am amazed at how many people are ready to find their inner teacher or already have some sense of it" (61:85).

There is little doubt that Reid's text and his own dream workshops are an effective means toward introducing people to the world of the occult. And yet he makes the standard claim that this kind of activity is really a "divine" work because dreams "are manifestations of the Spirit of the living God. As for me, I insist on testing those spirits with the highest standard I know. As I am by choice a Protestant Christian, I test the spirits by the spirit of Christ as best I know it. . . . [Nevertheless,] I believe that the task of Spiritual leaders today is to instill trust of the inner teacher into our people" (61:86).

Reid believes that those who think such activity may involve demonic deceptions are simply uninformed as to how God works: "Historically, religious authorities have feared such inner leading as the work of the devil. Today we are much more ready to trust that God works from deep within us. When we learn to trust the inner teacher, and to check our dreams with that teacher, our lives begin to flow with the divine intention" (61:75).

### Joan Windsor

Another illustration of New Age dream work is found with Joan Windsor, an author who holds workshops on dreaming, parapsychology, healing, and creativity topics. One of her mentors is the spiritist and New Age leader, Ruth Montgomery (335:VI). Windsor is the author of *The Inner Eye: Your Dreams Can Make You Psychic* (Prentice Hall, 1985) and *Dreams and Healing: Expanding the Inner Eye—How to Attune Your Mind-Body Connection Through Imagery, Intuition and Life Energies* (335). Dreams are utilized for and associated with all sorts of New Age topics: auras, Edgar Cayce, channeling,* reincarnation, astral projection, psychic development and guidance, intuitive* diagnosis and psychic healing, psychic counseling, absent healing, crystal work,* visualization,* positive affirmations, and meditation.*

For example, dreams can be utilized for physical healing by "asking for direction from higher realms":

Not only is the dreamer able to invoke physical guidance and healing for himself, but given that all minds are in contact with one another, we are often assigned the task of personally healing our friends and acquaintances. This is accomplished through the medium of dream revelations which contain transmissions commenting on aberrant conditions regarding their physical health.

Through intensive review and interpretation of dreams, expanding minds realize that not only are dreams soul flights into higher realms in an unquenchable thirst for esoteric knowledge, but they may also be the vehicle for achieving physical healings for others while the body lies at rest. . . . To quote Phyllis A. Koch-Sheras, author of *Dream On*, "You don't have to wait for your dreams to offer you health advice spontaneously. You can educate them to provide this advice when you need it, through dream incubation (335:110,114).

*New Age "Christian" Dream Work*

Most but not all "Christian" dream work is really New Age dream work using Christian terminology. The influence of the following text among Christians is great enough that we will use it as an illustration. In *Dreams and Spiritual Growth: A Christian Approach to Dreamwork* (65), we discover that so-called "Christian dream work" is not derived from Scripture itself. Rather, it comes from secular psychotherapy and culture, such as the Jungian analysis and dream work of those who endorse shamanism,* such as John Sanford and Morton Kelsey (65:64-69).

The book repeatedly stresses that dream work leads to "wholeness" and "holiness" (65:70-71,188). "Wholeness" is supposedly achieved by the technique of Jungian "individuation," and "holiness" is a subjectively determined state of spiritual growth based upon psychological completeness or integration. In other words, this book basically deals with psychological experimentation, defined subjectively and then interpreted as spiritual growth. Despite its title, it does not deal with Christian theology or Christian sanctification.

This kind of dream work may also be used as a means of spirit contact, although the spirits contacted are believed to be Christian saints:

One of the significant doctrinal beliefs in the Christian Church is called the communion of saints. This doctrine teaches that persons in God's grace do not cease to exist after death, but live in a non-physical state joined to each other and to Christ in loving, soul-to-soul communion. Early Christian teachers proposed a variety of relations between the communion of saints and dreams.

For example, for many of the Church elders, the dream state gives us some idea of the life of the soul after death. Ambrose believed that dreams and visions were a means of contacting those who had died. More generally, Justin Martyr

believed that humans are capable of contact and spiritual communication with non-physical beings (65:41).

But were Ambrose and Martyr really spiritists or necromancers? Hardly! If some early Christians did believe such things, they were clearly wrong from a scriptural perspective. At least the early Christians warned that dreams could come from either God or Satan. Many of the current texts on "Christian" dream work don't go this far. Furthermore, as is true in the text under discussion, they reject biblical authority and deny or downplay the devil. In fact, no personal devil or demons really exist (65:208-12). By accepting *all* dreams as divine and by integrating dream work with Jungian presuppositions, they also open the door for demonic intrusion into dreams while inhibiting any process of biblical discernment:

In this book our general position is that since everything in the universe is God's, all dreams somehow reflect God's purposes and plans for our lives. Even the most demonic or terrifying presences in dreams can be worked with and their energy transformed.

We are not as concerned with where dreams come from as we are with what we do with the dreams which do come to us. Our methodology and spiritual perspective of commitment to wholeness and holiness should be able to encompass any kind of dream and offer ways of working with it toward transformation and meaning (65:41).

This book on "Christian" dream work accepts contact with the dead through dreams (65:42), and it masks spiritism under its Dream Work Technique 5: "Dialogue with the Dream Figure" (cf. Inner Work). All in all, the book provides some 37 different dream work techniques:

It is also possible to dialogue with dream characters, meditatively, after the dream. Dialoguing with figures or symbols from our dreams is a very powerful and basic dreamwork technique with a wide variety of uses.

We need to establish relation to the energies in a dream in order for them to work for us toward healing and wholeness. Almost all dream work techniques suggested in this book invite us to relate to the dream and its energies.

Dialoguing [with dream entities] is ... especially powerful in releasing spiritual energy and insight. ... On the other hand, dialoguing is an exercise in surrender, in letting go of control.

Dialoguing with dream figures puts us in touch with both the invitation and the energy to change and grow. Dialoguing is the beginning of transformation.

Dialoguing in dream work is quite simple. ... To get started, we ask the dream figure a question and let the dream figure's response come. Usually this response leads us to respond in turn, or perhaps to ask another question. In this way a dialogue may continue (65:56-57).

As noted earlier, there is little doubt that this process can and does lead to spiritistic contact. Although the dream figures are normally interpreted as part of a person's "unconscious," they are nevertheless part of spiritual reality: "As you practice dream work, you grow comfortable in working in non-rational realms. You soon realize these realms have their own reality, which is fundamentally a spiritual reality. In time, you find it natural to work with spiritual energy" (65:59).

Consider the following example about alleged angels:*

Once when we were explaining the dialogue technique to a group, one woman told how as a child she used to dialogue with her guardian angel, especially at times when she was lonely or hurting. At these times she felt her angel responding and comforting her. Many people in the audience were familiar with the dialoguing experience, for they were nodding their heads in agreement. In dreamwork we are to be open like children, to allow two-way conversations between us and dream figures to happen in our imaginations (65:59).

The spiritually naive approach suggested in texts like this underscores why they can lead participants to spiritistic deception: Personal experience overrules critical thinking. Thus, we are told that the actual identity of the dream figure is really unimportant. Knowing whether it is merely a part of one's unconscious or an actual spirit entity is not as important as using the technique to "grow spiritually." The dream user is assured that questions of spiritual discernment are out of place and may actually harm the process of effective dream work. The proper approach is simply to trust in the process itself, wherever it leads. "[W]e are not suggesting source questions such as: 'Who are you? Are you a part of me? Are you someone outside me? Do you come from God? Are you a messenger? Are you a projection of my mind?' These are questions of theory. As such, they may distract from the main task of entering into a relationship with the dream figure. ... Our suggestion is: Trust the process" (65:58).

In other words, "From our perspective, *all* dreams are given for our growth, no matter how paranormal [occult] their content may seem. The ultimate source of the dream is God and its purpose is ultimately to bring about healing and wholeness" (65:207, emphasis added). Because "God is everywhere, and nowhere visible" (739:221) all invisible realities are assumed to be divine.

Once we assume that everything comes from God in such a manner, the question of demonic deception is ruled out by definition. Again, the authors of *Dreams and Spiritual Growth* don't believe in a personal devil (65:208-12). And they are fully open to working with any and all kinds of spiritual "energies." "Spirituality is one's way of responding to God's call, a style of living that is open to energies of God's spirit. ... For persons using dreamwork, their spirituality involves ways of channeling energy released from the inner world into the everyday world" (65:106-07). Here we encounter the development of psychic abilities under the aegis of working with supposedly divine energies. "We assume that truly telepathic dreams are a sign of latent psychic ability, and that dream work may be used to accept this ability as a gift from God to be used in deepening one's spiritual insight and direction in life. Dream work here is designed to help broaden the dreamer's life view and to develop tasks that use the [psychic] ability to serve others in healing ways" (65:213).

The authors also want occult powers to be used in Christian ministry: "Some people are able to use their psychic and intuitive abilities in their Christian ministry in situations where deep spiritual knowing and help can bring issues into awareness for healing and growth. It is with this orientation that we offer suggestions for working with dreams that reflect paranormal human capacity such as telepathy, ESP, synchronicity, prophecy, and the like" (65:214).

It seems clear that the several dozen dream work techniques suggested in this text, like the three dozen in *The Jungian-Senoi Dreamwork Manual* (739:219-25), can become a basis for developing psychic abilities, entering altered states of consciousness,* energy channeling,* or spirit contact. That the former book sanctifies spirit contact under the guise of encountering Christian saints or biblical personages hardly alters its occult potential. Indeed, one cannot distinguish the kind of dream work suggested in this book from the more openly spiritistic forms, such as those experienced by followers of medium Edgar Cayce:

Dreams came to Cayce's subjects to show them the kind of [spiritual] vehicle or body they might have after death, how they would know they were dead, how they would progress through various planes, and what sort of [spirit] helpers they would find. Much was unfolded in their dreams about communication with the dead. ... How they longed to speak through a psychic. ... One is ready for dreams of the dead when he is as ready to give aid to the dead as to receive it. When prayer for a discarnate [spirit] comes freely and naturally to mind, then visions of them may follow (64:189-90).

Here is a sobering thought. The number of occultists who utilize dream work for an endless variety of occult pursuits is legion. Yet the same dream techniques used by these occultists are now employed by some or many Christian dream workers within the church.

Because the therapeutic application of dream work is not proven, and because its occult potential outweighs its possible benefit, we believe that using dream work techniques and workshops in the church is spiritually hazardous.

## DREAM RESEARCH AND NEW AGE GOALS

Psychophysiologist Dr. Stephen LaBerge, noted authority and pioneer in dream research, is currently engaged in lucid dreaming research at Stanford University. His book *Lucid Dreaming* is one of several which shows how even secular, scientific research into dreams can be used in support of New Age beliefs and goals.

His research, and that of others, reveals that to develop the potential for lucid dreaming is *also* to develop the potential for the occult practice of astral projection (338:228-58). LaBerge's work with lucid dreams further reveals a reason why the spirit world may be so interested in encouraging people toward dream work, particularly lucid dream work. The phenomena of lucid dreams are so real that those enamored with them, like those who use drugs, may find it difficult to separate objective and subjective reality. Even Dr. LaBerge's own work in this area has led him to question what is real:

According to the traditional psychology of Tibetan Buddhism, all of our experiences are subjective and thus, by their very nature, no different in substance from what we call 'dreams.' This is also the point of view of the cognitive psychology of the modern West. Granting this premise—and scientifically speaking, it is impossible to argue with it—it would be difficult to name any experience that was not a sort of dream (338:234-35).

What you see is not "what is out there"; in fact, it isn't even "out there." What you see is only a mental model inside your head of what you perceive or believe is "out there. ... " I recommend the working hypothesis that your experiences are necessarily subjective (338:274).

Of course, if objective and subjective reality are the same, where does anyone find a scorecard? One guess about reality is as good as the next, and no guess is authoritative. This perspective can lead to any number of conclusions supported by New Age, Eastern, and occult philosophy. Perhaps our normal waking experience is only a dream, as Hinduism teaches. Perhaps no reality exists outside our own minds, and we create our own reality, as various spirits

("Seth," "Ramtha," "Lazaris"), certain mind science philosophy, and much of the New Age
Movement teaches. Perhaps lucid dreams reveal
that we are normally only "half-awake," living in
a "lower state" of consciousness, and that we
must pursue a path of "higher consciousness" in
our daily lives in order to live in "true reality," as
the occult teaches. Or perhaps if we create reality,
then "death" is our own creation, or even our
own spiritual awakening. "[F]rom the point of
view of dreaming, death and transcendence are
the same thing" (338:272) (cf. *A Course in Miracles*). Of course, these four conclusions are
taught by the spirit world, and for good reason
(refs. 63,507), because if reality is uncertain, then
the idea of the "subjectively" supernatural (e.g.,
spiritistic guidance in dreams) may just as easily
be considered objectively real.

If we create our own reality *entirely*, then
every influence of the spirits in our lives is really
something *we* created. And if we are divine
beings, then such influence is divine by definition. Spiritual deception becomes a myth. The
work of actual spirits outside of us is internalized
and the traditional spirit guide, for example,
becomes our "higher self," or a Jungian archetype, or a manifestation of the collective unconscious, "superconsciousness," or whatever. Once
we accept that spiritistic phenomena are our
own objective creation, then all bets are off; we
are at the mercy of the spirits. They are part *of*
us, an aspect of our own *internal* consciousness.
If so, it is then impossible to view the spirits as
separate entities, let alone entities who might
seek our spiritual destruction.

Finally, consider LaBerge's discussion of
Buddhist "dream yoga." This is a practice in
Buddhism and Hinduism that uses dreams to
confuse subjective and objective reality in order
to recognize the "illusion" of the creation and to
help prepare the yogi for death and the realization that he is one with God, or ultimate reality
(Brahman or Nirvana). The purpose of dream
yoga is to awake from the illusion that what we
see around us is real:

Dream yoga is not merely intended as a
rehearsal for the final sleep of death. The serious
follower of dream yoga is attempting to awaken

before death: "The whole purpose of the Doctrine of Dreams is to stimulate the yogin to arise
from the Sleep of Delusion, from the Nightmare
of Existence, to break the shackles in which
maya [illusion] thus has held him prisoner
throughout the aeons, and so attain spiritual
peace and joy of Freedom, even as did the Fully
Awakened One, Gautama the Buddha."

The first steps toward the dream yogi's goal of
awakening involve becoming proficient in "com-
prehending the nature of the dream state." Once
the yogi has become an accomplished lucid
dreamer, he proceeds to the next stage, "trans-
muting the dream-content" . . . (338:261-62).

This next step involves the conscious "control"
of the dream, including, as we saw with Castaneda's sorcery, astral projection to visit other
spiritual realms. "After gaining sufficient skill in
controlling his reactions to the contents of his
lucid dreams, the yogi goes on to more advanced
exercises, and by means of these he masters the
ability to visit—in his lucid dreams—any realm
of existence desired" (338:262).

Later the yogi uses dream work to realize the
illusion of his own body. "After becoming 'thoroughly proficient' in the art of transforming
dream content, the yogi turns his attention to his
own dream body: this, he now sees, is just as
illusory as any other element of his lucid dream.
The fact that the fully lucid dreamer knows he is
not his dream body plays a crucial role in self-
transformation" (338:262-63).

After this, the yogi encounters spirits and gods
who play a role in his progress toward "higher"
consciousness, although by now he recognizes
them as his own dream creations, not as objective spiritual beings:

The fourth and final stage of dream yoga is
enigmatically termed "meditating upon the
thatness of the dream-state." The text tells us
that by means of this meditation, "the dream
propensities whence arise whatever is seen in
dreams as appearances of deities, are purified."
It is, ironically, by means of these "appearances" that the ultimate goal is reached. The
yogi is, of course, aware that these "deities" are
his own mental images. Bearing this in mind,
he is instructed to concentrate in the lucid

dream state, focusing on the forms of these deities, . . . (338:263).

The final stage is the yogi's realization that he is one with ultimate reality, or God itself:

A final step brings the yogi to "the Great Realization" that nothing within the experience of his mind "can be other than unreal like dreams." In this light, "the Universal Creation . . . and every phenomenal thing therein" are seen to be "but the content of the Supreme Dream." And for the one upon whom "this Divine Wisdom" has dawned, "the microcosmic aspect of the Macrocosm becomes fully awakened; the dew-drop slips back into the Shining Sea, in Nirvanic Blissfulness and at-one-ment, possessed of All Possessions, Knower of the All-Knowledge, Creator of All Creations–the One Mind, Reality Itself" (338:263-64).

As the Hindu would say, "atman (the individual soul) is Braham (the highest God)," or more simply, "I am the only incarnation and representative of the Supreme One" (338:265). Actually this is also Dr. LaBerge's own tentative personal conclusion: that individually, in our true nature, we are one with God. From this perspective, the value of lucid dreaming is that it helps us to realize that we are "identical with the nature of ultimate reality":

Lucid dreaming can be a point of departure from which to understand how we might not be fully awake—for as ordinary dreaming is to lucid dreaming, so the ordinary waking state might be to the fully awakened state. This capacity of lucid dreams, to prepare us for a fuller awakening, may prove to be lucid dreaming's most significant potential . . . (338:279).

. . . Our individuality is not our truest being, . . . [Y]our essential being transcends space and time: your transpersonal identity transcends your personal identity. This, your transpersonal individuality, may in the end prove identical with the nature of ultimate reality . . . Creator of All Creations—the One Mind, Reality Itself (338:272).

In conclusion, modern dream work is an overrated and questionable practice at best. Its effectiveness in therapy is unestablished, and it often promotes a variety of occult pursuits. It easily confuses important spiritual and metaphysical issues, and even its scientific research can become tainted by New Age influence.

Perhaps dreams are better left to the dreamer.

# Eastern Gurus

- Info at a Glance
- Introduction and Influence
- Hinduism Defined
- Leading Gurus
- *Advaita* Vedanta
- Nihilism
- Common Practices
  - Altered States of Consciousness
  - Yoga and Meditation
  - Occultism
- Theology
  - God
  - Man
  - Jesus Christ
  - Salvation (Enlightenment)
  - Afterlife
- Philosophical Consequences
  - Spiritual Authoritarianism
  - The Mind as Enemy
  - Personhood as an Illusion
  - Morality as Counterproductive
- Personal Consequences
  - Insanity and Possession
  - Family Life
  - Murder and the Spiritually Enlightened?
- Other Hazards

## Info at a Glance

**Description.** Eastern gurus constitute a large class of Hindu occultists who have come to America to spread the teachings of Hinduism, especially its necessary spiritual practices for achieving enlightenment.*

**Founder.** Different schools of Hinduism have different founders. Shankara (9th c. A.D.) founded the *advaita* school, which is the teaching of most Hindu gurus in America.

**How does it claim to work?** Through practices such as altered states of consciousness,* meditation,* and yoga,* disciples are told they will achieve a form of spiritual "enlightenment"* and thereby realize their true nature as being one essence with the highest Hindu God, Brahman.

**Examples of occult potential.** Psychic development, spirit contact, and possession. The gurus accept a wide variety of occult practices.

**Major Problems:** The gurus' claims to represent, or incarnate, God and to offer higher forms of spirituality, which they say are desperately needed in the West, is contradicted by their teachings. Collectively, the gurus are a powerful vehicle for spreading dangerous forms of pagan spirituality and practice in America.

**Biblical/Christian evaluation.** Despite their claims to represent God or Jesus, and to not contradict Christian belief, the gurus' teachings and practices are implicitly hostile to biblical theology and instruction.

**Potential Dangers.** Social withdrawal, moral compromise, psychological damage, demonization.

*Note:* This chapter is based on the authors' *The Facts on Hinduism in America* (cf. Enlightenment).

Once embarked on this [spiritual] journey, we are advised to seek the guidance of those who have been there before and know it well: teachers, gurus, roshis, swamis . . . and adepts of every description. But with common sense set aside, how can we judge the credentials of our teachers? What criteria can we use to determine the suitability of this man or this woman to guide us along the path . . . ?

—*Yoga Journal* Editorial (1353:4)

## INTRODUCTION
## AND INFLUENCE

The purpose of this chapter is to briefly evaluate the teachings and practices of many of the major Hindu gurus or "spiritual leaders" in America. We will seek to determine whether the gurus are a positive or negative religious and social force in the nation.

Hinduism is, of course, Hinduism, wherever it is found. However, it should be noted that certain differences exist between Indian and American Hinduism. Hindu influence in India pervades the entire culture; in America, Hinduism is only one part of a growing pagan religious culture. Thus, the pervasive idolatry of India, illustrated in thousands of temples and idols paraded throughout the streets, is currently lacking in America. Also, Hinduism in America is sometimes "secularized," "Christianized," or otherwise toned down or made palatable for Western consumption. For example, Maharishi Mahesh Yogi's Hindu practice of Transcendental Meditation claims (falsely) that it is a true science and not a religion; and the spiritistic revelation called *A Course in Miracles*\* is merely a novel form of Hindu philosophy (*advaita* Vedanta) with a "Christian" veneer.

Nevertheless, the East has indeed come West and the impact of Hinduism in America is unmistakable. In the minds of millions of Americans, Hindu gurus represent a positive and godly spiritual trend in the fabric of American religious and cultural life. The gurus are viewed as:

1. Enlightened spiritual masters and authoritative representatives of God.

2. Morally pure individuals.

3. Men with great wisdom and compassion, with gentle and dignified personalities.

4. Often as "incarnations" of God, or as having divine attributes, such as omniscience (all knowledge), omnipotence (all power) and eternality (as having existed forever). Therefore, they are worthy of worship.

Why do so many Americans view the Hindu gurus like this? One reason is because this is how the gurus present themselves. Another reason is because they claim to be like Jesus Christ, and therefore, people may innocently transfer the characteristics of Christ to them.

In Western culture, Jesus Christ is the only illustration of a divine incarnation with whom people are familiar. When the gurus claim to be the incarnation of God, this portrait of Jesus may be unsuspectingly transferred to them. But if we examine and compare the teachings and practices of the Hindu gurus with the biblical Jesus, it is a study in stark contrasts.

Years of research have led us to conclude that virtually all the individual claims of the gurus should be viewed critically, particularly their spiritual claims. Indeed, from the perspective of traditional Western values in general, and Judeo-Christian philosophy and religion in particular, the American guru phenomenon is a genuine threat to society, the family, morality, and the vitality of the church and her influence in culture.

We came to two major conclusions from our study:

1. Practically speaking, the guru phenomenon comprises a revival of occult practice and philosophy. We repeatedly encountered themes of shamanism,\* spiritism, psychic development, modified aspects of witchcraft practice, and other forms of paganism. Such methods do not lead to an alleged spiritual "enlightenment,"\* but rather to harmful spiritual states, including the distinct possibility of mental illness or demon possession. Thus, the gurus are not divine incarnations as they claim, but spiritually possessed occultists whose philosophical and occult teachings are consequential for human society and welfare.

2. Theologically, the gurus are an anti-Christian force; their religious instruction is not in harmony with biblical or Christian teaching as claimed, but actively opposes it.

Had the average disciple of a Hindu guru known his guru's true teachings, and their potential moral, psychological, and spiritual consequences, we suspect that most would never have followed. After surveying some of the recent tragedies among followers of the gurus, even Dio Neff, a book review editor for the *Yoga Journal*, wonders, "Are many Western seekers just fools" (1354:21)?

In all its forms, including direct and indirect influence, Hinduism and its practices have tens of millions of followers in America. By itself Maharishi Mahesh Yogi's Transcendental Meditation, a form of *advaita* Vedanta Hinduism, has some four or five million graduates (468). Hinduism is influential upon college campuses, in particular in schools of psychology, such as the transpersonal school, and in a wide variety of religious movements (1365:9-15). The "large majority" of several thousand transpersonal psychologists are involved in Eastern forms of meditation,* and "one of the long-held goals of transpersonal psychology has been an integration of Western science and Eastern practice" (439:69).

The New Age Movement, with a collective following in the tens of millions, has also been powerfully influenced by Hinduism. In many respects the philosophy of the New Age Movement parallels that of Hinduism.

In addition, there are scores of modern religious cults and sects that have been influenced by Hinduism to varying degrees. Werner Erhard, founder of "Landmark Education's 'The Forum'*," and "est"* seminars, which have about 700,000 graduates, was influenced by Hinduism through Swami Muktananda, one of Erhard's principal gurus (1366). The occult religion of Theosophy was influenced by Hinduism (1366), as were many of the New Thought religions, such as Science of Mind and Divine Science, which actively promote Hindu teachings (1366). Mary Baker Eddy's Christian Science and Charles and Myrtle Fillmore's Unity

School of Christianity were also influenced by Hinduism. Much of the popular occult religion of Eckankar is a plagiarism of a Hindu sect known as Radhasoami. Scientology,* a powerful and controversial new religion, has also been influenced by Hinduism (1366).

In addition, literally millions of Americans have taken up Hindu practices, such as yoga,* meditation,* developing altered states of consciousness,* and seeking Hindu "enlightenment."*

If we were to combine the influence of Hinduism in the guru movements, in American colleges, in the New Age Movement, in yoga and meditation, and in various modern religious cultisms, Hinduism has influenced tens of millions of Americans.

Unfortunately, ignorance is widespread concerning the true practices and teachings of Hinduism. If Hinduism in America is often packaged as one thing when, in fact, it is something else entirely, then people have a right to that information. For example, many gurus claim their spiritual path is compatible with Christian faith. But most Hinduism views Christianity as a harmful influence, which it seeks to undermine. Many gurus think biblical Christianity is "dangerous nonsense," "psychologically manipulative," or "spiritually destructive" (1367:196-97).

Some Hindu organizations allegedly espouse (secretly) the destruction of Christianity in America and its replacement with Hinduism (cf. 2817:52). Yet at the same time they may claim to offer the world the genuine teachings of Jesus Christ. When the gurus claim that their teachings follow Jesus', and yet when they undermine His teachings, people also have the right to know where the Hindu path will ultimately take them.

## HINDUISM DEFINED

In its most simple definition, Hinduism may be defined as the religious beliefs and practices common to India. Defining Hinduism in a more precise manner is difficult because of its wide number of practices and teachings. To illustrate this, here are selected definitions from authoritative sources. Hinduism is:

The Way of the majority of the people of India, a Way that is a combination of religious belief, rites, customs, and daily practices, many of which appear overtly secular but in most cases have religious origins and sanctions. Hinduism is noted as being the only one of the major beliefs that cannot be defined, for any definition is inadequate, contradictory, and incomplete (1355:166-67).

The name used in the West to designate the traditional socioreligious structure of the Indian people. As a religion based on mythology, it has neither a founder (as do Buddhism, Islam, and Christianity) nor a fixed canon. Myriad local cults and traditions of worship or belief can be distinguished (1356:130).

The variety of religious beliefs and practices making up the major religious tradition of the Indian subcontinent (302:306).

... a complex product of [the] amalgamation of various cults and beliefs within a common social framework [e.g., the caste system] (1357:330).

In spite of its diversity, Hinduism reveals a number of common themes. Some of these include pantheism (the belief that all is God, God is all), polytheism (a belief in many lesser gods), and a reliance upon occult ritual and practices.

Hinduism originated from a body of conflicting and contradictory (1358) literature called the *Vedas* (ca. 1500-1200 B.C.). Hindus claim that this body of literature was supernaturally revealed by the Hindu gods (759:21). Thus, these basic religious texts "make a special claim to be divine in their origin" (1359:3).

The four Vedas are the *Rigveda, Samaveda, Yajuraveda,* and the *Artharvaveda.* They are divided into two parts: the "work" portion (basically polytheistic ritual) and the "knowledge" portion (philosophical speculation). This latter portion comprises what is called the Upanishads or Vedanta: "Since they brought to a close each of the four Vedas, the Upanishads came to be spoken of often as the Vedanta—the *anta* or end of the Vedas" (1359:21).

The Vedas are mostly a collection of ritualistic hymns to various Hindu gods. The *Rigveda* comprises the foremost collection of these hymns. The *Yajurveda* is a collection of various mantras,* or special words used to evoke occult power. The *Samaveda* combines verses from the *Rigveda* to melodic chants. The *Artharvaveda* is basically a collection of occult spells, incantations, and hymns (1360:375).

The Vedas are really the "Bible" of Hinduism. They can be divided into the Samhitas, Brahmanas, Aranyakas, and Upanishads. The visual chart below may help the reader see the relationships here.

Only 108 Upanishads remain and, of these, ten are of central importance. They are the tsa, kena, katha, prasma, mundaka, mandukya, chandogya, brhadaranyaka, aitareya, and taittiriya. As far as the Upanishads themselves are concerned, "[T]heir variety of thought has allowed considerable latitude in their interpretation, so that scriptural orthodoxy has not led to a single viewpoint. Thus, Hindu metaphysicians range in their adherence from ... theism to atheism" (1361:155).

The entire collection of Vedas is held to be supernaturally inspired. "The entire corpus of Vedic literature—the *Samhitas* and the exposition

| 4 Vedas | Rig | Ritual ("work" portion) | Samhitas—collections of mantras or hymns to pagan deities |
| | Sama | | Brahamnas—details of sacrificial rites and duties |
| | Yajur | | Aranyakas—spiritual/occult interpretations of religious rites and ceremonies |
| | Artharva | Philosophical (commentaries; "knowledge" portion) | Upanishads (Vedanta) |

that came to be attached to them, the *Brahmanas*, the *Aranyakas* and the *Upanishads*—was considered *sruti* or divinely heard" (1361:155). But who was it that heard and received this supernatural inspiration? It was the Hindu *rishis* or *seers*—powerful occultists who interpreted their revelations as divine communication from the gods (1362:251). For reasons that will soon become clear, we cannot accept the idea that such literature had a *divine* origin, because it bears the marks of spiritistic inspiration.

Hindu influences in America are not new. They were felt earlier through the New England Transcendentalists, and through a variety of religious movements such as Theosophy, Christian Science, Unity School of Christianity, and through the spiritualist revival that began in 1848. An important role for introducing Hinduism to America was played by the World Parliament of Religions Congress in 1893. At that Congress, the brilliant disciple of Sri Ramakrishna, Swami Vivekananda, gave a powerful oration that dramatically affected many who were present. Subsequently, liberal clergymen were instrumental in helping Vivekananda to get a social platform from which to spread his Hindu teachings. This lead to the establishment of the Ramakrishna Mission in New York and a dozen other centers, which even today "carry on a vigorous propaganda" for Hinduism (1363:201).

In 1920, Paramahansa Yogananda spoke before the International Congress of Religious Liberals in America, sponsored by the American Unitarian Association. Again, religious liberals were instrumental in giving a Hindu leader a wide public platform. From 1920-30 he single-handedly led tens of thousands of Americans into yoga practice and other aspects of Hindu belief (1364:405-08). And his *Autobiography of a Yogi* was well read during the 1960s counterculture movement. Thus by the time of the social revolution of the late 1950s and 1960s, the soil had already been prepared for a significant planting of Hindu gurus throughout the nation.

## LEADING GURUS

Below is a list of some of the Hindu gurus having the most influence in America. They have each had, or still have, at least 20,000 followers. In terms of direct and indirect impact (writings, cassettes, videos), most of the gurus have reached hundreds of thousands; several have reached millions of people. Since a significant number of dropouts and new converts exchange places each year, and because figures for the rest of the world are not included, their overall influence would be considerably enlarged:

*Bhagwan Shree Rajneesh*
Rajneesh founded the Rajneesh Foundation International, and is one of the most controversial of modern gurus. In 1981 he was deported from Oregon under a bevy of serious criminal charges associated with his ashram, or spiritual community. His recent death did little to stem his influence in Europe or America.

*Swami Muktananda*
Muktananda founded Siddha Yoga Dham of America (SYDA), and was also a highly controversial guru. He is especially popular among some of the Hollywood jetset.

*Sai Baba*
Sai Baba is the founder of the Sathya Sai Baba Society, and is perhaps the dominant guru in India, having over 20,000,000 followers in that nation; through his writings he is also having an impact in America.

*Maharishi Mahesh Yogi*
Maharishi Mahesh Yogi is the founder of the popular Hindu practice of Transcendental Meditation, also known euphemistically as the "Science of Creative Intelligence."

*Paramahansa Yogananda*
Yogananda founded the Self-Realization Fellowship, which attempts to blend ancient pagan Hinduism and the teachings of Jesus.

*A. C. Bhaktivedanta Prabhupada*
Prabhupada was the founder of ISKCON, the International Society for Krisha Consciousness, whose followers are more popularly known as "Hare Krishnas," who can be frequently seen in public, dancing, chanting, and begging for money. ISKCON is a Vishnuite sect that makes the Hindu god Krishna the supreme deity.

*Ram Dass (Richard Alpert)*
Ram Dass is the founder of the Hanuman Foundation. [Hanuman is the Hindu monkey god.]
He is a former Harvard professor who worked
with Timothy Leary. He became a Hindu guru
as a result of his experiences under LSD and his
travels to India to study under his own guru,
Neem Karoli Baba. His checkered spiritual
odyssey is recorded in his multimillion bestsellers *Be Here Now* and *Grist for the Mill.*

*Swami Kriyananda (Donald Walters)*
Kriyananda is the founder of the Ananda Cooperative Village. Before becoming a guru on his
own, he was a devoted disciple of Paramahansa
Yogananda and the Self-Realization Fellowship.

*Da [Bubba] Free John (Franklin Jones)*
Free John is the controversial founder of the
Free Communion Church/Dawn Horse Fellow-
ship and Laughing Man Institute. He is another
Westerner who became a guru by studying
under Hindu gurus such as Nityananda,
Muktananda, Rudrananda, and others.

*Charan Singh and Sawan Singh Ji*
Founders and leaders of Radhasoami Satsang
Beas, a religion based on what is called Surat
Shabd Yoga (the yoga of "divine sound and
light"), from which much of the American cult
of Eckankar was derived.

*Kirpal Singh*
Singh is the founder of Rhuani Satsang, a further development of Radhasoami.

*Maharaj Ji*
Maharaj Ji is the rotund guru who founded the
Divine Light Mission, whose followers are
known as "premies."

*Sri Aurobindo*
Aurobindo founded the Sri Aurobindo Ashram/
Integral Yoga fellowship. His intellectual synthesis of Eastern occultism and Western philosophy has received wide acclaim.

*Jiddhu Krishnamurti*
Krishnamurti founded the Krishnamurti Foundation of America, and was once best known as
the one whom Anne Besant, then president of
the Theosophical Society, proclaimed as a new
Christ. Krishnamurti rejected this role and
began his own spiritual path.

*Swami Rama*
Swami Rama is the controversial founder of
the Himalayan International Institute of Yoga
Science and Philosophy. He became famous
through biofeedback research conducted with
biofeedback pioneer Dr. Elmer Green at the
Menninger Institute.

*Sri Chinmoy*
Sri Chinmoy founded Sri Chinmoy Centers and
is a spiritual adviser at the United Nations.

*Yogi Bhajan*
Yogi Bhajan founded the "3HO" (Happy Healthy
Holy) organization which stresses a combination of Hindu and Sufi practices such as yogic
kundalini arousal.

Ramakrishna, Vivekananda, Sivananda,
Satchidananda—the list of gurus who continue
to influence America goes on and on. Yet many
Americans have little idea of the powerful impact
these men have had.

## ADVAITA VEDANTA

In America, the dominant Hindu belief is
called Vedanta.

Of all the schools of Hinduism, Vedanta has
had the most profound overall influence:

Vedanta ("the End of Vedas") was the school
which gave organized and systematic form to
the teaching of the Upanishads. While the other
schools are almost or wholly extinct, Vedanta is
still very much alive, for nearly all the great
Hindu religious teachers of recent centuries
have been Vedantists of one branch or another
(1368:237).

The influence of Vedanta on Indian thought has
been profound, so that it may be said that, in
one or another of its forms, Hindu philosophy
has become Vedanta (1369:375).

Hinduism is, truly speaking, the religion and
philosophy of Vedanta (1370).

Since the texts of Vedanta are contradictory
and impossible to interpret uniformly (1371),
three primary schools of Vedanta have arisen.
The most influential Vedantic school in America
is called *advaita,* or the "non-dual" school. This

monistic belief teaches that there is only one impersonal God called Brahman. Brahman alone is real—everything else is considered a dream of Brahman—an "illusion." This form of Hinduism teaches that as part of its "sport" or "play" (*lila*), Brahman exuded or emerged the universe as part of itself, but then "covered" it with what is called *maya* or illusion. This illusion is the entire physical universe that we see around us, including all stars and planets, the sky, trees, rivers, mountains, and all people as well (1372). Essentially, the idea that the world is an illusion "hiding" Brahman is a key teaching of Hinduism in America. This teaching aims at supposedly revealing one's inward divine nature by "contacting" Brahman through occult practices such as yoga,* meditation,* and altered states of consciousness.*

Hinduism also teaches that Brahman exists "beneath" this illusory universe. In other words, Brahman resides "in" and "underneath" the material creation, including man. This explains why the goal of Hinduism is to go inward, into one's consciousness, to mystically discover that one's true nature is one essence with God, or Brahman. Yet as we will seek to demonstrate, this philosophy has profound practical implications.

## NIHILISM

Because *advaita* teaches that the world is ultimately an illusion, a "dream" of Brahman, its basic philosophy can be described as nihilism. The *Oxford American Dictionary* defines "nihilism" as: "(1) a negative doctrine, the total rejection of current beliefs in religion or morals; (2) a form of skepticism that denies all existence" (414:601). Thus, in the end, Hindu practice leads to nihilism: "The experience of *samadhi* is, literally, a death to the things of this world" (1373:20).

Nihilism is exactly what the Hindu gurus in America teach:

*Swami Vivekananda*—The world . . . never existed; it was a dream, maya (1374:64).

*Paramahansa Yogananda*—I don't take life seriously at all. . . . It's all a dream (1375:218-19).

*Ram Dass*—What responsibility? . . . God has all the responsibility. I don't have any responsibility (1376:179).

*Meher Baba*—Mere mind and mere body do not exist (1377:146).

*Da Free John*—All of this life, past and future, up and down, in and out, is just an hallucination. . . . What is that great universe? . . . It is absolutely nothing. . . . In our [spiritual] enlightenment, the entire appearing universe is impotent, no longer the intentional creation of holy God at all. . . . Birth, the world, and the whole affair of life become nonsense, no longer impinge on you, have no implication whatsoever, absolutely none. . . . Ultimately, there is no world (1378:226-27, 238-48).

*Bhagwan Shree Rajneesh*—Your so-called society . . . is a conspiracy against man. . . . Whatever you call real life is not real. . . . Society is rotten. . . . I am not at all concerned with society . . . [We are] escaping from illusions and escaping into reality [through "enlightenment"]—hence it's not really escapist (1379:3-5).

There is no purpose in life. . . . The questions are meaningless, the answers are even more so. . . . [Life is a] meaningless, fruitless effort leading nowhere. . . . This whole [life is] nonsense . . . you simply live: there is no purpose (1380:5-6).

*Sri Aurobindo/The "Mother"*—One lives in Auroville [the spiritual community] in order to be free of moral and social conventions (1381:24).

According to Hinduism, Brahman is wholly indifferent to what goes on in the world. Brahman is *impersonal*; it does not speak, it does not feel, it is unconcerned with good or evil. It is unconcerned with men and women. It has no cares because it has no emotion. It is unconcerned with morality because it has no moral attributes. The one who "knows" Brahman knows that there is no right or wrong, and that good and evil deeds do not actually happen. In Hinduism the truly "enlightened" individual is indifferent to *all* actions. As Maharishi Mahesh Yogi says, "[I]ndifference is the weapon to be used against any negative situation in life." And because the enlightened are "far above the boundaries of any social bond or obligation," the true self of such persons is "uninvolved in every way—it is uninvolved with activity and it is uninvolved with the *selves* of individual beings" (469:157,212/1426:183). And so the guru declares, "This world of joys and sorrows, of man's great enterprise and ambition, is for them [the enlightened] like a world of dolls and toys with which children play and amuse themselves. Toys are a great source of excitement for children, but grown-ups remain untouched by them" (469:157).

These are just some of the beliefs of Hinduism in America concerning the world we live in. Ultimately, the world is an "illusion," having no ultimate value. Nevertheless, the Hindu gurus claim to offer people transcendence and meaning to life, which Western materialism has cruelly denied them. In truth, however, both Hinduism and materialism end in exactly the same place: nihilism. This is why influential guru Da Free John, speaking of the despair of nihilism, asserts, "Upon this absolute Truth [nihilism] we must build our lives" (1378:238-48). Noted atheistic philosopher Bertrand Russell affirms this: "Only on the firm foundation of unyielding despair can the soul's habitation henceforth be safely built" (1382:107).

Nevertheless, people who seriously adopt a nihilistic philosophy should realize that it can profoundly affect them. Consider the description of the truly "enlightened" soul as given by the great Hindu saint Ramakrishna:

But the man who always sees God [Brahman] and talks to him intimately has an altogether different nature. He acts sometimes like an inert thing, sometimes like a ghoul, sometimes like a child, and sometimes like a madman. . . . He is not conscious of the holy and the unholy. He does not observe any formal purity. To him everything is Brahman. . . . People notice his ways and actions and think of him as insane (489:405).

Any culture that adopts such a philosophy will also be profoundly affected. India is living proof that what a people are committed to inwardly is powerfully manifested outwardly. India's "Wis-

dom from the East" carries a heady price tag. A small part of this cost is discussed by Paul Molnar. Writing in the *National Review,* he recalls his feelings after a visit to India:

It's the utter degradation of the scene; the squalor, defecation, hashish, the pus-filled wounds on the backs of the holy men, pilgrims pushing and crowding into temples where a sweetish stench dominates—all that, plus the dead.

It was hard, afterward, to sort out my impressions, to pull them together. Paul Claudel once wrote to friends, during his travels and ambassadorships in the Far East, that oriental religion is the devil's invention. In these ecumenical times one is not supposed to say such things. Yet that is my inescapable conclusion. The faith of the worshippers is, without any doubt, sincere, even fervent. . . . But the objects of worship are brutal, inhuman deities who know how to scare, punish, avenge, mock and cheat, not to elevate and forgive; and the environment surrounding the worshippers repels rather than attracts: horrid, grimacing idols with cunning or cruel stares; incredibly gaudy vulgarity, copulating monkeys, defecating cows, mud, stench, garbage. Hippies are drawn to this witches' brew, and the reason is not far to find.

What attracts and keeps them here is the degradation: of reason, of self-esteem, of vital forces, of faith in God and man. Here they find innumerable gods and none at all; everybody may do this thing just like the monkeys and the cows, sinking slowly toward the Ganges or Nirvana. Intelligence and purposefulness dissolve on the trashheap, the body rots until it becomes one with the road, the grass, the dung. The great nothingness envelops all, and the ashes go into the river (1385:22).

What gave India all this—and more? No one can logically deny it was the religion of Hinduism, a religion millions of Americans are now welcoming with eagerness.

## COMMON PRACTICES

In this section, we will briefly examine some of the common practices within Hinduism.

*Altered States of Consciousness*

Altered states of consciousness* (ASCs) involves a variety of categories, including hypnosis* and other trance conditions, yogic kundalini* arousal, shamanism,* lucid dreaming,* drug states, meditation,* biofeedback induced alterations. In Hinduism, as in most Eastern practices, the development of altered states of consciousness is encouraged, and people today are pursuing them thinking that they will produce a condition of spiritual "enlightenment."*

Pursuing altered states can be dangerous because they tend to open the doors to spirit possession. As we commented in our chapter on altered states:

Historically the linkage between pagan cultures and the manipulation of consciousness for occult purposes, such as spirit possession, has been strong. This indicates that the spirit world has a vested interest in encouraging the exploration of altered states of consciousness along specific lines, especially those devoted to spirit contact. The history of Eastern religion, Western occultism, modern parapsychology, etc., constantly reveal the importance of developing altered states of consciousness for contacting other dimensions. Revelations of the spirits themselves often stress their importance for this very purpose (cf. 1386).

Nobel scientist, Sir John Eccles once commented that the human brain was "a machine that a ghost can operate." His statement illustrates the truth that given the proper conditions, the human mind can become an open door permitting the influence of spirits. Altered states of consciousness are one principal method offering the proper conditions (cf. 1387).

A major study on ASCs revealed that of almost 500 societies observed, over 90 percent considered trance states and spirit possession as socially acceptable (297:16-17). In America, the Hindu gurus and their occult practices are making trance and possession states socially acceptable. Today, in many quarters what was once called spirit possession is now simply termed an altered state of consciousness. This can be seen in the research of Tal Brooke, the former premier Western disciple of India's super guru Sathya Sai Baba. In *Riders of the Cosmic Circuit,*

Brooke offers a powerful examination and critique of Eastern philosophy, including the altered state of consciousness found in the meditative disciplines of many gurus. Altered states of consciousness are revealed as common ways to foster spirit contact and possession, which is then viewed as an experience of "higher" states of consciousness (249:39-50,107-39,165-208).

When Hindu gurus claim that their practices will produce enlightened states of consciousness, the practitioner should beware. These meditation-induced altered states frequently lead to periods of social withdrawal, mental illness, and demonization, as we have documented elsewhere (see Shamanism, Meditation, Altered States, Enlightenment, Yoga).

*Yoga and Meditation*

Other typical practices within Hinduism include the interrelated disciplines of yoga* and meditation.* Due to space restrictions, we will limit the discussion to yoga, keeping in mind that all yoga practices involve meditation.

Over the years more and more health professionals have advocated yoga as a "safe and effective" method for procuring physical and mental health. Today, millions of people in America use this ancient Hindu practice.

Yoga has one specific goal: allegedly to unite the practitioner to the Hindu God Brahman through experiences of mystical consciousness. The individual is brought to realize that he is one essence with God, i.e., Brahman itself. "The aim of yoga, then, is to achieve the state of unity or oneness with God, Brahman, [and] spiritual beings [spirits] . . ." (592:14). Yoga authority Gopi Krishna observes, "All the sytems of yoga . . . are designed to bring about those psychosomatic [mental and physical] changes in the body which are essential for the metamorphosis [change] of consciousness" (592:15) that is required to "realize" Brahman.

This is why yoga authorities say that Eastern meditation, including yogic postures and breathing practices, awaken occult energies and induce a psychic alteration that can lead to dramatic changes in consciousness, changes so powerful that many people seem permanently altered. As in many other forms of occult practice, the old person ceases to exist and is replaced by an entirely new personality (e.g., 759:85,127,131,137; cf. "Spiritual Authoritarianism" and "Personhood as an Illusion" pp. 228-29; also see: Tal Brooke, *Riders of the Cosmic Circuit*).

Although many Americans practice yoga as mere exercise, few have any idea of where true yoga may take them. In the literature, we have read numerous accounts of yoga-induced insanity and demonization, even from "innocent" yoga practice (see Yoga). But, incredibly, the altered states that yoga produces—even the periods of madness—are now frequently defined as positive spiritual experiences, capable of leading one to spiritual "emergence" or "enlightenment" (759).

That yoga practice can "break down" the mind and body is not surprising. The true goal of real yoga is to "destroy" the person (who is only a false self, an illusion) so that the impersonal Brahman (the alleged Real Self) may be experienced. Moti Lal Pandit states that "the aim of Yoga is to realize liberation from the human condition. To achieve this liberation, various psychological, physical, mental, and mystical [occult] methods have been devised. All those methods are anti-social (sometimes even anti-human) in that yoga prescibes a way of life which says: 'this mortal life is not worth living'" (1383:41).

Because yoga is ultimately an occult practice (e.g., it develops psychic abilities), the charactistic hazards of occult practice, such as physical problems and disease, mental illness and demonization, may be encountered (1069). We believe these hazards are encountered *because* yoga is an occult practice, not because yoga is, allegedly, performed in an incorrect manner.

Most people (including most medical doctors) wrongly assume that yoga is harmless. They rarely consider yoga per se as relevant to any illnesses in their patients. But we are convinced that many perplexing conditions, including some deaths, are related to yoga (see Yoga for examples).

*Occultism*

As noted, Hinduism is an occult religion. Hinduism began from occult practice and the alleged supernatural revelations given to the *rishis*, or seers. Thus, considering the American gurus as a whole, it is not surprising that occult practices are widely accepted. Typically, they not only include various forms of spiritism, but also astrology,* magic, sorcery, necromancy, development of psychic abilities, shamanistic* practices, the transference of occult power in initiation *(shaktipat diksha)*, and so on. Rajneesh, for example, stated that witchcraft was "one of the greatest possibilities of human growth" (482:364). As veteran researcher Brooks Alexander says of Rajneesh, Muktananda, and Sai Baba: "All of these gurus espouse a similar philosophy, and they all turn it into practice in a similar way. It is a pattern that we find not only in tantra (Indo-Tibetan occultism), but in European satanism, antinomian gnosticism, and ancient pagan sorcery as well" (1388:39).

A disciple's required obedience to a guru includes following the guru's *sadhana*, or spiritual path. By definition, this places one on the path of occultism. Psychic powers (1389:218) and spiritism are to be *expected*. For example, spirit contact frequently occurs with what are believed to be various Hindu deities, "nature" spirits, the guru himself after his death, or the guru while he is alive via his alleged "spiritual form."

Muktananda tells his students that they will encounter various Hindu gods and other spirits, as well as the alleged dead (467:XXIII, 155-61). His spiritual autobiography, *Play of Consciousness* (467), is full of occult phenomena and practice. Occult preoccupation is also true for other gurus, such as Paramahansa Yogananda, whose spiritual autobiography, *Autobiography of a Yogi*, is replete with occult phenomena and experiences—astral projection, psychometry, astrology,* psychic healing, spiritistic materializations and apportations, amulets, and so on (1390). Yogananda taught, "True spiritualism [mediumism] is a wonderful science ... [and] it is possible by meditation and spiritual [occult] development to contact departed loved ones ... " (1391:6-7). The text *Sri Aurobindo and the Mother on Occultism* claims that true occultism is "dynamic spirituality ... an indispensable instrument along the spiritual path" (1392:17). Aurobindo and his companion, called "the Mother," emphasize that "to talk about occult things is of little value; one must experience them" (1393:273).

When the gurus endorse occultism they are clearly violating God's instructions warning against such things: "Let no one be found among you ... who practices divination or sorcery ... engages in witchcraft, or casts spells, or who is a medium or spiritist or who consults the dead. Anyone who does these things is detestable to the Lord ..." (Deuteronomy 18:10-12). Unfortunately, the gurus' endorsement of the occult is only a small portion of their overall rejection of Christian faith. To document the gurus' incompatibility with Christianity, we will now examine several theological views of the gurus.

## THEOLOGY

*God*

Hinduism in America usually teaches that God is an impersonal divine essence called Brahman. Brahman is described as *satchitananda*, infinite being, consciousness and bliss. Brahman has two aspects, one called "Nirguna" and another called "Saguna." Nirguna Brahman is God as It exists in Its ultimate reality; unmanifested and unknown. Saguna Brahman involves the "illusory" manifestations of Nirguna Brahman, as seen in various Hindu deities such as Brahma, Vishnu, Shiva, Kali, and Krishna. The technical distinctions between these "forms" of Brahman are too detailed to discuss here (see 1372). For our purposes we only need know that the gurus teach that everything is God or part of God (1372). This is known as pantheism. Thus, the gurus teach that "there is nothing that is not God" (1394:355).

In *The Gospel of Sri Ramakrishna*, we read: "It is God Himself [Brahman] who has become all this—the [physical] universe, maya [the illusion] and the living beings.... It is God alone who has become everything" (489:395). Nevertheless, because the Hindu concept of God includes so many contradictions, the gurus say that nothing concrete can be said about God. Thus, in a final sense, "no one has ever been able to say what

Brahman is" (489:102). Furthermore, "the nature of Brahman cannot be described. About it one remains silent" (489:218). The common phrase used by Hindus to describe Brahman is "neti neti"—"not this, not that."

As noted, the Hindu God is also impersonal: "The idea of a Personal God is not a true generalization. We have to go beyond, to the Impersonal [God] ... the Personal God ... is not absolute truth" (1394:740). Hinduism also teaches that Brahman cannot be worshiped: "God in His absolute [nirguna] nature is not to be worshiped. Worshiping such a God would be nonsense.... It would be sin to worship that God" (1374:195,199-200). Worship is reserved for the "illusory" manifestations of Brahman; that is, the gods and gurus who "incarnate" or represent Brahman, such as Brahma, Vishnu, Shiva, and Krishna.

In *Teachings of Swami Vivekananda*, it is said that Brahman does not know anything. He is described as "an impersonal, omnipresent being who cannot be called a knowing being.... He cannot be called a thinking being, because that [i.e., thinking] is a process of the weak only. He cannot be called the reasoning being, because reasoning is a sign of weakness. He cannot be called a creating being, because none creates except in bondage" (1395:91-92).

Thus, the ultimate God of Hinduism in America is: 1) pantheistic, 2) impersonal, 3) unknowing, and 4) unknowable. It cannot love or show mercy, or know or be known, because these are personal attributes. What Brahman finally is or isn't, no one knows.

By contrast, the biblical God is personal, loving, and holy. He *can* be known and experienced personally. Because He is personal, and because we are created in His image, our personhood has meaning and dignity. There is no need to view ourselves as illusions, or to seek to destroy our personhood in our attempt to know God.

The Bible also teaches that God is a God who loves us, even though we are sinful. In fact, "God is love" (1 John 4:8). Nowhere is God's love better demonstrated than at the cross, where in human nature, and, in one act of unparalleled self denial, He took all the world's sins upon Himself and was judged in our place.

He did this because of His great love for people and His desire that "none should perish" (Philippians 2:1-8; John 3:16; 2 Peter 3:9).

## Man

Hinduism teaches that man outwardly is an illusion, i.e., in his body and personality. But in his true inward nature, he is one essence with Brahman. The common phrase used to describe this assumption is "Atman is Brahman." In other words, the individual human soul, the *atman*, is ultimately one essence with *Brahman*:

- Muktananda teaches, "The Guru is God Himself..." (483:98-99; cf. 103-06). Thus, "Muktananda ... is the God of the universe" (1396:158). And, "As you worship God, you become God..." (1397:5; cf. 467:203-04).
- Swami Satchidananda refers to our "true nature which is God" (1398:6).
- Sai Baba teaches, "You are the God of this universe" (1399:112). He emphasizes, "You *are* God in reality" (1400:68). And, "You are not a man, you are God..." (1400:184).
- Rajneesh teaches, "As you are, you are God" (486:362).
- Swami Vishnudevananda's yoga meditation, intended to help disciples realize that they are God, is also illustrative: "I am the light of lights; I am the sun; I am the real, real, sun. ... In me the whole world moves and has its being.... I existed before the world began.... I permeate and pervade every atom. . . . Oh, how beautiful I am.... I am the whole universe; everything is in me....I am That [Brahman]" (1402:351).

The Bible teaches that this religious philosophy is wrong. In his own heart every person knows he is not God. Man is a creation of God, not God Himself: "So God created man in his own image, in the image of God he created him; male and female he created them" (Genesis 1:27). "The Sovereign LORD says: 'In the pride of your heart you say, "I am a god; I sit on the throne of a god." ... But you are man and not a god, though you think you are as wise as a god'" (Ezekiel 28:2).

The Bible also teaches that our true inner nature is not divine, but sinful. "For from within,

out of men's hearts, come evil thoughts, sexual immorality, theft, murder, adultery, greed, malice, deceit, lewdness, envy, slander, arrogance and folly" (Mark 7:21-22). People are not to look within themselves for salvation. Rather, they are to look to God, their Creator, for salvation. "This is what the LORD says: 'Cursed is the one who trusts in man, who depends on flesh for his strength and whose heart turns away from the LORD'" (Jeremiah 17:5). In essence, what the Bible says is created (mankind), Hinduism says is God itself, and what the Bible says is sinful and imperfect (fallen human nature), Hinduism says is divine.

## Jesus Christ

The Hindu gurus typically redefine Jesus Christ after their own likeness. Jesus becomes a teacher of Hinduism, a guru of the past who has been greatly misunderstood by Christians. The only Jesus the gurus praise is a Hindu Jesus. The biblical Jesus is either ignored or ridiculed, or even condemned as a false Christ. Rajneesh taught, "To tell you the truth, Jesus is a mental case.... He is a fanatic. He carries the same kind of mind as Adolf Hitler. He is a fascist. He thinks that only those who follow *him* will be saved. ... And the fools are still believing that they will be saved if they follow Jesus. Even Jesus is not saved. And he knew it" (1403:9-10). "Jesus is just a salesman, saying, 'Come follow me, because those who will follow me will find God, and will find heaven.'... Now, this man is not going to help anybody" (1403:26-27).

Swami Vivekananda asserts, "The Trinitarian Christ is elevated above us; the Unitarian Christ is merely a mortal man. Neither can help us" (1394:511). And, "Every worm is the brother of the Nazarene.... The range of idols is from wood and stone to Jesus and Buddha" (1374:XII). Da Free John emphasizes that the Jesus of Christian faith is a cultic "false idol" and "a perversion of the truth" (1404:212/1405:472).

What Hinduism teaches about Jesus Christ is wrong. Jesus never taught He was a Hindu guru. He taught He was the promised Jewish Messiah (1406) and the only incarnation of God, the one and only Son of God (John 3:16-18; cf. John 5:18;

19:7). Jesus claimed He was God (John 10:30; 14:9), and He proved it by resurrecting from the dead. In all of history, no Hindu guru has ever resurrected from the dead, which places Jesus miles apart from all the gurus of history. The entire New Testament emphasizes that Jesus Christ is God Himself. "For in Christ all the fullness of the Deity lives in bodily form . . ." (Colossians 2:9). Christians everywhere "wait for the blessed hope—the glorious appearing of our great God and Savior, Jesus Christ . . ." (Titus 2:13).

Jesus is not a guru from the past, someone now dead and gone. The Bible teaches that Jesus is alive and exalted above everything. Because of His atoning death on the cross and His resurrection, "Therefore God exalted him to the highest place and gave him the name that is above every name, that at the name of Jesus every knee should bow, in heaven and on earth and under the earth, and every tongue confess that Jesus Christ is Lord, to the glory of God the Father" (Philippians 2:9-11). "He is the image of the invisible God, the firstborn over all creation. For by him all things were created: things in heaven and on earth, visible and invisible, whether thrones or powers or rulers or authorities; all things were created by him and for him. He is before all things, and in him all things hold together" (Colossians 1:15-17).

The Hindu gurus reject the biblical Jesus Christ when they deny His nature as the unique God-Man (Philippians 2:1-8), and His mission as atoning Savior (1 John 2:2).

### Salvation (Enlightenment)

The gurus define "salvation" as: 1) the realization of our own godhood; 2) the progressive "working out" of that realization throughout our life; 3) the final merging with—a complete dissolution into—the impersonal God Brahman. This process may require millions of lifetimes of reincarnation as we strive to earn our own salvation by working off our "karma" ("unenlightened" thoughts and actions) in accordance with Hindu requirements.

For example, Hinduism teaches that all men and women are now living in a great delusion; that is, people think this world is ultimately real

when it is only a dream. This delusion leads them into false perceptions, harmful ideas, and destructive ways of living. In other words, it adds more and more karma to their lives. The gurus seek to save them from this great deception and bad karma.

The goal of Hindu "salvation" is an alleged enlightenment*—a denial of the world as it is and the "realization" of spiritual reality as Hinduism defines it. And as we have seen, a key part of that realization is that the world is an illusion, and that in our true nature we are God.

But if one is already God, then to seek a God outside oneself is foolish and spiritually destructive. One must turn inward, not outward. This is why Rajneesh taught, "The greatest deception is the deception of devotion to God" (1380:16). In other words, people must be devoted to themselves, for they are God inwardly; they must not be devoted to an independent Creator God, a false idol they think exists apart from them. According to Hinduism, this will damage them spiritually.

The Bible teaches something entirely different about salvation. It teaches that men and women are sinful and require *redemption* (forgiveness of sins), not so-called "enlightenment." If any person's sins are not forgiven in this life, he will pay the divine penalty and judgment on his sins after death—eternal separation from God. This is why Jesus Christ came to earth: to provide salvation for sinners. At the cross, Jesus was judged by God in our place: "He himself bore our sins in his body on the tree so that we might die to sins and live for righteousness; by his wounds you have been healed" (1 Peter 2:24). "He is the atoning sacrifice for our sins, and not only for ours but also for the sins of the whole world" (1 John 2:2). God did this because He loves us and does not desire that anyone should perish. "He is patient with you, not wanting anyone to perish, but everyone to come to repentance," and, "For God so loved the world that he gave his one and only Son, that whoever believes in him shall not perish but have eternal life" (2 Peter 3:9; John 3:16).

Salvation is therefore a *free* gift that God offers all those who will confess their sinfulness before

Him, acknowledge that Christ died for their sins on the cross, and then receive Christ as their personal Savior. "For the wages of sin is death, but the gift of God is eternal life in Christ Jesus our Lord" (Romans 6:23). "Yet to all who received him, to those who believed in his name, he gave the right to become children of God ..." (John 1:12). "For it is by grace you have been saved, through faith—and this not from yourselves, it is the gift of God—not by works, so that no one can boast" (Ephesians 2:8-9).

*Afterlife*

The basic teaching of Hinduism concerning the afterlife involves believing in reincarnation. The idea is that we have many lifetimes to perfect ourselves, to work off our karma (spiritual imperfections) until we finally merge back into Brahman. Millions of Americans believe in reincarnation today largely because of the influence of Hinduism and other forms of occult practice. Polls reveal that as many as one in four adult Americans believes in this occult doctrine. Another reason for this is the thousands of reports of alleged "past lives" episodes, which have convinced many that reincarnation is true.

After an in-depth investigation into reincarnation historically and philosophically, we see no genuine evidence to support such a doctrine. We are convinced that "past-life" experiences are really self-deceptions, or even demonic deceptions; they are hypnotic-like experiences which cause people merely to think that they have lived before (see Hypnosis).

The leading secular reincarnation researcher in America is probably parapsychologist Ian Stevenson of the University of Virginia. Yet he denies that there is any proof of reincarnation, and he also accepts that one explanation for reincarnation experiences is that they are implanted into the mind by deceiving spirits (1401:374-77). This is the conclusion of many other researchers who have studied reincarnation, such as Walter Martin, Mark Albrecht, John Synder, Robert Morey, Norman Geisler, and J. Yutaka Amano (1384). Furthermore, we

have yet to encounter a claimed reincarnation experience that is not best explained by recourse to natural theories or to demonic power and deception.

Why would demons be interested in encouraging a belief in reincarnation? Simply because it is such an effective barrier to the Christian gospel. If men live through many lifetimes, then there is no biblical judgment at death, but Hebrews 9:27 teaches that there is. If men must work out their own salvation over many lifetimes, then Jesus Christ did not have to die on the cross for our sins, but 1 John 2:2 and Luke 24:25-26 teach that he did. If all men will eventually be saved and absorbed into the impersonal Brahman, then there is no eternal heaven or hell, but Matthew 25:46 and Revelation 20:10-15 teach that they are real.

These and many other factors reveal why it is logical to conclude that the teaching of reincarnation involves spiritual deception. Biblically, of course, if Jesus Christ paid the full divine penalty for all our sin at the cross, there is no more karma, so to speak, for us to work off over many lifetimes. In other words, if Christianity is true, then reincarnation must be false. The Bible is very clear at this point: "He forgave us all our sins" (Colossians 2:13), and "by one sacrifice he has made perfect forever those who are being made holy" (Hebrews 10:14).

## PHILOSOPHICAL CONSEQUENCES

We now turn to examining some of the philosophical, spiritual, and ethical consequences of the gurus' teachings. In this section we will briefly address some of the gurus' practices in America.

*Spiritual Authoritarianism*

A characteristic common to most cults is that the guru or leader requires unquestioning obedience from his disciples. Right or wrong, disciples are to obey the guru just as they would obey God. Disobedience is cause for immediate expulsion from the spiritual community:

*Sri Aurobindo*—There must be total and sincere surrender.... The surrender must be total (1408:3).

*Bhagwan Shree Rajneesh*—You are nobody to judge what is right and what is wrong.... This is none of your business.... Whatsoever I decide is absolute. If you don't choose that way you are perfectly happy to leave (1409:33).

*Sai Baba*—I will insist on strict obedience (1410:186).

*Meher Baba*—I am for the selected few who ... surrender their all, body, mind and possessions to me. Those who have today willingly chosen to become my slaves will become true masters tomorrow (1411:351).

It is frightening to realize that some followers of Eastern gurus have admitted that they would do anything, even commit murder or suicide, if their guru told them to (1412). This is because, right or wrong, the disciple must not hesitate or question the will of the guru. If the guru is the enlightened manifestation of God, then the guru must be obeyed as God. Da Free John teaches, "When I approach you, I ask you for this, I ask you for that.... I ask you for everything. The longer you stay with me, the more things I will ask you for. I will ask you for *all of it*. You must yield everything to me. You must yield yourself in every function. Your very cells must yield. Only then are you fit for the Divine Yoga" (946:276).

*The Mind as Enemy*

Obeying the guru "right or wrong" is made easier because of another teaching. The Hindu gurus instruct their disciples that their *mind* is their enemy. If they desire true "liberation," the mind must be undermined and even "destroyed."

According to the gurus, the human mind is not a gift from God but a form of spiritual poison. The mind and its normal thoughts are trapped in delusions. Because the mind perceives only falsehoods, it is really a spiritual enemy and must be undermined to permit the experiencing of "higher" consciousness. Thus, logic, common sense, and reason are rejected as "lower" forms

of consciousness that prevent more spiritual forms of "knowing."

Normal consciousness is equated with spiritual ignorance, or being "unenlightened." Because spiritual truth is, allegedly, only understood in an altered state of consciousness,* specific spiritual (occult) techniques (yoga,* meditation*) are the means to the needed "restructuring" of the mind. Below we present several illustrations of such teachings:

*Bhagwan Shree Rajneesh*—I am for the death of [the] mind.... (1413:80)

I'm not here to strengthen your mind. I'm here to destroy it.... Much will have to be done to destroy your mind (1414:52,150).

If you go on nourishing the mind, you are poisoning yourself.... The mind becomes almost like a cancerous growth (1415:15).

*Sai Baba*—[You must achieve] elimination of the mind, which is the arch obstacle in the [spiritual] path (1416:206).

Do not listen to your mind [but] ... to my voice ... (1417:15).

Give [your minds] to me ... but it must be a complete handing over; no reservations; the mind is the source of delusion (1418:473).

*Meher Baba*—As long as the mind is there, the real "I am God" state cannot be experienced.... Therefore ... [the] mind must go. ... Mind has to destroy itself.... The mind has to die in this body.... [We must] attain this ... annihilation of the mind during this life (1419:38).

*Sri Aurobindo*—We can do very well without the mind ... [and] in truth, we are the better for it (1410:44).

*Radhasoami (Charan Singh, Sawan Singh, Swami Ji)*—Our mind leads us astray (1421:41).

Fear the devil, your own mind (1422:128).

But should anyone be surprised that a rejection of the mind as one's "enemy" might produce an irrational approach to life in general? In her critique of Hindu spirituality, *Karma Cola: The Marketing of the Mystic East*, Indian author Gita

Mehta observes the following of those who travel East in search of alleged "wisdom":

> The early Christian missionaries were not paranoid. Heathens do dabble in the irrational, and none more elaborately than Indian heathens, who have in their long evolution spent a couple of thousand years cultivating the transcendence of reason, another couple of thousand years on the denial of reason, and even more millennia on accepting reason, but rejecting its authenticity. To be cast adrift in this whirlpool of differing views on the validity of simple mental activity seems a very high price to pay for cheap air fares (1423:18-19).

Thus, not unexpectedly, even the gurus frequently confess to their own irrationalism:

> *Bhagwan Shree Rajneesh*—What I am doing here is absurd, it is not logical. You will have to put logic aside . . . (1424:38).

> Many times you will find my statements contradictory—they are contradictory, they *are* absurd because I will say one thing one moment and I will contradict it another moment. . . . I am only consistent in one thing—my inconsistencies . . . (1425:5).

> The energy of love and hate . . . are one energy. . . . [Hate] is not a different thing [than love] (1403:79).

> *Maharishi Mahesh Yogi*—It is only childish and ridiculous to base one's life on the level of thinking. Thinking can never be a profound basis of living. Being [living in "higher" consciousness] is the natural basis [of living]. . . . Thinking on the other hand, is only imaginary (1426:99).

Rejecting the mind, however, is only the *first* step on the road to "enlightenment."

### Personhood as an Illusion

As we have seen, the gurus in America teach that the individual person (body, mind, personality) is a false self that has no ultimate reality. Since Hinduism teaches that the only true reality is the impersonal God Brahman, and that the entire creation is an "illusion," then the individual person must also be considered an illusion (1427:11,178). In fact, it is the individual *person* who is the enemy of spiritual enlightenment*—in Da Free John's words, just so much "garbage" (476). This is why the goal of most Hindu and Buddhist sects is to destroy *the person*, so that one's alleged inner, *impersonal* divine reality may "emerge," be revealed, and take over.

There are at least three consequences to this teaching. First, this Hindu methodology is finally reduced to an assault upon the image of God in man, an image that is clearly personal. It seeks to destroy that which God Himself has created and identified as good (Genesis 1:31). Second, what replaces the reamed-out human personality is, paradoxically, often a new personality—an evil spirit the Bible identifies as a demon. Thus, what is incorrectly interpreted as something "demonic" (the person) is finally replaced by that which truly is demonic (an evil spirit). We will discuss this later. Third, whenever this process of alleged enlightenment involves physical or spiritual brutality, a convenient rationalization is now available. No genuine harm is perpetrated since no true person exists to be harmed:

> *Bhagwan Shree Rajneesh*—You have been thinking that you are something unique, something special. . . . You are nobody (486:200).

> To me the person does not exist. . . . The person is not existent, a nonentity . . . (1407:1).

> As you are you cannot become enlightened. Great chunks of your being will have to be cut and thrown away. It will be almost like committing suicide (1428:16; cf. p. 18).

> *Da Free John*—But the process in which the guru involves you in the meantime is destroying the separate self-sense and destroying the viewpoint of conventional cognition and perception (476:310-11).

In other words, the path of Hinduism involves a destruction of the disciple by one who has already been destroyed himself—that is, the guru, the "enlightened" spiritual master. The path of yoga is acknowledged as constituting "a progressive dismantling of human personality ending in a complete abolition. With every step of yoga what we call "man" is demolished a little more" (593:8). This is why Rajneesh taught, "I am going to destroy you *utterly*. Only then can I help you" (1429:34).

The purpose of the destruction is a temporary insanity that allows a new "mind" to emerge. "A master is utterly destructive; a Master creates a chaos. He drives you insane as far as your mind is concerned—because when the mind has been driven insane, it stops,... and suddenly a new consciousness arises" (1430:3). Thus, Rajneesh taught, "Around great Masters you will see many people who look like zombies. [This is] something immensely valuable" (861:11).

According to Da Free John, everything that attaches us to our separate individual, personal existence must be annihilated. In *Garbage and the Goddess*, he argues:

> Among devotees there are no marriages, there are no brothers, sisters, husbands, wives, mothers, fathers, cousins, karmic friends, there is none of that. All of that is obsolete.... Spiritual life is leading to the absolute undermining of your separate existence. Absolutely. That is what this work is all about.... You are not going to go to heaven from here. You are going to die: literally and absolutely (476:10-12).

Da Free John, who presumably experienced enlightenment* himself, informs his disciples that all "contracts" (contracts are our beliefs about many things—personal morals, standards, relationships, marriage, and so on) must deliberately be violated and undermined. "One of the 'secrets' of spiritual life is continually to violate your own contracts. If you do that with intelligence, with understanding, you will continually be free.... Do not assume any contracts to be invalid. Do not assume any contracts to hold" (476:23).

In the words of a devoted disciple, Da Free John provides the following advice to his spiritual students:

> But the maturity that the disciple's sadhana [path] requires is a matter of becoming grounded enough in the life of Satsang [spiritual growth] that the guru can begin to really throw you around, undermine you, disorient you to the point of the absolute impossibility of any form of orientation whatsoever. That is what God-Realization amounts to. *You* disappear, along with every vestige of your attempts to make sense out of existence. Bubba once described looking forward to the appearance of his first disciples so that he could start really "punch heads"! (946:274).

No one should doubt that this destruction of the personality can be frighteningly real, or that such destruction, in reaming out the original personality, can open the door for the body to be inhabited by a new and foreign personality. If God's gift of personhood is rejected and tossed away as so much garbage, if the human mind is deliberately emptied and becomes a vacuum, we should not be surprised that the "new consciousness" that enters and fills the vacuum could be something unexpected, even something evil (see p. 233).

This annihilation of the old personality is another link to occultism. Only when the old personality is somehow removed can the new personality take over. Thus, in the tortures of shamanism,* "the suffering has annihilated all former characteristics of the personality" (759:85). In many UFO close encounter and contactee cases, the individual personality is also taken over. "Many who have had such [UFO] initiations feel that they have ceased to exist" (759:131). In the words of the noted UFO celebrity, Whitley Streiber, author of the bestsellers *Communion* and *Transformation*, "I do not think that my ordinary humanity survived the transition" (759:85).

*Morality as Counterproductive*

Ultimately, in *advaita*, morality is merely a reflection of "unenlightenment" consciousness. Charles Manson once stated, "If God is One, what is bad?" He rejected the categories of good and evil on the basis of monistic philosophy. Hinduism also teaches that "God is One"—that ultimate reality is One impersonal, undifferentiated divine essence. What this means is that just as humanity itself is ultimately meaningless (as separate individual persons) then humanity's morality must also be meaningless. Human morality is simply a product of "unenlightened" and "deluded" thinking; morality per se does not exist.

Thus, in Hinduism in America we find not only the rejection of the image of God in man concerning his personality, but the attempt to *defile* the image of God in man concerning his morality, his conscience. "Moral" thinking is held to be as destructive of "higher" consciousness and true reality because it too is an illusory activity. But if we really believe that man as man is only an illusion, and that morality is irrelevant, then is it surprising to discover that those who hold such views are willing to accept the mistreatment, brutalization, or even demonization of men and women?

While few disciples live these spiritual "truths" consistently, such Hindu philosophy can become the means to justify selfish, unethical, immoral, cruel, and criminal behavior, particularly on the part of the guru, who can view such actions through any number of alleged rationalizations. The guru may justify himself on the basis of his claimed inability to commit evil (e.g., on the basis of evil's ultimate nonexistence), or on the basis of his own divine authority (e.g., all his actions are spiritual, regardless of contrary appearance), or as a spiritual "test" or lesson for the sake of the disciples' spiritual "growth" in apprehending metaphysical "truth" (e.g., that evil has no reality).

Virtually any evil, from deliberate deception to criminal activity, is capable of rationalization within a monistic ("All is One") system. Thus, "What you would normally think to be right or wrong no longer has any place. The underlying premise is that everything that the guru does is for your own good. The guru does no wrong" (1431:110).

If morality is ultimately part of the illusory nature of all things, then to achieve true enlightenment,* to inhabit true Reality, one must logically go beyond the idea of good and evil. Theoretically, once a disciple becomes truly enlightened, any action, even evil actions, become "spiritual" actions, for the "enlightened" person is, by definition, *incapable* of committing evil. He cannot possibly commit that which does not exist:

*Swami Muktananda*—Our concepts of sin and virtue . . . alienate us from our true Self. . . . That which you see as impure is pure. . . . You imagine [ideas of] sin and virtue through ignorance (1432).

*Swami Satchidananda*—If you are possessed by that higher sense of wisdom, nothing is bad (477:156).

*Paramahansa Yogananda*—[God] sees your good and evil thoughts and actions but they do not matter to him (1375:332).

*Bhagwan Shree Rajneesh*—My ashram [spiritual community] makes no difference between the Devil and the Divine. . . . I use all sorts of energies. And if the devilish energy can be used in a divine way, it becomes tremendously fruitful (482:382).

Obedience [to God] is the greatest sin (1403:368).

I don't believe in morality . . . and I am bent on destroying it. . . . I believe in consciousness, not conscience (1429:34).

The person who has deep compassion is not going to be bothered about whether he tells a lie or a truth. . . . All [spiritual teachers] have lied. . . . Through lies, by and by a master brings you toward light (482:153).

To emphasize morality is mean, degrading; it is inhuman (567:22).

*Da Free John*—Divine life itself . . . is entirely separate from all of the usual moralistic horse [expletive deleted] (476:18).

*Swami Adbhutananda*—Good and evil have no absolute reality (1451:160).

*Vivekananda*—Really, good and evil are one and the same. (979:512)

## PERSONAL CONSEQUENCES

Given the above teachings, no one should be surprised when they hear of gurus or their disciples caught in immoral or criminal behavior. Even in light of the modern AIDS plague, the teachings of the gurus concerning sexual permissiveness continue. Rajneesh taught, "[Homosexual love] is natural . . . far easier, far more convenient" (1414:35). Da Free John teaches, "It is not suggested that homosexuals in the ashram abandon their sexual life" (946:55). He also teaches, "Sex relations are [a divine process, in or out of marriage] . . . a random and loving occasion without [any] contracts [obligations]" (476:32-33).

Most people today entertain the common misconception that the gurus live morally celibate lives. However, our own research and that of others indicates most are not celibate, even when they claim they are. The research of Buddhist teacher and psychologist Jack Kornfield, in the article, "Sex Lives of the Gurus," reveals, "Deception has proven to be the greatest source of disappointment and pain in spiritual groups. The discovery of covert or inappropriate sexual relations between teachers and students is not an infrequent occurrence. In recent years such discoveries have caused major upheavals in nearly a dozen of the largest Eastern spiritual communities in America" (1452:28).

Of 54 gurus researched, 39 were found to be sexually active—over 70 percent. Close to 90 percent of the sexually active gurus had "at least occasional sexual relationships with one or more students" (1452:27). Of the married, many were adulterers, and "some are homosexual and some are bisexual in preference" (1452:27-28). In those cases where gurus had sex with their women disciples, approximately 50 percent of the women were in some way damaged by the incident. Being seduced by the guru was "a source of great suffering" (1452:28). Guru Ram Dass states that when Eastern teachers first came to the West they "fell like flies" to sexual license (759:179). In the intervening years, not much seems to have changed.

Our own research uncovered the following allegations, which were made principally by eyewitnesses, the victims themselves, or their friends. Although such charges are unproven legally, we could find no reason to doubt the integrity of the sources (1450):

| | |
|---|---|
| • Ram Dass | bisexuality |
| • Sai Baba | homosexuality, possible child molestation |
| • Swami Rama | rape, threats of murder |
| • Yogi Bhajan | homosexuality, rape, rumors of drug investments |

| | |
|---|---|
| • Muktananda | rape, voyeurism, fornication, violence, child molesting |
| • Da Free John | pornography, rape, adultery |
| • Maharishi Mahesh Yogi | fornication, violence |
| • Rajneesh ashram | rape, violence, attempted murder, murder, drug abuse, adultery, fornication |
| • ISKCON community | drug trafficking, murder, wife beating, child abuse |

According to the Associated Press, on June 2, 1986, Guru Prem Paramahansa, 38, was found guilty in Torrance, California, of eight counts of unlawful sex, over a 17-month period, with an eight-year-old girl (in 1982 to 1983). The *Chicago Tribune* of August 16, 1982, ran an article on the 400,000-member Ananda Marga Yoga Society titled "Guru Sect Is Probed for Terrorism, Murder," which detailed CIA and FBI investigations into the sect. The writer, Bernard Bauer, noted that for 27 years "the cult has left a trail of blood around the world."

The ISKCON community was also under federal investigation for some time. Over the years, many reports appeared in the *Los Angeles Times* and other papers on the community's alleged criminal activity at the sect's various headquarters; for example, the Gurukula school in Dallas, Texas, and the "New Vrindaban" community in West Virginia. Concerning the latter, the investigative news show "West 57th Street," on October 31, 1987, reported allegations concerning the murder of former members, wife beating, child molesting, and the sale of illegal drugs, such as cocaine and heroin.

Proponents cite such incidents as "aberrations," but again, given the forceful denial of absolute standards of right and wrong, is any of the above surprising? But there is more. In some forms of Hindu enlightenment,* the basic ethical categories of right and wrong must be transcended in another manner: through the *intentional* violation of moral values by the *deliberate* practice of evil (see Enlightenment, "Tantrism").

The goal here is to completely erode the conscience. In that man is created in God's image, and because a strong part of that image involves conscience, it is not unexpected that the destruction of the conscience is part of the process of the destruction of the individual. Once the individual is reamed out and his conscience seared, only a "void" remains: Is it therefore surprising that what enters and sets up house could be demonic? In other words, the practice of spiritual evil leads to further spiritual evil:

> The effect of this level of practice becomes chillingly clear in the inner rings of the Rajneesh camp. We listen to ex-Neeshlings unfold horrific tales of breaking the boundaries—of bizarre behavior, of beatings, rapes, and worse in the intensive training courses. We see a shockingly effective effort to break down human identity through a calculated violation of the taboos of human morality. . . . This is more than random vileness. Such thorough-going violation of taboos eventually erodes one's humanity—it "reams out" the physical envelope of a human being and leaves a void where the person should be. This extinction of identity makes possible the entry of demonic entities in a unique and total way (1388:39).

We emphasize again: to deliberately reject God's handiwork (persons) as something demonic and then to defile it opens the doors to that which truly *is* demonic. And once possessed of evil spirits, of course, anything is possible.

### Insanity and Possession

The gurus frequently teach that insanity and spirit possession are indications of higher, "divine" consciousness and enlightenment* (cf. Shamanism). They also frequently admit their own spiritual (spirit) possession. They also say that this is their desire for their disciples. Characteristically, however, such spirit possession is defined in more "spiritual" terms, in light of the respective tradition. For example, it is interpreted as a spiritual manifestation of enlightenment, as kundalini arousal (see Yoga), as possession by their own gurus' "spiritual form," as "God possession," "divine companionship," or "union with the Divine."

Nevertheless, in light of historic and biblical demonology, not to mention the gurus' own experiences, it is impossible to classify such experiences as anything but demonic: all the facts suggest possession by an evil entity.

And these states of possession are often accompanied by temporary insanity, usually involving what can only be described as torturous states of madness. Here is one of many links to the tradition of the shaman and occult magic as well, where adherents typically encounter possession and insanity as the means to spiritual enlightenment or authority (1407). (See Enlightenment, Meditation, Yoga, Shamanism.)

We believe that in many cases the guru is a type of revolving door for an invading spirit (or spirits), who comes and goes as it pleases, inducing whatever physical, mental, or spiritual phenomena suits its purposes. The following are several illustrations of this from leading gurus.

*Ramakrishna.* During his duties as a priest in the temple of Kali, Ramakrishna went insane:

> Kali was waiting for him. Hardly had he crossed the threshold than divine delirium in its most violent form was rekindled. . . . The legion of Gods swooped upon him like a whirlwind. He was torn in pieces. . . . His madness returned tenfold. He saw demonic creatures emerging from him. . . . Horror paralyzed his limbs. . . . Two years went by in this orgy of mental intoxication and despair (1433:41).

*Da Free John.* In describing his own *sadhana*, or work along the spiritual path, Free John openly confesses the insanity of his own gurus. They were indeed mad. They were also possessed by spirits. That Da Free John represents the logical culmination of their teaching and influence speaks for itself. His principal gurus were Nityananda, Muktananda, and Rudrananda ("Rudi"). In *No Remedy*, Da Free John tells of his personal "sanctification":

> Those who have served my function as guru, those who I worked with in my own sadhana, have been wild and powerful men. . . . True yogis are living, forceful beings. They are madmen, absolutely mad–and absolutely dangerous. You should know that, and you should not approach me if you are not willing to be undone. . . . My experience with people like

Rudi [Rudrananda], Muktananda, Nityananda, and others, was like this: I would be sitting in my house in New York by myself, and this force would enter me, it would practically break my neck, and my body and mind would be taken over.... That is how I learned [of spiritual truth] in these vehicles [gurus].... So these wild men serve that process. And they served it in exactly the same way I serve you. They *acquired* me ... (946:174-76).

*Shree Purohit Swami and Gopi Krishna.* Concerning meditation-induced kundalini arousal, a practice often promoted by the gurus, Shree Purohit Swami experienced near-insanity, madly ate the leaves of two entire nimba trees, devoured mudra leaves, and could not sit or stand. He mentions one yogi who had the "fire" rage for six to eight months, and another who had to sit under cold tap water eight hours a day (600:58-59).

Gopi Krishna, founder of one of the several Kundalini Research Centers in the world, records his own yoga-induced kundalini experiences:

It was variable for many years, painful, obsessive, even phantasmic. I have passed through almost all the stages of different mediumistic, psychotic and other types of mind, for sometime I was hovering between sanity and insanity. I was writing in many languages, some of which I never knew [the mediumistic ability of automatic writing; 491:124].

*Swami Muktananda.* The popular Swami Muktananda described his own possession in some detail in his spiritual autobiography *Play of Consciousness.* In the chapter titled "My Confused State of Mind" and elsewhere, he describes this terrible experience of madness as the "blessing and grace" of his own guru, Nityananda. Muktananda goes on to state that his disciples can expect similar experiences, and that such are merely the normal workings of kundalini arousal: "By now it is after 9:00. Someone had seated himself in my eyes and was making me see things.... It seemed that I was being controlled by some power which made me do all these things. I no longer had a will of my own. My mad-

ness was growing all the time.... My intellect was completely unstable" (467:76; cf. pp. 75-89).

Describing his "tandra" state of meditation (an alleged experience of omniscience), he recalls:

Every day I had meditation like that. Sometimes my body would writhe and twist like a snake's, and a hissing sound would come from inside me.... Sometimes my neck moved so violently that it made loud cracking sounds, and I became frightened.... Sometimes my neck would roll my head around so vigorously that it would bend right below my shoulders so that I could see my back.... Later, however, I learned that this was a Hatha Yogic process affected by the Goddess Kundalini in order for Her to move up through the spinal column ... (467:88-89).

*Swami Rudrananda:*
Slowly Swami Nityananda [in spirit form] came toward me and entered into my physical body. For three hours I felt nothing of myself but that the saint had possessed me. It was a terrifying experience and it required all my faith not to fight it (449:13).

*Swami Satchidananda:*
I felt myself fall into a sort of trance.... I was overjoyed with the feeling that my master [Sivananda] had entered into my own system [body] (477:119-20).

*Ram Dass:*
Some of the times when I'm speaking, it isn't me speaking. [I'm not there, my guru] Maharaji was teaching you using my body to do it. It would be like possession, except that it's an invitational possession.... He actually moves in and out of my body (1434).

We could continue on down the line, but the point is made: The gurus often admit to possession by an alien spirit being and the accompanying phenomena which often include various forms of madness. Does what we have been describing so far sound like something divine?

And the gurus are not the only ones possessed. The spiritual path they offer to their disciples frequently leads them to possession as well. "Anyone who goes deeply into these

[Eastern] disciplines taps mystery. Wall Street's Adam Smith, ruthlessly rational, reports in *Powers of Mind* on an invisible 'it' or presence that he feels on several kinds of meditative trips" (1435:4). Here are several examples:

*Da (Bubba) Free John:* Da (Bubba) Free John (Franklyn Jones) illustrates the state of a disciple possessed by the alleged "spiritual form" of the guru or master. His text *Garbage and the Goddess* describes the experiences he and his disciples underwent at his Persimmon, New York, ashram. While Free John describes normal everyday living as being "possessed by the most insidious demonic force in the universe," one would hardly suspect it from the following descriptions of, as he calls it, "life in God" (476:51).

Here are several descriptions given by several disciples:

> ... The Guru *literally* enters and transforms. It is a kind of possession. It is God-Possession. Bubba animates this body (476:151).

> People were screaming and howling and weeping, emitting strange grunts and snarls, their bodies jerking, writhing, and assuming yogic mudras ... (476:71-72).

> I felt utterly possessed, my body was possessed, and my hands started to move, and I couldn't control them. I had no control at all. My face started taking on expressions (476:263).

> My body wasn't mine. I didn't even *feel* my body as mine. There was only this sensation I've had before in Bubba's Presence, the feeling that this body is being used.... I went in and at first I was totally out of my mind. I was screaming for a long time.... I was making very strange sounds.... It is God-possession. It is God totally taking over your form (476:282-83,285).

> I was so insane I didn't know what was happening at all ... (476:66).

> Last night I was led to this spontaneous experience of conducting the force, and I felt possessed, really possessed. Then suddenly I wasn't my body any more (476:312).

Perhaps Free John is correct: "True wisdom is the capacity for perfect madness" (478:1).

*Rudrananda:*
There are times when the psychic system of the teacher will seem to control the student. He will feel possessed by his teacher. There is nothing to fear from this. It is only a stage of growth through which he [the student] is passing (449:103).

*Sri Chinmoy:*
If you remain calm and quiet, and allow your spiritual Guide to enter into you, you will become flooded with Peace. This kind of turning in is not only a valid and correct practice, but is essential for one who has placed himself under the guidance of a spiritual Master (480:113, emphasis added).

One disciple asked, "During meditation I have the feeling that there is a stranger inside me looking out. It is not me looking out through my eyes, but someone else. Is that usual?" [Chinmoy answers with], "It is quite usual. It is nothing abnormal.... It is very healthy good experience, very inspiring" (1436:23).

*Bhagwan Shree Rajneesh:*
Whenever a master wants to help you ... he simply possesses you. He simply descends into you.... If the disciple is really surrendered, the master can possess him immediately (482:168).

*Family Life*
According to many of the Hindu gurus, the family unit is also a spiritual evil. It engenders too many natural human attachments, which of necessity bind one to illusions. Because the family can be so harmful spiritually, the goal for those who are truly committed is to transcend the family, to forsake the family for purposes of enlightenment.* The following reveal several of the Hindu gurus' views toward the family:

*Rajneesh:*
Marriage is the death of love (1403:406).

Marriage is one of the ugliest institutions man has invented (1403:416).

Your childhood—an education in psychological slavery ... from the very beginning. (1403:211; cf. p. 214).

"Husband" and "wife" are going to become ugly and dirty words (1437:13).

The family creates a very, very ill human being.... I am against the family.... If families disappear churches will disappear automatically, because families belong to churches (1437:11,14-15).

*Da Free John:*
Motherhood ... is an illusion. Giving birth is no more divine than taking a crap.... Motherhood is garbage. It is all garbage.... The whole drama of existence ... is garbage (476:199-20).

Don't get the impression there is anything serious about loving someone (476:30).

It is the responsibility of the [spiritual] community to ... continually undermine "marriages" (476:7-8).

*Aurobindo/"The Mother":*
In Auroville [the spiritual community] there will be no marriages (1381:254).

What makes a woman "a pitiable slave" is "attachment to motherhood," "desire for home life and its security" and "attraction" towards the male and his strength (1393:227).

*Rajneesh on Children's Discipline:*
I am not for order at all. Disorder is perfectly beautiful.... Order is one of the most dangerous calamities.... They should be allowed all chaos (1438:20).

*A. C. Bhaktivedanta Prabhupada:*
No one can be happy in family life (1439:230).

[Commenting on a verse in the *Srimad Bhaga-vantam*, Hindu holy literature]: During the daytime the wife is compared to a witch and at night she is compared to a tigress. Her only business is sucking the blood of her husband both day and night.... The children are also like tigers, jackals and foxes.... The family members may be called wives and children but actually they are plunderers (1439:101).

*Murder and the Spiritually Enlightened?*
If good and evil are ultimately meaningless categories, and if life itself is an illusion, and if acts of evil must sometimes be deliberately undertaken in order to "prove" to oneself that there is no evil, then on what logical basis can even murder be condemned? Ritual murder has been condoned in many ancient and modern traditions, from the ancient Aztecs to modern Satanism, from ancient (and some contemporary) Hinduism to modern witchcraft. Throughout history a countless multitude of people has been sacrificed on pagan altars (825).

The tradition of human sacrifice has always been justified on fundamentally pagan religious grounds. Human sacrifice is condoned on the basis of appeasing the gods, protecting spiritual integrity, or personal enlightenment gained from the alleged death-energy transferred to the initiate when it is released at the point of sacrifice.

So why should even murder be condemned if it is part of the process of spiritual enlightenment? Even so, it is hard to believe that, as in the words of one authority on shamanism,* some possessed shamans confess "the urge to kill... [comes] to them with a strength and frequency similar to that of hunger" (862:17-20). For the reader's consideration, we cite the following statements without comment:

*Rajneesh:*
Even if you kill someone consciously ... it is meditative. This is what Krishna [in the *Bhagavad Gita*] was saying.... Kill, murder, fully conscious, knowing that no one is murdered and no is killed.... You are only destroying the forms. So destroy the forms (567:399).

[You have ignored your own deity.] *This* is the sin—not that you have murdered somebody or stolen; that is nothing. Those are minor sins (567:399).

*Swami Rama:*
If the killer thinks that he kills [he is ignorant] (1440:67).

*Ramakrishna/Vivekananda:*
The murderer too is God (1394:530).

*Krishna (Hindu deity):*
Even if a devotee commits the most abominable actions he is to be considered saintly because he is properly situated (1441).

One who is [enlightened], even killing in this world, he is not killing, and neither is he [karmically] bound by such action (1442).

*Maharishi Mahesh Yogi:*
Maharishi says of Arjuna in the Bhagavad Gita, "[He has to] attain a state of consciousness which will justify any action of his and will allow him even to kill in love, in support of the purpose of evolution" (469:26).

*Indra (Hindu deity):*
The man who knows me as I am loses nothing whatever he does. Even if he kills his mother or his father, even if he steals or procures an abortion; for whatever evil he does, he does not blanch if he knows me as I am (1443).

Without very much effort we can switch from the amoral philosophy of the gurus to the amoral philosophy of serial killers or the Manson clan. Vincent Bugliosi, the prosecutor of Charles Manson, observed that Manson enjoyed killing as an end in itself, and that had he not been caught, he would have murdered as many people as possible (1444). Consider the comments of some of his "family": "Whatever is necessary, you do it. When somebody needs to be killed, there's no wrong. You do it, and then you move on. . . . You kill whoever gets in your way. That is us" (1445:624). "You really have to have a lot of love in your heart to do what I did to [Sharon] Tate" (1446). In fact, it was Manson's adoption of Eastern philosophy that help encourage his brutal crimes (1447).

The majority of gurus, however, do not publicly condone murder. Usually, they are merely describing the spiritual ignorance of those who would assume that anyone who really doesn't exist can ever be killed. Of course, that was also Manson's argument: There is no death. Nevertheless, such teachings can be abused, and they can open the door for a form of murder that *is* spiritually justified: ritual sacrifice. As noted, human sacrifice has been an acceptable practice of paganism throughout history. Once again human sacrifice is on the increase, and the rationale given is that of pagan teachings: the placating of the gods, or that ritual murder releases the great amounts of energy needed for ritualistic purposes (1296:247; cf. ref. 1069). Enlightenment doesn't care how you get there; only that you arrive.

## OTHER HAZARDS

There are other dangers. When men and women reject their minds, follow religious leaders blindly, undercut and demean moral values and open themselves to occult forces, it's not surprising that people will be hurt or killed. When men and women are taught to see themselves as worthless illusions and to adopt a nihilistic outlook, and when they reject moral standards as "unenlightened" and enter abnormal states of consciousness, who can be surprised when there are casualties? What *is* surprising are the number of people who accept such things as insanity or demonization uncritically, and then naively proceed to interpret them as "true spirituality," "higher consciousness," or "divine enlightenment." The following are representative statements concerning possible hazards along the Eastern path.

*Rajneesh:*
The experience of deep meditation is exactly like death. . . . [But] when it happens so suddenly, either the body suffers or the mind . . . some people can go mad (1448:371; cf. 373).

This [temporary madness] is going to happen to many. Don't be afraid when it happens (861:11).

Either you will become enlightened or you will go mad—the danger is there. One has to take the risk (1449:5).

*Sri Chinmoy:*
Many, many black magicians and people who deal with spirits have been strangled or killed. I know because I have been near quite a few of these cases (810:62; cf. 71).

I know of a case in India where the hostile forces used to take the form of a particular Master and ask the disciples to commit suicide. "If you commit suicide, I will be able to give you liberation sooner" it would say. They tried to commit suicide even though the Master told them outwardly that he had never said that. These hostile forces are very clever (810:94).

237

*Aurobindo.* Aurobindo and his co-guru "the Mother" have warned the yoga aspirants of hazards they may face. There may be attacks on them by "cosmic forces"; there are often "disastrous results" (1393:142/1392:2). The Mother also warns about the hazards of astral projection, here being attacked by otherworldly entities who "like amusing themselves at the cost of human beings" (1392:2). "As soon as they see that someone is not sufficiently protected, they rush in and take possession of the mechanical mind and bring about all kinds of disagreeable happenings—nightmares, various physical disturbances—you feel choked, bite or swallow your tongue, and even more serious things" (1392:2).

A brief summarization indicates that to one degree or another many of the gurus in America directly or indirectly:

1. Discard the mind and independent thinking.
2. Demand an absolute, unquestioning obedience.
3. Reject moral standards.
4. Demean and cheapen human life as maya (illusion).
5. See family life as a perversion or a concession to evil.
6. Reject Christianity as a spiritual hazard or abomination.
7. Offer teachings leading to despair and nihilism.
8. Offer an occult path that may lead to insanity, serious physical ailments, possession, or death.

Are such teachings truly "Wisdom from the East," or are they really the "doctrines of demons" referred to in Scripture (1 Timothy 4:1)? All this leads to one basic conclusion: Far from dealing with a benevolent form of spirituality or of godly wisdom, "This wisdom is not that which comes down from above, but is earthly, natural [unspiritual], demonic" (James 3:15 NASB).

What justifies this assessment? In part, the growing number of tragedies reported by former disciples, including the published accounts of blatant deception, grave immorality, criminal activity, physical assaults, murder and threats of murder, cruelty, drug trafficking, rapes, and other forms of sexual violence, not to mention even worse things on the part of some gurus (1450).

# ENLIGHTENMENT

## INFO AT A GLANCE

**Description.** Enlightenment involves an allegedly higher state of consciousness and existence leading to a potentially profound personal alteration that radically, and often permanently, changes one's perception of self and the world.

**Founder.** Unknown, but the goal of seeking alleged enlightenment is a central characteristic of much pagan religion, such as Hinduism, Buddhism, and Taoism.

**How does it claim to work?** By various occult practices and disciplines (altered states of consciousness,* meditation,* magical practice, yoga,* and so on), one allegedly realizes the divine or monistic nature of all reality—self, world, universe—and lives in accordance with such a perception.

**Scientific evaluation.** New Age scientists and other researchers who are attempting to examine "higher or enlightened" states of consciousness are having little success. This research is usually conducted through the disciplines of parapsychology and New Age consciousness studies.

**Examples of occult potential.** Psychic development, spirit contact, or possession.

**Major problem.** The goal of occult enlightenment is not merely a new perspective; it is usually to destroy and replace the old personality and consciousness with a radically new level of being. Unfortunately, that which is alleged to be a higher state of existence is usually a state of spiritistic manipulation of consciousness or actual spirit possession. It is not an advanced spiritual state, but one that is primitive and regressive, and consequentially results in bondage to spiritistic powers.

**Biblical/Christian evaluation.** Enlightenment is a phenomenon stressing the need for occult practice, the acceptance of psychic development, the experiential realization of occult philosophy (e.g., pantheism), and it has traditional associations to spiritism. As such, seeking a state of New Age enlightenment is prohibited biblically.

**Potential dangers.** Occult bondage, demonization.

*Note:* In other chapters, e.g., Eastern Gurus, Altered States of Consciousness, Shamanism, Meditation, Yoga, Intuition, and New Age

Inner Work, we have discussed related issues or documented that states of enlightenment are characteristically spiritistic encounters involving manipulations of consciousness or spirit possession.

## INTRODUCTION AND INFLUENCE

Enlightenment is realization of the truth of Being. Our native condition, our true self is Being, traditionally called God, ... the Supreme Being ... (843:xv).

The value of mystical and transformative states is not in producing some new experience, but in getting rid of the experiencer (843:xiv).

In the New Age Movement, "enlightenment" is one of those words that everyone respects. It suggests something very good. For anyone to say that it is something negative would seem harsh, for such a polite-sounding word should speak of something noble and sublime.

But just what *is* "enlightenment," this concept that allegedly describes a higher order of existence, a grander state of being, which for many New Agers represents the emerging prototype of a new species of humanity? This is the fundamental question, a question which in some ways answers other important questions about New Age metaphysics, occultism, and Eastern mystical religion in general. It is also an important question because the final goal of almost all serious New Age practice, as well as of many within occultism, Hinduism, Buddhism, Sufism, Sikhism, and other forms of mysticism is "enlightenment," however it is conceptualized. And whatever occurs along these spiritual paths is designed to nourish the process of enlightenment; whatever is endured or achieved is inescapably linked in some fashion to that final goal. And if we can determine the nature of the goal, we can also learn something about the nature of the path.

Because it is in harmony with Hindu, Buddhist, and most mystical metaphysics, New Age "enlightenment" teaches the internal recognition by the individual that he or she is one essence with God or ultimate reality, with all

that this implies. All mysticism is not the same, of course, nor are all categories of religious enlightenment, but sufficient commonalities exist to warrant extrapolation for the focus of our study here. For example, the development of monistic consciousness, the acceptance of spiritism and other forms of occultism, and a pragmatic amoralism typify the general process of mystical enlightenment. Our own research on many occult traditions and on some 25 Eastern mystical sects bears this out. Not all are equally potent or radical, but all set up shop in the same spiritual house, so to speak. Different rooms may be occupied, but the fundamental environment is consistent.

What enlightenment means in the New Age Movement can be gauged through editor John White's text *What Is Enlightenment?: Exploring the Goal of the Spiritual Path.* White is an authority on consciousness exploration and related areas, having authored or edited numerous books, such as *What Is Meditation?*, *Frontiers of Consciousness*, *The Highest State of Consciousness*, *Psychic Exploration*, *Other Worlds, Other Universes*, and *Kundalini, Evolution and Enlightenment.* White holds degrees from Dartmouth College and Yale University, is on the boards of several academic and New Age organizations, and is an editorial contributor to a variety of national publications.

He writes, "So widespread is the urge to know about enlightenment that, for the first time in history, people and organizations claiming to understand it have developed into a thriving field of commerce. The enlightenment industry is big business.... Today, enlightenment is for everyone" (1528:XIII). But the kind of enlightenment White discusses is not new; it is the age-old enlightenment of Eastern religion and occultism: that people are, in their true nature, one essence with God. As noted in the introductory quote: "*Enlightenment is the realization of the truth of Being. Our native condition, our true self is Being, traditionally called God ...*" (1528:XV).

According to this view, the fundamental problem is that most people do not know that they are God. The common way of viewing things (that we are limited egos, personal selves) must thus be transcended until people recognize that they are "enlightened" as to their true nature. White emphasizes, "But the critical point to be understood is this: the value of mystical and transformative states is not in producing some new experience but in *getting rid of the experiencer.* Getting rid, that is, of the egocentric consciousness which experiences life from a contracted, self-centered point of view rather than the free, unfettered perspective of a sage who knows he or she is infinity operating through a finite form" (1528:XIV).

The false perception of one's limitations and isolation must be replaced with a new, direct experience of pantheism: "The limitation is in you—your consciousness—and when that limitation is transcended, you perceive existence differently and therefore relate to it in a new way. Your sense of identity changes. You experience the cosmos as unified and intimately one with your own essential being, rather than experiencing yourself as a separate, isolated physical form apart from all the rest of existence" (1528:XVIII).

But through what means is individual perception so radically altered that the person now views his true nature, and the nature of the universe, as deity? This change in perception occurs by means of various occult practices found in both Eastern and Western spirituality. These practices lead the seeker of enlightenment into contact with the spirit world—what the Bible identifies as the realm of deceiving spirits or demons. As we will see, these practices permit the interfacing of the human and the demonic such that individual consciousness becomes manipulated toward delusions of personal godhood. For example, as we have shown in the chapter on Eastern Gurus ("The Problem of Personhood"), the goal of enlightenment is not only to alter one's perspective but to destroy one's basic identity so that it may be replaced with a new, alien consciousness.

Before we move into our analysis, it might be helpful to consider the individuals in White's anthology who write about enlightenment. Many of these names will be familiar to readers of other chapters of this book. Their backgrounds and interests here reveal the typical Eastern or occult orientation of New Age enlightenment:

*Sri Aurobindo* is the Hindu occultist who attempted a synthesis of Eastern and Western thinking. He said that the central spiritual experience was "the descent of the Supermind"—an experience that parallels spirit influence or possession. He is perhaps best known for his two-volume text, *The Life Divine.*

*Meher Baba* is an Eastern guru who underwent periods of insanity and possession on his personal route to enlightenment, as indicated in the biography by Purdom, *The God-Man.*

*Richard Maurice Bucke, M.D.* authored the occult classic *Cosmic Consciousness.* It was written in 1901, and has significantly influenced consciousness research and the field of transpersonal psychology. It was Bucke's own brief mystical encounter that impelled him to write on mystical consciousness.

*Allan Y. Cohen* has his doctorate in clinical psychology from Harvard and has worked with radical LSD explorer Timothy Leary. He is currently adjunct professor of parapsychology and mysticism at the John F. Kennedy University in Orinda, California. He is also a committed disciple of Sufi guru Meher Baba and has written widely in the field of mysticism.

*Da Free John* is another controversial guru who was previously a disciple of radical Hindu gurus Swami Muktananda, Rudrananda, and Nityananda. Free John's anarchistic spirituality centers upon such themes as "God-possession," which is indistinguishable from classical demonization (for examples, see Meditation).

*Lex Hixon* is a devotee of meditation,* which he practices under the guidance of Swami Nikhilananda and Swami Prabhavananda of the Ramakrishna Order. He has also practiced under Zen,* Tibetan Buddhist, and Islamic meditation masters.

*Aldous Huxley* was the popular mystic who, in some ways, is one of the principal fathers of the consciousness research movement. His widely read books include *The Doors of Perception, The Perennial Philosophy, Heaven and Hell,* and *Brave New World.*

*Gopi Krishna* is a well-known yogi who seeks to advance the cause of kundalini enlightenment around the world as an experience with divine energy (see Yoga). He is author of the spiritual autobiography *Kundalini, the Evolutionary Energy in Man*, in which he recounts his experiences with insanity and spirit possession as typical results of his kundalini experience. He has also written *The Secret of Yoga, Higher Consciousness*, and *The Dawn of a New Science*.

*Jiddhu Krishnamurti* was the internationally known teacher whom Annie Besant of the Theosophical society attempted to introduce to the world as the new Christ and World Teacher. Repudiating this role, he pursued his own path of occultism and wrote *The Awakening of Intelligence, The First and Last Freedom*, and *Freedom from the Known*. Mary Lutyen's two-volume biography, *Krishnamurti*, indicates that Krishnamurti also became demonized on the path of enlightenment.

*Dane Rudhyar* is a prominent humanistic and transpersonal astrologer and occult psychologist who has been awarded several honorary degrees for his work. Among his best-known works are *The Planetarization of Consciousness, Rhythm of Wholeness, The Astrology of Transformation*, and the 1936 classic *The Astrology of Personality*.

*Satprem* is the disciple of Sri Aurobindo and author of a 13-volume set on the personal conversations he had with Aurobindo's spiritual partner, "The Mother."

*Houston Smith* was a professor of religion and philosophy at Syracuse University for 15 years. He is author of the well-known text, *The Religions of Man*, which has sold over two million copies. He has produced documentary films on Sufism, Hinduism, and Tibetan Buddhism that have won international film festival awards. He has also written *Forgotten Truth: The Primordial Tradition*, and *Beyond the Post-Modern Mind*.

*Evelyn Underhill* was a well-known authority on mysticism and author of such books as *The Mystic Way, Practical Mysticism, Man and the Supernatural, The House of the Soul, Essentials of Mysticism and Other Essays*, and her classic text *Mysticism: A Study in the Nature and Development of Man's Spiritual Consciousness*.

*Roger Walsh* trained in medicine, psychiatry, and neuroscience, and he is a practitioner of Buddhist *vipassana* meditation. He has attempted to integrate modern forms of transpersonal psychology into therapy. He is the coauthor of *Beyond Ego: Transpersonal Dimensions in Psychology*, and of the authoritative text *Meditation: Ancient and Contemporary Perspectives*.

*Alan Watts* was the famous mystic and Western popularizer of Zen Buddhism and a promoter of psychedelic drug use. Among his books on mysticism are *Psychotherapy East and West, The Supreme Identity, Behold the Spirit, The Way of Zen, Beyond Theology*, and *The Book*.

*Ken Wilber* is regarded as among the foremost theorists in transpersonal psychology and has been a practitioner of Zen Buddhism for over 20 years, studying under several Zen masters. Although he completed his course requirements for the Ph.D. in biochemistry, his interest in mystical states caused him to leave the academic world and devote his time to personal exploration in consciousness research. He is author of *The Spectrum of Consciousness, No Boundary, The Atman Project, Up From Eden*, and *System, Self and Structure—An Outline of Transpersonal Psychology*. He is also editor-in-chief of *Revision: A Journal of Consciousness and Change*.

The above describes the typical spiritual orientation of leaders of the search for spiritual enlightenment. Obviously, this "modern search" is nothing new; it is fundamentally a throwback to ancient pagan practices, usually reconstituted for contemporary Western consumption. Nevertheless, the essence and consequence of paganism remains. Indeed, modern enlightenment is an extended experimentation with occult states of consciousness. Thus, the severe consequences found in this modern search for supposedly higher states of being are not unexpected (cf. 278), as we will now document.

## DEMONIZATION AS ENLIGHTENMENT

It is our conviction that the experience of enlightenment isn't what proponents claim it to be: an exalted and divine state of consciousness permitting experiential awareness of the pantheistic reality of all existence. We think it is just the opposite. Far from being a spiritual evolutionary leap for mankind, we think enlightenment is a rather unprogressive encounter with the demonic, which ultimately leads to possession. If it can reasonably be shown that the process of enlightenment results in a condition of spiritual *evil*, then at least from a moral and spiritual viewpoint we have discovered that enlightenment is neither what it claims to be nor seems to be.

Such a judgment is perhaps unimaginable to most New Age practitioners because enlightenment gravitates around the context of spiritual growth and an alleged encounter with the divine. To complicate matters, the experience itself, whatever negative elements also exist, can be indescribably profound and pleasant. Nevertheless, the experience is about the impersonation of the divine by the demonic for purposes of spiritual deception and enslavement, offered under the ageis of profound divine evolution.

To even suggest this may seem incredible to some people. Yet the devil's primal rebellion was precisely about his desire to be "as God," and his first communication to man offered the same tantalizing perspective (Genesis 3:4-5; Isaiah 14:12-14). To us, it is not surprising that Satan would weave the mechanics of human demonization to look like godhood, and call it an enlightened state of being. From his perspective, it is an enlightened state—so enlightened that in the end it lusts to be worshiped as God (Matthew 4:9) or even for the worship of God Himself!

Is "true enlightenment" really a form of demonization, of possession by a hostile entity imploding the consciousness toward deceptive perceptions of inner divinity? Most definitely. Many Eastern gurus, including Muktananda and Da Free John, actually describe it as possession, denoting awareness of being taken over by an alien intelligence. True, they may interpret this as possession by divine forces or entities, but the associated phenomena and consequences clearly suggest the demonic.

*Examples of*

Consider the comments of Tal Brooke, formerly a practitioner of Eastern metaphysics and the premier Western disciple of India's most famous guru, Sai Baba. After personal experience and study of the phenomenon of enlightenment, and then conversion to Christian faith, he wrote *Riders of the Cosmic Circuit* (249). His con-

tention is that enlightenment as an ancient spiritual tradition is really a form of demonization:

How do you explain enlightenment? Enlightenment is the ultimate initiatory giving over of the identity—the mind, spirit, and soul—to another power to become the occupant. It is a self-annihilating surrender. The new occupant is no longer human. It is operating on a superhuman level of intelligence. And it has strategy, deception, and power—this is the timeless theme. That final rite of surrender has a recurrent configuration before the cosmic possession becomes irreversible (249:200-01).

In a statement he wrote specifically for this chapter, Brooke discusses his personal experience to answer the question of why he wrote his book. His insight is worth quoting at length:

"It was the most incredible feeling I've ever had in my entire life"—These are the familiar words western adepts use to describe their experiences of "altered states" of consciousness. The guru touches them on the forehead and they are blasted into realms of bliss that pales any "high" they have ever experienced before.

Swami Anand Virendra, the former Echart Flother, once Senior Editor of *German Business Week* magazine, describes a Rajneesh encounter group in Germany prior to his departure to Poona where he surrendered his life to Rajneesh. "It felt like a waterfall of electricity shooting through my entire body, more powerful than any drug or orgasm I have ever had. Yes, it was sexual in a way, but it was more than just that. It took possession of me, this force. And nobody even touched me. It was with this group of Rajneeshies, in the middle of this encounter group, just standing alone. Then . . . WHAM . . . it hit."

His name is once again Echart Flother, but he has been through a profound and overpowering experience in India. That initial ecstasy he felt disarmed him completely. Echart's agnostic materialism was suddenly meaningless. The motivation of his career oriented life was now paled in light of what he now knew. Western ambitions seemed trivial. And what the Church offered seemed empty and irrelevant in comparison. The Lutheran State Church could not provide this magnitude of experiential "Zap." It was like comparing a discharged flashlight battery—the Church—with a modern hydroelectric plant.

Indeed, the initial experiences seemed to be "very good." What could be wrong with such feelings of elation, such epiphanies of supernatural surety?

Now consider the same words we heard initially. "It was the most incredible feeling I've ever had in my entire life"—This time these words are coming from a heroin addict describing the first time the "spike" went into his arm. The feeling of euphoria was overwhelming . . . initially.

How could something that feels so good subjectively, heroin, produce something that in time becomes a monster of self-destruction from the objective viewpoint—cracking teeth, yellowing pale skin, a vacant stare, physical emaciation, and finally death? Socially, the addict becomes alienated from other people who are now objects to be manipulated and used for one end alone—more heroin. He is no longer the person he was before. He has lost his innocence in a profound sense. Yet its initial feeling was incredibly good!

Malcolm Muggeridge, among others, encouraged me to write *Riders of the Cosmic Circuit* after he had read my first book, *Lord of the Air,* the contents of which had spurred us into an intense discussion in his living room in Robertsbridge. He challenged me as a former adept to look closer at the pattern I was unearthing and flesh this stuff out. It was a fascinating and alarming revelation that needed to be sounded out as a warning, Muggeridge admonished me. I had, after all, been an Eastern adept myself.

Ten years prior to Muggeridge's 1981 challenge to me about this present book, I too had been in India going through enormous inward changes. I had been for several years in the inner circle of India's premier guru, Sai Baba, who is renowned for his miraculous powers. And on numerous occasions I felt myself experience radical and startling states of altered consciousness in his presence. But like Echart Flother in Poona under Rajneesh, I eventually encountered a dark side to Sai Baba, the complete story of which is recounted in my book *Avatar of Night,* which was a best seller in India. I broke away suddenly from Baba after having a dramatic Christian conversion in South India.

In my present book, I name Sai Baba and Rajneesh among the *Riders of the Cosmic Circuit.*

They are far from being ordinary people. Each has gone through an absolutely radical change of consciousness beginning at an historically traceable moment in time. I call this point "explosion." Incredibly, most major gurus who carry the credentials of "enlightenment" have been through what seems to be an irreversible experience beginning at "explosion." The self seems to have been obliterated and a new cosmic occupant seems to have invaded them and taken over—they say, and others believe, that it is God.

Now we find there is a strange logic behind what the "Riders" do as self-proclaimed deities in their own realm. But it is a pattern with a radically new figure-ground. It is easy to miss this pattern and be stuck on one side of an optical illusion.

Most people have experienced standing in a novelty store and being intrigued by the various optical illusions. For a while you can see it only one way, then there is a brief thrill, and you can see it a totally new way. Take for example the common picture of the full page champagne glass. One keeps seeing a "champagne glass." Then suddenly that disappears and is replaced by "two faces" staring at each other that are equally as real and discernible as the champagne glass. The illusion flips back and forth, but you never see both at the same time.

Similarly, if the observer can be brought around to the new perspective, then the Rider's prior acts take on a completely new meaning. And this can be shocking. It is a perspective that the twentieth century has only just begun to wake up to once again. I am referring now to the reality of demonic possession—the other explanation for the cosmic occupant with the Rider.

Richard Foster of Cambridge has demonstrated that there is now once again room in our postmodern world for mystery. That the "closed universe" concept in vogue till the middle of this century, which did not acknowledge forces beyond those of materialistic mechanism, has given ground to new post-modern paradigms, stemming, in part, from discoveries in physics. Modern thought is once again faced with the possibility of the supernatural—including such raw-boned biblical concepts as possession.

There is indeed a darker side to what the Riders are really doing inside the souls of their closest devotees. In Poona, I saw human wreckage much worse than that of our heroin addict. But more than that, there was a pattern to this systematic dehumanization within the subjects. They were being prepared for something that would catch them fully unawares, as shocking and tangible as when a woman is raped suddenly with no forewarning. In seconds she has gone from the quiet awareness that comes from strolling in familiar territory along a neighborhood street to the terror of being raped in the darkness by a psychopathic killer. Both situations can exist only seconds apart with no forewarning.

What I found in India, after closely observing Rajneesh, was a spiritual reality that carried the chill of a Dennis Wheatly novel. The figure-ground of the optical illusion suddenly switched, leaving the naked force of something fully occult—like looking into a colored laser hologram that switches faces and stares out at you from its own three dimensional world. The hologram of Shiva suddenly flickered and resembled Satan. Is so-called "superconsciousness" or "enlightenment" in reality "perfect possession," a unique form of demonic possession? I am afraid that the facts suggest exactly this.

To determine if an experience is either divine or demonic is to determine the personal and, if encultured, the social consequences that flow from such a condition. From a biblical perspective, confusing the divine and the demonic has always been the goal of Satan for purposes of spiritual deception (2 Corinthians 11:14-15; 2 Thessalonians 2:3-4). And the devil has indeed achieved a significant measure of success. The epistemological gulf that lies between public adoration of the allegedly "enlightened" gurus and the underlying demonic reality behind them represents a distorted perception of massive proportions (see Eastern Gurus).

If "enlightenment" is demonization, then the hallmarks of possession will be present. Eastern gurus often claim that they can possess their disciples through their "spiritual form." Sri Chinmoy states, "The disciples sit in front of me and meditate. At that time I go into my highest consciousness and enter them. I enter into each individual soul . . ." (2772:89). Tal Brooke uses the metaphor of "explosion" in his description of the process:

When a guru, a Rider, emerges from Explosion, you have his revelations, his claimed experiences, and his non-human personality operating behind a poker face. Like a good screen actor, he can manipulate every button of human reaction, but behind it is a cold, unknowable, non-human intelligence. Who is the Rider? Who or what is occupying the body? . . . He says he is one with God. He says a lot of things. Clearly, if he is truly Enlightened and has passed all the tests, he is an enigma within a riddle and you can either believe or disbelieve his claims. But make them he does. They all do, all the Riders— "I am God," they say.

If we cannot peer into the black hole of the "static-eternal" and are faced with the well-known psychologist's dilemma of assessing subjective private experience, we are forced into looking into a lot of associated areas. One key lies in the initiatory signs, the flavor or essence of those signs, leading to the barrier of the Explosion. And we begin to see a pattern. The pattern may wrap itself in varying semantic packages, but the flavor is there. And this is true whether the initiation is Tantric, Mahayana Buddhist, by means of *kundalini, shakti-pat,* or the spontaneous Explosion of Rajneesh in the garden at midnight under the maulshree tree, or Sai Baba's spontaneous and powerful character change.

Curiously, when the heavy-hitting gurus, the Riders, emerged from the Explosion, close associates and family usually used the term "possession" in describing the change that they saw. Rajneesh prepares his highest adepts by readying them emotionally to do the same thing—sink into the infinite abyss, and drop away and keep dropping away. His words are a juggling act. Along with this comes the admonition, "Don't worry about what fills you or enters you. Let it happen. Surrender. Lose your identity forever."

The only Scripture on earth that deals with this phenomenon is the Holy Bible. Period. It talks about massive evil intelligences operating behind the scenes of our world. It talks about Possession. It has live historical instances of demonic possession and exorcism. . . .

It became vivid, this new class of creatures— superhumanly-energized figures proclaiming to be God in human form, yet in a state of Perfect Possession. Not ordinary demonic possession, but perfect. The original human inhabitant now fully obliterated out of the body, blow-torched as it were. The new resident consciousness not your standard comic-book demon, but a massive, baleful intelligence that is ageless, that has witnessed cosmic creation, that is extremely powerful and extremely evil (249:170–71).

Irrespective of the fact that enlightenment comes in many forms and guises, when all the prerequisites for demonization are present, demonization occurs. Furthermore, the "Riders' " religious methods and paths are designed to replicate their unique "state of consciousness" within their disciples. *Shaktipat diksha*, or the energy transfer and possession by the guru's "energy force" at initiation, puts another twist to the process. According to Rajneesh:

Whenever a Master wants to help you, cleanse your energy channels, your passage [*kundalini* spinal channel] if it is blocked, he simply possesses you. He simply descends into you and his energy, which is of a higher quality . . . moves into your energy channels. . . . This is the whole art of *Shakti-pat* [when he touches the forehead at initiation]. If the disciple is really surrendered, the Master can possess him immediately. And once you are possessed by the energy of the Master, once his *prana* surrounds you, enters you, much is done very easily which you cannot do in years. . . . But if a Master can enter you like a waterfall, many things are washed away. And when the Master has gone out of you, suddenly you start to be a totally different person (482:68).

## A NEW MORALITY

In the following material, we will see where this "totally different person" is taken by the occult path and the experience of enlightenment.

According to biblical teaching, God is a holy and righteous God. "The LORD is righteous in all his ways and loving toward all he has made" (Psalm 145:17). "There is no one holy like the LORD" (1 Samuel 2:2). Hence no one should be surprised that God Himself declares to us, "Be holy because I, the LORD your God, am holy" (Leviticus 19:2).

Because it is God's desire to exalt righteousness in the world, the devil does his best to promote sin and evil. One of the most effective means to accomplish this is to obliterate the categories of good and evil. This is done by promoting an amoral worldview and through having people experientially perceive that ultimate reality, or God Himself, is *beyond* good and evil. Demonized people are amoral and frequently express varying degrees of sociopathic behavior. However, the changes in moral perspective do not occur overnight, but are gradually induced by the ongoing mystical experiences. In the end, the state of enlightenment becomes a subjective, experiential *condition* hostile to moral standards and behavior. By the time one attains "enlightenment," moral standards have been virtually "blowtorched" out of the individual. Conventional morality is now perceived as mere remnants of an unenlightened consciousness. The evil and immorality one uncovers in the camps of the "enlightened" aptly illustrates this.

When prideful men with supernatural powers believe that they are God and sit with absolute authority over thousands of trusting devotees, stories such as the following can be expected, no matter how seemingly meek, enlightened, or spiritually powerful the guru or spiritual "master" appears. The tales of violence and sexual immorality condoned by Rajneesh and Muktananda are only the tip of the iceberg (249). Spiritual abuse comes in many forms, but sexual abuse is common. Here is an illustration from the *Yoga Journal* (some readers may find the following offensive):

I once knew a charming, radiant, charismatic teacher who successfully taught most of his small following to connect clairaudiently with the "Higher Self" so they could better receive inner advice and become calm and centered at will. The teacher had remarkable *siddhis*, or [psychic] powers. He was clairaudient, and sometimes clairvoyant. He claimed to call on angelic beings for wisdom and healings, and several followers were indeed healed. He claimed to experience ecstatic communion with these beings for days on end and would emerge from his retreats more radiant than usual, almost visibly surrounded by light. On several occasions I and several others observed him insert large needles through the skin of his cheeks and arms without pain or bleeding, and chew up and swallow razor blades with no apparent harm.

This teacher believed that stressful confrontations were useful in helping his students to evoke the Higher Self. He therefore collected "collateral"—the student's most prized possession—to be forfeited if the student did not obey him implicitly. He then took groups of students on hikes and threatened to hurl one or two of them off a cliff if they didn't summon their Higher Selves and become immediately calm. As a further confrontation, he would ask students to masturbate in front of the group. And as an ultimate confront, he would ask students (both male and female) to engage in one or another sexual activity with him. When they finally agreed (perhaps remembering the collateral), the teacher would either withdraw the request or go through with it, sometimes in the presence of other group members (1354:21–22).

Most Eastern gurus* appear to have an active sex life and, given human nature and the esoteric occult teachings which condone abuse or immorality, the results can be very degenerative. One two-year study by a sympathetic practitioner reported the following, indicating that some 70 percent of the gurus and other spiritual masters were active sexually:

According to this survey—which includes information on 54 teachers, six females and 48 males—sexual relations form a part of the lives of 39 of them. Only three out of 15 Zen masters, three of nine Hindu and Jain swamis, less than half of the Tibetan lamas, and five of the 24 Theravada Buddhist teachers considered in this survey are celibate. The rest (including myself) have chosen to involve themselves in sexual relationships. Significantly, 34 of 39 teachers who are not celibate have had at least occasional sexual relationships with one or more students. Sometimes these were straightforward and open, sometimes more covert (1452:27).

The study also mentioned additional experiences of adultery and homosexuality among the gurus:

Some teachers who are not celibate have spouses and families; of these, some live monogamously, while many others do not. Among non-celibate teachers, some are sexually very active, others only occasionally so. Some are heterosexuals, some are homosexual, and some are bisexual in preference. . . . Clearly, many of those who are generally acknowledged to be accomplished meditation masters and teachers are sexually active. Indeed, as a group these teachers seem to represent the whole range of human sexuality (1452:27–28).

This study also noted abuses, which were not uncommon, and that there was often an attempt to cover up immoral behavior:

Nevertheless, some have involved the exploitation of the teacher-student relationship and have, in a number of cases, contradicted the teachings of the tradition. We have to acknowledge that such incidents have occurred and that in many cases they have been harmful.

Compounding the problem are the situations that involve secrecy or deception, for deception has proven to be the greatest source of disappointment and pain in spiritual groups. The discovery of covert or inappropriate sexual relations between teachers and students is not an infrequent occurrence. In recent years such discoveries have caused major upheavals in nearly a dozen of the largest Eastern spiritual communities in America. . . . Of the students with whom I have spoken, most of whom were women, approximately half report that such sexual relationships have undermined their practice, their relationship with their teacher, and their feelings of self-worth (1452:28).

Indeed, when one really gets to know a person who claims to be enlightened—either personally, or by reliable firsthand reports, or through an autobiography—the term "spiritually enlightened" hardly seems appropriate. "Moral anarchist" seems to be the only appropriate term.

Many spiritual leaders today are indeed enlightened, but in an occult sense, which is the opposite of what it means in a biblical sense, to be regenerated and sanctified by repentance and faith in Christ. In our postbiblical culture, people fall prey to "the enlightened" because of being fascinated by their spiritual power, or because they do not understand fallen human nature or the mechanics and dimensions of spiritual deception as revealed in the Bible. Scripture declares that Satan is "the god of this world" (2 Corinthians 4:4 NASB), who "deceives the whole world" (Revelation 12:9 NASB; 13:14; 20:3,8,10), and indeed that "the whole world is under the control of the evil one" (1 John 5:19; cf. Matthew 4:8–9).

From a biblical perspective, those enlightened through the path of occultism, far from incarnating divine power and holiness, are simply living according to their fallen nature. They are manifesting the deeds of the flesh (Galatians 5:19-21) or the individual purpose of the spirit (demon) entity living within them. In John 13:27 and Luke 22:3, we are told that "Satan entered Judas" in order to use Judas to betray Jesus (see John 13:2; Acts 5:3). In addition, the monistic and amoral teachings within the traditions they follow become the religious and spiritual justification for what "the enlightened" do. A sympathetic commentator on Swami Muktananda's violence and seduction of young girls was forced to confess that "the enlightened are on an equal footing with the ignorant in the struggle against their own evil" (1353:30; cf. 1431). To the contrary, we would suggest the ignorant are better off. But even for the ignorant, it is easy to rationalize such evil. For example, when one bewailer of the abuses commented that the "ignorant" cannot be blamed for being deceived by the "enlightened," he was neglecting personal responsibility. Ignorance of the law, social or spiritual, has never been an acceptable excuse for condoning evil.

One of the arguments ran as follows: "But in the case of spiritual teachers, who can really blame us? We have nothing in our [American] cultural context in which to place them [the enlightened]" (1354:22). But this is not true at all. By far the most astute commentary on spiritual issues of this sort is the Bible, and the Bible is found in virtually every household and hotel room in the nation. American culture has been profoundly influenced by biblical teaching. A large part of it deals with issues relating to good and evil, and one of its principal themes is spiritual deception and the consequences of

idolatry—of forsaking the true and living God for false and demonic gods. The Bible repeatedly warns against men who claim to speak for God and yet lead people to worship false gods (Deuteronomy 13:1-5; Matthew 7;24; 2 Peter 2; Jude).

To walk off a cliff in the dark has never been good advice, yet millions are advised by their "enlightned" masters to do just that, spiritually and morally speaking. From our research and discussion with former devotees, the alleged accounts of evil committed among the gurus and the "enlightened" are legion: rape, fornication, drug smuggling, adultery, beatings, murder threats, and worse.

For example, the *San Francisco Chronicle* of April 3 and April 4, 1985, ran a front-page story titled, " 'Sex Slave' Sues Guru," where former members including a former director of the sect's Laughing Man Institute accused Western guru Da Free John, a former member of the Church of Scientology,* of encouraging "drunken sex orgies," and, "indulging in long drinking binges, public sex and humiliation, assault. . . . Women devotees were dressed in naughty lingeries for the guru's pleasure and subjected to nights of psychological and physical abuse." One devotee claimed she was "compelled, over a prolonged period of time to accept physical and sexual abuses [including beatings], confinement, degrading acts, inadequate diet, and the surrendering of her children" to Da Free John.

Former members have said that at times they became like zombies, and that even a guru's most bizarre activity, such as ordering devotees to make pornographic films, were justified as being "religious teachings."

Another example is from Swami Nityananda, who claims to be the late Swami Muktananda's legitimate successor. *The Illustrated Weekly of India* (March 16-22, 1986) ran a cover article, "I was Abducted," in which Swami Nityananda alleged he was forced to abdicate his guru status and abducted by a "gang" of foreign devotees involving a "reign of spiritual terror." The response of the official Muktananda organization in the United States was quite different. In a special Report of March 23, 1986, the Siddha Yoga Dham of America organization (SYDA) denied all charges and claimed that it was Nityananda's own evils which forced his retirement from gurudom.

In the report, American swamis said:

> This path is not an easy one—it is like a razor's edge. Because a swami is so visible, his actions must be spotless and beyond reproach. This is not so with Swami Nityananda, now known as Venkateshwar Rao. Having publicly renounced the world he privately embraced it. Ignoring his duties and the spiritual needs of his devotees, he pursued sense pleasures, misled seekers and broke his vows of chastity and obedience time and time again. In short, he abused his position as a spiritual teacher, betraying the love and trust of thousands of devotees. (1587)

In light of the serious charges leveled against Muktananda by three dozen former disciples (see "The Secret Life of Swami Muktananda," *Co-Evolution Quarterly*, Winter 1983), Nityananda, it would appear, was not behaving all that differently from his own guru. It was Muktananda's own disciples—and some of those closest to him—including those who had witnessed or been participants in such acts that stated Muktananda had engaged in lies and deception, sex with young girls, had some of his own disciples beaten, and worse things.

Note also a few descriptions of self-styled gurus who claim enlightenment, as given in the *Yoga Journal*. Here we see that the consequences of "enlightenment" can range from spiritual pessimism to gross immorality to extreme self-aggrandizement. "Guru Rama," aka Frederick Lenz, Ph.D., states: "Enlightenment simply means that you've run out of questions and that the answers don't matter anymore" (1354:35). On the other hand, Barry Tellman offers the world the boastful invitation: "This letter is an invitation to live with me. I am the Supreme Being, the sole source of everything and everyone that ever was or will be" (1354:32). I. M. Nome claims that he has "no personality" at all, period (1354:33). Lee Lozowick may choose to use methods that are arbitrary, foolish, unjust, contradictory, and irresponsible, since "all his actions are God-motivated" and as such, potentially *any* behavior is "proper . . . for a Godman" (1354:34).

The following assessment concerning Rajneesh, who wanted to "blow apart" all that is human seems to sum it up:

> As has been said, one of the key innovations of this guru above the others is his synthesis of advanced contemporary psychological techniques in the peeling off of layer after layer in the onion-skinned defenses of his disciples—rolfing, rebirthing, primal scream, encounter groups, sex encounters, the deprivation tank, and so on. And then synthesizing this with *kundalini* yoga, *shakti-pat*, and far more subtle and esoteric forms of possession, mind-bending, and hidden initiations geared at blowing apart that most basic barrier, the barrier of the conscience, the sense of good and evil. Here is where Advaita and Tantra remain supreme. Not the popularized Tantra, but the cryptic North Indian Kashmiri variety. Here is where all the seals of what we call a human being are blown apart (249:138–39).

## A New Personality

A radical new morality would hardly be possible without a new personality to go with it. Rajneesh once described the importance of the state of catalepsy and insanity for dismantling all that is truly human, in effect prepping the interim vessel for takeover:

> Just the other day Divyananda came to me—he works in my garden—and he said, "What is happening to me? I have become almost a Zombie, and I am afraid. Should I go and do something else?" And I told him, "You be a Zombie. Be a perfect Zombie, that's all. You continue your work." Now something immensely valuable is happening, but he cannot understand it yet. This is what is happening: catalepsy. He's open to me, and working in my garden. He has become even more open to me. He is in a shock, he is forgetting who he is. He is losing his old identity, he is paralyzed! Why paralyzed? Because the old cannot function and the new has yet to be born. So he is in the interval (1589:11).

To Rajneesh, this was a normal part of the process for destroying the person, the individual ego:

This is going to happen to many. Don't be afraid when it happens. . . . This is a state of not knowing; you don't know what is what, all your knowledge is lost, all your cleverness is gone. You become idiotic. You look like an idiot! People will say that you have become hypnotized or something, that you are no longer your old self. That is true; but it is a kind of shock. And good, because it will destroy the past. . . . That is the whole meaning of sannyas and discipleship: that your past has been completely washed away—your memory, your ego, your identity—all has to go (1589:11).

Thus, the enlightened master does whatever is necessary to achieve a disciple's own enlightenment. No mercy is permitted. Rudrananda, Nityananda, Rajneesh, Da Free John, and many others are utterly pragmatic and amoral. Rajneesh continues:

And each Master beheads you, cuts your head mercilessly, destroys your reason, destroys your logic, brings you down from the head. And the only way is to cut the head completely. This is the third state: catharsis. When the head is no longer functioning, its control is lost and the prisoner is set free. . . . That's why a real disciple passes through a kind of insanity around a Master (1589:11).

A special *Yoga Journal* issue on "Perils of the Path" is devoted to the problems and abuses among so-called enlightened teachers and masters. The editorial states:

Ever since I left the Zen community I'd been involved in for years, I've been reflecting on the perils of the spiritual path. At first torn by conflicting loyalties and then, later, angry at how I'd been manipulated and misled, I've come over the years to realize that the issues involved . . . penetrate to the core of the spiritual endeavor itself. . . .

The spiritual traditions propose a hidden, deeper, more fundamental reality that is available to most of us only in "altered states" of consciousness. . . . We must pass through a period—often quite lengthy—in which "mountains are no longer mountains, and rivers no longer rivers." A period, that is, in which "com-

mon sense" no longer provides an accurate map of unfamiliar and often frightening terrain. . . .

What about the great Tibetan guru Marpa, who spent years abusing his disciple Milarepa. . . . What of the great Chinese Zen master Bokuju, who enlightened his disciple Ummon by slamming the door on him and breaking his leg! Nor have teachers eschewed unconventional sexual behavior in their attempts to awaken their students, as both Zen and Tibetan records reveal . . . (1588:4).

In this journal, however the various authors not only bemoan the abuses, but they tend to justify them as well. Unfortunately, they never ask the right questions, such as, What is the real source of the spiritual teacher's power? Is there widespread evil and immorality because the spiritual traditions of the enlightened reject morality as a form of "unenlightened consciousness"? Are such traditions fundamentally evil? Does the evidence suggest these gurus might be demon possessed and manipulative of others because they themselves are being manipulated? Are they aligning themselves with a spiritual rebellion against the "only true God" (John 17:3), courting his judgment (Romans 1:21-24), and thus opening the doors to demonization? Is the Eastern and occult path merely a clever spiritual ruse to lead people away from the true God and His salvation by replacing it with the devil's own brand of "salvation"—demonization as enlightenment?

Perhaps disciples rarely ask these questions because they are too difficult. Perhaps it is because, in spite of the tragedies, they prefer to believe otherwise. Whatever the case may be, the abuses continue because the strongest medicine within their worldview merely warns seekers to be less naive, but by all means stay on the path. Unfortunately, the path itself is the real problem because of the nature of its spiritual dynamics, occult practices, and philosophy (see 278).

Furthermore, most gurus and spiritual teachers know what they are doing. They have deliberately rejected the Christian message and the Christian God and sought the path of occultism. In their writings they declare that the God of the Bible is a false God and that it is a sin to worship

Him. Rajneesh called Jesus "a mental case" and Christians "fools." He said he preferred to do the work of the devil and that "obedience [to God] is the greatest sin" (see Eastern Gurus*). So most spiritual teachers are not unaware of the truth; they have deliberately suppressed it.

People seeking enlightenment might also want to ask other questions. Are "divine lila," "ruthless compassion," or "crazy wisdom" valid justifications for violent and immoral behavior? Is the teacher really enlightened, and what makes us think so? How does one determine what an "enlightened" state of existence is? Apart from occult tradition, what evidence exists for concluding that enlightenment is a divine state? Does the presence of spiritual power and charisma necessarily mean that an individual is enlightened? What criteria indicate classical demonization, and how do they relate to enlightenment? Do any criteria distinguish so-called "God possession" from demon possession? How does anyone know such possession is *not* a form of demonization?

These are important questions because the enlightened freely admit something else controls them at least part of the time, if not most of the time. Distinguishing between a divine or demonic reality is relatively easy on either biblical or common-sense grounds. One good way is to examine the "fruit" of the spiritual master—his teachings, influence, and practices.

## DARK TEACHINGS AND PRACTICES

Consider the teachings and practices of the enlightened. These may or may not be ascribed to spiritistic inspiration, but they are nevertheless consistent with the teachings of the spirit world in many historic and contemporary occult traditions. The Bible describes such teachings as the "doctrines of demons" (1 Timothy 4:1 NASB). For example:

1. The acceptance of sexual immorality, unethical or criminal practices or teachings, justified on the basis of an amoral philosophy, monistic presuppositions, or the absolute authority of the enlightened individual.

2. The rejection of independent, critical thinking and the demand for unquestioning obedience, right or wrong. This is usually justified on the basis of the disciple's ignorance in the face of the "omniscient wisdom" of the master; failing this, psychological manipulation usually achieves the same results.

3. Brutal practices such as beatings, rapes, sexual perversions, dehumanization, and cruel intimidations.

4. Certain types of bizarre behavior as illustrated, for example, in Muktananda's *Play of Consciousness,* cited in our chapter on meditation.

5. Antibiblical teachings that involve rejecting or perverting the nature of God, Jesus Christ, the Bible, salvation, and Christian doctrine in general; occult practices and teachings; teachings and practices that degrade the "image of God" in man (for example, amoral views, monistic consciousness).

6. The existence of supernatural occult powers.

7. Practices that open the door to spirit influence and possession in others; for example, altered states of consciousness,* meditation,* and kundalini arousal (see Yoga, Eastern Gurus).

The teachings and practices of the enlightened are basically the age-old endorsements of the spirits, cleverly accommodated to a variety of religions or worldviews. The spirits' teachings exist in all times and cultures but provide the necessary adaptations to maximize their influence in a particular religion or practice.

It seems evident to us that the conscious rejection of the true God, the blatant idolatry, sexual perversion, and so on, which are part of the path of "enlightenment" describes the spiritual degeneration given in Romans 1. How can this be harmonized with true spiritual enlightenment? Isn't it just the *opposite*? Here's how the apostle Paul puts it:

The wrath of God is being revealed from heaven against all the godlessness and wickedness of men who suppress the truth by their wickedness, since what may be known about God is plain to them, because God has made it plain to them. For since the creation of the world God's invisible qualities—his eternal power and divine nature—have been clearly seen, being understood from what has been made, so that men are without excuse. For although they knew God, they neither glorified him as God nor gave thanks to him, but their thinking became futile and their foolish hearts were darkened. Although they claimed to be wise, they became fools and exchanged the glory of the immortal God for images made to look like mortal man and birds and animals and reptiles. Therefore God gave them over in the sinful desires of their hearts to sexual impurity for the degrading of their bodies with one another. They exchanged the truth of God for a lie, and worshiped and served created things rather than the Creator— who is forever praised. Amen. Because of this, God gave them over to shameful lusts (Romans 1:18–26).

## TANTRISM

To further unveil the nature of the demonic, let's consider a more in-depth illustration provided by the occult practice of tantrism as seen in the late Rajneesh and other modern gurus.**

Tantra is a practice found in Hinduism, Buddhism, and certain other religions. It is primarily based upon the teachings of the Hindu *Tantras*, or holy books. Despite its esoteric nature and historical confinement primarily to Tibetan Buddhism and Shivaite Hinduism, the influence of tantra in various forms and ways has increased in the West significantly in the last generation. Even the immensely popular movie *Indiana Jones and the Temple of Doom* involved tantric themes largely unnoticed by its millions of viewers. (Indiana Jones was really combating a "left-hand" tantric sect for possession of a primeval *shiva-lingam* in order to return the talisman to its proper owners, presumably a "right-hand" tantric sect, 2813.)

To further illustrate, aspects of tantra can be found in many of the guru movements and the

new religions as well as in segments of the New Age Movement and the occult in general.

The world of the occult has been considerably influenced by tantra through its Eastern connections: "Almost all forms of occult teaching make direct use of eastern philosophical notions. The image of the East in western occultism borrows heavily from tantric lore, especially where the emphasis is on mystical powers and magical abilities" (2813:10).

Examples of tantric influence among Eastern gurus include earlier leaders such as Ramakrishna, Vivekananda, and Paramahansa Yogananda, as well as modern prominent gurus including Ram Dass, Muktananda, and many others. However, because of its notorious reputation, many proponents do not directly advertise what they are selling. Thus, "most of the Indian gurus in the West have been delivering tantra, whatever they may be advertising.... As Aagaard says, 'most gurus explicitly deny their own tantric roots.' No doubt they wish to evade the taint of tantra's still seamy reputation" (2813:11).

Indeed, many, or perhaps most, of the deepest secrets of tantra are not written in any Eastern scripture. Or, if so, they are deliberately discussed in ambiguous and obscure language to protect the secrets. This explains why the secret oral teachings of the spiritual master or guru is a necessity for the survival and transmission of tantra (2813).

A final influence of tantra in America comes through the field of humanistic and transpersonal psychology where Hinduism and Buddhism have found powerful friends. For example, as indicated by the journals in transpersonal and humanistic psychology, it is probably true that among American Buddhist disciples, psychologists, as a class, represent the largest single grouping.

All this indicates that tantra is not an obscure, irrelevant occult practice without influence in America, but is a slowly increasing presence in American life.

The term "tantra" has numerous meanings and may refer either to particular scriptures of Tibet and India, certain practices and techniques

---

**Most of our initial discussion is excerpted from 2813.

taught by those scriptures (primarily involving yoga* practice), the religious and philosophical traditions based on those scriptures, or all of this considered as a collective phenomenon (2813:1).

Although worldwide, tantric beliefs and practice vary, a common theme is the belief that in its true, indivisible nature, everything is divine. As we noted, this is known as monism. A corollary belief is that all duality—or experience in the world—is seen as an illusion or *maya*. This harmonizes well with the *advaita* philosophy of Vedanta and New Age belief in general. Tantra cannot be properly understood unless one recognizes that all of its actions are designed to transcend all dualities and achieve enlightenment through manipulation of consciousness: "Tantrism above all is what one does to produce certain states of consciousness. The tantric doctrines are simply interpretations of those states" (2813:6-7).

However, tantra is unique in how it employs the world of duality. It is not seen as merely an illusion to escape from, but as an actual *vehicle* for spiritual enlightenment. In other words, the illusory mind, body, and physical universe can actively (indeed, amorally) be employed in the very process of liberation itself. For example, the cosmic dualities of light and dark, male and female, are believed to function at all levels of existence. One can transcend these illusory dualities and arrive at liberation through particular acts—as we will see, even acts of evil such as perverse sexuality, violence, ritual human sacrifice, or other practices aimed at manipulating the energies of the universe toward the goal of transcending illusory categories. The goal is to use the physical body and universe in such a powerful or extreme way as to literally force a radical alteration of consciousness such that enlightenment is achieved *through* the vehicle of duality.

Concerning the body, a number of bodily functions are used in tantra as a basis for achieving enlightenment. The sexual act is the best known of these. In addition, tantra uses posture and breathing (cf. yoga*), sight (mandalas,* yantras), speech and hearing (mantras*).

To the tantric, the universe is a mystical tissue of consciousness, held in form by the tensions of duality—the polar opposites of positive and negative, light and dark, male and female, yang and yin, etc.—that appear throughout all levels of existence. Tantra is a way to the mastery of these fundamental cosmic dualities—through the mastery of one's sexual function.

The connection between sex and cosmic sorcery is based on the theory of *occult correspondence*. Polarity is the key to existence; its tensions give unity and structure to all of manifest reality. The human body, as part of manifest reality, is caught in this network of polarity and existence. The body is a microcosm, a miniature version of the cosmos. Polarity in the body—sex—is therefore the key to our own existence. It is also an antenna, tuned to energies of polarity that span the universe. By learning to control the energies of polarity in the body (i.e., the sexual function) the tantric taps the powers of matter and mind, and masters the secrets of space and time.

Tantra thus *embraces illusion* as a means to reality, baptizes duality as a path to the One, and affirms the human body—particularly the sexual function—as our most reliable connection with the divine.

But even in its affirmations, tantra is haunted by paradox. The naturalness of human life is affirmed, but only as a means for its ultimate dissolution. Human existence is validated but only as a platform for leaving humanity behind (2813:5).

It should be noted that physical sex in tantra is *not* used primarily for pleasure, but rather for spiritual enlightenment through occult exercises that immobilize the breath, consciousness, and semen as a means to achieve mystical union with the One impersonal divine consciousness. (As far as sexuality is concerned, tantric practitioners are termed "left-hand" or "right-hand" based on their literal or figurative interpretation of the *maithuna* ritual. Right-hand or "white" tantrics interpret the passages figuratively while left-hand or "red" tantrics take the scriptural instructions literally and engage in actual sexual acts during ritual performances.)

The sexual aspect of tantra (along with its connection to drugs; see 2813:11), is what has fascinated many New Age and counterculture Westerners. Tantra's "alchemical ecstasy," in which the body becomes a sexual "clearinghouse of interdimensional energies," can be seen in such literature as *Sexual Secrets: The Alchemy of Ecstasy.*

But Western experimenters are urged, even by tantrists, to exercise caution. Tantra traditionally is held to be a fast path to enlightenment, and tantric texts warn that the dangers are considerable—including permanent physical disability, insanity, and death (2813:6; cf. yoga*).

Whether considered from the perspective of Christianity, religion in general, or common sense, tantrism is a truly revolutionary spirituality, and carries all the consequences of a revolution. Because tantra, like many Eastern religions, seeks the destruction of what is truly human, its approach to life is both contradictory and consequential: "Tantra . . . embodies all the extremes and contradictions that it thrives on. It is simultaneously erotic and ascetic, self-indulgent and self-denying. Its rituals invoke demons and deities indiscriminately, yet its doctrine dismisses them all in the name of radical monism. Tantra's adherents range from the respectable to the scandalous, from the credentialed scholar pursuing sanskrit etymology to the illiterate yogi practicing unspeakable graveyard rituals in the dead of night" (2813:5).

In essence, tantric belief and practice are fundamentally hostile to every aspect of the creation—including humanity made in the image of God. In the end, what tantra destroys is everything of value according to biblical teaching: "Christianity and tantra face each other as virtual mirror images. Each system exalts what the other devalues and affirms what the other denies" (2813:9). "Every level of tantric practice constitutes an assault on the realm of normal experience by literally disintegrating it—by dissolving it into its occult (hidden) components, then using those elemental forces of creation as links to forces that are beyond creation altogether. Tantra unravels the normal world of perception and understanding and reweaves it into an intricate network of occult correspondences

that ultimately vanishes into the One. . . . Tantra is how the world looks as it disappears" (2813:9).

As noted, in hidden corners, tantra and related philosophies have been influencing the West for decades. Today, the influence of tantra continues to be seen in Eastern and Western forms of witchcraft, in aspects of modern Satanic practice, and in controversial gurus like Da Free John and, again, the late Rajneesh who also incorporated modern psychotherapeutic methods with his tantric philosophy.

But tantric initiation and practice may involve things like extreme sexual perversion, violence, and even human sacrifice as a means of experientially shattering moral sensibilities in order to experience the union of opposites (male/female; good/evil). Again, this is the means to the enlightened state in which one realizes "all is one" and that all actions, good or evil, in the end, are only the actions of the ultimate impersonal God who exists beyond primitive notions of right and wrong. As Tal Brooke recalled of his experience with the Rajneesh ashram in Poona, India, "The initiate must become blasé about the lessor taboos of good and evil such as rape and assault and perversion" (249:150-53).

Thus, all acts of evil and all forms of perversion are *potential* means of spiritual advancement. When used properly, such acts are to be considered holy. As Rajneesh once stated, "For tantra, *everything* is holy, nothing is unholy" (567:36-37).

Thus, in a clandestine mission to India, Brooke documented the horrors in the Rajneesh ashram at Poona, India, cataloging the delicate souls who were raped, abused, shattered—all in the name of tantric "enlightenment." He also discusses the indescribably blissful experiences produced by spiritistic manipulation of the mind, as well as the suicides and the violence (e.g., 249:141-53). Following we present three illustrations which encapsulate the end reality of darker forms of occult enlightenment.

*Illustration One—Violence*

Rajneesh had been asked by a frightened woman disciple why he permitted [the favored disciple] Teertha the freedom to do anything in these groups with such savage authority. His answer was, "I only send people to the Encounter group when I see that now they understand that they have to go beyond all boundaries—boundaries of sex, boundaries of violence, anger, rage. They have to break all the boundaries. . . ."

Richard Price, famed founder of Essalen, later repudiated his sannyasin status. He wrote the ashram a private letter that was later published in the Indian and American media (23 February 1978): "The ashram encounter group is an abomination—authoritarian, intimidating, violent—used to enforce conformity. . . ."

Price gave specifics.

A woman who had her arm broken was repeatedly kicked. A young man twice hit a sixty-year-old woman in the face. There were eighteen fights in the first two days alone—when I stopped counting. I did prevent one young man from hitting a sixty-one-year-old man with his fist. Stopping him was strictly against the "rules." After the end of the "Encounter" group, a woman in the so-called "Primal" group had her leg broken. On inquiry many other incidents came to light—injuries physical, mental, and spiritual.

Yet what baffled Eckart [a disciple] were the immense ecstasies he had experienced. But just because they were ecstasies, did that mean they had God's seal of approval? He knew then that heroin is supposed to be the supremely euphoric ecstasy. Who could deny the incredible desirableness of it? Did that make it good? One had to look a little deeper, at the fruits, the effects (249:145-47).

*Illustration Two—Moral and Sexual Perversion*
Brooke discusses additional details of the ashram, correlating them to the logical consequences of Eastern tantric occultism.

The language would become more and more pornographic, as taboos were systematically shattered. People's minds would bounce all over the place. It became for some a kind of shock-orgasm. Abuse and degradation would deepen in new and more creative ways. This was liberation with a vengeance. The groups usually spent days and days locked up together with no escape.

It was exactly the kind of experimenting that Charles Manson did on his girls and his gang. When they had gang orgies, it was the same sort of thing as on the ashram. The Manson girls were making love with God and the Devil at the same time, wrapped up in one man, Charlie Manson. That is what he claimed and that is what they believed. . . .

Allen Edwards, in *The Jewel and the Lotus,* has given an extraordinary insight into Tantric Eastern Yoga. He shows that its orgies are identical to the way in which medieval witches are said to have regarded their Devil, the "Man in Black," when he presided over the coven wearing his ritual grand array, the Satan-head, horned mask. A number of lesser Tantric Indian gurus watched and coached the sexual unions of their following. I had known a New York couple twelve years back who were both driven insane by something the guru did when he oversaw them. He was now in New York, furthering his ring of adherents. (249:206-07)

*Illustration Three—Satanism and Witchcraft Motifs*
Finally, consider the more obvious parallels to Satanism, witchcraft, and biblical demonology that are found in tantrism. An anti-moral pragmatism is a strong feature of Satanism and witchcraft on the one hand, and much Eastern religion on the other. For example, in a standard text entitled *Yoga: Immortality and Freedom,* the late yoga authority and University of Chicago professor Mircea Eliade observes the amoral orientation of much yoga:

The tantric texts frequently repeat the saying, "By the same acts that cause some men to burn in hell for thousands of years, the yogin gains his eternal salvation." . . . This, as we know, is the foundation stone of the Yoga expounded by Krishna in the *Bhagavad Gita* (XVIII,17). "He who has no feeling of egoism, and whose mind is not tainted, even though he kills (all) these people, kills not, is not fettered (by the action)." And the *Brhadaranyaka Upanishad* (V. 14, 8) had already said: "One who knows this, although he commits very much evil, consumes it all and becomes clean and pure, ageless and immortal" (601:263).

Further, the goals of the sexual union in tantra and witchcraft and in magic/Satanism are also similar (e.g., 237:129-33/601:263-67/

429:107-08). For example, in tantra and witchcraft we find the predominance of the feminine energy theme. In both categories we find occasional cannibalism, ritual cruelty, a preoccupation with death, ritual sacrifice, ritual insanity, anarchy, and horrible degradations in general (601:202-06,261,272,294-307/429:10-11,22,35-36,84-86,107-12).

Only now is the true purpose of such practices discerned and the penetratingly evil nature of this "enlightenment" revealed. As Brooke states of the initiate who has surrendered his mind and body to the radical tantric path:

What happens within the surrendering vehicle? The total desecration, degradation, defamation of a soul during the ritual. That is the recurrent theme. Ecstasies may appear, but the rites have a certain definite pattern.

For years I had studied North Indian Tantra and seen that it was the original model of European Satanism.... [The theme involved] surrender by degradation (249:201-02).

Brooke proceeds to mention such things as the ingestion of human waste, necrophilia, and human sacrifice (249:200-07). He also explains the rationale for all this, and illustrates the satanic themes by citing the philosophy of Rajneesh:

Why is man degraded? If man is made "in the image of God," that likeness has to be once and for all smeared and defaced beyond recognition as an act of surrender on the part of the man and as an act of cosmic blasphemy.... At times, Rajneesh has been brazenly revealing from his throne. The bearded Godman would leak out such revelations as, "God has to take the help of the Devil to run the affairs of the world. Without the Devil, even He cannot run the affairs. So I had to choose devils, Beelzebubs, so then I thought why not with style? Why not with taste? Devils there are going to be. I decided for women, more are wanted. Also, my ashram makes no difference between the Devil and Divine. I absorb all. So whoever you are, I am ready to absorb you. And I use all sorts of energies... the devilish energy can be used in a divine way.... And this is only a beginning. When more devils come, you will see....

What emerged in the Charles Manson case was that when the level of fear in the victims was raised to a peak, another energy-presence became operative in the field. The Encounter groups on the ashram raised the energy field by shock and "blowing the lid off" (249:200-01)

At this point, considering a few relevant citations from books on witchcraft and Satanism helps one to understand the potential of this radical spirituality, even for murder: "The object of ritual, including the Black Mass, is to raise power to implement and strengthen the mental force of its practitioners.... There is no doubt that the emotions generated by the Black Mass constitute a considerable energy potential" (526:47). Wouldn't human sacrifice raise the temperature of the ritual all the more? Consider a statement from an authority on the occult, Richard Cavendish, in his *Black Arts*: "In the later grimories the sacrifice is done... to increase the supply of force in the circle. In occult theory a living creature is a storehouse of energy, and when it is killed most of this energy is suddenly liberated.... The amount of energy let loose when the victim is killed is very great, out of all proportion to the animal's [or victim's] size or strength" (1296:247).

The same book continues: "The spirit or force which is summoned in the ceremony is normally invisible. It can appear visibly to the magician (occultist, yogi, witch, Satanist) by fastening on a source of energy on the physical plane of existence. It may do this by taking possession of the human beings involved in the ritual" (1296:248).

And finally, "The most important reason for the sacrifice, however, is the... charge which the magician obtains from it.... It would obviously be more effective to sacrifice a human being because of the far greater psychological kick involved. Eliphas Levi said that when the grimories talk about killing a kid they really mean a human child.... There is a tradition that the most effective sacrifice to demons is the murder of a human being" (1296:248). "If this [sacrifice] is combined with the release of sexual energy in orgasm, the effect is to heighten the magician's frenzy and the supply of force in the circle still further" (1296:249). This is the other "sacrifice" which Crowley (the Satanist) and other modern magicians skirt mysteriously around— "with regard to which the Adepts have always maintained the most profound secrecy" and which is the "supreme mystery of practical Magick" (1296:249).

In a concluding segment, Brooke discusses the common themes found in tantra and much pagan occult practice:

Death, orgasm, sacrifice, energy, power, entity-presence, possession—this is the ancient chemistry.... Mircea Eliade, in probing into the history of witchcraft said, "All features associated with European witches are . . . claimed also by Indo-Tibetan yogis and magicians." And, along with a range of occult powers common to both, the Indians "boast that they break all the religious taboos and social rules: that they practice human sacrifice, cannibalism, and all manner of orgies, including incestuous intercourse, and that they eat [human waste], nauseating animals, and devour human corpses. In other words, they proudly claim all the crimes and horrible ceremonies cited *ad nauseam* in the Western European witch trials."

It was hardly new in India. In Assam, a Tantric haven over the long centuries, the temple of Kamakhya (Durga) was famous for human sacrifices. In the 1500s they had 140 people beheaded at a single mass sacrifice. The members of that group, the Aghoris, were famous for their cruelties and their orgies. There, subjects volunteered to be sacrificed to the goddess Kali. The Aghoris ate from human skulls, haunted ceremonies, and practiced cannibalism, up until and including this century . . . (249:205-06).

The violence and abuse of the Rajneesh ashram, as well as Rajneesh's own predilection for death themes, fit well with the tantric worldview. In Hinduism, the god of death and dissolution is Shiva, and Shiva is the sponsoring deity of most tantrism.

And when one actively worships a god of death, it is not surprising that occasional murders and human sacrifices might enter the picture. In India, historically, this has happened on a regular basis. For example, there are various tantric sects who actively seek the death of others in order to worship their god. Among such tantric cults are the *Pindaris, Thugee,* and the *Dacoits*—all of whom have turned random murders into acts of ritual worship (the Dacoits worship Shiva's wife, Kali, the goddess of death, who also requires human sacrifice).

But as noted, sex and mystical ecstasy are also part of tantra. Not surprisingly, Shiva is also considered the god of ecstasy and divine madness. "He personifies *lila* [the divine sport] as the insanity of god. Tantrics worship Shiva, and they accept their existence as the insanity of god with no questions asked. The tantric's novel response is to get gleefully insane along with god, as god, in the midst of existence and thereby penetrate beyond existence altogether" (2813:6). [One need only think of the philosophy of Sufi guru Meher Baba, and his lifelong work with the insane (the *masts*) of India, whom he interpreted as the truly enlightened or God-realized.] Nevertheless, tantra's fascination with the bizarre and the crude is one reason it "often seems like systematic insanity with a thin religious gloss" (2813:5).

And in the 1990s, such practices continue. The Chingons, in the Santa Ana mountains above Los Angeles, now practice this branch of ancient tantrism, eating living hearts of sacrificed animals. Several groups in the Topanga Canyons of the Hollywood Hills also combine black magic, drugs, orgies, and (animal?) sacrifice (249:206).

We find similar incidents among some Caribbean immigrants to the United States who practice santeria and other forms of witchcraft magic. And the number of adherents continues to increase, as more and more people join the modern neo-pagan revival.

However, as tantrists would argue, everything depends on *how* the practitioner engages in these individual acts of evil—what state of mind the act is committed in. The *Vajrayana Tantra* cites the common teaching, "By the *same* acts that cause some men to burn in hell for thousands of years, the yogi gains his eternal salvation."

Apparently, enlightenment doesn't care how you get there. So where will it all end? Who can say? Most Western New Agers would recoil at the radical path to enlightenment seen in tantra. On the other hand, it cannot be denied that New Age philosophy and practice helps condition the soil for just such extremes. For those willing to experiment with more radical forms of enlightenment, the path has already been prepared:

The New Age [is very much] into the idea of initiation, but milder, sweeter, more aromatic ones. The vicious and obvious path of Rajneesh and the Tantrics was a far more radical initiation than most New Agers would ever consider. That was too blatantly "evil" to most people.

The majority needed a far more gradual incline. The implications of "there is neither good nor evil," driving them the route of experimentally "blowing the roof off," on the fast-track of "Explosion techniques," that comes in way down the path (249:207).

In conclusion, after examining so-called New Age enlightenment, what seems apparent to us is that this enlightenment is really darkness. Though occult enlightenment has a long-standing tradition, it clearly reveals its true nature (cf. 1069). Unfortunately, thousands of searching people are being thrust onto a path promising enlightenment—but they are wholly unaware of just where it will lead them.

# Est, The Forum, and Related New Age Seminars

## INFO AT A GLANCE

**Description.** New Age seminars are 50–to–60-hour intensive programs designed to unleash human potential and achieve "enlightenment."* Many New Age seminars are offshoots of the philosophy of Werner Erhard or Jose Silva (Silva Mind Control).* So in this chapter we have concentrated on Erhard generally as a means to evaluate a larger number of seminars that cannot be included here.

**Founder.** Werner Erhard (est/The Forum); John Hanley (Lifespring); Stewart Emery (Actualizations). Related seminars include founders John-Roger (Insight Seminars); Dennis Becker (Impact Seminars); Bob White and Duncan Callister (Life Dynamics); William Patrick (the now-defunct Mind Dynamics).

**How do they claim to work?** The founders of these seminars alleged their methods have the ability to radically empower individuals through unleashing the untapped powers of the mind. Because each individual's mind determines and shapes reality, once people experience their true (divine) potential, they are allegedly able to influence all areas of their lives for the better.

**Scientific evaluation.** Few, if any, comprehensive and independent studies have been conducted.

**Examples of occult potential.** Altered states of consciousness,* psychic development, spiritism.

**Major problems.** The generally monistic and solipsistic worldview of these seminars assumes a false view of man, a false view of the world, and a false view of how people are to live in the world.

**Biblical/Christian evaluation.** In general, both the anti-Christian teachings (e.g., monism, humanism, occult philosophy) and practices (e.g., visualization,* meditation,* self-hypnosis,* psychic development) mean that participation in these seminars is prohibited.

**Potential dangers.** Self-deception over one's abilities; possible occult influences, conversion to Eastern-occult worldviews.

*Note:* The seminars discussed in this chapter are all by-products of est and contain a similar approach and philosophy. As a result we have concentrated on est but also included brief treatments of the Forum, Lifespring, and Actualizations. Reading the entire section in one sitting will reveal the similarities among these seminars. One major difference is that Actualizations does not promote the destructive est theory of absolute personal creatorship. Lifespring did for many years, but has now, apparently, either toned down this philosophy or abandoned it.

Although est was retired in 1985, this does not mean that the material we provide is outdated or irrelevant. Many of the beliefs of Werner Erhard and est live on in The Forum, Lifespring, Actualizations, and in other ways and places in society. The Forum has been renamed "Landmark Education's The Forum," but we will be using "The Forum" for brevity.

Because we have frequently cited Erhard in the following material on est, reading only the shorter sections on related seminars will *not* provide an understanding of Erhard's philosophy necessary to comprehend its full implications. Therefore, we encourage reading the entire section on est. Also, the chapter on Silva Mind Control* may be read for another illustration of New Age seminars.

Readers should be aware that name changes of these seminars, or their proponents' claims that substantial alterations have been made in content, should be taken skeptically. For example, we asked Forum graduate Jude C. Peck to offer his comments on the relationship between est, The Forum, and Landmark Education's The Forum. His important observation was that such seminar name changes are more cosmetic than substantive, for purposes of public relations and proselytization. Here is what he told us in a statement prepared for this volume:

> After going through Adelaide Bry's book "est" [a standard, accurate text on est (ref. 1467)] and talking with several "est" graduates, it is abundantly obvious that although the name of the seminar has changed, the Landmark Education's Forum Seminar that I attended contained basically the same content and worldview. They have also changed terms and techniques of presentations to make them less objectionable and easier for an unsuspecting audience to swallow.

> After discussions with a number of close relatives who attended several seminars several times, and who have volunteered many hours assisting instructors and enrolling people, it became evident that such name changing enables them to disassociate themselves from the responsibility of embarrassing errors of the past and to enroll previous graduates in repackaged—new and improved—seminars.

> Although names, terms, and techniques have been changed and cloaked to be more appealing, they are still, if not more so, deceptive, fundamentally destructive, and diametrically opposed to basic Christian beliefs (letter dated August 10, 1995).

## INTRODUCTION AND INFLUENCE

In the last 20 years, millions of people have been exposed to personal growth "New Age seminars." These are usually one or two weekend, intensive "relearning" programs designed to foster the specific goals or beliefs of the seminars' founder(s). To accomplish this, the seminars employ didactic teaching, experientially oriented psychological exercises such as visualization,* and radical confrontative sessions one-on-one with the seminar leader. Appropriately, the leader is usually termed a "trainer." These seminars stress: 1) advancing "human potential"; 2) psychic development; 3) restructuring of the participant's worldview, allegedly leading to psychological or spiritual "enlightenment."* The originators of these seminars seem to have an intense dislike for biblical Christianity, and thus their seminars also insulate participants against a Christian worldview.

Est (Erhard Seminars Training), Landmark Education's The Forum, Lifespring, and Actualizations, despite their differences, share a similar worldview, philosophy, and religious perspective. This is largely because the latter three, The Forum, Lifespring, and Actualizations, are all offshoots of est. Erhard Seminars Training was developed by Werner Erhard, and Landmark Education's The Forum is his remolding of est philosophy in order to make it more palatable and hence more influential among a wider audience. Both Lifespring and Actualizations were developed by est graduates; most of the basic est philosophy is found in their seminars and literature.

Collectively, these powerful New Age seminars alone have graduated about two million people. Yet this figure hardly reveals their true influence. Because their founders want to transform society, these seminars and their offspring try to reach the most influential people. For example, Erhard started a company called Transformational Technologies, which "claims that its clients include 25 of the Fortune 100 companies and that its eight-week Executive Excellence program 'has attracted executives from some of the largest corporations in the world' " (2687:71).

Many of the popular cable network TV programs that emphasize personal power, prosperity, health, self-actualization, dysfunctional families, overcoming fear and sexual problems, and so on, reflect the basic teachings and goals of these New Age seminars, albeit in commercialized, toned-down form. Thus, beyond their two million graduates, these seminars impact contemporary American society vastly by means of indirect influence.

To varying degrees, these personal growth seminars attempt to produce a Western form of enlightenment,* which builds upon a platform of human potentialism, Eastern mysticism, and, to an extent, occult practice. Each of them erects an eclectic edifice derived from a large variety of sources, both religious and secular, and are largely tailored to reach the populace of mainstream America.

There is little doubt that a major purpose of these seminars is to transform a person's worldview from a Western to more of an Eastern or occult perspective. Often through intense psychological manipulation, the seminars are in part designed to help people realize that they are part of ultimate reality or God and, to varying degrees, literal creators of their world and their experience (see *A Course in Miracles*).

Although such seminars are slickly packaged and can produce extremely powerful transformations, by breaking down people psychologically and emotionally, they are also potentially destructive processes psychologically and spiritually. Because they are nihilistic or solipsistic, we think they are a social evil. Nor are we alone in this judgment. In response to a critical article on est, even Erhard himself once responded with, "So est is evil, what's the point? Yeah, I got that, now what? So what?" He proceeded to tell est graduates:

> You do not *have* to accept any of the responsibility for any of the evil in the organization, nor do you have to make anyone else responsible. Everybody is absolved of *having to be* responsible for any of the evil. I have already taken 100% of the responsibility. . . . I have already acknowledged being 100% causer and creator of every speck of evil in this organization. . . . I am willing to have created all the evil in the est organization. I am willing to and experience that I have (1088:10).

For reasons that will become clear as we proceed, we have seen nothing in est or its offshoots that would cause us to question the continuing relevance of Erhard's judgment. In our opinion, est/The Forum, Lifespring, and Actualizations, and other offshoots, because of the powerful transformations they produce in people and because of the anti-Christian perspective that people adopt as a result, bear significant responsibility for instilling a destructive philosophy and approach to life into the maintsream and upper echelon of American society.

Although these seminars allege that they do not interfere with anyone's religious beliefs and that Christians can participate in them in good conscience, this is not the case. Though it is claimed that these seminars are supposedly non-religious, one of their major purposes is to alter a person's epistemology and instill a monistic or pantheistic belief; hence they qualify as religious. Biblical Christianity is assumed to be *detrimental* to personal growth and enlightenment.* Erhard once stated, "In a seminary, I would have been burned as a witch," and, "Had I been in any religious order, or any church monastery, I definitely could not have done any of this. It would have been heresy" (2730:30/1346:5). He also once emphasized, "In est training *you* are God. . . . Therefore you cannot look to any supreme being for special treatment, goodness, or award" (1347:131). Obviously, such a perspective is anti-Christian and, therefore, claims to compatibility with or neutrality toward the Christian faith are probably a recruitment technique.

Because est/The Forum, Lifespring, and Actualizations are designed to subtly undermine the validity of the Christian worldview (or almost any worldview one brings to the seminar), they are explicitly hostile to the Christian faith. As we will see, John Hanley, the founder of Lifespring, believes that all people are part of God; he also encourages occult practices and views Christianity as a symptom of unenlightened thinking. Stewart Emery, founder of Actualizations and a "profound psychic," teaches that it is an illusion to think that God is going to save man because man is already God (1348:6,11,21,45,101/1349: 165, 207,99).

New Age seminars of this genre often deliberately manipulate people in a manner that, from a biblical view, is clearly evil. Indeed, there is a carefully engineered attempt to dismantle people *deceptively*. People often don't understand the consequences of the seminars until it's too late. They end up transformed by what, to many critics, is a form of brainwashing. And the manner in which they are transformed can profoundly alter their lives destructively.

All this is particularly of concern when it is understood, again, that the leaders of society are often the ones targeted: college graduates, clergy, business leaders, professionals in all walks of life, and those in government, law, and education. In the following material we will evaluate the background, philosophy, and methods of Werner Erhard and est in some detail and then discuss The Forum, Lifespring, and Actualizations.

## ERHARD SEMINARS TRAINING

Est was once described as having the top of your head blown off and then being pacified with an aspirin. Dr. Herbert Hansher, professor of psychology at Temple University, called it "one of the most powerful therapeutic experiences yet devised" (1467:200). Est confrontations involved participants in fainting, uncontrollable trembling and vomiting, hysterical screaming, temporary confusion about reality, and various psychopathological reactions, some quite serious. Before est was "transformed" into The Forum in 1985, over half a million people had paid an estimated 150 million dollars to have the est experience. Between 1971 and 1980 some 500 articles had been written on est, and a dozen books on the topic sold well over a million copies (1499:10).

Est was an intensive 60-hour seminar of psychological indoctrination designed to restructure a person's worldview. During its 15-year history, est made a notable impact on American society. Just four years after its inception, *San Francisco Magazine* stated that est was "making a serious bid to affect basic American institutions" (1531:22). In some ways, it succeeded.

Indeed, those of us who are familiar with California's Esalen Institute will recognize est as a comrade in arms. Although Esalen sparked the human potential movement and has had a major impact on modern culture, in certain ways, est alone has had equal or greater influence than Esalen. (Esalen's impact is documented in some-times-fascinating studies like Walter Truett Anderson's *The Upstart Spring: Esalen and the American Awakening;* 1532.) For example, "Erhard *Americanized* the human potential movement in a way that Esalen had never done or tried to do," and thus helped it to emerge from the radical fringe of society into the mainstream (1532:254).

The est seminar, conducted by an est trainer, was comprised of three basic parts: lectures, mental exercises sometimes involving altered states of consciousness,* and group "sharing" of feelings and experiences. During the sessions, the trainer maintained a rigid, authoritarian at-mosphere, both physically and psychologically. Est staffer Dr. William Bartley stated that "the training provides a very highly controlled con-tent which opens people to certain kinds of expe-riences" (1533:180). These sometimes-dramatic experiences were part of the overall package of helping participants to achieve Erhard's brand of enlightenment. The first three days were de-signed to prepare or condition the person for the fourth day when "it" (enlightenment) was achieved. Erhard wrote that "all the first three [days] do is to open people's consciousness up so they can get it" (1534).

"Getting it" was also the term used by gradu-ates to describe particular realizations learned from the seminar. Since est was a subjective ex-perience, people learned different things. For ex-ample, a woman who was raped was made to "get" that this was her way of punishing her hus-band or inducing sympathy. She was the creator of her own rape. To be enlightened is to recog-nize that you are God and the source or author of everything you experience.

The underlying concept here is that people create their own experiences and circumstances; therefore they must have *wanted* whatever hap-pens to them to happen because, after all, it hap-pened! All people literally create their own reality and destiny, their own life-conditions and events. A recognition of this allows them to "take re-sponsibility" for it. Thus, they are never really victims but rather "gods" who create their own reality and destiny.

Before we discuss the philosophy of est/The Forum in more detail, we need to examine the background of the man who created it. If we un-derstand the experiences and basic perspective of Werner Erhard, we will understand the true nature of est/The Forum.

*Werner Erhard: A Man Transformed*

The official biography of Werner Erhard was compiled by est graduate and advisory board member William W. Bartley, the philosopher whose intellectual sleuthing had gained him some acclaim. Of particular interest is the extent of Erhard's occult activities. Erhard was involved in a powerful and dangerous form of yoga* (hatha yoga) at the tender age of 11 (1707:19). This led him into hypnosis* experimentation, whereby he gained the ability to hypnotize people (1707:75-76). Eventually he became in-volved in many occult disciplines. It seems he investigated nearly everything, including chan-neling,* or spiritism. He spent a year with Subud, a potent occult movement (1707:145). He partici-pated in Subud's main spiritual exercise, the *lati-han*, which can easily be described as opening oneself to the spirit world to allow temporary possession. (See p. 94 for a description.)

Erhard eventually entered Scientology,* an-other occult religion, and graduated to the fifth level where he had "past lives" experiences (1707:146-58; see Hypnosis). While an instructor for the now-defunct but cruel and manipulative Mind Dynamics, he became acquainted with techniques cultivated from the medium Edgar Cayce, Silva Mind Control,* Rosicrucianism, Theosophy, and other occult groups (1707:158-62). (The "Personality Profile" given to est trainees seems to be derived from Edgar Cayce and Silva Mind Control.) However, it appears that of all the disciplines Erhard went through, Zen Buddhism and Scientology* provided the crucial turning points in the development of est (1707:118-20,147/2226:142).

For eight long and difficult years Erhard searched and studied intensively, only to eventu-ally realize, "I knew nothing" (1707:167). Yet, after his eventual experience of occult enlightenment* in 1971, he was radically and permanently transformed (1707:166-70). He came to believe that the morality of the Mind state, which people normally experience, is *irresponsible* when compared to the morality of the Self, which assumes the experience of enlightenment and the truth of est's philosophy. In other words, the Mind state refers to the normal experience of living and is supposedly concerned only with defending itself and its false beliefs. Hence, it cannot understand "true" morality. When the mind is transformed into a divine state (an experience of the Self), a superior understanding of morality develops. That "superior" understanding is: true responsibility realizes that absolute moral values *do not exist*. In discussing Erhard's view that "*irresponsibility* gives rise to [moral] values," Bartley writes, "This distinction between the transformed and the untransformed, between the responsible and the irresponsible, between those at cause [i.e., creators, the enlightened] and those at effect [i.e., victims, the unenlightened], is only sketched briefly here. When fully set out, it has profound implications for the history of morality and religion, and for all questions of social reform (1707:214).

Such a view does indeed have profound implications. For example, in direct contrast to Jesus' teachings in Matthew 5:6, we are told, "The responsible person does *not* hunger and thirst after righteousness" (1707:212, emphasis added). Also, the responsible person does not recognize any ultimate validity to concepts of good and evil. Obviously, this has profound implications. This is why Erhard believes that he must transform society as a whole, and not just individuals. The world as it is, in an untransformed state, is "evil"; that is, it exchanges aliveness (participation in the godhead) for "survival" (defending yourself and being the victim). Thus, transformed people (est/The Forum graduates) returning to an untransformed, evil society were reentering a restrictive environment. "Hence, the environment to which transformed individuals return after an experience like the est training is usually not one where the truth can be told. It is a restrictive econiche that is deadly dangerous to transformation, having been created by individ-

uals in the [evil] Mind state to foster the [evil] Mind state" (1707:214).

Erhard is thus radically antisocial in his perspective and aims at a fundamental revolution in human consciousness and society to foster "social aliveness and health." Erhard himself, through the usual route for such transformations (the Eastern-occult path), abandoned conventional morality and now exists in a state beyond good or evil. In such a transformed state, he thinks that whatever he does is, by definition, perfect.

Before we consider more fully the views of est/The Forum, let's look at some of those it has changed. Est had special programs for children, teenagers, parents, college students, professors, blacks, prisoners, clergy, scientists, lawyers, psychiatrists, and others.

*Worldwide Influence*

Among est graduates are scores of famous people. John Denver not only wrote a song about est ("Looking for Space") but also dedicated one of his albums to Werner Erhard. Est changed Denver's life so much that he donated a large sum of money to the est foundation, and he sat on est's advisory board. Valerie Harper praised est during the Emmy Awards, before a national audience of 36 million. The "Dinah Show" had a 90-minute special on est, also seen by millions in dozens of cities. Other celebrity graduates include Yoko Ono, Taryn Power, Carly Simon, Harvey Korman, Anthony Zerbe, Olympic ski champion Suzy Chaffee, gold medalist John Curry, George Maharis, Richard Roundtree (of "Shaft" fame), Joanne Woodward, Jerry Rubin, Gary Wright ("Dream Weaver"), Roy Scheider, Cloris Leachman, Cher, Buzz Aldrin, Marion Javits, John Dean, Herb Alpert, Jerry Stiller, and Ann Meara (of the award-winning team for the "Blue Nun" commercials), Polly Bergen, *Vogue* editor Kate Lloyd, John Davidson, Stan Getz, Norman Lear, Judy Collins, Diana Ross, the co-chairman of Warner Brothers, all of Lloyd Bridges' sons, Beach Boy Carl Wilson, and four members of the Fifth Dimension. (There were reportedly enough executives at Warner Brothers who had taken est that the studio was termed by some "Werner" Brothers!) *Star Wars'* filmmaker, Robert Black, and special-effects man, Paul Roth, are est graduates, as are Valerie Singleton (a household name in Britain), John Ritter, Sim Van der Ryn (the California State architect and appointee of Governor Brown), Louis Kislik (president of Publishers Clearing House), and many, many others (1344).

The collective influence of est's prestigious advisory board also contributed to its growth (2728:15-17). The board was chaired by Roger Sant (energy consultant, Washington, D.C., former assistant administrator, Federal Energy Administration), and Phil Lee (M.D., former chancellor of University of California's medical school; he was also a former assistant secretary of the United States Department of Health, Education and Welfare). Others on the board included: Frank Berger, M.D., D.S.C., consultant to the Surgeon General and U.S. Army; Enoch Callaway III, M.D., chief of research at the Langley Porter Neuropsychiatric Institute, San Francisco; Jack Thayer, president of NBC Radio; Don Cox, president of est, was the former vice president of Coca-Cola, USA; Helen Nahm, R.N., Ph.D., dean emeritus at the School of Nursing, University of California, and former consultant to the World Health Organization, Geneva; Frances Petrocelli, a former principal staff assistant to three chancellors of the University of California; Eugene Stevens, a former mayor of Lompoc, California, and former correspondent for UPI and the *Los Angeles Times*; George Brecher, M.D., former president of the American Society of Hematology; Douglas Engelbart, Ph.D., former director of the Augmentation Research Center, Stanford Research Institute; Peter Lenn, Ph.D., former president of American Analysis Corp., a firm that develops educational training materials. This is only a small portion of est's 50-plus board members. Nearly all have taken the training.

Many of est's grants went to Eastern religious groups or gurus like the Naropa (Tibetan Buddhist) Institute in Colorado, and Tibetan Buddhist leader, Gyalwa Karmapa the 16th. Est also sponsored the United States tour of the late controversial Hindu guru Swami Muktananda, one of Erhard's mentors, who was finally exposed as being anything but enlightened (see Eastern Gurus; Enlightenment). Jerry Rubin appropriately remarked that est was "an important

part in the Easternization of America" (1759:44). *East West Journal* noted, "People who graduate from est usually end up with an Eastern teacher" (1346:6).

Werner Erhard has personally addressed numerous prestigious professional organizations, including Stanford University, University of Munich, and the University of California Medical Center. He participated in the Sixth World Congress of Social Psychiatry in Yugoslavia, and met with officials of several international organizations in Paris and Geneva. Many showed an interest in est. In Paris he delivered a lecture to UNESCO members and delegates and talked with John Forbes (then secretary-general of UNESCO) and other influentials. In Geneva he spoke with "high-ranking members of the World Health Organization, International Labor Organization, the University of Geneva and the U.S. Mission to the United Nations" (2057:15).

## EST (THE FORUM) THEORY**

"I am here to explain what can't be explained," says Erhard. In an est publication, "What So" for October, 1974, there is the following box:

---

**RULES ABOUT LIFE**
BY
Werner Erhard

1. Life has no rules

2.

---

Indeed, as we will see, that "life has no rules" is precisely what Erhard tries to explain, for reasons that will become obvious. Many people

---

**Most of this material can be found in early issues of *The Graduate Review*, an est publication, and Luke Rhinehart's authoritative *The Book of est*, which has a foreword by Werner Erhard and had every page checked for accuracy by an est trainer (2067:cover).

went to est to "improve their lives," but this was never the purpose of est Erhard stated, "Sometimes people get the notion that the purpose of est is to make you better. It is not. I happen to think you are perfect exactly the way you are" (2064:1).

So what was the purpose of est? Erhard himself has told us, "In est, the organization's purpose is to . . . create an opportunity for people to experience transformation, enlightenment . . ." (2065:3). "We want nothing short of a total transformation—an alteration of substances, not a change in form" (2731:1), and "all we want to do is change the notion of who you are" (2730:35).

One of est's main purposes was to destroy a person's existing belief system. According to est (and Scientology*), people's problems result in part from living mechanistically in and from the past, rather than directly experiencing the here-and-now as it truly is. The mind, in order to survive, has imposed false meanings and purposes on the world and, hence, deceives people into reacting as if reality conformed to those self-imposed belief systems. Thus, every belief system from an outside source—parents, church, or society—is an illusion. Only true experience is meaningful. But what one normally thinks of as experience is really non-experience, according to Erhard. "True" experience is what he calls transformation: the continual manifestation of the divine Self that lies behind one's illusory body and personality. This is why he says, "I don't think that you and I experience, I think we non-experience. Any time we truly experience, it is a spiritual experience because true experience is spiritual" (1346:6). True experience is spiritual because one is in touch with his divine Self. Est attempts to alter not the *content* of one's life but the *context* in which a person lives his experiences. The idea is not to change *what* one is doing but to change how he *views* what he is doing (1467:186-87). In the following pages, we will see how this is accomplished.

*Mystical Illumination*

What est attempted to achieve for participants was direct experience of the mystical or occult way of knowing. Rather than knowing by the normal medium of language, thought, rationality, and experience, one was to know by a psy-

chic perception outside time and space, which, once achieved, redefined the context of experience. This was Erhard's occult conversion experience in 1971. It is similar to Hindu or Buddhist enlightenment.* It is even similar to drug-induced monistic states of consciousness. Radical activist Jerry Rubin recalled, "On LSD I felt separate from myself, free of my ego, united with all energy. I felt everyone and everything as one. Sitting in that training room without any sense of time gave me a drug-like feeling of timelessness and spacelessness" (1759:34).

Most people react to their current situations based on beliefs and past experiences, but est removes this tendency and replaces it with a mystical experiencing (not reacting), and a total acceptance of whatever happens. Once an event occurs (good or bad), instead of reacting like a programmed machine (because of past conditioning), one simply accepts what occurs and chooses it. And, the theory goes, in choosing it one gains control over the situation rather than having the situation gain control over oneself. As Erhard states, "Happiness is a function of accepting what is" (2066).

Erhard carries the idea of "choosing what is" to the extreme of creatorship. If one gets robbed, beaten, raped, or murdered, one chose it; that is, one created the situation entirely and perfectly. According to Erhard, one creates literally everything one experiences—good, bad, and neutral. Also nothing is really good or bad; these are merely concepts that keep one's life from working. Things just are: Accept this, choose it, and life will be full of satisfaction. In conformity with Scientology* beliefs, Erhard thinks that all people consensually created the world simply because, as immortal gods, they got bored and needed a game to play. Thus, whatever is, was already created. As Erhard says, "You don't get to vote on the way it is. You already did" (2066).

The purpose of est, therefore, was to transform the manner in which a person views the world and his experience in it. "You will walk out of here turned around 180 degrees," promised the trainer (1759:34). And, in harmony with the purpose of many Eastern gurus,* "We're going to help you throw away whole belief systems, totally tear you down so you can put yourself back together in a way that lets life work" (2067:22).

*Experience Is Non-Experience*

To further understand Erhard's beliefs, one first needs to know that Erhard argues that only one's *experience* is real. However, as noted, what one normally thinks of as experience is really non-experience. Hence, if one lives totally in the realm of non-experience, one's life won't work. Erhard states, "Now what you and I normally call experience is that stuff that comes in from the outside [perceptions, etc.], but that is part of the experience which I call non-experience" (1346:2).

True "experience" is being in touch with and living from the mystical inner Self, which is beyond description. In other words, people are wrong in thinking that true experience involves perception, sensations, and cognitive processes. What people call normal experience is an illusion, at best just a reflection of true experience. It is merely an *effect* of one's inner self. This inner self is where one knows true experience and is "at cause" as creator, i.e., the cause of everything rather than "at effect" (at the mercy of) everything.

*Levels of Experience*

In est there were various degrees of "experience" ranging from non-experience (or, perhaps better, misperceived experience) to genuine experience, or understanding life and reality as it truly is, which puts the former in its proper perspective. The following est scale illustrates the est differences between true experience and non-experience. Notice that reasonableness ranks as one of the lowest forms of non-experience (cf. 2067:29).

This chart is based on the unique est philosophy and terminology. Providing definitions and explanations of each term at this point would be too cumbersome; however, much of the chart will become clear after finishing this chapter. Our intention here is merely to show Erhard's

| Scale of Experience | |
|---|---|
| *Source*<br><br>Realization<br>Clearing (participation)<br>Purpose<br>Ability<br>Correction<br>Enlightenment**<br>Understanding<br>Communication<br>Acceptance | These are the degrees of fully experienced experience in an ascending scale. "Acceptance" (of truth, self, and so on) begins the process of the genuine experience of life. As one matures in experience (upwards from Acceptance), one eventually reaches the level "Source" where thoughts and actions emerge as a natural function of one's divine Self. |
| 0 (ZERO)<br><br>Help<br>Hope<br>Demand for Improvement<br>Need of Change<br>Fear of Worsening Effect<br>Ruin<br>Dispersal<br>Disconnection<br>Unexistence<br>Reasonable<br>False Cause | These are the degrees of non-experience in a descending scale. We experience them as real because we are deluded, but they are not true experience. "Helping" someone begins the condition of "non-experience," which may end at "false cause," where one is at the mercy of one's self-induced delusion, powerless, and a victim of other people's realities. |

**Erhard is apparently using the term "enlightenment" in this chart for an incomplete form of the ultimate enlightenment one experiences as Source, where one mystically perceives oneself as creator of all things.

point that most people who think they experience life actually live in the realm of "non-experience," or delusion. To understand the chart fully should not concern the reader. (For purposes of argument, "0" [zero] on the chart is considered a neutral area between "experience" and "non-experience.")

In est, helping someone, hoping for something, or trying to make up one's mind about something is "evil" and should be avoided. Being reasonable (meaning, to use logic) about anything is one of the lowest forms of non-experience. Being reasonable ruins one's life. Being *unreasonable* makes it work. Sourcing, where one sees oneself as God, is the highest experience.

Notice that to go from a state of false cause, or non-experience, to the state of true experience, one must pass through zero. This is why a trainer explained that one must go through nothing to get something. Erhard states, "One creates from nothing. If you try to create from something, you're just changing something" (2067: 255).** In other words, one is just rearranging what is there, not changing its essence. When one rearranges the form of a piece of dough, one is not changing the nature of the dough, only its form. "So in order to create something, you first have to be able to create nothing" (2066). In other words, to create yourself as God, you must

realize that you are now in an unconscious state—you are unconscious of your divinity. As the chart below reveals, you must progress up the scale through zero to the state of natural knowing, where you intuitively experience your divine nature.

Thus, in est there were also "levels of certainty," which everyone, unfortunately, has also confused to no end. For example, when one believes or thinks he knows something, he really does not. In the following est diagram, note that feelings, actions, thinking, and belief represent "decreasing certainty." Note also that such an idea runs contrary to the way most people normally live their lives. Not surprisingly, Erhard says that he does not *think* much anymore; he observes and experiences (1533:26).

*Three Notions of Est*

Three basic "notions" were central to est. These are, first, that one is perfect, but that barriers prevent one from experiencing and expressing this perfection. Second, when one tries to resist, control, or change something, one only causes it to endure. Third, the re-creation of an experience makes it disappear; that is, if one keeps going over it, re-experiencing it and "being" with it, it will eventually go away. To get rid of something (for example, a bad habit), one

| Natural knowing or certainty (ineffable) <br> Certainty of not knowing <br> Certainty one knows something (realization) <br> Observation (the Eastern concept of "witnessing") | Increasing certainty (reliable experience) |
|---|---|
| 0 | + (PLUS SCALE) |
| (ZERO) | – (MINUS SCALE) |
| Feel about/sense of (emotions) <br> Do about/experiment; effort <br> Think about <br> Believe about <br> In mystery about <br> Unconscious about | Decreasing certainty (unreliable experience) |

**The term "nothing" is used in its neutral or "zero" meaning as here, but also as a metaphor for sourcing on page 275.

should just let it be and experience it fully. Get
into it, create it, allow it. (Obviously, such a concept has serious implications for conventional
morality.) Because belief is the lowest form of
certainty and "understanding is the booby prize"
(2730:37), trainees were told not to understand
or believe these three notions. They were simply
to experience them in the seminar.

*Reality and Unreality*

During the seminar, a trainer would have had
a long discussion on distinguishing reality from
unreality, involving classic doublethink logic. A
trainer would have had defined reality in an incomplete, but normal manner and then persuaded participants that it is actually not real.
Trainees would have been told that the test
for reality is physicalness, measurability (time,
form, distance), and agreement or consensus
(we all agree this book is real, hence it is real).
Now, if reality is comprised of that which is
physical, measurable, and agreed upon, the *un*-
reality must be the opposite, that which is non-
physical, nonmeasurable, and not agreed upon,
i.e., an individual's subjective *experience* of life.

Now according to this line of reasoning, the
trainees are faced with a serious problem. They
know that their experiences are not illusions;
their experiences are the most real thing they
know. Therefore, they must conclude that, in
truth, what most people call reality (e.g., the real
world—that which is physical, measurable, etc.)
is in fact *not* real, and that what most people call
unreal (e.g., that which is nonphysical, etc.) is
truly real (one's individual experience).

Trainees, therefore, were brought to understand that only experience as defined by est was
real. Furthermore, the goal for trainees was to
reach the realm of divine experience and to experience oneself as creator. Once reached, true
experience, though ineffable and mystical, supposedly overflowed into the realm of daily experience. Thus, the est goal was to subjugate the
realm of non-experience (i.e., that realm of one's
daily living where one exists at the *effect* of
things, a victim of circumstances) to the realm of
"real" experience as defined by est, where one is
the source or *cause* of all things and is in control
of all things.

According to Erhard, *true* reality and experience are tied to the concept of creatorship. The
major source of people's problems is that they let
something called "false cause" run their lives.
False cause says everything that happens to one
(his daily experiences) is the result of some other
person, thing, or circumstance, instead of something he himself created. Erhard also calls this
non-experience. Since one is really one essence
with God, to live as if one were not the creator of
all things, but rather as if one were at the mercy
of circumstances, is a betrayal of one's divine nature: It is not one's true nature or true experience. Erhard wants trainees to see that "true"
experience does not originate from *any* outside
effect but results entirely from one's sovereign
choice as creator. Trainees are the cause, the creator, of *all* their experience. If so, then one's daily
experiences are not non-experiences, but fully
experienced (self-created) experiences.

Now, if they were to "get" this, est graduates
would view all experiences as originating from
within their divine self, as part of its manifestations. And further, even though normal daily experience is unreal, since it is nevertheless part of
the game one has chosen to play, one lives it accordingly. Graduates could live as the creator of
their experiences and circumstances, not as victims of them. They could see themselves as
being literally in control of their lives, even of the
universe itself. They are its maker, sustainer,
and destroyer.

Their perception of the world was totally altered. While the world (content) is the same,
their view of it had been radically transformed
(context). It is totally the same, and yet totally different. This, then, is the transformation Erhard
wants people to experience.

A diagram of est's view of reality and unreality would look like the one on the next page.

Luke Rhinehart, a Zen teacher and author of
the most complete book on the est training,
records the trainer's statement cautioning participants about reality and unreality:

And try telling people that the only real thing is
your experience. Lots of luck. No, we'll have to
stick to the code words society accepts. When
we talk about the unreal physical universe we'll
have to call it by its code word: "reality." And

| Unreality | Reality |
|---|---|
| How the world sees reality | How the world sees unreality |
| Physical | Nonphysical |
| Measurable | Nonmeasurable |
| Agreement | Non-agreement |
| Necessitates a world of effect, living as a victim in a world of problems outside your control. | Source or cause of all things. Living in a world where you are fully in control, living from your divine nature. |
| Non-experience | Real experience |

when we talk about our real experience of the training we'll have to call it "unreality." After all, according to society the "real" training must be something we can measure, something typed up in this notebook, maybe, something we can all agree upon (2067:133).

Trainees were also warned that illusions can have serious consequences. If an unreal bus hit a man, est never denied it would kill him. "The unreal physical universe is solid, it can kill," says the trainer. Even though this is so, life "should be a little easier knowing what's real and unreal instead of operating in the world of illusion, in the world of effect, effect, effect" (2067:134).

Trainees thus discovered that each person, alone, is 100 percent responsible for his experience. If reality exists only by one's agreement to create it, and is ultimately subjective, then each individual is responsible for his or her particular reality, and *no* experience exists for which the individual is not entirely responsible. Although graduates are assured they should not feel a sense of blame, guilt, or morality, they nevertheless created 100 percent of their experience. Be it cancer, rape, robbery, or murder, the individual is responsible for it precisely because of his experiencing it. Notice the following dialogue between a trainer and trainee:

Trainee (t): But I'm not the source of *everything* I experience. When I get hit by a bus, the bus is a partial source of my experience.

Trainer (T): That bus is an *agreement* and you have to agree that that hunk of matter is a bus before you can experience getting hit by a bus.

t: But I'll get killed whether I agree that it's a bus or not!

T: You'll get killed all right. But *your* experience will be determined by what agreements you've entered into about the unreal physical universe we inhabit. *You* are the source of these agreements and of your subsequent experience (2067:135).

Let's back up a bit. At one point in the seminar, trainees would have been influenced to experience that they were just machines. At this point they were either depressed or resisting what has been said. But the argument would have been presented powerfully in an authoritarian atmosphere, and few trainees who have bought it would have been able to escape the implications. The trainer concluded:

You're all machines—you've never been anything else—your lives are meaningless—machines don't have morals, goals, ideals—machines aren't meaningful, they just chug away, just are, just exist. You don't have any control in your life—you never did. Your tragedies are just you playing your tapes. This is it. This is it. You're a machine before the training and you're a machine after the training. There ain't no more. Three hundred-fifty big ones for no change. That's all there is. I hope you get it. There's nothing to get. Nothing matters. Nothing is important. Nothing to worry about. Everything is as worthless as everything else. Now you can find out what "Enlightenment" is. It's all a cosmic joke. That's it. There's nothing to get. Get it? Enlightenment is saying "yes" to what is, taking what you get. What is, is (2068).

Whatever the reaction to the above (acceptance, anger, resistance, depression), people were told to take what they get, it does not matter what. What they get is what they get. Most people seemed to take it and accept the message. And they experienced great relief because nothing has any meaning anymore. After all, if everyone's a machine and nothing has meaning, *nothing* is ever consequential. Trainees described the release as having a great weight lifted off their shoulders. Erhard says, "There's an enormous freedom in experiencing that realization" (2069:2).

Now, since everyone is a machine with no choice or control and no moral responsibility, then, goes the reasoning, if one accepts and *chooses* it, one can view himself *not* as an effect of things but as the cause of them. One goes from being an automaton to the realization of godhood. By choosing to accept *responsibility* for being the cause of literally everything in one's experience, one realizes that all along one has been the creator of all these things. *Now* the trainees will *always* get what they want, *if* they want what they get.

### Altered States of Consciousness

Because people found it difficult to encounter so-called est enlightenment* in the normal state of consciousness, est used various relaxation and meditation* techniques to alter the normal state and make the mind more receptive. Like most Eastern religions, the desired goal is reached only through an abnormal state of consciousness (see Altered States of Consciousness). Normal consciousness is, in fact, a barrier to "enlightenment" in the East (see Enlightenment and Eastern Gurus). In a similar fashion, to be successful in est one had to get out of, or go out of, one's mind. In the words of Bhagwan Shree Rajneesh (explaining one of Erhard's aphorisms), "Truth is not something of the mind. When the mind is no more, truth is" (2070:12). Erhard asserts, "Hypnosis and trance states can be used to transcend the mind, to go beyond it to . . . the Self. They can also be used—as they very often are—to operate simply on [the normal] Mind" (1707:81). Because the normal mind has to be "removed" by altered states of consciousness, Er-

hard declares, "It is as legitimate to make use of trance states as it is to make use of normal states of consciousness" (1707:81-82). In an interview found in *The est Experience*, Erhard biographer Dr. William Bartley said, "Various altered states of consciousness play an important role in the training. . . . Certainly one can enter an altered state of consciousness through a number of the est processes" (1533:175).

According to est trainers, "People have to have the experience of nothing. . . . Your mind sort of empties out. . . . So that there's nothing there" (2192:2). In this state, "transformation" or "enlightenment" or "getting" (see below) can be experienced. For example, in the following encounter, the trainee is told that she is the real source of her vandalized apartment, and that unless she gets out of her mind, she will never understand the truth.

Trainer (T): Do you take responsibility for not having created friends who might have stayed in the apartment most of the times?

Victim (V): Maybe, but . . .

T: Whose idea is it that because you come home and find things missing from your apartment that you were robbed?

V: My idea!

T: Precisely.

V: D--- it! Precisely what!

T: Precisely you created the idea that you were robbed.

V: But I didn't cause the robbery.

T: There was no robbery unless you created it. If your stereo was stolen you did it.

V: You're out of your mind!

T: That's what est is all about. GET OUT OF YOUR MIND, BARBARA! YOU'RE THINKING IN CLICHES AND LETTING OTHER PEOPLE DICTATE REALITY when you actually create it yourself (2067:139-40).

Luke Rhinehart, a Zen teacher with a Ph.D. from Columbia and author of *The Book of est*, remarked, "One can rarely have an enlightenment experience except under the impact of nonsense. Est's attack on man's belief systems during the first weekend of the training is essential to the later 'getting it.' Sense is our disease, the barrier to our full experience of life" (2067:249).

Hence, the est "processes," working in conjunction with the severe physical and mental strain, were designed to alter normal consciousness until a person became receptive and open to new experiences such as enlightenment.* The 45- to 90-minute "processes" involved various exercises in meditation,* visualization,* and self-hypnosis.* Through some of these exercises, trainees also experienced the release of symptoms brought on by the training (e.g., headache, nausea, backaches). Thus, they were prepared or conditioned by their own experience to accept one of est's basic principles: Since consciousness can alter bodily states, one can see that one is the cause of one's own experience.

Some processes involved the participant in consciousness projection (projecting one's consciousness into other things or people), which may precipitate out-of-the-body experiences.

Several of the est processes come from the occult methods of Zen, Scientology,* Silva Mind Control,* Mind Dynamics, and Tibetan Tantric Yoga* (cf. 226:142-45/2067:42). For example, in both Scientology* and the "Truth process," discussed below, the initiate is told over and over to locate a space in different parts of his body, e.g., "Locate a space in your left foot.... Fine.... Locate another space. Locate a space in your left leg.... Good" (2734:54). This is right out of Scientology founder L. Ron Hubbard's *The Creation of Human Ability.* According to Dr. Elmer Green of the Menninger Foundation, this technique also comes straight from the hypnosis manuals (2226:144). It can produce the effects of a drug high or a deep meditation trance (cf. 2067:42). Award-winning film producer Nathaniel Lande noted, "It is particularly effective upon people who have willingly accepted agreements (suggestions) and then been totally exhausted by hours of sitting on a hard seat while feeling bored and hungry" (2226:144).

The est processes we will discuss below (truth, fear, and danger) are still employed in the Forum, albeit in a somewhat subdued form.

### The Truth Process

In this exercise, trainees go into a meditative state and start locating spaces in their body for 20 to 30 minutes. Initially, this relaxes and conditions them; then it can produce a trance state. A poem by Erhard is read that assures everyone they are perfect and good. Next, initiates are told to directly experience a specific situation or item that is a problem or barrier to them, such as fear or anger. ("What feelings does it bring up, what images are associated with it, what bodily sensations, what emotions? Dive in and experience them. Take what you get.") In *Est: 4 Days to Make Your Life Work,* we read, "Taking everyone through specific situations, the trainer skillfully manages to reach the inner emotional depths of practically everyone present" (1347:67). The effect is far more traumatic in person than any description of the process can indicate. One graduate summarized, "Soon the room was filled with moans, sobs, whimpers, and cries. Then there was an earsplitting scream. A man cried out, 'It's on my chest—get it off!' I felt I was the only normal person in the place. I sat up and saw hundreds of people writhing and flailing the air. I was in a snake pit and I wanted out—to h— with the money! I might never get it, but I had had it" (2227). Another said, "This process evoked crescendos of harsh weeping, agonized shouts and guttural grunts as dozens of trainees completely broke down, turning the Sutton Hotel's ballroom into almost unbearable bedlam" (2725:98). Another reported, "Two hundred and fifty people in every form of emotion, giving free vent to vomiting, shaking, sobbing, hysterical laughing, raging—recreating experiences in a safe space. No one paid the slightest attention to anyone else. Each person there was concentrating wholly on his own mind/body experience" (1467:85).

### The Danger and Fear Process

In the fear process, groups of trainees have been marched up onstage to stand in a straight line in front of the audience, and they are instructed to make eye contact with the audience. They are to experience their reaction at "being with" the audience, while the trainers confront their "acts" which prevent their lives from working. While onstage they are unmercifully harassed and confronted by est staff. As in the truth process, some cannot manage; they may vomit, weep hysterically, pass out, or shake uncontrollably. "The first row is told to go to the platform and make eye contact. Watching this process is somewhat like being transmitted to a combination insane asylum/torture ward. What happens to the trainees is absolutely incredible. . . . Like a scene from a horror movie, people began to fall apart right before your eyes" (1347:68-69).

Some say the danger process makes the truth and fear processes seem like a calm sail on the lake. After the fear process, all the trainees are told to lie on the floor. They are instructed to go into their "spaces." (These "spaces" are mentally constructed fantasy environments where a person can supposedly go and experience anything "safely.") Then they are told to pretend to be fearful and terrified of the person lying next to them. Next they are to fear those all around them who, they are informed, really *are* their enemies. The trainer then says that everyone in the room is out to kill them. Soon their enemy is the whole city; then the entire world is out to murder them.

The mental state the trainer places them in makes it all seem very real. "A lot of people take the instructions to heart and scream and throw up and curl into the fetal position. Some black out and finally faint. The hotel room had become a madhouse. Many people are obviously not pretending. It is as if they are in a deep hypnotic trance and living out their fears" (2226:139). Rhinehart observed, "After a slow, repetitious buildup the whole room is filled with writhing, groaning, moaning, screaming, shrieking, crying—some acted, and some very real" (2067:106). Another participant remarks, "On and on it goes. The noise is frightful. People are crying, some are vomiting into bags produced for just that purpose. It is chaos unleashed. Bodies thrash upon the floor. Sobs and groans rend the stale air which is laced with the aroma of sweat and fear and now and again vomit" (2228:87).

With many people thinking they are about to *die*, the process ends when the trainer brings the people back to reality and tells them the big joke. If they were afraid of everybody in the room,

then everybody in the room—indeed, the world—must be afraid of *them. They* are powerful. "There is nobody in the universe more *powerful* than you. So go outside and scare some people." It is about 3:00 A.M., and the trainees march ecstatically out into the darkness, awed with their newfound sense of power.

There are other processes. For example, reluctant trainees are told during one process: "Every man has a little girl in him somewhere, and if he's got a barrier to expressing it, he's got an area of stuckness" (which is bad). The trainer continues, "Every heterosexual has a repressed homosexual element in him someplace, and every homosexual has a repressed heterosexual inside" (2067:153). The implication is that one should not be stuck in his sexual "role," and should have the freedom to experience his homosexuality if he so chooses. (In the est "About Sex" seminar, pornographic films were used to supposedly help break down barriers to sexual fulfillment (2229:153). One pornographic magazine noted approvingly that "est has enabled many to face and accept their fears of homosexuality or has given them the freedom to choose whatever form of sexuality they want" (2227). Another reported some of the training sessions were said to have attracted a large number of homosexuals for just this purpose (2227).

*Playing the Game*

On the first day of the sessions, a trainer barks: "You can't win in here. Nobody wins in here except me. Unless I decide to let you win. It ought to be perfectly clear to everyone now that you're all — and I'm God. Only an — would argue with God. I may let you be Gods too, but that'll come later" (2067:47).

Apparently, in eternity past, everyone as a god grew bored sitting around experiencing perfection, so we collectively created games to play: We consensually made a universe, and in it each of us arbitrarily made some things more important than others (because all things were equally meaningless). Individually, this universe is each person's experience in life. This concept (sometimes also found in occult religions and in channeled revelations) explains why everyone now has "problems" (cf. Scientology). We created problems as part of our game; most of us even created our own ignorance that made us forget we are gods. As Erhard states:

> You're God in your universe. You caused it. You pretended not to cause it so that you could play in it, and you can remember you caused it any time you want to (2066).

> The point is that you lose your ability to play the game, to master the game, when you forget that a game is a game. In order to master life, we need to recover the realization that life is truly a game. . . . To have a game you have to agree that something is more important than something else (2069:2).

For example, Christians would be playing the game that the Person of Jesus Christ was more important than self-oriented New Age seminars. Only it would not be true—it would only provide an interesting game. Likewise, police are playing the game that criminals are more antisocial than law-abiding citizens. According to Erhard, all things are equally unimportant or equally important; it doesn't matter what. Words don't mean much, but who wants to sit around forever being bored with perfection? As a trainer stated, "But we Gods get bored with this perfection, and so we always end up pretending that something which ISN'T [important] is more important than what is, and that's a game. . . . As long as we're sitting here feeling perfect, being fully aware of our being Creator, then all is equally important. There's nothing to do, no game to play, we can sit for a while in bliss examining our navels. But we get bored. We decide to begin playing again" (2067:217).

Yet, even if we choose to think that everything is equally important, this does not make it intrinsically meaningful. As Erhard states, "The truth doesn't mean anything. It just is" (2066).

In fact, the world itself is only imaginary. Again, we gods created it merely to amuse ourselves. But we choose to either play in someone else's world or to make up our own:

> The only question is who is going to do the imagining. Most people passively absorb the imaginary structures and game rules of others. The wise man creates his own. All games, all

goals, all events are the creation of imagination. You can accept the world as others have created it, accept their goals and rules and play their games, or you can consciously create your own. In both cases, however, you and you alone are responsible for everything that happens (2067:218).

Hitler played his game. So did Jim Jones. And the pimps and drug dealers and Mafia bosses are all playing their games. So do the American president and the medical doctors. So does everyone. Any search for an absolute truth, or God, or beauty beyond ourselves is all just part of the game to escape boredom:

> The search for Enlightenment or Reality with a Capital R, for God with a big G, for Ultimate Truth is an interesting game . . . until it's won. It's interesting until one has grasped Enlightenment, Reality, God, or Ultimate Truth. Then, as soon as you have, you find THAT game is over. . . . What you decide is Ultimate Truth probably seems to your neighbor to be trivial illusion. . . . What we humans want is interesting problems and games, no more, no less. Not pleasures, not truths, not moral codes, not a state of happiness, but interesting games (2067:218-19).

At the end of day four, Rhinehart records the trainer's words: "And now I'm going to step down from the platform and return to playing the game of Michael, God pretending He's a human, interacting with you other Gods, also pretending you're humans" (2067:219).

This in a nutshell is a key ingredient in the philosophy behind est: gods creating universes to play in because nothing really matters. As we will see, with a few alterations, this and what follows also seems to be the philosophy behind The Forum. However, "playing the game" was only one aspect of the philosophy underlying Erhard's views. "Transformation" is the real key to understanding his worldview.

*Transformation*

"Transformation" a la Erhard explains how people can realize they are gods. Everything in est revolves around this key word: transformation. Not to be confused with change, transformation is said to take place on a deeper level than a mere reordering of actions. As an example, consider the difference between the *change* and the *transformation* of a criminal. In est, to change the criminal would be to reform him by changing the *content* of his life (his actions), but not the *context* (how he sees things—his worldview). As a "reformed" man, his actions would be changed, e.g., he would no longer steal or murder. Consequently, his "form" would be changed so that he would be a respectable moral member of society.

But to Erhard this is not what is ultimately important. He declares, "I want to be clear with you that est and transformation are not a matter of getting better. I support things that make people better; I support things that contribute to the content of people's lives. But est is not about getting better. Est is about transformation" (1088:3). Erhard wants transformation; that is, an alteration of a person's context, or *how* he looks at the world, rather than mere content, or *how* a person acts. Est would want to alter the criminal's essence of who he is, not necessarily how he acts. Why? Because "change" will only alter the form (be it outward appearance, behavior, or morals), which is essentially useless. A criminal is already "okay" in content (actions),** but until he is transformed, he is seriously deficient in *context* (epistemology).

According to est, in change there is only a meaningless alteration of form; the man will still persist as man, which is not his true identity. He may no longer be a killer, but that is relatively unimportant. He must be transformed; he must experience the self (his real personality) as the Self (God). He must experience his true nature as

divine. This true experience of the Self causes him—the man as limited personality (representing a false epistemology)—to "disappear," and then he sees who he really is: God, the *context* in and from which all existence arises. As Erhard explains, "The ecstasy I'm telling about is a loss of *persona*, a loss of personality, in which you realize something more profound, more magnificent than that which you've been calling yourself," and thus, "I didn't just experience Self [God]; *I became Self* [God]" (2276:4/1707:167).

As noted earlier, when anything is truly experienced, it "disappears," whether it is body pain, cancer, the personality, or the universe. Trainers say that this is why headaches, backaches, and even stuttering or allergies are (allegedly) cured. This is why the concept of one's identity is tied to true experience. "To make sure a person doesn't find out who he is, convince him that he can't really make anything disappear. All that's left then is to resist, solve, fix, help or change things, which is useless and causes it to persist" (2066).

Thus, the worst thing possible is to try to reform, change, or help someone, such as a criminal, in the way we normally think of these words. It will not work. This is resistance, which leads to a persistence of the condition. To create something in a true sense, it must be done through "nothing," the experience of mystical reality that is beyond communication. Again, this is why Erhard teaches that "one creates from nothing. If you try to create from something [e.g., a moral society from the Bible], you're just changing something. So in order to create something, you first have to be able to create nothing" (2192:2). As est trainer Ron Bynum explains, "The training and the experience of the training don't come out of the world. They don't come out of any form. They come directly out of true experience. Therefore it's nothing." He went on to say that pretrainees cannot understand this because, "They're all there in their minds. They're in their thoughts. They don't know that there's a thing called experience or 'no thinking' or 'nothing' that's before all that stuff" (2192:2).

When a criminal is est-transformed, he experiences himself, which causes "him" (as body and personality) to "disappear"; nothing is left. And within this ineffable experience, he "discovers"

---

**As one graduate remarked, "It seems that no matter how unlovable, anti-social, bigoted or uncivilized a person is, it's still 'all right' with est (2275:15). In an "Evening with the Clergy," a graduate asked Erhard, " 'What do we do about killers?' He had a hard time accepting such people as being OK." "In brief [Erhard] answered that it is perhaps unwise to take this to its brutal extreme. 'It must work in the extreme, yes, but it is hard to take it right off. . . . You were forgiven in the first place, you have to realize that,' he said. 'Make the world be God, don't make part of it be God and part be not-God'" (2724:2).

that he is God. As God, he created the universe in which to play, this universe which only appears to be real. After the criminal recognizes who he is—the source of everything—he can then choose to stop his game or to continue playing the criminal. At least he will now know who he really is (his context), and will no longer be tied to his actions (his content), or be burdened down by unrealities (such as morality or decency)—unless, of course, he wants to play those particular games.

In essence, Erhard-style transformation alters one's perception; it has little concern with one's behavior. Here is how Erhard defines it:

... "Transformation" doesn't have the properties that things do. No position or location, no time, no form, no beginning, and no end. It doesn't look like anything and it doesn't feel like anything. And it does not happen. Transformation just is and you can create it and you can know it. It just is, and while you can know that it is, you can't perceive it or sense it or feel it.

To explain it (and it can't really be explained), you could say that transformation is the shift in the definition or focus of self from content to context, from identifying one's self as point of view, story, personality, body and so on, to recognizing one's self as the context in which all things occur. It is not an event; it's a context for events to occur in—a space (1088:2).

And, with Zen eloquence:

Transformation is the self as the self, the self as the context of all contexts, everything/nothing. The self itself is the ground of all being, that from which everything arises. The self is pure context, it is everything/nothing, it is pure space. And out of the self emerges a manifestation of it. That is, the self (context) *is* complete; the self manifests itself by being complete, and the manifestation is process or content (1088:3).

However, one big problem with a philosophy like this, which is, technically speaking, solipsistic and nihilistic, is that people cannot live it out. Those who try to keep running into reality. Even Erhard had a problem here, because even such enlightened and transformed beings as est staff degenerated to such an extent that even Erhard

called it evil (although evil does not exist). Erhard admitted this happened throughout the est organization. Some of the best staffers were engaging in dirty tricks (although these do not exist). But regardless, Erhard was still frustrated with "the game" some staffers had created and were playing, because "it was the absolute best I had ever seen in the universe, the best I could imagine, that was crystallizing into evil. It was not the worst of people, it was the best of people. Can you get the kind of hopelessness and frustration of that?" (1088:3, cf. pp. 5-7,10).

Why was Erhard frustrated at all? In light of his philosophy, so what? In the end, however, he was true to est philosophy. Nothing mattered anyway. It was just more games, and evil had no relevance. Erhard had already defined "perfection" as simply "what is." The est organization was thus perfect, even with all the evil.

Erhard did not seem to recognize his own betrayal of his philosophy in initially expressing a frustration over evil, or the relation of his own philosophy to the emergence of evil in people's lives.

But let's get back to "transformation." How did participants come to understand that before the creation—as gods—they got bored sitting eternally in the light? In order to experience this boredom, one of the est processes had trainees imagining brilliant light for a long period of time. It was boring, and trainees got the message. In the training one also "experienced" that the person himself, as God, created his own mind, body, and personality in order to play in his game. Erhard says, "My notion is that what happens in the Training is that the individual is given the opportunity to . . . re-experience the fact that he created himself" (1346:2). Erhard explains that transformation is valuable because it leads to *nurturing* even the illusions of life, i.e., the context of the game:

In fact, no matter what you do after the training, you can be nurtured. When what your life is about shifts from trying to get satisfied to being satisfied, then [literally] any content [anything in your life] is satisfying, nurturing and complete. So est isn't improving the content of one's life—it isn't about "getting better" though you may have the experience of getting better. It's about shifting the context in which all events occur [i.e, your way of viewing them].

Est's purpose is to create the space in which you can get that your self is context rather than content—which enables you to CREATE the story of your life rather than BE the story or events. So that everything becomes the completion of your transformation (1088:2).

Erhard also expands on his philosophy in different terms: "life" versus "living." "Life [content] is a totally different thing from living [context]." Life is "the drama, the story, the illusion, the lie." "Living is just what's happening right this instant, and that's all perfect. Perfect means what is—is, and what isn't—isn't, and that's flawless" (2069:2).

Ultimately, perfection (what is) exists only in the realm of divine reality—in est jargon, the context, everything/nothing. This is *living*. Our *life* is the unreal realm of day-to-day occurrences, concepts (time, space, history), morals (good and evil). This is the game. Erhard states that "when all is said and done, life is a game. Some of the games have enormous consequences. However, if you get stuck in the importance of it, then you no longer see that it's a game. Even when the consequences are enormous, you need to realize it's a game. *Everything* in life is a game, *except living*. Living is not a game. Living is simply what is [i.e., perfect]" (2069:5).

In other words, *living* is not the unreal game we invent to play in; it is reality. Living is *not* the game. Our purpose is to become *aware* of living, i.e., to be enlightened. But this is not the goal of *life*, which is the game we create. With life, the only goal is to win, since there is nothing else to do. "Your total purpose in life is *LIVING* [being enlightened]. That's the real purpose in life, but that's not the goal in the *GAME*. The goal in the game is always to win" (2069:3). Thus, Erhard explains the value of *living*:

What is, IS, and what ain't, *AIN'T*. So what! That's precisely what people say when they find out. Enthusiastically—So what! There's an enormous freedom in experiencing that. When you can really observe and experience that, it transforms your ability to *experience living* (2069:1-2, emphasis added).

This may explain why some graduates' "experience" of problems "disappear," for they no longer exist as significant entities. At this point Erhard says they've got the truth, and they "could just sit there and dig the experience of it," i.e., its perfection. But there's a problem. They've handled the truth, but what about the lie, the creation? They must do something with it. Again, they handle it by constructing a game. After all, if, as he states, *"Nothing is intrinsically important"* (2069:3), they had better make some things important unless they want that eternal boredom.

Erhard says that "the truth is that all of life IS a game." This includes wars, which are merely bigger games with bigger "consequences," but games just the same (2069:2). In *est: Playing the Game (of life) the New Way*, Carl Frederick called "the point of absolute truth" the following est belief: "Right now, everything that's 'out there' in the world, you constructed from your notion of what ought to be out there, consciously or unconsciously you did it. It's also perfect, because it exactly reflects what you wanted" (2337:161). Frederick also said, "Take wars, you get a notion of wars before wars exist. . . . You construct wars. You agree to have a war, or wars wouldn't exist. Period. Don't lie about it" (2337:155).

In other words, it's only one's agreement to have a game that makes it perceptually "real." Nothing is really "out there" objectively. Even war has no real consequences, only unreal ones. Like Arjuna's battles in the *Bhagavad Gita*, they are fought in the realm of illusion. As R. H. Blyth remarks, "[The] 'enlightened' person [is put] into a complacent state of mind in which he 'enjoys every day' and feels calm and undisturbed among screams of agony, physical and spiritual" (1533:262).

Now, in looking over Erhard's entire theory, several things become clear. A murderer or rapist could be transformed—could achieve the ultimate goal of est—and remain as he is, and even gain satisfaction and "completion" from his brutal acts. Such a person would be a fully enlightened soul as long as he "lived self as context." Everything the enlightened do in life (content) is fine. That is their game, what they want. Erhard states, "To master life, you simply need to know what you want. There's nothing you SHOULD want. Whatever you want's fine. There's no intrinsically valuable importance.... Wake up in the morning and make up a goal. It doesn't make any difference" (2069:3).

Such an outlook would never have been accepted by ordinary people apart from the seminar. This is the insidiousness of it all. It transforms people into its own nihilistic and solipsistic image (2727). As Erhard remarks, "Self is all there is" (1346:4). *Whatever* game one wants is fine; rules don't matter. This philosophy is not concerned about rules or morals, only victory. In est, people were taught to play whatever game they chose, and to win. That was the only goal. As Erhard stated, "Est is our game and we wholeheartedly invite you to participate with us in playing our game" (1088:12). And, as we will see, the game continues to be played in The Forum.

Erhard's own "game" is to transform the world. He's playing it vigorously. People can laugh when Erhard says that everyone has to give up their resistance to being conned. But the implications of millions of people "getting it" aren't humorous. As Stan Mieses once wrote: "The whole process of breaking down a personality . . . and then rebuilding it, almost by intimidation, seems to lie at the heart of est" (1779:46).

## THE HUNGER PROJECT

If Erhard is in part nihilistic, supporters ask, why did he create the social "Hunger Project"? Why, indeed. It must be remembered that a game is a game; if we wish to escape boredom, some things will be arbitrarily considered more important than others. One does indeed wonder how any promoter of his philosophy can really care about helping the starving. As a trainer explained: "I don't care about you anymore than gravity cares about you when it knocks you on your a—: it doesn't offer you any help either. Hey! Know what I do when someone asks me for help? I kick 'em right in the groin; help someone, and he becomes helpless" (2229:88). For those "unenlightened" to Erhard's ideas, his public display of concern over world hunger masks a deeper reality.

As we saw earlier, one should never "help" anyone. Individually, it is either sink or swim. "Assisting," however, might be proper action. "Assisting" means to make a task easier for someone else, who could just as easily get along perfectly well without you. But to "help" implies taking away another's responsibility as creator.

Since Erhard teaches that people must claim authorship for their own particular circumstances in life, it may sound strange to hear Erhard and his followers say that they are personally taking responsibility to end world hunger. Remember, though, that est's "responsibility" does not involve a moral obligation to do anything.

Suzanne Gordon, author of *Lonely in America* (2333), wrote "Let them eat est," an exposé of the Hunger Project. Not surprisingly, sending money to feed relief organizations was considered by the Hunger Project to be a dehumanizing act, so almost none of the large sums of money collected by the Hunger Project has actually helped the hungry. Instead, the money is used to tell more Americans about the Hunger Project. Lester Brown, who is widely respected in the field of world food problems, says that the Hunger Project has "probably collected more money in the name of hunger and done the least about hunger than any group I can think of" (2729). Gordon claims the Hunger Project is a thinly veiled recruitment arm for est. And the hunger issue itself has been used to gather money for est. A "Hunger Project Seminar Series," for instance, costs 30 dollars per enrollment, with the proceeds going directly to the est organization (2729).

## REVERSAL OF VALUES

Another consequence of Erhard's worldview is its dehumanizing nature, which has led to a fatalistic attitude in untold numbers of people. A mother reports, "Est changed my life. I used to think everything was so important. So now I don't worry. A few weeks ago, my son and some friends were in a car accident, and several of them were hurt. Before est I would have thought it was very important and worried. But I didn't worry about it at all" (2333:294). After suffering from insomnia after est, another graduate stated, "Nothing matters. I feel like a machine, I feel hollow. I feel like what Landon [the trainer] said I was—a mechanical a——h——. I try to remember what I was like before the training, but I feel like a collection of empty spaces" (2227). Another reported, "The differences I can measure in myself are mostly attitudinal. Nothing overwhelms me as before: nothing seems tragic or permanent" (1534:205). Adelaide Bry reported about another est graduate: "During the training, she got that she was frigid. She subsequently left her high-status and well-paying job to work full time producing pornography films" (1467:71).

*Time* magazine interviewed an individual who "took est a year ago, got the Zen message and plunged into depression. 'I was in a black hole for weeks. Nothing mattered, nothing would change' " (2334:54). Other personal accounts include:

> JANE: It certainly isn't nearly as important for me to be right anymore as it used to be. . . . What is important to me is what is happening to me right now. And I don't give a f— about tomorrow (1533:57).

> PHIL: It becomes apparent to you that the people whose lives aren't working are those who don't support that which supports them (1533:94).

> HANS: I am so lazy these days. . . . I don't care that much if people don't buy my work. . . . That is their problem. . . . For the first time I am running into a problem about paying the rent. And it doesn't really bother me (1533:62).

The above citations show the personal impact of Erhard's nihilistic and solipsistic philosophy. It removes the "burden" of social responsibilities. And people can indeed experience a sense of freedom when they think they do not need to be concerned about life's problems. In a high-pressure society, people could be expected to feel some sense of release upon believing that nothing is really significant. All at once, some social, financial, family, or job pressures would completely "disappear." But that would be a false sense of freedom.

In his ironically titled book *est: Making Life Work*, Robert Hargrove recalls that when he

began to understand the unreality of the world, he had the sensation of someone lifting an enormous rock off his head (2229:102). If nothing is real, or finally important, then a person is free to do whatever he wants, and he has no commitments, obligations, or values, unless he chooses them. This is nectar to the ears of sinners.

Of course, even though everything is an illusion, one can still agree to play the game (in est, "take responsibility"). But as a god, one can do whatever one wants, unhampered by the thought of any *ultimate* consequences that may result from his actions. One can play the game without worry. Although one created the laws of society, one can also just as easily ignore them. It is not morally wrong to do so. This might not work too well, but *so what?* Nothing is important unless a person decides to pretend that it is.

This helps to explain why people who were often justifiably critical of est before the training came out of it enthusiastically when their commonsense values had been undermined. Author Marcia Seligson recalled that initially she was skeptical. Indeed, after talking with est graduates and hearing Erhard speak, she had thoughts about Hitler, mass hypnosis, cultism, and Manson. She said, "It didn't seem just cuckoo; it seemed damn dangerous. . . . As far as I was concerned, est was the biggest rip-off . . . and I would expose it" (1534:165). But after the est training, her initial impressions were radically altered: "I think that est has been one of the truly powerful experiences in my life. And I love Werner Erhard" (1534:165). She became a member of est's advisory board.

Journalist Peter Marin hit the nail on the head when he said that est represents "a retreat from the worlds of morality and history, an unembarrassed denial of human reciprocity and community." He saw est and other narcissistic cults, like Arica and Scientology,* as "the growing solipsism and desperation of a beleaguered class, the world view emerging among us centered solely on the self and with individual survival as its sole good" (2335:46). His personal interviews with over a dozen est graduates strongly supported his views. He begins his analysis by referring to one woman graduate who said:

... that because of the training she now understood: (1) that the individual will is all-powerful and totally determines one's fate; (2) that she felt neither guilt nor shame about anyone's fate and that those who were poor and hungry must have wished it on themselves; (3) that the North Vietnamese must have wanted to be bombed, or else it could not have happened to them; (4) that a friend of hers who had been raped and murdered in San Francisco was to be pitied for having willed it to occur; (5) that in her weekend at est she had attained full enlightenment; (6) that she was God; (7) that whatever one thought to be true was true beyond all argument; (8) that I was also God, and that my ideas were also true, but not as true as hers because I had not had the training; and (9) that my use of logic to criticize her beliefs was unfair, because reason was "irrational," though she could not tell me why.

There is no telling whether or not this is precisely what she learned at est, and no doubt other adherents would deny it, but I have talked by now to at least a dozen of its enthusiasts, and each one of them has blankly recited to me, word for word, the same ill-taught and ignorant catechism (2335:46).

The success of the seminar rests largely on the deliberate emotional and psychological manipulation of its trainees. And it teaches them to do the same thing to others. Richard Farson comments on the "unconscious" message delivered by est:

My main concern about est comes from the fact that in any educational program, public schools included, people tend not to learn much about what is in the subject matter or content of the program but, at a deeper level, they learn the method by which the program is taught.... When people learn, as I believe they do in est, that it is acceptable, perhaps even necessary, to coerce, abuse, demean, incarcerate and exhaust people "for their own good" we have a classic means/ends dilemma and I'm afraid, the precondition for fascism (1476:202).

This sentiment is backed up by some graduates:

The training, carried to its natural conclusions philosophically and politically, makes it an almost fascistic organization. There are all the accouterments that one finds in fascism and other right wing ideologies. I have had trouble discussing this subject with other graduates because either they don't agree with me or they don't get what I am attempting to say (1533:205).

Erhard himself once stated in response to an article that referred to est as a "crypto-fascist, neo-Nazi organization" that "a free press was a small price to pay for full communication in a democratic society" (2229:45). One graduate remarked, "I see that they try to get you to do what they want you to do without letting you do what you want to do. And that's their game" (2336:76). Carl Frederick, in his book on est, said one may notice "that you're actually manipulating others. And you'll be right again. And at that point, you'll have another choice to make: whether to be the manipulator or to return to being manipulated. Because that's all there is" (2337:50). It is either win the game or lose it.

Thus, according to Erhard, social evil does not exist. If people want to play the "hunger game," let's play along. As for murderers or rapists, each has created the experience. Victims? They created that experience too. Nevertheless, the cruelty of such a perspective is evident.

## SOCIAL APATHY

With its insistence that everything is perfect the way it is, and that the truth ("what is so") is unimportant ("so what?"), est produces social apathy. Erhard states, "Perfection is a state in which things are the way they are, and are not the way they are not. As you can see, this universe is perfect. Don't lie about it" (2066).

But in America, concerned citizens need to be involved socially and morally, *especially* today. However, examine what Erhard's philosophy does to social involvement: To change something is counterproductive. As a trainer stated, "If you try to resist something or change something, it will become more solid. The only way to get rid of something is to just let it be. That doesn't mean ignore it.... To let something be means to observe it, stay in touch with it, but make no effort to change it (2067:44-45). Notice the following dialogue between a trainer and trainee:

Trainee (t): You seem to be saying that a good person should stop trying to avoid the bad.

Trainer (T): That's right, David.... Good people have been trying to eliminate badness for a million years and it doesn't work.

(t): It works better than not doing anything.

(T): Not so, David. I know the myth is that if we all believed in doing good and avoiding evil that all would be well. It's doing nothing that works (2067:58).

Erhard believes "happiness is a function of accepting what is" (2066). After all, what is, is; and what is, is perfect. Why be upset over anything, even if others in their ignorance assume it is evil or immoral? Anyway, trying to change society is futile. And since, as Erhard says, "In life, understanding is the booby prize" (2066), attempting to understand social problems is only getting the booby prize. One graduate clearly exemplifies the impact est has on a person's concept of social responsibility: "Since est, the world can be any way it wants. Fine with me.... So, I don't understand it. So what?" (2338:11).

The best est staff could do when confronted about the negative implications of their philosophy was to rationalize them away. One trainer said, "Being enlightened is choosing what happens when it happens.... Being enlightened is saying yes to what happens.... It doesn't mean that because everything is perfect as it is, we don't protest against war, or work to end poverty. ... No. Enlightenment means saying yes to what is for us, and if society is sick and needs changing, then we choose to work to change the sick society (2067:210).

Only the person who *thinks* society is sick (i.e., imperfect) will try to do something about it. But the est person is told that whatever is, is perfect, and that to try to change it makes it persist. And anyway, as trainers explain, each person sets up the whole game of making some things more important than others because this is necessary in order for a game to be a game. No won-

der so many graduates are socially apathetic! No wonder its founder could start a hunger project that is not really about feeding the hungry. The path of least resistance is always easiest. Graduates are so enthralled with flying the plane, they can't see the mountain ahead!

Should a trainer say that some people can work for social change, he is contradicting Erhard who teaches, "A thing is perfect when it is the way it is. When it is not the way it is, then it is flawed" (2338:12). Pat Marks, in her book on est, shows the practical result of Erhard's philosophy:

What about the evil in the world? And the sickness? And all the rest? Well, Werner says, "Perfection is a state in which things are the way they are and are not the way they are not." So the universe is perfect. I don't say it's always easy to agree with what's so, but it IS so, nevertheless. And I have come to the point now where my only prayer is to have the wisdom to choose the way things are, to embrace instead of to resist what's so (2336:49).

## EST AND CHILDREN

Another unfortunate consequence of est was its children's training. By training them young, est hoped to prevent the supposed "damage" they would encounter while growing up. In the first five years, est influenced more than 2000 children in California, Colorado, Hawaii, and New York. Thousands more attended trainings in the next decade. The Forum also has trainings for children.

In *A Look at est in Education*, Dr. R. W. Fuller and Z. Wallace sympathetically analyzed the impact of est on one private and four public elementary schools, two special education facilities, one public high school, and three universities. They discovered the following facts:

1) Children learn to experience their true Self, i.e., God-nature:

The activities of the est Children's Training, like those of the est Standard Training, are designed so that the participants begin the process of experiencing through these blocks and barriers [to the Self] and begin to experience and express this *SELF* (2339:7).

2) Via the training, children learn, "They know it doesn't matter if they're wrong" (2339:14).

3) The children are told by the trainer that "it's totally OK with me that you do these things." "These things" include insulting others, lying, not caring, committing suicide, and rebelling (2339:34). [The idea is supposedly to show the children these things don't "work"; but is it wise to imply that one does not care what they do? And in Erhard's philosophy, why wouldn't they work?]

4) The children's training also involves the following: "The experience of despair and nothingness intensifies throughout the rest of the day, as the trainer demonstrates that adults are in the same spot, in short, that *nothing works,* and that there is no escape. The training has been consciously designed so that at this point, the children feel that this is the way life is, and assume there is nothing they can do about it. After all, the students have experienced deeply that this is the way it is and they are feeling that there is simply no way out, the trainer points out that although life is that way, it can nonetheless be experienced as satisfying, by changing one's attitude toward it, a theme to be developed in the next two days of the training" (2339:34-35).

5) Scientology techniques, such as the following, were also used on the children for three to four *hours* (and could easily induce hypnotic states):

   1) "Touch your elbow. Good. Let go of your elbow. Fine. Touch your shoulder. Good. Keep touching your shoulder. Good. Let go of your shoulder. Thank you." This may continue for three to four hours.

   2) "Locate a spot. Thank you. Touch the spot. Good. Let go of the spot. Thank you. Locate another spot. Good. Touch the spot. Fine. Let go of the spot. Thank you." Again, this may continue for several hours (2339:38-39).

One wonders—since many adults become seriously depressed (some psychotic and suicidal) from est practice—what is the final impact on impressionable children? Think of the values: "Life is a game, NOTHING matters."

Yet est has a consuming interest in spreading its philosophy via the educational system. Erhard once stated, "My plans could be said to make est as public as possible. My notion on how to do that is through the educational system" (1346:6). By 1976, almost 15 percent of est graduates worked in areas of education, and at least 4000 of them desired to work with est to get it into education (1467:132; by 1995, the figure may have been as high as 30 percent).

At the Sydney School in Castro Valley, California, teachers who were est graduates instigated est seminar training for their second and third graders. *San Francisco Magazine* reported: "The reaction of parents and children was mixed. Parents reported discipline problems with children after the training" (1531:22). Surprise! According to Dr. Fuller, as a result of the training, children are "less into concepts of right/wrong as the basic orientation of life" (1533:171). Also, because of their perspective, trainers view even very troublesome children "as functioning perfectly" (1533:172).

Est graduate Carl Frederick, author of *est: Playing the Game the New Way,* believes that schools should be created for only one purpose: teaching children to follow their natural inclinations (2337:63). He instructs parents to "set up very few rules with kids," and to "get yourself out of the right/wrong game with your kids" (2337:118-19). Children already know where they are going, he says, and they will "get" that they are fine "unless you tamper with them" (2337:121).

Again, we see the influence of Scientology in est. The late L. Ron Hubbard, the founder of Scientology,* believed:

A child is a man or woman who has not attained full growth. Any law which applies to the behavior of men and women applies to the children. The child's possessions must remain under his exclusive control. So he tears up his shirt, wrecks his bed, breaks his fire engine. It's none of your business. In raising your child you must avoid "training" him into a social animal. Your child begins by being more sociable, more dignified than you are. Train him, control him, and you'll lose his love. . . . Care for the child?—Nonsense! He's probably got a better grasp of immediate situations than you have.

Only when he's almost psychotic with aberrations will a child be accident-prone (2342).

After all, the Self in the child is equal to the Self in the adult: omnipotent, omniscient God. Phyllis Allen, who conducted the children's training, stated that during the training, children discover, "They are limitless, they are infinite" (2346:4). Frederick closes his advice on children with the following "absolute truth" for adults: "Finally, you'll get to the absolute truth: that you CREATED the game called kids, and that you're winning that one too. What else is there?" (2337:122).

This "game" could get rough for parents who are foolish enough to permit their children to take the training. One eight-year-old boy who went through est was asked by his mother what he had gotten from the training. She said, "He just looked at me calmly and said, 'I don't really need you' " (1467:140). The mother had a *real* hard time with that.

At the beginning of our chapter, we cited one of est's top staff members, Dr. William Bartley, describing est as "a way of teaching philosophy . . . more effective than anything else I've encountered" (1533:174). We think it was also effective on children, and that the training the schoolchildren received damaged their psychological and spiritual health. No one should think children were never affected by est, or that they aren't being affected by The Forum. Children are more impressionable than adults and can be influenced much easier. Est/The Forum and Erhard talk a lot about "love." We believe that love of children demands concern over any program that feeds them Erhard's philosophy.

## THEOLOGY

The est organization claimed that est did not interfere with anyone's religious beliefs, and that it was not at variance with the Bible or Christianity (so does The Forum). Letters of recommendation from Christian pastors, Catholic priests, and Jewish rabbis were and still are quoted in support of the seminars. Erhard's philosophy may not interfere with the beliefs of New Agers and others who are like-minded religiously, but we will now document that est does interfere with most religious beliefs, particularly if one is Jewish, Catholic, or Christian. And, since Erhard's philosophy is at issue here, the same is true for The Forum. (Another section illustrates contrasts between Erhard's views and biblical teachings.)

*Christianity*

Above we cited Erhard's admission that "in a seminary, I would have been burned as a witch" (2730:35). It is not hard to see why. In est there is no meaning or reason behind a person's choices. People choose to do something because and *only* because they choose to do it (2067:212-15). A person who chooses to make Jesus Christ his Lord and Savior is not doing so out of love for God to be saved from God's wrath against sin, or because it is right. Choosing to follow Jesus is equal to choosing something in any other area. The personal decision is made only because of one's choosing. In est the concept of the choice to believe in Jesus Christ for personal salvation, for forgiveness of sins, represents a very unenlightened attitude, to say the least:

*Concepts* are meaningless and keep one's life from working.

*Choices* are made only because they are made.

*Beliefs* exist at the highest level of untruth and uncertainty. Belief systems are what one gets stuck in to prove he's "right."

*Christ* never existed until man thought Him up.

*Personality* is illusion.

*Salvation* is a belief. Nothing will ever save man because there's nothing to be saved from.

*Forgiveness* is not needed. Everyone already has it.

*Sin* is a useless concept. Good and evil are just concepts that have no meaning.

As Kevin Garvey noted in *Christianity Today*, "Est hammers away at previously held perceptions of reality, particularly a Christian world view. . . . Erhard is adamantly opposed to Christianity, to the need for repentance, and forgiveness" (2347:15). A Christian working in est/The Forum would immediately face a conflict over obeying either Erhard or Christ, for "Erhard, despite his occasional disclaimers, is to est what Christ is to Christianity" (2691:54).

To be successful in est/The Forum, the Christian must abandon trust and belief in God and Christ, moral views, and views on salvation—in other words, everything Christian. If he is unwilling to totally abandon Christ, he is "stuck" on Christ, and this is evil (2192:4). Est author William Green affirms that "part of the purpose of the est training is to break away from this sense of being right" (1347:29).

In est/The Forum, a strong faith in Jesus Christ is a serious barrier to discovering one's true self. Est aimed at breaking down all barriers that cover or hide one's supposedly divine nature. Est "means throwing away all of the beliefs, concepts, and logic that you have heretofore known and understood" (1347:153).

Since est and The Forum are opposed to Christian principles and doctrine, one expects the training to move people away from, or insulate them against, Jesus Christ:

I've read the Bible a lot, and now I see that the church totally misinterpreted what Jesus said. He kept telling everyone over and over that everybody was like he was: perfect. He was experiencing life, like Werner. He knew he was total source, living moment to moment, and was spontaneous.

Jesus is just another guru who happens to be popular here in Western civilization. I can't go into a church and praise Jesus. But I really got where he is coming from. He wants to let everybody know "I'm you." So my whole point of view about religion has been totally altered (1467:182).

*The Washington Star* presented one Episcopal clergyman's reaction to est as follows:

The est training validly tries to jar us from a common religious mistake—to reduce God to words, belief systems and credal formularies and to pass that on as enough! . . . In the est

process of going to my inner center, I became more acutely aware of the all-knowing, God aspect of myself. So the Christ I try to tap is the Christ within me, rather than the one projected out onto somebody else. . . . I don't think he (Jesus) would want us all to look at him and adore him and magnify him, but rather to look and discover that power within ourselves (2070:13).

Unfortunately, several Christians have told the authors that the effect of est impoverished their spiritual lives for years. Est confused or spiritually impacted even apparently relatively mature Christians.

Several Christians who had participated in the early est trainings were kind enough to answer brief questions in multiple-choice fashion. All expressed concern as to how long it would take for the powerful effects of est to wear off. Even today, years later, some of these people still suffer the negative consequences of est on their Christian lives. Their answers are starred.

1. How did the training effect you emotionally?

   a. positively
   b. no effect
   c.* negatively

2. In what ways did the training obstruct or hamper your Christian life and walk?

   a  no effect
   b.* in subtle ways almost too hard to explain
   c.* personal morality
   d.* Bible study and reading habits
   e.* fellowship
   f.* by thinking of the world and myself in est terms rather than biblical terms

3. By what percent did est interfere with your growth as a Christian?

   a. zero percent
   b. 10 to 30 percent
   c. 30 to 60 percent
   d.* 60 to 90 percent

4. How long did it take for the anti-Christian effect of the est training to wear off entirely?

a. one month
b. six months
c. one year
d. two years
e. three years
f.* four years or more
g. it will never entirely be gone

5. How long did it take for *most* of the effects to wear off?

a. six months
b. one year
c. two years
d. three years
e.* four or more years

6. What is the most destructive effect of est in your experience?

a.* general morality
b.* business and social life
c.* family and married life
d.* inner life (psychological-emotional)
e.* spiritual life

7. What has been the effect of est on your friends who have taken the training?

a. they are better people, morally and socially
b.* they act more selfishly
c.* they are less able to cope with reality
d.* they show an increase of energy
e.* they use est to justify doing what they want

In the following material we will briefly examine Erhard's view of God and salvation, which help to explain the above answers.

*God and Jesus Christ*

Erhard's concept of God is primarily Eastern religious. This philosophical orientation demands contradictory statements, "As a matter of fact, the heart of est is spiritual people, really. You see, I don't know anyone who is not spiritual.... That's all there is, there isn't anything but spirituality, which is just another word for God, because God is everything.... Of course, I think *not* being spiritual is also being spiritual" (1346:4).

Luke Rhinehart, whose book on est "had each page ... checked by an est trainer" to ensure ac-

curacy, notes that his est trainer made several points about God:

• Having a belief in God kills God. (Remember, in est "beliefs" are the lowest level of knowledge.) As long as a person lives in his "belief" in God, it causes God to cease to exist.

• In order to experience God, you must not have a belief about God.

• Man is the true God (2067:25-27,38,216-17)

Hence, the trainer stated in one of his conversations with a trainee: "Look Jerry, don't give me your G— d— belief systems. They don't work. If you want to share with me your actual experience of God, that I would be interested in, but ideas about God are deadly. They're so deep in the scale of nonexperience, they're less substantial than ghosts" (2067:25).

Elsewhere the trainer states: "*ALL* belief is the least reliable form of knowing. Belief represents UNcertainty. People believe in God because they have no real certainty about Her. Where there is a [mystical] natural knowing of God, there is no need for belief. The highest form of certainty is something you know so thoroughly and so naturally that it's impossible to put into words" (2067:38).

The trainer also wants to know, "What do you know about God? Any of you? Who's God? Don't give me your religious s—" (2067:137). And, "[You] don't know Him, never experienced Him, wouldn't know Him if you met Him, and besides, she's black" (2227). Erhard states: "When you *think* you have experienced God, you haven't" (1467:199; cf. 2067:113). No wonder Erhard claims, "To pay attention to personality [e.g., as the Bible speaks of God] is to pay attention to an illusion" (1346:2).

By comparison, Scripture declares that one can both *think* about and *know* that he has experienced God. Jesus said to "love the Lord your God with all your heart and with all your soul and with all your *mind*" (Matthew 22:37). And if we *believe* in Jesus, "The Spirit Himself *bears witness* with our spirit that we are children of God" (Romans 8:16 NASB). The apostle John wrote, "But you have an anointing from the Holy One, and *you all know*. I have not written to you because you do not know the truth, but because you do know it, and because *no lie is of the truth*" (1 John 2:20-21 NASB). The Bible also teaches:

> And it is the Spirit who bears witness, because the *Spirit is the truth*. . . . The one who believes in the Son of God has the witness in himself; the one who does not believe God has made Him a liar, because he has not believed in the witness that God has borne concerning His Son.

> And the witness is this, that God has *given* us eternal life, and this life is *in His Son*. He who *has* the Son has the life; he who does *not* have the Son of God does not have the life. These things I have written to you who believe in the name of the Son of God, in order that you may *know* that you have eternal life (1 John 5:7,10-13 NASB).

Biblically, it is impossible for a person to come to know and experience God apart from belief in Jesus Christ. But Erhard declares in *The East-West Journal*, "I believe that the 'belief' in God is the greatest barrier to God in the universe—the single greatest barrier. I would prefer someone who is ignorant to someone who believes in God. Because the belief in God is a total barrier, almost a total barrier to the experience of God" (1346:2). To the contrary, in Hebrews 11:6 we read, "And without faith it is impossible to please God, because anyone who comes to him must *believe* that he exists and that he rewards those who earnestly seek him."

In the same journal, Erhard, in so many words, blasphemously implies that Jesus Christ is dog excrement, though he uses the four-letter equivalent (1346:4). This is the same man who, incredibly, declares, "I consider myself one of Christ's staunchest supporters" (2724:3). He has even suggested that he is the reincarnation of Jesus Christ (2697:42).

The following statements from several est graduates also show est's anti-Christian view of God:

> Jim: It is a belief in yourself as God creating everything. . . . You are God and you create everything around you and you create the universe (1533:101).

Alan: To get at the [est] concept of your "sourcing" . . . where you can recognize yourself as the source of everything, you are in effect recognizing your own Godhood (1533:212).

Carol: We created this universe. It is just ideas. . . . My experience with est was enlightenment and that I am the center of the universe. I emanate it, I create it continually (1533:66,69).

*Salvation*

According to Erhard, man is already perfect the way he is and needs nothing. He just does not yet realize that this is his true spiritual condition. This is why Erhard says, "Est *IS TRYING TO ACCOMPLISH WHAT IS ALREADY SO*. . . . Actually the four days of training are wasted. It [enlightenment]* happens like that (snap fingers)" (1346:3). Est argued that since people are already divine and perfect just as they are, they certainly have no need of salvation in a biblical sense. They are already "saved:—fully and completely" (2229:53,55). All they really need is est-enlightenment as to their true spiritual condition.

Obviously, this is not the biblical view, because "all have sinned and fall short of the glory of God" (Romans 3:23). Because only Jesus Christ paid the divine penalty for sin on the cross (1 Peter 2:24; 1 John 2:2), only He can provide salvation. "Now this is eternal life: that they may *know* you, the *only* true God, and Jesus Christ, whom you have sent" (John 17:3). "For God so loved the world that he gave his one and only Son, that whoever *believes* in him shall not perish but have eternal life" (John 3:16).

Apart from personal faith in Jesus Christ, no one can be saved. Jesus Himself said, "I am the way, and the truth, and the life; no one comes to the Father, but through Me" (John 14:6 NASB). He also emphasized that "unless you repent, you too will all perish" (Luke 13:5). And, "if you do not believe I am the one I claim to be, you will indeed die in your sins" (John 8:24). Acts 4:12 (NASB) declares that "there is salvation in no one else; for there is no other name under heaven that has been given among men, by which we must be saved."

Werner Erhard denies what Jesus taught about salvation. He writes:

We've been conditioned to look for answers outside ourselves. But that's not what people get from us. What they get is an experience of enlightenment, which is different from the belief system called salvation. If I get the idea that God is going to save me, therefore I'm all right, that's salvation; if I get the idea that nothing's going to save me, therefore I'm all right, that's enlightenment (1534:204).

Here we can see that the philosophy of Erhard is opposed to the very core of Christianity. Anyone who accepted such views would conclude that they have no need whatsoever to turn to Jesus Christ for personal salvation from sin. Remember, according to Erhard, truth and reality are found in est-experience alone. "Belief" is detrimental. "Belief" is defined as "the act of placing trust or confidence in a concept or conviction and accepting it as Truth." According to Erhard, this "makes it a lie" (2066), because "beliefs prevent an individual from experiencing life" (1347:29).

Of course, this is only the *belief* of Erhard, isn't it? Regardless, according to est, Christian faith or belief prevents one from experiencing life and is fundamentally opposed to truth and reality. In essence, Christians are living a lie. As one est trainer put it, est attempts to "systematically cut off all hope . . . that any external sources will ever save you" (2693:2). One graduate learned that "est is not going to save mankind; mankind is going to have to save itself. I got this point so clearly that I won't forget it ever again" (1759:46).

*Eastern Religions and the Occult*

Several graduates told us that the est training opened their understanding of the metaphysical concepts in Eastern and occult literature, and that as a result they seriously considered pursuing the Eastern path (see 2336:66,77). In an interview with Erhard, *The East-West Journal* asked, "Some people say that est is a bridge between the traditional churches and the Eastern masters. People who graduate from est usually end up with an Eastern teacher. How do you feel about that?" Erhard replied, "I think it happens to some people. Once you know that you can play any game well, once you are guided, all nurtures. I just happen to like Eastern games, so est is a lot of that kind of thing: but it is done so that it is to-

tally acceptable to Westerners, so they come out of the Training and they begin to hear little things that come from Eastern things and they say, 'Oh, that came from est, I'll look into that' " (1346:6).

Erhard has long had close friendships or associations with a number of Eastern gurus,* and he supports their work wholeheartedly. This includes Hindu gurus like the late Swami Muktananda, Satya Sai Baba, and Tibetan Buddhist leaders such as the Gyalwa Karmapa and the Dali Lama (1899:274/2694:2-7). In recalling the purpose of his many trips to Asia, he writes that it was to acknowledge his spiritual parents. Here we again see the importance of Eastern metaphysics to Erhard's philosophical worldview. "It was very much like the purpose of other trips I've made to visit Yogi masters in India and Zen masters in Japan. The fundamental purpose was an acknowledgment and a completion of my relationship with my spiritual ancestors. . . . With my spiritual parents" (2694:2).

Tibetan Buddhism is a powerful occult religion whose teachings and practices may easily lead to spiritism or demonization. This can be documented from the literature of Tibetan Buddhist gurus. In the following statement by Erhard, therefore, we think it is significant that he recognizes the similarity between the experience of enlightenment* in Tibetan Buddhism and est. Commenting on his visits with Gyalwa Karmapa the sixteenth and the impact of est, Erhard states, "One of the things we spoke about was my interest in Tibetan Buddhism—because part of my understanding of Tibetan Buddhism is that its principles are closely related to the realizations which people have as a function of their experience in est. . . . It seems that graduates learn for themselves, out of their experience, things that are very close to what's said in Tibetan Buddhism" (2694:3).

Erhard also states: "I would say that whatever the experience of Buddhism is, it is certainly consistent with the experience of est" (2694:4). And he reveals his personal commitment to the expansion of an Eastern spirituality when he states, "We [graduates] all have a responsibility, those of us who have the opportunity to make masters from the East available to other people, to support the whole tradition" (2694:7).

In developing est, Erhard incorporated a great deal from the occult religion of Scientology.* In *Mindstyles, Lifestyles,* Nathaniel Lande points out some of the connections:

> Many est graduates are going to find it hard to accept that almost everything est teaches about communication, acknowledgment, agreement, and responsibility comes directly from Scientology.
>
> Intimates of Erhard like [Charles] Manson acknowledge that before starting est he completed the Scientology communication course and the first four grades of Scientology training. Any est graduate who really wants to remember those seemingly forgotten lectures of the training only has to look at the Scientology textbooks for those grades and the axioms from L. Ron Hubbard's *Creation of Human Ability* to recapture the experience (2226:142-43).

Erhard's discussion on ethics also closely parallels Scientology* ideas, such as given in founder L. Ron Hubbard's *Introduction to Scientology Ethics.* Ethics has no concern about being right or wrong, or with morality, but "exists to get technology [results] in." If an est staff member had "low stats," that is, he was not getting enough recruits, he became an ethics target. "Proper ethics action" is always to first look up a person's statistics, and then judge his case in light of them. A staff person who has been reported to the ethics officer for misdemeanors or crimes is "judged" in light of his production output. He may have committed immoral deeds, but if his statistics are up, it is of little concern to ethics. The following section of the est *Basic Staff Book* contains the essence of an L. Ron Hubbard "HCO letter" for September 1965:

> We are not in the business of being good boys and girls. We're in the business of producing results and serving human purposes. Nothing else is of any interest then to Ethics but getting production up and the enterprise roaring along. Therefore, if a member of the enterprise is getting the enterprise's production up . . . Ethics sure isn't interested [in anything else]. But if a member isn't producing, shown by his bad stats for his post, ethics is fascinated with his small-

est misdemeanor. In short a person can get away with murder as long as his stats are up, and cannot sneeze without a chop if they're down.**

Part of the est teaching also involved a discussion of the occult concept of the "Akashic Records," purportedly a "psychic storehouse" of data on everything that has ever happened. Only people who develop psychic powers can "tune into" these "records" to read past lives or see into the future (2229:112-13/1347:163). Occult aspects of est can also be found in est's use of hypnosis,* consciousness projection, employment of psychic advisers (probably developed from Silva Mind Control;* 2695).

During one session, trainers had each person construct a mental space, or center, that they could enter to meditate, gain power, see into the past, do telepathy, go out of the body, and so on (2067:155). Coming out of this "space" requires a gradual desensitization, much like in hypnosis* and other altered states, presumably to avoid a shock to the body (2067:40-41,79-93). Trainees were eventually given instructions on how to psychically create a male or female helper who would then be invited into their center, who, much like the traditional spirit guide, would advise them on matters and do other things for them (2067:155-61/1347:30). Again, much of this appears to be borrowed from Silva Mind Control.* And, as in SMC, these advisers are not always imaginary. One est participant found two real entities in his mind. They said that they were there to serve him and to give him power, which is what mediums' and occultists' spirit guides claim as their function (2067:158-59). Sometimes even the alleged dead would appear to graduates and give messages (2067:161).

This reveals that some people were able to open themselves up to spiritism or channeling* because all the needed ingredients were present: passivity, hypnotic-like altered states of consciousness,* and the "helpers." Spirits would

---

**The only copy of the *Basic Staff Book* we could obtain was a poor Xerox without bibliographic data; however, its condition was sufficient to quote from.

enter a person's life under various guises (for example, a dead family member), and then start influencing and subtly controlling the person. Obviously, the participants were not always controlling these "exercises," because even when they constructed a particular person, sometimes someone else would appear.

Est trainers themselves apparently have some degree of occult power similar to that of gurus, mediums, and other occultists. Robert Hargrove, former editor and publisher of *The East-West Journal*, describes the presence of his trainer as akin to the "influence of a supernatural or divine spirit felt to be present" (2229:83). In Erhard's own life, supernatural incidents have occurred that are common to mediums and occultists (2067:243-44/2229:168-69,183-84).

For our research on est, we asked the most knowledgeable graduate that we knew about est in general and the occult in particular. Mary was an early est convert and a very good friend of Stuart Emery, the first est trainer and founder of Actualizations. After attending the third est training in Aspen, Colorado (John Denver was present), Mary began preparing to be a trainer. She assisted with the first children's course, and then took the training six more times. She taught the "Be Here Now" seminar and helped manage the Aspen office for several years. She knew all the est staff well, including Erhard. One of her problems was, "I could never quite understand that I was God; I fought against that, called it self-defeatism, etc." Here are several questions we asked Mary:

Q: Is it clear that among the est staff the teaching is that each person is God?

A: It is. That's what Werner taught.

Q: What's the goal of est?

A: Werner wants to reach millions of people with est, until it "dies out" naturally as a phase of the expanding planetary consciousness. Est will then have been given over or assimilated into the environment. . . . But it led me down a tunnel of darkness. It was getting very, very bad, and I was experiencing spirits and oppression that had not happened before.

Q: Was Werner very close to Muktananda?

A: Yes, oh yes. Oh yes. Oh yes . . . it was a very tight relationship . . . very good friends.

Q: Looking back as a Christian, do you think est is something a Christian should do?

A: NO, definitely not. I hung onto est for a long, long time because est gave me power and security, but with the Lord, it is the opposite—a real submission to Him, not a desire for power. Est led me down a path that was unfruitful. It led me toward looking to myself, and it didn't produce any love in me. It produced a hunger after power, a thirst after strength that I could do it all, and I could manipulate others as needed, and there was nothing I couldn't do. In est, to look to Christ for help is blasphemy. I never questioned their morality. I was so wrapped up in est. People just don't see the moral implications. Anyway, it's all just a game.

Q: In the est philosophy, you create whatever happens to you. If you get raped, robbed, you did it to yourself.

A: Yes. You created it. You did it. I remember when (skier) Spider Savitz (whom I knew personally) was killed. That morning I broke down and cried, but my girlfriend said, "So what. He got it! He created it!" There's just no compassion. One of our friends, Patti, committed suicide and we all felt she created it. That was what she wanted. Another died from a drug overdose. That was *her* fault. On a scale of 0 to 100, I think est is 100 percent bad. It takes you away from the Lord. It's deceitful. . . . Est did not lead me into a fuller experience of love.

Q: That's interesting, because Erhard is always talking about love.

A: I don't believe it. I don't believe he knows what real love is, or has any realization of true love. It's a counterfeit.

Q: Do you feel est could open people to the spirit world?

A: Yes. It led me to the spirit world, and there are incidents of people making spirit contact from the practice of inviting "people" into their [mental] center.

Q: The training, it seems, can be very cruel to some people. Can you give an example?

A: There was a boy in a training who broke his back in a ski accident and was paralyzed from the waist down. Werner spent two hours trying to convince him it was his fault that he landed the way he did because he chose to, and that if he would accept creatorship of the situation and experience it, he would walk again. The boy wanted desperately to walk again, but became very upset over this. I don't know whatever happened to him.

In conclusion, if est/The Forum and related New Age Seminars are anything, they are a symptom of what's wrong with our society. When a nation rejects the one true God, it logically opens itself to anything and everything, even the perverse as it seeks blindly for that which only God can provide.

*Comparing est and the Bible*

The following are comparisons between biblical passages and statements by Werner Erhard, est trainers, and est graduates. They indicate how consistently the ideas of Erhard oppose biblical teachings. (All Bible verses here are taken from the New American Standard version.)

| EST | BIBLE |
|---|---|
| **BAD LANGUAGE** | |
| *William Green, est graduate and author*: Foul language is ever present in the training (1347:139). | Let no unwholesome word proceed from your mouth, but only such a word as is good for edification according to the need of the moment, that it may give grace to those who hear. And do not grieve the Holy Spirit of God, by whom you were sealed for the day of redemption (Ephesians 4:29-30). |
| **CHRISTIAN RESPONSIBILITY** | |
| *Est graduate*: You can't change the world. Things are the way they are (2227). | You are the salt of the earth.... You are the light of the world.... Let your light shine before men in such a way that they may see your good works, and glorify your Father who is in heaven (Matthew 5:13-16). These men who have upset the world have come here also (Acts 17:6). |
| **LOVE** | |
| *Werner Erhard*: In other words, when submission or resistance are the only two alternatives, there isn't any love. I can't love you if I submit to you (1533:195-96). [In est, loving a person means being perfectly willing to let them be any way they want.] There is the nonjudgmental, nonevaluative acceptance in Zen of everything that is, as it is. I call this love, and in the Orient it is sometimes called compassion (1707:123). I might *have* love for you or *do* love for you but I *am* not loving you. Having or doing love can be gratifying, need-fulfilling, [but] cannot be satisfying, whole or complete (2696:121). | For God so loved the world, that He gave His only begotten Son, that whoever believes in Him should not perish, but have eternal life (John 3:16). And this is love, that we walk according to His commandments (2 John 6). Do nothing from selfishness or empty conceit, but with humility of mind let each of you regard one another as more important than himself (Philippians 2:3). Let love be without hypocrisy. Abhor what is evil; cling to what is good. Be devoted to one another in brotherly love; give preference to one another in honor (Romans 12:9-10). |

| EST | BIBLE |
|---|---|

### HEAVEN

| | |
|---|---|
| *Pat Marks, est author and graduate:* There is no plateau of forever-after, where there is nothing that goes wrong, and nothing to upset us and everything is perfect (2336:99). | But lay up for yourselves treasures in heaven, where neither moth nor rust destroys, and where thieves do not break in or steal (Matthew 6:20). <br><br> Then the righteous will shine forth as the sun in the kingdom of their Father. He who has ears, let him hear (Matthew 13:43). <br><br> But according to His promise we are looking for new heavens and a new earth, in which righteousness dwells (2 Peter 3:13). |

### STRIVING FOR HOLINESS

| | |
|---|---|
| *Werner Erhard:* That's what people do with their [behavior] patterns; they submit to them or they resist them. . . . It doesn't make any difference whether you submit or resist. It's exactly the same (1533:195). <br><br> TRYING is a belief, a concept that does not exist in experience, and is employed for self-defeat (2227). | Only conduct yourselves in a manner worthy of the gospel of Christ; so that whether I come and see you or remain absent, I may hear of you that you are standing firm in one spirit, with one mind striving together for the faith of the gospel (Philippians 1:27). <br><br> And for this purpose also I labor, striving according to His power, which mightily works within me (Colossians 1:29). <br><br> Now I urge you, brethren, by our Lord Jesus Christ and by the love of the Spirit, to strive together with me in your prayers to God for me (Romans 15:30). |

### GOD'S WILL

| | |
|---|---|
| *Werner Erhard:* What[ever] you're doing is what God wants you to do (2066). | I urge you therefore, brethren, by the mercies of God, to present your bodies a living and holy sacrifice, acceptable to God, which is your spiritual service of worship. And do not be conformed to this world, but be transformed by the renewing of your mind, that you may prove what the will of God is, that which is good and acceptable and perfect (Romans 12:1-2). |

### SELFISHNESS

| | |
|---|---|
| *Est graduate:* I take responsibility for the people that let me step on them, and don't feel guilty (1531:26). | Let no one seek his own good, but that of his neighbor (1 Corinthians 10:24). |

### THE SPIRITUAL CONDITION OF MAN

| | |
|---|---|
| *Werner Erhard:* I happen to think you are perfect exactly the way you are (2066). <br><br> *Carl Frederick, est graduate and author: You* are the supreme being (2733:171). | There is none righteous, not even one; . . . for all have sinned and fall short of the glory of God (Romans 3:10,23). <br><br> Because your heart is lifted up and you have said, "I am a god. . . . yet you are a man and not God (Ezekiel 28:2). |

| EST | BIBLE |
|---|---|
| **MAN CREATED IN THE IMAGE OF GOD (THE DIGNITY OF MAN)** ||
| *Est trainer*: You're machines.... You've never been anything else except machines.... Your lives are meaningless.... Machines don't have goals... ideals... morals. Nothing's important. Everything is as worthless as everything else (2067:195,197). | And God created man in His own image (Genesis 1:27). Yet Thou hast made him a little lower than God, and dost crown him with glory and majesty (Psalm 8:5). I will give thanks to Thee, for I am fearfully and wonderfully made; wonderful are Thy works, and my soul knows it very well (Psalm 139:14). |
| **JESUS CHRIST** ||
| *Werner Erhard*: How do I know I'm not the reincarnation of Jesus Christ? You wouldn't believe the feelings I have inside me (2697:42). | And Jesus answered and said to them, "See to it that no one misleads you. For many will come in My name, saying, 'I am the Christ,' and will mislead many" (Matthew 24:4-5). |
| **WITNESSING** ||
| *Werner Erhard*: The truth believed is a lie. If you go around preaching the truth, you are lying. The truth can only be experienced (1467:55). | Go therefore and make disciples of all the nations, baptizing them in the name of the Father and the Son and the Holy Spirit, teaching them to observe all that I commanded you; and lo, I am with you always, even to the end of the age (Matthew 28:19-20). |
| **REPENTANCE** ||
| *Werner Erhard*: Realize you're all right the way you are and you'll get better naturally (2066). | I tell you, no, but unless you repent, you will all likewise perish (Luke 13:3). |
| **HUMILITY** ||
| *Werner Erhard/Trainer*: If you accept what you call your ego and ride with it it's okay. It's no more necessary to get rid of what you call your ego than it is to get rid of your bald spot: let them both shine forth. If you've got an ego, ride with it, let it go (2067:89-90). | But He gives a greater grace. Therefore it says, "God is opposed to the proud, but gives grace to the humble" (James 4:6). |
| **COMPASSION** ||
| *Werner Erhard*: We in the West have this really strange notion that it's "good" to be compassionate and therefore it's "bad" not to be compassionate. And the whole meaning of compassion is lost if you make it "good" or "right," to put it in more accurate terms—if you make it righteous (2694:7). | But love your enemies, and do good, and lend, expecting nothing in return; and your reward will be great, and you will be sons of the Most High; for He Himself is kind to ungrateful and evil men. Be merciful, just as your Father is merciful (Luke 6:35-36). |

| EST | BIBLE |
|---|---|
| **GOD/PRIDE** ||
| *Est trainer*: God is a CONCEPT. God is b———. There is nobody in the universe more powerful than you (2227). | Do you say, "My righteousness is more than God's"? (Job 35:2). Where were you when I laid the foundation of the earth? Tell Me, if you have understanding (Job 38:4). |
| **ON SEEKING/SEARCHING FOR GOD** ||
| *Werner Erhard*: What the f— are you looking for? This is it! There is nothing to find! You've found it! There is nothing in life but this! There is no tomorrow! Tomorrow is today. There is nothing, nothing, nothing! This is it! (2698:34). | Seek the Lord while He may be found; call upon Him while He is near. Let the wicked forsake his way, and the unrighteous man his thoughts; let him return to the LORD, and He will have compassion on him; and to our God, for He will abundantly pardon (Isaiah 55:6-7). |
| **THE RESURRECTION** ||
| *Est trainer*: ALL belief is the least reliable form of knowing. Belief represents uncertainty. People believe in God because they have no real certainty about her. . . . A belief is a statement that does *NOT COME OUT OF EXPERIENCE*. "Christ died and on the third day rose from the dead." . . . It's a belief (2067:38,46). | For we did not follow cleverly devised tales when we made known to you the power and coming of our Lord Jesus Christ, but we were eyewitnesses of His majesty (2 Peter 1:16). To these He also presented Himself alive, after His suffering, by many convincing proofs, appearing to them over a period of forty days, and speaking of the things concerning the kingdom of God (Acts 1:3). |
| **RESISTING SATAN AND SIN** ||
| *Est trainer*: If you try to resist something or change something, it will become more solid. The only way to get rid of something is just to let it be. . . . To let something be means to observe it, stay in touch with it, but make no effort to change it (2067:44-45). | Resist the devil and he will flee from you (James 4:7). Do not be deceived: "Bad company corrupts good morals." Become sober-minded as you ought, and stop sinning; for some have no knowledge of God. I speak this to your shame (1 Corinthians 15:33-34). |
| **FAITH** ||
| *Werner Erhard*: If you experience it, it's the truth. The same thing believed is a lie (2066). *Est trainer*: Belief is a disease. A belief system is a myth (2227). | And without faith it is impossible to please Him, for he who comes to God must believe that He is, and that He is a rewarder of those who seek Him (Hebrews 11:6). |
| **ON MAN AS CREATOR** ||
| *Werner Erhard*: You're god in your universe. You caused it. . . . [The] individual created himself, and in the Training, he gets an opportunity to re-experience the fact that he created himself (2066/1346). | Know that the LORD Himself is God; it is He who has made us, and not we ourselves (Psalm 100:3). |

| EST | BIBLE |
|---|---|
| ON EVIL | |
| So EST is evil, what's the point? Yea, I got that, now what? So what? (1088:10). | Do not be overcome by evil, but overcome evil with good (Romans 12:21). |
| TRUTH | |
| *Werner Erhard*: The truth doesn't mean anything. It just is (2066). | God [is] Truth (Psalm 31:5). If you abide in My word . . . you shall know the truth, and the truth shall make you free (John 8:31-32). |

## PSYCHOPATHOLOGY AND PSYCHOSIS

In *Biosciences Communications*, Erhard made the following claim: "In our research, we have asked independent investigators to look very carefully at the issue of harm. And while I am not fully qualified to discuss the intricacies of research, I can report that none of the research has shown any evidence that est produces harm" (2696:113).

Erhard was wrong. Although some therapists enthusiastically supported est as a treatment modality, others had serious reservations. New York certified clinical psychologist Herb Michelson stated that est was "faddish, potentially dangerous, experimental and dehumanizing" (2227). *Psychology Today* editor T. George Harris wrote: "Bruce Ogilvie in the Counseling Center at San Jose State University and a few other clinicians are treating est casualties. The stripping down of defense and belief leave some people in serious trouble" (1759:25). Psychiatrist Lloyd Maglen confirms, "I've also seen several people who have become psychotic and had to be hospitalized" (1759:356).

Dr. Elayne Kahn, assistant professor at City University of New York, encouraged several of her patients to take est, thinking it might help them. "After having observed the results of the training, Dr. Kahn now feels that 'the dangers outweigh any benefits—and, in any case, I don't see any lasting effectiveness: I see increased rigidity and a self-deprecatory dependence on est. The totalitarian methods employed by the trainers breed self-centeredness; est fosters psychopathic attitudes'" (2227).

Psychologist Dr. Sheridan Fenwick, who is with Columbia University, discussed est casualties who were under psychiatric care. She gave an interesting account of the est organization's reactions to those therapists who openly expressed critical attitudes: "An internal memorandum from a staff member to the president of the est corporation describes plans to 'handle' certain psychologists and psychiatrists who have been publicly critical of est" (2699:159,174).

The first published study in professional literature on the harmful effects of est training is found in the March and November 1977 issues of the *American Journal of Psychiatry*. Part One, "Psychiatric Disturbances Associated with Erhard Seminars Training: 1. A Report of Cases" details five cases, which were said to "represent a segment of est trainees who came to our attention in a variety of emergency psychiatric settings." Part Two examined two other cases. One reason for the article was to warn psychotherapeutic professionals of potential hazards resulting from est. Leonard Glass, one of the three psychiatrists who authorized the articles, warned that "there's enough possibility of a real connection between est and psychotic breaks to cause us to want to alert psychiatrists and psychologists." Part One stated that "the spread of the est 'movement' and the gravity of the cases that have come to our attention contribute a sense of urgency and importance to the communication of these preliminary findings" (2700:245-47).

The findings also noted that 1) the est lectures "borrow heavily from psychoanalytic theory, Jungian psychology, transactional analysis and Eastern philosophy," and that 2) the processes utilize "Gestalt, relaxation, guided imagery and psychodrama techniques." Of the seven cases discussed, six people developed psychotic reactions, some life-threatening. Five of the seven people had no previous psychiatric illness or treatment and neither was it found in their family history (2700:245-47). This report and others showed that est was psychologically damaging to some people. But est was also dangerous in other ways.

## SUICIDE

Suicide was also a potential problem, as some est leaders themselves acknowledged. Former est trainer Stewart Emery, the founder of Actualizations, remarked, "I had one person in a workshop who was considering committing suicide because he believed he had created the suicide of a member of his family" (2701:12). Pat Marks details an interview with an est staff member, who noted, "One of my roommates took the training because I had been so high on it, and she had a totally different reaction. And at one point she got so depressed that she tried to commit suicide" (2336:126-27).

William Greene tells of one man who said "he had seriously considered committing suicide during the week because . . . est had really made him realize that he hadn't done a single thing of importance in his life. He didn't see how he could justify going on under those circumstances" (1347:83). Philosopher-historian Dr. Rousas Rushdoony wrote that "est is a popularization of a very crude existentialism and is likely to leave some of its adherents with a suicidal hopelessness when they are finished with it" (2702). Indeed, those who became "very depressed" as a result of the first weekend were told to "stay with that feeling," since this is what they "got" from the training (1347:75-76). Greene reveals that "many trainees attend the midweek training in a terrifically depressed state" (1347:76). But how many people are left in this

state? Greene noted that "many people came away from the training very depressed and remained that way" (2229:30). How many are now emotional cripples—or dead? One person said that since est he had "been unable to control my thoughts and feelings and it's frightening." And, "much of the time I am feeling tremendous sadness, tremendous depression, and I am so confused that it is unbelievable. I don't have any ambition to do anything" (2703:13).

Are such incidents as psychosis and suicide really so surprising? In light of the dehumanizing and depressive philosophy of est, they are not. As Carl Frederick, author of *est: Playing the Game the New Way*, emphasized, "To repeat: the truth is that there is no inherent significance to anything you are, you do, or you have. That's why it's a game. It truly doesn't matter what notion you got last, or the one you get next. The game just is. Period. Money is not significant. Your mother is not significant. . . . Junk your mind. It's of no value to you in the game" (2337:187-89). The est graduation booklet states that "obviously the truth is what's so. Not so obviously, it's also so what."

Several graduates have also voiced concerns that some or many trainees might do anything they were told to do, even evil things. This amount of control over people worried them (1533:58/2703:11). Terri Schutz, writing in the *Village Voice*, mentioned that she had seen people give up their freedoms and become like robots (2703:13).

Here are other examples of statements made by the trainers that could have led to problems:

*Trainee:* I can't go through another process. It's too painful. Too much terrible stuff comes up. I've had two heart attacks, and my doctor says that it's bad for my heart for me to go through this.

*Trainer:* Your heart? You don't even know where your heart is, a——h——. Can you feel it? The only way to know something is experientially. Are you experiencing a heart attack right now? You're walking out of this room because of a b—— concept. You're leaving because of your b—— doctor. You don't know your heart from your a——h—— (2227).

My wife gets cancer. I experience her getting cancer. That makes me *responsible?* Right, Fred. (2067:144).

## MORALITY

Since the entire universe is an "illusive game" created by bored gods who need to amuse themselves, absolute morality has no significance in Erhard's philosophy. Some est graduates reported that they now "look forward to playing with people instead of just relating to them" (2704). Donald Porter and Diane Taxon indicated the amoral pragmatism of est when they wrote, "There is no right and wrong in the est vocabulary, no good and bad, no judging. There is a lot of pragmatism, a lot of watching the universe to see what works and what doesn't work" (1533:55). Ignoring the reality of evil in the world, Erhard states, "Life is always perfect just the way it is. When you realize that, then no matter how strongly it may appear to be otherwise, you know that whatever is happening right now will turn out all right. Knowing this, you are in a position to begin mastering life" (2704). Why? Because "if you keep saying it the way it really is, eventually, your word is law in the universe" (2066). Regardless, "as you can see, this universe is perfect" (2066).

The various books written by graduates also illustrate that within est philosophy is a basic pragmatism. For example, stealing does not work, but not because it is *wrong* to steal, only "inappropriate" because it might not work. However, stealing "with a free mind" could be appropriate (2229:70). Premarital, extramarital, and homosexual affairs were permissible and in some cases encouraged. Trainees were told that whatever they are unwilling to experience controls them, and that the only way to deal with "upsets" is to experience them (2229:133/1533:158).

Furthermore, there is nothing wrong with breaking up a marriage if spouses are having difficulty, or even if they just do not want to be married any longer. "My best friend divorced her husband after fifteen years of marriage. She says est gave her the courage to do it" (1347:41). "My wife told me that if I didn't attend a Seminar and sign up for est that she would divorce me" (1347:41).

This was part of estian "ethics," to give up beliefs of right and wrong and stop making others "wrong." Just experience. An issue of *The Graduate Review* carried a poem sent to Erhard by his friend Seung Sahn Soen-sa, a Zen master. Its first stanza reflects est views: "Good and bad have no self nature, holy and unholy are empty names" (1499:12). Of course, a lot of this philosophy also rebounded on Erhard:

> The next thing that happened was that other staff members began to leave. Many who didn't leave were thinking about leaving. Not only were many graduates making the est organization wrong, many staff members also were making it wrong—complaining about it, griping about it, being at the effect [i.e., being a victim of circumstances] of it.
>
> There were staff members—people with whom I had an absolutely complete relationship, people to whom I would give my life without worrying about it, people I would trust with anything—who did the most incredibly treacherous things that you could imagine (1088:5).

## HOPELESSNESS

In the end, what did est really offer people? Having thoroughly studied its teachings and effects, the authors conclude that it offered nothing more than betrayal and a life without meaning. As one examines the following statements, one has to wonder about the overall cost to society of millions of people following Erhard's philosophy. In reading the citations, keep in mind that in est a person should always be able to get on and off a position or point of view, because to be stuck in something is bad. Remember also that people created the universe merely to play in, and so made some things "more important" than others. That gives them problems to solve, something to do. So here is what Erhard offers:

> *Werner Erhard:* Now there's a very ugly fact in life. It is, perhaps one of the ugliest facts that I know of: *Nothing* is ever over. *Nothing* is ever handled [resolved]—and it's also true that there are no ultimate solutions (2727:11).

*est trainer:* There's only one thing you can do when you get it, and that is to lose it. And that creates the space to get it again (2229:131).

*est trainer:* This is what life is all about—getting it, losing it, getting it. I want to tell you there are no ultimate answers and that you can't hold onto anything (2229:160).

*est trainer* (at the end of the training): Life doesn't work, it never has, and it never will—I know that may be hard to get, but no matter what you do, it won't work, and no matter what you think, it won't work, and no matter who you become—it's never going to work.

But you know what. . . . It doesn't even mean anything that life doesn't work. It isn't even bad that life doesn't work.

So here's a suggestion and it's one of the most valuable ones I've picked up from Werner.

Stop trying to make life work. When you stop trying to make life work, you won't have to struggle anymore; you will have nothing to do; you will have literally nothing to do.

And that creates the space for you to discover that you are. That's the only thing there is to get (2229:122-23).

*est trainer* (graduate seminar): You're gonna find that instead of being stuck solving the same old problems over and over again, you'll have some new ones to deal with; and when you solve those, you'll get some more; and when you solve those, you'll get some more (2192:4).

That is what est offers. No answers. Just games to play and "problems" to solve. If est trainer Jerry Joiner's perspective was any indication of what five years with est did for a person, the training was better omitted. "I can't *see* anything else, you know, I mean, I don't *see* anything else. All I see is being on it and getting off it, being on it and getting off it, and I think that if I was to look at myself today and look at myself five years ago, the only difference I would see is my ability to get off it [i.e., his point of view]" (2192:4).

The philosophy of est continues to live on in The Forum, Lifespring, and Actualizations, and we will now look at these.

## THE FORUM

When Werner Erhard began est in 1971, few expected he would one day run a significant corporate empire. In addition to the half million graduates of est, The Forum has now attracted approximately 200,000 participants around the world, primarily in the United States. Yet The Forum is only one of some two dozen seminars, businesses, and enterprises founded by or affiliated with Werner Erhard. There is also The Hunger Project, Hermenet, Inc., Transformational Technologies, The Education Network, The Holiday Project, Paradigm 3 Satellite Network, and, not surprisingly, given Erhard's interest in influencing the clergy, The Mastery Foundation, which is described as "an interdenominational group of clergy and lay people whose purpose is to empower those who minister" (2705:45).

Although one often hears that The Forum is not merely est repackaged, this is, for the most part, incorrect. Those who have had extensive est training and also been through The Forum have said that the two are very similar. There are some differences. For example, for 625 dollars and two weekends, individuals can get all the est philosophy they want *without* all the trauma and dehumanization of est.

After officially retiring est, even Werner Erhard stated on March 27, 1985, "The Forum is *all that the training was in terms of the results that it produces in people's lives* and, in addition, offers results produced by more than two years of intensive research on accessing the source of human effectiveness and accomplishments" (2706:47). In describing the relationship between est and The Forum, *The Network Review* (a Forum publication) declared, "The philosophy of the training *has not changed*. . . . These trainings are not mere modifications of the original training. They are, as [designer] Arnold [Siegel] puts it, 'an opportunity to accelerate the mastery of the principles of transformation that the [est] training contains so that a lasting difference . . . is realized' " (2735:1).

Thus, like est, The Forum is clearly a world-view having religious and philosophical beliefs and implications. Consider the astute analysis of former Spiritual Counterfeits Projects researcher and writer Robert Burrows:

> Erhard . . . does more than conceal his ideology, he openly denies he offers any. That was true of est and it continues to be true of the Forum. . . . But Erhard's view of the world remains a world view. It is as religious and philosophical as the monism that informs it, which is to say through and through. It is also patently irreconcilable with Christian faith simply because monism is irreconcilable with theism. Monistic traditions don't distinguish between God and creation; theistic traditions do. Monistic traditions believe that to believe in anything, God or otherwise, is to attribute reality to something that is ultimately unreal. To theistic traditions, distinctions are critical, and the most critical is that between Creator and creature. That distinction is the basis for theistic belief in God, a belief Erhard's monism cannot tolerate: "I believe that the 'belief' in God is the greatest barrier to God in the universe." . . . [B]eliefs and barriers are what Erhard attempts to dismantle in his seminars, theistic beliefs included. When the demolition is complete, according to Erhard's assumptions, experience, or Being itself, blooms into view, bringing with it this direct gnosis: the world is self-created, reinvented and structured at every moment from every source of pure Being that Erhard's "technology" invokes.

That gnosis is the religious and philosophical cornerstone of Erhard's empire. Est, the Forum, and the Hunger Project can only be understood if that foundation is kept in mind—which isn't always easy. Erhard's denial of ideology suggests the reason. Erhard uses language that means one thing to the outside world and quite another to him and his fellow gnostic initiates. That is true of the terms "religion" and "philosophy" and is also true of other words Erhard often uses. . . . Shifting the sense of terminology to suit the audience is a common tactic in New Age circles. It's called equivocation and is as frustrating to penetrate as it is aggravating to encounter. . . . For New Age religionists, equivocation also functions as a conduit for future indoctrination (2707:34).

The point is well taken. In general, The Forum is est in a slick new suit. It incorporates minor changes to make it appear different and seem all the more attractive (2758:12). Again, graduates of both seminars know this. Carol Giambalvo took the est training in March 1978 and remained in its graduate seminar program for five years. She was extensively involved in The Hunger Project as a briefing leader and then took The Forum training. She believes The Forum does not differ significantly from est. Supposedly, The Forum no longer has the confrontational, intrusive, abusive nature of the est training. But Giambalvo asserts that the abusive language of est and the intimidation of people remains. The Forum has more breaks than est, every 2 1/2 to 3 hours, and sessions do not continue into the wee hours of the morning. "Nevertheless, the overload of abstract ideas and information drains, confuses, disorients and tires many participants" (2706:48).

According to Giambalvo, the major difference between the two is that the hypnotic processes of est have been removed. Nevertheless the est processes known as the "Truth Process," "Fear Process," and "Danger Process" remain, although in somewhat subdued forms. The language has also been altered in certain ways, for example, "rules" are no longer employed, only "requests"—however the requests still function as rules (2706:48). Thus, although Forum argot has replaced a certain amount of the est argot, the sense is largely the same. "The Forum has largely abandoned the *language* of 'total responsibility' and the description of reality as 'self-created.' But those *premises* are still central" (2706:48, emphasis added).

Forum advertising contends that the seminar is not a new belief or philosophy, but after taking the seminar, Giambalvo was convinced that this was not the case:

> "By the second weekend, it was clear that The Forum was working with some basic premises that were both philosophical and religious. Those premises were about the nature of being—what in philosophical and theological circles is known as ontology. . . . The Forum offers its own brand of salvation. [The trainer states,] 'By creating out of nothing a stand [i.e., an affirmation] that I am my word, my word

becomes law in the universe—when it does. Or it doesn't when it doesn't. Consider the possibility that the universe is within you. Or did I create that?' " (2706:48-49).

Giambalvo concludes that The Forum "cloaks its agenda in misleading rhetoric. We were told that The Forum presents no philosophy, yet people emerged from the sessions with a new view of reality, which is reinforced by the ongoing seminar program and network groups. The Forum's philosophy of no philosophy is pushed with religious fervor. To say it is a hard sell is to put it mildly. We were pressured to share The Forum with others and to bring guests to the evening event and the seminars. . . . *The faltering est empire has been revived*. A few alterations in externals and the new clothes of the emperor are again on parade" (2706:49, emphasis added).

With some 200,000 graduates, The Forum now has a good start toward surpassing est in influence, albeit not in basic philosophy.


## LIFESPRING

In 1992, we received one of many letters written by concerned Christians about the impact that Lifespring was having on their friends, Christian and non-Christian. One Christian was concerned about six friends who had completed the basic Lifespring training and another who had completed the basic training, the advanced course, and "enhancement" courses. The writer told us that this particular individual "now believes the following": in omens, reincarnation, seances, palmistry;* that we create reality in our minds, and "all is one and one is all"; that world peace can be achieved if everyone *thinks* world peace because all things are possible through the power of the mind; that there is no right or wrong and no morality "and many other strange things."

Lifespring, with est and Actualizations, is part of the human potential movement. Lifespring was founded in January 1974 by John P. Hanley and four other human potential experimenters. One was John Enright of the Gestalt Institute. Hanley, like Erhard, was a teacher in Mind

Dynamics, the occult group referred to earlier (2226:143/2715:5). Hanley was the national field director. In 1969, he had been convicted on six counts of mail fraud and sentenced to five years in prison. Because he was under 21, the judge suspended the sentence (2710:3).

Before starting Lifespring, Hanley was also involved with a company called Holiday Magic, a cosmetics firm owned by the late William Penn Patrick, another leader in the human potential movement. He also attended Patrick's Leadership Dynamics Institute which, according to a 1987 article published in the *Washington Post*, was a motivational sales training program with a vengeance. Enrollees were allegedly beaten, whipped, tied to crosses, and forced to eat garbage and feces (2708:70). Hanley distinguished himself among his peers, and LDI hired him as a staffer. As noted, Hanley was a leader in Mind Dynamics, another venture begun by Patrick, which apparently also used brutal methods.

As with Actualizations, the size of the Lifespring group is reduced (150 people), and the experience is allegedly more mild, although it can still be very traumatic. The 450-dollar Lifespring seminar basic training is conducted over a 50-hour, five-day period. The seminars are currently held in over a dozen cities, and plans are under way to open centers in more cities. As of 1990, over 300,000 people had taken the training, and Lifespring had grossed over 25 million dollars a year.

Like other New Age human potential seminars, Lifespring boasts its list of famous and notable persons, including North Carolina Congressman Charlie Rose; the San Francisco Forty-niners safety Ronnie Lott; the former assistant to President Carter for public liaison, Midge Costanza; marketing specialist Peter Bogdonoff; and "many Capitol Hill staffers" (2708:26).

As with est/The Forum, various Lifespring trainings are also offered for special groups: children 6 through 12, teenagers, businessmen, the family, prison inmates, and others. Hanley is particularly concerned about the family (their monthly periodical is *The Family News*), and he hopes to have a strong impact on the families of America.

Along with est/The Forum, Lifespring is also attempting to infiltrate education:

Some colleges offer university credit for the seminar (e.g., California State University, Fullerton); the entire staff of one of the largest elementary schools in Los Angeles (Pacoima) has taken the training; the Lifespring Foundation, a non-profit agency (apparently "separate" from Lifespring) "will be making a significant impact on education in the years ahead." Currently, accountants, dentists, administrators, police officers, nurses, pharmacists, MD's, family counselors, and teachers can use the Lifespring seminars as education credits. On August 23–27, the Lifespring Foundation provided special "Teacher Trainings" to the 60 staff members of the Institute for Teacher Leadership, a joint effort of the United Teachers—Los Angeles and California State University, Fullerton (2722).

After a graduate has taken the Lifespring Basic Training he may then take the Interpersonal Experience (IPE) for 900 dollars, a far more intensive five-day seminar, which is a more advanced, in-depth training. Beyond this is the advanced leadership training called TC, the Training Coordinator Program. This is a 70-day "session" calling for three weekend trainings, weekly early-morning meetings, and a "service" commitment to Lifespring heavily involved in recruitment. About half of Lifespring's graduates take the IPE, and a significant number complete the TC program. As with est/The Forum, various additional enhancement workshops are offered. These 20-hour two-day sessions involve such topics as finances, sexuality, relationships, health, prosperity and abundance, "illusions and your personal subjective reality," "loving your body," creativity, "turning on personal power," and communication.

Just as est has cloned Lifespring, Lifespring has cloned itself. Former trainer Dennis Becker began "Impact Seminars," and recently Lifespring spread to Tokyo, Japan, in the form of "Life Dynamics." Bob White, one of the co-founders of Lifespring, started the Japanese trainings with Duncan Callister, a lawyer who left his profession in the early seventies to join Lifespring. They hope eventually to expand to Hong Kong and Australia (2711). There is apparently another course that is almost identical to Lifespring started by a former Lifespring trainer, John-Roger, titled "Insight Seminars," which is a kind of sanitized and glitzy human potential outreach. (We might even expect these offshoots to produce their own clones in the years ahead.) As we note below, there is even an allegedly Christian version of Lifespring begun by Daniel Tocchini, a Lifespring trainer for seven years. It goes by the name "Momentus," "Mashiyach Ministries," and "Grace Training Company."

*Compatibility with Christianity?*

Why should Christians be concerned about New Age seminars? The following illustrations show how they may touch the life of the church. (Reliable sources have told us the following material is accurate based on their personal knowledge or research. However, since the authors have not personally confirmed such material or attended the training, the following should be considered provisional.)

Daniel Tocchini claims that he became an evangelical Christian in 1979. In spite of this, he became a Lifespring trainer from 1981 to at least 1986. He concluded that he could no longer remain with Lifespring because it was not based on Christian principles. (Apparently it required at least five years to discover this.) Tocchini next began a training for evangelical Christians called "Momentus," which also goes under the name of "Mashiyach Ministries" and "Grace Training Company." Supposedly, Tocchini Christianized Lifespring. He removed the monistic philosophy, the abusive methods, bad language, and so on. And, apparently, thousands of Christians have gone through this training and many have given extremely positive reports. Indeed, when one hears these testimonies, one assumes this must be a legitimate forum for enhancing the Christian lifestyle.

But just because someone has powerful experiences that seem to be Christian or encourage one's Christian walk does not mean that allegedly Christian trainings like this are legitimate. Perhaps Christians have been taken in by the profundity of the experience without thoroughly evaluating that experience or even asking the right questions. Even with its monism, etc., removed, one cannot just take the principles and/or techniques of Lifespring and "Christianize" them. According to critics, there is still too much passivity and manipulation, the techniques are still mind altering, and some of the radical "shock therapy" methods can hardly be advocated without analysis and critique.

Consider another illustration. One California pastor, the Rev. Winston C. Gould, an ordained minister with the United Church of Christ, said that as a result of his participation in Lifespring:

> Lifespring builds on points of view common to Christianity. . . . I was able to deal with some obstacles inside me that were in the way of my achieving a deeper Christian faith. In addition, my ministry was enhanced and as a result I became more open to God. . . . [M]y faith as a Christian is more central to my life than ever. . . . I write this letter to you as a Christian minister who sees that Lifespring's experiential approach in its trainings reaches people with the values Christianity teaches. Christians can benefit from the training without fear or losing faith and without having to give up essential Christian convictions (2712:4).

Of course, many mainline and liberal Christian ministers have endorsed est, Actualizations, The Forum, Silva Mind Control, and all sorts of things. And many genuine Christians have innocently or naively taken these trainings. The question is, Are claims of compatibility with the Christian faith valid? We will see that they are not.

First, the humanism in Lifespring is evident from its view of man as an inherently perfect being whose major problem is not sin but ignorance of his own perfection: "At the essence, or core, of each of us is a perfect, loving, and caring being," and, "Come and experience beyond self-esteem and self-worth to a sense of awe and veneration for who you are just as self-love is the greatest love . . . ," and, "people [have] unlimited knowledge and potential within them" (2689). In essence:

> Lifespring emphasizes the idea that truth is a subjective enterprise whose source lies within the "core" of the human soul. Within the core lies all truth, love, and identity. The goal is to tap

the core, that is, to discover the potential that lies within and to actualize that potential. Part of the training is to have the trainees pair off in groups of two called "diads" for the purpose of sharing and confrontation. They attempt to discover the "space" inside the mind of the other, thereby discovering the potential that is latent within. Actualizing one's potential then becomes possible with further training.

> All problems and difficulties in life arise from the fundamental errors of one's thought process. The solution, therefore, is to undergo a radical change in the way one thinks or conceptualizes reality. Even sickness, disease, and all forms of physiological malady are attributed to problems within the mind (2381:176).

Second, the anti-Christian monistic philosophy of est is found in Lifespring. As SCP former researcher Dean C. Halverson remarks, "Monistic philosophy is at the core of Lifespring's teachings. The reason a person can depend only on himself or herself is because there is nobody else. We are all one. Only the self exists. The reason each individual is perfect is because there is no standard outside ourselves. The Absolute within transcends all dualities, including good and evil. Because the source of reality is within, each person's potential is infinite" (2713:25).

Finally, the occult aspects of Lifespring are also opposed to Christian faith and practice. According to *The Lifespring Family News*, "The seminars make use of the most effective principles, intellectual concepts and techniques of . . . parapsychology . . . and Eastern disciplines" (2714:2). In addition, Lifespring training involves individual meditations* and guided fantasies with occult potential (see Visualization). Elliot Miller, author of *A Crash Course on the New Age Movement* and senior editor of the *Christian Research Journal* reveals, "We have interviews on tape with advanced Lifespring graduates who say that powers of ESP, soul travel, and the 'third eye' were cultivated, and a practice of wearing people's shoes in order to absorb their vibrations (and thus take on their characteristics) was employed. The Hindu occult doctrine of the seven chakras or psychic centers in the human body was also taught" (2715:5). Miller later noted that "some of the practices and beliefs that are a part of the training have a definite relationship to the world of the occult. . . . Not only do we have testimonies of graduates to the effect that these practices go on, but Lifespring trainers actually boasted to us about the various psychic and mystical aspects of the trainings" (2716:4)

*Est Revisited*

A 1993 dictionary of religion stated, "The teachings of Lifespring remarkably parallel estianism" (2381:176). One journalist participant in Lifespring (1990) noted that "est and Lifespring have far more similarities than differences" (2687:70). An earlier "thorough inquiry into Lifespring" conducted by the Christian Research Institute revealed, "Lifespring instructors have consistently informed us that their program is based upon the same basic concepts and ideas as *est*, although their approach in attaining these mutual goals differs to some extent" (2715:5).

In our own discussion with Lifespring graduates and staff in the late 1980s, we were told that despite differences in style, the worldview was very similar to est's. One staff member said that graduates who have taken both est and Lifespring agree that the two are the same in basic philosophy.

In an early article in *The Family News*, John Hanley discussed various states of perception. Above the state of "accountability" ("the acknowledgment that we set everything up, that we're the ones that did it") comes the highest level of all, sourcing. As we saw earlier, "sourcing" is experiencing oneself as creator of all things. Hanley states:

Accountability is an after-the-fact acknowledgment that we did it, it's ours, we made it happen. Sourcing is the before-the-fact creation, the conscious involvement in making something happen. In order to source we have to be willing to give up the notion that somebody or something is going to do it for us. . . . Sourcing is not about being accountable. It's not about accepting and it's not about surrender. Sourcing is really about transformation. But in order to source we have to get clearly, at the experiential level, that nobody out there can make us happy. . . . It is me alone who can from within deliver happiness to

me. Period. . . . Sourcing is really a very spiritual experience (2717).

As one trainer said, "You are accountable for everything that happens to you, from the moment you pick your own parents till you choose the moment of your death" (2720:2). ("Choosing your own parents" is a theme common to some Westernized reincarnation theories.)

This concept of sourcing has now apparently been revised due to tragedies and lawsuits among graduates (see pp. 303-04). Regardless, besides the concept of creatorship in all situations, Lifespring and est are also similar in their rejection of critical ("nonacceptable") thinking and in the nature of the transformative experience. Both also claim not to conflict with one's religious faith. For both, nothing is immoral; there is no ultimate right or wrong, only "viewpoints." The argot is similar, too; one cannot "help" people, only "assist" them. Both are roughly equivalent in format: half the program is processes (guided imagery, meditation), half is lectures, confrontations, and discussion or "sharing." It is not surprising that a brochure about Lifespring's purpose could just as easily have been about est's:

The purpose of the Lifespring training is to create an environment where you can alter the way you see yourself and the world. . . . You don't need the training. At a deeper level you are perfect just the way you are. If you are not experiencing your perfection, we are convinced you will find the training valuable.

The Basic Training is a blend of various approaches found in the human potential movement today . . . meditation . . . Zen . . . mind power methods (2718).

Lifespring "views people as having unlimited potential and knowledge within them" because, "We are all a vast source of creativity, knowledge and vitality" (2719).

The authors interviewed a recent graduate, "Tim," who shared the following about Lifespring philosophy and practices. Within oneself, one is all-knowing. There is no transcendent God because God is within each person.

Part of the training on the last day is called "OPV," and the idea, as in est, is to provide "evidence" of innate psychic potential. Partners are selected, and one person goes into his (or her) workshop, the mentally constructed fantasy space, and invites a psychic "adviser," selected by his partner, into his mind. Previously, part of the workshop had involved instruction on how to psychically invite other advisers or people into one's life. This includes even the dead, and, as was true for est, can provide the basis for spiritism. In fact, in "Tim's" workshop, some of the participants did invite dead family members to enter their consciousness. After inviting the "advisers" in, "Tim" said they had conversations with them to learn more about them. Often the knowledge the "adviser" gave was unknown except to the person, but highly accurate. Clearly, as in est, enough people are successful in this to suggest spiritistic collusion.

"Tim" also said that Lifespring was not Christian, and that a Christian could not possibly take the seminar in good conscience. He felt it could insulate a person against Christianity and cause severe emotional problems. Another parallel to est is that even though most graduates are very "high" right after the seminar, a severe depression may soon set in, as happened with this graduate.

### Hazards at the Lifespring

Like est, Lifespring has had its cases of psychosis, suicide, and other serious outcomes. Consider a brief history. The ABC news program "20/20" spent ten months in "rigorous investigation" of Lifespring, involving hundreds of interviews and examining thousands of documents. In their 1980 broadcasts on Lifespring, they noted that it utilizes very "powerful psychological techniques," including high-pressure confrontation and exhaustive group therapy. They also stated that the Office of the Surgeon General concluded that Lifespring "has considerable potential for emotional harm." Among their findings (2721):

- The Lifespring trainers are unlicensed amateurs.
- Pam Munter, a psychologist in Portland, Oregon, has treated over 40 graduates [revised figures] who had become casualties. She commented that she had no doubts that Lifespring was "destructive."
- Gail Renick of Seattle suffered a severe asthma attack on the fifth day of the training

and died soon after. Since Lifespring teaches that people are responsible for their own problems, the Lifespring Trainer made no attempts to help her. While she could hardly breathe, the calloused trainer merely said, "Gail, what's causing this attack?", and walked away.

- "Bruce A." suffered a broken blood vessel in his brain during the training. But again, for the trainers, it was merely a psychological problem, a way of "getting attention," despite its serious nature. No attempt was made to help. Moreover, Bruce believed them. The condition worsened and he spent months in the hospital in a paralyzed condition.

- Linda Smith of Los Angeles was committed to a mental institution within two weeks after the training. Days after the training ended, her personality began a drastic change which became so bizarre that institutionalization was necessary. After her release, months of psychiatric care were necessary. One day she stayed home, listening to Lifespring music over and over. That afternoon she picked up a gun and shot herself in the head. (Before Lifespring, she had no mental problems.)

- The "Holy Grail" teaching. A person's darkest fears are labeled one's "Holy Grail," and the person is to confront them. Artie Barnett of Portland, Oregon, had a lifelong fear of swimming. It goes without saying that he could not swim. The trainer apparently suggested that Barnett swim the quarter mile stretch across the dangerous Willamette River in Portland, in order to prove that he had been victimized by his "limiting beliefs" that he really couldn't swim. Attempting it, Barnett drowned (2708:68). Covington Vego, afraid of heights, jumped off a bridge and nearly died. One woman, a former mental patient who had a fear of being locked up, spent a full day locked up inside a wire chicken cage.

- On the 20/20 program John Hanley admitted two other cases, in which a woman attempted to drown herself, and a veteran went psychotic.

- Lifespring graduates currently work at the CIA, defense installations, the Defense Communications Agency, leading defense industry contractors (TRW, IBM), in police departments, and other highly sensitive jobs. The authorities interviewed saw such individuals as a clear and potentially serious risk factor.

- An undercover reporter who went through the training reported that at times people were "ranting and raving and screaming and cursing and spitting. It was like bedlam . . . like being in a mental institution."

- A Washington, D.C., engineer with no history of mental problems, landed in a psychiatric ward.

Research from other sources indicates:

- David Priddle of Eugene, Oregon, apparently committed suicide within 12 hours after completion of the seminar (2710:3).

- Susan Gilmore, a psychologist in Eugene, has treated a number of Lifespring casualties, including one who was "psychotic and extremely suicidal" and spent eight months in a hospital (2710:4).

- Barbara Long took an overdose of propoxyphene during the training and "suffered a fatal heart attack" (2710:4).

In a 1983 issue of the journal *Psychiatry*, psychologists Janice Haken and Richard Adams, after they participated in the seminar, concluded that the impact of the Lifespring training was "essentially pathological." They felt that the training "reduced the ability of the participants to think critically," and that attendees became "increasingly reliant upon the trainer to interpret reality" (2708:71). In 1990, *Boston Business* ran an article by Paul Keegan, who decided to take the Lifespring seminar in order to do an objective report. He notes that Lifespring's legal problems have cost it millions of dollars. "About 30 lawsuits have been filed against Lifespring since its quiet beginnings in 1974, six of the claims charging that trainees died as a result of the course and most of the others claiming that the course had caused severe psychosis. Lifespring has settled almost all the cases out of court for as much as $500,000 apiece" (2708:26). He also noted the processes were reminiscent of those in est, where people were manipulated into drastic emotional catharsis. During one session, "People were screaming at full volume. The noise was deafening. I opened my eyes and saw a darkened room full of what looked like raving

maniacs." During another, "It was like being in an insane asylum . . . or Hell itself" (2708:69,72).

This power of the seminar to impact people emotionally in very dramatic ways surprised Keegan. The editor of *Boston Business*, in his "Letter from the Editor" column, wrote, "What is dished out by Lifespring is shocking doses of brain bashing. One need only look into the glazed eyes of those emerging from the basic Lifespring course to get to see they've been through something powerful" (2708:4). Keegan himself reported, "Like some grade-B horror movie, about half of these ordinary, accomplished citizens will be turned into glassy-eyed automatons" (2708:26).

Despite some positive impact that Keegan felt at moments throughout the seminar, at the end he concluded that he had been the victim of an extremely powerful manipulation:

The warmth and openness I have felt one-on-one disappeared. I realized what had happened. One hundred and fifty people, manipulated into having the same utopian vision, following the same thought process and communicating with the same buzzwords meaningful only to them, were no longer a collection of individuals in search of "personal growth," but automatons, human cogs in a highly sophisticated machine whose ultimate goals were unknown (2708:76).

In one est-like process, participants reversed sexual roles. After the instructor asked them, "Wasn't that fun?" Keegan reports:

Everyone cheered in agreement. I was shocked. We were essentially programmed to act insane, irrational—at their command. And we thought we were being spontaneous! That's the absolute brilliance of Lifespring. In this bizarre world Hanley has created, white becomes black and black white. Control is considered spontaneity. We had given up control of our lives and yet we felt liberated. We reported feeling great, but that's how we'd been conditioned to feel (2708:77).

Even Keegan, who had taken the seminar as a skeptic and fully intending not to be swayed, was forced to conclude that based upon the power of the manipulation present, "My values were powerless in this bizarre world" (2708:73). Indeed, he was frightened with what the seminar did to him: "I wouldn't have believed it, either, had I not witnessed it and actually felt the undertow myself" (2708:26).

The casualties and lawsuits against Lifespring have forced some changes. Lifespring now requires all participants to take their medicine if they are following a doctor's prescription. The strict concept of personal creatorship has been abandoned or at least revised. Every participant must sign a legal document stating they understand that Lifespring is "not psychotherapy," that "trainers are generally not licensed psychiatrists or psychologists," and that they "may experience deep emotions and possibly emotional stress, anxiety, tears, physical discomfort or exhaustion." In the document participants also declare, "I do not have any doubts about my mental health, emotional stability or physical ability to handle the Basic Training." And (get this) that they "forever discharge" Lifespring from any legal liability in case of "personal, physical, psychological or emotional injuries, distress or death" (2708:29).

Lifespring has also funded its own studies, usually hiring Dr. Morton Leiberman, a University of California San Francisco psychiatry professor, who has long been an advocate of large group awareness training programs. Leiberman stresses what he believes are the positive aspects and results of Lifespring, although he does admit there is still some risk in the training (2708:72). Lifespring's Director of Corporate Affairs, Charles Ingrasci, likens participation in Lifespring to driving a car: "It's your obligation to weigh the value of driving the car against the risk" (2708:72).

## ACTUALIZATIONS

Actualizations is another offshoot of Erhard Seminars Training (est). It was begun by Stewart Emery, the first est trainer, in 1976. Emery apparently could never completely accept the entire philosophy of est. In a December 15, 1975, *East West Journal* interview, he stated that he initially thought much of the training "was non-

sense" although he supported it for many years. "I still think that to tell people they create everything is not the thing to do." He also had problems with the idea that anything the staff does "is a function of Werner's grace" (cf. 1349:167-68).

In Actualizations, Emery has softened aspects of the est training. We have been told by graduates that the 300-dollar, 100-member, 48-hour seminars are less brutal. While it is encouraging to see at least one former trainer recognize that est philosophy and brutality didn't always "make the world work," it is nevertheless true that much of the est philosophy and worldview remains in Actualizations. In our view, far too much, such as the basic monistic philosophy, which remains intact.

The first published book on Actualizations was Stewart Emery's *Actualizations: You Don't Have to Rehearse to be Yourself: Transform Your Relationships* (1348). While the est philosophy is very present, the form and delivery is somewhat different, and unless one had spent a good deal of time studying est, the parallels would not be easily noticed in the book.

According to Emery (and est), one of mankind's basic problems involves people's false perception of reality. People wrongly think they are separate from themselves, from others, and from the universe, when everything is really part of one united Essence, the Divine Self. Emery writes, "Our reality is a part of everything." And, "We really *are* each other" (1348:88,222).

Along with Erhard, Emery intends to produce drastic changes in people, "nothing short of a complete transformation." This happens not only in the area of relationships, but with a person's self-image, his view of life, morality, work, the world, and everything else (1348:2). The process of transformation attempts to have people realize the *illusion* of separation and experience monistic enlightenment.* "Separation is an illusion that we have made real by agreement. The fundamental nature of the universe is one of balance and harmony in relationships. There is *no* separation. . . . All our efforts to end our sense of separation are the attempt to solve a problem we do not have in the first place. Our life has become a collection of solutions to a problem we do not have! (1348:4-5).

However, "When we have the experience of being one with everything, we have the experience of being related to everything. All the separation disappears; all the conflict disappears, and we are left with a sense of fullness, joy, serenity. In short, an experience of love. It is love beyond attachment—what the yogis call the fourth chakra" (1348:114).

Obviously, if one really believes in a monistic unity, then life becomes free and easy because nothing matters. The Actualizations view of love is love *beyond* attachment. Separationist (dualistic) ideas—pleasure versus pain, love versus hate, God versus man, Creator versus creation, good versus evil—are no longer real. Problems can "disappear" by the power of our minds. "Every time you remove and dissolve the illusion of conflict and dissolve the experience of separation, revealing the experience of unity, production goes up" (1348:177).

Pressing his monism to its logical conclusion, Emery rejects concepts of good versus evil. "It would be nice if we could stop talking to children in terms of Good and Bad. The notion of Good and Bad is one of the most devastating biases we pass along" (1348:162). He also argues, "We are so busy laying our trip on our children that we overlook the greatest gift we could give: no trip. If we could simply break the tradition of parenthood, which seems to be nothing more than passing our insanity and biases along to our children as our parents passed their insanity and biases along to us—if we could break that chain, that would be a contribution that would alter the course of human history" (1348:157).

Of course, without a strong ethical commitment to morality and children, a society will perish. To teach parents to disregard their children's morality is to not only rub against the grain of human conscience, it is to reject human history, to say nothing of what God thinks on the subject. Thus, in Actualization, a true friend supports (not only accepts) one in *all* that he is and will not settle for anything less. No judgments are allowed about a friend's moral direction because this is the game he has chosen to play (1348:26,93-94). To Emery, usually what "passes for friendship is really a pool of quicksand." And,

"For me, love is insufficient grounds for a friendship" (1348:148-53). To this, one might compare Proverbs 27:5-6 NASB: "Better is open rebuke than love that is concealed. Faithful are the wounds of a friend, but deceitful are the kisses of an enemy."

Emery also admits his nihilism. He is not "certain of the purpose of our existence," but regardless, "there is no hope." He teaches that "no hope is needed" because nothing matters (1348:12,43). Emery also offers a similar approach to transformation as in est. "Transformation means housing a different essence [now divine] in the same form. To the person who has undergone a transformation, the world is exactly the same as it was before. When you are transformed, the immediate circumstances of your existence are the same. What is altered is how you feel about it" (1348:45).

There are other est concepts in Actualizations besides the experience of monistic unity and consciousness transformation. These include the notions of men functioning almost entirely by conditioned responses, and the belief that life is merely a game (1348:99,187-99,214). However, Emery does teach that reality is real, and he denies the est extreme of personal creatorship of *every* circumstance (1348:200,212).

From a Christian perspective, Emery's philosophy involves a low view of marriage, the family, and morality, and it is ultimately nihilistic—all features of est. Thus, Emery can believe that each individual is to embrace their experience, no matter what it is: moral or immoral (1348:134-46). In one seminar, according to writer and graduate James Martin, he told a wife named "Marva," "Do anything you want to do, so long as it brings you joy. And if that means joining a group of swingers, then do that too." She responds with, "Well, I just might. . . . I know what I have to do now. I have to go back and start doing the things that bring me joy. And if that means kicking my husband in the a— and getting it on with someone else, then I will. After all, it's never really too late to have fun, is it?" "No, Marva, it ain't" (1349:95-96).

Even sex with animals may be all right (1349:130), and "it may even be more all right to be gay" (that is, better to be into homosexuality than bestiality; 1348:137). Like est/The Forum, therefore, Actualizations encourages the homosexual lifestyle if the partners are enjoying it (1349:191-92). "Sex is nothing more than bodies at play with each other.... Only too many people take their minds along for the ride" (1349:196). He advocates the unrestricted "pure joy available in the sharing of yourself sexually with another person" (1348:144). Elsewhere he says, "I personally have found that I can have sexual relationships with a variety of people and that it is not a problem for me" (2723:80). "People have thought I was against marriage. It's not true: marriage has been an odyssey for me. I'm just against marriage as it exists for most people, because it's so destructive" (2723:80).

*Actualizations and the Bible*

Actualizations is obviously opposed to biblical teachings. Not surprisingly, Emery teaches that it is an illusion to think that God is going to save man, or that there is a battle between God and Satan, or good and evil. He says, "None of this is happening, of course" (1348:6). The concept of monism leaves no room for Jesus Christ's atonement that reconciled us to God. "Hope is the expectation that some source external to ourselves is going to save [us] so we will live happily ever after.... Hopelessness is finding out it's up to you" (1348:37).

In Emery's view, people are not sinners in need of redemption but gods in embryo (1348:11,21,101). With a "proper" awareness of reality, people can be totally self-sufficient. According to Emery, all people are part of God. If "life is the experience of moving along the path toward Godhood...then life is about expansion" (1348:45).

The previous statements leave no room for salvation through Christ or a meaningful life of service to God. Goals themselves are meaningless; they serve only as an excuse to play the game of life that one has created. "A goal [in life] is nothing more than the excuse for the game.... Goals do not work until we see them as merely an excuse for the game" (1348:208,218).

To the contrary, the apostle Paul admonishes Christians to press on toward the goal for the prize of the upward call of God in Christ Jesus" (Philippians 3:14 NASB).

The first book about Actualizations was published by James Martin, an enthusiastic graduate. He tells us that Stewart Emery (along with Werner Erhard and Jack Hanley) was also a trainer for Mind Dynamics, the destructive psychic potential seminar that seems to have multiplied itself time and again (1349:56). Martin said that Emery is "profoundly psychic," and that when Emery took the Mind Dynamics course he "discovered that he had profound psychic powers lying dormant within him" (1349:165,207). Martin also noted psychic aspects of the Actualizations training (1349:136), as well as the est influence (1349:36,77,148), its amoral views (1349:95-96, 130-31,190-94), and its human potentialism (1349:25,181,190). "You only need to have faith *in yourself*, Claire" (1349:53). "Only *you* can help yourself. God won't" (1349:99). But according to the Bible, trust in one's self is not the way of life, but the way of destruction.

Emery's dislike for Christian principles was also evident in Martin's book. "The world was sold that most misguided and pessimistic concept known as original sin" (1349:33). "If you go around making others wrong, you won't win. [This attitude] invariably leads to psychoneurosis" (1349:74-75). "Righteousness is a pain in the a—" (1349:187).

Like est/The Forum and Lifespring, Actualizations speaks of love and commitment but ends up grinding one's face in the dirt. These seminars know nothing of true love and forgiveness; they can only mask them with false philosophies (cf. 1349:207). Biblically, love is infinitely more than the perverted caricature such New Age seminars continue to resurrect (1349:97-100,104,122):

This is how God showed his love among us: He sent his one and only Son into the world that we might live through him. This is love: not that we loved God, but that he loved us and sent his Son as an atoning sacrifice for our sins. Dear friends, since God so loved us, we also ought to love one another.... And so we know and rely on the love God has for us. God is love. Whoever lives in love lives in God, and God in him.... This is love for God: to obey his commands. And his commands are not burdensome (1 John 4:9-11,16; 5:3).

Love is patient, love is kind. It does not envy, it does not boast, it is not proud. It is not rude, it is not self-seeking, it is not easily angered, it keeps no record of wrongs. Love does not delight in evil but rejoices with the truth. It always protects, always trusts, always hopes, always perseveres. Love never fails (1 Corinthians 13:4-8).

# HYPNOSIS AND HYPNOTIC REGRESSION

## INFO AT A GLANCE

**Description.** Hypnosis is a deliberately induced condition of deep mental relaxation, passivity, or trance, in which a person becomes highly suggestible and flexible within a state of consciousness capable of dramatic manipulation. Hypnosis in therapy seeks to deal with current problems by employing hypnotic states or information to change behavior. Hypnotic regression in psychotherapy usually takes a person back into the past or childhood to buried memories, in order to uncover and resolve hidden conflicts. In New Age and occult applications hypnosis and hypnotic regression are used for a wide variety of psychic purposes, including developing "human potential" and uncovering "past lives" for "therapeutic" and occult purposes.

**Founder.** Unknown. The practice can be traced to antiquity. The noted hypnotist and psychic (767:189-98) Anton Mesmer (1734-1815), from whom we derive the term "mesmerism," is often considered the "father" of modern hypnosis.

**How does it claim to work?** The exact process by which hypnosis works is unknown; however, widespread claims are made for its application to medicine, psychotherapy, education, and many other fields. Self-help promoters make claim that it can be used to treat or cure an endless variety of physical ailments and personal problems (from allergies and low self-esteem, to smoking, cancer, obesity, and guilt), and that its application to personal growth, learning abilities, human potentialism, and self-transformation is endless.

**Scientific evaluation.** Scientific research has been conducted, and much information about hypnotic trance and susceptibility to it is available; nevertheless, a generally accepted scientific theory about it is still lacking.

**Examples of occult potential.** Hypnosis is a unique altered state of consciousness* that can be used for a large variety of occult pursuits, including psychic development, spirit contact, automatic writing, astral travel, past-life (reincarnation) regression or "therapy," and many others.

**Major Problems.** Releasing one's mind to the suggestions and control of another; possible uncertainties as to the nature and long-term implication of the hypnotic state.

**Biblical/Christian evaluation.** Hypnosis may be related to the biblically forbidden practice of "charming" or "enchanting"; to the extent this relationship holds true, the practice should be rejected. The Christian is to be filled with and controlled by the Holy Spirit; to permit one's mind to be controlled by another person is, in the least, a questionable practice. Clearly, it is forbidden for a Christian to permit his mind to be influenced by spirit entities as occurs in certain occult applications of hypnosis.

**Potential dangers.** Occult influences, unexpected problems arising from the trance state, abuse by the hypnotist.

## INTRODUCTION AND INFLUENCE

Hypnosis seems to be one of those subjects that everyone knows about but few know what to do with. Although many articles have appeared in the popular press, from *Time* and *Newsweek* to women's magazines and self-help publications, many people don't know what to think about hypnosis. The term itself conjures up images of everything from stage entertainment to dangerous Svengali types. Most people seem to assume that because it is so widely used, it must generally be safe. This may not be a wise assumption.

What is hypnosis? One encyclopedia defines it simply as "an artificially induced mental state characterized by an individual's loss of critical powers and his consequent openness of suggestion" (1591:600). The term itself comes from Hypnos, the Greek god of sleep, and was coined by physician James Braid, an early investigator and promoter of "mesmerism," or "animal magnetism," which were earlier terms for hypnosis.

In attempting to determine the basic characteristics of hypnosis, researchers have used a variety of terms: "partial sleep," "atavistic regression," "hypersuggestibility," "lowered criticality," and even "a primitive psychophysiological state in which consciousness was eliminated" (1046:136)! But researchers are still puzzled.

Gerald Jampolsky, M.D., states the common problem: "No agreement has been reached on

what constitutes a hypnotic state" (1034:257). Psychologist and associate editor of *Psychology Today*, Daniel Goleman, who has a Ph.D. in clinical psychology from Harvard University, observes, "After 200 years of use, we still cannot say with certainty what hypnosis is nor exactly how it works. But somehow it does" (374:60). A modern encyclopedia on psychology states that "divergent psychological and physiological theories exist to explain [hypnotic] phenomena" (536:545). Nevertheless, "Hypnosis has historically been considered an altered state of consciousness, often called 'trance.' [It is] initiated by a set of procedures called 'induction techniques.' When this altered state has been achieved, then various therapeutic maneuvers in the form of suggestions or other psychological interventions are performed and are called the practice of 'hypnotherapy.' This altered state is characterized by increased suggestibility and enhanced imagery and imagination, including the availability of visual memories from the past. There is also a lowering of the planning function and a reduction in reality testing" (1046:133).

According to psychologist and parapsychologist Dr. Charles Tart, about 10 percent of people do not react at all to attempts to hypnotize them, 20 percent respond to almost any attempt, and the remaining 70 percent vary in their degree of susceptibility** (373:30). One physiological psychologist gives similar but not identical statistics when she writes that "only about 5 percent of the population can be deeply hypnotized: about 20 percent or so can scarcely be hypnotized at all. Everyone else falls somewhere between these two extremes" (2659:64). Nevertheless, the level of trance, at least in many cases, is apparently unrelated to efficacy: "Most practitioners of hypnotherapy have felt that the deeper this depth, the more likely it is that suggestions will be acted upon. . . . [But] excellent results can often be achieved when patients are only in a light or relaxed state" (1046:134).

What we can say is that hypnosis, in large part, involves a deliberately induced heightened state

---

**Perhaps this varies by culture. For example, since mediumism is known to heighten the psychic potential of hypnosis, countries where spiritism is predominant could exhibit different percentages: The more occult oriented a culture, the higher percentage of more easily hypnotizable subjects.

of suggestibility that produces an extremely flexible state of consciousness, often giving the hypnotist dramatic power over the person hypnotized.

Historically in the United States, the practice of hypnosis appears to occur in periodic cycles from acceptance to rejection. First, it is "discovered" and heralded as a panacea, then it is debunked when its failings are realized, and it passes from favor; later it is rediscovered, and the process begins all over. Rediscovery tends to occur in periods of occult revival, which may help to explain why we are currently in the phase of rediscovery and fascination.

Hypnosis has now almost come "of age" in the United States, and it appears to be with us for the foreseeable future. It is widely utilized in the New Age Movement, where autohypnosis is among the most popular forms of self-treatment or spiritual growth (cf. Visualization). Hypnosis is also the principal means for uncovering alleged UFO abductions, a practice whose dangers are clearly outlined in Philip J. Klass' *UFO Abductions: A Dangerous Game.* And *Harper's Encyclopedia of Mystical and Paranormal Experience* points out, "Hypnosis is the most popular means of past-life recall. Self-hypnosis is used in behavior modification, and by mediums and channelers to communicate with spirits" (1526:276).

The application of hypnosis to many other fields, including education, holistic health, psychotherapy, and medicine has been established (cf. New Age Education and Medicine). For example, in *Modern Scientific Hypnosis,* Richard N. Shrout, president of the International Institute of Hypnosis Studies in Miami, Florida, justifies the relevance of hypnosis for modern education:

Hypnosis is of value to educators in the same way it can be of value to psychologists; in both experimental and applied ways. Enough hypnotic experimentation in perception and memory has been done to demonstrate its potential usefulness in applied education. Certain findings in hypnotic research, such as the time-distortion phenomenon could have a revolutionary impact on the learning process....

Since teachers and lecturers are faced with such problems as stimulating students to learn, overcoming their mental blocks about certain subjects, rapid learning of increased amounts of material, instilling studious habits, etc., as well as developing situations in which the curriculum can be mastered and creativity fostered, it should be obvious that they cannot afford to ignore the possibilities of scientifically applied hypnosis....

Of course, it would require teachers especially trained in proper [hypnotic] techniques, and various types of "learning laboratories" would be ideal for educational hypnosis, whether it is called hypnosis or something else.... There is no real reason why hypnological principles could not be applied effectively with beneficial results in all phases of education, even if some other name were used for them....

Experimental and clinical hypnotics have also proven the feasibility of "automated hypnosis" with technological aids....

Every student, beginning at the first year of schooling, should be taught self-hypnosis as a method of self-involvement in goal-seeking activities.... Research that has been done with hypnosis and students indicates that the most dramatic effects are with the "under-achievers." In other words, although all students benefit to some degree, the degree of improvement is most noticeable, most measurable, and most astounding in those who have the most room for improvement (1048:104-07).

According to psychiatrist Dr. George Twente, who was interviewed on "The John Ankerberg Show," September 1992, hypnotic techniques are used in the widely distributed "Pumsy" and DUSO programs, which are curricula in use in thousands of school systems (cf. 1064/1985). Interviewed on the same program, Dr. William Coulson said, "The Michigan Model of Comprehensive Health Education" employs hypnotic methods to place seventh graders into a trance state. Project SOAR is another educational program that uses hypnosis; it is being based upon a book by psychic William Hewitt, *Beyond Hypnosis: A Program for Developing Your Psychic and Healing Power.* In *The New Age Masquerade: The Hidden Agenda in Your Child's Classroom,* Eric Buehrer devotes a chapter to exposing the hypnotic methods and blatant spiritism of this program.

Holistic health care is another avenue for potential exposure to hypnotic methods. Writing in *The Holistic Health Handbook,* psychic Freda

Morris, director of the Hypnosis Clearing House in Berkeley and former assistant professor of medical psychology at the UCLA Medical School, stresses the importance of hypnosis for New Age medicine* when she writes, "Hypnosis, practiced in many societies for millennia by shamans and priests, ... holds great promise as a holistic-health technique ..." (197:241). She states its application to what is often termed "inner work." "Your consciousness is your own and you have a right to do anything you want with it. By going into hypnosis ... you get in touch with a wiser, deeper part of yourself from which you can gain information" (197:241).

Hypnosis and hypnotic regression also play an important role in modern medicine and psychotherapy. Since the American Medical Association approved hypnosis as a legitimate form of treatment in 1958, hypnosis has been increasingly accepted by the medical community. Today, courses in hypnosis are often taught in medical schools, and the practice is used in conjunction with most medical fields.

In *Exploring Hypnosis*, Donald S. Connery observes the impact of modern hypnosis in the medical field:

> ... There is greater interest in and employment of medical hypnosis than ever before in history. ... [M]ore than ten thousand physicians, dentists, psychologists, and psychiatrists in the United States employ hypnosis as a clinical tool. Thousands of other doctors, while not identified with hypnosis, use relaxation techniques and other hypnotic-like methods.
>
> The courses and workshops for clinicians conducted by the major hypnosis professional societies are more popular than ever, and there has been a steady rise in the number of medical and dental schools teaching hypnosis. More and more hospital administrators are recognizing the value of doctors and nurses being proficient in activating the trance capacity of their patients (684:31).

Hypnosis is used to help treat cancer patients who are in pain, to assist patients in dying, and to treat a wide variety of ailments in children. It is also used in anesthesiology, in dentistry and surgery, in the treatment of drug and alcohol abuse, for numerous psychosomatic conditions,

and for hypnotic regression where an individual is taken back to his childhood (or to a supposed past life) to relive traumatic events that are presumably causing present problems. These are only several of its contemporary applications.

The role that hypnosis plays in the field of modern health is also noted by Dr. Gerald Jampolsky, a New Age physician who uses a spiritistic writing (*A Course in Miracles**) in his professional treatment of children:

> Originally limited to [treating] phobic and hysterical states, it [hypnosis] has since been used in conjunction with virtually every medical specialty. With increased enlightenment regarding the role that the mind plays in all illnesses, whether functional or organic, it became clear that hypnosis could assist in the treatment of all illnesses.
>
> [Furthermore] the growing trend toward using hypnosis is explained by the fact it can serve as a shortcut to other, more standard psychotherapeutic techniques. Moreover, by teaching autohypnosis, professionals have been able to assist patients to play a more active role in their own healing process, while gaining a more wholistic viewpoint of the relationship of mind, body, and psychological and spiritual self-concepts. Through hypnotherapy patients can participate in a positive health profile (1034:257-58).

An estimated 20,000 medical and psychological specialists use hypnosis with their patients. Several thousand police officers have been trained to use it in their profession. Numerous professional societies exist to investigate the phenomenon, such as the Society for Clinical and Experimental Hypnosis. A wide variety of self-help or personal growth seminars instruct people in the techniques of self-hypnosis to achieve their desired goals. And, of course, stage hypnosis has been a popular entertainment for millions of people. This means that in modern America millions of people have been hypnotized in varying depths.

Many of the popular claims made for hypnosis are similar to those made for most New Age therapies: 1) Proponents claim it can cure almost anything; 2) it has wide occult application; 3) it has alleged potential to uncover one's so-called "divine mind" or "higher consciousness."

Potentials Unlimited of Grand Rapids, Michigan, and their "World Congress of Professional Hypnotists" offer dozens of how-to tapes on hypnosis that illustrate these claims. The following is a small sampling of claimed benefits:

- how to develop psychic abilities
- past-life (reincarnation) regression therapy
- discovering parallel lives or separate lives
- astral projection or travel
- mind projection
- chakra meditation
- psychic healing
- visualization or guided imagery
- reading auras
- losing weight
- freedom from allergies, acne, or migraines
- calming hyperactive children
- attracting love
- freedom from sexual guilt of any kind
- how to divorce yourself mentally, emotionally, and physically
- how to prepare for death
- generating higher consciousness
- preparing to enter new worlds after death
- subconscious sales power
- money and prosperity
- birth control or conception
- how to be better at sports
- meditating for world peace
- triggering out-of-body experiences (e.g., 710:4-14,29)

The previous list is not exhaustive, but it gives us an idea of the wide variety of uses claimed for hypnosis. Furthermore, the "World Congress of Professional Hypnotists" conventions have keynote speakers such as reincarnation therapist Helen Wambach, parapsychologists, instructors in Silva Mind Control* and related New Age seminars,* as well as authorities on consciousness research and the exploration of "mind power" in general.

## ITS SAFETY?

A large number of organizations offer how-to instruction in hypnosis, and many, if not most of them, also have New Age, Mind Science, or psychic orientations or emphases. This underscores our concern over the modern use of hypnosis, but it is not our only concern. Before writing this chapter, we examined the arguments for the use of hypnosis in medicine and psychotherapy. We have talked with people who have undergone hypnosis in secular and Christian psychotherapy. We agree that in some cases it appears to be helpful. We admit the possibility of a therapeutic use of hypnosis; nevertheless, we have yet to see a convincing set of arguments that answers all the questions which we feel are germane. Thus, we are not willing to give an unqualified or even a tentative endorsement to hypnosis for reasons which should become clear in this chapter.

One way we can illustrate our concerns is through a rough parallel to professional racing. For the moment, let us accept the common belief that competently handled hypnosis is effective and relatively safe. For the qualified professional, so is high-speed racing. But there are still some risks at every turn, even for the professional. Hypnosis is like that. Even when it is safe, there are still risks and potential unknowns; a large number of variables enter into play, and these must be carefully weighed.

However, our concern over hypnosis is dramatically increased when we consider the non-professional, unregulated, and unqualified therapists, as well as New Age or other experimenters that abound in the field. But even professionals are capable of misusing hypnosis and can be deceived by the power it gives them over other people. Even professionals can become subject to its occult trappings and deceptive allurements.

If the alleged moral and safe use of hypnosis is subject to some risk, its amoral and occult use is all the more risky. And it is this segment of hypnosis that appears to dominate the marketplace. Digging for clams may be safe, fun, and perhaps even therapeutic. But no one goes digging for clams in a mine field, even if only a few mines are present. In the following material we will examine hypnosis in the light of the following topics: 1) psychotherapy, 2) science, 3) moral issues, 4) the occult (e.g., hypnosis and the development of psychic powers and spirit contact or possession), and 5) Christian psychotherapy.

## PSYCHOTHERAPEUTIC ASSUMPTIONS

Hypnosis is widely employed in psychotherapy. But in many quarters it is being used under false assumptions, of which we mention three: 1) that the hypnotic state is a normal state of consciousness; 2) that it should be used merely because it works, or because hypnosis is required for effective psychotherapy; 3) that hypnosis can never be used in psychologically or spiritually harmful ways. Let's briefly examine these assumptions.

First, many hypnotherapists, parapsychologists, and some psychotherapists would have us believe that artificially induced, abnormal mental conditions are really normal. In their minds, this premise alone justifies the practice of hypnosis. To them, the hypnotic state is actually a rather "ordinary" experience within a "normal" state of consciousness, one which all of us undergo daily in times of concentration, relaxation, or suggestion (watching TV commercials). Another assumption is that "normal" is something neutral or even good.

We believe that only superficial similarities exist between ordinary waking consciousness and hypnotic states, because the average person certainly does not perform daily activities in a state of hypnotic trance! And is it without question normal or good to allow someone else to control your mind in the dramatic manner called hypnosis? Just because hypnosis can be learned or experienced does not necessarily make it good. Life is full of learned behaviors and personal experiences that are evil or destructive. People can learn to develop psychic abilities if they join a psychic development circle or seek to become a channeler. They can also experience possession. But none of this is normal, good, or neutral because psychic abilities and spirit possession represent a defective, abnormal spirituality rife with unforeseen negative consequences. In a similar manner, we believe hypnotic states are subnormal conditions that potentially open doors to the world of the occult. Therefore, we reject the argument that the hypnotic state is necessarily a normal or natural mental condition.

Second, to accept hypnosis in psychotherapy simply because it is effective is faulty logic. A terrorist's bomb is "effective" when it explodes and

maims people, but does that make it acceptable? If hypnosis is to be accepted solely on the basis of pragmatism (it works; therefore, it is good), we must also accept virtually every form of occult and psychic methodology on the basis of pragmatism—they can be effective, therefore, they are good. But given the psychological and spiritual wreckage in the occult, who would logically argue in such a fashion (277/278)?

Since hypnosis is a questionable procedure, then it should not automatically be accepted merely because it "works." Other factors and issues should be weighed up and the risks balanced against benefits. Regardless, some have questioned whether hypnosis has any necessary value to psychotherapy at all. The truth is that hypnotic methods are not necessary for results in psychotherapy. Martin and Deidre Bobgan, authors of *Psychoheresy* and *Hypnosis and the Christian,* cite Alfred Freedman and others in the *Modern Synopsis of Comprehensive Textbook of Psychiatry II* (2nd ed., 1976, p. 905) as stating, "Everything done in psychotherapy with hypnosis can also be done without hypnosis" (376:47). If hypnosis is really unnecessary in psychotherapy, then the question becomes, "Are the potential risks worth the benefits?"

The third assumption—that hypnosis can never harm anyone—we will discuss in more detail later. For now we will say that psychotherapy either masks or redefines the occult phenomena that may occur during hypnosis. This is because most secular psychologists are rationalists and materialists: They use hypnosis on pragmatic grounds. They do not believe in the spiritual realm, let alone in the possibility of demonic entanglements. What is demonism to the Christian, the secularist explains by natural means. Thus, all spiritistic manifestations that may occur in hypnosis (such as occult "past-life" experiences, certain cases of multiple personalities,** or developing psychic powers) are seen as aspects of the subconscious mind. As a result, these spiritistic manifestations become the

---

**The phenomenon of multiple personality is difficult to evaluate; granting a natural explanation related to childhood abuse in many cases does not invalidate the seemingly spiritistic nature of other cases (1086). (See p. 107-109.)

means for spiritual deception and harm in both the client's and psychotherapist's life (278).

Because the rationalistic psychotherapists do not believe in the potential for demonic intrusion, they are unable to discern or defend against spiritual deception when it occurs in hypnosis. In light of the above, we question their "normal," "pragmatic," or "safe" arguments to justify their use of hypnosis.

## SCIENTIFIC CONCERNS

Clients often submit to hypnosis because of its allegedly scientific nature and medical-therapeutic benefits when in the hands of a qualified professional. The idea is that, while it may be occult or dangerous in the hands of a psychic or charlatan, it is scientific and safe in the hands of a qualified M.D. or a competent psychologist, Christian or otherwise.

But when does an operator ever alter the nature of what he uses? He only alters its *use*. Thus, the person who performs hypnosis may change only the phenomena of hypnosis, not its nature. A parapsychologist using it to explore "past lives" or to increase psychic ability finds different uses than does a materialistic M.D. exploring past traumas, and who is uninterested in psychic phenomena. However, the M.D. could use it for the same purpose as the parapsychologist. And, as we will see, psychic phenomena can occur spontaneously even when these are not being sought. So the issue is not only the operator of hypnosis but the potential problems of the hypnotic state itself.

Hypnosis does have many scientific associations. The problem is that hypnosis itself is not a scientific technique. Martin and Diedre Bobgan claim that hypnosis in the hands of a qualified psychiatrist or therapist is about as scientific as a dowsing* rod in the hands of an engineer (376:46). They assert: "We cannot call hypnosis a science, but we can say it has been an integral part of the occult for thousands of years" (376:43). They give several illustrations of parallels between hypnosis and witchcraft:

E. Fuller Torrey, a research psychiatrist, aligns hypnotic techniques with witchcraft. He also says, "Hypnosis is one aspect of the yoga techniques of therapeutic meditation."

Medical doctor William Kroger states, "The fundamental principles of Yoga are, in many respects, similar to those of hypnosis."

Donald Hebb says in "Psychology Today/The State of the Science" that "hypnosis has persistently lacked satisfactory explanation." Kroger and Fezler say, "There are as many definitions of hypnosis as there are definers." At the present time there is no agreed-upon scientific explanation of exactly what hypnosis is. Szasz describes hypnosis as the therapy of "a fake science ... " (376:42-43).

One illustration of the problems faced by the "scientific" use of hypnosis is its application to memory enhancement. Hypnosis has become popular as a method of helping uncover traumatic memories, particularly where a violent crime is involved. At one time, such testimony was accepted in courts of law, but now experts are questioning the accuracy and validity of this approach. Hypnosis may indeed produce information that helps solve a crime, but that does not make it sufficiently reliable for court testimony.

An expert in hypnosis, Dr. Bernard Diamond, professor of clinical psychiatry at UC Berkeley, wrote in the *California Law Review*, "I believe that once a potential witness has been hypnotized ... his recollections have been so contaminated that he is rendered effectively incompetent to testify. Hypnotized persons, being extremely suggestible, graft onto their memories fantasies or suggestions ... (and) then cannot differentiate between a true recollection and fantasy" (372).

Martin Orne, coauthor of the *Encyclopaedia Britannica* article on hypnosis and director of the Unit of Experimental Psychiatry at the Institute of Pennsylvania Hospital, believes, "Hypnotic memory is clearly less accurate than normal waking recall" (424:35). It is simply not possible to verify the accuracy of memory that is enhanced by hypnosis (372). Martin and Diedre Bobgan cited Diamond's conclusions:

Bernard Diamond, a professor of law and a clinical professor of psychiatry, says that court witnesses who have been hypnotized "often develop a certitude about their memories that ordinary witnesses seldom exhibit." . . . Diamond then reveals that "after hypnosis the subject cannot differentiate between a true recollection and a fantasy or a suggested detail. . . ."

Research shows that hypnosis is just as likely to dredge up false information as true accounts of past events. In addition, studies have shown that individuals *can* and *do* lie under hypnosis. Because memory is so unreliable, any method of cure which relies upon memory is generally unreliable (376:24-25).

The previous facts, and the fact that the subject under hypnosis is, typically, extremely sensitive to leading questions and what the hypnotist expects from him, call into question all "therapy" of the type which seeks to relate present problems to alleged "past-life" incidents, birth or childhood experiences, or subconscious material based solely on hypnotic memory:

[H]ypnotized subjects apparently are very sensitive to subtle cues coming from their therapist or experimenter. Orne (1979) has called attention to the fact that inadvertently hypnotists can transmit their expectations to their subjects, who then give back to the hypnotist the desired behavior. It is not surprising that investigators often report contradictory results. Very little seems to have been done in controlling the beliefs, theories, and expectations of researchers. . . . While most of the major controversies in the field have been extensively studied, to date few of them have been completely and satisfactorily resolved (1046:135).

## MORAL ISSUES AND POTENTIAL DANGERS

Robert A. Baker has taught psychology at Stanford University and the Massachusetts Institute of Technology. He is the author of *They Call It Hypnosis,* in which he argues that hypnosis does not exist as a unique state of awareness or consciousness. He argues that what is called hypnosis is merely a normal state of creative imagination, relaxation, and suggestion (1735:288-89) and that

it is not dangerous at all in the hands of a qualified therapist. "In fact, almost no one believes the use of hypnosis constitutes any danger." He also cites authorities on hypnosis who claim that the procedure is harmless (1735:269-70).

Nevertheless, prior to this he points out that dangers *do* exist in hypnosis, but that they are no worse than those associated with psychotherapy in general. The real dangers, he insists, arise with the therapist, not with hypnosis:

Just about anything and everything can be dangerous if it is misused or misapplied. . . . There are no deaths on record due specifically to hypnosis. In spite of this fact, a number of years ago Harold Rosen launched a nationwide campaign against hypnosis, on the premise that it could endanger a patient's physical and emotional health and life through serious adverse sequelae such as incapacitating substitute symptoms, suicidal depression, and psychotic episodes. In an article in the *American Journal of Clinical Hypnosis,* A. Meares (1961) pointed out nine possible areas of difficulty the hypnotist or his client might encounter. These were:

1. Perverse motivation; either the patient or the physician may misuse the situation to satisfy ulterior needs.

2. Untoward personality effects; hypnosis can increase a subject's suggestibility and overdependence; conversely, continued use of hypnosis may exaggerate unfortunate facets of the physician's own personality.

3. Traumatic insight; sudden confrontation with repressed material intolerable to the subject.

4. Precipitation of a psychosis.

5. Development of disabling substitute symptoms when the original symptoms have been removed by hypnotic suggestion.

6. Sudden panic reactions occasioned by the experience of hypnosis.

7. Complications arising from misunderstandings of communication.

8. Possible unscrupulous use of hypnosis.

9. Difficulty in waking a subject and unfortunate effects of incomplete waking.

Meares concluded that the use of hypnosis by an unskilled person can represent a real danger, but the dangers, he felt, are minimal in the hands of a trained physician. It is obvious, however, that most of the dangers listed above are by no means peculiar to hypnosis. They are intrinsic to all intimate interpersonal relationships that develop during any type of psychotherapy. In fact, if there is any danger at all with regard to the use of hypnosis, it resides almost wholly in its use as a therapeutic tool, and the danger in that case is primarily to the hypnotist rather than the client.

Sydney Pulver (1963) called attention to the fact that many patients suffer from delusions following a hypnotic session, and the delusions are usually the result of the interplay of three factors: 1) the heightening of transference fantasies due mainly to the regression of the hypnotic state; 2) the presence of major ego defects, projective defenses, or other predisposing factors in the patient's character; 3) countertransference reaction on the part of the hypnotist which touch on a specific area of conflict within the patient.

The delusions most commonly take the form of the patient accusing the hypnotist of violating the patient's person, property, or privacy, of unduly influencing him, of rendering him helpless against the sexual or financial influence of others, etc. Pulver recommends that anyone using hypnosis should be careful to conduct a good preliminary evaluation and select patients who are free from dispositions to delusions, and also be aware of his own emotional responses to the patient. . . .

As for hypnosis being of any danger to the client, other than in a few rare and isolated instances, hypnosis has proven to be one of the safest tools in the armamentarium of the healing professions. This was the conclusion of a special symposium devoted to hypnotic complications that was published in the January 1987 *American Journal of Clinical Hypnosis*. J. H. Conn (1972), among others, has also minimized the complications related to the use of hypnosis and concluded it is a very safe procedure. According to Conn, "There are no significant dangers associated with hypnosis *per se* and the actual dangers are those which accompany every psychotherapeutic relationship. . . .

In his book *Hypnotism: Its Powers and Practice*, Peter Blythe (1971) notes that even trained professionals make mistakes in their use of hypnotherapeutic procedures. In his words, "My intention has been to illustrate that there are no dangers inherent in hypnosis itself, and any dangers which do arise are created by the hypnotist, and not hypnosis" (1735:268-69).

Thus, the argument is advanced that hypnosis itself is harmless and that potential complications arise only from the therapist who misuses the practice. But even granting this claim, concerns must still be raised over the widespread use of hypnosis when incompetence and abuse among therapists *are* so frequent. After all, it is conceded that "even trained professionals make mistakes in their use of hypnotherapeutic procedures," and that such mistakes can result in serious complications for the patient. The argument that hypnosis is safe seems unestablished if the dangers of hypnosis cannot easily be separated from the expertise of the hypnotist. And if even the experts make mistakes, what about the majority of hypnotherapists who are not expert? And even some experts in hypnotic procedures may be immoral or abuse hypnosis for personal reasons.

Dr. Baker also points out, and it is becoming increasingly evident to many, that psychotherapy itself has certain risks; indeed, entire books have been written on this subject, such as Dorothy Tennov's *Psychotherapy: The Hazardous Cure* (see 1736/2491). But if therapy itself has potential dangers, then to introduce hypnosis into the equation complicates problems.

To concede that hypnosis has similar risks to those found in therapy in general is to concede that hypnosis is potentially dangerous. This is especially true given the large number of amateur or unqualified hypnotherapists, and the equally large number of humanistic, Jungian, and transpersonal therapists, whose experimental, eclectic, and frequently occult approach to therapy does indeed constitute a risk factor.

Dr. Baker also cites Dr. Frank J. MacHovec's *Hypnosis Complications*, which details a large number of problems and complications related to hypnosis. While Baker is convinced that these result from preexisting personality disorders of the patients, rather than from hypnosis, we are not so convinced. But even if it were true, it would still show that hypnosis is dangerous for *some* people. And who doesn't have at least *some* degree of preexisting personality disorder that they bring into therapy? How can therapists know they determined the real extent of a patient's problem or the effect hypnosis may have?

We think at least five distinct variables must be considered when evaluating the risks of hypnosis:

1. The religious, ethical, and philosophical orientation of the hypnotherapist.

2. The emotional history and condition of the client.

3. The degree of technical expertise and past experience of the therapist.

4. The motive and purpose for engaging in hypnosis.

5. The hypnotic state itself.

In the material following, we will cite a number of authorities. We will briefly examine the potential dangers of hypnosis in popular and psychotherapeutic methods, and then we will document the dangers arising from the occult potential of hypnosis.**

A popular belief is that a hypnotized subject cannot be made to do something against her will or to commit an evil act. But this is simply not true. Dr. J. Meerloo, a psychiatric consultant in the geriatric department of the Municipal Health Service of Amsterdam, the Netherlands, discusses how and why hypnosis can be used to manipulate people to commit evil acts. He is supportive of professionally administered hypnosis, but he seeks to dispel certain myths:

Several textbooks on hypnosis inform us that the patient's superego is strong enough to protect him against immoral suggestions given in a trance. Experimental hypnosis has shown that this is not the case. The art of moral seduction is based on repeated fragmentized suggestions that gradually permit the other party to give in to what he or she would never have done without those repeated suggestions.... The act of suicide, especially, can be suggested by an aggressor with daily nagging admonitions or in semi-hypnotic trance. In a previous study I

called this criminal suggestive strategy *psychic homicide....*

Indeed, hypnosis is a means whereby one can manipulate the conscience of other people. ... At the close of the Second World War, one of my tasks was to investigate SS officers. I discovered that several of them had participated in the most outrageous, unthinkable crimes while in a kind of collective trance. Indeed, they broke down when a more realistic awareness took hold of them.

There are numerous other examples to indicate that a person can be induced to commit antisocial acts while under the influence of hypnosis or under collective suggestion, or because of servile dependency. He would have considered these deeds unacceptable to him had circumstances allowed him to remain an independent thinking individual (375:1-2; cf. pp. 22-24).

In theory, there is no immoral act that a hypnotized subject could not be tricked into committing:

---

**Documentation concerning the potential dangers and/or misuse of hypnosis can be found in e.g., Eugene E. Levitt, et. al, "Testing the Coercive Power of Hypnosis: Committing Objectionable Acts," *The International Journal of Clinical and Experimental Hypnosis*, Vol. 23, No. 1 (1975); Campbell Perry, "Hypnotic Coercion and Compliance to It: A Review of Evidence Presented in a Legal Case," *The International Journal of Clinical and Experimental Hypnosis*, Vol. 27, No. 3 (1979); Steven Starker, "Persistence of a Hypnotic Dissociative Reaction," *The International Journal of Clinical and Experimental Hypnosis*, Vol. 22, No. 2 (1974); Josephine R. Hilgard, "Sequelae to Hypnosis," *The International Journal of Clinical and Experimental Hypnosis*, Vol. 22, No. 4 (1974); Moris Kleinhauz, et. al, "Some After-Effects of Stage Hypnosis: A Case Study of Psychopathological Manifestations," *The International Journal of Clinical and Experimental Hypnosis*, Vol. 27, No. 3 (1979); Doris Gruenewald, "Failures in Hypnotherapy: A Brief Communication," *The International Journal of Clinical and Experimental Hypnosis*, Vol. 19, No. 4 (1981); Moris Kleinhauz and Barbara Beran, "Misuses of Hypnosis: A Medical Emergency and Its Treatment," *The International Journal of Clinical and Experimental Hypnosis*, Vol. 29, No. 2 (1981); Moris Kleinhauz and Barbara Beran, "Misuses of Hypnosis: A Factor in Psychopathology," *American Journal of Clinical Hypnosis*, Jan. 1984.

Since reality becomes distorted during a trance, the subject cannot properly evaluate which actions make sense and which ones do not. Hilgard says that in the trance state there is a trance logic that accepts "what would normally be found incompatible." . . . If reality is distorted and the person is not able to make reality judgments, his means of responsible choice have been impaired. He is unable to exercise his own will responsibly.

A well-known textbook of psychiatry states: "Hypnosis can be described as an altered state of intense and sensitive interpersonal relatedness between hypnotist and patient, characterized by the patient's nonrational submission and relative abandonment of executive control to a more or less regressed, dissociated state."

. . . A hypnotist *can* deceive a person into committing an act which would be in violation of his normal range of choice. A hypnotist can even lead a person into committing murder by creating an extreme fear that someone is attempting to kill him. The patient would discern it as an act of self-defense. Through hypnotic deception, it is possible to cause one to do something against his will by disguising the act into one which would be within his choice.

Because hypnosis places responsibility outside the exercise of objective, rational, full conscious choice, it does violate the will. The normal evaluating abilities are submerged and choice is made according to suggestion without the balance of rational restraint. The will is a precious treasure of humans and shows forth the indelible hand of our Creator. The human will requires more respect than hypnosis seems to offer. Bypassing the responsible state of reason and choice just because of the hope for some desired end is bad medicine and, worst of all, bad theology (376:34-36).

Most people falsely assume that hypnosis can never be misused professionally. But there has been more than one case where therapists have confessed to hypnotizing patients to take advantage of them sexually. With the expected use of hypnotic suggestions to *forget* the sexual encounter, one wonders about how many unreported cases there are.

Psychologist and leading parapsychologist Dr. Charles Tart acknowledges that when hypnosis was "reintroduced" into America through mesmerism "much of its emphasis was on power over people" (373:28). He also confesses, the "god-like" power the hypnotist exerts over his client is "what attracts a lot of us into the field" (373:30). Although Dr. Tart uses hypnosis clinically and experimentally, he acknowledges that the power of hypnosis:

. . . horrifies me every time I see it done. . . . You can induce total analgesia. . . .

You can have people hallucinate. . . . You can tamper with their memory in certain ways so they do not remember what went on in a hypnotic session or they remember selected parts of it or you can induce false memories of one sort or another. These sorts of things can happen after the hypnotic session, post hypnotically. . . . [S]o it's what I might call a very strong phenomenon. . . . The phenomena are pretty striking (373:27-28).

The following statement by Dr. Tart underscores the occult quality of hypnosis (in spite of its scientific image) as well as an apparent motive of many hypnotherapists for entering the field, that of seeking power over others:

Now, I've talked about these kinds of cycles in terms of hypnosis being used for too many things, to cure everything. But, in point of fact, it's actually more than that. Because while I run with a bunch of people who are the scientists in this field and we talk very scientific language and all that, if you think about it there's a tremendous magical quality to hypnosis and this never ceases to amaze me. It doesn't work well with everybody, but for about 20 percent of people in general it works extremely well.

And for these people I can sit down, and in the course of talking to them for half an hour or sometimes less I can change their whole perceptual world. And it really blows my mind to think that I can talk to somebody for a half an hour and tell them Marilyn Monroe is floating through the window, and they really see it. As far as I can tell from anything they say, they really see it.

This is a phenomenal change in somebody's experience. *And this smacks very much of magic.* In fact, if you look at a lot of old magical procedures, a lot of the techniques were similar to the kinds of techniques we use in hypnosis now. Now, this is something that isn't discussed very often in modern scientific hypnosis. . . .

In a sense, the hypnotist acquires a certain amount of god-like power over the subject. He can simply restructure his reality. This attracts a lot of us into the field. I came into it for that. I really dug having all this power over people. I hope I've changed. I'm not sure sometimes, but at least I've got a good set of rationalizations now. Being a hypnotist can be a marvelous ego trip. You can bend men's wills and change their reality and even give them good experiences and that's really an ego trip. A number of charlatans come into hypnosis, of course, because of that . . . (373:29-30).

Dr. Meerloo, quoted earlier, also discusses some of the problems and dangers that may occur during psychotherapeutic hypnosis:

As long as the hypnosis is applied incidentally to initiate anesthesia or soothe pain, not much harm will be done. But in repeated hypnotherapy, the therapist's feelings of omnipotence (of which he is not always aware) may be aroused too much in response to the patient's infantile dependency without either participant escaping from this delusional labyrinth. While working with future psychotherapists I learned that especially those whose infantile magic thinking is not sufficiently under control like to use hypnosis as a means of therapy. . . .

I have also seen patients who after a hypnotic session lived for days in a kind of hysterical fugue, roaming around without finding the initiative to resist influences from outside. . . .

Acceptance of hypnosis by the therapist as a method of cure unobtrusively influences his option for a patient's free, independent, individual mind, or a state of mental dependency. The therapist's choice of hypnosis as a means of cure almost always implies a preference for passivity and obedience on the patient's part and a non-acceptance of the challenge of uniqueness, loneliness, and isolation.

Inadvertently, hypnosis holds out the lure of a quick cure while ignoring the complexity of complications and involvements that follow in its wake. Because everybody can learn how to hypnotize in a few lessons, the danger of over-simplified, panacea-like attitudes is very real. The disappearance of symptoms, rather than an understanding and working through of them, becomes the sole aim.

Hypnosis unwittingly tends to propagate man's living by proxy. Indeed, people with a feeble will may temporarily borrow the strength, goals, aims, and illusions of the hypnotist. It may at the same time be an exercise in detachment and withdrawal. From this breeding ground of dangerous, passive mental defenses, often no return is possible (375:23).

The Bobgans stress the problems involved in treating symptoms rather than the underlying problems:

Immediate positive results from hypnotism should especially be dismissed as evidence for validity of the practice, since many who gain initial victory over problems later suffer defeat. The pain which was "cured" may return, the sleep turns again into sleeplessness, and the temporarily improved sex life deteriorates.

Besides this possibility of the quick cure, short-term change with later failure, there is the possibility of symptom substitution. For example, those who are relieved of migraine headaches through hypnosis may end up with ulcers. A study conducted at the famous Diamond Headache Clinic in Chicago revealed the strong possibility of symptom substitution. They found that of those migraine patients who had learned to control headaches through biofeedback, "two-thirds reported the development of new psychosomatic symptoms within five years" (376:46).

In his *Demonology Past and Present*, noted theologian and counselor Dr. Kurt Koch also refers to the possibility of symptom substitution or transference:

Hypnotism is a highly controversial subject. The famous psychologist, Dr. Paul Tournier of Geneva in Switzerland rejects its use entirely. He argues that hypnotism illegally interferes with the subconscious mind and the soul of man. On the other hand I have met missionaries who have regarded hypnotism as a means of obtaining healing.

I will quote an example concerning the head doctor of the Cruz Blanca Sanatorium, Esquil, Argentina.

One of the doctor's patients was a woman suffering from a pronounced complex. . . . Hypnotizing her, the doctor told her that when she regained consciousness the spiders would be gone. The experiment was successful. Yet from that time onwards the woman began to develop a strong alcoholic addiction, something she had never suffered from before. The doctor told me that because this transference had taken place, he now had reservations about using hypnotism in his practice.

A similar example to this was told me in the Swiss canton of Berne while I was counselling a person there. A Christian woman was hypnotized by a doctor while she was suffering from a gall-stone colic. The hypnosis was surprisingly successful and the almost unbearable pain disappeared within minutes. Afterwards, however, the woman began to suffer from terrible outbursts of rage. . . . In this case the hypnosis had triggered off a lack of self-control, and the many similar examples I have come across in my work have led me too to reject the use of hypnosis as a means of therapy. . . .

I can quote an example of occult hypnosis to help us understand the problem more clearly. It comes from a Baptist minister in the United States. . . . [At college his] son had taken part in one of the school's entertainment evenings. The highlight of the evening came when a hypnotist invited 25 of the students to come up onto the stage and then hypnotized them. He suggested to them that they were all taking part in a horse race.

When the act ended, the hypnotist told the students to come back out of their hypnotic states. The minister's son, however, remained in a trance. The college president was extremely worried. In the end they were forced to call the hospital, and the boy was taken away in an ambulance. The doctors attempted again to bring him out of his hypnotic state, but with no success. It was only after five days had passed that his father was finally notified as to what had [really] happened.

Immediately he had his son transferred to his own home. Together with his wife and some friends they began to pray for the boy. Yet even then the hypnotic effect was not broken.

In the end, when a few more days had elapsed, the father felt constrained to command his son in the name of Jesus. To his amazement, his son responded at once. The hypnotic effect was broken.

I could quote many examples like this involving so-called harmless hypnotists. People must be warned of the dangers involved in allowing their children to take part in what they think are only harmless hypnotic games.

The unfortunate thing is that occult hypnosis is often used as a means of obtaining healing. The apparent success of the hypnosis, however, is accompanied without fail with all sorts of mental and emotional disturbances. As the previous example shows, even qualified doctors are unable to undo the damage done by occult forms of hypnosis. The problem is not a medical one, but rather a religious one (271:114-15,127-28).

## Occult Potential

Our next concern with hypnosis is its promotion of the occult. We will introduce the relationship here and then proceed to a more in-depth analysis.

*Altered States of Consciousness**

In our chapter on altered states of consciousness,* we documented why we were concerned over the great amount of experimentation in this area. ASCs were shown to be excellent doorways to spiritistic phenomena and possession. Hypnosis is, after all, an altered state of consciousness* that has marked similarities to occult ASCs, particularly in its more profound states. For example, the deeper levels of hypnosis have a number of parallels to ASCs produced in the practices of occult Eastern religions, such as Hinduism and Buddhism, which often culminate in possession (see Eastern Gurus and Enlightenment).

In 1971, one of the earliest scientific studies on this was reported by parapsychologist Dr. Charles Tart, who apparently first coined the term "altered states of consciousness." Dr. Tart discussed the mystical potential of deep hypnosis, which he correctly perceived was a future direction in research. Significantly, these descriptions are strikingly similar to the occult, spiritistic, and pantheistic states of consciousness found in many occult religions, cults, and mystical practices. Common characteristics include: 1) an entire alteration of one's sense of identity; 2) the disappearance of the self and replacement with a sense of infinite potential existing in infinite consciousness; 3) unthinking awareness, i.e., no awareness of the process of individual consciousness or the physical world environment; 4) transcendence of space/time concepts, which become meaningless; 5) pantheistic sensations and feelings of monistic oneness with the universe (373:34-37). Dr. Tart observes, "I think what we have here is a transition to a new state of consciousness. In many ways it sounds like what's traditionally been called the [Buddhist] Void" (373:37).

In "Measuring Hypnotic Depth" in *Hypnosis: Developments in Research and New Perspectives* (1979, p. 59), Dr. Tart discusses "the possibility of using hypnotic states to induce and/or model mystical states" (376:29). In *Divided Consciousness: Multiple Controls in Human Thought and Action* (1977, p. 168), Ernest Hilgard, who has studied hypnosis over a quarter of a century, comes to an identical conclusion about deep hypnosis and Eastern mysticism: "The passage of time becomes meaningless, the body seems to be left behind, a new sense of infinite potentiality emerges, ultimately reaching the sense of oneness with the universe" (376:30). Clinical psychologist Peter Francuch in *Principles of Spiritual Hypnosis* (1981, pp. 79-80) describes the higher levels of hypnosis where "one goes through various states and levels that reflect different states and levels of the spiritual world and its conditions.... Here is [also] a state that corresponds to the state described by Eastern mystics" (376:30).

As our next section will indicate, the fact that hypnotism and Eastern mysticism share much in common is hardly surprising. The occult potential of hypnosis is probably its greatest hazard.

*Occult Associations Historically*

In various forms, hypnotism can be found in every culture in every age. Historically, it is typi-

cally associated with the occultist or psychic, the one who exercises power over things or persons, such as the shaman, magician, witch doctor, medium, witch, guru, or yogi. In our own country, hypnosis was first called mesmerism, where it was frequently associated with the occult. And its association to spiritism and early mind science religion (2639) was pervasive:

In America, an initial proponent of mesmerism named Andrew Jackson Davis began leading supporters of mesmerism into the new faith of spiritualism. At about the same time, mesmerism was developed into a new healing system by Phineas Parkhurst Quimby (1802-1866), a professional mesmerist who felt that many diseases could be cured by suggestion and were therefore essentially illusory. Eventually drawing the conclusion that all diseases are illusory, Quimby in 1859 began teaching the system that he called Science of Christ, Science of Health, and occasionally Christian Science. His system later developed into the New Thought movement, and led by Mary Baker Eddy, who began her career as a mesmerist and a spiritualist medium, into Christian Science (1525:59).

The writings of such spiritists as A. J. Davis and Mary Baker Eddy (2639) are all pervasively anti-Christian (cf. *Science and Health with Key to the Scriptures; A. J. Davis and the Arabula*; 1857), as are the writings of occultists in general. The fact that it was mesmerism which helped lead such individuals into occult philosophy and practice is noteworthy.

According to neurosurgeon and occult advocate Dr. Norman Shealy, the first formal study of clairvoyant diagnosis began around 1847 with the British physician John Elliotson and his work with mesmerism, or "animal magnetism," as it was termed by its founder Anton Mesmer who was also an astrologer and mystic. Actually, mesmerism was the source for the nineteenth-century development of psychic diagnosis, and it was used for decades prior to Elliotson's study in both Europe and America. In the United States at the time of Elliotson's study there was a great deal of interest in mesmerism, which culminated in the spiritist movement that began in 1848. In part, modern parapsychology seems to have begun with mesmerism, which before the 1800s had become a worldwide fascination (2027:4-6).

Examination of historical accounts of mesmerism disclose obvious ties to occultism (2028), including many spiritistic phenomena—contacting the dead in mesmeric trances, occult psychometry, occult personality alterations, and astrology.* In fact, the mesmerist trance is strongly linked with, if not identical to, the trance state of shamans and mediums (2032). The term used to describe the trance state was "somnambulance." Slater Brown, in his study of 19th century spiritism, states:

> The Swedish magnetists, under the influence of their own great seer, Emanuel Swedenborg, almost at once turned their attention to the invisible world and soon were receiving messages from identifiable spirits through magnetized clairvoyants. As early as 1788, sixty years before spiritualism initiated the general practice of communing with the recently deceased, a Stockholm society devoted to the study of animal magnetism reported to a sister society in France a number of cases in which somnambulists, acting as mediums, had transmitted messages from the spirit world (463:11).

A well-known magnetist, J. P. F. Deleuze (author of *Practical Instruction in Animal Magnetism*, 1846), wrote to another prominent magnetist, French physician G. Billot, that "a great number of somnambulists have affirmed that they have conversed with spiritual intelligences and have been inspired and guided by them" (463:11). Billot stated that somnambulists had, in the words of Brown, "produced flowers and other objects presumably out of thin air.... Some of the spirits who appeared were tangible, one not only saw but could touch them....I [Billot] have seen the stigmata rise on magnetized subjects, I have dispelled obsessions of evil spirits with a single word. I have seen spirits bring those material objects I told you of, and when requested make them so light that they would float" (463:12).

Even today mediums use hand (or healing) passes physically similar to the early mesmerist hand passes (2033). Also, the early "cures" associated with mesmerism were not infrequently accompanied by symptoms of spirit possession (hysterical fits, severe convulsions, and so on) which, incidentally, were also reminiscent of the mass possessions of the Shaker community during 1837-44 (463:8). Clearly, the somnambulists did experience marked personality changes while in trance, as if another being were inside them (468:3).

The similarity of mesmerism to mediumism is obvious, and so it is not surprising the mesmerist movement laid the basis for and was absorbed by the spiritist movement that followed it. In his authoritative *Encyclopedia of Psychic Science*, psychoanalyst and psychic researcher Dr. Nandor Fodor writes: "The conquest by spiritualism soon began and the leading Mesmerists were absorbed into the rank of the spiritualists" (389:241).

J. P. Rindge, founder and director of the Human Dimensions Institute, also observes the parallels, many of them reminiscent of modern procedures in various forms of New Age healing (psychic healing, "Touch for Health," therapeutic touch, and so on):

> Hand passes and suggestion frequently entranced the patients, some of whom in this somnambulistic state "saw" what their physical eyes were incapable of seeing including, reportedly, their own internal organs with diagnosis (often erroneous) and prognosis (often correct) of cure. Further, many claimed to see, converse with and be healed by departed spirits. This trend mushroomed into the rapidly spreading Spiritualist movement, and was accepted by millions. It absorbed many of the Mesmerists who claimed collusion with departed spirits for the purposes of healing (2029:17).

One of the authoritative volumes on parapsychology says of spiritism: "No doubt its passage had been eased by the earlier conquests of the Mesmerists. The role of the trance medium fitted neatly the niche previously occupied by the somnambules, and not a few of those who began as mesmerists made the transition to Spiritualism" (2027:5).

Mesmerism, then, paved the way for occult revival. And there is an ominous parallel today in the great upsurge of interest in hypnotism as both an occult method and a medical-diagnostic tool. In many ways, we are again being fascinated by mesmerism. Whatever their differences, one fact is admitted by all: The phenomenon of mesmerism is today known as hypnotism.

It is perhaps worth noting that the aforementioned Andrew Jackson Davis, a powerful medium with an unrelenting antagonism toward Christianity, developed his clairvoyant diagnosis and other occult powers by mesmerism, just as today hypnosis has helped to produce a great number of mediums and psychics. Davis was known as the "John the Baptist" of the spiritualist movement, and his life and teachings bear many parallels to those of Edgar Cayce, who similarly first developed his abilities in psychic diagnosis from hypnosis (2031).

Nevertheless, in our modern scientific age, hypnosis also has recurring cycles of association with the scientific community, such as with the psychiatrist, psychologist, physician, and dentist. The *Encyclopedia of Occultism and Parapsychology* reveals that though most authorities no longer classify it as an occult phenomenon, its correlation to the occult historically cannot be denied (cf. 764):

> *Hypnotism* is no longer classed with the occult sciences. It has gained, though only within comparatively recent years, a definite scientific status, and no mean place in legitimate medicine. Nevertheless its history is inextricably interwoven with occultism, and even today much hypnotic phenomena is classed as "spiritualistic"; so that the consideration of *hypnotism* in this place [encyclopedia] is very necessary to a proper understanding of much of the occult science of our own and former times.... [A]t a very early date phenomena of a distinctly hypnotic character were ascribed to the workings of spiritual agencies, whether angelic or demonic, by a certain percentage of observers (377,I:448,453).

*Occult Phenomena*

Hypnosis can produce a wide variety of occult phenomena. For example, it takes four volumes just to survey nineteenth-century cases (1087). The following are some of the more spectacular, which may occur in deeper hypnotic states: past-life experiences, multiple personalities, speaking in unknown languages, automatic writing, vari-

ous psychic powers (clairvoyance, psychometry, telepathy), committing acts against one's will, seizures, spirit possession, astral projection, and psychic diagnosis (380; cf. 1087). It is significant that all of these phenomena also occur in or through the mediumistic trance state where a person is possessed by demons. In light of this, we question the advisability of widespread use of hypnosis.

The occult application of hypnosis can be found in many modern articles and texts on the subject, such as *Beyond Hypnosis: A Program for Developing Your Psychic and Healing Powers* (713).** The author is William W. Hewitt, a Silva Mind Control* graduate, who is also a psychic, a professional astrologer, and a member of the American Association of Profession Hypnotherapists. He encourages visualization* and self-hypnotic exercises to develop altered states of consciousness, psychic powers, and channeling,* or spirit contact. As noted earlier, this text influenced the project SOAR educational curriculum.

---

**Additional examples include Mylan Ryzl, *Hypnosis and ESP* (763); Dr. Hiroshi Motoyama, *Hypnosis and Religious Super-Consciousness,* Tokyo, Japan, The Institute of Religious Psychology, 1971; Erik J. Dingwall (ed.), *Abnormal Hypnotic Phenomena: A Survey of Nineteenth-Century Cases,* 4 vols., New York: Barnes and Noble, 1967, 1968; V. L. Raikov, "Theoretical Analysis of Deep Hypnosis: Creative Activity of Hypnotized Subjects into Transformed Self-Consciousness," *The American Journal of Clinical Hypnosis,* April 1977, pp. 214-20; R. Douglas Smith, "Hypnosis, Multiple Personality, and Magic: A Case Study," *Voices: The Art and Science of Psychotherapy,* Spring 1981, pp. 20-32; Richard J. Davidson, Daniel J. Goleman, "The Role of Attention in Meditation and Hypnosis: A Psychobiological Perspective on Transformations of Consciousness," *The International Journal of Clinical and Experimental Hypnosis,* October 1977, pp. 291-308 (cf. Erika Fram, "Altered States of Consciousness and Hypnosis: A Discussion"; David Akstein, "Terpsichoretrancetherapy: A New Hypnopsychotherapeutic Method," *The International Journal of Clinical and Experimental Hypnosis,* Vol. 21, No. 3 (1973, pp. 131-43); Thelma Moss, et. al, "Hypnosis and ESP: A Controlled Experiment," *The American Journal of Clinical and Experimental Hypnosis,* July 1970, pp. 46-56; R. L. Van De Castle, "The Facilitation of ESP Through Hypnosis," *The American Journal of Clinical and Experimental Hypnosis,* July 1969, pp. 37-56; Isaac Gubel, "From Hypnosis to Sophrology—Eleven Years of Teaching," *The American Journal of Clinical Hypnosis,* April 1973.

Clinical psychologist Leslie M. LeCron is a member of the American Board of Psychological Hypnosis. In *Self-Hypnotism: The Technique and Its Use in Daily Living*, he explains how to use hypnosis in conjunction with the occult pendulum, and how to develop the occult practice of automatic writing for self-healing (712:28-32). In using the pendulum he states, "This technique has been taught to several thousand physicians by a small group of physicians, dentists, and psychologists known as Hypnosis Symposiums. It has been used in many thousands of cases to great advantage, its users including a number of psychiatrists" (712:31; cf. Dowsing).

In the following pages we will document two aspects of the occult potential of hypnosis: how it can develop psychic abilities and its connections to spiritism (demonism), including the possibility of demon possession through hypnosis. We document this in some detail because so many people today believe that hypnosis is merely an innocent pastime and has no spiritual implications whatever.

*Psychic Abilities.* Many articles in standard parapsychological texts and journals indicate that psychologists and parapsychologists with an interest in hypnosis often use it to uncover and explore so-called human psychic potential.

Drs. Stanley Krippner and Leonard George are well-known researchers of consciousness. (Krippner is with the Center for Consciousness Studies, Saybrook Institute, San Francisco, California.) In "Psi Phenomena as Related to Altered States of Consciousness" in the *Handbook of States of Consciousness*, they observe: "Of the sixteen comparisons between hypnosis and waking conditions in these sixteen studies, ten showed overall significant psi performance in hypnosis.... Honorton concluded, 'The conclusion is now inescapable that hypnotic induction procedures enhance psi receptivity.... In a meta-analysis of twenty studies in which psi tasks were compared in this manner, sixteen showed higher scoring for the hypnotic condition, with seven attaining statistical significance'" (1046:337-38).

Leslie LeCron, co-author of *Hypnotism Today*, editor of *Experimental Hypnosis,* and a member of the Academy of Psychosomatic Medicine, observes that the only discernible differences between earlier hypnotism (mesmerism) and modern clinical hypnotism is the method of induction (hand passes over the body versus verbal suggestion) and the depth of trance. Modern hypnosis may involve either a light, medium, or deep trance. The deep trance may be termed a somnambulistic state. In mesmerism more time was spent on induction, which seems to have produced a deeper state of trance, (378:70; cf. 765-74).

However, it appears that only a relatively small percentage of persons can reach the state of deep trance, and even a smaller percentage slips easily into this state (1526:275/378:70-71). A deeper state may be termed "plenary trance," and LeCron urges that the deep "plenary" trance states be used to produce psychic phenomena and for experimental psychotherapy (378:71). However, he sees psychic abilities merely as powers of the unconscious mind, as something latent and normal, and therefore not related to anything supernatural or demonic. For example, though the use of pendulums clearly involves spiritistic powers (cf. Dowsing), LeCron believes pendulum phenomena reflect a human ability. In speaking of a hypnotized subject answering questions psychically, using a pendulum device, he claims this illustrates that "much information can be gained from the subconscious" (378:73). He also states that this method "is now used rather extensively in hypnotherapy" (378:73 cf. 379).

LeCron concludes by noting the connection between hypnosis and other phenomena, such as automatic writing, which is a practice frequently used in psychotherapy to uncover alleged unconscious material:

These [pendulum] techniques are, like the Ouija board, variations of automatic writing. ... The late Anita Muhl [author of *Automatic Writing*], a psychiatrist, was undoubtedly our leading authority on automatic writing. She claimed that four out of five persons could learn to automat, although many would require long hours of training to succeed.... But almost any hypnotic subject capable of reaching the somnambulistic state will automat readily. Probably the best results in research as to ESP abilities would be found in this method.... Automatic writing and other experiments with subjects in plenary trance hypnosis might teach us much and aid in promoting ESP faculties (378:73-74).

It appears true that the deeper the trance, the greater the chance of encountering occult and spiritistic manifestations. But is it wise to be placed along a continuum so close to the occult? Biblically speaking, we are to avoid the occult entirely, not see how closely we may safely approach it.

Martin and Diedre Bobgan cite a study in *Psychology Today* (January 1981, p. 81) which revealed that good trance subjects (for deeper states) all encountered psychic experiences. The Bobgans conclude:

Hypnotic trance at the deeper levels can and usually does result in the above descriptions, which will be easily identified by Christians as occult, but these obvious manifestations of the occult may not appear at the shallow levels. We can only warn that the deeper the induction, the greater the danger; the deeper the trance, the more potential for harm. However, this raises a question: What is the relationship between the various levels of hypnosis and at what level does a person enter the danger zone? (376:30-32).

It seems that as the hypnotic trance deepens, the possibility of demonic danger grows. Paradoxically, some claim it is at the deeper levels of hypnosis that the most beneficial work can be done (376:29-32).

In *Hypnosis: Key to Psychic Powers*, Simeon Edmunds reveals one method by which hypnosis can be used to develop psychic ability:

Dr. Milan Ryzl, of Prague, has recently reported success in developing psychic powers in a large number of subjects by the use of hypnosis. Dr. Ryzl's method of "training," as he calls it, is a progressive one. The first step is the development of the desired depth of hypnosis and the highest possible degree of suggestibility. When this is achieved suggestions are given designed to convince the subject that he is able to develop psychic powers and that he *will* develop them. . . .

Finally the subject learns to use his clairvoyant powers on his own initiative and independently of his teacher (382:39-40).

Edmunds concludes that "there is no doubt that hypnosis induced by a hypnotist . . . often assists the development and functioning of psychic powers" (382:63). Professional writer and hypnosis enthusiast L. E. Levinson observes that Ryzl's method can be allegedly used "to train extrasensory abilities in all people" (382:120).

Almost anywhere we look, research into hypnosis ties it to the occult. Again, the four-volume *Abnormal Hypnotic Phenomena*, a worldwide compendium, is full of occult phenomena (1087). Occultist J. H. Brennan confesses in his *Astral Doorways* that "hypnosis is a major key to the Astral Plane. . . . It can produce striking results" (386:65).

The popular text by Clayton Matthews, *Hypnotism for the Millions* (one of 20 volumes on the occult in the "For the Millions" series), lists numerous cases of hypnotism-induced psychic powers (astral projection, psychic diagnosis, clairvoyance, telepathy, and mediumism; 387:35-61), and he also gives a few cases of hypnotism that led to spirit possession (387:101-28). These allegedly "subconscious" personalities contacted through hypnosis clearly have a personality and will independent of both the hypnotist and hypnotized (387:101-09).

In *Reliving Past Lives*, psychologist and psychic Dr. Helen Wambach discusses the results of nearly 1100 hypnotically induced "past-life" (reincarnation) recalls. She states, "One aspect of right brain functioning that I have found manifesting itself in every group I have hypnotized is the phenomenon of telepathy" (388:80; see "Past-Life Therapy" on page 336).

L. E. Levinson writes about using hypnosis to develop psychics, including child psychics:

I believe that hypnosis is a catalyst for unlocking latent psi faculties. There seems to be a personality and physical pattern that is part of the somnambulistic state. . . .

The natural tendency of a somnambulist to perform with psi awareness in both the trance and waking states allows for serious consideration of training somnambulists to develop their powers through the self-hypnotic condition.... This technique may be realized once the subject develops a rapport and attunement with his inner self via the autohypnotic state.

Since there is general agreement that almost everyone possesses latent psi abilities, it would seem most logical to begin training with the youth. This idea is further supported by the fact that children are highly suggestible and that, in the waking state, they possess the innate qualities of the trance somnambulist.

Telepathic experiments were conducted by Dr. W. H. C. Tenhaeff with 1,188 Utrecht kindergarten children....

The experiment proved that telepathy occurs in the classroom....

I propose that children, who are natural paragnosts during their formative years, are capable of being trained to develop their psi faculties; their minds are malleable and highly suggestible at an early age . . . (381:139,143-45).

The previous material clearly indicates that hypnosis may induce psychic abilities. But as we attempted to document elsewhere, from both parapsychology and the Bible, man does not possess innate psychic ability as commonly found among occultists (1522:257-81). From where, then, do such powers originate? The best explanation seems to be found in spiritism.

*Spiritism and Possession.* Having documented the connection between hypnosis and psychic development, we can document the connection to more overt spiritism and spirit possession. We stress that the relationship between the three categories (psychic development, spiritism, and spirit possession) can be fluid.

In recent years channeling,* or voluntary spirit possession, has become increasingly popular. And, significantly, many, if not most, channelers employ self-hypnosis. They use hypnosis as a means to enter the trance state, which facilitates the spirit guide in taking over the mind and body. New Age psychologist Jon Klimo, formerly a professor at Rutgers University and the author of a standard text, *Channeling*, states that spirit channelers "are in a hypnotic altered state that allows them access to messages from transmitters or operators to which they would not have access under normal mental conditions" (574:221).

For example, John C. White became a modern channeler through the practice of Transcendental Meditation, Silva Mind Control,* and self-hypnosis. He argues that hypnosis is an excellent way to train for channeling:

> I believe a way to train yourself to go into trance would be through hypnosis. There would be a certain point when the guide, the control spirit, would take over. I try to be quite disciplined. If you can set up the environment, by changing your brain waves, the phenomena has a possibility of happening. By doing meditation, Yoga, or whatever you do as a "discipline," you can set up your environment so the spirits can come and work with you (2225:147).

This is one reason the spirits themselves endorse the use of hypnosis—because it frequently serves their purposes. For example, Robert Bradley, M.D., the developer of the Bradley method of natural childbirth, has long had an interest in spiritism. He recalls a time in his life when he was hesitant about using hypnosis. It was "Fletcher," the spirit guide of the famous trance medium Arthur Ford, who convinced Bradley not to worry, claiming that he and other spirits would "assist" him in the hypnotic process. Bradley recalls how the spirit soothed his fears over using hypnosis:

> This man Arthur Ford was really something. I went to a hypnosis convention in Philadelphia, sneaked down the street to where I knew he lived in a little apartment nearby. Because I didn't have much confidence in myself as a hypnotherapist, in spite of my little certificate on the wall certifying that I had the trance induction training, I still was hesitant to use this new tool. Should I enter into this? I had some twenty questions listed on an index card in my shirt pocket. I never told Arthur why I came. He went into his trance. Fletcher immediately, brightly, cheerfully said, "Well, I see you have the following questions." He then answered them in proper sequence. He gave me the reassurance that we put in the last chapter of the book, *We*

*Are Never Alone.* He was patting me on the back saying go ahead and do hypnotherapy, we in the spirit world will guide you and protect you and help you.

I personally feel that there are two people in the trance when doing hypnotherapy, and that's the hypnotist too. I'm a great believer in spirit guidance. I think it is the only logical explanation for some of the things that have happened to me (517:100-01).

The spirit guide of the late Jane Roberts, "Seth," also endorsed hypnosis (796:324), as do many other spirits. As noted, one reason the spirits promote hypnosis is because it may facilitate their possession of an individual. Citing a study reported in *Psychology Today*, January 1981, the Bobgans note the occurrence of two cases of possession in hypnotic states. One individual became possessed by the Hindu "monkey god," the other subject could call upon various spirits who would possess him and then answer questions (376:32).

Edwin Zolik is codirector of the North Virginia Mental Health Project and former professor of the Department of Psychology, graduate division of Marquette University, Milwaukee, Wisconsin. In his article "Reincarnation Phenomena in Hypnotic States," he writes that "psychologists and psychiatrists have long been familiar with the various phenomena which occur during the hypnotic state, such as age and time regression, the manifestation of multiple personalities, and the elicitation of foreign languages not voluntarily learned" (384:66). One five-year study of 6000 hypnotized subjects found that fully 20 percent of them reported "earlier lives" (376:23).

Why should hypnotic subjects experience such things at all? Past lives, other personalities, and knowledge of other languages never learned are things commonly found among trance mediums possessed by spirits. In fact, one of the leading reincarnation researchers in this country, parapsychologist Dr. Ian Stevenson, M.D., has stated his belief that spirit possession is a legitimate explanation for some reincarnation experiences (858:374-81).

Even parapsychologist Dr. Shafica Karagulla, M.D., a neuropsychiatrist and member of the prestigious Royal College of Physicians in Edinburg, warns against possession from hypnosis in

her *Breakthrough to Creativity* (711). This text, which unfortunately advocates the "safe" use of psychic development (cf. 278), is used in several universities. Still, she warns that hypnosis can open ". . . the door to your mind which can be influenced by other intelligences, some greater than your own. In such a passive state, an entity can get in and obtain control of you" (385:60).

In *Hypnosis: Key to Psychic Powers*, hypnotist Simeon Edmunds indicates the potential of hypnosis to permit spirit possession. He cites the following case of spontaneous possession from his own clinical practice:

Most of my sessions with Nora were given up to long conversations with the alleged spirit of a young soldier, killed in Korea, who purported to speak through the entranced girl. Although no evidence that could be verified was ever given, the statements and descriptions were most dramatic and impressive. They showed knowledge and command of words which Nora, a domestic servant of limited education, would be unlikely to possess, and I am sure many people would have accepted them as genuine communications from the dead. . . .

So far as I could learn, Nora had no knowledge or experience of spiritualism. The "communications" began when, hypnotized, she was told to sit quietly for half an hour, to describe anything she seemed to see, and to repeat any words she seemed to hear (382:57).

In *Reliving Past Lives*, psychologist Dr. Helen Wambach reports on a hypnotic "past lives" subject, "Anna," who progressed to becoming a trance medium from her experiments with hypnosis (388:49). One scholarly text that attempts to normalize hypnosis as merely a state of creative imagination, relaxation, and suggestion—not a unique or altered state of consciousness—nevertheless concedes its strong ties to the occult:

There was also a strong link between the mesmeric movement and the modern Spiritualist movement, which began around 1848. . . . Meanwhile, in 1847 in the United States, Andrew Jackson Davis, another follower of Swedenborg, published his 800-page spiritualistic classic *Principles of Nature*. According to Davis, this book was dictated by him at the age of nineteen while he was in a mesmeric trance. . . .

What became known as the "mediumistic trance" clearly evolved out of the "mesmeric trance," and the concept of magnetic flux from the operator to the subject was obviously extended to include the "control" exercised by the spirits. In this manner, the mesmeric movement merged with and became the Spiritualist movement (1735:219-20).

But hypnotism is related to more than the American revival of spiritism. Brazilian spiritism began in the same general period, the mid-nineteenth century. Yet in Brazil, this movement, which now encompasses tens of millions of followers, began when French educator Leon-Denizarth-Hippolyte Rivail was influenced toward spiritism from his interest in hypnosis. Eventually his spirit guide told him to assume the name of "Allan Kardec," supposedly a former druid master whose body Rivail's spirit had occupied in a past life. The publication of Rivail's *The Book of the Spirits*, under the pen name Allan Kardec in 1857, caused a sensation in France, England, and later in Brazil. It can be argued that this book was instrumental in establishing spiritism among the Brazilian educated class, guaranteeing a prosperity that continues to this day (91:22-23; cf. 981).

In *Hypnotism and the Supernormal*, Edmunds observes that "much of the early literature of psychical research is devoted to detailed, substantiated reports of experiments in which hypnotic subjects became highly psychic" (383:81). Even today "many of the most famous spiritualistic mediums began their psychic careers as hypnotic subjects, and hypnosis has been used with marked success in the development of a number of others. Outstanding among the latter is Mrs. Eileen J. Garrett . . . " (383:114-15). As noted earlier , the modern "father" of New Age medicine,* Edgar Cayce, is another example, as is the powerful nineteenth-century medium, Andrew Jackson Davis (772:158).

Significantly, Edmunds cites a paper published in *The Proceedings of the Society for Psychical Research* which actually concludes that the *mediumistic* trance is almost indistinguishable from the *hypnotic* trance. "In these cases we have

obviously states very nearly and probably quite identical with the hypnotic sleep" (389:118). He also discusses the "remarkably similar" methods of inducing hypnosis as it is found among modern hypnotists and ancient and modern shamans (383:155).

Respected parapsychologist Dr. Stanley Krippner and psychologist Albert Villoldo also point out that spirit-possession resembles a state of deep hypnosis in their *Healing States: A Journey into the World of Spiritual Healing and Shamanism* (91:197-98; cf. 574:219-27). L. E. Levinson is another researcher who notes parallels to the hypnotized subject and the medium: "[I]t is no less well established that hypnosis increases cryptesthesia. Various persons quite incapable of any transcendental manifestations when their senses are awake, become lucid when hypnotized. . . . The hypnotized somnambule undergoes in deep trance a physical change comparable to the state of trance mediumship" (381:119-20).

The point should be obvious. The hypnotic state is not only conducive to spirit possession, it can closely resemble spirit possession. And this linkage is not merely a modern conclusion. The relationship between early hypnotism (mesmerism) and spiritism is abundantly documented in mediumistic, mesmeric, and psychical literature (463:1-100; refs. 765-74). Cases of spirit possession resulting from hypnosis frequently occurred. This is why many of the best-known mediums of the nineteenth century first started their careers as mesmeric or hypnotic subjects (727:51-154). Mesmerism was used for psychic development and could also lead to contact with the spirits (refs. 765-73):

The earliest reliable report of the enhancement of psychic powers by hypnosis seems to be by the Marquis de Puysegur, a pupil of Mesmer, who in 1807 published a book, *Du Magnetisme Animal*, containing a number of examples. One of his subjects, a normally rather stupid peasant lad, when mesmerised showed not only increased intelligence but remarkable powers of clairvoyance. De Puysegur found that several subjects with no medical knowledge were able to make accurate diagnoses of disease. He noted that sometimes another personality would seem to emerge, possessing higher faculties and clearer vision (382:29-30).

*The Encyclopedia of Occultism and Parapsychology* discusses how often mesmerism and hypnotism and spiritism converge, and how often hypnotists actually became spiritists or mediums as a result:

Though the movement known as "modern spiritualism" is usually dated from 1848, the year of the "Rochester Rappings," the real growth of spiritualism was much more gradual, and its roots were hidden in animal magnetism [mesmerism].

Emanuel Swedenborg, whose affinities with the magnetists have already been referred to, exercised a remarkable influence on the spiritualistic thought of America and Europe, and was in a sense the founder of that faith. Automatic phenomena were even then a feature of the magnetic trance, and clairvoyance, community of sensation, and telepathy were believed in generally, and regarded by many as evidences of spiritual [spirit] communication.

In Germany, professor Jung-Stilling, Dr. C. Romer, Dr. Werner, and the poet and physician Justinus Kerner, were among those who held opinions on these lines, the latter pursing his investigations with a somnambule who became famous as the "Seeress of Prevorst"—Frau Frederica Hauffe. Frau Hauffe could see and converse with the spirits of the deceased, and gave evidence of prophetic vision and clairvoyance.

Physical phenomena were witnessed in her presence, knockings, rattling of chains, movement of objects without contact, and, in short, such manifestations as were characteristic of the poltergeist family.

She was, moreover, the originator of a "primeval" language, which she declared was that spoken by the patriarchs. Thus Frau Hauffe, though only a somnambule, or magnetic patient, possessed all the qualities of a successful spiritualistic medium.

In England, also there were many circumstances of a supernatural character associated with mesmerism. Dr. Elliotson, who, as has been indicated, was one of the best-known of English magnetists, became in time converted to a spiritualistic theory, as offering an explanation of the clairvoyance and similar phenomena which he thought to have observed in his patients.

France, the headquarters of the rationalist school of magnetism, had, indeed, a good deal less to show of spiritualistic opinion. Nonetheless even in that country the latter doctrine made its appearance at intervals prior to 1848. J. P. F. Deleuze, a good scientist and an earnest protagonist of magnetism, who published his *Histoire Critique deu Magnetisme Animal* in 1813, was said to have embraced the doctrines of spiritualism before he died.

Dr. G. P. Billot was another believer in spirit communication, and one who succeeded in obtaining physical phenomena in the presence of his somnambules. It is, however, in the person of Alphonse Cahagnet, a man of humble origin who began to study induced somnambulism about the year 1845, and who thereafter experimented with somnambules, that we encounter the first French spiritualist of distinction. So good was the evidence for spirit communication furnished by Cahagnet and his subjects that it remains among the best which the annals of the movement can produce.

In America, Laroy Sunderland, Andrew Jackson Davis, and others who became pillars of spiritualism in that country were first attracted to it through the study of magnetism. Everywhere we find hypnotism and spiritualism identified with each other until in 1848 a definite split occurs, and the two go their separate ways.

Even yet, however, the separation is not quite complete. In the first place, the mediumistic trance is obviously a variant of spontaneous or self-induced hypnotism, while in the second, many of the most striking phenomena of the seance-room have been matched time and again in the records of animal magnetism.

For instance, the diagnosis of disease and prescription of remedies dictated by the control to the "healing medium" have their prototype in the cures of Valentine Greatrakes, or of Mesmer and his disciples. Automatic phenomena—speaking in "tongues" and so forth—early formed a characteristic feature of the induced trance and kindred states. While even the physical phenomena, movement without contact, apports, rappings, were witnessed in connection with magnetism long before the movement known as modern spiritualism was so much as thought of (377,I:453).

Nevertheless, whatever similarities exist between mediumistic and hypnotic trance states, they are, strictly speaking, not identical. By definition the mediumistic trance involves spirit possession; hypnosis does not, although as noted, it may certainly lead to possession. Psychoanalyst-psychic researcher, Dr. Nandor Fodor discusses some of the differences between these states in his *Encyclopedia of Psychic Science,* while also commenting, "The nature of the hypnotic trance is unknown. Its relation to the mediumistic trance is of absorbing interest" (389:179).

In conclusion, the occult potential of hypnotism should leave us uneasy. In some ways the hypnotized person is playing Russian roulette with such potential. No one can tell when or under what conditions spiritistic or occult manifestations may emerge.

The use of hypnosis by Christian psychotherapists, therefore, presents us with a dilemma. Can we be certain of the final outcome of hypnosis in clients' lives? It is to this issue we now turn.

## HYPNOSIS IN CHRISTIAN PSYCHOTHERAPY: A CRITIQUE

Many Christian therapists use hypnosis on pragmatic grounds, maintaining that it is useful for helping their clients. It works for them, and they see positive results. Nothing occult happens, and they feel comfortable with the practice.

There are certain reasons why hypnosis would be used by Christian therapists. First, there is a genuine desire to help people (775:169-70). Second, the hypnotic state is therapeutically useful. A standard encyclopedia on psychology written by evangelical Christian psychologists offers the following endorsement:

Hypnosis is also extremely valuable in psychotherapeutic activities. The hypnotically achieved relaxation can often enhance rapport and facilitate conversation. The dissociative aspects of the hypnotic state can facilitate cathartic experience as well as the exploration of material too psychically painful for immediate conscious awareness. The hypernesic effect can permit recall and, on occasion, revivifica-

tion of past, forgotten material, while the amnesic effect can allow the forgetting of material discovered through hypnosis but too threatening for conscious retention at the moment. Hypnotic imagery can create the situation for projection of psychic material into fantasy or hypnotic dreams either explored or used profitably in ways that will advance therapy.

Hypnosis is very effective and valuable in pediatrics. By their nature children are generally better hypnotic subjects and can use hypnosis very naturally for pain control, to alter symptoms or habits, to imagine and change situations or outcomes, or to adjust physical functioning (536:547-48).

After a brief mention of a possible, though unlikely, spiritistic aspect to hypnosis, an evangelical Christian encyclopedia on ethics concludes, "Perhaps a better view is that hypnosis is in itself a spiritually neutral phenomenon that may be used for good or evil purposes.... Provided it is practiced by a reputable medical practitioner for legitimate therapeutic purposes, hypnosis may be of significant benefit to a patient" (896:193). Yet this text also states:

Despite their long history and current popularity, however, remarkably little is known about either hypnosis itself (the hypnotic state) or of the means by which it is induced (hypnotism).

Over the years more than a dozen distinct theories have been advanced to explain the workings of hypnosis, and there is still little consensus in the academic literature on the subject (896:192).

If we don't know what hypnosis is or how it works, can we be assured that it "is in itself a spiritually neutral phenomenon"? It *may* be, but even so, does this fact by itself answer all the questions raised by an endorsement? For example, it could be argued that *all* trance states are spiritually neutral. Yet though one could argue this, it is false, as in the case of spiritistic trance channeling.* As one text on channeling observes, "A trance is a state of consciousness that allows you to connect with a guide" (575:25). Not all trance states do this, but clearly many do. So all trance states are not the same. Thus, if all states of hypnosis are

331

not the same, how can anyone know that all hypnotic states in general are ultimately neutral? If deeper hypnotic states are far more prone to occult phenomena, can it still be argued that the hypnotic state per se is spiritually neutral?

Even if hypnosis is a neutral mental state, it is nevertheless a state easily prone to abuse and manipulation. The NBC evening news of April 8, 1995, thought it important to report on stage hypnosis as a growing but dangerous entertainment fad in Britain. What wasn't so funny was the problems some people encountered as a result of using this "innocent, neutral" technique. One young woman, Sharon Tabam, mysteriously died just five hours after coming out of a hypnotic trance. Others could not be rid of hypnotic suggestions. One man continued to eat up to eight onions a day, thinking they were apples. After almost nine months, no one was able to convince him otherwise, with or without hypnosis. What if a hypnotic suggestion dealt with a more serious mental, physical, or moral area? Just because counselors or entertainers claim to be authorities in hypnosis doesn't answer all the questions.

A Ph.D. in psychology does not automatically grant one spiritual discernment, wisdom, or biblical commitment. After eight years of secular education in pursuit of their Ph.D.s, one wonders how many Christian therapists have given sufficient attention to the possibility of spiritual harm through hypnosis. As we have seen, it is easy to accept something on pragmatic or personal grounds alone without thinking through other implications. Aren't there cases of Christian professionals who are authorities in given areas (sociology, biology, psychology), yet who also pursue questionable practices or teach spiritual error? Isn't it true that many Christian professionals have never been trained theologically or biblically? Don't others have a preexisting bias or emotional investment in a false practice or belief? Aren't some Christian professionals in the academic community subject to intimidation by secular colleagues? As a result, even Christian scholars have accepted such false and harmful teachings as universalism, parapsychology, evolution, higher criticism, and so on, simply because their secular learning was never critiqued bibli-

cally. To use hypnosis, therefore, merely because it helps people does not necessarily justify it.

Because hypnotherapy is being practiced by many Christian psychologists, the church needs to take a hard look at the issues. This is not something we can do here. But we can say that Christian scholars are divided over the issue. One of the leading Christian authorities on the occult, the late Dr. Walter Martin, accepted the medical practice of hypnosis, while warning against its occult use (776). Noted psychiatrist Paul Tournier, on the other hand, is opposed to any use of hypnosis (642:95).

Perhaps the leading authority on Christian counseling and occultism in this century was Dr. Kurt Koch. His conclusion of a lifetime of study and counseling is: "If asked for my opinion, I would have to admit that I have heard so many ill effects of hypnotism that I am opposed to it" (642:95). "For the Christian, it is a good rule not to use any dubious forms of help" (642:100). He also observed an interesting phenomenon, that prayer could apparently counteract hypnotic suggestibility.

Again, most Christian therapists seem to use hypnosis merely because it is a powerful and effective method; the hard questions that might temper its acceptance seem to be raised too infrequently. But are good motives or practical results sufficient justification for endorsing a practice that involves numerous unanswered questions and historic and contemporary associations with the occult? When so little is actually known about what hypnosis really is, and when it has strong associations with occultism, we believe that everyone should seriously question the advisability of using the technique. We provide the following questions for people who want to think through the issue more fully.

1. Does the hypnotic trance state differ within the 1) medical, 2) psychotherapeutic, or 3) occult use of hypnosis?

2. Why is it that as evangelicals we can easily reject cultivating occult trance states but just as easily accept them in medicine or psychology? How has the church viewed hypnosis, and Christian participation in it, historically? For example, how did the church view Christian participation

in hypnotism in the nineteenth century, when it was termed "mesmerism"?

3. If hypnosis can induce psychic sensitivity, what percent of the hundreds of thousands who are being treated with hypnosis in psychotherapy are becoming more psychically active? If repeated hypnosis increases one's sensitivity to hypnosis, does repeated hypnosis also increase one's sensitivity to psychic experiences? Does it really help people to induce their openness to the psychic realm or to produce psychic experiences in them? Is the depth of the hypnotic trance proportional to the degree of susceptibility to the psychic realm? If so, can that depth be carefully regulated?

4. How do we distinguish the possible spiritual or psychic impact of hypnosis on different populations: a) the "average" person; b) occultists; c) people marginally interested in the psychic realm; or dabblers; d) people with an occult or psychic family history; e) Christians who have had psychic involvement prior to conversion; f) among Christians who are backslidden? In other words, does a person's previous "exposure" to the occult, or does his spiritual health, affect the outcome of hypnosis?

5. If hypnosis is a neutral tool, with either scientific or occult application or potential, how do we determine the conditions under which it actually becomes one or the other?

6. If we accept the trance state of hypnosis for solely therapeutic reasons, where do we draw the line in accepting similar methods, such as other altered states of consciousness for therapeutic reasons, or the questionable techniques of Jungian and other potentially occult psychologies?

7. Does the worldview and lifestyle of the therapist affect the outcome of hypnosis in his patients? Would a qualified psychotherapist or hypnotherapist who is an occultist have a different effect on the same person than a Christian therapist would? Why or why not? For example, would more power be exerted over the patient in terms of susceptibility in trance by an occult hypnotherapist or by a Christian one? Or would there be no difference?

8. Does the worldview or lifestyle of the client affect the outcome of hypnosis? Would a Christian counselee have a different experience

under deep hypnosis than an occult practitioner would?

9. Are there any dubious interests or practices in the background or training of many therapists who use hypnosis?

10. Why do so many Christian practitioners of hypnotherapy recommend that it be performed only by a Christian, if it is really a scientific and neutral practice? If it is not a scientific and neutral practice, then what is it?

11. If "occult hypnosis" leaves one open to the influence of the demonic, what is there about the medical and scientific use of hypnosis that may prevent this influence? Could it be context, environment, motive, prayer, or other factors? Is the occult use of hypnosis really a different form of hypnosis than the medical and therapeutic varieties? If not, does this mean its scientific use is automatically void of occult potential? Doesn't the parapsychologist attempt to use hypnosis in a scientific manner? We know that most parapsychologists study mediums and occult phenomena in a scientific context and with good motives; but does this really alter the nature or potential consequences of such activity (5:331-40)? So, is it true that whatever hypnosis is, it is by virtue of its nature, regardless of context or motive?

12. What about the long-term impact of hypnosis? Are there negative effects spiritually or emotionally? Are the alleged benefits of hypnosis long-term or short-term benefits? How often does it merely treat symptoms, leaving the person to deal with the root problems later on?

Clearly, these are tough questions to answer, but they need answering.

## AGE REGRESSION

Another potential problem of hypnotherapy is age regression. This is where a person is taken back into childhood to reexperience an alleged trauma which is said to be causing problems in the present. And then there is age regression into "past lives" or "other personalities." The latter, in particular, presents significant problems.

What does a therapist do when his patient seems to spontaneously regress to a "past life," or when the patient becomes "another person," or persons, under hypnosis? The strange phenomenon of "multiple personalities" and multiple personality disorder (MPD), which occur under hypnotic suggestion, are increasingly drawing public attention. In fact, multiple personalities and hypnosis are strongly linked in therapy. But distinguishing the natural from the supernatural in this phenomenon can be difficult at best (574:237-38/1086; see Channeling).

Although there are differences between MPD and channeling, there are cases where MPD sounds like channeling. In an interview with Jon Klimo, New York City therapist Armand DiMele stated:

> In dealing with multiples you need to call on the highest possible powers a person has, and you actually invite that thing in through a hypnotic state. But when it comes in, it comes in so clearly, so beautifully, so filled with information one couldn't have had any idea about it. I have spoken to "spirit voices" who have come through multiples that have told me things about my childhood. Specifics, like things that hung in the house (574:238).

Other cases exist where the MPD phenomenon can only be described as spiritistic channeling (cf. 2394:119-20). And one common denominator in both cases is hypnosis. Therapists characteristically use hypnosis in the treatment of MPD and, as we have seen, many or most channelers use hypnosis to channel their spirit guides. Thus hypnosis may be the condition responsible for inducing spiritism in both cases.

In light of the above, is it wise to manipulate a person's consciousness to begin with, especially when a therapist is uncertain as to what he might be opening a person to?

## FALSE MEMORY SYNDROME

Hypnosis, visualization,* and other methods are often used to uncover alleged past histories of sexual or satanic ritual abuse, which is another popular interest in much psychotherapy. Indeed, repressed memory therapy is now advocated "among the cream of the crop of psychiatrists and clinical psychologists" (2230:55). While such

abuse does exist, with children as its victims, using hypnosis for therapy in this area is problematic because it is impossible to finally separate reality from fantasy, or from spiritistic influences in hypnosis. Therapists can rarely be certain of what they are dealing with.

Dr. Elizabeth Loftus is author of *The Myth of Repressed Memory: False Memories and the Allegations of Sexual Abuse.* She is considered an authority on the malleability of memory, and for 25 years she has conducted laboratory studies, supervised graduate students, and written technical papers. Listen to what she says about the growing fad among therapists to uncover "repressed" memories:

> Poorly trained therapists and therapists who operate under a fixed belief system (for example, "All MPD patients have been ritually abused"; "memory operates like an interior video recorder"; "healing comes only when the client assesses buried memories, resolving and integrating the trauma experience") are at greatest risk for confusing fact and fiction. Through tone of voice, phrasing of questions, and expressions of belief or disbelief, a therapist can unwittingly encourage a patient to accept the emerging "memories" as real, thus reinforcing the patient's delusions or even implanting false memories in the patient's mind.... [S]uch therapists may be doing a great deal of harm to their patients and their profession (2644:85-86).

In response to therapists who use either hypnosis or other methods to uncover alleged repressed memories, she writes:

> To complicate reality even further, hypnotized patients tend to be extremely confident that such pseudomemories represent real events and experiences. Once a patient has convinced herself that certain events occurred, she'll believe it so completely that if she took a polygraph she'd pass. All a polygraph measures is a person's conviction that something may be true or false, not the accuracy or authenticity of the event being described.... Many [therapists] invest hypnosis with magical healing powers. Hypnosis is considered a function like a sort of truth serum.... This misconception, coupled with the fact that most therapists have only a rudimentary knowledge of the reconstructive nature of

memory, can lead to the creation of false memories within the therapeutic environment.

"I never use hypnosis!" a therapist might object. But as the Paul Ingram case demonstrates, you don't need formal hypnotic induction techniques to induce a trance state; all you need is a suggestible client with a problem (2644:254-55).

The truth is that almost any fantasy can be experienced as reality under hypnosis, from the humorous stage pranks of hypnosis entertainers to supposed UFO abductions and past lives. Thus, fantasies about satanic abuse and multiple personalities may also be encountered as entirely "real."

When an otherwise normal person living a normal life is hypnotized to deal with a weight problem and the result is *years* of therapy dealing with alleged multiple personalities or satanic abuse, one wonders if there isn't a problem with the psychotherapy. In such cases, we believe hypnosis, and frequent therapist coaching, is the real culprit. University of California, Berkeley, social psychologist Richard Ofshe goes so far as to say, "Recovered-Memory therapy will come to be recognized as the quackery of the 20th century" (2230:55).

A tragic case was reported on the "Maury Povich" show, May 11, 1993, which also noted there were some 15,000-20,000 diagnosed cases of MPD in the United States. In this story, Susan Houdelette was a normal woman who went to a therapist to quit smoking. The counselor used hypnosis, and out popped 239(!) different personalities that proceeded to make Susan's life miserable. One personality even engaged in self-mutilation, and Susan showed the marks and scars on national television. And her story gets worse because while she sued her first therapist, another was kept busy for years trying to "reintegrate" or otherwise manage the 239 personalities—personalities that no one knew "existed" prior to hypnosis. By all accounts, Susan would have continued to live a normal life were it not for the application of hypnosis.

In addition, there are thousands of victims today who, because of hypnotic regression, only *think* that they were subject to sexual or satanic abuse as children. This has resulted in great tragedies, including ruined families (where parents were the alleged abusers or Satanists) and patients who committed suicide. Because thousands of families have been torn apart by things like this, a national organization has been formed specifically to draw attention to the problem and to help victims of what is termed the "false memory syndrome" (2221). In its November 29, 1993, issue, a *Time* cover story that asked, "Is Freud Dead?" warned that repressed memories were alive and well. It noted: "Repressed-Memory therapy is harming patients, devastating families and intensifying a backlash against mental-health practitioners."

John Weldon has experienced firsthand the destructive potential that such false memories can have. A Christian member of his extended family went to a therapist who concluded that this person's current problems may have resulted from childhood sexual abuse. In order to test this theory and to uncover possible repressed memories, hypnosis was employed. The result was several months of therapy uncovering supposed childhood sexual abuse by this individual's father, mother, and uncle. Yet none of the abuse had occurred, and no "memory" of it ever existed until hypnosis was used. Because the "revelations" and perceptions of having been abused were so devastating, the result was the person's admittance to a psychiatric ward and a great deal of grief for all concerned. Thankfully, proper intervention prevented a worse scenario, and when it was soon realized that no abuse had occurred, the process of healing began. Today, this person is, thankfully, fully recovered and a committed Christian.

But who is the real culprit here? Dr. Elizabeth L. Hillstrom, a physiological psychologist, comments that based on "statistics compiled by the False Memory Syndrome Foundation (formed by a distinguished group of psychologists and psychiatrists to combat this problem), the origin [of the problem of repressed memories is a subgroup of psychotherapists who call themselves 'traumatists' " (2659:66). The problem is that the hypnotist's suggestions "literally shape the subject's reality when they are in [this] hypnotic state."

Hillstrom also describes the basic premise of this group of therapists which, incidentally, in part coincides with the auditing or "counseling" premises of the Church of Scientology:*

These therapists share the conviction that childhood sexual abuse is very common. They believe that the memories of such events get repressed into "the subconscious," where they cause all sorts of problems until they are consciously recalled and dealt with. These therapists assume that the offending memories can be dislodged from "the subconscious" through hypnosis, dream interpretation, sodium amytal, trance writing, reading self-help books, participating in "survivor" groups or massage. Yet there is no scientific evidence to support their assumption that these techniques produce accurate memory recall. In fact, the evidence points strongly in the other direction (2659:66).

The fact that trance (automatic) writing, hypnosis, dream interpretation, and related methods are employed not only underscores the subjective and potentially manipulative nature of this "therapy," it also reveals the possibility of spiritistic influences (see Dream Work).

Again, once hypnosis is employed, separating truth from fiction can be impossible. Compounding the problem, once hypnosis is employed, it is usually impossible to separate purely human suggestion from spiritistic suggestion when the latter is present.

What we have discussed about hypnosis so far suggests the spirit world may take advantage of *any* altered state of consciousness,* if it has the opportunity to do so. False memories seem to be a key method for taking advantage, whether the memories are of sexual abuse, satanic ritual, past lives, UFO abductions, or others. The purpose is to deceive and destroy, and the spirits could care less what someone believes, or whether he has good motives, or a Ph.D. in psychology or theology. For example, some patients experience past-life recall or encounter spirit entities without warning, even when hypnotized by therapists who reject reincarnation and the occult. Can the Christian therapist automatically assume God's protection against such things? He may be engaging in a practice that is unwise to begin with, or the patient may be dabbling in the occult. In Fisher's *The Case for Reincarnation*, even reincarnation skeptic Dr. Gerald Edelstein, a staff

psychiatrist at Herrick Memorial Hospital in Berkeley, California, discovered that "several of his patients have slipped into past lives" in spite of his personal skepticism, and with uniformly "positive" results emerging from the "past life" or "reincarnation" encounter (392:37-38).

## PAST-LIFE THERAPY

Past-life therapy (PLT), or so-called "reincarnation" therapy, is more widely practiced than most people might think. Clinical psychologist and hypnotherapist Jonathan Venn writes, "Past-life hypnosis has become a common practice in the United States and Western Europe" (950:390). Hundreds—possibly several thousand—therapists use this method. The field has professional societies and journals, such as the Association for Past-Life Research and Therapy, and the *Journal of Regression Therapy*. Numerous texts have been written on the subject by clinical psychologists, and literally thousands of people have been hypnotically regressed to experience their alleged "past lives." Illustrations include Helen Wambach's *Reliving Past Lives: The Evidence Under Hypnosis* (1027), based on a thousand subjects; her *Life Before Life* (1026); Morris Netherton and Nancy Shiffrin's *Past Lives Therapy* (1028); Dr. Edith Fiore's *You Have Been Here Before: A Psychologist Looks at Past Lives* (1029); Brian L. Weiss, *Many Lives, Many Masters* (1801); Roger Woolger's *Other Lives, Other Selves* (1800).

"Past-life" therapy employs hypnosis to place the individual into a trance state for a specific purpose. That purpose is to send the individual "back" into his supposed former lives in order to resolve hidden emotional or spiritual conflicts that are allegedly affecting his physical, emotional, or spiritual health today. Yet the results of such therapy typically support occult New Age philosophy and goals (922; cf. Scientology).

The basic conclusion of our own research into reincarnation* is that its experiences and phenomena result from several factors: 1) suggestions of the therapist; 2) inventions or delusions of the patient; 3) spiritistic manipulation of the mind.

Perhaps it is significant that past-life therapy began to take form as a psychological treatment after the sanctioning of hypnosis by the British Medical Association in 1955 and by the AMA in 1958. However, its roots can be traced to the depth psychology of Freud and Jung:

> PLT goes beyond traditional psychotherapy. Psychiatrists Carl G. Jung and Sigmund Freud both said that the individual's worst fears, pain, and trauma are buried deep within the unconscious mind. Freud believed the roots of those problems could be uncovered in early childhood experiences. Psychoanalyst Otto Rank advocated going back further, to the time spent in the womb. With the increase in hypnotherapy, some therapists discovered that many patients *automatically regressed* to what seemed to be previous lives when asked to identify the source of a problem, thus prompting experimentation with regression.

> The use of PLT as an alternative therapy led to the formation of the Association for Past Life Research and Therapy (APRT) in Riverside, California, in 1980. It is estimated that roughly 80 percent of patients who seek PLT do so in order to eliminate a phobia, habit, or negative tendency (1526:435 emphasis added).

How do we explain "past-life" experiences? Because hypnosis induces a state of trance conducive to spiritistic manipulation, and because the entire purpose of past-life regression is to encounter alleged previous lives, spiritistic influence is certainly one logical explanation because reincarnation philosophy is so antibiblical.

Few authorities on reincarnation experiences match the stature of parapsychologist Dr. Ian Stevenson of the University of Virginia. Even he has accepted spirit possession as one of the possible explanations for reincarnation phenomena (858:374-77). In terms of the episodes he considers, ". . . We can grade the cases along a continuum in which the distinction between reincarnation and possession becomes blurred" (858:376). Although he finds possession problematic in some ways, he does not rule it out; furthermore, the dilemmas surrounding his view of possession are solved when the biblical Christian interpretation of demons is allowed.

People who have these experiences, which are similar in impact to near-death experiences (2642) and alleged UFO abductions (2643/393),

can be profoundly affected by them. They may produce dramatic life and worldview changes that harmonize with occultism:

> Twenty-five therapists reported taking their patients through past-life deaths. Seventy-two percent of those who went through the experience observed it while floating above their bodies; 54 percent perceived a white light and moved toward it; 15 percent reported a tunnel. Of those whose physical problems were connected to death experiences, 60 percent reported relief of symptoms after going through the death.

> The apparent ability to relive death experiences may hold the most promise for PLT. Most patients discover that though circumstances leading to death are sometimes traumatic, death itself is pleasant. The past-life death experience is used in alternative treatment of the terminally ill to help them overcome their fears of dying. It also seems to help people who are not terminally ill to overcome fear of death, and in some cases helps patients realize how to better fulfill their soul's purpose. In regression a great deal of pain in past-life death is associated with regret over opportunities not taken.

> People who undergo PLT say they come into contact with their own inner wisdom, which continues to guide them long after the therapy. They also often change their view of their life, seeing it as part of a spiritual progression in which the soul constantly strives for perfection. They say they become aware of certain universal laws, such as karma, self-responsibility, and the right of others to progress in their own fashion. They learn there is no "good" or "bad," but that everything is relative, an opportunity to learn and advance (1526:436).

Individuals who come to believe in reincarnation through PLT are convinced that when they die, they will not encounter divine judgment like the Bible clearly teaches (Hebrews 9:27), but simply other lifetimes in which to continue their spiritual evolution and goal of self-perfection. If so, there is no need for any person to receive Jesus Christ as their personal Savior from sin and judgment. Reincarnation is an ancient Hindu idea based upon the concept of karma, that we slowly "atone" for and eliminate our own "sins" in each successive life until we finally achieve perfection at some distant point in the future.

Reincarnation insulates those who accept it against the basic gospel message. The apostle Paul tells us, "By this gospel you are saved.... For what I received I passed on to you as of first importance: that Christ died for our sins according to the Scriptures, that he was buried, that he was raised on the third day according to the Scriptures" (2 Corinthians 15:2-4). However, one who believes in reincarnation cannot logically accept his need to believe in Christ as Savior from sin. If he is going to atone for his own sins (pay off his "bad karma") over many lifetimes and achieve his own perfection, why does he need to believe in Jesus Christ? Indeed, Christ could not have atoned for our sins if we are to atone for them ourselves.

On the other hand, if through His death on the cross, Christ atoned once for all, for all sin (Hebrews 10:10,14), then reincarnation could not possibly be true. If Jesus Christ paid for all sin, what sin (or "karma") remains for us to atone for? "He himself bore our sins in his body" (1 Peter 2:24). "In him we have redemption through his blood, the forgiveness of sins, in accordance with the riches of God's grace" (Ephesians 1:7). "He forgave us all our sins" (Colossians 2:13).** In essence, past-life "therapy" often becomes a form of questionable or occult practice leading patients to adopt an occult worldview and to seek out such activities as developing altered states of consciousness,* psychic powers, or spirit contact.

Because of the subtlety of the spiritual implications involved, past-life therapy is no less profound in its destructive potential than are similar areas where spiritual warfare is unsuspected but just as pervasive, as in clinical or near-death experiences (2642), or in UFO phenomena, particularly the categories of close encounters, abductions, and the "contactee" experience (2643/393).

Furthermore, are Christian therapists who utilize hypnosis immune to "past-life" phenomena by definition? Are they immune to other subtleties of spiritual deception when they place their clients into trance states? What if the client has been dabbling in the occult? How does the patient know that she will remain free from spiritual deception when she allows herself to be placed into a trance state?

That past-life episodes can spontaneously occur in routine therapeutic hypnosis is clear from Raymond Moody's *Coming Back: A Psychiatrist Explores Past-Life Journeys*:

> When asked about past lives, it was difficult for me to hide my skepticism.... There the matter stood until I met Diana Denholm. She is a lovely and persuasive psychologist who used hypnosis in her practice. Originally she used it to help people stop smoking, lose weight, and even to find lost objects. But some strange things had happened, she said. Every once in a while, a patient would start talking about experiences from a past life. Most of the time these events occurred when she took people back through their lives to recover a lost, traumatic memory, a process known as age regression therapy. This technique would help them find the source of phobias or neuroses that were creating problems.... The intention of regression therapy was *not* to go beyond the date of the patient's birth certificate, just far back in their current life.

> But occasionally, patients would slip back even further than seemed possible. They would *suddenly* begin talking about another life, place, and time as though it were right there before their very eyes.... At first these experiences frightened Denholm. She thought she had done something wrong in her hypnotherapy, or perhaps she was treating someone with multiple personalities. But when this happened a few times, Denholm began to realize that she could use these experiences to help treat the patient's disorder.

> With research and practice, she became quite proficient at eliciting past lives from people who would allow it. Now she uses regression therapy regularly in her practice because it frequently cuts through hours of therapy by plunging right to the heart of the problem (2433:12-13).

Moody himself allowed her to elicit nine of his own alleged past lives (2433:13-25), which soundly converted him to a belief in

---

** Good critiques are found in John Snyder's *Resurrection Vs. Reincarnation*, Norman Geisler and J. Yutaka Amano's *The Reincarnation Sensation*, and Mark Albrecht's *Reincarnation: A Christian Appraisal*.

reincarnation. Psychologist Edith Fiore, author of *You Have Been Here Before,* relates MPD to past lives. She first observes that "sometimes multiple personalities emerge under hypnosis." Then she theorizes they may be "nonintegrated" past-life personalities, or split personalities, in this life (714:12-15). But she also accepts that "they could also be [spirit] entities of some sort" (391:71-72).

So is the Christian who practices yoga,* or other occult forms of meditation,* or who plays with the Ouija* board, or who experiments in seances with "good motives," immune from spiritual deception during hypnosis?

In his study of channeling, Professor Jon Klimo states, "Many hypnotherapists help the client contact an 'inner advisor' for gaining access to information that the normal waking self does not have" (574:223). Apparently, many Christian therapists do something similar. But in our chapters on New Age Inner Work, Visualization, Dream Work, Intuition, and Silva Mind Control, we have shown how difficult it is to distinguish supposed "inner advisors" from spirits. So what should a Christian psychotherapist do if "entities" or "past lives" or "multiples" appear as a result of the hypnotic trance state? Again, should Christian psychotherapists believe that they will never, under any circumstances, encounter spiritual deception or bring unforeseen problems into a person's life when they toy with a person's consciousness and induce trance states in them?

Martin and Diedre Bobgan also have a number of questions about the Christian use of hypnosis:

An occult practice in the hands of even a kind-hearted doctor can still leave the Christian open to the works of the devil. Why would occult hypnosis leave a person open to demonism and medical hypnosis not? Does the doctor have spiritual authority to keep Satan away? Is Satan afraid to interfere with science or medicine? When is the Ouija board merely a parlor game? Where is the boundary between a parlor game and the occult? When is hypnosis merely a medical or psychological tool? Where is the boundary between the medical or psychological and the occult? When does hypnosis move from the occult to medicine and from medicine to the occult? Why is it that some in the church who know that hypnosis has been an integral part of

the occult nevertheless recommend its use? Paradoxically and sadly, though the experts cannot agree on what it is and how it works, hypnosis is being cultivated for Christian consumption (376:53-54).

## BIBLICAL PROHIBITIONS?

The various hypnotic methods may lie within the biblically prohibited practices of "charming," "enchanting," and general magic, in the sense of the exercise of hidden, or occult, power over another person. In fact, the magician in ancient times (an occultist, not a performer) is described as "one who tries by certain prescribed words and actions to influence people and events, bringing about results beyond man's own power to effect" (2030, IV:37).

In addition to concern over its occult potential, we believe that consideration should be given to whether or not hypnosis fits within the biblical prohibition against charming or enchanting. Concerning the prohibitions in Leviticus 19:26,31 and Deuteronomy 18:10-12, the Bobgans state:

The words from the Old Testament which are translated *charmers* and *enchanters* seem to indicate the same kinds of persons whom we now call *hypnotherapists.* Dave Hunt, author of *The Cult Explosion* and researcher in the area of the occult as well as the cults, says:

"From the Biblical standpoint, I believe that in such places as Deuteronomy 18, when it speaks of 'charmers' and 'enchanters,' the practice involved anciently was exactly what has recently become acceptable in medicine and psychiatry as hypnosis. I believe this both from the ancient usage of this word and from occult traditions" [letter to Walter Martin, January 13, 1982, p. 5].

Just because hypnosis has surfaced in medicine does not mean that it is different from the ancient practices of charmers and enchanters or from those which have been used more recently by witchdoctors and occult hypnotists (376:50).

The *Zondervan Pictorial Encyclopedia of the Bible* refers to an enchanter as "a person who influences people or things through charms, enchantments and spells. . . . Although practice of the art was forbidden to the Hebrews (Deuteronomy 18:10,11), the Old Testament shows acquaintance with several kinds of 'charming' " (390,II:304). In Deuteronomy 18:11 the condemnatory reference is to a person who "casts spells"; in Isaiah 19:3 the root word for "charmer" is sometimes translated as a "spiritist" or "sorcerer." In Daniel 1:20 the word "enchanter" refers to the occult practitioners of Nebuchadnezzar's court.

*Wilson's Old Testament Word Studies* defines the various Hebrew words for "charmer" as, in part, referring to one who speaks in a soft, gentle manner or who uses soft, silent motions (much like the hypnotist); also, as "to join together, to bind, to fascinate" (1049:74). Some have translated the "interpreters of omens" or "observer" as relating to a whispering magician or as one "who fascinates through an evil eye" (1051, II:148). *The Hebrew-Greek Key Study Bible* defines "enchanter" (*nachash*) in part as "to hiss, to whisper (a magical spell), to practice sorcery or enchantment . . . " (1050:1613). A "charmer" (*cheber*) is defined, in part, as "a spell, a charm, an enchantment," and it has the added connotation of "to unite" or "to tie a magic knot" (1050:1590).

Exactly what these ancient words and practices involved is sometimes debated, and some argue whether their direct application to hypnosis is established. However, there are certainly important similarities, and if it can be established that such words encompass the practice of hypnosis, then hypnosis would be biblically forbidden, and for Christians, at least, the issue would be settled.

We asked Tim Rake, assistant editor of *The Complete Word Study Old Testament* (AMG Publishers) to research the Hebrew words having possible relevance to the practice of hypnosis. Here are his findings:

Of the several Hebrew words used in the Old Testament in connection with divination, none directly or explicitly refer to Mesmerism or hypnosis. The more general terms, *'ōb qāsam nāhash* , and *kāshaph,* are too broad for making a specific reference to hypnotism.

However, words with a more narrow connotation—*lākash* (to charm, enchant), *nākash* (to whisper sorceries, to take auguries), and *hābar* (to charm), (Deut. 18:11)—may very well involve activity which was designed by its esoteric and secretive nature to induce various states of mind by the power of suggestion, i.e., hypnosis. In such cases, the audience becomes captivated and influenced by the very spell itself.

In fact, commentator R. E. Clements noted that the term "expert enchanter" in Isaiah 3:3 (NJKV) "was a person skilled in incantations, and who was believed thereby to be able to cast spells on people and so undermined their strengths and rational faculties" (R. E. Clements, *The New Century Bible Commentary*, Isaiah 1-39, Grand Rapids: Erdmans, 1980, p. 48).

Of interest also is the fact that in 2 Kings 21:6 and 23:24, the LXX [Septuagint] uses *thelētēs* for the Hebrew *'ōb.* One older authority observed that *thelētēs* "meant perhaps a person with a strong will who could act upon the feelings of others" (Rober Girdlestone, *Synonyms of the Old Testament*, Grand Rapids: Erdmans, 1951, p. 299).

In conclusion, hypnosis is a questionable method at best. We do not think the practice ultimately serves the best interest of Christians or non-Christians who are seeking physical or emotional healing. We do not think it should be used or taught in public school curricula. And a number of important, unanswered questions remain concerning its occult potential, whether in secular Christian psychotherapy.

What should a person who has been hypnotized do? If no adverse reactions were encountered, he or she should let the matter rest and not be concerned. But if one is still in hypnotherapy, it should not be assumed that the practice is safe. If adverse circumstances are encountered or problems continue, the practice should be immediately stopped and professional help should be sought. If the problems are spiritual in nature and occult phenomena were encountered, the person should renounce the practice and seek professional Christian spiritual guidance.

# Mantras and Mandalas

## INFO AT A GLANCE

**Description.** Mantras are sacred sounds and mandalas are sacred pictures (usually four-sided) employed for specific spiritual purposes such as occult forms of meditation, enlightenment,* and contact or union with various gods and deities.

**Founder.** Use of mantras and mandalas is most frequently associated with traditional Hinduism and Buddhism. Many mantras and some mandalas are held to have originated as a supernatural revelation from the gods or spirits with which they are associated.

**How do they claim to work?** Mantras and mandalas function as a means of "focusing" the mind, e.g., in meditation* and visualization,* and thus to assist the seeker along a given spiritual path.

**Scientific evaluation.** Not applicable.

**Examples of occult potential.** Mantras and mandalas are often part of a larger program of occult instruction and may help in developing psychic powers, occult enlightenment, or contact with spirits.

**Major Problem.** Traditionally, mantras and mandalas have clear connections to the spirit world and present other hazards, such as the development of altered states of consciousness.* Unfortunately, the false perception of most Westerners who use these methods is that they are relatively innocent or harmless forms of spiritual practice.

**Biblical/Christian evaluation.** As pagan implements or forms of idolatrous worship, use of mantras and mandalas is biblically prohibited.

**Potential dangers.** The hazards of occult practice in general (278).

*Note to Reader:* The terms "mantra" and "mandala" are phonetically similar and may be confused while reading this chapter. When using this material, please be aware of this.

## INTRODUCTION AND INFLUENCE

The dramatic rise of occult practices, New Age religions, plus Hindu, Buddhist, and Sufi gurus* in America has brought the magical and symbolic acoustic and visual accompaniments associated with such religions. Among these are mantras and mandalas, both of which, once consecrated, offer a representational form of worship common to much paganism.

*Mantras* are sacred utterances thought to mystically represent the essence of religious literature or the deities they invoke, thus conveying supernatural knowledge and/or power. They are used in religious worship, ritual, and meditation.*

*Mandalas* are complex circular and usually four-sided diagrams offering a symbolic representation of a larger cosmic reality or aspects of it. Mandalas are also used in religious worship, ritual, and meditation.

Although mantras are more well known in America through such Hindu practices as transcendental meditation, mandalas also play a key role in the New Age revival of Eastern religious practices. In this section, mandalas and mantras are considered together because of their similarity in purpose and effect. Both are religious methods having similar goals: ultimately, to help achieve occult enlightenment.* To do this, they frequently invoke various gods and deities. Ultimately, both forms of occult practice seek to unite the individual with the larger cosmic order. The primary difference is that while mantras are believed to achieve their efficacy through sound and vibrations, mandalas attempt to achieve the same through visual and symbolic means. And both methods may be used together; for example, a person employing a mandala in Buddhist meditation may also be chanting a mantra for a similar purpose.

Mandalas and mantras are frequently employed in Eastern religions, such as Hinduism and Buddhism. Mandalas, for example, are "fundamental to the ritual and meditation of Hindu and Buddhist Tantrism" (302:455). However, one or the other may also be used by individuals in various magical practices or occult religions, such as the Church Universal and Triumphant. Mandalas may be used in Jungian psychology and other forms of potentially occult, occult, or fringe psychotherapy. For example, in Jung's analytical psychology, "the mandala conforms to the microcosmic character of the psyche" (302:456). Among his patients, Jung felt that the spontaneous production of a mandala was a step along the path in what he termed the individuation process, a central concept of his psychological theory. Mandalas are also found in the sand paintings of some Native Americans and in Hindu

and Buddhist architecture (a Hindu temple viewed from the top is often a mandala).

Mandalas and mantras have almost infinite variations. In referring to some 70 *million* mantras, *Harper's Dictionary of Hinduism* points out that "*mantras* are of infinite diversity and are thus all things to all men" (2379:181). In a similar fashion, mandalas have an unlimited diversity since their complex symbolic designs are capable of endless variations (2379:178).

Both practices have a long and complex history, the detailing of which exceeds the scope of an introductory work. Our major purpose is to document the pagan or occult nature of these methods. Along the way we will briefly discuss similarities between these techniques, including the following: their relationship to a) the alleged spiritual structure and purpose of the cosmos; b) meditation and visualization; c) magic, occult practice, and the development of psychic powers; d) occult enlightenment; e) the spirit world, i.e., various "gods" and "deities" of occult and pagan religious traditions. We will close with a brief assessment of the potential dangers that these practices represent to adherents.

## RELATION TO PAGANISM

Standard descriptions of mandalas and mantras show a relationship between their use and pagan gods or supernatural cosmic forces. Concerning mandalas, *Harper's Dictionary of Hinduism* describes them as follows:

> Basically they consist of a circular border enclosing a square divided into four triangles; in the center of each triangle, as well as in the circle at the center of the *mandala* a deity or its emblem is depicted (2379:178).

The *Encyclopaedia Britannica* describes mandalas as follows:

> The *mandala* is basically a representation of the universe, a consecrated area that serves as a receptacle for the gods and as a collection point of universal forces (2383:555).

Mantras are also associated with pagan gods and deities:

A properly repeated hymn or formula used in ritual worship and meditation as an instrument for evoking the presence of a particular "divinity" (*devata* [god]); first uttered by an inspired "seer" (Rishi) and transmitted orally from master to disciple in a carefully controlled manner (302:457-58).

Mantras may also be the actual name of the god being invoked; many advocates believe the mantra is one essence with the deity, or that it contains the essence of the "divine" guru's teachings.

That mantras are (or can mystically "become") the essence of the deity, or the mystical essence of religious teaching, underscores the reverence in which they are held. A contemporary mantra, "nam-myoho-renge-kyo," in Nichiren Shoshu Buddhism, is believed to mystically represent and inculcate the entire essence of the Lotus Sutra, the central scripture. In other words, in these few syllables the "doctrinal" teaching of an entire Sutra is believed to be mystically embodied. In Hinduism even a single syllable is believed to mystically convey the teaching of an entire Veda, or major scripture:

The most potent mantras are those embodied in a "seed," or monosyllabic form, and such seed mantras are held to be the quintessence of complex teachings. For instance, an elaborate doctrine of occult knowledge set forth in a work of 100,000 verses can be reduced by a rishi [occult seer] to a single short chapter; this may be further condensed into a single verse; and the verse finally concentrated into a single syllable. This syllable if correctly transmitted to a pupil can, it is thought, communicate to him the substance of the entire doctrine contained in the 100,000 verses (2382:1728).

In the *bija* (seed) mantra just mentioned, this "is the most powerful of all *mantras*, for it potentially can become the concept or the deity it represents. Thus the sacred symbol *om* is said to evoke the entire Veda or . . . the three greatest Hindu gods, Brahma, Visnu, and Siva" (2383:582). Because mandalas and mantras are held to invoke, represent, or contain the essence of the gods, such magical application ultimately qualifies their use as a form of spiritism. Plainly, mandalas and mantras are vehicles through which supernatural

forces can be contacted for occult knowledge and power. Their source of power is said to be the spiritual forces contacted through proper practice.

Although this theme of contacting personal spiritual forces—gods or spirits—may be lacking in an official definition, the source of power is always assumed to be supernatural. For example, one definition of a mantra states that while no single definition is entirely adequate to convey its full significance, the mantra is "a formula, comprising words and sounds which possess magical or divine power" (2379:180).

## COSMIC SYMBOLISM

Mandalas and mantras are said to symbolically represent or embody the true spiritual essence of the universe or ultimate reality. In other words, the sound of the mantra or the diagram of the mandala, once consecrated, mystically embodies ultimate reality and/or spiritual potency of the entire macrocosm:

Typically a mandala presents a central Buddha figure, who is surrounded by a pantheon of subordinate deities, positioned in a geometric composition. This galaxy of supermundane beings is to be interpreted as a manifestation of the Universal Buddha or the Brahman of Hinduism, the primordial One from which the universe emanates and to which it returns. In short, the mandala serves as a cosmoplan, a spiritual blueprint of the universe. As such, it schematically maps the origin, operation, and constitution of the cosmos by disclosing its pattern of spiritual forces (302:455).

In pagan religion, typically, the spiritual powers of the universe are the various gods and goddess who act as subordinate deities regulating certain universal functions. The purpose of the mandala is not merely to portray these deities but to link the one who visualizes the mandala to the spiritual power it represents. The number of deities in a mandala may vary from a few to 100 or more:

Because the mandala is understood as a microcosm which embodies the various divine powers that work in the universe, the number of deities is limited only by the imagination and industry of the artist. Thus, many mandalas present the viewer with a bewilderingly intricate configuration, a composition which must be carefully read . . . (302:456).

Regarding mantras, some are "convinced that the *mantra* is a form or representative of God himself, the phenomenal world being the materialization of the *mantra* . . ." (2379:181).

In occult theory, sound is said to be one of the most primitive and powerful forces in the universe. Consider the following about how the mantra, sound vibrations, and universal forces may interact:

> . . . Mantras derive their most consistent and plausible rationale from an emanationist metaphysics in which all levels of reality come forth from, and continue to be permeated by, the same source or power. In this scheme sound (*sabda*) has a primary place. . . . Thus, sound and its vibrations (*spanda*) are able to interrelate and interact with all elements and all levels, stimulating resonance or sympathetic vibrations among them. Moreover, every emanation or manifest form, every distinct type or class of reality or being, is produced by and corresponds to a specific configuration of sound-vibration which in turn corresponds to and is expressible by a simple linguistic and cognitive form. This precise correspondence of being, sound, thought, and language is a key assumption underlying this rationale for a mantra's effectiveness.
>
> Also basic is the assumption of a correspondence between each microcosm and the macrocosm. All individuals, having come forth from and continuing to exist within the same sacred power, have the potential to experience, manifest, or become any being or "divinity" by reforming their psychic power (*cit-sakti*) through the concentrated, intentional repetition of the proper mantra (302:458).

Because of their alleged cosmic power, the use of mandalas and mantras in occult meditation,* visualization,* magic, and psychic development is common.

## MEDITATION AND VISUALIZATION

Both mandalas and mantras are frequently used in occult meditation and visualization practice. For example, "Continuous repetition of mantras is practiced as a form of meditation in many Buddhist schools" (2380:220). A standard definition of the mandala is "a symbolic diagram used in the performance of sacred rites and as an instrument of meditation" (2383:555). Because the mandala is a visual symbol of the macrocosm, the one who meditates on a mandala can visualize himself absorbing cosmic knowledge and power through meditation. Mandalas are thus often used to assist the meditative process through visualization upon its symbolic pictorial representation.

Just as visualization is a key component in the use of mandalas, so it is for mantras. In many religious traditions, "Recitation of mantras is always done in connection with detailed visualizations and certain bodily postures," e.g., *mudras* (2380:220).

## MAGIC, OCCULT PRACTICE, PSYCHIC POWERS

Mandalas and mantras are also related to or incorporated as part of magic ritual and occult theory and power:

> The mantra functions as a magical incantation, conjuration, invocation, evocation, and all the varieties of spells that comprise the armory of words of power. It is said before, during and after all important ceremonies. It is used as a curse, a blessing, a prayer, a way of remembrance. There is hardly an activity for which there is not a mantra (2468:139).
>
> The word "spell" is perhaps the nearest approach to the Sanskrit word *mantra*. It is a form of words or sounds which are believed to have a magical effect when uttered with intent. . . . A sound is a vibration, and when we consider that the family of vibrations include not only the things we hear but all material objects seen (which may be said to be patterns of vibrations), we can appreciate why the magician has always laid great emphasis on words of power. Sound is the foundation of all magic, and an armory of mantras forms part of the equipment of the magician in all countries.
>
> Mantras can create, sustain and destroy. The ancients believed that miracles could be

performed by means of magical formulas, and they made extravagant claims for the powers of such formulas. . . . The real power of the mantra resides in its effect on the invisible world. A mantra repeated often enough can penetrate the dense barrier of the material sphere and draw power from the occult planes (2382:1727-28).

The power of the mantra also functions to facilitate altered states of consciousness.* "Humming mantras . . . lead to a kind of intoxication which results in trance. Such mantras are ideal for magical purposes" (2382:1728). Consider the following description of witchcraft and other neopagan practices in Margo Adler's *Drawing Down the Moon*:

> Chants, spells, dancing around a fire, burning candles, the smoke and smell of incense, are all means to awaken the "deep mind" . . . and facilitate entry into an altered state. . . . "Mandalas," "sigils," "pentacles," and "yantras" are all pictures to stimulate the sense of sight; "mudras" or "gestures" stimulate the kinetic sense; "mantras" or "incantations" stimulate the sense of hearing (429:154).

Thus, proper use of the mantra is believed to internalize the power of the gods for attaining altered consciousness,* and for securing occult goals such as the development of psychic powers. Mantras are therefore mental tools "for manifesting particular 'divinities' within the reciter, i.e., for transforming his or her consciousness into specific forms of psychic power leading to the attainment of various worldly or transcendent ends" (302:458).

In *Magic: An Occult Primer*, occult magician David Conway soberly describes how the use of a mantra evokes the ritual "madness" leading to the sought-after spirit possession and the successful completion of the ritual intention:

> The aim of such unreason will be to receive the deity that is being invoked. The method adopted to induce this frenzy will be the one which the adept's experience has shown him to be the best. . . . Some magicians cultivate the sweet madness by reciting one word over and over again. The adept begins by heaping incense on the charcoal and then, kneeling before the altar,

he starts his verbal repetition or mantra. Any word will do for this purpose; it may be one of the words of power, an euphonious word of the adept's own invention or even a keyword associated with his ritual motive, a crude example being the word "money" in a ritual intended to procure wealth. While engaged in this, the adept imagines that the god-form . . . is materializing behind his back. . . . Slowly, as the altar candles flicker, he will sense with a sureness which precludes all doubt that the visualized form is in fact towering inside the circle behind him. . . . At last—and he will certainly know when—the god-form will take control of him. . . . As this happens, and while the power is surging into him, he forces himself to visualize the thing he wants his magic to accomplish, and wills its success (237:130-31).

Like mantras, mandalas are also used for magical purposes:

> Properly drawn and duly consecrated it becomes a focus of occult energy, drawing down hidden powers and itself sending forth magical emanations like a talisman. . . . Within the boundaries of the mandala various other geometrical shapes are drawn, lesser squares, circles and triangles, dividing the whole into a series of zones which are treated as sacred areas, each reserved for the spirit entities who will be called down to occupy the places allotted to them. Some mandalas are rich and complex works of art, whose pictures, colours, patterns and orientation all have a correspondence with the occult planes. . . . The mandala is regarded as a cosmogram, a map of the universe, with the regions marked out for the spiritual guardians of the cosmos. The patterns are traditional and many are said to have been captured in the past by adepts meditating on the planes. Special rites go into the drawing of a mandala, special invocations call the deities down, and in the sacred area a high-powered operation is believed to take place in a confrontation with the self. Meditation on a mandala calls forth not only the beneficent deities, but also the terrifying apparitions, bloodthirsty demons and images of putrefaction and death. . . . In Western occultism its analogue is the magic circle whose exact demarcations are given in medieval grimoires. The difference between the two is that after the magic circle is drawn the Western magician steps inside its protective boundary so that the

spirits he summons cannot invade his territory to molest him, whereas the Eastern practitioner remains outside the mandala while the spirit powers remain within (2468:137).

Clearly, mandalas and mantras are integrally related to occult practice and philosophy. It is not surprising, therefore, that these methods are also involved in the development of spirit contact or psychic abilities. Because mantras and mandalas can result in identification with the divine power or deity they represent, the inculcation of the power of that spirit and the production of psychic powers (*siddhis*) or mystical illumination will occur (302:458/2382:1727).

## Occult Enlightenment

We have seen that mantras are allegedly capable of mystically or psychically transmitting or "infusing" the contents of an entire teaching or comprehensive religious scripture. This is one purpose of the mantra: to transmit occult knowledge intuitively rather than cognitively. And the mantra or mandala can as easily invoke the presence, assistance, and *union* with its relevant god or spirit. Thus, psychic transmission of knowledge involves the participant in some form of spiritistic illumination or inspiration.

Such occult knowledge and power are merely a precursor to the ultimate purpose of these methods, which is occult enlightenment.* For example, after proper meditation* and use of the mantra, "one awakens to his divinity and realizes his identity with Absolute Brahman of Hinduism or the Void of Buddhism" (302:456). In Hinduism, "The mantra, which is held to be one with God, contains the essence of the guru's teaching.... Regular repetition of the mantra ... clarifies thought and with steady practice will ultimately lead to God-realization ..." (2380:220). Furthermore:

The sounds of *mantras* constituted a secret, initiatory language, to be uttered according to particular rules if their esoteric meaning and power were to be assimilated and the initiate fully "awakened" [enlightened].... In particular circumstances *bija-mantra* is repeated 100 or

even 1,000 times ... or inscribed in the center of a *mandala* as a focal point in meditation.... As a type of prayer they are linked with *sraddha* (faith) *bhakti* (devotion) and together constitute the means by which the devout Hindu achieves *moksa* (liberation) and union with *Brahman* (2379:180-81).

Because the deity "indwells" the mantra, "A true mantra has its own life" (2468:139), and it can be used for the same purposes that spirit guides are used for. The following description reveals that the functions of the mantra and its indwelling spirit can be virtually one and the same. In other words, distinguishing between the mantra and the spirit guide is difficult at best. The mantra is an occult vehicle

whose vibrations are first concentrated and then projected, either inward into oneself, or outward in the form of invocations, commands, blessings or curses, to function as protective instruments, healing potencies, defensive or destructive missiles.

The mantras directed internally are aimed at a particular part of the body such as the head, between the eyebrows, the solar plexus or the sex organs, and at these points they set up vibrations that create specific energies. Thus those directed to the cranium set up resonances in the chambers of the head, resulting in a kind of mystic illumination. Sometimes a mantra is sent on a journey in a circuit round the body and its reverberations cause the old bodily tissues to fall off and make place for new. They may be directed to a part of the body that needs strengthening or healing. It is believed that there exists a mantra for every condition and every illness (2468:137-38).

The mantra also appeals to the occultist's quest for power, whether such power is to be used for good or evil:

It penetrates the supernatural realms and in a way coerces the gods into granting one's requests.... If a person repeats a given mantra 100,000 times, men and women will obey him implicitly; if he repeats it 200,000 times, he will be able to control all natural phenomena; if a million and a half times, he will be able to travel over the universe. Special rosaries are used to keep a tally of the number of repetitions made. They usually consist of dried seeds on a string, but when sinister powers are sought the smaller bones of men and animals take the place of seeds (2468:137-39).

Now, in the case of mandalas, mandalas are highly complex symbolic and pictorial designations that must be "read" or "penetrated." The goal is to use the mandala to influence the mind in order to establish altered states of consciousness,* psychic development, mystical experiences, and so on, by "opening" the alleged chakras, or psychic centers. "The adept penetrates the *mandala* by certain yoga techniques which re-activate the *chakras* (circles or planes), regarded as points of intersection of the cosmic and the mental life" (2379:178).

Some mandalas have various "levels," each one representing different states of consciousness, with the final level signifying enlightenment:

But after spiritual progress, one transcends these penultimate interpenetrations and identifies the five principle emanations with types of wisdom. Thus the larger [mandala] figure is associated with enlightened consciousness and the remaining four with subsidiary states of consciousness. Repetitions of the quintuplet pattern signify the interpenetration of all things and lead one away from dualistic thinking (302:455-56).

Thus, "Hindu and Buddhist mandalas are basically alike in that both are inspired by the quest to recapture primeval consciousness, that integrity of being which only rapport with the One [e.g., Brahman, Nirvana] can restore" (302:456).

## SPIRITISM

Although traditional Hinduism and Buddhism perceive the mandala and mantra as related to the gods who bestow psychic powers and enlightenment,* in many ways these "gods" function in a similar manner to the spirits of both ancient occultism and modern channeling, and are indistinguishable from them.

When the practitioner refers to contacting the "gods," or to having one's being or essence infused by the gods, or to achieving *siddhis* (psychic powers) from the gods, religious tradition may lead the person to interpret this as contact with an actual deity. However, from the Christian perspective, that person is contacting a powerful spirit entity which the Bible identifies as a demon. The pagan world, past and present, has long worshiped its "gods," but the apostle Paul identifies these gods as demons. "The sacrifices of pagans are offered to demons, not to God, and I do not want you to be participants with demons" (1 Corinthians 10:20).

To understand the real nature of mandala or mantra use is to understand why such practices are ultimately dangerous. The consequences of such practices can bring one's life under the influence or control of an evil spirit, which may lead to demon possession. God warns us, "Let no one be found among you who . . . practices divination or sorcery . . . or casts spells, or who is a medium or spiritist. . . . Anyone who does these things is detestable to the LORD. . . ." (Deuteronomy 18:10-12). The Bible also exhorts: "Be . . . alert. Your enemy the devil prowls around . . . looking for someone to devour" (1 Peter 5:8). We are also commanded to "stand against the devil's schemes" (Ephesians 6:11) and not to be "unaware of his schemes" (2 Corinthians 2:11).

Unfortunately, the millions of people today who are employing mantras and mandalas are really toying with demonic powers. Whether or not a given practitioner internalizes, naturalizes, or psychologizes the supernatural is irrelevant. The consequences of occult involvement will still make themselves felt:

Given the abundance of spiritual beings portrayed in mandalas, one might naturally raise the question of the ontological status of these creatures. Some practitioners regard them as mere symbols, but others conceive of them as objectively existing entities. Those who subscribe to idealism are able to view all entities as creations of mind and as ontologically equal (302:456).

Unfortunately, redefining spiritistic influence as merely internal and psychological functions, or as cosmic realities, does nothing to change the malevolent purpose of demonic entities who may operate behind such constructs.

We should also note that whether we are dealing with mandalas or mantras, both function as methods involving the *worship* of deities. As such they foster idolatry, something God has warned against. "You shall have no other gods before me," and "Do not worship any other god . . . ," and "Do not follow other gods . . . ," (Exodus 20:3; 34:14; Deuteronomy 6:14). Indeed, under various guises, demons have always sought the worship of humans; Satan himself sought the worship of none less than Jesus Christ, the Son of God (Matthew 4:9).

*Mandalas and Spiritism*

The following citations reveal how mandalas function as a forms of worship, contact, and/or invocation of the "gods":

On a popular level, however, mandalas commonly function as objects of worship. . . . [W]orshipers offer prayers to the deities of the mandala in order to insure prosperity and protection from adversities. On a magical plane mandalas transcend symbolism and are actually used to conjure up deities (302:456).

In Tantric meditation chanting and contemplation can produce a "mandala" world which is populated by a host of divinities (302:456).

In many traditions, it is the "deity" itself that helps the aspirant along the spiritual path, whether through entering altered states of consciousness,* developing psychic abilities, performing difficult yoga* postures, and so on. "Here an empowerment to practice a particular *sadhana* [spiritual path] is required, since the mandala is the environment of a particular deity who dwells at its center. The ritual objects or offerings are connected with a particular quality of the deity, which the ritual action invokes" (2380:219).

*Mantras and Spiritism*

From time immemorial mantras have also been said to invoke the "gods," and their function today in modern occultism, Hinduism, Buddhism, and the New Age Movement is no differ-

ent. In fact, the mantras and the gods can become one and the same. The close association between mantras and the deities can be seen in the fact that the mantra "can *become* . . . the deity it represents" (2383:582, emphasis added), and in the fact that some mantras "are traditionally held to be revealed by the deities themselves, whose name vibrations are latent within them, so that a god can be summoned, or at any rate his power drawn down, by uttering his particular mantra. The mantra in this case represents more than a sound, it is the vibration of the divine emanation; *the deity is identical with it*, and like the deity it remains eternal" (2382:1727, emphasis added). "Mantras are formed in several ways. They can come as a result of inspiration, sent direct by the deity to the devotee" (2468:137).

*Harper's Dictionary of Hinduism*, observing that mantras were used for "ensuring communication with the chosen deity" (2379:180), briefly discusses the occult and magical purposes of the mantras according to the Hindu vedas:

In the RV [Rig-veda] the gods were invoked by means of *mantras* to ensure success in impending battles (I.100), to avert drought (V.68), to grant long life (I.89,9), and in the AV [Artharvaveda] to ensure escape from all danger and difficulty (XIX.7), and to grant the fulfillment of all needs. The AV *mantras* also served to expel the demons of fever and other diseases (V.22;III.31), to bewitch and destroy enemies (IV.18), and to stimulate love in unresponsive lovers (VI.130) (2379:180).

In the following citation, note how thoroughly the mantra is connected to the deity it symbolizes or evokes:

The efficacy of a mantra depends on its being or containing either a true name (nama) of the "divinity" or, . . . an equivalent esoteric "seed" (*bija*) syllable (e.g., Om), which is held to be essentially related to the being itself and to embody it when uttered. A mantra is accepted as having been revealed through the "vision" of a "seer" who directly experiences the "divinity" within his or her consciousness and whose mind (*manas*) then formulates a composition (*mantra*) that perfectly captures the name, character, and power of the "divinity." Such a mantra can be used as an instrument for continued evocation of the "divinity" if, and only if, heard ... from the mouth of a master (Guru) or teacher (Acarya) who knows how to repeat it correctly, including the proper mental concentration and intention. ... The student must undertake a long discipline of repetition ... until the rhythm of its sound-vibrations transforms his or her consciousness into the likeness of the "divinity" (302:458).

To conclude this discussion, we will cite a section from John Weldon's critique of transcendental meditation, *The Transcendental Explosion.* In an appendix to the book, he listed the common TM mantras and showed that they were not "meaningless sounds," as claimed by TM promoters, but that they are clearly related to Hindu gods. Notice again the close association between the mantra and the god it represents, and the ease with which the worshiper's personality can be taken over by the god:

Sir John Woodroffe, a recognized authority on Hindu tantrism, states, "Each mantra has its devata (god); and each devata has its mantra. ... The most potent way of realizing a devata is with the help of the bija-mantra," and, *"The Mantra of a Devata is the Devata"* (Woodroffe, *The Garland of Letters,* Madras, India, Ganesh Company, 6th edition, 1974, pages VIII, 260-61).

Allegedly, the rhythmical vibrations of the mantra's sound transform the worshiper and by striving he can raise the god's form.

Woodroffe equates the following bija mantras with particular Hindu gods: *Hrim* is related to Siva and Prakriti (Vishnu as Purusha) and worships the god Bhuvanesvari; *Krim* is related to Brahma and worships Kali; *Ram* is a mantra of the fire god Agni; *Ing* is a variant spelling of "Aim," the mantra of Sarasvati, and worships Vani; *Shirim,* a derivative of Srim is the mantra of the god Laksmi and worships it; *Thim* is related to the god Siva and Bhairava and worships them. *Shyama* is possibly related to Krishna. (Woodroffe, Ibid., chapter 26; personal correspondence with former meditators).

M. H. Harper observes, "For the Hindu a *mantra* is not a mere formula or a prayer ... *it is the deity itself.* ... The purpose of *japa,* the frequent

repetition of the mantra, is to produce the *gradual transformation of the personality of the worshiper into that of the worshiped.* The more a worshiper advances in his *japa* the more does he *partake of the nature of the deity whom he worships, and the less is he himself"* (M. H. Harper, *Gurus, Swamis and Avatars,* West Philadelphia, Westminster, 1972, pages 97-98, emphasis added).

Woodroffe agrees that the mantra of a god actually reveals the god to the consciousness of the one invoking it and the mantra is a symbol of the god itself and its power. The one who uses the mantra of the god is transformed into the likeness of that god (Woodroffe, *The Garland of Letters,* p. 277; *The Serpent Power* (Dover, 1974), p. 88). ... Patanjali says, "Repetition of sacred words brings you in direct contact with the God you worship," and that psychic powers are acquired by mantra-repetition. Repeating its name over and over awakens or transfers these powers. ... (Shree Purohit Swami, trans., *Aphorisms of Yoga by Bhagwam Shree Patanjali* (London: Faver & Faver, 1973, rpt., pp. 54, 79-80).

Maharishi [Mahesh Yogi] himself says that achieving cosmic consciousness through worship is done by "taking the name or form of the god and experiencing it in its subtler states until the mind transcends the subtler state. ..." This is also a description of the process of TM (M. M. Yogi, *On the Bhagavad Gita,* pages 293-94). ... The yoga authority Mircea Eliade, in describing the mantra as the very *being* of the god remarks, "By repeating the bija mantra in conformance with the rules, the practitioner *incorporates its ontological essence (nature) to himself, assimilates the god ... into himself in a concrete immediate fashion"* (Mircea Eliade, *Patanjali and Yoga* (NY: Schockem, 1975, p. 183, emphasis added).

Mantra yoga theory teaches an occult correspondence between the mystical letters and sounds of the mantra and certain areas of the body on one hand and these body areas and divine forces in the cosmos on the other. By repeating a mantra you "awaken" all its corresponding forces in the cosmos. Hence each body area has its god and mantra. Gods are said to reside in the chakras (psychic centers) and their powers assimilated as kundalini rises through each chakra (Ibid., page 183; Wood, *Sevens Schools of Yoga* (Wheaton, IL: Theosophical, 1973, rpt., p. 92).

There should be no doubt that mantras bear a direct and essential relationship to the gods of pagan religions, gods which, again, the Bible identifies as demons.

## PROTECTION AGAINST EVIL?

The demonic potential of these practices can also be illustrated through the literature's acknowledgement that *evil* deities can appear during the use of mandalas or mantras. These may appear even if the practitioner thinks he is involved with mere words, symbols, or supposedly good deities:

> Certain mandalas are marked by the prevalence of wrathful figures who exhibit hideous grimaces and enhance their gruesomeness by wielding terrifying weapons.... Familiarity with these awesome beings also has a virtue of preparing one for any malevolent deities which he may encounter as forms emerging from his own consciousness (302:456).

The fact that the circle of the mandala allegedly "gives protection from malevolent forces" (2379:178) illustrates not only its similarity to magic ritual but also to the possibility of having uninvited nasty guests. Many of the mantras used in the Atharva-veda are actually "brief incantations or magical spells meant to ward off evil..." (302:458). And in certain traditions, mantras are held to be a necessary means of "protecting the mind" (2380:220) from the evil spirits associated with these practices. Unfortunately, the alleged ritual "protection" offered against evil forces is no guarantee of success, as occult history itself demonstrates. Also, Buddhist authority H. V. Guenther and leading Tibetan Buddhist guru Chogyam Trungpa warn in their book *The Dawn of Tantra* that "practicing visualization [e.g., with a mandala] without the proper understanding is extremely destructive.

... Tantric scriptures abound with warnings about using visualization" (705:49).

Mantras are also potentially dangerous. "Some Hindu and Buddhist mantras are regarded as extremely dangerous if uttered incorrectly or with misplaced intent.... Such mantras require a very precise knowledge of their pronunciation, intonation and timing, and frequently several days preparation and purificatory rituals before they can be uttered" (2382:1727). In other words the same ritual preparations and potential risks surrounding some mantras are similar to those used in occult magic ritual itself.

In addition, it is known that occultists who are unable to transmit their powers to another person at death often suffer hellish death throes. But we also find this phenomenon with the mantra user who is unable to pass on his mantra:

> In India there is a belief that every sorcerer is in possession of a mantra of terrible malignancy which is the source and focus of his success and power. Such a mantra can be known to only one person at a time, and it is this last bearer of the knowledge who possesses the power of the mantra. As the time of his death approaches it begins to build up a terrifying tension and becomes an unbearable burden on the mind of the magician, causing him untold anguish. It is said that the magician cannot die until he has passed on the mantra to someone else. Stories are told of magicians of great repute dragging out their end in excruciating torment, in a state of living death because they could not unburden themselves of the mantra, since they were unable to find anyone willing to accept the secret from them, even though it bestowed material benefits (2382:1727-28).

In conclusion, mantras and mandalas may be widely used in American religious life, but people have little idea of their history, purpose, and potential consequences.

# THE MARTIAL ARTS

## INFO AT A GLANCE

**Description.** The martial arts are systems of physical discipline stressing the control of mind and body for self-defense, health, physical conditioning, and enlightenment.*

**Founder.** Different practices have different founders. For example, Tai Chi Chuan originated with Chang San-Fen, in fourteenth century China. China is often considered the dominant wellspring for the ideas and practices that have shaped martial arts practices. India and Japan have also contributed to their development.

**How do they claim to work?** The martial arts claim to work by unifying mind, spirit, and body chiefly through meditation and physical discipline. In Eastern forms this allegedly helps to regulate the flow of mystical energy throughout the body (*ki* in Japanese; *chi* in Chinese) and to enable one to attain the state of mind-body oneness. Both of these qualities are said to be important to effective performance of self-defense techniques or spiritual enlightenment.* Nonreligious forms of the martial arts can be found when the basic stress is strictly upon physical development. Although, even when they are considered as regimens of physical development only, they can be adapted to any religion.

**Examples of occult potential.** Occult meditation, development of psychic powers, spiritism.

**Major problem.** People who practice a martial arts program primarily for physical purposes can still be converted to its underlying religious philosophy. Because most methods incorporate Eastern teachings and techniques, the martial arts are easy doorways into Taoism, Buddhism, Confucianism, and other non-Christian religions.

**Biblical/Christian evaluation.** Any program having Eastern or occult beliefs or methods should be avoided; however, the truly nonreligious martial arts program may, in some cases, prove profitable. This is not to endorse all martial arts, nor is it to say nonreligious forms can be developed in every system. Even among Christian practitioners it is easy to become sidetracked into Eastern mysticism and to compromise or hinder spiritual growth in Christ (see last two sections, this chapter). And we do not wish to ignore the issues involved when a person is converted to Christian faith. Such a person may find it essential to forsake association with the martial arts as a requirement of spiritual growth.

**Potential dangers.** Occult influences and physical hazards resulting from martial arts techniques.

*Note:* See also Meditation* and Yoga.* This chapter is principally a critique of Eastern forms of the martial arts.

## INTRODUCTION AND INFLUENCE

In the award-winning, nationally televised 1993 PBS series "Healing and the Mind," host Bill Moyers discussed the popularity of the martial arts and the amazing powers they offer. In one segment, both Moyers and the martial arts students were astounded as a 90-year-old Tai Chi master used the mystical energy called *chi* to send an entire line of adepts tumbling to the ground by merely "throwing" "*chi*" at them from a distance of some 20 feet. Interviews with the students afterward revealed they felt forced down by a mysterious and irresistible power. This was the power they themselves were seeking, although they were warned it would take many years of austere discipline to acquire.

Perhaps few Oriental systems have become as widely accepted in the West as the martial arts, which are now part of the American mainstream. Most U.S. cities have at least one gym, or *dojo*, where people can learn judo, aikido, karate, Kenpo, Ninjutsu, Tai Chi Chuan, Hwarang-Do, Tae Kwon Do, Kyudo, Kuk Sool, Pa-Kua, Shaolin, Kendo, Eskrima, or any of the 60 other forms of the martial arts currently practiced in America. A discussion of the martial arts is important today for several reasons: 1) their relation to the renewed emphasis in our culture upon physical fitness and health; 2) their claim to utilize the same mystical energies so frequently encountered in New Age occult practices; 3) their stress upon meditation* and enlightenment*; 4) their potential relationship to other areas of the occult; 5) their increasing influence in mainstream America, especially among children and teenagers.

The rising interest in the martial arts over the last two decades may be attributed to several reasons. First, there has been the popularity of television programs emphasizing the martial arts, such as the "Kung Fu" series with David Carradine or the "Ninja Master" series with Lee Van Cleef. (Carradine also sells nationally advertised videotapes on how to learn Tai Chi.)

Second, the martial arts have been widely advertised to tens of millions of people through cinema. The immense popularity of motion pictures stressing martial arts adventures includes the Chuck Norris and Bruce Lee movies, and the many Ninja films. Aikido advocate Steven Seagal and Jean-Claude Van Damme have wide appeal through their martial arts films, which have earned well over 100 million dollars. The "Karate Kid" films have also grossed over 100 million dollars, and the pizza-gulping "Teenage Mutant Ninja Turtles" merchandise has raked in well over a *billion* dollars!

Third, the martial arts are often advertised as physical fitness and health programs, able to improve everything from blood pressure to length of life. The martial arts have taken advantage of the increasing American participation in physical fitness and exploration of alternate health methods (see New Age Medicine).

Fourth, the dramatic rise of crime has sparked people's interest in the martial arts as a respected means of self-defense. Both law-enforcement agencies and the military are increasingly incorporating such practices into their regimen, as are college and university campuses.

Fifth, revival of interest in Eastern ways in general (e.g., Taoism, Buddhism) has caused a corresponding interest in the martial arts, which are usually associated with Eastern religions (see Eastern Gurus).

All this leads Herman Kauz, a teacher of the martial arts for over 25 years, to say, "In the last 20 years, the United States—and the entire Western world, for that matter—has seen a tremendous growth in the Asian martial arts" (935:13). From 1987-92, the number of martial arts schools in the United States rose from 4650 to over 7000, providing an average income of 60,000 to 70,000 dollars a year for each school. With two to three million practitioners in the United States (almost 40 percent are children aged 7-14), one can see how the American martial arts industry is now a billion-dollar-a-year enterprise (cf. 2403:27). Worldwide, of course, interest runs even higher. Tae Kwon Do alone claims an international membership of over 250 million in some 140 countries (2403:32).

## HEALTH AND FITNESS CONCERNS

As noted, in health-conscious America, the martial arts are often advertised as an excellent means to overall physical fitness and vitality (916:111). And they are increasingly promoted by the health arm of the New Age Movement, which is the multi-billion-dollar industry of holistic or New Age medicine.* The connections to health concerns are evident. For example: 1) the martial arts are said to stress "natural" methods; 2) traditionally, they claim to regulate mystical energies of health in the body; 3) New Age health practices, such as meditation,* yoga-like breathing exercises, and visualization* may be offered; 4) they may offer mystical "enlightenment" as a means to physical well-being. Thus, in America today, a principal means of exposing people to the martial arts is through health concerns.

Tai Chi, for example, is usually promoted as a "health secret" from ancient China. One alternate health guide comments, "Tai Chi has come to be prescribed by some cardiologists for patients who have had, or are threatened with heart disease—patients with palpitations, angina or hypertension—because it is a form of exercise which imposes no strain" (727:146). The guide also claims that Tai Chi "tones" the mind and body in such a way that most people will "remain immune to everyday disorders" (727:146).

And in tandem with New Age medicine* is the claim that the martial arts awakens, regulates, or directs the same mystical energies which are found in numerous holistic health methods. Many of the energies *(chi, ki, prana)* of New Age medicine were derived from the traditions in which the martial arts developed, or by which they were influenced: Taoism, Buddhism, Shinto, and so on. When this energy is blocked, disease is said to result. Proper manipulation of this energy will unblock it and allegedly cure illness and bring health (976:38).

An article by Tai Chi practitioner Jerry Mogul states that the essence of Tai Chi is manipulation of the psychic energy within: "... The essence of Tai Chi is ... [in] controlling and sensing the energy within us.... Just by touch the teacher can diagnose [energy] imbalances and [physical] tensions ..." (977:43-44).

The martial arts discipline of aikido also claims to produce health benefits. Proponents assert that it improves blood circulation and generally, the nervous system. "General overall fitness is often claimed to be a by-product..." (727:149). Leading aikido master, Koichi Tohei, in *Aikido in Daily Life*, teaches that "... we can overcome an illness if we learn the Aikido rules of spirit and body unification and if we manifest the ultimate [reality] in our life power by practicing so that all physical motion is correctly done" (931:23).

And personal health benefits may be emphasized indirectly as well. For example, Ninjutsu master Harunaka Hoshino, the founder of the San Francisco Ninja Society comments, "... Indirectly, I will be emphasizing health care. This will involve primarily diet (nutrition through traditional ninja recipes) and physical fitness (through exercise and shiatsu)" (922:56).

Many martial artists also use this alleged mystical energy for more than health concerns. The energy may also play an important role in martial arts combat, meditation,* occult aspects of the practice, and in the cultivation of so-called enlightenment.* (We will discuss these later.) As one article observes, "Tai Chi has flourished in the increasing health conscious American environment" because "by maintaining a balance of energy in the body, and by moving [*chi*] energy through [alleged meridian] blocks, Tai Chi is a way of both preventing and healing disease" (913:25,26). And Tai Chi meditation supposedly allows one to become spiritually "enlightened" and move in harmony with the Tao, which is the Way, or mystical Path of the Universe.

## EASTERN PHILOSOPHY AND AMERICAN MARTIAL ARTS

The martial arts are ancient methods of self-defense that are traditionally based upon Eastern philosophies or religions, especially Taoism and Zen Buddhism (cf. 2403:27-30).

Jujitsu, karate, kyudo, and kenpo are strongly influenced by Zen Buddhism. Tai Chi is influenced by Taoism and to a degree also by Buddhism. Aikido is related to Japanese Buddhism and is influenced by Shinto. One writer exploring the history of Ninjutsu ties its development to various Mahayana Buddhist religions (926:34-42).

There are also many Western offshoots of martial arts that carry an eclectic or novel approach and incorporate other religious traditions or practices. As Dr. J. Gordon Melton, one of the preeminent chroniclers of religious movements in America, points out, *traditional* martial arts practices are religious: "... It is presently difficult to find a traditional martial art that is not somehow associated with a religious vision of the world" (1525:335).

On the other hand, they have continued to evolve to the present day, and many non-traditional martial arts practices may not be religious at all. In large measure, the religious or nonreligious nature of martial arts instruction depends more on the instructor than on any other factor:

It has been our finding that the degree to which any form of Eastern religion finds its way into regular training regimens of the martial arts has more to do with the approach of the individual instructors themselves, whose opinions are as varied as the arts they teach.... Yozan Dirk Mosig, 8th-degree black belt and chairman of the regional directors for the United States Karate Association (USKA), makes no qualms that Eastern philosophy should be the focal point of all martial arts curricula: "Karatedo, aikido, kyudo... and many others are ways of... extending the meditative experience of

zazen [Zen meditation] to daily life." Indeed, Mosig says, "he who practices martial arts without the mental discipline of zazen is... like a fool who comes to eat without a chopstick." Yet, many disagree with Mosig. Louis Casamassa, head of the Red Dragon Karate System, is representative in saying that today "the martial arts and religion are as far apart in ideology as Albert Schweitzer is from Adolph Hitler." Likewise, keichu-do karate founder Karl Marx, a 50-year veteran of the martial arts and an avowed Christian, [claims] that "the average American [martial arts] instructor doesn't even bother with the mental/spiritual aspect of his art" (2404).

Nevertheless, we must remember the increasing influence of Eastern philosophy and religion in our culture, and how quickly and easily the martial arts can be adapted to them by an instructor. The complexity of the situation is illustrated in the following attempt to sort out a "rule of thumb" method for discerning religious aspects of a given martial arts program:

Christians considering participation in the martial arts must be extremely discerning and select an art located *only* on the purely physical/sportive side of the spectrum. Here is a good rule of thumb: generally speaking, the "internal" or "soft" martial—such as t'ai-chi ch'uan and aikido—tend to emphasize Eastern philosophical and religious concepts more so than the "external" or "hard" martial arts, such as kung fu and judo. Put another way, most "internal/soft" martial arts fall on the mystical side of the spectrum while most "external/hard" arts fall on the physical/sportive side of the spectrum.... Having said this, however, we must make a few important qualifications. On the one hand, while "internal/soft" martial arts generally involve Eastern philosophical/religious elements, in some cases the physical aspect of the art *may be isolated* from the philosophical/religious context. This is the case with the so-called Koga method employed by several law enforcement agencies.... [C]ommon aikido concerns—such as learning to utilize the *chi* force, and attuning one's spirit and body with the universe—are *not* part of Koga, which focuses strictly on physical techniques and their proper application.

On the other hand, while most "external/hard" martial arts avoid or minimize Eastern religious elements, in some cases an "external/hard" art retains some religious trappings. The Indonesian-based style pentjaksilat, for example, is oftentimes colored by an eclectic blend of animism, shamanism, occultism, Hinduism, Buddhism, and Sufism.

What, then, can we conclude? The "internal/soft" and "external/hard" designations can be helpful in choosing an art as a *general* rule, but in select cases the designations may prove problematic, especially since elements of one occasionally overlap into the other. More often than not, the chief instructor of a given school—whether "external/hard" or "internal/soft"—becomes the deciding factor (2404).

Choosing a proper instructor is crucial for those who wish to avoid the religious aspect of the martial arts.

## BODYWORK, ENLIGHTENMENT, MEDITATION

In this section we will briefly examine three important aspects related to traditional martial arts practice: 1) the premise of mind-body unity; 2) the goal of spiritual transformation, or enlightenment; 3) the accompanying practices of meditation, visualization, and yogic breathing methods. It should also be noted that because of the large variety of forms and methods and their continuing evolution, we are merely giving a general analysis of the martial arts; not everything stated will hold true for every method.

*Mind-body Unity*

The martial arts along with yoga,* constitute perhaps the most original forms of what are now frequently termed "bodywork" methods, such as Rolfing, Orgonomy, the Alexander Method, and Traeger work. A fundamental premise of most bodywork is to bring about the unity of the mind-spirit with the body. The goal is to work on the body to influence the 'mind-spirit,' or vice versa.

In contrast to much Western thinking, and also to biblical teaching, the martial arts usually assume that the "mind-spirit" and physical body are one with a supermundane or divine consciousness, or complementary aspects of universal consciousness.

Koichi Tohei is the author of the *Book of Chi: Coordinating Mind and Body in Daily Life* (930). He is a Zen Buddhist and an aikido teacher, and he has established aikido training halls in more than 20 different states. He is also the founder and president of the Chi Society International and has a black belt in Judo. He states that, "Ultimately, mind and body are one—no borders exist between them. The mind is a refined body, the body unrefined mind. It is foolish to consider them two separate things. I have attempted for many years to introduce Mind Body Unification into academic circles.... In America, the University of Hawaii and Lewis & Clark College have paid attention ..." (930:10).

Peter Payne is an instructor in the Alexander Method whose main interests are aikido, Tai Chi Chuan, and Pa Kua (a martial arts style). In his *Martial Arts: The Spiritual Dimension* he writes, "[W]e may acknowledge the body as the external manifestation of spirit or consciousness ..." (920:9). In essence, for many martial arts practitioners, what other people normally think of as mind, body, and spirit are really just different manifestations or facets of a higher, unitary spiritual consciousness.

Understanding this belief in the unity of mind, spirit, and body is usually fundamental to understanding the true purpose of those martial arts that have religious goals. For example, potentially, the body contains great power because it is the *external manifestation* of the mind-spirit, and thus the visible revelation of spiritual consciousness. The inherent "divine" power, or energy underlying the universe (*ki* or *chi*) flows through the mind and body, waiting to be unleashed by proper instruction. It is this mystical power that many of the practitioners of the martial arts seek to develop. And if the spiritual consciousness and essence of man are defied, as they are in many martial arts programs, then potentially both mind and body are capable of manifesting divine, supernatural power.

Furthermore, because the body is only one part of the mind-spirit, it is impossible by the very nature of things that martial arts programs having this assumption could *only* be concerned with the physical body. This exposes the false conclusion made by thousands of Westerners who think that the martial arts are necessarily merely programs of physical discipline and development.

Thus, by recognizing that mind and body are one with, or merely different aspects of, the same spiritual and divine consciousness, we can see that the purpose of the martial arts may proceed far beyond physical disciplines alone. To regulate the mind-spirit, as in meditation, is to help transform and empower the body. In a similar manner, to regulate the body, as in the physical disciplines of the martial arts, is to also help transform and influence the mind-spirit. Indeed, martial arts practice is frequently about spiritual transformation, as we will document following. The goal common to many modern bodywork methods, such as Reiki, Lomi-work, or Arica is also the goal of many martial arts: transformation and enlightenment* of the mind-spirit by manipulation of the body, or transformation of the body by the spiritual disciplines of the mind.

Herman Kauz has been an instructor in the martial arts for over 25 years. He has a fourth degree black belt in judo, a second degree black belt in karate, and is author of the bestselling, *Tai Chi Handbook*. In his *The Martial Spirit: An Introduction to the Origin, Philosophy and Psychology of the Martial Arts*, he discusses the influence of martial arts practice on the mind. "As we practice martial arts, we find that our training has a strong effect upon our mind as well as on our body.... Acceptance of the concept of body-mind unity makes us more concerned than previously with ways the body effects the mind and vice versa" (935:25), and "the various aspects of training designed specifically to work upon the mind have their effect" (935:113).

*Spiritual Transformation and Enlightenment*

As we have said, the purpose of the martial arts may not be merely physical discipline. Traditionally, the martial arts are forms of spiritual *education* (921:46-47) that function as a means toward self-realization or spiritual enlightenment.* It is true that the spiritual dimension of

the martial arts can be downplayed or ignored, but this is not consistent with their ultimate purpose historically. This should not be forgotten. One standard text makes the following important comment:

The martial arts all have their origin as part of a total system of training, the ultimate aim of which was a *radical transformation of the very being of the practitioner.* Often these roots have been neglected, underemphasized or totally abandoned; nevertheless *their spiritual dimension is the heart of the martial arts....* To understand the martial arts properly, it is necessary to take account of the psychological and metaphysical as well as the technical aspects. Above all, it is vital to understand how a physical activity, seemingly closely related to the fields of pure sport such as prize fighting or wrestling, can come to deal with such matters as psycho-spiritual [e.g., occult] transformation and the nature of reality (920:5, emphasis added).

Richard J. Schmidt is assistant professor of health, physical education, and recreation at the University of Nebraska in Lincoln, Nebraska. In an article in *Somatics* Magazine, "Japanese Martial Arts as Spiritual Education," he observes two facts. First, that the Japanese martial arts are traditionally vehicles for spiritual education and enlightenment. Second, as to underlying ethos, their spirit and beliefs remain fundamentally the same, regardless of particular approach. Thus, Dr. Schmidt argues that the traditional martial *arts*, i.e., practices employed for military combat, are connected to what is termed the martial *ways;* that is, modern cognate forms practiced as methods of sport, self-defense, physical education, aesthetics, and meditation:

The purpose of this paper is to describe how Japanese martial arts [*kobujutsu;* military combat] and ways [*budo*] serve as vehicles for spiritual education [*seishin, kyoiku*] or self-realization [*jitsugen*] for practitioners of both East and West.... While the martial arts and ways differ widely with respect to purpose, technique, and method, the underlying intrinsic martial ethos [character, guiding beliefs] of both remain essentially the same (921:46).

Consider the following description of the fourth stage (the "do") of Japanese martial arts practice: ". . . This level is the final and ultimate stage of self-realization, the 'do,' the equivalent of Zen enlightenment or satori" (921:48). Writing in the *Yoga Journal*, Buddhist scholar and aikido instructor John Stevens, now living in Sendi, Japan, states that "martial ways are spiritual disciplines to be practiced *for the sake of enlightenment . . .*" (940:62, emphasis added). But anyone familiar with Zen Buddhism and other Eastern disciplines will recognize that the purpose of such "enlightenment" is ultimately to destroy the individual, and that their methods and end goals are fundamentally occult (941; see Enlightenment, Yoga, Eastern Gurus).

The problem faced by uninformed Western practitioners, especially children and teenagers, is that when they enter the martial arts primarily or exclusively for physical discipline and development, they may still be converted to Eastern religions or occult practices. In this regard, the martial arts function as a subtle form of proselytism for the occult religions of Taoism, Buddhism (such as Zen), or Shinto. The eclectic system of Jeet Kune Do, developed by the late Bruce Lee, is one example. Based on Taoism, and described by Lee as "a way of life" and "a means to enlightenment" (2403:34), many of Lee's students converted to mystical religion as a result of his martial arts program.

Herman Kauz, the martial arts authority cited earlier, has been a student of the martial arts for over 30 years and an instructor for 25. He has studied or taught judo, karate, aikido, Zen, Tai Chi Chuan, and others. In this regard, he observes how easily students can get more than they bargained for:

Most students come to the martial arts for self-defense training or for exercise. . . . But as their training progresses they may find that their teacher considers of primary importance such intangibles as self-knowledge and, ultimately, self-realization. . . .

Western students of Asian martial arts are usually unaware that the Eastern view of man differs from their own. . . . Therefore when a Western student begins to notice that his teacher seems to be concerned with more than his physical development, he should not be surprised. . . . Students in the West sometimes . . . feel the study of martial arts should be concerned only with its practical application. . . . Such thinking seems to view martial arts too narrowly and is usually held by beginners and by students whose teachers themselves think this way. However, those who have practiced some years and are still unaware of anything beyond the physical miss the vast potential in their training that can contribute to self-knowledge (935:28-29).

Kauz later observes that "relevant ideas from Taoism, Buddhism and Confucianism were incorporated into the philosophy of the martial arts as they developed through the centuries," and that the teachers of various martial arts disciplines "usually *attempted to originate training methods* that would enable their students to *directly apprehend* the *content* or spirit of these philosophical concepts. Their intention was to help students understand important truths *intuitively*, to develop their insight, rather than to have contact with these ideas only intellectually" (935:94, emphasis added). In other words, the purpose of a martial arts program may be the direct apprehension or experience of ultimate spiritual reality as defined by the pagan Eastern religion with which it is associated.

George Leonard, a former president-elect of the Association for Humanistic Psychology and author of the bestselling, *The Ultimate Athlete*, which was inspired by his practice of aikido, testifies that his teacher was concerned with much more than physical discipline. The instructor was an accomplished martial artist with experience in judo, karate, Tai Chi, and aikido:

Yet he told us that he considered himself primarily a meditation teacher, and he spent about half his time leading us in various forms of meditation, centering, and "energy awareness" exercises. Nadeau taught us to think of ourselves and of our fellow students as fields of "energy." . . . One day we spent a half hour imbuing our "energy bodies" with the quality of slabs of granite (939:54).

357

*Meditation, Visualization, and Breathing*

In an interview on "Larry King Live" (August 28, 1991), "Kung Fu" practitioner and TV star David Carradine stated that if a person wants to be successful in the martial arts, a meditation* program is essential. In "Kung Fu—the Legend Continues" series, Carradine has made it clear that the character he plays, "Cain," is a shaolin priest whose occult powers are unleashed by martial arts meditation and mind-concentration practices. Indeed, one of the principal methods for spiritual instruction and transformation within the martial arts is the practice of Eastern forms of meditation. We should also remember that the purpose of such meditation is often spiritual (i.e., occult) enlightenment:

> Within the context of the martial arts, meditation has generally referred to those practices that involve "the focusing of attention non-analytically in either a concentrated or expansive fashion, the outcome of which can lead to an alteration in consciousness, an increase in awareness and insight, or a combination of such psychological factors. It is said that diligent practice of meditation "leads to a nondualistic state of mind in which, the distinction between subject and object having disappeared and the practitioner having become one with 'god' or 'the absolute,' conventions like time and space are transcended ... [until] finally that stage is reached which religions refer to as salvation, liberation, or complete enlightenment" (2404).

Ninjutsu master Ashida Kim argues that *all* the Far East martial arts require meditation for efficient practice and that this is particularly true for Ninjutsu:

> The emphasis on meditation to cultivate the mind and the body *is characteristic of all the Far East martial arts.* Nowhere is this more true than in Ninjutsu.... Ninja places much importance on the spiritual and mental aspects of their art as on the physical.... Breath control is the key to proper meditation, which may be defined as *the art of consciously altering the state of mind* (918:5-6; cf. 922:55, first emphasis added).

A standard text on the martial arts declares, "The fundamental state of meditative practice is also the prerequisite for mastery in the martial arts" (920:94). James W. DeMile, one of the original students of Bruce Lee, comments on the importance of meditation in his *Tao of Wing Chun Do*, stating that various forms of meditation, visualization, yoga* breathing, and energy channeling* are considered fundamental (915:27-36).

Another authoritative text on the martial arts acknowledges that one more "aspect of martial arts considered of major consequence is meditation" (935:27):

> In the Middle East the Sufis and in the Far East the Buddhists, Taoists, Shintoists, and Indian Yogis all depend upon meditation to achieve their particular ends. Members of primitive tribes throughout the world engage in one or another form of meditation for spiritual [i.e., occult] development. The meditation practiced by all of these groups has certain mental and physical methods in common.... The individual practice of form in martial arts, when it is used as mental training, also relies upon some of the foregoing methods to bring about in its students *various changes in the way they view the world....* Despite the occasional failure of their teacher to point the way, students *will notice a change in themselves* nonetheless (935:55-56, emphasis added).

Tai Chi is also described as a form of meditation having a spiritual purpose. An alternate health guide comments:

> T'ai chi has been described as "meditation in motion." It can be regarded as a civilian version of some of the ancient eastern martial arts such as kung fu, and it has some affinities with dance therapy. Unlike dance therapy, however, it is ritualized into a succession of flowing movements, with relatively little scope for individual variations. Each movement or exercise has a symbolic interpretation, and emphasis is laid upon the psychological or psychic element involved.... [The purpose of Tai Chi] is about finding the center of balance, with the physical center gradually leading to the spiritual center. It teaches the individual containment, the way to build up energy in the body, and then to direct and control its release through movement (727:144-45).

One practitioner confesses that Tai Chi can heal a person physically, mentally, *and* spiritually (976:36), and that it can do this because Tai Chi meditation is inextricably bound to the mystical Tao:

> It is the meditation which places T'ai Chi beyond a physical exercise or a technique of self-defense, and coordinates the conceptual framework of Taoism with the reality of the healing energy. The key to the system of T'ai Chi Ch'uan, as emphasized by all masters and the classics, is the total reliance on the mind. The consciousness directs; it is that simple. Without it, there is nothing. . . . It is the meditative state which allows us to move in accordance with the Tao (977:44-45).

But as we discussed in another text, the philosophy of Taoism is anything but neutral (1590:110-18). Because its beliefs and practices are anti-Christian, Tai Chi programs based on Taoism are unlikely to be spiritually productive, and they can easily lead a practitioner into occult philosophy.

In seeking the spiritual goals of martial arts, we are told that "various forms of meditation are perhaps the most important of these methods. The martial arts can be taught with primary emphasis on their meditative character. Those martial arts teachers with the requisite skill in this area do what they can to help students penetrate their self-created veil of illusion about themselves and the world" (935:96).

One aspect of the "veil of illusion" would be the student's belief that he is separated from God. In Eastern religions, man (in his true nature) is seen as one essence with ultimate reality, however such reality is defined (Tao, Brahman, Nirvana, and so on). The goal of Eastern meditation and its accompanying enlightenment is to enable the student to recognize that he is ultimately one essence with God or ultimate reality (see Enlightenment and Meditation).

That this is also the goal of many martial arts systems is evident. Aikido master Koichi Tohei states that "our lives are a part of the life of the universal" (931:17), and that the methods of aikido lead to spiritual enlightenment. "Sink your spirit into the single spot in your lower abdomen and you will become unconscious of the act of breathing. You will then forget yourself, become one with the universal, and enter the realm in which nothing but the universal exists. . . . In the first stages of practicing seated Zen, this method is often used because it is extremely good in leading one to a deep enlightenment" (931:36). Another text states, "The secret of Aikido is to harmonize ourselves with the movement of the universe and bring ourselves into accord with the universe itself. He who has gained the secret of Aikido has the universe in himself and can say, 'I am the universe'" (920:36).

In some martial arts, the ancient goal was immortality itself. "The search for immortality, a constant theme of Taoism, may be considered under two aspects, the first positive and the second negative. In its *first aspect*, what is envisaged is an abnormal longevity leading to an actual physical immortality, a goal obtainable by observing the moral law, by magical means (via *magica*), and by mystical elevation (via *mystica*)" (936:51).

While many instructors incorporate Eastern forms of meditation into martial arts practice, this does not mean that all use of the term "meditation" is necessarily religious. For many instructors "meditation" only involves concentration upon one's lessons, placing all distractions aside so that full effort may be expended on the physical technique being mastered. Athletes do this on a regular basis, whether it be the concentration required of the high jumper, the freethrow of the basketball player, or a golfer putting.

Meditation is not the only accompaniment of martial arts practice. In some martial arts forms, one also finds similarities to the religious goals of various yogic* practices that stress proper physical posture and movement, or the proper regulation of one's breath. Concerning physical postures:

> In all martial arts teaching (as in all movement systems), great attention is paid to detail in posture and gesture. This is not because what is desired is a certain precise technique; rather the master's correction says to the student, "If your

spirit were in the right state it would manifest in your movement, and it would be *thus.*" What is important is the spirit.... The above explanation deals with Tai Chi in particular, but it conveys the principles behind body movement systems in general as means toward spiritual change.... In Hatha Yoga, for instance, it is said that in each asana [posture] a yogin obtained enlightenment; through entering into the [spiritual] essence of the asana [posture] the practitioner will attain communion with the energy of this enlightened being [i.e., state or condition] (920:43).

Breathing methods also perform an important part of the meditation practices leading to enlightenment (cf. Yoga). For example, "Breath and Body are vital to the pursuit of both spiritual unfoldment and the mastery of the martial arts. It is vital to understand the basic structure of Breath and Body accurately and in detail. This understanding may be gained intuitively in the presence of the true master over a long period of time; this has been the traditional way of teaching" (920:38).

One aikido manual discloses: "Breathing methods [are introduced] as a method of spiritual unification," and the "ultimate aim of breathing practice and quiet seated meditation in both Zen and Yoga is a comprehension of our basic essence, which is one with the universal, and a manifestation of the divine soul" (931:24,103).

In these methods, yogic* breathing techniques are used to regulate the flow of mystical energy (*ki* or *chi*) within the body, to "draw" it within (from the universe) or to project it outward into the environment for physical power or even psychic healing, as Steven Seagal does. In "the Asian systems of martial arts, *chi* is directed by will power to specific points of the body, resulting in apparently paranormal feats of strength and control" (2404).

## MYSTICAL ENERGIES

The martial arts are traditionally tied to the regulation and manipulation of mystical energies such as *chi* (Chinese) and *ki* (Japanese). *Harper's Encyclopedia of Mystical and Paranormal Experience* points out:

Regardless of style the key to all martial arts is skillful use of the universal life force (ch'i in Chinese and ki in Japanese), which permeates all things and can be directed throughout the body.... The force is controlled by uniting it with mind and body in physical movement, breathing techniques, and meditation (1526:344).

In the martial arts, physical movement alone, whether the gentle, harmonious exercises of Tai Chi, or the powerful defensive maneuvers of Kung Fu, can be a meditation* in itself and, with proper training, intended to stimulate mystical energy. It is this supposed universal life energy which many hold to be so valuable to martial arts performance, training, meditation, and enlightenment.

The following statements and descriptions will show that the manipulation of this energy in the martial arts is frequently indistinguishable from its use in the world of the occult in general. For example, it can be developed by certain techniques such as meditation and yogic* breathing; it can be directed outward by the will in order to perform difficult or even miraculous feats; it is said to be a divine force (2403:28/2404). One book on Kenpo observes that, "Mind development of 'ki' or 'chi' is an excellent martial art technique" (916:3).

Obviously, since *chi* is a mystical force or power that can be generated and controlled by the martial artist through meditation and breathing exercises, the connection between *chi* development, breath control, and the powerful physical feats of martial arts displays is evident (2404).

A book on Ninjutsu explains that the *inner* strength developed through the cultivating of *chi* energy is far more powerful than any "outer" physical strength. "The Chi is a force within all people that can be forged to perform the will. But not one in ten thousand will ever know the true Chi. This cannot be explained, but it can be experienced. The practice is known as *Kuji Kiri*" (918:5).

An article on Tai Chi explains, "Without *chi* development," tai chi would be merely an external martial arts exercise. *Chi* development comes from "passive meditation and stance training." Thus:

Students practiced special standing meditation postures and breathing exercises before learning anything else. Each training session began with an hour of standing meditation to build up *chi* (often written *qi*).

Only when their chi was sufficiently developed did they start learning tai chi's martial art stances. As they progressed, they eventually combined their training sessions to include meditation, breathing and martial art stances. . . . Each posture developed jing (energy) in different parts of the body, while externally strengthening their arms and legs (1058:30,34).

Martial arts master Koichi Tohei claims that *chi*, or *ki*, is ultimately part of the energy of God: "This is Ki. Christians call it 'God' " (930:10).

Aikido, like many martial arts, places great emphasis upon developing *ki*. Westbrook and Ratti in *Aikido and the Dynamic Sphere* discuss the nature of *ki* and its historic centrality to almost all the martial arts:

This power has been called by many names, but the one that appears most often in these accounts, especially in Japan, is *ki* and the seat of that power is said to be the *hara*, or [psychic] Centre.

Almost all of the martial arts at some point in their development mention this power and the various means by which it may be developed. It is held to be "Intrinsic Energy" or "Inner Energy" and possessed by everyone although developed consciously by only a few. . . . Many scholars and practitioners of the martial arts, as well as monks and medical men have spoken of and demonstrated this Inner Energy and the ofttimes almost unbelievable results of its development and use. One frequently mentioned method of developing this Inner Energy is by the regular practice of deep or abdominal breathing. . . . Every beginner who steps on the mat in an Aikido Dojo soon encounters examples of Inner Energy (932:21,23).

This energy is said to be the power behind the dramatic feats of martial arts practitioners:

Most martial arts have feats of incredible power, such as powerbreaking, which is the breaking of thick pieces of wood, layers of tile or bricks, and so on with the hand, foot, elbow, head, or even fingertips. In Kung Fu the "iron palm" is a single blow with the hand that kills.

Other amazing feats are immunity to fire, cuts, severe blows, and the like. The purpose of these feats is to make the student aware of the power within. The feats are accomplished by directing the *ch'i* or *ki* to various parts of the body. When the body is full of *ch'i*, it is exceptionally strong.

Ueshiba often demonstrated his command of *ki*. He was five feet tall and weighed only 120 pounds, yet by directing his *ki* down to the ground could remain rooted to the spot and resist the efforts of several men to pick him up. Likewise, he used *ki* to send several assailants flying, while barely moving himself (1526:344-45).

In *Aikido in Daily Life*, Koichi Tohei explains that *ki* is ultimately the divine, universal energy which can be manipulated at will. He reports that most people do not recognize that the "everyday" *ki* is connected with the universal *ki*. Nevertheless, the very name of "aikido" literally means "to unite with *ki*":

Aikido is literally the road (*do*) to a union (*ai*) with *ki*, particularly with the *ki* of the universal. It is the way to the enlightenment that is our nature to be one with the universal. The entire reason for all of the techniques in our daily training is to refine our *ki*. For this reason we use such expressions as, "to send forth *ki*," "to lead *ki*," "to put *ki* into," "to repress our opponent with *ki*." Apart from *ki*, Aikido cannot exist (931:86).

Tohei again describes *ki* in divine terms:

*Ki* has no beginning and no end; its absolute value neither increases nor decreases. We are one with the universal, and our lives are part of the life of the universal. . . . The Christian Church calls the universal essence "God." . . . Our lives were born of *ki*, to which they must some day return. . . .

*In Aikido we always practice sending forth ki, because when we do so the ki of the universal can enter our bodies and improve the conflux between the two. If we stop the flow of ki, new ki cannot enter, and the flow becomes poor. For this reason, practice in Aikido emphasizing the sending forth of ki aims [not] only at improvement in the Aikido* techniques, but also at facilitating the conflux of our ki with that of the universal [ki]. . . .

If the basic essence of the body is *ki*, so is the basic essence of the spirit. . . . Aikido is a discipline that helps us unite the spirit and the body and become one body with the *ki* of the universal. In other words, Aikido is, as its name implies, the way to union with *ki* (931:86-89,98, emphasis added).

Another text describes the results of the martial arts as "the emergence of a new dimension, a new kind of energy, a new principle, symbolized by the 'Centre,' which is a generating force in itself" (902:8). And it describes this energy as follows:

Internal energy is stored centrally and can be directed to wherever it is required. It is flexible and changeable, and it integrates the body into one coordinated unit. . . . Internal energy is also the primary factor in maintaining good general health. . . . Internal energy is developed in many ways. It cannot be acquired mechanically (920:11).

In essence, in those martial arts stressing a religious program we are dealing with the manipulation of *chi*, or *ki*, which is the same old mystical energy of traditional occult practice as well as the modern New Age Movement. For example, a standard text on the martial arts and Oriental methods of health relates the channeling* of *chi* to the Hindu *prana* (936:55). A practitioner of Tai Chi connects *chi* to several related mystical energies, such as *ki*, *prana*, and Wilhelm Reich's *orgone* (976:44).

Another standard text also discusses how *ki* is related to a variety of occult energy concepts, such as the Hindu *prana*, Polynesian *mana*, shamanistic *n/um* (cf. Yoga), orgone, od, and magnetic fluid:

The word for *ki* in different cultures usually carries implications of both "breath" and "spirit" linking the material and the immaterial. . . . In Sanskrit [it is], *prana*, in Chinese, *chi*; in Polynesian, *mana*. . . . In bushmen [tribes] *n/um*. . . . Anton Mesmer's "Magnetic Fluid," Von Reichenbach's "Odic Force," and Wilhelm Reich's "Orgone Energy" all deal with *ki*.

*Ki* is an energy which is inherently linked with life and consciousness, and which can produce direct effects on physical energies and matter. . . . *Ki* can be directed by conscious intention. . . . The *ki* is developed through conscious linking of physical movement, breathing and focused attention. . . . The *ki* thus developed, may be stored, usually in the *hara* [psychic center], or lower abdomen and pelvis, and may be directed at will to whatever task is undertaken. Many healing methods use the direction of *ki* to the effected part [of the body]. . . . *Ki* comes in different "currents" and "voltages." . . . So as well as the task of accumulating the *ki* there is also the process of "refining" it, raising its "voltage" and establishing connections to more expanded penetrative levels of consciousness (920:44-45).

In conclusion, there appears to be little difference between the mystical energy used in the martial arts and the psychic energy used by the occultist, whether shaman,* witch doctor, medium, spiritistic channeler,* or psychic healer. This use of mystical energy brings us to a fuller discussion of the occult aspects of the martial ways.

## OCCULT POTENTIAL AND SPIRITUAL DANGERS

In this section we will examine three concerns: 1) the occult origin of some of the martial arts; 2) the spiritistic potential of the traditional *dojo*; 3) the ability of martial arts practice to develop psychic powers by "generation" and manipulation of psychic energy (*ki*, *chi*, etc.). These three facets underscore the occult nature and dangers of much martial arts practice (278).

### Occult Origins: Two Illustrations

At least some of the martial arts were influenced by or developed from occult experiences. For example, although its origins may be traced to twelfth-century Japan, the modern developer of aikido was Morihei Ueshiba (1883-1969). An article in *Yoga Journal* by Buddhist scholar and aikido instructor John Stevens states, "Morihei Ueshiba, founder of Aikido, looked like a Taoist immortal, acted like a Hindu swami and spoke like a Shinto shaman" (940:47).

Aikido was developed out of Ueshiba's experience of enlightenment.* In the spring of 1925, when Ueshiba was walking alone in the garden, suddenly, "a golden spirit" sprang up from the ground. "I was bathed in a heavenly light; the ground quaked as a golden cloud welled up from the earth and entered my body. I felt transformed into a golden being that filled space—I am the universe" (940:47-48). Further, "At the same time, my mind and body turned into light. I was able to understand the whispering of the birds, and was clearly aware of the mind of God.... At that moment I was enlightened.... I have grown to feel that the whole earth is my house, and the sun, the moon and the stars are all my own things" (920:46).

Ueshiba's meditation* practice had produced in him an occult enlightenment* typical of Eastern gurus* and other occultists. It also produced dramatic psychic powers. Such was the occult form of "enlightenment" from which aikido sprang.

The development of Tai Chi is often credited to Chang San-Feng (ca. 1260-1368), who was apparently a Taoist hoping to discover the secret of immortality by occult means. His strong interest in the I Ching* and other occult pursuits were well known and, in part, eventually led him to develop Tai Chi. The Chinese emperor himself described San-Feng as "the wise and illustrious spiritual man who understands the occult [i.e., the Tao]" (934:183).

### The Dojo and the Spirits

The occult potential of traditional Eastern martial arts is evident from the religious value and spiritistic function assigned to the *dojo*, or hall, in which the martial arts are to be practiced. The aspiring student may even be told that he practices under the watchful eye of the *dojo*'s spirits and that he must gain their approval:

*Dojo* is the name given to a place devoted to religious exercises, and its original Sanskrit meaning, *bodhimandla*, is the place of enlightenment.... [T]he focal point of the *dojo* is the *"Kamidana"* or deity shelf. It is here that the *"mitama"* (spirits) of the deities reside and

under whose cognisance the exponents diligently train in hope of seeking their approval. For this reason the *dojo* is considered to be a "shinsei" or sacred space (921:48).

One wonders how many Westerners are aware of this traditional occult function of the *dojo*. Nevertheless, all actions within the *dojo* are conducted according to a rigid code of etiquette. The front of the *dojo* is known as the *"shomen."* This is where the "deity shelf" resides and "all actions and references take place in relation to the *kamidana* [deity shelf]" (921:49). To the left of the *kamidana* is the sitting place of the senior-ranking students, for opening and closing salutations, and to the right is the area for the lower-ranking students. Most significantly, the position given to the instructor allegedly symbolizes his closeness to the spirit world. "The instructor is seated in front of the *dojo*, near the kamiza, signifying not only close physical contact with the *"mitama"* [the spirits] but spiritual [closeness] as well" (921:49).

### Psychic Powers and Spiritism

Psychic powers are developed through spiritistic contacts. The martial arts often claim to have the potential to develop psychic powers, and by implication, spiritistic encounters, whether these are perceived or not.

Many examples can be cited. Given the proper conditions, *ki* or *chi* in general is said to "become a supernatural power" (1526:346). The Korean *Hwarang-Do*, which came to the United States in 1972, stresses internal and external power, including "training in controlling the mind and developing psychic powers ... " (1526:346).

In the same manner that yogis speak of *prana*, which is associated with the development of *siddhis* (psychic abilities), martial artists may speak of *chi*. For example, *chi* cannot be accumulated in the body quickly, but must be built up slowly. It is regulated through breathing and meditation* (1526:346).

A text on alternative medicine discusses the potential of martial arts practice for inducing meditative "harmony" and the ability of *ki* to extend awareness into psychic realms. It notes the parallel to the nineteenth-century mesmerists (who were often spiritists cf. Hypnosis) and their dependence on "magnetic fluid" or "animal magnetism" for clairvoyance:

> As in t'ai chi, the element of the vital force is strongly emphasized. The assumption is that when the "wrestlers" are in full harmony, their powers are increased, and not just their physical strength. The *ki* is thought to extend awareness, so that the practiced performer can sense where any adversaries are and what they are doing, even if they are behind his or her back or at a distance, and can take the appropriate moves to anticipate them.
>
> Interestingly, this ties in with what the mesmerists reported from their research during the nineteenth century. Certain susceptible subjects, when mesmerized, could "see objects held behind their backs, and react to signals from the mesmerist even when he was out of their sight." The mesmerists also had the same explanation; animal magnetism was simply another version of *ki*, or *chi*. Later James Braid, who introduced the concept of hypnotism, ... claimed that there was no need to think in terms of any such vital force: It was simply that individuals in the trance had an increased physical awareness, and some aikido teachers today prefer to think in these terms (727:148).

Many other books describe the psychic powers that can be developed through the martial arts. One text discusses a variety of psychic abilities that can be achieved through solely internal means, with little or no physical power being employed. Again, the point of such abilities is to enable the martial arts students to be aware of the alleged tremendous power within them. It admits that these techniques "border on the supernatural" (920:12). Supernatural, indeed. Listed are such abilities as throwing an opponent without touching him, knocking down opponents at a distance, the breaking of bricks with a slight hand motion, and making the skin strong enough to resist a sword thrust (920:12/1526:346). Such claims of physical defense are reminiscent of the supernatural protection that shamans and other occultists may receive from their spirit guides or demon helpers. As comparative religion expert Mircea Eliade, a noted authority on shamanism, states, "After a man

[shaman] has obtained a guardian spirit he is bullet and arrow proof" (583:100).

Another supernatural manifestation is the use of so-called "repelling energy," in which an attacker is automatically thrown away from the master's body "with no conscious attention on the master's part" (920:12). The text discussing this observes that these abilities are still demonstrated by contemporary masters and that there are even deeper levels of power to be obtained.

Then there is the alleged ability of some martial arts practitioners to cause death by occult means. This, too, is reminiscent of shamanism* and the more virulent forms of occult magic. The so-called "death touch" supposedly sends a lethal charge of *ki* or *chi* energy to damage the internal organs in mortal ways. Ashida Kim, in *Ninja Mind Control* and in *Ninja Death Touch*, claims that *chi* can be used as a psychic power or for producing death by "touch." In Mashiron's *Black Medicine I: The Dark Art of Death*, the claim is made that *ki* can be manipulated in order to kill a person (924:27). The similarity to black (and even so-called "white") magic, hex death, and so on, is evident.

Also practiced are various forms of telepathic hypnosis*; for example, the art of putting an opponent to sleep at a distance, or hiding oneself from an opponent by distorting his perceptual ability or by inducing hallucinations. These techniques are claimed to be employed by the ninja (920:13). An illustration involving aikido master Ueshiba shows him on film, at the age of 75, being charged from both sides at top speed by two large judo black belts. When projected in slow motion, the successive frames show the master standing calmly while the charging attackers close in on him. However, at the very moment they are about to reach him, between *two* frames, Ueshiba allegedly has moved several feet out of the way and is facing the other direction. The black belts collide violently while the master watches in amusement. "Such a movement, which from the film testimony must have taken *less than 1/18th of a second*, demonstrates a transcendence of normal laws of time and space, a penetration of this world by the magical world of the eternal..." (920:32).

George Leonard describes a similar incident in his own experience with aikido. "As the four of us attacked her, repeatedly, I had a sample of that quality of Aikido that so often is called 'magical' or 'occult': *I simply could not get to her.* It was as if she were surrounded by the kind of force field you see in Star Trek" (939:50). Leonard says that he is "at a loss for words" to explain these kinds of experiences he has encountered (939:58).

In other words, the traditional mystical (*ki* or *chi*) energy developed in the martial arts is equivalent to occult energy in general. This *chi* or *ki* energy can be used for the standard occult powers developed in other occult systems. It can be used to turn the hand into a powerful or deadly weapon, to heal wounds and diseases, to break bricks and boards without even touching them. It can be used as a shield to prevent attacks and to strengthen the body to such a degree that allegedly no amount of physical attack by hand or sword can leave even a bruise or scratch. It can be used to read the past or predict the future (919:16), or even to kill: "Kung Fu practitioners widely believe in a traditional death touch called *dim mak.* If a body is struck at a certain point in a certain manner at a certain time of day, a delayed death inevitably follows. At first the victim feels unharmed, then later becomes ill and dies" (1526:344).

In MGM's "Ninja 3—The Domination," the starring role is played by Sho Kosugi, one of the world's most proficient martial artists. He plays the character "Yomada," a martial arts expert who is possessed by an evil spirit. Through the spirit's power, Yomada commits mass murder on a crowded golf course. He also kills about 40 policemen, taking dozens of bullets in the process. Before he dies he passes his occult abilities on to a young woman he meets by chance. Tormented by Yomada's spirit, she is driven to killing; she also develops psychic abilities.

The film's writer, James Silke, has obviously connected the martial arts (here, the Ninja) and the spirit world. But even some books on the martial arts hint at connections to the spirit world. One text, *Ninja: Warrior Path of Togakuri*, Volume 3, mentions the master's seeming reliance upon the assistance of spirits. "It is as though the spirits of all the past grand masters stand behind the man who now carries the title, and guide him through these dangers in ways that the master himself admits that he cannot explain scientifically" (933:11).

The potentially spiritistic nature of the martial arts can also be seen in their precipitation of kundalini* arousal (976:40; see Yoga). One text, explaining the dependence of Tai Chi Chuan on the Chinese system of divination* known as the I Ching,* discusses "the flow of psychic energy (*chi*) along these two channels" (917:9). One psychic channel runs along the spinal column from the base of the spine, where the psychic center called *Wei Lu* is located, to a psychic center at the top of the head called *Ni Wan* (917:9). Here are clear parallels to the psychic anatomy of kundalini.

Another text states that the Taoist psychic anatomy "is worth comparing with that of kundalini energy and Indian yoga" (936:54). In traditional religious Taoism, reliance on the spirits, both internal and external, was commonly accepted (936:52-53); therefore, it is not surprising to find spiritistic manifestations (e.g., kundalini arousal) in those practices based on such a philosophy. Thus, *prana*, the Hindu "energy" term, is sometimes paralleled to *chi*, with both being equated to kundalini energy (759:99).

Another example of psychic development in the martial arts is seen when Tai Chi, visualization,* and meditation* are used to develop psychic power:

> The use of visualization serves a double purpose of cultivating the psychic power of imagination. In order to feel the ch'i, we must first imagine it to be real. We must imagine it circulating through the energy channels, gathering in the psychic centers.... In this way we are employing a meditative technique, which allows the ch'i to take root, and we are actually hastening its development. The psychic energy cannot but have an effect on the object of its imagination. Two criteria are necessary—the energy must be positive and we must have a deep and abiding faith that it is real (977:46).

The end result of the visualization induced psychic energy is the recognition of the alleged truth of occult philosophy that "All is One." "T'ai Chi Ch'uan (the form and discipline) is organized specifically to discover that unifying essence or soul (the T'ai Chi) which is present in everything... [reflecting] the living connection and life-affirming oneness of all things in the universe" (977:48).

In *The Martial Spirit* the author mentions how practice of the martial arts might encourage students to admit "the possibility of psychic or clairvoyant ability. He might even visit a psychic when he seeks the solution to an important problem" (935:66). The book also discusses the importance of divination* methods such as the I Ching. "Consulting the *I Ching* when faced with the need for a decision on some difficult subject can help the student toward greater insight.... Other members of the occult fraternity such as astrologers, graphologists and hand analysts, also can help the serious seeker after self-knowledge.... Another method the student might employ to gain greater self-knowledge is the analysis of his dreams" (935:66-67).

In other words, the mystical aspect of martial arts self-development can lead the aspiring student into other forms of occult practice. If Tai Chi is actually based upon the I Ching, this would seem logical: "[T]he movements of Tai Chi Chuan and the [I Ching] hexagrams upon which they are based are both methods of describing the circulation of psychic energy in the body of the meditator" (917:v). "The I Ching also gives practical advice on matters not directly connected with divination or philosophy. It includes information on government, numerology, astrology, cosmology, meditation..." (917:7).

Furthermore, in many of the traditional martial arts there is an unhealthy interest in confronting death, another feature common to the occult (249:105-20). Professor Schmidt, cited earlier, quoting an unpublished doctoral dissertation on the martial arts, notes that "meeting or confronting one's death has been a central teaching in the martial ways..." (921:46).

Another authority observes that one of the most important "learning situations for self-discovery" used to advance spiritual endeavor is "the confrontation with death." He explains:

All spiritual systems set up a confrontation with death.... In the Chod rite of Tibetan Buddhism, practitioners visit a Tibetan graveyard at night ...and invite the demons to come and take them.... In the martial arts, of course, death is a constant presence, the whole activity revolves around it.... The confrontation with death is perhaps the most important element of spirituality.... The fear of death is the greatest of obstacles for martial artists.... But freedom from this incapacitating fear releases great powers. ...In the Buddhist tradition, the preparatory practices of the remembrance of death are regarded as being the great motivators on the path; this is why they are essential.... Don Juan, the [shaman*] Yaqui Indian teacher in Castanada's books, makes the same point with great clarity and power (920:29-31).

What this approach supposedly reveals is the "importance of death as the source of life" (920:29-32).

As a final illustration of occult potential, we cite *Secrets of the Ninja*. The author, a Ninja master, observes the shamanistic* nature of Ninjutsu in words similar to the sorcerer Don Juan, who educated Carlos Castenada in the ways of Yaqui shamanism.* He asserts, "To be a Ninja one must be a wizard. This means that he can 'stop the world' and see with the 'eyes of God'" (918:2).

The first part of the book discusses the nine occult power centers that are to be used in Ninja practice. The first center is described in terms parallel to kundalini philosophy:

There are nine basically significant centers of power. The first of these is located at the base of the spine.... This is the occult center of the body, which holds the serpent power.... You will feel a sensation stirring at the base of the spine. It will grow, double, redouble, and race up the spine to the base of the skull.... Once in this state, begin sensory withdrawal exercises to isolate the mind and develop conscious control of the body (918:10,12).

The second center, also reminiscent of the yogic chakras, is said to "develop power generation in the psychic centers" (918:12). The third center regulates and controls the flow of psychic energy, or *chi.* "The practice of Kuji Kiri is the art of transmitting this energy" (918:17). And at this stage, we are able "to passively withdraw into ourselves, to become one with the universe. This is sometimes known as the state of trance contemplation" (918:17).

In the fourth power center one learns other exercises for transmission of psychic energy, plus "in combat, the *kiai* or spirit shout is drawn from this source" (918:17, 19). In the fifth power center, special exercises help one to "develop the power to relieve pain through psychic means. The yogic concept of *prana* is useful in understanding this. *Prana* is not the consciousness or the spirit, but is merely the energy used by the soul in its material and astral manifestations. . . . One who can learn to control this pranic energy has the power to bring it to a state of vibration that can be conveyed to others, causing them to vibrate harmonically" (918:20-21). In other words, this power center is about psychic healing (918:22).

In the sixth power center, various techniques assist practitioners to "develop the psychic sense of hearing allowing one to hear the inner voice. Further, it stimulates the proximity sense which allows one to feel the presence of the enemy and locate him in total darkness" (918:24). This center "also serves as the psychic force which separates the astral body from the physical at the time of death. Meditation on this center leads to the philosophical concept of one-self—'I am that I am' " (918:24).

The seventh power center leads to extraordinary occult strength, knowledge, and willpower. And through this center, one can apparently achieve the goals of occult magic ritual.

Each of the centers so far experienced is also a center of consciousness which may be activated by the sound energy of a chant or by meditation. For each center there is a specific chant, and for each a specific mandala in the form of the visualized ideogram. By these means, the force may be channeled to perform the will. The magic of the serpent from the lowest to the site of the seventh center constitutes the first third of the journey. From here the energy rises to the Lotus and

merges with the consciousness of the Infinite. At this level, one overcomes the limit of time and space, and gains the ability to control the actions of others without physical contact (918:24-25).

In the eighth center, kundalini energy can be consciously directed at will, and there is a "marriage of spirit and matter" as "the individual consciousness unites with the universal consciousness" (918:26). Furthermore, the eighth and ninth centers represent acquisition of occult knowledge that cannot be publicly described but only be passed from master to student (918:27-28).

It should be evident by now that the martial arts can be systems of occult practice. And many of the other martial arts techniques and methods not discussed may also have occult elements. All of this is why the widespread practice of Eastern forms of martial arts should be of concern to our society. As we thoroughly documented in *The Coming Darkness: Confronting Occult Deception* (278), occult practices are anything but inconsequential.

## POTENTIAL PHYSICAL DANGERS

Besides occult dangers, there are other hazards for the martial arts practitioner. Martial arts practices can be exceptionally rigorous, taxing the body to its limits. It is hardly surprising that a practice of breaking bricks and boards—with all the punching, tumbling, and kicking—could cause injuries or, in the long run, health problems such as arthritis or other chronic pains (See closing section, "Three Testimonies").

A master of aikido observes that those who attempt to cure a serious illness from the Zen meditation used in aikido "should be aware that rather than always cure, such procedure can be very dangerous. The likelihood is that an illness will get worse . . . " (931:22; cf. Yoga). A text on Ninja exercises points out that they "are strenuous in the extreme—some may produce unconsciousness. The shock to the body could be quite severe unless proper precautions are taken" (918:6).

Another potential danger is physical damage to the head. An article in the *Taekwondo Times*, "Neurological Disorders in the Martial Arts" by Dr. Michael Trulson, cautions, "I would now like to discuss injury to the nervous system in the martial arts. Head injuries are the most commonly ignored serious injuries in the martial arts. Often they are not taken seriously and *fatalities occur that could easily have been prevented.* Concussions occur frequently in contact martial arts, and may occur even when the contact is relatively light" (937:84, emphasis added).

Violence is another problem. Until recently, many of the martial arts were used defensively. However, in recent years the tendency has been more toward an offensive approach. One code espoused in some programs is "do not provoke attack, indeed, do all you can to avoid it. But if you can no longer avoid it, retaliate with total power: kill with one blow" (920:35). What are the implications of teaching this philosophy to people, especially to children or teenagers? Some people deliberately use the martial arts only for offensive purposes.

The death of the late Bruce Lee at the young age of 32 appears to have resulted from a brain aneurysm. Lee was hypersensitive to meprobamate, a drug used in painkillers, and this sensitivity apparently caused a fatal reaction in the brain (2405). But it is also possible that a cofactor in his death was trauma to the head from vigorous martial arts practice. Futhermore, there is speculation among some practitioners and masters concerning the possibility of a more esoterically induced death. A reliable source told us that several masters boasted (independently of one another) that *they* were the ones who had put the "touch of death" upon Lee.

Other theories were also put forth. One text said that "his early death was a tragedy. Speculations on the true cause of his death by cerebral hemorrhage are rife, but it seems possible that one factor was his misuse of breath-holding *ki* exercises . . . " (920:22-23). Because the martial arts may deal with the same kinds of "psychic energies" found in the occult and yoga,* they may lead to the same hazards associated with such practices. Just as yogis have unexpectedly died from manipulating this occult energy, the possibility would seem to be present in martial arts practice as well.

## CHRISTIAN PARTICIPATION

According to Scot Conway, founder of the Christian Martial Arts Foundation, over 50 percent of practitioners and some 20 percent of instructors consider themselves Christians (2403:27).

The question of Christian participation in the martial arts is easy to resolve at one level and less easy at another. On the one hand, there is no doubt that Christians are to avoid any system that encourages or requires occult practices of meditation,* breath control, visualization,* manipulation of mystical energies such as *ki* or *chi*, or the adoption of Eastern philosophy. This would therefore rule out participation in many forms of the martial arts.

On the other hand, meditation, the manipulation of psychic energies, and occult breathing techniques are not necessary to the physical conditioning required for effective mastery of the body. The mind and body can be disciplined to produce many (although not all) of the more extraordinary abilities seen in the martial arts without recourse to any kind of occult or supernatural power. However, any time something supernatural occurs in the martial arts, such as breaking a pile of bricks by light touch or throwing an opponent at a distance, we have left the realm of natural human ability.

Christian groups which teach the martial arts, or employ them as evangelistic methods, stress that they can satisfactorily remove the Eastern philosophy and the occult practices and still produce favorable results. For example, Robert Bussey is regarded "as one of the most dynamic fighting technicians of our day," according to *Ninja Masters* (923:67). He has the largest and best-equipped Ninjutsu hall in the world. Yet Mr. Bussey appears to be a committed Christian. "I enjoy working hard to be the best that God wants me to be—and I have hundreds of dedicated students that feel the same way" (923:91). "As a Christian, it is important that I see people in the same way Jesus did" (923:91). Another example is Raul Ries and Xavier Ries, pastors of Calvary Chapel in Diamond Bar and Pasadena, California, respectively, who both hold eighth-degree black belts in Kung Fu, a discipline they have been teaching for over 20 years. They believe that the mystical or occult potential of the martial arts can be avoided (2404).

We are not saying that it is always easy to practice the martial arts as a Christian. Theoretically and practically there are pitfalls to be avoided, and for a variety of reasons not everyone could be expected to avoid them (See closing section, "Three Testimonies"). For example, novices must be careful to evaluate the true nature of a martial arts practice. Is it practiced traditionally or as a hybridization? If toned down in religious content, will some practitioners, upon learning this, desire the real thing? A book on Tai Chi states: "The great majority [in China] . . . have always engaged in it, and do so still, quite without mystic or religious purpose" (934:8). But traditionalists claim that this is not true Tai Chi. "[O]ne school of traditionalist thought strongly resents the spread of what it regards as a very superficial version of t'ai chi, as taught in most classes. Teachers in this mold refuse to take pupils except on a long-term basis, and require them not just to learn the dance, but also to study Taoism, the I Ching, and their general philosophies" (727:146).

Sometimes, even in the allegedly nonmystical, nonreligious Tai Chi, the manipulation of *chi* can still remain. In other words, *chi* itself is defined nonmystically and its manipulation is not perceived as a religious or mystical practice, but as a "natural" communion with the essence of the universe. How then can Tai Chi or Tai Chi Chuan be "nonreligious" if *chi*, deeply rooted as it is in Eastern religion and philosophy, remains a central element in its practice?

It does not, however, require . . . a long apprenticeship to appreciate the difference between t'ai chi and most western forms of exercise, and to reach at least the beginning of an understanding of the significance, in this context, of *chi*, the life force, which in Chinese metaphysics is held to permeate the atmosphere. The aim is to tune in to chi. In Chinese metaphysics, the assumption is that mind and body in combination can be opened up to it, *so that the energy itself takes*

*over,* as it were. Instead of having to go through the motions, the dancers find the motions going through them (727:146, emphasis added).

This kind of "energy possession" is also encountered in yoga,* where difficult postures are effortlessly achieved by the indwelling spirit, and in occult meditation.* Nevertheless, because of its supposedly "nonreligious" forms, some Christian organizations have endorsed the practice of Tai Chi Chuan (974), despite the fact that the manipulation of *chi* is intrinsic to its purpose:

The ancient and elegant system of Chinese exercise known as T'ai Chi Ch'uan is designed primarily to maintain and enhance health by giving full expression to the life-force, or ch'i, of the universe, embodied in each of us. . . . Tai Chi is more than a mere physical exercise. As a system devoted to wholeness and unity, it is truly an integrative experience—it is a silent meditation, an energizing exercise, a joyful dance, a precise system of self-defense, a daily ritual and prayer, and a living expression of a way of being in the world.

It embodies the vibrant philosophy of Taoism through its emphasis on the gentle strength of centering and yielding. The binding force of all these elements is the ch'i, which is harnessed and utilized by T'ai Chi Ch'uan in order to perform its intrinsic healing function (976:37).

The occult potential of Tai Chi is evident not only from Taoism (976:38-39) but because *chi* is equivalent to kundalini energy (see Yoga), and because Tai Chi, like yoga, arouses such energy:

The T'ai Chi Ch'uan exercise is the choreographed movement, the discipline, the ritual, which gives shape to the living breath of the ch'i and allows the healing to take place. . . . It rouses the ch'i "as a dragon rising from hibernation" and then channels, as a river bank, the latent force of that energy into specific articulations of the body. . . . [Chi] adheres to the base of the spine. . . . [I]t rises to the top of the head. . . . [I]t travels through the meridians and energy channels, and it is mobilized by the will and imagination. In order to cultivate the ch'i we must be sensitive to its presence. . . . It can manifest as heat, as surges of energy, as tingling, as a certain heaviness to the limbs . . . (976:39-40).

Tai Chi is not nonreligious just because its religious elements are said to be absent. Indeed, when conducted in a religious atmosphere (however defined), the exercises *alone* are allegedly able to assist in the arousal of kundalini. As we have seen elsewhere, this phenomenon is related to spiritistic intervention or possession (see Yoga).

Can anyone guarantee that the claimed "nonreligious" practice of Tai Chi will never have spiritual implications? Claims to having removed mysticism from martial arts practice must be critically evaluated. Again, much depends on the instructor. What is religious, mystical, or occult can be called mere psychological dynamics, and thus wrongly interpreted as something entirely "natural" (cf. parapsychology).

Again, none of this is stated to deny the reality of nonreligious programs of martial arts practice. For example, through personal concentration, strong discipline, and intensive conditioning, the normal human body can, after years of effort, be trained to perform many of the dramatic physical feats in the martial arts. The removal of the meditation,* mysticism, *chi*, and Eastern philosophy may restrict the potential range of abilities, because occult power may not then be present, but it will not prevent considerable human physical strengths from being developed.

At this point we should note there are divergent opinions on the subject of Christian participation in the martial arts. In order to acknowledge both sides, we asked representatives to defend their particular views.

Bruce L. Johnson, a former practitioner of the martial arts, has lived in China, Japan, India, and in other countries in the Far East. He has studied many Oriental religions and philosophies and was greatly enamored with the various martial art styles of these countries. As a result he became involved in Taoism and trained at the Kodokan Institute of Judo in Tokyo, Japan. Eventually, he studied "Chinese Wand Exercise" in Shanghai, under the great Chinese Grand Master, Dr. Ch'eng, who later bestowed the title of Grand Master on him. After Dr. Ch'eng's death, Johnson became the only living Grand Master teaching these exercises. He eventually taught them to several famous movie stars, including clients of Bruce Lee who had previously been instructed in the martial arts. Johnson also lived for a while in the South Pacific and Caribbean, where he witnessed authentic voodoo and macumba ceremonies.

He now argues against Christian participation in the martial arts. He is not convinced that "you can fully learn the physical aspect without at least dabbling in the metaphysical," and, practically speaking, he questions how effectively the two can be separated. He also feels that the tendency to violence in many of these practices raises issues for active Christian practice. Here we cite part of his views at some length from a statement prepared for this chapter:

"I remember being taught, actually *commanded*, to never use the techniques I had learned, unless, as one wise sensei told me, 'Use them only if your very life is hanging by the golden thread . . . and then, if at all possible, make your moves defensively.' Learning how to defend oneself is what the martial arts used to be about. But in today's world the emphasis is on offensive maneuvers. Full contact in both sparring and contests is encouraged. Gone are the beautiful defensive moves, such as in aikido, so aptly demonstrated by the old masters.

"Most forms of the martial arts can be traced back to some form of Buddhism, especially Zen, which originated in ancient India, and eventually spread to the Orient. Since meditation is such an integral part of the martial arts, it cannot be dismissed or ignored. Ancient practitioners knew their power was of a spiritual nature and not merely physical. It is this balance and harmonization of the opposite poles of yin and yang, that allegedly produces the mysterious *ch'i*, permitting a 'flow' from one move to another. Can practice and theory be so easily separated when the 'flow' of movement is dependent on *chi*? Further, becoming 'enlightened' or entering 'altered states' of consciousness are not normal Christian practices.

"Buddhism teaches transmigration (reincarnation) and Zen meditation is the spiritual heart of the majority of all forms of martial arts. You cannot separate out the raw Taoism of the martial arts just as you cannot separate yoga from Hinduism.

"The ultimate goal in the martial arts was to perfect one's capability toward superhuman, supernatural feats. The martial arts are steeped in mysticism and frequently boast of these supernatural, occult abilities.

"The Orientals also practiced the martial arts for other reasons besides defense. The deep spiritual disciplines allowed the practitioner to 'shake hands with nature' so to speak, and tap into the energy of the universe, to get in touch with their mysterious inner 'life force.'

"Our nation is now being bombarded from the Far East with Transcendental Meditation, Buddhism, Zen, Taoism, yoga, reincarnation, and now the martial arts, which are also promoting the metaphysical and supernatural. Christians who endorse martial arts are indirectly helping promote the cultural emergence of Eastern ways.

"In the last several years, I've watched the dramatic changes in the martial arts in the United States, again, noting an emphasis being put on the offensive aspect. This has led to full contact sparring, kick boxing, the teaching of weaponry, etc. I see no reason at all for Christians to teach youngsters how to use the variety of 'crafted' weapons that are so dangerous and potentially deadly. Pick up any martial arts magazine and one can see for themselves how 'self-defense' has been tossed by the wayside, and deadly kicks, punches, and the mastery of all types of lethal weapons are now the vogue. Isn't there enough violence in America, without Christians participating and instructing in offensive martial arts? For example, would Jesus approve of Christians teaching deadly fighting/combat techniques including weaponry? Regardless of how many say they want love and peace, the human heart still appears to be fascinated with violence.

"Jesus was basically a gentle man. He never physically harmed anyone, even though He was brutally beaten, tortured, and crucified on a cross. He forgave even His enemies. By not teaching students to 'turn the other cheek' and walk away from unpleasant situations, the offensively oriented martial arts of today promote violence by default. Students aren't taking martial arts lessons to learn self-control or peace.

Rather than learning to defend themselves, many are itching to practice offensive moves on someone. Notice the many youngsters on the corners, waiting for their school buses, practicing their karate kicks and punches on other classmates. Even the 'touch of death' is being taught, including to children. In fact, some top Masters have argued among themselves which one had put the 'touch of death' on Bruce Lee. Even when I was practicing the martial arts, this seemed incredible.

"I have refused countless numbers of parents, who've asked me to teach their boys the martial arts, since 'they know little Johnny would never, ever use this on anybody, as he only wants to know how to defend himself.' I don't know these youngsters and what they would do with this knowledge. I would be indirectly responsible for their actions, if they were to do bodily injury to another. It would be analogous to teaching a child about guns, then handing him a loaded pistol and telling him never to use it.

"There are teams that travel around, such as 'Judo for Jesus' and 'Karate for Christ' who draw crowds curious to see their demonstrations. Christians who break boards, bricks, blocks of ice, etc., tend to also feed the practitioner's ego. Further, the 'Judo for Jesus' and 'Karate for Christ' groups that witness for Jesus Christ, are also witnesses for the martial arts.

"Even though the martial arts look physical on the outside, as I have said, Oriental philosophy is at their heart. It is raw metaphysical discipline. These things are not from God, as God is not in the business of mystical energies or the occult. Christians who participate or instruct in the martial arts usually justify their practices by claiming they do so only for self-defense, exercise value, or for the sport of it. They never intend to hurt anyone. But since martial arts masters are known for their supernatural feats and in their practices there is a direct parallel to the occult/psychic powers of spirit mediums I question whether Christians have any place in this realm. The master 'is known to perform acts of magic. The master performs . . . miracles' (976:42). Further, God calls a man to humility and dependence on Him whereas the martial arts emphasize human self-sufficiency and this may also foster pride.

"One might get the impression that I am a pacifist, and would never defend myself or my family. That would not be the case. What was said before, 'Use only if your very life is hanging by the golden thread,' remains true. But when I was saved years ago, the Lord made me a new creature; the old things were passed away, and all things became new. I no longer practice the martial arts because I am certainly accountable for the witness I extend to others and as a Christian, I cannot in good conscience, teach or recommend the martial arts to others" (980).

To present the other side, we had several Christian experts in the martial arts evaluate this chapter. All agreed that the martial arts could be Eastern or occult. But they also stressed that martial arts practice can be neutral forms of discipline that anyone may engage in safely and effectively. Mark Pinner, a gold medalist and an instructor in karate, also gave us the following comments:

"The main problem with karate and the spiritual association with it stems from the practitioners themselves, not karate. . . . I am often frustrated with members of the church who would immediately assume that all karate or martial arts are occult or of Satan, simply because some practitioners are!

"I am an instructor of karate and that is how I support myself. I teach from the first day under my own spiritual beliefs as did the first practitioners. I have both saved and unsaved students and I make no secret of my love for Jesus. I wish that all Christians had the freedom and opportunities to reach such a variety with the witness of Christ that I do through this sport. Unfortunately, we have many opportunities to expose ourselves to occult potential, and I am sure that there are those who have adopted the religious practices of their martial arts mentors, but isn't that exactly what I myself am attempting for the Body of Christ?

"I feel that Christians can practice karate according to the same caution and biblical applications with which they live their lives in general. . . . I think this approach is far more

discerning than to reject all martial arts and forget that many godly men and women are teaching karate. Nor should we forget that many pupils will benefit from the skills the practice of karate will develop. This includes control of one's body which can prevent the problems of premarital sex, smoking and drugs; the achievement of discipline which is related to job, school and home duties; and developing a humble temperament and submission to authority. Certainly, these are Christian virtues and perhaps we should not forget that although Christ was the most humble man who ever lived, He was also the most powerful. In essence, if the martial arts are practiced wisely, they can be of great benefit."

In offering a biblical case for self-defense in general, one article on the martial arts said:

Though the Bible is silent regarding the Asian martial arts, it nonetheless records many accounts of fighting and warfare. . . . God is portrayed as the omnipotent Warrior-leader of the Israelites. God, the LORD of hosts, raised up warriors among the Israelites called the *shophetim* (savior-deliverers). Samson, Deborah, Gideon, and others were anointed by the Spirit of God to conduct war. The New Testament commends Old Testament warriors for their military acts of faith (Heb. 11:30-40). Moreover, it is significant that although given the opportunity to do so, none of the New Testament saints—nor even Jesus—are ever seen informing a military convert that he needed to resign from his line of work (Matt. 8:5-13; Luke 3:14).

Prior to His crucifixion, Jesus revealed to His disciples the future hostility they would face and encouraged them to sell their outer garments in order to purchase a sword (Luke 22:36-38; cf. 2 Cor. 11:26-27). Here the "sword" (*maxairan*) is a "dagger or short sword [that] belonged to the Jewish traveler's equipment as protection against robbers and wild animals." It is perfectly clear from this passage that *Jesus approved of self-defense.*

Self-defense may actually result in one of the greatest examples of human love. Christ said, "Greater love has no one than this, that he *lay down his life for his friends*" (John 15:13). When protecting one's family or neighbor, a Christian is unselfishly risking his or her life for the sake of others.... Scripture allows Christians to use force for self-defense against crime and injustice. If self-defense is scripturally justifiable so long as it is conducted without unnecessary violence, then so are the martial arts (the *physical* aspects only) (2404).

Divergent opinions. Different perspectives. Certainly, this underscores the need for Christians to be aware of the issues involved. Christian instructors also need to assess carefully their teaching methodology with discernment.

For those who decide to begin a martial arts program, the following guidelines from an article in the *Christian Research Journal* may prove helpful: "Because the question of whether a Christian should participate in the martial arts involves gray areas, we believe it is worthwhile to consider some guidelines for discernment.... Christians must be honest with themselves, evaluating *why* they desire to participate in the martial arts. Negatively, some reasons might be to become 'a tough guy,' to get revenge against someone, or perhaps to pridefully 'show off.' Positively, some reasons might relate to staying in shape physically, practicing self-discipline, or perhaps training for self-defense against muggers or rapists. The Christian should not get involved in the martial arts with unworthy motives.

"Christians must realize that practicing the martial arts will teach them maneuvers, blows, and kicks that could severely injure a person when actually used in a hostile confrontation. For this reason, they must examine their consciences regarding the potential use of force against another human being.

"Not only is a commitment of time required to practice the martial arts, but Christians must also decide whether they will be able to endure the discipline needed to be an effective student. Such arts are generally very strenuous and demanding.... Certainly Christians should not allow a martial art to overshadow or detract from their religious commitments (Heb. 10:25). They should weigh whether they can afford to spend the time and money needed each week in practicing the martial arts. Could these resources be better spent in another endeavor?

"The Christian should ascertain whether the instructor under consideration is himself (or herself) a Christian, a *professing* Christian with an Eastern worldview, a nonreligious non-Christian, or a religious non-Christian. If the trainer subscribes to an Eastern worldview, this will likely carry over into his teaching of the martial arts.... We believe that the choice of the right instructor is probably the single most important consideration for the Christian contemplating participation in the martial arts.

"The Christian should keep an eye out for Eastern religious books, symbols, and the like, that might be in the training hall. This may help one discern what practices and beliefs are being espoused during training. Many schools start new students on a trial basis. Such a trial could help the Christian solidify his or her decision.

"It may also be prudent to observe an advanced class. This will help the prospective student determine whether Eastern philosophy is taught only as the practitioner progresses" (2404).

In conclusion, we believe some mature and informed Christians may participate in the martial arts to benefit *if* they have carefully evaluated their motives and the particular program being considered. Parents especially need to evaluate thoroughly any program for their children. On the other hand, if such precautions are not taken, the martial arts may become more of a snare, spiritually and otherwise, than expected. In the next section, we will see how easily this will occur.

## THREE TESTIMONIES

The following material is used with permission and further clearly highlights the complexities and delicacy of Christian participation in the martial arts. While it does not alter our fundamental conclusions, it provides some very important information that needs consideration.

Bill Rudge is the founder of the Christian Martial Arts Association (CMAA). He acknowledges that there are many committed Christians who feel justified before the Lord to remain in the martial arts. However, he also realizes that many others clearly feel led by the Lord to discontinue involvement (2757:1). In 1994, he published information about his background in the martial arts and the specific reasons he decided to forsake all involvement with these methods. He says that one reason for writing was due to the large number of Christians around the world, both students and instructors, who had been contacting him to discover why he had left the martial arts, or who were struggling with the issue of their continued personal involvement. Rudge had traveled throughout the country and had "spent considerable time researching and interviewing" a significant number of martial artists, Christians and non-Christians, involved in a diversity of martial art styles. He cites five personal reasons for leaving the martial arts and, subsequently, in their own words, he offers the explanations of three other former martial arts experts who are Christians. What these testimonies reveal is that different Christians have different experiences in, and responses to, the martial arts. The testimonies also reveal that for many, perhaps most, it may be difficult to tell just how an experience will turn out.

The first reason Rudge gives for leaving the martial arts is both psychological and spiritual. He refers to particular attitudes easily developed by martial arts practice: egotism, self-sufficiency, pride, a desire for power and control, and even arrogance. These:

> are often developed by adherents. Many claim humility, but I believe it is usually a false, deceptive humility. I began to think I was god and almost invincible. I became haughty and egotistical and had an air of superiority when dealing with people. And I saw the same attitude in almost every student and instructor (even Christians) I met. Many impressionable students (even many advanced practitioners) idolized and practically worshiped their senseis and masters (2757:2).

His second reason surrounds the violent nature of the practice. He notes that while self-defense and the use of force are scripturally justifiable, "many of the techniques being taught transcend self-defense" and are offensive, aggressive methods "designed to maim and cripple one's opponent. These tactics are not as much defensive as they are retaliatory. . . . One time

before I quit karate, a man got so obnoxious with me that I actually considered taking his eyes out" (2757:2-3) (cf. Romans 12:19).

A third reason is the physical dangers that may be involved, and how this relates to the Christian's body being the temple of the Holy Spirit and, as such, to be treated respectfully. "I frequently had black-and-blue marks all over my arms, legs, and chest from being an uke or from sparring and training. . . . I have injuries that can be traced directly to those days of rigorous conditioning, training, sparring, and breaking wood and cement blocks. Many practitioners eventually develop arthritis, joint injuries, and various other debilitations and health problems because of martial arts involvement" (2757:3).

His fourth reason involves the martial arts connection between Eastern mysticism and the occult. He observes that many people who begin innocently, using the martial arts merely for self-defense, physical discipline, health benefits, or sports competition, eventually become involved in occult practice and philosophy (2757:3).

The fifth reason he gives for leaving the martial arts concerns his changed conviction about his personal testimony before others. Rudge first points out that during many years of martial arts demonstrations to Christians, he believed that he was giving a wonderful testimony for the Lord. But he started noticing that Christians being introduced to the martial arts as a physical discipline still became involved with mysticism. And some seemed to be transferring their allegiance from Christ to the martial arts:

> I thought I could (and many Christians claim to be able to) remove the mystical/occult elements and limit my training to only the physical aspect. But those following my example (and yours) might not be able to maintain that separation.
>
> I tried to justify teaching karate classes and doing self-defense clinics and demonstrations in churches, schools, and detention centers because of the tremendous impact I was having and all the fruit I was bearing for the Lord. But now I realize that far more people got into the practice and philosophy of the martial arts than were genuinely led to Christ. People would respond to the altar calls, but a few days later they

would also sign up at the local dojo. As I evaluated many of the people influenced by myself and other Christian martial artists, I discovered they were becoming more and more committed to the martial arts and less and less committed to Jesus Christ.

Even Christian students and instructors are often not aware of how affected they are by the Eastern/occultic practices and beliefs that are the basis of the martial arts. In fact, when first asked, most will initially indicate that they are not involved in any questionable practices nor have they been philosophically influenced. But after a more thorough consideration, many admit that some of their involvements were Eastern and occult in nature and the philosophy has had some effect upon them. It is alarming that most of them honestly do not recognize the potential danger of some of their practices and how their world view is being subtly influenced (2757:4-5).

He also points out that many professing Christians who were his karate associates later took up:

Yoga, meditation, or TM, and some even consider themselves Zen Buddhist or Taoists.

And perhaps more significant:

It also became apparent that Taoist and Buddhist overtones cannot be conveniently separated and discarded because in reality they are the foundational principles of martial arts training and philosophy, whether the practitioners and instructors realize it or not. In some styles it is very visible, while in others it is more subtle and covert. Nevertheless, in every style I researched—even those practiced only for physical fitness and self-defense purposes—there were definite Eastern/occult influences (2757:5,7).

Rudge also recalls a particularly tragic and frightening incident that was apparently related to the occult aspects of the martial arts. He interviewed a fifth-degree black belt in Poekoelan, an Indonesian style, whose father was a ninth-degree black belt who, at the time, was one of the highest-ranking martial artists in the country. The father went berserk and attacked his son with a samurai sword. The son had to fight with his father to prevent his father from killing him and, he feared, his family as well. The gruesome battle lasted almost an hour. In the end, the son "had some 40 cuts on his body and had his throat ripped open. Finally, he killed his father with a pair of nunchucks. The son was tried for murder but released on the basis of self-defense. Investigations revealed that his father had voodoo dolls with pins stuck in them. He had a black candle which he used when meditating and he was involved in other occult practices" (2757:8). The son's explanation for this horrible tragedy was that his father had become demonized through the martial arts.

Rudge also confirms the spiritistic potential of martial arts. He refers to a man he met who had been involved in a particular Chinese style for numerous years. They got into a discussion about the mystical energy *chi*, and Rudge noted that both this man and his instructor could, allegedly through *chi*, move objects "with their minds." Supposedly, his instructor could extend his arm and point his finger at someone, and by concentrating on extending his *chi*, he could knock them down without touching them—and do many other seemingly superhuman feats" (2757:10).

This same individual noted that the spirits of the dead could also become involved in assisting one's martial arts performance. Rudge recalls, "He told me that sometimes as they performed kata (pre-arranged patterns of fighting imaginary opponents), if they were totally yielded, the spirits of dead masters possessed their bodies and controlled their movements—greatly increasing their skill, performance, speed and power. He also said they can put hexes and spells on people, and told of other occult powers and phenomena . . ." (2757:10-11).

Rudge's own practice was fully accepted by Christian parents, students, and teachers, who all told him to remain in the martial arts and to warn others about its occult aspects. In particular, a Bible college professor and a minister whom he respected, as well as several other Christian leaders, encouraged him to continue "teaching [martial arts] at the Bible college and at churches" (2757:13). In other words, Bill

Rudge was involved in what most Christians would consider a distinctively *Christian* use of the martial arts:

> After graduation from Bible college, I founded the Christian Martial Arts Association (CMAA). I developed some impressive demos for churches and schools during which I demonstrated and shared numerous biblical principles: balance, commitment, courage, self-control, discipline, and determination. I also illustrated through demo and message the evidence for biblical Christianity and how to grow in Christ, be available to God, glorify Him with every aspect of our lives, overcome peer pressure, and be proficient in spiritual warfare, as well as many other biblical truths. I explained why I, as a Christian, was involved; I warned about the Eastern/occult teachings associated with the advanced stages of the martial arts. I also developed innovative and total fitness and defense clinics that became very popular (2757:13).

If his use of the martial arts was Christian, why did Rudge finally leave the discipline? Basically, it was the result of his own research and critical reflection upon how he had used the martial arts even as a Christian. Because of its impact upon him, he eventually felt convicted by the Lord that he could no longer continue:

> But the more I researched, the more I became convicted and the more Christ's Lordship in my life became threatened by my continued involvement. So began the gradual discontinuing of all my karate involvement—a process that took several years. At first I was convicted about developing the power of ki and mental powers, so I discontinued that mode of training. Years later, in one of my file cabinets, I discovered some of the old training materials I had used for my classes. Before destroying them, I read them. I was shocked to discover what I had innocently taught my students years before when I was a new Christian. I realized I had begun to teach occult techniques to develop mental powers and the power of ki ... all in the name of Christ!
>
> And few, if any, ever questioned what I was teaching. Nor did any Christian leaders I consider credible rebuke me. In fact, most loved it and encouraged me (2757:14).

It was difficult for Rudge to break off from what had become a love of his life. Even after having quit his personal practice and having stopped teaching classes, "For several more days I continued to pray about it because it was a difficult decision—I loved these things—they gave an excitement and credibility to the ministry" (2757:15). However, in Bill's case, one result of leaving the martial arts was "that instead of being less effective, my speaking engagements had even more power" (2757:18).

We included Rudge's testimony because it reveals several things: 1) how easy it is for new Christians to become sidetracked through the ego-boosting or mystical or occult aspects of the martial arts; 2) the lack of discernment of many Christians in this field, who continued to encourage his involvement; 3) that even Christian experts and leaders in the martial arts may be led by the Lord to discontinue all involvement.

The above illustrates that there are indeed subtleties involved, and that Christians need to think through this area very critically, especially if they are considering personal involvement. Spiritual maturity and much prayer are required and, hopefully, discussion with those on both sides of the issue before anyone starts training. Our concern here is twofold: 1) how the Christian church generally reflects largely uncritical attitudes toward the martial arts; 2) how the degree of spiritual maturity at the individual level is essential to making the right decision about involvement.

The following two testimonies point out several other issues involved. The first is about Bob Brown, who had 20 years' experience in the martial arts, including black-belt ranking in three separate systems. He received his first-degree black belt in Shoto-kan karate. During his military service in the Army he was trained by a third-degree black belt who ran a Shoto-kan Karate Do school that was associated with the Nippon Kobudo Rengokai of Japan. After military service and attending college for a year, he accepted Jesus Christ as his Savior. He immediately went to Bible college and afterward began training with a seventh-degree black belt in Kwon Mu Do Taekwondo. He received a second-degree black belt in Tae Kwon Do from the founder and president of the Central Tae Kwon Do Association. He then began studying under a sixth-degree black belt, who subsequently became the master of the Goshin Jutsu Karate system following the death of the previous master. After this he took lessons based on Escrima, Jeet Kune Do, and Wing Chun Kung Fu, in which he received his third black belt degree in 1990 (2757:20). Brown also conducted martial arts tactics training for several police agencies, and he is certified as a Defensive Tactics and ASP Tactical Baton instructor with the Oregon Board on Police Standards and Training.

The significant point concerning Brown's experience is the apparently negative influence of the martial arts on his spiritual growth in Christ. Even though he had accepted Christ as His Lord and Savior in 1975, he continued martial arts training until November of 1991. He recalls:

The years slipped by. My martial arts skills were developing, but my life in Christ never got off the ground. There were many recommitments to Christ which would last about a month or two, but no lasting relationship.

During the final years of my training in the martial arts, several things happened that I feel God used to bring me to a point of decision. I was intensely working out to develop skills in the use of sticks and knives (escrima). The movements involved in this training put a serious strain on my joints, primarily my knees and shoulders. To overcome these debilitating developments I began to spend more and more of my training time in visualization techniques.... My skills improved dramatically as a result of this type of training. But as I became more adept at the technique and as my objectives in escrima became more defined, I began spending greater amounts of time practicing mentally. It was not uncommon for me to sit in a chair and visualize defending myself against several attackers for one and a half to two hours twice a day.

These images became increasingly violent. ... [M]any people claim that they have become more peaceful as a result of their training. On the contrary, I found my visualizations taking a very morbid turn.... In the end, the issue that brought me back to God was that I came to a place where I could not distinguish between training and real life, between visualized actions

and reality. Training and visualization of self-defense situations dominated my life. I had fits of rage for no reason. Patience was nonexistent, and I became unable to "turn off" the visualizations, especially when I needed to sleep. The visualization would start the moment my head touched the pillow and would not stop for three or four hours, even though I was exhausted. In the end I became suicidal (2757:22-23).

Brown's testimony reveals that not only did his Christian life suffer as a result of his martial arts training, but that his martial arts visualization* practices became a destructive influence.

The martial arts, therefore, can be a substitute for spiritual growth in Christ. Brown recalls, "If anyone had asked me if I believed that Christ was Lord, I would have answered yes! Is He Lord of my life? Yes. Was I yielding to Him? Yes. But in fact, I was not yielding and I had not yet died to the old life of sin. I had held on to a god I had found in my former life that I was not willing to be without" (2757:24).

The third testimony comes from Michael Allen Puckett, who was a national free-style and Grecco-Roman wrestling champion. He had won numerous trophies for competition in the martial arts, was a brown belt in Kajukempo Karate, and close to a third-degree black belt in Tae Kwon Do. He also ran two Tae Kwon Do schools that enrolled over 100 students.

After receiving Christ as his Lord and Savior, he made a public confession of this to his students in an attempt to make his martial arts school Christ-centered:

In all my years within the system, I explained to them, no one had ever approached me about Christianity.... The reality of the martial arts training was that the God of the Bible was not a priority, and the instruction was contrary to the Scriptures. In order to be a higher ranking belt, a study of Eastern philosophies was required. All of my spare time was spent keeping up on karate skills. I didn't go to church, I didn't spend time in prayer. But now I wanted to put Christ in His proper position, as the only Truth worth knowing (2757:33).

The result of his speech was that many of his students boycotted the class, but he began to get

377

calls from Christians who had heard of his idea to begin a Christ-centered dojo, and who wanted to join. He thought he could build up his previous practice perhaps even bigger than before. "Then a strange thing happened. When I tried to practice my karate skills, a weakness overcame me. I felt like praying instead. Something was still wrong" (2757:34). After three days of prayer and fasting, he said the Lord spoke to his heart, "You must lay down your martial arts because you covet them and put them above me" (2757:35).

These testimonies reveal that there is more that inhibits the spiritual growth and more self-deception of Christian practitioners of the martial arts than many people might think. Again, we are not saying that Christians should never practice the martial arts. We are saying that this is a complex issue, and that Christians who are interested in this field, as well as the church as a whole, need to take it more seriously in terms of critical evaluation. Clearly, God has led these and other instructors and students to forsake involvement with the martial arts. In such cases, the primary issue seems to be that the martial arts became a substitute for the Lordship of Christ, or that it has in other ways hampered spiritual growth. This also indicates that Christians who want to join the martial arts should make absolutely certain that their spiritual life does not become compromised. Maybe Jesus is *not* leading them to involvement or to retain involvement.

On the one hand, we cannot say absolutely that some Christians should never practice the martial arts. If they do this wisely and are sufficiently informed, it could be useful. On the other hand, it seems that for many Christians it is not right to get involved. One issue, then, is, What is God really saying to the individual? Another issue is one of how much wisdom the individual Christian and church currently has on this issue.

How much spiritual wisdom do pre-teenage, or even teenage, Christians have? As a parent, are you willing to shoulder the possible spiritual or physical risks involved in having your son or daughter trained in the martial arts? The trainer may be a Christian, but does he really know what he is doing? What has been his own experience in the martial arts? Is your child going to be trained by other instructors at the dojo who are not Christians? What happens if your child

begins to enjoy the excitement and power of the martial arts more than his love for Jesus or the discipline of Christian living?

To conclude this chapter, we asked a Christian mother who had read the chapter for her thoughts about whether she would let her son join a martial arts program at a Christian school if he became interested:

> As far as I can see, a martial arts program with the Eastern philosophy supposedly removed is represented by proponents as an opportunity for a child to develop physically, mentally, emotionally, and spiritually. As a parent who wants her child to enjoy life and be successful, the martial arts appear to allow a child the capacity to advance and improve on an individual level, unlike being involved in team sports. However, the testimonies we have just read disturb me. Even for Christian adults, who have researched this area, and who know first-hand what involvement in the martial arts entails, it was still difficult and even impossible for them to keep the priority of their relationship with Jesus Christ where it should be.

> So, if my child had a strong desire to become involved in a martial arts program, we would first consult personally with the instructors and/or leaders of the program. We would study the background of the style being taught and ask the instructor pertinent questions. Just because something is labeled "Christian" or offered at a Christian school does not necessarily make it biblically correct. We would also read their literature critically and not just accept what they claim they will be doing. Further, we would speak with parents whose children are currently enrolled in the program, and personally observe training sessions at several different levels.

> As a parent it is my God-given duty to look after my child's well-being and, with prayer and study, to help him make wise and informed decisions. With so many different other sports and ways for a child to develop in all areas, should I take a chance on damaging or inhibiting his spiritual growth—which is and will be the most important area of his life? Why should I intentionally risk my son's involvement in something that could be to his detriment? So, unless the martial arts program we investigated proved to be one with no Eastern or questionable connotations whatsoever, I would seek another avenue of physical development for my child.

# MEDITATION

## INFO AT A GLANCE

**Description.** New Age meditation comprises many forms and involves the control and regulation of the mind for various physical, spiritual, and psychological purposes. New Age meditation is derived from Eastern or occult methods, which seek a radical transformation of the consciousness. This altered state of consciousness* leads to an alleged "self-realization" or spiritual "enlightenment," which has as its final goal union with ultimate reality and the resulting dissolution of the individual personality. There are many forms of religious meditation in the world, and the New Age Movement seems to have adopted most of them. Almost all forms of meditation practiced today produce similar results in the individual.

**Founder.** Unknown; the practice is ancient and cross-cultural.

**How does it claim to work?** New Age meditation claims to work by profoundly "stilling" or otherwise dramatically influencing the mind. Through this process the meditator is allegedly able to perceive "true" reality, his own "true" divine nature, and finally achieve spiritual enlightenment.* Meditation promoters also claim the practice has numerous health benefits.

**Scientific evaluation.** Apart from the documented effects of simple relaxation, scientific studies have confirmed other psychophysiological influences of meditation, but their meaning and value is variously interpreted. Science cannot comment on the spiritual claims made by proponents.

**Examples of occult potential.** Psychic powers, altered states of consciousness, astral projection, spiritism, kundalini arousal, and other occult phenomena.

**Major problem.** Although widely perceived as a harmless form of relaxation, New Age meditation is far more than this because it brings a variety of spiritual and other consequences. New Age meditation uses the mind in an abnormal manner to radically restructure a person's perceptions of self and the world in order to support occult New Age philosophy and goals. In the process, regressive states of consciousness are wrongly interpreted as "higher" or "divine" states of consciousness, and meditation-developed

379

psychic powers are falsely interpreted as evidence of a latent divine nature. Unfortunately, meditators often do not realize the possible long-term consequences of these practices, such as the extremely dangerous kundalini arousal (see Yoga).

**Biblical/Christian evaluation.** The nature, context, purpose, and type of meditation determines its validity and outcome. Biblical meditation (Psalm 19:14; 77:12; 119:97,99) is a spiritually healthy practice; Eastern or occult (e.g., New Age) meditation is harmful and has negative spiritual outcomes.

**Potential dangers.** The form and duration of meditation will influence the outcome. A daily 20-minute period of transcendental meditation is quite different from eight hours a day of Buddhist *vipassana*, or "mindfulness" meditation. However, adverse responses are not infrequently encountered even in milder forms of meditation. For example, the dangers in Transcendental Meditation were documented in coauthor Weldon's earlier critique of this practice (468), and since then scientific studies have continued to document the possible dangers of this Hindu practice. It seems that when altered states of consciousness* are entered for even a short period of time, day after day, month after month, year after year, that some or even many of the same adverse phenomena found in more extensive meditative programs are encountered. Among these are philosophical conversion to the occult, demon possession, and various forms of physical, spiritual, and psychological damage (278).

*Note:* The chapters on Altered States of Consciousness, Yoga, Enlightenment, and Eastern Gurus may be read in conjunction with this chapter. Meditation typically induces altered states and is often a form of yoga or used with a yoga program to progress toward enlightenment.

## INTRODUCTION AND INFLUENCE

Meditation is one of the most popular of all modern religious practices. Meditation techniques have assumed a prominent place in large numbers of physical, spiritual, and health therapies where relaxation is a primary goal. A recent article titled "Unwind and Destress" in *Prevention*, America's leading health magazine, endorsed Maharishi Mahesh Yogi's transcendental meditation (see 468) as well as a form of Buddhist "mindfulness" or *vipassana* meditation (762:85-86). Herbert Benson, M.D., is the author of a bestselling text, *The Relaxation Response*, which also emphasizes the stress reducing benefits of meditation (903).

Meditation is increasingly found in schools and is an important pillar of transpersonal, or New Age, education.* Wilson Van Dusen, a psychologist with an interest in the psychic realm and the occult Swedenborgian religion (see his *The Presence of Other Worlds*), points out that "meditation is one of the foundations of transpersonal education" (1090:98; cf. p. 101).

Because meditation is widely viewed as a positive practice with a wide variety of applications, almost any topic in this volume may employ meditation as an adjunct. This is why Eastern, occult, and other New Age forms of meditation are increasingly used in our society among both laypeople and professionals. Such meditation, however, is typically combined with a particular religious perspective. This perspective sees the purpose of meditation as inducing a form of spiritual enlightenment, one that harmonizes with the occult goals and beliefs of the religious view advocated. Spiritual goals aside, meditation is also recommended enthusiastically for its alleged mental and physical health benefits. But as we will see, such meditation is far from healthful.

Given the number of people who are practicing meditation today, we believe it has become a significant social problem. In 1975 William Johnston warned in his *Silent Music: The Science of Meditation*, "Anyone with the slightest experience of meditation knows about the uprising of the unconscious and the possible resultant turmoil, to say nothing of the increased psychic power that meditation brings. All this could have the greatest social consequences if meditation becomes widespread" (438:26).

But today meditation has become widespread. Meditation is practiced by 10 million to 20 million people in this country (cf. 949:135). Almost four million people have been initiated into Maharishi Mahesh Yogi's occult system of transcendental meditation alone (468). Dozens of Hindu and Buddhist gurus or groups all require meditation practice in conjunction with their religious programs. Examples include: Nichiren Shoshu Buddhism, Swami Kriyananda, Bhagwan Shree Rajneesh, the Siddha Yoga Dham of America (SYDA) Foundation (Swami Muktananda), Sai Baba, Yogi Bhajan, Swami Rama, Maharaj Ji, Kirpal Singh, Self Realization Fellowship (Paramahansa Yogananda), Chogyam Trungpa, Sri Chinmoy, the International Society for Krishna Consciousness (ISKCON), and Da Free John. These all stress the importance of occult meditation. For example, Rajneesh's "chaotic meditation" is particularly bizarre—and dangerous (249/1040).

Hundreds of relatively new spiritistic religions also have meditation agendas: the Association for Research and Enlightenment (based on the psychic readings of Edgar Cayce), the Church Universal and Triumphant (founded by Mark and Elizabeth Claire Prophet), Eckankar (begun by Paul Twitchell), the Gurdjieff Foundation, the Rosicrucians, Theosophy, Anthroposophy, Astara, and many more.

Established traditional, mystical, and occult religions in America, such as Sufism, Sikhism, Taoism, and Tantrism stress the importance of their meditation procedures. Scores of New Age therapies, such as those found in the growing field of transpersonal psychology, require or recommend some form of meditation in conjunction with the therapy (943/860). And endless occult practices, such as witchcraft, druidism, cabalism, and mediumism offer their own brand of meditation.

Meditation is also offered in many new contexts: at the local YMCA, at churches, in schools, in sports clinics, and even in some hospitals. The United Nations has an unofficial meditation adviser, guru Sri Chinmoy, who is a practiced meditator and spiritist (810:53-68/811:9-20,26-29). Chinmoy conducts meditation sessions for government officials in the United States, Congress, and the British Parliament (565:311).

If our view of New Age meditation is correct, then it will not offer the benefits claimed by promoters. However, before we proceed to examine the goals, nature, practices, and potential consequences of meditation, we must first discuss its influence in the church and in other areas of society. We will begin by looking at its influence on children.

## SCHOOLCHILDREN AND MEDITATION

Maureen H. Murdock is a classroom teacher, educator, and therapist who conducts teacher workshops nationally and is the author of *Spinning Inward: Using Guided Imagery with Children for Learning, Creativity and Relaxation.* In her article "Meditation with Young Children," she describes her pupils' experiences with meditation. Utilizing Deborah Rozman's approach (1092), itself based in part on the Hindu practice of transcendental meditation (see 468), Murdock describes the following results with elementary schoolchildren who practiced so-called "energy meditation." This is where the child is to "feel the top of your head and now your whole head disappears into light. Now there is no body, only light. Now in that stillness, go deep inside the real you, that which is you without your body." This is what some of the children experienced:

- "I felt like I dissolved part by part."
- "I looked down from the ceiling and saw my body here."
- "My body disappeared."
- "I am the world."
- "The white light was real big like a wave. Air added on to it and it went through my body. The wave went through my body. The light went away like night and I started to feel cold."
- "I had lights all around me.... I was shimmering with white light...."
- "When it came up to my neck, it went back down and I couldn't let go of my head."
- "When all of my body vanished into white light I felt there was a rainbow going all over me" (1091:35-36).

Because of the religious nature of her meditation program, Murdock does not use the term "meditation" when talking with parents. She is careful to use a "neutral" term like "centering":

We discussed how we would broach the subject to parents, and I told them that I had decided to use the term "centering exercises." This was a more specific description of the exercises than "meditation." Also, the school, St. Augustine's, is non-sectarian, serving families of diversified religious backgrounds, and I did not wish to advocate or appear to advocate an ideology, religion, or identification with a guru or organization. We began meditating with the children from the first day onward (1091:30).

Thus, "The parents were informed at the beginning of the year at a parent meeting of my intention to use 'centering' exercises at the beginning of each day with the children" (1091:40). She also noted that the "parents were *very* pleased" about her use of "centering" in the public classroom with their children (1091:40). Yet when asked whether the children were actually meditating, she said, "My observation of the children over a nine-month period convinced me that most were, indeed, meditating" (1091:21).

Deborah Rozman is an educational consultant who teaches workshops nationally and is the author of *Meditation for Children* and *Meditating with Children: The Art of Concentration and Centering*. (As noted, Maureen Murdock uses Rozman's approach.) In *Meditation for Children*, Rozman admits that children may encounter "frightening experiences in meditation," and she offers this advice: "If you ever feel scared that there are bad vibes, monsters or evil forces attacking you, immediately call on your higher Self, . . ." (1092:15).

Rozman also encourages public schoolchildren with telepathy exercises, and how to see auras and feel colors, and in psychic divination* (e.g., dowsing* where she tells teachers, "Make pendulums for everyone"). She also promotes "channeling energy" (1092:129-37), in which children close their eyes and send energy from their right palm into their left palm. Children are to practice this and to concentrate on it until they actually feel psychic energy traveling between their palms. Then they are to transfer this energy into other students. For example, "Imagine the energy flowing into the top of the head through the heart and out the arm into the heart of the person in the center" (1093:136). Children

are also instructed to chant, "Ooooommmmm as you concentrate and send energy from your hands and voice. Direct the energy in your mind to someone you know. . . . By sending energy through the palm of our hand into the hurt in another or in ourself we can help heal it. . . . We can channel energy to plants and animals as well as people" (1092:137). And, "Keep the imaging and visualization going. Energy won't flow out your hand unless you send it out, which means concentrating" (1092:137).

In essence, Rozman, Murdock, and teachers like them are preparing children to develop psychically and to be open to becoming psychic healers and occultists. Maureen Murdock is correct when she says, "The implications of using meditation in the classroom are vast" (1091:38; see also New Age Education).

## MEDITATION IN THE CHURCH

Unfortunately, Eastern and other questionable forms of meditation are practiced by many church members. The modern interest in Christian mysticism (Catholic, Protestant, or Eastern Orthodox) has sparked a renewed interest in meditation among Christians. But the practices recommended often involve more than simple biblical meditation, which is conscious meditation on the content and application of Scripture. Unfortunately, Christians often draw upon forms of meditation that are Eastern or similar to Eastern varieties. Because most Christians are insufficiently instructed in these areas, we think this presents a potential problem.

Richard Foster is the evangelical author of *Celebration of Discipline*, a long-time Christian bestseller. His chapter on meditation stresses discovering "the inner reality of the spiritual world [which] is available to all who are willing to search for it" (431:18). Foster is careful to distinguish between Eastern meditation and Christian forms, noting they are "worlds apart" (431:15). His commitment to Christian faith also modifies his basic approach. Unfortunately, his methods are sometimes similar to New Age or Eastern techniques, such as his suggested use of the imagination and dream work.* Concerning the imagination and dream work he asserts:

The inner world of meditation is most easily entered through the door of the imagination. We fail today to appreciate its tremendous power. The imagination is stronger than conceptual thought and stronger than the will. . . .

Some rare individuals may be able to contemplate in an imageless void, but most of us need to be more deeply rooted in the senses. Jesus taught this way, making constant appeal to the imagination and the senses (431:22).

In learning to meditate, one good place to begin is with our dreams, since it involves little more than paying attention to something we are already doing. For fifteen centuries Christians overwhelmingly considered dreams as a natural way in which the spiritual world broke into our lives. Kelsey, who has authored the book *Dreams: The Dark Speech of the Spirit*, notes, ". . . every major Father of the early Church, from Justin Martyr to Irenaeus, from Clement and Tertullian to Origen and Cyprian, believed that dreams were a means of revelation."

. . . If we are convinced that dreams can be a key to unlocking the door to the inner world, we can do three practical things. First, we can specifically pray, inviting God to inform us through our dreams. We should tell Him of our willingness to allow Him to speak to us in this way. At the same time, it is wise to pray a prayer of protection, since to open ourselves to spiritual influence can be dangerous as well as profitable. We simply ask God to surround us with the light of His protection as He ministers to our spirit.

. . . That leads to the third consideration—how to interpret dreams. The best way to discover the meaning of dreams is to *ask*. "You do not have, because you do not ask" (Jas. 4:2). We can trust God to bring discernment if and when it is needed. Sometimes it is helpful to seek out those who are especially skilled in these matters (431:23-24).

In our chapters on New Age Inner Work, Intuition, and Dream Work we illustrated the potential dangers of such an approach. Foster also encourages "centering" exercises and concentrating on one's breath, also a common Eastern technique:

Another meditation aimed at centering oneself begins by concentrating on breathing. Having

seated yourself comfortably, slowly become conscious of your breathing. This will help you to get in touch with your body and indicate to you the level of tension within. Inhale deeply, slowly tilting your head back as far as it will go. Then exhale, allowing your head slowly to come forward until your chin nearly rests on your chest. Do this for several moments, praying inwardly something like this: "Lord, I exhale my fear over my geometry exam, I inhale Your peace. I exhale my spiritual apathy, I inhale Your light and life." Then, as before, become silent outwardly and inwardly. Be attentive to the inward living Christ (431:25).

Dr. Foster is convinced the above methods may be used by Christians, especially as part of a program of spiritual growth. He cites their use in church history (including Christian mystical traditions) as an affirmation of how believers have used them in the past. "Nor should we forget the great body of literature by men and women from many disciplines. Many of these thinkers have unusual perception into the human predicament. [For example,] Eastern writers like Lao-Tse of China and Zarathustra of Persia . . ." (431:62).

Thankfully, Dr. Foster does warn that practicers are engaging in a "serious and even dangerous business" (431:62). But we don't think his approach answers all the questions that may be raised over such practices. The reason for our concern is twofold: 1) because Christians are usually insufficiently instructed in these areas, they may slip into more Eastern and occult forms of meditation; 2) our conviction that these methods are questionable to begin with (431:16). We do not doubt Dr. Foster's Christian commitment or sincerity. We appreciate his desire that Christians be more committed to Christ. We simply disagree with his basic approach to meditation and sanctification.

Secular psychotherapy in the church has also encouraged the use of "novel" spiritual practices (cf. 2491). For example, clinical psychologist E.S. Gallegos works at the Lutheran Family Service in Klamath Falls, Oregon, and he is coauthor of *Inner Journeys: Visualization in Growth and Therapy* (957). In "Animal Imagery, the Chakra System and Psychotherapy," he offers a psychotherapeutic approach that uses occult theory and technique plus imagery or visualization* for attaining an "assessment" of the chakras (according to Hindu theory, chakras are psychic centers in the body).

By a common technique of occult meditation, each chakra is "contacted" and then permitted to "represent itself" in animal form within the counselee's imagination. The function of the animal is to guide and counsel the person. This is similar to the shaman's "power" animal— a spirit guide who assumes the form of an animal to help, guide, protect, and instruct the shaman in his occult quest (see Shamanism). "This therapeutic process was initially developed when the author observed similarities between the chakra system and the totem poles of the Northwest Coast American Indians. This therapeutic process also acknowledges a relationship between those tribal [shamanistic] Indian transformation rituals and modern psychological transformation" (900:136). Here we have a licensed psychologist, working in a Lutheran Family Service Center, who has combined elements of occult yoga*/meditation theory and shamanism* in his counseling practice.

But what if the therapist happens to be an occultist who transfers occult power into his clients (like a true shaman can)? Or what if he brings his spirit guide into the therapy session (knowingly or not)? Or what if the person seeking help pursues shamanism as a result? Such "therapy" has then become a vehicle for introducing people to the occult, with all that implies in terms of consequences (278).

While such "therapy" is not common in the church, neither is it rare. We have no idea of how widespread such practices are in the mainline churches, but we are convinced that hundreds of illustrations could be cited, and that the evangelical church itself is being impacted, for several reasons: 1) the pragmatic orientation of modern evangelicalism; 2) the current state of occult revival and naïveté in our culture; 3) the church's partial accommodation to surrounding pagan culture; 4) occultism (in modified and "mild" forms) entering the field of psychotherapy, which itself has infused Christianity (2491);

5) the rejection of biblical authority in some quarters of evangelicalism.

To cite an illustration, the occult-oriented *Yoga Journal* ran an article by two evangelicals titled "Christians Meditate Too!" These evangelicals teach courses on "Christian" meditation at their evangelical church, and they run seminars on "Christian" meditation at other evangelical churches:

Last year the two of us taught an eight-week seminar on meditation—a fairly bold offering at our conservative evangelical church. The course was an enthusiastic success, and we'd like to share its highlights with *Yoga Journal* readers.... Our own background includes practicing yoga, t'ai chi and aikido, and studying the *Bhagavad Gita*, the *Upanishads*, Lao Tzu, and the teachings of Buddha and Confucius (901:27).

They observe correctly that "in both East and West, meditation is introspective: we learn to look within to discover spiritual realities" (901:27). Thus, not surprisingly, "We of the West stand to gain by learning discipline and spiritual awareness from the East.... The new age movement in this country is already moving toward a personalizing of Eastern disciplines" (901:28).

Yet there was no critique of New Age philosophy or practice and no mention of the dangers or occult nature of most meditation. There was no warning about the hazards or implications of yoga practice (see Yoga*). There was no awareness of the anti-Christian philosophy underlying Eastern systems or the reality of spiritual deception and warfare that operates in pagan religion. The article only presented the "benefits" of Eastern spirituality and an endorsement of "Christian" meditation involving, among other things, questionable exegesis and an uncritical acceptance of Christian mysticism,* such as the mindless repetition of certain phrases found in many Christian mystical traditions. They told readers of the *Yoga Journal*, "Christians meditate, too. When they do, they are falling behind Isaac and David, Ignatius and Francis and Christ himself" (901:45).

Yet, we do not see Jesus in the New Testament sitting in yoga positions, or encouraging people to "practice yoga, t'ai chi, and aikido" or to study the pagan *Bhagavad Gita*, the *Upanishads*, Lao Tzu, or the teachings of Confucius and Buddha. These evangelicals may have been attempting to "reach" readers of the *Yoga Journal* with some kind of Christian influence. While that motive would be noble, we question the efficacy.

The authors of the previous article recommended three books. The first was Thomas Merton's *New Seeds of Contemplation*. Merton (1915-68) was an influential ascetic Catholic monk who incorporated Eastern beliefs and practices into his Catholicism and led many Catholics into contemplative Eastern traditions. He believed he had found genuine spiritual truth in many Eastern scriptures and practices, including Hindu, Buddhist, Sufi, and Zen* traditions. The second book recommended was Evelyn Underhill's *Mysticism*, which supports a variety of mystical practices and encourages belief in pantheism (2041:XIV,XV). The authors also recommend Richard Foster's *Celebration of Discipline*, which is described as being "prominent in the revival of interest in Christian meditation" (901:45).

## MEDITATION AMONG PROFESSIONALS

Many professional people, among them scientists and academics, practice meditation. For example, Roger Walsh, who has both the M.D. and Ph.D. and works in the Department of Psychiatry and Human Behavior in the College of Medicine at the U.C. Irvine campus, is a committed student of Buddhist *vipassana* ("mindfulness") meditation and the spiritistically inspired *A Course in Miracles** (439:69,81-82).

Deane Shapiro also has impressive academic credentials and was recipient of a Kellogg National Fellowship to study meditation. He has served on the faculty of the University of California and the Stanford University Medical School, and he is president of the Institute for the Advancement of Human Behavior. He is the author of *Precision Nirvana: An Owner's Manual for the Care and Maintenance of the Mind*, and an edi-

tor of *Meditation: Self-Regulation Strategy and Altered States of Consciousness* (439:69,81-82).

Together, Walsh and Shapiro edited *Meditation: Classic and Contemporary Perspectives* (566). This text has over 700 pages containing 60 chapters by 30 authors. It includes almost all Eastern Asian systems now practiced in the West, involving dozens of methods and techniques. Their bibliography is extensive (over 600 items), including many articles relating to empirical studies and interacting meditation with psychology, psychiatry, biochemistry, psychophysiology, the neurosciences, and more.

Yet elsewhere Shapiro states that "the most promising future meditation research may lie in the model of a personal scientist, using ourselves as subjects—and combining the precision of Western phenomenological science with the vision of Eastern thought and practice" (440:128-29). In part, he is referring to the field of Transpersonal Psychology, the so-called "fourth" school of modern psychology, behind psychoanalysis, behaviorism, and humanistic psychology. According to Walsh, in "A Model for Viewing Meditation Research," apparently the "large majority" of transpersonal psychologists meditate. "The number of Westerners who have learned to meditate now number several million, and surveys of transpersonal psychologists suggest that the large majority are involved in some form of this practice. . . . One of the long-held goals of transpersonal psychology has been an integration of Western science and Eastern practice" (439:69).

The research bibliography on meditation compiled by Steven Donovan and Michael Murphy also illustrates the large impact that meditation is having in our culture. Murphy is a former psychologist and well known cofounder of the New Age Esalen Institute. The bibliography concerned research data on meditation from 1931 to 1983 and contained 776 English language entries. This was *not* a bibliography of the religious, philosophical, or metaphysical literature on meditation; it dealt with scientific research only (434:181-229).

What does all this mean? It means that Christians can no longer afford the luxury of being uninformed about meditation. Because most people see meditation merely as a form of relaxation, this has masked its true nature and sparked the interest of researchers who would ordinarily avoid the occult. Clinical psychologist Gordon Boals, who has taught at Princeton and Rutgers universities, points out:

> Viewing meditation as a relaxation technique has had a number of consequences. One result has been to make meditation seem more familiar and acceptable to the Western public so that subjects are willing to learn and practice it and researchers and psychotherapists are interested in experimenting with it. Another outcome is that therapists have been able to find a variety of ways of using it as a therapeutic technique. If meditation is relaxation, it should serve as an antidote to anxiety (898:146).

However, as we will now see, New Age and related meditation is far more than a relaxation technique and its goals encompass far more than anxiety reduction.

## CLAIMS AND GOALS

The goals of Eastern and occult meditation are to change a person's view of "self" and the world. In the end, as far as the meditator is concerned, "It lastingly changes his consciousness, transforming his experience of himself and his universe" (442:118). Dr. Roger Walsh, cited above, authored several books on meditation, and he was an editor for the *Journal of Transpersonal Psychology*. Frances Vaughan is a past president of the Association for Transpersonal Psychology and a psychology professor at the California Institute of Transpersonal Psychology. These two authors describe the impact of meditative practice:

> The rewards of meditative practice tend to be subtle at first.... Old assumptions about oneself and the world are gradually surrendered and more finely tuned, comprehensive perspectives begin to emerge.
>
> Such immediate benefits, however, are only tastes of what is potentially a profoundly transformative process, for when practiced intensely, meditation disciplines almost invariably lead

into the transpersonal realm of experience. ...A progressive sequence of altered states of consciousness can occur, which may ultimately result in the permanent, radical shift in consciousness known as enlightenment or liberation (949:136-37).

Standard meditation texts claim that in our normal state of mind we misperceive and misunderstand ourselves (our true nature) and our world (its true nature). The purpose of meditation is to correct these false perceptions and to replace them with a true perception of reality, which is mystically induced by the procedures involved. This is why almost all forms of meditation involve the deliberate cultivation of altered states of consciousness* and the subsequent development of psychic powers.

These altered states of consciousness, however, are wrongly interpreted; that is, they are viewed as "higher" states of consciousness, presumably divine states, and the psychic powers developed are often seen as the awakening and developing "god-nature" of the individual.

For example, yoga* meditation, which is typically Hindu, and "mindfulness" meditation, which is typically Buddhist, are powerful forms of meditation designed to radically alter the meditator's state of consciousness. When practicing them, people have the religious teachings "confirmed" by the occult mental experiences they have. Meditators may become intellectually convinced they are one nature with God or with ultimate reality, with all that this implies. This change of perception can occur not only through cultivating altered states of consciousness* but also by meditation-developed psychic abilities, or by meditation-induced spirit contact. And such experiences lead to conclusions that are hostile to biblical faith. To believe that we are one essence with God is to undermine the basic Christian doctrines of creation, the atonement, redemption, and personal salvation by faith in Jesus Christ.

If people are already divine, and if they do not yet understand this, then the major issue is personal ignorance requiring the proper knowledge. This is at odds with what the Bible teaches, that the issue is one of personal sin requiring forgiveness through Jesus Christ. If people are divine, they have no need for a Savior from sin. Yet in the Bible we read, "For all have sinned and fall short of the glory of God" (Romans 3:23). "For God so loved the world that he gave his one and only Son, that whoever believes in him shall not perish but have eternal life" (John 3:16). Eastern and occult meditation denies biblical teaching by assuming that we are one essence with God and have no need to seek a God outside ourselves.

Because Eastern and occult meditation confirms occult beliefs and denies biblical beliefs, we often suspect the presence of demonic involvement through meditation-induced altered states of consciousness.* Most of our subsequent discussion will document this.

## SPIRITISTIC ENERGY MANIFESTATIONS

One of the principal features of New Age practice is the belief in a universal or cosmic energy circulating throughout the body (e.g., *prana, chi, mana, orgone,* or *ki*; see New Age Medicine, "Acceptance of Spiritism and Mysterious Body Energies"). This energy can be manipulated for various spiritual or psychological purposes, and it is even palpable.

Energy "manifestations" are a principal characteristic of meditative experiences as well. Although it is widely accepted in the East that psychic powers are a natural by-product of meditation, the vehicle through which these psychic abilities are produced is often viewed as a form of "cosmic" energy.

A major study on meditation asked respondents to check characteristics of their meditative experience. One description was: "I felt a great surge of energy within me or around me" (437:121). Meditators whose experience could be described in this manner were to check this item. Significantly, it received the highest "loading score" of all 16 items in the category of "Intensification and Change of Consciousness"** (437:127).

Experiencing a "great surge of energy" was therefore *a dominant characteristic* of the meditative experience (1849; cf. Yoga). The authors related this to the spiritistic *mana* of Polynesian shamanism and the occult *prana,* or kundalini, of Hinduism (437:132-33). Consider other characteristic descriptions: "The force went through and through my body. . . . It was absolutely wild and intense. . . . I felt possessed by the energy" (1850). One woman described the supernatural power as "entering me and taking over my being. . . . I was completely possessed. . . . [It was] taking me over completely. . . . There was nothing left of the person I thought to be Marie" (476:76).

The experience of a surge of energy or power is also related to the cultivation of altered states of consciousness* (437:132-33). Thus, "[Meditation is] a profoundly transformative process, for when practiced intensely, meditation disciplines *almost invariably* lead into the transpersonal [occult] realm of experience. . . . A progressive sequence of altered states of consciousness can occur, which may ultimately result in the permanent, radical [occult] shift in consciousness known as enlightenment or liberation" (949: 136-37, emphasis added).

For us, the key issue is to determine the nature of this energy. Transpersonal psychotherapist Dr. Frances V. Clark, who wrote her Ph.D. dissertation on "Approaching Transpersonal Consciousness Through Affective Imagery in Higher Education," refers to our culture's modern fascination with occult energies. "In recent years we have learned much about releasing energy, raising energy, transforming energy, directing energy, and controlling energy flow. Yet the energy we are talking about remains undefined" (448:163).

In the preface to "Kundalini Casualties," an article discussing the dangers of yogic kundalini arousal during meditation and other New Age therapies, *The New Age Journal* points out:

> Traditionally, spiritual teachers have warned their students of the dangers and possible side effects of meditative techniques and helped practitioners deal with these difficulties as they arose. Now that meditation is being marketed as a mass commodity, the information concerning

---

**The method used was the Verimax Orthogonal Factor Analysis; the loading score was .66.

the dangers and the necessary help is often not part of the package. Moreover, certain body therapies and human potential techniques appear to be triggering off the Kundalini syndrome completely outside the context of spiritual training, and often the therapists themselves have no idea what this energy is, let alone how to deal with it (897:47; cf. Yoga).

We are convinced that the mysterious, dramatic energy experienced in New Age meditation is characteristically the result of spiritistic influence. That meditation produces energy manifestations clearly associated with primitive shamanism,* the occult, and Eastern or Western spiritism, is undeniable. Meditation-induced "energy manifestations" are so often associated with spiritism, that we have no doubt that this energy is not human, and certainly not divine, but demonic (refs. 1039/1040/249; see New Age Medicine*).

Whether the phenomena are described in terms of the Eastern guru's* *shaktipat diksha* (transfer of occult energy), classical shamanism,* kundalini arousal, or something similar in other traditions, we are dealing with one and the same energy. Many primitive traditions attribute this energy to the spirit world (cf. the *num* of the Kalahari !Kung tribe); others see it as an internal manifestation of divine power residing potentially within all people. Even if this energy is not directly attributed to the spirit world, the spiritistic associations and manifestations are so blatant and pervasive one would be hard-pressed to conclude that he was dealing with anything other than spirit influence or possession. Great surges of energy are typically felt by Eastern and Western gurus, who freely confess they are possessed by spirits, demons, or gods (249). Occultists also admit the same condition (237:129-32), as do many practitioners of yoga* (479).

Swami Rudrananda, in *Spiritual Cannibalism*, writes that while in meditation his master touched him, and "I immediately felt within me a surge of great spiritual force.... [M]ovements similar to those of an epileptic controlled my body for about an hour. Many strange visions appeared and I felt things opening within me that had never been opened before" (568:85). In another experience, "Slowly [the spirit of my guru] Swami Nityananda came toward me and

entered into my physical body. For three hours, I felt nothing of myself but that the saint had possessed me" (449:13). A leading popularizer of Tibetan Buddhism in this country, Chogyam Trungpa, states, "I will say that for beginners, it is extremely dangerous to play with [this] energy, but for advanced students such work becomes relevant naturally" (450:74).

One of the dangers is temporary or permanent insanity. Here are a few illustrations from meditators who follow guru Da (Bubba) Free John:

Bubba's eyes rolled up, and his lips pulled into a sneer. His hands formed mudras [yogic movements] as he slumped against Sal, who also fell back against other devotees sitting behind him. Almost immediately, many of those present began to feel the effects of intensified Shakti [power], through the spontaneous internal movement of the life-force. Their bodies jerked or shook, their faces contorted, some began to cry, scream, and moan. The whole bathhouse seems to have slipped into another world....

I saw Bubba just enter into Sal, just go right into Sal. From there he went out over everybody else, and then everybody else started going crazy (476:47).

My hands were glowing and vibrating. It felt like electricity, like they were on radar or something, and they were just being directed to all of the people around me. I felt like I was conducting the Force through me to the others there. People were screaming and howling, crying and yelling out . . . (476:60).

As soon as I went into the room, I felt the Force. My head started jerking, and I sat down next to Billy Tsiknas and Joe Hamp. The Force went through and through my body, at first warm, then hot. It started to hurt. I was in a sitting position. My hand was raised, and I couldn't move it because of the Force moving through it. My head was bent down. I was so full of intensity, I started to cry (476:61).

I was so insane I didn't know what was happening at all.... Everybody sitting here started to have incredible Shakti [power] manifestations, and other things. It was absolutely intense. ...When I was sitting here with everybody, I was shaking, and it felt sort of like I was possessed, . . . the "terror of being destroyed, totally destroyed" (476:66).

Suddenly his body exploded with movement, his arms and legs flying outward, his head rolling around and snapping. Force seemed to be flung from his body into the others present (476:72).

What is called "intensification," or possession by energy, is a core experience in the historical literature of meditation and many occult practices. This "energizing" is experienced as a dramatic and even overwhelming influx of spiritual power. It can be wild or uncontrollable, even deadly. And, irrespective of the interpretation placed on it, it shares characteristics with spirit possession. Abundant literature illustrates this, such as Bhagwan Shree Rajneesh's *The Book of the Secrets* (567); Swami Muktananda's *Play of Consciousness* (467); Swami Rudrananda's *Spiritual Cannibalism* (449); Da Free John's *Garbage and the Goddess* (476); Tal Brooke's *Riders of the Cosmic Circuit* (249).

What is troubling is the pervasive denial that what is really operating here is, in fact, demonic influence or spirit possession. The following cartoon illustration underscores our concerns:

> There is a cartoon by Feiffer that illustrates some of these component aspects of meditation, and it proceeds something like this: Harry is sitting meditating; Madge walks in and asks, "Harry, what are you doing?" "I am concentrating on my mantra." "A mantra? What's a mantra?" "It's a secret. I cannot tell." "Harry, what is a mantra?" "I cannot tell." "Harry, I must know what a mantra is. Tell me what is a mantra? It's either me or the mantra." Harry doesn't tell and she packs up her bags and leaves, and Harry says, "See it works; no stress." Meditation may be working for a variety of reasons other than the ones that the literature cites, and I think we need to research these reasons (451:128).

Though no one really knows how meditation "works," given the historic and contemporary associations to spiritism, it is by far the most logical theory as to how it "works." On the "Merv Griffin Show," July 25, 1986, Griffin interviewed New Age channeler Jach Pursel and actor Michael York and his wife. They, along with Griffin and many other top Hollywood stars, were described as disciples of "Lazaris," the spirit entity who possessed Pursel and spoke through him while on television.

On the show, Pursel described how he met his spirit guide while engaged in his normal practice of simple meditation. In October of 1974, he recalled, he was meditating as usual; there was nothing abnormal in his experience. But all of a sudden—totally unexpectedly—he became possessed. The entity took him over entirely, completely controlling him and using his vocal chords to speak through him. His wife recorded the entity's statements, and Pursel's career as a medium was launched.

The significant fact here is not the birth of another medium, but how easily Pursel became demon-possessed (he had been practicing 20-minute sessions of a simple and widely practiced form of meditation twice daily).

## OCCULT NATURE

Millions of people today do not realize that most meditation is occult in nature. The practices (some form of daily meditative discipline), results (altered states of consciousness,* psychic powers, kundalini arousal,* spirit contact), and goals (some form of cosmic consciousness, enlightenment,* or development of the "higher self") may all be classified within the sphere of the practices, results, and goals of the occult world in general. In this section, we will document the occult nature of the vast majority of the forms of meditation practiced in America today.

*Occult Phenomena in Meditation*

Almost all forms of meditation involve three similar occult phenomena: 1) the cultivation of altered states of consciousness*; 2) the eventual development of psychic powers; 3) the possibility of spirit possession. We will look at each of these following.

*The Cultivation of Altered States of Consciousness.* Meditation-induced altered states of consciousness* are our first illustration of the occult nature of meditation. Following we will note the

389

research of parapsychologist Dr. Karlis Osis and others which reveals that the most central factor in meditation is an altered state of consciousness (ASC). Parapsychologist Dr. Gertrude Schmeidler, former president of the Parapsychological Association, states "Trance shows many similarities to meditation . . ." (443:30).

Trance states and ASCs have been traditionally associated with the occult world, demonism, and other forms of spirit contact, such as shamanism,* witchcraft, neo-paganism, magic ritual, Satanism, mediumism, and yogic* disciplines). Whether one is a short- or long- term practitioner, meditation is designed to change one's view of "self" and the world by altering one's consciousness. Noted parapsychologist Karlis Osis and others observe in "Dimensions of the Meditative Experience" that their own research reveals that "the most central and complex factor" of the meditative experience is an "intensification and change of consciousness"; that is, an altered state of consciousness (437:121). They also write:

> In spite of the almost universal claim that the meditation experience is ineffable [indescribable], clear dimensionalities [characteristics] emerge. Even more, these dimensions seem not to express everyday states of consciousness: The way of experiencing [reality] definitely changed. . . . The subject's free comments support the view that successful meditation leads to altered states of consciousness (437:130).

They conclude, "Effective meditation induces radical changes in a meditator's way of experiencing [reality]" (437:109).

Further, additional studies prove that meditation induces ASCs:

> Ludwig (1966) pointed out that ASCs have both maladaptive expressions (for example, acute psychotic reactions and manifestations of organic lesions) and adaptive expressions (for example, the shamanic trance for healing purposes and new experiences of knowledge and growth in mystical states). . . . Meditation of any denomination or persuasion has been the religiously sanctioned method for the induction of the highest state of consciousness or Meditative ASC. A re-

view of the psychological and philosophical analyses provided by many authors (James, 1902; Susuki, 1952; Stace, 1961; Deikman, 1966; Prince & Savage, 1972) revealed a commonality of features. . . .

> These experiential characteristics permitted the categorization of meditative experiences as ASCs (455:78).

The ASCs that meditation typically develops tend to result in a radically restructured, and false, view of self and society. Characteristically, one ends up thinking that the material universe is a dream or an illusion and that one's true nature is one essence with God. Haridas Chaudhuri writes in his *Philosophy of Meditation:* "On attaining cosmic consciousness a person's world view undergoes a radical transformation. The consensus of all mystics and sages . . . is that the world of normal experience is now revealed as unreal, as phenomenal, as a mere appearance, as a bad dream from which one wakes up with a sigh of relief . .." (435:59). Another authority correctly points out, "Decisive behavior changes follow from this state of consciousness, and the full realization of nirvana actuates a *permanent alteration* of the meditator's consciousness per se. With the meditator's realization of nirvana, aspects of his ego and of his normal consciousness are abandoned, never to arise again" (949:148, emphasis added). In other words, the individual *person* is radically affected, and aspects of his being are destroyed, "never to rise again" (for examples, see Eastern Gurus, Yoga, Enlightenment).

Dr. Jack Kornfield trained for six years in Southeast Asia and teaches Buddhist *vipassana* meditation. As a *result* of his experiences, he eventually became a Theravadin Buddhist monk. He also has a doctorate in psychology and is the author of *Living Buddhist Masters*. He states, "One articulation of the purpose of spiritual practice and a viewpoint that is a product of it as well is to come to understand *that we don't exist*" (949:15, emphasis added). In other words, our body and personality are illusions and the goal of meditation is to escape from or "transcend" them in order to discover our "true" inner nature, which is supposedly one essence with God or ultimate reality.

There are many personal and social consequences to such a view. In the words of Maharishi Mahesh Yogi, the guru of transcendental meditation, the true self of the enlightened meditator "is uninvolved with activity . . . and it is uninvolved with the *selves* of individual beings" (469:212). For the meditator, the entire world and all its activities is "like a world of dolls and toys" which he long ago discarded as an adult (469:157).

Gurus and meditators often think that they are one nature with God as a result of their meditation practices. Muktananda says, "The Guru is God Himself . . ." (483:98; cf. pp. 99-106); Sai Baba tells his followers, "You are the God of this universe" (484:112), and "You *are* God in reality" (485:68); Rajneesh says, "As you are, you are God" (486:382).

Since the result of New Age meditation is a reinterpretation of reality as an "illusion," such meditation perceives normal consciousness itself as *maya* (illusion), that is, as a "trap" to be escaped if one is to find true liberation and spiritual enlightenment. Dr. Walsh states:

> . . . To date, I have seen no explanations other than the almost universal ones among the meditative—yogic traditions that normal man is an automaton, more asleep than awake, etc.
>
> . . . A remarkably wide range of meditation and yogic disciplines . . . assert that whether we know it or not, untrained individuals are prisoners of their own minds, totally and unwittingly trapped by a continuous inner fantasy-dialog which creates an all-consuming illusion or *maya*. . . . "Normal" man is thus seen as asleep or dreaming. . . . When the individual permanently disidentifies from or eradicates this dream he is said to have awakened and can now recognize the true nature of his former state and that of the population. This awakening or enlightenment is the aim of the meditative-yogic disciplines . . . (441:156-57).

Thus New Age meditation is properly classified as an occult practice because it induces ASCs that support occult philosophies and goals.

*The Eventual Development of Psychic Powers.* Almost all forms of meditation lead to the development of psychic abilities. This is acknowledged by researchers and practitioners alike. *Psychology Today* associate editor and psychologist Daniel Goleman has the Ph.D. in clinical psychology from Harvard and is an authority on Buddhist *vipassana* [mindfulness] meditation. In his article "The Buddha on Meditation and States of Consciousness," Goleman observes that "every school of meditation acknowledges them [psychic powers] as by-products of advanced stages of mastery . . ." (434A:218).

A popular teacher of meditation says:

> . . . Psychic power expresses itself in many forms. It is known as intuition, clairvoyance, clairaudience, precognition, mental telepathy, telekinesis, cosmic perception and spiritism. The techniques for developing all these various forms of psychism are the same. Mystic meditation is the means by which you may reach into the higher psychic centers of consciousness and channel the tremendous forces that await your joyous discovery (447:91).

Leading consciousness researcher John White acknowledges that "psychic development is likely in the course of one's [meditative] practice" (444:48). Television personality and parapsychologist Patricia Mischell says that "one of the unforeseen bonuses of meditation is that many people experience an increasing or unfolding of their mental-telepathy abilities, clairaudience, and clairvoyance through meditation" (445:126).

Several experimental studies concluded, "Meditation is an effective means of producing controlled psi [psychic] interactions" (446:339). And a three-year study by Karlis Osis and Edwin Bokert also revealed a correlation between meditation and psychic ability (902). One writer explained the ability of meditation to induce astral projection and spirit contact:

> Transcendental meditation is used as the means for releasing the soul from the physical body and projecting it into the astral realms. While you are out on the astral [plane], your soul may acquire knowledge from [dead] ancient masters.

391

You may become instructed in the arts, music, languages, history or the mystical secrets back of the cosmos. When you enter that mysterious fourth dimensional world of spirit, you can tap unlimited powers and soar to mystic realms where the immortals dwell (447:153).

But psychic powers, however they are mediated in men, are spiritistically induced and not the result of some allegedly "divine" human potential. Whenever spiritism is found, psychic powers are also found (904). The individual who develops psychic powers invariably involves himself in the world of spiritism, knowingly or unknowingly. Because New Age meditation develops psychic powers, it is proper to classify New Age meditation as a form of occult practice.

*The Possibility of Spirit Possession.* One problem with ASCs and psychic abilities is not only the false ideas that they produce, but that they can easily lead to demonic influence or possession (see Altered States of Consciousness*). Even advanced meditators freely confess this. For example, Rolling Thunder, a shaman leader in the Shoshone and Cherokee tribes, states, "If it is not done correctly, evil spirits can get into people while they are meditating" (436:110).

But the problem is that when meditation is done *correctly*, ASCs foster spiritistic influence or possession. Channeler Laeh Garfield writes in *Companions in Spirit: A Guide to Working with Your Spirit Helpers*, "Meditation simultaneously calms you down, uplifts you and sharpens your awareness, so that discarnate teachers can come through to you with the messages they convey" (349:36).

Because of modern reluctance to deal forthrightly and responsibly with the category of the demonic, meditation is one of the common methods available for becoming possessed by spirits who are really demons. Endless numbers of gurus, psychics, mediums, other occultists, and even scholarly authorities testify to this. For example, Dr. Weldon's Ph.D. dissertation researched over 20 different Hindu and Buddhist gurus, and every one had been spirit-influenced or possessed, apparently during their meditative practices (610/249; see Eastern Gurus).

Should we believe that the spirits' will *not* make use of meditative practices that alter people's consciousness? Should we believe that this will *not* facilitate the spirits' ability to possess individuals, when this is what serves their purposes? Indeed, the very nature and goals of meditation suggest the *probability* of spiritistic involvement. In *Spirit Communication for the Millions,* Doris H. Buckley correctly observes that through meditation "greater power [becomes available] so that the [mediumistic] channel develops more quickly" (452:156).

Furthermore, the spirits themselves endorse New Age meditation. The books the spirits dictate through their human mediums enthusiastically recommend meditative practices as a means to contact them. For example, Ruth Montgomery, a former hard-nosed, skeptical newspaper reporter who eventually became a medium, has single-handedly interested millions of people in the spirit world through more than a dozen books inspired or dictated by her spirit guides. In one of her books, *A World Beyond,* the alleged spirit of a famous trance medium, Arthur Ford, endorses New Age meditation: "Now let's speak of the value of meditation. . . . Remember in meditation to breathe deeply at first . . . use the mantra . . . and feel yourself melding with the universal whole. . . . [S]pend at least fifteen or twenty minutes each day in this stillness" (453:141).

Here we cite several authorities to show that meditation can and does lead to demon possession. India-born Douglas Shah, the grandson of Yogi Ishwar Dayal, observes, "I have watched Hindu worshipers by the scores chanting for hours before idols during a special *Puja* (worship) Season, and I have literally felt the supernatural presence of the gods they were invoking" (487:98). He comments that "being taken over by an evil spirit . . . is a very real possibility" in meditation (487:102). British scholar Os Guinness states: "Many . . . who practice yoga or Zen Meditation have found they have opened their minds to blackness and spiritism, seeing themselves as mediums and describing themselves as possessed" (488:298).

Consider an experience of Swami Muktananda, who describes the results of his meditation. In his spiritual autobiography he writes that "when I sat for meditation [my] own body acted as if [it] were possessed by a god or a bad spirit" (467:122). Muktananda details an entire chapter of such experiences, including more bizarre encounters than we list below. We quote at length to give the reader an accurate feel for the potential consequences of meditation:

> I was assailed by all sorts of perverse and defiling emotions. My body started to move, and went on like this in a confused sort of way.... After a time, my breathing changed, becoming disturbed. Sometimes my abdomen would swell with air, after which I would exhale it with great force. Often the breath that I took in would be held inside me. I became more and more frightened.
>
> My mind was sick with fear. I called Babu Rao and said to him, "Babu, go home now. The rhythm of my heart and the state of my mind are not good. I feel sure that I am going to die tonight of heart failure.... I don't think I shall live through this night, and if I do, it will be to go mad. I am losing my mind...."
>
> My thoughts became confused, meaningless. My limbs and body got hotter and hotter. My head felt heavy, and every pore in me began to ache. When I breathed out, my breath stopped outside. When I breathed in, it stopped inside. This was terribly painful, and I lost my courage. Something told me that I would die at any moment.
>
> By now it was after 9:00. Someone had seated himself in my eyes and was making me see things. It seemed that I was being controlled by some power which made me do all these things. I no longer had a will of my own. My madness was growing all the time. My intellect was completely unstable.
>
> My fear increased every second. I heard hordes of people screaming frightfully, as if it were the end of the world. I looked out of the small window of my hut and saw strange creatures from six to fifty feet tall, neither demons nor demigods, but human in form, dancing naked, their mouths gaping open. The screeching was horrible and apocalyptic. I was completely conscious, but was watching my madness, which appeared to be real.
>
> Then, from over the water, a moonlike sphere about four feet in diameter came floating in. It stopped in front of me. This radiant, white ball struck against my eyes and then passed inside me. I am writing this just as I saw it. It is not a dream or an allegory, but a scene which actually happened—that sphere came down from the sky and entered me. A second later the bright light penetrated into my *nadis* [psychic channels]. My tongue curled up against my palate, and my eyes closed. I saw a dazzling light in my forehead and I was terrified. I was still locked up in the lotus posture, and then my head was forced down and glued to the ground. ... Afterward I sat down in the lotus posture and once again started to meditate on the Guru. As soon as I sat down, my mind became completely indrawn. My body, fixed in lotus posture, began to sway.... This Meditation went on for an hour and a half, and then a new process began.
>
> I started to make a sound like a camel, which alternated with the roaring of a tiger. I must have roared very loudly, for the people around actually thought that a tiger had gotten into the sugarcane field.
>
> I am in a terrible state. I have gone completely insane.... My body began to twist. Now, it was not I who meditated; Meditation forced itself on me. It came spontaneously; it was in all the joints of my body. All the blood cells in my body were spinning, and *prana* flowed through the *nadis* at an astounding speed. Then, suddenly, a red light came before me with such force that it seemed to have been living inside me. It was two feet tall and shone brightly. I clearly saw myself burning, but I did not feel the heart of the fire on the outside. Every part of my body was emitting loud crackling and popping sounds (467:75-79).

After it was all over, Muktananda concluded that he had been spiritually enlightened (see Enlightenment). Like endless gurus with similar experiences, he teaches his students that while following the meditative path, they too will experience what he did. But, he tells them, they should not worry, for it is all part of the normal results of meditation leading to spiritual enlightenment. He also observes how easily their meditation will lead them to spirit contact: "They talk to and receive instruction from gods and goddesses" (467:xxii).

Da (Bubba) Free John (Franklin Jones) also illustrates various kinds of possession, in particular being possessed by the "spiritual form" of the guru or master. His book *Garbage and the Goddess* describes the experiences he and his disciples underwent at his Persimmon, New York, ashram from March to July, 1974. While Free John describes normal everyday living as being "possessed by the most insidious demonic force in the universe" (476:51), one would hardly suspect it from the descriptions of, as he calls it, "life in God." In light of the experiences described, perhaps Free John is correct: "True wisdom is the capacity for perfect madness" (478:1). We cite several examples by different individuals who encountered this phenomenon of mass possession, as given in Free John's *Garbage and the Goddess*. The descriptions are reminiscent of the mass Shaker possessions in the 1840s and related spiritistic incidents (see 463:75-83):

The most significant thing about this event is that contrary to the usual beliefs, even of traditional spirituality, the Guru *literally* enters and transforms. It is a kind of possession. It is God-Possession. Bubba animates this body (476:151).

People were screaming and howling and weeping, emitting strange grunts and snarls, their bodies jerking, writhing, and assuming yogic mudras . . . (476:72).

I felt utterly possessed, my body was possessed, and my hands started to move, and I couldn't control them. I had no control at all. My face started taking on expressions (476:263).

My body wasn't mine. I didn't even feel my body as mine. There was only this sensation I've had before in Bubba's Presence, the feeling that this body is being used. . . . I went in and at first I was totally out of my mind. I was screaming for a long time. . . . I was making very strange sounds. . . . It is God-Possession. It is God totally taking over your form (476:282-83,285).

I was so insane I didn't know what was happening at all . . . (476:66).

. . . Last night I was led to this spontaneous experience of conducting the Force, and I felt possessed, really possessed. Then suddenly I wasn't my body any more (476:312).

Muktananda's and Free John's experiences and teachings are not unique; they are the norm

among gurus and their followers. Consider several other examples:

*Swami Rudrananda*
Slowly Swami Nityananda [in spirit form] came toward me and entered into my physical body. For three hours I felt nothing of myself but that the saint had possessed me. It was a terrifying experience and it required all my faith not to fight it (449:13).

*Swami Satchidananda*
I felt myself fall into a sort of trance. . . . I was overjoyed with the feeling that my Master [Sivananda] had entered into my own system [body] (477:119-20).

*Rudrananda*
. . . There are times when the psychic system of the teacher will seem to control the student. He will feel possessed by his teacher. There is nothing to fear from this. It is only a stage of growth through which he [the student] is passing (449:103).

*Sri Chinmoy*
. . . If you remain calm and quiet and allow your spiritual Guide to enter into you, you will become flooded with Peace. This kind of tuning in is not only a valid and correct practice, *but is essential for one who has placed himself under the guidance of a spiritual Master* (480:113, emphasis added).

*Rajneesh*
Whenever a master wants to help you, cleanse your energy channels, your passage [kundalini spinal passage], if it is blocked, he simply possesses you. He simply descends into you. . . . If the disciple is really surrendered, the master can possess him immediately (482:68).

From all of the above, we conclude that New Age meditation is generally occult in nature because it cultivates altered states of consciousness,* psychic abilities,* and fosters demonic influence and possession.

*Occult Goals in Meditation*
Another indication of the occult nature of meditation is that almost all forms have a similar occult goal. Our own study of meditative systems and occultism has convinced us that the end result of meditation is a goal similar or

identical to occult self-transformation. Other researchers have made similar conclusions. In other words, most meditation systems, despite different external characteristics, all lead to the same end state: a psychic merging with "ultimate reality."

This supposed ultimate reality is usually defined either as a merging into the "One" (an impersonal God such as the Hindu Brahman) or as merging into the "void," as in Buddhist *nirvana*, or their equivalent in various forms of Western occultism. In all cases, the end result is the same: the destruction of the individual personality which, after all, was only an illusion (see Yoga).

As noted earlier, Dr. Daniel Goleman has studied meditation systems extensively. He teaches courses on meditation at Harvard University and is a committed Buddhist with a Hindu guru, Neem Karoli Baba—the guru that Ram Dass made famous in his multimillion-selling text *Be Here Now* (639). In Goleman's *The Varieties of the Meditative Experience*, we discover that (biblical meditation aside) almost all forms of meditation are strikingly similar. For example, he discusses a dozen different meditative systems which are representative of all varieties of meditation in general. Goleman says that a remark by Joseph Goldstein, that "all meditation systems either aim for One or Zero—union with God or emptiness," became a type of guideline in his research (442:xix). And so Goleman wrote, "At this [their] most universal level, all meditation systems are variations on a single process for transforming consciousness. The core elements of this process are found in every system, and its specifics undercut ostensible differences among the various schools of meditation" (442:106).

While it is true that "the meditator's beliefs determines how he interprets and labels his meditation experiences," nevertheless, "all [systems] seem to refer to a single state [of consciousness] with identical characteristics. These many terms for a single state come from Theravadan Buddhism, raja yoga, Sufism, [the] Kabbalah, kundalini yoga, Zen, and TM [transcendental meditation], respectively" (442:112). In other words, regardless of the system of meditation, all aim at the same end state: a radical, occult transformation of the individual and how he perceives himself and the world. Dr. Goleman concludes:

> The literature of every meditation system describes an altered state. . . . Virtually every system of meditation recognizes the awakened state as the ultimate goal of meditation. . . .
>
> Each path labels this end state differently. But no matter how diverse the names, these paths all propose the same basic formula in an alchemy [transformation] of the self: the diffusion of the effects of meditation into the meditator's waking, dreaming and sleep states. At the outset, this diffusion requires the meditator's effort. As he progresses, it becomes easier for him to maintain prolonged meditative awareness in the midst of his other activities. As the states produced by his meditation meld with his waking activity, the awakened state ripens. When it reaches full maturity, it lastingly changes his consciousness, transforming his experience of himself and his universe (442:115-18).

Indeed, in almost every major and minor meditative system, this transformation of personal identity and perception of the universe is achieved principally along occult, non-Christian lines and at the expense of biblical truth. Despite outer differences between these systems, all of them are potentially harmful due to their anti-Christian worldview, occult techniques, and spiritistic elements.

Having now examined the characteristics and goals of most meditation as it is practiced today, there is little doubt that most meditation systems should be classified as occult training. To view them otherwise is simply a delusion.

## RISKS TO PHYSICAL AND MENTAL WELL-BEING

Transformation of consciousness, psychic powers, and spirit possession are not the only dangers of meditation. There are many studies which show that physical and psychological harm can occur from meditation training (458; see Altered States of Consciousness). And these consequences, like those discussed previously, mirror the effects produced by occult practices in general.

A symposium report by a number of authorities, some of whom practice meditation, "Spiritual and Transpersonal Aspects of Altered States of Consciousness," comments: "Recently the 'fringe benefits' of meditation regarding health, vitality, and cognitive functioning have been broadcast, and increasing numbers of people practice meditation for these purposes. . . . [But] there are many dangers in this journey" (457:62-63). One authority states, "There can arise a clear vision of the dissolution of the self from moment to moment, and this often leads to a realm of fear and terror, and a kind of inner death" (949:153).

In "Psychiatric Complications of Meditation Practice," Mark Epstein, M.D., and Jonathan Leiff, M.D., discuss potential hazards. Leiff is a graduate of Yale College and the Harvard Medical School and is currently with the Boston University School of Medicine. Epstein, a psychiatrist at Cambridge Hospital, Harvard Medical School, wrote his undergraduate thesis on Theravadin Buddhist psychology and has practiced *vipassana* meditation for over a decade. The authors note the lack of public awareness concerning meditation hazards:

What has not been made clear, however, is the range of side effects of meditative practices that may present to the clinician as psychological disturbance. Some of these complications have already been noted by Western health professionals, others are only too well known within the meditative traditions. The most obvious misuses of meditation were hinted at by early psychoanalytic investigators, while the more subtle abuses and psychological crises of the advanced practitioner have traditionally been handled by the meditation teacher (454:137).

The authors' conclusions are based on their ten years of experience observing literally "hundred of meditators." They note that "practitioners of meditation, often swimming in the rhetoric of transformation, may fail to recognize the regressive nature of much of their experiences" (454:139). After a long discussion of the psychiatric complications noted in the literature,

they conclude with a significant observation: "Meditation may be conceptualized as a developmental process that may produce side effects anywhere along the continuum. Some of the side effects may be pathological in nature while some may be temporary distractions or hindrances," and they ask, "How can innocuous side effects of meditation be differentiated from debilitating ones?" (454:144-45).

The point is that they *cannot* be differentiated. The person who meditates in the Eastern or occult manner takes risks with his bodily health, his mental health, and his spiritual health, as a great deal of research and literature demonstrates (455/456/468/1064:182-84).

The following are some of the characteristics experienced at the deeper levels of a particular type of Buddhist *vipassana* meditation, but they are not unique to it. They include spontaneous movements, experiencing dramatic "energy flows," unusual breathing, dream and time changes, out-of-the-body experiences, and psychic phenomena. The descriptions given in the "spontaneous movement" category included much twitching, involuntary jerks, violent shaking, spontaneous yoga stretching, jerking, weird faces, drooling, pain, arms dancing, head rolling, falling over, violent shakes, loosening, and arms flapping like wings (456:41-45). On his own meditative journey, *vipassana* practitioner Jack Kornfield said, "[M]y arms started to involuntarily flap like I was a chicken or another bird. I tried to stop them and I could barely do it, and if I relaxed at all, they would flap. . . . For two days I sat there watching my arms flap" (759:155).

Meditators also described many other experiences, such as loss of body awareness, the body disappearing, leaving the body, the head detaching itself, the body growing huge, LSD-like visions, hallucinations, and visions of Buddha. Almost half of those completing student questionnaires reported "especially dramatic mood swings." These included huge releases of anger, "screaming mind trips," depression, fantastic mood swings, "turbulence of mind," "days of acute anxiety," "violent crying," restlessness, and "hellishness" (456:47-49).

It is hardly surprising that one hears about meditation-induced casualties, when the very process of meditation is *designed* to radically dismantle the divinely instituted functions of human perception. After all, if one refuses to play by the rules, one might expect problems.

Many of the horrors experienced by committed meditators are also revealed by Tal Brooke, the former leading Western disciple of India's premier guru, Sathya Sai Baba. Before receiving his graduate degree in religion from Princeton University, Brooke wrote *Riders of the Cosmic Circuit* (249), a little-known but urgently needed exposé unveiling much Eastern metaphysics for what they really are: forms of Satanism. But the power of the book also lies in documenting the hazards of many Eastern paths, including the radical breakdown of personal morality, suicides, and insanity (249:140-54,190-202).

These kinds of profoundly regressive states of consciousness are one reason for the confusion surrounding so-called "enlightenment,"* and how to properly evaluate it and distinguish it or its components from psychopathology (e.g., madness or insanity). Experiences of Eastern and occult "enlightenment" and mental illness are often so similar that even some New Agers are baffled at their correspondence (cf. Shamanism).

## PSYCHOPATHOLOGY

Properly evaluating the relationship between enlightenment* and psychopathology has been difficult for some people because what we commonly define as mental illness in the West is actually a sign or component of "enlightenment" in the East. In other words, many Eastern gurus* teach that periods of insanity *indicate* spiritual enlightenment! This is why it is called "divine madness." The Hindu guru Bhagwan Shree Rajneesh once quaintly remarked that many of his disciples were going to become zombies, and all to the good:

You be a Zombie. Be a perfect Zombie. . . . This is what is happening: catalepsy. . . .This is going to happen to many. Don't be afraid when it happens. . . . You become idiotic. . . . And [it is] good, because it will destroy the past. . . . That is the whole meaning of sannyas and discipleship:

That your past has been completely washed away—your memory, your ego, your identity— all has to go (861:11).

Meher Baba teaches that many of India's insane, the *Masts,* who in the West would be treated in mental hospitals, are in various stages of spiritual evolution. They are mad precisely because they are so spiritually committed to God (492:137-39). Meher Baba calls them the "God-intoxicated" ones. In the words of biographer and disciple C.B. Purdom:

They are in a state of mental and physical disorder because their minds are overcome by strong spiritual energies that are far too much for them, forcing them to renounce the world, normal human habits and customs, and civilized society, and to live in a condition of chaos. They are psychological cases beyond the reach of psychoanalysis, because their condition is too advanced and obscure for any known procedures. Their minds are in some way shattered and their brains cannot fully function. Only a spiritual Master, says Baba, who is aware of the divine spirit that possesses them, which causes them to be unfit for normal society, can be of any help to them, and even his help reaches them with difficulty as they are virtually shut off from human contact. They are in the world but not of it. In Baba's terms they are "God-intoxicated souls" (492:137).

Significantly, the *Masts* became mad from *meditative* practices, and during some of these practices it was "by sudden contact with a highly advanced spiritual being" (492:137). It is supposedly a "*divine* spirit that possessed them which causes them to be *unfit* for normal society" (492:137, emphasis added).

The famous Ramakrishna experienced insanity while undertaking his duties as a priest in the temple of Kali, and at many other times. During meditation he would experience a "divine delirium" and see demonic creatures emerging from him. For him, the truly enlightened soul often acts, in his words, "like a madman" (489:405; cf. p. 548).

Biographer Romain Rolland described part of Ramakrishna's experiences:

He was no longer capable of performing the temple rites. In the midst of the ritual acts he was seized with fits of unconsciousness, sudden collapses and petrifactions, when he lost the control of the use of his joints and stiffened into a statue.... Minute drops of blood oozed through his skin. His whole body seemed on fire.... He became the Gods himself.... He *was* the great monkey [god], Hanuman.

The legion of Gods swooped upon him like a whirlwind. He was torn in pieces. He was divided against himself. His madness returned tenfold. He saw demonic creatures emerging from him.... He remained motionless, watching these manifestations issue from him.... He felt madness approaching.... Two years went by in this orgy of mental intoxication and despair (490:36-37,41).

On his own path to enlightenment,* Gopi Krishna "passed through almost all the stages of different, mediumistic, psychotic, and other types of mind; [and] for some time [he] was hovering between sanity and insanity" (491:124). Da Free John extols the "divine madness" of his own gurus, Nityananda, Muktananda, and Rudrananda:

True yogis are living forceful beings. They are madmen, absolutely mad—and absolutely dangerous.... Look at Nityananda—he severed heads all his life.... Those who came to him ... were wiped out, torn apart.... My experience with people like Rudi, Muktananda, Nityananda, and others was like this: I would be sitting in my

house in New York by myself, and this force would enter me, it would practically break my neck, and my body and mind would be taken over. And I would walk around as Nityananda, as Rudi, as Muktananda, literally.... [T]hese wildmen served that process [of enlightenment] (946:275; cf. 945:256-58).

Such stories could be multiplied ad nauseam. This modern penchant to reinterpret demonism and insanity as "true spirituality" is illustrated in numerous books, such as by consciousness researchers Stanislav and Christina Grof (eds.) in *Spiritual Emergency: When Personal Transformation Becomes a Crisis* and *The Stormy Search for the Self.* Chapter titles from *Spiritual Emergency* include such items as "When Insanity Is a Blessing: The Message of Shamanism" (759:77-97). The introduction to the book informs us that pathological states of consciousness, when "properly understood and treated supportively," can produce "healing and have very beneficial effects on the people who experience them" (759:x). All of this illustrates the deep spiritual confusion now coursing throughout our nation. The East has indeed come West and the church must be prepared to deal with the consequences.

In conclusion, meditation today is almost universally seen as a positive path bringing physical or mental health and spiritual wholeness. Unfortunately, many of those who suffer from such an interpretation have little knowledge of either the occult tradition behind meditation or the dynamics of spiritual deception.

# MUSCLE TESTING

- Info at a Glance
- Introduction and Influence
- Nature and Use
- Psychic Connection
- Behavioral Kinesiology
- Chiropractic Influence
- Occult Potential

## INFO AT A GLANCE

Applied Kinesiology (AK), Touch For Health (TH), Behavioral Kinesiology (BK)

**Description.** Muscle testing is often a combination of chiropractic and Chinese acupuncture theory plus "muscle-testing" practices. It involves physical diagnosis, e.g., testing the supposed "strength" or "weakness" of muscles which are believed to be related to organ systems. And it may employ treatment or healing by acupressure, meridian tracing, "cosmic energies," or other dubious methods.

**Founder.** George Goodheart (AK), John Thie (TH), John Diamond (BK).

**How does it claim to work?** Muscle testing claims that disease can be evaluated, at least in part, through specific patterns of muscle weakness. It also claims to manipulate alleged body energies to produce and maintain healing. By supposedly "unblocking" congested energy along meridian pathways, or by infusing energy into deficient organs or bodily areas, practitioners believe that physical health can be maintained.

**Scientific evaluation.** Discredited.

**Examples of occult potential.** Manipulating invisible energies can easily become an occult practice, e.g., a form of psychic healing. In addition, many muscle testers employ pendulums, dowsing* instruments, and other radionics devices (276:117-18).

**Major problems.** Muscle testing rejects the known facts of human anatomy by accepting undemonstrated connections between muscles and specific organs and diseases; it also claims to regulate bodily energies whose existence has never been proven.

**Biblical/Christian evaluation.** Muscle testing is often based, in part, upon Taoist philosophy or other Eastern metaphysics, is scientifically discredited and potentially occult. It should be avoided on this basis.

**Potential dangers.** The attendant hazards of misdiagnosis and occult influences.

*Note:* This material is general and introductory. Modern "New Age" muscle testing methods must be distinguished from the scientific discipline of kinesiology proper. *Webster's Third New International Dictionary* and the *Encyclopaedia Britannica* both define formal kinesiology as "[the] study of the principles of mechanics and anatomy in relation to human movement" (1005). *Webster's New Twentieth Century Dictionary* defines it as "the science or study of human muscular movements, especially as applied in physical education" (1004:1002). While New Age muscle testing may or may not employ some of the methods of formal kinesiology, scientific kinesiology never employs the methods of New Age muscle testing. The two disciplines are based on an entirely different approach to physiology and health.

## INTRODUCTION AND INFLUENCE

On a windswept Sunday morning in Los Angeles, an articulate young Chinese woman surveys an audience of 2500 and asks for three volunteers. She has just concluded a message on the energy systems of the universe and their application to classical Chinese acupuncture. In return for braving the elements and leaving behind the Sunday *Times*, the audience now will be treated to a most unusual demonstration.

Two young women and an older man stand somewhat nervously onstage as the Chinese woman explains how applied kinesiology, or muscle testing, can demonstrate changes in one's life energy. With arms stretched forward and hands clasped, the first volunteer easily resists the speaker's efforts to pull her arms downward. Quickly, the speaker touches a few points around the head, and the startled volunteer's arms are pulled down without resistance. More points are touched, and strength returns as before.

The second woman is tested for arm strength. The speaker then places her hands in front of and behind the volunteer's head. Suddenly she passes her hands downward to the floor, like an illusionist making a magic pass over a box whose contents are about to disappear. After this is done, the second volunteer's arms drop with an apparently effortless pull. Then with a quick upward sweep of her hands, the Chinese woman restores the volunteer's strength as easily as she apparently drained it.

The third volunteer easily resists the arm pull, then waits as the woman walks behind him. Twice she gives a thumbs-up gesture behind him for the audience to see, followed by unchanged tests of strength. After a thumbs-down gesture, the surprised volunteer's arms

drop with an easy pull. Another thumbs-up signal, and complete resistance returns. The woman ends her presentation with an admonition to use such abilities for good. Later she informs a small group of bystanders that she did indeed lower the third volunteer's energy level simply by willing it to be done. "Is this magic?" one bystander asks.

"Only if you call it that," she answers.

The Chinese woman is Effie Poy Yew Chow, Ph.D., who has served as president of the East-West Academy of Healing Arts, as an appointed member of the former National Advisory Council to the Secretary of Health, Education and Welfare, and as organizer of a major conference on holistic health and public policy in Washington, D.C. (1:3-4).

The previous paragraphs began coauthor John Weldon's book with Dr. Paul and Teri Reisser, *New Age Medicine*, as an illustration of the "muscle testing" technique of holistic medicine. In its most basic form, "muscle testing" is one of the simplest to learn and most popular of all New Age health practices. Three kinds of muscle testing dominate the marketplace—applied kinesiology (AK), "Touch for Health" (TH), and behavioral kinesiology (BK).

AK was developed for health professionals by chiropractor George Goodheart in the 1950s. According to at least one source, Goodheart allegedly received some of his data on AK by psychic means (35:310), although we have also been told that he denies this. In the early 1970s, AK was popularized and made available to laymen by New Age chiropractor, John Thie, through his "Touch for Health" method. The third form, behavioral kinesiology, is an extended, if bizarre, application of AK, developed in the late 1970s by psychiatrist John Diamond.

In essence, applied kinesiology and "Touch for Health" are very similar. Behavioral kinesiology is a related but separate discipline that has greatly expanded the application of applied kinesiology while incorporating additional strange theories of diagnosis.

Muscle testing is often employed in conjunction with other New Age treatments. Because it is easily integrated with a wide variety of New Age health practices, it is frequently combined with other techniques as part of a "comprehensive" health treatment program. For example, naturopaths, chiropractors, reflexologists, iridologists, psychic healers, acupuncturists, and those using various forms of yoga* and bodywork techniques may all incorporate muscle testing in their treatment programs (188:85). And the "muscle testers" themselves often employ one or more additional methods of New Age health practice.

Like most New Age therapies, muscle testing is used for both diagnosis and treatment and stresses its "natural" approach to health by assisting the body's "innate" ability to heal itself through the "proper" regulation and maintenance of mystical life energies.

## NATURE AND USE

In part, muscle testing assumes that physical illness and disease result from a blockage or deficiency of psychic energy within the body. Thus, muscle testing claims to work by manipulating this mystical life energy (called *chi, prana,* the life force, and so on), which is supposedly circulating within the body. The purpose of manipulating these alleged energies is to cure illness and maintain health.

Muscle testing is also based on certain beliefs of chiropractic (including, in some forms, D.D. Palmer's theory of "Innate Intelligence"), and on ancient Taoism, in particular the meridian structures of classical Chinese acupuncture. It teaches that, if left untreated, blockages or imbalances of the body's "energies" (the "life force," or *chi*) eventually result in physical illness or aberrations.

One way to examine the condition of the "life energy" it is said, is through the body's muscles. Because specific organs are allegedly "connected" to specific muscles through the Chinese acupuncture meridian system, when these muscles are "tested" and discovered to be in a "weakened" condition, this is said to indicate that the muscle and its corresponding organ are deficient of *chi.* Thus, various methods of physical, intuitive,* or even psychic manipulation are

used to "test" muscle strength and to treat alleged energy imbalances.

Muscle testing is used in two basic ways: for prevention of illness and for treatment of existing problems. For example, muscle testing may be used to treat current specific symptoms. A patient may complain of back trouble or a stomach pain. By applying pressure against the corresponding muscle(s) thought to be related to the illness, the muscles may test "weak," indicating the underlying deficiency, or blockage, of cosmic energy. Treatment would employ acupressure methods (finger pressure applied to acupuncture points), or "hand passes" above the skin along specific acupuncture meridian lines related to the problem, which supposedly "unblocks" or "realigns" the energy imbalance and so restores health (see below). Muscle testers also claim that their methods can detect food allergies, dietary deficiencies, structural problems, and other physical maladies.

Muscle testing also purports to be used preventively to detect preclinical problems. In this case patients are encouraged to have a general diagnostic checkup, even when they feel fine. Here the therapist tests all major muscles to discover which ones are "weak." Proper treatment is then applied *before* the underlying "problem" has a chance to manifest outward illness on the physical level. Because it is believed that months, or even years, may pass before the blocked energy causes an illness, disease, or other problems, muscle testers encourage regular checkups.

## PSYCHIC CONNECTION

Some aspects of muscle testing may be indistinguishable from psychic diagnosis and healing. In applied kinesiology, chiropractor George Goodheart recommends a method called "therapy localization." Here, the hand is placed on the body over an alleged point of energy imbalance so that the practitioner can diagnostically "test" an area for a suspected problem. The hand is thought to become a sort of psychic "conduit," able to locate the point of impaired function, allowing the practitioner to successfully "treat" the symptom. Some practitioners claim that they use their hands to "sense" various energy imbalances in different organs, much in the manner used by practitioners of psychic healing. Goodheart calls "therapy localization" the "most astounding concept in applied kinesiology" (988:78) because it "is capable of identifying virtually all faults and dysfunctions that have an effect on the nervous system. These encompass everything from [chiropractic] subluxations of the spine to imbalances in the body's energy fields" (988:78).

Chiropractor John Thie teaches that "Touch for Health" can be performed in virtually the same manner as psychic healing. For example, in so-called meridian tracing, one can apparently regulate mystical energy flows by mental power alone. "In fact, you do not even have to make contact with the body. You can simply follow the meridians in your mind's eye, through concentration, and produce much the same effect" (34:36). He further teaches a common New Age belief that "we are all one with the universe, the universal energy. . . . Our bodies are literally this universal energy in some of its various forms" (34:99).

Most muscle testing, therefore, is simply a combination of or variation upon classical chiropractic/acupuncture theory and the ancient Chinese practice of acupressure, plus the novel approaches to muscle "weakness" developed by George Goodheart or John Diamond.

## BEHAVIORAL KINESIOLOGY

Behavioral kinesiology (BK), an outgrowth of George Goodheart's applied kinesiology, is the novel brainchild of John Diamond, M.D. *Family Circle* magazine is one of many popular newsstand periodicals that has carried glowing comments about its alleged "miraculous" powers (267). Famous personalities use it, and many athletes, dentists, artists, and New Agers swear by it.

Dr. Diamond himself argues that BK's magic is applicable to literally every area of life, which explains its wide appeal:

It provides us with the means of assessing and evaluating the effects of nearly all stimuli, internal or external, physical or psychological, on the body. Furthermore, it gives us a new understanding of the comprehensive action of the entire body energy system. There is no area of life to which BK does not apply. It even sheds light on such diverse topics as instinctive behavior, the creative process, the origin of language, anthropology, ethnology, the aesthetic experience, and modes of communication such as gesture (37:123).

BK is established on the basic philosophy of applied kinesiology: "Every major muscle of the body relates to an organ" (37:100), and that muscles and organs can be "tested" to determine the condition of the "life energy" flowing through the supposed meridians related to them.

By "muscle testing," BK claims that it is able to determine the "strengthening" or "weakening" effect of a vast array of objects upon a person's "life energy," from foods and other items to symbols and thoughts.

The centrality of the thymus gland is Dr. Diamond's unique contribution to applied kinesiology. His book is subtitled "How to Activate Your Thymus and Increase Your Life Energy." He calls the thymus gland "the seat of the Life Energy," and relates the supposed powers of the organ to knowledge derived from expanded consciousness and the ancient "gods." He even claims that his system "ushers in the Third Golden Age of Thymology" (37:29,128-30). "A major discovery of Behavioral Kinesiology is that the thymus gland monitors and regulates energy flow in the meridian system" (37:28).

The thymus is a lymphoid organ beneath the breastbone at heart level. In infants and children, it regulates the production of the lymphocytes, or white blood cells, that fight infection. After puberty, the gland atrophies and continues to do so until death. Its role in the immune system of infants and children is established, and it retains that function in adults. It might even be a more important organ than we know. Yet, despite Diamond's claims, it is not known to regulate mystical energies:

I have come to believe that all illness starts as a problem on the *energy level*, a problem that may exist for many years before it manifests itself in physical disease. It appears that a generalized reduction of body energy leads to energy imbalances in particular parts of the body (37:2).

What is the "life energy" that Diamond claims BK can regulate? It is the same old occult energy found in many different cultures:

Our Life Energy is the source of our physical and mental well-being . . . throughout recorded history it has had many names. . . . Paracelsus called it the *Archaeus*; the Chinese, *Ch'i;* the Egyptians, *Ka;* the Hindus, *Prana;* the Hawaiians, *Mana.* It is all the same thing (37:23).

Dr. Diamond believes we can use our thymuses to properly regulate our "life energy." Indeed, everything in our personal world—from objects, to emotions and habits, to environments, lifestyles, and even beliefs—can and probably should be tested to determine if they "increase" or "decrease" our all-important "life energy." For example, we can "test" the effect of the type of music we listen to, how to walk or swim properly, the color to paint our house, which tooth to have pulled, which medicine to use, which foods to eat, and which vitamins or homeopathic treatments to take. Apparently, we can even use BK tests to prevent or detect heart disease or cancer (37:8-13,47) and treat them— the list seems endless. We can even test for individual lifestyles:

For many years I have used BK to investigate the environments, lifestyles, and personal habits of a wide variety of people. My findings have been generally consistent . . . by all means test them for yourself. . . . If the muscle goes weak, then you know that the stimulus has interrupted the energy flow to your thymus gland and thereby reduced the energy in your entire body-energy system (37:74).

The quack aspect of BK is easy to document. Consider the following claims, as reported on pp. 74-106 of Dr. Diamond's book. Thymus tests supposedly reveal that your life energy is:

| Increased By: | Decreased By: |
|---|---|
| Head nods (vertical) | Head shakes (horizontal) |
| Smiling (or merely seeing a drawing or picture of a smile) | Frowns (or merely seeing a drawing or a picture of one) |
| Seeing normal faces | Seeing "sanpaku" eyes (with three sides of white visible around the eye) |
| The swastika | The Roman cross |
| Organic foods | Synthetic or refined foods (the more foods are processed, "the less, if any, Life Energy will remain in them") (37:107) |

*Life energy is also decreased by:*

The musical note C

Sunglasses

Electric wristwatches
(but only in certain positions)

Most hats

High-heeled shoes

Ice water/cold showers

Microwaves

Police "speed gun" detectors
(effective within 100 feet)

Perfume

Artificial light

And (surprise!) people do not respond well to breathing gas fumes!

If you want to find out whether you are affected by cooking gas, just go over to the stove and see whether the indicator muscle goes weak first before and then after you turn on the front burner. It's as simple as that. Your body's answer is immediate and direct (37:80).

And according to BK, not just cooking gas, but most things in our modern technological world are conspiring against us, depleting our "life energy" (37:7). Anyone who believes all this is welcome to his views. But consider the following incredible claims and explanations offered by Dr. Diamond.

Concerning the Nazi swastika (a symbol which BK says will *increase* our life energy!), "Even Jewish concentration camp survivors test strong in its presence..." (37:91). Goodness, can the people who survived the torments of Nazi Germany's death camps really have their "life energy" *increased* while looking at the symbol of their destruction? And why on earth would the Christian cross supposedly deplete our life energy? Furthermore, the clockwise swastika will supposedly have a different result on people than the counterclockwise swastika (37:91).

Dr. Diamond also thinks that facial gestures, such as smiles and frowns, are related to the ancient Chinese acupuncture meridians. Smiles or frowns supposedly regulate life energy because "all gestures relate to specific meridians; these gestures of acceptance and rejection relate directly to the thymus, the monitoring center for energy imbalances of the entire meridian system" (37:49). Perhaps the National Academy of Sciences should look into all this.

If the previous ideas are not silly enough, consider that people with depleted energy can deplete others' thymus energy just by being in their presence, even through the television set!

Somehow the Life Energy of the "strong" person was diminished by his coming into personal contact with someone with a weak thymus. Not only this: If you test various meridian (energy system) test points throughout the bodies of the interacting subjects, you will find that a specific imbalance can be transmitted from one person to another (37:60).

To be weakened by another person, you need not be face to face or even one to one. Your involvement can, for example, be over television. ...If a public figure has a specific energy (meridian) imbalance or an underactive thymus, he can adversely affect a large number of people [i.e., the TV audience]. An emotional state, negative or positive, can spread through a community and even a country from its primary source, the television personality, to the viewers, to their neighbors, and to all the people with whom they come in contact. If we are susceptible—of low Life Energy—we can pick up like an infection the emotional attitudes that are "going around" (37:65).

A photo of Adolf Hitler will "destroy your thymus" but, remember, the Nazi swastika energizes it (37:66,88-91). Advertisements can weaken you, and two slightly different portraits of the same person can have exactly opposite effects on your thymus, depending on whether you are looking at the original or a copy (37:66). Symbols must also be carefully evaluated. "Through the techniques of BK I have been able to demonstrate the effects of hundreds of symbols on the body. Each affects a specific energy system" (37:86). And although most rock music greatly decreases life energy, "In contrast, the Beatles never do" (37:100). Amazing. And refined white sugar is *always* bad. "*A poison is a poison!* So get out of the habit of thinking: 'Well, a little sugar won't hurt me.' A substance either raises your energy or lowers it. It is one way or the other" (37:115).

Occasionally, even Dr. Diamond runs into trouble with his theory. For example, sometimes people will test strong with refined sugar and weak with raw honey. "This paradoxical finding is hard to explain" (37:107), as are other even more bizarre BK principles than the ones we have discussed (37:40-43,54-55,70-73,83).

It should again be stressed again that the use of the term "kinesiology" in muscle-testing practices involves an entirely different application than in formal kinesiology, which is the scientific study of bodily movements and the muscles which control them. Applied kinesiology, "Touch for Health," and behavioral kinesiology are a distortion of scientific kinesiology, although they may employ its methods and insights. New Age kinesiology and scientific kinesiology are opposed to one another in the same way that New Age medicine* and scientific medicine are opposed to one another. The former is based on mystical energy concepts and various novel, even bizarre, practices; the latter restricts itself to physical medicine regulated by the scientific method. Confusing them will be consequential.

## CHIROPRACTIC INFLUENCE

Chiropractic can be safe and effective for a number of muscular and related conditions when used responsibly by adequately trained chiropractors. Unfortunately, there is another side to chiropractic, as we documented in *Can You Trust Your Doctor?* (1590). Not unexpectedly, the chiropractic profession is almost single-handedly responsible for the introduction and promotion of muscle testing in America. John Thie, the developer of "Touch for Health," states that "most of these [Touch for Health] methods and techniques have been exclusively the province of the chiropractic profession" (36:4). A text on applied kinesiology confesses, "Most applied kinesiologists are chiropractors" (276:9).

Muscle testing was developed by chiropractors and is often taught at chiropractic schools. We have mentioned that George Goodheart was the chiropractor who may have used psychic methods to develop his system of applied kinesiology, that New Age chiropractor John Thie popularized it (with Goodheart's help; 36:2), and that John Diamond, an understudy of Goodheart (276:139), took applied kinesiology and extended its principles into his strange system of behavioral kinesiology (37:6-7).

It is important to understand the logical connection between chiropractic, the potential for dabbling in the psychic world, and muscle testing. Classical chiropractic theory easily lends itself to the acceptance of a psychic realm as related to health. (We documented this in *Can You Trust Your Doctor?*; 1590). That Goodheart might have used psychic means to develop his system of applied kinesiology would not be surprising. Furthermore, although elements of the chiropractic profession are scientifically oriented and practiced responsibly, chiropractic itself often rejects the safeguards of the scientific method; historically, it has opposed medical science and rejected any findings disproving its theories. Chiropractic, for example, was founded upon a false theory of subluxations being the cause of all disease, and its early concept of the "Innate" is difficult to distinguish from psychic energy in general.

Thus, the two characteristics that have strongly influenced chiropractic historically—the rejection of medical science and an openness to the psychic—help explain the unscientific and New Age orientation of much modern chiropractic practice. It is hardly surprising, then, that chiropractic would be the principal agent for advancing the practice of an unscientific and/or psychically based system of muscle testing in the United States.

The ease with which chiropractic and New Age muscle testing are blended can be seen in the many books advocating a union of the two, such as the Valentines' *Applied Kinesiology* (276), chiropractor David S. Walther's *Applied Kinesiology: The Advanced Approach in Chiropractic* (Pueblo, CO: privately published, 1976), and Chiropractor Fred Stoner's *The Eclectic Approach to Chiropractic* (Las Vegas: privately published, 1976). Walthers is author of the "definitive textbook" on AK, *Basic Procedures and Muscle Testing*:

> Goodheart's original research is now being expanded, and more investigations are being carried out by many of his fellow chiropractors, hundreds of whom are finding applied kinesiology of inestimable value in their practices as a diagnostic aid. It is a fast and reliable way to discern where structural imbalances lie, to access dietary deficiencies and allergies, to detect organ dysfunctions, and even determine the extent to which psychological factors are involved (987:44).

## OCCULT POTENTIAL

Each of these systems variously accepts the occult idea of a mystical "life energy" flowing through the body. Although promoters may attempt to explain it scientifically, they accept the unproven premise of ancient Chinese Taoism and of much occultism, which teaches that psychic or mystical energy (*chi, prana, mana,* and so on) flows along energy pathways in the body called meridians.

As a result, applied kinesiology, "Touch for Health," and behavioral kinesiology are based upon an unfounded and unscientific concept, involving the same mystical life energies promoted in the occult and Eastern religion. Because these methods claim to manipulate invisible energies, some of the practices employed are indistinguishable from those used by psychic and spiritistic healers. This is why muscle testing may introduce people to psychic or spiritistic practices under another name, or influence them to seek out practitioners of these other forms of so-called "natural healing."

We believe that any system which claims to regulate or manipulate "invisible energies" is, at least potentially, an introduction to occult energies and should be avoided. Since these methods are not based upon the findings of scientific medicine, they are unscientific, whether or not they introduce someone to the occult (1:79-89).

In *New Age Medicine*, Reisser, Reisser, and Weldon discuss why AK, BK, TH, and related methods should not be accepted uncritically, and why they should be avoided:

We strongly urge that patients avoid any therapists who claim to be manipulating invisible energies (Ch'i, life energy or whatever), whether using needles, touch, hand passes, arm-pulling or any other maneuver.

Why do we take such a hard-nosed stand? For two reasons. First, we have seen how the invoking of life energy, especially in the spin-offs from applied kinesiology, throws critical thinking to the wind. Therapists who use such techniques have strayed far from the mainstream of objective knowledge about the human body. Their "science" is based on conjecture, subjective impressions, unreliable data and, most importantly, the precepts of Taoism. They stand separate from the scientific community. You will never see muscle testing written up in *Scientific American* or recognized by the National Institutes of Health. We challenge anyone who is involved in this therapy to take a hard look at its origins, its underlying assumptions, and its supporting evidence (or lack thereof).

Our look at Jin Shin Do provided an example of our second objection: the general orientation of the literature which promotes the doctrines of Ch'i and meridians. The overwhelming majority of authors express a distinct spiritual perspective which is some variation on Eastern

mysticism or the New Consciousness. We have seen no exceptions to date. John Thie, originator of Touch for Health, proclaims in *Science of Mind* magazine that "we are all one with the universe." Iona Teeguarden and her spirit guide tell us how Jin Shin Do can open our psychic centers to experience the universal flow which is love and magic. Hiroshi Motoyama, a Japanese physician, acupuncturist, and psychic researcher, is actively seeking to unify ancient Chinese medicine, East Indian kundalini yoga, and virtually all other psychic or mystical experiences into a single "science of consciousness." Psychic healer and medium Rosalyn Lee Bruyere, mentioned previously, claims to "see" auras, chakras, and meridians, and manipulates the latter two in her practice. Under the direction of two spirit guides who instruct her regularly, she teaches a blend of psychic healing, spiritism, reincarnation, and Eastern mysticism. The pattern is unmistakable. There is no neutral "science" of life energy and meridians, but rather a highly developed mystical system with strong ties to the psychic realm.

What does all this mean? It means that energy therapists, whether they realize it or not, are carrying out a form of religious practice and conditioning their patients to accept its teachings. Indeed, some therapists enter a trancelike state in order to become a channel to direct Ch'i (or whatever they choose to call life energy) into the patient. The idea of the healer's injecting invisible energy into another person may seem innocuous to most (and silly to some), but the results may be anything but trivial. Brooks Alexander, co-director of the Spiritual Counterfeits Project, warns:

It is not difficult to see that . . . psychic manipulation could turn an otherwise benign form of treatment into a spiritual booby trap. The nature of the doctor-patient relationship implicitly involves a kind of trust in and submission to the healer on many levels. For a Christian to accept the passive stance of "patient" before a practitioner who exercises spiritual power (either in his own right or as a channel for other influences) could easily result in spiritual derangement or bondage.

We find it particularly unsettling to see members of the Christian community having their energies balanced by chiropractors and other therapists who claim a Christian commitment and who feel that they are not involved in any questionable practices. These practitioners may claim that Ch'i, yin and yang, and meridians are neutral components of God's creation (similar to electricity and radio waves), available for anyone to use; but they ignore the roots of these ideas.

The products of natural science—the technologies of electronics, biochemistry and so on—can be validated by controlled experiments whose results are not tied to the religious beliefs of the researcher. But the "technology" of life energy is totally defined by the belief system of its promoters: the mystics, the psychics and the leaders of the New Consciousness.

Christian energy balancers present us with a paradox. They claim reliance on Scripture, but they carry out the practices of an occult system. Most are sincere in their desire to help their patients. Unfortunately, they lack discernment, failing to see the implication of the ideas they promote. Some are even dabbling in the psychic realm, diagnosing disease through hand passes or over long distances, claiming that this is a natural by-product of their sensitivity to life energy.

To these therapists we offer a challenge and a warning. Take a long look at the world of Chinese medicine and then decide whether you belong there. Do you feel comfortable as a part of the New Consciousness movement, promoting Taoist philosophy, supporting a system whose basic message is that "all is one," and helping usher in the New Age of miracles and magic? If not, then it is time to stop participating in therapies which lend credence and support to a world view which is antagonistic to the most basic teachings of Scripture (1:93-95).

In conclusion, muscle-testing practices are scientifically unestablished or discredited and potentially occult. Therefore, they are not true healing methods. And due to their reliance on "mystical energies," they are vehicles for introducing ancient pagan concepts or irrational approaches to medicine into modern health care.

# NEW AGE EDUCATION

## INFO AT A GLANCE

**Description.** Transpersonal or "New Age" education (the terms are not necessarily equivalent) incorporates spiritual methods into children's learning that are characteristically based on Eastern mysticism and certain aspects of occult practice. Various forms of transpersonal and humanistic psychology may also be advocated.

**Founder.** None per se. Transpersonal education seems to have developed as a result of 1) the terrible crises in modern education, which has opened the doors to experimentation with new methods, and 2) the revival of Eastern and occult practices in American culture.

**How does it claim to work?** Transpersonal educators claim that their methods will improve the children's self-esteem, their learning abilities and potential, and, among other things, expand their horizons and help them become better citizens of a global community.

**Scientific evaluation.** Subject to interpretation. In some areas of research (e.g., humanistic education) a good deal of work has been done. However, this must be evaluated carefully from a biblical perspective to understand both the reasons for and implication of favorable outcomes. Teaching or counseling children by means of Eastern or occult practices and psychotherapeutic or humanistic methods may "work," but in what manner and at what cost spiritually?

**Examples of occult potential.** It appears that a large number of different Eastern religious and occult methods are utilized throughout New Age education.

**Major problems.** 1) The promotion of religion in the public school classroom is a violation of federal law; 2) the disguising of religious methods and beliefs under secular or neutral terminology; 3) the use of unsubstantiated and inappropriate psychotherapeutic methods is a violation of the Hatch Amendment; 4) self-esteem programs, values clarification methods, affective education, and related trends are either ineffective, morally bankrupt, or potentially harmful.

**Biblical/Christian evaluation:** Educational philosophies or methods based on Eastern or occult philosophy, or inappropriate psychotherapeutic methods, are to be avoided.

**Potential dangers:** Emotional or spiritual harm may come to the child through the use of either questionable psychotherapeutic techniques or Eastern or occult practices (278).

*Note:* The following material is excerpted and condensed (with new material added) from the authors' *Thieves of Innocence* (Harvest House, 1993, with Craig Branch), which evaluates and documents areas not discussed or not fully discussed in this chapter (e.g., Quest, DUSO, Pumsy, DARE, and other programs, as well as affective education and psychotherapy in the classroom, countering objections, parental strategies, and so on).

This chapter primarily documents the increasing influence of New Age or transpersonal education in modern public schools and critiques this dangerous approach scientifically, biblically, and legally. Further descriptions and evaluations of the practices advocated in New Age education can be found throughout other chapters of this text, such as altered states of consciousness, astrology, channeling, dream work, hypnosis, martial arts, meditation, New Age inner work, shamanism, and visualization.

## INTRODUCTION AND INFLUENCE

A 1992 U.S. Department of Education press release observed the following: "In spite of the increased investment in education spending by all levels of government in recent years, there has been no corresponding improvement in student achievement" (2234). For example, in 1960 we spent 16 billion dollars on education, and our schools were the envy of the world. In 1990, a short 30 years later, we spent 200 billion dollars and our schools ranked among the worst of the industrialized nations. Significantly, a 1995 report on "20/20" and additional research have documented that the traditional educational methods used a generation ago are much more effective for teaching children than modern approaches. Unfortunately teachers and especially administrators have intentionally rejected reintroducing these effective methods because they aren't considered "progressive" enough! It is a sad commentary when educators summarily dismiss methods that work for those that don't, merely because of unfounded perceptions.

What happened to the quality of our education? In *The Devaluing of America*, former Secretary of Education William J. Bennett argues that the inferiority of American public school education is also partly a result of our modern scorn for the public expression of religious values and our abandonment of morality. And the result is that in the last 30 years we have turned our schools into secularist institutions that have demeaned the very principles that work in society's best interests. Thus, today, "The extreme to which educators go to deny the place of religion in American life is mind-boggling. . . . [Yet] we cannot deny in our public schools that from the Judeo-Christian tradition come our values, our principles, and the spirit of our institutions. That tradition and the American tradition are wedded. When we have disdain for our religious tradition, we have disdain for ourselves" (2235:79,81).

To abandon the values and principles of the past is to leave empty that which was once occupied. What has replaced traditional American principles? Almost anything. And in large measure this explains the direction—and problem—of education in our nation today. This also explains why many parents are surprised when they discover what their children are being exposed to in public schools.

In the end, classroom education reflects the values of the culture. If national polls reveal that

70 percent to 80 percent of adults reject the idea of moral absolutes, then this perspective, and all its consequences, can't help but find its way into children's education. If our culture is increasingly turning to the occult and Eastern practices, this will also impact education.

This chapter takes a critical look at certain trends in education as they relate to particular occult, religious, psychological, moral, or scientific issues. Our basic concern is to evaluate two key trends, which may be termed the *transpersonal* ("beyond the person") and *humanistic* approaches to education. The transpersonal method is sometimes known as "New Age" education and employs various Eastern or occult beliefs and techniques to allegedly help children develop their "full potential." The humanistic trend incorporates a secular and/or psychological approach that usually stresses: 1) "values clarification," or an allegedly morally neutral approach toward helping children develop their own values independently; 2) the importance of fostering a child's self-esteem; 3) the use of various psychotherapeutic techniques, such as those incorporated in affective education or hypnotic methods.

But the fact that transpersonal education is "religious" and humanistic education is "secular" does not mean that these approaches operate independent of one another. What we find is a significant degree of overlap so that transpersonal and humanistic approaches are often used together. The question is whether either approach is in the best interests of our children.

For example, by opening children to certain New Age methods and beliefs what else are we teaching them about how to live their lives? Consider that popular techniques like guided imagery and progressive relaxation are also methods encouraged by the spirit world as ways to become channelers or mediums. By teaching children to use these procedures are we also preconditioning at least some of them to be open to contacting spirits?

Our basic concern is that educational programs and methods, which may not be in the student's best interest, be examined critically by all concerned. For example, according to James Dobson's "Focus on the Family" publication, *The Arkansas Citizen*:

The DUSO and Pumsy programs are by far the most prevalent New Age curricula as of yet uncovered in Arkansas.... Both DUSO and Pumsy have been removed from schools in other states for "their religious" nature. ... [S]chool administrators fail to see the Hinduistic traits in these [programs'] relaxation techniques [even though any] encyclopedia of Hinduism will show the uncanny resemblance Hatha yoga steps have to the relaxation exercises in DUSO and Pumsy. Tensing and relaxing of muscles, deep breathing, meditation, and even the lotus and cobra positions are all identical (2236:1; cf. 2243:51–76).

What can concerned parents do? It is important to remember that effective influence starts by having accurate information. It is also important to become acquainted with the members of the board of education and your child's teachers and principal. What are their qualifications? What are their backgrounds? Have they made statements that would indicate what their personal philosophies are? What do they see as the role and function of education? Are they aware of any covert spiritual or religious ideas in programs or methods? What is the history and mind-set of the school system itself? What about other unconventional educational methods that may constitute undiscerned aspects of a school's philosophy? For example, the occult-oriented Waldorf schools have a unique set of educational presuppositions and methods that radically condition their educational approach. Also, the New Age interpretation of Montessori education must be warned against.

Introduce yourself to school board members, teachers, and the principal. Let them know who you are. Acquaint them with your concerns. Do everything you can to establish good rapport. Unless it is relevant, don't approach secular school officials on religious grounds; evaluate each controversial curriculum on its own merits. Always approach school officials with the attitude that this is a cooperative effort between parents and school administrators to improve the quality of the school and of children's education. There is nothing as refreshing as an informed, concerned parent who has something of substance to offer when a school or board is facing a challenge.

When you do find programs, teachers, resources, or other features of the educational system which are good, be certain to express your approval. This can be done in many ways, such as writing letters of commendation or thank-you letters to all involved. In essence, your best support for the school system should include a continuing active interest in your child's daily education (2237).

## PROGRESSIVE RELAXATION, GUIDED IMAGERY, INNER COUNSELORS

"You can only have a new society, the visionaries have said, if you change the education of the younger people. . . ."

Marilyn Ferguson in
*The Aquarian Conspiracy;* 301:280

"What did you do in school today?" used to be asked without fear by parents. But if some parents dropped in at school during the week and listened in, they might have good reason to be alarmed. They may find something like the following scene:

It is 1990 and the kindergarten class sits eagerly on the floor. They are going through a visualization exercise created by the Science Research Associates. Lesson 10 is called *The Witches Ride.* Bobo, the central figure in the story, wakes up and sees 12 witches in a hut across from his window. Each witch in turn mounts a broom crying, "Fly me faster than a fairy, without God, without Saint Mary" and soars "gracefully" off.

Bobo goes over and imitates the 12 witches with the same chant using the remaining broomstick. As he chants, "Without God, without Saint Mary," he, too, soars gracefully off.

Soon the object lesson comes: "But, alas, he was not called a bobo for nothing. In his great glee he muddled the words, and said to the broomstick "Fly me faster than a fairy—Fly *with* God and *good* Saint Mary." No sooner were these words out of his mouth than the broomstick began to fall (2239:11).

Here Bobo found power from rejecting God; he also found impotence and fear by speaking about God, even innocently. The lesson seems obvious, though never directly stated.

In November of 1988 we received a letter from a couple involved in researching a program used in elementary schools in Florida and other states. This program used tapes called "Quieting Reflex and Success Imagery." A mother had told this couple that her little girl had contacted an inner guide through the hypnotic techniques used in this program. The daughter commented, "My 'wise person' told me not to pray in the name of Jesus anymore." Furthermore, this "wise person" was not the guide that the little girl had chosen for herself but rather someone that had appeared unexpectedly and spontaneously in her consciousness. It claimed that it resided in the corner of a "safe place" in her mind. But it proceeded to command her to do "mean and nasty things." The mother was distraught and had no idea what to do.

Consider a less blatant but more widespread illustration of some of the latest trends in classroom education. The guidance counselor comes into the second grade class and the regular teacher leaves. The counselor is there as part of the mandatory requirement by the state, to enhance the children's self-esteem and their ability to solve problems. The counselor turns off the lights and begins to play an audiotape. A deep, slow, soothing voice comes in saying, "Hello—today I am going to teach you how to relax. First find a comfortable place to lie down where you will not be disturbed. (Pause) Be sure your clothing is not tight. (Pause) Now let's start our new adventure." The voice begins telling the children to slowly tighten and loosen their muscles alternately.

"Now I'm going to teach you how to relax your whole body. (Pause) Being relaxed is such a nice feeling—it's just like floating on a cloud. (Soothing harp music begins.) Take a deep breath—hold it (Pause) and now let it go," the voice whispers.

The voice continues to instruct the children to tighten their muscles and relax, take deep breaths and let them go. "It feels so good to relax

411

and let go—the more you do this, the more peaceful and calm you will become. Now while you are relaxed and your eyes are closed, take a deep breath—hold it—let it go." The voice leads the children to repeat this in a slow-rhythmic cadence.

"You are now in a deep state of relaxation. (Pause) Remain there for a few seconds, deeply, totally relaxed. (Pause) Now you will go still deeper. Imagine yourself going down a staircase. Starting at the top, you will slowly go down ten stairs, one at a time, each stair going into a deeper state of relaxation.

"Remember this feeling of being deeply relaxed so that in the future you can return to it in a matter of seconds. (Pause) Today we are going to a magic mountain. (Pause) The sun is warm and bright and it feels so good on your face. (Pause) There is no wind and the mountains are calm and still. (Pause) They have been here for so many years—longer than you, your father or your mother. (Pause)

"The mountains seem so sure of themselves—just as you do with your own self-power.

"It's so quiet way up here—you are very safe here—it's your very own mountain for no one else can come up here. (Pause) Look over to your right to the mountain next to you. (Pause) Use your own mind self-power to take you there.

"Now I want to share with you a secret. (Pause) The secret is called believing in yourself—in your self-power. (Pause) With it you can do anything—it works like magic.

"Now take a deep breath and say to yourself, 'I am peaceful.' (Pause) Feel peace flow all through you. (Pause)

"Today as you travel to your safe secret place in the mountain, you find something new waiting for you. (Pause) A little white rabbit with pink eyes and long ears watches you from nearby grass. (Pause) He wants to be your friend. (Pause)

"We know that rabbits don't talk but this rabbit is very special. (Pause) You don't actually have to use words between you, but you can understand each other's thoughts. (Pause) He is a very wise rabbit and he has answers to any questions. (Pause) If you have a question to ask him, ask him in your mind. (Pause) Stay very relaxed and you will hear his answer. (Pause)

"Why don't you ask him how he knows so many things—how he got so wise. (Pause) He answers, 'Let me take you to my secret place and I'll tell you.' (Pause)

"As you both sit in a white light coming through the trees, you watch bubbles gurgling up in a pond. (Pause) White rabbit tells you that these bubbles come from underground springs, deep below the surface, and they feed the pool. (Pause) He tells you that you too have deep underground springs and this is where answers to your questions come from. (Pause)

"And then you ask, 'How do you ask your questions and how do you get your answers?' (Pause) Friend rabbit says, 'First I come to my secret place and get very quiet. (Pause) I make my body very relaxed and my mind very quiet, and then I ask my question. (Pause) Sometimes I hear the answer in words, and sometimes I just feel the answers.' (Pause) It's getting late now and you must soon return to the outside world—but you can return here anytime you wish."

What you have just read is a portion of a transcript from a program being used in elementary schools all over the country, titled "Peace, Harmony, and Awareness" (2240). Does this technique, known as progressive relaxation and guided imagery, sound at all familiar?

Perhaps you saw the "Oprah Winfrey Show" when she had Shirley MacLaine on, explaining her spiritual journey into the New Age Movement, channeling, and Eastern mysticism. Oprah asked Shirley, "What questions were you asking yourself, that needed answers?"

Shirley responded with, "Who am I, where am I going, what is life all about, where do I go when I die?"

"And when you asked the questions," Oprah said, "how did the answers come?"

"Well," MacLaine said, smiling, "first I had to learn how to meditate. I had to be very quiet, to be still, and then BOOM, the answers would come to me."

What you read above is also common to induction techniques for meditation* and hypnosis.* In fact, meditation, hypnosis, progressive relaxation, and guided imagery or visualization have more commonalities than many people realize. A leading authority on hypnosis, Dr.

Martin Orne, coauthor of the *Encyclopaedia Britannica* article on hypnosis, points out that "guided imagery is just another term for hypnosis" (2283). Patricia Carrington of Princeton University says, "It is possible that in the broadest sense of the term, meditation is a form of hypnosis" (844:496). Yet young children all over the country are having these hypnotic techniques imposed on them, even by well-meaning educators.

However, these techniques are also taught by the spirit world as a means to become a channeler, i.e., one who is possessed by spirits in order to allow the spirits to "channel" information out of them. Many examples can be seen in books like *Opening to Channel*, a text dictated by two spirits, "Orin" and "DaBen," through their human mediums specifically to teach people how to become channelers (see Channeling). What these spirits encourage is no different than what New Age educators are now teaching children. In the example below, we cite a guided imagery and relaxation exercise. (For an example of hypnosis, meditation, and visualization exercises recommended by the spirits, see the respective chapters.) Remember, what you read below are the words of the spirits themselves:

*Exercise from Orin and DaBen*

### Achieving a Relaxed State

**Goal:** This exercise is basic preparation for going into trance. We want your experience of channeling to be relaxing, easy, and joyful. . . .

Steps:

1. Find a comfortable sitting position, either on a chair or the floor, which you can easily hold for ten or fifteen minutes.

2. Close your eyes and begin breathing calmly and slowly, taking about twenty slow, rhythmic, connected breaths into your upper chest.

3. Let all your concerns go. Imagine them vanishing. Every time a thought comes up, imagine it on a blackboard, then effortlessly erase it, or imagine putting each thought into a bubble that floats away.

4. Relax your body. Feel yourself growing serene, calm, and tranquil. In your imagination, travel through your body, relaxing each part. Mentally relax your feet, legs, thighs, stomach, chest, arms, hands, shoulders, neck, head, and face. Let your jaw be slightly open, and relax the muscles around your eyes.

5. Put up a bubble of white light around you. Imagine its size, shape, and brightness. Play with making it larger and smaller until it feels just right. . . . [U]sually it is sufficient to practice every day for twenty minutes or so for one to two weeks to grow accustomed to deeper relaxation and inner stillness. This regime is not absolutely essential, but helps you become accustomed to the state of mind that is best for a guide's entry (575:68-69).

While directed relaxation and guided imagery are not necessarily occult practices in themselves, they are common tools for learning to channel spirits. So what exactly are we teaching our children when these methods are practiced in a New Age or human potential context? Are we preparing them to become comfortable with channeling exercises? If children are simultaneously taught about contacting "inner guides or counselors," "inner wisdom," and one's so-called "wise self" or "higher self," are we not preparing them to accept the possibility of spirit guides operating under another name? (In some ways, the "wise rabbit" in the exercise cited above is not so different from the "power animal" who becomes the sorcerer's spirit guide in shamanism*.) And if educators discover that such methods "work" and are "educational," will they fail to use them on children?

The following five sections give examples to prove that the influence of New Age methods in education is substantial. (Note to reader: Because so many people remain unconvinced that there really is a New Age agenda in public schools, the following material is primarily for purposes of documentation. Some readers may wish merely to peruse this material and then to proceed to the next section, "Evaluation.")

## NATIONAL CONFERENCES

The first national conference on holistic education, "Mind: Evolution or Revolution? The Emergence of Holistic Education," was held in 1979 and was sponsored by the Mandala Society and the National Center for the Exploration of Human Potential in cooperation with the University of California, San Diego.

Consider what the conference speakers said and did. New Age humanist George Leonard, past president of the Association for Humanistic Psychology and the author of *Education and Ecstasy*, led 600 educators in energy centering and channeling exercises, altered states of consciousness,* and "crystalline exercises" (2232:21-27). Family therapist Virginia Satir led them in directed visualization* (2232:71-73). New Age scientist and educator Robert Samples spoke on planetary consciousness, "holonomic knowing," and how New Age education "encompasses all the spheres of knowing, validated or not" (2232:54). Psychiatrist and transcendental meditation promoter Harold Bloomfield spoke about the importance of educators to engaging in personal self-transformation in order to radically transform school systems because we are now "in the dawn of an Age of Enlightenment" (2232:90-93). Educator Marc Robert, administrative consultant and management trainer for the Los Angeles Unified School District, spoke about the importance of first changing *parents* as the means to implement New Age education into school systems (232:108).

At the second annual conference, held in 1980, occultist and educator Joseph Chilton Pearce, author of *The Magical Child* and *The Bond of Power*, castigated conventional childhood education as a sickness and proposed that children be taught the principles of yoga* and occult meditation* (2233:13-18). Educator Anastas Harris, executive director of the National Center for the Exploration of Human Potential, argued that New Age education "is the ultimate tool in preventative health care" (2233:22). The late noted educator Beverly Galyean received numerous federal and private grants to implement what she termed "confluent education" in Los Angeles city schools. She spoke on the importance of confluent education, which uses experience-oriented, inner-directed psychological methods, such as meditation,* visualization,* guided imagery, and self-esteem exercises (2233:55-59). (Elsewhere, Galyean also promoted astrology, Eastern mysticism, and spiritism.) Afred A. Bar-

rios spoke on Self-Programmed Control (SPC), which has been used in many primary and secondary schools. SPC teaches children how to use teachings like occult pendulums (cf. Dowsing), rapid breathing, and hand levitation as ways to expose them to the power of their minds (2233:74-76). Creative education teacher Patricia Gordon encouraged the use of altered states of consciousness,* meditation, dream work,* self-hypnosis,* visualization, centering, and psychic development in college curriculums (2233:83). The above is only a small sampling of the kinds of methods advocated at such conferences.

## EDUCATIONAL TEXTS

The philosophy of transpersonal education is characterized by viewing schools and other learning environments as places to develop "spiritual potential." Spiritual potential is defined as an extremely broad set of philosophies and practices that include Eastern religion,* meditation, spiritism, and so on. In fact, most aspects of the occult can be incorporated under the transpersonal umbrella.

Consider an earlier standard text, *Transpersonal Education: A Curriculum for Feeling and Being*, edited by James Fadiman and Gay Hendricks. In the chapter "Transpersonal Psychology and Education" educators Thomas B. Roberts and Francis V. Clark concede that the domain of transpersonal education involves a new image of man and a new worldview incorporating such things as altered states of consciousness, meditation, self-realization, parapsychology, and psychic phenomena, as well as other cultures and their psychologies (especially Eastern psychologies), and "newly discovered forms of energy" (2261:4). Transpersonal education is thus heavily influenced by both humanistic education and transpersonal psychology, again, an Eastern or occult approach to human psychology and development.

One definition of transpersonal education given by Hendricks and Fadiman is "an approach that aims at the concurrent development of the logical and the mystical, the analytical and intuitive" (2261:1). We are told that exploring altered states of consciousness* can become a "natural" alternative to the student's "natural" desire to use illegal drugs: "Open discussion of altered states of consciousness can throw some light on this mysterious topic and inform students that there are effective non-drug ways of exploring and controlling consciousness. A complete drug education program should recognize the natural human desire for exploring consciousness and should provide acceptable alternative routes" (2261:10).

Dream work* is also advocated: "Dreaming is an altered state that is being used successfully by teachers both as technique and as content. From a transpersonal point of view, dreams are important because they give us messages from the unconscious, and they afford easy access to a different reality. Dreaming is one door to our 'inner selves'" (2261:10).

Roberts and Clark believe, "No education of man can be complete which leaves these potential forms of consciousness undeveloped" (2261:12). They observe that "centering" exercises (often used to "contact" the "inner self") provide a good introduction to meditation* and the inner flow of mystical energy: "In many Eastern traditions, including the Japanese martial arts, the center of physical energy is located in the belly, about two inches below the navel, and two inches in front of the spine. Focusing attention on this center while noticing the movements of breathing in and out is an easy and widely used method of centering" (2261:13). They also advocate the scientific study of the occult: "Parapsychological topics make excellent class reports. Students enjoy learning about parapsychology and doing their own experiments. . . . Subjects which were formerly taboo for 'respectable' psychologists are opening up, and they provide an excellent example of how fields of knowledge change with the times" (2261:15).

Significantly, these educators point out that research on psychic healers indicate that they tap into some kind of power or force, and that perhaps biofeedback training or other self-controlled altered states of consciousness* may enable other people to become psychic healers (2261:17). But as coauthor Weldon demon-

strated years ago in *Psychic Healing: An Expose of an Occult Phenomenon* (Moody Press, 1982), the only power psychic healers tap into is the power of the spirit world—spiritism is the lowest common denominator of all forms of psychic healing.

Nevertheless, these educators say that transpersonal education is so popular because students enjoy turning inward. "Teachers are often surprised at how eagerly students respond to transpersonal teaching techniques. Some of these approaches seem to awaken the natural desire in each of us to explore our inner selves" (2261:18).

If this exploration of the inward self for wisdom and power is the essence of transpersonal education, it is also the essence of the problem. Turning inward in the ways described above is not only a terribly poor excuse for academic education, it is also an open door for indoctrination into the religion of the occult. We will see that this is true as we now sample some of the leading transpersonal educators in this country and the practices and beliefs they advocate.

## TRANSPERSONAL EDUCATORS

How prevalent are these New Age techniques in the public schools? Who are some of the leading contemporary educators promoting them? According to Dr. Stewart B. Shapiro and Louise F. Fitzgerald of the University of California at Santa Barbara, "A transpersonal orientation to learning was detected in the writings of 89 well-known representatives of humanistic education" (2265:375). In testimonials before the U.S. Department of Education in 1984, among the examples of New Age influence in classrooms were how to do astrological* horoscopes, conduct seances, use a Ouija board,* meditate,* role-play characters such as spiritists and warlocks, cast a witch's circle, and do occult readings (2266).

### Jack Canfield

Jack Canfield is director of Educational Services for Insight Training Seminars in Santa Monica, California. He is a founder and past director of the Institute for Holistic Education in Amherst, Massachusetts, past president of the Association for Humanistic Education, and he has been a consultant to over 150 school systems, universities, and mental-health organizations. Canfield is both well liked and highly influential in the field of education, especially in the popular if ill-advised self-esteem field, which is now a multibillion-dollar industry in America. For example, he is president of Self-Esteem Seminars, which boasts over 400 school districts as clients. He is also chairman of the board of the Foundation for Self-Esteem and sits on the board of the National Council for Self-Esteem. He is the author of numerous books and articles on education, such as *A Hundred Ways to Enhance Self-Concept in the Classroom* and *Self-Esteem in the Classroom.*

According to his 1991-92 Self-Esteem Seminar newsletter, Dr. Canfield has been conducting in-service training to teachers and delivering conference keynote speeches on the topic of self-esteem for over 20 years. He speaks or conducts seminars in 250 public schools a year. He has also practiced psychotherapy for five years.

In one article Canfield and Paula Klimeck discuss the importance of transpersonal education. Almost the entire gamut of the occult is endorsed as being applicable to children's education, including dream work,* mandalas,* meditation,* Arica psychocalisthenics, yoga,* occult "centering," "sacred" dances such as those found at the spiritistic Findhorn community in Scotland and the anthroposophical* eurythmy/sufi dances, teaching children to psychically see their chakras, auras, and healing energies, magic circles, and psychic chanting. He also advocates such books as Robert Masters and Jean Houston's *Mind Games*, which has a section on "raising spirits." (See p. 420.)

Canfield's *The Inner Classroom: Teaching with Guided Imagery* and his *Self-Esteem in the Classroom*, teach that spirit guides are an important element of self-esteem or other educational programs (2267). Indeed, he sees one of the most important aspects of New Age education in general is to help students contact their own spirit guide:

One of the most central concepts in New Age education is working with "life purpose." After doing some centering activities, students are asked to review their life in reverse, starting in the present and going backward over time until they come to the time before they were born. Here they meet a guardian spirit whom they ask, "What is my life purpose?" They then review their life in the other direction, coming forward in time and reconsidering the events of their life in the light of their life purpose. We recently conducted this exercise with a group of seventh graders (2260:38).

In other words, after the "softening up" methods of relaxation techniques, the teacher guides the children back through the year, to the previous year, to being a young child prior to entering school, to being a baby, to birth, to the mother's womb, and then to the time *before conception.* "You are about to meet a special guide, your own special guide. A guide whom you may ask what the purpose of your life is. . . . Feel your guide's unconditional love, and strength and beauty. . . . Let whatever happens, happen. . . . Communicate with your guide. . . . Listen to your guide" (2268:39). Elsewhere, Canfield and Klimeck write:

In a growing number of classrooms throughout the world, education is beginning to move into a new dimension. More and more teachers are exposing children to ways of contacting their inner wisdom and their higher selves. . . . New Age education has arrived . . . an influx of spiritual teachings from the East, combined with a new psychological perspective in the West has resulted in a fresh look at the learning process (2260:27).

Part of this "new psychological perspective" for learning utilizes the occult psychology of Roberto Assagioli, as can be seen in Canfield's 1980 paper *Psychosynthesis in Education: Theory and Applications.* Assagioli was the Italian psychiatrist who developed psychosynthesis and who was a prominent student of New Age medium Alice Bailey. He even directed her Lucis Trust organization in Italy for two years (2269:224-25). Bailey was the author of *Educa-*

*tion in the New Age* and 21 other occult books. Actually, almost all her books were received by inspiration from her spirit guide "Djwhal Khul"—"The Tibetan" (2270). Bailey's spirit guides influenced Assagioli, who, in turn, influenced Canfield. Thus, much of Canfield's educational approach is based on Alice Bailey's material filtered through Roberto Assagioli (2232:33-35). Canfield's interest in spiritism is hardly surprising, since his educational theories are themselves influenced by revelations from the spirit world.

Canfield and Klimeck also write: "Our work began in the mid-60's with the emergence of the field of 'humanistic education.... Within the past five years we have also witnessed the birth of 'transpersonal education,' the acknowledgement of one's inner and spiritual dimensions, through working with such forms as dreams, meditation, guided imagery, centering, mandalas and so forth" (2260:8). They also say, "Learning how to center one's self is one of the most important processes of all the New Age educational tools" (2260:30). And they describe how "centering" is to be accomplished: through progressive relaxation techniques and guided imagery, for which they recommend Hendricks' and Roberts' *The Centering Book* and *Second Centering Book* (see Hypnosis, Visualization). Canfield state, "When students are participating in a guided imagery experience, they are in an altered state of consciousness" (2268:29).

Also described is the theory behind using guided imagery, which is intended to prove to children that they have a spiritual nature through their exposure to psychic or mystical energies. Canfield and Klimeck believe that "it becomes very important to validate the spiritual essence of children to help them discover their own unique inner qualities... [e.g.,] a special inflow of super conscious energy which can be tapped into—indeed must be tapped into if New Age children are to be fully educated" (2260:32).

In conclusion, Dr. Canfield may indeed be a leader in the field of nontraditional education, but his preference for occult methods can only damage children in the long run (278).

## Stewart Shapiro

Dr. Stewart Shapiro is a noted educator with the University of California. In the *Educational and Psychological Measurement* journal he states that "according to the transpersonal approach, schools and other learning environments should be used for the development of spiritual potential as well as academic, vocational and socio-personal learning" (2271:47,375). Shapiro describes this transpersonal philosophy as "spiritual/mystical," and as "being based on transpersonal psychology which is concerned with those ultimate human capacities and potentialities..." (2271:376). He believes that in this philosophy, "Intuitive and receptive modes of consciousness are equal in importance to cognitive, rational, logical and active modes" (2271:376).

But how does Dr. Shapiro see these "intuitive and receptive modes of consciousness," which have *equal* importance to cognitive and logical modes of thinking, as being produced? He describes them as being produced by the "use of various psychological techniques [e.g., fantasy, guided imagery] ... relaxation techniques," and other methods which "at times border on the occult" (2271:381).

Shapiro initially sought objectively to measure the alleged effectiveness of transpersonal methods of learning because of their growing impact. He felt that these approaches, being so widespread, were controversial, and therefore that scientific evidence was needed to demonstrate their validity. "Since various practices in the public schools, ranging from the so-called religion of secular humanism on the one hand, and to meditation, the use of fantasy and imagery, and references to magic, the occult, or witchcraft on the other, have become so controversial of late ... an objective, reliable and valid measure ... was considered both practically and theoretically timely" (2271:377).

Dr. Shapiro recommends we look at "children and youth in schools" who have been "taught how to induce altered states of consciousness in themselves, such as those states in psychic healing, parapsychological phenomena, yoga, biofeedback, and meditation" (2271:383). He calls our attention to "twenty-five well-known representative writers in transpersonal/humanistic psychology and education" (2271:377), especially Thomas B. Roberts. He also recommends leading New Agers, occultists, and transpersonal psychologists such as Marilyn Ferguson, Ken Wilber, Roberto Assagioli, William James, Gay Hendricks, Krishnamurti, Ken Keyes, and Michael Murphy (2271:377/2272).

*Thomas Roberts*

Dr. Roberts is a graduate of Stanford University who now teaches development and special education at Northern Illinois University. He gained prominence in education circles in 1977 when he coauthored *The Second Centering Book* with Gay Hendricks. (Dr. Hendricks had coauthored the original *The Centering Book* in 1975.)

In the preface to *The Second Centering Book*, Roberts and Hendricks discuss the value that New Age education has for them personally in reconceptualizing human nature: "We see transpersonal education as part of a larger progression that society is going through.... [Those who are] explorers of consciousness, or 'inner space,' indicate that our ideas of human nature are vastly wrong" (2273:XX). What the authors suggest is that our "true" nature is not limited and human but almost infinitely knowledgeable, powerful, and perfect, i.e., godlike. our higher self, or divine intuitive self, can supposedly be accessed through Eastern mystical and other religious techniques.

Again, we see the common theme that we must bypass the logical, rational, cognitive mind and move into an alternate state of consciousness* if we are to "properly" understand ourselves, to know things correctly, and to enhance our individual performance and grow spiritually. Roberts explains, "The consciousness revolution is permeating education, too. This book is part of it. Teachers, administrators, and parents who are concerned with optimum learning are introducing transpersonal techniques into the classroom.... It expands our knowledge of not only where we are, but when we are, what we know and who we are" (2273:XVIII,XX).

In "States of Consciousness: A New Intellectual Direction, a New Teacher Education

Direction," Roberts writes, "New principles of learning based on the research on states of consciousness offer opportunities for teacher educators to re-structure curriculum, to modify content, and to revise instructional methods" (2274:55). In other words:

An enormous amount of curriculum development stands waiting to be accomplished at all educational levels. In terms of methods, teachers continue to use consciousness methods... that increase student learning of existing content and at the same time give practice in using advanced mental abilities. In terms of professional standards, there is strong evidence that biofeedback, meditation, yoga and similar exercises result in enhanced mental development, physical health, and social responsibility.

From a states of consciousness perspective, the future of education is wide open. It concludes the intelligent use of all states and their resident abilities. (2274:57-58).

*Barbara Clark*

Dr. Clark is a professor of education at Cal State University, Los Angeles. She is a well-known educator of those who teach gifted children and author of the graduate-school text *Growing Up Gifted: Developing the Potential of Children at Home and at School.* Here, Clark also advocates a variety of Eastern and occult methods for the educational curriculum.

Her concept of "integrative education" is intended to create what she calls "transpersonal learning." She suggests that students learn to find the "hidden teacher/artist" within them and that the philosophies of East and West merge. "Guided fantasies and dreams, recognition and use of altered states of consciousness, and centering activities will develop more of our intuitive [e.g., psychic] abilities.... All of this and more lie ahead as we seek to bring all of our knowledge, feelings, talents, and creativity into the classroom in the service of actualizing and transcending" (2259:592-93).

In discussing psychic energies and parapsychology in general, including out-of-body experiences and "healing energies," Clark says that current research into such subjects contains "valuable content for the education of human beings" (2259:593). She also suggests that an occult and Eastern monistic view of reality is beneficial for educational advancement:

> Reality is seen as an outward projection of internal thoughts, feelings, and expectations. Energy is the connector, the center.... Western pragmatists will join Eastern mystics, and all humans will benefit. Human potential, as yet unknown, will have a chance to develop.... It may be, as Bentov said, that "we are all part of this great hologram called Creation which is everybody else's SELF.... You create your own reality. It's all a cosmic play, there is nothing but you!" (2259:582-83).

This philosophy is a form of *advaita* Vedanta Hinduism, and it is the teaching of most of the New Age, as well as of innumerable spirits, such as "Seth" (see *A Course in Miracles*).

Barbara Clark also encourages the exploration of the mystical and spiritistic energies associated with occult traditions, such as *mana, chi, kaa,* and *prana*. She believes that we need to tap into and "balance" this psychic energy within ourselves. In part, this is because, "the ebb and flow of human energy has been central to many belief systems—the Yin/Yang of ancient China, the Ka of the ancient Egyptians, the Chi of the Eastern Indians, the Kaa of the American Indians . . . " (2259:387-88). Thus, she states, "We are all affected by the differing amounts of energy available in our lives and by what inhibits or facilitates our energy supply" (2259: 387-88). But as we have documented in the chapter on New Age medicine and elsewhere, this so-called "universal" or "mystical energy" is fundamentally occult and frequently indistinguishable from the spirits or spiritistic energy itself. To encourage children to "tap into" it is extremely irresponsible.

If we consider what Dr. Clark advocates, we can see how easily Eastern and occult ideas and practices can be incorporated into educational curricula. Clark asserts that Eastern and Western philosophies are merging today in a climate of acceptance. She views creativity in the classroom as serving students in the process of self-actualization and transcendence. The more we discover through an integration of East and West,

"the more we can validate the ancient wisdom that has come to us from the Chinese, Hindu, Egyptian and other age old teaching" (2259:583).

Among the things advocated in her text are parapsychology and psychic abilities, Eastern forms of "enlightenment,"* channeling* psychic energy, the use of fantasy, progressive relaxation, autogenic training, centering, guided imagery, and visualization* (2259:387-410,576-96). Yet this book is widely used as a textbook for those who teach gifted children! Until recently it was the required textbook for teachers at the University of Alabama in order to maintain their certification through continuing credits in the graduate program, and it still remains on the recommended supplemental reading list (2493).

*Deborah Rozman*

Deborah Rozman is an educational consultant and has taught at workshops and related educational programs throughout the country. She has also taught visualization, transpersonal psychology, centering, and meditation "to all age groups in California Public Schools. Her books have been sponsored by superintendents of several school districts and by church leaders as effective learning tools" (2494:149). Rozman is the author of *Meditating with Children* and *Meditation for Children*, having cumulative sales of over a quarter million copies.

Her *Meditating with Children: The Art of Concentration and Centering* is described on the title page as "a workbook on New Age educational methods using meditation" (2495). Rozman believes that her meditative educational methods will lead to an unfolding expansion of "awareness" for both teacher and child alike (2495:1). She encourages teachers to remain at least "one step ahead of the children" by researching the subject beforehand "and practicing the meditations and exercises before the class" in order to be more effective (2495:130). Her personal philosophy is basically New Age, e.g., she accepts the idea that we are all part of God. "Meditation takes us back to the Source of all Life. We become one with ALL" (2495:134). She defines "ultimate reality" as "the Source" or as "existence, consciousness, and bliss," a standard designation for transcendental meditation and other Hindu groups' descriptions of the impersonal Hindu God Brahman (2495:134).

Thus, it is not surprising that Rozman describes her educational philosophy and goals in New Age categories and that she emphasizes the importance of meditation* to further these goals:

Education, like religion, is in the process of undergoing radical transformation to accommodate the growing recognition of the need to eliminate outworn forms that are no longer effective in providing for the optimal growth of children. New breakthroughs ... are bringing new light into the consciousness of man. This light some have called the dawning of the New Age. It is slowly leading to regeneration in the educational system. . . .

Eastern researchers, who for thousands of years have studied the nature of consciousness ... have developed [meditative] processes for building bridges in consciousness to close . . . [these educational] gaps (2495:134).

Nor surprisingly, both Rozman's books contain complete instruction in meditation, using the typical methods of progressive relaxation and guided imagery. She says that the ultimate goal of meditation is to tap into the "Source," or God. By doing so, the child will lose all self-identity as he awakens to his "true" nature—oneness with the true reality underlying the universe—including a oneness with the true (divine) reality of all people, vegetables, animals, and minerals (2495:134). Of course, this has always been the goal of Hinduism, Buddhism, and other Eastern and occult religions.

"Much of the knowledge from which we draw, in learning to use meditation to get in touch with the great wisdom inside us, comes from Eastern meditators, many Hindu or Buddhist, who have researched deeply into the soul" (2494:1).

After discussing karma, Rozman states that one purpose of meditation is to permit our real self to emerge, i.e., our God-self. She tells children that there is "no real separation between ourself and others," and she believes that children can expect to encounter "miracles, psychic experiences, visions, etc., [which] are all part of the unfoldment" (2494:27). She even encourages

children to apply specific biblical phrases, blasphemously making them personally applicable to themselves. Among the phrases listed are "I and my Father are one," "before Abraham was I am," and "I am that I Am" (2494:27).

*Jean Houston*

The name, Jean Houston, continually surfaces as a prime mover and inspirational force for transpersonal educators. Houston was the keynote speaker at the 1989 conference for the prestigious Association for Supervision and Curriculum Development in Orlando, Florida, where over 6000 educational curriculum developers were present. Robert Caldwell, founder of a QUEST educational program (not Quest International), praises Houston as one of the best workshop leaders he has ever seen (2496). She has served on faculties of psychology, philosophy, or religion at New York University, the University of California, and Columbia University and is past president of the Association for Humanistic Psychology. In 1985 she was awarded the National Teacher-Educator Association's award as Distinguished Educator of the Year (USA).

Not only is her influence felt by curriculum writers; it is also felt by school guidance counselors. For example, she was the featured speaker at the 1982 American Association of Counselors Development National Conference. In the brochure's advertisement she is depicted as the premier presenter in the field of New Age human potential and altered states of consciousness.*

Houston is also the author or coauthor of many books on occult subjects, including *Mind Games, Life Force,* and *The Possible Human.* Any parent who takes the time to read Houston's books will discover that what she proposes for education is nothing less than exposing children (many of whom she views as "natural visualizers") (2497:135) to dangerous occult philosophy and practices (278). In *The Possible Human,* she reports that researchers, herself included, are "rediscovering what the early Sanskrit psychophysical [i.e., occult] philosophers had always known—that the key to transpersonal realities lay in the expansion of physical awareness" (2497:xix). This research, she says, is helping us gather "the momentum for bringing new forms into being ... evolving the self, and finally, growing God-in-us" (2497:200).

Houston instructs her readers in a progressive relaxation exercise and guided imagery in order to become what she calls a "co-creator" in the evolutionary process. The guided imagery takes the participant down deep into his own body and eventually to a door, behind which "is someone who understands all about you.... [T]his wise being ... can become a powerful ally for you.... [H]owever you must act on the advice given" (2497:26-27). This, of course, is a spirit guide, something Houston advocates contacting in other books, such as *Mind Games*, which is another of her "educational" endeavors in which she confesses that "trances, ASCs and hypnoid states should prove relaxing and beneficial ..." (1854:5,13).

In *Mind Games*, coauthored with her husband, Robert Masters, of Masters and Johnson sex researchers' fame, she tells people how to contact what she terms "the Group Spirit." She discusses how this spirit is to be raised in classic seance terms: "We are beginning to go now into trance together. We are going to experience deepening together, and, finally, each of us will contribute to the pool of consciousness out of which the Group Spirit will draw its substance and arise to exist once again" (1854:199). She describes this Group Spirit as a literal spirit entity: "an actual, intelligent being, conscious, and powerful," and that the participants of the seance are to permit the "spirit to inspire us" (1854:202). The Group Spirit will continue to be with people *after* the "seance" has ended. For example, "The Group Spirit will appear to you in a dream, and you will be able to gain a clear and detailed impression of its appearance, and you may be able to enter into a conversation with it, and various things might be revealed to you" (1854:202).

*Maureen Murdock*

Maureen Murdock is an educator and therapist who conducts teacher workshops across the Unites States. She is the author of *Spinning Inward: Using Guided Imagery with Children for Learning, Creativity and Relaxation*. She asks, "How do we learn? How do we expand creativ-

ity? How do we know those things which we know intuitively?" She then describes the development of her own theory after research into the New Age Movement: "I began meditating ... [and] introduced this technique to my own children.... Encouraged by their response, I then tried short centering exercises with my kindergarten class" (2257:1).

Murdock also writes, "We used to think of the newborn child as an empty cup waiting to be filled with knowledge by its wise parents and an all-knowing society. That theory no longer holds. ... Their inherent knowledge is such that they see the present and the future more clearly than we do.... For this reason, present learning techniques are inadequate for them" (2257:5). She then describes the presuppositions behind her strategy, premises which also refer to contacting one's "inner guide." For example: "The search for a deeper connection to self helps older adolescents to realize their own inner wisdom and recognize that they have all the answers within if they take the time to center ... to find a wise being within who gives guidance and support and who may have answers to personal questions" (2257:137).

## ORGANIZATIONAL SUPPORT

In the 1980s, the Holistic Education Network was organized at local and national levels "to bring about transformation in education ... [and] to assist educators to make the transition from traditional education to holistic education" (2232:3). The first two volumes in its "Holistic Education Series," *Mind: Evolution or Revolution? The Emergence of Holistic Education* (2232) and *Holistic Education: Education for Living* (2233) became primers for educational change by various means, including incorporating Eastern and occult practices and beliefs into the classroom. Following their lead, many professional organizations now support transpersonal education to one degree or another. One example is cited below.

The American Personnel and Guidance Association is the major professional organization for elementary school guidance counselors and functions as a division of the American School

421

Counselor Association (ASCA). Their professional journal is called *Elementary School Guidance and Counseling*. This journal devoted an entire issue to transpersonal approaches to learning. Among the authors of 12 articles were leaders in the area of transpersonal or humanistic education, including Thomas B. Roberts, Beverly Galyean, Gay Hendricks, and significantly, Dinkmeyer and Dinkmeyer, the former editors of the journal and originators of DUSO (Developing Understanding of Self and Others; 2498). These articles also demonstrate that techniques used in education, such as affective decision-making, progressive relaxation, and guided imagery/fantasy, are not only linked together but may intentionally be a part of the transpersonal and New Age strategy.

Guest editor Jon Carlson, professor in the Educational Foundations and Counselor Education Department of the University of Wisconsin, begins this special issue by writing, "I hope that this special issue of the *Elementary School Guidance and Counseling Journal* jars you from your current role and helps you realize the long term futility of traditional approaches to counseling. . . . This issue intends to expose the reader to the multitude of approaches available to help counselors help youngsters grow and move toward developing their true potential" (2498:84).

Among the surprising guidelines Carlson lists as being useful in pursuing optimal development are those that encourage children to, "learn to empty your mind on a daily basis through centering, meditation, or relaxation. An empty mind has room for new learning and change" (2498:88-90). (One would also think that an *empty* mind is one primed for indoctrination.)

Dr. Carl Rogers, who advocated spiritism in his *A Way of Being* (1068:82-92), is quoted as saying, "The basis for values will need to be recognized as discoverable within, rather than in dogmas or the material world . . . [perhaps in] our growing use of psychic forces and psychic energy" (2498:91).

An article by Herbert Otto, president of the National Center for the Exploration of Human Potential, argues, "There is every indication that children have extrasensory capacities [i.e., psychic abilities] that are progressively extin-

guished or suppressed as they grow older. . . . The school system and especially the counselor play a crucial and formative role in the development of [this] potential" (2498:93-94).

In his article, Dr. Thomas Roberts presents a systematic attempt to help counselors operate within altered states of consciousness.* He writes:

> Counseling is entering one of the most exciting stages of its development, that of consciousness counseling. It consists of helping people to develop their full capacities in every state of consciousness. . . . What makes consciousness counseling most distinctive and exciting to me is that it recognizes states of consciousness that have not been recognized by most western psychological theories (2498:103).

Roberts also lists his mentors and other leaders in the consciousness movement: Timothy Leary of LSD fame, Aldous Huxley, Jean Houston, shamans, and other participants in the occult or researchers in psychic phenomena. Noting that psychedelic users and cult leaders are also explorers of altered states of consciousness, he warns counselors to encourage the "responsible exploration" of these "inner frontier" areas (2498:105). And he instructs school counselors that "imagery, dreams, biofeedback, relaxation, [and] beginning meditation . . . should be studied and practiced before they are used. . . . [H]ypnosis and advanced meditation should be attempted with oneself and with clients only after specified training in those methods" (2498:107).

Don Dinkmeyer and Don Dinkmeyer, Jr. are the developers of the popular self-esteem drug and alcohol prevention program, DUSO. In the issue they write:

> Affective education has helped us get more in touch with the child's feelings and attitudes. Education needs to place more emphasis on the affective area and more attention on developing affective curriculum. . . . The move toward positive wellness has been accompanied by a great increase in the interests of relaxation response and the renewed interest in Yoga. It is believed that these two activities may stimulate inner healing power. There are many research studies

that indicate the positive effect of meditation on physical health (2498:108).

Dinkmeyer recommends Deborah Rozman's TM-based *Meditation with Children* as an example of "meditation for teachers and students" (2498:110). "If education is to be conducted in a milieu that is growth producing, we must recognize that there is a need for retraining of educators. . . . If children are to become able to cope with stress and tension and to learn how to relax, they must learn the concepts of help from teachers who model positive wellness" (2498:109).

Beverly Galyean, the pioneer of confluent education (the merging of Eastern mystical and Western approaches to education) encourages guided imagery methods in the classroom because "on the affective plane they enable students to discover the resources of their inner wisdom, their 'higher Self,' and to source themselves from within rather than depend on outside persons and events for nurturance" (2498:118). As James Fadiman of Stanford University and the California Institute of Transpersonal Psychology had remarked in his article, "The transpersonal approach encourages children . . . to consider alternative truths" (2498:113).

There is also an article by Dr. Deane Shapiro, Dean of Academic Affairs at the Pacific Graduate School of Psychology and clinical instructor in the Department of Psychiatry and Behavioral Sciences at Stanford University Medical School. The article begins by quoting the Hindu scripture, the *Bhagavad Gita*, and then asks the question, "How does the person of enlightenment gain this discipline? And how, as counselors and educators, can we encourage the pursuit of this discipline in children?" (2498:125). He believes:

A new model, a new vision of our human potential is necessary. . . . This vision may come from the eastern esoteric and mystical tradition; others may come from our western scientific research laboratories and field experiments. Parents, teachers and educators are in a pivotal position to transmit aspects of this vision to future generations, to offer them a vision of an enlightened life . . . (2498:126).

In another of the articles, Gay Hendricks, professor in the School of Education at the University of Colorado, believes that the "quiet, compassionate revolution underway in our schools" is laying "the groundwork for a truly holistic curriculum." He points out that "centering activities" and other affective education materials are now "a trend in which several hundred thousand teachers and counselors participate on a daily basis. . . . The activities I advance to accomplish this are largely relaxation activities, communication skills, meditation, movement and fantasy journeys . . . " (2498:130). Concerning children he writes:

Children take to relaxation, meditation, and other centering activities like proverbial ducks to water. . . . I would like centering and other affective educational activities used on a more regular basis in our schools. . . . What I would most like to see is a curriculum that fully integrates centering, communications, values clarifications and other key affective skills. . . . To equip students with the skills of communicating about their inner experience (2498:131-33).

Popular teacher and workshop leaders Jack Canfield and Paula Klimeck also have an article. They begin with a "message of inner wisdom," written by a seventh-grade student after a guided imagery session. "My [inner] guide was a voice and it still is. Many times I feel like a failure, like report cards, and it (the voice) speaks not with a roar, but with a gentle call, like my grandmother who died one year ago: 'Press on. Don't give up. Press on. Don't give up'" (2498:135). And so the authors write, "One of the most exciting aspects of our work has been in the areas of centering, fantasy, imagery, and meditation. . . . Techniques such as eye and ear centering, breath relaxation, chanting, mandala work, meditation, and receptive imaging are particularly useful" (2498:136-37).

Finally, Marianne DeVoe, an educational consultant for the county schools of Knoxville, Tennessee, concludes:

For the transpersonal educator, spiritual growth includes discovering an expanded view of man, experiencing altered states of consciousness, developing in terms of self-realization and self-transcendence, accepting subjective experiences, and realizing inner states. Specifically, the transpersonal educator is committed to helping individuals focus internally as well as externally in an effort to effect personal growth and improve learning potential. Relaxation, concentration, guided fantasy, dreams, meditation, centering, biofeedback, and parapsychology (ESP, dream telepathy) are all components of the transpersonal approach. A variety of these techniques are being introduced into the traditional classroom setting and are being pursued by students outside the school environment (2498:143).

The contents and message of this journal issue are characteristic of the field of New Age transpersonal education. Today, 15 years later, this discipline has merely expanded and "matured." Just as national chain bookstores are now abandoning their "New Age" sections and incorporating this material into conventional disciplines—psychology, sociology, biology, business—so the educational establishment is in the process of integrating these New Age education methods into conventional curricula.

## OTHER IMPORTANT INFLUENCES

With transpersonal educators calling for a merging between East and West, the influence of other prominent individuals on educational theory should not be neglected. Scientology,* Psychosynthesis, Theosophy, Krishnamurti, Aurobindo, and many other similar influences have impacted segments of today's education.

### Sri Aurobindo's "Integral Education"

Sri Aurobindo was a noted Hindu occultist and spiritist who developed what is termed "Integral Yoga." His Eastern and occult philosophy is an essential part of his educational method. For example, altered states of consciousness* "are of key importance in Aurobindo's system. They relate essentially to the growth of the soul, or the unveiling of the inner center, and of developing its union with Being [i.e., Brahman]" (2499:15). In Sri Aurobindo's Integral Education, "The first principle of true teaching is that nothing can be taught" because the teacher is merely a facilitator who helps draw out the student's

own divine potential from within. Students learn by themselves, and the role of a teacher is "not to impose knowledge but rather to guide, suggest, and demonstrate by the example and influence of their own being" (2499:14).

### Krishnamurti

Krishnamurti was a novel Hindu "guru" whom Annie Besant, then president of the Theosophical Society, had groomed to become a new "Christ." Krishnamurti eventually rejected this role and began his own path. On education he comments, "Another function of education is to create new values. Merely to implant existing values in the mind of the child, to make him conform to ideals, is to condition him without awakening his intelligence" (2676:30). Like Aurobindo, Krishnamurti believed that "nothing can be taught and that true education is a process of mutual exploration" (2499:16). From his viewpoint, the individual student is "already whole and everything is already integrated [therefore] education is [merely] coming to realize [that] situation" (2499:16).

### Rudolf Steiner's Waldorf Schools

Rufold Steiner was a noted occultist who left Theosophy to begin his own religion. Although Steiner's educational philosophy is based on the occult system of anthroposophy, students at the Waldorf Schools are not taught the philosophy directly. Nevertheless, like Aurobindo and Krishnamurti, he saw the purpose of a holistic approach to education as the education of the whole child which included instruction in occult ideas.

### Edgar Cayce

Edgar Cayce, like Steiner, was a spiritist and not a formal educator. Nevertheless, the spirits who spoke through him encouraged children to be educated in typical New Age fashion. The psychic readings of Cayce outlined several key aspects to children's education; among them was dream work* (to explore the inner self), regular use of the imagination,* and pre-sleep "hypnotic" or other autosuggestions to stimulate the child's "higher self" during the night. Not surprisingly, "The Edgar Cayce Readings suggest a relationship between the faculties of intuition, imagination and psychic ability, as they play a part in the [spiritual] awakening of the soul. . . . [This may] increase the importance of the parent or teacher providing the child with . . . particular periods for exposure to creative imagination" (2677:296).

*Est*

Est, now called "Landmark Education's The Forum," has also played a significant role in education. Est founder Werner Erhard once said, "My plans could be said to make est as public as possible. My notion of how to do that is through the educational system" (1346:6). An estimated 20 percent to 30 percent of est/The Forum graduates work in education many seeking to incorporate Erhard's theories into education. For an evaluation of Erhard Seminars Training, The Forum, and the impact of related human potential seminars in education and other fields, see the appropriate chapter.

In conclusion, what was once strange and even bizarre to our culture is now part of accepted educational procedure. If we wait another 20 years, the battle for quality education will be lost. This is why concerned parents and educators must begin to work now to retain both the integrity and credibility of our children's learning.

## EVALUATION

According to Dr. J. Gordon Melton's *New Age Almanac*, some 300 colleges and educational institutions (over 75 are accredited or state-approved) now offer programs or degrees on New Age topics (1525:384-99). And the 1995 *Common Boundary Education Guide* lists over 600 transpersonal psychological and New Age-related degree and nondegree programs. Obviously, as we have seen, this has influenced many educators who have introduced these topics into their schools.

Brooks Alexander, noted authority on New Age philosophy, observes why the New Age movement has targeted education:

In the ideological contest for cultural supremacy, public education is *the* prime target; it influences the most people in the most pervasive way at the most impressionable age. No other social institution has anything close to the same potential for mass indoctrination (2241:14).

Children especially are targeted because most New Agers (such as prominent educator Jack Canfield) believe that the innate innocence and sensitivity of children render them much closer to the influences of the spiritual world, such as to the spirits who reside there. These spirits seek to direct the course of human "evolution" into a New Age of peace and prosperity. By reaching children *before* they have been "corrupted" by Western culture and Christian values, New Agers hope they can educate an entire generation around the spiritual values of New Age philosophy. In other words, if children can be indoctrinated in New Age techniques and beliefs, as adults they will become powerful agents of change, helping to move society toward a supposed new era of global harmony.

How did those of a New Age or transpersonal perspective manage to slip their ideas into the public school curricula? In part, they have often brought in their beliefs under the disguise of neutral, academic, psychological, or scientific-sounding terminology (see "The Hidden Agenda" on p. 430). If parents want to protect their children in public schools, they should become familiar with the new terminology used by these educators (e.g., see the glossary in 1064:311-17). For example, "transpersonal psychology" sounds pretty impressive. So does adjusting one's "left brain/right brain" equilibrium. What could be wrong with such harmless-sounding concepts as "guided imagery" or "centering"? And who would think that "human potential" or imaginary "inner guides" might lead to a more sinister reality?

Although New Age educators believe that these disciplines are truly helping students and society at large, there are sound reasons to question this assumption. Because of underlying philosophies and potential dangers, whether physical or spiritual (278), these practices and techniques are not promoting the best interest of our nation or its children.

Occult techniques and philosophy are effective; they do work, as pagan and occult history demonstrates. Yoga* and Eastern meditation* may calm nervous students; visualization,* guided imagery, and fantasy practices might help to improve creativity; teaching psychic development* may enhance self-esteem and increase a sense of power; but what is the ultimate cost of exposing our children to the occult? Those persons integrating Eastern and occult methods and ideas into school curricula will exact a great cost and lay a heavy burden on our children and future generations.

Unfortunately, educators who really care for children and educational excellence may not understand all that is involved in occult practice. We will look at two illustrations.

First, it is important to realize that in visualization,* guided imagery, and hypnosis* we are not merely dealing with the natural or innocent use of the imagination. In normal use of the imagination, there is a discriminating, or fairly controlled, use of internal thoughts. The person is in control of how he uses these thoughts, whether it is in visualizing winning a race or what it would be like to marry another person. This natural use of the imagination is not what we find in New Age visualization, guided imagery, or hypnosis.

Characteristics that distinguish these methods from a normal use of imagination may include the use of relaxation, auto-suggestion, creating new realities, an altered state of consciousness,* being directed by another person so that the participant is not ultimately in control, and having to be carefully brought out of the internal condition into which one has been placed. These can all be powerful methods for introducing children to the occult, something not true of a person's own unaided imagination.

New Age visualization often attempts to use the mind to control reality outside oneself. For example, the visualizer might attempt to influence events, objects, or even people through a supposed psychic power of the mind, which "travels" outside the mind to have an influence. Guided imagery and hypnosis share many similarities. Here we also find the use of relaxation and psychological suggestions in order to produce a new reality. For example, when a child reaches a suggestible state of mind (one without discrimination and in which he is not in control of his inner environment), and if he starts to do, remember, or believe things that ultimately

aren't real, and if he has to be brought out of that state of mind by another person, then this is guided imagery or hypnosis. Again, there may be hidden psychological and spiritual consequences to these methods (see Hypnosis).

Prominent New Age educator Jack Canfield creatively uses guided imagery and the popular TV series "Kung Fu" to help children contact their own personal "inner guides." In his article "The Inner Classroom: Teaching With guided Imagery," he lays the foundation for employing guided imagery with children:

To me the most interesting use of guided imagery is the evocation of the wisdom that lies deep within each of us. The most exciting experience I ever had with this grew out of a discussion of the television show *Kung Fu* with a group of six graders. We were discussing how it was that Cain always knew the right thing to do in any situation no matter how difficult or hopeless it may have appeared. They told me that each time he was in an emergency situation, he could close his eyes and flash back to a time when his teacher had told him something very wise and important. I asked them what this was called. One girl said, "It was like meditation." I agreed and said that it was. I then asked them what kind of teacher Cain talked to. Was he like their sixth grade teacher? They all agreed that he was a different kind of teacher, somehow more special, more wise and more able to be trusted. They all agreed they would like to have a teacher like that.

I then asked the kids if they would like to have a wise old teacher whom they could consult for advice in times of pressure and confusion. They all said yes they would but they weren't sure where they'd find one. Most of them decided they'd have to go to China or Japan or India. I asked them where David Cain went when he needed help. They finally realized that he had closed his eyes and gone inside himself. At this point I suggested that we all try that and see if we could find a wise old teacher inside our minds who could share his or her wisdom with us. They excitedly agreed to try. Here is what I asked them to visualize:

"Close your eyes, take a few deep breaths to relax. I want you to imagine that it is a pleasant day and you are walking in a friendly foreign land, a place where you've never been before . . ." (2223:38).

During an extended guided imagery exercise, Canfield led these sixth graders to their "wise old person," leading to "remarkable transformation" in the children. "You are about to meet a special guide, your own special guide., . . . Let whatever happens happen. . . . Communicate with your guide in whatever way possible. . . . Listen to your guide" (2223:39). The children's response in this exercise and others indicates that they can and do contact genuine spirits (see also the last section of this chapter, "Teaching Children to Hear Spirits p. 442).

A second example of how new educational methods can be counterproductive is "values clarification". Educator Eric Buehrer recalls how he initially failed in his role as a teacher to instruct his inner-city students that it was wrong to steal. Why? Because he had adopted a values clarification approach. During his first year of teaching, he told his students that he was going to help them to grow in decision-making through values clarification exercises. He asked his students how many of them believed that stealing was okay. Half the class thought it was fine. So he attempted to "clarify those values." What he found was that the kids clarified for *him* what *their* values were, and they had endless justifications for their belief that stealing was right.

Buehrer discovered that in values clarification it is impossible for a teacher to bring his or her own value judgment into the education process because there are no moral absolutes. This means that the students' values, regardless of what they are, are just as valid as the teacher's. All a teacher can do, ultimately, is affirm to students that it is okay to believe whatever they want to believe. He became convinced that values clarification was a terrible thing to teach impressionable youngsters. He concluded that not only should we teach students absolute values, but that we *must* teach them absolute values:

If we don't, then we can write off all these other issues, whether it's abortion or euthanasia or promiscuity or drug abuse—it doesn't matter. If at the root of it, the child believes that whatever he chooses is right simply because he *chooses* it—then we've lost the battle (2242).

*Thieves of Innocence*

In his book *The Original Vision: A Study of the Religious Experience of Childhood*, Edward Robinson selected and arranged significant anecdotes from among 4000 first-person accounts of religious experience in childhood. His study proves what many people have forgotten: that children are innately religious, and that they can and do have "profound, mature religious experiences" (2244:xiii). In the words of the Reverend Dr. John H. Westerhoff, professor of religious education at the Duke University Divinity School, "Religious Awareness, the religious imagination, the experience of the holy or sacred, is natural to childhood" (2224:xiii). "Children should be affirmed as persons who can and do have significant experiences of the divine which, while only recollected and described later in life, are still mature, mystical, numinous experiences of the holy" (2224:xiii).

God tells His people, "Impress them [My instructions] on your children. Talk about them when you sit at home and when you walk along the road, when you lie down and when you get up" (Deuteronomy 6:7). The Proverbs tell us, "Even a child is known by his actions, by whether his conduct is pure and right" (Proverbs 20:11), and "Train a child in the way he should go, and when he is old he will not turn from it" (Proverbs 22:6). In the Gospels, Jesus tells us to be as little children, and he sternly warns those who would lead children astray from Him: "Therefore, whoever humbles himself like this child is the greatest in the kingdom of heaven. And whoever welcomes a little child like this in my name welcomes me. But if anyone causes one of these little ones who believe in me to sin, it would be better for him to have a large millstone hung around his neck and to be drowned in the depths of the sea" (Matthew 18:4-6).

Jesus also said, "'Let the little children come to me, and do not hinder them, for the kingdom of God belongs to such as these. I tell you the truth, anyone who will not receive the kingdom of God like a little child will never enter it.' And he took the children in his arms, put his hands on them and blessed them" (Mark 10:13-16). And, the apostle Paul reminded Timothy that he had known the Scriptures from infancy. "But as for you, continue in what you have learned and have become convinced of, because you know those from whom you learned it, and how from infancy you have known the holy Scriptures, which are able to make you wise for salvation through faith in Christ Jesus" (2 Timothy 3:14-15).

All of this shows that children can be influenced spiritually, for either good or evil. Indeed, untold numbers of Christians first accepted Jesus Christ as their Savior when they were children. But children being taught New Age methods and beliefs often become insulated against the gospel. Decades ago children were usually exposed to a Judeo-Christian worldview. As God has been increasingly taken out of the classroom (and many other aspects of society), children have been stifled in their religious awareness. The "original vision" of children— that is, their innate perception of God and religious intuition—is something that late twentieth-century education has increasingly obstructed through its secularist orientation. Today, however, religious influence is making a major comeback in education and throughout society in the form of pagan practices and philosophies which are often, though not exclusively, associated with the New Age Movement.

Because children are innately religious, they are "naturally" susceptible to any religious ideas. With traditional religion now effectively removed from the school system, "natural" religion (e.g., pantheism) in all its various forms is emerging. Dr. Hardy argues that the most important thing to stress in the schools today is that the discussion of religious feelings "is no longer to be dominated by conventional ideas of what constitutes religion, or by theological orthodoxies of one kind or another," but rather by observational study (2244:5). In other words, religious experience itself, of whatever form, is what is important.

Supposedly, occult and mystical experiences of children are valid precisely because they are legitimate experiences worthy of reflection and study. The problem here is not the innate sensitivity of children to God and spirituality, which is a blessing from God and, properly nurtured, trains a child in the things of God and in a sensitivity to His will. The problem is the corruption of

this natural tendency by New Age mystical experience and Eastern and occult forms of religion.

This brings up the vital question: In what spiritual direction are we educating children? The current bias against even considering the possibility of demonic realities are deception in the study of "religious experience" in children means that the spiritual direction is increasingly tunneled or skewed away from a biblical direction. "*True* spirituality" becomes any spiritual experience—mystical, Eastern, occult, New Age, or whatever. And these experiences are becoming interpreted as statistically predominant, hence *normal.* Furthermore, children do what Mommy and Daddy do. And if Mommy and Daddy meditate, do yoga, practice visualization, or contact spirits, children will usually want to emulate them.

Books such as Joseph Chilton Pearce's *Magical Child*, James W. Peterson's *The Secret Life of Kids: An Exploration Into Their Psychic Senses* (see p. 445), and Samuel H. Young's, *Psychic Children* prove that children's religious sensibilities can be corrupted by exposure to occult philosophy and practice. Some of the consequences are seen in books like Johanna Michaelsen's *Like Lambs to the Slaughter: Your Child and the Occult*. Michaelsen writes:

> The children have by no means been left untouched or ignored by the spiritual "transformation" of their elders. The question of how occultism is affecting the children of this country is no longer one that parents can afford to ignore. The children, in fact, are the key targets. It is, after all, the little ones who will be the leaders, teachers, politicians, law makers, and parents of tomorrow. What they are taught today as young children about who or what God is and about who they are, what the nature of reality is, what happens to a person after death, and what morality and ethics are based on must necessarily have a tremendous impact on the direction the society of the future will take. It is staggering to realize to what extent the answer they are developing to these crucial questions is firmly entrenched in occult philosophy (2245:12).

Consider also the following from the New Age leader Marilyn Ferguson in her *The Aquarian Conspiracy: Personal and Social Transformation in the 1980s*:

Of the [New Agers] surveyed, more were involved in education than in any other single category of work. They were teachers, administrators, policy makers, educational psychologists. Their consensus: education [must be transformed].... Subtle forces are at work, factors you are not likely to see in banner headlines. For example, tens of thousands of classroom teachers, educational consultants and psychologists, counselors, administrators, researchers, and faculty members in colleges of education have been among the millions engaged in *personal transformation*. They have only recently begun to link regionally and nationally, to share strategies, to conspire for the teaching of all they most value ... (1547:280-81.

Ferguson also points out that *Phi Delta Kappan*, perhaps the most influential journal for school administrators, stated that the field of transpersonal education not only offers tremendous potential for enhancement of learning and for solving the nation's serious social crises, but that it is "perhaps the dominant trend on the educational scene today and presages a momentous revolution" (1547:288).

Because New Age educators are convinced that their techniques are effective and can solve the world's problems, they are convinced that schools must be revolutionized in order to incorporate their methods. "Because of its power for social healing and awakening, they conspire to bring the philosophy [of transpersonal education] into the classroom, in every grade, in colleges and universities, for job training and adult education" (1547:288).

## Consequences of Occult Education

It's probably true that most educators and parents do not yet understand the ramifications of teaching occultism to children, or even introducing it to them in an offhand manner. As our book on the dangers of the occult documents (278), occult practices are dangerous to adults, and to encourage children toward occultism in any manner is extremely irresponsible. Children are impressionable; they want to please their parents and other authority figures around them. They are innately trusting. To precondition or expose them to the psychic realm is simply not in their best interest.

Children exposed to the occult become excellent subjects for conversion to the occult. For example, little Dora Kunz "began to meditate from the age of five and has been interested in various forms of meditation all her life. 'My mother,' she laughs, 'did not care what her children ate or whether they ate, as long as they did not skip meditation'" (2246:289). Today Dora Kunz is a leading spiritist, psychic healer (a codeveloper of the form of psychic healing known as Therapeutic Touch), and former president of the occult Theosophical Society.

Mantak Chia was exposed to Buddhist meditation* at the age of six, while in grammar school in Hong Kong. He also learned the martial arts,* such as T'ai Chi Chuan and Aikido, and Hatha yoga.* Today he is a practicing occultist specializing in the martial arts and "taoist esoteric yoga" (2247:42).

Thomas Armstrong's article "Transpersonal Experience in Childhood" and many other sources prove that children who are exposed to the occult in a systematic manner (including through altered states of consciousness,* visualization,* New Age inner work,* meditation,* yoga,* and psychic development) are influenced to choose that way of life after childhood. Indeed, some of the most powerful and influential occult figures in modern American life were thrust into the occult path by the powerful spiritistic experiences they had as young children. Examples include Paramahansa Yogananda, founder of the Self-realization Fellowship;* Guru Meher Baba, founder of Sufism Reoriented; medium Helena P. Blavatsky, founder of the Theosophical Society; "guru" Jiddu Krishnamurti; noted shaman Black Elk; and famous psychic healer Olga Worrall (2248). Some of these individuals, such as Ramakrishna and Yogananda, became spirit possessed or demonized as young children.

Unfortunately, numerous articles in *Gifted Child Quarterly,* and in other periodicals on the subject of children with creative abilities, indicate that psychic powers have often been placed in the category of children's gifted abilities (2251). For example, *Learning: The Magazine for Creative Teaching* has on its cover a child's drawing of her teacher's "aura." The child's words are printed on the cover: "I see white light coming out of your head and fingers. There are bright colors around your face and body." Below that we read, "Is Jessie hallucinating? Or is she one of many children with extrasensory abilities?" The article cites Rudolf Steiner's anthroposophical education, noting, "This system serves as a foundation for his remarkable theories of child development, which are parallel to those of Jean Piaget's" (2252:13).

*The Hidden Agenda*

One of the most disturbing aspects of transpersonal education is the apparent legerdemain or subterfuge of those educators who seem to have their own agenda, even regardless of parents' wishes.

Most New Age theorists and curriculum developers acknowledge problems of implementation because of parent resistance. New Age educator Gay Hendricks and Northern Illinois University educator Thomas B. Roberts write, "Often, schools that are ready to adopt new ways of teaching hesitate because they expect the parents will not understand what is going on" (2256:XIX). Nevertheless, New Age educators are pressing on. In *Spinning Inward*, Maureen Murdock encourages teachers, "You may receive resistance from some family members, but don't be deterred" (2257:14).

After heaping praise on the "heroes" in New Age education who are pioneering their methods, Marilyn Ferguson quotes Mario Fantini, former Ford consultant on education who is now at the State University of New York, as saying, "The psychology of becoming [i.e., enlightenment] has to be *smuggled* into the schools" (1547:281, emphasis added). Deborah Rozman's *Meditating with Children* is a good example of the "smuggling" going on. This book was distributed to all California public school teachers, many of whom began to implement its occult techniques in their classrooms. Rozman describes how she hides the real nature of her Eastern and occult forms of meditation:

> Due to fear of parent criticism, I call it centering and concentrating our energies.... I tell the parents and my classroom's volunteers that centering was a relaxation exercise for increasing the children's concentration. ...

The process of integrating these meditations into a classroom has been left to the teacher. This is intentional because so many changes are now occurring in classroom policy.... If you don't see how you can possibly integrate them into your particular situation, pick out the elements you feel you can use ... (2494:130).

In a question-and-answer section of *Growing Up Gifted*, Barbara Clark asks, "Can we really use altered states of consciousness in the classroom? What will the parents say?" Her answer is revealing: "The phrase altered states of consciousness may sound too strange so you need to use other terminology that better communicates what you intend to do ..." (2259:601). Thus, these educators don't often use potentially emotive or controversial terms like "meditation," "hypnosis," or "spirit guides." As Jack Canfield comments, "If you're teaching in public school, don't call it meditation, call it 'centering'" (2260:36). At a plenary session during a conference titled "Education in the 80's," the late Beverly Galyean said this about spirit guides: "Of course, we don't call them that in the public schools, we call them imaginary guides" (2492).

In *How to Help Your Child Have a Spiritual Life: A Parent's Guide to Inner Development*, psychiatrist Annette Hollander believes that a *secular* approach to New Age practices is useful for their implementation:

> A revolution is happening in education.... Transpersonal educators believe we can learn to experience the divine within ourselves. In practice, this usually means teaching children how to alter their consciousness in order to be able to relax and "center" at will, and to contact inner wisdom.... Transpersonal educators have found *secular ways* of teaching children to work on their inner lives (2254:47, emphasis added).

She points out that although altered states of consciousness* and occult rituals used to be taught only in various religions, "Now there are secular disciplines, nonreligious 'trainings' to reach those [same] goals'" (2254:63). As an illustration in the purely psychological realm, she observes, "When Chogyam Trungpa Rinpoche set up a pre-school for his Buddhist community in Boulder, Colorado, there were no Buddhist 'teachings.' The spirit of Buddhism was conveyed by the psychological state of the people who worked with the children" (2254:64).

The book *Transpersonal Education: A Curriculum for Feeling and Being* begins by noting, "Transpersonal education *is* for the whole person, and views the school as a place where this wholeness can be supported and encouraged" (2261:vii). This "wholeness" involves an essentially *religious* view. In other words, transpersonal education promotes religion in the classroom. And it has entered the classroom because its religious practices have been "stripped of their jargon":

[Transpersonal educators] are incorporating practices from a dozen fields into the teaching/learning situation. Insights gained from the upsurge of interest in meditation, biofeedback, martial arts, Eastern thought, and altered states of consciousness are finding their way into the classroom. *Stripped of their jargon,* these fields of study are accelerating and improving conventional learning, as well as bringing new and more personal areas of learning into the classroom (2261:vii).

Taking out the religious jargon supposedly means that these practices are no longer religious and therefore can be used in our public schools. But removing the Eastern and occult terms and replacing them with secular "counterparts" does not affect the essence or outcome of the practice at all. As Shakespeare observed, "A rose by any other name would smell as sweet." For example, the Hindu practice of transcendental meditation may be termed the "Science of Creative Intelligence;" the religious practice of yoga* may be called "psychophysiological exercise," and meditation* may be called "centering" and visualizing.* Spirit possession may even be called "divine companionship," and contacting pagan deities may be called contacting one's "higher self."

Christian author Charles Strohmer calls this "changing the nouns of the game" in his book, *The Gospel and the New Spirituality* (Oliver-Nelson, 1996), which is about communicating to and evangelizing New Age seekers. Strohmer

believes that the New Age penchant for renaming mystical and occult-sounding words creates semantic distortions and a whole range of communication headaches. And just as importantly, he also shows that even Carl Jung (who renamed religious, spiritual, and occult concepts with psychological terms) thought people were stupidly gullible if they believed that changing the nouns of the game in any way changed the nature of the game. For example, regarding Jung's popularizing the term "archetype," Strohmer (pp. 2814:75-77) cites Jung in *Memories, Dreams, Reflections*:

I did all in my power to convey to my intimates a new way of seeing.

[If] by employing the concept of archetype, we attempted to define more closely the point at which the daimon grips us, we have not abolished anything.

The concept of them as demonia is therefore quite in accord with their nature. If anyone is inclined to believe that any aspect of the *nature* [his emphasis] is changed by such formulations, he is being extremely credulous about words. The real facts do not change, whatever name we give them.... [T]he change of a name has removed nothing at all from reality.

This is important because the reality and methodology remain the same and have similar psychospiritual results no matter what you call it. And regardless, exposing children to religious methods without the religious words is certainly a preconditioning for those practices when they are encountered in their true context.

In *The Humanist,* John Dunphy states what everyone knows, that to a large degree the battle for the future is a battle for the minds of children. And he is perfectly clear about his particular agenda: Christianity and humanism are in a war to the finish. "I am convinced that the battle for humankind's future must be waged and won in the public school classrooms by teachers who correctly perceive their role as the proselytizers of a new faith.... [One that recognizes] Divinity in every human being.... The classroom must and will become an arena of conflict between the old and new—the rotting corpse of Christianity, together with all its adjacent evils and misery, and the new faith . . ."(2262).

In an article in the *Rocky Mountain News,* June 3, 1992, economist Thomas Sowell of the prestigious Hoover Institute discussed the bias of some modern educators and the consequences it has brought to schoolchildren. Sowell underscores what many parents seem unwilling to concede:

> The zealots know what they are doing, and are well aware of its illegitimacy. One teacher's manual for a widely used program includes instructions on how to evade complaints and how to deal with students who don't go along. A mother who complains individually is almost certain to be told that she is the only one who has ever objected. There may be controversies raging from coast to coast, and even lawsuits filed over the program, but you will still be told that you are the only one who has complained. Complain in a group and they will cry, "censorship." . . .
>
> The glib gurus who set the trends are at war with all the fundamental values of this country. . . . To such people, our children's education is a small sacrifice on the altar of their vision (2263).

This flood of new curricula did not spring up overnight. It resulted from an incremental process over the past three decades. Initially, these programs surfaced in rather blatant forms in receptive pockets of the country, such as California, but now they are widespread due largely to their cleverly disguised nature.

This strategy has also been articulated by New Age leader Dick Sutphen. "One of the biggest advantages we have as New Agers is, once the occult, metaphysical and New Age terminology is removed, we have concepts and techniques that are very acceptable to the general public. So we can change the names and demonstrate the power. In so doing, we open the New Age door to millions who would not be receptive" (2264:14).

Now stop for a moment and consider all you have read. How far have we "progressed" with this supposed enlightenment of education? Haven't we just retreated backwards into an-

cient pagan beliefs? And isn't it true that what was considered a lunatic fringe not long ago has now moved into mainstream culture?

Yet everyone knows that the quality of education has significantly deteriorated. College PSAT and ACT scores continue to fall, illiteracy continues to rise, and other indicators reflect an ongoing decline. Shouldn't this tell us something? Many educators, especially the National Education Association, have put the blame on parents and on children's low self-esteem and on behavioral problems generated from the growing number of dysfunctional homes. But it is our belief that too many educators have been promoting what might be termed an "experimental mysticism" and psychotherapy in the classrooms. We think this reflects a serious problem and that it, much more so, is responsible for the decline in education. So what can we do about it?

## PARENTS' RIGHTS

Parents must become informed about these issues. Their children's education and future are at stake, and parents have the right to be involved in what their children are taught. Happily, many parents' groups supporting traditional values have begun to emerge across the country to respond to New Age issues. And just as happily, some school boards and administrators have responded by either removing the objectionable material or, more importantly, by introducing policies to prevent new occurrences. However, many, if not most school systems have not addressed such issues, or they have reacted defensively and continue to expose students to potentially harmful curricula.

The courts have held that parents have the primary right of education for their children (see next section). Schools should be academic institutions, as they have been traditionally. "Families and communities err when by neglect or design, they transfer to the school, responsibilities that belong in the home and in the community. Schools were created to help and strengthen families, not to undermine or substitute for them" (2678:20).

In order to help change education back to an academic labor, parents and educators need to be responsive, but in an informed and intelligent manner. We provide the following summary points toward that end.

1. The New Age Movement is a spiritual and sociological phenomenon in our country, whose beliefs and practices are being established in many areas of culture.

2. It can be demonstrated that many educators and curriculum developers are personally involved in a New Age perspective, or that they have accepted New Age practices, techniques, and theories without knowledge of their true source.

3. It can be demonstrated that the adoption of New Age and occult ideology and practice is not sporadic and random, but that an underlying philosophical current moves large numbers of these curricula into American public schools.

4. These programs tend to enter the classroom through counseling, self-esteem, stress reduction, health, gifted programs, creative writing, global education, and literature curricula.

5. A frequent form that these programs take involves: deep breathing relaxation or progressive relaxation exercises, guided imagery, and visualization.* These are sometimes associated with value-free or affective-learning programs, which are inappropriate and ineffective (2243: chs. 2,3,6).

6. The techniques and the presuppositions on which such programs are based are intrinsic to Eastern and other mystical religious traditions and practices (e.g., Hinduism, meditation*). They are frequently synonymous with the techniques of hypnosis* and trance induction. And they are probably disguised so as to project a secular or nonreligious appearance.

7. Religious practice in the public schools is a violation of the Establishment Clause of the First Amendment, as public schools cannot promote the practice or ideology of religion.

8. Even if administrators refuse to acknowledge this connection to Eastern occult religions, the further problem of using hypnosis* and dissociative techniques or other psychotherapeutic methods and psychological techniques without the informed consent of parents may constitute a violation of the Hatch Amendment, and if so, is illegal.

9. It can be established that there are genuine risks and liabilities for both school and children if unlicensed teachers are involved in administering speculative or unproven therapeutic techniques. The resulting psychiatric problems that can occur may be considered malpractice.

10. Many self-esteem-oriented curricula, as well as drug or alcohol prevention and sex education curricula, utilize a "nondirective" decision-making process without empirical justification. Evidence suggests these methods have actually produced a rise in drug and alcohol abuse and promiscuity.

11. Parents should not only be well informed but closely involved with their children and teachers to make sure such practices are not occurring in the classroom.

12. Because of the frequency of incidents, we recommend that state or local school boards adopt official policy prohibiting the use of these techniques. This would prevent the costly political, emotional, educational, and financial consequences of litigation (2243:193-220).

## LEGAL AND SCIENTIFIC ASPECTS

In this section we will discuss the legal and scientific problems surrounding the controversies mentioned previously. We will discover considerations that warrant the removal of religious and psychotherapeutic-oriented curricula from the classrooms, and we will demonstrate that state board regulation (or state government legislation) is needed to provide screening guidelines for curricula selection.

### Church and State Issues

It might be helpful to start with a basic grasp of the background of the church/state issue as it relates to education. The Supreme Court has interpreted the Establishment Clause of the First Amendment to mean that a government agency, or an agency that receives funds from the government, cannot promote the ideology or practice of religion.

Our public schools have encountered problems here because of the expansion of government control over education and the compulsory nature of school attendance. A tension exists between the

Establishment Clause, which prohibits the governmental establishment of religion, and the Free Exercise Clause, which permits the free exercise of religion and prohibits government interference in religion. For example, the courts have had a difficult time distinguishing state involvement with religious symbols and activity, on the one hand, and the individual right to freedom of expression for students and teachers on the other. This right certainly includes the right of students to not have their own religious beliefs abused or prohibited by the schools.

In the end, our schools and students are left with a seemingly irresolvable dilemma: Ethics, morals, and values are ultimately and logically derived from some religious foundation, but if the courts conclude that public education is to be "religionless," they will also make them "valueless," which, by its nature, nurtures a philosophical position hostile to the Judeo-Christian tradition.

Of course, this has not always been the case. In *The Rights of Religious Persons in Public Education*, John Whitehead explains the "historic logic" of our problems today by reminding us that early America had a general acceptance or "prevalent value" of Christianity, producing a social homogeneity. This is why prayer and Christian-oriented textbooks or readers were commonplace in the schools (2679:19). But today "modern society is a collection of races, creeds, and religions not present within early American culture. Contemporary cultural diversity militates against any inculcation of 'common' values" (2679:19). For example, Christians who support the idea of school-sanctioned prayer worry that this opens the doors to all concepts of prayer, which, in today's diversified marketplace includes everything from meditation and chanting to yoga and spirit contact.

Because court decisions have been a bit unclear in resolving the tension between free exercise and the Establishment Clauses decisions are being increasingly left up to individual school boards. "The Supreme Court has recently directed the lower courts to show deference to the judgments of school boards when considering board policies or practices" (2679:147). Nevertheless, even though the trend is toward

deference, the Supreme Court also stated that deference should be given "absent any suggestion [that a school board's rule] violates a substantive Constitutional guarantee" (2679:147). This means that the courts should not unnecessarily entangle themselves in normal school operations except where there is a substantial violation of the Constitution. Although the courts are also showing an inclination to move away from parental rights, they have clearly made an exception when it comes to a violation of Constitution law, and this presents problems for the new curricula.

In brief, these problems may involve: 1) a violation of the Constitution of the United States, principally but not exclusively the First Amendment (the Establishment Clause), and the Fourth and Fourteenth Amendments, which have been interpreted as dealing with parental rights and freedom of religious rights; 2) a violation of the Protection of Pupil Rights (or Hatch) Amendment; 3) a violation of the Federal Drug Free Schools and Communities Act Amendment of 1989; 4) the resulting vulnerability to malpractice lawsuits; 5) the unfortunate wasting of valuable time and funding on programs with little or no scientific credibility.

If a public school program promotes either the ideology or practice of religion or religious philosophy, it violates the Establishment Clause prohibiting the governmental teaching of religion. Courses designed to engage a student in psychological treatment or experimentation without his or her parents' informed consent violate the Hatch Amendment. Any program or course that is clearly psychotherapeutic in nature and may be psychologically harmful is vulnerable to a malpractice lawsuit. This is especially true when psychotherapeutic methods are performed without a parent's consent and by teachers who are not licensed mental-health professionals.

Finally, can any school system justify spending scarce human resources and funding on New Age or other unsubstantiated programs that have little or no scientific credibility, or when their own objectives are vague and ambiguous? What would happen if even a reputable scientist came to a school district announcing he had developed a "smart pill" to make children 50 percent more intelligent and dramatically enhance their performance? What if he claimed the pill was completely safe and would only have to be taken three times a week? Wouldn't the Federal Drug Administration require appropriate testing to prove the claims? Wouldn't the school want to see and carefully examine the test results for themselves? Would you allow your child to take the pill without solid, long-term, established research results concerning its safety and effectiveness? And even if it were effective, is that reason enough to take such a pill automatically? Then why should our children's emotional and educational future be subject to dubious religious experimentation?

In *Thieves of Innocence*, we examined several legal and scientific issues that parents need to be informed on (1064). For example, the First, Fourth, and Fourteenth Amendments have been interpreted to provide for basic rights, including the right of parents to be the primary controllers of their child's education, and the right for one's own freedom of religion to be pursued without interference (U.S. Supreme Court decisions: *Griswold vs. Connecticut*, 1965; *Pierce vs. Massachusetts*, 1944; *Abington vs. Schempp*, 1963; *Wisconsin vs. Yoder*, 1972; *Stanley vs. Illinois*, 1972; *Mercer vs. Michigan*, 1974).

Furthermore, in 1988 the Equal Employment Opportunity Commission (EEOC) issued a policy statement intended to guide employers in handling cases where an employee refuses to participate in a training program because it conflicts with his religious beliefs. Initially, this was part of the Civil Rights Act of 1964, Title VII. But the EEOC and its attorneys deemed it important enough to make it law, and the explanation of the policy is relevant to current public school curricula. The policy begins by noting:

> Employers are increasingly making use of training programs designed to improve employee motivation, cooperation, or productivity through the use of various so-called "New Age" techniques. ... Most of the nation's major corporations and numerous government agencies have hired some consultants and purveyors of similar inside "personal growth" training programs in recent years. The programs utilize a wide variety of techniques: meditation, guided visualization, self hypnosis, therapeutic touch, biofeedback, yoga, and inducing altered states of consciousness. These programs focused on changing individual employees' attitudes and self concepts by promoting increased self-esteem, assertiveness, independence, and creativity in order to improve overall productivity (2279).

What happens if we substitute the word "schoolchildren" for "employees"? It is equally appropriate. This means that legal precedent has been set to exclude not just employees but children from practices that conflict with their religion.

In another case, *Malnak vs. Yogi*, February 2, 1979, United States Court of Appeals, Third District, parents had objected to their children being exposed to transcendental meditation as part of the regular school curriculum. But the New Jersey school district would not drop the program, requiring parents to resort to litigation. The concepts of TM had been cleverly camouflaged under neutral wording and the practice itself was given a new name, the "Science of Creative Intelligence," even though it was a Hindu practice. The judge in the federal district court found for the parents, declaring that SCI was a religious practice and therefore in violation of both the separation of church and state and the Establishment Clause of the First Amendment. The school board took their case to the U.S. Court of Appeals, where the court reaffirmed the earlier decision.

Finally, the Hatch Amendment is a Federal Law enacted under the title *Protection of Pupil Rights*, Public Law 95-561, Sec. 1250, Section 439 of the General Education Provisions Act, 20 USC 1232 g, enacted 11/2/78. It requires "prior written consent of the parent" for psychiatric or psychological "examination, testing or treatment." For example, consider Section 439:

> Sec. 439. "(a) All instructional material—including teachers' manuals, films, tapes, or other supplementary instructional material—which will be used in connection with any research or experimentation program or project shall be available for inspection by the parents or guardians of the children engaged in such

program or project, (b) for the purpose of this [section] research or experimentation program or project means any project in any [applicable] program under 98.1 (a) or (b) that is *designed to explore or develop new or unproven teaching methods or techniques"* (2280).

Sec. 439. "(b) No student shall be required, as part of any applicable program, to submit to psychiatric examination, testing or treatment, in which the primary purpose is to reveal information concerning:

(1) political affiliations;

(2) mental and psychological problems potentially embarrassing to the student or his family;

(3) sex behavior and attitudes;

(4) illegal, anti-social, self-incriminating and demeaning behavior;

(5) critical appraisals of other individuals with whom respondents have close family relationships;

(6) legally recognized privileged and analogous relationships, such as those of lawyers, physicians, and ministers; or

(7) income (other than that required by law to determine eligibility for participation in a program or for receiving financial assistance under such program), without the prior consent of the student (if the student is an adult or emancipated minor), or in the case of an unemancipated minor, without the prior written consent of the parent" (2280).

The following official definitions applicable to the Hatch Amendment also apply to many of the specific programs, beliefs, and practices which we are concerned about. These are included in the Final Regulations to implement Sec. 439 as printed in the *Federal Register,* Vol. 49, No. 174, Thursday, September 6, 1984, Rules and Regulations, pp. 35318-21:

(1) " 'Psychiatric or psychological examination or test' means a method of obtaining information, including *a group activity, that is not directly related to academic instruction* and that is designed to elicit information about attitudes, traits, opinions, beliefs or feelings;

(2) '[p]sychiatric or *psychological treatment'* means an activity involving the planned, systematic use of methods or techniques that are not directly related to academic instruction and that is *designed to affect behavioral, emotional, or attitudinal characteristics of an individual or group"* (2280).

*Malpractice*

The use of progressive relaxation, guided imagery, visualization,* and other religious or psychotherapeutic methods in the regular classroom presents another legal issue: malpractice vulnerability.

Despite disclaimers, many of the new educational methods are a form of hypnotherapy or religious meditation. We elsewhere documented that such approaches are frequently rooted in Eastern religious philosophy (1064). Even if school board members disagree, these methods still include potentially harmful psychotherapeutic techniques. And consulting the professional literature on subjects like hypnosis,* autogenics, or meditation* will show that progressive relaxation, guided imagery, and visualization methods do involve hypnosis or meditation.** Such studies indicate that the words "hypnosis" and "meditation" are frequently interchanged.***

If one consults the bibliographic citations to these studies, one consistently encounters treatments on psychotherapy and behavior modification, which brings guided imagery and visualization* under the Hatch Amendment.

---

**For the professional educator, refer him to studies in one of his own professional journals, *Elementary School Guidance and Counseling,* "Imagery in Counseling" (October, 1987, p. 5); "Imagery: Painting of the Mind" (December, 1986, p. 150); "Discipline: Can It Be Improved with Relaxation Training?" (February, 1986, p. 194); "The Effects of the Relaxation Response on Self-Concept and Acting Out Behaviors" (April, 1986, p. 255); "Relaxation Training with Intermediate Grade Students" (April, 1977, p. 259), and many more.

***In "Meditation as an Access to Altered States of Consciousness" Patricia Carrington of Princeton University points out that while meditation and hypnosis have different characteristics, "It is possible that in the broadest sense of the term, meditation is a form of hypnosis" (in 844:496; B. B. Wolman and M. Ullman (eds.), *Handbook of Altered States of Consciousness*).

Easier still, a parent or educator need only to consult the *Encyclopaedia Britannica* for the definition, methodology, and relative appropriateness of hypnosis and related methods. The *Encyclopaedia Britannica* describes various methods of hypnotic induction, including those of progressive relaxation and guided imagery. It also notes that the hypnotic subject is one who becomes highly suggestible, whose perceptions are distorted, and whose distinction between reality and fantasy becomes blurred. The articles also point out, "The induction of hypnosis requires little training and no particular skill, a tape recording often being sufficient." Thus it warns that the person leading a hypnosis session should "have the necessary training or skill to treat medical or psychological problems." This is because "improperly used, hypnosis may add to the patients' psychological or medical difficulties" (2282:133-40).

The coauthor of the article is Dr. Martin Orne of the University of Pennsylvania Medical School, one of the foremost American experts on hypnotherapy. When interviewed for a television report on parents' objections to certain programs in public schools, specifically Pumsy and DUSO, Dr. Orne was very concerned about the extensive use of these fantasy techniques in the classroom. "You can raise issues that the child is not ready to deal with—guided imagery is just another term for hypnosis. . . . You have to be very careful because an individual who is confused or troubled may require treatment, and hypnosis may not be the treatment of choice—it may encourage different thoughts which are not necessarily helpful" (2283).

Ross S. Olson, M.D., is a Minneapolis pediatrician who has expressed his own concerns over the use of guided imagery in the classroom. He believes that by turning inward, children may discover a more attractive world than that found in normal reality. Olson also believes:

There is the possibility of psychological injury to participants. . . . I am acquainted with a woman who began to have uncontrollable "out of body" experiences after a similar program. . . . [T]he [program] leaders are inadequately

prepared to deal with this possibility. [This is why] physicians using guided imagery for therapy stress that it is a powerful technique requiring proper psychological training. Finally, it is completely consistent with New Age religion and therefore should not be promoted by public schools (2285).

Dr. Olson also expresses concern because some secondary students are being taught to visualize diseases away, and that these programs may be antieducational, antirational, and medically dangerous (2286). Professional, educational, and psychological journals are also indicating potential problems with these approaches. An article in *Elementary School Guidance and Counseling* warns, "There are some situations where use of fantasy may be inappropriate. Children with serious emotional problems that tend to retreat from reality would not benefit and can be harmed by such fantasy exercises. Counselors need to screen students before they begin fantasy activities" (2287:46).

In the same journal, another article describes research findings on the Magic Circle, which is part of the Human Development Program (HDP). The Magic Circle is described as a "comprehensive, sequential, developmentally based, affective education curriculum designed for use with the general classroom population." But the question was asked, "Can psychological education be required of all students if the possibility of detrimental effects is as distinct as these results suggest?" The study revealed that there was "sufficient general and specific dissatisfaction by students with HDP to question the appropriateness" of the program for students in all cases. And the results of this study, and that of Gerler and Tupperman, "raised an important philosophical issue as to whether all children should be unquestionably exposed to developmental guidance or psychological education" (2288:137-45).

*Scientific Evidence: Wasted Resources*

The question must be raised whether these programs are cost-effective and whether there may be currently unknown side effects for

437

children. Just because a percentage of parents and educators are not concerned about the religious or psychotherapeutic aspects but only the alleged results of these programs, what if scientific testing is demonstrating the ineffectiveness of these methods? What if our children are being used as "guinea pigs" of sorts for experimental programs?

Particularly damaging to a number of New Age claims about "scientific validation" for their methods is a recent metanalysis conducted by the National Research Council and published by the National Academy Press (2289). The report was prepared by the Committee of Techniques for the Enhancement of Human Performance and the Commission on Behavioral Social Sciences and Education. It was prompted by the Army Research Institute, which asked the National Academy of Sciences to examine the value of certain techniques that had been alleged to enhance human performance and had been presented with strong claims for high effectiveness. The value of this report is that it provided a systematic approach to evaluate the *studies* that claimed that these methods enhance human potential. The range of investigation included techniques in learning, improving motor skills, altering mental states, stress management, and paranormal phenomena.

Some of the techniques or programs studied included S.A.L.T. suggestology, neurolinquistic programming (NLP), Sybervision, hemispheric brain studies in learning theory (right brain/left brain), meditation,* and subliminal self-help tapes. Their final conclusion was that the claim to enhance human performance was greatly exaggerated. Either no real research base existed to support the relationship between a given technique and subsequent performance, or the bodies of research that did exist were too poorly done or too conflicting to make valid scientific claims (2289).

Dr. Charles Heikkinen is director of counseling services at the University of Wisconsin. Although the excerpt from his article below involved a discussion of *adult* counseling methods, it is these techniques that are now being used on public school *children*! In the *Journal of Counseling and Development*, he warns, "Coun-

selors increasingly appear to be using visualization, relaxation training, and hypnosis. . . . I have also seen more people who have gone through these approaches, especially in group formats, and then had hours and even days of unusual mental functioning." For example:

In my experience, counseling strategies such as visualization, relaxation, meditation and hypnosis almost always induce a qualitatively different type of consciousness, typified by changes in emotion, increases in suggestibility and alterations in logical thought. . . . [T]hey can also induce persistent, undesirable aftereffects, including panic and confusion, unless counselors take time to re-orient clients after each session. . . . Be extremely careful when using altered states of consciousness experiences with groups whose members you do not know (2290:520-21).

Meditation* in the schools has very dubious results. Today, transcendental meditation is by far the most widely practiced form of meditation in the country. Thousands of schoolteachers have become meditators through this system and many have encouraged their students to practice TM as well. Although TM has legally been expelled from the classroom (*Malnak* vs. *Yogi*), in some school systems its procedures continue to be taught.

TM proponents claim that hundreds of research studies to validate the alleged benefits of meditation. What they don't say is that these studies have usually not been independently established through rigorous scientific testing. Even though Maharishi Mahesh Yogi's TM enterprise is worth between three billion and four billion dollars and continues to influence education, many teachers are unaware of the dozens of studies showing the harmful effects of meditation. Some of these have been annotated by an organization called the Ex-Transcendental Meditation Members Support Group in Arlington, Virginia. They state:

Suppressed by MIU [Maharishi International University] and the TM movement are many independent research studies with tighter controls which have uncovered the following actual effects from the practice of TM:

1. No specific or broad-scale benefits

2. Impaired mental faculties

3. Depersonalization

4. High percentage of psychological disorders

5. Aggravation of preexisting mental illness

6. The onset of mental illness (2291).

We might also add that in many cases TM has also actually led to outright spirit possession, as Dr. Weldon documented in his 1975 exposé *The Transcendental Explosion* (468). Social scientists Drs. Singer and Ofshe express their concerns about

> Groups relying more on the use of meditation trance states, and dissociative techniques.... A program relying heavily on meditation trance and dissociation techniques is likely to include elements of emotional arousal devices... [which] can be produced by guided imagery and other trance inducing procedures.... Groups that used prolonged mantra and empty-mind meditation, hyperventilation and chanting appear more likely to have participants who develop relaxation induced anxiety, panic disorders, multi dissociative problems and cognitive inefficiencies (2292:190,193).

As noted, a number of independent research studies have proven the use of Eastern and occult meditation can be harmful. Drs. Heide and Borkovec indicate that 54 percent of anxiety-prone subjects tested experienced increased anxiety during the TM-like mantra meditation (2293:1-12). Dr. Arnold Lazarus shows that serious psychiatric problems can ensue from the practice of TM (2294:601-60). Meditation researcher Dr. Leon Otis refers to a Stanford Research Institute study involving 574 subjects, which revealed that the longer a person practiced meditation the greater the number of adverse mental effects; indeed, 70 percent of subjects recorded mental disorders of one degree or another (2295:204).

The sad thing is that none of this is necessary if all we are seeking is stress reduction and relaxation. Five issues of *American Psychologist*, 1984-87, detailed an exhaustive TM research review and further controlled testing which demonstrated that what TM produces is no more beneficial for physical relaxation than merely sitting with one's eyes closed (2296).

Having concluded a discussion of some of the legal and scientific issues, we are now ready to look at practical remedies for a solution.

## FINDING SOLUTIONS

When a conflict occurs over educational curricula, how should a parent respond? We recommend the following.

*Understand your rights.* Tradition and the courts have consistently demonstrated that parents have *primary* rights and responsibilities in educating their children. By law, children must be educated, but parents have primacy in this. No one can force your child to participate in programs you object to.

*Be firm, but gracious.* Avoid a reactionary, emotive response. This creates a defensive atmosphere in which it is difficult to find constructive resolutions.

*Be informed.* Occasionally a parent will hear a rumor and go to the school with false accusations based on incomplete or inaccurate information. This reinforces certain stereotypes some educators have about Christians and other people with so-called "old-fashioned" values. It serves to discredit the parent and not only hinders personal respect but also communication.

It is very important to understand the school's perspective. Today schools encounter a wide variety of problems. There are children who come to school suffering from abuse and neglect. The school genuinely wants to be able to help them. This is why they are struggling for solutions. But unfortunately, conflict arises when the school initiates pro*active* programs, usually psychotherapeutic (developmental) in nature, which involve children in a way that may not be in their best interest and may conflict with parents' beliefs and values.

*Be active politically.* Be aware of local or national legislation that may affect educational issues and work toward passing or defeating it as it relates to the needs of quality education.

*Go to the teacher.* Many schools recommend or require parents to express their concerns first to the teacher. This is appropriate in many situations. Using the first three suggestions, try to arrive at an agreeable solution. Understand that the parent has a legal right to inspect any instructional material required for their child.

*Go through channels.* Be aware of the school board's policy concerning complaints. Be sure to follow *reasonable* procedures. We say "reasonable" because it has been our experience that sometimes the procedures are, unfortunately, purposely obstructive. For example, some professional journals give advice to make the complainant go through bureaucratic procedural hoops, apparently to frustrate or weary the parents.

*Make appeals.* Discover if there is any local process of appeal. If there is none, push to install one. It is important, at least in the appeal process (if not in the regular review process), that parents, as well as educators, are involved in the decisions.

The previous recommendations are standard suggestions for dealing with normal complaints over instructional methods or materials. However, because the issues raised in this chapter are broad, we also recommend the following.

*Setting Policy.* Since current educational philosophy has produced a large volume of New Age or psychotherapeutic-oriented curricula, we recommend that parents' focus on setting policy, guidelines, or regulations, not necessarily with one particular curriculum, program, or instructional material, but to cover a range of them. Even though there may now be only one particular dubious program being used, others on the market may get in. Also, programs have been known to change names and emphasis. To pass appropriate guidelines for the overall methodology and content, and not just for specific programs, is a good strategy.

The best place for challenging and setting policy is with the local or state school board. According to Howard Kirschenbaum, whose paper "Democratic Procedures for School-Community

Relations" was excerpted for the *Elementary School Guidance and Counseling* journal, the rights and responsibilities of the school board are "to set goals, objectives, policies, and standards for the school district... *to set specific guidelines for adopting school curricula and reevaluating curricula* and due process procedures for handling complaints or controversy from the community" (2680:38). Thus, school boards ought to consider issuing policies concerning religious and psychotherapeutic issues *before* disputes arise, not after they find themselves embroiled in controversy, which generates mistrust, costly litigation, and emotional, educational, and perhaps political consequences.

Opponents to family rights and traditional values will often counter with a cry of "censorship." Simply remind them that this is not the issue. The purpose of the school board is to set guidelines in evaluating curricula. There is no logical basis on which parents can be prohibited from expressing legitimate concerns over curricula. Because educators are implementing *their* ideas and methods on the children of *others*, parents have the fundamental right to question their appropriateness.

If what the parents are doing is "censorship," then what is the appropriate term for what these educators are doing? Aren't some of them engaging in their own form of religious "indoctrination"? To cry "censorship" to parents while you yourself are engaged in indoctrination seems a bit much.

Even though parents may have a legitimate complaint, there are, unfortunately, certain factions in the educational community (as well as political groups) who are causing deliberate resistance. In light of this we recommend the following additional steps.

1. In the information-gathering stage, take advantage of the materials available and the resources of groups like the American Family Association (601-844-5036), Gateway to Better Education (714-486-5437), Eagle Forum (618-462-8272), Focus on the Family (719-531-3400), Watchman Fellowship (817-277-0023), The John Ankerberg Show (615-892-7722), Citizens for Excellence in Education (714-546-5931), The

Rutherford Institute (804-978-3888), The Research Council on Ethnopsychology (707-937-3934), and the Spiritual Counterfeits Project (510-540-0300). When you approach educators, be certain the information you are presenting is accurate for the program you are examining, because programs with the same name can vary in content.

2. Begin to draw in other parents to build a coalition. One parent can have an influence, but often the amount of attention given is proportionate to the number of parents expressing strong concern. Also, reproduce materials, hold meetings, and get the information out. Some communities have effectively held large-scale informational meetings so that everyone hears both the information and recommendations at the same time. This helps to minimize uninformed and inappropriate emotional reactions, which do more harm than good. In some cases, organizing a non-profit "parents' rights" group has also been appropriate and helpful.

3. Maintain a cooperative spirit. Always assume the best on the part of your child's teacher. Parents and educators should be reminded that they are working together. A cordial face-to-face meeting can do wonders. If an adversarial position is taken, let it be on the part of the educators and not the parents.

4. Make it clear that these instructional methods and their content raise multiple concerns, any one of which would require removing the harmful curricula and setting standards to screen out other potential problems, such as: a) the underlying religious philosophy of these materials, b) the use of inappropriate psychological methodologies, c) the lack of scientific verifiability, d) their potential dangers (278).

5. Make sure documentation is available to school board members and all concerned parties.

6. Know the political landscape. Ideally, school boards are serving their constituents (the parents) and, therefore, should appropriately instruct the superintendents and teachers about parents' concerns, but this does not always happen. Some school districts are run by the superintendents, who may be either elected or appointed. Determine the best approach to maximize passage of your policy recommendation. Also keep

in mind that a few dozen or a few hundred votes can radically change the makeup of a school board. Most school board elections have such a low turnout that the votes in a large Sunday school class can determine who is or isn't elected.

7. Try to recruit and select the most articulate and influential representatives from among parents to meet individually and collectively with board members or superintendents.

8. If there is resistance, devise a well-organized plan to involve the media and to generate public support. But be circumspect about giving interviews to the news media, e.g., communication through press releases will lessen the chance of misrepresentation, but a story written up by a journalist who works for the newspaper may increase chances of misunderstanding.

9. It is crucial to be aware of the arguments and tactics of certain professional educators' groups that actively seek to forward their own agenda and oppose those who disagree with it (see 1064:193-209).

10. Obviously, a parent's own school district is of immediate concern, but we should not neglect policy enactment on a statewide level. We recommend parents or a coalition of parents' groups meet with each state school board member to formulate policy or regulations covering all state school districts. (A proposed Policy Statement is found in 1064:297-99.) Be aware that educators will acknowledge parents' rights to exercise domain over their own children but not over others' children. In other words, they believe the teacher or school has the right of greater influence.

11. Some parents believe that a better route is to have legislation enacted. Watchman Fellowship in Birmingham, Alabam, can assist here.

12. If all of these measures fail, then the last resort would be litigation. This is costly both in terms of money and community-school relations, but the issues involved and our children's futures are important enough to seriously consider it.

In conclusion, remember that parents have the legal right to remove their children from programs that conflict with their values. However, this, too, can have liabilities. A teacher or other children can make the child feel ostracized. It may be better for a child to remain in the classroom and be assigned other activities, such as reading a book or homework. In fact, the other students may actually be jealous of those who are excused from these programs, since many of the students don't like the programs.

In certain cases, older children are, with their parents' help, able to discern the issues and participate in these programs using them to good advantage—asking questions of the teacher, seeking to point out their implications, weaknesses, or problems. Ideally, parents should only pull their children from programs when the children are forced to participate in something destructive, or if so young the children will be swayed by the teaching. Make sure removal is done with kindness, respect, and discretion. And even if parents remove their children, they should continue to work for implementation of new policies.

All of this underscores an important fact: current priorities are upside down. The current approach is an "opt out" option, in which the burden is on parents to remove their children from programs that should, in all probability, never have been adopted in the first place. This has allowed educators to control education for their own purposes without parental input. A school's approach should involve an "opt in" philosophy. Here schools would be required to have parental permission *before* a curriculum is adopted, and it would have to involve full disclosure of what a program consists of philosophically and educationally. This would result in most controversial programs being rejected before implementation.

Be encouraged that there are many good educators who are not agenda-conscious but have introduced these dubious programs innocently. When presented with appropriate documentation regarding one's concerns, they are usually reasonable and will comply. But there are segments in the educational establishment like the National Education Association, People for the American Way, and others who may strongly resist family rights and traditional values. We agree with Pearl Evans in *Hidden Danger in the Classroom*:

You resist because you're working for the good of the child, sound principles and practices, excellence in education, the rights of parents and citizens, and free access to information. . . . But be forewarned: If you don't put your whole heart and head into this effort, you'll lose this fierce and long term battle; it's not for cowards. You'll have to overcome and outlast. . . .

Even though it may not seem so at first, remember you [can] have the public on your side. One or two may have to work alone until others gain hope and courage. In the end, however, you'll find that parents of all backgrounds and beliefs care about the good of their children and will join you (2640:77).

In other words, "Fight the good fight of the faith . . .", and "Let us not lose heart in doing good, for in due time we shall reap if we do not grow weary" (1 Timothy 6:12; Galatians 6:9 NASB).

## TEACHING CHILDREN TO HEAR SPIRITS

Mediums and other channelers or spiritists continually report how their spirit guides show concern for the children's "education" through psychic development. In her book on how to contact and use your own spirit guides, Laeh Garfield states, "Parenting had been one of the the important activities Johannah [the spirit guide] helped me with" (349:116). She claims that when mothers take their young children to spirit guide workshops, "Newborns and infants who attend these workshops have bubbled and cooed with excitement upon the appearance of their mother's guide" (349:98).

One reason Garfield encourages children to contact their own spirit guides is because "the majority of our celestial friends have worked out their human negativity and have no plans to abuse us in any way" (349:96). Nevertheless, she also reports:

Young children often encounter their totem animals [spirit guides] in dreams, dreams which are sometimes frightening. The animal may appear extra-large; it may try to come closer and closer. When a child awakes from a dream like this, the well-meaning parent tends to rush in and provide assurance of ordinary reality. What the child needs, however, is the reassurance that it's natural, when small, to be scared of communicating with the agents that foster one's higher self. Children commonly have such visions between the ages of four and seven, a period of time when their guides are reaffirming the life and work they are to do and the path that they are to take (349:52).

In other words, if your child is encountering spirits, let the process continue, even if it's frightening. This is why Garfield emphasizes:

Guides are of particular importance to the well-being of children. In many instances your child's imaginary friends are actually his guides, so don't deny their existence or try to send them away. One of the worse things that children go through is being told to give up what they know, especially concerning their connections with the world of spirit. Your child needs his guides as surely as he needs you, and as surely as you need guides of your own (349:44-45).

Not surprisingly, Seth, the spirit guide of the famous medium Jane Roberts, has "written" a book specifically to encourage children to develop psychic powers and to encounter their own spirit guides, *Emir's Education in the Proper Use of Magical Powers*. Seth is not the only popular spirit who has "written" books for children; so has "Ramtha." Ramtha requested Douglas James Mahr, who was later converted to Christianity, to write a child's book under his guidance, *The Ominous Dragon of Dothdura*. These are only two of many children's books on the occult (often dictated from the spirit world) that parents can purchase at bookstores or check out from libraries. Some publishers concentrate stongly on occult and spiritistic books for children.

For example, the spiritistic publisher Stillpoint's Spring/Summer 1987 catalog offered the following children's books: Kathleen J. Fonti, *The Door to the Secret City* (spirit guides for children); Chuck Hillig, *The Magic King* (building the child's inner kingdom); Shaun deWarren,

*Harris Visits the Garden of Everything* (bringing the child's "dream reality" back to "awake reality"); Jane Roberts' *Emir's Education in the Proper Use of Magical Powers*.

The Spring 1987 catalog for Celestial Arts publishers offered the following as children's books: Joyce Petschek, *The Silver Bird*, which is described as "a book of teachings, disguised in the form of a fantasy" and covering inner guides, astral projection, reincarnation, the power of crystals, dream work, "archetypes of the superconscious," and Tibetan Buddhism; Richard M. Koff, *Christopher* (children's psychic powers); spiritistic thanatologist Elisabeth Kubler-Ross, *Remember the Secret* (spirit guides who teach that there is no death); Vernon Brown, *Return of the Indian Spirit* (shamanism for children).

Following we describe several other examples of actual or potential spiritism in modern education.

*Jean Porter.* Jean Porter is the author of the book *Psychic Development*. She had her own psychic abilities "awakened" through the same techniques she describes in her article on how to use psychic development in the classroom:

Everyone has psychic abilities. Not everyone has explored some of the ways to develop them. . . . The first step involves going inward to find a place which for you is experienced as an inner sanctuary, a retreat, or a place of inner peace. This is a real place in the inner environment of your mind and is to be explored with care, delight, and offensive discovery. You will use the psychic abilities of seeing, hearing, and sensing as well as telepathic communication (2311:77-78).

She also describes how to use the imagination and visualization* (active imaging and receptive visualization) to develop children psychically. There is little difference here between the kind of visualization techniques and experiences used for psychic or non-psychic purposes. This indicates that when visualization is used for "educational" reasons, it is laying the same groundwork that psychics lay in preparation for their own psychic development.

Through visualization, Porter teaches how to contact spirit guides. After visualizing the proper

443

environment, the participant is approached "mentally" by a spirit guide: "You now are aware as to whether this being is masculine in appearance and energy or feminine.... In a warm, friendly manner this being approaches you.... [T]his being is your guide..." (2311:81). She even identifies it specifically as a spirit guide: "What has happened is that this spirit guide, a non-physical part of yourself but not a product of your imagination, is perceived by your receptive visualization as a form to which you can relate as you would to a friend. It is the expression of your higher consciousness..." (2311:82).

*Thomas Armstrong.* Thomas Armstrong is director of Late Bloomers Educational Consulting Services in Berkeley, California, and has taught undergraduate courses in childhood and adolescent development. In his article "Children As Healers," he discusses his belief that children can be trained to become sensitive to psychic energy and become psychic healers, allegedly because "children have access to healing energies which are not available to the average adult..." (2312:16). He believes that children "are healers on many levels" because they have an innate openness to "subtle energies, alternative cultural realities, and developmental shifts of awareness" which permits the process of psychic healing to occur unimpeded by rigid or self-limiting belief systems (2312:18).

As an example of how to help children become healers, he cites the shamanistic* tradition. Here youngsters will receive their "guardian spirit" (often in the form of a power animal), which serves as a guiding principle or "healing factor" in their future role as a shaman. "The youngster then joins the shaman and over a period of years is taught the outward rituals and the inward principles of healing..." (2312:18). Armstrong has proposed a Center for the Study of Childhood Consciousness where researchers, parents, and teachers can "gather with children to explore those dimensions" within a child's experience that open them to become psychic healers (2312:18-19).

*Gerald Jampolsky.* Gerald Jampolsky is the author of *Children As Teachers of Peace,* a book

based upon the spiritistic writings found in *A Course in Miracles.** He also shows how children can become psychically attuned to alleged healing energies.

*Joseph Chilton Pearce.* In "Freeing the Mind of the Magical Child," educator Joseph Chilton Pearce says that one of our false assumptions which is "particularly damaging to children" is that children must be "civilized" by being taught "adult ideas about the world and reality" (2319:23-25). In the article he encourages parents and teachers to accept the potential of powerful occult powers which reside within children.

*Jan Ehrenwald.* Writing in the National Education Association Journal, *Today's Education,* psychiatrist Jan Ehrenwald comments that psychic phenomena, spiritism, astrology, yoga, various forms of divination, magic, and parapsychology may hold forth the promise of revitalizing our culture (2313:28-30).

*Georgi Lozanov.* Hypnotist and psychotherapist Dr. Georgi Lozanov of the Suggestology Institute in Sophia, Bulgaria, developed the educational method known as Suggestopedia, which attempts to accelerate learning through relaxation, hypnosis, meditation, concentration, and suggestion. This approach, also known as the Lozanov method, has gained attention throughout the world and was popularized in America in Ostrander and Schroeder's 1979 book *Super Learning.* The Lozanov method in the United States is referred to as Suggestive/Accelerative Learning and Teaching Techniques (SALTT, also SALT; 2314:326).

*New Age* magazine observed that in formulating "suggestology," of which Suggestopedia is a branch, Lozanov and his coworkers garnered insights from hypnosis,* parapsychology, autogenics, and especially yoga*: "Suggestology's deepest roots lay in the system of raja yoga" (2315:28). Raja yoga involves altered states of consciousness,* visualization* training, mind concentration exercises, yogic breathing methods, and so on, which help to develop psychic powers, or *siddhis.*

What is also significant is that Dr. Lozanov developed his "super learning" techniques in part by studying people with psychic abilities. Then he selected out "appropriate" learning methods from those having such spiritistic powers (2315:29-30).

The University of Iowa in Des Moines is a leading research and development center for the SALTT method, and Picayune, Mississippi, elementary schools use the SALTT method. SALTT illustrates how a program may evolve over the years and how persons concerned with transpersonal approaches need to carefully evaluate not only a program's origin but also its modification.

*James W. Peterson.* James W. Peterson's *The Secret Life of Kids: An Exploration into Their Psychic Senses* reveals that if encouraged to do so, children can become excellent subjects for the development of psychic awareness and psychic abilities. Peterson has taught elementary school children for many years in both public and private settings. He has been director of a middle school at Concordia Montessori School in Concord, California, and teaches courses in "Psychic and Spiritual Development in Children" and "New Age Education Movements in America" at the New Age oriented John F. Kennedy University at Orlinda, California.

Joseph Chilton Pearce, noted above, states in the foreword to Peterson's book that "psychic capacities are an integral and early part of a general development which is always by nature spiritual. When we grasp how these early psychic abilities are designed by nature to be integrated into and put to the service of higher realms of intelligence later in life, the mature spiritual intuitions, we are then well on the road to realizing what this divine play of development of consciousness is of all about" (2316:XI).

In his book on the psychic lives of children, Peterson discusses various psychic senses: telepathy, clairvoyance, spirit playmates, past-life experiences, and others. He cites noted spiritist Olga Worrall, who has had encounters with spirits since the age of three, as an illustration of the potential "abilities" of children. He concludes that such things are either emerging evolutionary advances or the natural products of transpersonal forms of education that have the capacity to bring

out children's "human potential." This is why Peterson says that parents and teachers must help children who are psychically sensitive:

> Since many children seem to be sensitive to hidden dimensions of life [psychic realities], those charged with their care should themselves become more aware of these dimensions. The secret life of kids compels us to see effective child care in new, non-traditional, and even non-physical ways. Learning to cope with the psychic world can be an adventure in itself, in which parents and teachers discover new realms of life as they learn new ways to meet the needs of these children (2316:205).

But what is significant is that even Peterson is worried at the current trend of encouraging children with a wide variety of New Age practices. He warns parents and teachers:

> The child care-giver who nurtures an interest of the psychic life of children is quickly inundated with trendy practices and techniques: guided imagery, visualization, yoga, meditation, breathing exercises, psychic expansion, psychic channeling, chakra awareness, aura balancing, dream research, past life journeys, out-of-body trips, color counseling, music therapy, visionary art, crystal sensitization, and the list goes on. My personal view is that the psychological development of a child, as seen from the spiritual perspective, indicates that many of these "New Age" practices may be less appropriate for children than one might think (2316:207).

Again, many are not listening to warnings of this sort and continue to advocate these methods, especially for children they consider gifted, advanced, or creative.

Peterson's point is that children are simply not able to handle the powerful psychic realities that they may encounter in these practices. As an occultist, he believes that these practices are all to the good. But he points out that even occult theory suggests—if not requires—that such occult practices must be utilized at the *proper* stage of individual and spiritual development:

> Many teachers who advocate meditation for children will argue that it does work, that

children love it, and that it can help keep psychic channels open. From the perspective of the present discussion, these three statements are true. Meditation can "work" for children, but it works completely differently from the way it does for adults. Furthermore, I am suggesting, it is more often than not counterproductive and sometimes even dangerous. . . .

Meditative and spiritual practices for children can encourage the psychic permeability of [their] *chakra* membranes . . . and interfere with correct development of [psychic] filtering processes. Children can thus be trained to remain open to the psychic world, but is this helpful for them? The astral world is a realm of duality; it contains negative as well as positive influences. A child rendered more open and vulnerable to astral impressions may not be in an enviable position, especially during adolescence. Children are not sufficiently in control of their minds to protect themselves from the powerful, negative currents in the astral. Nightmares, terrifying visions, obsession and possession can be the eventual outcome (2316: 211-12).

To think that transpersonal education is innocuous is considered naive even for some occult educators. As more and more children are exposed to the occult and the damage increases, more and more people will become aware of the folly of encouraging children in occult practices. And as transpersonal and other forms of occult education continue to increase in our culture, we may frequently be forced to deal with demon possessed children. Even Peterson admits, "I have been told that children can be particularly vulnerable to [spirit] possession at the ages of four, five and six" (2316:213). Although stated in an occult and not Christian context, he comments that "incarnate beings" sometimes deliberately attempt to "cause psychic trouble for a child" (2316:214). And so he warns:

Any "spiritual" training children receive which makes their minds blank and passive can, in my view, render them more open and vulnerable to possession. Ouija boards can be particularly dangerous. . . . Furthermore, any training in telepathy or past-life reading, in which children

are told to open to inner images, seems to me risky. . . . And once they passively allow outside energies to be consciously channeled through them, possession could be the outcome. I am even suspicious of art training in which the child is taught to leave himself open to his "intuition" before beginning a drawing or painting.

There are schools that attempt to train children in these passive abilities, including a "seminary for psychic children" in Northern California that attempts to open kids up to the astral world. This group also offers seminars for adults on topics such as "how to allow a child to express psychic abilities" and "how to meditate with your child." The view expressed is, "If your child is not already psychic, he ought to be and, with our help, he most certainly will be!" (2316:215).

Peterson also argues that developing psychic abilities as a child can be contrary to natural growth processes and may "seriously undermine, proper intellectual and emotional development." He also believes that psychic development in children "can be dangerous" for another reason: the possibility of childhood schizophrenia (2316:215).

He also questions the validity of psychic development at any school age because "the overwhelming majority of informants found their paranormal experiences confusing and distracting, or even frightening. Another frequent theme is that these experiences interfered with the ability to make friends, to do well in school, and generally to feel happy and comfortable" (2316:216).

We should emphasize that Peterson, despite his concerns and criticisms, does not advocate that children are never to be educated in the psychic realm. To the contrary, education must simply be done with regard for the potential dangers and with due concern to prevent problems, and thus to make the emerging "spiritual or psychic awareness of the child" a positive, life-nurturing process:

The recognition of the secret life of children might well be another revolutionary development in child psychology. Although these widespread, atavistic psychic abilities of children reveal a great deal about the natural relationship of children with inner spiritual realms of existence, one cannot understand them by studying the functioning of corresponding psychic abilities in adults. The mechanism of childhood psychism is unique to children, and it is for this reason that one should not start tampering with and developing additional psychic channels in the child by training them with essentially adult practices of yoga and meditation. Rather, the secret life of kids should be acknowledged in a quiet, relaxed, and natural way (2316:220).

Another one of his chief concerns is over how many of these techniques are used:

Guided imagery and visualization techniques are popular these days. Often these techniques are used to take children on bizarre astral journeys, to confront projections of their inner being, "spirit guides," or other astral creatures. Although I do not recommend these exercises for young children, there is no reason visualization activities should be neglected. Modern education is far too reliant on auditory memory, and educators do not take proper advantage of other facets of the child's consciousness (2316:217-18).

*Frances Vaughan Clark.* Frances Vaughan Clark is a transpersonal educator and former president of the Association for Transpersonal Psychology. She defines "transpersonal education" in the following manner:

Transpersonal education is concerned primarily with the study and development of consciousness, particularly those states commonly called higher states of consciousness and with the spiritual quest as an essential aspect of human life. . . . [In this quest the belief that] all things are seen as one Reality, remains central to the transpersonal approach. . . . [T]ranspersonal education challenges the mind to revise outmoded conceptual structures, discarding those belief systems, be they rational or revealed, which do not account for the full range of human potential. . . . [T]he objective of transpersonal education is the realization and maintenance of higher states of consciousness . . . (2317:1,3,4,7).

When Vaughan refers to human potentialism, she includes a wide range of fields and beliefs, including parapsychology, people as possessing latent divinity, and many forms of psychic practice. She believes that the regular practice of meditation is key to transpersonal education (2317:6).

She also underscores a point which many have neglected to fully understand. Transpersonal education rejects Christian beliefs as innately inferior. In most forms of transpersonal education, the concept of revealed religion—one which supplies man with absolute truths—is seen as an extremely rigid, "lower form" of education and knowing. Transpersonal education encourages "discarding those belief systems" that reject the concepts of occult philosophy and human potential.

Thus, the educational philosophy of transpersonal approaches is concerned with the promoting of subjective "spiritual" experience. For example, Vaughan states:

Unlike religious education, transpersonal education is not concerned with teaching a particular doctrine or inculcating a particular belief system. It focuses, rather, on the process of discovery and transcendence of self which results from spiritual practice, affirming subjective experience as valid and even essential for determining the nature of reality and the relative validity of revealed truth. . . . [T]ranspersonal education [is] a process to balance knowledge about a subject with direct intuitive knowing of particular states of being [i.e., ]. . . . Without self-awareness knowledge of facts may be of little value (2317:1,4,5).

In other words, children are taught that subjective experiences derived from altered states of consciousness* are "essential" not only for determining the nature of reality, but also for ascertaining "the relative validity of revealed truth." Thus, transpersonal education sees biblical revealed truth as having only "relative validity" at best. But the experience of some form of pantheism, where all things are seen as one divine reality, is supposedly the "final experience" by which everything else is to be judged.

*Hugh Redmond.* Hugh Redmond is a faculty fellow at Johnston College in Redlands, California, and the codeveloper of undergraduate and graduate programs in transpersonal education. He has taught courses in parapsychology, altered states of consciousness, and transpersonal psychology. He believes, "An expanded image of man is evolving out of the literature and work in transpersonal psychology, one which has deep implications for educational philosophy and practice.... Transpersonal education is committed to the expansion of all human abilities.... Experience, intra- and interpersonal, is the major mode of learning" (2318:9).

Thus, Professor Redmond espouses the transpersonal education view that experience is an essential, if not *the* essential, form of learning. But what are the experiential techniques to bring about this alleged learning? Professor Redmond identifies them as meditation,* biofeedback, psychosynthesis, various spiritual practices, dream studies, guided fantasies, yoga,* physical discipline such as the martial arts,* and practices such as from Buddhism (2318:9). In the transpersonal

education programs that he has developed, he also includes altered states of consciousness, Zen, psychic self-regulation, parapsychology, Jungian psychology, Western mysticism, and human energy systems (2318:9).

In other words, the means by which the core aspect of transpersonal education (i.e., learning by mystical experience) is activated is through various forms of New Age, Eastern, and occult practices. Redmond also sees the following as goals for transpersonal education: 1) the exploration of altered states of consciousness, 2) an atmosphere that will stimulate the psychic and creative growth of students, 3) the development of a paradigm for higher education that enlarges the awareness of reality and permits the experience of deeper levels of reality, 4) providing a forum for the merging of Eastern and Western spiritual traditions, 5) the encouragement of intuitive and spiritual abilities (2318:9).

All of this is further evidence that common spiritistic practices and New Age philosophies are being used in various educational programs and seminars.

# NEW AGE INNER WORK

## INFO AT A GLANCE

**Description.** New Age inner work involves turning inward to seek the "wisdom" of alleged inner guides, "sanctified" or empowered imagination, the power of the unconscious mind, "archetypes," and other information sources. Concepts from Jungian psychology in particular are employed in New Age inner work.

**How does it claim to work?** For New Agers, every person has a divine "inner core" or "higher self" that can be contacted by the proper methods (meditation,* visualization,* dream work,* yoga,* Jungian active imagination, shamanistic practice,* and so on). This inner core is said to be a reservoir of wisdom and information on any number of subjects.

**Scientific evaluation.** Discredited; neither brain research nor the objective study of the mind offers evidence for the claims of New Age inner work.

**Examples of occult potential.** Psychic development, spiritism.

**Major problems.** Spiritism is masked under neutral categories (e.g., the unconscious mind or "higher self") and redefined as latent human potential.

**Biblical/Christian evaluation.** The inner nature of man is not a storehouse of tremendous divine wisdom and power; rather, man's true inner nature is sinful and self-serving (Jeremiah 17:9; Matthew 15:19-20).

**Potential dangers.** Psychological hazards (e.g., forms of psychopathology); problems resulting from self-deception or the reception of false information from the inner work in any number of areas (e.g., finances, doctrine, health; occult influences).

*Note:* See chapters on Intuition, Visualization, Shamanism, Dream Work, Yoga, and Channeling for discussions of related issues.

## INTRODUCTION AND INFLUENCE

For many people, the answer to many of their problems is to turn inward to a so-called "higher self," "intuitive wisdom," the unconscious mind, or "inner guides," however these may be conceptualized. In the New Age Movement, the number of inner guidance methods, self-help therapies, and self-medication treatments is legion. We could not begin to catalog and evaluate them all here.

We are concerned with these supposedly "harmless" inner work methods, which are frequently employed in various forms of psychotherapy, medicine, and religion, because they make it difficult to properly or authoritatively evaluate the information received. In other words, where does one get reliable information from subjective inner processes? And just how reliable is one's unconscious mind, intuition,* or an alleged "higher self" or "inner guide"? Furthermore, if the "inner guide" acts of its own volition, independently of a person, how can one be certain not to have contacted a spirit entity who may have ulterior motives?

Many people today scoff at the idea of a real devil and demons:

> There is a supernatural world, which is real: a world in which not only God and His angels exist but also Satan and his demons. Many today doubt the existence of a real Satan or real demons. Yet if one were to honestly consider the positive consensus of history and religion—the testimony of active occultists as to the reality of evil spirits, the documented cases of demon possession, the hostility to historic biblical Christianity displayed in virtually all spiritistically inspired literature, and the claims of the Bible and the testimony of Jesus Christ as to the reality of Satan and demons—one would find it difficult to deny their existence and involvement in our world. In light of the vast amount of evidence, to reject the possibility of the existence of Satan and demons solely on the basis of rationalistic or materialistic presuppositions would at best be foolish and at worst very dangerous (433:74).

In this chapter, we will examine this tendency to turn inward for help and counsel and show that this method often becomes the means to receive spiritistic information under other names.

Given the influence of practices such as visualization,* occult meditation,* shamanism,* altered states of consciousness,* Jungian psychology, using psychic powers, plus the hundreds of transpersonal or fringe psychotherapies

stressing inner potential (860), it is evident that New Age inner work is being practiced by millions. Indeed, many people argue that unless we actively engage in transformational inner work, achieving psychological health will not be possible and the end result will only be neurosis. In other words, inner work keeps us psychologically healthy; failing to engage in inner work results in psychopathologies. Consider the following statement by Robert A. Johnson, a noted Jungian analyst who has studied at the Jung Institute in Switzerland and at the Sri Aurobindo ashram in India. In *Inner Work: Using Dreams and Active Imagination for Personal Growth*, he asserts that it is a psychological *necessity* to establish contact with the unconscious mind and to communicate with its "enormous" power:

> To get a true sense of who we are, become more complete and integrated human beings, we must go to the unconscious and set up communication with it.... Jung showed us that the conscious and the unconscious minds both have critical roles to play in the equilibrium of the total self. When they are out of correct balance with one another, neurosis or other disturbances result.... [Thus] we need to consult the unconscious and cooperate with it in order to realize the full potential that is built into us.... The unconscious is an enormous field of energy.... The purpose of learning to work with the unconscious is ... [that] we learn to tap that rich load of energy and intelligence that waits within.... If we go to that realm consciously, it is by our *inner work:* our prayers, meditations, dream work, ceremonies, and Active Imagination. If we try to ignore the inner world, as most of us do, the unconscious will find its way into our lives through pathology: our psychosomatic symptoms, compulsions, depressions, and neurosis (2472:3-6,8-11).

As we will document, the problem here is that people repeatedly confuse spiritistic influences with psychological processes. This largely occurs as the result of our culture's turn to the occult, the psychologization of occult powers, and the indiscriminate acceptance of dubious mental processes (e.g., Jung's active imagination) as a means to spiritual or psychological empowerment and enlightenment.*

## HAL BENNETT AND
## INNER GUIDES

Hal Bennett is the cofounder of "PATH: Inner Resources" and a leading author and spokesman for New Age human potentialism. In *Inner Guides, Visions, Dreams and Dr. Einstein*, he states how easily many people are persuaded to trust their "inner wisdom":

> I know of business people, artists, teachers, salespeople, doctors, college professors, psychotherapists, and health practitioners who never make a major decision without going into the privacy of their inner worlds to consult with their inner guides.
>
> I think it is not exaggerating to say that throughout Western society we are experiencing a major shift in our understanding of the self (426:141-143).
>
> Until the past two decades, techniques for getting to know the inner world, to travel safely within it, have been in the hands of an elite—the priest, the oracle, the guru, the shaman, and more recently the psychologist.
>
> We are living in a time of vast change, a time when greater and greater numbers of people are asking for information and tools to expand their understanding and mastery of their own inner worlds. In the Reformation of the sixteenth century, mankind claimed and won the right to *private judgement* in interpreting the Bible.... [W]e are claiming and winning our rights to private judgements about our own inner worlds (426:19).

However, *Inner Guides, Visions, Dreams and Dr. Einstein* is about the spiritistic potential of a directed use of the imagination and related psychological practices. (The text is one in a series of the Celestial Arts "Field Guide to Inner Resources" book, intended for "tapping the reality of our inner worlds"; 436:iv). In his annotated bibliography, Bennett describes six books which influenced the writing of *Inner Guides* (426:160). They include Aldous Huxley's *The Island*, a utopian novel about a society where the norm is to draw upon one's "inner resources"; occult therapist Roberto Assagioli's *The Act of Will*, which discusses his inspiration by an "inner

voice"; Hyemeyohsts Storm's *Seven Arrows*, which "has done more than most to introduce shamanic techniques in a way that is entertaining, responsible, clear and usable in contemporary life"; and occult psychologist (340; cf. 339:10-11) Carl G. Jung's autobiography, *Memories, Dreams, Reflections*. Bennett is "especially grateful to Jung" for introducing certain concepts germane to his own work (426:162).

As noted, Bennett is a leader in the human potential and holistic health movement (cf. New Age Medicine). He is also a spiritist and co-author of three books with spiritist-physician Mike Samuels, M.D.: *The Well Body Book*, *Well Body, Well Earth*, and *Spirit Guides: Access to Inner Worlds*. The latter was channeled by a spirit guide, as was a great deal of information for their other books. Consider the importance Bennett and Samuels place on contacting inner guides while writing:

> *The Well Body Book*...became a highly respected and loved basic text for the self-help health movement, eventually to be published in five languages and distributed worldwide. I mention this because while writing that book, Mike and I turned time and again to our inner guides. At one point, there was a long poem or song that was dictated to me by an American Indian shaman I met through the inner guide I called Hilda.... [I]t provides me with a very solid philosophy of medicine and healing that would be an important influence in my life forever after (426:60).

Bennett explains how they wrote their book on spirit guides:

> Because inner guides were so important to Mike and I, we decided that we would like to write a book about them. That was in 1972, soon after completing *The Well Body Book*. We called the new book *Spirit Guides: Access to Inner Worlds*. It was channeled to us through a guide called "Kishah."
>
> *Spirit Guides* was a tiny book, a scant 50 pages in length, that provided basic information about inner guides. Judging by the mail we got and the feedback we received from people in workshops who used it, the book was instrumental in

encouraging people all over the country in making use of inner guides in their lives.

Indeed we received praise from a number of physicians, including a long letter from a Jungian analyst who told how the book described "some successful approaches toward experiencing the helpful resources which are present in those events of fantasy, daydreams, hunches, intuition, and feeling which we call our inner life."

In the years since writing that little book, I have learned a great deal more about the use of inner guides. My expanded work on the use of guides, as well as Zuni fetiches, healing circles, dreams, and visions carried me quite beyond what we had been able to accomplish in that first book on spirit guides (426:60-61).

What is germane to our discussion is the subtle manner in which Bennett met his initial spirit guide and the end results, partially indicated above.

## INNER GUIDES AS PERSONAL IMAGINATION AND OTHER PSYCHOLOGICAL STATES

Bennett met his first spirit guide while driving down the freeway, and he was initially unaware it was anything other than his own imagination. "In the drive between West Marin [county] and Berkeley, I began talking with what I took to be an imaginary character who appeared in my mind.... He introduced himself to me as Alex.... Certainly it had never occurred to me that he might be an entity separate from myself" (426:149-50).

It did occur to him when "Alex" began to display his own volition, will, and personality. Bennett soon realized that he had carried on a conversation with a real spirit for several *months,* all the time thinking that it was only "an imaginary character who appeared in my mind"—one that he had simply "made up."

If nothing else, this shows the folly of assuming that all inner guides are merely "imaginary." It also reveals that spirits have the capacity to "blend into" or otherwise utilize human consciousness (see the New Age Intuition chapter for additional illustrations). Thus, once occult

practices enter the picture, distinguishing the normal workings of the mind from spiritistic influence is not always easy.

This may also hold true even when serious psychological disturbances enter the picture. Dr. Arthur Hastings is a former acting president and dean of faculty at the California Institute of Transpersonal Psychology in Menlo Park, California. He is also a member of the Parapsychological Association, an adjunct professor of Parapsychology at John F. Kennedy University, and past president of the Association for Transpersonal Psychology. He believes that there appears to be no known objective method for distinguishing psychic phenomena such as spirit influence from the abnormal workings of the mind: "Some psi phenomena can be mimicked by psychopathology. As indicated above, a person may hear inner voices purporting to come from discarnate beings—but these may also be parts of his or her personality that are separated from the main system of consciousness. So far as I now there is no objective means of distinguishing between these two possibilities" (944:145).

Of course, from a biblical and Christian perspective spiritistic influence and mental illness *can* be distinguished, although there are sometimes overlapping areas (see 270). The point is that the interface of spiritistic influence and human consciousness, normal or abnormal, is an area that is difficult to evaluate.

Although the reality of spiritistic contacts operating under the guise of psychological categories such as the imagination is now a popular and growing phenomenon, it is hardly a novel idea. Similar concepts can be found in many occult traditions, such as shamanism,* witchcraft, Western magic, and in various New Age practices such as visualization* and dream work.* In all this the spirits may either be conceived as real entities or psychological constructs, and they may be contacted by ordinary psychological processes modified for such purposes.

For example, in her book that intersects shamanistic principles with modern medicine, Dr. Jeanne Achterberg describes how shamans use a directed imagination (e.g., visualization*) to contact the supernatural world and to call on "good" and evil spirits (143:14-27). In other forms of healing, such as witchcraft and dream incubation, actual spirits—though they are often perceived as psychological inner guides—are contacted through psychological methods. The question is, when so many traditional occult practices maintain that the spirits are real, why do so many Americans think that they are "imaginary" inner guides? As one anthropologist and researcher of shamanism reflects, "Whatever else they are, spirits are certainly hypotheses used to explain what we would regard as psychological states . . ." (586:192).

One advantage of the "imaginary" assumption is that it permits access to these guides under a neutral construct, and this glorifies an alleged "higher self" without ever having to ask hard questions about the real nature of what is occurring or worrying about the consequences of involvement with evil spirits (278,280). Those who redefine spiritistic contact into neutral psychological constructs think that they are merely partaking in an "expansion" of normal psychological processes. Consider Dr. Achterberg's own approach to spirit guides and spirit possession. For her, the spirits "only symbolize the intuitive," and their functions are equivalent to brain hemispheric interaction. She soothes fears concerning the abnormality of spirit possession:

"Spirit possession," as described in the anthropological literature on shamanism, should be carefully distinguished from demonic possession. The spirits do not induce the shaman to perform evil acts, but are instead teachers. The periods of discomfort when the spirits are said to "take possession" are intended to be necessary learning experiences for the healing vocation.

Noll, in reviewing the opinion on this matter, concludes that "Much of what is summarily labeled as possession by trained observers may be a willful visionary experience for the shaman. Now, it is possible to analyze the use of spirit guides with the tools of science, and derive perfectly sane and acceptable communication."

If the spirits only symbolize the intuitive, then communication would be akin to the left side of the brain asking the right side, "What's happening?" The shamans would be those individuals who could best combine logic and intuition (143:47).

Today, we also find the incorporation of spiritism under several "newer" psychological constructs such as the "higher self," and Jung's "active imagination," "shadow," "anima," "animus," and "archetypes." In many cases, spiritism is being remade into a "scientific" method for psychological self-evaluation, and yet this often becomes a vehicle for achieving the same pagan goals of its ancient counterparts. Again, Jungian psychology is especially valuable in this approach (2472:137-221/339:10-11), and we will later cite contemporary illustrations in documentation.

Because our culture today has opened the doors to the occult on a wide scale, this seems to have given the spirits permission for more aggressive contacts. Esoteric inner directedness is a major cultural pastime and, increasingly, even our children learn imagination exercises for spirit contact from occult textbooks (see New Age Education and refs. 1064/572:127-46). Perhaps then, we should not be surprised at the outcome: that the imagination itself is increasingly being utilized as a vehicle for occult purposes, including outright spiritism.

## MATERIALIST MAGICIAN: CARL JUNG AND ACTIVE IMAGINATION

C.S. Lewis' warning about the birth of the "materialist magician" was prophetic. In *The Screwtape Letters*, the elder devil, Screwtape, instructs his underling, Wormwood, on the quintessential spiritual camouflage:

My dear Wormwood, I wonder you should ask me whether it is essential to keep the patient in ignorance of your own existence. That question, at least for the present phase of the struggle, has been answered for us by the High Command.

Our policy, for the moment, is to conceal ourselves. Of course this has not always been so. We are really faced with a cruel dilemma. When the humans disbelieve in our existence we lose all the pleasing results of direct terrorism, and we make no magicians. On the other hand, when they believe in us, we cannot make them materialists and skeptics.

At least, not yet. I have great hopes that we shall learn in due time how to emotionalise and mythologise their science to such an extent that what is, in effect, a belief in us (though not under that name) will creep in while the human mind remains closed to belief in the Enemy. The "Life Force," the worship of sex, and some aspects of Psychoanalysis may here prove useful. If once we can produce our perfect work—the Materialist Magician, the man, not using, but veritably worshipping, what he vaguely calls "Forces" while denying the existence of "spirits"—then the end of the war will be in sight.

But in the meantime we must obey our orders. I do not think you will have much difficulty in keeping the patient in the dark. The fact that "devils" are predominantly *comic* figures in the modern imagination will help you.

If any faint suspicion of your existence begins to arise in his mind, suggest to him a picture of something in red tights, and persuade him that since he cannot believe in that (it is an old textbook method of confusing them) he therefore cannot believe in you (294:32-33).

Screwtape's advice illustrates the approach to spiritistic phenomena of many modern psychologists, parapsychologists, and even spiritists. By incorrectly assuming that genuine spiritistic contacts are merely internal psychological processes, the result is a validation of whatever a spirit or demon chooses to do within the person's own subconscious, intuition, imagination, or alleged "higher wisdom." Conversely, in some modern expositions of cabalism, internal psychological processes (e.g., Jungian archetypes) are deliberately "reinvented" as independent spirits and gods, revealing again that once we enter the domain of the occult, distinguishing internal processes from external spirits can be difficult.

In *Occult Psychology: A Comparison of Jungian Psychology and the Modern Quabala*, cabalist Alta J. LaDage shows how Jungian concepts (here archetypes) are used for successful spiritism:

In the Qabalistic method the practitioner assumes the attitude that the "archetypes" are objective beings—gods or angels or autonomous entities of some sort, rather than components of his own psyche. By taking this attitude, he establishes a one-to-one relationship with them, and this has effects that are quite different than it would be if he tried to deal with them as instinctive forces in his own psyche. Each such "Being" such as Zeus or Kali has its images and its own complex history. This technique is one of the tools in the armory of the occult arts, in Magic, and therefore beyond the scope of this book. The imagination is a far more powerful tool than we know! One reason we are not aware of this is because of the negative connotation put on fantasy by most Western psychiatrists, especially of the Freudian school.

I have heard my own teacher say of the Higher Self, "I have seen Him and He is a Being of such grandeur and beauty as to defy description" (369:122-23).

Jung's dangerous practice (687:5-12) of "active imagination" is also relevant. For example, in the process described below, the production of ectoplasmic phenomena through "active imagination" is reminiscent of mediumistic and seance phenomena:

Jung's active imagination technique is one method that has been used by the Western occult orders since long before we ever heard about psychology in its modern sense, and there can be no argument to using this technique if sufficient caution is given about the possible involuntary outpouring of vital energy in the form of ectoplasm when one lets one's attention be held on visualized images. . . . [I]f enough ectoplasm is released by letting energy flow out to the images, we can get some startling physical phenomena.

This is not as uncommon as one may think, and the phenomena are not confined to the spiritualists' seance room. If one is using active imagination in the presence of heavy incense smoke it is quite easy to get physical phenomena. It is not quite as easy to banish it however! I therefore do not recommend the indiscriminate use of active imagination.

Dr. Jung did not recommend an indiscriminate use of it either. He very carefully warns about the unfavorable results one may obtain. It depends on who is using it, under what controls, etc. When we find occult techniques such as this one, coming into use by psychologists who may, but also may not know exactly how occult anatomy functions (or even that we have such an anatomy!) we cannot help but regret the unfortunate circumstances that drove our Western Tradition underground in the Third Century.

Madam David-Neel tells about the thought-form she deliberately made when on one of her journeys to Tibet, and how it became exteriorized and visible and tangible to not only herself, but to anyone who was with her. One should have considerable understanding of the "making of thought forms" before one lets one's energy flow out to images by means of the imagination. In Madam David-Neel's case it took her many months and a great deal of very grave trouble to banish the little monk she had "made" by means of active imagination. The little monk she had made took on a life of its own and eventually became quite ugly and disagreeable with her (369:126-127).

In another example, from leading Jungian analyst Barbara Hannah, a teacher at the C.G. Jung Institute, Jung's "active imagination" is said to be a method for exploring the unknown. But whether we consider the unknown "as an outside god" or "an entirely *inner* experience," Hannah points out that the essence of Jung's active imagination process has been used "from the dawn of history" to contact gods and spirits (687:3-4). She also writes that the inner world, in which the gods and spirit entities are encountered, "is just as real as the outside world . . . in fact it is more real . . ." (687:5). Furthermore, once the conscious mind is deliberately switched off, the "unconscious" is given the "opportunity to express itself" in such a manner that inner dialogues and conversations with it become "personified" (687:19). In essence then, these and other descriptions of Jung's "active imagination" process are similar, if not identical, to conversations occultists have with their own spirit guides.

In *Healing and Wholeness*, Christian Jungian therapist John A. Sanford, author of *The Invisible Partners* and *The Kingdom Within*, recommends the process of "active imagination" for his

patients. He describes it as a powerful technique that "brings into focus an image, voice, or figure of the unconscious and then [one] enters into an interaction with that image or figure" (799:140). He also states, "The ancients used to call such a figure a 'spiritus familiaris'"—a familiar spirit (799:143). "If a relationship with this inner figure can be developed, we are greatly helped. It is like having an inner analyst or spiritual director" (799:144).

Yet how does a therapist distinguish a so-called "inner analyst" from a cunning demon? The fact that many other Christian psychologists have also recommended "active imagination" and related processes is cause for real concern. One can only wonder about the final result in the lives of some of their patients. Again, how can one be certain spiritism is not entering the picture?

In *Invisible Guests: The Development of Imaginal Dialogues*, psychologist Mary Watkins, also the author of *Waking Dreams*, observes that "the imaginal other may have as much autonomy as the so-called real others I meet in consensual space" (802:92). She cites Jung himself, who asserted that it was not we who personify these figures, but they who "have a personal nature from the beginning" (802:99). One of Jung's own spirit guides, "Philemon," whom he mostly considered an archetype, is cited as an illustration, as are two of the characters in Alice Walker's bestselling novel, *The Color Purple*, whom she experienced as "trying to contact" her and attempting "to speak through her" (802:98-99).

In *Inner Work: Using Dreams and Active Imagination for Personal Growth* by Jungian analyst Robert A. Johnson, we also see how difficult it can be to separate real spirits from psychologically constructed inner characters. Through the process of dream work* and Jungian "active imagination," Johnson advises clients and other interested persons to seriously establish personal contact with their inner characters:

Entire personalities . . . live inside us. It is best if we get acquainted with our inner personalities *as persons in their own right* . . . (2472:29,77).

Active Imagination is a dialogue that you enter into with the different parts of yourself that live in the unconscious. . . . In your imagination you begin to talk to your images and interact with them. They answer back. You are startled to find out that they express radically different viewpoints from those of your conscious mind. They tell you things you never consciously knew and express thoughts that you never consciously thought (2472:138).

. . . An example of one of the finest uses of Active Imagination [is] *to personify an unseen content of the unconscious* and bring it to the surface, in image form, so that you can dialogue with it and deal with it. . . . [Y]ou can go to the unconscious in your imagination and ask the unseen content to personify itself (2472:143).

Above all, we keep going to the inner characters, day by day, and talking with them. Pour out your feelings; ask for information; ask for guidance (2472:205-06).

What is clear from books like this again confirms our primary concern that there is really no manner by which to distinguish between interaction with the internal characters of "active imagination" and traditional spirit guides. As we will later document, the actions and advice of these inner characters is often similar or identical to that of spirit guides. And like spirit guides, these "inner characters" can even alter their appearance at will to conform to the needs of the client: "The inner figure will almost always cooperate and alter his or her appearance" (2472:197). Again, this occurs regularly in spiritism.

And, as in spiritism, one is instructed to be open to the "psychological" guides but *not* to seek to control them. For example, Johnson encourages the reader to let "the inner figures have a life of their own," but he warns, "One precaution must be observed: Once you have found the image and started the inner dialogue, you must relinquish control" (2472:168,179).

Regardless of how innocently this image has appeared in the mind, why should anyone relinquish control to an internal character who has its own will and personality, whose ultimate nature is unknown, and who may be demonic? Yet clients are urged to be passive and pliant. Johnson says that as people seek out their inner guides for their advice, they "must be willing to say: 'Who are you? What do you have to say? I

will listen to you. You may have the floor for this entire hour if you want; you may use any language you want. I am here to listen.'" And, "We make no plan or script. We simply begin, and then let come what will" (2472:183,185).

But how can we really know that this kind of psychological experimentation with the inner realm can lead to genuine spiritistic contact? Because it has led to that on innumerable occasions, according to practitioners themselves, and because even so-called experts can't finally distinguish between the two realms. Johnson himself considers the unconscious realm to be the *same* realm that the ancients used to contact the spirit world. His discussion of shamanistic power animals, kundalini (see Yoga), and other occult themes, and the illustrations he gives of inner dialoguing, indicate that one can just as easily be dealing with spirit guides (2472:14, 26,101-04,117,144-47,174).

Johnson himself sometimes has difficulty distinguishing what is interpreted as a psychological construct from an actual living entity (2474:181,219-21). He even cites experiences of possession by inner characters, as in the case of one woman who described an experience in "active imagination," e.g., "What is happening here? I've been taken over by an unknown force" (2472:144 cf. p. 34). In addition, contact with the dead is also said to occur under active imagination (2472:165-66).

Regrettably, the argument of many therapists and practicing occultists is that it doesn't matter *who* appears but that *something* appears:

The first step in Active Imagination is to *invite* the creatures of the unconscious to come up to the surface and make contact with us. We invite the inner persons to start the dialogue. How do we make this invitation? We begin by taking our minds off the external world around us and focusing on the imagination. We direct our inner eye to a place inside us, then we wait to see who will show up (2472:165).

With most of his colleagues, Johnson also warns about the dangers of "active imagination." The inner characters, like the demons of old, have few moral scruples (e.g., 2472:142,192-94), and it is possible to become "lost" inside one's own consciousness, to become overwhelmed and "unable" to get back out. Or the creatures themselves may begin to take over one's life, and a person may begin to use the "energies of the unconscious" as a form of sympathetic magic to influence others against their will (2472:17, 174,184,190,198). Thus, Johnson warns that precautions *must* be observed. "Things can get out of hand if you are not careful. If you fail to take this process seriously, or try to turn it into mere entertainment, you can hurt yourself. You need to be particularly careful with Active Imagination" (2472:17). He also points out, "When people first learn to honor the voice of the unconscious and to take it seriously . . . [t]here is a tendency to take everything the inner figures say as final authority" (2472:184).

Finally, there is the risk of "possession" by the inner characters. He supplies an example of an "inner archetypal figure [who] demanded absolute control over a woman's life." She eventually gave in to the demands of the entity and turned "herself over completely," ending up "possessed by an archetype" (2472:190-91)—or, perhaps something else.

Following we will supply five brief examples to document that people may indeed get more than they bargained for on their psychological inner quests. These illustrations show that the use of New Age, Jungian, and other "therapeutic" methods to contact a source of inner wisdom is just as likely to become an invitation for spirits to enter one's life (see also Silva Mind Control).

## ANGELS OF LIGHT

*The Inner Guide Meditation: A Transformational Journey to Enlightenment and Awareness* is a book that seeks to help the reader meet spirit guides through the imagination. In the book, occultist Edwin C. Steinbrecher answers a query as to the subjective or objective nature of the spirit guide. In this case, the spirit guide introduces the person to the archetypes (which are actually other spirits) and proves his reality by the sensations of love and protection he gives:

How can I be sure that the Guide and the contact with him and the archetypes are real?

If you really feel love and protection coming from him, work with him. Have him take you to the archetypes within. See what happens in your outer world as you work with him. The test of the real Guide is what happens in your daily life, what happens around you. . . . A technique I recommend to firm up the Guide contact is to ask the Guide to take *both* of your hands into his, and then to give him permission to let you *feel* his feelings for you. With the true Guide you will *always* sense his love and protectiveness and care (427:100-01).

The cases are legion, however, in which a once "loving" spirit guide became vicious, cruel, and evil, and sought to destroy its host. Many former spiritists testify that their own "benevolent" spirit guides were ultimately demons, who were impersonating the dead, or psychological constructs, or "higher beings" in order to deceive them (278/241-45; 148). Even spiritists and Eastern gurus* such as Sri Chinmoy often confess that once you attempt to exert your own will over these "loving" entities, they will "try to cut your throat" (811:19).

In *Living in the Light: A Guide to Personal and Planetary Transformation,* a text on visualization* and intuition,* psychic Shakti Gawain refers to "imaginary" guides who are indistinguishable from the traditional spirit guide:

Imagine that you have a wise being living inside there. You might have an image of what this wise being looks like, or you might just sense that it is there. This wise being is really a part of you—your intuitive self. You can communicate with it by silently talking to it, making requests, or asking questions.

It takes practice to hear and trust your intuition. The more you do it, the easier it will become. Eventually you will be able to contact your intuition, ask yourself questions, and know that in that "wise being" within you, an incredible source of power and strength is available to answer your questions and guide you (398:14).

Once again, throughout the book we see that the phenomena described and the results of such imaginary contact with one's "intuitive self" or "higher self" are indistinguishable from spiritistic contacts in general. Consider also the following description of the "higher Self" by John Rowan, chairman of the Association for Humanistic Psychology in Britain and vice president of research for the European Association for Humanistic Psychology:

This is the sense of being in touch with my higher Self, or inner teacher. This often comes about in transpersonal or psychosynthesis groups, but again it can happen in many other ways. It may be seen as a guardian angel, a spirit guide, a high archetype, a guru, a Jesus-figure, a Yidam, an Ishtadeva, a god or goddess. At first it appears to be outside of us. . . . If we take it seriously and try to get closer to it over a period of time, getting to know it better and fulfilling its demands upon us, we may be encouraged to put our own identity into it. It becomes us; we become it (2631:16).

In *Creative Visualization,* Ronald Stone, author of *Autohypnosis* and *Advanced Autohypnosis,* discusses how the psychological inner guide can provide a wealth of information to the willing student:

Because inner guides belong to the areas of consciousness outside our conscious experience, they have knowledge beyond what is known at the conscious level.

They are persons from the past, present or future who belong to spheres of consciousness outside the conscious sphere. They can be of either sex and can be young or old. They are extremely knowledgeable, especially about ourselves.

When calling on an inner guide, which we shall discuss in the next section, you can decide which sphere of consciousness you would like the inner guide to come from.

After some time you will be able to recognized your inner guides very easily, you will know which sphere of consciousness they belong to and what type of advice or information they will be able to supply you with (461:34-35,38).

In the book *The Intuitive Edge: Understanding Intuition and Applying It in Everyday Life,* human development consultant Philip Goldberg describes "a mental journey" in which the person travels to an imaginary destination to reach a personal, sacred sanctuary:

Within the sanctuary is a source of wisdom. This too should be something with personal relevance—a disembodied voice, a symbol, an altar, a machine or device, a person. This source is really part of yourself; you can trust it and be perfectly honest with it.

Ask this source your question, or present it with your problem. Then let it respond. Don't force anything or impose anything. Just see what happens (411:191-92).

Again, can anyone who takes this approach be certain that he will not encounter a real spirit? A similar process has been used by the eight million graduates of Silva Mind Control,* and many of them have gone on to become spiritists or possessed.

In *Drawing Down the Moon,* a book on modern witchcraft and neo-paganism, Margot Adler (granddaughter of the famed psychiatrist Alfred Adler) discusses the fantasy and imagination games of her childhood, which were promoted by the "progressive" grammar school she attended. This school encouraged students to immerse themselves so deeply in historical periods it was as if they were living there:

At the age of twelve, a traditional time for rites of passage, that historical period was ancient Greece. I remember entering into the Greek myths as if I had returned to my true homeland.

I wrote hymns to gods and goddesses and poured libations (of water) onto the grass of neighboring parks. In my deepest and most secret moment I daydreamed that I had become these beings, feeling what it would be like to be Artemis or Athena. I acted out the old myths and created new ones, in fantasy and private play. It was a great and deep secret that found its way into brief diary entries and unskilled drawings. But like many inner things, it was not unique to me.

Religion had no official place in my childhood world. I was brought up in a family of agnostics and atheists (429:15-16).

As she looks back, Adler describes this period of imaginative encounters as the means of her later entry into feminist spirituality and her stressing of witchcraft. She describes it as "my own entry into this same world [of witchcraft]."

The imagination, not surprisingly, is crucial in all forms of paganism, neo-paganism included. For example, upon describing a modern witchcraft ritual she had attended:

> A feeling of power and emotion came over me. For, after all, how different was that ritual from the magical rituals of my childhood? The contents of the tape [a tape on witchcraft rituals she had earlier listened to] had simply given me *permission* to accept a part of my own psyche that I had denied for years—and then extend it.

> Like most Neo-Pagans, I never converted in the accepted sense—I never adopted any new beliefs. I simply accepted, reaffirmed, and extended a very old experience. I allowed certain kinds of feelings and ways of being back into my life (429:20).

Adler also refers to various interpretations that are given to the spirits:

> Others will tell you that the gods and goddesses are "ethereal beings." Still others have called them symbols, powers, archetypes, or "something deep and strong within the self to be contacted," or even "something akin to the force of poetry and art." As one scholar has noted, it is a religion "of atmosphere instead of faith; a cosmos, in a word, constructed by the imagination . . . " (429:20-21).

Nevertheless, this "imaginary cosmos" often assumes a reality of its own, replete with genuine "gods" and spirits who begin to influence the practitioner.

All of this shows that spiritism and internal psychological processes are increasingly confused today. But it is not only in the fields of visualization,* intuition,* neo-paganism, and Jungian psychology that confusion exists. Many texts on meditation,* hypnosis,* dream work,* and other inner work methods also stress contact with inner guides and imaginative encounters, which may be demonism under another name.

All too often, what was initially a simple technique undertaken for purposes of counseling or spiritual growth becomes an open door to that world of "principalities and powers" that the Bible classifies as the realm of demonic spirits (Ephesians 6:10-18).

Regrettably, we discover the same situation in the field of modern medicine. Indeed, literally hundreds of authorities in holistic medicine are open to spirit contact either directly or indirectly under another name. Following are two examples.

## INNER GUIDES AND MEDICAL TREATMENT: THE SIMONTONS

Thousands of people with serious illnesses today are treated by various kinds of inner "self-help" therapies. Even a modern form of cancer therapy utilizes the imagination to conjure inner guides. In *Getting Well Again*, cancer therapists O. Carl Simonton and Stephanie Matthews-Simonton do not believe that these imaginary guides are real. They believe the "inner guide" is merely a useful part of the patient's unconscious, even though these guides are indistinguishable from traditional, occult spirit guides. Yet this is surprising, considering the origin of this (and related) treatments.

The Simontons developed their system of therapy in part by: 1) extensive research into modern psychologies having occult potential (e.g., Jungian therapy and Roberto Assagioli's psychosynthesis, which both utilize the "inner guide"); 2) the spiritistic psychic development seminar, Silva Mind Control* (884); 3) occult meditation* and visualization* techniques; 4) aspects of shamanistic practice, such as its use of "power animals" or spirits who appear in the form of animals. In spite of all this, portions of their work have been praised in the prestigious *New England Journal of Medicine* (460:1640-44/3:276).

The following citation by the Simontons is identical to passages in occult literature that describe spirit contact. The only difference is that here the guide is *assumed* to be part of the unconscious mind and not a separate entity, whereas in the occult it is often assumed to be a separate entity:

> For many people, the Inner Guide takes the form of a respected authority figure—a wise old man or woman, a doctor, a religious figure—with whom the patient is able to carry on an internal conversation, asking questions and

hearing answers that seem to be wise beyond the individual's conscious capacities. . . .

Furthermore, patients are often more responsive to insights achieved in consultation with their Inner Guides than they are to the observations of a group leader or a therapist. Because the Inner Guide is an aspect of their own personalities, relying on such a guide is a healthy step. . . .

The steps described below are designed to help you establish contact with an Inner Guide, whatever form it takes. Once you have found it, you may call upon it whenever you wish during your regular, three-times-a-day mental imagery. . . .

In your mind's eye, see yourself in a natural setting. . . .

Notice a path emerging near you, which winds toward the horizon. Sense yourself walking along this path. . . .

Notice that in the distance there is a radiant blue-white glow, which is moving slowly toward you. There is nothing threatening about the experience. . . .

As the glow comes closer, you realize it is a living creature—a person (whom you do not know) or a friendly animal. . . .

As the person or creature comes closer, be aware of the details of its appearance. . . .

If this person or creature makes you feel warm, comfortable and safe, you know it is an Inner Guide. . . .

Ask the guide's name, and then ask for help with your problems. . . .

Engage the person or creature in a conversation, get acquainted, discuss your problems as you would with a very close friend. . . .

Pay careful attention to any information you receive from your guide. . . .

Establish an agreement with your guide about how to make contact for future discussions. . . .

If you feel uncomfortable or embarrassed consulting an Inner Guide, remember that the figure you are calling upon is merely a symbol for your inner self, an intuitive, wise, responsive part of your personality with which you are generally out of touch. If you can establish a strong relationship with your Inner Guide, you

may receive an extraordinary amount of information and advice about your feelings, motivations, and behavior (428:187,195-97).

In light of our discussion thus far, no Christian or other concerned individual should ever endorse the Simonton method of imagination therapy for cancer treatment. Not only is there a potential for patients to become occultly influenced, even the medical effectiveness of their method is questionable. In "Dream Your Cancer Away: The Simontons," Edward R. Friedlander, M.D., assistant professor of pathology at Quillen-Dishner College of Medicine, East Tennessee State University, observes, "Like many other systems of alternative medicine, the Simontons' imagery has its origins in magic" (3:277). He points out that "the Simontons have failed to provide such evidence" as would substantiate the claim that their methods are useful in cancer therapy (3:279; cf. pp. 273-85).

A second example of "inner advisors" in modern health practice is found with Dennis T. Jaffe (UCLA School of Medicine, Psychiatry Department) and David Bressler (UCLA School of Medicine). They also emphasize the value of "inner guides," which are interpreted as "creative parts" of the human mind or aspects of the unconscious (the popularizers they cite are all spiritists—Irving Oyle, Mike Samuels, and Mike Bennett):

Clinicians like ourselves are experimenting with many creative and highly experimental uses of mental imagery. One of the most dramatic techniques we have used involves what is known as "the inner advisor." This technique, popularized by Irving Oyle (1976) and Samuels and Bennett (1973), is utilized by many health practitioners. By creating and interacting with an inner advisor, a person learns to gather important information from their subconscious. . . . As clinicians, we have been surprised, not only by the immense value of guided imagery, but at how receptive most patients are to the technique as part of medical treatment. . . . It is important to wait until the advisor appears in human, animal, or other life form. . . . When the advisor arrives, the person is asked to greet it, and to begin the process of getting to know the advisor. This might include introducing themselves, and learning the advisor's name. ... People usually have the experience of receiving surprising or unexpected information from this inner oracle.... After patients develop a strong relationship with an advisor, we recommend they find other advisors as well. We suggest the patients invite their advisors to bring mates or other acquaintances to the next meeting (658:54,56-58).

The advice given by these alleged "inner advisors" is consistent with that of traditional spirit guides, what the Bible identifies as deceiving spirits or demons. For example, "One of the new advisors was a rabbit named Rachel, who told Terry, 'You only live once, and life is very short. Why not make it as sweet as you can? Have as many different sexual experiences as possible, and don't worry about attachments. Just live loose and free!' ... It is our hope that health professionals from all disciplines will begin to utilize them [inner advisors] to help their patients more effectively help themselves" (658:58).

## CHRISTIAN ENDORSEMENT AND AGGRESSIVE SPIRITS

Unfortunately, a similar use of the imagination has been endorsed or utilized by some Christians without any warnings as to potential misuse. In *Self-Talk: Key to Personal Growth*, Christian counselor Dr. David Stoop refers to Dr. David Bressler of the UCLA pain clinic, whom we just cited:

One of the successful forms of therapy involves the use of visual images in the mind. In this process of mental imagery, Dr. Bressler sometimes introduces the patient to an imaginary "inner adviser." This inner adviser may be an animal, such as a sea gull or a rabbit. The advisor has the ability to communicate with the person through the imagination. While they are relaxed, the patient will carry on an imaginary conversation with this "inner adviser."

Sometimes the inner adviser will make a suggestion to the patient, which is passed on to the doctor. The suggestion may involve a form of treatment, which is usually successful. Some-

times the inner adviser alone is able to give the patient freedom from the pain for the first time in years. The conversations with the inner adviser are carried on within the mind. These inner conversations are a form of Self-Talk, and some of the results have been amazing (430:53-54).

Similarly, bestselling Christian author Richard Foster discusses the use of the imagination to relive biblical events, which is fine up to a point. Unfortunately, the process is extended, and when he encourages contacting an "inner Jesus," no warnings of potential spiritism are given. The fact is that people have entered into spiritism as the result of contacting a spirit guide who claims to be Jesus. In *Celebration of Discipline*, Foster discusses how Christians can use their imaginations to allegedly contact the real Jesus:

As you enter the [imaginary] story, not as a passive observer, but as an active participant, remember that since Jesus lives in the Eternal Now and is not bound by time, this event in the past is a living present-tense experience for Him. Hence, you can actually encounter the living Christ in the [imaginary] event, be addressed by His voice and be touched by His healing power. It can be more than an exercise of the imagination: it can be a genuine confrontation. Jesus Christ will actually come to you.

A fourth form of meditation has as its objective to bring you into a deep inner communion with the Father where you look at Him and He looks at you. In you imagination, picture yourself walking along a lovely forest path.... After awhile there is a deep yearning within to go into the upper regions beyond the clouds.

In your imagination allow your spiritual body, shining with light, to rise out of your physical body. Look back so that you can see yourself lying in the grass and reassure your body that you will return momentarily. Imagine your spiritual self, alive and vibrant, rising up through the clouds and into the stratosphere. Observe your physical body, the knoll, and the forest shrink as you leave the earth. Go deeper and deeper into outer space until there is nothing except the warm presence of the eternal Creator. Rest in His presence. Listen quietly anticipating the unanticipated. Note carefully any instruction given (431:26-27).

We stress that neither Foster nor Stoop intend to encourage anything occult, and both are Christians. And Foster later amended the above passage. However, this is no guarantee that Christians or non-Christians who have had some previous occult exposure in this area may not have used their material in print and received more than they expected. Either one's previous history or personal ignorance, or an aggressive spirit, may turn a potentially neutral situation into an opportunity for occult contacts. Here are two examples:

In *The Seduction of Christianity*, Dave Hunt describes the experience of prominent positive thinker Napoleon Hill's encounter with the "imagination":

Napoleon Hill was convinced that his nine "Counselors," though so real that they frightened him at first, were only imaginary: Hill wrote: "These nine men [from the past] were Emerson, Paine, Edison, Darwin, Lincoln, Burbank, Napoleon, Ford and Carnegie. Every night ...I held an imaginary council meeting with this group whom I called my "Invisible Counselors."

In these imaginary council meetings I called on my cabinet members for the knowledge I wished each to contribute, addressing myself to each member.

After some months of this nightly procedure, I was astounded by the discovery that these imaginary figures became apparently *real*. Each of these nine men developed individual characteristics, which surprised me.

These meetings became so realistic that I became fearful of their consequences, and discontinued them for several months. The experiences were so uncanny, I was afraid if I continued them I would lose sight of the fact that the meetings were purely *experiences of my imagination*.

I still regard my cabinet meetings as being purely imaginary, but ... they have led me into glorious paths of adventure ... [and] I have been miraculously guided past [scores] of difficulties.

I now go to my imaginary counselors with every difficult problem which confronts me and my clients. The results are often astonishing. . . .

. . . . In seminars called "The Power of The Imagination" sponsored by Marquette University, psychologists have trained thousands of persons across America to visualize "inner guides" similar to Hill's and with equally astonishing results (432:32-33).

And here is a case from coauthor Weldon's book on fantasy role-playing games:

Today, classes in psychic and spiritual development use imagination and visualization techniques in their methodology to achieve out-of-body experiences, develop occult powers, and foster contact with spirits. Many of the most popular books on various occult themes allude to these same techniques. Whether one likes to accept the fact or not, simple imagination has been used to establish spiritistic contact (e.g., when an imaginary counselor suddenly becomes a real being).

There are numerous cases in occult literature where demons have actively sought out human contacts because of their "imagined" patron god, ascended master, counselor or spirit helper.

Regardless of the difference between reality and imagination, a word of caution such as the following by Elliot Miller is necessary:

However real this distinction may be in the minds of the players, though, I feel no assurance that the spirit world will not respond when it is beckoned.

When I was of high-school age I was extremely skeptical about anything reputedly supernatural. I recall engaging in a mock seance with a group of friends. Our lightheartedness was turned to fear when suddenly the "medium," my best friend, began to convulse, his eyes rolled back in his head, and a strange voice emerged from his throat. For the following two years this young Jew was tormented by spirits. Withdrawing from all social contacts, he haunted graveyards until he was delivered through the power of Jesus Christ (433:72-73).

If *imaginary* spirits can become real, and if *mock* seances can bring demonization, we think the imagination is no area to recklessly experiment with. After all, in the guise of an intensified form of ordinary imagination, the spirit world today is taking advantage of human gulli-bility. What is of greater concern is that, given our current spiritual climate, innocent children are being affected by the spirits (see New Age Education).

## IMAGINARY PLAYMATES IN CHILDHOOD?

Through extensive reading in spiritistic liter-ature for some 20 years, the authors have noted that many adult spiritists, such as psychic heal-ers Edgar Cayce and Olga Worrall, mediums Eileen Garrett and Rosalyn Bruyere, and psy-chic surgeon Tony Agapao, played with "imagi-nary" friends as children. These were not like most children's invisible playmates that were truly imaginary. They were actual spirit beings, revealed as such by the particular *kind* and *depth* of relationship that existed. It appears that these initial spirit contacts laid the foundation for full-blown spiritism later in life.

Through transpersonal, or New Age, educa-tion,* children are being encouraged to estab-lish contact with invisible playmates or helpers (572:109-25,141-46/1064). Even Hal Bennett, whom we mentioned at the beginning of this chapter, discusses his own "imaginary" friend, "Alex," and how Jung's theories later helped him accept the importance of "Alex," which made it possible for "Alex" to become his real life spirit guide later on:

When I was a small boy growing up in Michi-gan, I had an imaginary friend who I called Alex. . . . Alex was like a trusted older brother. . . . When Alex and I were together, we talked. Walking down the street in the suburban neigh-borhood where I lived, we carried on lengthy inner dialogues and, to me, Alex was as "real" as any other person in my life.

My parents were *tolerant* when I told them about Alex, though I am certain that had they understood how important he was in my daily life, they might have been more concerned.

In my twenties, I became interested in C.G. Jung's writings, which gave me at least a hint of support and confirmation for my experiences with inner guides. Jung spoke of the *anima* and

*animus,* figures that appear in our unconscious and which seem to us to be autonomous—that is, spirit beings with personalities that are sepa-rate from our own.

Jung said that his theories about the anima and animus were "not a question of anything *meta-physical.*" Yet, he admitted that the spirits or inner guides could be "as rich and strange as the world itself," and that as we begin "making them conscious we convert them into bridges to the unconscious." For Jung, the anima and ani-mus represented male and female functions or personal characteristics that, for highly individ-ualized reasons, were important to the person's overall vision of life.

He claimed that these spirits and their functions had been noted by people in "primitive" soci-eties for centuries.

Jung believed that we could transform these guides from being sources of conflict in our lives to becoming real helpers (426:44-47; cf. pp. 62-69).

Although anima and animus can be inter-preted as psychological concepts, Bennett sug-gests that they could also be independent spirit personalities. Given the occult revival in Amer-ica, there is no reason to think that there are not often spirit guides who use Jungian ideas to cover their true nature and influence. Jung's own concepts of anima, animus, and archetype seem to have been derived from his personal ex-periences with the spirit beings who appeared to him in his consciousness (340:182-92). Even Bennett describes modern spirit guides like "Seth" and "Ramtha" as having similar func-tions to anima and animus. Although he also sees mediumistic spirit guides as being *beyond* the psychological constructs of anima and ani-mus, he offers little basis for distinguishing be-tween them, and he suggests that even Jung had wrongly categorized independent spirit beings as internal psychological processes:

Often, the entities that Jung called anima/ animus appear spontaneously in dreams, or through the use of *active imagination* (guided imagery or visualization), but in no way do these entities or their histories appear to be re-lated to other issues that the person is dealing with, and so would appear quite separate from the person perceiving them.

For example, "channeled" entities such as Seth, or Ramtha, whose wisdom and personal histories appear to be quite outside the everyday realms of the persons receiving their words, would have to be viewed as something other than anima/animus.

In his memoirs, Jung described a conversation he had with his own spirit guide, Philemon, which should help shed some light on this subject: "I observed clearly that it was he (Philemon) who spoke, not I. It was he who taught me psychic objectivity, the reality of the psyche . . . "

The mystery about the source of these entities remains, but we do know that there are many records of conversations with such beings, most of them highly beneficial, which in many cases continued for many years (426:49-50).

To the contrary, such experiences are not ultimately beneficial, whatever they may seem to be initially. One of many reasons we give for this, as we now discuss, is the inner guides' seemingly universal aversion to biblical morality.

## AMORAL ENTITIES AND THE PROMOTION OF THE OCCULT

Many people who seek these "entities" sooner or later discover that the spirits are so morally flawed as to be demonic (e.g., 280:35-43). But most people are grateful for the seeming benefits of "inner guides" and refuse to entertain questions as to their real origin, nature, and motive. Bennett describes how, in spite of their moral flaws, his relationship with them evolved to complete acceptance:

I found that my task with at least some of the inner guides I encountered became one of accepting their importance in my inner life, and then allowing myself to learn from them, setting up the same kinds of sometimes skeptical, sometimes fully trusting relationships that I had with people in my outer world.

And I found, indeed, that as I grew to know them, to recognize and accept their *human*

strengths and weaknesses, my own personality took on their functions.

That which was *imagined* could have as dramatic affects on the body and the conscious mind as that which was experienced in the *real world through the senses*.

What bearing did this discovery have on inner guides? For me it was a great revelation: it indicated that in the final analysis it did not matter what the inner guides really were. . . . [O]ne had a responsibility to himself to weigh the value of whatever these beings brought to our lives. Sometimes they were right, sometimes they were wrong. Sometimes they were kind, sometimes cruel.

Whether they were real or not, one had to treat them as being, after all, "only human," just as capable of vanity and folly and error as the rest of us (426:52-53).

Like people with physical bodies, the inner guides can provide knowledge, comfort, counsel—in short, nearly all the qualities that we seek in our every day human relations. . . . The same things are true of inner guides as are true of the people in our outer worlds (426:75).

In *Inner Work*, Robert A. Johnson also admits to the inner guides' moral flaws:

The archetypes burst into consciousness with all the pent-up instinctual power of the primordial jungle, and like wild animals in nature, they can have little concern with human ideas of fairness, justice, or morality. . . . They are also [like] impersonal forces of nature, each a law unto itself, following nature's impersonal and amoral laws, unqualified by human considerations of pity, kindness, identification with the victim, love-relatedness, or a sense of fairness (2472:194).

Biblically, one might expect that a forceful encounter with the unconscious was more evil than good, for people are fundamentally sinful.

But what we find occurring through "active imagination" and other such techniques is often similar to the actions of spirit guides who have turned on their human hosts and engaged in a capricious and amoral manner. The many warnings given of the psychological dangers of "active imagination" and related techniques could also provide a cover for what demons might wish to accomplish:

> The great powers of the collective unconscious are so overpowering that we can be suddenly swept away by a flood of primitive energy that seizes the conscious mind—an energy that races towards its instinctual goal, heedless of the effect that it may have on ordinary human life or on the people around you. Inevitably a powerful figure will appear in your Active Imagination and constellate this raw power drive. It may advise you in the strongest terms to drop all scruples that stand in the way of getting what you want, to drop the commitments and responsibilities that "hold you down" (2472:192).

As Johnson argues, the unconscious and its components are amoral and therefore, "By itself it cannot put moral or ethical limits on what it does or what it demands" (2472:193-94). So whether we are dealing merely with a fallen human consciousness *or* with some kind of spiritistic interaction, the problem with "active imagination" and related techniques is that they have no moral limits. "The object is to experience and record whatever flows out of your unconscious honestly in its raw, spontaneous form. . . . let it be as rough, crude, incoherent, embarrassing, beautiful or unregenerate as it may be. . . ." (2472:142). Contrast this to Philippians 4:8: ". . . whatever is true, whatever is noble, whatever is right, whatever is pure, whatever is lovely, whatever is admirable—if anything is excellent or praiseworthy—think about such things."

Another reason to question the nature and advisability of these internal contacts is because these "psychological" entities may promote occult practices in the same manner as demons. Animistic tribes, of course, believe that virtually everything has its own living spirit—rocks, weather phenomena, insects, animals, rivers, crops, and so on. Such spirits must be placated or worshiped if men are to derive proper benefits from them. But the end result is bondage and manipulation by the spirit world (291/583/585/586). Significantly, we also find the "inner advisers" promoting animism and things like fetishes. The fetish is a symbolic representation of the entity whose likeness it bears. Thus, a "fox" fetish contains the "spirit of the fox." In New Age inner work, pagan fetishes may become an important part of one's relationship to these guides, helping to "externalize" them and, if nothing else, making the idolatry more potent.

According to Bennett, each fetish "contains a living power, which, if treated properly and with veneration will give its help to its owner" (426:115). Thus, by "modernizing" pagan (here, Zuni) and shamanistic (here, American Indian) metaphysics, Bennett adapts fetishes to contemporary psychological interests. He encourages people to engage in personal inner dialogue with each fetish in order to get to "know" it thoroughly. Readers are told to wait patiently for answers from the fetish to any of their questions (426:138):

> It is my belief that in modern times fetiches can serve as *templates* for creating meaningful mental holograms.

> I cannot emphasize strongly enough the importance of getting to know and recognize each fetich as an individual character or *persona* before you sit down to work with them. Here's how I recommend you do that:

> Choose fetiches to which you feel strongly attracted. If possible, begin with objects that have been in your life for a considerable period of time.

> Get to know it in a variety of circumstances. Set the fetich on your desk at work. Put him or her on the dashboard of your car. Place it on the table beside your bed. Carry on internal dialogues with them. Ask them their names, what they consider to be their most valuable traits, and how they think they can serve you.

> Each of my fetiches has a long history for me. Except for one, all came to me as gifts. Some have been with me for fifteen years or more, one for over thirty years. . . . For example, in working with the Tomahawk Head, which is one of my fetiches.

> I can also recall numerous "consultations" I have had with the inner guide who is associated with this object. . . . Every object for which we feel a strong personal attachment is a potential "channel," a key unlocking the door to our inner resources.

I use my six fetiches in a conference framework, organized around what the native Americans call a Medicine Wheel.

When I am feeling comfortable and open, I present my question or problem to the fetiches, asking them, for example: "I am having trouble seeing the inner resources of a particular client. I would like help seeing into him."...I allow myself the luxury of following whatever happens (426:118,126-35).

But again, these so-called psychological "inner guides" and fetiches perform many of the traditional functions of occult spirit guides: psychic diagnosis, revealing secret knowledge, giving spiritual and practical advice on health and other issues, and so on (426:75,90).

Bennett admits that using actual physical fetiches has its practical problems, and that secret "inner guides" are clearly more "portable" than a tomahawk fetish! As a result, he discusses how closet occultism may be expedient:

...Using these skills will become as common as reading and writing in our society. But let's be realistic. If you're the CEO of a large corporation you probably won't feel comfortable about bringing your fetiches with you to your next stockholders' meeting, announcing that they will help you make a decision about correcting slumping sales.

However, if you are working with your fetiches on a regular basis in the privacy of your home or office, their holographic correlatives in your mind will always be present. You can turn to them whenever you wish and no one but you will be the wiser. Some people find inner guides more "portable" and adaptable to their needs than are fetiches (426:141-42).

Finally, Bennett encourages a variety of other potentially spiritistic and divinatory*

methods, such as through dream figures (see Dream Work*):

...Guides may also appear spontaneously in dreams....If there are people in the dream, strike up conversations with them. In your imagination, ask them what business they have with you. Treat them as if they were real people. Play in this imaginary world. Remember, it is your territory, solely yours, and you can do whatever you wish to do here (426:73,110).

Strike up an imaginary dialogue with the image, especially if it is a living thing—an animal, a person, or even a "personified" object. Ask it what it is doing in your life. You may be very surprised by its answers. Ask it how it might be of service to you.

Work with the image just as you might do if the real object or animal or person represented by the image appeared in your life.

For a more deliberate and systematic way of looking at your dreams and visions, I suggest working with one of the many *oracle* systems that are available. This might be the ancient *I Ching* or the *Runes* or the *Tarot* cards, or *Star + Gate* or my own system, *Mind Jogger,* or any other system of oracle that appeals to you (426:97,99).

When we have studied the oracle systems he recommends (see Divination), we see that invariably the real power of the oracle is a spirit entity who works through the system of divination to guide and influence the practitioner. Whatever pagan method is chosen, the power is spiritistic, and in the end the mind is used for occult purposes.

But the Scriptures teach that the mind and the imagination are wonderful gifts of God to men. They should be honored as such and used for godly purposes, not for pagan ones.

# New Age Intuition

## Info at a Glance

**Description.** Occult New Age intuition is a euphemism for a wide variety of psychic abilities or spiritistic inspiration.

**How does it claim to work?** "Intuition" is often developed in the same manner as psychic abilities (for example, through meditation,* concentration, visualization,* and altered states of consciousness*). Once developed, a person seeks out his "intuitive" abilities and relies on them for guidance and instruction.

**Examples of occult potential.** Psychic diagnosis, spiritism, telepathy, clairvoyance, and other psychic abilities.

**Major problems.** The normalization of psychic powers as mere intuitive abilities masks their true reality as supernatural abilities originating in the spirit world. Occult abilities and spiritistic powers are thereby internalized as latent "human potential," and a normal human process, intuition per se, becomes a cover for occult revelation. Distinguishing normal human intuition from psychic powers becomes difficult or impossible.

**Biblical/Christian evaluation.** Occult practices are forbidden (Deuteronomy 18:9-12), no matter what they are termed.

**Potential dangers.** Fostering occult development under the guise of enhancing normal human intuition; the normal physical, mental, and spiritual hazards associated with occultism (278).

*Note:* The chapters on Inner Work and Visualization should be read alongside this material.

## Introduction and Influence

Most of us have experienced flashes of intuition, whether we call it insight, instinct, gut feelings, surmise, or something else. Sometimes insights about this problem or that situation come to us unbidden. And these insights often prove useful or even resolve a matter. But intuition is such a nebulous, intangible thing that one is hard-pressed to deal with this phenomenon in a satisfactory manner. Indeed, its mercurial nature is the reason for wide disagreement in discussions on the topic. As New Age human development consultant Philip Goldberg states in *The Intuitive Edge*:

> In his 1968 book, *Toward a Contemporary Psychology of Intuition*, Malcolm Westcott ended his introduction by writing, "The last word on intuition is as far in the future as the first word on intuition is in the past." Fifteen years later, I must echo the same sentiment. We are dealing with a complex and elusive subject, one that

many great minds have wrestled to a draw and on which there is much disagreement. Intuition has been a peripheral subject in science, a difficult one to study even when interest is high. Hence there is not much by way of a research tradition or accepted body of knowledge (411:13).

Nevertheless, no discussion of the New Age Movement would be complete without an evaluation of New Age "intuition."

We are not speaking of normal human intuition, which the *Oxford American Dictionary* defines as "the power of knowing or understanding something immediately without reasoning or being taught" (414:467). For example, a person may intuitively sense that she is in danger; a boss may intuitively know his employee is not telling the truth; a wife may intuitively sense her husband's needs or concerns. According to the Bible, man intuitively knows that God exists, which is one reason he stands "without excuse" at the judgment (Romans 1:19-20). There is nothing supernatural or magical about normal intuition, which is often based on human instinct, or on subtle clues picked up from the environment (person, places, things), or as the result of accumulated past experience.

Human intuition, however, is neither infallible nor particularly concrete. It can be fleeting and uncertain. It can be just plain wrong. In fact, intuition is often incorrect. To illustrate, most people would intuitively assume that if you drop a bullet from your left hand and at the same time use the other hand, held at the same height, to shoot another bullet straight across an open field, that the bullet leaving your left hand would reach the ground first. Here, people assume that not only must the bullet from the gun travel the same distance from the height of the hand to the ground, but that it must also travel the entire distance across an open field, which should take it longer, therefore to hit the ground. But in fact, both bullets will hit the ground at the same time (2446). Here is another illustration:

One day, after leaving an anthropology class that I particularly liked, I was walking downtown and happened past a pet store. My mind still abuzz with the material from the class, I looked through the window, up into the face of a small new-world monkey. I can't recall what species he was, but it's the one with the tiny little ears that look exactly like human ears. He stared at me. I stared at him. And we reached an understanding.

At that instant evolution stopped being a theory to me and became a "truth." Those ears proved it. It was a highly emotional experience (1089).

This intuitive realization of the "truth" of evolution, assisted by the power of monkey ears, resulted in the adoption of a scientific philosophy that is clearly false (see 2641). Because intuition may be correct or incorrect, it is therefore not a reliable basis for decision making in important matters, particularly spiritual, economic, or medical ones.

Unfortunately, many New Age authors think intuition is accurate by definition. Even *Harper's Encyclopedia of Mystical and Paranormal Experience* somehow claims that "intuition invariably proves to be right" (1526:286). For many New Agers, intuition can become a kind of "divine inspiration," and in the process, rational thinking and spiritual discernment are often discarded. In such cases, not only is there danger of leading one's life on the basis of intuitive impulses in disregard of critical thinking and careful planning, there is also the possibility of psychic involvement under the guise of intuition. As we will show, spiritistic revelations often stress the importance of trusting one's "intuition." This is hardly surprising; its mercurial nature means it can easily become a mask for spiritistic inspiration. Popular books on intuition clearly show the influence of Eastern religion, psychic phenomena, and occult practices in this field.

As recourse to New Age intuition increases and as discernment remains marginal, the greater the opportunity for psychic abilities to be redefined as normal human processes. For example, based on the misapplication of Robert Sperry's work, we are told repeatedly that our "right brain" has been greatly neglected and that we must correct the imbalance by developing our "right brain," which is said to be the intuitive, psychic side of our nature. Goldberg (who, thankfully, at least sets the record straight on Sperry's work) nevertheless observes:

> The emergence of intuition is part of a more global shift in values.... Contributing to the new attitude is a resurgence of respect for the world within ... a more positive, often sublime vision. The growth of cognitive research, theoretical advances in humanistic and transpersonal psychologies, provocative brain studies, the remarkable acceptance of Eastern philosophies and disciplines—such developments have led large numbers of people to believe that there is untapped power and wisdom within us (411:16).

And so we should not underestimate the growing interest in this field of going inward. More and more, counselors, health therapists, executives, and professors, are encouraging the development and use of intuition in medicine, business, psychology, education, and other fields. We find professional texts like Weston Agor's *Intuitive Management*, Mihalasky and Dean's *Executive ESP*, and Jeremy Brauerman's *Management Decision Making: A Formal-Intuitive Approach*.

A standard encyclopedia on mystical experience points out how channelers and psychics are now being used as "intuitive" oracles:

> Intuition, along with other psychic skills, has been applied on an increasing basis since the early 1970s to a wide range of scientific and business endeavors. Kautz developed a technique called "intuitive consensus," in which highly skilled channelers and psychics are given questions related to problems or situations; the information is validated as much as possible by empirical methods. The process has been shown to be effective and save time and money over traditional methods of validating hypotheses. Similar problems have been employed in California by the Stanford Research Institute of San Francisco (SRI) and the Mobius Group of Los Angeles (1526:286).

Furthermore, the field of what is termed "applied psi," which many New Agers label "practical intuition," has been incorporated into over 30 different disciplines. "Applied psi," or "psion-

ics," is a discipline of parapsychology that seeks to apply the utilization of psychic abilities to all facets of modern life (1526:28):

> By 1984 applied psi had become an informal part of at least twenty-eight fields: archaeology, agriculture and pest control, animal training and interspecies communication, contests and gambling, creativity, education and training, entertainment, environmental improvement, executive decision making, finding lost objects, future forecasting, geological exploration, historical investigation, investigative journalism, medicine and dentistry, military intelligence, personnel management, police work, psychotherapy and counseling, safety inspection, scientific discovery, social control, and weather prediction control (1526:29).

## NEW AGE MEDICINE

Dr. Lynn Rew, assistant professor in the School of Nursing at the University of Texas in Austin, wrote an article for *Advances in Nursing Science* entitled "Intuition: Concept Analysis of a Group Phenomenon." She concludes her article by endorsing mind-quieting exercises and visualization* as means to develop intuition for practicing nurses:

> The application of intuitive skills is needed in basic, graduate, and continuing nursing education. The task of building a comprehensive science of nursing depends on acquiring and applying knowledge from rational and intuitive cognitive processes. Students can learn to develop their intuitions through mind-quieting exercises, and these intuitions must then be validated through analytical reasoning.
>
> In contrast to the regimentation of nursing students, which stifles intuition, group brainstorming sessions, group visualization, and quiet thinking time are necessary if nurses are to respond creatively to the changing needs of human beings.
>
> The evidence that collective intuitions carry much power is just beginning to accumulate. Perhaps the survival of such organizations depends on a willingness to "look within."

Intuition should be considered a respectable cognitive skill characteristic of the science of nursing (459:26-27).

Unfortunately, those involved in occult activities who unquestioningly follow their "intuition" are just as likely to be wrong as right, and they are just as likely to be recipients of spiritistic influence or inspiration. When it comes to medical diagnosis and treatment, following such "intuition" can be dangerous.

Even so, endless numbers of New Age therapists and healers claim to use intuition in both diagnosis and treatment. It is through "intuition" that many New Age therapists claim to be able to "diagnose" physical problems and prescribe methods of treatment or remedies.

An illustration is found in the text, *The Creation of Health: Merging Traditional Medicine with Intuitive Diagnosis* by Dr. C. Norman Shealy and Carolyn Myss (108). Dr. Shealy, who has taught at Harvard, is a neurosurgeon by training. He is founder of the American Holistic Medical Association, director of the Shealy Institute for Comprehensive Pain and Health Care in Springfield, Missouri, and president of the Holos Institute of Health. He is the author of such New Age books as *Occult Medicine Can Save Your Life* (77). Carolyn Myss is a psychic who regularly receives guidance (including, presumably, her "intuitive" diagnostic ability) by means of her spirit guide, "Genesis" (732:5-6). She is a consultant to numerous physicians, Dr. Shealy included, and co-publisher of Stillpoint Publishing Company, which specializes in publishing "channeled" works (732:1-15; also see chapter on Channeling).

In Shealy's preface to *The Creation of Health*, he discusses the importance of "intuition" for his own practice:

In 1970, I developed an intense interest in the possibility of intuitive diagnosis as an assistance to medical practice. In the ensuing years, I have had the opportunity to evaluate a wide variety of intuitive [i.e., psychic] individuals and to work very closely with a small number of them. I have become aware of the numerous instances in which intuition has allowed me to make a diagnosis or to get a therapeutic message through to a patient.... I am convinced that intuition is

the essential ingredient in the growth of human consciousness.

[Spiritist] Robert Leichtman, M.D., further strengthened my enthusiasm for the benefits of intuitive diagnosis and has served as counselor and friend for many years. [Leading biofeedback researcher and spiritist] Elmer Green, Ph.D., has also provided me with more opportunities to expand my own consciousness than any other teacher or friend.... Carolyn Myss, M.A., has provided a far greater share of this work than have I, and without her intuitive abilities, this book would not even have been begun (108:xxii-xxiv).

Even though Myss regularly receives inspiration from her spirit guide, she, too, defines her powers as "natural" and "intuitive":

During the years I spent studying spirituality, I realized that the skill of intuition is a natural attribute of the human spirit that can be developed and disciplined to benefit one's life. I specifically focused the development of my intuition on learning to do intuitive diagnosis.

This skill enables me to perceive a person's energy, or life force, to such an exact degree that I can intuitively identify and locate the presence of a physical disease within a person's body. More importantly, however, I am able to recognize and identify the patterns of an emotional, psychological and spiritual stress within a person's life (108:5-6).

Other psychics claim the same abilities strictly because of the power of their spirit guides. In other words, what one psychic calls "normal human intuition," another psychic relegates to the powers of the spirits. This is one reason why courses that seek to develop New Age intuition, typically through meditation* and visualization* are often forms of psychic development. Thus, people today take classes in developing their "intuition," when just a few years ago these courses would have been labeled as classes in psychic development.

## PSYCHIC DEVELOPMENT

Philip Goldberg is a consultant in human development and lectures widely on human consciousness. He is the author of *The Intuitive Edge: Understanding Intuition and Applying It in Everyday Life* (411). Dr. Frances Vaughan is a humanistic and transpersonal psychologist who has served as President of the Association of Transpersonal Psychology and is on the board of the *Journal of Humanistic Psychology*. She is the author of *Awakening Intuition* (412).

These and many other books show that "developing intuition" is indistinguishable from developing psychic abilities. Intuition becomes the means to expand one's consciousness in order to enter altered states or experience occult transformation. Goldberg writes that "the relationship between intuition and psychic phenomena frequently comes up, and it is not an easy one to sort out. Some people use the terms almost interchangeably" (411:40). Dr. Vaughan believes that psychic abilities are part of intuition:

Learning to use intuition is learning to be your own teacher, and getting in touch with your own inner guru.... Extrasensory perception, clairvoyance, and telepathy are part of the intuitive function. In recent years new methods have been developed for educating and training the neglected intuitive faculties. Indeed, many believe that everyone has the potential for psychic experiences and that these experiences represent a type of intuitive knowing (412:3,4,46).

Dr. Vaughan also believes that intuition allows one to contact a realm of "infinite" knowledge, which Jungian psychology calls the collective unconscious and which occultists often refer to as the "Akashic records." "Intuition allows one to draw on that vast storehouse of unconscious knowledge ... [including] the infinite reservoir of the collective or universal unconscious ..." (412:4).

*Harper's Encyclopedia of Mystical and Paranormal Experience* points out, "Intuition is integral to all forms of divination and psychic consultation" (1526:286). This encyclopedia also equates the cultivation of intuition with psychic development. In the citation below, note the recommended employment of yoga* and meditation,* which characteristically develop psychic abilities, as well as the reference to medium

Edgar Cayce, who received his information from the spirit world:

An individual may cultivate and strengthen intuition by paying closer attention to whole-body responses to information, people, and situation; by relaxing both body and mind through diet, exercise, yoga, meditation, and prayer; by working with dreams; and by becoming attuned to spiritual forces.... Edgar Cayce, who lived in a constant flow of intuition, said one must "know thyself," be close to the Maker, and trust what comes from within. Cayce said that impressions obtained from the physical/mental self, rather than the spiritual self, were not intuition.

According to William Kautz, founder (1979) and director of the Center for Applied Intuition in San Francisco, intuitive information comes from the superconscious mind (1526:286).

The reference to Edgar Cayce is apropos, since he typifies the confusion between spiritistic inspiration and human intuition. So many people today are being led into spiritism by means of this confusion that we think it is necessary to document this and discuss the implications.

## SPIRITISTIC INSPIRATION

In the New Age Movement, intuition and spiritistic inspiration are often confused both semantically and phenomenally. In this section and the next, we will show this and reveal some of its sobering implications. We will document that even seasoned spiritists may not be able to distinguish their own intuition from the influence of their spirit guide. Some New Agers, of course, do not wish to confess to involvement with spirits. A significant number of channelers, mediums, and spiritists who *know* their inspiration proceeds from personal spirit guides, nevertheless claim that they are only using latent "intuitive abilities" that are within everyone.

One reason for this is because in certain social contexts it just sounds better. It is far more acceptable, especially in scientific or academic circles, to speak of one's intuition, rather than to risk ridicule by confessing to guidance from nebulous spirits. Although it is also true that more and more people are willing to openly admit to their spiritism in academic circles. And those who contact the spirits say that the spirits themselves stress the importance of "intuition."

But would spirits be interested in promoting "intuition" if it didn't serve their purposes? One popular spirit with millions of followers is "Lazaris." This creature has dictated a cassette on intuition through its human medium, Jack Pursel. In "Lazaris on Intuition," the spirit teaches that "intuition is the vehicle that moves you closer to God/Goddess/All That Is." In other words, intuition becomes the means to experience a pantheistic God and to help people to discover their own godhood (574:306).

Sociologist Earl Babbie is the author of some of the leading texts used today in social science research (574:6). Educated at Harvard and University of California, Berkeley, he was a professor at the University of Hawaii for 12 years. Recently, he began conducting interviews with leading spirit entities through their human mediums or "channels." He told educational psychologist and New Age channeling researcher Jon Klimo:

> A lot of the entities say that much of their purpose is simply to train us to use our intuition and creativity—that we have all this material available to us, and we're not using it and not trusting it. And their purpose, they say, is to get us more in touch with that so that we're not getting dependent on entities, but are learning to trust our own intuition (574:304).

A similar example of the connection between channeling* or mediumism, and intuition is seen in William Kautz (founder of the Center for Applied Intuition in San Francisco) and Melanie Branon's *Channeling: The Intuitive Connection* (1738).

We think the spirits' goal in all of this is to equate their influence and revelations with normal human intuition. Once a person is indoctrinated by the spirits, psychic abilities and various paranormal or supernatural inspirations become a natural aspect of the psychological powers of human consciousness. Once trained by the spirits, a person is often incapable of distinguishing normal intuition from occult suggestion. The spirits want people to think that by using intuition in the manner they suggest, people are only engaging in a safe, natural process unencumbered by occult trappings and dependence on "entities." Of course, the spirits are lying. People who follow their advice not only become victims of spiritistic inspiration, they become dependent by degrees on the entities as well.

Furthermore, the spirits themselves have the capacity to mimic the process of normal human intuition, making it impossible to detect their influence. One's intuition appears entirely natural and yet it is really spiritistic inspiration. We know this by examining the experiences of those who claim to receive spiritistic inspiration. Most cannot determine when such inspiration comes from their own mind and when it comes from the spirit world. (Additional examples are given in the chapter on Inner Work.)

## SPIRITISTIC INFLUENCE AND FALSE PERCEPTION

Once a person enters the world of spiritism and the occult, he or she encounters the problem of knowing just where intuition ends and where something supernatural begins. True intuition does not carry the signs of spiritual deception that we find in psychic development. True intuition exists "by itself." Psychic development gives all the evidence of nonhuman personalities operating behind the scenes to confuse matters of spiritual truth, cause dependence on psychic power, bring occult enslavement, and so on.

Indeed, it is the very idea of "developing" intuition which takes us outside the domain of true intuition. By "developing" intuition, one is leaving normal intuition behind and opening the doors to the psychic world; one is abandoning the region of mind alone, along with its normal internal functions and sensitivity, and moving into a realm where one can interface with the supernatural world.

Furthermore, human intuition does not seem to be generated in the same way psychic powers are generated. We would expect that a universal human ability (as opposed to a human talent, e.g., for mathematics or music) could be developed by anyone. But intuition is a human ability that probably *cannot* be developed, at least in the manner of psychic development. By contrast, psychic powers do *not* represent normal human capacity (1522:268-81), and yet given the right circumstances and conditions, they can be developed.

But, "developed" is probably not the best word to use despite its prominence. It is more appropriate to say psychic powers are increasingly encountered in various ways and then utilized, rather than to say they are developed. In the context of this discussion, a term like "psychic development" is misleading. Intuition cannot be developed because it cannot be controlled by the human will. But psychic powers *can* be controlled. It is true that psychic powers are not subject to *human* control. However, they are subject to spiritistic control. They can be "developed" (i.e., encountered and utilized) because they are somehow induced and regulated by the spirit world. Psychic powers interface with extra-dimensional entities who somehow influence the process according to their own purposes.

Thus, psychic powers are much more than merely "developed" intuition. Intuition is simply a faint mental process, but psychic abilities involve supernatural power. Psychic powers are consistently associated with spirits; intuition is not. This is why "developing intuition" leads so often and so logically to involvement in the psychic and spiritistic realm.

Since intuition is natural, goes the reasoning, so must be its "extension" into the psychic realm. That, of course, is the error. It is the very fact of "extension" that removes one from the realm of intuition. Notice how easily the two are blended:

Psychic phenomena not only exist, but are currently considered by increasing numbers of people to be the next step in the evolution of human potential. Science fiction has for some years been exploring through fantasy the possibilities of expansion of psychic powers, and when you begin to pay attention to your intuition you will find that what you once considered strange, and perhaps a little weird, is perfectly ordinary, and within the normal range

of human potential.... Intuition is a way of knowing that transcends both time and space (412:98).

The simple truth is that when the spirits wish to mimic human intuition, no one who receives their inspiration can distinguish it from normal intuition. In our files, we have many cases where psychics, mediums, spiritists, and other occultists admit to times when it is impossible to distinguish between their own intuition and what they receive from their spirit guides. Clearly, it may become impossible for New Age people to separate direct spiritistic inspiration from their own conceptual thought processes. And this situation is compounded by the complex intellectual discussions on intuition by academically inclined spiritists or other professionals who have been influenced by the occult, such as Carl Jung, Roberto Assagioli (founder of Psychosynthesis), and P. D. Ouspensky who popularized the work of Russian occultist Gurdjieff (1526:287).

Nevertheless, the indistinguishability of spiritistic inspiration and intuition is admitted by leading scientists, such as parapsychologist Dr. Andrija Puharich, by prominent psychics, such as Uri Geller (281:50), and by spiritists and New Age psychic diagnosticians, such as Robert Leichtman, M.D. (395:40). It is also admitted by those who have done in-depth study on both human intuition and psychic or spiritistic inspiration.

Obviously, there are many cases when spiritistic inspiration is direct and can easily be perceived. But when the spirits choose to, they can influence the human mind so that their influence remains hidden, and this is where the problem lies. How does any New Age healer using what he thinks is "intuition" *know* that it is really intuition as opposed to spiritistic, that is, demonic, inspiration? Following we present specific examples.

In his article "Clairvoyant Diagnosis" Robert Leichtman, M.D., comments that the spirits were very interested in proving to him that their existence was real, because at first he didn't believe in them. He says that the spirits were his real teachers, both in instructing him about the occult and about healing. "What they did was to give me a whole bunch of ideas. And of course, I thought well, my mind has suddenly become brilliant. I was already great before, but now it is absolutely brilliant. I was getting all kinds of ideas from time to time and of course, the spooks [Leichtman's term for the spirits] said they were giving them to me and I said, Uh-Uh" (395:40).

In the book *Eileen Garrett Returns*, Leichtman records conversations with a spirit claiming to be the famous trance medium Eileen Garrett, now speaking through a mediumistic friend of Leichtman's, D. Kendrick Johnson. In response to the question, "Mediumship does not have to involve spoken communication from spirits, does it?" the spirit entity told Leichtman, "Good heavens, no! You [i.e. Leichtman] practice, for example, a kind of open-eye mediumship when you are writing or thinking. Sometimes this includes speaking, too, but you may not even be aware of the mediumistic aspects of your inspiration. Particularly, when you are lecturing, you are often helped mediumistically. Sometimes you are aware of it, but other times it just happens" (396:46). The spirit also told him, "There are many forms of mediumship which entail transfers of subtle energy and pure ideas, as opposed to words and concepts" (396:48).

In his book *The Art of Living*, Dr. Leichtman states that "often, we will not be aware that we have made contact with a particular Muse [spirit]. The inspiration occurs at the deepest level of our unconscious being" (397:78). Another spiritist physician, Dr. Arthur Guirdham, also confesses that many spiritistically influenced persons "are unaware that they are so inspired" (557:219).

One Christian psychologist who attended one of scientist John Lilly's seminars at a professional symposium in Chicago in 1981, which was titled "The Healing Potential of the Human Brain: Exploration of a New Frontier," recalls how Lilly discussed his contact with spirit entities, what they did to him, and how he was unable to distinguish their influence from that of his own mind:

> He described how these beings would take over his body and use it to communicate with other

people when it suited their purposes, and how they had roughed him up quite a bit when he didn't want to join their cause. In a book written in 1972 Lilly had been very enthusiastic about his spiritual adventures, but at the conference nine years later he seemed disillusioned, mechanical and devoid of any hope or joy. He commented ruefully that *many times he could no longer tell whether he was really in control of his body and mind or not*. My impression was that he had either slipped over the edge psychologically or completely surrendered to demonic control. Whatever the case, the other professionals in attendance did not seem shocked or incredulous. Judging by their comments, they were taking what he had to say quite seriously (2659:63, emphasis added).

Neurologist and parapsychologist Andrija Puharich and world-famous psychic Uri Geller recall a time when the power of the spirits to manipulate their minds was revealed so dramatically that it shook the very foundations of their ability to trust their own perception. Dr. Puharich explains how, given the existence of "IS," a term for the alleged Intelligences from Space (the spirits, cf. 393), he could never again know what was real:

> These two days' events numbed me. Sarah and Uri experienced one sequence [of events], and Ila and I experienced another, in the same timeframe. I had discovered the truth about Uri's deepest secret, had had a gun in my hand that felt real, and had had a phone call experience that is real in my mind to this day. But most of all I realized that the four of us had had an experience imprinted on our minds by what could only be the agency of IS. I finally learned that, given the existence of IS, I could never again know which of my experiences were directly imposed upon me by IS and which were not.
>
> I have never been so deeply shaken in my life as when I realized the full implication of this power . . . (394:112).

Here is another illustration from a different realm of the occult. Although they are not often classified as such, most Eastern gurus* represent a variation upon the ancient phenomenon of the shaman* or the spiritistic medium (610/759:86-

# NEW AGE INTUITION

87). The spirit world is the source of their power, and yet many of them admit that when lecturing or writing they receive inspiration from their spirit guides (see 249). New Age guru Ram Dass says, "Some of the times when I'm speaking, it isn't me speaking. [I'm not there, my guru] Maharaji was teaching you using my body to do it. It would be like possession, except that it's an invitational possession.... He actually moves in and out of my body" (425:27). While this inspiration is sometimes obvious, it is sometimes so subtle that the gurus cannot distinguish it from their normal thought processes (610).

Parapsychologists Drs. Albert Villoldo and Stanley Krippner disclose in *Healing States: A Journey into the World of Spiritual Healing and Shamanism* that they really cannot distinguish normal intuition from communication with the spirit world:

We were struck with the thought that communications from the spirit world could be happening all the time, and that we might simply not be aware of them. Is it possible that many of our intuitions and creative thoughts come from outside ourselves? Although most scientists believe that contact with spirits are fantasies of the unconscious mind, a small but growing number of investigators believe that the human brain may behave like a complex transmitting and receiving apparatus, which under certain conditions can pick up thoughts from other minds, even across space and time (399:18).

The same holds true for Dr. Robert Bradley, M.D., developer of the Bradley method of natural childbirth. A long-time student of the occult (544), he is never certain when his thoughts and ideas are his own or those of the spirit world:

I'm a great believer in spirit guidance. I think it is the only logical explanation for some of the things that have happened to me.... I personally think spirit communication is going on constantly, that we are never alone. The talks I give, the ideas I have on natural childbirth came to me either in sleep or from direct spirit communication.... I can't give you absolute proof of anything on a sensory level, but I think certainty comes from altered states of consciousness which are spirit controlled (517:100-01).

Silva Mind Control* graduate and psychic Shakti Gawain, author of *Creative Visualization* and *Living in the Light: A Guide to Personal and Planetary Transformation*, discusses the use of intuition to contact a wise "inner being" that is indistinguishable from a spirit guide (see Inner Work, Visualization):

Now focus your conscious awareness into a deep place into your body.... This is the physical place where you can most easily contact your intuition.

Imagine that you have a wise being living inside there.... This wise being is really a part of you—your intuitive self. You can communicate with it by silently talking to it, making requests, or asking questions.

Eventually you will be able to contact your intuition, ask yourself questions, and know that in that "wise being" within you, an incredible source of power and strength is available to answer your questions and guide you. As you grow more sensitive to this guidance from the intuitive feelings within, you will gain a sense of knowing what you need to do in any situation.

To whatever degree you listen to and follow your intuition, you become a creative channel for the higher power of the universe.

[Soon] your body will become capable of channeling more energy.

Your body's expanding its capacity to channel the universal energy (398:14-16,22,74).

There is little doubt that New Age "intuition" and spiritistic inspiration are not so easily distinguished. And for those who understand that the spirits contacted are really demons, the ramifications are sobering indeed.

## DANGERS

Nothing could be more irresponsible or potentially dangerous than elevating subjective hunches or spiritistic inspiration as a source of reliable or infallible information.

For example, even using normal human intuition, a person making a physical diagnosis and giving treatment on this basis is on dangerous

475

ground. If engaging in medical practice by normal intuition is hazardous, how much more so when the intuition is really spiritistic inspiration! What would you do if your physician said that he really didn't know for certain, but he had a "hunch" that you may have cancer? What if he also had a "hunch" that you should undergo radiation treatment and chemotherapy?

What you would do is find another physician. But what if your physician actually used and trusted New Age intuition in diagnosis (as some do), but never told you? What if you trusted his decisions and they were wrong? Worse still, what if such diagnosis was really coming from demons? Anyone familiar with spiritism's trail of human deception and destruction does not re-

quire intuition to consider the possibilities (see 278). Whether a false diagnosis leading to tragedy or a true diagnosis resulting in conversion to occultism, neither consequence is insignificant (see 278 and New Age Medicine). If even normal intuition is often unreliable, how can anyone trust New Age practitioners who openly confess they rely on psychic "intuition" in their practices?

The term "intuition" is today often only a euphemism for such things as psychic development, spiritistic inspiration, and so-called "higher" (occult) consciousness. In the New Age Movement intuition is anything but a neutral term. There is indeed "a way that seems right to a man, but in the end it leads to death" (Proverbs 14:12).

# NEW AGE MEDICINE

## INFO AT A GLANCE

**Description.** New Age medicine is the "health" branch of the New Age Movement that involves the application of generally Eastern/occult methods to healing while stressing treatment of the whole person—body, mind, and spirit. The term is frequently used interchangeably with "holistic medicine," although the two are not necessarily equivalent. The term "alternative medicine" is also used interchangeably, but it may or may not include New Age approaches; for example, it may involve novel methods or new approaches to standard treatments which are not fully tested or demonstrated.

**Founder.** None per se. The term "holistic" (from the Greek *holos*, meaning "whole" or "entire") was apparently first coined by South African prime minister Jan Smuts in his 1926 book *Holism and Evolution*, a philosophical work not connected to medicine. Today, the term "holistic" is applied to many different fields, e.g., holistic psychology, but usually in connection with a spiritual or cosmic perspective.

**How does it claim to work?** Proponents claim that reliance on allegedly "natural" and "spiritual" methods of healing offer medical care superior to that of modern orthodox medicine. Recourse is often made to various concepts about so-called invisible "life energies" as the reason it "works."

**Scientific evaluation.** Discredited, despite numerous and vocal claims to the contrary.

**Examples of occult potential.** Altered states of consciousness,* psychic healing, channeling,* divination,* shamanism,* and many additional forms of occult practice.

**Major problem.** Leading people into ineffective, dangerous, or occult practices and philosophy in the name of healing and health.

**Biblical/Christian evaluation.** Due to its generally fraudulent or occult nature, the entire realm of New Age medicine, with few exceptions, is biblically or ethically prohibited. On

477

the other hand, a truly Christian holistic medicine is possible where a scientific medical basis is maintained and emotional or spiritual problems that may affect physical health are dealt with on the basis of biblical presuppositions and teachings.

**Potential dangers.** False diagnosis and treatment; worsening of a physical condition or death; fraud; occult hazards: physical, psychological, spiritual harm (see 278).

*Note:* Much of this is excerpted with updated material from *Can You Trust Your Doctor?* (1590). The Comprehensive New Age Health Listing in the Appendix offers a categorized evaluation of some 700 alternative/New Age practices.

"Practicing medicine is serious business because it has a major impact on people's quality of life, and, at times, deals directly with life or death."

—Medical writer *Kurt Butler* (1143:93)

## INTRODUCTION AND INFLUENCE

One reason for the burgeoning crisis in health care, financially and otherwise, is that we are often our own worst enemies. Millions of people live lifestyles that damage or ruin their health. A healthy lifestyle is much more important to overall health than many people, some physicians included, are willing to admit.

A good illustration is AIDS. This single illness has the capacity to swamp and destroy our national health care system. Before this plague ends, tens of millions of people worldwide are going to die. Yet AIDS was almost entirely a preventable disease. And it still is. Apart from innocent victims, whether a person ever gets AIDS is largely a matter of one's personal lifestyle. If a person is sexually chaste and avoids intravenous illegal drugs, getting AIDS is nearly impossible.

Another reason for our health crises is that American society overvalues expensive medical care (as it does litigation) to the exclusion of a more commonsense approach, and we all pay the price. The advocacy of quality medical care for people *is* important (when it is needed), but too many individuals demand too much of the profession and have unrealistic expectations of its role in their lives. The truth is that most illnesses are self-limiting. In other words, our bodies are so well designed they are able to handle many illnesses without outside intervention. The important role of modern medicine in preventative health-care, diagnostic procedures, and the necessary use of drugs and surgery is beyond question, but in many cases both patients and health-care providers abuse the system.

There are three reasons for the revival of holistic alternatives, or New Age medicine in our culture. The first is a new realization (or perception) of some of the unavoidable problems of orthodox medical care, which we briefly discussed elsewhere (1590:35-39). The second is the revival of occult practice and Eastern philosophy in America. The third is a renewed and positive emphasis on lifestyle and personal responsibility for one's health.

However, that many people are generally more health conscious today, does not necessarily make them more health wise, though it makes them ripe for influence by New Age medicine. Thus, as more and more people retreat from the perceived or real problems of conventional medicine, they are turning in droves to more "natural" methods of healing—those which claim to treat them as "whole" persons and do not rely on drugs, surgery, or other "invasive" methods. It should be noted, however, that good physicians have always been "holistic" in that they are concerned about their patients' overall health. But they have also recognized their role as *physical* specialists, and therefore where necessary made referrals to counselors or ministers for non-physical problems. On the other hand, New Age medicine's promoters often claim the expertise to treat the whole person—body, mind, and spirit.

The problem in the approach of New Age medicine is twofold: 1) New Age health providers are usually not experts in biological medicine; 2) their treatment of body, mind, and spirit is based on occult presuppositions and practices. In both cases, this can *damage* a person's health.

By the early 1990s the influence of New Age medicine on American culture was unmistakable. *Time* magazine's cover story for November 4, 1991, "The New Age of Alternative Medicine: Why New Age Medicine Is Catching On," stated that 30 percent of people questioned in a *Time*/CNN poll had tried an unconventional therapy, and that alternative medicine was a 27-billion-dollar-a-year industry.

Television specials and books on the subject have fascinated millions, such as Bill Moyers' 1993 PBS special "Healing and the Mind" and its companion volume by the same name. Moyers notes that New Age therapies have taken hold in many U.S. hospitals, which now offer practices such as Buddhist meditation* and "therapeutic touch" to their patients. Says Moyers, "I know people by the tens of millions are using alternative medicine. If established medicine doesn't understand that, they're going to lose their clients" (2348:51). Even prominent medical schools like Emory and Harvard University Medical School now offer courses on "non-conventional and unorthodox medical techniques" (see 2348:49).

With the U.S. population aging, funds significantly declining, and "technological life" continuing to increase, the cultural turn to and social acceptance of less expensive, more "personal" holistic methods can only increase, perhaps dramatically, in the next generation. The issue is whether there will be greater spiritual cost—*and* health cost—if these methods are not sufficiently critiqued and evaluated from a comprehensive scientific, biblical, religious, and occult perspective before they are widely accepted.

Alternative medicine courses are also being taught at one-third of other leading American medical schools, such as Boston University School of Medicine, Columbia University College of Physicians and Surgeons, John Hopkins School of Medicine, Mount Sinai School of Medicine, Stanford University School of Medicine, University of California Los Angeles School of Medicine, University of California San Francisco School of Medicine, Yale School of Medicine, and many others (2811:111-13).

Are these medical schools on to something? The answer is both yes and no: "New Age medicine" and "alternative medicine" do not neces-sarily refer either to similar approaches to medical practice or to the same methods employed. But clearly there is a great deal of overlap, and this *is* a problem. However, it should not be forgotten that it is possible to have a truly scientific approach which combines legitimate or promising alternative medicine along with the established benefits of contemporary medicine. Despite its obvious benefits, medicine can rely too much on drugs and surgery. Of course, when it comes to illness, especially as we grow older, medical decisions are frequently of a "lesser of two evils" nature, e.g., prescription medicine to alleviate constant pain may come with some undesirable long-term side effects. And, in certain instances, use of drugs and surgery should be reconsidered if and when there are milder but equally effective methods that allow the body to heal itself, rather that taking drugs that have serious side effects or which may interfere with the body's own ability to heal itself.

Contemporary medicine also has a number of additional problems that could at least be alleviated, if not solved, by taking a second look at what *is* valuable in alternative medicine. For example, a scientific examination and approach to diet and nutrition (which, along with exercise, are far more important to health than most people seem to realize), or the rational use of herbal remedies, massage, scientific chiropractic, biological rhythms (especially as they relate to the taking of medicines), psychoneuroimmunology, vegetarianism, biofeedback, light therapy, and others are worth consideration.

Of course, the safety and efficacy of any procedure must be established before it can be rationally advocated. This is part of the problem since the time and cost involved in this process is very significant. Obviously, however, it's better to be safe than sorry. There is thus a large new area in which medical researchers need to sift the wheat from the chaff.

Unfortunately, the general problem in society, and even in medical schools, is that unscientific, New Age approaches are being accepted without adequate analysis and testing merely because they seem to work. What this means for the consumer is that it is important to learn how to be more involved in one's own health care—on the one hand to be cautiously open to promising new approaches, but on the other hand to studiously avoid disproven, occult, or suspect practices (refs. 1387/278).

In 1993 the *New England Journal of Medicine* revealed that one in three Americans had tried at least one form of alternate medicine in the last year, and that survey's extrapolations "suggest that in 1990 Americans made an estimated 425 million visits to providers of unconventional therapy" (2023:246). The article emphasized that "...unconventional medicine has an enormous presence in the U.S. health care system," that its use is widely distributed "across all sociodemographic groups," and that its frequency of use "is far higher than previously reported" (2023:246, 251). In addition, "unconventional therapies are frequently used by patients" with such conditions as cancer, arthritis, chronic back pain, AIDS, gastrointestinal disease, kidney failure, and eating disorders (2023:246). Among the "sixteen commonly used interventions" studied in this survey were relaxation methods, acupuncture, homeopathy, visualization,* self-help groups, herbalism, chiropractic, energy healing, and hypnosis* (2023:248).

Orthodox physicians are also being swayed. The 700-member American Holistic Medical Association is only one of several national organizations which indicate that a significant number of medical professionals are turning to occult New Age teachings and practices. Indeed, the influence of alternate medical practices among physicians appears significant:

Testimony and further refinement of statistics given in a joint hearing of the House Subcommittee on Health and Long-Term Care in 1992, given by Dr. John Renner, M.D., head of the Consumer Health Information Research Institute in Kansas City, Missouri, showed that: Of the 630,000 M.D.s in America, 6,300 to 12,600 M.D.s engage in purely quack activities. An additional 12,600 to 31,500 M.D.s use some kind of unproven alternative technique in their medical practice. And further, 31,500 to 63,000 additional M.D.s occasionally use an unproven alternative technique (personal conversation with Dr. Renner).

According to the influential New Age physician and bestselling author Dr. Deepak Chopra, some 6000 American medical doctors have now learned Transcendental Meditation (TM) and "many prescribe it to their patients" (2369:124). Dr. Chopra's principal occult medical method is "Maharishi Ayur-Veda" (a Westernized form of Hindu ayurvedic practice), and it has in some instances been approved by the American College of Preventive Medicine for the American Medical Association's Physicians Recognition Award category 1 Continuing Medical Education credit (2370:1744). We personally confirmed with administrator Sandy Hale of the Sharp Chula Vista Medical Center that it is also utilized by such prominent medical groups as the prestigious Sharp Health Care in San Diego, California. Indeed, TM itself is sufficiently accepted so that even "some insurance carriers now pay for TM instruction when prescribed by a physician" (2373:1).

According to Sharon Fish, R.N., Ph.D., "Conservative estimates are that close to 100,000 nurses have been trained to perform the techniques called Therapeutic Touch" in over 65 countries (2812:30), although most of the 100,000 practitioners are in the United States. Therapeutic Touch is a form of psychic healing (1590:391-406).

In light of all this, it is not surprising that in 1993 a new National Institutes of Health "Office of Alternative Medicine" (OAM) was established to begin testing a variety of New Age and unconventional therapies. Unfortunately, charges of bias in favor of New Age medicine at the OAM have been raised (see 2219). For example, Dr. Deepak Chopra is one of several New Age enthusiasts who work with the OAM. He sits on the advisory council. Another example is Dr. Cathie E. Guzzetta, who was appointed to the study section of the OAM. She is the coauthor of *Cardiovascular Nursing: Holistic Practice* and *Critical Care Nursing: Body, Mind, Spirit* and similar texts that variously accept practices like channeling* energies, hypnosis,* visualization,* meditation,* shamanism,* psychic healing,* and Therapeutic Touch. To many observers, such bias of the council has undermined the credibility of the entire project.

Even that bastion of conservative American ideals, *Reader's Digest,* now publishes the *Family*

*Guide to Natural Medicine.* This volume claims that its purpose "is to examine these [New Age] therapies under the lens of objective inquiry" (1456:26). Yet the topics it discusses and often *endorses* include shamanism* and spiritistic healing (e.g., Native American healing), acupuncture, ayurvedic medicine, mandalas,* homeopathy, iridology, visualization,* dream work,* primal therapy and rebirthing, body work, mystical energies, reflexology, polarity therapy, yoga,* herbal remedies, hypnosis,* charms and talismans, chiropractic, auras, meditation,* autogenics, martial arts,* and macrobiotics.

Objective inquiry should presumably include rationality. To say that such subjects have been examined objectively, but then to find them endorsed with little concern as to the issue of truth or scientific analysis, is a sign of the times we live in. It shows that the American acceptance of New Age medicine and its influence is probably here to stay.

So why is New Age medicine an important issue that both the church and society itself must deal with? (Some people wrongly have argued that New Age medicine is a passing fad and hardly relevant at all.) The subject of New Age medicine is important for many reasons:

- Because our health and our family's health is important. For example, homeopaths, naturopaths, and many chiropractors *oppose* children's immunization against serious or even fatal diseases (1143:44-45,140/1093:111).

- Because the physical and spiritual health of the nation as a whole is important.

- Because it is important to know if our doctor is using a method that may be quackery or occult, whether or not it "works."

- Because New Age medicine is a major vehicle for spreading the occult. Those treated with New Age health methods often become converts to New Age philosophy and practice (301:257-58).

- Because New Age medicine is undergirded by a New Age worldview that is anti-Christian.

- Because New Age medicine can promote an irrational attitude not only toward medicine but toward other areas of life as well.

## INFLUENCE IN THE CHURCH

In what would have been unthinkable only a generation ago, Christian practitioners and clients are today found endorsing many New Age health techniques, especially in chiropractic, homeopathy, dowsing,* applied kinesiology,* Therapeutic Touch, iridology, dream work,* hypnosis,* and visualization.*

For example, in 1986 Dr. Weldon received a letter from a member of a Baptist church who was concerned because "over forty families are involved in applied kinesiology [muscle testing]* and iridology, including our pastor, deacons, and Sunday School teachers." Since the 1982 publication of an earlier book he coauthored on New Age medicine, *The Holistic Healers* (818), many such letters have been received. By the mid-1990s, matters had not improved. What Paul Reisser, M.D., Teri Reisser, M.S., and John Weldon had written in 1987 remains true:

> ... Although awareness of this movement has grown, discernment among Christians has remained marginal in the area of health care practices which are at one level or another hostile to biblical teaching. ...
>
> More than half of the headquarters personnel of a highly-respected, worldwide evangelical organization have been treated with applied kinesiology, homeopathy and other holistic therapies. Guests on national Christian TV shows have endorsed similar practices. A best-selling Christian author uses and promotes a "Christian form" of acupressure, iridology, etc. The promoter of a healing program whose textbook was dictated by a "spirit guide" [*A Course in Miracles*]* was given a friendly interview on Sunday morning at a well-known California church. We have continued to hear ... stories of churches embroiled in controversy, divided and quarreling after an alternative therapist wins some enthusiastic converts. A large Midwestern Baptist church has been split down the middle over the practice of iridology. ...
>
> An example: segments of *The Holistic Healers* were reprinted in three consecutive issues of the *Journal of Christian Nursing* in 1986. Our critique of Therapeutic Touch ... elicited a significant amount of mail from Christian nurses who saw nothing wrong with this practice ... (1:iv-v).

481

Despite its lack of credibility, a significant number of Christians have now accepted New Age medicine because some professed evangelicals have taken the lead in promoting these methods. Dr. Monte Kline is one example. Dr. Kline is the founder of "Total Living" in Bellevue, Washington, and author of *The Christian Health Counselor*, a bimonthly newsletter on supposedly Christian holistic health. We are going to take some time to evaluate Dr. Kline's arguments here because they illustrate the basis on which New Age medicine is often accepted by Christians.

Dr. Kline disagrees that many of these methods are necessarily occult. He thinks that they can be used effectively by Christians with proper safeguards. He claims, "... Quite a controversy has developed over the subject of 'wholistic' and 'holistic' health therapies among Christians. Several popular Christian books are assailing various natural, non-invasive therapies as being 'occult.' Included in the list is Applied Kinesiology, as practiced by myself and thousands of other Christian practitioners. ... *[T]he witch hunt is on*" (826:1).

Dr. Kline claims that he was led by the Holy Spirit into "Christian" New Age medicine (826:1). He explains how he was introduced to the subject:

I was introduced to my first true wholistic therapy nearly three years ago. This therapy was built around Applied and Behavioral Kinesiology—determining body energy levels by testing muscles. ... I learned how to determine nutrient deficiencies, supplement dosages, organ and gland imbalances, how to correct cranial faults, atlas, axis, temporomandibular joint dysfunction and a whole lot more. ... [R]esults have been dramatic. I have seen person after person for the first time discover the root emotional and spiritual causes of their health problems, from obesity to stiff necks, and be set free by the power of God's Spirit. ... (826:1)

Dr. Kline argues there are two possible responses to the phenomena of holistic health therapies. First, "I don't understand it, therefore it's Satanic." Second, "I don't understand it, therefore it must be something in God's creation I haven't known before."

But this kind of arguing represents a logical fallacy known as "faulty dilemma"—only two options are presented when there may be more than two. For example, another equally valid possibility is that New Age treatments are neither Satanic, nor based upon God's creation, but simple quackery. Nevertheless, Dr. Kline sets forth his argument as to why Christians should accept "invisible energies":

It amazes and amuses me when someone, particularly someone of scientific background, is concerned with "invisible energies." What about electricity, magnetism, gravity, centrifugal force and the whole gamut of classical physics, none of which we can "see," all of which we can observe and measure the effect of though. Kinesiology is no different. How arrogant can we be to assume that anything we don't understand is occult? We are so finite! We don't know one millionth of what God has built into His creation. Instead of presuming everything strange or different is occult, it makes a lot more sense to assume it is part of God's creation *unless* scripture *clearly* speaks to the contrary (which it does on many occult practices). I wonder how many Christians a hundred years ago upon hearing a radio or watching a television or seeing a motion picture would have thought them occult? I can just imagine! And why would they label them occult? Because of scripture? No, because of ignorance. And things haven't changed any today as evidenced by the Kinesiology controversy (826:1).

But why should anyone be amazed and amused that Christians are concerned over "invisible energies"? Such a concern is healthy and reflects a legitimate desire to express spiritual discernment. The Bible tell us, "Test everything. Hold on to the good. Avoid every kind of evil" (1 Thessalonians 5:21-22). The Bible also tells us to be aware of the devil's schemes and to stand against them (2 Corinthians 2:11; Ephesians 6:11). We are also warned, "Do not give the devil a foothold" (Ephesians 4:27).

The existence of invisible energies that science can measure does not automatically mean that *all* invisible energies are legitimate or neutral. Nor does it prove that the energies of New Age medicines are either natural or divine. The alleged principles on which applied kinesiology* operates are certainly different than the known energies science measures and investigates. And no one can deny that many New Age health practices based on invisible energies are clearly occult, that is, spiritistic and demonic.

In addition, the argument based upon human understanding needs qualification. It is one thing for a therapy to actually work on some unknown but natural and legitimate principle. If so, its effectiveness could be demonstrated to anyone's satisfaction by double-blind testing, even though *how* it worked might still remain a mystery. But it is quite different to say a therapy that can never be demonstrated works on natural and neutral principles. At that point, how does one prove anything? (In fact, New Age methods can often be evaluated on the basis of the *claims* they make. Their failure to work, or to work on the basis of their stated principles, is the real problem.)

No one is arguing that everything we don't understand is occult. However, isn't it possible that *some* things we don't understand may be? And isn't it a non sequitur to argue that merely because we don't understand something, we ought to probably or necessarily accept it as a neutral aspect of God's creation? On what basis should we accept Dr. Kline's argument that all mysteries should be assumed to be natural and part of God's creation, unless Scripture clearly speaks to the contrary? Aren't there many issues that can be decided scripturally even though Scripture never comments on them directly, such as abortion, drug abuse, and biblically unreferenced occult practices? And in a fallen world, with Satan as its god (2 Corinthians 4:4), and with the whole world lying in his power (1 John 5:19), isn't it more likely that mysterious energies related to occultism are more likely to be demonic than neutral or godly?

Still, Dr. Kline suggests that certain evangelical critics of New Age medicine are engaging in "paranoia." "This tends to be the position of those Christian brethren promoting paranoia over the New Age Movement.... Their assumption is that anything outside their knowledge of the creation is supernatural in the demonic sense and therefore to be denied. Thus, the ch'i energy of acupuncture, auras, and chakras could not possibly be just another part of God's creation, only unknown to them" (283:4).

Kline and many others believe that most of what occurs in New Age medicine is explainable under natural but as yet undiscovered laws of the universe. He believes that the universe is so infinite, and that God is so infinite, that Christians who criticize New Age medicine as a whole are "naive." For who can really judge what hidden things lie within the creation?

But this is the problem. Hidden things are just that—hidden, or occult. Like "things that go bump in the night," they are mercurial, uncertain, difficult to ascertain. On what basis does one judge a thing when little or nothing can be known about it? Unknown things can also be dangerous. In Russian roulette, the location of the bullet is unknown. But who would pull the trigger six times to find the proper chamber?

Furthermore, would Mr. Kline believe that the apostle Paul was "paranoid" when he stated that Satan was the *god* of this world (2 Corinthians 4:4)? Or would he think that the apostle John was "paranoid" when he stated that "the whole *world* lies in the power of the evil one" (1 John 5:19 NASB)? Don't these apostles and the rest of the Bible grant the devil a significant degree of authority and power? Didn't Jesus (Luke 4:5-8)?

Are evangelical critics of New Age medicine really throwing the baby out with the bathwater? Or are they engaging in proper spiritual discernment? After all, who really has the wisdom of a Solomon to sort out the complexities of what "might" be hidden in God's creation? And when occult realities and spiritistic powers at a certain level become indistinguishable from certain *alleged* neutral aspects of creation, is it wise or foolish to assume that those aspects of creation really are neutral? Is anything in the creation finally neutral? The burden of proof should rest with the one who makes the claim. In this chapter and in other books we have shown the occult and pagan nature of New Age medicine. Where is Dr. Kline's evidence that prana, mana, chi, auras, and chakras are a neutral part of God's creation?

And isn't it the spirit world itself which argues that mystical energies are a natural part of the creation? In other words, Dr. Kline's arguments are the same arguments given by the spirits. This does not necessarily make them false, but it certainly means such arguments should not be accepted uncritically. It does mean that we should question why the spirits would want to promote these concepts. For example, the spirit guide of medium Alice Bailey promoted the idea of mystical energy flowing through the chakras as being responsible for all physical diseases and even personality problems. This demon argued that once men recognize God as energy and themselves as energy, and once they learn to manipulate these energies, then they will be healthy and progress spiritually (313:135-40,155,483,723-26,733).

Dr. Kline also seems to believe that merely because he is a Christian he is automatically protected from spiritual deception. "Because I am in Christ, under His blood, keeping Him central in all I do, my [applied] kinesiology practice cannot be occult. But a practitioner not in Christ and centered on Him could easily express the occult" (862:2). But if we substituted "Ouija board" for "kinesiology," would the argument still hold true?

It is a mistake to assume that being a Christian precludes one from spiritual deception. As an illustration, Mineda J. McCleave was disillusioned with her church but "could not reject Christ or the Bible" (890:400). When she could not understand certain Bible passages relating to "mysteries" (Luke 8:10; 1 Corinthians 4:1), she sought occult interpretations in hopes of understanding them. Her acceptance of occult literature began a process of terrible self-deception:

> Most of the religious books I had read warned me against studying occult literature. They claimed that such material was the work of the devil; it was demonic, satanic, evil, and filled with black magic. However, by the time I had progressed to reading occult books, I had already made a covenant with God. It was simple. I would *trust* him and he would *protect* me. I prayed for guidance in the selection of my reading material. I discovered there were good occult books and bad ones, and trusted God to help me choose the good ones (890:400-01).

But the result was not a deeper biblical understanding; it was a perversion based on occult philosophy. Today she remains a Christian mystic who thoroughly integrates Christianity and the occult. Instead of forsaking the occult entirely as

God had instructed (Deuteronomy 18:9-12; Acts 19:19), McCleave attempted to discover the "good" in the occult. She had trusted God to protect her, even while she studied and engaged in practices He has forbidden. The final result was that her meditative* practices led to kundalini* arousal, mental illness, and ten years of unrelenting pain and suffering (see Yoga).

Christians, like all people, will be harmed by entering occult practices. In both the Old and New Testaments, why would God have given so many warnings to His people against occult practices if the mere fact of being a believer was an automatic protection against them?

Spiritual healing can either be legitimate or illegitimate—that is, either divine or demonic. In the Bible we discover that God does heal supernaturally according to His will and wisdom (Psalm 103:3; Exodus 4:11). In the Gospel accounts we find that Jesus repeatedly healed people (Matthew 4:23-24; 8:16). We also see that there is a divine gift of healing that God may give to some of His people (1 Corinthians 12:9,28,30). But there are also occult (demonic) miracles and healings. Scripture warns that *genuine* spiritual miracles can occur and yet still be false. For example, God Himself sternly cautioned against a false prophet who would work genuine miracles and then counsel rebellion against Him by enticing people to worship a false god (Deuteronomy 13:1-5). Such miracles are described in the Bible as deceptive miracles and lying wonders because they lead people to worship false gods.

Jesus also warned about people who claimed to perform "many miracles" in His name, but at the final judgment they were found to be false professors and "evildoers" (Matthew 7:22-23). He acknowledged that false Christs and false prophets would perform "great signs and wonders" to try to lead even God's elect astray (Matthew 24:24). Such false miracles come from the devil (2 Thessalonians 2:9).

The previous verses underscore much of what occurs in modern New Age medicine: spiritual claimants performing "miracles" and then counseling people to follow false gods. At its heart, New Age medicine is fundamentally idolatrous. In fact, spiritual deception within the New Age

Movement is a reason why even practitioners of scientific medicine may become converted to New Age beliefs. After they encounter an occult miracle, which undermines their faith in materialistic medicine, they may join forces with occult medicine and its pagan philosophies.

All this is why we think that Christian promoters of New Age medicine are in serious error when they advocate the use of fraudulent or occult methods.

## New Age Medicine Versus Orthodox Medicine

The general differences between New Age medicine and scientific medicine can be seen in the chart on the next page, which we stress is for purposes of general contrast only. (Please examine chart now.)

The obvious differences between scientific and New Age medicine are why Drs. Stalker and Glymour observe in their excellent text, *Examining Holistic Medicine* that " . . . holistic medicine is not a scientific tradition. It has no paradigmatic work, no recognized set of problems, and no shared standards for what constitutes a solution to those problems; it also lacks the critical exchange among its practitioners that is characteristic of the sciences" (3:26).

These authors discuss how the very existence of New Age medicine is undermining medicine in general and, to that extent, the nation's health. They write:

> The shared aims that tie so many diverse people together are to institutionalize holistic medical practices, and, furthermore, to loosen the demands of evidence that we, as a society, impose on those who claim to cure or prevent disease. The first aim requires the second. . . . Only by abandoning the usual criteria of scientific evidence, and even the usual demands of rational thinking, can the claims of holistic medicants be established and made legitimate. . . .
>
> [However,] the science of holistic medicine is bogus. . . . [T]he philosophical views championed by this movement are incoherent, uninformed, and unintelligen. . . . [M]ost holistic therapies are

crank in the usual sense of that word: they lack any sound scientific basis (3:10).

Dr. Thomas Chalmers is Distinguished Service Professor of Medicine as well as president emeritus and dean emeritus of the Mount Sinai School of Medicine. He is the author of over 250 publications and head of the Clinical Trials Unit at the Mt. Sinai Medical Center. Dr. Chalmers examined the scientific quality of articles found in perhaps the most scientifically oriented New Age medical journal, *The Journal of Holistic Medicine*.** This is the official journal of the American Holistic Medical Association, founded by neurosurgeon and New Age practitioner Dr. Norman Shealy, author of *Occult Medicine Can Save Your Life* (103), and with spiritist Caroline M. Myss, *The Creation of Health: Merging Traditional Medicine with Intuitive Diagnosis* (108).

After examining 47 articles from four different volumes, Dr. Chalmers discovered only nine trials of therapies, and of these only two were randomized control trials (both by the same author). Yet AHMA proponents had claimed that their journal published empirical studies similar to those in standard medical journals. But the scientific tests were few and far between and "generally not well done." They suffered from errors such as "a lack of adequate control with regard to measurements and separation of investigative agents" (3:14). This is why Dr. Chalmers concluded that the "*Journal of Holistic Medicine* has a long way to go to achieve the same standards of scientific reporting as the more orthodox medical journals . . ." (983:163).

In a similar fashion, after we personally examined 153 articles from the *Journal of Holistic Health*, an early publication in the field, it became obvious that this was not science but primarily Eastern, occult religion (210-218).

It is vital to understand why a scientific approach to medicine is important and the difference that can make when compared with New Age medicine. Let's say that you or your child has a persistent sore throat. How does the diagnosis

---

**A newcomer in 1995 to the field is the *Journal of Alternative and Complementary Medicine*.

## CONTRASTS BETWEEN ORTHODOX AND NEW AGE MEDICINE

| | *Scientific Medicine* | *New Age Medicine* |
|---|---|---|
| PREMISE | Disease operates at the physical level and should be treated physically. (We do note, however, that in many disorders there are emotional components that must be treated as well.) | Disease begins at an energy level and should be treated energetically. |
| WORLDVIEW | Holds most or all premises of materialism and/or naturalism, although it is not incompatible with the worldview of Christian theism. | Holds many premises of general occultism, pantheism (all is God; God is all) and/or philosophical spiritualism (that all reality is, in essence, spiritual). |
| MEDICAL ORIENTATION | The scientific disciplines: biology, anatomy, physiology, chemistry, pharmacology, etc. | The metaphysical disciplines: a) Eastern-occult philosophy and practice: Chinese (e.g., Taoism, acupuncture); Hindu (e.g., Vedanta, ayurvedic medicine); Buddhist, (e.g., Mahayana, *vipassana* meditation); shamanistic (e.g., American Indian, spiritual possession); b) Western occult vitalistic philosophy and practice (e.g., anthroposophical medicine; homeopathy) |
| BASIS FOR METHODOLOGY (why its methods are used) | Rational scientific inquiry (techniques are used because they are scientifically shown to work on the basis of their stated principles). | Pragmatic, empirical inquiry (techniques are used primarily because they seem to work, not because they have been demonstrated to work on the basis of their stated principles). |
| SAFEGUARDS | Preexisting scientific data base of confirmed medical testing; double-blind clinical trials; peer review, skeptical attitudes toward research findings; methods not adopted until validated for their effectiveness. | Little or no data base; no safeguards against irrational and scientifically unproven methods; uncritical attitudes often permit a large variety of false therapies to be accepted. |
| MEDICAL FINDINGS | Generally consistent by discipline and consistent across disciplines. | Often contradictory by disciplines (e.g., iridology, reflexology charts) and across disciplines. |
| DIAGNOSTIC METHODS | Physically based; consistently used. | Psychically based; contradictory use. |
| STATUS RE: EFFECTIVENESS | Scientifically validated. | Scientifically disproven or unproven. |

based on scientific medicine prove its usefulness? First, you go to the doctor and tell him your symptoms. He examines you, asks questions, and because he is medically trained, he suspects it may be more than an ordinary sore throat. How does he find out whether his suspicion is true? He will probably order a blood test to reveal white cell count and bacterial infection. He suspects you have strep throat. How does he determine what kind of bacterial infection you have, whether you are infected with the streptococcus bacterium, and which kind of streptococcus bacterium it is? He determines this by scientific results from a simple culture which proves the existence of the bacterium and identifies it.

Because your doctor knows that antibiotics such as penicillin will kill the strep bacteria, he will write you a prescription. If you take the drug according to his instructions, in a few weeks you will no longer have strep throat.

Now, let us say you have a sore throat and you go to a New Age healer. Because she is not medically trained, she wrongly assumes you have a simple cold or flu. She decides that your supposed "life energy" (*prana, chi*) is blocked or slightly out of balance, and thus producing your cold or flu symptoms. By acupuncture treatment or applied kinesiology,* she "unblocks" your life energy and prescribes rest and herbal tea. No blood test is given to determine infection level. No culture is taken to determine if bacteria are present.

After a week or so your sore throat subsides and you conclude that New Age medicine is wonderful. Not only are you cured, but you never had to pay for any of those expensive medical tests. But two months later you feel tired, feverish, and have painful, swollen joints. You go back to your New Age therapist. By "muscle testing"* or reflexology, the practitioner concludes that your "life energies" are blocked. Using Therapeutic Touch, she claims to transfer her own life energy into your body to assist your own *prana* (life energy) to heal your illness. She also prescribes homeopathic remedies. You go home, still feeling rotten.

A month later you are no better. In fact, your speech is slurred and you experience involuntary jerking movements of the hands, arms, and face. You visit your conventional doctor and to your horror you discover that you have streptococcus-induced rheumatic fever and chorea. You also have valvular heart disease—a condition you will live with for the rest of your life.

You learn a hard lesson about New Age medicine. Your New Age therapist never knew that an untreated streptococcal infection, which often has no more symptoms than a common sore throat, could temporarily damage your brain and permanently damage your heart. (The strain that allegedly killed the Muppets' inventor Jim Henson can be deadly within 48 hours.) Your New Age therapist had no access to a medical lab to test your blood levels, no medicine to prescribe. She had little interest in scientific medicine at all and was merely concerned with manipulating your supposed life energies.

When it comes to the area of health practices, the safeguards of the scientific method are that before a given treatment can be offered to the public, it must have undergone intense scrutiny in order to make sure that the treatment is effective based upon its stated principles. Penicillin must really have been proven to kill streptococcus bacteria. It's not good enough to *think* that it does, or merely to *claim* it does this. It must really kill the bacteria. Scientific medicine works because it is based upon proven facts.

We may define scientific medicine as the practice of diagnosis and treatment by a medically qualified, scientifically oriented specialist using methods for which effectiveness has been established by rigorous and independent clinical testing. We may define New Age medicine, generally, as the practice of diagnosis and treatment by a medically unqualified and often psychically oriented practitioner using methods for which effectiveness has never been established or may even have been scientifically discredited (see 959). And even when a practitioner is medically qualified, this does not by itself validate a New Age treatment.

Those who practice New Age medicine usually do not have the medical skill, let alone the qualifications, of a regularly trained physician. Their methods will neither diagnose accurately nor cure disease. Thus, acupuncturists, iridologists, psychic healers, chromotherapists, applied kinesiologists,* practitioners of astrologic medicine, and so on rarely have four or more years of rigorous postgraduate medical education and internship, nor will their techniques diagnose or cure illness. (When genuine spiritistic power is present, accurate diagnosis or healings can be produced, but they are produced by the spirits, not the method. Furthermore, they are not true healings but "transfer" the illness to the psychological or spiritual level. See "Dangers" on p. 504.)

*Quackery*

The U.S. House of Representatives Select Committee on Aging defines a quack as "anyone who promotes medical remedies known to be false, or which are unproven, for a profit" (31:411). But one does not have to actually promote techniques or remedies for a profit to be a quack. The essence of quackery is false or unproven remedies, thus the *Oxford American Dictionary* defines a quack as "a person who falsely claims to have medical skill or to have remedies that will cure disease" (414:732).

Is New Age medicine quackery? The definition of "quack" or "quackery" varies only slightly in medical dictionaries. To the extent the definition includes the idea of *deliberate* misrepresentation concerning diagnostic and healing ability, an individual New Age practitioner is not necessarily a quack. Most sincerely believe that their diagnostic and healing treatments work. But if these methods do not work, practitioners are still engaging in misrepresentation, deliberate or not. And misrepresentation of a remedy's effectiveness is the heart of quackery, as proven by standard definitions in medical dictionaries and encyclopedias, e.g., "Quack—One who misrepresents his ability and experience in diagnosis and treatment of disease or the effects to be achieved by his treatment" (675:947).

The standard definitions of "quackery" include the following items:

- misrepresentation of diagnostic or treatment ability
- false claims regarding experience in diagnosis and treatment
- ignorance or dishonesty concerning medical skill

- the practice of medicine by unlicensed individuals
- the use of methods not generally recognized by the medical profession (675/678/679/680/681).

In light of such definitions, there is little doubt that New Age medicine in general should be classified as quackery. What is worse, the doors are now open for official government recognition of quackery, thanks in part to the Office of Alternative Medicine and the U.S. Department of Education (1143:143).

But isn't it true that many people report being cured by holistic therapies? And doesn't this prove New Age medicine cures disease? No, because even when these healings are genuine, they are not produced on the basis of the stated principles of New Age technique themselves. New Age medicine does not work on the basis of its stated principles but upon psychological factors, or through the body's natural ability to heal itself, or through spiritistic powers.

When New Age medicine claims it is scientific, no one should be fooled. New Age medicine is essentially a spiritual practice that treats its patients on the basis of religious (Eastern or occult) principles, not scientific ones. In light of this, we present some general guidelines to help patients determine whether their physician is adopting New Age methods.

## PRINCIPLES OF DISCERNMENT: CAVEAT EMPTOR

How can a person tell whether a doctor is practicing scientific medicine? Informed and attentive listening is important. Ask the doctor to explain things in simple English; critically think through what a doctor says. If you believe it is necessary, do not hesitate to bring up the subject of New Age medicine. What does a doctor think about it, and why? Has a doctor ever considered adopting New Age medical treatments? Which one(s), and why? What is the doctor's religious worldview? Does he have a spiritual leader or guru? Does he follow an Eastern religion or practice a form of Western occultism? Is he frustrated from some of the problems in conventional medicine and looking for alternate ways of treating his patients? Has a personal crisis in his life led him to explore alternate spiritual lifestyles?

Unfortunately, the occult nature of New Age treatments may be camouflaged by scientific, neutral, or spiritual-sounding euphemisms. Because of this, it is often necessary to investigate the background of a given treatment thoroughly before placing one's physical or spiritual health at risk. Certainly anyone who suspects any unusual or unorthodox method or therapy should investigate the matter before treatment begins or continues.

How did the practice originate? Who was its founder? What was his worldview and spiritual orientation? Is the method or practice accepted in the medical community, and if not, why not? Does a method require a psychic sensitivity to operate successfully? Is there any evidence to substantiate that this method really functions on the basis of its stated principles? If it claims to function on spiritual or mystical principles, what is the worldview tied to those principles, and how are they related to the occult? Does accepting the method *require* adopting a new worldview? Does the method require faith: Does it "work" only if one believes in it?

In Reisser, Reisser, and Weldon's *New Age Medicine*, a number of principles are discussed for determining which therapies or techniques should be avoided (1:147-52). We have reproduced these principles below, added others, and provided illustrations with various New Age therapies. In recognition of the ancient Latin phrase "caveat emptor," that is, "let the buyer beware," they are listed as "caveats."

*Caveat #1.* Beware of therapies that are energy based and claim to manipulate invisible or mystical energies or that rely on psychic anatomies. Examples are acupuncture, muscle testing,* ayurvedic medicine, reflexology, and color therapy. Be aware, also, that a practice which appears entirely innocent, such as passing a hand over the body (as in therapeutic touch), may not be innocent at all. Therapists who claim to manipulate invisible energies may harm a person spiritually by such a method (271:104-30/272:142-54/270:42-56; see also "Dangers" on p. 504 and 278).

*Caveat #2.* Beware of those who seem to use psychic knowledge, power, or abilities, as in clairvoyant diagnosis, psychic healing or surgery, crystal healing,* therapeutic touch, radionics and psychometry, channeling energies,* and shamanistic* medicine. Those having psychic abilities are ultimately linked to the spirit world, and their methods and practices are consequential.

*Caveat #3.* Beware of a practitioner who has a therapy that almost no one else has heard of. We could cite something called Terpsichoretrancetherapy or TTT. This is a "hypnopsychotherapeutic" method which claims that "the ritual kinetic trance existing in primitive Afro-Brazilian spiritual [spiritist] sects may be used therapeutically," noting that "under [both] TTT and during a ritual [spirit] possession, the subject undergoes [allegedly therapeutic] regression" (715:131).

*Caveat #4.* Beware of any technique that is promoted before it has been validated by mainstream science. This includes New Age medicine in general. To accept such practices is unwise because responsible persons do not publicly promote techniques whose value and safety is undemonstrated. Such practices are typically quack methods whereby people lose their money through experimentation and do not get better.

*Caveat #5.* Beware of anyone claiming that the therapy will cure almost anything, as in color therapy, acupuncture, homeopathy, and some forms of chiropractic. Those who maintain that the therapy will cure almost anything will probably cure almost nothing.

*Caveat #6.* Beware of someone whose explanations are bizarre or don't make sense, as in astrologic medicine, behavioral kinesiology,* homeopathy, and color therapy. A practitioner of astrologic medicine may tell you that the influence of Jupiter or Pluto has affected your nucleic acids. A homeopath may claim that the more diluted a "medicine" is, the greater its power to heal. A color therapist may ask you to drink water bathed in "yellow rays" to cure indigestion. (Never hesitate to ask your doctor to explain in simple English, and to offer scientific evidence,

489

why the therapy works on the basis of its stated principles.)

*Caveat #7.* Beware of therapies whose primary "proof" is the claims of satisfied clients. Again, this includes New Age medicine in general. In fact, the only "evidence" we have that New Age medicine works comes from testimonials which are better explained by other means. Of course, satisfied clients (at least initially) are found in everything from con schemes to witchcraft, but that hardly validates them. Therapies can seem to work and still be false (see "Nature of Cures" and "Pragmatism" on p. 503).

*Caveat #8.* Beware of therapies that rely upon entering altered states of consciousness,* such as hypnotic regression,* therapeutic touch, meditation,* and visualization* techniques. Altered states of consciousness* are notoriously deceptive, unreliable in health matters, and frequently open the doors to spiritistic influences (see Altered States of Consciousness).

*Caveat #9.* Realize that a practitioner's sincerity is no guarantee of scientific or medical legitimacy. This holds true for all practitioners, including Christian ones. Even noted evangelical health therapists and pastors have employed or endorsed questionable or discredited techniques.

*Caveat #10.* Beware of any method that has been scientifically disproven, such as iridology, homeopathy, applied kinesiology,* astrologic medicine, radionics, and many chiropractic claims.

*Caveat #11.* Beware of a therapist or physician who claims to diagnose or treat patients on the basis of "intuition."* In New Age medicine, "intuition" is often a euphemism for psychic and spiritistic inspiration or ability (see New Age Intuition).

*Caveat #12.* Beware of spiritual imperialism. Avoid any therapist who thinks his or her methods are specially connected to God. For example, many of these therapists will attempt to treat clients psychically without their knowledge or permission. Some nurse practitioners of therapeutic touch have admitted this (e.g., 2812:28). Such therapists may assume the divine "right" to

do so because "divine" intuition tells them such treatment is "needed." Also, it is always wise to make certain a physician has attended an accredited medical school. This is no guarantee that he or she will practice legitimate medicine. But it will weed out those who are medically untrained, to help you determine whether the therapy offered is commensurate with their educational background. And be wary of a practitioner who will not directly answer your questions or seems evasive. Even some physicians are closet spiritists or psychics. When directly asked if they are practicing energy manipulation or have spirit guides, they will evade the issue in order to retain respectability and credibility. Or they will redefine their occult beliefs and practices so that they sound scientific. Continue to pursue the issue until you have a definite answer concerning their orientation.

Finally, if the buyer is to beware, the seller of questionable therapies should also beware. Those who deal in the realm of health, not to mention the human spirit, have a responsibility to others not to promote therapies which may endanger the physical, emotional, or spiritual health of their clients. Those who offer therapies that are not scientifically established, and which may harm their patients, need to realize they can be held legally accountable for their actions.

## COMMON FEATURES OF NEW AGE MEDICINE

Despite the large number and variety of New Age health practices, common themes emerge, and we present some general characteristics below. Not every New Age medical technique fits every characteristic, but the following features are frequently encountered.

### A Magical Worldview

New Age Medicine lives within the confines of a world of its own special rules. It is a kind of "magical" world where anything is possible, no matter how implausible or irrational. And once we believe such things, we can believe almost anything. For example:

- "Medicines" can heal even though not a single molecule of the "medicine" is taken (homeopathy).

- The iris of the eye can diagnose preclinical and other disease even though this is anatomically impossible (iridology).

- A physician can diagnose the patient's problem by consulting a psychic a thousand miles away (clairvoyant diagnosis).

- A physician can diagnose the patient by consulting dead objects *millions* of miles away (the stars and planets of astrologic medicine).

- Ordinary rocks and stones can heal (crystal* and amulet healing).

### Altered States of Consciousness and Psychic Anatomies

Altered states of consciousness* are used in therapeutic touch, psychic diagnosis and healing, hypnotic regression,* shamanism,* radionics, dream work,* crystal healing,* visualization,* and other practices. They appear in health training, diagnosis, treatment, and for health maintenance after treatment.

Altered states have played a vital role in occult medicine since the dawn of history. They are believed to "properly" orient the healer or the patient toward optimum physical, mental, and spiritual "health." For example, they are essential in all forms of psychic diagnosis and healing. Altered states help a therapist to develop psychic abilities so that the "healer" can receive information from his "higher mind," "cosmic wisdom," or spirit guides. They appear in the development of clairvoyant vision so a person, allegedly, can see "psychically" within the body to make diagnoses. They can also be used to diagnose the patient "spiritually" by supposedly psychically examining the "aura" or "astral and etheric bodies."

Altered states may also appear in conjunction with almost any New Age health technique, as a means of developing so-called "intuitive" abilities in diagnosis (see New Age Intuition). They may even be recommended to the patient as part of an ongoing health treatment program.

"Psychic anatomies" are also important in New Age medicine. Indeed, it seems that it was through altered states of consciousness that the alleged psychic anatomies were first discovered, such as the *chakra* system in Hinduism or the meridian system in Chinese acupuncture. Thus, numerous New Age healers, from mediums and spiritists, to psychics and yogis, to energy manipulators and acupuncturists, may claim to see the invisible anatomy psychically and its energy "blockage." The particular remedy-technique employed is supposed to "realign" or "unblock" the energy, thereby permitting it to flow freely through the body and so restore health.

### Spiritism and Mysterious Body Energies

Because New Age medicine is characteristically an Eastern and occult form of medical treatment, the predominance of spiritistic influence is not surprising. Just as spiritism is at the core in the revival of pagan religions and new cults in America (716), it is also at the core of New Age medicine. Spiritistic influence is found in New Age health practices as diverse as acupuncture, dream work,* meditation,* psychic diagnosis and healing, hypnosis and hypnotic past-life regression,* color healing, radionics, rod and pendulum dowsing,* visualization,* homeopathy, and crystal healing.*

But can we accept the reality of spirits on the one hand and deny the reality of New Age energies on the other? This question raises two concerns. First is the issue of evidence: What genuine evidence exists to substantiate the particular spiritual *claims* of New Age medicine? Second is the issue of interpretation: How do we know that the interpretation New Age medicine places on spiritual phenomena is correct? Though sufficient evidence exists for the fact of a spiritual world (which we have cited elsewhere; see 278), no evidence exists to substantiate the particular *claims* of New Age medicine concerning the function and nature of its alleged mystical energies. We do not reject the possibility of spiritual energies; we reject the claims, interpretations, and use/abuse of them by New Age medicine.

Nevertheless, this raises another issue. Why would the spirits be interested in medicine? When historically considered, they always have been. For example, a number of researchers, such as Walter Addison Jayne, M.D., in his *The Healing Gods of Ancient Civilizations* (230), have chronicled the dramatic influence of the "gods" and spirits in ancient medicine. In mediumism and much other spiritism of the past and present, "The spirit-guides supply constant medical advice ... and even give treatment in case of illness" (389:235). And listen to Dr. Michael Harner, a graduate professor at New York's New School for Social Research, visiting professor at Columbia, Yale, and the University of California, Berkeley, and a practicing shaman. He points out how ancient pagan shamanism* is influencing New Age medicine:

> The burgeoning field of holistic medicine shows a tremendous amount of experimentation involving the reinvention of many techniques long practiced in shamanism....
>
> A current example of a mutually supportive combination of shamanism with Western technological medicine is the well-known work of Dr. O. Carl Simonton and Stephanie Matthews-Simonton in treating cancer patients....
>
> One day, and I hope it will be soon, a modern version of the shaman will work side-by-side with orthodox Western physicians. In fact, this is already starting to take place (142:175-77).

Throughout history, the spirit world has sought to influence the affairs of people through areas over which people have little or no control. People have little control over the future, so endless systems of divination* exist. People have little control over disease and none over death, so occult healing is found everywhere.

The reason we think that spirits work through many New Age healers, even without their recognizing it, is because New Age health practices are characteristically occult. Spirits and the occult go hand in hand. New Age medicine fulfills numerous spiritistic goals, such as the dissemination of occult philosophy and practice in society. To think that the spirits would not be involved in that which promotes the moral and spiritual disintegration of society is to be ignorant of the mechanics of spiritual deception. What is also significant is how spiritistic mani-

festations are increasingly relabeled as latent human powers, psychological phenomena, or the alleged "energies" of creation: powers from "the higher mind," "collective unconscious," "inner teachers," "archetypes," "bioplasma," "prana," "life energy," and so on.

Perhaps it is this concept of a cosmic, universal, mystical, or "divine" life energy (supposedly uniting people, God, and the universe) that is most frequently associated with spiritistic phenomena. For example, New Age medicine teaches that in order to really understand health and disease, we must switch our thinking from a model of health based on matter to one based primarily on energy. In the end, this is an open door to spiritism under another name. It is difficult, if not impossible, to distinguish the use of "energy" in most New Age techniques from the manipulation of "energy" found among psychic healers, mediums or spiritists, and magic rituals where the magician is possessed by his familiar spirit.

This mystical energy is invariably associated with pagan religion and occult practitioners and, some claim, has up to 90 different designations, depending upon the time and culture. In ancient and modern Hinduism, it is called *prana*. In Taoism and ancient Chinese medicine, it is called *chi*. In Japanese culture it is called *ki*. In Hawaiian shamanism* and Polynesian religion, it is called *mana*. The developer of modern hypnotism,* Franz Anton Mesmer, called it *animal magnetism*. D. D. Palmer, the founder of chiropractic, called it *innate*. Wilhelm Reich, founder of orgonomy, called it *orgone* energy. The American Indians call it *orinda*. Parapsychologists give it a variety of different designations, such as *psi*. Samuel Hahnemann, the founder of homeopathy, called it *vital force*. In yoga* theory it is prana or kundalini* energy. Various modern psychics and mediums, such as spiritist Ambrose Worrall and radionics leader George de LaWar, define it as paraelectricity, biomagnetism, psi plasma, or other terms. Occult magicians define it as *elemental* energy. And the list goes on.

It is essentially psychic energy, as many psychics will admit. For example, R. M. Miller and J. M. Harper state in their *The Psychic Energy Workbook:* "We refer to this substance as psychic energy. The same substance is called 'Prana' by yogis, 'Chi' by practitioners of the martial arts, and 'bio-energy' by therapists" (265:9).

Certain aspects of this variously named energy are influenced by the broader context of the system in which they occur. They are not, therefore, necessarily strict equivalents in the sense that all characteristics of one energy will fit those of another. But again, distinguishing between the manifestations of this energy and the manifestations of spiritistic energy in general, or the spirits themselves, can be virtually impossible. This means that those who seek out energy manipulators may be opening themselves to spiritistic powers and influence.

To illustrate, we will show how a New Age healer can heal through spirit guides and yet never be aware of it; furthermore, even when aware of it, the patient may never be told. Then we will show the spiritistic or other origins of selected New Age techniques. (In the chapters on New Age Intuition and New Age Inner Work, we have cited several additional examples, showing that a person can unsuspectingly be dramatically influenced by a spirit entity.)

Barbara Brennan has the M.S. degree in physics and was a research scientist for NASA at the Goddard Space Flight Center for five years. She spent two years in neo-Reichian bioenergetic counseling, one year in massage therapy, two years studying and experiencing altered states of consciousness,* one year in homeopathy, three years in Core Energetic training (a radionic-based analysis of astral/etheric bodies based on the psychic work of Dr. John and Eva Pierrakos), five years in "Pathwork Helpership Training," and several years studying privately with psychic healers and shamans. She is founder and director of the Gaiabriel Foundation in New York City and lectures and conducts New Age workshops throughout North America and Europe. She also channels the spirit guide "Heyoan," among many others:

As my life unfolded, the unseen hand that led me became more and more perceptible. At first I vaguely sensed it. Then I began seeing spiritual beings, as if in a vision. Then I began to hear them talking to me and felt them touch me. I now accept that I have a guide. I can see, hear, and feel him.... "He" says that his name is

Heyoan... His introduction to me was slow and organic. The nature of our relationship grows daily, as I am guided to new levels of understanding (95A:14).

Although often aware of her spirit guides, she nevertheless cannot always determine when they are working through her. For example, she confesses, "There are times when my guidance is more obvious than other times" (95A:15).

Brennan's major text, *Hands of Light: A Guide to Healing Through the Human Energy Fields* (95A), is a standard New Age work. It links auras, chakras, "opening" acupuncture meridians, etheric/astral bodies, chiropractic, yoga,* reflexology, homeopathy, herbal cures, energy balancing, past lives, psychic surgery, meditation,* color therapy, and visualization.* In fact, *Hands of Light* connects all these methods to potential spiritism. Brennan believes spirits can operate behind the scenes through all these techniques—indeed any method—to psychically influence the patient. Furthermore, her discussion reveals that those who visit New Age healers may "innocently" pick up a spirit guide in the process. Because she can "see" her patients' guides, she assumes the guide came in the door with the client. But who can say the person had a guide before they entered her office? She says:

I usually have about three [spirit] teachers that guide me. The person who has come to me for help will usually be accompanied by his guide or guides (95A:171).

Later in the book, she writes:

The guides of the patient always come to healings and assist. If you are alert, you will see them walk into the healing room with the patient. At this point in the healing they usually pull the patient out of his body and care for him so that a deep relaxation can take place and allow for the template [occult] work to be done. Usually the patient's experience is that of floating in a peaceful state. He usually is not aware of how deeply he has moved into an altered state of consciousness until he gets up or tries to stand up at the end of the healing.... The guide's hands work directly through the healer's hands in an overlay manner. The guides come down over the shoulders and into the hands and arms of the healer (95A:222).

Brennan also describes how her guides heal through her; for example, in verbal channeling:

I feel it kinesthetically. I see the guide behind my right shoulder, and I hear the first few words from that direction. When I and the guide are ready to begin, I lift my hands and hold [my] fingertips together in front of my solar plexus or my heart. . . . At this point, I usually begin to channel verbally. At first the words come from the right shoulder area. The more connected to the channelling process I become, the closer-in the words are. The guide also appears to come closer. Soon, there is no lag time between hearing and speaking the words, and the apparent direction they are coming from moves to above and inside my head. The guide also visually appears to fit over me like a glove. The guide begins to move my arms and hands in coordination with the conversation. "He" also uses my hands to balance my energy field and to run energy into my chakras while "he" is talking. This keeps the energy high and focused. My personality self seems to be floating off and above, listening and watching it all. At the same time, I feel merged with the guide, as if I am the guide. As the guide I feel much bigger than the personality me, Barbara.

At the end of the conversation, my experience is one of the guide lightly disconnecting and lifting off, while my consciousness sinks downwards into my body and my personality self (95A:172).

Brennan also supplies several illustrations from various healing methods:

*Reflexology:*
In channelling for the healing itself, you allow the guides to utilize more of your energy field. . . . [T]he guidance and hand movements are general and may begin as soon as you put your hands on the patient's feet. . . . Many times the guide will reach his hand through the healer's hand and beyond, going right into the body of the patient (95A:203).

*Auric/chakra healing:*
As the energy is flowing, clearing, charging and generally rebalancing the energy field of the patient, you will probably feel it flowing through

your hands. . . . You can direct energy like a beam of light deep into the body. It can fill, or it can knock things loose. The guides will direct you as to what is needed and run the appropriate energy through (95A:206,217).

*Crystal healing:*
A crystal is a very powerful tool. . . . It goes in, cuts and collects the energy which . . . the guides turn to white light. . . . The healer can scan the auric layers to see if the chakras or organs need restructuring. . . . If the guides decide to do ketheric template work (seventh layer), the healer must take the crystals away from the patient . . . (95A:218).

During all of this, the patient may never know that the healing was performed spiritistically. All the client may experience is a relaxed condition, with or without various energy sensations. "The patient . . . will be curious as to what you did. At this point, it is important not to go back to the linear mind too much since that would pull her out of the altered state of consciousness. Explain in brief terms what you did, just enough to satisfy her, but not enough to disturb her relaxed state" (95A:230).

Barbara Brennan is not unique. In America there are thousands of "healers" like her, who, though they admit that spirit guides work through them in healing, also say that they cannot always determine when this is occurring and that the spirits can work undiscerned (see New Age Intuition and New Age Inner Work).

Our question for New Age healers is this: How can they be certain a spirit is not working behind the scenes in their own practices? And if one is, how do they know its real nature or motives? We are concerned about this because when we examined the founders and leaders in modern New Age medicine, we usually found spiritistic influence. (Topics not documented here were documented in 2673,1590.)

Many acupuncturists and acupressurists are occultly involved or have spirit guides. The founder of anthroposophical medicine was occultist Rudolph Steiner, who practiced and encouraged necromancy, or contacting the spirits of the dead (792:232-33/782:35). Astrology* and astrologic medicine are replete with spiritistic influence (83:201-55). Attitudinal therapy* has been dramatically influenced by the spirit-written text *A Course in Miracles*\* and medium Jane Roberts' *The Nature of Personal Reality: A Seth Book.* Modern leaders in the field of biofeedback, such as Elmer and Alyce Green, are both scientific investigators and promoters of occult phenomena (Elmer Green has a spirit guide he calls "the Teacher"; 46:289-90). The "father" of modern body work, Wilhelm Reich, was occultly involved. Body-work techniques are frequently based on Eastern philosophy or practice and may be used in conjunction with occult methods. Channeling is spiritistic by definition. "Edgar Cayce methods" were developed by medium Edgar Cayce, through whom the spirits dictated thousands of pages of information on health issues and "past lives." D.D. Palmer, the founder of chiropractic, was involved in psychic practices and a lifelong spiritist (54:17/58:33/59:48-49). Although chiropractic per se is not a New Age practice, it is frequently used among New Agers in conjunction with a wide variety of occult or pseudoscientific practices. Many leaders in the field of color healing are spiritists and occultists (498/750/48/95A). Many leaders in crystal work\* have spirit guides (203:V,2,22/202:1/205:8,23). Popular divination\* methods that are occasionally used for diagnosis, such as the Ouija board,\* runes,\* Tarot,\* I Ching,\* palmistry,\* and numerology\* often involve spiritistic influences. Some leading medical dowsers\* are spiritists (514:44/627:151), and dowsing\* itself is a spiritistic practice. Many leaders in dream work\* also have spirit guides and use dreams to help others contact the spirit world (739:166-219/61:85; cf. 63/64). Shamanism\* is spiritistic by definition. Iridology, the martial arts,\* and muscle testing\* may all involve the occult. Meditation,\* parapsychology, psychic healing, radionics and psychometry, "past-life"\* counseling, visualization,\* and yoga\* also often include spirit guides.

Many other founders and leaders of New Age medicine have spiritistic contacts or are variously involved in the occult (compare Appendix). Even modern herbalism can have spiritistic associations. Hypnosis\* is frequently an occult practice. Naturopath Bernard Jensen, the modern founder of iridology, is a member of the occult sect the Rosicrucians, which encourages spirit-istic contact (285:226-29). Chiropractor George Goodheart, the modern founder of applied kinesiology,\* may have connections to the psychic world (35:310). Wilhelm Reich, the founder of orgonomy, was involved in the occult and the spirit world (170/286:279/169:161-201). Sources tell us that Samuel Hahnemann, the founder of homeopathy, may have been a spiritist (419). He was, at least, a follower of the famous spirit medium Emanuel Swedenborg, as well as a Mason (25:14/2:67). Leaders in the field of radionics, such as George De la Warr and its founder Albert Abrams, have been involved in spiritism or the occult (420:5/6:53-63). Randolph Stone, founder of polarity therapy, was an occultist and a member of the spiritistic Hindu sect Radhasoami (287:314-24/197:99). The founder of psychosynthesis, Roberto Assagioli, was an occultist and a leader in Alice Bailey's Lucis Trust and Arcana workshops in Italy (288:224-25). Dolores Krieger and Dora Kunz, founders of therapeutic touch, are both psychics. Kunz is a spiritist and the former president of the spiritistic Theosophical Society (144:13/ 90:111). One prominent leader in modern visualization,\* Mike Samuels, M.D., is a confessed spiritist and author of the text *Spirit Guides* (289), and visualization itself is frequently used for spirit contact.

Space does not permit us to list or research the personal history of every founder of a New Age health method or therapy. But well over 90 percent of those we did examine were in some way involved in the occult. We think such a fact speaks volumes about the nature of New Age medicine, and why it is so permeated with occultism. The history of occult practice is littered with human wreckage; it is therefore ironic to see it so thoroughly linked to human *health.* If the Bible did not plainly state that the spirits of the occult world are demons, one would almost be forced to that conclusion solely based on its own history and the damage it has caused mankind.

*Eclectic Nature*

It is the purpose of this section to show that clients of New Age medicine may be treated with methods other than those they expected or sought. New Age health practitioners use a variety of methods for several reasons.

First, the philosophy of New Age medicine encourages such an approach. For example, New Age medicine claims to be "holistic." By this it means it can supposedly treat the "whole" person—body, mind, and spirit. Thus, it does not restrict itself to treating only a physical problem because it sees mind, body, and spirit as interrelated. Therefore, to treat a mental or physical problem, a spiritual treatment is probably also required. To some degree, then, New Age health practitioners imply that they are physician, therapist, and minister wrapped into one.

If a problem is more spiritual than mental, or more mental than physical, then more than one approach may be suggested or required. For example, a person with headaches may be treated with chiropractic spinal manipulation for his physical problem (pain in the back or head), while yoga* meditation* may be prescribed for the more underlying and "serious" condition of emotional tension that is causing the pain. But because mind, body, and spirit are all interrelated, treating a given illness by emotional and physical means alone may be deemed ineffective. Physical illness may be a symptom of a deeper spiritual illness requiring spiritual treatment. Backache or headache may not only result from stress; it may supposedly result from a "blockage" of one's "life energy." Thus, applied kinesiology,* acupuncture, or therapeutic touch may be prescribed to unblock the flow of energy and thereby "cure" the problem. While a conventional physician may simply prescribe penicillin for a viral infection, a New Age practitioner may think it necessary to prescribe astrological* counseling, crystal therapy, or hypnotic regression* into a past life.

A second reason for employing a variety of techniques may be because the methods of diagnosis chosen are as abundant as the methods of treatment. Thus, in addition to a variety of possible *treatment* practices, New Age medicine offers a variety of different *diagnostic* methods, such as iridology, applied kinesiology,* clairvoyant diagnosis by a spirit guide, or diagnosis through a "radionics" instrument.

Third, employing a variety of treatments may be a financial necessity. Concentrating on one particular therapy, such as reflexology, may not pay all the practitioner's bills. Thus, the more treatments, the greater the number of clients, the greater the income, the better the opportunity to remain in business.

Fourth, by using different methods of diagnosis and treatment, New Age practitioners think that this improves their public image as effective healers. The more methods used, the more "holistic" or "comprehensive" one appears. Anyone who employs so many different "medical" practices must be all the more "medically" competent. Consider how treating a person "holistically" may require the use of all the following different methods:

*Iridology:* diagnoses the problem; e.g., asthma, liver trouble, ulcers

*Astrology:* determines the correct time for treatment

*Herbal teas:* treats the physical symptoms

*Occult meditation:* treats the mental symptom, perhaps anxiety or depression

*Acupuncture:* treats the spiritual problem of unbalanced or blocked life energy

*Hypnotic "past-life" regression:* treats the ultimate cause of bad "karma" from one's past life, e.g., where the patient is told she had lung cancer and renal failure.

Any number of different techniques could be used in diagnoses and treatment of any given health condition. Because almost all New Age therapies work at least to some degree on the basis of the placebo effect (people's faith and trust in the therapy or therapist), almost any techniques will work for some people some of the time, so all methods are equally valuable.

Techniques can even be combined in an unusual manner. To illustrate, an acupuncturist may employ what is known as "homeoacupuncture," which is a combination of homeopathy and acupuncture. In this process, homeopathic solutions are injected into acupoints. Or the acupuncturist may also employ auricular acupuncture, which is also termed "earology" by some. The idea is that the external human ear corresponds section by section, or point by point, to the inner organs and functions of the human body. (In the same way, the iridologist assigns different organs and functions of the human body to the iris of the eye, and the reflexologist assigns them to sections of the hand or foot. In fact, throughout history the human body has been miniaturized and stuffed into numerous parts of the body: the eye, the ear, the head, the face, the foot, the hand, even the nose and anus; 256:26,39,59,65,84,101.)

The following chart of 22 alternate therapies is intended to show how easily a given New Age therapist can incorporate other techniques or methods. All the following were encountered in the literature. The most common additions are the use of altered states of consciousness,* occult meditation,* and some form of psychic diagnosis or healing. If you seek out a practitioner in the left-hand column, you may also be treated with a therapy from the right-hand column.

This list is not exhaustive and, in theory, almost any New Age practice could incorporate almost any other practice.

The reason for this is because New Age medicine is not based upon scientific principles and so anything goes. And there are dangers in such

| *If you seek this principal method* | *You may also receive this additional therapy* |
| --- | --- |
| Therapeutic Touch | Occult Meditation<br>Altered States of Consciousness<br>Radiesthesia/Rod and Pendulum Dowsing<br>Yoga<br>Psychic Energies<br>Psychic Diagnosis and Healing |
| Color Therapy | Radiesthesia/Rod and Pendulum Dowsing<br>Astrology<br>Psychic Diagnosis and Healing<br>Occult Meditation |
| Biofeedback | Altered States of Consciousness<br>Occult Meditation<br>Psychic Diagnosis<br>Yoga |
| Chiropractic | Applied Kinesiology<br>Iridology<br>Reflexology<br>Crystal Healing<br>Radiesthesia/Rod and Pendulum Dowsing<br>Acupressure<br>Psychic Diagnosis<br>Kundalini Yoga<br>Rolfing<br>Ayurvedic Medicine |
| Homeopathy | Radiesthesia/Rod and Pendulum Dowsing<br>Psychometry<br>Astrology<br>Psychic Diagnosis |

| *If you seek this principal method* | *You may also receive this additional therapy* |
|---|---|
| Acupuncture and Acupressure | Homeopathy<br>Kundalini Yoga<br>Astrology<br>Occult Meditation<br>Spiritism<br>Psychic Diagnosis and Healing |
| Endogenous Endocrinotherapy<br>(a naturopathic method to allegedly<br>"normalize" a malfunctioning<br>endocrine gland) | Acupuncture<br>Homeopathy<br>New Age Osteopathy<br>Applied Kinesiology<br>Herbal Treatment<br>Shortwave Irradiation |
| Astrologic Medicine | Chiropractic<br>Homeopathy<br>Radiesthesia<br>Muscle Testing<br>Occult Meditation, Yoga<br>Spiritism<br>Rod and Pendulum Dowsing<br>Psychic Diagnosis and Healing<br>Iridology<br>Crystal Healing |
| Body Work (a general term for such disciplines<br>as Rolfing, the Alexander Method, Functional<br>Integration, Orgonomy, Bioenergetics, Arica,<br>and many more) | Yoga<br>Psychic Diagnosis and Healing<br>Occult Meditation<br>Altered States of Consciousness |
| Psychic Healing | Radiesthesia/Rod and Pendulum Dowsing<br>Spiritism<br>Occult Meditation<br>Altered States of Consciousness |
| Reflexology | Astrology<br>Radiesthesia/Rod and Pendulum Dowsing<br>Occult Meditation<br>Altered States of Consciousness<br>Psychic Diagnosis |
| Herbal Medicine | Astrology<br>Radiesthesia/Rod and Pendulum Dowsing<br>Psychic Diagnosis and Healing<br>Spiritism<br>Homeopathy<br>Occult Meditation |
| Yoga and Visualization | Spiritism<br>Occult Meditation<br>Altered States of Consciousness |

| If you seek this principal method | You may also receive this additional therapy |
|---|---|
| Naturopathy | Iridology<br>Acupuncture<br>Herbal Medicine<br>Radiesthesia/Rod and Pendulum Dowsing<br>Homeopathy<br>Biofeedback<br>Chiropractic<br>Astrology |
| Dowsing | Altered States of Consciousness<br>Radiesthesia/Rod and Pendulum Dowsing<br>Occult Meditation<br>Psychic Diagnosis and Healing |
| Polarity Healing | Psychic Diagnosis and Healing<br>Spiritism |
| Applied Kinesiology and Touch for Health | Aromatherapy<br>Reflexology<br>Yoga<br>Psychic Healing<br>Iridology<br>Shiatsu |
| Iridology | Astrology<br>Psychic Diagnosis<br>Naturopathy<br>Applied Kinesiology<br>Radionics<br>Rod and Pendulum Dowsing |
| New Age Osteopathy | Homeopathy<br>Iridology<br>Radionics<br>Color Therapy<br>Edgar Cayce Methods<br>Occult Meditation |

extensive cross-pollination. First, a practitioner whose primary treatment method is relatively harmless may incorporate additional treatment methods which can be harmful. Second, the more exposure to a variety of treatments, the greater the chance *something* will "work," thereby converting the person to New Age philosophy as well as practice. Third, most of these methods are designed to work on not only the body but the mind as well. For example, in *Mind Therapies Body Therapies*, shaman-instructed author and naturopath George Feiss examines some 50 alternate or unconventional or new self-help therapies, such as autogenic training, Silva Mind Control,* reflexology, polarity therapy, the Alexander technique, bioenergetics, and aikido. Many of them are based on the mystical life energy concepts of the East. Feiss writes, "In actuality there are no hard and fast boundaries for any of these disciplines; all of them affect the whole (mind-body) organism to varying degrees" (166:vii).

The worldview of these therapies, and the openness to the psychic realm that is evident in many of them, bring subtle spiritual implications. Any systematic technique that is seriously pursued and that works on the mind-body system within an Eastern or occult context may become the vehicle for spiritual entrapment. One may become more open to the psychic realm, or be treated psychically, or develop psychic powers. Or one may develop an alien worldview that insulates against Christian truth. One may even become demonized (see "Dangers" on p. 504).

## NATURE OF CURES

Perhaps the strongest endorsement for New Age medicine is the claim by thousands of followers that it "works." Glowing testimonies can be multiplied for the diagnostic or curative powers of almost any technique. Because of this, three important facts need to be recognized: 1) given enough time, a degree of success is guaranteed for all quack treatments; 2) New Age health practices may operate merely as a placebo; 3) pragmatism is not the only issue: There may be hidden costs in New Age therapies. We will discuss these three areas in turn.

### The Time Factor

*Any* fraudulent treatment can seem to work most of the time because most ailments, given sufficient time, will go away naturally. The simple fact is that most people do not die from their pains and illnesses. Thus, virtually *any* treatment, no matter how irrelevant (say, adding pulverized tree bark to one's cereal), is certain to have its "success" stories. All a therapist has to do is make a treatment *sound* good. When a New Age method is "packaged" correctly with charts, machines, and scientific-sounding explanations, people may attribute a cure where none is deserved, and thus the treatment gets credit for the body's natural recuperative power.

If we invented and correctly packaged a new treatment for certain common illnesses and *claimed* scientific backing, we could sell almost anything. If we claimed that sucking ice cubes at 75-minute intervals for 15 days would lower body metabolism one percent, reverse cell dehydration, cure inflammation, and bolster the immune system, some gullible people would believe us.

Surely some, perhaps many. Testimonials would even come in for curing every ailment that would have gotten better in two weeks regardless.

It is hardly insignificant that New Age therapists usually tell their clients that in order to cure a given problem, a period involving weeks or even months of treatments may be needed. Because these healers are granted authority which they usually do not deserve, most people will begin treatment, not realizing that in the same amount of time the problem would disappear anyway.

### The Placebo Factor

For New Age therapies to "work," patients often must have dedication, the will to believe, and lots of patience. Clients who believe that a treatment will work, and therapists who are good counselors, account for an endless variety of "healings" that have nothing to do with a given New Age healing practice. Thus, New Age health techniques that do not work on the basis of their stated principles may nevertheless work on the basis of other principles. If a physical problem is emotional or psychological in nature, such as tension headaches, it may respond to psychological treatment, regardless of which New Age technique is employed.

Psychosomatic medicine and placebo research indicate that many complaints which are not organic will respond virtually to any treatment that helps a person believe he will be cured, or that promises to otherwise relieve the psychological or emotional conditions which produced the ailment. Anything from aromatherapy to Zen could be effective if the patient believes the "medicine" will work:

> Two things distinguish alternative medicine. The first is that it does not derive from any coherent or established body of evidence. The second, that it is not subjected to rigorous assessment to establish its value.... The variety and absurdity of "alternative" cures is a tribute to the power, largely unrecognized and unacknowledged, of the placebo effect... (1142:103).

In their *Follies and Fallacies in Medicine*, medical researchers Dr. Peter Skrabanek and James McCormick, M.D., with the Department of Community Health, Trinity College, Dublin, make some interesting observations about placebos. They point out that there are three possible explanations for an association between a given health treatment and cure. The first is that the treatment is actually beneficial. The second is the body's own healing ability, in which case a person would have returned to health in the absence of any intervention. The third possibility is the placebo effect. They point out that placebos are more potent than generally assumed. For example, among physicians who employ the placebo, their faith that placebos work plus the patient's faith in the physician "exert a mutually reinforcing effect; the result is a powerful remedy that is almost guaranteed to produce an improvement and sometimes a cure" (1142:13).

As a way of gauging the function of a placebo, they distinguish between the terms "illness" and "disease." "Illness" is what people feel, whereas "disease" connotes the existence of a pathological process. They note that placebos do not affect the outcome of disease, but rather of illness. "Disease may or may not be accompanied by illness. Many diseases, including some that are potentially serious, are often symptomless. On the other hand, feeling unwell is not always the result of disease. Placebos have no effect on the progress or outcome of disease, but they may exert a powerful effect upon the subjective phenomena of illness, pain, discomfort, and distress. Their success is based on this fact" (1142:13-14).

Skrabanek and McCormick also point out that placebos need not be a particular substance, but may be entirely verbal. One British physician tested 200 of his patients and divided them into two groups. The first group received a highly positive consultation, and were given a firm diagnosis and a strong reassurance they would speedily recover. Members of the second group were told by the physician that he was uncertain as to the cause of their symptoms, and that if the symptoms did not cease within a few days, to return for another appointment. "At the end of two weeks, 64 percent of those who had received a positive consultation were better as compared with only 39 percent of those who were offered uncertainty" (1142:14).

They report another study of 56 students who were given either a pink or blue sugar pill and told that the pills were either a sedative or stimulant. Only three of the 56 individuals reported that the pills had no effect. Those who received the blue pills thought they were taking a sedative, and 72 percent reported they felt drowsy. (Those who took two pills felt more drowsy than those who had taken one pill.) Also, 32 percent of the students who had taken the pink stimulant placebo said that they felt "less tired." Fully one-third of the students reported side effects, including headaches, watery eyes, abdominal discomfort, dizziness, tingling extremities, and staggering gait (1142:17).

Here are some other characteristics noted by Skrabanek and McCormick:

- Possibly as much as one-third of modern-day prescriptions are unlikely to have a specific effect on the diseases for which they are administered (1142:13).

- Sir Douglas Black, a past president of Britain's Royal College of Physicians, estimated that "only about 10 percent of diseases are significantly influenced by modern treatment" (1142:17).

- In one study, patients suffering from angina that was limiting their physical activities agreed to participate in a particular experiment. (This took place in 1956 and would not be accepted by ethical committees today.) Half received a sham operation, and half received a ligation of the internal mammary artery. "During the first six months after the operation, five out of eight of the ligated patients and five out of nine of the patients who had the sham operation were much improved according to their own evaluation. Striking improvement in exercise tolerance occurred in two patients who had had the sham operation" (1142:19).

- The placebo effect is actually powerful enough to "raise doubts about the validity of many double-blind therapeutic trials" (1142:21).

- In some cases, the effect of placebos can actually counteract the physical effect of certain drugs (1142:22), and "a placebo can imitate a true pharmacological effect" (1142:23).

• "Placebos may in some circumstances increase rather than decrease pain, depending upon the expectations of those administering the placebo" (1142:20).

All of this leads Skrabanek and McCormick to conclude, "The placebo response is a complex phenomenon that is still little understood. The placebo effect contributes to every therapeutic success by helping to alleviate the symptoms of disease, and it is often the sole cause of the 'cure' of illness. Since the success and reputation of medicine is based upon its ability to cure, it is perhaps not surprising that doctors refer so seldom to the placebo effect, as a same effect underpins the success of every charlatan and quack" (1142:25).

Their book also has an important chapter, "A Fist Full of Fallacies," in which the authors explain 29 separate examples of faulty reasoning, arguments, and logic as they apply to medical treatment and cure. Perusing these fallacies shows how easy it is for people to assume that a particular New Age method has produced a cure when in fact it did nothing of the sort.

Because the power of the mind works in some cases, it would be a mistake to conclude that it works in all cases or to neglect the distinction between illness and disease mentioned above. For example, of the 6000-plus individuals oncologist Dr. Saul Silverman treated for cancer over a 25-year period, he has seen only about a dozen cases of spontaneous remission from true terminal cancer. These patients should have been dead within months, but they recovered and lived for many years without evidence of recurrence. When Silverman studied these cases to determine why the illnesses reversed themselves, he concluded that placebo, positive thinking, visualization, and suchlike had little or nothing to do with it. Why? One reason was because many of his patients progressed relentlessly to death even though they were extremely positive and expressed an absolutely heroic determination to live. On the other hand, he has also seen terribly depressed patients who had terminal cancers remitted. In the case of one individual, six years after his cancer was gone, "he was just starting to cheer up and admit that maybe he was going to be okay" (1143:117).

Thus, if positive attitudes or the placebo factor were always important in the prevention or cure of most disease in general, large-scale studies should be able to find evidence that depressed people or those who disbelieve in placebos would have a higher incidence of disease. But this correlation has never been verified. Indeed, if faith per se is a truly powerful medicine that can cure virtually anything in the manner some proponents claim, then it is unlikely modern medicine would ever have developed to begin with. Instead, healing temples devoted to building people's faith would exist where hospitals do now (1143:117).

Some people may respond by saying that as long as a person's symptoms are relieved, nothing else matters. If certain New Age methods act as placebos then, in their own way, they are still effective. Yes, but this misses the point. A truly neutral placebo administered by an orthodox medical doctor for legitimate medical reasons and a New Age treatment operating as a placebo are worlds apart.

New Age methods are generally fraudulent or unproven, and they may cause spiritual harm. But when a health-care service or a product is marketed, the public has the right to be assured of its safety and quality. When we purchase a cereal for its vitamin content, we should expect a nutritious product, not sawdust or nicotine manufactured to look and taste like cereal. No one would purchase a cereal labeled "100% sawdust." Likewise, no one would pay 50 dollars for a bottle of sugar pills, unless they believed that the pills were effective medicine. Does anyone think that New Age therapists could effectively market their products as placebos? As a result, the therapies are sold on the basis of a variety of claimed principles that makes them sound legitimate.

Furthermore, it is one thing for a doctor to employ placebos occasionally for normal aches and pains if, based on his knowledge of the client, this would be as effective as an actual medicine and would prevent possible side effects. But it is courting disaster to employ only placebos in serious organic illness. Thus, when an M.D. administers a placebo, the patient is still under the supervision of a qualified physician. But when patients are given New Age treatments that operate as placebos, they may get more than they bargained for.

Many things work and yet are still dangerous: terrorism, drugs like heroin and cocaine, nuclear bombs, consumer fraud, prostitution, abortions. All these are effective. They "work," but they are also dangerous. Whether it is drug addiction, jail terms, unexpected complications, or death, a price is paid. The same is true for New Age medicine. It may "work" and still be dangerous. A delayed diagnosis or a misdiagnosis may cost a person dearly in permanent injury or even death, even though initially the technique seemed to be working.

Thus, widespread use of these methods not only endangers the nation's health quality and health standards, but it also promotes an irrationalism that can spill over into other areas of people's likes. Realizing that New Age medicine is comprised of 1) highly questionable techniques, 2) irrational methods, and 3) occult philosophies and practices, the idea that it "works" is irrelevant. What one receives in exchange for the "cure" may not be worth the price.

*Pragmatism and Its Problems*

Because New Age medicine is undergirded by pragmatism ("it works"), this forces an irrational and often self-justifying approach to New Age treatments.

Since publication of coauthor Weldon's *New Age Medicine*, he has received numerous letters from Christians and non-Christians who take issue with his critical approach expressed toward unorthodox or fringe methods of treatment, such as unsound chiropractic, homeopathy, iridology, therapeutic touch, and applied kinesiology.* The common elements in most of these letters are instructive:

- People accepted the irrational aspects of a method without asking whether it could be effective on the basis of its stated principles.

- They ignored scientific information that disproved the medical effectiveness of the treatment.

- They redefined the occult aspects of a practice as something divine, or they appealed to supposedly unknown "scientific" laws or phenomena of the creation.

- They claimed to know that the treatment was sound because it worked for them personally, and they appealed to alleged miraculous cures that conventional scientific medicine was unable to produce.

These responses indicate four false approaches to New Age medicine:

- an unwillingness to research a practice before adopting it—laziness

- the will to believe in spite of contrary scientific data—blind faith

- a rationalizing and legitimizing of the mystical and the occult on the basis of entirely unknown factors—speculation

- a personal bias in favor of the method merely because it "worked"—pragmatism

An article by Karl Sabbagh, author of *The Living Body*, discusses the issue of why fringe medicine "works." In his article "The Psychopathology of Fringe Medicine," he correctly affirms that "when it works, it works for none of the reasons given by fringe practitioners themselves" (266:155).

Almost overnight almost anyone could be guaranteed a successful New Age healing practice, regardless of the method used or its effectiveness, because of three undeniable facts: 1) the relatively benign nature of most illnesses treated, 2) the natural variability of disease, 3) the psychosomatic aspect of many ailments that respond to a placebo.

Furthermore, as Sabbagh notes, even with genuinely serious disease there are usually periods of remission when a patient feels better and has actually improved. This is also true even for fatal diseases, like cancer, when the overall trend is usually downward. Disease variability like this can be used to great benefit by New Age practitioners, *regardless* of the short- or long-term outcome. Thus, if the patient begins to improve from natural remission, the therapist can claim the treatment is effective. If the patient remains stable and doesn't get worse, the therapist can claim the treatment has arrested the disease. If the patient gets worse, the therapist can claim that either the treatment or dosage must be increased or revised, or that the patient hasn't been treated long enough for the treatment to work. After all, unless it is a fatal illness, the patient will get better sooner or later anyway. And even if the patient dies, the therapist can claim that he started the treatment too late, or that the patient must not have been following instructions properly. The New Age therapist always wins.

Sabbagh also observes that there is a natural tendency in each of us to ascribe cause and effect where none exist. This may be related to simple ignorance about the nature of disease, which in turn can lead to a false perception about the nature of a cure. "Most of us are just not familiar enough with probability figures or the natural history of disease to make the sort of informed judgments that apply in the assessment of therapeutic effectiveness" (266:158).

By now it should be obvious that any person with any ailment could walk into the office of a reflexologist, homeopathist, acupuncturist, iridologist, applied kinesiologist,* unsound chiropractor, or shaman* and all the methods employed could be "effective." But because each of these techniques claims to work on entirely different, or even conflicting principles, it must also be obvious that the methods themselves are not producing the cure.

When a treatment works or seems to work, it is vital to know why. If we fail to answer that question, we may waste valuable time and money, encourage an irrational approach to medicine, support a form of institutionalized dishonesty, encourage dangerous forms of occult practice and philosophy, or even cause our own death or that of another.

## PHYSICAL DANGERS

Many people have died as a result of some irresponsible "faith" healer or New Age therapist who has assured them that their life-saving medical treatment can now be dispensed with because all that is needed is for them to follow what turns out to be a dubious treatment.

When a child with leukemia is taken off chemotherapy and placed under the supervision of a homeopath or a chiropractor, and the child dies as a result, who can be unconcerned? When a man with a highly infectious form of tuberculosis refuses hospital treatment and goes to a New Age practitioner, who diagnoses constipation and supplies a herbal remedy, and then the man dies after a period when he distributed TB-laden sputum to those around him, who can be indifferent (266:163-64)?

New Age medicine, here, is reminiscent of certain cultic views of medicine. Cultic medicine deliberately withholds vital medical treatment on the basis of antiscientific prejudice or irrational religious doctrines. For example, Jehovah's Witnesses prohibit blood transfusions, and Christian Scientists avoid medical treatment altogether. Because of these practices, thousands of people have died unnecessarily. Something similar can occur in New Age medicine. To the degree New Age health techniques 1) misdiagnose a serious illness, or 2) prescribe ineffective treatments for a serious condition or otherwise delay proper medical care, they can be and have been deadly (see 356:4).

New Age medicine is  physically hazardous because it also leads people into the occult. Abundant documentation exists concerning the dangers of New Age occultism; the works of a dozen researchers can be cited (270/277/273/280/662). The various texts circulating that are attempting (quite incorrectly) to treat what are termed "spiritual emergencies" is one indication of the problem (274). Occultists themselves warn of the dangers here, noting that various practices can lead to physical disease, suicide, or death. We documented this in *The Coming Darkness* (278). Dr. Kurt Koch notes that numerous cases of suicides, fatal accidents, emotional disorders, diseases, strokes, and insanity are found among occult practitioners, and that "anyone who has had to observe for 45 years [as Koch did] the effects of spiritism can only warn people with all the strength at his disposal" (642:238; cf. pp. 261-82/270:30-31/273:184-87).

## SPIRITUAL DANGERS

New Age medicine is dangerous spiritually as well because occult philosophy is anti-Christian and amoral. Occult philosophy leads people away from salvation in Jesus Christ and justifies a variety of sinful behaviors (278/280).

New Age medicine is also spiritually dangerous because when healing occurs through spiritistic power, it may only reflect a psychic transference of the condition from one symptom to another. Again, the lifetime research of Dr. Kurt Koch may be cited. Dr. Koch counseled thousands of individuals who were involved in occult New Age healing and similar practices. His observation is that no genuine healing occurs, but rather merely a transference of the condition from the physical to the emotional or to the spiritual realm. In exchange for a physical healing, the illness switches to a higher level:

[D]emonic healing always results in an engram taking place, i.e. a transference from the lower to the upper levels. The original organic illness is shifted higher into the psychical realm, with the result that while the physical illness disappears, new disorders appear in the mental and emotional life of the person concerned, disorders which are in fact far more difficult to treat and cure....

Firstly, one does not realize the force with which these transfers are accompanied.

Secondly, the transfers cannot be reversed, the wheel cannot be turned back, except through the power of Christ.

And thirdly, these magical transfers act as a blockage to a person's spiritual life (271:121).

New Age medicine is spiritually hazardous because it also may lead one into spiritistic entanglements, which may or may not be discernible, but which will be costly.

Thus, New Age medicine involves more profound matters than most people realize. The issue is not merely physical health and illness, or scientific medicine versus quackery, or the moral responsibility of health practitioners to provide safe and effective health treatment. If we think of New Age medicine only on a "physical" level, we misunderstand the more fundamental issue of its spirituality and the implications and consequences.

Studies in diverse fields relating to demonism, such as missiology, cults, and occult counseling, reveal that occult practices harm people spiritually. And Christians are not immune from these hazards, as the works of Drs. Kurt Koch, Merrill Unger, Fred Dickason, and others show (270-273/275/806/807/851). Here are two illustrations known to the authors.

A nurse and missionary among the Nduga people of Mapnduma in Irian Jaya, Indonesia, had won numerous awards for her medical work in training nationals and in setting up health clinics. Two years ago she suffered an attack of dengue fever, an infectious tropical disease, which forced her to come home on furlough. After a year of medical treatment, she returned to the mission field, still weak, with a "heaviness" over her, but supposedly recovered because medical tests revealed nothing wrong.

Six months later she had a relapse and came home again. Chronic fatigue and other problems proved intractable. The best efforts of a tropical disease specialist and several other physicians proved fruitless. She was prayed over many times, but also to no avail.

Finally, a pastor she happened to meet suspected a heretofore unaddressed spiritual cause of her problems. During counseling he asked her whether she had ever used alternate medicine. She explained that as a health-conscious nurse, when normal medical means did not help, it was her custom to turn to alternate health care: naturopathy, homeopathy, acupuncture, reflexology, and other New Age techniques. After counseling concerning the nature and implications of these methods, the missionary forsook them and before the Lord confessed her involvement in such practices as sin. As a result of confession and forsaking these activities, the oppression, chronic fatigue, and other medical problems vanished, and she returned to the mission field in good health.

The second example is about a hospitalized Christian man. A group of Christian men went to pray over him, but he was restless, spiritually oppressed, and unable to find peace with God. No amount of prayer or counsel would help this man's spiritual condition. Someone noticed he wore a Masonic ring. Counsel as to the nature of

Masonry (496) and the man's repentance bore no fruit until he also removed his Masonic ring. This simple act produced a dramatic change in his spiritual condition. He went from a state of depression and spiritual oppression to one of peace and reconciliation with God. Incidents such as these are not unique; scores of similar situations are chronicled in the writings noted previously.

But what is their meaning? What could a Masonic ring have to do with one's spiritual condition? How could visiting an acupuncturist or homeopathist produce intractable physical problems that would not respond to medical treatment? Why the dramatic physical and spiritual changes over seemingly insignificant actions, such as confession and renunciation or removing a symbolic ring?

Obviously, these were *not* insignificant actions. They were necessary actions to break the power that the spiritual forces held over the person; even "small" things may be significant when it comes to spiritual realities.

The Scripture reveals that God is a jealous God. His love for His people is zealous and pure and requires that they cling to Him alone; double-mindedness in spiritual matters cannot be blessed (James 1:6-8). Consider the following passages:

> Or do you think that the Scripture speaks to no purpose: "He jealously desires the Spirit which He has made to dwell in us?" (James 4:5 NASB).

> You shall have no other gods before me. . . . You shall not bow down to them or worship them; for I, the LORD your God, am a jealous God, punishing the children for the sin of the fathers to the third and fourth generation of those who hate me, but showing love to thousands who love me and keep my commandments (Exodus 20:3-6; cf. Deuteronomy 4:24; Joshua 24:19; Zechariah 8:2).

The above passages reveal that God takes a person's spiritual walk seriously. The problem with Christian involvement in New Age medicine is that it can easily compromise the purity of a person's spiritual life.

One particular form of disobedience that God has warned against is idolatry, a practice asso-ciated with the powers of darkness (Psalm 106:34-39; 1 Corinthians 10:14,20). Because God knows the consequences of idolatry—revealed so profoundly throughout Old Testament history and in anthropological studies—He has warned that those who practice it will suffer its consequences.

In essence, this is the fundamental reality of New Age medicine—it is a form of idolatry. Only this can explain its spiritual philosophy and consequences: "They exchanged the truth of God for a lie, and worshiped and served created things rather than the Creator—who is forever praised. Amen" (Romans 1:25).

Why do we say New Age medicine is a form of idolatry? Simply because its practices reflect an underlying religious philosophy that promotes a false god; that is, New Age practices consistently underscore variations on New Age pantheism. When one involves himself in practices whose philosophy is idolatrous, practices which lead one away from the true God and into the realm of false gods and demonic spirits, can we be surprised there may be harmful consequences?

God lamented in Hosea, "My people are destroyed from lack of knowledge" (Hosea 4:6). The "lack of knowledge" that had destroyed His people was a lack of knowledge concerning God and His ways (Hosea 4:1-6). As a result, the people turned to other gods, and their idolatrous practices became a snare and delusion. Because they did not know the true God, they became the prey of false gods, even while thinking that their lifestyle was pleasing to God.

Often we need to be reminded that spiritual warfare exists (Ephesians 6:10-18). When God's people do not make knowledge of Him a priority and His glory preeminent, is it really surprising that some are led astray by false practices and deceitful spirits, or that there are consequences to such deception?

> The Spirit clearly says that in later times some will abandon the faith and follow deceiving spirits and things taught by demons (1 Timothy 4:1).

> Be self-controlled and alert. Your enemy the devil prowls around like a roaring lion looking for someone to devour (1 Peter 5:8).

Put on the full armor of God so that you can take your stand against the devil's schemes. For our struggle is not against flesh and blood, but against the rulers, against the authorities, against the powers of this dark world and against the spiritual forces of evil in the heavenly realms (Ephesians 6:11-12).

No one who has experienced pain enjoys it. And yet pain is one of the necessary accompaniments to a fallen world. It teaches us to avoid things that are dangerous to our health. Without it, we would engage in activities that could injure or destroy us. The same holds true in the area of spirituality. There are consequences for sin and idolatry in order to admonish people about healthy spiritual living:

The sorrows of those will increase who run after other gods (Psalm 16:4).

For rebellion is like the sin of divination, and arrogance like the evil of idolatry . . . (1 Samuel 15:23).

Therefore, my dear friends, flee from idolatry. . . . The sacrifices of pagans are offered to demons, not to God, and I do not want you to be participants with demons (1 Corinthians 10:14,20).

Dear children, keep yourselves from idols (1 John 5:21).

The major issue of New Age medicine is fundamentally a spiritual one. Christians are to flee practices which are false, which promote idolatry, lies, pagan gods, and which lead people astray and harm them spiritually. To fail to recognize the spiritual implications of New Age medicine is to fail to understand New Age medicine.

By leading people into the occult, New Age medicine may eventually result in their being demon-possessed (278/291, Meditation, Channeling, Hypnosis, Psychic Healing, Shamanism, Yoga). This process can happen gradually and almost imperceptibly, as revealed by specific case histories (718). Spirit influence is not always obvious. Indeed, the authors' research into spiritism indicates that spirits have the ability to operate unnoticed behind the scenes in such a way that even occultly involved individuals may

not discern their influence; they may think it's the natural functioning of their own mind or their intuition. (See New Age Intuition and New Age Inner Work for examples.)

Those who seek out New Age health methods need to realize that initial appearances can be deceptive. The full consequences of an activity may not be felt until years or decades later, as in the physical impact of smoking, or the psychological impact of abortion (973), or the spiritual impact of a religious cult.

## COMPREHENSIVE NEW AGE HEALTH COMPARISON

Jack Raso, M.S., R.D., who is a board member of the National Council Against Health Fraud, has developed an excellent listing of alternative health practices. After our discussion with Mr. Raso regarding alternative medicine, he graciously gave us permission to use some of his material (found in Appendix). Following is a short summary he provided with his list that explains part of his approach:

The word "alternativism," which I coined in 1994, refers to a motley accumulation of movements whose central thesis seems to be the following: faith—based on common sense, subjective experience, or revelation—preempts rational understanding. Medical alternativism comprises three divisions, which overlap one another: 1) alternative healthcare, 2) occult medicine, and 3) sectarian religious "healing." The ascendant division, alternative healthcare, is a phantasmagoria of systems and methods that goes by more than a dozen names. Its doctrines posit more than a score of forms of energy alien to physics, and its overall aims are to make health science a sham and to desecularize healthcare.

Since the late 1950s, nearly 700 health-related methods—i.e., freestanding methods, multimethod systems, component methods, and general "approaches"—that I consider mystical or supernaturalistic have been subjects of uncritical public discourse in English (most since 1980). Broadly, mysticism is belief in realities accessible only through subjective experience. Supernaturalism is belief in entities, or forces,

507

that are outside of, yet affect, the universe. The vast majority of the systems and methods of alternative health care are mystical or supernaturalistic. It may be cavalier to judge methods solely on the basis of the theories that underlie them, the methods' contexts, their histories, and the credibility or implausibility of claims for the methods. However, such information furnishes valuable clues, especially when pertinent scientific findings are nonexistent, meager, or discrepant.

Alternative health care is a "melting pot" of folklore, occultism, parapsychology, pop psychology, religion, pseudoscience, and medical guesswork.

Raso's list includes most of the mystical and/or supernaturalistic health-related methods he described in his books *Alternative Healthcare: A Comprehensive Guide* (1994), *Mystical Diets: Paranormal, Spiritual, and Occult Nutrition Practices* (1993), and *Nutrition Forum* newsletter.

Many of the alternative medicine methods are clearly supernatual, but even the innocent-sounding ones, according to Raso, are mystical or relate to the supernatural. Certain therapies, depending on use, run the gamut from neutral practices to occult applications (biofeedback is an example), so any listing has to be considered a general guide. Nevertheless, we urge readers to use the material in the Appendix to exercise discernment based on placement of material that should be generally valid.

We want to emphasize: 1) Consumers are urged first to critically study *any* alternative medical practice before employing it, 2) secure second (or third) opinions concerning medical advice in serious matters, 3) read the latest medical literature on a diagnosed condition concerning treatment options.

## In Summary

From our study we conclude:

1. Physically, as a whole, New Age medicine uses highly questionable techniques that are scientifically unfounded (959:67). Most of its methods involve quackery.

2. Spiritually, New Age medicine is permeated with spiritistic influence and occult philosophy; this means it is both physically and spiritually dangerous.

But the quest for physical health is not the final issue in any person's life. Good health is precious, yet it is not the ultimate gift. Even if New Age medicine could cure all illness, in the end everyone dies. So what is the final purpose in life?

The purpose of life is to inherit eternal life. The purpose of life is to know and honor the one true God. Jesus said, "And this is eternal life, that they may know Thee, the only true God, and Jesus Christ whom Thou hast sent" (John 17:3 NASB). The ultimate gift is the gift of eternal life by God's gracious forgiveness of our sins through Christ's death on the cross.

"For God so loved the world, that He gave His only begotten Son, that whoever believes in Him should not perish but have eternal life" (John 3:16 NASB).

# New Age Physics

- Info at a Glance
- Introduction and Influence
- The Priority of Mysticism
- Implications and Consequences
- Beyond Science
- Cultural Transformation
- Professing Themselves Wise?

## Info at a Glance

**Description.** Quantum physics adopted in support of New Age beliefs or Eastern mysticism in general.

**Founder.** Fritjof Capra's *The Tao of Physics* (1975) offered the first major attempt at the above synthesis.

**How does it claim to work?** Proponents allege that the new discoveries of particle physics and various theories proposed by physicists to understand them lend strong scientific support to ancient mystical religions such as Buddhism, Taoism, and Hinduism and to the modern movements based on them, such as New Age religion, transpersonal psychology, and various practices in the occult and holistic or New Age medicine.*

**Scientific evaluation.** Discredited; science is being misused to support Eastern and occult metaphysics, mysticism, parapsychology, and so on.

**Examples of occult potential.** The alleged scientific support of Eastern mysticism and New Age occultism has personally justified such practices in the minds of thousands.

**Major problems.** Physicists in general reject the alleged associations to mysticism and the occult; this even includes physicists whose personal worldview is New Age. Some leading New Age theorists also confess that the associations are nonexistent, contrived, or the result of misinterpretation.

**Biblical/Christian evaluation.** New findings or paradoxes uncovered in physics research may indeed reveal additional information about the structure of the creation, assuming interpretation of the data is accurate. However, alleged parallels to New Age beliefs based solely on what are still often theories in physics hardly validates Eastern mysticism scientifically or otherwise, nor does it discredit biblical metaphysics, cosmogony, or cosmology. Whether science can ever adequately conceptualize or understand the nature of the creation at the subatomic level is not known; however, factual scientific discoveries that are made can only confirm, and will never deny, the truth of the biblical worldview (Colossians 1:15-17; 2 Corinthians 13:8).

**Potential dangers.** The misuse of science in the support of an occult or Eastern mystical philosophy of life.

## Introduction and Influence

Quantum mechanics (QM) is a division of mathematical physics dealing with the motion of protons, neutrons, electrons, and other subatomic particles (e.g., the meson) found in atoms. The subject is as fascinating as it is confusing to the layman, who occasionally hears such terms as the Heisenberg uncertainty principle, bootstrap philosophy, wave particle duality, Schrodinger's wave mechanics, the Pauli exclusion principle, or references to the works of J. S. Bell, Eugene Wigner, and Niels Bohr.

Quantum mechanics has been with us for over 70 years, although its ultimate meaning is still debated. For example, if you were to ask ten physicists the meaning of quantum mechanics you might get several different answers. Yet while its meaning is debated, its value is not; the theories and methods of QM have had tremendous impact. According to the *Encyclopaedia Britannica*, they "have dominated all progress in atomic, nuclear, and molecular physics and chemistry" since 1925 (2406:793).

However, in the past two decades proponents of certain mystical and occult traditions of the East, such as *advaita* Vedanta, Mahayana Buddhism (e.g., Zen), and Chinese Taoism have claimed their worldview has been offered new support from science; that is, from quantum mechanics, or elementary particle physics. Beginning with New Age physicist Fritjof Capra's *The Tao of Physics* (1975), dozens of books have offered the thesis that modern physics is now validating the Eastern religious, occult, mystical, and monistic traditions (2206:3). Among these books are Michael Talbot's *Mysticism and the New Physics*, Amaury de Reincourt's *The Eye of Shiva: Eastern Mysticism and Science*, Gary Zukav's *The Dancing Wu Li Masters*, Itzhak Bentov's *Stalking the Wild Pendulum*, psychical researchers John White and Stanley Krippner's *Future Science*, psychic Lawrence LeShan's *The Medium, the Mystic and the Physicist*, and others (2205-16). Parapsychologists have also jumped on the bandwagon with books like *Quantum Physics and Parapsychology* (2211). Although these books are often written by non-physicists, they have collectively had wide public distribution and impact. Capra's books alone have sold over a million copies.

## THE PRIORITY OF MYSTICISM

In light of such claims, are we dealing with a new branch of science which, in the end, will support the search for mystical enlightenment,* or instead are we being confronted with individual worldviews that would like it to be a "science"? Put another way, are those who promote these ideas more concerned with fulfilling personal religious yearnings and attempting to use science to support them, rather than being concerned with the scientific method itself? If we see mystical leanings in their works or the belief and practice of occultism, it is hardly surprising to discover "similarities" advocated between physics and mysticism. Surface similarities could excite the religious imagination, leading some proponents to stress the purported association.

Thus, if we look at the promoters of New Age physics, we see that they are often oriented toward Eastern religions or the occult, and that their approach toward science reflects their religious commitment.

Lawrence LeShan is an admitted psychic healer who teaches others the practice of psychic healing (614). Gary Zukav has been associated with the Eastern-oriented Esalen Center in Big Sur, California, and is a devoted student of Buddhism (2212:25,31). Fritjof Capra is a Taoist who has been interested in Eastern mysticism for years and whose Tai Chi master is Liu Hsiu Ch'i (2210:13). Capra encourages his readers to become personally involved with the Eastern mystical path. "All I can hope to do is generate the feeling that such an involvement would be highly rewarding" (2210:11-13). The late Itzhak Bentov was a mystic who believed in psychics and reincarnation, and who engaged in astral travel and kundalini* experiences. His occult and Eastern views are evident in his works (2208:122-51). Not unexpectedly, he "spent several hours a day in deep meditation, during which he received many of the insights behind his theories and inventions" (2217:1/2208:xi, 4). Michael Talbot has had a "lifetime involvement with the paranormal ..." (2213:211).

In other words, those who promote a mystical physics have a preexisting commitment to the world of Eastern religions, mysticism, or the occult. One might ask whether we could always expect objectivity from men who have a particular metaphysical perspective to defend. For example, if we examine statements from these authors, we see that forages are being made far beyond science and physics per se. Gary Zukav's *The Dancing Wu Li Masters* is a case in point:

> Do not be surprised if *physics* curricula of the twenty-first century include classes in *meditation* (2212:327, emphasis added).

> The ideas of the new physics, when wholly grasped, can produce extraordinary *experiences.* The study of relativity theory, for example, can produce a remarkable experience that space and time *are only mental constructions!* Each of these different experiences is capable of changing us in such ways, that we never again are able to view the world as we did before (2212:43, second emphasis added).

> A powerful awareness lies dormant in these discoveries: an awareness of the hitherto-unsuspected powers of the mind to mold "reality," rather than the other way around. In this sense, the philosophy of physics is becoming *indistinguishable from the philosophy of Buddhism,* which is the philosophy of *enlightenment* (2212:296, emphasis added).

> We are approaching the end of science.... [T]he "end of science" means the coming of Western civilization, in its own time and in its own way, into the higher dimensions of human experience.

> A vital aspect of the enlightened state is the experience of an all-pervading unity. "This" and "that" no longer are separate entities. They are different *forms* of the same thing.... *We* are the manifestations of that which is.... It is neither well nor not well. It simply is what it is. What it is is perfectly what it is. It couldn't be anything else. It is perfect. I am perfect. I am exactly and perfectly who I am. You are perfect (2212:297-98).

## IMPLICATIONS AND CONSEQUENCES

Of course, ideas have consequences. The idea of applying a New Age interpretation of physics to the larger world has significant implications. In the following material, we will briefly illustrate this in the areas of science, medicine, and the occult.

We will begin by offering a few introductory comments on one of the relevant New Age themes here: that consciousness affects, and ultimately molds and determines, reality. Previously, we saw that Zukav expressed the occult idea that time and space are perhaps mental constructions, and that therefore the mind has powers to re-create and mold reality. New Agers claim that modern physics support this idea, an idea which is simply not true.

The actual source for this New Age concept is not the legitimate or logical extension of theories in modern physics, but occult revelations from the spirit world (e.g., "Seth," "Mafu," and other spirit guides; see also *A Course in Miracles** and religious or medical concepts in ancient pagan religions such as *advaita* Vedanta and *ayurveda*).

Zukav's idea is in harmony with the philosophy of the mind sciences generally (2639). The individual human mind has divine power because it is one in essence with God or ultimate reality, which is viewed as divine Mind or divine Consciousness. Of course, if the mind of man is also the mind of God then it can do what the mind of God does. In other words, once "awakened" to its true nature and power, the human mind can manipulate and control reality because the mind itself, being one essence with God, is actually the Creator of the universe and the Author of reality. Just as a disciplined human mind controls its thoughts and bends them to its own will, New Agers teach the divine Mind (God) controls its own thoughts (the Creation) and bends them to its own will.

Here we also find the common occult belief in monism: All reality is reducible to one substance (i.e., divine Consciousness), and that therefore divine Mind is all that exists or is real. The phenomenal world, the real world about us, is merely an "illusory" manifestation of divine Mind and subject to its power. In the words of Science of Mind philosophy, "Thought controls the image of thought," that is, divine Consciousness (Thought) has the power to generate and manipulate the phenomenal world (the image of Thought).

Now, people may claim that quantum mechanics "proves" that human consciousness has the potential to manipulate reality, but this is nonsense in both practical and scientific terms. For example, would New Agers bet good money that the combined consciousness of even a million humans meditating upon a brick all day would change its shape an inch or turn it to gold? The argument that consciousness affects reality at the subatomic level is not the only possible interpretation to explain quantum phenomena, nor is it the most credible. "Wigner's solution [that consciousness affects the outcome of the position of elementary particles] is not the only possible one, and it is not even a very popular one among experts on the interpretation of the quantum theory" (719:116). Furthermore, "Holistic writings about quantum mechanics sometimes mention a proof attributed to J. S. Bell. Just why they cite it is unclear, since the proof has nothing to do with consciousness or the like" (719:117).

So what would be the implications of a "science of consciousness" wherein monistic enlightenment* is interpreted as the determiner of reality? If unitary consciousness is the ultimate or only reality, and if it is divine, how might such a worldview alter a culture that adopted this philosophy? Would it change moral concepts, theology, science, and other areas? Of course it would.

If monism is ultimately true in an Eastern mystical or occult sense, then things like conventional reality, absolute morality, and Christian theology are radically altered or dismantled. In the monistic view, the phenomenal world and all the activity that occurs in it are not part of ultimate reality; material reality and events are mere "illusion" (see Eastern Gurus). So what then is their ultimate relevance or value? Whatever it is, it is not biblical, and its cultural acceptance would destroy both individual and societal purpose in life. As one guru recluse acknowledged, "If everyone lived as I do, how would the world go on" (2417:61)?

Consider that the monistic (*advaita*) philosophy of Hindu religion has had a profound impact on both the individuals who live in Indian society and the overall culture itself. This is seen in the lives of followers of many Eastern gurus* and many cultural practices in India. Even if physics were to prove Eastern monism as true, it would only prove a philosophy that is impossible to be lived out in daily life, and one that is highly

destructive besides. As a reviewer of Talbot's *Mysticism and the New Physics* wrote, "[I]t surely cannot be denied that if the first purpose in life is to maintain existence on this planet, then such ideas are singularly at variance with what is necessary in order to do so" (2218:233-34).

Indeed, India itself is supposed to be the land of perpetual spiritual enlightenment,* where sages and gurus offer the means to live perfectly within the harmony of our own God-realization. Yet Gopi Krishna states, "In India, the number of enlightened during the last 100 years can be counted on the fingers of one hand" (491:81). Perhaps something is missing in New Delhi. And perhaps it has something to do with the philosophical nihilism (see Eastern Gurus) so prevalent in monistic systems.

Our view of reality is not the only thing to be sacrificed. Ethics are also at risk. To take an extreme example, serial killer Charles Manson once argued that if "all is one" what could possibly be evil? Concepts of "right versus wrong" and "good versus evil" are merely the dualistic categories of a "lower" order of knowing. Such "primitive" thinking can be overwhelmed by the dramatic power inherent in monistic occult experience. This unhappy dismantling of moral values through occult experience is illustrated only too well in texts such as R. C. Zaehner's *Our Savage God*, and the implications can be frightening (see Eastern Gurus, Enlightenment).

And according to a monistic worldview, Christianity is reduced to irrelevance because it is primarily concerned with a personal God, concepts of sin and morality, the existence of heaven and hell, and the necessity of Christ's atonement for individual salvation. Monism considers these an illusion. Indeed, few religious philosophies are as anti-Christian as the mystical Eastern religions that deify man, depersonalize God, make the creation an "illusion," and justify and promote social apathy, to name just several serious consequences (see Eastern Gurus, 2681).

Adopting a monistic philosophy, then, would affect how people viewed themselves and how they lived among themselves. Inner man would indeed be granted divine status; outer man would become an "illusion." But this would place him back at the Fall. It was the desire to be "like God" that brought judgment, sin, and imperfection into the world to begin with (Genesis 3:5).

From a Christian perspective, in perceiving one's true nature as divine, one denies one's ultimate creaturehood. In perceiving the outer world, body, and personality as an "illusion," one denies the creation itself, not to mention one's creation in the image of God (Genesis 1:26-27). In other words, overall, to adopt the philosophical monism of mystical physics, especially in Eastern forms, is to repudiate and destroy the biblical concept of God as Creator. One needs only to examine the cultures in which the concept of God as a personal Creator has been rejected to see the unhappy results.

## BEYOND SCIENCE

One implication of New Age physics is to encourage a "science" of consciousness, which by definition would open the doors to mysticism and the occult. Capra observes:

The explicit inclusion of human consciousness may be an essential aspect of future theories of matter.

Such a development would open exciting possibilities between physics and Eastern mysticism. The understanding of one's consciousness and of its relation to the rest of the universe is the starting point of all mystical experience. The Eastern mystics have explored various modes of consciousness throughout the centuries, and the conclusions they have reached are often radically different from the ideas held in the West. If physicists really want to include the nature of human consciousness in their realm of research, a study of Eastern ideas may well provide them with stimulating new viewpoints (2210:300).

Capra quotes a speculative physicist who theorizes that a "new form" of intellectual endeavor may be on the horizon, "one that will not only lie outside of physics but will not even be describable as 'scientific' " (2210:301). Capra himself speculates that the end point will be to "go beyond science" into the realm of "the unthinkable," conceptually speaking, wherein complete

but ineffable knowledge is attained, as summarized in the words of Lao Tzu, "He who knows does not speak, He who speaks does not know" (2210:301). While some New Agers might think this a quaint description of the scientific method, such enlightenment* is unlikely to do much for either laboratory research or scientific progress. Apparently, we can go from science to mystical experience straight into the Void—all by way of allegedly modern physics.

Capra is aware of the difficulties involved in his thesis, and he suggests not the actual merger of science and mysticism but a "dynamic interplay" (2210:299-307). But the damage has already been done:

The principal theories and models of modern physics lead to a view of the world which is internally consistent and in perfect harmony with the views of Eastern mysticism.

For those who have *experienced* this harmony, the significance of the parallels between the world views of physicists and mystics is beyond any doubt (2210:303 emphasis added).

The proof of this harmony, then, comes not from science but from mystical experience. Thus, *advaita* Hinduism is allegedly confirmed scientifically. "The harmony between their views confirms the ancient Indian wisdom that *Brahman*, the ultimate reality without, is identical to *Atman*, the reality within" (2210:305).

But if science and mysticism were ever truly to unite, as so many New Agers hope, science as we know it would be destroyed and we would therefore all be denied its benefits. The Western world would begin to reap the fruit of Eastern metaphysics as it filtered down into daily life. If, to quote Capra, "physics can be ... a way to spiritual knowledge and self-realization," and if "man's scientific discoveries can be in perfect harmony with his *spiritual aims* and religious beliefs" (2210:25), then what we have is a "mental" science, a "science" of occult enlightenment,* not true science at all. Dean Halverson notes some irony in this:

It is curious that the New Agers claim scientific support for a world view which destroys the validity of doing science. It is also curious that New Agers claim scientific support for a view that says the mind creates material reality, when science itself says the physical universe existed long before anybody was around to see it (2216:23, prepublication transcript).

Nevertheless, Capra states:

To free the human mind from words and explanations is one of the main aims of Eastern mysticism.... *As long as we try to explain things, we are bound by karma: trapped in our conceptual network. To transcend words and explanations means to break the bonds of karma and attain liberation.*

The world view of the Eastern mystics shares with the bootstrap philosophy of modern physics not only an emphasis on the mutual interrelation and self-consistency of all phenomena, but also the denial of fundamental constituents of matter. In a universe which is an inseparable whole and where all forms are fluid and everchanging, *there is no room for any fixed fundamental reality* (2210:291, emphasis added).

What Capra implies is that science "supports" the goal of attaining monistic enlightenment,* as understood in Hinduism, Buddhism, Taoism, mysticism, and the occult in general. No wonder physicists are disturbed by this kind of thinking! Others should be as well, for whatever the underlying reality of matter turns out to be, the Eastern approach to man and the cosmos is fundamentally hostile to a Western worldview, not to mention human welfare itself.

An example would be the problems associated with applying New Age quantum mechanics to the field of medicine. An article by Drs. Douglas Stalker and Clark Glymour, "Quantum Medicine," offers an excellent illustration of the errors and dangers of misapplying quantum mechanics to the larger world:

If you pick up any respected medical journal and examine papers intended to defend specific therapies, whether vitamin C therapy or bypass surgery, you will not find discussions of the interpretation of quantum mechanics, or philosophical disquisitions on reductionism. Presumably the authors of such essays on medical

research do not think quantum mechanics or philosophy have any bearing, one way or the other, on such questions as to whether bypass surgery relieves angina or whether vitamin C prevents colds or cures cancer. Holists, in contrast, really do seem to think that quantum mechanics and philosophy of science have a bearing on whether Rolfing, acupuncture, visualization, chiropractic, iridology, homeopathy, and the like, cure or prevent disease (719:107).

Stalker and Glymour demonstrate that advocates of New Age medicine* have little understanding of the scientific process, and that, their assertions concerning the structure of contemporary and recent physical science and the conclusions that can reasonably be made from that science "are false and absurd." In fact:

There is no alternative holistic paradigm for scientific medicine. There is only an insistence on abandoning every feature of scientific medicine, including experimental controls and experimental design generally, careful statistical analysis, use of the best relevant conclusions drawn from other sciences, and the practice of rational criticism and response to arguments (719:109-10).

After examining a number of arguments and claims by holists, who attempt to subjectivize reality and apply QM theory to health and medicine, Stalker and Glymour respond:

This is noxious falsehood. The quantum theory has nothing to do with the "subjectivity of all diagnostic judgements." The "conventions of objective research" have not been altered by the quantum theory. The *uncertainty relations limit predictability—they are limitations on the powers of the mind, not enhancements of it.* Theoretical physics has not become touchy-feely—anything goes, you have your particles, I'll have mine—pseudoscience. Ask the teams of physicists who spend tens of thousands of hours, and millions of dollars designing reliable apparatus, reproducing experimental results, checking for errors in calculations and in physical arrangements. Ask them if they have abandoned the "conventions of objective research."

Moreover, quantum theory has not led physicists to place any emphasis on "consciousness" as a causal factor in experimental outcomes. States of consciousness do not appear as variables in any of the papers published in *Physical Review* nowadays. Physicists have not found that in order to do particle physics they must first do psychology. Consciousness plays *only a minor role in one rather implausible solution to the measurement problem*; and even if that solution is embraced, there is nothing to be learned about the physical structure of the universe from speculations about the mind (719:119, emphasis added).

The authors also show how the standard approaches to integrating New Age medicine* with quantum mechanics consistently violate the principles of careful evaluation:

There is a pattern to holistic writing about quantum mechanics. Some half-truth about the theory is vaguely stated, some controversial interpretation is taken as the subtle judgment of the scientific community, the half-truth is widely exaggerated, and the exaggeration is used to justify an absurdity about biomedical research and clinical practice. The repeated litany is that orthodox medicine is in error because is it not *consistent* with this exaggerated and distorted account of fundamental physics (719:123).

They also point out that most of the arguments put forth by New Age quantum promoters are really just bluff:

Any medical researcher can call the bluff with one challenge: *give us a single quantum mechanical calculation that contradicts our biomedical findings.* Holists cannot and do not do it, exactly because—save in rare cases—quantum mechanics simply cannot be applied to the levels at which biomedical researchers work. No one knows how to apply the theory, or approximations of it, to bacteria and viruses. When the theory can be applied, it is taken account of in conventional scientific practice (719:124).

## CULTURAL TRANSFORMATION

No one denies that the approach of physics mysticism has implications. Unfortunately, the promoters of the new paradigm frequently travel beyond emphasizing mere personal enlighten-

ment.* What many advocates really seek is a much larger cultural transformation wherein "unenlightened" attitudes are "refined" or, in some cases, even done away with. In other words, a profound cultural revolution is preached:

Science points . . . towards a oneness of the universe which includes not only our natural environment but also our fellow human beings. . . . To achieve such a state . . . a radically different social and economic structure will be needed: a cultural revolution in the true sense of the word. The survival of our whole civilization may depend on whether we can bring about such a change. It will depend ultimately, on our ability to adopt some of the yin attitudes of Eastern mysticism . . . (2210:307).

Capra has outlined this cultural revolution in *The Turning Point*, where he advocates radically different perspectives on reality, life, consciousness, and society. Indeed, we can see that the signposts are already here. New Age concepts and philosophies are everywhere having an impact to one degree or another and, in many areas, promoters are thinking globally. For example, Maharishi Mahesh Yogi, founder of the popular Hindu religion known as transcendental meditation, advocates a new TM-controlled "world government." He states plainly that there will be no room for the "unfit"—e.g., the "unenlightened"—according to his standards (2419:47). Gopi Krishna works for the day when the earth will be ruled by a new race of beings, kundalini-induced "supermen" whose occult consciousness will set the standard of "proper" behavior (491:128; see Yoga). These are only two of many sobering examples that could be given.

Whatever *orthodox* physicists are doing, and wherever their science is headed, we may be certain of one thing. They are not concerned with personal occult enlightenment* and dramatic worldwide cultural revolutions in that direction.

## PROFESSING THEMSELVES WISE?

It should be obvious that there is more than science going on in the realm of New Age physics. A major problem is that its promoters often engage in oversimplifications and distortions of science, which undermine their position. Such theories may impress and titillate some spiritual seekers, but not many scientists. The vast majority of physicists remain unmoved by the physics/mysticism paradigm. Even Albert Einstein once noted, "I cannot seriously believe in [the quantum theory] because it cannot be reconciled with the idea that physics should represent a reality in time and space, free from spooky actions at a distance" (2471:51).

What "spooky actions" was Einstein concerned about? For one, the idea that a particle does not possess certain properties (e.g., location) until measured by an observer. How can this be? According to Newtonian or classical physics, it could not be explained.

Let's try to simplify this. When physicist Niels Bohr formulated the "complementarity principle" in 1927, he was attempting to evaluate the fact that sometimes subatomic phenomena behaved like waves and sometimes they behaved like particles. Bohr concluded that we should accept these paradoxical characteristics instead of attempting a more "rational" explanation that would violate observed data.

The man regarded as the father of quantum mechanics, Werner Karl Heisenberg, next rejected a "model" approach to the atom and instead used algebraic matrices to describe its characteristics. In 1927 he developed the "uncertainty principle," which revolutionized modern physics. This principle asserted that subatomic phenomena in the quantum realm were unpredictable and therefore, among other things, incapable of objective measurement. And it soon appeared as if the very process of observation influenced the position or state of a subatomic particle.

New Agers have now interpreted the findings of modern physics under the two major themes of "interconnectedness" and "consciousness." If the mere act of observation affects basic reality, there must be a significant interconnection between the microscopic and macroscopic worlds. So is there really any final distinction between the observer and that which is observed? Perhaps, then, all creation really is one basic essence, like the mystics have taught:

At the subatomic level, matter does not exist with certainty at definite places, but rather shows "tendencies to exist," and atomic events do not occur with certainty at definite times and in definite ways, but rather show "tendencies to occur." . . . At the subatomic level, the solid material objects of classical physics dissolve into wave-like patterns of probabilities, and these patterns, ultimately, do not represent probabilities of things, but rather probabilities of interconnections. A careful analysis of the process of observation and atomic physics has shown that the subatomic particles have no meaning as isolated entities, but can *only be understood as interconnections between* the preparation of an experiment and the subsequent measurement. *Quantum theory thus reveals a basic oneness of the universe.* It shows that we cannot decompose the world into independently existing smallest units. . . . [P]*roperties of any atomic object can only be understood in terms of the object's interaction with the observer.* This means that the classical ideal of an *objective description* of nature is no longer valid (1558:68, emphasis added).

The argument is essentially: Because we cannot objectively measure subatomic phenomena, they do not objectively exist as discrete, isolated entities but only as "probabilities of interconnections" whose properties or reality are based upon the act of observation itself. In *The Dancing Wu Li Masters*, Gary Zukav writes, "This is the primary significance of the uncertainty principle. At the subatomic level, *we cannot observe something without changing it*" (2212:134).

Consciousness itself is then brought into the picture. If the process of conscious observation *influences* subatomic reality, perhaps it is because subatomic reality is itself *part of* consciousness. And perhaps everything, then, is just one divine consciousness after all; again, like the mystics have taught. In *Mysticism and the New Physics*, Talbot extends the argument to its New Age conclusion: "The entire physical universe itself is nothing more than patterns of neuronal energy firing off inside our heads!" (2213:54). Thus, "there is no physical world 'out there,' consciousness creates all," and, "Our consciousness is all-powerful. *We* are not all-powerful because we are not in complete control of the consciousness" (2213:152).

In essence, according to New Agers, all reality is merely consciousness and, by implication, divine consciousness. This implies that *our* true reality is also divine consciousness. And thus New Age philosophy is "confirmed" by the latest discoveries of modern physics. Or is it?

The problems with New Age interpretations are multiple. For example, we are dealing with objects at the *quantum* level, where our knowledge is meager at best. Things don't operate as we expect them to because we don't have enough knowledge to understand *why* they operate as they do. These particles are so infinitesimally small that we must spend billions of dollars on gigantic accelerators just to gain even a minuscule amount of information about them. By electromagnetically accelerating particles to near speed-of-light velocities, the particle beams can be focused to break up atomic nuclei or to interact with other elementary particles in order to reveal their structure and properties. But no one can logically assume such knowledge of this realm is sufficient to support New Age conjectures.

Furthermore, the alteration at the quantum level is not a result of consciousness but of the objects of measurement. For example, when we attempt to measure big objects, like a chair, we do not alter their basic nature because chairs are so large that they cannot be affected by the photons that are bounced off them from artificial light. But at the subatomic level, photons and detection apparatus (not our consciousness) do impact what is being observed. Thus, "since the position of the electron inside an atom cannot be measured without destroying the atom, the [dominant] Copenhagen Interpretation holds that an electron has no definite position in an atom" (2471:53). But if it has no definite position, does this mean that it is not objectively real or that consciousness "determines" its "reality"? Of course not.

But here is one way in which New Agers attempt to assert their beliefs:

Extending this idea [that subatomic phenomena do not possess certain properties until measured] to all other physical quantities, we conclude that they become real only upon their being measured. Now this may sound like ancient Hindu idealism, with everything in our heads, or the New Age: "Reality is whatever you want it to be." [But the] fact that reality rarely is what you want it to be is the best evidence that a world beyond our heads does indeed exist (2471:53).

In other words, consciousness does not determine reality because reality is rarely what "consciousness" would like it to be. What's more, consciousness *cannot* determine reality because even at the quantum level all sorts of events are happening all the time entirely apart from any direct observation or "intervention" by consciousness. And although mysteries and paradoxes exist at the quantum level, it is not as if this realm has no consistency or comprehensibility at all. Halverson refers to

the consistency of the quantum realm. No matter who observes it, its behavior is consistent. Although you cannot predict the outcome of a single event in the quantum realm, you can statistically calculate the percentage of what does occur. For example, after you shoot 100 particles of light at a screen, you might observe that 10 percent of those particles hit in one area and 90 percent hit in another area. The same percentage will occur no matter how often the experiment is repeated and no matter who is doing the observing (2682:83-84).

The real issue, then, is whether the legitimate findings of quantum mechanics actually support New Age, parapsychological beliefs. What recent scientific experiments conclude is that Einstein may have been wrong—there are "spooky" actions at the subatomic level. Nevertheless, such experiments just as clearly force us to reject New Age interpretations and applications of quantum physics as being false:

The conventional interpretation of quantum mechanics ... provides no mechanism for psychic phenomena or simultaneous connections between events. On the contrary, [it is] paranormal phenomena [that] violate the foundational principles of twentieth-century physics—relativity and quantum mechanics. These principles are confirmed by countless empirical tests, having withstood every challenge every scientist and pseudoscientist have been able to mount (2471:51).

Now consider an example of how things do not operate the way we would expect them to at the atomic and subatomic levels. Experiments such as the apparently definitive ones done by Alain Aspect and his coworkers at the Institute for Applied Optics of the University of Paris in 1982 empirically demonstrated that the spin components of photons cannot be both local and definite (cf. 2471:58). However, notice what is *not* said here. What is not said is that the spin components cannot be both local and *real*. This is where New Agers and even some philosophers and scientists misunderstand or misuse Heisenberg's Uncertainty Principle.

All physics is saying here is that there is *indefiniteness* at the subatomic level. But to say a particle or its properties are indefinite in terms of location and mass is *not* to say they are unreal—to the contrary. They are as real as anything else. Put another way, just because something cannot be precisely defined does not mean it should be considered unreal.

So nothing in modern physics requires or even suggests that nature is unreal, either in the sense of the ancient Hindu notion of *maya* (illusion) or any other sense. New Age arguments in this important area, therefore, are false. In the words of Victor Stenger, "[T]he true reality of the universe is not necessarily manifested by objects possessing [definite] attributes, such as position and mass, that we assign them in the process of doing physics. These variables, after all, are human inventions with no precisely definable meaning beyond their measurements as performed with specific instruments like clocks and meter sticks" (2471:58).

The point is, if we must accept some level of indefiniteness at the subatomic level, this has *nothing* to do with notions of reality and unreality. And, obviously, no orthodox physicist will conclude that the larger world is *unreal* just because incomprehensible phenomena exist at the subatomic level. Nor will he conclude that everything is divine consciousness or that a subatomic "interconnectedness" exists that permits a natural, physical explanation for psychic phenomena:

Paranormalists are dead wrong when they claim that modern physics supports their proposal of extrasensory channels in some kind of underlying ethereal reality. The opposite is true. Einstein's relativity destroyed the continuous ether and the instantaneous connection between events. Quantum mechanics destroyed the notion of continuous matter and energy. Twentieth-century science provides a picture of a universe of discrete material objects, interacting with each other within the light cone, with nothing further required by any existing data.

Quantum mechanics does not provide a mechanism for supersensory phenomena. Experiments fully support the conventional statistical interpretation of quantum mechanics, with the nonlocal and nonreal ["nonreal" should be read "indefinite"] wave-function describing ensembles rather than individual particles.

Quantum effects are certainly beyond normal experience. They are weird. But it does not follow that every weird idea is consistent with quantum mechanics (2471:60).

Indeed, it may even be possible that Einstein was correct and that future discoveries will confirm his initial judgment. The fact is, science will never know the absolute truth about anything. That is not what science is about. It simply does the best it can with the tools it has. (Einstein also stated that 10,000 experiments could not prove him right if one good experiment proved him wrong.) At the quantum level, one wonders if the tools we have are sufficient to make conclusions about the nature and functions of subatomic reality that will always hold true. We doubt it. And physicists themselves do not agree on these issues. Indeed, in the minds of some astute commentators, "particle physics is becoming more like myth than science because its mathematical constructions are so distant from any conceivable experimental confirmation" (2767:55).

Dr. Joseph Hamilton is Landon C. Garland's Distinguished Professor of Physics with the Physics and Astronomy Department of Vanderbilt University. He has authored over 550 scientific journal publications and is one of the leading physicists in the country. Hamilton has discussed the New Age interpretation of physics with one or more of the world's leading physicists, and he was kind enough to read our chapter for accuracy. It was he who pointed out to us that even philosophers and a few physicists, besides New Agers, may misstate and misuse the Heisenberg Uncertainty Principle. We asked him to comment on this issue, and he gave us the following statement:

I do not concur that modern physics provides support for New Age beliefs and/or mysticism based on an analysis of the quoted works. Their proposed support rests on several misunderstandings of modern physics, especially of the Heisenberg Uncertainty Principle. All of the New Age/Mysticism (Eastern religions) writers make a common misinterpretation of the Heisenberg Uncertainty Principle whereby a measurement is taken as the cause of (or introduces) the uncertainty. This is not what the Heisenberg Uncertainty Principle says. It says that there is a basic uncertainty or indefiniteness in two complementary variables such as the position and momentum in a given direction, eg. $x$ and $p_x$, or energy and the time interval a system has that energy so that $\Delta \times \Delta p_x \geq \hbar/2$ or $\Delta E \; \Delta t \geq \hbar/2$. According to quantum theory, no system can exist with a definite $x$ and a definite $p_x$. It is true that our measurement may perturb a system and make the uncertainties greater than $\hbar/2$, but there are precise and careful experiments where we can show that our experimental uncertainty introduced in a measurement is less than that expected by the uncertainty principle and yet the uncertainty principle spread is what is observed. The statement "we cannot observe something without changing it" is sometimes true but is a misinterpretation of the uncertainty principle. While all of our knowledge in empirical sciences can only be understood as interconnections between the object observed and subsequent observation or measurement, this does not mean that consciousness plays any special role in subatomic physics. In particular, it does not mean that consciousness determines reality. Finally, there is an erroneous mixup in exchanging the words "uncertainty" and "indefiniteness" with "unreality" or "non-real." In physics for something to be "uncertain" or "indefinite" does not say or imply it is in any sense "unreal," i.e. aspects of "reality" may be indefinite. The French experiments demonstrate that the spin components of photons cannot be both local and definite, not "both local and real." Thus again the exchange of "unreal" for "indefinite" is misleading, and the New Age/Mysticism inferences drawn from this exchange have no basis.

Thus, when New Agers (or scientists) use language that implies that the universe is fundamentally contradictory or unreal, one can assume they are confused or that they really don't know what they are talking about. To say quantum physics is paradoxical is true—there seems to be a contradiction, but it is only an apparent one and with sufficient knowledge can be resolved.

But to say that the universe is contradictory or unreal is something that science cannot recover from. "It is one thing to say that reality is paradoxical. It is quite another to say that reality is contradictory. If it is paradoxical, we can hope for resolution. If it is contradictory, there can be no resolution and science is reduced not only to linguistic confusion but to unintelligibility. . . . It is time for scientists to stop speaking in contradictions. They are as confusing as they are meaningless" (2809:73).

Thus, "Statements [by physicists] like 'chaos is an agent of order' are examples of linguistic confusion. Such confusion is a serious problem. Indeed it may be *the* problem between classical physics and quantum physics. Linguistic problems will continue to plague us as anomalies continue to appear that do not fit existing paradigms. Until the paradigm is revised or expanded to accommodate the anomalies, we will tend to attempt to squeeze or force the anomalies into old categories, giving rise to linguistic confusion and even nonsense statements. Here is where great caution is required plus at least a basic understanding of the function of language" (2809:65).

In *God and the Cosmologists* (2810:118), Stanley L. Jaki comments, "Yet if modern scientific cosmology has reached the point where it may be deprived of its very object, the universe, it is because the champions of the Copenhagen philosophy of quantum mechanics, hardly ever distinguished from the science of quantum mechanics, have succeeded in selling the idea that doing very good science justifies doing philosophy very badly" (2809:97).

In light of all this, we again suggest that Einstein may not have been wrong, or at least not entirely wrong. At one point in a discussion with his colleague, Max Born, he suggested that the voice of his own reason gave him qualms that quantum mechanics was not yet the real thing. "Quantum mechanics is certainly imposing. But an inner voice tells me that it is not yet the real thing. The theory says a lot, but does not really bring us any closer to the secret of the 'old one.' I, at any rate, am convinced that *He* [God] is not playing at dice. . . . I am quite convinced that someone will eventually come up with a theory whose objects, connected by laws, are not probabilities but considered facts. . . ." (2809:60)

Even promoters of the occult and mysticism may see the errors of the New Age approach to physics. In *The Holographic Paradigm and Other Paradoxes,* leading New Age theorist Ken Wilber offers a critique of New Age physics mysticism. He points out that the mystic and physicist aren't even talking about the same worlds. The "new physics" has nothing to do with the so-called "higher" levels of "mental" reality that mystics claim to encounter, and, practically speaking, it is obviously irrelevant when it comes to living in the day-to-day world. Thus, the alleged agreement between physics and mysticism on the level of physical reality is naive. For example, the physicist sees a "oneness" (granting that interpretation) at the subatomic level, but not in the real world, yet the real world is precisely where the mystic perceives his oneness (2209:157-86).

Wilber also points out:

The "new physics" is far from a grand consensus as to the nature of even subatomic reality. To hook transpersonal psychology/mysticism to the consensus of the new quantum physics is not possible, *because there is no consensus.* Those connections that have been drawn between physics and mysticism are of the pick and choose variety. . . . [I]n the words of physicist Bernstein, "a travesty and a disservice" to the theories involved (2209:178, emphasis added).

The reason that quantum mechanics is never applied to the larger world is because quantum reality has no practical relevance to the larger world, and physicists are the first to emphasize it:

In the rush to marry physics and mysticism, using the shotgun of generalization, we tend to forget that quantum reality has almost no bear-

ing whatsoever in the actual world of macroscopic processes. As physicist Walker puts it, in the ordinary world of "automobiles and basketballs, the quanta are inconsequential." This has long been clearly recognized by physicists. The quantum level is so submicroscopic that its interactions can for all practical purposes be ignored in the macro world. The intense interactions between subatomic mesons, which sound so mystical, are not observed at all between macro-objects, between rocks and people and trees. . . .

. . . The physicist and mystic aren't even talking about the same world. The physicist says: "The ordinary Newtonian world is, for all practical purposes, separate and discrete, but the subatomic world is a unified pattern." The mystic says: "The ordinary Newtonian world is, as I directly perceive it, one indivisible whole; as for the subatomic realm, I've never seen it" (832:166-67).

If the phenomena and implications of quantum mechanics were as true as the advocates of the New Age movement claim, then why aren't *physical* scientists jumping on the mystical bandwagon? Perhaps it could be argued that they know something New Agers don't. In fact, with the rise in popularity of the alleged synthesis between physics and mysticism, physicists are increasingly denouncing the entire matter in their published books. For example, the eminent physicist Heinz R. Pagels has labeled the attempts to link physics and Eastern mysticism as misleading "nonsense" and "fantasy" in his *The Cosmic Code: Quantum Physics as the Language of Nature.* Yet bestselling New Age ayurvedic physician and transcendental meditation supporter Deepak Chopra, M.D., listed this book as supplemental reading for those who wanted to learn more about the amazing connections between physics and Eastern mysticism (2369:131-32,323/2370:1750). Dr. Chopra claims that the antirealist "vast assumptions" of Eastern mysticism "all are grounded in the discoveries of quantum physics" (2368:7), and that this includes the Hindu philosophy of Transcendental Meditation.

But Dr. Pagels was sufficiently incensed to file an affidavit repudiating claims like these:

In his capacity as executive director of the New York Academy of Sciences in 1986, Pagels submitted an affidavit on behalf of a former TM member who was suing the movement for fraud. "There is no known connection between meditation states and states of matter in physics," Pagels wrote. "No qualified physicist that I know would claim to find such a connection without knowingly committing fraud. . . . The presentation of the ideas of modern physics side by side, and apparently supportive of, the ideas of the Maharishi [Mahesh Yogi] about pure consciousness can only be intended to deceive those who might not know any better. . . . To see the beautiful and profound ideas of modern physics, the labor of generations of scientists, so willfully perverted provokes a feeling of compassion for those who might be taken in by these distortions" (2370:1750).

We stress again that most *physicists* who are sympathetic or converts to New Age philosophy reject New Age claims about theoretical physics. Perhaps we need to remember that theoretical physics is, after all, dealing in the realm of physics *theory.*

Reviews in the literature, therefore, indicate that much is left to be desired. Consider that reviews of the leading text on the subject, *The Tao of Physics*, by Fritjof Capra, remain valid for the field in general:

The most that Eastern religious philosophy and elementary particle physics seem to have in common is that they are both hard to understand. . . . I find the intellectual thesis—that these two subjects represent a similar view of the world to be completely without merit or credibility (*Contemporary Sociology*, July 1979, p. 587).

Superficial and profoundly misleading . . . (*The American Scholar*, Winter 1978-79).

This simplistic view of both science and Eastern thought possibly results from a fascination for the metaphysical, an eagerness to bridge a gap, and a search for emotional satisfaction . . . (*Choice*, June 1976, p. 541).

A muddling of distinctions. . . . Arguments never develop beyond an analogy (*Library Journal*, October 15, 1975, p. 1933).

. . . Overall lack of balance [in] its cursory examination of mysticism, and its nimiety of enthusiastic attempts to relate ideas of quite different origins and meanings . . . (*San Francisco Review of Books*).

. . . making mountains out of molehills. . . . The effort to harmonize the two is not only very thin, but downright wrong . . . (review of Zukav and Capra quoting two physicists, *Newsweek*, July 23, 1979, p. 86).

Almost from the point of publication, promoters of the new physics have been criticized by physicists and by many popular lay science writers. So by what leap of the imagination does anyone conclude that quantum physics provides a justification for Hindu and Buddhist metaphysics, as is often claimed? Again, because indeterminacy exists at the level of particle physics, is it logical to conclude the creation is an illusion? Why should anyone surmise that because mysteries are found at the substratum of matter, this is sufficient reason to deny the reality of matter? The real miracle is not the mysteries of quantum physics; it is the marvel of all creation: the beauty, profundity, and orderliness of the universe even given its so-called "ephemeral" foundation. Ephemeral indeed. One can only wonder if "ephemeral" is the proper term for matter in outer space that is so dense a piece the size of a bowling ball weighs 5000 tons! Only an infinite God could have so arranged things (1666).

New Age promoters may cite God Himself as the "Creator" of the illusory world. Yet when God visited this planet in the person of Jesus Christ, He clearly acted as if the world were real and as if beliefs and actions of people mattered. Not once did He hint that the world was ultimately an "illusion," even though God knows more about quantum mechanics than New Age synthesizers!

Again, no one really knows the ultimate meaning of particle physics. Researcher Dean Halverson wonders on what basis we should assume that either physics or mysticism deals with the nature or character of God; or, even granting the existence of a universal oneness—that we are dealing with ultimate reality rather than a *lower* level of reality? Halverson quotes Ian Barbour in *Issues in Science and Religion* (1971, pp. 289-90) as pointing out that the "primary significance of modern physics lies not in any disclosure of the fundamental nature of reality, but in the recognition of the *limitations of science.* . . . [T]he new physics is no more adequate for the exhaustive description of all existence than was the old" (2216).

As the *Encyclopaedia Britannica* reminds us, the scientific endeavor is by nature limited (and more fickle than most people realize):

> Science is a human enterprise, carried out by human beings, employing sense organs, muscular structure, and a nervous system, as well as auxiliary tools of manipulation and observation, which are enormously large compared to the atoms of which they consist. When scientists seek to learn details of atomic structure by observation, they are limited to what can be learned through observations made with such large instruments. Some of the features of quantum mechanics have to be understood in terms of this limitation on human observational powers (2406:793).

All of this is why both physical scientists and many promoters of mysticism themselves have rejected the so-called "new paradigm" marrying physics and mysticism. Over a decade ago one of the principle theorists for New Age thinking, Ken Wilbur, observed that attempts at union were futile. In both camps, those who knew what they were talking about were in agreement:

> From one end of the spectrum: already certain mystically or transpersonally oriented researchers—Tiller, Harman, W.I. Thompson, Eisenbud—have expressed disappointment in or total rejection of the new paradigm.

> From the other end: already many physicists are furious with the "mystical" use to which particle physics is being subjected. Particle physicist Jeremy Bernstein recently unleashed a broadside on such attempts, calling them "superficial and profoundly misleading" (1978). And no less an authority than John Wheeler—whose name is always mentioned in the "new paradigm" and in a way he finds infuriating—recently released two scathing letters wherein, among several other things, he brands the physics/mysticism

attempts as "moonshine," "pathological science" and "charlatanism." "Moreover," he states, "in the quantum theory of observation, my own present field of endeavor, I find honest work almost overwhelmed by the buzz of absolutely crazy ideas being put forth with the aim of establishing a link between quantum mechanics and parapsychology" (1979)—and transpersonal psychology, for that matter . . . (832:184-85).

New Age theorists who apply the ideas of quantum mechanics to justify their occult practices are misleading others; they are not justifying either their methods or their theories. We conclude with Stalker and Glymour:

> As for scientists who do physiology, sociology, organic chemistry, fluid dynamics, and biomedicine without regard to quantum mechanics, they are not betraying scientific standards or being illogical or old fashioned. They are doing science the way it is supposed to be done, and the only way it can be done. . . .

> We do not believe that the holists are really concerned to make science consistent with quantum theory. Instead, their aim is to establish their credentials on the cheap. It usually requires a lot of work to establish new therapies, new sciences, and new approaches to old and well investigated problems. They must be shown, by the usual canons of evidence and arguments in science, to explain better and to predict better. In medicine the standard is found in the clinical trial, which requires careful design, careful selection of subjects, accurate and specific descriptions and definitions, and close statistical analysis.

> Holistic practitioners do not really care to provide any of these things. Nor do they even care to provide weaker forms of scientific evidence such as statistical ex post facto studies. They rely instead on attempting to undermine the very concept of rational science, and present their wholism as the only apparent alternative. Were they to succeed, the result would not be better and more exciting science. It would be no science at all (719:124).

Precisely.

# Scientology

## Info at a Glance

**Description.** Scientology is a novel and eclectic religion drawing from Eastern philosophy, modern psychology, and occult practice. It seeks to release human potential, free the soul, and restore people to their original state as pure, immortal spirit.

**Founder.** L. Ron Hubbard (1911-86).

**How does it claim to work?** Through its "counseling" procedures (termed "auditing"), Scientology alleges to offer the only final solution to mankind's problems. Auditing "locates" and "resolves" "engrams," or past traumatic experiences that allegedly inhibit true spiritual enlightenment.* Scientology claims it can eventually free the human spirit from its bondage to the material world.

**Scientific evaluation.** While the specific religious tenets of Scientology are incapable of scientific evaluation, many of its stated beliefs that are capable of evaluation run contrary to most basic data in the natural and social sciences.

**Examples of occult potential.** Development of psychic powers, out-of-body experiences, and other occult practices.

**Major problems.** The specific claims of Scientology in many different fields of study are inconsistent with known data; the extent to which Scientology has or has not reformed its past methods of dealing with critics; the rejection of the material world as an "illusion."

**Biblical/Christian evaluation.** As an occult religion having specific theological beliefs contrary to biblical teaching, membership in the Church of Scientology is prohibited for Christians.

**Potential dangers.** The acceptance of false data carries its own consequences; the physical, psychological, and spiritual hazards associated with occult practice; psychological harm from auditing.

*Note:* This material originally appeared in the *Christian Research Journal,* Summer 1993.

## INTRODUCTION AND INFLUENCE

The last generation has seen the proliferation of "New Age" religions that stress common themes, such as human potentialism, spiritism, psychic development, Gnosticism, occult enlightenment, and Eastern philosophy and practice. Examples include The Church Universal and Triumphant, begun by Mark and Elizabeth Claire Prophet; Eckankar, invented by Paul Twitchell; Astara, started by Robert and Earlyne Chaney; Silva Mind Control,* developed by Jose Silva and the Church of Scientology, founded by L. Ron Hubbard. Scientology is arguably among the most powerful and the most influential of new religions.

In *Faith Founded on Fact*, Dr. John Warwick Montgomery accurately described our own era when he wrote:

> Ours is an age of religious cacophony, as was the Roman Empire of Christ's time. From agnosticism to Hegelianism, from devil-worship to scientific rationalism, from theosophical cults to philosophies of process: virtually any world view conceivable is offered to modern man in the pluralistic marketplace of ideas. Our age is indeed in ideological and societal agony, grasping at anything and everything that can conceivably offer the ecstasy of a cosmic relationship or of a comprehensive *Weltanschauung* (2550:152-53).

The Church of Scientology is certainly one of the most intriguing and controversial of the new religions to illustrate Dr. Montgomery's assessment. It promises its adherents complete spiritual freedom and authoritative knowledge concerning the true nature of man and the universe (2547:III/2548:99). The church was founded by Lafayette Ronald Hubbard in California in the 1950s as an extension of his earlier non-religious theory of Dianetics (2549). Dianetics is believed to deal with mind and body; Scientology with the human spirit, although they necessarily overlap in places. According to the church, technically "para-Scientology" is that branch of "Scientology" involving past lives, mysticism, the occult, etc. (2551:189). For our purposes, the term "Scientology" is employed in its broadest sense.

Drawing upon ideas from Buddhist and Hindu religious philosophy, science fiction, and Western concepts in psychology and science, L. Ron Hubbard produced a new religion that sees everyone as immortal spirits (thetans) who have forgotten their true identity and became deceived by the very universe they mentally emanated in order to amuse themselves. (This latter view and others are similar to those of est* inventor Werner Erhard, a student of scientology). Scientology claims that it can free the "thetan" to realize its own "godhood" through certain procedures (controversial ones) that heal the mind and free the spirit.

Although the church claims its beliefs are not incompatible with Christian faith, an evaluation of Scientology and major Bible doctrines show that this assessment is incorrect. Scientology teachings are inconsistent with the beliefs of orthodox Christian faith.

Today, Scientology boasts over 700 centers in 65 countries, with seven million followers. And it is one of the wealthiest new religions claiming assets of over one billion dollars. Screen stars and famous individuals such as Tom Cruise, John Travolta, Kirstie Alley, Priscilla Presley, and performer Sonny Bono are only a handful of the Hollywood faithful who actively endorse Scientology. But this new religion also has strong critics, as issues of many popular magazines reveal (e.g., *Reader's Digest*, May 1980, September 1981; and *Time* magazine, May 6, 1991.

## PHILOSOPHY

The basic tenets of Scientology result from an eclectic mixture of Eastern philosophy and Hubbard's personal research into a variety of disciplines, as well as the "data" uncovered from "auditing." Auditing is Scientology's "counseling," an extensive examination of the present or "past lives" of the "preclear" thetan, or initiate. In one of its many definitions, Hubbard has said that Scientology is "the Western anglicized continuance of many earlier forms of wisdom" (2551:177). These include the Vedas, Taoism, Buddhism, Judaism, Gnosticism, early Greek civilization, and the teachings of Jesus, Nietzsche, and Freud. According to Hubbard, "Scientology has accomplished the goal of religion expressed in all Man's written history, the freeing of the soul by wisdom" (2551:180/cf. 2552:3-17).

Scientology divides the mind into two components, the analytic and the reactive, roughly parallel to the conscious, or rational, mind and unconscious, or "irrational," mind. Experience of extreme shock, pain, or unconsciousness causes "engrams," or sensory impressions, to be recorded in the reactive, or unconscious, mind. These mental pictures are the cause of our emotional and physical problems today (2553). They can be dislodged only through Scientology procedures (2554).

While these memory pictures are perfectly recorded, they lie dormant in the brain until restimulated by a similar incident. When restimulated, they cause conditioned, stimulus-response behavior that is counterproductive to a person's well-being. Thus, when the brain sees a situation similar to a past negative experience, even if it is not a threat to survival, it responds as if it were, producing a form of inappropriate and self-defeating behavior. For example, a boy falls out of a tree just as a red car passes by and is knocked unconscious. Later, even as a man, red cars (even red things) may restimulate the episode in various ways and cause irrational reactions. This man may thus refuse to ride in a red car and may even get ill or dizzy when confronted with the possibility.

In this sense, we are all, more or less, conditioned beings, "machines" that simply respond to their "operator" (i.e., the reactive mind). Scientology believes this restimulation is fairly automatic. In other words, we are not free beings; we are slaves of, in Scientology terms, an "aberrated" (reactive) mind. Scientology maintains that through Dianetic and Scientology therapy, we can be directly exposed to our engrams, "erase" them, and become "clear," or get in control of our behavior ("at cause") rather than be at the mercy of a damaged reactive mind ("at effect").

According to Scientology, we have all been accumulating engrams for trillions of years through reincarnation,. Thus, in order to resolve hidden engrams, the initiate must be mentally whisked back to reexperience the damaging events of this life or previous lives. This fits in nicely with each person being a thetan, an immortal spirit who has been so damaged by engrams that he has forgotten he is immortal and even that he is a thetan. Thetans have absolute control over bodies, but, sadly, they think they are bodies (a terrible fate) and hence are bound by the MEST (matter, energy, space, time) universe. Each time a body dies, a thetan must enter another body, but this brings with it all its trillions of years' accumulation of engrams. Thetans thus are no longer free but bound to the material universe (2555). Thus, Scientology claims that it can free the thetan.

## THEOLOGICAL BELIEFS

In light of the religious claims of Scientology, we have chosen to emphasize its theological presuppositions in six fundamental categories: God, Man, creation, salvation, death, and the supernatural.

### God

In the Church of Scientology, the concept of God would appear to be partly panentheistic and perhaps polytheistic. Panentheism refers to the belief that the world and all finite entities are within God but that God is more than the world. When Scientology defines God as "all Theta" (life), it indicates at least partly a belief in panentheism. However, Scientology also seems to grant thetans the status of ontologically real, independent existence. If thetans, who are eternal, are considered to have divine attributes, or at least "infinite creative potential," and if in some sense each thetan is a "god," then a polytheistic classification could also seem appropriate. Interestingly, the official 1965 Australian government inquiry into Scientology observed that the scores of Scientology axioms (certain stated beliefs) undergird a polytheistic rather than a monotheistic theology, and hence they are thus "quite the reverse of Christian belief" (2556).

What the church refers to as "the Supreme Being" is purposely left undefined and not particularly relevant in Scientology theory or practice. It is variously implied to be or referred to as "Nature," "Infinity," "the Eighth Dynamic," "all Theta" (life), and so forth. Usually the individual Scientologist is free to interpret God in whatever manner he wishes (2557).

*Man*

Scientology maintains that, in their true nature, people are not the limited and pitiful body and ego that they mistakenly imagine themselves to be. They are thetans, whose fundamental nature is basically good and divine. They are not morally fallen but simply ignorant of their own perfection. Their only "fall" was into matter, not sin.

How did this fall occur? Apparently, trillions of years ago thetans became bored, so they emanated mental universes to play in, to amuse themselves. Soon, however, they became more and more entranced by their own creation until they were so conditioned by the manifestations of their own thought processes that they lost all awareness of their true identity and spiritual nature (see 2555/2557). In a scholarly analysis, *The Road to Total Freedom: A Sociological Analysis of Scientology*, Roy Wallis describes the process:

> Progressively they became absorbed into the games they were playing, permitting further limitation of their abilities, imposing limitations upon other thetans, forgetting their spiritual nature, and becoming more dependent upon the material universes that they had created. While the MEST universe began as the postulation of thetans it gradually acquired an overwhelming sense of reality. The thetans became so enmeshed in their creation they forgot their origins and true status, lost the ability to mobilize their spiritual capacities, and came to believe they were no more than the bodies they inhabited (2558:104).

In other words, thetans became hypnotized and trapped by MEST. Compounding the entrapment was the accumulation of endless "engrams" throughout trillions of years of existence. The final result was a pitiful creature, indeed—a materially enslaved entity existing as a mere stimulus-response machine. Today, only slavery to the reactive mind and bondage to the MEST universe (i.e., the physical body and environment) are what remain of once-glorious spiritual beings who ruled the heavens.

In an official church publication, *Scientology: A World Religion Emerges in the Space Age*, we find the Scientology concept of man described as follows:

The THETAN is the *individualized* life force, *. . . the person himself, . . .* the identity that is the Being, per se. . . .

The PERSON in Scientology is (and discovers himself to be) a Thetan (spiritual being) of infinite creative potential who acts in, but is not part of, the physical universe. . . .

The Eternal Indestructible Self (Atman) of the Hindu Upanishads early foreshadowed the Scientology concept of the Thetan. . . .

The Thetan is also considered to be the innate source of his own projected universe, which overlaps the created universes of other Thetans in a great community of souls. Thus is formed the world of the senses, in relation to which, like the Hindu "Lila," or "Divine Play," each Thetan plays the Game of Life in concert with its spiritual partners. . . . As a Being descends . . . into Materiality, the manifestations of his communication become heavier and more dense, and his experience of reality deteriorates (2552:21-24).

*Creation*

The universe was not, as the Bible teaches, created by a single Supreme Being *ex nihilo*, thus having a separate existence of its own. The Scientology universe is a subjective, mental emanation, or "projection," of the thetan, having merely an agreed-upon (not actual) reality. Thus, the entire physical universe is a game, a product of thetan ingenuity (apparently designed for escaping boredom) that allegedly emanates from an original thetan consensus to "create" in prehistory (2559). As a product of thetan minds, the physical universe is capable of endless manipulation by an aware or spiritually "enlightened" thetan. Thus, Scientologists may view psychic powers developed through church practices as a confirmation of this teaching. But for a densely ignorant thetan (principally, all non-Scientologists), the universe is a deceptive and deadly spiritual trap. Ignorant thetans are bound by engrams and think they are only physical bodies. As a result, they are weak, impotent creatures enslaved to a material universe that inhibits self-realization of their true nature as an immortal spirit (2559).

In essence, the material creation as we know it is not only an illusion but also a positive evil, a powerfully destructive barrier one must overcome in order to advance spiritually (2560).

## Salvation

The pitiful thetan slavery to MEST, ignorance, and imprisonment in a body remained until L. Ron Hubbard discovered the secret nature of humankind and pioneered a universal plan of salvation. Through Scientology auditing processes, engrams can be neutralized and the thetan made increasingly self-aware, or "enlightened." By various techniques, a practical methodology (a "technology of enlightenment") was developed to enable the initiate to recognize his spiritual existence, to separate from the MEST body, and to begin to exert mental control over the MEST universe. In other words, the initiate can eventually achieve a state of "clear" and then, by progressing through numerous levels of "Operating Thetan," increasingly achieve self-realization. (An "Operating Thetan" is one who is more and more aware, or increasingly "operating," in terms of his true thetan abilities; see notes 2559/2560). Eventually, he can return to his former existence and glory.

## Death

Death for Scientology is sometimes a positive blessing, for it may permit the release of the soul from the prison of the body, and this would mean the evolution of the thetan (soul) into a higher state of awareness. Nevertheless, in another sense, death is an event so appallingly ordinary (indeed, one which each person has passed through trillions of times) that it is, in effect, an irrelevant incident, almost inconsequential in the larger scheme of things (2561).

## The Occult

The employment of psychic powers and out-of-body episodes (these are means by which thetans re-realize their true powers) is indicative of the church's acceptance of the realm of the supernatural. Hubbard's son goes so far as to claim that occultism played a significant role in the development of Scientology. For example, he wrote that "black magic is the inner core of Scientology" (2562). Hubbard himself allegedly confessed that a spirit entity guided him throughout his life (2563:256). And a number of scholarly researchers have verified the occult nature of Scientology (2558:122/2564:582).

## CRITIQUE

In spite of many successful legal attempts by the Church of Scientology to inhibit criticism against it (2565), there remains a sizable literature of material available to the researcher. Particularly helpful are: 1) government investigations and reports; 2) transcripts of innumerable court proceedings (whether Scientology functions as plaintiff or defendant); 3) scholarly review in any number of fields related to Scientology theory (e.g., philosophy, medicine, psychology, sociology, theology, ethics); 4) analysis by the popular press and investigative reporting, in both printed and visual media; 5) the published literature of current and former members (2566).

Scientology and Dianetics are certainly not without testable claims, even though the church alleges that Hubbard has at no time made any claims for them (2567:5). Still, Hubbard believed, among other things, that his philosophy and methodology are 1) superior in mental health expertise, 2) (Dianetics) can be a hundred percent successful and increase one's I.Q., 3) can solve humankind's major problems, and 4) are a rational and proven science, except where they impinge upon the study of the spirit (2568). But before Dianetics had evolved into Scientology, it had been examined and critiqued by many experts who questioned the validity of its basic claims (2569).

This is true for Scientology itself. For example, one of the great legal minds of our century is Oxford-educated Lord Chancellor Haisham. He has twice held the highest office open to lawyers in England, that of Lord Chancellor, as well as being the Minister of Education and Minister of Science and Technology. He comments, "I do not feel [Scientology's] philosophical conceptions [are] adequate to support [its] theories. . . . [T]he factual basis on which they claim to have produced good results on individuals do not seem to me to be fully substantiated" (2570:51).

As to its mental-health claims, the application of Scientology techniques has allegedly harmed some people. Problems can arise from occult activity (cf. 278), Scientology processes, and auditor inexperience (2571). They include hallucinations and irrational behavior, other strange symptoms, severe disorientation, physical sickness, unconsciousness, mental illness, and even suicide (2572). (As the notes will reveal, most of the above hazards were admitted by Hubbard himself, although he maintained they only occurred through misapplication of the "technology" of Scientology.)

Hubbard also claimed that Scientology is a proven science that is rational and utilizes scientific principles. Unfortunately, Hubbard's often subjective or arbitrary methods contradict this assertion and reveal that, scientifically, his research methodology is questionable or unreliable (2573). Even his son claims that for the multimillion bestseller, *Dianetics: The Modern Science of Mental Health,* he did

> no research at all. . . . [W]hat he did, really, was take bits and pieces from other people and put them together in a blender and stir them all up—and out came Dianetics! All the examples in the book—some 200 "real-life experiences"—were just the result of his obsessions with abortions and unconscious states. . . . In fact, the vast majority of those incidents were invented off the top of his head. The rest stem from his own secret life, which was deeply involved in the occult and black magic. That involvement goes back to when he was sixteen (2574:113/cf. 2563:270-71).

Furthermore, researchers who have examined the only "scientific" instrument in Scientology, which is allegedly capable of producing "data" (i.e., the "E-Meter," which is used to "locate" "engrams"), have concluded it is useless as to its claimed abilities. The E-meter is an electric meter which accurately measures variations in the electrical resistance of the human body, like a galvanometer. However, "None of the scientology theories associated with, or claims made for, the E-meter is justified. They are contrary to the expert evidence which the Board heard . . ." (2556:97/2575:63-66/2558:197).

*Ethics*

Scientology maintains a strong position outwardly on ethical issues:

> The practice of Scientology results in a higher level of ethics and integrity . . . (2567:77).

Millions already believe the Ethics of Scientology carry more weight and honesty than the traditional and confused laws of nations (2576:132).

The Church of Scientology International [is] your link to other honest, ethical people (2577:1).

Unfortunately, Scientology does not always live up well to its own ethical confessions because, in part, its ethics seem to be valid only for those it deems worthy of them. For example, critics of the church may be treated as enemies (2578). We should also note that Scientology has its own unique definition for terms. Words used in the previous quotations, such as "ethics" and "integrity," carry not only accepted meanings but also Scientological ones (2579).

*Subjectivism*

This brings us to discuss Scientology's subjective use of terms, by which data is manipulated to conform to the alleged discoveries and truths of Scientology. Perhaps the most fruitful seedbed for this was Hubbard's expertise as a science-fiction writer. Many of the themes in Scientology can also be found in his science-fiction works (2580).

For Hubbard, "life is a game," and this is about the only thing that gives it any real meaning (2581). The various exploits of thetans in the past trillions of years are their *lila* (or sport)—the games they play to keep eternal boredom at bay. Certainly many critics would contend that the adventures of thetans as chronicled in Hubbard's *A History of Man* and *Have You Lived Before This Life?* should be ranked among his best science-fiction work. But there's not much difference between fact and fiction in Scientology. Consider one alleged "past-life" incident of a Scientology counselee, as uncovered by a Scientology auditor using his "E-meter":

> The preclear was on Mars without a body 469,476,600 years ago, creating havoc, destroying a bridge and buildings. The people were called by an alarm to temple. PC went and broke the back pew, and the Temple tower. He wandered in town and saw a doll in a window, and got entrapped [inside the doll] trying to move its limbs. People seized it, beat it up, and threw the doll out of the window (30 ft. drop).

The doll was taken roughly to the Temple, and was zapped by a bishop's gun while the congregation chanted "God is Love." When the people left, the doll, out of control, staggered out and was run over by a large car and a steamroller. It was then taken back to the Bishop, who ordered it to be taken (in a lorry with others) to dig trenches or ditches for 2,000 years. (The whole incident took nearly 2,000,000 years.) Then it was taken and the body was removed and the PC was promised a robot body. The thetan (PC) went up to an implant saucer and was dropped at Planet ZX 432 (2582:63-64).

Hubbard himself confesses that truth is so strange one cannot actually distinguish between science fiction and science fact, and he found this principle useful for rejecting or manipulating the "illusions" of conventional knowledge. For example, Hubbard once noted, "One of the closest pieces of work to a thetan is *Alice in Wonderland.* . . . He can mock up [invent, make] white rabbits and caterpillars and Mad Hatters. He'd find himself right in his element" (2583:6). And, "When you look at man's location in the MEST Universe and what he has or has not been through the picture is just incredibly wild . . . it's just too fantastic for words, so of course, nobody would believe it" (2584:4).

If we recall Hubbard's teaching on the material creation, we remember it is an illusion: "The MEST universe can be established easily to be an illusion . . ." (2585:133). It is not that the universe does not exist; rather, it has no objective, independent reality. It is a frivolous mental game of thetans. Conventional reality simply results from the primordial thetan agreement ("mock-up") and no more (2585:107; cf. pp. 106-08/2551:249). Thus, "objective" reality is simply a temporary subjective manifestation of the mind of thetans.

Such a universe, of course, cannot give true objective knowledge about things, for things that per se have no independent existence of their own are capable of endless manipulations and meanings by an aware thetan. For Hubbard, only an unaberrated thetan (one who by means of Scientology is truly enlightened) knows things as they really are and, apparently, Hubbard was the most enlightened thetan of all. Thus, for many Scientologists, *whatever Hubbard says is true*

*really is true*, no matter how fantastic or disharmonious with currently accepted knowledge (see 2576:28-42/2558:249-50).

The end result is that valid information is rejected from almost every category of conventional knowledge Scientology happens to touch upon that rejects its ideas. Thus, Scientology may reject data in medicine, physics, psychiatry and psychology, logic, historical theology, and so on. Why? Perhaps because at best such disciplines only provide us with the largely uncertain or irrelevant data of an illusory material world and, if they conflict with the truths of Scientology, they are doubtful or harmful by definition (see 2586 for illustrations).

## SCIENTOLOGY AND CHRISTIANITY

As late as 1974 (20 years after the Church of Scientology was founded), at least one book by Hubbard carried the straightforward claim: "Scientology . . . is not a religion" (2587). Nevertheless, it has become a religion, and one in competition with the Christian church.

A survey conducted by the Church of Scientology (the poll involved over 3000 members) determined that the background of Scientologists is predominantly Christian (41 percent Protestant, 26 percent Catholic, 21 percent with no religious affiliation, 7 percent Jewish, 5 percent other). A full 70 percent report that they still considered themselves a practicing member of their Christian faith, which means that almost half of those polled still considered themselves Christian (2567:246-47; cf. 2558:72). That 37 percent had received college degrees, and 80 percent were from the middle class, indicates that Scientology also appeals to an educated class of people.

And yet, with many being recruited from Christian churches, the response of Christianity has been almost nonexistent. Just as the Scientologist who considers himself a Christian does not recognize the inconsistency of that position, the Christian church has not yet recognized the risk Scientology poses to its own fold.

In a rational universe two contrary religions might be false, but both cannot be true. Thus, if the Christian worldview is true (we have shown elsewhere how this may be reasonably established on revelational-empirical grounds using the strict measure of legal criteria; see 798), then that which contradicts it cannot be true.

In the area of theology, several key issues are pondered continually and quite personally. They concern the areas of theology proper (the existence and nature of God), revealed theology (Does God exist for me?), anthropology (Who or what am I?), soteriology (Why am I here?), and thanatology (What happens when I die?).

These questions raise issues about the nature of God, man, salvation, and death. No issues are more fundamental or important. To answer these questions in error will, like a philosophical leaven, spread corruption throughout one's entire worldview. Following we will briefly compare and contrast the Scientology view with the Christian view in these four areas.

*God*

As noted, Scientology is fundamentally panentheistic (2557). This contradicts the biblical teaching that there is only one sovereign and perfect Creator God from all eternity. God is immutable, without beginning or end, exists in three Persons, and is infinitely holy, just, and loving (Genesis 1:1; Isaiah 43:10-11; Acts 5:3-4; Isaiah 61:8; Malachi 3:6; 1 Timothy 2:5; Titus 2:13; 1 John 4:8-10).

Scientology has relatively few comments about Jesus Christ; however, it does not accept the biblical teaching that Jesus Christ was the only incarnation of God and divine Savior of the world. In fact, Jesus was rather ordinary. "Neither Lord Buddha nor Jesus Christ were OTs [Operating Thetans, i.e., enlightened as to their true spiritual nature] according to the evidence. They were just a shade above clear" (2588).

*Man*

Scientology teaches that a person is an immortal spirit, similar to the *atman* in Hinduism. And, as in Hinduism, a person may be considered a deity of sorts, who has forgotten he or she is divine.

The Bible rejects the idea that people are ignorant gods who need only enlightenment,*

or self-realization. People are a creation of God, made in God's image, and their problems do not result from engrams or boredom but from sin and self-centeredness (Romans 3:10-18; Ephesians 2:1-3).

If there is one supporting pillar of Scientology upon which everything rests, it is the thetan concept. If there is no thetan, the practices of Scientology are without justification, for nearly everything of importance in Scientology is predicated upon the existence of thetans as Hubbard defines them.

In the biblical view the one eternal God (Isaiah 43:10-11) created man (body and spirit) as a finite creature (Genesis 2:7) at a specific point in time. Hence it is impossible that divine beings such as Scientology's thetans could exist. Therefore, Scientology's philosophy, techniques, solutions to problems, and final goals are based upon underlying presuppositions that are biblically incorrect. Put simply, if no thetan exists, then most of Scientology is based on error, for "almost the entirety of Scientology consists of discovery and refinements of methods whereby the Thetan can be persuaded to relinquish his self-imposed limitations" (2576:31). And, if no thetan exists, what may a rational inquirer to Scientology conclude?

*Salvation*

Salvation in Scientology takes a thetan from personal ignorance and bondage to matter into Gnostic enlightenment and freedom from the MEST body and universe. One is progressively "saved" from engrams by *knowledge* (Scientology beliefs) through good works (Scientology auditing and practice) to arrive at the highest level of "operating thetan." (By the way, the cost of this ongoing sojourn easily reaches tens or hundreds of thousands of dollars.)

The Bible, on the other hand, teaches that salvation is a free gift. One is redeemed from sin by God's grace through faith in Jesus Christ (Ephesians 2:8-9; John 6:47; Hebrews 11:1; 1 John 2:2). Scientology, however, clearly rejects the atonement of Jesus Christ. Scientology alleges that to believe in and trust in Christ's atonement on the cross for forgiveness of sins is to "keep man in chains."

In Hubbard's *Volunteer Minister's Handbook*, we read, "We have proven conclusively that man is basically good—a fact which flies in the teeth of old religious beliefs that man is basically evil.... Man is basically good but he could not attain expression of this until now. Nobody but the individual could die for his own sins—to arrange things otherwise was to keep man in chains" (2589:348-49). To the contrary, the Scripture teaches of Jesus Christ, "He is the atoning sacrifice for our sins, and not only for ours but also for the sins of the whole world" (1 John 2:2). Jesus Himself taught, "For God so loved the world that he gave his one and only Son, that whoever believes in him shall not perish but have eternal life" (John 3:16). And, "just as the Son of Man did not come to be served, but to serve, and to give his life as a ransom for many" (Matthew 20:28).

### Death

Scientology claims that death is endlessly repeatable through reincarnation and hence almost inconsequential, although at least potentially beneficial in that one is released from the prison of the body.

Biblically, death is a one-time event that carries either the most sublime of blessings (eternal heaven) or the most horrible of consequences (eternal hell). Death leads to an irreversible fate for both the saved and the lost. People have one lifetime only to make their peace with God (Hebrews 9:27; Matthew 25:46; Luke 16:19-31; Revelation 20:10-15).

To summarize, Scientology does not conform in basic worldview or particular theological teachings to Judeo-Christian revelation in any sense. Indeed, examined as a whole, it fundamentally rejects Christian faith. For example, Hubbard rejects Christ's deity and mission as figments of an "unenlightened" mind. Therefore Hubbard's philosophy "is not interested in saving man, but it can do much to prevent him from *being* 'saved' " (2590:105; cf. p. 408).

We may observe that Scientology does entertain a noble goal in attempting to improve the world and man's lot within it, whether materially or spiritually. Many practitioners are dedicated and selfless in seeking such ends. Nevertheless, each Scientologist must weigh the scales of his own conscience to determine the best manner in which to achieve such goals. If man is not a thetan but a fallen being in need of redemption, what will have been the fruit of a lifetime of work for Scientology? It would be wise for those Scientologists with a Christian background (indeed, for all Scientologists), to listen afresh to the words of Jesus:

For what will a man be profited, if he gains the whole world, and forfeits his soul? Or what will a man give in exchange for his soul? (Matthew 16:26 NASB).

This is eternal life, that they may know Thee, the only true God, and Jesus Christ whom Thou hast sent (John 17:3 NASB).

531

# SHAMANISM

- Info at a Glance
- Introduction and Influence
- Shamanism in Contemporary Medicine
- Characteristics
- Dangers and Degradations
  - Amorality
  - Sexual Immorality
  - Drug Use
  - Death Magic and Other Forms of Murder
  - Spiritual Blackmail
  - Psychopathology
  - Demonism and Health

## INFO AT A GLANCE

**Description.** Shamanism is an occult path claiming contact with supernatural entities for a variety of religious or, today, even secular purposes. *Traditional* shamanism is where the shaman functions as healer, spiritual leader, and mediator between the spirits and people. Shamanistic *psychotherapy*, a novel form of modern fringe psychology, is where shamanistic techniques are employed allegedly to produce "psychospiritual integration," explore the unconscious, contact one's "higher self," and so on. Shamanistic *medicine* includes the application of animistic and various ancient witchcraft techniques to health care. It may involve either shamanism itself as a means to health and enlightenment* (shaman initiation and following the shaman's "life path"), or the varied use of specific shamanistic

techniques in conjunction with a particular health program (e.g., visualization,* altered states of consciousness,* dream work,* or the use of "power animals," which are spirits that appear in the form of animals, birds, or other creatures in order to instruct the shaman).

**Founder.** Unknown; the practice is found in almost all cultures throughout history. In the United States, the Native American religious tradition is representative.

**How does it claim to work?** Modern shamanism claims its methods will bring personal power, spiritual enlightenment, greater harmony with nature, psychological insight, and physical healing.

**Scientific evaluation.** Because of its occult nature, science has little to conclude concerning shamanistic claims. However, the methods and occult powers of shamans are studied parapsychologically, as is true for the spiritual cousins of shamans such as psychic surgeons, mediums, channelers,* and Eastern gurus.*

**Examples of occult potential.** Spiritism, spirit possession, kundalini arousal, psychic healing, and various occult practices (see Yoga, Channeling, Enlightenment, Eastern Gurus, Meditation).

**Major problems.** Shamanism leads to spirit possession and other forms of occult bondage. For example, in shamanistic healing the acquiring of true health demands both the practitioner and patient to be "energized" by his or her "power animal," or spirit guide. Possession by one or more spirits for empowerment, enlightenment, personal health maintenance, and healing abilities is fundamental.

**Biblical/Christian evaluation.** Shamanistic practices involve pagan methods and beliefs that are forbidden (Exodus 20:3-4; Deuteronomy 18:9-12).

**Potential dangers.** Temporary insanity, demon possession, and tremendous physical suffering are some of the effects. Those treated with shamanistic techniques or methods may become converted to the occult.

*Note:* It should be said that using shamanistic techniques and methods in any given program (e.g., visualization,* altered states of consciousness,* sensory manipulation, dream work)* is not equivalent to following the shamanistic path. Shamanistic methods can be used independently in a variety of ways; they may or may not introduce one to pursuing the path of the shaman. Shamanism also bears a significant relationship to modern cultism. In the last generation the revival of new American cults and religions illustrates a number of shamanistic motifs.

## INTRODUCTION AND INFLUENCE

The term "shaman" is apparently a derivative of the vedic *sram*, meaning "to heat oneself or practice austerities."

Shamanism is, in some form, indigenous to nearly all cultures. However, in technologically advanced Western nations, the influence of Christian belief, science, and rationalism has suppressed or muted its development, at least until recently. Today, shamanism is making a significant resurgence.

*Reader's Digest* says of shamanistic healing methods that "these alternate systems merit our attention," and yet it realizes that the purpose of the shaman is to "mediate between the ordinary world and the world of the spirits" (1456:31). A number of periodicals (e.g., *Shaman's Drum*) and organizations (e.g., "Shaman Pharmaceuti-

cals" in California) now promote shamanism in sundry ways. For example, *Shaman's Drum* combines accounts of contemporary experiential and experimental shamanism and related practices (e.g., voodoo) as well as historic anthropological reports, and is a clearinghouse of sorts for dozens of shamanistically oriented enterprises.

Several organizations seek to integrate shamanism with contemporary American life. These include Shamanic Journey Counseling in Oakland, California; the Center for Shamanistic Studies in Norwalk, Connecticut; the Church of Loving Hands in Eureka, California; Four Winds Circle in Mill Valley, California; Hawaiian Shaman Training in Santa Monica, California; and Transformative Arts Institute in Albany, California.

In addition, literally thousands of "vision quests"—shamanic wilderness retreats conducted by Native Americans—have introduced shamanistic concepts and practices to untold numbers of teens and adults. "The most famous method of acquiring a guardian spirit is the vision quest or vigil conducted in a solitary wilderness location, as among the Plains tribes of North America" (142:81).

Throughout the country, the renewed interest in Native American cultural and religious life is introducing aspects of shamanism to thousands of adults, and even to children. (Over 500 federally recognized Native American communities now exist.) One example is the "As the Indians Lived" day camps that are held in various places to teach children ages 6-15 the traditions and culture of Native Americans. Such camps are usually taught by Indians or sometimes even by shamans themselves. One camp in Chattanooga, Tennessee, was led by "Flaming Warrior" (Michael Ziegler) of the Lakota Sioux Nation.

Despite its primitive, animistic nature, the direct and indirect influence of shamanism is significant in many areas of modern American culture (570). Veteran spiritual counterfeits researcher Brooks Alexander comments, "A variety of shamanistic forms and images pervades contemporary art, literature and music at all levels,"—especially rock music (2490:28).

Dr. Robert S. Ellwood of the University of Southern California is a well-known authority on the resurgence of new religions and cults in America. He points out there are "striking parallels" between modern cults and shamanism and suggests that the modern revival of scores of new cults "could almost be called a modern resurgence of shamanism" (561:12). Many of the founders of these new religions experienced a type of shaman initiation in their quest for the occult empowerment, which granted them the spiritual authority and charisma necessary to institute and lead the new religion. Examples include L. Ron Hubbard, founder of Scientology; Rudolph Steiner, founder of anthroposophy; Werner Erhard, founder of est/The Forum*; Rajneesh; Sri Aurobindo; Swami Muktananda; and many or perhaps most other Eastern gurus (especially in Tantrism, Hindu, or Buddhist). Our detailed research into some two dozen Eastern gurus repeatedly uncovered shamanistic motifs (610).

Shamanistic techniques are also being incorporated into segments of modern psychotherapy (562/860/91:200/586:197-99/846:1-26). Some people have suggested that shamanism has "a crucial role to play in preventive psychiatry" (586:192). Even the National Institute of Mental Health and other U.S. government agencies occasionally award grants "to finance the training" of shamans (e.g., 91:200). In *Inner Work*, Jungian analyst Robert Johnson, a disciple of Sri Aurobindo, suggests the importance of shamanism for psychological self-insight:

> We have begun to rediscover [shamanistic] ritual as a natural human tool for connecting to our inner selves, focusing and refining our religious insights, and constellating psychological energy. . . . Jung anticipated this new awareness decades ago when he demonstrated that ritual and ceremony are important avenues to the unconscious. . . . Without thinking about it in psychological terms, ancient and primitive cultures have always understood instinctively that ritual had a true function in their psychic lives. They understood ritual as a set of formal acts that brought them into immediate contact with the gods (2472:101,103).

Unfortunately, shamanism is also influencing some segments of the church (570). Many Native American shamans were formerly active in Protestant or Catholic churches. After conversion to their birth religion, they now seek to "enlighten" the churches. Other shamans have visions of "Jesus" and believe that their ministry is to be directed toward Christians. Still others combine elements of Christianity with shamanism (2488). To varying degrees, some ministers, theologians, and psychologists of a Christian persuasion variously endorse shamanism. In *The Christian and the Supernatural*, Morton Kelsey, a Jungian analyst and Episcopal priest associated with the charismatic movement, argues that Jesus and His true disciples were either shamans or exercised the power of shamans (342:16-17, 69,92-95). Jungian therapist and Christian author John A. Sanford also argues that shamanistic motifs were common among the Old Testament prophets and that Jesus was a shaman. Sanford believes shamanism is a legitimate form of spiritual healing (779:75,80-81; see Dream Work).

Doran C. McCarty is Professor of Ministry at Golden Gate Baptist Theologian Seminary in Mill Valley, California. In his convocation address to the seminarians titled "The Making of the New Shaman," he spoke of the need for Christian ministers to adopt aspects of a more refined shamanism, and that this shamanism should become "a model for Christian ministry." Indeed, "The New Testament picture of Jesus was that of a shaman," and, "Seminaries now face the task of creating 'the new shaman,'" who is to become "the minister of Jesus Christ" (2489:5-6,25-28)!

Although many people are unaware of the fact, many practices of the New Age Movement and of New Age medicine* are shamanistic in nature. Shamanism, both traditional and modern, involves such practices as:

- meditation* and visualization*
- deliberately cultivating altered states of consciousness,* trance, and out-of-body experiences
- contact with the spirit world (see Channeling)
- spirit-possession
- psychic-spiritistic healing
- dream work*

- crystal work*
- certain aspects of psychotherapy
- occult ritual
- sensory stimulation or deprivation
- body work methods
- hypnosis* (refs. 142/585/586/583).

In addition, shamanism has influenced, or is part of a significant number of, religious traditions which are, to degrees, experiencing revival in America. This includes various forms of witchcraft, voodoo, Tibetan Buddhism, and Hindu Tantrism (2487). Although shamanism, Eastern religion, and witchcraft are distinct categories, there is nevertheless a strong correlation between them—a fact admitted to by anthropologists, shamans, witches, and gurus. Consider that ancient pagan nature worship and witchcraft practices "were essentially shamanistic" (cf. 586:221). "Anthropologists with cross-cultural information on shamanistic health practices have concluded the wise women (witches) were acting within the long-standing pagan tradition of European tribes whose practices were essentially shamanistic" (143:61). And, "The ancient shamanic traditions of the West African peoples are the source of many of the practices and beliefs of Lucumi, Santaria, Condumble, Umbanada, Haitian Voodoo, and other New World spiritist traditions" (2479). The relationship between witchcraft on the one hand and yoga* and other Eastern practices on the other is noted by Mircea Eliade in his "Observations on European Witchcraft":

As a matter of fact, all the features associated with European witches are—with the exception of Satan and the Sabbath—claimed also by Indo-Tibetan yogis and magicians. They too are supposed to fly through the air, render themselves invisible, kill at a distance, master demons and ghosts, and so on. Moreover, some of these eccentric Indian sectarians boast that they break all the religious taboos and social rules: that they practice human sacrifice, cannibalism, and all manner of orgies, including incestuous intercourse, and that they eat excrement, nauseating animals, and devour human corpses. In other words, they proudly claim all the crimes

and horrible ceremonies cited *ad nauseam* in the western European witch trials (564:71).

If much witchcraft practice is "essentially" shamanistic, then it should not surprise us that the practice of many Eastern yogis and gurus—who claim "all the features associated with European witches"—would bear marked resemblance to shamanistic practices as well. There is a closer relationship between Eastern gurus,* psychic surgeons, black magicians, witches, and shamans than many people realize. For example, the spirit possession, temporary insanity, kundalini arousal, bizarre animal sounds and grunts, and occult transfer of energy found among magicians, voodooists and Hindu and Buddhist gurus are all found among the shamans as well. In the latter instance, "[the shaman] Matsuwa... touched his prayer feathers to objects that had become infused with life energy force *(kupuri)* and transferred the precious substance to those who were in need of it, a transmission similar to the communication of shakti between Hindu guru and disciple" (585:21; cf. 2474:42, Eastern Gurus, Meditation). Harner points out that in dancing or "exercising" their guardian spirits (to supposedly keep them happy) shamans are transformed into the animal, making its own movements and noises: "Shamans, in dancing their guardian animal spirits, commonly not only make the movements of the power animals but also the sounds. In Siberia, native North and South America and elsewhere, shamans make bird calls and the cries, growls, and other sounds of their animal powers when experiencing their transformations" (142:80).

Shamanism is not only pervasive in pagan religion, it is increasingly found even in scientific circles. Today there are literally hundreds and possibly thousands of what can be termed "shaman scientists"—men and women in a variety of scientific disciplines who are employing shamanism or shamanistic methods as forms of personal transformation or enlightenment* and incorporating shamanistic techniques into their professions. The eminent scientist John Lilly, famous for his research with dolphins, is one of many illustrations (836; cf. 91:198-201/846:1-26;

see Altered States of Consciousness). A number of universities have practicing shamans as professors, such as Robert Lake with Humboldt State University, Dr. Albert Villoldo of San Francisco State University, and Dr. Michael Harner at New York's New School for Social Research. Increasingly today, anthropologists and anthropology professors are turning to shamanism, and in the process converting some of their students to it (2473). Anthropologist Dr. William S. Lyon, a shaman apprentice who works closely with the well-known shaman Wallace Black Elk, has "a particular interest in the incorporation of Native American values into contemporary educational systems" (2478; cf. New Age Education).

In addition, converts to shamanism usually become ardent promoters of spiritism in the national culture. Examples include Laeh Garfield, coauthor of *Companions in Spirit: A Guide to Working with Your Spirit Helpers*, and psychologist Albert Villoldo, coauthor of *Realms of Healing* and *Healing States*, a text about shaman healing. Well-known shamans like Carlos Castaneda, Rolling Thunder, Sun Bear, and shamaness-voodooist (Yoruba Lucumi) Luisah Teish, author of the spirit-written *Jambalaya: A Natural Woman's Book of Personal Charms and Practical Rituals* (2474:43, are often speakers or lecturers at universities and colleges around the country (2475:20/2476:40).

In the field of modern literature (and cinema; 2485), we also discover the impact of shamanism. Hyemeyohsts Storm's popular *Seven Arrows* has allegedly "done more than most to introduce shamanic techniques in a way that is entertaining, responsible, clear and usable in contemporary life" (426:162).

The many books of influential American shamans such as Carlos Castaneda and Lynn Andrews have remained on national bestseller lists for many months at a time (563). Castaneda's own journey into shamanism began when he was an anthropology student. His subsequent tutelage by a Mexican sorcerer named Don Juan is a story known to millions. Proof of his popularity can be seen in the fact that his books have been read by well over ten million people. Among his books are The *Teachings of Don Juan:*

*A Yaqui Way of Knowledge; Journey to Ixtlan; Tales of Power; A Separate Reality; The Eagle's Gift; The Fire Within; The Second Ring of Power; A Way of Dreaming* (see Dream Work for brief comments).

Castaneda is not alone. A minority of anthropologists and other scientific professionals, who initially sought only to study shamanic culture academically, have been converted to shamanism. For example, Mike Plotkin was a botanist who went to study plants in the Amazon. In *Tales of a Shaman's Apprentice*, he tells how he became enthralled with shamanism as a result of the shaman's "expertise" with the medicinal properties of certain plants and, as a result, "logically" converted to shamanism.

Lynn Andrews is one of the feminine counterparts to Carlos Castaneda. She has chronicled her own modern shamanistic journeys with Native Americans. Like anthropologist Castaneda, it began innocently enough: She was a simple art dealer looking for a sacred Indian marriage basket. However, that innocent search led her deeper and deeper into shamanism until today she is a leading U.S. recruiter, along with Michael Harner (*The Way of the Shaman*), Taisha Abelar (*The Sorcerer's Crossing*), Castaneda, and others.

Andrews is recasting the sorcery of Native American shamanism specifically for modern American consumption, especially feminism, and characteristically doing it under "orders" from her spirit guides. In correlating a radical feminist spirituality, already saturated with witchcraft and neopaganism, to shamanistic motifs and power, her place as a leader within the American feminist tradition seems assured. She states that her books "stress the ancient [occult] powers of woman" (842:IX). Several of her books have also achieved sustained recognition on *The New York Times* bestseller list (*Jaguar Woman, Medicine Woman, Star Woman, Flight of the Seventh Moon*).

And the connection to radical feminism and shamanism is noted by many others as well. Shamaness Vicki Noble is described as "a healer working with snake power for the healing and empowerment of women" (shades of the Garden incident?). She states, "The current interest in and attraction to shamanism runs parallel to the emergence of a feminist spirituality" (2483:20).

Then there are other indicators of the influence of shamanism. A number of journals, such as *Shaman's Drum: The Journal of Experiential Shamanism*, have sprung up and are gaining a respectable following. This is somewhat surprising because articles in these journals often reveal the truly dangerous nature of shamanistic practices (736). Also, many states around the country offer "workshops" on shamanism for a variety of purposes, especially to teach people how to contact their spirit helpers (737/571:27).

## SHAMANISM IN
## CONTEMPORARY MEDICINE

The influence of shamanism in New Age medicine* is significant. As leading American shaman Michael Harner says, "The burgeoning field of holistic medicine shows a tremendous amount of experimentation involving the reinvention of many techniques long practiced in shamanism, such as visualization, altered states of consciousness, aspects of psychoanalysis, hypnotherapy, meditation" (142:175).

Shamanistic medicine per se may involve either a traditional approach, which is entirely occult and opposed to the scientific principles of modern health care, or it may involve a blending of the techniques of ancient shamanism with modern science and medicine. In the former, Rolling Thunder observes it is *always* true that "the healing comes from the spirit world" (2476:43). Concerning the latter, Harner, who has personally trained many orthodox physicians to accept shamanistic methods into their practice, comments:

In fact, in some hospitals . . . visits by native healers are being increasingly encouraged as the Western medical staff becomes more aware of the benefits produced and there is no conflict between shamanic practice and modern medical treatment. Every North or South American Indian shaman I have ever asked about this matter has agreed there is no competition whatsoever. Jivaro shamans [into which Harner was initiated] are perfectly willing to have their patients go to see a missionary doctor, for example. . . . One day, and

I hope it will be soon, a modern version of the shaman will work side-by-side with orthodox Western physicians. In fact, this is already starting to take place (142:130,176-77).

One example of the incorporation of shamanistic techniques into modern medical health care can be found in O. Carl Simonton, Stephanie Matthews-Simonton, and James Creighton's *Getting Well Again: A Step by Step Self Help Guide to Overcoming Cancer for Patients and Their Families* (428). This book not only incorporates several shamanistic techniques, it also encourages patients to contact their own "inner guide" or "power animal" (see New Age Inner Work for examples).

Another illustration is the book by psychologist Dr. Alberto Villoldo and noted parapsychologist Dr. Stanley Krippner, *Healing States: A Journey into the World of Spiritual Healing and Shamanism* (91). They propose the adoption of a shamanistic worldview, the acceptance of shamanistic practice, and the integration of shamanism and modern medicine (91:147-48). They point out that worldwide only 15 percent to 20 percent of all people are treated allopathically, and that for over a decade the World Health Organization has given its blessing to shamanistic and other pagan systems of medicine (91:187). Indeed, in the United States, the AMA has followed the trend. "In 1980 the American Medical Association revised its code of ethics and gave physicians permission to consult with, take referrals from, and make referrals to practitioners without orthodox medical training. This move opened the way for physicians to initiate some degree of cooperation with shamans, herbalists, spiritists, homeopaths, and other non-allopathic practitioners" (91:188).

Not surprisingly, then, shamanistic techniques are now increasingly used at modern medical health centers. Jeanne Achterberg is associate professor and director of research and rehabilitation science at the University of Texas Health Science Center in Dallas. Her text *Imagery in Healing: Shamanism and Modern Medicine* reveals how easy it is for modern medical practitioners to incorporate shamanistic techniques like altered states of consciousness* and visualization* into their health-care delivery. But however else she conceptualizes it, she concedes that the essence of shamanism is spiritism:

The focus of the shamanic journeying is on obtaining power or knowledge. . . .

. . . The shaman is identified as one who has guardian spirits (also sometimes called power animals, helping spirits, tutelaries, totems, or fetishes), from whom power and knowledge is gained. . . .

The shaman, then, is defined both by practices and intent: Shamanic practice involves the ability to move in and out of a special state of consciousness, a notion of a guardian spirit complex and has the purpose of helping others (143:13).

Many Americans think shamanistic health practices are "superior" to conventional treatment because shamanism supposedly not only "cures" health problems but "properly" aligns them with the environment and universe. In other words, like ayurveda (Hindu medicine) and other pagan methods, shamanism at its heart is much more than merely a medical practice; it is a spiritual quest that seeks to answer fundamental questions about man's place and purpose in the world. Because these are questions that gnaw deeply at the soul of modern man, shamanism is attractive.

Introducing shamanism into modern medicine is ironic because of its essentially antiscientific nature, such as its occultism and irrationalism. The following accounts are typical of the bizarre world of shamanistic "healing" procedures. (Readers may find some of the following quite offensive.) Shamans will do such strange things as "placing spirits" in their mouth and sucking out the "poison" from the body, which is believed to symbolically represent the person's illness. Or they may rub a patient's body with guinea pigs or gerbils believing that a transfer of the illness takes place into the hapless creature. Here is an illustration from the personal experience of Michael Harner (who, remember, is a chairman at the New York Academy of Sciences):

If the patient has a harmful power intrusion [causing the illness], the shaman suddenly [occultly] sees one of the following: voracious or dangerous insects, fanged serpents, or other reptiles and fish with visible fangs or teeth. He immediately stops the [occult] journey [that he has been traveling in his mind or the spirit world] to deal with these intrusive powers. . . . [T]he sight of one of these creatures . . . involves a complete certainty by the shaman that it is eating away or destroying a portion of the patient's body. At that moment, one may experience an incredible revulsion and an awareness that the insect or other creature is evil and the enemy of the shaman as well as of the patient. . . . The shaman must locate the harmful, intrusive powers within the patient. To this end he uses a divinatory technique. In the absence of taking [the drug] ayahuasca to [clairvoyantly] see into the patient, the shaman may use a technique that is something like employing a divining rod. . . . By passing his hand a few inches above the body slowly back and forth, an experienced shaman gets a definite sensation in his hand when it is over the place where the intrusive power lies. Another technique is to pass a feather over the patient to pick up any vibration.

When the shaman senses a particular location, he calls the two spirit helpers, either silently or in song, as he shakes his rattle steadily over the patient. When he clearly sees the helpers approaching in the darkness, with his eyes still closed he wills them into his mouth. There they will capture and absorb the power intrusion as he sucks it out of the patient. When he definitely sees the two in his mouth, he wills all his other spirit helpers to assist him in the sucking. Now he is ready to begin the work of abstraction.

At the location in the patient's body where he has sensed the harmful intrusion, the shaman sucks with all his might. . . . *The shaman has to be very careful in this process not to permit the voracious creature he saw from passing through his mouth and throat into his stomach.* . . . The shaman repeatedly sucks and "dry-vomits" as many times as necessary. It is important not to swallow the sucked-out power, but to expel it after each sucking into the container on the floor or ground. This is done with powerful, sometimes involuntary, violent wretching that gives the shaman a real sense of cleansing, of being emptied of the emotionally disgusting power that he has extracted. As he removes the power intrusion from the patient, the shaman may feel engulfed in waves of extracted power that almost stun him and cause his body to tremble. . . . He keeps up such cycles of sucking until finally, in passing his hand back and forth above the patient, he no longer feels any localized emanations of heat, energy, or vibration.... [T]hen he stops the sucking process.... Finally, when he is convinced that the patient is spiritually clean, he shakes his rattle around the patient's body in a circular fashion four times to provide a definition of the unity of the cleansed area, demarcating its boundaries for the spiritual world [e.g., so that no more evil spirits can enter] (154:151-57).

That such a spectacle can, to observers, be odd indeed is seen from the following recollection of a shaman-initiate present at a "healing" ceremony conducted by Peruvian shaman Don Edwardo Calderon: "The apparent suffering of my dear friend, whose guts were being sucked and puked out, was hard to reconcile with the serene sense of love and compassion seeming to envelop me. I had never participated in a ceremony where the medicine nauseated so many, yet there was an orderliness about it that defies description. At one point that night the only sounds I could hear were various members of the [shaman] circle clearing their throats, belching or vomiting—an oddly comforting euphony in the desert darkness" (2481:26).

One of the most famous North American Indian shamans who used the sucking method was the late Mormon leader Essie Parrish, who healed Indian and non-Indian patients. Because of a vision from her spirit guides that she should reveal her shaman methods to non-Indians in order to "benefit" them as well, she cooperated in making the Sucking Doctor film (142:161). In the Kalahari !Kung Tribe, the shaman "pulls out the sickness with eerie, earth-shattering screams and howls that show the pain and difficulty of his healing." This involves the shaman in several hours of exquisite torment (142:173).

This kind of irrational "healing" attempts to transfer the patient's illness in other ways as well. In the case of Don Calderon:

The act of diagnosis is not separated from the act of healing, as they are in Western allopathic medicine. They occur together at the same time.... For example, when the guinea pig used in diagnosing is rubbed over the areas of the body associated with the spiritual energy

centers, it may manifest physical symptoms correlating to the problem of the person [denoting the manifestation or transference of illness].... [T]he guinea pig makes externally apparent what may be invisible to the person experiencing it (2481:26).

Finally, if oral spirits, fanged serpents, sucking out energies, vomiting diseases, and guinea pig transfers aren't strange enough, consider the process of "restoring" a power animal into a person who, for various reasons, has lost it and has become "sick" as a result. The shaman must descend into the "lower world" to capture the spirit and return with it clasped in his hands. As Harner states, he proceeds to "blow" the spirit back into the person's body through the chest and head. "Immediately place your cupped hands containing the guardian spirit on your companion's breastbone, and blow with all your strength through your cupped hands to send it into the chest of your partner.... Forcefully blow again to send any residual power into the head" (142:104,108). Now the shaman must assist the client to "dance his animal" in order to make the spirit feel welcome. This gives "it the reward of experiencing its movement in material form." The client is instructed to dance with his animal regularly so that it will remain content and stay within him (142:108).

What practices such as these have to do with scientific medicine is not clear, to say the least! Neither is this explained by its shaman promoters or persons in the AMA who endorse a degree of cooporation with shamans. Unfortunately, however, many modern scientists and physicians who incorporate aspects of shamanism in their practices usually redefine its spiritistic realities in scientific or psychological terms, thereby masking the occult methods promoted. Dr. Achterberg naturalizes much of shamanism into supposedly universal laws that function in accordance with psychodynamics, such as visualization* (cf. 142:16,71-77,107,210-11). The result is that many people are unaware that they are being treated with shamanic techniques.

Achterberg, who also codirects the Professional School of Biofeedback in Dallas, shows how the use of biofeedback can be related to shamanism: "Biofeedback involves healing in the imaginary realms and fits well within the rubric of proverbial healing using the imagination. It contains aspects of shamanism: Rituals are conducted, the subject goes into an altered state of consciousness, takes an imaginary journey, and enters into a territory where healing information is available" (143:100).

Other more direct associations between shamanism and medicine can be seen in dream work,* visualization,* and meditation.* For example, the therapeutic use of dream work illustrates one manner by which shamanistic methods are being incorporated into American culture. Dream work is a component of New Age medicine,* much modern psychotherapy, and also important in shamanism, as standard texts and periodicals reveal. Numerous modern books on dream work, including some Christian books, are also ultimately based on shamanistic techniques and goals. The pagan Senoi dream methods are an example (739). These shamanistic connections are one reason so many modern texts on dream work utilize altered states of consciousness* and lead to spirit contact. It is also significant that within the shamanistic tradition, visualization* and the directed use of the imagination may lead to spirit contact and even possession. In other words, spontaneous spirit contact results from what appears to be an entirely neutral technique (143:98; see Dreamwork, Visualization, New Age Inner Work, and Intuition).

To summarize, hundreds if not thousands of health-care practitioners are experimenting with shamanistic techniques. Some are even using them on their patients without patients' knowledge. Shamanism is also being camouflaged by a "scientific" reclassification of its characteristics, with even the spirits being redefined into neutral psychological categories (see 586:192). That old adage "let the buyer beware" is quite relevant here.

Space does not permit detailing the full influence of shamanism in modern American life. For further information, popular books such as Dave Hunt's *America, The Sorcerer's New Apprentice: The Rise of New Age Shamanism* may be consulted (570). What concerns us more is the innocence with which thousands of people are being

drawn into shamanism and the consequences this will bring them to personally.

In the following pages we will examine the characteristics, nature, and dangers of this ancient but increasingly influential practice.

## CHARACTERISTICS

First of all, what exactly is a shaman? A shaman is a religious leader who usually functions in an animistic culture to contact the spirit world in order to be empowered by it. He is expected to protect the tribe, cure illness, predict the future (divination*), and offer practical advice. Initially, certain occult rituals are prescribed for the shaman initiate, which culminate in spirit possession and the resulting empowerment for whatever tasks may be at hand.

Throughout the world, shamanistic practices and experiences are highly uniform. In North and South America, Australia, Africa, and Asia, the shaman functions in a similar fashion, using the same techniques, achieving the same results. Anthropologists have long recognized this "remarkable" worldwide consistency of shamanism.

Michael Harner received his Ph.D. in anthropology from the University of California, Berkeley and has been a visiting professor at Columbia, Berkeley, and Yale. He is described as "an authentic white shaman" and teaches anthropology courses in the graduate faculty of the New School for Social Research in New York. Founder of the Center for Shamanistic Studies and currently chairman of the anthropology section of the prestigious New York Academy of Sciences, Harner observes, "One of the remarkable things about shamanic assumptions and methods is that they are very similar in widely separated and remote parts of the planet.... [O]ne anthropologist notes: "Wherever shamanism is still encountered today, whether in Asia, Australia, Africa, or North and South America, the shaman functions fundamentally in much the same way and with similar techniques ..." (142:52)

Following are some common characteristics or features of shamanism.

- The shaman works in darkness.

- The shaman must enter a trance state in order to "control" the spirit world and function effectively. The shaman employs specific methods for entering this trance state, or altered state of consciousness,* which is necessary to contact the spirits. Two of the more common methods are ritual dancing with drum music or ingesting hallucinogenic drugs, although visualization,* self-hypnosis,* dream work,* and other methods will also suffice (2474:42/2486:38-39,49).

- The shaman employs "spirit flight" or out-of-the-body travels, into the spirit world, the "upper," "lower," and other occult realms. He enters these worlds as part of his initiation and regular occult work.

- The shaman is equally proficient in the practice of "good" or evil, e.g., "healing" or cursing work ("white" or black magic; 583:184).

- The power the shaman claims to use is either that given by the spirits themselves, or a force conceptually differentiated from the spirits but which is indistinguishable from them. And either may be said to be spiritistic manipulations of energy. Notable similarities exist between the power the shaman uses and that of many New Age energy concepts, such as *chi, mana, kundalini* (see Yoga), *kupuri* (585:21), and *prana.* "*Mana* represents a supernatural impersonal power, also present in today's so-called primitive religions; the *manitou* of the Algonquins, *wakonda* of the Sioux, *orenda* of the Iroquois—which could be appealed to for good or ill. The shaman or medicine man, by virtue of his special gifts and acquaintance with the supernatural world, was able to harness this force" (948:3; cf. 583:475; cf. New Age Medicine).

- It is essential for the shaman to contact one or more (sometimes dozens or hundreds) spirit guides. These are often viewed as nature spirits of various types, such as the spirits of plants, animals, or inanimate objects. "Spirit helpers" related to plants are often used in "healing" and are distinguished from the more powerful "guardian spirits." The latter are often a personal "power animal," from which the shaman derives his psychic abilities, spiritual assistance, and "protection" from evil forces. Basically, the power animal becomes the shaman's alter ego (142:54).

- Shamans acknowledge that spirit possession supplies their magical powers. In other words, apart from the spirits, shamans are impotent. As Harner observes, "Whatever it is called, it is the fundamental source of power for the shaman's functioning . . . Without a guardian spirit, it is impossible to be a shaman, for the shaman must have this strong basic power source . . ." (142:54). In his impressive study and standard work on the subject, *Shamanism,* no less an authority than comparative religions expert Mircea Eliade points out, "All categories of shamans have their helping and tutelary spirits . . ." (583:91). Anthropologist I. M. Lewis says the shaman is one who "permanently incarnates these spirits" into his own body, and thus "the shaman's body is a 'placing' or receptacle, for the spirits" (586:51).

- The shaman experiences temporary or extended periods of mental illness similar to psychosis and schizophrenia; extended periods of acute physical suffering and torture are also common. I. M. Lewis is professor of anthropology at the London School of Economics and author of *Ecstatic Religion: An Anthropological Study of Spirit Possession and Shamanism.* He observes that, in all cases studied, those experiences constituting shaman initiation "are certainly viewed as dangerous, even terrifying, experiences or illnesses. Experience of [mental] disorder in some form is thus an essential feature in the recruitment of shamans" (586:187).

How do shamans enter their strange vocation? As Eliade points out (in common with other forms of the occult), the most powerful shamans are produced either by heredity or election. The vocation is passed from generation to generation, creating a shamanic lineage from parents to children or, as we will see, the spirits personally choose the shaman such as during a traditional vision quest. "In Central and Northeast Asia the chief methods of recruiting shamans are: (1) heredity transmission of the shamanic profession and (2) spontaneous vocation ('call' or 'election'). There are also cases of individuals who become shamans of their own free will.... But these 'self-made' shamans are considered less powerful than those who inherited the profession or who obeyed the 'call' of the gods and spirits" (583:13). And this situation appears true for other forms of the occult as well (278:207-15).

If we were to summarize the essentials of shamanism, it would include at least four basic themes: 1) altered states of consciousness* or trance, 2) spirit possession, 3) experiences of severe physical and mental illness, 4) spirit travel. Although these are not limited to shamanism and, collectively, are found in much occult practice, without them, no one can become a shaman.

## DANGERS AND DEGRADATIONS

Shamanism is one of the most dangerous and potentially consequential of modern New Age practices. Anyone who reads the standard works on shamanism, such as those of perhaps the world's leading authority on the subject, Mircea Eliade (583/584), or those of I. M. Lewis (586) and Joan Halifax (585), or the books of popularizers like "white" shamans, Michael Harner (142), Lynn Andrews (563), and Carlos Castaneda (e.g., 740) will soon discover the potentially savage hazards of such a path. Even many anthropologists who have investigated shamanism "scientifically" have paid a costly price in the process (e.g., 846:1-16). Botanists, herbalists, and medical doctors likewise.

Horrors surrounding shaman initiations are common:

Tales of frightening initiations are not unusual ... with visions of physical dismemberment and reconstruction being quite common....

The Salish shamanic initiation includes first a period of torture and deprivation: being clubbed, bitten, thrown about, immobilized, blindfolded, teased, starved. When the initiate "gets his [shamanic] song straight," or the slate that is the mind is wiped clean, the guardian spirit or power animal appears [to possess the shaman] (143:22).

[Kinalik's] own initiation had been severe; she was hung up to some tent poles planted in the snow and left there for five days. It was midwinter, with intense cold and frequent blizzards, but she did not feel the cold, for the spirits protected her. When the five days were at an end, she was taken down and carried into the house, and Igjugarjuk was invited to shoot her, in order that she might attain to intimacy with the supernatural by visions of death.... Igjugarjuk asserted that he had shot her through the heart.... [Another student of Igjugarjuk, Aggjartoq] actually stood on the bottom of the lake with his head under water. He was left in this position for five days and when at last they hauled him up again, his clothes showed no sign of having been in the water at all and he himself had become a great wizard, having overcome death (585:9-10).

Shamans also usually undergo terrifying symbolic experiences of death, while experiencing mystical initiation during spirit-flights.

The often terrifying descent by the shaman initiate into the underworld of suffering and death may be represented [to him] by figurative dismemberment, disposal of all bodily fluids, scraping of the flesh from the bones, and removal of the eyes. Once the novice has been reduced to a skeleton and the bones cleansed and purified, the flesh may be distributed among the spirits of the various diseases that afflict those in the human community (585:12).

Through such means the shaman is said to not only relinquish his fear of death but to gain the secrets to healing his fellow tribe members.

Other shamans have real-world experiences of being horribly maimed in various accidents as part of their initiation. Others are poisoned with snake venom or other substances. Some experience diseases such as smallpox, and a few report miraculous phenomena such as a ball of fire that comes down from heaven and strikes them sense-less (585:13). "Kundalini" arousal is also not infrequent (see Yoga). Some American shamans specialize in helping initiates deal with what is apparently shamanically induced kundalini diffi-culties, including psychoses (2482:40-41/2477:37).

Because so many people are turning to shamanism, we think that stressing the dangers of this practice will help them reconsider their commitment and hinder the merely curious from future involvement. Suffice it to say that shamanism often involves the shaman in tremen-dous personal suffering and pain (magically, he often "dies" in the most horrible of torments), and that it often involves the shaman in demon pos-session, insanity, sexual perversion, and so on (585:7-27). Why anyone would consider shaman-ism or shamanistic initiation as *healthful*, spiri-tual or otherwise, is difficult to imagine.

*Amorality*

Obviously shamanism lacks moral standards. It is characteristically amoral, using the spirits for either good or evil purposes. As shamanistic counselor Natasha Frazier, director of Transfor-mative Arts Institute points out, "There are four ways to use shamanic power—for healing, for manipulation, for acquisition and for malevolent action. . . . Manipulatory shamanism is [sic] to do with manipulating the environment for per-sonal gain and without regard for the conse-quences. Malevolent shamanism is tied up with intentionally causing injury, illness or death and can be applied to people, places and the environ-ment" (2477:37). In other words, the shaman is one who acquires knowledge of both good and evil spirits, often attempting either to use both or to bring both into "harmony" (2480:20). The powerful Native American shaman, "Thunder Cloud," for example, was known as both "a great healer and adept poisoner" (585:175). Like witches, some shamans, of course, claim to con-centrate on "good" forces, while others deliber-ately use evil powers. Yet it is the amoral perspective in general that is part of what makes shamanism per se evil, regardless of any practi-tioner's claim to use shamanism benevolently. In the end, the "good" and evil spirits and forces cannot logically be separated, and therefore *all*

shamans must utilize a source of power that is as comfortable being used for evil purposes as allegedly for good ones.

In shaman training, "the forces of both light and dark [are] summoned" (2480:22), and the very process of accepting shamanic power also involves "accepting the ancient darkness" (2481:27). As one initiate recalled:

> Although I sat in the cave of light, my experi-ence that night was very dark. At times I felt myself to be a channel through which all the destructive and entropic forces of the universe were flowing. [My shaman later] explained that the darker forces . . . in that evening's work were seeking to restore balance in the circle, making themselves apparent to those able to perceive them. . . . While most of the group focused on the light . . . experiencing radiant visions of power animals or guides, three of us struggled with darkness. In this way the balance of the circle was maintained (2481:28-29).

Of course, any tradition, spirit, or power that is equally at home employing evil can never logi-cally be considered good. To accept or employ evil as a necessity to supposedly "balance" the occult circle or spiritual world is not wise.

*Sexual Immorality*

As an illustration of sexual perversion, many shamans become androgynous, homosexual, or lesbian at the insistence of their spirit guides. In an age of worldwide AIDS, can anybody con-sider this sound advice? As in forms of monistic Hinduism, the rationale is allegedly to unify the "illusion" of opposites (good with evil, male with female, dark with light). But the result is perver-sion or even suicide. As the following illustration reveals, the source behind such degradation is the spirit world:

> The dissolution of contraries—life and death, light and dark, male and female—and reconsti-tution of the fractured forms is one of the most consistent impulses in the initiation and trans-formation process as experienced by the shaman. . . . During mysteries of initiation such as those of shamanic election, androgyny can appear at two very significant moments in this sacred continuum: at its inception and at its

termination.... Among Siberian peoples, androgynous shamans appear to be unusually prevalent.... The spirit ally, or *ke'let*, demands that the young man become a "soft man being." Many instances of suicide among adolescent shamans occurred as a result of their refusal to meet this requirement. Nonetheless, most neophytes complied in spite of their profound social and psychological ambivalence. The transformation process is heralded by the spirits guiding the young man to braid his hair like a woman's. Next, the spirits, through dreams, prescribe women's clothing for the young man.... The third stage of this initiation entails a more total feminization of the male shaman. The youth who is undergoing the process relinquishes his former male behaviors and activities and adopts the female role.... His spirits are guiding and teaching him the woman's way. His mode of speech changes as well as his behavior, and on certain occasions, so does his body.... Even his physical character changes.... Generally speaking, he becomes a woman with the appearance of a man.... The "soft man" comes to experience himself sexually as a female. With the help of his spirit allies, he is able to attract the attention of eligible men, one of whom he chooses to be his husband. The two marry and live as a man and wife, often until death, performing their appropriate social and sexual roles (585:23-24).

In similar fashion, female shamans may become lesbians (585:25). We also find the horrible experiences of the demonic incubi and succubae or sex with male and female demons (583:80; cf. 273:162-64).

Sexual perversions occur because the shaman is controlled by *evil* spirits from beginning to end. "The initial experience of possession, particularly, is often a disturbing, even traumatic experience.... Where the successor shows reluctance in assuming his onerous duties, the spirits remind him forcefully of his obligations by badgering him with trials and tribulations until he acknowledges defeat and accepts their insistent prodding" (586:66). Indeed, I. M. Lewis's description of a particular amoral class of spirits that shamans may associate with is actually descriptive of shamanic spirit guides in general. "It is I believe of the greatest interest and importance that these

spirits are typically considered to be amoral; they have no direct moral significance. Full of spite and malice though they are, they are believed to strike entirely capriciously and without any grounds which can be referred to the moral character or conduct of their victim" (586:31).

Once inside their host, the spirits have the capacity to produce either a "divine" ecstasy or horrible, demonic torment. Perhaps only the occasional spiritual ecstasy of the shaman can explain the willingness of some to enter such a horrible profession (585:31-32/583:108-09,221; cf. ref. 291). Here, the spirits will entice their hosts with intense mystical joy, which may make their infliction of torture more acceptable. Nevertheless, the spirits are capricious:

> ...These maligned pathogenic spirits are regarded as being extremely captious and capricious. They strike without rhyme or reason; or at least without any substantial cause which can be referred to social conduct. They are not concerned with man's behavior to man. They have no interest in defending the moral code of society.... [T]hey are always on the look-out for a convenient excuse to harass their victims, and they are inordinately sensitive to human encroachment. To step on one inadvertently, or otherwise unwittingly annoy it, is sufficient to so inflame the spirit's wrath that it attacks at once, possessing its trespasser, and making him ill or causing him misfortune.

> ...They show a special predilection for the weak and downtrodden, ... indeed for all those whose circumstances are already so reduced as to make this additional burden seem a final, crushing, injustice (586:71-72).

### Drug Use

Many authorities also note the importance (if not necessity) of drug use for shaman enlightenment* (cf. 583:221-23). We also find this in the world of the occult generally, and among many Eastern gurus (610:71-73). But with millions of people now exploring shamanism and other kinds of occultism and Eastern paths, one can only hazard a guess as to what degree pagan religion in modern America fosters drug usage and its attendant problems.

## Death Magic and Other Forms of Murder

Harner, Eliade, and others discuss parallels between shamanism and occult death magic. Harner observes the following practice among the category of the so-called "bewitching" shaman: "Shamans send these spirit helpers into the victims' bodies to make them ill or kill them. . . . [T]he urge to kill felt by bewitching shamans came to them with a strength and frequency similar to that of hunger" (862:17-20). According to Eliade, "when the shaman wants to poison someone, he sends a *damagomi* [spirit]: 'Go find so-and-so. Enter him. Make him sick. Don't kill him at once. Make him die in a month'" (583:106).

However, because there are no absolute moral values exercised by shamans (or their spirit helpers), one discovers allegedly "good" shamans also use their powers for evil, whenever it suits their purposes (e.g., 583:184). This is exactly what we find among so-called "good" witches (278:136-37,298).

Another illustration of how shamanism is used in killing or murdering others is seen in that the spirits which shamans cavort with enjoy "taking the heads" of tribal enemies, or even of innocent victims. Indeed, primitive shamanistic communities may undergo a crisis when civilization comes and takes hold of their social life and head-hunting becomes outlawed. "Head-hunting had been outlawed, and the people feared that the spirits would consume them because they were not able to feed the hungry spirits the heads of slain enemies" (585:24-25).

A television special on the subject was produced by Douchan Gersi, who had led the first successful expedition in history that crossed central Borneo through uncharted territory. Five previous expeditions had failed, and even in this one Gersi almost lost his life. On the TV special, one of the more understated personal sentiments he gave was, "*Everywhere*, invisible dangers." At one point of incredible hardship, near death, he recalled, "*Believe me*, I started saying all my childhood prayers."

Gersi discovered that the head-hunting tribes he encountered, in common with most pagan religion, justify murder on the basis of the spirits' own interests and perverted religious principles. He encountered some 350 of these shamanistic tribes and spent years living among them as a convert. One such tribe, the "Iban," gather heads from other tribes and from explorers like Gersi. Why? Because the heads are believed to confer "social status" and occult power. Reminiscent of Western gunslingers, one native had 250 notches proudly carved out on his spear—one notch for each head. Indeed, for every major event (moving, marriage, etc.), a head must be sacrificed and publicly displayed on a pole. Thus, as the ritual ceremony for displaying the severed head approaches, "the people sense the presence of a thousand spirits" hovering around them, ready to relish the gruesome spectacle.

The religious justification for this is that human skulls are believed to be the home of living spirits, hence the supposed reason for the spirits' interest in the displayed head. Human skulls are further thought to symbolize life, and so the tribe must be kept "healthy" by ritual sacrifice—the human sacrifice itself symbolizing life-giving power for the tribe. In harmony with other occult traditions of human sacrifice, it is also believed the person taking off the head of the victim receives the power from the spirit of the dead man. Gersi himself came close to having his own head removed—even after having been accepted by the tribe. He was spared only by a tortuous shamanistic initiation. Being placed in a deep pit with flesh-eating ants was only one of his many ordeals.

Perhaps the most incredible part was Gersi's pagan conversion and proud membership in the community. He no longer believes such people are primitive, but now is convinced they are spiritually advanced because of their "harmony with nature." He concluded his television show by criticizing modern viewpoints and the encroachment of civilization for destroying such important cultures, using the wry phrase, "Progress is beheading Borneo."

Consider that here are hundreds of tribes that engage in ritual murder—a theme so common in demonic religion—and yet an intelligent, world-renown explorer complains that they are being forced to change their ways by the encroachment of civilization—as if changing the "natural order" of things for such tribes were the real sin! In a similar vein, those who criticize Christian missionaries for "destroying" pagan cultures apparently have little comprehension of how evil and demonic pagan culture can be. Perhaps the more enlightened among them would care to join the local coven and ritually sacrifice a baby—and then see how they feel about preserving paganism. It is right that Christians are financially supporting missions that seek to share Christ with such peoples.

To summarize, there is no such category as a "benevolent" practicing occultist, whether shaman, witch, medium, psychic, or guru. First, because the urge to use power amorally is always present and people sooner or later succumb to it, even when their motives are good. Second, the Bible makes no distinction between "good" and "evil" practices of the occult. God calls all occult practice evil and an abomination to Him (Deuteronomy 18:9-12). That the spirits themselves are evil leads us to conclude that they will influence people in that direction, albeit often in subtle ways. Once people turn to the spirits, the spirits always get their way, sooner or later.

### Spiritual Blackmail

The phenomenon of spiritistic intimidation is common to all categories of occultism. Thus, shamans who are "chosen" by the spirits as "healers" must either submit to the spirits or become ill, or even die. "The person called to be a shaman must learn to shamanize, that is, must take his powerful experiences and find a way to share the power with his people. If he does not shamanize, he will become ill again and may die, for the shaman is called to a certain kind of life, and if he does not lead it properly, his power will turn against him and kill him" (799:67).

In other words, to the spirits, human life is cheap. If their chosen host will not obey their wishes, they will destroy it and find another. Dr. Nandor Fodor discusses a similar condition among mediums. He observes that when a person neglects his mediumistic powers, illness results. Thus "mediumship, if suppressed, will manifest in symptoms of disease" (389:235). He cites the following illustration:

The spasms seized the whole body; even the tongue was affected, blocking the throat and nearly suffocating her. When the patient mentioned that in her youth she tried table tilting, the doctor thought of the possibility that the mediumistic energy might block his patient's organism. A sitting was tried. The lady fell into trance and afterwards slept well for a few days. When the sleeplessness became worse again the sitting was repeated and the results proved to be so beneficial that the chloral hydrate treatment previously employed was discontinued (389:235).

This woman discovered that, like many shamans, she too had been "called" to her profession, and that unless she gave in to the process, she would suffer immeasurably.

Such spiritistic intimidation is common (e.g., 1069:223-38). Once the door has been broken down to permit spiritistic influence, whether by heredity, occult transfer, or personal choice, the spirits may aggressively pursue their evil agenda. Whether in mediumism, shamanism, or witchcraft, the person "has been caught by the spirits and must serve the spiritual world" (759:97). The following shamanistic examples, from Swiss psychologist, anthropologist, and ethnologist Holger Kalweit show the true nature of the spirits. These examples, which come from a chapter having the incredible title, "When Insanity Is a Blessing: The Message of Shamanism," reveal how dangerous it is to open the doors to the occult, and why those trapped often find it so difficult to escape (278). "Among the Siberian Tofa, too, shamans become sick before their initiation and are tormented by spirits. ... [S]haman Vassily Mikailovic ... could not rise from his bed for a whole year. Only when he agreed to the demands of the spirits did his health improve" (759:83). The wife of another shaman recalled the terrible experience of her husband's call to shamanism. She warns, "He who is seized by the shaman sickness and does not begin to exercise shamanism, must suffer badly. He might lose his mind, he may even have to give up his life. Therefore he is advised, 'You must take up shamanism so as not to suffer!' Some even say, 'I become a shaman only to escape illness.'" Another shaman added, "The man chosen for shamandom is first recognized by the black spirits. The spirits of the dead shamans are called black spirits. They make the chosen one ill and then they force him to become a shaman" (759:81). And a shamaness reports, "Sometimes I say to them, 'I do not want to go with you.' Whenever I turn down such an invitation I develop a fever and become very ill" (759:93).

Kalweit comments that, in harmony with occult healing generally, the "healer" must suffer the illness of the patient:

> Resistance to psychophysical change and a disintegration of the normal structure of existence has always been part and parcel of the transformative process. Because of this, it forms at least a partial aspect of every rite of transformation.... Frequently the shaman enters a patient's state so thoroughly that he himself experiences the symptoms and pains of the illness.... In the course of their painful existence, many shamans have physically experienced countless illnesses ... (759:93-94).

Either way, the shaman cannot win. If he pursues his spiritistic calling, he suffers. If he does not, he suffers. The shaman who refuses his call in all probability "will be plagued by sickness the rest of his life" (759:87). Even one's own family members may be tortured by the spirits as a means of forcing compliance:

> Often not only the shaman himself but his whole family are visited by misfortune.... The Koreans talk about a "bridge of people" (*indari*) that comes into being when a member of the family is chosen to be a shaman and another member has to die as a result of this.... A God has "entered into" the shaman and, in return, demands another human life.... But most families are unwilling to have a shaman in their circle, so the *indari* phenomenon occurs quite frequently. According to the investigations made by Cho Hung-Youn, *indari* occurs on average seven or eight times in every twenty cases of shamanic vocation (759:95-96).

In a parallel to life of famous trance medium Edgar Cayce, we read:

The Yakut shaman Tusput, who was critically ill for more than twenty years, could find relief from his suffering only when he conducted a seance during which he fell into a trance. In the end he fully regained his health by this method. However, if he held no seances over a long period of time he once again began to feel unwell, exhausted, and indecisive. In general, the symptoms of an illness subside when a candidate for shamanism enters a trance (759:91).

In the end, because of their power, the spirits will have their way. "In the end I became so ill that I was close to death. So I began to shamanize, and very soon my health improved. Even now I feel unwell and sick whenever I am inactive as a shaman over a longer period of time" (759:92).

Clearly, horrible torments, paralysis, drownings, insanity, extended sickness, being maimed, poisoned, and worse are the shaman's lot (585:7-66/2475:18,22). Perhaps this explains why even those sympathetic to the practice may issue warnings. Dr. Achterberg writes:

> Any current thrust toward romanticizing shamanic medicine or folk medicine in general should be tempered with the knowledge that often the remedies prescribed were clearly wrong and harmful from the standpoint of physical well-being. Jilek-Aall describes birthing procedures dictated by custom in parts of Africa that defy the course of nature. The result is high infant mortality and a high incidence of epilepsy....
>
> The practice of shamanism is always regarded as being fraught with grave risk to the life and well being of the practitioner.... One particularly dangerous aspect of shamanism, "soul raising" is almost always practiced by women....
>
> A long standing debate has existed in anthropological writings on whether shamanism is a shelter for deranged personalities (143:18-20).

*Psychopathology*

The obvious reason for the debate over the shaman's psychological health, as mentioned by Achterberg, is that shamanism usually involves the practitioner in psychotic and schizophrenic-like episodes (see 741:22-27). But because shamanism is now often interpreted as a form of "higher" spirituality by many psychologists, especially transpersonal psychologists, its accompanying mental states are also being reinterpreted in a benign fashion.

In other words, what was once considered a psychological state of depraved insanity is today considered a spiritual state of higher consciousness (741:23,27)! What was once dangerous and feared is now *preferred* as a method of spiritual empowerment and enlightenment* (742:40-41). As Achterberg writes, "Newer theories of personality development . . . all include the notion that 'normal' [consciousness] is by no means the most evolved possibility" (153:31). The East has indeed come West: temporary insanity as a potentially higher or elevated state of consciousness is a premise of Hindu and Buddhist thinking, more than many people realize (610; see Meditation and Eastern Gurus).

Of course, not all agree that states of insanity are spiritually desirable. "Among those most frequently cited are Devereux, who steadfastly maintains there is no excuse for not regarding the shamans as neurotic or even psychotic, and Silverman who likens the SSC [Shamanic State of Consciousness] to acute schizophrenia" (143:30). (Silverman is the author of "Shamanism and Acute Schizophrenia," *American Anthropologist*, Volume 69, 1967, pp. 21-31, and Devereux is the author of *Basic Problems of Ethnopsychiatry*, University of Chicago Press, 1980.)

One of the biggest problems that surrounds ethnopsychiatry, or "transcultural" psychiatry, is the confusion of normal and abnormal states of consciousness. Because states of mental illness are considered "normal" in shamanistic and other subcultures, and because modern secular psychiatry and anthropology have no absolute standards by which to judge such things, many scholars are concluding that even occult-induced mental illness can be simply part of a continuum along the "normal" range of transpersonal consciousness.

The implications of this are anything but minor. Consider Michael Harner's first experience with shaman initiation—an experience that resulted in his becoming a shaman. He

employed the sacred drug made from the ayahuasca plant or "soul vine":

I could make out large numbers of people with the heads of blue jays and the bodies of humans, not unlike the bird-headed gods of ancient Egyptian tomb paintings. At the same time, some energy-essence began to float from my chest. . . . Although I believed myself to be an atheist, I was completely certain that I was dying and that the bird-headed people had come to take my soul away. . . .

Starting with my arms and legs, my body slowly began to feel like it was turning to solid concrete. I could not move or speak. Gradually, as the numbness closed in on my chest, toward my heart, I tried to get my mouth to ask for help, to ask the Indians for an antidote. Try as I might, however, I could not marshal my abilities sufficiently to make a word. Simultaneously, my abdomen seemed to be turning to stone, and I had to make a tremendous effort to keep my heart beating. . . . I was virtually certain that I was about to die. . . . I was dying and therefore, [it was] "safe" [for me] to receive [new] revelations. These were the secrets reserved for the dying and the dead, I was informed. I could only very dimly perceive the givers of these thoughts: giant reptilian creatures. . . . I could only vaguely see them in what seemed to be gloomy, dark depth.

Then they projected a visual scene in front of me. First they showed me the planet earth as it was aeons ago. . . . [They said] they had come to planet earth to escape their enemy.

The creatures then showed me how they had created life on the planet in order to hide within the multitudinous forms and thus disguise their presence. . . . They were the true masters of humanity and the entire planet, they told me. We humans were but the receptacles and servants of these creatures. . . .

I knew I had only a moment more to live. Strangely, I had no fear of the bird-headed people; they were welcome to have my soul if they could keep it. . . .

[Later] I began to struggle against returning to the ancient ones, who were beginning to feel increasingly alien and possibly evil. . . .

I frantically tried to conjure up a power being to protect me against the alien reptilian creatures.

One appeared before me; and at that moment the Indians forced my mouth open and poured the antidote into me (142:4-6).

When native or naive Americans seek out such encounters, on what basis does anyone logically conclude there will never be casualties? Harner himself admits people may go insane, "become seriously ill or even die" from shamanistic experiences (142:2,19,125). The number of people who might never come back from such experiences is unknown, but the risks are certainly not less than those encountered in mind-expanding drugs such as LSD.

It is true that the mental states of what may be termed "shamanic consciousness" and those of schizophrenia and psychosis are not entirely identical. The shaman often has more volition and control during his altered state of consciousness,* and it is a "voluntarily" induced insanity similar to that found in the spiritistic Eastern guru* traditions (610). Nevertheless, while this state is controlled to some degree by the shaman, it seems to be controlled to a much larger degree by his spirit guides, and certainly it is manipulated by the spirits for their own purposes, whatever these might be. Regardless, the very fact of a debate among ethnopsychiatrists proves that the "state" of insanity and that of shamanistic consciousness are similar enough that they are not easily distinguished. Shamans themselves admit, "There is a fine line between the shaman and the psychotic" (2477:37).

As we will now seek to show, the unfortunate result for those who seek shamanistic states of consciousness is only that they will encounter their own demonically manipulated consciousness—and despite the claims of promoters, this is anything but "healthy" or spiritually "evolved." Because shamanism *requires* spirit possession and because one cannot become a true shaman-healer without it, demon possession is also required. How many shamanistically fascinated Americans realize that?

*Demonism and Health*

Any individual who decides to practice shamanism soon realizes he has contacted gen-

uine spirit beings who exist entirely apart from his own personality, at least initially (743:38-39/744:41-45).

Of course, modern Western scientists who employ shamanistic techniques may scoff at the idea of personal, independent spirits or demons. Many psychologists and shaman initiates may redefine spirit manifestations in more "neutral" categories, such as "archetypal consciousness," "higher self," and "cosmic consciousness." But such interpretations only underscore an anti-supernatural bias, which does nothing to protect one from the spirits themselves, who easily hide behind such "naturalistic" designations.

As is true for much Eastern religion in general (249:165-208; 610, see Yoga, Meditation, Eastern Gurus), the end result of the shamanistic path, whether it is used for spiritual or health purposes, is almost always the spirit possession of the seeker (or patient). As Harner explains,

When a power animal is restored to a person, he usually feels better immediately, and then gradually experiences a power flowing into his body over the next few days. . . . You should begin a weekly routine to retain the power by keeping your power animal content, for the spirit has entered your body, not only to help you, but also to help itself. You gain its power; it gains the joy of again experiencing life in a material form (142:124).

For almost all shamans, the entrance point to spirit possession is altered states of consciousness.* Indeed, this is precisely how many professional anthropologists and other social scientists become shamans. By personally engaging in the rituals and practices they are seeking to study academically, they use drugs or other means to "test drive" altered states of consciousness, trance, and spirit contact. Then they become shamans. This was true for Carlos Castaneda (740:13-99), Michael Harner (142:63), and others (846). Harner admits, "What *is* definite is that *some* degree of alteration of consciousness is necessary to shamanic practice" (142:62).

Shamans find that even a light trance is effective for their spiritistic work. Harner, refers to "the light trance in which most shamanic work is done" (142:64-65). This would seem to have implications for a good deal of modern experimentation, popular and scientific, with hypnosis* and related methods of altering consciousness (142:62; see also New Age Inner Work and Visualization). In fact, as Drs. Villoldo and Krippner note, "Spirit-incorporation according to Peters and Price-Williams [975] resembles 'deep hypnosis' . . ." (91:197; see Hypnosis). In addition, use of sweat lodges, sacred pipes, and even ritual alone may lead to spirit contact and possession (142:84-86/2475:21-22). Because the intent of the ritual is to deliberately contact the spirits, it is hardly surprising that the spirits who desire such contact will respond.

Sadly, as noted earlier, advocates do not recognize that the supposedly "good" spirits contacted in shamanism are really demons imitating good spirits for purposes of influence and control (see refs. 278/241-46/249). This indicates a gross contradiction within a shamanistic worldview, for shamanism freely admits that it *employs* "demon helpers" in its work (see 142:30). American shamans may prefer to term their spiritual possession as the more polite "divine companionship" (2474:42), but this hardly changes the facts. Indeed, some of the perceptual problems inherent in contemporary America's fascination with shamanism are illustrated by Harner's work *The Way of the Shaman.* Harner makes shamanism sound like the best thing since modern electricity. He calls it "a great mental and emotional adventure" (142:xiii) and emphasizes its physical and spiritual benefits. Displaying an inexcusable ignorance of his own field, not to mention the history of spiritism itself, he claims that spirit guides *never* harm those they possess (to the contrary, see 278/280/241-44/291). "Remember, guardian spirits are *always* beneficial. They never harm their possessors. And you possess the guardian spirit; it never possesses you. In other words, the power animal is a purely beneficial spirit no matter how fierce it may appear. It is a spirit to be exercised, not exorcised" (142:88).

Why, then, does Harner devote an entire chapter to the shamanistic practice of exorcising *demons* from patients (142:145-52)! As Eliade correctly observes, "In order to extract the evil spirits from the patient, the shaman is often obliged to take them into his own body; in doing so, he struggles and suffers more than the patient himself" (583:229; cf. 746:17-19).

Clearly, the spiritual naïveté of our culture is aptly demonstrated in the subject of shamanism. As a result, what is so demonic and dangerous is frequently accepted, uncritically and without question, as a method for securing physical health and healing, psychological adjustment, and spiritual advancement.

Harner points out the depth at which Americans want to get into shamanism: "I have been continually surprised to discover how many Westerners who are ill or injured immediately accept the possibility of their power animal [spirit guide] and happily enter into contact with it" (142:132). Not surprisingly, therefore, many of the spirits who work through shamans want their hosts to establish training centers so that more and more people can be instructed in the ways of spirit possession through shamanism. Don Edwardo Calderon was told by his spirits in a vision that "it was important to reveal this knowledge of healing and shamanism to outsiders" (2480:19). The same was true for shamaness Skyhawk, founder of the Church of Loving Hands (2484:45). Sun Bear, the founder and medicine chief of the Bear Tribe Medicine Society, recalls, "I have established an apprenticeship training because the spirits told me to do it" (745:22). He also notes, "If the spirits accept you, then you become a medicine man. . . . They are the ones who determine whether you actually have the power to practice" (745:21).

The irony of using shamanism as medicine is magnified when we consider what is involved in "healing" according to shamanism. It is not just the shaman who becomes demon-possessed. Why? Because shamanism assumes that most or all people already have a guardian spirit within them. That spirit has come and gone as it wished throughout the person's life (142:54-55,87,90). Illness and psychological or emotional problems are merely indications that, for various reasons, one's spirit guide has left one's body, and the illness or other condition is the final result. Eliade observes that "it is often the case that the illness is due to a neglect or an omission in respect to the infernal powers . . ." (583:216).

As noted earlier, to retain one's spirit guide or power animal one must keep it "happy." This illustrates another form of bondage to the spirits:

If one wishes to maintain shamanic practice, one has to change into one's animal regularly to keep the animal contented enough to stay. This involves exercising the animal through dance, singing songs of the animal, and recognizing "big" dreams as messages from the guardian, the power animal. Dancing your animal is an important method for keeping it content and thus making it reluctant to leave you. The guardian animal spirit resident in the mind-body of the person wants to have the enjoyment of once again existing in material form. . . . [A]s I learned from the Jivaro years ago, guardian spirits usually stay with you only a few years and then depart. So, in the course of a long, powerful life [as a shaman], you will have a number of them one after another, whether you know it or not (142:87).

According to shamanism, when a spirit leaves a person, physical, psychological, or spiritual illness results:

Thus possession of guardian spirit power [i.e., retaining the spirit within you] is fundamental to health. Serious illness is usually only possible when a person is dis-spirited, and has lost this energizing force, the guardian spirit. When a person becomes depressed, weak, prone to illness, it is a symptom that he has lost his power animal and thus can no longer resist, or ward off the unwanted power "infections" or intrusions (142:90).

In other words, shamans wish us to alter our perception to harmonize it with their spiritistic philosophy, to believe that the mere presence of illness, physical or psychological, or being in a serious accident, or even certain mundane problems, mean that one has *automatically* been "dis-spirited" and therefore, by definition, a spirit must be *reintroduced* into the body. Harner states, "The specific treatment, if the victim is not in a coma, is to recover or obtain his guardian spirit to re-energize him" (142:126). And "if your power animal's messages are ignored, or if it is not exercised through dancing, it may become discomforted, discouraged, and want to leave your body. Its discomfort may unintentionally flow into your own consciousness causing tension and anxiety. If you do nothing to remedy the situation, it will shortly leave you and you will again be dis-spirited" (142:129).

Again, *any* illness is evidence a person has been "dis-spirited." So the only possible way to recover "health," is for the spirit to be "reintroduced" into the mind/body. Of course, if the diagnosis is wrong, and illness is *not* related to a loss of one's pre-existing spirit guide, then shamanistic methods serve as a cover for the demonization of persons previously *not* demonized. This vital importance of the spirit guide to the health of the patient is why modern books about using shamanism for health purposes instruct people to meet or to be reintroduced to their spirit guides (142:146).

Because hundreds or thousands of practitioners are now adopting shamanism to varying degrees in their health and therapy work, it is hardly inconceivable that patients may become demon-influenced or demonized in the process:

The urgent healing work of the shaman . . . is to restore one of the person's lost guardian spirits as soon as possible. Since ours is not a shamanic society, it is usually not possible to do the necessary work in the same room as a hospitalized person. Exceptions are sometimes tolerated in this country if both shaman and the patients are American Indians. . . . In some hospitals, such as on the Navajo reservation, visits by native healers are being increasingly encouraged as the Western medical staff becomes more aware of the benefits produced. . . . Meanwhile, you can use the following long distance technique to restore guardian power (142:130).

Harner discusses how a spirit may be "restored" to a person at great distance through shaman ritual. The shaman merely calls upon his power animal, transfers its power to the patient's guardian spirit, and then visually and mentally sends the spirit "to the patient as visualized in the hospital room" (142:131).

As our American society increasingly turns to the occult, we can expect many more such "health" procedures in the future. An important point to remember is that even shamans (like other mediums and spiritists), are not always aware of the presence of their spirit guides. Their spirit guides may be right next to them, or even inside of them, and yet they may have no conscious awareness of that. And this means that people can become demonized unaware (see New Age Intuition and New Age Inner Work for illustrations).

In summary, the essence of shamanic "health" is possession by one or more spirits: "A power animal or guardian spirit ... not only increases one's physical energy and ability to resist contagious disease, but also increases one's mental alertness and self-confidence.... Being powerfull [spirit possessed] is like having a force field in and around you.... Thus, possession of guardian spirit power is fundamental to health" (142:89-90).

Once a person adopts shamanism, then by definition any illness, mental or physical, requires the following diagnosis: The person has lost his power animal (or spirit guide) and the only solution is to "restore" that person's spirit guide into his mind and body.

Even children can become novice shamans and spirit-possessed (142:82-83). Some of the modern practices in "transpersonal education" are useful for shamanistic instruction here (572:109-46; see New Age Education). Shamans themselves may help introduce power animals and other spirits to their children (583:22). As shamanism increases within our culture, the children of American shamans will become as demonized as their parents. As Harner explains of his own experience among the Jivaro, "Parents of a newly born infant, in fact, typically gave it a mild hallucinogen so that it could 'see' and hopefully thus acquire an *arutam wakanI* or guardian spirit. The parents, of course, wanted the baby to have as much protection as possible in order to survive into adult life" (142:82).

And shamanistic practice in America has many other fruits.

- Because it encourages demon contact, shamanism leads to occult bondage; that is, subjection to and dependence upon the world of demons.

- Because it is a form of spiritual warfare, shamanism brings powerful personal experiences that insulate a person against biblical teaching and the gospel message.

- Because it is irrational, shamanism produces a denial of cause and effect in the realm of medicine, leading to a rejection of scientific methods and an acceptance of occult methods. In that the spirits have subtle powers and persuasions, even "scientific" harmonizers may end up abandoning orthodox medicine.

- Because it stresses magical ability, shamanism exalts and glorifies the one with occult powers.

- Because it is animistic, shamanism breaks down three vital distinctions of the created order: 1) material; 2) plant/animal; 3) human. Rocks, trees, and animals become just as "alive" and therefore as important as man; in the process, humanity is reduced to the lower or lowest levels of the creation.

The result of all this keeps the shamanistic practitioner in a primitive state spiritually and often morally, with little hope of escape. The ritual and practices of shamanism reinforce its belief system and vice versa through powerful supernatural manifestations that are difficult if not impossible to counter.

Only the power of Jesus Christ can break into the dark world of shamanism and deliver those held in its bondage. Shamans and shaman apprentices who desire deliverance must turn to the living Jesus Christ, for He and He alone can save them.

# SILVA MIND CONTROL

## INFO AT A GLANCE

**Description.** Silva Mind Control (SMC), is a spiritistic New Age "self-help" seminar that claims to represent "the next phase of human evolution on this planet." It alleges that it is "the first and only fully guaranteed method known to be effective in developing and controlling Effective Sensory Projection," i.e., "mind projection" for psychic purposes (2624:1).

**Founder.** José Silva (1914– ).

**How does it claim to work?** Silva Mind Control claims that by developing the "unused potential" of the mind and by learning how to function psychically, individuals can dramatically improve the quality of their lives in virtually every area.

**Scientific Evaluation.** Although SMC claims cannot, strictly, be evaluated scientifically, they are sometimes done so parapsychologically in accordance with Silva's lifelong interest in this field.

**Examples of occult potential.** Psychic development, spiritism, and other forms of occult activity.

**Major problems.** Although Silva Mind Control is effective for developing psychic powers in many people, such instruction will not lead to genuine spiritual enlightenment but to occult bondage. The SMC claim that its seminars will change the destiny of mankind and usher in a millennium is naive at best.

**Biblical/Christian evaluation.** As an occult human potential method specifically designed to generate ESP and establish contact with "inner counselors" (frequently spirit guides), SMC is prohibited for Christians. Because of Silva's emphasis on human self-perfection, he rejects key biblical doctrines. Also, since SMC believes it can literally bring paradise to the earth, in that SMC itself is part of the "second phase of human evolution" on this planet, it contradicts Jesus' teaching about the millennium and heaven.

**Potential dangers.** The usual spiritual, psychological, and physical problems inherent to all forms of occult activity (278); basing important decisions upon alleged psychic information one only assumes is trustworthy.

*Note:* SMC has influenced a number of human potential seminars, including Mind Dynamics and est* that have utilized SMC techniques. According to Silva, both Alex Everett, founder of Mind Dynamics, and Werner Erhard, founder of est/The Forum, are SMC graduates (personal conversation). A number of popular books also utilize SMC principles. Jess Stearns' bestselling *The Miracle Power of Alpha Thinking* is basically SMC (2596:158).

## INTRODUCTION AND INFLUENCE

In 1979 a group of people got worldwide press coverage for their attempt to use "ESP" to affect the orbit of the faltering Skylab, which later came crashing to earth. After their failure, the project founder stated the obvious: "Apparently the height of the orbit was not influenced by the mental projections from earth" (2592:5). This vainglorious effort was the brainchild of Silva Mind Control International, a large occult "human potential" organization that had earlier attempted to psychically influence astronauts in space (2591:238ff).

Since Silva Mind Control (SMC) claims that it is designed to develop psychic powers in anyone within only four days, perhaps SMC attempts at such stalwart projects are comprehensible; then again, perhaps not. Regardless, thousands of professionals have been through SMC and utilize some of its principles in their professions. Executives at RCA use it, and so do directors in the Mary Kay Corporation. Physicians and psychiatrists use it, as well as allegedly, some ten million others in every American state and 71 countries around the world (cf. 2593).

Founder José Silva hopes to see tens of thousands of ministers, physicians, psychologists, government leaders, law enforcement officials, engineers, archaeologists, meteorologists, astronomers, industrialists, financiers, executives, pilots, and others become clairvoyant and psychic and change the world into a paradise (2591:11A-24A/2594:11). Allegedly, "His work signifies and has become one of the first steps taken toward the second phase of human evolution on this planet" (2595:5-6). Since, it is claimed, José Silva, is "recognized as a genius

in the fields of business, education, athletics, science, art and philosophy," perhaps we can take their word for it (2596:i). Silva himself states unabashedly, "Before we developed this method, there had been no such training since the time of Christ" (2596:161).

In order to help secure Silva's goals, SMC followers have undertaken various ambitious projects to reach all levels of society. Thus a number of specialized texts have been printed; for example, *The Silva Mind Control Method Book for Business Managers* (Prentice Hall):

> The goal of Silva Mind Control International is to take this discovery to every nation in the world to help human beings on this planet learn to use their minds better and to use more of their brains for the elimination of ignorance and human suffering (2595:62-63).

Silva Mind Control began in Laredo, Texas, in 1944, the brainchild of José Silva, a "lay research scientist" and self-developed psychic. Silva is a somewhat rotund and jovial man with a genuine concern to solve the world's problems and turn the earth into a Garden of Eden; he truly believes he has found the way to do it. It began with his interest in hypnosis* and parapsychology, which led him to begin experimentation with so-called "powers of the mind." He first began psychically testing his own children, using hypnosis and mind-control methods to help them do their homework. From 1953 to 1963, he trained 39 other Laredo children in psychic abilities. He then felt he was ready to expand operations (2597:24-25). In 1963, the Laredo Parapsychology Foundation, Inc., was established, and within three years the basic 48-hour Silva Mind Control course had become a reality.

Today, the organization is a large corporate structure. For example, there is the Institute of Psychorientology, which is the central organization and manages "research and development," although most of its power has been turned over to Silva Mind Control International, Inc. Silva defines "psychorientology" as "the study of orienting Mind in the subjective world of the [psychic] Mind dimension" (2598:82). Another branch, Silva Sensor Systems, coordinates parapsychologically oriented bookstores and provides continuing programs for graduates as well as tape distribution and SMC lecturers for the general public.

As of 1996, SMC had been taught, often with academic credits available, in scores of colleges and high schools and in numerous elementary schools. Hundreds, if not thousands of clergy, teachers, businessmen, and others have taken the course, which is specifically designed to make them psychic. A number of holistic health practitioners and physicians use it for psychic diagnosis. Harvard-trained neurosurgeon Dr. Norman Shealy, who is director of the influential Pain Rehabilitation Center at the LaCrosse, Wisconsin, hospital and author of *Occult Medicine Can Save Your Life* and *The Creation of Health: Merging Traditional Medicine with Intuitive Diagnosis*, is a prominent SMC graduate. Famous cancer therapists Carl O. Simonton and Stephanie Matthews-Simonton are also SMC graduates, and they use the concept of SMC "psychic advisors" in their cancer therapy (2597:73-76/2599:ch. 15).

SMC appears to have a large financial base. The ten million graduates worldwide have generated perhaps three-quarter billion dollars in revenue. SMC also supports the psychic research of numerous parapsychologists, and is associated with the Mind Science Foundation in San Antonio, Texas—one of the few scientifically oriented and academically "respected" psi laboratories in the country.

Like every other psychic, occult, or human potential group, SMC has its list of "stars" who add prestige to the organization. One SMC graduate is Richard Bach, who psychically produced the occult-flavored national bestseller *Jonathan Livingston Seagull*, which apparently even outsold *Gone with the Wind!* Carol Lawrence, Loretta Swit, Celeste Holm, Vicki Carr, and at least 14 of the Chicago White Sox have, SMC claims, all publicly spoken of their involvement in SMC. SMC also offers special lectures and courses for a variety of professionals—lawyers, doctors, executives, and others. And SMC even targets children.

Perhaps reflective of Silva's work with his first pupils, he has every intention of exposing young people to the "benefits" of psychic development. Grade-school children are especially targeted.

Many elementary schools have used the SMC course for their pupils, such as, the Blessed Sacrament Elementary School in Johnson City, New York (2602). Silva states; "Our ultimate goal is to see that all children are trained to use more of their minds in this concept, to help them become superior human beings in every aspect of science and art" (2603; cf. 2596:24). If he has his way, the SMC course will be *compulsory* in all school systems from elementary level to university. Harry McKnight, a director of the Institute of Psychorientology, says, "We are looking forward to the day when Mind Control Method will be available in all school systems and universities" (2598:58).

Since children are a prime target, SMC lectures are offered specifically for them (e.g., MC101-404 CLS), and again, the goal is to reach as many as possible. Reaching the youth will allegedly help transform the world all the quicker. Mr. Silva's daughter, Laura, has written a text specifically designed to help children become psychic:

> To correct... wrong conditioning or wrong programming done by our parents, one can follow the instructions as indicated in my daughter's book, *For Parents Only: The Silva Method of Mind Control*.... [S]he explains how and what to program, before conception, after conception and before birth, and after birth, so as to have and to raise clairvoyant geniuses (2591:appendix,9A).

However, as we documented in *Thieves of Innocence* (1064) and *The Coming Darkness* (278), developing children psychically is not at all in their best interests. It will damage them spiritually and emotionally.

## THE PSYCHIC LIFE OF JOSÉ SILVA

As we indicated in *The Coming Darkness* (278), in the life of psychics and occultists generally, occult involvement can frequently be found in the person's family history, indicating that a predisposition to psychic capacity may be hereditary or inborn (278:207-15). This was true for José Silva. He explains in his two-volume autobiography *I Have a Hunch*:

I had an aunt who liked very much to go to spiritist mediums, to their seances and so forth. I was the driver. . . . [M]y grandmother got sick one time, and a spiritist medium came from Mexico City to heal her. . . . [T]he medium made my aunt an assistant medium of some kind, and gave her instructions in what to do. Then she came and did it all. So I had experiences like that before learning of the Rosicrucian healing methods. There was a lot of that kind of thing going on (2591:265-66).

As noted, one result of such a familial history of occult involvement is that one may be "born" psychic. As Silva said on our televised debate, "I was a natural [psychic] . . . one of those ten per-centers" (2600:PRG.2; cf. 2598:10).

He also discusses his involvement with the Rosicrucians, an occult sect specializing in "astral projection," saying that "after I got into my research, and was having some success as a healer, I wanted to join the Rosicrucians to learn more about their methods . . ." (2591:265-67, 269,274). Rosicrucianism is apparently where Silva first began his out-of-body travels and met his first spirit guide, a charming little Chinese fellow who always seemed to be present (2593). Besides Rosicrucianism, Silva told us that he has studied psychic healers all over the world; he has also studied psychometry, auras, and similar topics (2595:17/2594:46). In light of his exten-sive psychic involvement, it is hardly surprising that the SMC organization generally reflects these interests of its founder.

Other leaders in SMC also have occult back-grounds or interests. For example, SMC leader Harry McKnight, author of *Silva Mind Control Key to Inner Kingdoms Through Psychorientology,* has interests in Edgar Cayce, the Urantia Book, and other spiritistic literature (p. 4); he, too, claims he was psychic since childhood (2598:8).

Unfortunately, José Silva was "born psychic" because of the sins of occult practice within his own family. As a result, he adopted a lifelong interest in the occult and converted his own chil-dren. Before it is over, he may influence tens of millions of people, including children, to adopt dangerous occult practices. This is the real "fruit" of psychic involvement and one of the terrible legacies of SMC. Indeed, to emphasize the psy-chic training of children will exact a heavy price on them and society itself (278/1064), not to men-tion the psychic promoters themselves, as even Jesus warned (Matthew 18:6-7; Revelation 21:8).

## REASONS FOR SUCCESS

Thousands of people wish to develop them-selves psychically today, which is probably the primary reason they attend SMC seminars. And people also attend because of SMC's many self-help claims (more energy, efficiency, happiness, weight loss, improving studies and memory, and so on). Nevertheless, a good number of these individuals get more than they bargained for because SMC is really an occult primer—in the guise of a self-help human potential seminar (2619:7).

Yet given its claim to control common human maladies (obesity, illness, smoking, addictions) and to unleash "natural" powers of the mind, it is no wonder that SMC has a significant worldwide following. For example, in a society where mil-lions of people are fearful of cancer, the following claim cannot help but arouse interest among the uncritical: "[C]ancer is mind-made and mind-developed. We have had people in class who have had cancer and who have used Mind Control's methods and have gotten enormous results" (2601). And for the lovelorn, Silva has instruction on "how to find an ideal mate" through SMC:

We know that for each person, there is a perfect partner somewhere, and each is looking for the other. . . . reenter your [psychic] level and imagine you are communicating with High Intelligence at the center of the galaxy. . . . Select the day, the date, and the place you will meet your perfect partner. . . . [A]llow suffi-cient time, then High Intelligence will know how to get this person to come in contact with you (2604:25-26).

People are also told SMC is "down to earth, scientific, fast, effective, simple, economical and just right for the world" (2598:90). They are told that *all* graduates can "change problems to solutions, illness to health, poverty to abun-dance, hate to love" (2598:78,42). They learn that

SMC is a vanguard group "providing the world with the attitudes and tools necessary for the continued survival of mankind" (2605:2), and that it comprises "one of the most significant planetary forces in existence today" (2606:2). Of course, similar claims are made by scores of other groups who, like SMC, have yet to supply any actual proof of their claims. Nevertheless, lack of proof does not inhibit droves of people from believing the publicity and flocking to such self-help seminars. SMC is indeed a sign of the times.

Note, too, that semantics play an important role in creating a positive image for SMC. Silva avoids negative terms like "the occult," substituting terms like "spiritual." The preferred term for psychic power is "mental power"; when the term "psychic" is used, it is interwoven with spiritual concepts, e.g., "Praying is psychic. Praying is the use of the mind" (2600:PRG. 6).

Silva also claims that his activities and the psychic powers he promotes are divine endeavors—that is, "good" by definition. By assuming this position, he has no need for concern with other more negative possibilities, such as the spiritistic or demonic duplicity that is so evident in all psychic involvement (278). Note, for example, the following statement, which transforms his promotion of an occult dimension into a "holy" realm: "This spiritual, mental dimension is sacred and divine because it was created by God. Being sacred and divine makes it holy" (2607:93). SMC is successful because many people today are interested in such things.

## THE SMC COURSE: MENTAL POWER THROUGH POSITIVE THINKING, VISUALIZATION, AND HYPNOSIS

Despite claims to uniqueness, the SMC method is merely a variation on numerous common forms of human potentialism and meditative psychic development, often with a "Christian" flavor. In the following promotion, for example, one thinks of the literature of Christian "faith" teachers:

You will learn how to make health an automatic process rather than something we have to work for. And wealth. And success. And happiness, too. You were born to be a winner, to be healthy, wealthy, successful, and happy (2594:10).

Likewise, according to SMC, "negative thinking"—using negative terms such as "can't," "won't," "hate"—is forbidden. SMC believes that even when we use certain "negative" cultural phrases ("He burns me up"), we are slowly programming ourselves into sickness, pain, and death. Hence, a central premise, again, as in the modern Christian "faith" movement, is the tremendous power of words to impact the psyche (see our *The Facts on the Faith Movement*).

Silva declares, "Words have special power at deep levels of mind" (2597:60), and, "Words do not just reflect reality, they create reality" (2597:56). The SMC course itself includes some of Emile Coué's concepts of the power of positive thinking, as given in his 1974 text *Self-Mastery Through Autosuggestion*. During daily meditation periods, graduates repeat some of his ideas: "Every day, in every way, I am getting better, better and better"; "Positive thoughts bring me benefits and advantages I desire"; "I will always maintain a perfectly healthy body and mind" (2608:17). These ideas are combined with specific meditation courses that tend to develop psychic abilities, particularly psychic "diagnosis" and "healing." Indeed, within the movement there is a great interest and hope extended toward incorporating SMC-developed psychic healers into the general medical profession. (As in Therapeutic Touch and related methods of psychic healing, SMC graduates claim to manipulate and place psychic energy into those they are trying to heal.)

As is also true for most psychic development courses, SMC utilizes visualization* techniques. Remember, Silva teaches that the psychic dimension is the spiritual dimension: "Visualization and imagination are faculties of human intelligence that function in a spiritual dimension, the world of the mind dimension" (2594:38). Thus:

A clairvoyant is a super human person, one who really has been created "in the image of God," and who functions God-like, correcting problems in the spiritual, invisible world of the mind with visualization and imagination.

Once the problems are corrected in the spiritual, invisible world of the mind, the effects will then be transferred to the physical, visible world of the body (2607:92).

Visualization seems to be the most powerful way to obtain the results you want from your programming (2604:19).

In keeping with his program of redefining occult terms into normal or neutral categories, Silva prefers to use the term "subjective communication," or "effective sensory projection," rather than "telepathy," "clairvoyance," or "ESP," because the latter are evasive and uncontrollable whereas, allegedly, his methods are not. Silva believes his methods allow students to accomplish what no one else has ever done: to learn to regulate and *control* psychic powers in only four days (2609:3). We will see later that this is not the case. Furthermore, as we cited in the chapter on New Age education, in "The Hidden Agenda" section, redefining your terms does nothing to alter the actual facts.

The basic thrust of the SMC program is to teach initiates how to use meditation to enter an "alpha" brain-wave state; that is, the mental state which corresponds to a predominantly alpha brain-wave pattern on an EEG machine (8 to 13 Hz). It is called "going to your level," or "going into Alpha."

Beyond this, of course, there are also deeper levels of the mind to be explored. For example, at the theta brain-wave level we are told, "Deep regression studies and reincarnation-type studies can be done when the subject is functioning in a controlled way at Theta frequencies" (2598:16).

The four-day program extends over two weekends, each day comprising 10 to 12 hours of lectures and guided meditations. This includes 19 psychic meditations, which constitute about 25 percent of the course. A brief summary of the 48-hour program is as follows:

*Day One—Controlled Relaxation.* Developing control over relaxation, sleep, dreams, headaches; increasing one's vitality and energy; "solving problems." According to Silva, the meditations

comprise "an altered state of consciousness used in virtually every meditative discipline" (2597:17).

*Day Two—General Self-Improvement.* Learning various techniques such as internally projecting a "mental screen" for clairvoyance and other psychic abilities; "memory pegs" for improved memory; "hand levitation" for greater awareness; "Glove Anesthesia" for "psychic blood clotting"; pain reduction for use in an emergency; the "Glass of Water Technique" for dream control and "subjective communication." The "mental screen" is used for visualization* purposes, and it is a central ingredient deemed vital to psychic development (2597:39-40).

*Day Three—Effective Sensory Projection.* Mental (psychic) projection into metals, plant life, animal life; the creation of a mental "laboratory"; meeting your "psychic counselors" (what would otherwise be understood as spirit guides).

*Day Four—Applied Effective Sensory Projection.* Mental projection into human life for psychic diagnosis and healing.

Note Silva's comments concerning psychic healing:

Detecting illnesses in persons you have never seen is astonishing enough, but we never let it go at that. Into the bodies where we project our awareness we also project healing.

Obviously there is an energy involved in mental projection, an energy aimed by the intentions of our minds. Change these intentions from information gathering to healing and we change what the energy does.... You can become an effective psychic healer simply by using your mental screen as you do in problem solving. In fact, even if you are in the early stages of meditation and visualization, you may still achieve some effective results...(2597:99,102-03).

In addition to the seminars, people are offered numerous books on personal psychic development, such as Silva's *Subjective Communication* and Emilio Guzman's *Mind Control: New Dimensions of Human Thought.*

The basic (if unfounded) parapsychological premise of the SMC course is that every person has latent neutral untapped psychic powers within. Time and space are barriers that restrict the physical senses but not the psychic senses Silva seeks to develop. In SMC, these "mental" abilities have such potential that the mind can become "divine" and literally create what it wants—if four "laws" are followed:

1. You must desire that the event take place,
2. You must believe the event can take place,
3. You must expect the event to take place, and
4. You cannot create a problem.

Supposedly, once developed, these powers can only be used for self-improvement and good or moral purposes. This, however, is an unfortunate premise which betrays a lack of understanding as to how psychic powers have been used historically.

While the power of positive thinking has certainly worked for many people (maintaining a positive attitude has biblical support, when properly integrated to the whole of biblical faith), on its own it is certainly no panacea. Few positive thinkers today seem to be familiar with the *negative* potential of positive thinking, some of which we discussed in our *The Facts on the Mind Sciences*. Of course, the concept also has a built in "safety valve." If it does not work, you were not desiring, believing, or expecting hard enough; you were not *really* thinking positively. You must have been in a state of "disharmony" with the laws of the universe. Regardless, because the world is a reflection of the "ideas" of God (a Science of Mind teaching), and since all persons are part of God, what you imagine, you *can* create. "Nothing is impossible to the conscious mind.... Whatever the mind of man can image [imagine or visualize], man can realize" (2610:6). "Our own personal world is our consciousness objectified" (2611:5).

SMC also utilizes certain principles of hypnosis,* although it denies that its techniques are hypnotic and lists certain differences. Although they prefer to see their program as superior to hypnosis:

There are many similarities between the two disciplines. The meditation exercises are accomplished with the use of a tape-recorded steady "clacking" or other rhythmic sound, while the students are instructed, as hypnosis subjects would be, to breathe deeply, relax, and listen to the soothing voice of the instructor as he repeats certain phrases. Graduates of SMC testify to the time distortion which accompanies these "mental exercises," a phenomenon which is familiar in hypnosis.... Many of the results obtained through SMC are also obtained through hypnosis. The parallels between the two are clear (2601:248-49).

José Silva does admit that he experimented with hypnosis for many years prior to beginning SMC (2597:107). Thus, Silva may claim that SMC does not involve hypnosis, but he cannot deny that hypnosis has played an important part in the development of SMC. In Silva's autobiography (volume 1) this becomes quite evident. Chapter 10 is titled "Hypnosis Fascinates Me." Chapter 15 is "Hypnosis in our Family." Chapters 16 and 17 deal with hypnotic age regression into alleged "past lives," and Silva admits, "I personally conducted hundreds of age regression experiments" (2591:197). Furthermore, the Silva Mind exercise "The Keys to the Kingdom of Heaven," published by the Ecumenical Society of Psychorientology of Laredo, Texas, 1985, is basically a 20-page booklet on how SMC instructors (here, "readers") can hypnotize others (2608:20).

## THEOLOGY

*José Silva and Christianity*

As a practicing Roman Catholic, José Silva claims to be a genuine Christian. In a personal conversation that we had with Silva, he claimed that the Roman Catholic Church had given its official blessing to his activities. In that the Catholic church, especially its mystical side, often accepts parapsychological research and has a "tradition" of spiritism in its own ranks (contact with alleged souls in purgatory, Catholic saints, Mary, and other biblical departed), this is not necessarily surprising (2434:195-209). At one point Silva was subject to a local church inquiry, but in the end, he claims, they accepted his work. As he retells the story in volume 2 of his autobiography, he was initially charged with fraud, superstition, delving in the supernatural, and engaging in activities displeasing to God. The fraud charge was not true, since (at least then) he was not charging for his services; and as for the other allegations, he replied to the church officials point by point. Thus, psychic activity must be pleasing to God because SMC utilizes it only for good purposes; Silva does not claim to deal in the realm of the supernatural, only the natural, hence he cannot be engaging in superstition or the occult (2596:43,44,46/2595:28).

Silva places a Christian imprimatur on SMC generally. In *Silva Reflections* he declares, "This book projects and exposes, exclusively, my own personal concepts and convictions as a researcher and as a Christian" (2595:8). He even claims to teach only what Jesus taught—therefore, he must also be considered a follower of Jesus:

In studying Christ's sayings and comparing them with our research findings we find very close similarities. . . .

Christ's saying, "He who believes in me the works that I do he also shall do," to us means that a Christian is not a person who just talks about Christ, but a person who does what Christ did (2595:32-33).

He also admits that his work is quite similar to that of mesmerist and psychic healer Phineas P. Quimby, whose work was instrumental in the founding of Christian Science, an anti-Christian religion. "The one who impressed me the most as a researcher in the field of the mind was . . . Phineas Parkhurst Quimby. . . . Dr. Quimby appears to have gone through everything we have experienced in our research with only minor differences" (2595:35-36).

Why is Silva so concerned with Christianity? The church is very important to Silva's goal of expanding the influence of SMC (2591:App. 11A). Not surprisingly then, one of his principal goals is to multiply the Christian population of SMC. So important is this to his plans that he offers the SMC course free to Christian pastors (2594:149).

In addition, Silva claims to receive psychic guidance from Jesus Christ, whom he believes has directed his life on the path it has taken (2594:93,105). He interprets this as divine revelation. In his autobiography he recalls how Christ "communicated" to him through a picture:

Christ was staring at me.

It was a large picture of Christ, just His head and shoulders, but as large as life, looking at me with dark piercing eyes, not judging, but full of love and compassion and I felt as though He was asking, "Why did you stop studying? Did I not tell you to study psychology?"

Tears came to my eyes and a feeling as though I had been a bad boy for not obeying. . . . Once again, I got out my psychology books. I framed the large picture of Christ, and it has been hanging in my office ever since. This last experience, with the picture of Christ, gave me more determination than ever before; I also consider this experience to be responsible for my method, developed through research, being brought to millions of people throughout the world . . . (2591:225,227,229).

The connection between "Christ and psychology" was eventually found in the study of parapsychology. "The study of hypnosis helped us to become better acquainted with the power of our phenomenal minds, and the study of parapsychology helped us to know what others had done in that field and how they did it" (2595:40).

The association between SMC and so-called "Christian" parapsychology here is a logical one. And due to the influence of SMC, many liberal theologians, priests, and pastors are accepting the unbiblical worldview of "Christian" parapsychology. For example an Episcopalian priest recommends SMC and uses SMC methods with his parishioners. He laments that in all his seminary studies he never learned to "pray." But "now because of the psychic training I had received, I was able to enter the inner kingdom." The SMC course was "what I had been seeking," and psychic prayer and meditation* coupled with SMC techniques "have become the basis of my ministry." Although, regrettably, he had "to go to a commercial ESP training course" to learn how to "pray in the Spirit," it was better late than never. As a result of SMC, he now sees the biblical gifts of the Holy Spirit as psychic gifts (2612), a common premise of "Christian" parapsychology.

This parapsychological restructuring of theology is the typical impact when SMC and nominal Christianity mix. We have discussed elsewhere why parapsychology is anti-Christian, and how it dismantles the gospel in its "Christian" form (1522:272-81). Our concern here is to note that SMC is part of that process. It has a theological outlook, and it attempts to influence the church, both Protestant and Catholic. A number of Roman Catholic sisters (with church approval) use it in their classrooms, and some nuns use their SMC-developed psychic powers openly (2613). For them the kingdom of God is none other than the "Alpha level" meditation that SMC promotes (2614). Of course, they claim to teach "Christian meditation," but this is not true, biblically speaking, as a study of the phrase "kingdom of God" and the word "meditation" in Scripture reveals.

SMC also makes a standard disclaimer here. Silva alleges, "Ours is not a religious movement, nor, for that matter, a movement dealing with the 'occult'" (2615:2). But as is true for est,* TM, and other allegedly nonreligious New Age Movement seminars, the commercial aspect simply makes it more accessible, but not necessarily less religious.

Because SMC originated as a spiritual technique rather than a theological system, we can acknowledge that its doctrinal structure is incomplete. But we can declare unequivocally that SMC has an inherently religious nature and that this nature is not Christian. Despite the claim that it "sits in any church pew," SMC is distinctly anti-Christian in its theological perspective. Although it has no "required" theology per se, there are references to seemingly polytheistic or monistic concepts of deity:

> Everything in some respect is the universal mind and the creation of that mind. . . . Each one of us is an idea in the universal mind. Man chooses to think of himself as a separate being . . . but actually we participate in this mind as an atom of water participates in the substance of the ocean (2611:4-5).

Reflecting this monistic premise, SMC graduates are to continue to "make [themselves] more consciously one with all that is" (2598:73).

McKnight, a leader of the organization, declares, "Jose wants people to find the guru within them . . . [a] self-orientation to their God-source within them," and, "In getting in touch with our own source, one definitely gets dependent on that source" (2614:7). How is this nonreligious? Silva himself boldly declares, "Our job on this planet is to take care of creation. We are, after all, extensions of our Creator" (2605:2). In emphasizing proper thinking, he argues that "thoughts that hinder and are negative [for example, thoughts "restricting" our psychic capacity] go against the Creator, which we sometimes call the Devil's side" (2605:2). Such statements betray SMC's theological dimension.

More or less, SMC adopts a New Age pseudo-Christian terminology that reflects a syncretistic and universalist theology. For example, through SMC the student is promised a higher state of consciousness:

> The Mind Control graduates will then have attained what is called *Christ Awareness*. And the experience is open to all alike—Christian, Jew, Moslem, Hindu, Atheist—after all, we are from the same Ultimate Source and we all live within the same system of law. We all call only One our Father. And the Father is within each of us (2598:77-78).

But Jesus Himself knew nothing of "Christ awareness" or the liberal theological concept of the universal Fatherhood of God and its corollary, universalism. Jesus taught that only true believers in Him, not humanity in general, have God as their Father. He told the hypocritical religious leaders of His day, "If God were your Father, you would love me, for I came from God. . . . You belong to your father, the devil" (John 8:42,44).

The biblical teaching, then, is that only some people have God as their spiritual Father (John 8:19;16:3;15:23;17:25). Why? Because God the Father only resides within His children: those who have believed on His Son, the historical Jesus Christ (John 1:12). Biblically then, there is a condition for having the Father within, that is, knowing God personally (John 17:3). To have God as one's Father and true "Christ awareness" is to have received Jesus Christ personally as one's Lord and Savior and to follow Him (John 1:11-12;12:26;14:23-24). But this has nothing to do with the Jesus of SMC. In SMC, the power of the mind is held to be so great that with proper training the mind *becomes* "the 'son' of God," hence everyone already has the son of God within them in a latent sense (2598:84-87).

Believing in "the Son" Jesus Christ means something entirely different for Silva Mind Control than it does for Christianity. We will document this in more detail below.

*God*

José Silva adopts a "unitarian" (as opposed to trinitarian) view of God, sometimes mixed with New Age concepts. God is the absolute Creator, but below Him exists a Gnostic-like hierarchy of "creative intelligences," which Silva apparently helps direct, all the way down to man (cf. 2591:15/2595:55-56). In Silva's *The Silva Mind Control Method*, God is loosely defined. Anyone can contact Him or "it" through SMC as sort of an omnipresent intelligent energy which we can "tap into" in order to develop psychic powers. According to Silva, man and matter appear to be simply different forms of the same universal intelligent energy we may call God (2597:106).

In our televised debate with José Silva on "The John Ankerberg Show" he defined the Holy Spirit as follows: "My personal definition of the Holy Spirit, to me, is a dimension that we can create, a state of mind to enter and make use of for problem solving situations." In other words, the Holy Spirit is the mental "dimension" of the alpha state produced by SMC. Since that dimension exists potentially within all men, the Holy Spirit is a potentially higher "state" of all men, and it "indwells" all men.

Since everything is part of the one intelligence ("God"), each of us is inherently divine. Of course "the Father" also dwells within us, but this says nothing about what Jesus taught, only what Silva believes. Thus, it is easy to see how New Age premises condition SMC theology.

Although sometimes Silva seems to distinguish God from the creation (2597:109), it appears that ultimately God is simply the most complex form of the universal energy underlying the creation:

I see various levels of intelligence *as a continuum*, going from inanimate matter to the vegetable to the animal, then to the human and to Higher Intelligence and finally to God (2597:109, emphasis added).**

Silva also speaks of his "scientific" (i.e., "psychic") contacts at each level: "I believe I have scientifically found ways of communicating with each level, from the inanimate to Higher Intelligence" (2597:109). And as noted earlier, there also seems to be a polytheistic element in SMC. McKnight teaches:

As you gain expertise at using the beautiful equipment *your creators* have given you to work with, you eventually learn to control with such intelligent management of energy that you attain more and more peak experiences of Christ Awareness until you eventually become a prominent citizen of the realm which is the second phase of human evolution on this planet. And you will do it all for yourself through the Silva Method (2598:78, emphasis added).

This idea of multiple "creators" may be associated with certain beliefs about extraterrestrial entities, although Silva has personally told us he is not a UFO contactee. SMC apparently views itself as being in the forefront of what will eventually culminate in a galactic citizenship for planet earth. In McKnight's book (2598), the dedication page by José Silva reads, "To: The honorable creators of our galaxy, the Milky Way, that through these works we creatures will now evolve to our full potential." Silva even claims to give a person the ability "to sense information impressed in neurons of any brain that is on this planet, or a brain that is on any planet within our solar system, any solar system within our galaxy or on any galaxy within our universe" (2598:84).

McKnight also speaks of our "new galactic citizenship," that is, our becoming on this planet what other planets have already achieved (2617).

---

**In another sense, "Higher Intelligence" begins with the human and extends throughout the intermediate spiritual higher intelligences (for example, SMC's psychic counselors) all the way to the absolute God. It is also defined, at least in part, as knowledge received by psychic means.

"We are the stuff of guidance for the planet. . . . We are the instruments of planetary uplift," he says referring to the leaders of SMC, whom he believes are similar to the "avatars" of history— "Christ," Buddha, Krishna (2617). Thus, "We are coming of age to join our stellar neighbors" (2617). "When we can control even Delta . . . we can do whatever needs to be done—we then will have arrived at the end of this earth plane mission" (2598:71).

*Jesus Christ*

It is from some of Silva's major teachings on Jesus Christ that we see the anti-Christian nature of SMC in particular.

*Christ did not come to die for human sin.* Silva clearly rejects the concept of a substitutionary, propitiatory atonement. Consider the dialogue between Silva and ourselves during week five of a 1986 debate on "The John Ankerberg Show":

*José Silva*: If anything that Jesus did cannot be duplicated [by us], it has no value for us today. . . . Doing it once in eternity and nobody can duplicate that, it has no value, because we're not going to be able to use it to continue solving more problems, so what value does it have? Just to know that it was done once?

*John Weldon*: How would you apply that to the death of Christ? That was only done once, it can't be repeated [Rom. 6:9], but Jesus said [it] was to forgive the sin of the world. That certainly has value!

*José Silva*: Can you imagine what would have happened if He didn't die? We'd all be Jewish today.

*John Weldon*: If He didn't die we would all have our sins unforgiven.

*José Silva*: Oh boy, that's [just] your thought (2600:Prg. 5).

To the contrary, it is what the Bible teaches (John 3:16). In 1 John 2:2 we read, "He is the atoning sacrifice for our sins, and not only for ours but also for the sins of the whole world." In 1 Peter 2:24 we read, "He Himself bore our sins in his body on the tree." Hebrews 9:28 states, "Christ was sacrificed once to take away the sins

of many people." Not surprisingly, Silva, denying what the Bible teaches, declares that man is to save himself:

Christ came with the message that we were created to be able to solve our own problems and do not need to turn to a supernatural power to solve them for us; we can solve our own problems if we will simply make a commitment to do so.

We do not need to constantly put God to work asking, "Heal this person," and *"Save that person,"* and "Do this," and "Do that." Who am I to put God to work? It is the other way: God has created *us to do such work.* And God expects all of us to help in solving problems on this planet. Then we will earn our rewards, through our demonstration of our faith and respect and reverence (2594:15 emphasis added).

To the contrary, the Bible teaches God "saved us, not because of righteous things we had done, but because of his mercy" (Titus 3:5). "For it is by grace you have been saved, through faith— and this not from yourselves, it is the gift of God—not by works, so that no one can boast" (Ephesians 2:8-9).

*Believing in Christ does not bring salvation.* Some of the clearest statements illustrating Silva's view of Jesus Christ are found in *The Mystery of the Keys to the Kingdom.* They unmistakably reveal both his misunderstanding of the central message of the New Testament and his evident rejection of and opposition to the gospel (cf. Luke 22:20; Acts 20:28; Revelation 3:20; Romans 10:9):

Many preachers have again and again recommended that we should have faith and believe in one of the great avatars of the past and that we will be saved or forgiven. Saved and born again for what? To continue making the same mistakes and continue hurting each other?

Just thinking about Jesus is not going to do it, nor allowing Him to enter your heart, or to be cleansed by His blood in hopes you will be saved. Jesus never said, "Being cleansed with my blood will save you," and He never said, "If you let me enter into your heart you will be saved" . . . (2594:162-63).

Again, Silva has denied biblical teaching. Silva claims that the blood of Christ does not cleanse from sin. But Scripture tells us, "In him we have redemption through his blood, the forgiveness of sins" (Ephesians 1:7), and "the blood of Jesus . . . purifies us from all sin" (1 John 1:7), and Christ Jesus "has freed us from our sins by his blood" (Revelation 1:5). Jesus Himself said during the last supper, "This is my blood of the covenant, which is poured out for many" (Mark 14:24). José Silva is wrong when he claims that the blood of Christ does not cleanse people from sin.

Silva also denies that Jesus Christ will physically return to earth:

We have been told, and are still being told, that He is coming back again. But why do we need Him to return again, when He fulfilled His mission and delivered His message to us [i.e., SMC]? We need only to heed the message. But instead of learning the method that Rabbi Jesus taught, instead of using the keys He entrusted to Peter, we are told to worship the man and expect Him to solve all of our problems for us and to correct what needs correcting on the planet . . . (2594:31-32).

Nevertheless, Jesus said, "And if I go and prepare a place for you, I will come back and take you to be with me that you also may be where I am" (John 14:3). And the angels told the apostles immediately after Christ's physical ascension into heaven, "This same Jesus, who has been taken from you into heaven, will come back in the same way you have seen him go into heaven" (Acts 1:11).

Of course, every religious cult and sect that wishes to replace the message of the New Testament with its own teachings must find a way to make such a transformation feasible. A common method is to claim that the "original" message of the New Testament was corrupted and that its "true" meaning has now been rediscovered. Following this lead, Silva teaches that the true message of the New Testament was later corrupted by unenlightened scribes. He then replaces its message with one of his own: "It could be that whoever put the information together, not being there when it happened and also not being a wise man and prophet himself, did not under-

stand the meaning or value of the keys to open the kingdom of heaven [i.e., SMC]" (2594:34).

One means by which Silva is able to reinterpret the Bible into conformity with SMC is his "rule of thumb" on hermeneutics (remember, SMC is the principal method for modern problem solving):

My rule of thumb on the interpretation of the scriptures is that the interpretation that offers the most information for problem solving is not only best, but is also the real and most truthful. Truth and reality, as I see them, are information that when applied solves problems. . . . My study of the Bible was the foundation that I built on for the development of the Silva Method. And a good source can produce only good fruits, I believe (2594:17).

One only need think of the endless cults that claim to be based on the Bible to question such a conclusion. Basing one's philosophy on the Bible will produce true spiritual fruit only if one interprets the Bible correctly to begin with, and then, as Jesus taught, only if we obey what we learn (see Matthew 7:21-22). Silva has neglected both.

*Jesus Christ was not incarnate deity.* José Silva also rejects the biblical teaching on Jesus Christ's deity, preferring to view Him as a physically advanced human whose abilities we can all emulate:

I believe that Rabbi Jesus, a highly evolved son of God, His Father, who is also our Father, was assigned to this planet as a Saviour of humanity, to save humanity from suffering due to ignorance. . . . Rabbi Jesus is a son of God, our God. We are also sons of the same God, not as evolved as Rabbi Jesus was, but still sons of the same God (2594:125-27).

Typical of "spiritual evolution" views, Silva believes that one day, in one sense, he will be greater than Jesus: "I for one believe that some day, when I become more evolved than the level of evolution that Rabbi Jesus demonstrated during his mission on earth, I could then do greater works, as He said I could" (2594:128). To the contrary, the Bible teaches that Jesus Christ is utterly unique because He alone is the only Son of God and the only incarnation of God. He is God's "one and only Son" (John 3:16,18), who has "the name that is above every name" (Philippians 2:9), who is "in very nature God" (Philippians 2:6; cf. Titus 2:13), and who has supremacy in all things (Colossians 1:18).

*SMC is Christ returned.* Silva rejects Jesus' physical return and teaches that the second coming of "Christ" involves using the "right brain" hemisphere to reach the "inner kingdom" (2594: 163,165). According to SMC, Christ taught SMC, and this was the most important aspect of His mission. Therefore, the "return" to the earth of SMC (Christ's most important work) is equivalent to the biblical doctrine of the second coming. SMC, of course, is not the first sect to claim that its activities comprise the second coming. Christian Science, the Unification Church, and many others make similar assertions (2595:7,55). While the arrogance of such a claim is not lost on everyone, it does help "legitimize" the activities of the organization to the undiscerning.

In yet another theological twist, since Jesus is not physically returning to earth, those who wish to meet Him must do so through visualization* in their own psychic "inner kingdom":

> Do always keep in mind that for me the correct interpretation is that Rabbi Jesus the Christ is not coming to the earthly level again in His physical form, but that He exists in the kingdom of heaven that is within us. To meet with Rabbi Jesus we must enter the kingdom of heaven, a spiritual kingdom that is within us. . . . Rabbi Jesus is not coming to us to solve our problems on this planet (2594:92).

On our televised debate, Silva stated, "Some of our students have Jesus as their counselor. . . . [T]hey were lucky that Jesus appeared for them, and they use Jesus as a consultant" (2600:Prg. 6). Thus Jesus is merely another psychic spirit guide to be used as a consultant; presumably He appears for the developing occultists at their command. This is hardly the biblical Jesus Christ who is God Almighty and who does not obey people's whims and "commands."

A friend of the authors, Johanna Michaelsen, wrote *The Beautiful Side of Evil*, which is repre-

sentative of the potential for spiritual deception here. She was a graduate of SMC and invited "Jesus" to be her "counselor." Things went fine for a while, but, as is true in many other cases (278), once she entertained doubts about the true identity of the guide and became convinced it was an evil spirit, "Jesus," her own guide, attempted to kill her! She offers one among many testimonies that belie the claim that going into the alpha state via SMC is harmless.

### Salvation

According to Silva Mind Control, the kingdom of God and being "born again" are about entering the "alpha state" and using your "right brain." Thus, the "gospel" to Silva means seeking the "kingdom of heaven" through developing our "right brain" hemisphere, going into our alpha level, and while in that altered state of consciousness* meeting our psychic guides, who will help us develop psychic abilities. And with these powers we will solve the world's problems and usher in a paradise on earth.

Alpha brain waves in the right-brain hemisphere, therefore, are vital. Silva thus claims that the kingdom of God corresponds to a brain-wave pattern of 8 to 13 Hz (alpha). Silva bases his views on Jesus' statement that "the kingdom of God is within you" (Luke 17:21 KJV). But the Greek term for "within," *entos*, can mean either "within" or "in your midst." Had Jesus really meant "inside," the more appropriate word would have been *eso*, which does not carry the dual meaning that *entos* does (2618:254,218). Thus, the New American Standard Bible, along with many other versions, translates this word "in your midst." Jesus was telling His listeners that the kingdom of God was among them, right there in their midst, because He Himself was present as King.

Although there is a sense in which the kingdom of God exists within believers, since Christ is Lord of their lives, Jesus would hardly have used the word *entos* to mean "inside." Why? Because He was speaking to the Pharisees who rejected Him and even tried to kill Him. The kingdom of God could not possibly have been inside such hypocritical, God-rejecting people. If they *hated* Christ, how could His kingdom of love be inside them? Jesus called them sons of hell and sons of the devil, so how could that mean that God's kingdom was inside *them*?

How then do we really enter the kingdom of God? Jesus never taught that it was by entering a particular brain-wave state(!) but through personally receiving Him as Lord and Savior. In John 3:3-5, Jesus emphasized that one could neither *see* nor *enter* the kingdom of God apart from the new birth, or spiritual regeneration. Thus, in John 3:8, one must be born of the Spirit of God, not of oneself or of one's mental powers and psychic development. Hence, He said, "That which is born of the flesh is flesh, and that which is born of the Spirit is spirit. Do not marvel that I said to you, 'You must be born again' "(John 3:6-7 NASB).

Silva has the same problem Nicodemus had—wondering how one can be born again from the womb, not realizing that Jesus was speaking spiritually of birth by the Holy Spirit. Thus, in John 6:63 (NASB) we read, "the Spirit... gives life; the flesh profits nothing." For Silva "the flesh"—at least its brain waves—profits everything. Consider Silva's definition of being born again. To be born again is the process of becoming a new person by using right-brain thinking through SMC (2600:Prg. 3):

When we enter the kingdom of heaven, once there we become centered and have access to the use of the right brain hemisphere. The first time we enter the kingdom of heaven and start for the first time to use the right brain hemisphere to think with would be like being born again.... This would truly be the concept of being born again (2594:162,164).

Thus, "salvation" for the mind-control devotee is primarily working your way into a "higher" state of consciousness and "retaining" it. The SMC graduate is to continually make himself "one" with the universe. Having done so, one becomes a superior person, a jump ahead of others who do not use psychic abilities. This is why, according to Silva, those who solve the most problems are the closest to God (who is the greatest problem solver of all). Given the rationale of SMC, therefore, Silva has solved more problems than anyone else on the planet and is therefore the closest to God.

Below alpha lies the theta and delta brainwave levels. Ultimately, the graduate is to have control over even his delta level, at which point he becomes a type of "god" (2598:77). "The Mind Control graduates eventually realize that they create their own destiny" (2598:73). Sooner or later, the various psychic or "unconscious" levels of the mind will merge into unity with the conscious mind, and we will not only have total use of our minds but will merge into (or perhaps experientially "realize") oneness with our divine Source (2598:76).

In comparing SMC with the Christian concept of salvation, we find that most of what is supplied by faith in Jesus Christ, biblically speaking, is *claimed* to be supplied by SMC. Thus, sin and guilt are *not* removed by the atonement and personal faith in Christ, but through positive thinking. "One of the beauties of meditation at the Alpha level is that you *cannot* bring your feelings of guilt and anger with you" (2597:28). In the mental laboratory which each initiate constructs, there are "baths for washing away guilt" (2597:85). No Savior from sin is necessary, since we can cleanse ourselves.

It should be obvious by now that according to the SMC worldview there is no source apart from man that can "save" him or fulfill his deepest spiritual needs. People must ultimately save themselves by tapping that infinite reservoir of power within (2598:73-75). Through SMC, "We start perfecting ourselves" as the "Mind Control Method helps people help themselves" (2598:48,68). Silva declares we must ensure that, individually and collectively, "The flow of the evolving process continues until peak PERFECTION is found" (2605:2).

SMC graduates are taught to rely entirely upon themselves for all of their spiritual needs. Biblically, however, such a doctrine comes under God's judgment, since it perpetuates rebellion against Him, and a prideful human self-dependence (Isaiah 2:22; Galatians 1:6-8; Romans 3:28; 4:4-5; 9:30–10:4; Ephesians 2:8-9; Galatians 2–3).

The Bible teaches that salvation is *freely* available to all who trust in Jesus: "Yet to all who received him, to those who believed in his name, he gave the right to become children of God" (John 1:12). And Jesus emphasized, "I tell you the truth, whoever hears my word and believes him who sent me *has eternal life* and will not be condemned; he has crossed over from death to life" (John 5:24). And, "I tell you the truth, he who believes *has* everlasting life" (John 6:47). All this is why the apostle John wrote:

> Anyone who believes in the Son of God has this testimony in his heart. Anyone who does not believe God has made him out to be a liar, because he has not believed the testimony God has given about his Son. And this is the testimony: God has given us eternal life, and this life is in his Son. He who has the Son has life; he who does not have the Son of God does not have life. I write these things to you who believe in the name of the Son of God so that *you may know* that you *have* eternal life (1 John 5:10-13).

### Man, Sin, the Fall

Silva teaches that man was created by God to be "a god," a cocreator with Him. "We have been created in the image of God our Creator for the purpose of serving as smaller gods to help with the creation of our planet" (2594:74-75). SMC views man as progressively evolving from his lowly animal origins—that is, from the original primitive condition—to his current advanced state, and eventually to a type of existence as gods. According to Mr. Silva, man is basically good. "[W]e are capable of no harm at all and a vast amount of good" (2597:106). Of course, if man is innately good, he cannot be innately sinful.

This contrasts with the biblical view that man was originally noble and great (because created in God's image), but due to the fall became sinful, selfish, and capable of great cruelty and evil. Thus man today is basically sinful, not good (Romans 3:10-18; Psalm 51:5). Indeed, "All have sinned and fall short of the glory of God" (Romans 3:23). The fall brought death, disease, decay, and self-centeredness to such a degree that the heart of man is "deceitful above all things and beyond cure" (Jeremiah 17:9), a truth Jesus also emphasized (Matthew 15:19).

SMC teaches that it can counteract even the fall. In our televised debate with Silva (week three) he stated, "Sin is error because of ignorance. If we knew better as what to do, we wouldn't commit

sin." In response to the question, "How do you get rid of true guilt?" he responded, "Learn to use both brain hemispheres." Sin and guilt, then, are not defined biblically; sin is mere ignorance and guilt is ultimately irrelevant. People would have no guilt and could be perfect if they just functioned with both brain hemispheres fully operating. "If Mind Control were perfect (it is not; we are still learning) I believe we would all have perfect bodies, all the time" (2597:68).

One wonders if Silva truly believes that people who learned SMC perfectly would never commit any wrong, that they would never sin again. If not, how would they be without true guilt before a holy God? " 'Although you wash yourself with soda and use an abundance of soap, the stain of your guilt is still before me,' declares the Sovereign Lord" (Jeremiah 2:22). "This is what the LORD says, 'Cursed is the one who trusts in man, who depends on flesh for his strength and whose heart turns away from the LORD' " (Jeremiah 17:5).

### Satan, Heaven, Hell

José Silva also rejects the biblical teaching on Satan, heaven, and hell. Of the devil he states:

> My concept about the devil is not an entity with horns and a tail, but an influence that keeps us from doing what is right, an influence that keeps us from correcting problems of creation.... This influence, "the devil," is just plain ignorance of not knowing any better what we should be doing (2594:70).

Hell is essentially pain produced in this life as a result of one's "ignorance." And Silva also adopts a mediumistic view of the afterlife:

> My concept about hell is not a place full of flames, but a situation that causes us to hurt because we had ears to hear and did not hear....
>
> My concept of what happens after we are dead is something I cannot be certain about, so I will use a phrase I like to use when I am not sure about something, "Could be." It could be that we are assigned to another dimension, plane of existence, or planet less evolved than the one we left behind so as to learn our lessons and evolve (2594:70-71).

Heaven is also redefined in mediumistic terms:

My concept of the heaven that we are supposed to go to when we die is not a place where we rest or loaf forever and ever. For me it is another dimension, plane of existence, or planet, that is more evolved than the one left behind (2594:71).

Silva's teachings conflict with what the Bible teaches concerning heaven and hell as real, eternal places, and of Satan as a real, personal being (Matthew 25:46; Revelation 20:1-10).

*Morality*

There is little doubt that SMC can be used without regard to ethical standards:

Some people [instructors] are in Mind Control only for the money. Jose [Silva] feels it doesn't really matter what your motive is when you start teaching; that once you've been in it long enough, you can't help but be affected [positively] by it (2627:140).

In response to a question about whether it is moral "to program other people" or "interfere with their 'free will,'" the response was that such things were moral actions:

As long as we are working to help correct things, to help relieve suffering, to make things right, we are doing what is "moral."

A person might feel he has a "right" to be ill, to suffer for some reason. We believe this is a mistaken attitude, and we should program [him] to help him understand this error in his thinking (2604:43-44).

During our debate with Silva on "The John Ankerberg Show," Dave Hunt referred to a former teacher to whom he had spoken. This person claimed that Silva convened a special session for SMC instructors in Laredo, Texas, who were *using SMC* to seduce women and for financial gain. Silva admitted that there *were* problems, but claimed *SMC* was not the cause of those problems (2600:Prg. 4).

Another problem concerns a basic premise of SMC that the mind is near omnipotence and can control almost anything. Biblically and rationally the human mind does not have anywhere near the power SMC attributes to it. Yet what are the consequences of granting the mind more power than it has? One result is that people tend to think and act unwisely in ways that are out of touch with reality, in ways which they would not do otherwise (1937:31). In *The Facts on the Mind Sciences,* we supplied illustrations.

Another problem concerns the malevolent motives behind the spirits who are guiding many SMC-trained people. What if a graduate *thinks* that something is wrong with her car and only "intuitively" examines the noise? And what if her psychic sense or counselor "tells" her everything is okay but a wheel is ready to fall off? Or could an airline pilot be so confident in his psychic sense that he would believe a cockpit warning light is merely malfunctioning because he is unable to psychically "locate" the trouble? "There is this Mind Control graduate who is a commercial pilot with a large airline. He is one of many. He now uses his Mind Control Method to sense his equipment before he takes it off the ground" (2598:56). (Incredibly, the March 30, 1995, "Nightline" program ran a critical story about air traffic controllers who had been influenced by the teachings of "Ramtha," channeler J.Z. Knight's spirit guide! To trust in the spirits' influence when other people's lives are at stake betrays the degree of deception to which people may subject themselves.)

*SMC and the Occult*

The admission by Silva Mind Control that its purpose is to develop psychic abilities is evidence enough of its fundamentally occult nature. "This whole process of psychic investigation we call *Psychorientology:* Science of Mind Control, or Science of Self-Guidance" (2598:49). "The Silva Method of Mind Control is the means to function psychically—clairvoyantly" (2619:7). Silva constantly attempts to point out the "benefits" for humanity of learning to function "at Alpha" rather than in a normal state of consciousness (2597:19).

In the major texts on SMC, in its newsletters, and at its conventions, the consumer is given a broad-based exposure to numerous occult topics, including divination,* numerology,* clairvoyance, psychometry, clairaudience, clairsentience, telepathy, psychokinesis, group psychic healing ("the gathering and focusing of directed healing energy"), precognition, and retrocognition (2598:16,33-34/2597:99-100,159). SMC also claims to be useful for reincarnation and spiritistic research (2598:63), and it tells us that we can, among other things, use SMC to:

play with clouds; psychically sense problems in machinery (2598:55/2597:146).

get rich through lotteries or the stock market (2597:50-55/2598:51).

influence the content of ours and others' dreams (2598:41).

become an effective psychic healer (2597:99).

read auras (2597:80).

Silva even credits much of the public acceptance of psychics to the work of his own organization—a claim that has some merit:

Psychics . . . are beginning to gain more recognition as truly legitimate and worthwhile practitioners. I feel that much of the acceptance of this new dimension of the mind is due to work we have carried out at Silva Mind Control thus providing credibility and legitimacy to the area (2621:2).

To the contrary, when members are "guaranteed that by the end of the course [they] would be trained in psychic awareness," SMC is, to that degree, guaranteeing that people may or will be harmed spiritually (2621:3/2612). Also since it has been documented (278) that occult involvement of any type may cause a proportionately higher rate of suicide, insanity, and other psychopathology, as well as physical and spiritual problems, we need to label SMC as physically, emotionally, and spiritually dangerous. Indeed, many of the psychic practices Silva Mind Control advocates are those things the Bible condemns:

Let no one be found among you who sacrifices his son or daughter in the fire, who practices divination or sorcery, interprets omens, engages in witchcraft, or casts spells, or who is a medium

or spiritist or who consults the dead. Anyone who does these things is detestable to the LORD, and because of these detestable practices the LORD your God will drive out those nations before you (Deuteronomy 18:10-12; cf., 2 Chronicles 33:2-6; Acts 13:6-11; Acts 16:16-19; 19:18-20).

When the Bible condemns divination,* spiritism, and contacting the dead, it includes SMC by implication.

*Spiritism*
SMC has tried to introduce every one of its ten million graduates to "psychic guides" or counselors. How did these first originate in SMC? Apparently, by spiritistic initiative. In a personal conversation with José Silva, he told us that many years ago, as he was formulating SMC and engaging in his own "spiritual" development, he noticed a curious phenomenon. Every time he went "out of the body," he encountered a little Chinese fellow to the back of his right shoulder. Eventually they became "friends," and this was one of Silva's first spiritistic encounters. And if we remember the conversation fully, Silva said that this fellow became the inspiration or "prototype" for the inner counselors contacted through the SMC program. In our debate, Silva made the following comments about the spiritistic (2596:170) inner counselors, or psychic guides: "I have had them all my life." "They have been my research for 42 years—all over the world, with psychic surgeons in Mexico, Central America." ("They help you in the psychic healings?") "They do, yes." "They are here . . . to help you evolve, to become as good as they are, whoever they are" (2600).

Supposedly, these entities are benign. Yet a former director of SMC in Pennsylvania told author Dave Hunt, who was also on "The John Ankerberg Show" SMC debate, that in the early days many people met counselors, spontaneously, who were demonic-looking beings, creatures, not humans, and that SMC had to place further controls on the practice. Even today graduates do not always get the guides they want or "mentally create." One graduate reports, "Rarely do you get who you think you will. My male counselor was an old Indian (Native American) and my woman counselor was a beautiful Chinese lady" (2621:8). Clearly, it is not mind *control* if you do not get the "counselor" you want!

On the program, Silva admitted: 1) He was not sure *what* the guides were but that they were very real to the graduates; 2) that participants cannot *control* them because they have a volition all their own; 3) that they give supernatural information—that is, information not otherwise known to the person. This dovetails neatly with spiritism, regardless of SMC's attempt to internalize, psychologize, and normalize the entities and their information as part of the unconscious mind. Again, as far as Silva is concerned, pragmatism is the key. At one point on the Ankerberg show he naively stated that if the information is good and people are helped, "Who cares where the information comes from, the idea is to get it any way you can to solve a problem and forget everything else." He has also said:

Counselors can be very real to Mind Control graduates. What are they? We are not sure—perhaps some figment of an archetypal imagination, perhaps an embodiment of the inner voice, perhaps something more. What we do know is that once we meet our counselors and learn to work with them, the association is respectful and priceless (2597:87).

The graduate relies heavily on these "counselors," and here also there is much in common with spiritistic practices and effects. In literature for SMC graduates only, we can see the parallels. "Directives for Orientologists" (MC-404-ESP) point 1b states, "Once at your laboratory level meet your counselors and say your welcome prayer." At the end of a psychic diagnosis, they are instructed, "Thank your counselors, say your farewell prayer" (point 4b).

A kind of friendly relationship between the "counselors" and graduates is developed in the same way a medium develops her relationship to her spirit guide(s). Continuing the spiritistic association, point 1b includes "placing your protective shield between you and your subject" (2634). Alluding to necromantic contacts, Silva teaches that the minds of SMC graduates "can tap any source in the universe for information, including the minds of other men—alive or

dead" (2634/2625:1). Silva reports on one grade-school teacher in Buffalo, New York, who uses SMC to teach her students to contact "the dead" to help them study history (2597:129). A college teacher has her students use SMC to tune into dead philosophers to clarify obscure points in their writings (2597:129).

A significant aspect of the "counselors" is that *they* often take the initiative. They are already present in your (mental) "laboratories" by the time you get there. Trainees are often amazed at the "reality" of these counselors, and the help and useful advice they provide. They are, seemingly, always "available" whenever the student needs them (2597:161). They have different functions related to their characters, and they are willing to give appropriate guidance whenever "called" upon. The trainees are told they can choose any persons living, dead, or fictional as counselors, although again, they often do not get the ones they chose. The guides (counselors) are "chosen" (or more properly, "invoked") while in the alpha state.

We agree that many of the "counselors" may simply be concoctions of fertile imaginations, wishful thinking, or just invented by the psychically "in" crowd. But the probability of having nonimaginary counselors is clearly real. Even genuine spirits may be interpreted as being imaginary, if this is how people have been taught to relate to them. If so, such persons truly will be amazed at their own "powers of mind" or their own "higher self." Dr. Walter Martin, the late authority on comparative religion, observed, "What are the counselors? Most . . . have attributed their existence to imagination, and it is probable that most of such counselors are imaginary. However, not all of the appearances of counselors in SMC can be attributed to fertile imaginations. The world of spiritism is dangerously close to that of SMC" (2601:245).

That a given spiritual technique employs "only imagination" is no guarantee that spirits will not have access to "open the door" to the real thing. Classes in psychic development routinely incorporate directed imagination and visualization* techniques to develop psychic powers and contact spirits. Innumerable cases exist in occult literature where demons actively sought out human contacts because of their "imagined" patron god, religious saint, ascended master, or spirit helper. When one is being instructed to open one's mind to "psychic counselors," one should not be surprised if they turn out to be spirits (see New Age Inner Work). Limiting visualization techniques to simple imagination does not thereby guarantee one's freedom from spirit influence: "I recall engaging in a mock seance with a group of friends. Our lightheartedness was turned to fear when suddenly the 'medium,'" my best friend, began to convulse, his eyes rolled back in his head, and a strange voice emerged from his throat. For the following two years this young Jew was tormented by spirits" (2635:10).

It is also possible that "imagination" can be a cover for occult activities in a different way, so that distinguishing the "normal" from the "supernatural" becomes difficult, if not impossible. "Actually, the entire Mind Control course consists of learning how to use the power of imagination to get what you want. 'Whatever you can visualize, you can actualize'" (2606:8). Here, the "power of imagination" can euphemistically describe what would otherwise be seen as the work of the spirits (see New Age Intuition and Visualization for examples).

The more we read of SMC, the more we are convinced that the guides, or counselors, are often real and that ultimately many SMC trainees become spiritists, perhaps unwittingly, because of this association. In fact, "counselors" are the source of much of the success of SMC graduates. Most of the participants are surprised, even astounded, to find themselves giving highly accurate "psychic diagnosis" of people they have never met, or in other ways receiving supernatural information (2623). It is even recognized that psychic feats cannot be undertaken apart from the presence and working of the "counselors": Trainees are told they will need the help of the "counselors" (2597:161). It is well known that psychics do not "perform" or function effectively when their spirit guides are "on vacation," so to speak. Neither can SMC graduates.

## A NEW MILLENNIUM

As in most new religions and cults, claims to being "special," "unique," and "new" abound in SMC. And in SMC literature, "lay research scientist" José Silva is compared with Socrates, Galileo, Christopher Columbus, da Vinci, Thomas Edison, and Jesus Christ. One SMC newsletter, in referring to Silva's discoveries as the beginning of the second major phase of human evolution boasts, "These are facts. These are philosophical and scientific facts. A new facet to the mind of man has been discovered. A new world of awareness in the psychic dimension beckons mankind" (2619:7). SMC, however, has discovered nothing new. The "new facet to the mind," that is, the so-called "controllable" psychic awareness, has been claimed for millennia but has never been controllable and never will be.

The SMC claim to have significant control over psi is simply false. Just talk to SMC graduates. Ask them to read your mind or to tell you how many walls there are inside the Pentagon. One outrageous SMC claim is that of the first 21,000 graduates there was not even *one* single failure (2625:1). Who is defining success and failure here?

"Success" and "failure" are defined subjectively in the SMC organization. Since no objective, independent, comprehensive testing has been or will be undertaken, the SMC claims will remain suspect. The unfounded scientific assertions of SMC are one reason that Dr. J. B. Rhine and other parapsychologists refer to SMC as fraudulent, and to Mr. Silva as a charlatan (2626:1-2). (Needless to say, some of the scientists and psychic researchers who receive sizable funding on research projects from SMC may have a more positive view of the organization.)

Even secular scientists have issued warnings. In "Mind Training, ESP, Hypnosis and Voluntary Control of Internal States," Drs. Elmer and Alyce Green share their concerns with SMC and related practices:

[T]hese advisors, however constructed or found, may serve as masks for "entities" who may attempt (now that the student has become amenable to suggestion at the unconscious level) to control the student's mental, emotional and physical behavior. The mediumistic concept will clearly be rejected by mind training teachers because, if accepted, it would imply that these teachers might be responsible for serious problems in the lives of some of their trainees. . . .

[O]ne of our friends in the Bay area, a counselor on psychological and religious problems, reports that at least a dozen of his clients are suffering from paranoid neuroses as a result of taking mind training courses. Another acquaintance, a psychiatrist who took one of the commercial courses himself, reported to us that four of the thirty who went through the program became psychotic. Two of them had to be hospitalized. . . . Another point: Mind training teachers often maintain that no harm can be done to another person by themselves or by their students, because they are programmed with the idea that if these "powers" are used for ignoble or selfish purposes they will be lost, but this is likely to be nonsense. Post-hypnotic suggestions are notorious for their impermanence, so if real psychic "powers" are developed in students it can be assumed that hypnotically-imposed restrictions on the use of such powers will not be long lasting. . . .

The examples given above indicate that whether one chooses to examine commercial mind training methods from either the traditional psychological point of view or from the parapsychological point of view, there is risk involved for students. . . . In view of the hazards associated with hypnotic programming in commercial mind training courses, the present writers believe that hypnosis as a technique for inducing self-awareness and parapsychological faculties is not adequately safe and should be discarded (2636).

Elsewhere Dr. Green declared, "Silva has no control over all of the oddballs who've gotten into this and are programming the public. He has no control over his own people" (2626). Obviously, all this is an issue for concern with some ten million graduates. The potential dangers of occultism are serious enough, but when those unknowledgeable of the occult, some with dubious motives, begin to experiment with people's minds, the potential exists for considerable risks indeed.

Psychic history is littered with human destruction and death. For SMC to declare that which has been documented as harmful as being entirely benevolent is morally intolerable. Yet Silva declares, "In all my experience with psychic healing, I have never experienced or seen or heard of a single harmful side effect" (2597:68). One can only wonder at such an assertion.

In conclusion, SMC does not represent the benign and advanced societal influence it claims. It is merely one of endless contemporary versions of age-old spiritism. Collectively, they are bringing ruin to innumerable people, and to modern culture as well.

# VISUALIZATION

## INFO AT A GLANCE

**Description.** New Age visualization is the use of mental concentration and directed mental imagery in the attempt to secure particular goals, whether physical, psychological, vocational, educational, or spiritual.

**Founder.** Unknown; the practice is ancient.

**How does it claim to work?** Visualization attempts to program the mind to discover inner power and guidance. For example, by using the mind to contact an alleged inner divinity or "higher" self, practitioners claim they can manipulate their personal reality to secure desired goals, such as occult revelations, financial security, health, or improved learning abilities.

**Scientific evaluation.** Scientific research on forms of imagery (not necessarily visualization) has provided some useful insights into brain/mind interaction and the ability of mental processes to affect the mind-body function. Unfortunately, modern science does not always separate legitimate from questionable research. And legitimate research is easily misused when tied to parapsychological and New Age premises or goals.

**Examples of occult potential.** Visualization is often used as a means to, or in conjunction with, altered states of consciousness.* It often accompanies occult meditation* and is frequently used to develop psychic abilities. It is used in channeling* to contact "inner advisors" or spirit guides. It has long been associated with pagan religion and practice such as shamanism* and Buddhism. Many human potential and occult New Age seminars, such as est* and Silva Mind Control* (884) employ it.

573

**Major problems.** New Age visualization assigns the human mind a divine or almost divine status. This not only represents a significant distortion of human nature, but it can also mask spiritistic manipulation of the mind, reconceptualizing this as a natural or divine endeavor.

**Biblical/Christian evaluation.** As an occult practice, New Age visualization is prohibited; but even alleged Christian forms are insufficiently critiqued, of dubious value, or subject to abuse.

**Potential dangers.** Chief hazards include occult influences and problems arising from the denial of reality by overreliance upon one's "divine" mind and its alleged power or "wisdom." For example, in the areas of medicine (physical self-diagnosis), education (e.g., tapping the knowledge of "inner counselors"), and religion (receiving psychic revelations), the process can produce a trust in false data that could result in foolish or harmful decisions.

*Note:* See New Age Inner Work, New Age Intuition, *A Course in Miracles*, Dream Work, Altered States of Consciousness, Meditation, Channeling, and Shamanism for discussions of associated practices and phenomena.

## INTRODUCTION AND INFLUENCE

The practice of visualization is a directed form of mental imagery and concentration, which is having broad and substantial impact in our culture. It involves the deliberate manipulation of the mind, individually or in conjunction with an assistant, to alter one's consciousness toward a specific goal—often the seeking of some form of secret knowledge or power. What is perhaps the most authoritative general text on the subject states, "If there are two important 'new' concepts in 20th century American life, they are meditation and visualization" (209:XI). "The growth of interest in visualization since the 1960's is part of a new climate of thought in the West. This new climate has manifested in an interest in all forms of imagery, in the experience of Eastern religions and philosophy, in hypnotism, and in hallucinogenic drugs and altered states of consciousness in general" (209:34).

Visualization is prominent in modern humanistic and transpersonal education and is increasingly finding its way into conventional educational curriculum (see New Age Education). Jack Canfield is Director of Educational Services for Insight Training Seminars in Santa Monica, California, past president of the Association for Humanistic Education, and consultant to over 150 schools, universities, and mental-health organizations. In "The Inner Classroom: Teaching with Guided Imagery" he asserts:

> Guided imagery is a very powerful psychological tool which can be used to achieve a wide variety of educational objectives: enhance self-esteem, expand awareness, facilitate psychological growth and integration, evoke inner wisdom, increase empathy, expand creativity, increase memory, facilitate optimal performance, evoke a more positive attitude, and accelerate the learning of subject matter (2233:27).

New Age visualization claims to work by using the mind to influence reality and one's perceptions. Proponents claim that by properly controlling each person's alleged mental power, they can influence and change a person's ideas, consciousness, or even their physical and spiritual environment. Visualization can supposedly be used to change one's self-image from negative to positive by holding a positive image of oneself in the mind. Visualization may also be used to uncover a claimed "inner divinity" that can allegedly manipulate reality. By creating the proper mental image and environment and then holding it or projecting it outward, practitioners claim they can exercise mental power over every aspect of their lives (see *A Course in Miracles*). (Related practices are used in magic ritual to call on spirits in order to secure such goals (see "Questions and Concerns" on p. 589).

Proponents say proper visualization methods can affect health, finances, educational abilities, relationships, vocation, and even one's destiny. For example, in many Hindu and Buddhist religions, the thought or image one holds at death is believed to powerfully influence one's supposed reincarnation. This is one reason for adopting mental training exercises such as visualization. In the Hare Krishna sect (ISKCON), devotees chant the name of the Hindu god Krishna thousands of times per day to infuse and influence their consciousness so at the point of death their thoughts will have been so conditioned by "Krishna consciousness" that they will immediately be ushered into Krishna's presence. On the other hand, if one is thinking of something like a pig or a worm at death, then one will reincarnate as that (883:52,57).

Because the mind is said to be so powerful and work so dramatically, visualization and imagery practices are being pursued by literally millions of people in America. These practices are having growing impact in diverse fields, from New Age medicine* and education,* to a variety of occult practices, to certain schools of psychotherapy such as the Jungian, humanistic, and transpersonal, to human potential seminars. A standard work on visualization comments:

> In the last hundred years specialists in different fields have begun to rediscover the existence and meaning of visualization. Historians, religious scholars, archaeologists, physicians, and psychologists have begun to study the nature of the inner image as it relates to their area of specialization. There is no widely accepted overview of visualization at this time. There is only a general striving toward understanding in many fields, from many viewpoints (209:21).

Many scientific journals on visualization have emerged, such as the *Journal of Mental Imagery.* These also document the impact of visualization in psychology, education, the arts and literature, linguistics, mythology, anthropology, sociology, religion, and even thanatology (e.g., 685:1-2). Of course, different forms of visualization exist, with different goals, but even the following brief perusal of its influence shows how widespread the practice has become.

## Medicine

Visualization is used widely in New Age medicine.* A central tenet of much New Age medicine is the manipulation of mystical life energies, such as *chi* and *prana.* Visualization promoters claim that the practice of visualization can "produce" and manipulate this energy:

> ... Physicists have also begun to study subtle body energies and their effect on the world outside the body. Throughout history, philosophers have recognized this energy and given it many names. The Chinese called it *chi*, and the Indians *prana* or *kundalini*, the Japanese *ki;* 20th century parapsychologists have referred to it as *bio-plasmic energy....* Russian and Czechoslovakian scientists have studied bioplasmic energy in association with healing, telepathy and psychokinesis. They have found that through visualization a woman named Nelya Mikhailoya can change her bio-plasmic energy fields.... Studies like this tend to confirm occult belief in such concepts as auras and astral bodies. These experiments demonstrate how a visualization [technique] can produce energy which directly affects objects in the external world (209:70-71).

## Education

Visualization is used in education, for example in counseling, creative writing, and problem-solving courses. It is also used to develop altered states of consciousness* in students, to help them reach "inner guides" or allegedly tap the "higher self" and its powers. It is used for enhanced learning potential, self-esteem, and stress reduction (see New Age Education).

## Occultism

Visualization is routinely used by shamans,* spiritists, magicians, and witches. Many people are familiar with American shamans Carlos Castaneda and Lynn Andrews, whose books have sold in the millions, and whose writings stress that visualization is a key ingredient for success as a shaman. According to hypnotherapists Richard Dobson and Natasha Frazier, "In the last few years shamanic trance techniques have been taught or explained almost entirely as a form of visualization" (2486:39).

Visualization is widely used in psychic healing. Psychic healers Amy Wallace (granddaughter of Irving Wallace) and Bill Henkin observe in *The Psychic Healing Book: How to Develop Your Psychic Potential Safely, Simply, Effectively:* "Visualization is one of the most potent and widely used techniques in [psychic] healing. It has been stressed for centuries in schools of Eastern mysticism and is used in nearly every contemporary school of 'consciousness-raising' " (104:43). Visualization is also used in numerous occult religions such as Rosicrucianism and Tantrism and in the mind sciences (such as New Thought, Divine Science, Unity School of Christianity, and Religious Science). Occult practitioners of all stripes use visualization. Even Kreskin, the psychic and famous "mentalist," admits that he "rehearses constantly through mental imagery" (688:14).

*Psychotherapy*

Visualization is also widely used in psychotherapy: "The use of the imagination is one of the most rapidly spreading new trends in psychology and education.... It is interesting to notice that many of the modern pioneers of imaginative techniques, Hans Karl Leuner and Robert Desoille among them, have stressed the compatibility of such techniques with all main schools of psychology" (693:119-20). A standard text on visualization is *Seeing with the Mind's Eye* by physician Mike Samuels, M.D., and his wife. Samuels is a committed spiritist and author of *Spirit Guides: Access to Inner Worlds* (289). In his book, he devotes almost 200 pages illustrating the use of visualization in modern psychology, medicine, parapsychology, art and creativity, and the occult, or, as he calls it, "the spiritual life" (209:162-323). Samuels also discusses visualization techniques used within many psychological disciplines and methods, including Freudian, Jungian, induced hypnagogic reverie, aversive training, implosion therapy, hypnotherapy* (the spiritistic ability of automatic writing is classified here), behaviorist systematic desensitization, induced dream work,* Kretschmer's meditative visualizations, Leuner's guided affective imagery, Gestalt psychodrama, psychosynthesis, and others (209:180-206).

The *Journal of Mental Imagery* is sponsored by the International Imagery Association, which conducts regular meetings for the academic community. The brochure for the Sixth American Imagery Conference held in San Francisco, "Timeless Therapeutic Images," observed:

A rapidly growing body of scientific findings from psychology, psychiatry and neuropsychol-

ogy has found that fast and extensive emotional, physiological and psychological change can occur through mental imagery.... The image resides at the core of consciousness.... It effortlessly joins the inner self with the outside world, permits the positive to confront and overcome the negative, leads us to an appreciation of art in Nature, [and] forges new paths in consciousness through new perception (689).

But as the Spiritual Counterfeits Project in Berkeley, California, warns, many such conferences:

...may best be described as an amorphous blend of secular scientific materialism and a (sometimes) disguised brand of occult philosophy.... [At one conference attended] the primary focus during the conference...was on the use of imaging in order to contact one's personal inner advisor or spirit guide (690:3).

For example, psychosynthesis is a fringe psychotherapy blending various Eastern and Western methods of self-awareness. It was developed by Roberto Assagioli, who for years was the Italian director of Lucius Trust, the occult organization founded by occultist Alice A. Bailey (288:224-25). It makes extensive use of visualization and imagery in order to contact the "higher self," which can become the means for psychic development and spirit contact.

Another example would be psychic Bob Hoffman who, with the help of a dead friend, Dr. Siegfried Fischer, and a psychiatrist, Ernest Pecci, developed a system of psychic psychotherapy called the Fischer-Hoffman technique, later renamed the Quadrinity Process. "This system involves imagining an inner sanctuary and a spirit guide in order to aid in receptive visualization" (209:276). One quadrinity teacher, Jean Porter, reveals its occult application in her book *Psychic Development*.

One of the early pioneers in the academic use of visualization was German psychiatrist Johannes H. Schultz. He developed what is called "autogenic training" from his clinical experience with hypnosis* (686:229). Autogenic training is therapy that uses autosuggestion, visualization, deep relaxation, and other techniques.

According to visualization authority Mike Samuels, M.D., it "is the most thoroughly researched and widely applied of all the systems of visualization in healing. Autogenic training has many characteristics in common with hypnotherapy (especially autosuggestion), certain psychic healing techniques, relaxation healing techniques . . . ancient yogic techniques, and the more recent healing techniques taught in mind-control courses" (209:226).

Autogenic training is promoted by some enthusiasts as a method of developing occult states of consciousness for those who don't want to take the time to follow an Eastern path:

Persons who, for whatever reasons, are not inclined to engage in any of the Eastern meditative techniques . . . might do well to consider autogenic training. It is a remarkably thorough and systematically designed practice with an end result comparable to that of diligent meditation. . . .

In essence, the final stages of autogenic training may be compared to the breakthroughs of consciousness obtained through meditative techniques of various kinds (686:229,233).

Wolfgang Luthe, one of Schultz's students, is "now the acknowledged authority on Autogenic Training" (686:237). He is author of *Autogenic Training* and with Schultz of the seven-volume *Autogenic Therapy*, which cites some 2400 case studies. Schultz states that the autogenic program of visualization exercises may be improved by the use of meditation.* According to Samuels, "All the positive effects of the standard exercises are reinforced by this meditative training" (209:225). One aspect of autogenic meditation has the patient "ask questions of his own conscious inner self" (685:225), a technique which has not infrequently become the means to spirit contact (see New Age Inner Work).

The influential psychoanalyst Carl Jung, a student of the occult (340:180-200), developed his own visualization method called "active imagination." This potentially dangerous technique is considered a "powerful tool in Jungian psychology for achieving direct contact with the unconscious and obtaining greater inner knowledge" (687:cover).

Jungian analyst Barbara Hannah is a teacher at the prominent C.G. Jung Institute. In *Encounters with the Soul: Active Imagination as Developed by C.G. Jung* (687), she frankly admits its danger and reveals in detail how it can powerfully influence the mind. She urges "great caution" before anyone employs this method (687:5-6,11-12,18-20,27). Hannah also says that it is a time-honored method for contacting the "gods" (687:3). Indeed, there is little doubt that it may facilitate contact with what can only be termed spirit guides (687:3-51). However, these spirits are typically internalized as powerful psychodynamics, that is, they are normalized as part of the internal "structure" of the unconscious mind (see New Age Inner Work).

*Human Potential Seminars*

Most popular "think yourself rich" (or healthy, or sexy, or happy) seminars and books endorse and use visualization. Modern New Age seminars have millions of graduates, such as Silva Mind Control* (884) and Landmark Education's The Forum* (formerly "est"), and employ visualization techniques. In one's mind, one can create "projection screens" on which to project desired images, such as greater self-confidence, losing weight, or even seeing one's white blood cells warding off viral invaders or specific illnesses. A secret inner sanctuary or mental laboratory may be created where one may contact "inner advisors," or spirit guides, for assistance in decision-making and direction.

Thus visualization practices are having substantial impact on modern culture, and people need to be informed on this important subject.

*In the Church*

The modern impact of visualization in health, science, education, psychotherapy, and other areas has resulted in visualization techniques being used by more and more Christians. Trott and Pement note that "visualization exercises are increasingly finding their way into Christian churches" (691:19). In *The Seduction of Christianity*, popular author Dave Hunt devotes two chapters to the harmful influence of visualization within the church:

"Visualization" and "Guided Imagery" have long been recognized by sorcerers of all kinds as the most powerful and effective methodology for contacting the spirit world in order to acquire supernatural power, knowledge and healing. Such methods are neither taught or practiced in the Bible as helps to faith or prayer (432:123).

The visualization we are concerned with is an ancient witchcraft technique that has been at the heart of shamanism for thousands of years, yet is gaining increasing acceptance in today's secular world and now more and more within the church. It attempts to use vivid images held in the mind as a means of healing diseases, creating wealth, and otherwise manipulating reality. Strangely enough, a number of Christian leaders teach and practice these same techniques in the name of Christ, without recognizing them for what they are (432:124).

Unfortunately, as we will shortly document, the worldview of the visualization promoters is rarely Christian. Instead, it is blatantly occult or humanistic. As researcher Stanley Dokupil comments: "Imagination is fast becoming the focus of much of New Age thought and method" (733:2).

## PURPOSES AND CLAIMS

Having established the modern impact of visualization, we may examine the claims proponents have made. These can be summarized under three dominant themes: 1) the quest for personal power, 2) the quest for inner knowledge or spiritual enlightenment,* 3) the quest for physical health.

*The Quest for Personal Power.* Psychic Harold Sherman says, "There is tremendous power in imagery" (112:99). Andrew Wiehl claims in *Creative Visualization*, "Wonders have been performed, seeming miracles wrought, through visualization. It is a God-given power available to anyone" (692:11).

*The Quest for Spiritual Enlightenment.* Jack Canfield remarks, "To me the most interesting use of guided imagery is the evocation of the wisdom that lies deep within us." He also discusses how students can contact their own spirit guides as "wisdom counselors" (2233:38-39). Visualization

authority and spiritist Mike Samuels observes, "Philosophers and priests in every ancient culture used visualization as a tool for growth and rebirth. . . . Most religions have used visualization as one of their basic techniques in helping people to realize their spiritual goals. Visualization intensifies any experience" (209:21,28).

In her book *Visualization*, Adelaide Bry writes that the power of visualization is to "reveal our hidden truths" and to allow us to experience personal connections to "cosmic consciousness" (701:14).

A journal devoted to Roberto Assagioli's method of psychosynthesis claims, "Imagination is superior to all nature and generation, and through it we are capable of transcending the worldly order, or participating in eternal life and in the energy of the super-celestial. It is through this principle, therefore, that we will be liberated from the bonds of fate itself" (693:119).

*The Quest for Physical Health.* Consciousness researcher Kenneth Pelletier of the Langley Porter Neuropsychiatric Institute in San Francisco teaches, "The greatest potential of autogenic training and visualization [is as] . . . a potent tool in a holistic approach to preventative medicine" (686:262).

In his *Positive Imaging*, the late popular "positive thinker" and sometimes occult promoter Norman Vincent Peale cites shamanistic researcher Jeanne Achterberg and G. Frank Lawlis as stating, "Imagery may well prove the single most important technique for modern health-care" (695:94).

Unfortunately, when people use visualization techniques for personal power, spiritual or educational enlightenment,* or physical or mental health, they may get more than they bargained for. Visualization programs usually come with the additional baggage of accompaniments, such as worldviews and physical and spiritual dangers. However, before we examine the accompaniments, we must first note the different types and varieties of imagery and visualization.

## TYPES

Visualization is essentially a powerful and directed use of the imagination with specific goals and methods that vary widely. One problem in writing briefly on this topic is that the different types of visualization make a general analysis difficult. The academic types of visualization do not have the same goals or necessarily the same methods as the occult or Christian types, so that a critique of one type may not supply a valid critique of another. For example, those interested in an occult use of the imagination do not have the same purposes or practices as Christians who may attempt to use the imagination for what they see as godly purposes.

In order to help distinguish the types of visualization, we have prepared the following generalized chart and subsequent discussion.

---

### FOUR TYPES OF VISUALIZATION

| 1 | 2 |
|---|---|
| **Academic:** e.g., | **Popular:** e.g., |
| Autogenic training | New Age therapies |
| Jungian methods | Mind science practices |
| Imagery studies | Personal or business-oriented |
| Secular or transpersonal | motivational/achievement |
| psychotherapy | programs and seminars |

| 3 | 4 |
|---|---|
| **Occult:** e.g., | **Christian:** e.g., |
| Ritual magic | Christian psychotherapy |
| Shamanism* | Inner healing |
| Psychic healing | Jesus visualization |
| Spiritism | Visualization with Scripture |
| Hinduism | (e.g., refs. 696,697) |
| Buddhist practice (such as the | |
| use of mandalas*) | |

Between types 1 and 3, and 3 and 4, some boundaries are concrete, but potential interrelationships exist.

Between types 2 and 3, boundaries are fairly fluid.

Between types 1 and 4, and 2 and 4, boundaries are more fluid; potential and actual interrelationships exist.

The chart reveals that concrete boundaries between the categories are rarely absolute, and that many categories interact.

## VARIETIES

There are three general varieties of visualization.

*Programmed Visualization.* This is an *active* process used individually; for example, the practitioner holds a positive image in the mind in order to "create" the desired object, situation, or reality. It can be performed on the couch or in magic ritual.

*Receptive Visualization.* This is a *passive* process; it (so to speak) "lets the movie roll" after an initial theme or setting is developed in the consciousness. The method is passive in that it receives whatever comes into the mind, which is usually interpreted as special guidance of some kind, such as instructions from one's "higher self," "inner guide," or "divine consciousness."

*Guided Visualization.* This is also termed "guided imagery," and it employs a friend, counsellor, or family member in either a therapeutic or occult New Age context. The therapist suggests a scene, such as a meadow or a forest, and the patient imaginatively elaborates upon the scene as a key to his own "inner processes" and "unconscious conflicts." Guided imagery may also be done by a leader of a New Age seminar,* or practitioner who helps the audience construct a particular mental environment for contacting a spirit guide. Silva Mind Control* is a case in point (884).

One may find that these general varieties of visualization can be described loosely under a number of terms: guided fantasy, mental imaging, active imagination, directed daydreaming, and inner imagery. But it should be remembered that visualization is not the same thing as imagery. Visualization involves imagery, but imagery purposely directed toward a particular goal.

How does imagery differ from visualization? There are many different forms of imagery, many of which we all experience. For example, a "memory image" is a reconstruction of a genuine past event tied to a specific occasion; for example, most of us remember what our first date was like. Or an "imagination image" is the construction of an imaginary image that may or may not contain elements of past perceptions or events, but it is arranged in a novel way. For example, we might imagine how we would look alongside a new car parked in front of our beach house, or how the living room would look with the furniture rearranged. We might imagine what it would be like to be in heaven (or hell), or how one of the biblical prophets dealt with a difficult situation, or what we would do in his place. This is similar to "daydream fantasy," in which there is a combination of memory and imagination images.

In dreams we find sleep imagery. And there is also imagery that is experienced only rarely, such as in hallucinations, in which internal imagery is wrongly believed to be external. In visions we find induced, internal imagery as, for example, revelations (or even projections) that may be either true or false; that is, from God and angels or from the devil and demons (Matthew 4:8; Ezekiel 1:1).

There are many other varieties of imagery, such as recurrent images, eidetic images, hypnagogic, and hypnopompic images. Typically, however, these kinds of imagery are not visualization; they lack the accompaniments, commitment, and trust involved in the visualization process and its specific techniques. All this is why it is important to distinguish imagination and imagery from visualization proper.

## ACCOMPANIMENTS

Visualization is never used by itself. Something always informs it. Typical accompaniments of visualization would include:

- relaxation
- meditation* (sometimes accompanied by yogic-like controlled breathing and postures)
- the cultivation of willpower
- various forms of self-hypnosis*

• faith or trust in the "guide" (whether human or spirit) and in the process of visualization itself

We will now briefly discuss these accompaniments.

*Relaxation*

Relaxation is, of course, a vital and necessary part of everyday living. But when combined with visualization and meditation* techniques, it can become transformed into an occult process. In "Relax Your Way to ESP," the late leading psychic researcher, D. Scott Rogo, refers to the research of parapsychologist Rhea White, who discovered that of the greatest psychics "by and large many of [them] began with relaxation" (698:18). These psychics stress the importance of suggestion and visualization (698:19).

In her popular book *Creative Visualization*, New Age psychic Shakti Gawain states, "It's important to relax deeply when you are first learning to use creative visualization" (699:24). Noted educator Jack Canfield encourages classroom students to practice a variety of occult, or potentially occult, relaxation techniques just prior to the visualization process; these include breath awareness, breath imagery, breath control (cf. Yoga), progressive relaxation, autogenic training, polarity, and chanting (2233:30-31).

In *Opening to Channel*, two spirit guides, "Orin" and "DaBen," offer specific advice for relaxation and visualization, which "helps you become accustomed to the state of mind that is best for a [spirit] guide's entry" (575:69). (See p. 413.)

Relaxation, then, is an important component of successful visualization.

*Meditation*

Another accompaniment of visualization is meditation.* Visualization is often conducted within a meditative environment; for example, within a structured program of internal concentration using a mantra* or word of psychic power. As we have shown elsewhere, almost all meditation* other than biblical meditation develops psychic powers and inculcates a nonbiblical worldview and can open the door to occultism and spirit contact (see Meditation). Gawain states,

"Almost any form of meditation will eventually take you to an experience of yourself as source, or your higher self" (699:57). What she means by "source" here is ultimate reality or God.

*Willpower*

Willpower is also important to visualization. The systematic use of willpower for effective visualization is stressed in magical and occult texts, particularly for ritualistic purposes, and to a degree parallels the popular usage, although often for different goals (700:244-45/693:120/237:60-69). In fact, without willful intent and commitment, visualization does not exist. Thus, "*Programmed visualization . . . is the deliberate use of the power of your own mind to create your own reality. . . .* [T]here is nothing too insignificant or too grand for you to visualize. *Our lives are limited by what we see as possible. . . .* A basic rule of visualization is: *you can use visualization to have whatever you want*, but YOU MUST REALLY, REALLY WANT WHAT YOU VISUALIZE" (701:40).

*Hypnosis*

Hypnosis* may be another accompaniment of visualization. In fact, some visualization and progressive relaxation methods are indistinguishable from hypnosis (2233:34). Hypnosis may be part of or joined with visualization in both the popular and the academic varieties. As far as the latter are concerned, interest in hypnosis is usually sparked by the fact that one's ability to visualize and one's susceptibility to hypnosis are related. "[I]maginative involvement, or absorption in fantasy experiences, and high imagery are known to be positively related to measured hypnotizability," and "today the intimacy between imagination and hypnosis are [sic] clearly recognized and studied by appropriate scientific methods" (694:63-64).

*Faith*

Finally, faith or trust is held to be an integral aspect regulating the effectiveness of visualization. As is clear from the material cited below, without such trust the person cannot expect much in terms of results. However, faith is rarely placed in the biblical God or Jesus Christ; faith is usually placed in one's alleged inner powers, mental capacity, "intuitive" abilities, cosmic energy, the universe, and so on. The following statements note the importance of faith:

> To put it another way, in attempting this or any other technique for self realization, one needs to trust that it can work (693:128).

> Have faith that it will materialize as you picture it, and never for a moment doubt it. . . . Just as an attorney must understand law in order to practice it . . . so must we understand the law of the Universe and co-operate with it in order to have our desires realized. The more faith and enthusiasm we put into our mental imaging, the sooner it will work out for us (692:72-73).

The previous introductory discussion on visualization suggests several conclusions:

- We all routinely experience certain types of imagery.

- Imagery is a component of visualization but may be studied in and of itself apart from visualization. In other words, imagery studies may be strictly scientific and neutral, or they may be placed into a larger metaphysical worldview.

- Imagery is not necessarily visualization. Visualization demands the exercise of will and faith within a context of relaxation, meditation,* and often self-hypnosis.*

- In general, the types, varieties, and methods of visualization can be, to one degree or another, fluid in their interrelationships.

- The accompaniments of visualization regulate its outcome. That is, they place it within a certain context, a certain worldview, and to that degree they influence the method's effectiveness, impact, and spiritual implications.

## WORLDVIEW

Because the practice of visualization can be adapted to almost any philosophy and uniquely colored by it, there is no well-defined worldview we could present that would be comprehensive. But if we restrict our discussion to classes 2 and 3 in the chart on page 579, recognizing the potential for cross-fertilization into the other divisions,

we can see a broad outline emerging. Some principal components include the following:

- Pantheism or monism: Everything is interconnected by divine energy, the One power, or ultimate cosmic reality.

- Man is divine in his true nature and controls his personal destiny; he is an integral part of this divine energy and can realize this experientially through proper technique and instruction.

- The mind of man has "infinite" potential; the "higher self" or unconscious mind provides the connecting link to the infinite and is believed to be the repository of vast wisdom and ability.

- Visualization is an important technique that initiates contact with the ultimate cosmic reality.

For example, Andrew Wiehl writes in his *Creative Visualization,* "In all the Universe there is but one power, the power within yourself" (692:81). Shakti Gawain claims that we are linked to "divine omnipresence and omnipotence," and that our "higher self" is "the God-like being who dwells within you" (699:55,81). Because of this, "There is no separation between us and God," in that we are "divine expressions" of God, the creative principle (699:149). Thus, "Imagination . . . empowers [us] to tap the endless and unborn potentials of universal mind" (702:126). And, "Visualization allows a person to travel into the mind to a space where the possibilities of matter, time and space are unlimited" (209:279).

Thus, when used in an occult program, visualization techniques become powerful instruments for securing New Age goals:

> At a practical level, visualization has an uncanny ability to improve the quality of our lives. It does this through its power to heal the body and spirit, to reconstruct the past and to reveal our hidden truths. . . . The most dramatic visualizations touch the deepest part of ourselves—our essence, our core, and allow us to experience connections beyond ourselves, what some describe as cosmic consciousness (701:14).

Indeed, the visualization process *itself* may alter a person's worldview. Dr. Mike Samuels discusses the mechanics of the process and the implications:

> When a person consciously visualizes he gains the ability to hold his mind on one object, to concentrate. This *one-pointedness of mind* is a state [of meditation] that has special properties: alertness, clarity of thought, identification with the object, and a feeling of participation in the visualization.

> The feeling of identification-participation causes the person to be less involved with himself as an entity separate from the world around him. He goes beyond the boundaries, the limitations of his physical body, beyond the awareness of his personality....

> Time and space disappear.... A person who has the experience feels that it unites him with the universe. He feels he is a part of creation rather than an observer of it.... This purity of vision ... is associated with tremendous energy surrounding both the visualizer and the image, and the unity of the two. Such energy cannot help but affect the world around it (209:65-66; cf. 192:100).

The "worldview" of visualization just discussed is obviously not Christian. The Bible denies that man is potentially one essence with God, the universe, or cosmic reality, because it declares that only God has inherent eternality—for He "alone is immortal" (1 Timothy 6:16), and only He is an infinite being. Furthermore, this one and only God (John 17:3), who existed from eternity (Psalm 90:2), created from nothing. God did not emanate something of Himself in the process of creation so that everything in creation is part of God. To the contrary, as the following biblical verses declare, God created the universe merely by speaking it into existence: "In the beginning God created the heavens and the earth" (Genesis 1:1), and "the universe was formed at God's command" (Hebrews 11:3). "By the word of the LORD were the heavens made.... For he spoke and it came to be" (Psalm 33:6,9).

Man cannot be one essence with God or a god because "You alone are God" (Isaiah 37:16), and,

"Did not one God create us?" (Malachi 2:10). "You alone are the LORD. You made the heavens, even the highest heavens, and all their starry host, the earth and all that is on it, the seas and all that is in them. You give life to everything, and the multitudes of heaven worship you" (Nehemiah 9:6). Deuteronomy 4:32 refers to "the day God created man on the earth," and Deuteronomy 4:35 declares, "You were shown these things so that you might know that the LORD is God; besides him there is no other."

We are not a part of God, nor does our mind have the "infinite" powers attributed to it by visualization philosophy. Neither is our mind a source of true spiritual wisdom, apart from spiritual regeneration or rebirth (Mark 7:20-23; Proverbs 28:26; Jeremiah 17:9; James 3:14-17). Visualization has no power to initiate contact with God or knowledge of Him. Biblically, those who wish to know the one true God personally must come to him by faith through the true Jesus Christ (John 17:2-3; Colossians 1:15-20; 2:9; 1 Peter 2:24; Hebrews 11:6).

People cannot know God by trusting in their own inner vision, a spirit guide masquerading as a false Christ, or by an alleged mystical union with some abstract impersonal concept of the divine. The Scripture declares, "Now this is eternal life: that they may know you, the only true God, and Jesus Christ, whom you have sent" (John 17:3). "We know that we have come to know him if we obey his commands. The man who says, 'I know him,' but does not do what he commands is a liar, and the truth is not in him" (1 John 2:3-4). "We know also that the Son of God has come and has given us understanding, so that we may know him who is true. And we are in him who is true—even in his Son Jesus Christ. He is the true God and eternal life" (1 John 5:20).

## THE OCCULT

Coauthor Weldon became interested in evaluating visualization a number of years ago while examining the latest semidivine trends at a local metaphysical bookshop. A large, bright, yellow text with a colorful caduceus had caught his eye: *The Well Body Book* (227), which was a New Age health home medical handbook. (It was right next to *The Well Cat Book* and *The Well Dog Book*.)

He began thumbing through the book and noticed that it stressed visualization exercises. In fact, the ability to visualize was said to be necessary "for understanding many parts of the book" (227:5). In the acknowledgments, author Mike Samuels, M.D., gave thanks to "Rolling Thunder," a well-known Native American shaman, "who taught me about healing," and to "Braxius, my imaginary doctor." However, "Braxius," it turns out, is Samuels' personal spirit guide and, quite obviously, *not* imaginary. The story of their meeting is found in Samuels' book *Spirit Guides: Access to Inner Worlds* (289), a text for utilizing visualization techniques to encounter spirits. (We relate this story in our chapter on New Age Inner Work.)

To date, *The Well Body Book* and *Spirit Guides: Access to Inner Worlds* have sold over half-a-million copies. The authors have received a "large number" of letters "from readers who have begun to use spirit guides in their [own] lives" (289:27,55). Visualization was the basic method used to contact the spirit world, and this is why the relationship between visualization and the occult is our greatest concern. If visualization can lead to spirit contact, it should concern everyone. As we will later document, the spirits themselves often recommend visualization practices as important components for securing occult goals, including spirit contact.

In the following material we will examine the occult potential of visualization by showing: 1) visualization can develop psychic abilities, 2) the use of visualization in occult ritual, 3) the relationship between visualization and spiritism.

*Psychic Development*

Visualization is often used to develop psychic powers. This fact is recognized by numerous experts in both the occult and visualization. For example, "The capacity to utilize visual imagination is a regular part of the training for psychics and healers in the Philippine spiritist churches" (118:41). And lifelong occultist J. H. Brennan acknowledges the importance of successful visu-

alization for contacting the astral realm where spirits dwell (386:11-17). As a leader in modern visualization observes, "People who have experienced astral travel say they do so by visualizing themselves separating from their physical body, then floating away from it" (209:282).

Parapsychologist Milan Rzyl states that "the ability to visualize sharply is central to good psychic performance" (209:274). And psychic Jack Schwarz utilizes visualization and creative imagery in a meditative context to develop and use his psychic powers (734:xiii,77,95-101). Mike and Nancy Samuels write, "The receptive visualization state is a state in which a person can receive extrasensory perceptions of another person's mind (telepathy), of objects or events (clairvoyance), of future events (precognition), and of psychic diagnosis" (209:270).

*Occult Ritual*

Occult magician David Conway devotes an entire chapter, "Visualization and the Training of a Magician," to the importance of visualization for magic ritual in his *Magic: An Occult Primer:*

> ... The technique of visualization is something you will gradually master, and indeed must master if you are to make any progress in magic.... It is our only means of affecting the etheric atmosphere. It enables us to build our own thought forms, contact those already in existence and channel elemental energy we need down onto the physical plane (237:59).

*Spiritism*

Conway also provides an example of a visualization practice used during magic ritual whose goal is to "produce, in reality, the spirit, god, or demon imagined through ritual." No one knowledgeable in occult ritual has any doubt about the dangers here, least of all Conway (237:180,196-201). Visualization at this point becomes an integral component fostering spirit possession:

> ... The adept imagines that the god-form or the most congenial of the planetary or sefirothic forms is materializing behind his back. He visualizes this in as much detail as possible. Slowly,

as the altar candles flicker, he will sense with a sureness which precludes all doubt that the visualized form is in fact towering inside the circle behind him. On no account must he turn his head to look at whatever is there; any temptation to do so must be sternly resisted: the form may be unbearably hideous or else possess a beauty that may literally be fatal.

In the meantime, the adept should endeavor to continue his mantra, although by now his heart will no doubt be beating furiously. Whatever else happens he must not move, even when he senses that the form is so close as to be almost touching him. Above all he must not panic [!] but should comfort himself with the thought that he is safe enough provided he stays where he is.

At last—and he will certainly know when—the god-form will take control of him. To begin with, the adept will feel an exquisite giddiness somewhere at the base of his skull and quickly convulsing the whole of his body. As this happens, and while the power is surging into him, he forces himself to visualize the thing he wants his magic to accomplish, and wills its success. He must put all he has into this [effort] and, like our friends the Bacchantes, must whip himself into a veritable frenzy.

It is at this point that the force evoked will be expelled to realize the ritual intention. As he feels the force overflowing inside him the adept, while still visualizing the realized magical intention, bids it go forth to fulfill his wishes (237:130-31; cf. 705:52).

In magic ritual we see the full power of visualization: directed imagery, meditation, force of will, and certainly(!), faith. What many do not realize is that although visualization can be used deliberately in magic ritual for spirit contact and spirit possession, the very same things can be encountered in normal visualization practice or even through purely make-believe fantasy rituals.

## FANTASY SPIRITS?

The story of "Philip" the "imaginary" spirit is illustrative of how the innocent use of the imagination may result in spirit contact and posses-

sion. Coauthor Weldon documented this principle in *Playing with Fire*, describing a young man who became possessed through an "imaginary" mock seance (433:73). Whether real or imaginary (in the mind of an individual), the spirit world may still respond when beckoned. The story of "Philip" has a similar theme and is reported in the book *Conjuring Up Philip* and elsewhere (706).

A group of psychic investigators and parapsychologists with the Toronto Society for Psychical Research came together to see if they could, through "collective mental power alone," that is, imagination and visualization, create the physical phenomena found in a seance and produce a materialized spirit. They named him "Philip" and gave him an imaginary past and personality.

They eventually succeeded—quite beyond their expectations—and remain puzzled to this day, indeed, awed over the subsequent events. What entered their parlor was not an imaginary spirit, but a genuine, living spirit being with its own personality and power, and which certainly was not part of the group's "collective" mind or energy. Incredibly, however, the group continued to believe that this independent spirit entity and the phenomena it produced were merely the result of their own "imaginative powers."

One result of this experiment—as knowledge of it spread through articles, a book, and a film— was the camouflaging of spiritistic phenomena in the guise of human potential. "Philip groups" began all over the world, attempting to duplicate the phenomena of the Toronto group. Thus, "the most important feature of this book is the fact that it specifies the method by which the physical PK [psychokinesis] force can be generated by ordinary people and thus made available for study" (707:xviii).

The only problem was that the "imaginary" spirits contacted "act with their own personalities and idiosyncrasies and not as though they were a part of your subconscious mind" (227:8). Therefore, many "Philip groups" ended up in actual spirit contact and necromancy.

Not surprisingly, then, in modern channeled literature the spirits actively endorse visualization, recommending specific exercises for learning how to contact them and become a channel.

ENCYCLOPEDIA OF NEW AGE BELIEFS

The spirit guide of the late medium Jane Roberts, "Seth," teaches that "the real work is done in the mind. . . . [Occult] beliefs automatically mobilize your emotional and imaginative powers. . . . Imagination and emotion are your great allies" (796:64-65,76).

The following instructions and advice given by two other spirits is typical:

Enter into the trance state you have practiced. . . . Imagine yourself going higher and higher, transcending ordinary reality and entering into a higher dimension of love, light, and joy. . . . Imagine that many beings of light are coming closer to join you. Feel their love and caring for you. Open your heart to receive them. Imagine the doorways opening between your reality and theirs. Sense the presence of many loving and high beings all around you. . . . Your guide and the guides are aware of you and hold a special welcome for you as you join more closely with them. Imagine that there is a doorway in front of you. . . . When you are ready, walk through this doorway. . . . Ask for the highest guide and teacher who is aligned with you to come forward. Imagine that your guide, a special guide, is coming forward. Sense this guide, feel his or her love for you. Be open to receive. Feel your heart welcoming this guide. Feel the response. Believe that it is really happening! Your imagination is the closest ability you have to channeling, and it is the easiest connection your guide has to you at first. . . . Greet your guide. . . . Mentally carry on a conversation with this guide. . . . Ask your guide to begin doing all that he or she can to open the channel, now that you are committed and ready to verbally channel (575:80-82).

Even cancer therapists O. Carl Simonton and Stephanie Matthews-Simonton, who employ visualization in a professional setting for cancer therapy, accept this theme of using "imaginary" spirit guides for supposed healing processes. An examination of their book indicates that they are encouraging nothing less than a form of spiritism. (For examples, see New Age Inner Work.)

Consider another illustration of how visualization can cause one to contact the spirit world. In *Mind Games: The Guide to Inner Space*, leading consciousness explorers Masters

and Houston tell others how to use visualization and trance to develop psychic awareness, monistic consciousness, and then to raise and contact what they term a "Group Spirit." This is all done as a means to advance the cause of psychic development. Participants actually offer "obeisance" to a materialized spirit masquerading in the form of the collective group consciousness of the "players" (708:198-206).

Yet, as in the case of "Philip," this "mental" group entity is described as "an entity with an independent existence of its own" (708:203), and as "an actual, intelligent being, conscious and powerful" (708:198). In actuality, the participants in such exercises hold a seance under another name:

We are beginning to go now into trance together. We are going to experience deepening together, and, finally, each of us will contribute to the pool of consciousness out of which the Group Spirit will draw its substance and arise to exist once again.

And we are going to cause to rise now, out of that pool, the entity we have called the Group Spirit. . . .

You will be aware of that emergence, and of the Group Spirit's location in space, there at the center. And you will concentrate on that space, focus intensely and remain focused on that space, and understand now we can and must materialize the Group Spirit, endowing that entity with a sufficiently material being that it can appear to us all. . . . But we can materialize this entity, by concentrating on the center and vividly imagining, powerfully imagining, the flow of substance, of material, from you and into that center, where the pool has been created by us (708:199-201).

This is little different from the visualization process described earlier, in which occult magician Conway described how magic ritual is used to conjure the spirit that possesses the magician. And the purpose is also similar: inspiration and guidance from the entity:

Go and stand before the place we have designated to be the residing place of this entity we have evoked. Request inspiration in the form of a dance or a song or a chant, something that can be performed by you now, as an offering and in celebration of the spirit of our group....

After that, as instructed by the guide, each player successively will stand near the center of the circle, receiving inspiration, and then carrying out whatever movements or sounds or other behavior the person feels motivated to do and experiencing this motivation as coming directly from the Group Spirit....

The Group Spirit will appear to you in a dream and you will be able to gain a clear and detailed impression of its appearance, and you may be able to enter into a conversation with it, and various things might be revealed to you (708:202).

Prominent educator Jack Canfield also recommends spiritism under another name. He encourages teachers to assist their students to perform a guided imagery exercise developed by Paula Klimek, who is with the Center for Holistic Education. This occult exercise is to be used by students as early as the *sixth* grade:

It is a very powerful experience which can help students become aware of their essential nature, their highest potential, their unique gift to the world, and their life purpose. Especially as kids enter adolescence, they often become confused and are usually unable to get clear answers from their parents or their teachers about many basic questions of life, such as Who am I? What difference does my life make? and What do I really want to do? My experience has been that when those core questions are addressed from within and when students experience recognition and affirmation of their essence, their core self, and their inner wisdom, remarkable transformations occur (2268:14).

But this exercise deliberately attempts to have children contact and develop a relationship with their "special guide" (see New Age Education):

You are about to meet a special guide, your own special guide. A guide whom you may ask what the purpose of your life is.... Meet this guide and pose your question.... Feel your guide's unconditional love and strength and beauty.... Let whatever happens happen.... Communicate

with your guide in whatever way possible. ... Listen to your guide ... (2268:15).

Another example of visualization-induced spiritism is found in Shakti Gawain's *Creative Visualization*:

Each one of us has all the wisdom and knowledge we ever need right within us.... The inner guide is known by many different names, such as your counselor, spirit guide, imaginary friend, or master. It is a higher part of yourself, which can come to you in many different forms, but usually comes in the form of a person or being whom you can talk to and relate to as a wise and loving friend....

[Through visualization] go to your inner sanctuary and spend a few minutes there, relaxing, getting oriented.... See in the distance a form coming toward you, radiating a clear, bright light....

Greet this being, and ask him or her what their name is.... Ask your guide if there is anything he or she would like to say to you, or any advice to give you at the moment....

Also your guide *may* change form and even name from time to time. Or you may have the same one for years. You may have more than one guide at the same time.

Your guide is there for you to call on anytime you need or want extra guidance, wisdom, knowledge, support, creative inspiration, love or companionship. Many people who have established a relationship with their guide meet them every day in their meditation (699:91-93).

The previous process is similar to those found in many other practices; for example, using the imagination to construct "imaginary advisors" in New Age seminars such as est* (The Forum*), Mind Psi Biotics, or Silva Mind Control* (884). Various cults and fringe or humanistic psychotherapies, which have reached millions, do the same.

Many of the "fantasy role-playing" games, such as Dungeons and Dragons,* may also use the imagination to foster an interest in the occult. In such cases "creative visualization" is used to guide the individual into encounters with allegedly imaginary nonmaterial entities, forces, or spirits (433). Again, it is often claimed that the entities are mere fantasies and have no basis in reality. But don't tell that to the people who ended up contacting real spirits.

## Medicinal Spirits?

Visualization spiritism is also becoming increasingly popular in health and medicine (see New Age Medicine). Popular osteopath and author Dr. Irving Oyle recommends the contacting of a personal "ally" or "guide" through visualization practices in his *New American Medicine Show*:

> Think of the most beautiful place you can imagine and pretend you are there. Mentally create the sounds, the smells, and the body sensations appropriate to being in that place....
>
> In your mind's eye, as you continue the previous steps, look around casually. You may be surprised to see or otherwise sense the presence of a living creature—a person, an animal, a plant, something which lives in the place you have recalled....
>
> This creature is your ally, your guide and advisor; your psychoanalyst, if you will. A hologram printed out by your biocomputer [mind], which pops spontaneously into your empty awareness....
>
> Befriend your guide in the best manner you know. Feed it, pet it, ask its name; find out if it's male or female....
>
> Ask your guide if he or she is willing to meet with you for fifteen minutes daily for a period of one week. (They always agree.)
>
> In return for your offering, and to seal your agreement, ask your ally to demonstrate a sign of its power. This may be immediate relief of a physical symptom or an answer to a thorny life problem.
>
> In the remaining steps your holographic ally tells you why you made your illness and suggests specific life transformations which will initiate the healing process.... The method is an adaptation of Carl Jung's method of active imagination ... (122:141-43).

Oyle also cites a case history in which "the ally appeared without being actually summoned" (122:145).

Dennis T. Jaffe of the UCLA School of Medicine Psychiatry Department (Ph.D., Yale), and David E. Bresler, director of the UCLA hospital's pain control unit, also stress the importance of inner advisers as an adjunct to medical diagnosis and treatment:

> Clinicians like ourselves are experimenting with many creative and highly experimental uses of mental imagery. One of the most dramatic techniques we have used involves what is known as "the inner adviser." This technique, popularized by Irving Oyle (1976) and Samuels and Bennett (1973), is utilized by many health practitioners. By creating and interacting with an inner adviser, a person learns to gather important information from their subconscious....
>
> As clinicians we have been surprised, not only by the immense value of guided imagery, but at how receptive most patients are to the technique as part of medical treatment ... (658:54-56).
>
> It is our hope that health professionals from all disciplines will begin to utilize them [inner advisers] to help their patients more effectively help themselves (658:58).

Jaffee and Bresler also describe how the patient is to wait upon and trust her "adviser":

> It is important to wait until the adviser appears in human, animal, or other life form.... When the adviser arrives, the person is asked to greet it, and to begin the process of getting to know the adviser. This might include introducing themselves, and learning the adviser's name.... People usually have the experience of receiving surprising or unexpected information from this inner oracle (658:56).

As the patient begins to know his inner guide, she is then supposed to ask other inner advisers into the mind. "After patients develop a strong relationship with an adviser, we recommend that they find other advisers as well. We suggest that patients invite their advisers to bring mates or other acquaintances to the next meeting" (658:57-58).

Paradoxically, the teachings of these "benevolent advisers" is not exactly healthful, especially in an era of AIDS. For example, "One of the new advisers was a rabbit named Rachel, who told Terry, 'You only live once, and life is very short. Why not make it as sweet as you can? Have as many different sexual experiences as possible, and don't worry about attachments. Just live loose and free!' " (658:58).

Jaffee and Bresler think that these advisers only "represent dialogues between different parts of one's nervous system" (658:58). Nevertheless, as they stated, this technique was developed by two spiritists, Mike Samuels, M.D., and Hal Bennett, who, as we noted, are the authors of *Spirit Guides: Access to Inner Worlds* (289).

There is little doubt that visualization techniques can and do result in the contact of genuine spirit beings, regardless of how they may be redefined as part of the human imagination or "nervous system" (289:29-33,53-55). Until recent times, visualization had been relegated to occultists and shamans. Today, new updated forms are being employed by medical doctors, athletes, teachers, artists, businessmen, and even some clergymen. Unfortunately, because many professionals have little understanding of the mechanics of spiritual deception, they have unknowingly allowed themselves to become pawns in a battle whose players are invisible to them (see New Age Medicine). The idea that some of our best-educated professionals are beginning to practice sorcery under the pretense of science and health is no longer the unimaginable concept it once was.

## QUESTIONS AND CONCERNS

It should be recognized that when the mind is manipulated into novel states of consciousness, there is always a potential for spiritual deception and danger (see Altered States of Consciousness). This is true regardless of a person's motive or environment—internal or external. The number of well-meaning people who embarked upon a visualization program merely for physical health, psychological understanding, or spiritual

advancement and who ended up involved in the occult is not small. Books on visualization carry numerous anecdotes of how even the innocent and benevolent use of visualization catapulted people into the New Age Movement, psychic development, or spirit contact. This includes academics and scholars. Because more and more professionals are also becoming interested in the psychic realm, in the exploration of human consciousness, in New Age techniques and therapies, and in allegedly neutral and scientific uses of visualization, the occult use of visualization in academic forms is now increasing.

Visualization may have a capacity to place the mind into a certain brainwave pattern conducive to the development of alleged psychic abilities (686:244-45/703:95-98/704:138-39). How then do we view the practice of visualization in Christian psychotherapy? What about visualization techniques practiced in education in general, or among children (686:262/693:151; cf. Hypnosis)? Educator Jack Canfield states, "When students are participating in a guided imagery experience they are in an altered state of consciousness" (2233:29). To what degree does a belief that is conditioned or manipulated by visualization affect our behavior and our worldview? What are the long-term effects of visualization itself, irrespective of the environment in which it occurs? How neutral is a systematic program of repeated visualization exercises?

Experts in both the theory and practice of visualization warn of its potential dangers. H. V. Guenther and leading Tibetan Buddhist guru Chogyam Trungpa assert in *The Dawn of Tantra*, "Certainly practicing visualization without the proper understanding is extremely destructive.... Tantric scriptures abound with warnings about using visualization" (705:49). Practicing occultist J. H. Brennan, whose *Astral Doorways* cites visualization as an "excellent doorway," warns that to mix certain things (for example, yoga postures and visualization techniques) without knowing exactly what one is doing "is asking for psychosis" (386:98). As noted, many people have embarked upon a visualization program and converted to occultism as a result. This is another of our concerns about the danger of visualization, because occultism is hazardous to people physically, emotionally, and spiritually (278).

Other questions and concerns surround variables that affect the specific outcome of visualization techniques. Unfortunately, neither good motives nor a neutral environment is a sufficient safeguard against spiritual deception or other dangers. The *context* of visualization—whether the therapist's office, personal meditation, or magic ritual—and the *content* of visualization (the worldview into which the practices are structured) are important for determining the potential degree of alignment with the occult. Furthermore, any claim to benevolence is ruled out when visualization is used to develop psychic abilities, enter altered states of consciousness,* magically control the environment, or channel* or other forms of spirit contact.

While some of the seemingly innocuous visualization techniques in some forms of psychotherapy are certainly not the same as visualization programs in the world of the occult, there are still unanswered questions about the possible impact of long-term visualization practices. For example, in education and Christian or secular psychotherapy, do we know the consequences of sustained visualization practice among children or patients? Can we be sure that long-term visualization practice will never open the door to the experience of so-called "higher consciousness"?

Is there really such a thing as neutral visualization in the long-term? When a person consecrates himself to an intensive program of visualization, does he really understand where this may lead? Many things which seem innocent are not necessarily so, for example, Ouija boards* (816). Practices that initially seem innocuous, such as transcendental meditation, can in the long run have considerable impact on a person physiologically, emotionally, and spiritually (468). For example, we might ask how a simple sound—that is, a mantra*—repeated 15 minutes twice a day could produce such dramatic changes as those sometimes brought about by TM (468). But we could ask the same thing of a simple visualization technique. Perhaps there is more going on here than meets the

eye. Perhaps spiritistic influence is a greater possibility than is usually supposed.

Consider someone using visualization to induce astral projection. What factors actualize the event? Intent? Occult environment? Psychophysical changes? The spirits? Indeed, it is the spirits themselves who often claim to induce and, to a degree, control out-of-body experiences (e.g., 63:193,350). So what are the parameters of the psychophysiology of visualization, and where do these end and spiritual warfare begin? To what extent does expectation condition or affect changes that occur from visualization?

## CHRISTIAN VISUALIZATION?

Many Christians have used forms of visualization. They argue that in rejecting visualization, the church is ignoring aspects of the creative imagination that are really legitimate. The comments of Stanley Dokupil, the author of a Spiritual Counterfeits Project critique of visualization, are perhaps relevant:

One of the reasons the New Agers are making such inroads is that the evangelical church has proven itself to be unimaginative, and overly linear in its thinking. The unconscious is real and there are powers there I believe that are not necessarily evil. Certain individuals by their nature are more inclined toward the full use of their imaginations than others, artists, therapists, certain other creative types, etc. If the church doesn't provide a discerning guidance for these people, other than outright dismissal of all borderline phenomena as satanic, then the church is not only poorer for having lost these people but will have to pay for it by having God's gifts used against His own church. The works of Jonathan Edwards, such as *Faithful Narrative of the Surprising Work of God, The Distinguishing Marks of a Word of the Spirit of God, A Treatise Concerning Religious Affections*, as well as Elizabeth Winslow's biography of Edwards are very informative here (709:1-2).

Obviously, we cannot recommend the kinds of visualization we have been discussing in this chapter. The spiritual risks are too clear. So if the church is going to accept some aspects of the practice of visualization, it will need to sort out the godly uses of the imagination from the counterfeit varieties. Otherwise, how does a Christian therapist using an "inner Jesus" as a guide, friend, and adviser ensure a client against spiritism? What safeguards can be provided to ensure that imagination will not lead to the appearance of a spiritistic Jesus? Spiritistic Jesuses appear all over the place in the occult, from dictating occult texts such as *A Course in Miracles,** to direct appearances in the temples of the Mormon Church, to various occultists (refs. 885/891).

Is a "Jesus" who truly manifests inwardly to guide and comfort or to erase bad memories, a "Jesus" who must appear at the beck and call of the emotionally needy in general? Is this not similar to the familiar spirit of the occultist?

Apart from the occult, how much power does visualization per se really have? If man *were* a god-in-embryo, with divine energy at his disposal, and if his thoughts actually *did* create reality, then visualization *should* produce literal miracles. But this is not the case. Given biblical teaching, visualization is mostly impotent and, even in its allegedly "neutral" or "Christian" therapeutic aspects, would only seem marginally useful at best. In other words, isn't it true that a) God's ordering of the world and how attentively we live in harmony with it, and b) obeying His moral standards, are vastly more important to any kind of physical and spiritual health than our mental pictures or manipulation of them through visualization, even in a Christian context?

Another issue is, Where is the Christian to derive a personal identity from? Is our self-image to be determined from our creative imagination or from the Word of God? Do the popular visualization techniques applied in a Christian context really conform to reality? Belief can certainly affect our behavior, but to be biblical it must be based on either reality or at least something possible. New Age and even much Christian positive confession imaging does not count as true what is true; it only imagines and visualizes as true what one *wants* to be true (cf. 2639).

If visualization truly puts us in contact with our inner being, our subconscious, what can we expect to gain but perhaps the upwelling of that

reality that Jesus spoke of: the sinful self? Perhaps this is the reason why some authorities have warned about the psychological dangers of using visualization to explore the unconscious. After all, as Jesus said:

"What comes out of a man is what makes him 'unclean.' For from within, out of men's hearts, come evil thoughts, sexual immorality, theft, murder, adultery, greed, malice, deceit, lewdness, envy, slander, arrogance and folly. All these evils come from inside and make a man 'unclean' " (Mark 7:20-23).

New Age theorists and many visualizing church members regard the biblical doctrine of depravity as anathema, as indeed they must. To find the "divine" within, with its suggestion of universalism, the words of Christ must be ignored or reinterpreted.

Is the visualization program that seeks to remold man's depravity into divinity really based on reality? Whose reality? If a Christian has been forgiven, regenerated, justified, joined to Christ, adopted, and positionally sanctified, how important is a spiritual program of Christian visualization? These biblical doctrines mentioned *are* spiritual realities. They are facts one need only *understand* and accept to integrate for major spiritual benefits (886). While the imagination might help a Christian to see such doctrinal realities as personally true, it is only by personal *study* of biblical doctrine and theology that the tremendous truths of Scripture are actually realized and applied. This is something visualization can't do.

God has promised Christians many things: He will finish the work He began in us (Philippians 1:6); our inner man is being renewed day by day (2 Corinthians 4:16; 3:18); and we will stand before Him, blameless, perfect in body, soul, and spirit, for "faithful is he who calls you, and He also will bring it to pass" (1 Thessalonians 5:23,24 NASB).

Christians are to be renewed daily by the Holy Spirit, prayer, and the Word of God. They are not to be renewed by a transpersonal psychology using Eastern metaphysics or inner work through visualization. The power of the Word of God to build a truly integrated person makes modern visualization pale by contrast. Jesus said, "Apart from me you can do nothing" (John 15:5). Where then is the spiritual power of visualization? Will an hour a day of our busy lives be better spent in visualization or in prayer? Will an hour a day be better spent on the therapist's couch talking to an imaginary "inner Jesus" or

in the Bible with the real Jesus? And what of our children? Will secular or New Age visualization methods in the classroom finally be in their best interests?

In our culture, visualization practices are here to stay. This underscores the necessity for Christians to bring a thoroughgoing and biblical critique to this subject.

# Yoga

## Info at a Glance

**Description.** The occult use of breathing exercises, particular physical postures, and meditation* for alleged improved mental functioning, health maintenance, and spiritual enlightenment.*

**Founder.** Unknown; one of the major developers is Patanjali, compiler of the classical *Yogasutras* of raja yoga.

**How does it claim to work?** The physical exercises of yoga are believed to prevent diseases and maintain health through bodily regulation of *prana* or mystical life energy. Furthermore, because the body is viewed as a crude layer of mind, various manipulations of the physical body (some severe) can affect the mind, bringing alleged enlightenment. In Hindu mythology, the serpent goddess *kundalini* "rests" at the base of the spine. She is aroused by yoga practice, travels up the spine while regulating prana and opening the body's alleged psychic centers (*chakras*), finally reaching the top (crown) *chakra*, permitting the merging of Shiva/Shakti and occult enlightenment.

**Scientific evaluation.** Yogic (e.g., psychic) powers and abilities have been scientifically studied, such as Elmer Green's widely reported research with Swami Rama. Because yoga is essentially an occult practice leading to the manifestation of *siddhis* (psychic abilities), such research is often parapsychological. Yoga, like meditation and visualization,* can have physical, psychological, and spiritual effects. Science may study these, but it cannot evaluate the spiritual or occult claims made for them (e.g., that they reflect evidence of "higher" consciousness or spiritual "enlightenment").

**Examples of occult potential.** Yoga practice involves occult meditation, the development of psychic powers, and may result in spirit contact or spirit possession.

**Major problems.** The public perception of yoga as a safe, spiritually neutral practice is false. It is difficult, if not impossible, to separate yoga practice from yoga theory. The one who engages in yoga practices for health purposes may also find himself converted to an occult way of life.

**Biblical/Christian evaluation.** Because yoga is an occult practice, it is prohibited.

**Potential dangers.** Authoritative yoga literature is replete with warnings of serious physical consequences, mental derangement, or harmful spiritual effects.

*Note:* See also Meditation, Shamanism, and refs. 249 and 278. Different Eastern or mystical religions practice different forms of yoga. Even in a given religion there are various kinds of schools, depending on the emphasis. In Hinduism, we find *hatha* (physical yoga), *raja* (mental yoga), *bhakti* (devotional yoga), *jana* (the yoga of knowledge), *siddha* (the yoga of psychic powers), *karma* (the yoga of action or social responsibility), *laya* or *mantra* (the yoga of sound), and other yogas. *Kundalini* may be labeled as a separate yoga; however, all yoga has the potential to arouse kundalini. Although the emphasis may vary, the basic goal in all yoga is the same: union with ultimate reality, however defined. In Hinduism this would be union of the individual self (*atman*) with the supreme self (*paramatman*), itself one with Brahman, the highest impersonal Hindu God; in Buddhism it would be union with Nirvana.

## INTRODUCTION AND INFLUENCE

For millions of Americans, yoga is a popular pastime. Yoga classes are regularly offered by the YMCA, the YWCA, in New Age and business seminars, on TV, and in church programs. Here the claim is often made that yoga practice is not religious and that members of any faith or persuasion can benefit from a yoga program. For example, several books attempt to integrate yoga practice and Christian faith (590). Promoters make such claims as, "Yoga and Christianity are founded upon a similar base of wisdom" (591:2).

More and more, health professionals are now advocating yoga as a safe and effective method for physical and mental health. Dr. Norman Shealy, who has taught at Harvard and is the founder of the American Holistic Medical Association, recommends hatha yoga along with "the power of crystals"* as an "essential component" of national health programs of the near future (108:58). Steve Brena, M.D., attempts to merge yogic concepts and modern medicine in his *Yoga and Medicine* (965).

A modern alternate health guide claims that "all the chronic diseases are specially amenable to yoga treatment" (727:144). The guide asserts that illnesses responding to yoga include asthma, backache, arthritis, bronchitis, high blood pressure, obesity, sinusitis, nervous disorders, constipation, dysmenorrhea, dyspepsia, and others. "The chief value of yoga . . . is in prevention of illness . . ." (727:143-44). With claims like this widely circulated and a growing health-care crisis, it is no wonder yoga is extensively practiced in America today.

In the new spiritual climate of America in general, the stress on yoga is both as a path to spiritual enlightenment* and a means to physical and mental health (so-called "therapeutic yoga"):

> The aim of therapeutic Yoga is to maintain healthy minds and healthy bodies, but its practices are being increasingly used to produce cures or alleviations of disease. Yoga works on the premise that most illness is caused by wrong posture, wrong diet and wrong mental attitudes, which imbalances are under the control of the student (patient) himself.

> Yoga is a philosophy embracing every aspect of human life, spiritual, emotional, mental and physical. It did not set out to be a therapy, but is being used as such today. It is a system of self-improvement, or "conscious evolution" (188:221).

Indeed, in modern America, people use yoga for a wide variety of purposes:

> People take up Yoga to reduce nervous tension by learning to relax, to slim and to become more agile mentally and physically. Eventually yoga leads them to meditation, thence to modifications of personal and social behavior. Students attending regular classes become more relaxed, more supple and clearer headed, and usually begin to question the purpose of life in a way they have not before. This holistic approach leads to better health, and the improvement or eradication of psychosomatic ailments.

> It is in the field of psychosomatic ailments that Yoga therapy can be most effective (188:221,222).

## YOGA AND CHILDREN

Today, yoga is increasingly advocated as a positive practice even for young children, such as an important adjunct to children's education or gym classes (2232/2243). Unfortunately, if yoga is ultimately an occult practice, such advocacy will not benefit children but will, in all probability, sooner or later harm them spiritually or otherwise (278).

Educator and psychic Deborah Rozman is the author of two books on meditation* for children, and she names her mentor as occultist Christopher Hills, developer of spirulina and founder of the University of the Trees in Boulder Creek, California (2261:dedication). After noting that puberty supposedly "opens new psychic energies," which result in experiencing psychic phenomena, she observes that classroom meditation helps to speed the process of evolution of the "higher Self." Here, she encourages children to do "physical yoga exercises to quiet and balance the rapidly growing and restless [psychic] energies . . ." (2261:74-76).

In her chapter "Yoga Exercises for the Young," she explains, "The real purpose of yoga exercises is to put the body in a state where meditation on the One is possible. . . . Physical yoga is called hatha yoga. . . . Hatha yoga is balancing the spiritual and physical and male and female energies (the polarities) in the body" (2261:85). Thus, using yoga exercises from the Hindu spiritist Paramahansa Yogananda, founder of the Self-realization Fellowship, she tells the child, "Use your will and your imagination to direct the [psychic] energy to flow down your whole body into your left foot as you tense the left foot and then relax it" (2261:86). This is also to be done for other areas of the body.

Today there are dozens of books specifically to instruct children on how to do yoga (cf. New Age Education). Among them are Rachael Carr's *Be a Frog, a Bird or a Tree*, and *Wheel, Camel, Fish and Plow: Yoga for You*; Ken Cohen's *Imagine That! A Child's Guide to Yoga*; Baba Hari Dass's *A Child's Garden of Yoga*; Eve Diskin's *Yoga for Children*; Else Klippner's *My Magic Garden*; Suzanne Schreiber's *Yoga for the Fun of It: Hatha Yoga for Pre-School Children*; and Susan N. Terkel's *Yoga Is for Me*.

Yoga is also becoming a popular approach to treatment for children with physical and learning disabilities (2448). Yet even noted New Age theorist Ken Wilbur admits, "The Path of Yogis can cause severe emotional-sexual upheavals . . ." (2449:160). As we will see below, yoga is not the safe or neutral practice its proponents claim and, therefore, it should not be used in public schools or advocated for children.

## THE PURPOSE OF YOGA

In this section, we will show that while yoga is a method of physical discipline, it always has distinct spiritual (occult) goals. We will examine the real purpose of yoga, its occult nature, and its physical, mental, and spiritual consequences because we think that people should be told that its alleged "health benefits" carry unforeseen risks. To begin, how is yoga defined? The *Oxford American Dictionary* defines "yoga" in the following manner: "1. a Hindu system of meditation and self-control designed to produce mystical experience and spiritual insight. 2. a system of physical exercises and breathing control" (414:1085).

Most people think of yoga only in terms of the second definition. We will show that this is a mistake. When examining the *true* goal of yoga, one sees why these two definitions ultimately cannot be separated. In other words, the one who practices yoga as "a system of physical exercises and breathing control" is also practicing a system "designed to produce mystical experience and spiritual (occult) insight." For example, Ernest L. Rossi of the Department of Psychology at UCLA states how yoga is designed to induce altered states of consciousness:

> If one considers the ancient yoga science of *pranayama* (controlled breathing) to have relevance, then one must admit that the manual manipulation of the nasal cycle during meditation (*dhyana*) is the most thoroughly documented of techniques for altering consciousness. For thousands of years these techniques for the subtle alterations of nasal breathing have been gradually codified into classical texts. Some of these are the *Hatha Yoga Pradipika* (II, 6-9,19-20), *Siva Samhita* (III, 24,25), *Gheranda Samhita* (V, 49-52), and *Yoga Chudamani Upsanisad* (V, 98-100). . . . A new tradition of psychophysiological

and experimental research exploring these ancient techniques has been developing during the past few decades (Hasegawa and Kem, 1978). The work of Vinekar (1966), Rao and Potdar (1970), Eccles (1978), and Funk and Clarke (1980) also provides a broad background of independent studies using Western laboratory methods in studying the relationship of this nasal cycle to the ancient yogic tradition of *pranayama* in achieving psychosomatic health and the transpersonal states of *dhyana* [deep contemplation] and *samadhi* [occult enlightenment] (1046: 113-14).

As we have said, many who recommend yoga claim it is an excellent way in which to loosen one's muscles, keep fit, and maintain health. For these people, yoga is simply physical exercise and nothing more; the practice has little to do with religion. Such persons, however, do not properly understand the nature and purpose of true yoga practice. Yoga is much more than merely an innocent form of relaxing the mind and body. One reason that yoga clearly belongs in the category of religion is because the classic yoga texts reveal that proper yoga practice incorporates many goals of occultism. Allegedly, it will not only result in a "sound" mind and a "healthy" body but also in spiritual (occult) enlightenment.*

However, a "sound" mind and "healthy" body, as defined in yoga, are different than what most people normally think of. Yoga philosophy teaches that mind and body are ultimately "one." In yoga theory, to influence the body through yoga practice will result in powerfully influencing the mind and spirit as well.

How does yoga theory maintain that the body can dramatically influence the mind and spirit, producing major experiences with altered states of consciousness* and spiritual enlightenment?* In yoga theory, the body is really a crude *layer* of one's mind, and both are aspects of the continuum of alleged divine consciousness that is "awakened" by yoga practice. Therefore, manipulation of the body is equivalent to manipulation of the mind and spirit. This is why the *physical* postures of yoga are *designed* to manipulate consciousness toward a specific occult goal. Yogi authority Gopi Krishna comments:

All the systems of yoga ... are designed to bring about those psychosomatic changes in the body which are essential for the metamorphosis of consciousness. A new [divine] center—presently dormant in the average man and woman—has to be activated and a more powerful stream of psychic energy must [be awakened] (592:15).

Yoga postures and breathing, then, are designed to *awaken* psychic energy and bring about dramatic changes in consciousness.

So what is the final goal of yoga practice and the altered states of consciousness that it generates? The end purpose is for the individual to realize that he or she is one essence with God, or ultimate reality, however this is defined. In other words, one must realize that he or she is God. Whatever school of yoga is used (*hatha, raja, bhakti*, etc.), whether it is Hindu, Buddhist, Taoist, Sufi, Tantric, or some other religious tradition, the goal is typically the same: occult enlightenment* achieved by internal manipulation of occult energies* (*prana, chi*) leading to altered states of consciousness* in order to produce awareness of one's inherent union with God, or ultimate reality (616).

Swami Rama, an accomplished yogi and founder of the worldwide Himalayan International Institute of Yoga, Science and Philosophy, affirms that "there are many different methods of yoga, all leading to the same goal of Self-Realization" (914:7). He describes this as "the union of man with Absolute Reality" (914:3). Swami Ajaya correctly affirms that "the main teaching of Yoga is that man's true nature is divine" (914:vi).

The physical exercises of yoga, then, are only a means to a much larger goal: attaining godhood. However, where the goal is to introduce yoga as a physical exercise only, this is probably not stated. Thus, some yoga teachers employ yoga *deceptively*. They know exactly what it intends, but hope to "enlighten" people on the sly. Yoga will achieve its own transformation in people, so there is no need to mention its controversial religious—especially occult—aspects. Judith Lasater, Ph.D., in her article "Yoga: An Ancient Technique for Restoring Health" states, on the one hand, that "yoga is widely used as a palliative for various physical problems" (197:37). But she agrees the *real* goal of yoga is to enable the individual to "perceive his true nature." The mind and body are *both* aspects of that nature, divine consciousness, and it is yoga which allows people to discover this as their true nature or essence:

One basic assumption of *Yoga Sutras* [a standard yoga text] is that the body and mind are part of one continuum of [divine] existence, the mind merely being more subtle than the body. This is the foundation for the yogic view of health. The interaction of body and mind is the central concern of the entire science. It is believed that as the body and mind are brought into balance and health, the individual will be able to perceive his true [divine] nature; this will allow life to be lived through him more freely and spontaneously (197:36).

In other words, yoga practice supposedly brings "health and balance" to mind and body. But defined properly, this means a developed awareness of one's own inner divinity and an allowing of one's divine nature to be "lived out."

## Innocent Yoga?

When Westerners employ yoga techniques as a means to improve their health, they should understand that they can also be producing subtle changes within themselves which will have dramatic spiritual consequences that will not be for the better. Regardless of the school or spiritual tradition, yoga practice tends to alter a person's consciousness in an occult direction.

Even when yoga is practiced innocently, it can eventually produce dramatic occult transformation. "Personality changes can be brought about in Hatha Yoga by changing the body so that it influences the mind" (188:223). Consider the experience of Christina Grof, who, prior to her experience with yoga, was an average housewife with normal plans for her life. She took up yoga entirely without suspicion as a practice that would help her physically during her pregnancy. After all, there are widespread claims that "during pregnancy, yoga exercises are extremely beneficial and will keep you supple and relaxed" (727:143).

What Christian Grof got was far more. She found herself transformed from a "conservative

suburban housewife" into a New Age leader by means of hatha yoga. All she had to do was "join a hatha yoga class for exercise" and the logical progression ensued:

During the birth of my first child, for which I had prepared with the Lamaze method of breathing (very much like yogic *pranayama*), this enormous spiritual force was released in me. Of course, I didn't understand it and was given morphine to stop it as soon as the baby was born.... Then the same thing happened when my second child was born. This all led to more and more experiences. I threw myself into yoga, although still not acknowledging it as a spiritual tool. My meeting with Swami Muktananda really blew the lid off everything. He served as a catalyst to awaken what I had been resisting, which was kundalini (the universal life force) (589:40).

Thus, an innocently practiced yoga-for-exercise routine led to numerous psychic experiences that had the cumulative impact of dramatically changing her life. She became a disciple of the Hindu guru* Muktananda and then, as we will see, a leader in the New Age Movement with a specific mission: to assist people who were having "spiritual emergencies" from their occult practices and help them to "properly interpret" and successfully integrate these "divine" experiences into their lives (759).

Initially, however, as the standard *kundalini* yoga symptoms emerged in her life, the prognosis was not good. (Hindu kundalini mythology is discussed later.) Grof herself was in the midst of a spiritual emergency and increasingly convinced of her own insanity. "I was convinced I was headed for a life of psychopathology. I was afraid I was going crazy" (589:41). Nevertheless, counseling through occult philosophy put matters in their "proper" perspective. Her marriage ended, "which it was destined to do anyway." And the late popular mythologist Joseph Campbell helped her recognize, "The schizophrenic is drowning in the same waters in which the mystic is swimming with delight." He also referred her to LSD and consciousness researcher Stan Grof for more counseling.

The rest is history. The couple were eventually married and today coordinate some 50 SEN

(Spiritual Emergency Network) regional information centers around the globe (cf. 759:227). They also publish a significant amount of literature in the field of occult metaphysics. Their reinterpretation of the pathological phenomena induced by occult practice—as a positive transforming spirituality (a spiritual "emergence")—not only helps undergird and legitimize the occult, but it also effectively inhibits discernment of the true issues involved.

For example, in the case of kundalini yoga, symptoms of mental illness and demonization are gratuitously redefined as emerging manifestations of "higher" or divine consciousness. Thus, we are not to question or fear the kundalini process but to surrender to it and trust it implicitly, for it is indeed part of that ageless wisdom of evolutionary transformation which is far wiser than ourselves. A chapter in a recent book edited by Stan and Christina Grof, *Spiritual Emergency*, reveals a basic approach of SEN counseling. The title is "When Insanity Is a Blessing" (759:77-97).

Thus, a slow but sure yoga-induced occult transformation catapulted Christina Grof headlong into the world of occultism. In the long run, her innocent flirtation with yoga altered her entire life and resulted in her becoming a leader in the New Age Movement, with influence over hundreds of thousands of people.

Consider one more example of the potential consequences of innocent yoga practice. While Christian Grof used yoga for help in her pregnancy, Carole, a friend of coauthor John Weldon, used yoga for medical and health reasons. We published her story in *The Coming Darkness: Confronting Occult Deception* (278). We first met Carole as a result of exchanging information on the famous Indian guru and yogi Swami Rama. The following information is taken from material sent to us.

Carole was very sick and doctors were unable to find the cause of her illness. When she went to a physician-nutritionist recommended by a friend, she found some literature in his office about the Himalayan Institute, of which the doctor was a staff member. The institute was founded by Indian Swami Rama, one of the most scientifically studied of the gurus, beginning with famous biofeedback researcher and spiritist

(2763) Dr. Elmer Green. Carole decided to attend the institute, where she began lessons in hatha yoga. Eventually, she was initiated and received her mantra, or word of occult power, from Swami Rama. As he laid his hands upon her head, the typical transfer of "occult energy" began (termed *shaktipat diksha*). Carole was in heaven:

Currents of electrical energy began to permeate my head and went down into my body.... It was as if a spell had come over me, the bliss that I felt was as if I had been touched by God. The power that had come from his hand, and simply being in his presence, drew me to him irresistibly.

The night after receiving her mantra, Carole was visited by a spirit being who claimed to be the spirit of Swami Rama himself. Although no one had ever mentioned the spirit world in her church (they did not believe in such things), Carole felt that this was the means of directly communing with God. She experienced wonderful powerful forces and energies, while thoughts entered her mind with a magnetic-like force:

Electrical currents were pulsating around my body and then moved into my hand, the currents were shaking my hand and strong, almost entrancing thoughts were impressed into my mind, "Meditate, meditate. I want to speak with you." It was a miracle. I was communicating with the spirit world. I had found God. Sitting in the darkness of my living room I began to repeat my mantra. A presence seemed to fill the room. I began to see visions of being one with the universe and the magnetic thoughts were now leaving and I was hearing a voice, which identified itself as Swami Rama, saying he was communicating with me through astral travel.

Within one week, after meditating many hours each day and still in constant communication with this spirit, forces began to come upon me and gave me powers to do yoga postures; I was floating through them, the forces giving me added breath even ... postures that before would be very painful to do.

However, after two weeks of daily yoga meditation, Carole became engulfed in a nightmare of utter dread and terror. Voices that once claimed they were angelic turned threatening, even demonic. She was brutally assaulted, both physically and spiritually by spirits. During meditation, in the midst of being violently shaken, she could sense that the same energy received at initiation, energy which was now felt to be *personal*, was attempting to remove her life-essence from her physical body—in her words, "to literally pull the life from my shell of a body." She sensed an overwhelming and implacable hatred directed toward her from this "energy," as if "monstrosities of another world were trying to take my very soul from me, inflicting pain beyond endurance, ripping and tearing into the very depths of my being."

The intermittent suffocation and torment seemed interminable; her fears increased as she realized there was no one to help her. Finally, the attack subsided. But it was merely the first of many.

It seems that nothing could stop the assaults. Her agonized pleas to the spirits were ignored; her husband was powerless. Her father wanted her to see a psychiatrist; others also doubted her sanity. In desperation, her mother contacted psychic friends from a local church of the Unity School of Christianity. They laid hands on Carole and commanded that "the divinity within" deliver her, but to no avail.

Dr. C. Norman Shealy, M.D., Ph.D., entered the picture. He is a noted neurosurgeon, a former professor at Harvard University, past president of the American Holistic Medical Association, and the author of *Occult Medicine Can Save Your Life.* Dr. Shealy also works in conjunction with psychics and spiritists such as Caroline Myss. When Dr. Shealy was unable to help, he referred Carole to Dr. Robert Leichtman, M.D., a spiritist who is coauthor of several dozen books received by revelation from the spirits.

Leichtman admitted that Carole's situation was not uncommon among followers of Eastern gurus.* He even told her some have died as a result of similar psychic attacks. But he, too, was unable to help. His instructions, such as visualizing herself in the white "Christ light" of protection, were useless. By this time, Carole was near the end:

I had to endure the torture, unable to free myself. To those around me I was insane. No one believed me and no one could free me. The hopelessness I felt was unbearable. No one believed me except the psychics . . . and they could do nothing.

I was defenseless against these never-ending attacks . . . hundreds of presences filling my room, which itself would be filled with thick, ice cold air, my body drenched with perspiration as my whole being fought against them.

After spending several weeks at my parents' we decided perhaps I could try returning home. But that night the spirits started to exert their full power.

First, against my skull. I felt as if they were trying to crack it open, like the air was being cut off to my brain. Incredible pressure was exerted upon my back and chest, pulling with a wrenchlike grip. It felt like they were trying to pull my shoulder from its socket, pressing on my eyes trying to blind me, pushing on my throat trying to choke me. Filled with fear and exhaustion, on the brink of death I screamed to my husband, "I'm dying; I can't take it anymore. Get me to the hospital."

I was taken to the hospital where I laid like a scared dog cowering on a cart. I could hardly speak but at least the spirits were gone—temporarily. . . . The doctor on duty recommended a psychiatrist who saw me the next morning. He told me I was covering up some deep problems with this "talk of evil spirits." "There is no such thing as the devil," he said coldly.

Carole admitted herself to the hospital, but once more no one could help. The attacks finally subsided and she was released. Upon returning home, the attacks began again. More unimaginable torment. Although she was terrified of dying, death was now her desire. Wishing to take her life but too fearful of dying, she readmitted herself to the hospital. Once again, she was placed in a locked ward. She felt that here she would die, alone and in torment.

But today, Carole is alive and well. Even her psychiatrist is amazed at the miraculous transformation. She is now in perfect health, both mentally and physically.

How did Carole get free? No one had been able to help her. Today, Carole attributes both her health and her life to a living Jesus Christ who delivered her from a desperate plight. Reflecting back on her predicament, she is awed that such terrible destruction could be purchased at the price of a simple, supposedly harmless form of yoga meditation.

Events like these reveal that there is more to yoga than meets the eye. Whether yoga can trigger some unknown psychospiritual, physiological response, or whether changes are produced spiritistically, or both, few can deny yoga is a powerful spiritual discipline that has been used for millennia to secure occult, pagan goals. As we proceed, we will better understand the reasons for this.

## THEORY AND PRACTICE: SEPARABLE?

The basic premise of yoga theory is the fundamental unity of all existence: God, man, and all of creation are ultimately one divine reality. An editorial in the *Yoga Journal* declares this basic premise:

We are all aware that yoga means "union" and that the practice of yoga unites body, breath, and mind, lower and higher energy centers and, ultimately self and God, or higher Self. But more broadly, yoga directs our attention to the unity or oneness that underlies our fragmented experiences and equally fragmented world. Family, friends, the Druze guerrilla in Lebanon, the great whale migrating north—all share the same essential [divine] nature (594:4).

This is why physical yoga and Eastern philosophy are mutually interdependent; ultimately, you cannot have one without the other. David Fetcho, a researcher with an extensive background in yoga theory and practice, states:

Physical yoga, according to its classical definitions, is inheritably and functionally incapable of being separated from Eastern religious metaphysics. The Western practitioner who attempts to do so is operating in ignorance and danger, from the yogi's viewpoint, as well as from the Christian's (725:2).

One of the leading contemporary authorities on kundalini yoga is Gopi Krishna. In his article

"The True Aim of Yoga," he says: "The aim of yoga, then, is to achieve the state of unity or oneness with God, Brahman, [and] spiritual beings . . ." (592:14).

Yoga authorities Feuerstein and Miller comment that the postures (*asana*) of yoga and its breathing techniques (*pranayama*) are much more than just physical exercises:

Again, we see that the control of the vital energy (*prana*) by way of breathing, like also *asana*, is not merely a physical exercise, but is accompanied by certain psychomental phenomena. In other words, all techniques falling under the heading of *asana* and *pranayama* as, for example, the *mudras* and *bandhas* [physical positions or symbolic bodily gestures utilizing *pranayama* and concentration for physical or spiritual purposes] of Hathayoga, are *psychosomatic* exercises. This point, unfortunately, is little understood by Western practitioners . . . (593:27-28).

Actually, yoga practice is *intended* to validate occult yoga theory. And as noted, yoga theory teaches that everything is, in its true inner nature, divine—not only divine but ultimately equal to everything else—everything from God and the devil to the athlete and the AIDS virus.

Yoga theory also teaches that in their outer nature, everything is *maya*, or illusion. For example, only in his inner spirit is man divine; his "outer nature," of body and personality, are ultimately a delusion that separates him from awareness of his real inner divinity. Thus, another purpose of yoga must be to slowly dismantle the outer personality—man's illusory part—so the supposed impersonal divinity can progressively "emerge" from within his hidden divine consciousness (see Eastern Gurus*).

This is why people who practice yoga only for physical or mental health reasons are ultimately the victims of a confidence game. *They* are promised better health; little do they suspect the end goal of yoga is to destroy *them* as individuals. As yoga authorities Feuerstein and Miller comment, yoga results in "a progressive dismantling of human personality ending in a complete abolition. With every step (*anga*) of Yoga, what we call 'man' is demolished a little more" (593:8).

In "Yoga as Methods of Liberation," Moti Lal Pandit observes that (as in Buddhism) "the aim of yoga is to realize liberation from the human condition. To achieve this liberation, various psychological, physical, mental, and mystical methods have been devised. All those methods are antisocial (sometimes even antihuman) in that yoga prescribes a way of life which says: this mortal life is not worth living" (595:41)

Yoga is, after all, a *religious* practice seeking to produce "union" with an impersonal ultimate reality, such as Brahman or Nirvana. If ultimate reality is impersonal, of what final value is one's own personality? For a person to achieve true "union" with Brahman, his "false" self must be destroyed and replaced with awareness of his true divine nature. That is the specific goal of yoga (again, see Eastern Gurus for examples). If we examine yoga theory in more detail, it is easier to understand why yoga practice has such specific occult goals.

One of the most authoritative texts on yoga theory within the Hindu perspective is Pantajali's text on raja Yoga titled *Yoga Sutras* (e.g., 596). In this text, he puts forth the traditional eight "limbs," or parts, of yoga. These are defined within the context of a basic Hindu worldview (reincarnation, *karma*, and *moksha*, or liberation) and intended to support and reinforce Hindu beliefs. Each "limb" has a spiritual goal and together they form a unit. These eight limbs are:

1. *Yama* (self-control, restraint, devotion to the gods [e.g., Krishna] or the final impersonal God [e.g., Brahman]

2. *Niyama* (religious duties, prohibitions, observances)

3. *Asana* (proper postures for yoga practices; these represent the first stage in the isolation of consciousness and are vital components for "transcending the human condition"; 601:54)

4. *Pranayama* (the control and directing of the breath and the alleged divine energy within the human body [prana] to promote health and spiritual [occult] consciousness and evolution)

5. *Pratyahara* (sensory control or deprivation, i.e., withdrawal of the senses from attachment to external objects)

6. *Dharana* (deeper concentration, or mind control)

7. *Dhyana* (deep contemplation from occult meditation)

8. *Samadhi* (occult enlightenment or "God [Brahman] realization" i.e., "union" of the "individual" with God).

Because the eight steps are interdependent, the steps of "postures" and "breathing" cannot logically be separated from the others. Thus, the interdependence of all eight steps reveals why the physical exercises of yoga are *designed* to prepare the body for the spiritual (occult) changes that will allegedly help one realize godhood status.

The concept of *prana* ("breath") is a key to the process. *Pranayama* refers to the knowledge and control of *prana*, or mystical energy, not merely to the control of one's physical breath (979:592). *Prana* is believed to be universal divine energy residing behind the material world (*akasa*). Prana is said to have five forms, and all energy is thought to be a manifestation of it. Swami Nikhilananada describes it in his *Vivekananda—The Yogas and Other Works* as "the infinite, omnipresent manifesting power of this universe" (979:592). Perfect control of *prana* makes one God. One can have "infinite knowledge, infinite power, now":

What power on earth would not be his? He would be able to move the sun and stars out of their places, to control everything in the universe from the atoms to the biggest suns. This is the end and aim of pranayama. When the yogi becomes perfect there will be nothing in nature not under his control. If he orders the gods or the souls of the departed to come, they will come at his bidding. All the forces of nature will obey him as slaves.... He who has controlled prana has controlled his own mind and all the minds... and all the bodies that exist... (979:592-93).

The aim of *pranayama* is also to arouse the coiled-up power in the *muladhara* chakra called *kundalini:*

Then the whole of nature will begin to change and the door of [psychic] knowledge will open. No more will you need to go to books for knowledge; your own mind will have become your book, containing infinite knowledge (979:605).

According to Vivekananda, all occult manifestations are accomplished through yogic control of *prana:*

> We see in every country sects that attempted the control of prana. In this country there are mindhealers, spiritualists, Christian Scientists, hypnotists, and so on. If we examine these different sects, we shall find that at the back of each is the control of prana, whether they know it or not. If you boil all the theories down, the residuum will be that. It is one and the same force they are manipulating.... Thus we see that pranayama includes all that is true even of spiritualism. Similarly, you will find that wherever any sect or body of people is trying to discover anything occult, mysterious, or hidden, they are really practicing some sort of yoga to control their prana. You will find that wherever there is any extraordinary display of power, it is the manifestation of prana (979:593,599).

In other words, *prana*, God, and occult energy are all one and the same. The one who practices yogic breathing (*pranayama*) is by definition attempting to manipulate occult ("divine") energy.

Consider a final statement as to why yoga practice and theory are inseparable. The Spiritual Counterfeits Project in Berkeley, California, publishes a relatively brief treatment on yoga, which we reproduce here with permission. The author was a former practitioner of yoga for several years with the Ananda Marga Yoga Society (726:31-36):

> Yoga exercises are taught as part of YMCA physical education programs, as health spa esoterica, on educational TV, and are incorporated into institutional church youth activities—all on the assumption that these techniques are nothing more than a superior brand of physical conditioning.
>
> Yet this assumption is really the worst presumption.... [E]ven physical yoga is inextricably bound up in the whole of Eastern religious metaphysics. In fact, it is quite accurate to say that physical yoga and Indian metaphysics are mutually interdependent; you really can't have one without the other. This point may be illustrated by referring to the two major traditional occurrences of physical yoga in the East.
>
> First of all, yoga postures (asanas) evolved as an integral part of Raja (royal) Yoga, also known as

*ashtanga* (eight-limbed) yoga. Raja Yoga is one of the more highly sophisticated systems of psychospiritual conditioning, and all the more so because it recognizes the profound influence of the body upon consciousness. (Indeed, its philosophical premise is that the body is but a crude layer of mind.) *Asana* (physical postures) is indispensable as one of the eight stages of Raja Yoga because the yoga postures are themselves specifically designed to manipulate consciousness, to a greater or lesser degree, into Raja Yoga's consummate experience of *samadhi:* undifferentiated union with the primal essence of consciousness, the monist's equivalent of 'God.' In his definitive work on Raja Yoga, Swami Vivekananda writes of *asana:* "A series of exercises, physical and mental, is to be gone through every day until certain higher states are reached. Nerve currents will have to be displaced and given a new channel. New sorts of vibrations will begin: the whole constitution will be remodeled, as it were."

In the context of Raja Yoga, then, the effects of the practice of *asana* are recognized as certainly going far beyond the merely physical and psychological results of Western systems of exercise. But does it necessarily follow that the Westerner practicing physical yoga will automatically have his or her consciousness manipulated into that experience of reality characteristic of Eastern metaphysics? Such a question has a great many ramifications. Some preliminary light may be shed on it, however, by examining the second major occurrence of physical yoga in the East— Hatha Yoga.

Because of widespread abuse in India, Hatha Yoga has there fallen into much disrepute, being considered a gross physical practice without spiritual value. Vivekananda, in comparing asana to hatha, summarily dismisses the latter as having no real worth at all: "This portion of yoga (*asana*) is a little similar to Hatha Yoga, which deals entirely with the physical body, its aim being to make the physical body very strong. We have nothing to do with it here, because its practices are very difficult... and, after all, do not lead to much spiritual growth."

It is this reputation, as well as the ready availability of certain teachers of hatha who would perpetuate it, which makes it easy for a Westerner to presume to use the techniques of yoga as but another form of physical self-culture. But, in reality, neither Vivekananda's partisan snobbery nor a lotus-cart full of Hatha gymnasts can mask the fact that Hatha is classically understood in much the same way as Raja Yoga.

In fact, the classic esoteric handbook of Hatha, the *Hatha Yoga Pradipika* by Swami Svatmarama states emphatically in the second and third slokas: "Having thus solemnly saluted his master, Yogi Svatmarama now presents Hatha Vidya (vidya = wisdom) solely and exclusively for the attainment of Raja Yoga. For those who wander in the darkness of conflicting creeds, unable to reach to the heights of Raja Yoga, the merciful Yogi Svatmarama has lit the torch of Hatha wisdom."

The meaning here could not be more plain. The techniques of Hatha are given so as to prepare a person's consciousness for the subtler metaphysics of Raja Yoga. Irrespective of belief, Hatha is regarded as a torch to experientially guide one out from that belief into the "wisdom" of Raja Yoga.

Alain Danielou, a recognized French scholar on the subject of yoga, states that "the sole purpose of the physical practices of Hatha Yoga is to suppress physical obstacles on the Spiritual or Royal path of Raja Yoga and Hatha yoga is therefore called 'the ladder to Raja Yoga.'" However for those who practice Hatha for purely physical ends, outside of a total context of spiritual discipline, most of the classic commentaries issue dire warnings. The Ananda Marga Yoga Society's manual for teachers sums them up well: "Indeed from the practice of Hatha Yoga, without a proper effort to the mind, mental and spiritual degeneration may ultimately occur."

The typical middle-class Westerner, taking yoga classes at the YMCA, has little or no idea of the how's and why's of yoga's seeming efficacy. In the traditional understanding, physical yoga has a great deal more to do with the practitioner's invisible, "subtle" body, than it does with the flesh and bones and muscles which encase it. While yoga does purport to first of all work on the muscular, glandular, and physical nervous systems, its real import, as Danielou says, is as "a process of control of the gross body which aims at freeing the subtle body." This subtle body is extremely complex, but can be superficially described as consisting of 72,000 invisible psychic channels called *nadis*, which constitute an other dimensional body which directly corresponds to the physical, or gross, body. The subtle body is connected to the gross body at several points, with the seven predominant ones located at distinct points ranging from the base of the spine to the top of the head. These are called *chakras*, and they are believed to control the various aspects of the consciousness of the individual. Physical yoga finds its most refined expression when it teaches postures which bring various channels within the subtle body into a specific alignment with one another and thus alter the consciousness of the practitioner in a specified way.

Whether or not this sort of thing is actually going on . . . it is important to understand that physical yoga, according to its classical definitions, is inherently and functionally incapable of being separated from Eastern religious metaphysics. The Western practitioner who attempts to do so is operating in ignorance and danger, from the yogi's viewpoint, as well as from the Christian's (725:2-6).

## THE OCCULT

The previous statement reveals that the physical practice of yoga is designed to alter one's consciousness and bring occult transformation. Thus, authoritative texts on both yoga and the occult reveal that yoga is a potentially profound occult practice (596:132-37,295-399/597:112-13/598:2-3,chs.17-19,26-27/386:29,98/435:50-51).Yoga is designed to awaken occult energies in the body, to lead to occult transformation, and to secure specific occult goals. Certain experiences under yoga (especially kundalini yoga) are similar to those found in shaman initiation and ritualistic magic, including experiences of spirit possession and insanity. Virtually all standard yoga texts acknowledge that yoga practice develops psychic powers and other occult abilities.

All this is why the yoga scholar and Sanskrit authority Rammurti Mishra can interpret yoga theory as laying the foundation for occultism. "In conclusion, it may be said that behind every psychic investigation, behind mysticism, occultism, etc., knowingly or unknowingly, the Yoga system is present" (596:138).

In his article "Kundalini and the Occult," occult authority John White observes that the essence of occultism is the attempt to gain "higher" knowledge and power or control of the forces of nature, especially the "life energy" (*prana*) which underlies the basis of true magic and psychic phenomena. "In its highest form, occult science merges indistinguishably with true mysticism.... [M]ysticism and genuine occultism are closely allied.... [T]he heart of genuine occult practices appear to be synonymous with aspects of the [yogic] kundalini concept..." (607:363-64). Yoga authority Sir John Woodroffe (Arthur Avalon), author of a standard text on kundalini yoga, *The Serpent Power*, agrees, and he supplies many additional reasons why yoga and occult magic go hand in hand (see 599:186-204).

Until his death, perhaps the leading authority on shamanism and comparative religion was Mircea Eliade. Note his observations of the similarities between yoga and witchcraft: "All features associated with European witches are ... claimed also by Indo-Tibetan yogis and magicians." Along with a range of occult powers common to both, some yogis:

> ... boast that they break all the religious taboos and social rules: that they practice human sacrifice, cannibalism, and all manner of orgies, including incestuous intercourse, and that they eat excrement, nauseating animals, and devour human corpses. In other words, they proudly claim all the crimes and horrible ceremonies cited *ad nauseam* in the Western European witch trials (564:71).

Because yoga is an occult system, the physical, mental, and spiritual dangers that accompany occult practices are also found in yoga (see 278). Thus, even standard yoga books warn of the serious dangers arising from supposedly "wrong" yoga practice. But we think such hazards are conceded because yoga is an *occult* practice, *not* because its techniques are allegedly done incorrectly.

## RISKS AND HAZARDS

The following citations taken from authoritative texts show many risk and hazards of yoga practice (including death).

Shree Purohit Swami's commentary on Patanjali's *Yoga Sutras* warns, "People forget that *Yama* and *Niyama* [limbs one and two] form the foundation [of yoga practice], and unless it is firmly laid, they should not practice postures and breathing exercises. In India and Europe, I came across some three hundred people who suffered permanently from wrong practices, the doctors on examination found there was nothing organically wrong and consequently could not prescribe" (600:56-57).

Because most people (including most medical doctors) wrongly assume that yoga is harmless, they rarely consider its possible relevance to any illnesses of their patients who practice yoga. But we are convinced that many perplexing diseases, including some deaths, are related to yoga. Richard Kieninger, a New Age educator, recalls, "A woman of my acquaintance upset her hormonal balance doing this yoga exercise, and it produced a malfunction in her adrenal glands. Doctors didn't know how to reverse the effects ... and she soon died.... Swami Rama warns that advanced forms of patterned breathing, which is a common yoga exercise, can cause a person to harm himself irreparably" (588:71).

United Nations spiritual adviser and spiritist Sri Chinmoy (810:53-68,87-89/811:9-20,26-33), author of *Yoga and the Spiritual Life* (617), admits, "To practice pranayama [breath control] without real guidance is very dangerous. I know of three persons who have died from it..." (618:8).

In *Yoga and Mysticism*, Swami Prabhavananda warns about the dangers of the yoga breathing exercises, which so many today think are harmless, when he writes:

> Now we come to breathing exercises. Let me caution you: they can be very dangerous. Unless properly done, there is a good chance of injuring the brain. And those who practice such breathing without proper supervision can suffer a disease which no known science or doctor can cure. It is impossible, even for a medical person, to diagnose such an illness.... [For example,] I had known a young boy of perhaps 16 or 17 years of age who had begun to practice hatha yoga. ... He was acting very strangely. He would prostrate fully on the ground, rise to full height, then

repeat the performance—over and over again. The Swami said that he had lost his mind. . . . Finally, however he became so unmanageable that he had to be confined. . . . As regards breathing exercises, I know that Sri Ramakrishna, Holy Mother, and all the disciples of Ramakrishna have warned us again not to practice them (604:18-19; yet Vivekenanda, Ramakrishna's disciple, encouraged them! 979:592-99).

Yoga authority Hans Ulrich Rieker admonishes in *The Yoga of Light*, "Yoga is not a trifling jest if we consider that any misunderstanding in the practice of yoga can mean death and insanity," and of *kundalini* yoga, he says that if the breath is "prematurely exhausted [withdrawn] there is immediate danger of death for the yogi" (603:9,134).

The practice of hatha yoga is often conceded to be dangerous. Gopi Krishna warns of the possible dangers of such practice, including "drastic effects" on the central nervous system and the possibility of death:

In Hatha yoga the breathing exercises are more strenuous, attended by some abnormal positions of the chin, the diaphragm, the tongue, and other parts of the body to prevent expulsion or inhalation of air into the lungs in order to induce a state of suspended breathing. This can have drastic effects on the nervous system and the brain, and it is obvious that such a discipline can be very dangerous. Even in India, only those prepared to face death dare to undergo the extreme discipline of Hatha yoga (592:13).

A standard authority on hatha yoga, *The Hatha Yoga Pradipika* (chapter 2, verse 15), warns, "Just as lions, elephants, and tigers are tamed, so the prana, should be kept under control. Otherwise it can kill the practitioner" (603:79).

As was mentioned earlier, so-called hatha yoga is not easily distinguished from other forms of yoga. And the same problems encountered in hatha yoga are encountered in almost all forms of yoga. Yoga authority Ernest Wood emphasizes, "I hold that all *Hatha* Yogas are extremely dangerous," and he therefore urges use of a "different" form of yoga, *Raja* Yoga (597:79). But another

authority on yoga, Hans Ulrich Rieker, claims, "Mastery of hatha yoga is *only a preliminary* to the mastery of raja yoga" (603:128, emphasis added). Furthermore, a standard work, the *Shiva Samhita*, argues, "There is no Hatha Yoga without Raja Yoga and no Raja Yoga without Hatha; therefore, the Yogi should start with Hatha Yoga, guided by a competent teacher" (597:77).

What this implies is that yoga is yoga; its various forms do not fundamentally alter its basic nature. For example, the Hindu holy book, the *Bhagavad Gita*, promotes at least five different systems of yoga, and yet all are acknowledged as potentially dangerous. Thus, Hindu master Sri Krishna Prem cautions in *The Yoga of the Bhagavat Gita*, "As stated before nothing but dangerous, mediumistic psychisms or neurotic dissociations of personality can result from the practice of [yoga] meditation without the qualifications mentioned at the end of the last chapter" (612:47). He warns, "To practice it, as many do, out of curiosity . . . is a mistake which is punished with futility, neurosis, or worse ['even insanity itself']" (602:XV,46).

The specific physical and mental consequences arising from yoga practice are also listed in other authoritative yoga texts. Sir John Woodroffe (Arthur Avalon) refers to "considerable pain, physical disorder, and even disease . . ." (599:12). Rieker lists cancer of the throat, all sorts of ailments, blackouts, strange trance states, or insanity from even "the slightest mistake . . ." (603:30,79,96,111-12).

In *The Seven Schools of Yoga*, Ernest Wood warns of "the imminent risk of most serious bodily disorder, disease, and even madness" (597:14). He observes that many people have brought upon themselves incurable illnesses or insanity by neglecting Hatha Yoga prerequisites, and "by any mistake there arises cough, asthma, head, eye, and ear pains, and many other diseases" (597:78).

From the above, we conclude that innumerable yoga teachers in the West are being irresponsible in promoting yoga as a safe physical regimen.

However, no discussion of yoga is complete without an evaluation of "kundalini yoga." By name, this is now practiced by tens of thousands of Americans, including many professing Christians in mainline churches.

## KUNDALINI YOGA

As mentioned earlier, *Spiritual Emergency* is one book that seeks to help people integrate pathological occult experience as a positive form of spiritual "emergence." It was edited by Stan and Christina Grof, who say "Kundalini awakening is becoming one of their most frequently encountered forms of spiritual emergency" (759:101). They noted that an analysis of the last 501 calls and 117 letters to their Menlo Park, California, office of SEN "revealed that a 'typical caller' was a forty-year-old female (69 percent) experiencing some form of kundalini awakening (24 percent)" (759:227).

In Hindu mythology and occult anatomy, the goddess Kundalini is thought of as a female serpent lying dormant at the base of the spine. Arthur Avalon comments that "kundalini is the Divine Cosmic Energy in bodies" (599:1). She represents the female half of the divine polarity in man. While lying at the base of the spine, she is separated from Shiva, her divine "lover" and masculine counterpart, who resides in the brain. When aroused by yoga practices, she uncoils, travels up the spine toward her lover, opening the alleged psychic centers called *chakras* in the process. When the crown or top *chakra* is reached, the union of Shiva/Shakti occurs, supposedly leading the practitioner to divine enlightenment* and union with Brahman. "Traditionally she is known as Durga the creatrix, Chandi the fierce and bloodthirsty, and Kali the destroyer. She is also Bhajangi the serpent. As Chandi or Kali she has a garland of skulls around her neck and drinks human blood" (491:13).

Kundalini arousal is not, as commonly thought, restricted to *hatha* yoga practice. Even yoga authorities have said that all yoga is ultimately kundalini yoga and that yoga is meaningless without it. This is why no less an authority than Hans Rieker concludes, "Kundalini [is] the mainstay of *all* yoga practices" (603:101, emphasis added).

Kundalini arousal or its equivalent is found not only in yoga; it is also encountered in scores of the new religions, many occult practices, and in some practices of New Age medicine.* Indeed, we have found no less than 15 different New Age health techniques in which proponents claim

that their methods may arouse kundalini. For example, certain body work programs such as the Alexander method may arouse kundalini (cf. Martial Arts).

In our study of 70 new religions, we found kundalini arousal, or something similar, in roughly 50 percent of them, particularly the mystical, New Age, occult religions (716). For example, Hindu and Buddhist gurus,* who account for scores of the new religions, are typically possessed by spirits. They often describe themselves in that manner, although they refer to it as a "divinizing"—not a demonizing—process (see below). But when describing their spirit, or "energy," possession, it is often directly linked to kundalini activity. This includes the experiences of Muktananda, Rajneesh, Rudrananda, Gopi Krishna, Ramakrishna, Sri Aurobindo, Vivekananda, Da Free John, and many others (610:1-2500); see Meditation). Whether it is called "supramental consciousness," "god-possession," "divine companionship," or some other euphemism, the reality is the same. Consciousness researcher John White concludes:

> Although the word kundalini comes from the yogic tradition, nearly all the world's major religions, spiritual paths, and genuine occult traditions see something akin to the kundalini experience as having significance in "divinizing" a person. The word itself may not appear in the traditions, but the concept is there nevertheless, wearing a different name yet recognizable as a key to attaining godlike stature (608:17).

For example, note the following account as cited by Richard Katz. Dr. Katz was personally involved with the Kalahari !Kung tribe and is the author of *Boiling Energy*, a book-length treatment on the tribe. He received his Ph.D. in clinical psychology from Harvard, where he currently teaches and is active in the field of Community Mental Health. In "Education for Transcendence: Lessons from the !Kung Zhin/Twasi" he writes of the occult energy that the !Kung tribe calls "n/um" (the exclamation and slash represent a "click" sound) which is activated by a trance state called "!Kia." And he describes how the tribe is socialized to accept the experience of it. We have here, as in the Bubba (Da) Free John spiritual community described elsewhere (see Meditation), socially legitimized mass demonization. Note the clearly shamanistic* and kundalini motifs:

The Zhu/twasi say that !kia is due to the activation of an energy, which they call n/um, or medicine. Those who have learned to !kia are said to possess n/um and are called "masters of n/um" or "n/um masters." N/um resides in the pit of the stomach. As the n/um master continues his energetic dance becoming warm and sweating profusely, the *n/um* heats up and becomes a vapor. It then rises up the spine, to a point approximately at the base of the skull, at which time !kia results.... The action and ascent of n/um is described by Tsau: "in your backbone you feel a pointed something, and it works its way up. Then the base of your spine is tingling ... and then it makes your thoughts nothing in your head."

This n/um is an energy which is held in awe and considered to be very powerful and mysterious. It is this same n/um that the n/um master "puts into" somebody in attempting to cure him. ... Through !kia, the Zhu/twasi participates in the religious dimension. Transcending himself, he is able to contact the supernatural, a realm where the ghosts of dead ancestors live.... Masters of n/um may struggle with the ghosts and may often win.... Socialization for !kia and seeking !kia are preparatory phases in education for !kia itself. There is consensual agreement and clarity about the concept of !kia and the action of n/um.... At its core, the education is a process of *accepting !kia experience for oneself.*

This is especially difficult because !kia is painful as well as unknown; it is a greatly feared experience.... In describing the onset of !kia, medicine men refer again and again to pain and fear. They describe searing pain in the area of the diaphragm and spleen, and at the pit of the stomach. A master of n/um recalling his first experience with n/um says: 'N/um got into my stomach. It was hot and painful, like fire, I was surprised and I cried." ... [A]s a person enters !kia the fear is that not only will he lose himself, but he may never come back.... One of the older n/um masters describes this death and rebirth: "(In !kia) your heart stops, you're dead, your thoughts are nothing, you breathe with difficulty. You see things, n/um things; you see ghosts killing people, you smell burning, rotten flesh; then you cure, you pull sickness out. You cure,

cure, cure, cure ... then you live. Then your eyeballs clear and then you see people clearly." ...

Though originally from the gods, n/um now passes regularly from man to man. Teaching is primarily by example. The teacher has been there before. He may !kia at that particular time; certainly he has had !kia many times before. He recognizes the student's progress, interprets his condition, and confirms that the student is in !kia.... The teacher is a spiritual guide in that he initiates the student into the cultural mysteries, probing the nature of his existence. He is like a priest in that he has had contact with the ghosts and can guide the student to that realm. He's very much a therapist in that he tries to help the student accept his fear rather than be overcome by it. And, he has been an academic teacher because he has taught the student the conceptual framework of !kia (899:140-44,148).

Thus, whether in the Eastern guru's* transmission of occult power termed *shaktipat* (see Meditation), the !Kung's !kia/n/um, classical shamanism,* kundalini, or similar phenomena in other traditions, one is dealing with basic occult energy. In the case of the !Kung tribe, it is attributed directly to the spirits, in the case of Muktananda, Bubba (Da) Free John, and other gurus, it may or may not be directly attributed to the spirits, but the spiritistic associations and manifestations are so pervasive one would be hard-pressed to deny them.

Kundalini arousal typically results in temporary states of insanity, radical changes in the physical body, and possession by a spirit (491:14,33,37; cf. 236). In *The Primal Power in Man or the Kundalini Shakti* (894), Swami Narayanananda describes some of the "exciting" possibilities:

These hot currents that reach the brain center heat the brain, make the mind fickle, bring insomnia, brain disorder, insanity and incurable diseases. For the hot currents keep the mind wide awake and if a person does not know how to check the currents and to bring down the partly risen kundalini shakti to safer centers, one suffers terribly and it may ruin the whole life of a person or lead one to insanity. This is why we see many become insane, many get brain defects, and many others get some incurable diseases after deep sorrow (895:356).

Gopi Krishna, founder of one of the many kundalini research centers throughout the world, records his own experience:

It was variable for many years, painful, obsessive, even fantasmic. I have passed through almost all the stages of different mediumistic, psychotic, and other types of mind; for some time I was hovering between sanity and insanity.

I was writing in many languages, some of which I never knew [the occult ability of automatic writing] (491:124; cf. pp. 14,33,37).

Krishna believes that most schizophrenics and manic depressives represent "malfunctioning" kundalini energy, thus noting the ease with which it produces mental derangement. When referring to his encounters with individuals who went mad, he says that it is widely known in India that hatha yoga practices can lead to insanity (491:14,33,37):

The power, when aroused in a body not attuned to it with the help of various [yoga] disciplines or not genetically mature for it, can lead to awful mental states, to almost every form of mental disorder, from hardly noticeable aberrations to the most horrible forms of insanity, to neurotic and paranoid states, to megalomania ... (491:14).

In spite of the admitted hazards of kundalini practice, many churchgoers in mainline liberal denominations are seemingly willing to experiment with it. Having received little or no discernment on occult issues from their liberal churches, they may find themselves open to experimentation in practices or traditions that claim to offer spiritual power, enlightenment,* and union with "God." Professing Christian Mineda J. McCleave is familiar with this. She became interested in the occult and, despite God's warnings against all such involvement (Deuteronomy 18:9-12), she naively trusted that God would protect her from anything evil (890:401). After immersing herself in occult literature, she began meditation.* The result was kundalini arousal, ten years of serious mental problems, and a thorough conversion to Christian mysticism. In the end, McCleave interpreted

her occult kundalini experience as the baptism of the Holy Spirit. Her story provides a powerful look at the consequences of occult practice in contemporary American spiritual life:

I plunged into meditative prayer. ... I began to have problems relating to the world around me. I had shifts in consciousness during my nonmeditative hours. ... I was again bothered by alternating periods of euphoria, anxiety, depression, and, sometimes, despair. I was surprised to find that my peaceful prayer life was often counterbalanced with thoughts of suicide. I could not understand these strange moods. ... This activity, added to long periods of prayer, was causing *changes*, painful ones, in my mind and body. The physical, mental, and emotional problems that surfaced were so dramatic that I had to quit working.

I withdrew from society and had to rely upon my family to care for and support me. ... I had begun a long "dark night of the soul," and it lasted for ten years. My peaceful prayers changed to frantic spiritual cries for help. ... Finally, in 1975, when I was thirty-seven years old, I was hospitalized three times in the psychiatric ward of the local hospital. ... I could no longer cope with my agitated mind. I was besieged with migraine headaches and no longer had any control over my life.

Reluctantly, I endured eight months of therapy. ... On April 6, 1976 ... I was jarred out of my prayer by what felt like a current of energy that seemed to enter my body through my left foot. ... This current was constant for four days and nights. With it there was an increased feeling of great body heat. I felt as though I were burning up from the inside out. Relatives could feel heat emanating from the front and back of my head while their hands were an inch away from me. It was a frightening experience. I knew, intuitively, that I had somehow triggered this current through intense prayer, but I had no knowledge of how to stop it.

My mind was *hyper*hyperactive. ... Physically, I went through a variety of symptoms. ... Emotionally, I went up and down the keyboard of euphoria, joy, bewilderment, anxiety, depression, and the familiar despair. I was, at times, deluded and often disoriented. On one occasion, I actually believed I had died. Such peace! I was almost disappointed to realize I hadn't. I was afraid to leave my apartment for fear someone would notice my schizophrenic-like behavior. I gazed into a mirror and observed a "wild" look—the same strange look I had noticed in 1973 after I took a week of biofeedback training.... Despite my discomfort, I believed that what was happening to me was *good*, regardless of contrary appearances. I believed, "All things work together for good to them that love God." Yet, while trying to adjust to this marvelous energy that was coursing through my mind and body, now intermittently, I exhibited so many psychiatric symptoms that the psychologist could no longer work with me....

Finally, in December 1976, by the grace of God, I was led to an open-minded, tolerant, compassionate, caring Christian psychiatrist, Bill Grimmer—an extraordinary man. He was not *afraid* of the occult. He was not *afraid* of kundalini.... My psychiatrist helped me to remember that I am still a Christian, not a yogi. He encouraged me to continue in my search—to reread the Scriptures and the writing of the mystics—to find the common denominator....

As I reread the Scriptures and the writings of the mystics, I was amazed at the new insights I gained.... The accomplished yogis explained their attainments in terms of kundalini. The Christian mystics, unaware of the Hindu term, described the same phenomenon, but named the animating, motivating spiritual force at work within them as the Holy Spirit.... The Christian experience [of kundalini] is described as the "baptism of the Holy Spirit" (890:403-07).

According to the Bible, however, receiving the Holy Spirit is not about having occult experiences. Unfortunately, as we saw earlier and also in the chapters on enlightenment, meditation, and shamanism, many people today not only discount the dangers, they also redefine yoga-induced psychopathology as genuine experience with Jesus Christ and God. Mediumistic healer and chakra/kundalini "energizer" Rosalyn Bruyere comments:

All the myths about the rising of the kundalini and the accompanying loss of sanity are associated with the inability of an individual to hold awareness on several levels of reality simultaneously. Many of the states which we consider psychotic may in fact be "ecstatic" ... (497:163).

## ENERGY PHENOMENA AND SPIRIT POSSESSION

Perhaps the dominant characteristic in kundalini arousal and other yoga practice is an experience of energy infusion, or possession (249:610). Gopi Krishna describes the following experiences of most yogic, meditative, and mystical practices. "During the ecstasy or trance, consciousness is transformed and the yogi, sufi, or mystic finds himself in direct rapport with an overwhelming Presence. This warm, living, conscious Presence spreads everywhere and occupies the whole mind and thought of the devotee ... " (592:14). Furthermore, this energy "is *invariably* experienced by all mediators and yogis as some kind of *supernatural* or divine energy" (2450:62, emphasis added).

Not surprisingly, we have yet to read a kundalini or yoga theorist who defines this energy infusion, or possession, as actual demon possession; however, there is often recognition of a possessing god or entity, and sometimes references to the demonic. The Taoist Master Chao Pi Ch'en observed that "as time passes, demonic states will occur to the practiser [sic] ..." (592:18). Significantly, yogic energy manifestations and possession are sometimes initially sensed by the experiencer as the work of an evil spirit. But this primary impression is "corrected" in accordance with Hindu theory, classifying the phenomena as a "divine process" (416 cf. 249).

But when we examine specific characteristics of kundalini arousal and its energy manifestations, we discover it is far more easily interpreted as a result of demonism than of anything divine. A perusal of the standard literature reveals the following characteristics: Kundalini energy is admittedly an occult energy; it is personal and supernatural; it can function independently of the person; it permeates and infuses the individual; it can *force* spontaneous yogic and other actions, including worship; it produces a form of consciousness and personality alteration hostile to Christian faith; it is related to evil pagan gods and deities; it is described as "being possessed" by those who experience it; it is dangerous and destructive not only to human life but to conventional societal values and morality.

In sum, kundalini arousal displays 1) an independent supernatural nature, 2) personal volition, 3) destructive potential, 4) an amoral or evil nature, and 5) a desire for "lordship," that is, the exerting of personal control over the practitioner, forcing compliance (889).

These facts do not suggest that we are dealing with an *impersonal* energy. The facts suggest that we are dealing with personal demonic spirit entities whose goal is spiritual deception and personal ownership. Sooner or later, the person who experiences kundalini arousal, experiences spirit possession. A leading guru, Swami Muktananda, reveals that he was violently shaken by a spirit as part of the divine "work" of kundalini within him. "A great deity in the form of my guru has spread all through me as *chiti* [energy] and was shaking me," and "when I sat for meditation, my whole body shook violently, just as if I were possessed by a god or a bad spirit" (415:84,122).

Yogi Amrit Desai warns that unless the experience is interpreted "properly" for the student, "he will become frightened, thinking it to be mental illness"—or "evil spirits" (611:70-71). But it gets worse. There is also the phenomenon of mass possession which can occur among disciples gathered to hear the guru.* This may end with the disciple finding himself in an involuntarily assumed position of worship of the guru, and, characteristically, worshiping the spirit entity possessing the guru:

> . . . As Amrit led us deeper into meditation, I began to realize that something unusual was happening to me. . . .
>
> Suddenly surges of energy-like electrical charges streaked up my spine. . . . Suddenly a scream from someone in the back of the room, then another. In a few moments the place was a mad house. People were crying hysterically, laughing uncontrollably, gasping for breath, even rolling on the floor. Apparently every one was experiencing some manifestation of the same energy I was feeling.
>
> Suddenly the whole thing stopped. . . . Amrit began to explain what had happened. We had just undergone what is called a *shaktipat* [power transfer] initiation. . . . [A]ll forms of yoga and consciousness development are aimed at even-

tually awakening the kundalini force. . . . [T]he psychic energy is transferred directly from guru to disciple.

> Simply by being in Yogi Desai's presence we had all experienced to some degree the awakening of the *Shakti* [power]. How this comes about is somewhat mysterious. Yogi Desai explains that the astral body of the guru merges with that of the disciple. . . . My body filled with a brilliant white light and I allowed myself to be absorbed in it. . . .
>
> When I opened my eyes again I noticed that my body had bent forward; my forehead was touching the floor. I do not remember assuming that position. I was actually bowing down to Yogi Desai! I had never bowed to anyone in my life but some inner unknown force had prompted me. . . . [H]e was surrounded by persons who only two hours before had never seen him but now sat on the floor around him, holding his feet, even kissing his feet . . . (612:185-87). (In our chapter on *meditation* we have quoted similar experiences by the followers of Da Free John).

Consider the following descriptions while under the influence of kundalini and other forms of yoga:

- I really felt frightened, as the Power seemed something which could consume me (599:21).
- Your mind gets influenced spiritually as if some spirit has taken possession of your body and under that influence different postures of yoga are involuntarily performed without the pain or fatigue (608:95).
- It seemed that I was being controlled by some power which made me do all these things. I no longer had a will of my own (467:76).

In conclusion, kundalini arousal, like shamanism,* typically involves some form of spirit possession or temporary or permanent insanity.

Because all yoga has the ability to arouse "kundalini," all yoga should be avoided. To offer it to the public as a form of *health* practice is highly irresponsible, if not perverse. To offer it to our children in our public schools is a betrayal of their trust.

# COMPREHENSIVE NEW AGE HEALTH LISTING

The following information should be considered as an illustrative analysis of alternative medicine based on the limited information available to the authors on many of these items and/or their lack of being subjected to scientific analysis or critique. Approximately 70 of the 170 topics in our original list were evaluated from earlier studies or brief material given in *Alternative Healing: The Complete A–Z Guide to Over 160 Different Alternative Therapies* (2752). In some cases, sufficient information about a therapy was not given to make probable category placement possible. Additional research could alter some of our conclusions. We are indebted to Jack Raso, M.S., R.D. for graciously allowing us to include his comprehensive listing of alternative therapies under "Occult, Mystical and/or Potentially Occult or Mystical Practices," which includes the topics in the author's original listing. Most New Age practices are given in this listing.

## OF SIGNIFICANT VALUE

1. Diet, exercise and sensible living
2. Judiciously applied consumer-informed use of contemporary scientific medicine, including consumer-informed use of prescription drugs and surgery where clearly medically justifiable. Diet, exercise, and lifestyle may reduce or alleviate the need for many prescription medicines and some surgeries.
3. Formal kinesiology, spinal manipulative therapy, osteopathy, physiatry and massage for certain injuries and/or musculoskeletal disorders.
14. A low-fat, high-complex carbohydrate diet and/or vegetarian diet (e.g., McDougal program

or modified vegetarian diet). (Note: Vegetarian diets are not necessarily healthy or low in fat.)

## OF LIMITED OR POSSIBLE VALUE

In a few (e.g., bodywork) of these practices, the practitioners and/or various forms of the practice may employ occult or dubious methods. (The term "limited value" does not imply some of these methods may not be of significant value for certain specific conditions.)

1. Nonvitalistic acupuncture and use of trigger or pressure points, although not necessarily acupressure, e.g., scientifically oriented trigger point work such as Bonnie Prudden Myotheraphy
2. Scientific biofeedback
3. Certain bodywork methods, for example, Rolfing, Alexander technique, Aston-patterning, Feldenkrais method, Benjamin System of Muscular Therapy, etc.
4. Scientific chiropractic
5. Rational nonvitalistic herbalism
6. Certain forms of light, magnetism and sound therapy
7. Massage (e.g., connective tissue massage, cross-fiber friction massage, deep compression massage, deep tissue massage, deep tissue sculpting)
8. Bee venom
9. Some forms of hydrotherapy
10. Hyperbaric oxygenation therapy
11. Aspects of visual imagery
12. Myofacial release therapy

13. Proprioceptive neuromuscular facilitation stretching
14. Nutritionally supervised vitamin therapy; however, megadoses of certain vitamins may be dangerous.

## SCIENTIFICALLY DISPROVEN METHODS

(Potentially dangerous for use in diagnosis and/or treatment)

1. Applied kinesiology (especially for diagnosis of certain conditions and evaluation of treatment or use of medicines)
2. Astrologic medicine
3. Ayurvedic (Hindu) and Tibetan (Buddhist) medicine
4. Behavioral kinesiology
5. Traditional chiropractic relying on manipulation of "innate" energy with the assumption that chiropractic manipulation can cure most or all disease; chiropractic that relies on additional New Age treatments for cure of disease.
6. Mystical, nonrational color therapy
7. Iridology
8. Reflexology
9. Subliminal therapy
10. Urine therapy (e.g., drinking urine)

## OCCULT, MYSTICAL PRACTICES

(Potential physical, psychological, and/or spiritual dangers whether or not they work or seem to work. In some cases, it is the context or worldview of the method rather than the method itself that is occult or occult-like.)

## MYSTICAL AND SUPERNATURALISTIC HEALTH-RELATED METHODS: A COMPREHENSIVE LIST

by Jack Raso, M.S., R.D.

The list below includes most of the mystical and/or supernaturalistic health-related meth-ods Jack Raso, M.S., R.D., described in *Alternative Healthcare: A Comprehensive Guide* (1994), *Mystical Diets: Paranormal, Spiritual, and Occult Nutrition Practices* (1993) and *Nutrition Forum* newsletter. We have added alternate names for the methods and put them in parentheses and constituent or related methods are indented. We have also made minor changes and added a few additional subjects. These are noted in brackets.

Absent healing (distant/distance healing, remote healing, absentee healing, teleotherapeutics)
Actualism (agni yoga, fire yoga, lightwork)
  Actualism bodywork
Acu-point therapy
Acupressure (*G-jo*)
  Acu-ball pressure self-treatment
  Do-in (*dao-in*, Taoist yoga)
  G-Jo acupressure
[Traditional] acupuncture (acupuncture therapy)
  Body acupuncture
  Electroacupuncture (electrical acupuncture)
Acupuncture anesthesia (acupuncture analgesia, anesthetic acupuncture)
Acupuncture energetics
  Acupuncture imaging
Acuscope therapy (electro-acuscope therapy)
Acu-yoga
Advanced energy healing
African holistic health
Agartha personal life-balancing program (Agartha program)
*Agni dhatu* (*agni dhatu* therapy, *samadhi* yoga)
Aikido
Alchemia
Alchemia breathwork
  Alchemia® heart breath
Alchemical hypnotherapy (alchemical work)
Alchemical synergy®
Alexander technique (Alexander method)
Alpha calm therapy
Alternative 12 steps
Amma therapy®
Amplified energy therapy
Amulet healing
Ancient Christian magic
Angelic healing
Annette Martin training

Anthroposophical medicine (anthroposophically-extended medicine)
  Therapeutic eurythmy (curative eurythmy; also spelled "eurhythmy")
Apitherapy (bee sting therapy)
Archetypal psychology
Arhatic yogasm
Aroma behavior conditioning (ABC)
Aromatherapy
  Subtle aromatherapy
Aromics™
*Astanga* yoga (*ashtanga* yoga, *raja* yoga)
Astara's healing science
Aston-patterning®
Astrological counseling
Astrologic medicine (astral healing, astrological healing, astromedicine, medical astrology)
Atlantean healing ray training
Attunement
Aura analysis (aura reading)
  Aura imaging photography (aura imaging)
  Kirlian diagnosis (Kirlian technique)
Aura balancing (auric healing, aura healing, aura cleansing, aura clearing)
  Auric massage technique
Aurasomatherapy
Auricular reflexology
[Autogenics
  Autogenic therapy
  Autogenic training]
Avatar®
"Awakened Life" program [from Dr. Wayne W. Dyer]
[Awareness Oriented Structure Therapy]
Awareness Release Technique®
Ayurveda (ayurvedic medicine, ayurvedic healing, Vedic medicine, ayurvedism)
  *Kalaripayat*
  Maharishi Ayur-Ved (formerly Maharishi Ayur-Veda)
  Marma therapy (ayurvedic massage, ayurvedic lymphatic massage)
  *Panchakarma*
  *Rakta moksha*
Ayurvedic acupuncture
Bach flower therapy (Bach flower essence method, Bach flower essence system)
*Baguazhang* (*pa kua chang*, circle walking)
Balance therapy

Barbara Brennan healing science
Barefoot shiatsu massage
Behavioral kinesiology (BK)
Bindegewebsmassage (bindegewebsmassage system)
Belly Bean diet
BEYOND MEDICINE
Beyond Therapysm
Bhramari
Bio-chromatic chakra alignment
Biodynamic massage
Bioenergetics
  Bioenergetic analysis
  Bioenergetic therapy
Bioenergy (bioenergy healing)
BioEssence therapy
  BioEssence bodywork
Biofeedback without machines
Biogram therapy
Biological Immunity Analysis™ (BIA, biological immunity system™)
Biomagnetics (biomagnetic medicine)
Biomagnetic therapy
Bioplasmic healing
Biorhythm(s)
BioSonic Repatterning™
Biosonics
Blood crystallization (diagnostic blood crystallization)
Blue water technique
Body harmony
Body integration
Bodymind centering
BodyMind therapy
  BodyMind breathwork
  BodyMind counseling hypnotherapy
  BodyMind shiatsu
Bodywork plus
BodyWisdom
Bodywork tantra
  Co-centering
  Tantsu
  Watsu
Breathwork
Breema
[Breath Awareness]
BRETH ("Breath Releasing Energy for Transformation and Healing" or "Breath Releasing Energy for Transformation and Happiness")

Bubble of light technique (bubble of light meditation)

C.A.R.E. (Chakra Armor Release of Emotions)

Cayce approach to health and healing

Apple diet (apple-cleansing regimen, apple-diet cleansing routine, apple-diet regimen, apple-diet therapy)

    Beyond Dieting

Cayce/Reilly massage (Cayce/Reilly approach to massage, Cayce/Reilly method, Cayce/Reilly technique)

    Weight No More

Cellular theta breath (cellular theta breath technique)

Chakra and cellular memory healing

Chakra energy massage

Chakra healing (chakra therapy, chakra balancing, chakra energy balancing, chakra work)

    Chakra breathing

    Chakra innertuning therapy

Chakra yoga

*Chan Mi gong*

Channeling (mediumship)

    Trance channeling

*Chi* (*ki*) energy flow

*Chi kung* meditation(s)

Chinese auricular therapy (Chinese auricular acupuncture, traditional Chinese auricular acupuncture, traditional Chinese auricular acu-points therapy, traditional Chinese auricular therapy)

    Auricular analgesia

    Auricular diagnosis

    Auricular magnetic therapy (magnetotherapy)

    Auricular massage

    Auricular moxibustion

    Auricular point injection

    Auricular point laser-stimulating method

    Bleeding manipulation (bloodletting therapy)

    Seed-pressure method

Chinese dietotherapy

Chinese hand analysis

Chinese Qigong massage

    *Amma* (*anma, pu tong an mo*)

    *Dian xue* (*dian xue an mo*)

    *Tui na* (*tui na an mo*)

Chinese system of food cures

Ching Lo

Chirognomy (cheirognomy)

Chi-Therapy™ (Gestalt energy work)

*Choi kwang do*

Christian positive thinking (CPT)

    Pealeism (Norman Vincent Pealeism)

    Possibility thinking

        Possibility thinking meditation (PTM)

    Positive confession (Word-Faith movement, faith movement)

[Christian yoga]

Clairvoyant diagnosis (psychic diagnosis)

Clean-Me-Out Program™

Color breathing

Color meditation (CM, color magick)

Colorology

Color psychology

Colorpuncture™ (colorpuncture system, Osho esogetic colorpuncture system)

Color synergy

Color therapy (chromotherapy, color healing, chromopathy)

    Color projection

Combine spirituality and psychotherapy

Concept-therapy® (concept-therapy technique)

    Suggestive therapy (suggestive therapy work, suggestive therapeutics)

    Suggestive therapy zone procedure (zone therapy diagnosis, health zone analysis, concept-therapy adjusting technique, zone testing)

Contact healing ([New Age] laying on of hands)

Connective tissue therapy (CTT)

Contact reflex analysissm (CRA)

Core energetics (core energetic therapy)

Core transformationsm

Core zero balancing

Cosmic energy chi kung (cosmic energy chi kung, cosmic healing chi kung)

Cosmic vibrational healing

*A Course in Miracles*

Cranial facial balancing

Craniosacral therapy (cranial technique, cranial osteopathy, craniopathy, craniosacral balancing, craniosacral work, cranial work)

Craniosacral-visceral balancing (craniosacral-visceral whole body balancing)

Creative concentration™

Creative Force Techniques (CFTs)

Creative meditation

Creative visualization (Terms for identical or

similar methods include: visualization, visualization therapy, guided visualization, imagery, guided imagery, guided fantasy, mental imagery, active imagination, imaging, creative imaging, dynamic imaging, positive imaging, positive thinking, positive visualization, directed day-dream, directed waking dream, waking dream therapy, led meditation, inner guide meditation, initiated symbol projection, imaginal medicine, and pathworking.)

Crystal therapeutics℠

Crystal therapy (crystal healing, crystal work, crystal therapeutics)

Cupping
  *Bu-hang*

Cymatics (cymatic medicine, cymatic therapy)

*Daoyin*

Dayan Qigong (wild goose breathing exercise)

Deep Emotional Release Bodywork System
  *Chi Kung* Empowerment
  Deep Emotional Breathwork
  Emotional Release

De la Warr system [radionics]

Diamond approach (Diamond approach to inner realization)

Diamond method

Dianetics

Dimensional clearing

Directed esoteric toning

Divine healing from Japan

Divine will healing

Dreamwork (dreamworking)

Dr. Lynch's holistic self-health program

EAV (electroacupuncture according to Voll)

Ecstasy breathing®

Ehretism
  Mucusless diet healing system
    Mucusless diet
  Rational fasting
    Superior fast (superior fasting)

Eighteen lohan tiger/dragon Qigong

Electrodiagnosis (electrodermal screening, bioelectric testing)

Electro-homeopathy

Electromagnetic healing

Electromedicine

EmBodyment

Emotional-kinesthetic psychotherapy (EKP)

Empyrean® rebirthing

Endo-nasal therapy

Energis™

Energy balancing

Enneagram system (enneagram)

Equestrian transformational expression

*Er Mei* Qigong (*Er Mei*)

Esalen massage

Esogetics

Esoteric Buddhism

Esoteric healing (seven ray techniques)

Etheric release

Etheric surgery

Etheric touch

Eutony (eutony therapy, Gerda Alexander method)

Exorcism
  Depossession (releasement)

Face modeling

Facial rejuvenation-Burnham system®

[Unbiblical] faith healing
  Christian Science
  [Word & faith healing]

*Feng shui*
  Black Hat tantric Buddhist *feng shui*

Ferreri technique

Firewalking

Five rites of rejuvenation

Flower essence therapy

Focusing (focusing-therapy)

Foot analysis (Grinberg method)

Future life progression

Gem therapy

Gerson therapy (Gerson treatment, the Gerson method, Gerson dietary regime [GDR])

Gestalt therapy

Going Home™

Grape cure (grape diet)

Graphochromopathy

Graphotherapy

Hakomi (hakomi method, hakomi therapy, hakomi body-centered psychotherapy)

Hakomi integrative somatics

Harmonics

Harner Method Shamanic Counseling (hmsc)

Hatha yoga

Healing tao (healing tao system, the international healing tao system, healing tao warm current meditation)

Bone marrow *nei kung* (iron shirt *chi kung* III)
*Chi nei tsang* (Taoist *chi nei tsang*, Taoist healing
   light technique, internal organ *chi* massage,
   organ *chi* transformation massage, organ *chi*
   transformation, healing light massage)
   *Chi* self-massage (tao rejuvenation-*chi* self-
   massage)
   Fusion meditations
   Healing light kung fu (healing hands kung fu)
   Healing love (healing love meditation, seminal
   and ovarian kung fu)
   Inner smile
   Iron shirt *chi kung*
   Microcosmic orbit meditation
   Six healing sounds
   Taoist five element nutrition (Taoist healing
   diet)
Healing touch
HealthWatchers Analysis™
HealthWatchers System™
Heartwood massage
Hellerwork
Hemi-sync™
Hippocrates health program
   Hippocrates diet (living foods lifestyle)
Herbal crystallization analysis (HCA, herbal identi-
   fication, herbal tracer test)
Holistic dentistry
Holistic gynecology
Holistic nursing
Holistic palpate energy therapy
Holistic reiki
Holoenergetic healing® (holoenergetics®)
Holotropic breathwork™ (holotropic therapy,
   holotropic breath therapy, holonomic breath-
   work, holonomic therapy, Grof breathwork)
Homeoacupuncture
Homeopathy (homeopathic medicine, homeother-
   apeutics)
   Classical homeopathy
   Contemporary homeopathy
Homeovitics
   Biogenic support (homeovitic support)
   Clearing
   Homeovitic detoxification
Homuncular acupuncture
   Auriculotherapy (auricular therapy, auricular
   acupuncture, ear acupuncture)
   Reflexotherapy

Ho'oponopono
Hug therapy (therapeutic hugging)
Human ecology balancing sciences
Human energetic assessment and restorative tech-
   nic (HEART)
Humanistic therapy
Human resources *chi gong*
Hydrochromopathy
Hydropathy (water cure)
Hypnoaesthetics™
[Hypnosis/"past-life" regression]
*I-Chuan*
Identity process
IIP Consciousness Development Program
Imagineering
Infantile *tuina* therapy (infantile *tuina*)
Inner bonding
Inner child cards
Inner child work (inner child therapy)
Inner guide work
Inner self-healing process
Integral counseling psychology
Integrated kinesiology
   Visceral meridian manipulation technique
   (VMM)
Integrative acupressure
Integrative therapy
Integrative yoga therapy
Interactive guided imagerysm
Inter-light kinesiology
Intuitive energy healing
Iridology (iridiagnosis, irido-diagnosis)
Iroquois medical botany
Iyengar yoga (Iyengar style yoga)
Jin shinn (jin shin)
   Jin shin do® (jin shin do® bodymind acupres-
   sure™)
   Jin shin jyutsu (also spelled "jitsu")
Johrei
Josephing
Jungian past-life therapy
Jungian psychology
Kelley/Radix® work
*Ki* breathing
Kinesiology (kinesiologies)
   Applied kinesiology (AK, kinesiology)
   Balanced Health
   BioKinesiology
   Clinical kinesiology

Creative kinesiology
Health kinesiology
Lepore technique (LePore technique)
Life care kinesiology (Life Care)
Optimum Health Balance
Professional Kinesiology Practice (PKP, PKP approach)
Psycho-kinetic health (PKH)
Self-help for stress and pain
Stress Release (Stress Release approach)
Touch for Health
Three in One (Three in One Concepts process, Three in One approach)
Ki-shiatsu®/oriental bodywork (ki-shiatsu/oriental bodywork therapy, shiatsu oriental bodywork)
Kneipping (Kneipp cure, Kneipp therapies, *Kneipptherapie*)
Kobayashi technique(s)
Kofutu system of spiritual healing and development
Kofutu absent healing
Kofutu touch healing
Kripalu bodywork
Kripalu yoga
Kriya massage
Kriyashaktism
Kriya yoga
Kulkarni naturopathy
*Kum nye* (*kum nye* relaxation)
[Kundalini yoga]
Lama yoga
Lane system of multilayer bioenergy analysis and nutrition (Lane system of 3-dimensional bioenergy analysis and nutritional healing)
Laserpuncture
Laura Norman method
Lemonade diet (lemon cleansing, master cleanser)
LeShan psychic training
L'Chaim yoga
Life energy analysis
Life force balancing
Life impressions bodywork
Life span nutrition (limbic eating)
Light energy implantations
Light ray rejuvenation system
Light work
Local healing
LooyenWork®

Love-powered diet
Macrobiotics
Magical aromatherapy
Magical diet(s)
Magical herbalism
Magnet therapy (magnetic therapy, magnetotherapy, magnetic energy therapy, magnetic healing, biomagnetics, biomagnetism, biomagnetic therapy, electro-biomagnetics therapy)
Magnetic healing
Magno-therapy
*Mahikari*
*Makko-ho*
Manifesting (manifestation, conscious manifestation)
Manual organ stimulation therapy (MOST)
MariEL
Marma healing (ayurveda marma healing)
Marma science (Dhanur Veda's science of marmas)
*Nadi Sutra Kriya*
Marrow cleansing *chi gong*
Medical graphology (grapho-diagnostics)
Medical palmistry
Chinese hand analysis
Medicine cards
MediPatch™ healthcare system (MediPatch™ system)
Mentalphysics
Pranic therapy
Mesmerism (magnetic healing)
Metal and gem therapy
Metamorphic technique (metamorphosis; originally called prenatal therapy)
Metaphysical hypnosis
Meta-Therapy™
Metta Touch™
Micromovement bodywork
Middle pillar meditation (middle pillar technique)
Morter HealthSystem
B.E.S.T. (bio energetic synchronization technique; originally called bio energetics)
Baby B.E.S.T.
Motherhand shiatsu
Moxibustion (moxibustion therapy)
Moxabustion
Nadi shodhanam (channel purification)
Natural Hygiene
Nature cure (nature care)

Naturology

Naturopathy (naturopathic medicine, naturology)

Neo-Reichian massage

NETWORK

Network spinal analysis (network chiropractic, network chiropractic spinal analysis, Network)

Neural therapy

Neural organization technique (NOT)

Neuro-bioenergetic treatment

New age shiatsu

Nichiren Buddhism (Nichiren Soshu [also spelled "Shoshu"] Nichirenism)

Numbers diet™ (Jean Simpson's numbers diet)

N.I.A. technique

Nichiren Buddhism

Nine Gates Training Program

Nsoromma body therapy

[Medical] Numerology

Nutripathy

Nutritional herbology

Nutrition kinesiology (NK)

Ohashiatsu®

Oki-do (okido, okido way of living)
    Chinese Chikwando

Okinawan karate (Shorin Ryu karate)

Omega

Omni-force

One Brain™

Open Mind™ programming (Open Mind advanced programming)

Original Ingham Method™ (Ingham method, Ingham method of foot reflexology, Ingham technique)

Organic process therapy (OPT)

Organismic psychotherapy

Orgone therapy (medical orgonomy, orgonomic medicine therapy)

Orionic healing system

Ortho-bionomy™

Osteokinetics®

Osteopuncture

Passion-for-life psychotherapy

Past-life therapy (past lives therapy, regression therapy, past-life regression therapy, transformational therapy)

Pathwork

P.E.E.R. (Primary Emotional Energy Recovery, P.E.E.R. counseling)

Pesso Boyden System/Psychomotor (psychomotor therapy, Pesso system)

Phoenix rising yoga therapy

Phrenology (head-reading)

Phreno-mesmerism (phreno-magnetism, phrenopathy)

Physiognomy

Pigeon remedy (pigeon therapy)

Planetary herbology (planetary herbalism)

Plant alchemy (spagyrics)

Polarity balancing (polarity therapy, polarity, polarity wellness®, polarity energy balancing, polarity energy balancing system, polarity system, polarity energy healing)

Plant alchemy

Pointing therapy

Polarity energy balancing massage

Polarity testing

Postural integration

Power yoga

*Prakrtika cikitsa* (naturopathy)

*Pranayama*

Pranic healing
    Advanced pranic healing
    Color pranic healing
    Distant pranic healing
    Invocative pranic healing
    Pranic psychotherapy

Prayer (metaphysical [e.g., New Age] healing)
    [New Age] Petitionary prayer
        intercessory
        personal

Pre-cognitive re-education

Primal therapy (primal scream therapy)

Process acupressure

Process psychology (process-oriented psychology)

Progression/regression therapy

Psionic medicine (psionics)

Psychic dentistry

Psychic healing (psi healing, psychic therapy)

Psychic self-defense

Psychic shield

Psychic surgery

Psychogenetics

Psychological astrology (astro-psychology)

"Psychology of evil" [M. Scott Peck, M.D.]

Psychometric analysis ("psychometric analysis of human character and mentality")

Psychometry (object reading)

Psycho-pictography

Psycho-regression

Psychospiritual holistic healing

Psychospiritual therapy

Psychosynthesis (and therapy)

Qigong (internal Qigong; also spelled "chi gong," "chi gung," and "chi kung")

    Taoist Qigong (Daoist *chi kung*)

Qigong meridian therapy (QGMT)

Qigong therapy (medical Qigong, *Qi* healing, external *Qi* healing, Qigong healing, external Qigong healing, *buqi*, *buqi* therapy, *Qi an mo*, *Qi* massage, *wai Qi liao fa*, *wai Qi zhi liao*)

Radiance breathwork

Radiance movement therapy

Radiance prenatal process

Radiesthesia (medical radiesthesia, medical dowsing)

    Pendular [pendulum] diagnosis (radiesthetic diagnosis)

    Telediagnosis (distant biological detection)

Radionics (psionics)

    Radionic diagnosis (radionic analysis)

    Radionic photography

    Radionic therapy (radionic healing, radionic treatment)

Radix™ (neo-Reichian therapy)

Rainbow diet

Raw juice therapy

Ray methods of healing

Rainbow diet

Rebirthing (conscious breathing, conscious connected breathing, circular breathing, free breathing, vivation)

Reflexology

    Body reflexology

    Ear reflexology

    Foot reflexology

    Hand reflexology

Reflexology workout

Reich blood test

Reichian therapy (Reichian massage, Reichian bodywork therapy, psychiatric orgone therapy; called vegetal therapy in Europe)

Reiki (Usui system of natural healing, Usui *shiko ryoho*, Usui *shiki ryoho*, reiki healing, reiki therapy; formerly called *leiki*)

Karuna reiki

Radiance technique® (TRT, real reiki®)

Reiki-alchemia®

Reiki plus® (reiki plus system of natural healing)

    Physio-Spiritual Etheric Body healing^sm (PSEB^sm)

    Psycho-therapeutic Reikism (Psycho-therapeutic Reikism healing)

Reimprinting with divine intervention

Rei-so (spiritual diagnosis)

Remote diagnosis

Resonant kinesiologysm

Rhythmajik

Rolfing® (structural integration, structural processing)

Rosen method

Rubenfeld synergy® method (Rubenfeld synergy)

Sacred psychology

*Seiki-jutsu*

Schuessler (also spelled "Schussler") biochemic system of medicine (biochemic system of medicine, biochemic medicine, tissue salts therapy)

Sclerology

Scrying (crystal gazing, crystal ball, crystalomancy)

Seichim

Seichim reiki

Seicho-No-Ie

Self-applied health enhancement methods (SAHEM)

Self-healing (direct healing)

Shiatsu (shiatzu, shiatsu therapy)

    Acupressure

    Shiatsu massage

    Zen shiatsu

Siddha (Siddha medicine)

Silva mind control (Silva method, Silva mind control method, Silva mind control system, Silva method of mind development, Silva mind control method of mental dynamics, Silva mental dynamics [Psychoorientology])

Simonton method

Self-expansion therapy

Seven keys meditation program

Shadow sound therapy©

Shamanic counseling

Shamanic extraction healing (extraction method of healing)

Shamanic psychotherapy

Shamanism (shamanic healing, shamanistic medicine)
   Huichol shamanism
   Kahuna healing
      Lomi-lomi
Shandra-chi
Shensm (Specific Human Energy Nexus Therapy, shen therapy)
Shinkiko
61-points relaxation exercise (61-points exercise, 61-points, *shavayatra*)
Soaring crane Qigong (crane style *chi gong*)
Somasynthesis
Somatic dialogue
SomatoEmotional Releasesm
Somatic emotional therapy
Song channeling
Sonopuncture
[Sophrology]
Sotai (sotai therapy, sotai treatment)
Soul amplification
Soul-centered psychology
Soul part integration
Soul retrieval
Sound energetics™
[Sound therapy, New Age]
Spinal balancing
Spirit healing (spiritual healing)
Spirit releasement therapy
Spirit surgery
Spiritual midwifery
Spiritual psychology
Stress pattern processingsm
Subatomic healing
Sufi healing
SuperShape psychological conditioning system
Swedish-Esalen
Synergy hypnosis
Syntonics
Systematic nutritional muscle testing (SNMT)
Tai chi (*tai ji*; tai chi chuan, *tai ji chuan, tai ji quan*)
   Chen style
Taido
Tanden breathing
Tantra [healing]
Taoist healing imagery
"Tap, Tap" system
Tatwa meditation
*Tenrikyo*

Tensegrity
Thai massage
Theotherapy
Therapeutic shiatsu
Therapeutic touch (TT)
   Non-contact therapeutic touch (NCTT)
Tibetan medicine (Emchi)
   Tibetan pulsing (Tibetan pulsing healing)
Tibetan reiki
Time Line Therapy™ (TLT)
TM-Sidhi (Transcendental Meditation Sidhi program, yogic flying)
Toning
Traditional Dhanur Veda diagnosis
Trager (Trager approach, Tragerwork, Tragering, Trager psychophysical integration®)
Trager mentastics (mentastics®)
Transcendental Meditation® (TM®)
Transformational counseling
   Psycho-neuro integration (PNI, psychic healing)
"Transformation" program [from Dr. Wayne W. Dyer]
Transformational bodywork
Transition method
Transpersonal hypnotherapy
Transpersonal psychology (transpersonal counseling psychology)
Triggers™ mind programming system (triggers)
Twelve stages of healing
Twelve steps
*Ujjayi* (*ujjayi* breathing)
UltraVit 7-day juice slimming program
Unani (Unani medicine, *Unani tibb*)
Unergi© method
UN systemsm
Urine therapy (uropathy, auto-urine-therapy, amaroli, shivambu kalpa)
Urine therapy
Vibrational medicine (vibrational healing, energy medicine, subtle-energy medicine)
Vita flex (reflex system)
Vitality fasting and rejuvenation
Viviano method
Vodou (vodoun, vodun, voudoun, voodoo, voodooism)
Warriorobics
White tantra
Whole health shiatsu
Whole person bodywork

Wise woman healing (wisewoman healing ways, wisewoman ways)

Witchcraft

Wu Ming Qigong

Yantra yoga (Tibetan yantra yoga)

Yoga of perfect sight

Yoga therapy

Zarlen therapy (Zarlen direct channelling)

Zen Alexander technique

Zen-touch™

*Zhan zhuang chi kung*

*Zhenjiu* (acu-moxibustion, acupuncture-moxibustion therapy, *chen-chiou* therapy, China zhenjiuology, zhenjiulogical therapy)

Zone therapy (reflex zone therapy, reflex zone massage)

Zulu Sangoma bones

19. Naturopathy–occult aspects
20. New Age nursing
21. New Age osteopathy
22. Polarity therapy
23. Postural integration
24. Psychic diagnosis healing & surgery
25. Psychometry, radionics, & radiaesthesia
26. Psychosynthesis
27. Quadrinity
28. Reflexology
29. Reiki
30. Shiatsu
31. Somatography
32. Sophrology
33. Sound therapy in some forms
34. Taoist self-massage
35. Therapeutic touch
36. Tibetan medicine
37. Touch for health

## UNSCIENTIFIC AND/OR ANTI-CHRISTIAN IN PHILOSOPHY OR PRACTICE

(The degree varies)

1. Traditional acupuncture and Acupressure
2. Aikido
3. Applied kinesiology
4. Arica
5. Astrologic medicine
6. Autogenic training
7. Ayurveda
8. Behavioral kinesiology
9. Bioenergetics
10. Body work in some forms
11. Breath work in some forms
12. Chiropractic, aspects of traditional and eclectic practice
13. Color therapy
14. Herbalism in some forms
15. Homeopathy–occult aspects
16. Iridology–occult aspects
17. Lomi work
18. Naprapathy

## GENERALLY DISPROVEN OR DOUBTFUL

(Some value may yet be found through future scientific research or heuristic effects)

1. Acupressure, certain nonvitalistic applications of
2. Applied kinesiology, (limited to legitimate interactions with formal kinesiology)
3. Body work (certain forms)
4. Chiropractic (visceral effects)
5. Color therapy
6. Nonvitalistic homeopathy, where low dilutions of homeopathic substances may exert a physical effect
7. Light, magnetism, and sound therapy, some forms
8. Bates method of vision training
9. Colon therapy
10. some applications of water therapy
11. Many aspects of dream therapy
12. Many aspects of naturopathy

# BIBLIOGRAPHY

References in the text are keyed to this select bibliography which is drawn from the authors' master bibliography. For example, 3:145 in the text would refer to reference 3 in the bibliography and page 145 in that specific work; 1215:18 would refer to reference 1215 in the bibliography and page 18 in that specific work. (The bibliographic references in this volume are *not* in sequential order because only those references actually cited in this volume were used in the production of this bibliography.)

Footnotes with slashes, for example, 35/18/93, refer to works as a whole, cited in general, with no required page numbers.

Footnotes with a limited number of references are separated by slashes and usually placed in the text (for example, 89:15/95:3). However, more extensive footnotes are given a single number with the full information at the bibliographic number given (e.g., see bibliographic numbers 536, 2763). Titles having more than one volume cite Roman numerals (I, II, III) after the text number to identify the volume number cited.

Because of the size and nature of this project in its original form (17,000 manuscript pages), there are occasional duplicate references in the bibliography. In rare cases, references having two numbers will refer to different editions of the same work; regardless, the bibliographic reference given should always refer to the proper source.

Sometimes secondary sources are used; therefore, the reader should not assume an error exists merely because an author cited in the text does not correspond to the stated author in the bibliography. One should assume the information cited can be found in the reference given. Also, where possible, primary source information is given in the text itself.

The following abbreviations are used: n.a. (no author given); n.p.p. (no place of publication cited); n.p. (no publisher cited); n.d. (no date cited).

The authors would appreciate any typographical or other (e.g. phonetic) errors being brought to their attention. (In a few cases, reference citations are inadequate due to lost, damaged, or stolen materials, or from circumstances beyond the authors' control.)

1. Paul C. Reisser, Teri K. Reisser, John Weldon, *New Age Medicine: A Christian Perspective on Holistic Health*, Downers Grove, IL: InterVarsity Press, 1988.
2. Samuel Pfeifer, M.D., *Healing at Any Price?* Milton Keynes, England: Word Limited, 1988.
3. Douglas Stalker, Clark Glymour, eds., *Examining Holistic Medicine*, Buffalo, NY: Prometheus Books, 1985.
4. Jane D. Gumprecht, *Holistic Health: A Medical and Biblical Critique of New Age Deception*, Moscow, ID: Ransom Press, 1986.
5. Clifford Wilson, John Weldon, *Psychic Forces and Occult Shock*, Chattanooga, TN: Global Publishers, 1987.
6. John Weldon, Zola Levitt, *Psychic Healing: An Exposé of an Occult Phenomenon*, Chicago, IL: Moody Press, 1982.
11. Iona Teeguarden, *Acupressure Way of Health: Jin Shin Do*, Tokyo, Japan: Japan Publications, 1978.
25. Andrew Weil, *Health and Healing: Understanding Conventional and Alternative Medicine*, Boston, MA: Houghton Mifflin, 1983.
31. Terence Hines, "High-Flying Health Quackery," *The Skeptical Inquirer*, Summer 1988.
34. John Thie, "Touch for Health: An Interview with John Thie," *Science of Mind*, September 1977.
35. William T. Jarvis, Edward Kravitz, in "Food, Fads and Fallacies," Robert L. Pollack, Edward Kravitz, eds., *Nutrition in Oral Health and Disease*, Philadelphia, PA: Lea & Febiger, 1985.
36. John F. Thie, *Touch for Health: A Practical Guide to Natural Health Using Acupuncture, Touch and*

*Massage...*, Marina del Rey, CA: DeVorss and Company, 1973.

37. John Diamond, *BK—Behavioral Kinesiology: The New Science for Positive Health Through Muscle Testing— How to Activate Your Thymus and Increase Your Life Energy*, San Francisco, CA: Harper & Row, 1979.

46. Elmer and Alyce Green, *Beyond Biofeedback*, San Francisco, CA: Delacorte Press, 1977.

48. Corinne Heline, *Healing and Regeneration Through Color*, La Cañada, CA: New Age Press Inc., 1976.

54. D.D. Palmer, *Textbook of the Science, Art and Philosophy of Chiropractic for Students and Practitioners*, Portland, OR: Portland Printing House, 1910.

58. Chittenden Turner, *The Rise of Chiropractic*, Los Angeles, CA: Powell Publishing, 1931.

59. B.J. Palmer, *The Philosophy of Chiropractic*, Davenport, IA: The Palmer School of Chiropractic Publishers, 5th ed., 1920.

60. James J. Donahue, *Enigma: Psychology, the Paranormal and Self-Transformation*, Oakland, CA: Bench Press, 1979.

61. Clyde H. Reid, *Dreams: Discovering Your Inner Teacher*, Minneapolis, MN: Winston Press, 1983.

62. Jeremy Taylor, *Dream Work: Techniques for Discovering the Creative Power in Dreams*, New York: Paulist Press, 1983.

63. Jane Roberts, *Seth: Dreams and Projection of Consciousness*, Walpole, NH: Stillpoint, 1986.

64. Harmon H. Bro., *Edgar Cayce on Dreams*, New York: Warner, 1968.

65. Louis M. Savary, Patricia H. Berne, Strephon Kaplan Williams, *Dreams and Spiritual Growth: A Christian Approach to Dreamwork*, New York: Paulist Press, 1984.

71. Samuel Hahnemann, *The Chronic Diseases, Their Peculiar Nature and Their Homeopathic Cure–Theoretical Part*, Louis H. Tafel, trans., New Delhi, India: Jain Publishing Company, 1976.

75. Robert Carl Jansky, *Astrology, Nutrition and Health*, Rockport, MA: Para Research, 1978.

76. Omar V. Garrison, *Medical Astrology: How the Stars Influence Your Health*, New York: Warner Paperback Library, 1973.

77. C. Norman Shealy, *Occult Medicine Can Save Your Life*, New York: Bantam, 1977.

78. Peter Damian, *The Twelve Healers of the Zodiac: The Astrology Handbook of the Bach Flower Remedies*, York Beach, ME: Samuel Weiser, 1986.

79. Marcia Stark, *Astrology: Key to Holistic Health*, Birmingham, MI: Seek It Publications, 1987.

80. Kathryn Davis Henry, *Medical Astrology: Physiognomy and Astrological Quotations*, privately published, 1978.

81. Robert C. Jansky, *Modern Medical Astrology*, Van Nuys, CA: Astro-Analytics Publication, 1978, 2nd rev.

82. Harry F. Darling, *Essentials of Medical Astrology*, Tempe, AZ: American Federation of Astrologers, 1981.

83. John Ankerberg, John Weldon, *Astrology: Do the Heavens Rule Our Destiny?* Eugene, OR: Harvest House Publishers, 1989.

84. Robert Eisler, *The Royal Art of Astrology*, London: Herbert Joseph, Ltd., 1946.

87. Sherman P. Kanagy II, and Kenneth D. Boa, *Astrology—Scientific, Philosophical and Religious Issues*, ms., 1986.

90. Dora Kunz, ed., *Spiritual Aspects of the Healing Arts*, Wheaton, IL: Quest/Theosophical Publishing House, 1985.

91. Alberto Villoldo and Stanley Krippner, *Healing States: A Journey into the World of Spiritual Healing and Shamanism*, New York: Fireside/Simon and Schuster, Inc., 1987.

95A. Barbara Brennan, *Hands of Light: A Guide to Healing Through the Human Energy Field*, New York: Bantam Books, 1988.

98. George W. Meek, ed., *Healers and the Healing Process*, Wheaton, IL: Quest/Theosophical Publishing House, 1977.

102. Paul Kurtz, *A Skeptic's Handbook to Parapsychology*, Buffalo, NY: Prometheus Books, 1985.

103. C. Norman Shealy, *Occult Medicine Can Save Your Life*, New York: Bantam, 1977.

104. Amy Wallace, Bill Henkin, *The Psychic Healing Book: How to Develop Your Psychic Potential Safely, Simply, Effectively*, New York: Delacorte Press, 1978.

108. C. Norman Shealy, M.D., Caroline M. Myss, *The Creation of Health: Merging Traditional Medicine with Intuitive Diagnosis*, Walpole, NH: Stillpoint Publishing, 1988.

112. Harold Sherman, *Your Power to Heal*, Greenwich, CT: Fawcett Publications, 1973.

118. Alfred Stelter, *Psi-Healing*, New York: Bantam, 1976.

120. Arthur Guirdham, *The Psyche in Medicine: Possession, Past Lives, Powers of Evil in Disease*, Jersey, Channel Islands, Great Britain: Neville Spearman, 1978.

122. Irving Oyle, *The New American Medicine Show: Discovering the Healing Connection*, Santa Cruz, CA: Unity Press, 1979.

142. Michael Harner, *The Way of the Shaman: A Guide to Power and Healing*, New York: Bantam, 1986.

143. Jeanne Achterberg, *Imagery in Healing: Shamanism and Modern Medicine*, Boston, MA: New Science Library/Shambhala, 1985.

144. Dolores Krieger, *The Therapeutic Touch: How to Use Your Hands to Help or to Heal*, New York: Prentice-Hall, 1986.

148. Martin Ebon, ed., *The Satan Trap: Dangers of the Occult*, Garden City, NY: Doubleday, 1976.

152. Albert Roy Davis, Walter C. Rawls, Jr., *The Magnetic Effect*, Hicksville, NY: Exposition Press, 1977.

153. Jack Schwarz, *Human Energy Systems: A Way of Good Health Using Our Auric Fields*, New York: E.P. Dutton, 1980.

154. Virginia MacIvor, Sandra LaForest, *Vibrations: Healing Through Color, Homeopathy and Radionics*, New York: Samuel Weiser, 1979.

161. Edward Russell, *Design for Destiny: Science Reveals the Soul*, Suffolk, Great Britain: Neville Spearman, 1978.

166. George J. Feiss, *Mind Therapies, Body Therapies: A Consumer's Guide*, Millbrae, CA: Celestial Arts, 1979.

169. W. Edward Mann, Edward Hoffman, *The Man Who Dreamed of Tomorrow: A Conceptual Biography of Wilhelm Reich*, Los Angeles, CA: J.P. Tarcher, 1980.

170. W. Edward Mann, *Orgone, Reich and Eros: Wilhelm Reich's Theory of Life Energy*, New York: Touchstone/Simon and Schuster, 1973.

182. Richard Cavendish, ed., *Man, Myth and Magic: An Illustrated Encyclopedia of the Supernatural*, New York: Marshall Cavendish Corporation, 1970.

188. Ann Hill, ed., *A Visual Encyclopedia of Unconventional Medicine*, New York: Crown Publishers, 1979.

192. Herbert A. Otto, James W. Knight, eds., *Dimensions in Wholistic Healing: New Frontiers in the Treatment of the Whole Person*, Chicago, IL: Nelson-Hall, 1979.

197. Berkeley Holistic Health Center, *The Holistic Health Handbook: A Tool for Attaining Wholeness of Body, Mind, and Spirit*, Berkeley, CA: And/Or Press, 1978.

198. Leslie J. Kaslof, *Wholistic Dimensions in Healing: A Resource Guide*, Garden City, NY: Dolphin/Doubleday, 1978.

202. Uma Silbey, *The Complete Crystal Guide Book: A Practical Path to Personal Power, Self-Development and Healing Using Quartz Crystals*, New York: Bantam, 1987.

203. Dael Walker, *The Crystal Healing Book*, Pacheco, CA: The Crystal Company, 1988.

204. Julia Lorusso, Joel Glick, *Healing Stoned: The Therapeutic Use of Gems and Minerals—A New Work Dealing with Gemstone Energies*, Miami Shores, FL: Mineral Perspectives, 1978.

205. George Frederick Kunz, *The Curious Lure of Precious Stones*, New York: Dover, 1971, rpt.

206. William Jarvis, "Chiropractic: A Skeptical View," *The Skeptical Inquirer*, Fall 1987.

207. Stephen Barrett, "Homeopathy: Is It Medicine?" *The Skeptical Inquirer*, Fall 1987.

208. Edmund S. Crelin, "Chiropractic" in D. Stalker, C. Glymour, *Examining Holistic Medicine* (ref. 3).

209. Mike Samuels, M.D., Nancy Samuels, *Seeing with the Mind's Eye: The History, Techniques and Uses of Visualization*, New York: Bookworks/Random House, 1983.

210. Leonard Pellettiri, ed., *Journal of Holistic Health*, San Diego, CA: Association for Holistic Health/Mandala Society, 1975-1976.

211. ———, *Journal of Holistic Health*, San Diego, CA: Association for Holistic Health/Mandala Society, 1977.

212. Michael Gosney, ed., *Journal of Holistic Health*, vol. 3, San Diego, CA: Association for Holistic Health/Mandala Society, 1978.

213. ———, *Journal of Holistic Health*, vol. 4, San Diego, CA: Association for Holistic Health/Mandala Society, 1979.

214. Anastas Harris, ed., *Journal of Holistic Health*, vol. 5, San Diego, CA: Association for Holistic Health/Mandala Society, 1980.

215. ———, *Journal of Holistic Health*, vol. 6, San Diego, CA: Association for Holistic Health/Mandala Society, 1981.

216. Alice DeBolt, Shelby Shapiro, eds., *Journal of Holistic Health*, vol. 7, San Diego, CA: Association for Holistic Health/Mandala Society, 1982.

217. ———, *Journal of Holistic Health*, vol. 8, San Diego, CA: Association for Holistic Health/Mandala Society, 1983.

218. ———, *Journal of Holistic Health*, vol. 9, San Diego, CA: Association for Holistic Health/Mandala Society, 1984.

222. The Edgar Cayce Foundation and the A.R.E. Clinic, *Proceedings: A Symposium on Varieties of Healing*, 6th Annual Medical Symposium, Phoenix, AZ: The Edgar Cayce Foundation, 1973.

226. Jeremy Kingston, *Healing Without Medicine*, Danbury Press/Grolier, 1975, n.p.p.

227. Mike Samuels, Hal Bennett, *The Well Body Book*, New York: Bookworks/Random House, 1982.

230. Walter Addison Jayne, *The Healing Gods of Ancient Civilizations*, New Hyde Park, NY: University Books, 1962, rpt.

232. C.W. Leadbeater, *Vegetarianism and Occultism*, Wheaton, IL: Theosophical Publishing House, 1972.

236. John White, ed., *Kundalini Evolution and Enlightenment*, Garden City, NY: Anchor/Doubleday, 1979.

237. David Conway, *Magic: An Occult Primer*, New York: Bantam, 1973.

238. Stanislav Grof, ed., *Ancient Wisdom and Modern Science*, Albany, NY: State University of New York Press, 1984.

239. Paul Solomon Readings, *A Healing Consciousness*, Virginia Beach, VA: Fellowship of the Inner Light, 1978.

241. Doreen Irvine, *Freed from Witchcraft*, Nashville, TN: Thomas Nelson Publishers, 1973.

242. Raphael Gasson, *The Challenging Counterfeit*, Plainfield, NJ: Logos, 1970.

243. Johanna Michaelsen, *The Beautiful Side of Evil*, Eugene, OR: Harvest House Publishers, 1975.

244. Victor H. Ernest, *I Talked with Spirits*, Wheaton, IL: Tyndale House Publishers, 1971.

245. John Ankerberg, John Weldon, *The Facts on Spirit Guides*, Eugene, OR: Harvest House Publishers, 1989.

246. Ben Alexander, *Out from Darkness: The True Story of a Medium Who Escapes the Occult*, Joplin, MO: College Press Publishing, 1986.

249. Tal Brooke, *Riders of the Cosmic Circuit: Rajneesh, Sai Baba, Muktananda. . .Gods of the New Age*, Batavia, IL: Lion, 1986. Available from *SCP*, P.O. Box 4308, Berkeley, CA 94702.

256. Mantak Chia, *Chi Self-Massage: The Taoist Way of Rejuvenation*, Huntington, NY: Healing Tao Books, 1986.

259. Garabed Paelian, *Nicholas Roerich*, Agoura, CA: The Aquarian Educational Group, 1974.

264. John Ferguson, *An Illustrated Encyclopedia of Mysticism and the Mystery Religions*, New York: Seabury Press, 1977.

265. R. Michael Miller, Josephine M. Harper, *The Psychic Energy Workbook: An Illustrated Course in Practical Psychic Skills*, Wellingborough, Northamptonshire, England: Aquarian Press, 1986.

266. Karl Sabbagh, "The Psychopathology of Fringe Medicine," *The Skeptical Inquirer*, vol. 10, no. 2, Winter 1985-86.

267. Walter Fischman, Mark Grinims, "The Muscle Response Test," *Family Circle*, Feb. 20, 1979.

270. Kurt Koch, *Occult Bondage and Deliverance*, Grand Rapids, MI: Kregel Publishers, 1970.

271.———, *Demonology Past and Present*, Grand Rapids, MI: Kregel Publishers, 1973.

272. ———, *Between Christ and Satan*, Grand Rapids, MI: Kregel Publishers, 1962.

273. ———, *Christian Counselling and Occultism*, Grand Rapids, MI: Kregel Publishers, 1982.

274. Stanislav Grof, Christina Grof, eds., *Spiritual Emergency: When Personal Transformation Becomes a Crisis*, Los Angeles, CA: Jeremy P. Tarcher, 1989.

275. Merrill Unger, *Biblical Demonology: A Study of the Spiritual Forces Behind the Present World Unrest*, Wheaton, IL: Scripture Press, 1971.

276. Tom and Carole Valentine, *Applied Kinesiology: Muscle Response in Diagnosis Therapy and Preventive Medicine*, Rochester, VT: Healing Arts Press, 1987.

277. See refs. 270–273, 275, 291–295, 317, and Merrill Unger, *Demons in the World Today*, Wheaton, IL: Tyndale House Publishers, 1973; Merrill Unger, *The Haunting of Bishop Pike*, Wheaton, IL: Tyndale House Publishers, 1971; Merrill Unger, *What Demons Can Do to Saints*, Chicago, IL: Moody, 1977; also, Carl A. Raschke, "Satanism and the Devolution of the 'New Religions,' " *SCP Newsletter* (Fall 1985); Carl A. Raschke, *The Interruption of Eternity: Modern Gnosticism and the Origins of New Religious Consciousness*, Chicago, IL: Nelson-Hall, 1980; John Warwick Montgomery, *Principalities and Powers*, Minneapolis, MN: Bethany, 1973; Gary North, *Unholy Spirits: Occultism and New Age Humanism*, Fort Worth, TX: Dominion, 1986; John Ankerberg, John Weldon, *The Coming Darkness: Confronting Occult Deception*, Eugene, OR: Harvest House Publishers, 1993; John Weldon, Zola Levitt, *Psychic Healing*, Chicago, IL: Moody Press, 1982; Johanna Michaelsen, *Like Lambs to the Slaughter: Your Child and the Occult*, Eugene, OR: Harvest House Publishers, 1989; Ted Schwarz and Duane Empey, *Satanism: Is Your Family Safe?* Grand Rapids, MI: Zondervan, 1988; M. Lamar Keene, *The Psychic Mafia: The True and Shocking Confessions of a Famous Medium*, New York: St. Martin's Press, 1976.

278. John Ankerberg, John Weldon, *The Coming Darkness: Confronting Occult Deception*, Eugene, OR: Harvest House Publishers, 1993.

280. John Ankerberg, John Weldon, *The Facts on Spirit Guides*, Eugene, OR: Harvest House Publishers, 1988.

281. Andrija Puharich, *Uri*, New York: Bantam, p. 112; Robert Leichtman, M.D., "Clairvoyant Diagnosis," *Journal of Holistic Health*, 1977, p. 40; Robert Leichtman, *Eileen Garrett Returns*, pp. 46-48; and Robert Leichtman, *Edgar Cayce Returns*, 1980, Columbus, OH: Atiel Press, pp. 50-52; D. Kendrick Johnson; *From Heaven to Earth* series; and Robert Leichtman, Carl Japikse, *The Art of Living*, vol. 4, Columbus, OH: Ariel, 1984, p. 78.

283. Monty Kline, *Christian Health Counselor*, March-April 1988.

285. "Health and Spirituality: An Interview with Dr. Bernard Jensen," *Rays from the Rose Cross*, May 1978.

286. John Keel, *UFO's: Operation Trojan Horse*, New York: G.P. Putnam, 1970.

287. Dr. Randolph Stone, *The Mystic Bible*, Punjab, India: Radha Soami Satsang Beas, 1977.

288. Alice Bailey, *The Unfinished Autobiography*, New York: Lucis Publishing Co., 1976.

289. Mike Samuels, M.D., Hal Bennett, *Spirit Guides: Access to Inner Worlds*, New York: Random House, Inc., 1974.

291. John Warwick Montgomery, ed., *Demon-Possession: A Medical, Historical, Anthropological and Theological Symposium*, Minneapolis, MN: Bethany House, 1976; cf. Malachi Martin, *Hostage to the Devil: The Possession and Exorcism of Five Living Americans*, New York, Bantam, 1977; T.K. Oesterreich, *Possession: Demonical and Other Among Primitive Races, in Antiquity, the Middle Ages and Modern Times*, Secaucus, NJ: Citadel, 1974; William M. Alexander, *Demonic Possession in the New Testament: Its Historical, Medical and Theological Aspects*, Grand Rapids, MI: Baker, 1980; John L. Nevius, *Demon Possession*, Grand Rapids, MI: Kregel, 1970.

292. Doreen Irvine, *Freed from Witchcraft*, Nashville, TN: Thomas Nelson Publishers, 1978.

293. M. Scott Peck, *People of the Lie*, New York: Simon and Schuster, 1983.

294. C.S. Lewis, *The Screwtape Letters*, New York: McMillan, 1971.

295. John Warwick Montgomery, *Principalities and Powers*, Minneapolis, MN: Bethany, 1973.

297. Erika Bourguignon, ed., *Religion, Altered States of Consciousness and Social Change*, Columbus, OH: Ohio State University Press, 1973.

301. Marilyn Ferguson, *The Aquarian Conspiracy: Personal and Social Transformation in the 1980s*, Los Angeles, CA: J.P. Tarcher, Inc.

302. Keith Crim, ed., *Abingdon Dictionary of Living Religions*, Nashville, TN: Abingdon, 1981.

313. Alice A. Bailey, *Esoteric Healing*, New York, Lucis Publishing, 1977.

317. Kurt Koch, *The Devil's Alphabet*, Grand Rapids, MI: Kregel Publications, 1969.

319. Dean C. Halverson, Kenneth Wapnick, "A Matter of Course: Conversation with Kenneth Wapnick," *Spiritual Counterfeits Journal*, vol. 7, no. 1, 1987.

319A. Dean C. Halverson, "Seeing Yourself as Sinless," *SCP Journal*, vol. 7, no. 1, 1987.

320. Frances Adeny, *Re-visioning Reality: A Critique of A Course in Miracles*, *SCP Newsletter*, vol. 7, no. 2, 1981.

321. Brian Van Der Horst, "Update on *A Course in Miracles*," *New Realities*, vol. 3, no. 1, August 1979.

322. *New Realities*, vol. 1, no. 1, lead article, 1977.

323. Gerald Jampolsky, *Teach Only Love*, New York: Bantam, 1983.

324. Gerald Jampolsky, *Good-Bye to Guilt: Releasing Fear Through Forgiveness*, New York: Bantam, 1985.

325. *A Course in Miracles, Volume 2: Workbook for Students*, Huntington Station, NY: Foundation for Inner Peace, 1977.

326. James Bolen, "Interview: William N. Thetford," *New Realities*, vol. 6, no. 1, July/August 1984, Part 1.

328. James Bolen, "Interview: William N. Thetford," *New Realities*, vol. 6, no. 2, September/October 1984, Part 2.

330. *A Course in Miracles, Volume 3, Manual for Teachers*, Huntington Station, NY: Foundation for Inner Peace, 1977.

331. *A Course in Miracles, Volume 1*, text, Huntington Station, New York: Foundation for Inner Peace, 1977.

332. E.g., the editors of *Psychic* magazine, *Psychics: In-depth Interviews*, New York: Harper & Row, 1972.

333. Sharon Begley, "The Stuff That Dreams Are Made of" *Newsweek*, August 14, 1989.

334. Norman MacKenzie, *Dreams and Dreaming*, New York: Vanguard Press, 1965.

335. Joan Windsor, *Dreams and Dreaming: Expanding the Inner Eye—How to Attune Your Mind-Body Connection Through Imagery, Intuition and Life Energies*, New York: Dodd Mead, 1987.

336. Ann Faraday, *The Dream Game*, New York: Harper & Row/Perennial, 1976.

337. ———, *Dream Power*, New York: Berkeley Books, 1986.

338. Stephen LaBerge, *Lucid Dreaming*, New York: Ballantine, 1986.

339. John Ankerberg, John Weldon, *The Facts on False Teaching in the Church*, Eugene, OR: Harvest House Publishers, 1988.

340. Carl Jung, *Memories, Dreams, Reflections*, New York: Vintage/Random House, 1965.

342. Morton T. Kelsey, *The Christian and the Supernatural*, Minneapolis, MN: Augsburg Publishing House, 1976.

347. Shirley MacLaine, *Dancing in the Light*, New York: Bantam, 1985.

348. Hugh Lynn Cayce, et al., *Dreams: The Language of the Unconscious*, Virginia Beach, VA: A.R.E. Press, rev. 1976.

349. Laeh M. Garfield, Jack Grant, *Companions in Spirit: A Guide to Working with Your Spirit Helpers*, Berkeley, CA: Celestial Arts, 1984.

356. Jerry A. Green, Steven Markell, "The Health Care Contract: A Model for Sharing Responsibility," *Somatics: Magazine-Journal of the Bodily Arts and Sciences*; cf. Jerry A. Green "Holistic Practitioners Unite! It's Time to Learn to Fly," *Somatics: Magazine-Journal of the Bodily Arts and Sciences*, Spring/Summer 1982.

369. Alta J. LaDage, *Occult Psychology: A Comparison of Jungian Psychology and the Modern Quabala*, St. Paul, MN: Llewellyn Publications, 1978.

372. David Savage, "Justices to Rule on Use of Hypnosis: Refreshing the Memory of a Witness Has Troubled Courts," *Los Angeles Times*, November 11, 1986, citing Bernard Diamond, "Inherent Problems in the Use of Pretrial Hypnosis on a Prospective Witness," *California Law Review*, March 1980.

373. Charles Tart, "Transpersonal Potentialities of Deep Hypnosis," *Journal of Transpersonal Psychology*, vol. 2, no. 1, 1970.

374. Daniel Goleman, "Hypnosis Comes of Age," Psychology Today, February 1977.

375. J. Meerloo, "Crime and Hypnosis," *Parapsychology Review*, vol. 1, no. 1, March/April 1970.

376. Martin and Deidre Bobgan, *Hypnosis and the Christian*, Minneapolis, MN: Bethany House, 1984.

377. Leslie Shepard, comp.-ed., *The Encyclopedia of Occultism and Parapsychology*, Detroit, MI: Gale Research, 1979, rev.

378. Leslie LeCron, "Hypnosis and the Production of Psi Phenomena," *International Journal of Parapsychology*, vol. 3, no. 3, Summer 1961.

380. See the following articles: "Reincarnation Phenomena in Hypnotic States"; "Hypnosis, the Key to Unlocking Latent Psi Faculties"; "Hypnosis in the Production of Psi Phenomena"; "Hypnotic Alterations in Time and Space"; and "Crime and Hypnosis" in *The International Journal of Parapsychology*, vol. 4, no. 3; vol. 10, no. 2; vol. 3, no. 3; vol. 10, no. 1, respectively; and *Parapsychology Review*, vol. 1, no. 1; cf. Thelma Moss, et al., "Hypnosis and ESP: A Controlled Experiment," *The American Journal of Clinical Hypnosis*, vol. 13, no. 1, July 1970; R.L. Van De Castle, "The Facilitation of ESP Through Hypnosis," *The American Journal of Clinical Hypnosis*, vol. 12, no. 2, July 1969; and refs. 376:53; 382:57; 386:65; 383:89-138; 389:179.

381. Lee Edward Levinson, "Hypnosis: The Key to Unlocking Latent Psi Faculties," *International Journal of Parapsychology*, vol. 10, no. 2, 1968.

382. Simeon Edmunds, *Hypnosis: Key to Psychic Powers*, New York: Samuel Weiser, 1972.

383. Simeon Edmunds, *Hypnotism and the Supernormal*, North Hollywood, CA: Wilshire Books, 1967.

384. Edwin Zolik, "Reincarnation Phenomena in Hypnotic States," *International Journal of Parapsychology*, vol. 4, no. 3, 1962.

385. In Margaret Gaddis, "Teachers of Delusion" in Martin Ebon ed. *The Satan Trap: Dangers of the Occult*, Garden City, NY: Doubleday, 1976.

386. J.H. Brennan, *Astral Doorways*, New York: Samuel Weiser, 1972.

388. Helen Wambach, *Reliving Past Lives*, New York: Barnes and Noble, 1984.

389. Nandor Fodor, *An Encyclopedia of Psychic Science*, Secaucus, NJ: The Citadel Press, 1966.

390. Merrill C. Tenney, gen. ed., *The Zondervan Pictorial Encyclopedia of the Bible*, Grand Rapids, MI: Zondervan Publishing House, 1975.

391. In Mark Albrecht, *Reincarnation: A Christian Appraisal*, Downers Grove, IL: InterVarsity Press, 1987.

392. Joe Fisher, *The Case for Reincarnation*, New York: Bantam, 1985.

393. John Weldon, Clifford Wilson, *Close Encounters: A Better Explanation*, San Diego, CA: Master Books, 1978.

394. Andrija Puharich, *Uri*, New York: Bantam, 1975.

395. Robert Leichtman, "Clairvoyant Diagnosis: Developing Intuition and Psychic Abilities in the Diagnostic Process," *The Journal of Holistic Health*, San Diego, CA: Mandala Society, 1977.

396. Robert Leichtman, *Eileen Garrett Returns*, Columbus, OH: Ariel Press, 1984.

397. Robert Leichtman, Carl Japiske, *The Art of Living*, vol. 4, Columbus, OH: Ariel Press, 1984.

398. Shakti Gawain, *Living in the Light: A Guide to Personal and Planetary Transformation*, Mill Valley, CA: Whatever Publishing, 1986.

399. Albert Villoldo, Stanley Krippner, *Healing States: A Journey into the World of Spiritual Healing and Shamanism*, New York: Simon and Schuster, 1987.

400. Joseph Millard, *Edgar Cayce: Mystery Man of Miracles*, Greenwich, CT: Fawcett, 1967.

403. Thomas Sugrue, *There Is a River*, New York: Dell, 1970.

411. Philip Goldberg, *The Intuitive Edge: Understanding Intuition and Applying It in Everyday Life*, Los Angeles, CA: J.P. Tarcher, 1983.

412. Frances Vaughan, *Awakening Intuition*, Garden City, NY: Anchor/Doubleday, 1979.

414. *Oxford American Dictionary*, New York: Avon, 1982.

415. Swami Muktananda, *Play of Consciousness*, New York: Harper & Row, 1978.

627

416. Da Free John, *Garbage and the Goddess*, Lower Lake, CA: Dawn Horse Press, 1974.

419. Personal conversation with Dr. Jane Gumprecht (ref. 4) who had a nurse practitioner relay this information to her.

420. Hugh Lynn Cayce, "The Variety of Healings," in ref. 222, p. 5.

424. Elizabeth Stark, "Hypnosis on Trial," *Psychology Today*, February 1984.

425. Ram Dass, interview, *New Age Journal*, no. 9; cf. his interview in the 1976 issue of *The Movement* magazine.

426. Hal Zina Bennett, *Inner Guides, Visions, Dreams and Dr. Einstein*, Berkeley, CA: Celestial Arts, 1986.

427. Edwin C. Steinbrecher, *The Inner Guide to Meditation: A Transformational Journey to Enlightenment and Awareness*, Wellingborough, Northhamptonshire, England: Aquarian Press, 1986.

428. O. Carl Simonton, Stephanie Matthews-Simonton, *Getting Well Again*, Los Angeles, CA: J.P. Tarcher, 1978.

429. Margo Adler, *Drawing Down the Moon: Witches, Druids, Goddess Worshippers and Other Pagans in America Today*, New York: Viking, 1979.

430. David Stoop, *Self-Talk: Key to Spiritual Growth*, Old Tappan, NJ: Revell, 1982.

431. Richard Foster, *Celebration of Discipline*, New York: Harper & Row, 1978.

432. Dave Hunt, T.A. McMahon, *The Seduction of Christianity*, Eugene, OR: Harvest House Publishers, 1984.

433. John Weldon, James Bjornstad, *Playing with Fire*, Chicago, IL: Moody Press, 1984.

434. Michael Murphy, Steven Donovan, "A Bibliography of Meditation Theory and Research, 1931-1983," *The Journal of Transpersonal Psychology*, vol. 15, no. 2, 1983.

434A. Daniel Goleman, "The Buddha on Meditation and States of Consciousness," in Charles Tart ed., *Transpersonal Psychologies*, New York: Harper Colophon Books, 1977.

435. Haridas Chaudhuri, *Philosophy of Meditation*, New York: Philosophical Library, 1974.

436. Cited by Stanley Krippner in *Song of the Siren*, San Francisco, CA: Harper & Row, 1975.

437. Karlis Osis, et al., "Dimensions of the Meditative Experience," *The Journal of Transpersonal Psychology*, vol. 5, no. 2, 1973.

438. William Johnston, *Silent Music: The Science of Meditation*, New York: Harper & Row, 1975.

439. Roger Walsh, "A Model for Viewing Meditation Research," *The Journal of Transpersonal Psychology*, vol. 14, no. 1, 1982.

440. Roger N. Walsh, et al., "Meditation: Aspects of Research and Practice," *The Journal of Transpersonal Psychology*, vol. 10, no. 2, 1978.

441. Roger Walsh, "Initial Meditative Experiences, Part One," *The Journal of Transpersonal Psychology*, vol. 9, no. 2, 1977.

442. Daniel Goleman, *The Varieties of the Meditative Experience*, New York: E.P. Dutton, 1977.

443. Gertrude Schmeidler, "The Psychic Personality," *Psychic*, March/April 1974.

444. John White, "What Is Meditation?" *New Realities*, September-October 1984.

445. Patricia Mischell, *Beyond Positive Thinking: Mind Power Techniques*, Englewood Cliffs, NJ: Prentice-Hall, 1985.

446. Stanley Krippner, Leonard George, "Psi Phenomena Related to Altered States of Consciousness," in Benjamin B. Wolman, Montague Ullman, eds., *Handbook of States of Consciousness*, New York: Van Nostrand Reinhold Co., 1987.

447. Anthony Norvell, *The Miracle Power of Transcendental Meditation*, New York: Barnes and Noble, 1974.

448. Frances Clark, "Exploring Intuition: Prospects and Possibilities," *The Journal of Transpersonal Psychology*, vol. 5, no. 2, 1973.

449. Rudi [Swami Rudrananda], *Spiritual Cannibalism*, Woodstock, NY: Overlook Press, 1978.

450. Chogyam Trungpa, "An Approach to Meditation," *The Journal of Transpersonal Psychology*, vol. 5, no. 1, 1973.

451. Roger Walsh, et al., "Meditation: Aspects of Research and Practice," *The Journal of Transpersonal Psychology*, vol. 10, no. 2, 1978.

452. Doris H. Buckley, *Spirit Communication for the Millions*, Los Angeles, CA: Sherbourne Press, 1967.

453. Ruth Montgomery, *A World Beyond*, New York: Coward McCann and Geoghegan, 1971.

454. Mark D. Epstein, Jonathan Lieff, "Psychiatric Complications of Meditation Practice," *The Journal of Transpersonal Psychology*, vol. 13, no. 2, 1981.

455. Komilla Thapa, Vinoda Murthy, "Experiential Characteristics of Certain Altered States of Consciousness," *The Journal of Transpersonal Psychology*, vol. 17, no. 1, 1985.

456. Jack Kornfield, "Intensive Insight Meditation: A Phenomenological Study," *The Journal of Transpersonal Psychology*, vol. 11, no. 1, 1979.

457. Mary Jo Meadow, et al., "Spiritual and Transpersonal Aspects of Altered States of Consciousness," *The Journal of Transpersonal Psychology*, vol. 11, no. 1, 1979.

458. Among them are Leon Otis, *Adverse Effects of Meditation*, Menlo Park, CA: Stanford Research Institute,

1979; J.A. Fahmy and H. Fledulisu, "Yoga Induced Attacks of Acute Glaucoma," *Acta Ophthalmologica*, 1973, 51, pp. 80-84; J. Hassett, "Meditation Can Hurt," *Psychology Today*, 1978, vol. 12, no. 6, pp. 125-26; A. Lazarus, "Psychiatric Problems Precipitated by Transcendental Meditation," *Psychological Reports*, 1976, vol. 39, no. 2, pp. 601-02; B. O'Regan, "Mind/Body Effects: The Physiological Consequence of Tibetan Meditation," *Newsletter of the Institute of Noetic Sciences*, 1982, vol. 10, no. 2.

459. Lynn Rew, "Intuition: Concept Analysis of a Group Phenomenon," *Advances in Nursing Science*, January 1986.

460. R.M. Mack, "Lessons from Living with Cancer," *New England Journal of Medicine*, vol. 311, 1984, pp. 1640-44.

461. Ronald Shore, *Creative Visualization*, Rochester, VT: Thorsons, 1984.

463. Slater Brown, *The Heyday of Spiritualism*, New York: Pocket Books, 1972.

467. Swami Muktananda, *Play of Consciousness*, New York: Harper & Row, 1978.

468. A critique is found in John Weldon, Zola Levitt, *The Transcendental Explosion*, Irvine, CA: Harvest House Publishers, republished by Zola Levitt Ministries, Dallas, TX, 1991.

469. Maharishi Mahesh Yogi, *On the Bhagavad Gita*, Baltimore, MD: Penguin, 1974.

473. Edwin Erwin, "Is Psychotherapy More Effective Than a Placebo?" in Jusuf Hariman, ed., *Does Psychotherapy Really Help People?* Springfield, IL: Charles C. Thomas, 1984.

474. John A. Sanford, *Dreams and Healing: A Succinct and Lively Interpretation of Dreams*, New York: Paulist Press, 1978.

475. John A. Sanford, *Dreams: God's Forgotten Language*, New York: J.B. Lippincott, 1968.

476. Bubba Free John, *Garbage and the Goddess*, Lower Lake, CA: Dawn Horse Press, 1974.

477. Sita Wiener, *Swami Satchidananda*, San Francisco, CA: Straight Arrow Books, 1970.

478. Da Free John, *A New Tradition: An Introduction to the Laughingman Institute and the Crazy Wisdom Fellowship*, Clear Lake, CA: The Laughing Man Institute, 1980.

479. Swami Bakta Vishita, *Genuine Mediumship*, n.p.p.: Yoga Publication Society, 1919, .

480. Sri Chinmoy, *Yoga and the Spiritual Life: The Journey of India's Soul*, Jamaica, NY: Agni Press, 1974.

482. Yarti, Swami Anand, comp., *The Sound of Running Water, a Photo-Biography of Bhagwan Shree Rajneesh and His Work*, 1974–78, Poona, India: Rajneesh Foundation, 1980.

483. Swami Muktananda, *Siddha Meditation: Commentaries on the Shiva Sutras and Other Sacred Texts*, Oakland, CA: Siddha Yoga Dham of America, 1975.

484. Sai Baba, *Sathya Shivam Sundaram*, Part 3, Whitefield, Bangalore, India: Sri Sathya Sai Publication and Education Foundation, 1972.

485. Sanathann Sarathi, ed., *Sathya Sai Speaks*, vol. 9, Tustin, CA: Sri Sathya Sai Baba, Book Center of America,. 1975. The Indian publisher is Bangalore, India: Sri Sathya Sai Publication and Education Foundation.

486. Bhagwan Shree Rajneesh, *The Mustard Seed*, San Francisco, CA: Harper & Row, 1975.

487. Douglas Shah, *The Meditators*, Plainfield, NJ: Logos, 1975.

488. Os Guinness, *The Dust of Death*, Downers Grove, IL: InterVarsity Press, 1973.

489. Mahendranath Gupta, *The Gospel of Sri Ramakrishna*, 6th ed., New York: Ramakrishna-Vivekananda Center, 1977.

490. Romain Rolland, *The Life of Ramakrishna*, vol. 1, Calcutta, India: Advaita Ashrama, 1979.

491. Gopi Krishna, *The Awakening of Kundalini*, New York: E.P. Dutton, 1975.

492. C.B. Purdom, *The God-Man: The Life, Journeys and Work of Meher Baba*, London: George Allen & Unwin, Ltd., 1964.

496. John Ankerberg, John Weldon, *The Secret Teachings of the Masonic Lodge*, Chicago, IL: Moody Press, 1990.

497. Rosalyn Bruyere, *Wheels of Light: A Study of the Chakras*, Sierra Madre, CA: Bon Productions, 1989.

498. a) Ann Nietzke, "Portrait of an Aura Reader," Part 1, *Human Behavior*, February 1979; b) Part 2, *Human Behavior*, March 1979.

500. Jeffrey Mishlove, *The Roots of Consciousness: Psychic Liberation Through History, Science and Experience*, New York: Random House, 1975.

501. Reviews, *Journals of Psychology and Theology*, (*JPT*) vol. 12, no. 3, 1984; see *JPT*, vol. 13, no. 3, (Fall 1985) [and Fall and Spring, 1983], Fall 1974; cf. Jeffrey Sobosan, "Kierkegaard and Jung on the Self," *JPT*, vol. 3, no. 1, Winter 1975; Jane Kopas, "Jung and Assagioli in Religious Perspective," *JPT*, vol. 9, no. 3, Fall 1981. (See refs. 502-04.)

502. Reviews, *Journal of Psychology and Christianity*, vol. 4, no. 4.

503. Ibid., vol. 3, no. 2.

504. John A. Walsh, "The Dream of Joseph: A Jungian Interpretation," *Journal of Psychology and Theology*, vol. 11, no. 1, 1983.

505. David Brenner, ed., *Baker, Encyclopedia of Psychology*, Grand Rapids, MI: Baker Book House,

1985, articles on Dream Therapy and Jungian Analysis.

507. Jane Roberts, *The Nature of Personal Reality: A Seth Book*, New York: Bantam, 1978.

514. Ben G. Hester, *Dowsing: An Exposé of Hidden Occult Forces*, 1982, rev. ed., 1984 available from the author at 4883 Hedrick Ave., Arlington, CA 92505.

517. Robert A. Bradley, "The Need for the Academy of Parapsychology and Medicine," *The Varieties of Healing Experience: Exploring Psychic Phenomenon in Healing*, Los Altos, CA: Academy of Parapsychology and Medicine, 1971.

518. D. Kendrick Johnson, Robert A. Leichtman, "From Heaven to Earth" series, Columbus, OH: Ariel Press, 1978-90.

520. Hugh Lynn Cayce, "The Varieties of Healings," in *Proceedings: A Symposium on the Varieties of Healing* (ref. 222).

526. Justine Glass, *Witchcraft—The Sixth Sense*, North Hollywood, CA: Wilshire Book Co., 1974.

530. Michael Howard, *The Magic of the Runes: Their Origins and Occult Power*, Wellingborough, Northamptonshire, England: The Aquarian Press, 1986.

533. Irving I. Zaretsky, Mark P. Leone, eds., *Religious Movements in Contemporary America*, Princeton, NJ: Princeton University Press, 1974.

535. E.J. Moody, "Magical Therapy—An Anthropological Investigation of Contemporary Satanism," in Zaretsky and Leone, Ref. 533.

536. B. Van Dragt, "Psychic Healing," in David G. Brenner, ed., *Baker Encyclopedia of Psychology*, Grand Rapids, MI: Baker Book House, 1985. E.g., "Viewed phenomenologically, the ability to heal psychically is just another human capacity, on a par with sensation, locomotion, and thought. It is not, therefore, the paranormal phenomena themselves [i.e., psychic healing] but rather the healer's philosophy that a Christian evaluation would address. . . . Both Christianity and psychic healing view human beings as related to a transcendent source, from which comes the power for healing. However, whereas a particular healer may equate this source with the personal God of the Bible, she may also see it as, among other things, a "loving energy field" or even some aspect of her own self. While this may seem problematic theologically, from an experiential standpoint the process is the same for both Christian and psychic healer alike. What is essential is that one surrender to some higher power than one's own ego or conscious self" (p. 889).

537. Morton Kelsey, *God, Dreams and Revelation: A Christian Interpretation of Dreams*, Minneapolis, MN: Augsburg Publishing, 1974.

538. W.B. Crow, *Precious Stones: Their Occult Power and Hidden Significance*, New York: Samuel Weiser, 1977.

540. Michale Harner, ed., *Hallucinogens and Shamanism*, New York: Oxford, 1973.

544. Dorothy Bradley, Robert A. Bradley, *Psychic Phenomena: Revelations and Experiences*, New York: Paperback Library, 1971.

549. Marilyn Ferguson, ed., *The Brain-Mind Bulletin*, October 26, 1981.

557. Arthur Guirdham, *A Foot in Both Worlds*, London: Neville Spearman, 1973.

558. W.J. Finch, *The Pendulum and Possession*, Sedona, AZ: Esoteric Publications, 1975.

559. Anne Yeomans, "Psychosynthesis," *New Realities*, vol. 1, no. 2, 1977.

561. Robert S. Ellwood, *Religious and Spiritual Groups in Modern America*, Englewood Cliffs, NJ: Prentice-Hall, 1973.

563. Carlos Castaneda's books include: *The Teachings of Don Juan: A Yaqui Way of Knowledge; A Separate Reality; Journey to Ixtlan; Tales of Power*, New York: Simon and Schuster/Touchstone; Lynn Andrews, *Jaguar Woman*, San Francisco, CA: Harper & Row, 1986; Lynn Andrews, *Medicine Woman*, San Francisco, CA: Harper & Row, 1986; Lynn Andrews, *Star Woman*, New York: Warner, 1986.

564. Mircea Eliade, *Occultism, Witchcraft and Cultural Fashions: Essays in Comparative Religions*, Chicago, IL: University of Chicago Press, 1976.

565. Sri Chinmoy, *Meditation: Man-Perfection in God-Satisfaction*, Jamaica, NY: Agni Press.

566. Deane Shapiro, Roger Walsh, eds. *Meditation: Classic and Contemporary Perspectives*, New York: Aldine, 1979.

567. Bhagwan Shree Rajneesh, *The Book of the Secrets, Volume 1: Discourses on Vigyana Bhairava Tantra*, New York: Harper Colophon, 1977.

568. Rudi [Swami Rudrananda}, *Spiritual Cannibalism*, New York: Quick Fox, 1973.

570. Dave Hunt, *America: The Sorcerer's New Apprentice*, Eugene, OR: Harvest House Publishers, 1989.

571. Brooks Alexander, "A Generation of Wizards: Shamanism and Contemporary Culture," *Spiritual Counterfeits Project Special Collections Journal*, Berkeley, CA: Winter 1984, vol. 6, no. 1.

572. Johanna Michaelsen, *Like Lambs to the Slaughter: Your Child and the Occult*, Eugene, OR: Harvest House Publishers, 1989.

574. Jon Klimo, *Channeling: Investigations on Receiving Information from Paranormal Sources*, Los Angeles, CA: Jeremy P. Tarcher, 1987.

575. Sanaya Roman and Duane Packer, *Opening to Channel: How to Connect with Your Guide*, Tiburon, CA: H.J. Kramer, Inc. 1987.

576. Robin Westen, *Channelers: A New Age Directory*, New York: Perigree Books, 1988.

577. Kathryn Ridall, *Channeling: How to Reach Out to Your Spirit Guides*, New York: Bantam Books, 1988.

578. Robert Leichtman, "Clairvoyant Diagnosis: Developing Intuition and Psychic Abilities in the Diagnostic Process," *The Journal of Holistic Health*, San Diego, CA: Mandala Society, 1977.

583. Mircea Eliade, *Shamanism: Archaic Techniques of Ecstasy*, Princeton, NJ: Princeton University Press, 1972.

584. ———, *From Medicine Men to Muhammad*, New York: Harper & Row, 1967.

585. Joan Halifax, *Shamanic Voices*, New York: E.P. Dutton, 1979.

586. I.M. Lewis, *Ecstatic Religion: An Anthropological Study of Spirit Possession and Shamanism*, Baltimore, MD: Penguin, 1975.

587. Sally Hammond, "What the Healers Say: A Survey of Healers in Britain," *Psychic*, July 1973.

588. Richard Kieninger, *The Spiritual Seekers' Guidebook*, Quinlan, TX: The Stelle Group, 1986.

589. Stan and Christina Grof, "Spiritual Emergencies," *Yoga Journal*, July-August 1984.

590. Thomas Matus, *Yoga and the Jesus Prayer Tradition: An Experiment in Faith*, Ramsey, NJ: Paulist Press, 1984.

591. Justin O'Brien, *Yoga and Christianity*, Honesdale, PA: Himalayan International Institute, 1978. For a critique of yoga see John Allan, *Yoga: A Christian Analysis*, Leicester, England: InterVarsity Press, 1983.

592. Gopi Krishna, "The True Aim of Yoga," *Psychic*, January-February, 1973.

593. George Feuerstein, Jeanine Miller, *Yoga and Beyond: Essays in Indian Philosophy*, New York: Schocken, 1972.

594. Editorial, *Yoga Journal*, May/June 1984.

595. Moti Lal Pandit, "Yoga as Methods of Liberation," *Update: A Quarterly Journal on New Religious Movements*, Aarhus, Denmark: The Dialogue Center, vol. 9, no. 4, December 1985.

596. Rammurti S. Mishra, *Yoga Sutras: The Textbook of Yoga Psychology*, Garden City, NY: Anchor Books, 1973.

597. Ernest Wood, *Seven Schools of Yoga: An Introduction*, Wheaton, IL: Theosophical Publishing House, 1973.

598. R.S. Mishra, *Fundamentals of Yoga*, Garden City, NY: Anchor, 1974.

599. Arthur Avalon [Sir John Woodroffe], *The Serpent Power: The Secrets of Tantric and Shaktic Yoga*, New York: Dover, 1974.

600. Bhagwan Shree Patanjali, *Aphorisms of Yoga*, trans. Shree Purohit Swami, London: Faber and Faber, 1972.

601. Mircea Eliade, *Yoga Immortality and Freedom*, trans. Williard R. Trask, Princeton, NJ: Princeton University Press, 1973.

602. Sri Krishna Prem, *The Yoga of the Bhagavat* [sic] *Gita*, Baltimore, MD: Penquin, 1973.

603. Hans Ulrich Rieker, *The Yoga of Light: Hatha Yoga Pradipika*, New York: Seabury Press, 1971.

604. Swami Prabhavananda, *Yoga and Mysticism*, Hollywood, CA: Vedanta Press, 1972.

607. John White, "Kundalini and the Occult," in ref. 608.

608. John White, ed., *Kundalini Evolution and Enlightenment*, Garden City, NY: Anchor, 1979.

610. John Weldon, "Eastern Gurus in a Western Milieu: A Critique from the Perspective of Biblical Revelation," Ph.D. dissertation, Pacific College of Graduate Studies, Melbourne, Australia, 1988.

611. Yogi Amrit Desai, "Kundalini Yoga Through Shaktipat," in ref. 608.

612. D. R. Butler, "Instant Cosmic Consciousness," ref. 608.

614. Lawrence LeShan, *The Medium, the Mystic and the Physicist: Toward a General Theory of the Paranormal*, New York: Ballantine, 1975.

616. E.g., on Taoist Yoga, see Dio Neff, "Taoist Esoteric Yoga with Mantak Chia," *Yoga Journal*, March-April 1986.

617. Sri Chinmoy, *Yoga and the Spiritual Life: The Journey of India's Soul*, Jamaica, NY: Agni Press, 1974.

618. ———, *Great Masters and the Cosmic Gods*, Jamaica, NY: Agni Press, 1977.

619. Norman Evans, "Dowsing: Its Biblical Background," *The American Dowser*, May 1979.

620. Ann Fleming, "Ideas About Dowsing," *The American Dowser*, August 1978.

621. Norman E. Leighton, "A Brief History of Dowsing," *The American Dowser*, February 1978.

622. "The Dowser's Prayer," *The American Dowser*, November 1977.

623. Frances Hitching, *Dowsing: The Psi Connection*, Garden City, NY: Anchor Books, 1978.

624. Raymond C. Willey, *Modern Dowsing: The Dowser's Handbook*, Sedona, AZ: Esoteric Publications, 1978.

626. Erwin E. Stark, *A History of Dowsing and Energy Relationships*, North Hollywood, CA: BAC, 1978.

627. William Vrooman, "Dowsing for Health: Mental and Spiritual Bodies of Human and Non-Human Entities," *The American Dowser*, November 1977.

631

628. Gordon MacLean, "Dowsing Experiences and Problems," *The American Dowser*, May 1976.

630. Raymond C. Willey, "Dowsing Basics," *The American Dowser*, November 1977.

631. F.A. Archdale, *Elementary Radiesthesia*, and *The Use of the Pendulum*, Christies Beach, South Australia: Radionic and Chirotherapy Centre of Australia, 1977, rev.

634. Gordon MacLean, *A Field Guide to Dowsing*, Danville, VT: The American Society of Dowsers, 1976.

635. Ann Fleming, "Ideas About Dowsing," and Harry Steinmetz, "Teleradiaesthesia: Fact or Fiction?" both in *The American Dowser* August 1978.

636. James Randi, "A Controlled Test of Dowsing Abilities," *Skeptical Inquirer*, vol. 4, no. 1, Fall 1979.

637. Michael Martin, "A New Controlled Dowsing Experiment: Putting the President of the American Society of Dowsers to the Test," *Skeptical Inquirer*, Winter 1983-84.

638. Evon Z. Vogt, Ray Hyman, *Water Witching USA*, 2nd ed., Chicago, IL: University of Chicago Press, 1979.

639. Ram Dass, *Be Here Now*, Boulder, CO: Hanuman Foundation, 1978.

640. James Randi, "The Great $10,000 Dowsing Challenge," *The Skeptical Inquirer*, Summer 1984.

641. Dick Smith, "Two Tests of Divining in Australia," *The Skeptical Inquirer*, Summer 1982.

642. Kurt Koch, *Occult ABC*, Grand Rapids, MI: Kregel, 1980 (retitled *Satan's Devices*).

643. T.E. Coalson, "Dowsing: The Eternal Paradox," *Psychic*, March/April 1974.

645. See *The American Dowser*, May 1976, p. 90; February 1977, pp. 20-21; February 1975, pp. 15-18; August 1976, pp. 101, 109, 118; May 1977, pp. 66-69; August 1977, pp. 10-111; November 1977, pp. 176-77; February 1978, p. 27; May 1978, p. 64; May 1979, pp. 53, 82-83. cf. ref. 514:3-4.

646. W. Brugh Joy, *Joy's Way*, Los Angeles, CA: J.P. Tarcher, 1979.

647. Susan Stewart, "What Is Dowsing?" *The American Dowser*, May 1975.

648. Christopher Bird, "Dowsing in Industry: Hoffman-La-Roche," *The American Dowser*, August 1975.

650. Egon E. Eckert, "A Dowser's Trip to West Germany," *The American Dowser*, May 1975.

651. See *The American Dowser*, February 1976, p. 15; May 1976, p. 87; August 1976, p. 118; November 1977, p. 176.

652. Augustus T. Nottingham, "Reaching into Space and Time," *The American Dowser*, February 1977.

653. *The American Dowser*, February 1976.

655. A.J. Soares, "My Pendulum Said 'No,' " *The American Dowser*, November 1977.

656. Raymond C. Willey, "Editorial," *The American Dowser*, May 1976.

657. Harvey Howells, "How We Came to Dowsing," *The American Dowser*, August 1976.

658. Dennis T. Jaffe, David E. Bresler, "The Use of Guided Imagery as an Adjunct to Medical Diagnosis and Treatment," *Journal of Humanistic Psychology*, vol. 20, no. 4 (1980).

662. John Ankerberg, John Weldon, *The Facts on the New Age Movement*, Eugene, OR: Harvest House Publishers, 1988.

674. Letter from Ben Hester, March 23, 1990. (See ref. 514.)

675. Benjamin F. Miller, Claire Brackman Keane, *Encyclopedia and Dictionary of Medicine, Nursing and Allied Health Care*, Third ed., Philadelphia, PA: W.B. Sanders, 1983.

678. *Dorland's Illustrated Medical Dictionary*, 27th ed., Philadelphia, PA: W.B. Sanders, 1988.

679. *Webster's Medical Desk Dictionary*, Springfield, MA: Merriam Webster, 1986.

680. *The American Medical Association Encyclopedia of Medicine*, New York: Random House, 1989.

681. *Fishbein's Illustrated Medical and Health Encyclopedia*, New York: H.S. Stuttman Co., 1977.

682. Otis Brickett, "The Gift of Healing," *The American Dowser*, August 1979.

683. Check any standard ASD supply list. Ours was received in 1983.

684. Donald S. Connery, *The Inner Source: Exploring Hypnosis with Dr. Herbert Spiegel*, New York: Holt, Rinehart and Winston, 1984.

685. A.A. Sheikh, editorial, "Mental Images: Ghosts of Sensations," *Journal of Mental Imagery*, Spring 1977, vol. 1.

686. Kenneth Pelletier, *Mind as Healer, Mind as Slayer: A Holistic Approach to Preventing Stress Disorders*, New York: Dell, 1979.

687. Barbara Hannah, *Encounters with the Soul: Active Imagination as Developed by C.G. Jung*, Santa Monica, CA: Sigo Press, 1981.

688. "Kreskin: Mind Star in a Universe of Realities: Who or What Is He?" *New Realities*, vol. 1, no. 6, February 1978.

689. International Imagery Association, Sixth American Imagery Conference, "Timeless Therapeutic Images," brochure describing proceeding of the November 5-7, 1982, conference in San Francisco, CA, distributed by Brandon House, Box 240, Bronx, New York, NY 10471.

690. Stanley Dokupil, "Seizing the Power; The Use of the Imagination for Healing," *SCP Newsletter*, vol. 8, no. 6 (1982).

691. John Trott and Eric Pement, *Cornerstone*, vol. 14, issue 74, Chicago, IL: Jesus People USA.

692. Andrew Wiehl, *Creative Visualization*, St. Paul, MN: Llewellyn, 1958.

693. James Vargiu, Ed., Psychosynthesis Institute, *Synthesis Two: The Realization of the Self*, San Francisco, CA: Psychosynthesis Institutes of the Synthesis Graduate School for the Study of Man, 1978.

694. K.P. Monteiro, et al., "Imagery, Absorption and Hypnosis: A Factorial Study," *Journal of Mental Imagery*, vol. 4, no. 2, 1980.

695. Norman Vincent Peale, *Positive Imaging*, Old Tappan, NJ: Fleming H. Revell, 1982.

696. Carolyn Stahl, *Opening to God: Guided Imagery and Meditation on Scripture*, Nashville, TN: The Upper Room, 1977.

697. C.S. Lovett, *Longing to Be Loved*, 1982.

698. D. Scott Rogo, "Relax Your Way to ESP," *Psychic*, vol. 7, no. 4, September/October 1976.

699. Shakti Gawain, *Creative Visualization*, Mill Valley, CA: Whatever Publishing, Inc., 1983.

700. Colin Wilson, *Mysteries: An Investigation into the Occult, the Paranormal and the Supernatural*, New York: G.P. Putnam's Sons, 1978.

701. Adelaide Bry, *Visualization: Directing the Movies of Your Mind*, New York: Barnes and Noble Books, 1979.

702. R. Eugene Nichols, *The Science of Mental Cybernetics: How to Lead a High-Voltage Life*, New York: Warner Paperback, 1975.

703. Robert L. Keck, *The Spirit of Synergy*, Nashville, TN: Abingdon, 1978.

704. Jess Stearn, *The Power of Alpha Thinking*, New York: Signet, 1977.

705. H.V. Guenther and Chogyam Trungpa, *The Dawn of Tantra*, Boston, MA: Shambhala, 1975.

706. I.M. Owen, "The Making of a Ghost," *Psychic*, July-August 1975; "Generation of Paranormal Physical Phenomena with an Imaginary Communicator" and "Philip's Story Continued," in *New Horizons*, Toronto Society for Physical Research, vol. 1, no. 3, and vol. 1, no. 4; I.M. Owen, M. Sparrow, *Conjuring Up Philip*, New York: Harper & Row, 1976.

707. A.R.G. Owen in I.M. Owen and M. Sparrow, *Conjuring Up Philip*, New York: Harper & Row, 1976.

708. Robert Masters, Jean Houston, *Mind Games: The Guide to Inner Space*, New York: Delta, 1981.

709. Letter to the author, May 1983.

710. "Self Hypnosis Tapes...for the Change in Your Life," Grand Rapids, MI: Potentials Unlimited, Inc., 1980.

711. Shafica Karagulla, *Breakthrough to Creativity: Your Higher Sense Perception*, Santa Monica, CA: DeVorss & Co. 1972.

712. Leslie M. LeCron, *Self-Hypnotism: The Technique and Its Use in Daily Living*, New York: Signet, 1970.

713. William W. Hewitt, *Beyond Hypnosis: A Program for Developing Your Psychic and Healing Powers*, St. Paul, MN: Llewellyn, 1987.

714. Edith Fiore, *You Have Been Here Before: A Psychologist Looks at Past Lives*, New York: Coward, McCann & Geoghegan, Inc., 1978.

715. David Akstein, "Terpsichoretrancetherapy: A New Hypnopsychotherapeutic Method," *The International Journal of Clinical and Experimental Hypnosis*, vol. 21, no. 3 (1973).

716. John Weldon, *A Critical Encyclopedia of Modern American Sects and Cults*, unpublished. (This ms. covers 70 groups and is 8,000 pages in length); cf. Robert S. Ellwood, *Religious and Spiritual Groups in Modern America*, ref. 561:12.

718. Malachi Martin, *Hostage to the Devil: The Possession and Exorcism of Five Living Americans*, New York, NY: Bantam, 1979.

719. Douglas Stalker, Clark Glymour, "Quantum Medicine," in ref. 3.

725. Dave Fetcho, "Yoga," Berkeley, CA: Spiritual Counterfeits Project, 1978.

726. Dave Fetcho, "David Fetcho's Story: Last Meditation/Lotus Reference," *Special Collections Journal*, vol: 6, no. 1, Berkeley, CA: Spiritual Counterfeits Project, Winter 1984.

727. Brian Inglis, Ruth West, *The Alternative Health Guide*, New York, NY: Alfred A. Knopf, 1983.

732. "Empowering Message from Genesis, a Universal Teacher," and "Applying Universal Principles for Spiritual Fitness," in *The Stillpoint Catalogue*, Walpole, NH: Fall/Winter 1987-88.

733. Stanley Dokupil, "Seizing the Power; the Use of the Imagination in Healing," *SCP Newsletter*, vol. 8, no. 6, 1982.

734. Jack Schwarz, *Voluntary Controls*, New York, NY: E. P. Dutton, 1978.

735. See Edmond Gruss, "God Calling: A Critical Look at a Christian Best Seller," *Personal Freedom Outreach Newsletter*, vol. 6, no. 3, (P.O. Box 26062, St. Louis, MO 63136); L.M. Arnold's text and *Oahspe* are much more blatantly anti-Christian.

736. E.g., articles in *Shaman's Drum:* Matthew Bronson, "Brazilian Spiritistic Healers" (Winter 1986, pp. 23-28); Knud Rasmussen, "The Shaman's Magical Drum," (Summer 1985, pp. 18-24); Frena Bloomfield, "Asking for Rice: The Way of the Chinese Healer" (Summer 1985, pp. 33-37); Naomi

Steinfeld, "Surviving the Chaos of Something Extraordinary" (Spring 1986, pp. 22-27).

737. Each issue of Shaman's Drum lists a "Resources Directory," with numerous workshops, retreats, shaman centers, shaman counseling, etc.

739. Strephon Kaplan-Williams, *Jungian-Senoi Dreamwork Manual*, Novato, CA: Journey Press, 1988.

740. Carlos Castaneda, *The Teachings of Don Juan: A Yaqui Way of Knowledge*, New York, NY: Touchstone, 1974.

741. Naomi Steinfeld, "Surviving the Chaos of Something Extraordinary," *Shaman's Drum*, Spring 1986.

742. Natasha Frazier, "A Model of Contemporary Shamanism," *Shaman's Drum*, Fall 1985.

743. E.g., David Quigley, "Spirits of the Wilderness," *Shaman's Drum*, Fall 1985.

744. Timothy White, "An Interview with Luisah Teish, Daughter of Oshun," *Shaman's Drum*, Spring 1986.

745. Alan Morvay, "An Interview with Sun Bear," *Shaman's Drum*, Winter 1985.

746. Knud Rasmussen, "Horqarnaq and Kiguina Subdue the Storm-Child: An Account of a Copper Eskimo Drum Seance," *Shaman's Drum*, Winter 1985.

750. C.W. Leadbeater, *Man Visible and Invisible*, Wheaton, IL: Theosophical, 1969, rpt.

755. Patricia Garfield, *Creative Dreaming*, New York: NY: Ballantine, 1985.

756. Good starters are ref. 2491; Thomas Szasz, *The Myth of Psychotherapy*, Garden City, NY: Anchor Press, 1978; Martin L. Gross, *The Psychological Society: A Critical Analysis of Psychiatry, Psychotherapy, Psychoanalysis and the Psychological Revolution*, New York: Random House, 1978.

758. Cf. Ken Wilber, *The Spectrums of Consciousness* and *The Atman Project: A Transpersonal View of Human Development*, Wheaton, IL: Theosophical, 1977, 1985; Ken Wilber, *No Boundary: Eastern and Western Approaches to Personal Growth*, Boston, MA: Shambhala, 1979; John White (ed.) *What Is Enlightenment?* Los Angeles, CA: J. P. Tarcher, 1984; Douglas and Barbara Dillon, *An Explosion of Being: An American Family's Journey into the Psychic*, West Nyack, NY: Parker, 1984.

759. Stanislav Grof, Christina Grof (eds.), *Spiritual Emergency*, Los Angeles, CA: J. P. Tarcher, 1989.

760. John White (ed.), *Frontiers of Consciousness*, New York: Avon, 1975.

761. Don Matzat, *Inner Healing: Deliverance or Deception*, Eugene, OR: Harvest House Publishers, 1987.

762. Porter Shiner, "Unwind and Destress," Part 1, *Prevention*, July 1990.

763. Mylan Ryzl, *Hypnosis and ESP*, Chene-Bouirg, Switzerland: Ariston-Verlag, 1976.

764. Maurice M. Tinterow, *Foundations of Hypnosis: From Mesmer to Freud*, Springfield, IL: Charles C. Thomas, 1970.

765. F.D. O'Byrne, *Reichenbach's Letters on Od and Magnetism*, London: Hutchinson & Co., 1926.

766. James Braid, *Neurypnology or the Rationale of Nervous Sleep Considered in Relation with Animal Magnetism*, NY: New York Times/Arno Press, 1976, rpt. of 1843 ed.

767. Vincent Buranelli, *The Wizard from Vienna*, New York: Coward, McCann & Geoghegan, 1975.

768. William Gregory, *Animal Magnetism or Mesmerism and Its Phenomena*, New York: New York Times/Arno Press, 1975, rpt. 1909.

769. Jerome Eden, *Animal Magnetism and the Life Energy*, Hicksville, New York, NY: Exposition Press, 1974.

770. George J. Block comp. ed., *Mesmerism: A Translation of the Original Medical and Scientific Writings of F. A. Mesmer*, Los Altos, CA: William Kaufman, Inc.,1980.

771. Allan Kardec, *The Book of Mediums*, New York: Samuel Weiser, 1978.

772. Frank Podmore, *Mediums of the 19th Century*, New Hyde Park, NY: University Books, 1963.

773. Emma Harding, *Modern American Spiritualism*, New Hyde Park, NY: University Books, 1970, rpt. 1870 ed.

774. Arthur Conan Doyle, *The History of Spiritualism*, New York: Arno Press, 1976, rpt.

775. Vance L. Shepperson, "Hypnotherapy," in David G. Benner, ed., *Psychotherapy in Christian Perspective*, Grand Rapids, MI: Baker, 1987.

776. Walter Martin, "Hypnotism: Medical and Occultic," cassette tape, El Toro, CA: Christian Research Institute, 1985.

779. Rudolf Steiner, "How We Can Help Our Dead," *The Christian Community Journal*, vol. 7, 1953, p. 48; Rudolf Steiner, lecture, "The Dead Are with Us," London, 1945.

780. Rudolf Steiner, *From Jesus to Christ*, London: Rudolf Steiner Press, 1973.

782. Rudolf Steiner, "The Relationship Between the Living and the Dead," *Journal for Anthroposophy*, Autumn 1978.

791. Rudolf Steiner, *Christianity and Occult Mysteries of Antiquity*, Blauvelt, NY: Steinerbooks, 1977.

792. Rudolf Steiner, *Building Stones for an Understanding of the Mystery of Golgotha*, London: Rudolf Steiner Press, 1972.

796. Jane Roberts, *The Nature of Personal Reality: A Seth Book*, New York: Bantam, 1978.

798. John Ankerberg & John Weldon, *Do the Resurrection Accounts Conflict?* . . . (Chattanooga, TN: Ankerberg Theological Research Institute, 1990.)

799. John A. Sanford, *Healing and Wholeness*, New York: Paulist, 1977.

802. Mary Watkins, *Invisible Guests: The Development of Imaginal Dialogues*, Hillsdale, NJ: Analytic Press, 1986.

806. C. Fred Dickason, *Demon Possession and the Christian*, Chicago, IL: Moody Press, 1987.

807. Merrill Unger, *What Demons Can Do to Saints*, Chicago, IL: Moody Press, 1977.

810. Sri Chinmoy, *Astrology, the Supernatural and the Beyond*, Jamaica, NY: Agni Press, 1973.

811. Sri Chinmoy, *Conversations with the Master*, Jamaica, NY: 1977.

812. Emmett Culligan, *Emmett Culligan on Water*, San Bernardino, CA: Crestline Books, 1965.

813. *The American Dowser*, November 1979, p. 187.

814. *The American Dowser*, August 1977 p. 68.

815. E.g., see *The American Dowser*, February 1976, pp. 3, 13; August 1978, pp. 118-19; May 1975, p. 68; November 1977, p. 177; May 1977, pp. 76-77.

816. Edmond Gruss, *The Ouija Board: Doorway to the Occult*, Chicago, IL: Moody Press, 1973, reprinted and expanded in 1995; cf. Stoker Hunt, *Ouija: A Most Dangerous Game*, New York: Harper & Row/Perennial, 1985.

817. G.W. Peters, "Demonology on the Mission Field," (ref 291).

818. Paul Reisser, Teri Reisser, John Weldon, *The Holistic Healers*, Downers Grove, IL: InterVarsity Press, 1982; expanded and republished in 1988 as ref. 1.

823. See New Age Physics in vol. 1 of this series; ref. 719 and Fritjof Capra, *The Tao of Physics*, Berkeley, CA: Shambhala, 1975, pp. 300-07; and Amaury de Riencourt, *The Eye of Shiva: Eastern Mysticism and Science*, New York: William Morrow & Co, 1981; Michael Talbot, *Mysticism and the New Physics*, New York: Bantam, 1981.

825. Nigel Davies, *Human Sacrifice in History and Today*, New York: William Morrow, 1981; also, ref. 249.

826. Monte Kline, "Guilt by Association . . . Are All Wholistic Health Therapies Occult?" two-page brochure, n.p., n.d., from "Total Living," ref. 827.

827. *Christian Health Counselor*, Is. 31, Bellevue, WA: Total Living, P.O. Box 3581, March/April1989.

832. Ken Wilber, "Physics, Mysticism and the New Holographic Paradigm: A Critical Appraisal," in Ken Wilber ed. *The Holographic Paradigm and Other Paradoxes: Exploring the Leading Edge of Science*, Boulder, CO: Shambhala, 1982.

835. See ref. 862; and Charles T. Tart, *On Being Stoned: A Psychological Study of Marijuana Intoxication*, Palo Alto, CA: Science and Behavior Books, 1971, pp. 195-96, 204-06, passim.

836. John Lilly, *The Scientist: A Novel Autobiography*, NY: J.B. Lippincott, 1978.

837. Illustrations can be found in the following magazines: *The Journal of Transpersonal Psychology; Revision; The Common Boundary; Shaman's Drum; Parapsychology Review*; and others.

838. R.C. Zaehner, *Zen Drugs and Mysticism*, New York: Random House/Vintage, 1974.

839. Arnold M. Ludwig, "Altered States of Consciousness," in Charles Tart (ed.) *Altered States of Consciousness*, Garden City, NY: Doubleday/Anchor, 1972.

840. Elsa First, "Visions, Voyages and New Interpretations of Madness" in John White (ed.), *Frontiers of Consciousness*, in ref. 760.

841. Kenneth Ring, "A Transpersonal View of Consciousness: A Mapping of Farther Regions of Inner Space," *Journal of Transpersonal Psychology*, 1974, no. 2.

842. Lynn Andrews, *Jaguar Woman and the Wisdom of the Butterfly Tree*, San Francisco, CA: Harper & Row, 1986.

843. John White (ed.), *What Is Enlightenment?: Exploring the Goal of the Spiritual Path*, Los Angeles, CA: J.P. Tarcher, 1984.

844. Benjamin B. Wolman, Montague Ullman (eds.) *Handbook of States of Consciousness*, New York: Van Nostrand Reinhold Co., 1986.

846. Larry G. Peters, "An Experiential Study of Nepalese Shamanism," *The Journal of Transpersonal Psychology*, volume 13, no. 1, 1981.

849. As told by his friend Colin Wilson, in *Mysteries*, New York: G.P. Putnam's Sons, 1978.

850. The editors of *Psychic* magazine, *Psychics: In Depth Interviews*, New York: Harper & Row, 1972; cf. Arthur Ford's autobiography, *Unknown But Known: My Adventure into the Meditative Dimension*, New York: Harper & Row, 1968.

851. Merrill Unger, *The Haunting of Bishop Pike*, Wheaton, IL: Tyndale House Publishers, 1971.

852. M. Lamar Keene, *The Psychic Mafia*, New York: St. Martin's Press, 1976.

853. Carl Wickland, *Thirty Years Among the Dead*, Van Nuys, CA: Newcastle, 1974, rpt.

854. Hereward Carrington, *Your Psychic Powers and How to Develop Them*, Van Nuys, CA: Newcastle, 1975, rpt.

855. David G. Benner (ed.), *Baker's Encyclopedia of Psychology*, Grand Rapids, MI: Baker, 1986.

858. Ian Stevenson, *Twenty Cases Suggestive of Reincarnation*, Charlottesville, VA: University Press of Virginia, 1978, rev. 2nd ed.

860. Raymond J. Corsini (ed.), *Handbook of Innovative Therapies*, New York: John Wiley, 1981. (This book discusses some 250 therapies.)

861. Bhagwan Shree Rajneesh, "God Is a Christ in a Christ," *Sannyas*, May-June 1978.

862. Michael Harner, "The Sound of Rushing Water," in Michael Harner, ed., *Hallucinogens and Shamanism*, ref. 540.

883. E.g., A.C. Bhaktivedanta Prabhupada, *On the Way to Krishna*, New York: Bhaktivedanta Book Trust, 1973.

884. A video debate between José Silva, John Weldon, Dave Hunt, and George DeSau is available from The John Ankerberg Show, P.O. Box 8977, Chattanooga, TN 37411.

885. The Christ, *New Teachings for an Awakened Humanity*, Santa Clara, CA: S.E.E. (Spiritual Education Endeavors) Publishing, 1986.

886. J.I. Packer, *God's Words*, 1981, and *Knowing God*, 1978. Downers Grove, IL: InterVarsity Press.

887. Stephan Schuhmacher, Gert Woerner (eds.), *The Encyclopedia of Eastern Philosophy and Religion: Buddhism, Hinduism, Taoism, Zen*, Boston, MA: Shambhala, 1989.

889. See refs. 236, 559, 894, and Lee Sannella, *Kundalini: Psychosis or Transcendence?* San Francisco, CA: H.S. Dakin Co., 1977; Swami Sivananda Radha, *Kundalini Yoga for the West*, Boston, MA: Shambhala, 1978.

890. Mineda J. McCleave, "Christian Mysticism and Kundalini," in ref. 236.

891. John Ankerberg, John Weldon, *The Facts on Mormonism*, Eugene, OR: Harvest House Publishers, 1991, and *Behind the Mask of Morminism*, Eugene, OR: Harvest House Publishers, 1996.

893. Gary North, *Unholy Spirits: Occultism and New Age Humanism*, Fort Worth, TX: Dominion Press, 1986.

894. Swami Narayanananda, *The Primal Power in Man or the Kundalini Shakti*, Rishikesh, India: Narayanananda Universal Yoga Trust, 1970.

895. John White, "Some Possibilities for Further Kundalini Research," in ref. 236.

896. R.K. Harrison gen. ed., *Encyclopedia of Biblical and Christian Ethics*, Nashville, TN: Thomas Nelson, 1987.

897. "Kundalini Casualties," *The New Age Journal*, March 1978.

898. Gordon Boals, "Toward a Cognitive Reconceptualization of Meditation," *The Journal of Transpersonal Psychology*, vol. 10, no. 2, 1983.

899. Richard Katz, "Education for Transcendence: Lessons from the !Kung Zhu/Twasi," *The Journal of Transpersonal Psychology*, vol. 5, no. 2, 1973.

900. E.S. Gallegos, "Animal Imagery, The Chakra System and Psychotherapy," The Journal of Transpersonal Psychology, vol. 15, no. 2, 1983.

901. Kirk Bottomly, Jim French, "Christians Meditate Too!" *Yoga Journal*, May/June 1984.

902. Karlis Osis, Edwin Bokert, "ESP and Meditation," *Journal of the American Society for Psychical Research*, January 1971.

903. Herbert Benson, *The Relaxation Response*, New York: William Morrow, 1975.

904. John Weldon, John Ankerberg, *The Facts on the Occult*, Eugene, OR: Harvest House Publishers, 1991.

913. Marsha Newman, "Tai Chi in America," *New Realities*, January/February 1985.

914. Swami Rama *Lectures on Yoga: Practical Lessons on Yoga*, Glenview, IL: Himalayan International Institute of Yoga, Science and Philosophy, 1976, rev.

915. James W. DeMile, *Tao of Wing Chung Do: Mind and Body in Harmony*, vol. 1, part 1, Kirkland, WA: Tao of Wing Chung Do Publishers, 1983.

916. Ed Parker, *Ed Parker's Infinite Insights into Kenpo, Volume 1: Mental Stimulation*, Los Angeles, CA: Delsby Publications, 1984.

917. Da Liu *Tai Chi Chuan and I Ching*, New York: Perennial/Harper & Row, 1978.

918. Ashida Kim, *Secrets of the Ninja*, Secaucus, NJ: Citadel Press, 1981.

919. Stephen K. Hayes, *Ninja: Warrior Ways of Enlightenment*, vol. 2, Burbank, CA: O'Hara Publications, 1985.

920. Peter Payne, *Martial Arts: The Spiritual Dimension*, New York: Crossroad, 1981.

921. Richard J. Schmidt, "Japanese Martial Arts As Spiritual Education," *Somatics*, vol. 4, no. 3, 1983-84.

922. Interview, "Humble Teacher, Deadly Master: The Thoughts and Techniques of Harunaka Hoshino," *Ninja Masters*, Winter 1986.

923. Interview, "The King of Combat: Robert Bussey's Unique and Devastating Approach to Ninjitsu," *Ninja Masters*, Winter 1986.

924. *Ninja* magazine, 1986.

926. Kirtland C. Peterson, "History: In Search of the Real Ninja: Exploring the Past to Better Understand the Present," *Ninja*, December 1986.

930. Koichi Tohei, *Book of Ki: Coordinating Mind and Body in Daily Life*, Tokyo, Japan: Publications, Inc., 1978.

931. Koichi Tohei, *Aikido in Daily Life*, Tokyo, Japan: Rikugei Publishing, 1973.

932. A. Westbrook and O. Ratti, *Aikido and the Dynamic Sphere*, Rutland, VT: Charles E. Tuttle Company, 1974.

933. Stephen K. Hayes, *Ninja: Warrior Path of Togakure*, vol. 3, Burbank, CA: O'Hara Publications, 1986.

934. Edward Maisel, *Tai Chi for Health*, New York: Dell/Delta, 1972.

935. Herman Kauz, *The Martial Spirit: An Introduction to the Origin, Philosophy and Psychology of the Martial Arts*, Woodstock, New York, NY: Overlook Press, 1977.

936. Pierre Huard, Ming Wong, *Oriental Methods of Mental and Physical Fitness: The Complete Book of Meditation, Kinesitherapy, and Martial Arts in China, India, and Japan*, Donald N. Smith, trans., New York: Funk & Wagnalls, 1977.

937. Michael Trulson, "Neurological Disorders and the Martial Arts," *Taekwondo Times: Martial Arts Fitness and Health*, vol. 7, no. 2, January 1987.

939. George Leonard, "Mastering Aikido: On Getting a Black Belt at Age 52," *New Age Journal*, April 1979.

940. John Stevens, "Japan's Traditional Martial Ways," *Yoga Journal*, September/October 1985.

943. We examined over 40 issues of the *Journal of Transpersonal Psychology*. This revealed that Eastern and occult forms of meditation have great importance to transpersonal psychologists.

944. Arthur Hastings, "A Counseling Approach to Parapsychological Experience," *The Journal of Transpersonal Psychology*, vol. 15, no. 2, 1983.

945. Franklin Jones [Da Free John], *The Method of the Siddhas*, Los Angeles, CA: Dawn Horse Press, 1973.

946. Bubba Free John, *No Remedy: An Introduction to the Life and Practices of the Spiritual Community of Bubba Free John*, rev. ed., Lower Lake, CA: Dawn Horse Press, 1976.

948. Walter Bromberg, *From Shaman to Psychotherapist*, Chicago, IL: Henry Regnery, 1975.

949. Roger N. Walsh, Frances Vaughan, eds., *Beyond Ego: Transpersonal Dimensions in Psychology*, Los Angeles, CA: J. P. Tarcher, 1980.

950. Jonathan Venn, "Hypnosis and Reincarnation: A Critique and Case Study," *The Skeptical Inquirer*, Summer 1988.

957. Eligio Stephen Gallegos, Teresa Rennick, *Inner Journeys: Visualization in Growth and Therapy*, Wellingborough, Northamptonshire, England: Turnstone Press, Ltd., 1984.

959. Merlin V. Nelson, "Health Professionals and Unproven Medical Alternatives," *Journal of Pharmacy Technology*, March/April 1988, pp. 60-69; The following methods "have been promoted without adequate scientific evidence to support their usefulness or safety": acupuncture, auriculotherapy, cellular therapy, homeopathy, hypnosis, iridology, naturopathy, nutrition quackery, and many others.

960. Wallace I. Sampson, "When Not to Believe the Unbelievable," and Elie A. Shneour, "The Benveniste Case: A Reappraisal," in *The Skeptical Inquirer*, vol. 14, no. 1, Fall 1989, pp. 90-95.

965. Steven F. Brena, *Yoga and Medicine: The Merging of Yogic Concepts with Modern Medical Knowledge*, NY: Penguin, 1973.

973. John Ankerberg, John Weldon, *When Does Life Begin? and 39 Other Tough Questions on Abortion*, Brentwood, TN: Wolgemuth and Hyatt, 1989. See the authors' *The Facts on Abortion*, Eugene, OR: Harvest House Publishers, 1994.

974. Migi Autore, "The Contemplative Way of Tai Chi Chuan," *Aeropagus*, vol. 3, no. 3, Easter 1990.

975. L.G. Peters, D. Price-Williams, "Towards an Experimental Analysis of Shamanism," *American Fthnologist*, vol. 7, pp. 297-418, 1980.

976. Jerry Mogul, "Tai Chi Chuan: A Taoist Art of Healing," Part One, *Somatics: The Magazine-Journal of the Bodily Arts and Sciences*, Spring 1980.

977. Jerry Mogul, "Tai Chi Chuan: A Taoist Art of Healing, Part Two," *Somatics: The Magazine-Journal of the Bodily Arts and Sciences*, Autumn 1980.

979. Swami Nikhilananda, *Vivekananda, the Yogas and Other Works*, New York: Ramakrishna and Vivekananda Center, 1953.

980. Personal letter, September 21, 1990.

981. Alan Kardec, *The Book of Mediums*, Emma A. Wood, trans., New York: Samuel Weiser, 1978, rpt.

983. Thomas C. Chalmers, "Scientific Quality and the Journal of Holistic Medicine," in ref. 3.

987. Brian H. Butler, "Applied Kinesiology," in ref. 188.

988. George J. Goodheart and Walter H. Schmitt, in ref. 198.

995. Edward Erwin, "Holistic Psychotherapies: What Works?" in ref. 3.

997. Sandy Newhouse, John Amoedo, "Native American Healing," in ref. 197.

1004. *Webster's New Twentieth Century Dictionary*, 2nd ed., 1978.

1005. *Webster's Third International Dictionary*, 1981, p. 1244.

1025. Robert Monroe, *Journeys Out of the Body*, Garden City, NY: Anchor/Doubleday, 1973.

1026. Helen Wambach, *Life Before Life*, New York: Bantam, 1979.

1027. ———, *Reliving Past Lives: The Evidence Under Hypnosis*, New York: Harper & Row, 1978.

1028. Morris Netherton, Nancy Shiffrin, *Past Lives Therapy*, New York: William Morrow, 1978.

1029. Edith Fiore, *You Have Been Here Before: A Psychologist Looks at Past Lives*, New York: Coward, McCann & Geoghegan, 1978.

1034. Gerald G. Jampolsky, "Hypnosis/Active Imagination," in ref. 198.

1039. Bhagwan Shree Rajneesh, "Energy," *Sannyas*, no. 1; January-February. See ref. 1040.

637

1040. See the kundalini issue, *Sannyas*, no. 2, 1976; also Bhagwan Shree Rajneesh, "Suicide or Sannyas," *Sannyas*, no. 2, 1978.

1046. Benjamin B. Wolman, Montague Ullman, eds., *Handbook of States of Consciousness*, New York: Van Nostrand Reinhold, 1986.

1047. Martin Gardner, "Marianne Williamson and 'A Course in Miracles,' " *The Skeptical Inquirer*, Fall 1992.

1048. Richard N. Shrout, *Modern Scientific Hypnosis*, Wellingborough, Northamptonshire: Thorson's 1985.

1049. William Wilson, *Wilson's Old Testament Word Studies*, McLean VA: MacDonald Publishing, n.d.

1050. Spiros Zodhiates, *Hebrew-Greek Key Study Bible*, Chattanooga, TN: AMG Publishers 1994.

1051. John Peter Lange, *Commentary on the Holy Scriptures*, vol. 2 on Deuteronomy 18:22, Grand Rapids, MI: Zondervan, 1980.

1058. Doc-Fai Wong, Jane Hallander, "Tai Chi's Internal Secrets," *Inside Kung Fu*, October 1991.

1062. J.M. Angebert, *The Occult and the Third Reich*, NY: McGraw Hill, 1975; Dusty Skylar, *Gods and Beasts*, NY: Thomas Crowell, 1977.

1063. Barbara Clark, *Growing Up Gifted: Developing the Potential of Children at Home and at School*, Columbus, OH: Merrill Co., 1988.

1064. John Ankerberg, John Weldon, Craig Branch, *Thieves of Innocence: Protecting Our Children from New Age Teaching and Occult Practices*, Eugene, OR: Harvest House Publishers, 1993.

1065. Annette Hollander, *How to Help Your Child Have a Spiritual Life: A Parent's Guide to Inner Development*. New York: A&W Publishers, 1980.

1066. Jane Roberts, *Adventures in Consciousness*, Englewood Cliffs, NJ: Prentice Hall, 1975.

1067. Bhagwan Shree Rajneesh, *The Discipline of Transcendence: Discourses on the 42 Sutras of the Buddha*, vol. 2, Poona, India: Rajneesh Foundation International, 1978.

1068. Carl Rogers, *A Way of Being*, Boston: Houghton Mifflin Co., 1980.

1069. John Ankerberg, John Weldon, *The Coming Darkness: Confronting Occult Deception*, Eugene, OR: Harvest House Publishers, 1993.

1070. John H. Manas, *Divination: Ancient and Modern*, New York: Pythagorean Society, 1947.

1071. Christopher Bird in *New Realities*, vol. 4, nos. 5, 56; and John White, ed., *Frontiers of Consciousness*, p. 244.

1072. *The American Dowser*, August 1975, p. 101.

1073. *The American Dowser*, February 1975, pp. 15-16.

1074. *The American Dowser*, November 1979, p. 90.

1075. *The American Dowser*, November 1974, pp. 132-40.

1076. *The American Dowser*, August 1979, p. 104; May 1976, pp. 57, 70, 87; May 1979, p. 56; August 1978, p. 103; February 1975, pp. 28-29.

1077. *The American Dowser*, August 1978, pp. 118-119.

1078. *The American Dowser*, February 1976, p. 13.

1079.*The American Dowser*, November 1977, p. 177; May 1977, pp. 76-77.

1080. *The American Dowser*, February 1979, pp. 5-6.

1081. *The American Dowser*, May 1977, p. 68.

1082. Holger Kalweit, "When Insanity Is a Blessing: The Message of Shamanism," in ref. 759.

1083. *The American Dowser*, February 1977, p. 31.

1085. John Ankerberg, John Weldon, Craig Branch, *A Parent's Handbook*, Chattanooga, TN: Ankerberg Theological Research Institute, 1992.

1086. John G. Friesen, *Uncovering the Mystery of MPD*, San Bernardino: CA, Here's Life Publishers, 1991.

1087. Erik J. Dingwall, ed., *Abnormal Hypnotic Phenomena: A Survey of Nineteenth Century Cases*, 4 vols., New York: Barnes and Noble, 1967, 1968.

1088. Werner Erhard,"The Transformation of Est," *The Graduate Review*, November 1976.

1089. Ken Ham, "Monkey Ears and Wasted Years," *Acts and Facts*, January 1993, no. 49.

1090. Wilson Van Dusen, "On Meditation" in James Hendricks and Gay Fadiman, eds., *Transpersonal Education: A Curriculum for Feeling and Being*. Englewood Cliffs NJ: Prentice Hall 1976.

1091. Maureen Murdock, "Meditation with Young Children," *The Journal of Transpersonal Psychology*, vol. 10, no. 1.

1092. Deborah Rozman, *Meditation for Children*. Boulder Creek CA: University of the Trees Press, 1989.

1093. David and Sharon Sneed, *The Hidden Agenda: A Critical View of Alternative Medical Therapies*, Nashville, TN: Nelson, 1991.

1095. John Ankerberg, John Weldon, *The Coming Darkness: Confronting Occult Deception*, Eugene, OR: Harvest House Publishers, 1993, appendix.

1096. Brooks Alexander, "Theology from the Twilight Zone," *Christianity Today*, September 18, 1987.

1097. G.H. Pember, *Earth's Earliest Ages and Their Connection with Modern Spiritualism and Theosophy*, New York: Revell, n.d.

1098. This is evident from any number of historical studies. See Paul Kurtz, "Introduction: More Than a Century of Psychical Research," in Paul Kurtz, ed., *A Skeptic's Handbook of Parapsychology*, Buffalo, NY: Prometheus, 1985, pp. xii-xiv; John Beloff, "Historical Overview," in Benjamin B. Wolman, ed., *Handbook of Parapsychology*, New York: Van Nostrand Reinhold, 1977, pp. 4-7; J.B. Rhine, "A Century of Parapsychology" in Martin Ebon, ed., *The Signet Handbook of Parapsychology*, New York: Signet, 1978, p. 11.

1099. E.J. Dingwall, "The Need for Responsibility in Parapsychology: My Sixty Years in Psychical Research" in ref. 102.

1100. Personal correspondence.

1101. Geoffrey Dean, "Does Astrology Need to Be True? Part 1: A Look at the Real Thing," *The Skeptical Inquirer*, vol. 9, no. 2, pp. 166-85.

1102. Lynn Smith, "The New Chic Metaphysical Fad of Channeling," *Los Angeles Times*, December 5, 1986, Part 5.

1103. Nina Easton, "Shirley Maclaine's Mysticism for the Masses," *Los Angeles Times* magazine, September 6, 1987.

1104. E.g., Mark Vaz, "Psychic!—The Many Faces of Kevin Ryerson," interview, *Yoga Journal*, July/August 1986, pp. 26-29, 92; ref. 1326:3, 20, 39, 64-69, 131-32, 167, 237-53, 205-320; Stephan Schwartz, *The Secret Vaults of Time: Psychic Archaeology and the Quest for Man's Beginning*, NY: Grosset & Dunlap, 1978; Gerald G. Jampolsky, *Goodbye to Guilt: Releasing Fear Through Forgiveness*, NY: Bantam, 1985, (based on *A Course in Miracles*); Jane Roberts, *Adventures in Consciousness: An Introduction to Aspect Psychology*, 1975; John Weldon and Zola Levitt, *Psychic Healing*, Chicago, IL: Moody Press, 1982, pp. 7-22, 42-46.

1105. A. Harwood, *Rx: Spiritist As Needed*, New York: John Wiley & Sons, 1977, cited in Albert Villoldo and Stanley Krippner, *Healing States: A Journey into the World of Spiritual Healing and Shamanism*, New York: Fireside/Simon and Schuster, 1987, p. 198.

1106. Walter Martin, *Kingdom of the Cults*, Minneapolis, MN: Bethany House, 1985, rev.

1107. E.g., ref. 574:1, 185; and Jane Roberts, *Seth Speaks*, Englewood Cliffs, NJ: Prentice Hall, pp. 1-2 and cover photo.

1108. E.g., gurus, Sri Chinmoy has produced thousands of paintings by automatic painting. In less than two hours on June 26, 1975, Sri Chinmoy painted 500 paintings according to the publicity booklet, *Sri Chinmoy*, Jamaica, NY: Aum Publications, n.d., pp. 15-18; Rosemary Brown, *Unfinished Symphonies*, New York: William Morrow & Company, 1971. Medium Rosemary Brown has composed hundreds of musical pieces in styles very similar to the famous dead composers she claims work through her.

1109. Mark Vaz, "Psychic!—The Many Faces of Kevin Ryerson," interview, *Yoga Journal*, July/August 1986.

1110. E.g., according to Merv Griffin on "The Merv Griffin Show," July 26, 1986.

1111. Orthodox Christianity and Judaism are almost alone in the universal condemnation of seeking to contact the spirit world. The practice is accepted, variously, among Hindus, Buddhists, Sufis, Sikhs, Muslims, cabalists, Taoists, Animists, etc. See the extensive discussion in James Hastings, ed, *Hasting's Encyclopedia of Religion and Ethics*, New York: Charles Scribner's Sons, n.d., vol. 4, pp. 565-636.

1112. This is proven beyond reasonable doubt by both the history of the occult and modern data from parapsychology. See e.g., Alfred Douglas, *Extra-Sensory Powers: A Century of Psychical Research*, Woodstock, NY: Overlook Press 1977, pp. 87-360; Alan Gauld, *The Founders of Psychical Research*, New York: Shocken Books, 1968, pp. 153-364; Naomi Hintze and Gaither Pratt, *The Psychic Realm, What Can You Believe?* New York: Random House, 1975, pp. 135-223; Norma Bowles and Fran Hynds, *Psi-Search*, San Francisco: Harper & Row, 1978, pp. 51-91.

1113. Elliot Miller, "Channeling—Spiritistic Revelations for the New Age" Part 1, *Christian Research Journal*, Fall 1987.

1114. Satprem, *Sri Aurobindo or the Adventure of Consciousness*, New York: Harper & Row, 1974, p. 199; cf. pp. 197, 201.

1115. Samuel M. Warren, *A Compendium of the Theological Writings of Emanuel Swedenborg*, New York: Swedenborg Foundation, 1977, p. 618; cf. ref. 463:63.

1116. Emanuel Swedenborg, *The True Christian Religion*, New York: E. P. Dutton, 1936, pp. 667-669; Emanuel Swedenborg, *Heaven and Its Wonders and Hell*, New York: Swedenborg Foundation, 1940, pp. 265-268; Rev. John Whitehead, *Posthumous Theological Works of Emanuel Swedenborg*, vol. 1, New York: Swedenborg Foundation, 1969, p. 452; Samuel M. Warren, *A Compendium of the Theological Writings of Emanuel Swedenborg*, New York: Swedenborg Foundation, 1977, pp. 376-77.

1118. Colin Wilson, *The Occult: A History*, New York: Vintage, 1973.

1119. Pat Rodegast, *Emmanuel's Book*, Weston, CT: Friends Press, 1986, pp. 132, 198-99, 200, 201, 227, 232, 205, 161.

1120. Ibid., XX, 88, 145, 151, 208, 223, 228.

1121. Ibid., 29, 30, 33, 39, 42, 44, 169-72, 243.

1122. Ibid., XIX, 71, 74, 76-77, 78, 138, 142-43, 153, 222, 239-41.

1123. Jane Roberts, *The Seth Material*, New York: Bantam, 1976.

1124. Robert E. Leichtman, Carl Japiske, *The Life of the Spirit*, vol. 1. Columbus, OH: Ariel, 1987.

1125. White Eagle Publishing Trust, *Wisdom from White Eagle*, Liss, Hampshire, England, 1978.

1126. Robert E. Leichtman, Carl Japiske, *The Life of the Spirit*, vol. 2. Columbus, OH: Ariel, 1987.

1127. The Christ, *New Teachings for an Awakened Humanity*, Santa Clara, CA: S.E.E. Publishing, 1987, pp. 2, 21, 35, 51, 53, 62, 72, 82, 92-95, 139, 188.

1128. C.S. Lewis, The Screwtape Letters, New York: MacMillan, 1969.

1129. Edmond Gruss, *The Ouija Board: Doorway to the Occult*, Chicago, IL: Moody Press, 1975, reprinted and expanded in 1995.

1130. On human sacrifice see Nigel Davies, *Human Sacrifice in History and Today*, New York: William Morrow, 1981, pp. 13-28, 84-87, 92-98, 275-289; *The Chattanooga Times*, March 25, 1988, where a seven-year-old girl is murdered by a Hindu priest in a ritual offering to a goddess; and Maury Terry, *The Ultimate Evil: An Investigation of America's Most Dangerous Satanic Cult*, Garden City, NY: Doubleday/Dolphin, 1987, introduction, ch. 25; on the Atlanta slayings, Sondra A. O'Neal, Emory University in Atlanta, *King City: Fathers of Anguish, of Blood: The True Study Behind the Atlanta Murders* (unpublished; for her synopsis see ref. 1095, appendix).

1131. Robert Somerlott, *Here, Mr. Splitfoot*, New York: Viking, 1971, p. 12; ref 1129 recommends Dr. Charles C. Cumberland's *Mexican Revolution: Genesis Under Madero*, which identifies Francisco I. Madero, the originator of the Mexican revolution, as a leader of spiritism in Mexico. According to a report in the Wall Street Journal, June 12, 1987, a similar situation may have existed in Panama.

1132. Ref. 389:266; Bhagwan Shree Rajneesh, "Suicide or Sannyas," *Sannyas*, no. 2, 1978, pp. 27-31; ref. 1129: 75; Martin Ebon, ed., *The Satan Trap: Dangers of the Occult*, Garden City, NY: Doubleday, 1976, pp. 232-236; Doreen Irvine, *Freed from Witchcraft*, Nashville, TN: Thomas Nelson, p. 121; J.D. Pearce-Higgins, "Dangers of Automatism," *Spiritual Frontiers*, Autumn 1970, p. 216; Morton Kelsey, *The Christian and the Supernatural*, Minneapolis, MN: Augsburg, 1976, p. 41.

1133. Elliot O'Donnell, *The Menace of Spiritualism*, New York: Frederick A. Stokes, 1920.

1134. Cited in *Human Behavior* magazine, September 1977.

1135. See our *Facts on Islam* for several original refs. cf. J.M. Rodwell, trans., *The Koran*, New York: Dutton, 1977, preface, pp. 5, 13-14.

1136. *Holistic Life* magazine, Summer 1985, p. 30. For another example, see Laeh Garfield and Jack Grant, *Companions in Spirit: A Guide to Working with Your Spirit Helpers*, Berkeley, CA: Celestial Arts, 1984, pp. 92-93.

1137. J. G. Bennett, *Concerning Subud*. NY: University Books 1959.

1138. Aleister Crowley, *Magic in Theory and Practice*, New York: Castel, n.d., pp. 127, 152-53, from ref. 893:286; Leslie A. Shepherd, *Encyclopedia of Occultism and Parapsychology*, vol. 1, Detroit, MI: Gale Research Company, 1979, p. 203; cf. J. Symonds, K. Grant, *The Confessions of Aleister Crowley*, New York: Bantam, 1971, pp. 575-76.

1139. Mary Lutens, *Krishnamurti: The Years of Awakening*, New York: Avon 1976.

1142. Petr Skrabanek, James McCormick, *Follies and Fallacies in Medicine*, Buffalo, NY: Prometheus, 1990.

1143. Kurt Butler, "A Consumer's Guide to 'Alternative Medicine,' " Buffalo, NY: Prometheus, 1992.

1163. J. Dover Wellman, et al., *The Christian Parapsychologist*, vol. 5, no. 7, Michaelmass, 1984.

1164. John L. Nevius, *Demon Possession*, Grand Rapids, MI: Kregel, 1970. See chs. 2, 8-10, 14-18.

1165. Charles and Frances Hunter (as told by Roland Buck), *Angels on Assignment*, Houston, TX: Hunter Books, 1979, pp. 22-24, 52, 29, 77, 81, 116-30, 142; James Bjornstad, "Angels on Assignment," in Institute of Contemporary Christianity newsletter, January/February 1980, pp. 2-3 (Box A, Oakland, NJ 07436); Christian Research Institute fact sheet, "Angels on Assignment" by Leah Grossman and Walter Martin, 1979, Box 500, San Juan Capistrano, CA 92693, pp. 1-2, 10-12.

1166. G. Don Gilmore, *Angels, Angels Everywhere*, NY: Pilgrim Press; 1981. See also ref. 574:63, 178-277.

1167. Kenneth Copeland, *The Laws of Prosperity*, Fort Worth, TX: Kenneth Copeland Publications, 1974.

1168. Gloria Copeland, *God's Will Is Prosperity*, Fort Worth, TX: Kenneth Copeland Publications, 1978.

1169. Charles Capps, *Releasing the Ability of God*, England, AZ: Charles Capps Publishers, 1978.

1170. Charles Capps, *Angels*, England, AZ: Charles Capps Publishers, 1984.

1171. Jerry Savelle, *Energizing Your Faith*, Fort Worth, TX: Jerry Savelle Ministries, 1983.

1172. John Osteen, *Unraveling the Mystery of the Blood Covenant*, Houston, TX: John Osteen Ministries, 1987.

1173. Robert Tilton, *Climb Your Ladder of Success*, Dallas: Robert Tilton Ministries, 1988.

1175. In *The Christian Sentinel*, vol. 1, no. 1.

1176. William Branham, *Footnotes on the Sands of Time: The Autobiography of William Marrian*

*Branham*, Jeffersonville, IN: Spoken Word Publishers, 1976; cf., pp. 55-91, 117, 177, 590, 647, 675.

1177. Edward W. Oldring, *I Work with Angels*, Vancouver, B.C.: Note of Joy Books, 1979.

1178. Kenneth Copeland, "Take Time to Pray," *Believers Voice of Victory*, February 1987, p. 9. In a subsequent issue, Copeland explained that he does believe in Christ's deity and that Jesus only meant to say He never claimed to be God while on earth (prepublication copy, p. 1). But this is not true: for example, the Gospel of John is full of Christ's claim to be God while on earth—John 8:58; 10:30; 14:9; 15:26; 20:28,29). Even the Kenneth Copeland Ministry staff admit in a letter dated February 9, 1988 (on file) that, while on earth, "Jesus revealed His deity only in a very limited number of situations." Copeland's own staff denies Copeland's statements.

1179. Kenneth Hagin, *I Believe in Visions*, Tulsa, OK: Kenneth Hagin Ministries, 1984.

1192. Nicholas deVore, *Encyclopedia of Astrology*, Totowa, NJ: Littlefield Adams & Co., 1976.

1193. Lawrence E. Jerome, *Astrology Disproved*, Buffalo, NY: Prometheus Books, 1977.

1195. Roger B. Culver and Philip A. Ianna, *Astrology: True or False, a Scientific Evaluation*, Buffalo, NY: Prometheus Books (1988 update of their *The Gemini Syndrome*).

1196. June Wakefield, *Cosmic Astrology: The Religion of the Stars*, Lakemont, GA: CSA Press, 1968.

1197. Jeff Mayo, *Astrology*, London: Hodder & Stoughton Ltd., 1978.

1199. Marcus Allen, *Astrology for the New Age: An Intuitive Approach*, Sebastopol, CA: CRCS Publications, 1979.

1200. David Pingree, "Astrology," *The Encyclopaedia Britannica*, 15th ed. vol. 2 Macropaedia, Chicago, IL: University of Chicago Press, pp. 219-23.

1201. Franz Cumont, *Astrology and Religion Among the Greeks and Romans*, New York: Dover, 1960.

1202. Keith Thomas, *Religion and the Decline of Magic*, New York: Charles Scribner's Sons, 1971.

1203. Manly P. Hall, *The Story of Astrology*, Los Angeles: Philosophical Research Society, 1975.

1204. John Anthony West and Jan Gerhard Toonder, *The Case for Astrology*, Baltimore, ME: Penguin Books, 1973.

1205. R.B. Culver and P.A. Ianna, *The Gemini Syndrome: A Scientific Evaluation of Astrology*, Buffalo, NY: Prometheus Books, 1984 Rev.

1206. Donald T. Regan, *For the Record: From Wall Street to Washington*, New York: Harcourt Brace Jovanovich, 1988.

1207. "Good Heavens!" *Time magazine*, May 16, 1988.

1208. "The President's Astrologers," *People Weekly*, May 23, 1988, and *Moody Monthly*, July-August, 1988, p. 10.

1209. Brooks Alexander, "My Stars!: Astrology in the White House," Spiritual Counterfeits Project, Berkeley, CA, 1988.

1210. John Weldon, "Astrology: An Inside Look," Part 1, *News & Views*, August 1988.

1213. Bernard Gittelson, *Intangible Evidence*, New York: Simon & Schuster, 1987.

1214. Derek and Julia Parker, *The Compleat* [sic] *Astrologer*, New York: Bantam, 1978.

1215. Letter from Dr. Atlas Laster, Jr., September 23, 1988, containing a copy of a letter by astrologer Harry Darling M.D., approving his Ph.D. dissertation on astrology submitted to the University of Pittsburgh ("On the Psychology of Astrology: The Use of Genethliacal Astrology in Psychological Counseling," 1976).

1216. Carol Cocciardi ed., *The Psychic Yellow Pages*, Saratoga, CA: Out of the Sky, 1977.

1217. American Federation of Astrologers, *50th Anniversary AFA 1988 Convention Program*, Tempe, AZ: American Federation of Astrologers, 1988.

1218. Sir John Manolesco, *Scientific Astrology*, New York: Pinnacle Books, 1973.

1219. In Kurt Goedelman, "Seeking Guidance from the Stars of Heaven," *Personal Freedom Outreach Newsletter*, July-September 1988. The figure is probably exaggerated, though a significant number of major corporations do use astrology in some fashion.

1220. Liz Greene and Howard Sasportas, *The Development of the Personality (Seminars in Psychological Astrology, Volume 1)*. York Beach, ME: Samuel Weiser, 1988.

1222. Dane Rudhyar, *From Humanistic to Transpersonal Astrology*, Palo Alto, CA: The Seed Center, 1975.

1223. Bernard Rosenblum, *The Astrologer's Guide to Counseling*, Reno, NV: CRCS Publications, 1983.

1225. Alice O. Howell, *Jungian Symbolism in Astrology*, Wheaton, IL: Quest/Theosophical Publishing House, 1987.

1226. Dr. Karen Hamaker-Zondag, *Planetary Symbolism in the Horoscope* (The Jungian Symbolism and Astrology Series Vol. 2). York Beach, ME: Samuel Weiser, 1985.

1233. Joanne Sanders, "Connecting Therapy to the Heavens," *The Common Boundary*, Janurary-February 1987.

1234. Owen S. Rachleff, *Sky Diamonds: The New Astrology*, New York: Popular Library, 1973.

1235. Cyril Fagan, *The Solunars Handbook*, Tucson, AZ: Clancy Publications, 1976.

1236. Richard Nolle, *Interpreting Astrology: New Techniques and Perspectives*, Tempe, AZ: American Federation of Astrologers, 1986.

1237. Doris Chase Doane, *Astrology: Thirty Years Research*, Tempe, AZ: American Federation of Astrologers, 1985.

1238. Jeff Green, *Pluto: The Evolutionary Journey of the Soul*, Vol. 1, St. Paul, MN: Llewellyn Publications, 1988.

1241. David and Gina Cochrane, *New Foundations for Astrology*, Alachua, FL: Astrological Counseling and Research, 1977.

1242. Mae R. Wilson-Ludlam, *Interpret Your Rays Using Astrology*, Tempe, AZ: American Federation of Astrologers, 1986.

1243. Udo Rudolph, *The Hamburg School of Astrology: An Explanation of its Methods*, England: The Astrological Association, 1973.

1244. Sabian Publishing Society, *Astrology Books by Marc Edmund Jones: A Commentary*, Stanwood, WA: Sabian Publishing Society, 1987.

1245. Marc Edmund Jones, *The Counseling Manual in Astrology*, Tempe, AZ: American Federation of Astrologers, 1982.

1246. James T. Braha, *Ancient Hindu Astrology for the Modern Western Astrologer*, North Miami, FL: Hermetician Press, 1986.

1247. Gouri Shankar Kapoor, *Remedial Measures in Astrology*, New Delhi, India: Ranjan Publications, 1985.

1248. Derek Walters, *Chinese Astrology*, Wellingborough, North Amptonshire, England: The Aquarian Press, 1987.

1249. K.C. Tunnicliffe, *Aztec Astrology*, Essex, Great Britain: L.N. Fowler & Co., Ltd., 1979.

1250. Pamela A.F. Crane, *Draconic Astrology: An Introduction to the Use of Draconic Charts in Astrological Interpretation*, Wellingborough, North Amptonshire, England: Aquarian Press, 1987.

1251. Margaret H. Gammon, *Astrology and the Edgar Cayce Readings*, Virginia Beach, VA: ARE Press, 1987.

1252. Edward K. Wilson, Jr., *The Astrology of Theosophy*, Tempe, AZ: American Federation of Astrologers, 1987.

1253. Jane A. Evans, *Twelve Doors to the Soul: Astrology of the Inner Self*, Wheaton, IL: Quest/Theosophical Publishing House, 1983.

1254. Sybil Leek, *My Life in Astrology*, Englewood Cliffs, NJ: Prentice Hall, 1972.

1255. Doreen Valiente, *An ABC of Witchcraft Past and Present*, New York: St. Martin's Press, 1973.

1256. Mary Devlin, *Astrology and Past Lives*, West Chester, PA: Para Research, Inc., 1987.

1257. Joan Hodgson, *Reincarnation Through the Zodiac*, Reno, NV: CRCS Publications, 1978.

1258. Alice A. Bailey, *Esoteric Astrology*, New York: Lucis Publishing, 1975.

1259. Max Heindel, *Your Child's Horoscope* Vol. 2, Oceanside, CA: The Rosicrucian Fellowship, 1973.

1260. Thomas H. Burgoyne, *The Light of Egypt or the Science of the Soul and the Stars*, Vol. 1, Albuquerque, NM: Sun Publishing, 1982.

1262. Edward Doane, *Aquarian Age Philosophy*, Tempe, AZ: American Federation of Astrologers, 1979.

1263. Richard Nolle, *Critical Astrology: Investigating the Cosmic Connection*, Tempe, AZ: American Federation of Astrologers, 1980.

1264. Joan McEvers, ed., *Spiritual, Metaphysical and New Trends in Modern Astrology*, St. Paul, MN: Llewellyn Publications, 1988.

1265. Doris Chase Doane, *How to Prepare and Pass an Astrologers Certificate Exam*, Tempe, AZ: American Federation of Astrologers, 1985.

1266. Sage Mantreswara, *Jataka Phaladeepika or Hindu Astrology's Light on the Fruits of Action*, Trans. K.N. Saraswathy, Madras, South India: Kadalangudi Publications, 1983.

1267. *The Los Angeles Times*, January 15, 1975.

1269. Michel Gauquelin, *Birth Times: A Scientific Investigation of the Secrets of Astrology*, New York: Hill and Wang, 1983.

1270. Mark Urban-Lurain, *Astrology as Science: A Statistical Approach*, Tempe, AZ: American Federation of Astrologers, 1984.

1271. Ivan W. Kelly and Don H. Saklofske, "Alternative Explanations in Science: The Extroversion-Introversion Astrological Effect," *The Skeptical Inquirer*, vol. 5, no. 4, pp. 33-39.

1272. Two articles: 1) Geoffrey A. Dean, I.W. Kelly, James Rotton, and D.H. Saklofske, "The Guardian Astrology Study: A Critique and Re-analysis," pp. 327-38; 2) James Rotton, "Astrological Forecasts and the Commodity Market: Random Walks as a Source of Illusory Correlation," pp. 339-47, *The Skeptical Inquirer*, vol. 9, no. 4.

1273. H.J. Eysenck and D.K.B. Nias, "Astrology: Science or Superstition," book review, *The Skeptical Inquirer*, vol. 7, no. 3, pp. 65-67.

1274. Four articles: 1) Paul Kurtz, Marvin Zelen, and George Abell, "Results of the U.S. Test of the 'Mars Effect' are Negative," pp. 19-25; 2) Dennis Rawlins, "Report on the U.S. Test of the Gauquelins 'Mars Effect,'" pp. 26-30; 3) Michael and Francoise Gauquelin, "Star U.S. Sportsmen Display the Mars

Effect," pp. 31-43; 4) Paul Kurtz, Marvin Zelen, and George Abell, "Response to the Gauquelins," pp. 44-63, in *The Skeptical Inquirer*, vol. 4, no. 2, Winter 1979-80.

1275. Dennis Rawlins, "Follow-up" [on the "Mars Effect"], *The Skeptical Inquirer*, vol. 6, no. 2, pp. 58-68.

1276. Michel Gauquelin, "Zodiac and Personality: An Empirical Study," *The Skeptical Inquirer*, vol. 6, no. 3, pp. 57-65.

1277. ———, *The Scientific Basis of Astrology: Myth or Reality*, New York: Stein and Day, 1973.

1278. Francoise Gauquelin, *Psychology of the Planets*, San Diego, CA: Astro Computing Services, 1987.

1279. Ralph W. Bastedo, "An Empirical Test of Popular Astrology," *The Skeptical Inquirer*, vol. 3, no. 1, pp. 17-38; cf. vol. 10, no. 2, pp. 129-43.

1280. Paul Kurtz and Andrew Fraknoi, "Tests of Astrology Do Not Support Its Claims," *The Skeptical Inquirer*, vol. 9, no. 3, pp. 210-12.

1281. John D. McGervey, "A Statistical Test of Sun-sign Astrology," *The Zetetic* [earlier title for *The Skeptical Inquirer*], vol. 1, no. 2, pp. 49-54.

1282. I.W. Kelly, James Rotton, and Roger Culver, "The Moon Was Full and Nothing Happened," *The Skeptical Inquirer*, vol. 10, no. 2, pp. 129-143.

1283. Douglas P. Lackey, "Controlled Test of Perceived Horoscope Accuracy," *The Skeptical Inquirer*, vol. 6, no. 1, pp. 29-31.

1284. Guy Playfair and Scott Hill, *The Cycles of Heaven: Cosmic Forces and What They Are Doing to You*, New York: St. Martin's Press, 1978.

1285. Various authors, "Special Report: Astrology and the Presidency," *The Skeptical Inquirer*, vol. 13, no. 1, pp. 3-16.

1286. Charles Strohmer, *What Your Horoscope Doesn't Tell You*, Wheaton, IL: Tyndale House Publishers, 1988.

1287. Joseph F. Goodavage, *Astrology: The Space Age Science*, New York: Signet, 1967.

1289. John Weldon, "Astrology: An Inside Look," Part 2, *News & Views*, October 1988.

1290. Charles E.O. Carter, *The Principles of Astrology*. Wheaton, IL: Quest/Theosophical Publishing House, 1977.

1291. Daniel Logan, *The Reluctant Prophet*, 1980.

1292. Sepharial [sic], *A Manual of Occultism*, New York: Samuel Weiser, 1978.

1294. Dane Rudhyar, *The Practice of Astrology as a Technique in Human Understanding*, New York: Penguin Books, 1975.

1295. Henry Weingarten, *The Study of Astrology: Book 1*, New York: ASI Publishers, 1977.

1296. Richard Cavendish, *The Black Arts*, New York: G.P. Putnam's Sons, 1967.

1301. Sylvia De Long, *The Art of Horary Astrology and Practice*, Tempe, AZ: American Federation of Astrologers, 1988.

1306. Tracy Marks, *The Art of Chart Interpretation*, Sebastopol, CA: CRCS Publications, 1986.

1309. Firmicus Maternus, *Ancient Astrology Theory and Practice* [original title: *Matheseos Libri VIII, 334 A.D.*], trans. Jean Rhys Bram, Parkridge, NJ: Noyes Press, 1975.

1310. Roy A. Gallant, *Astrology Sense or Nonsense?* Garden City, NY: Doubleday, 1974.

1311. E.g., P. Thomas, *Hindu Religion Customs and Manners*, Bombay, India: D.B. Taraporevala Sons & Co., 1960; Alain Danielou, *Hindu Polytheism*, New York: Bollingen/Random House, 1964; Nigel Davies, *Human Sacrifice in History and Today*, New York: William Morrow & Co., 1981; T.K. Oesterreich, *Possession: Demoniacal and Other Among Primitive Races, in Antiquity, the Middle Ages, and Modern Times*, Secaucus, NJ: Citadel Press, 1974; Felicitas D. Goodman, et al., *Trance Healing and Hallucination: Three Field Studies in Religious Experience*, New York: John Wiley & Sons, 1974; Paul Hawken, *The Magic of Findhorn*, New York: Bantam, 1976.

1315. Cynthia Bohannon, *The North and South Nodes: The Guideposts of the Spirit: A Comprehensive Interpretation of the Nodal Placements*, Jacksonville, FL: Arthur Publications, 1987.

1318. E.g., Sri Chinmoy, *Astrology: The Supernatural and Beyond*, Jamaica, NY: Agni Press, 1973; Elman Bacher, *Studies in Astrology* (9 vols.), Oceanside, CA: The Rosicrucian Fellowship, 1968; refs 28,42, 120,240, as given in ref. 83.

1320. Courses taken at the July 4-8, 1988, American Federation of Astrologers Convention in Las Vegas, Nevada. Statement is by the instructor: Irene Diamond, "Let's Talk About God"; Randall Leonard, "The Crystals & Astrology"; Capel McCutcheon, "Esoteric Astrology"; Sue Lovett, "Make Lemonade Out of Those Lemons"; Doris Chase Doane, "The Art of Transmutation"; Maxine Taylor, "Can I Rise Above My Chart?"; Terry Warneke, "The Archetype of Planets"; Karen Hamaker-Zondag, "Elements and Crosses."

1322. Former astrologer Karen Winterburn, personal phone conversation, August 1988.

1324. Letter from Dr. Atlas Laster, Jr., September 12, 1988.

1326. Jon Klimo, *Channeling: Investigations on Receiving Information from Paranormal Sources*, Los Angeles, CA: J.P. Tarcher, 1981.

1327. *Los Angeles Times*, September 14, 1975.

1328. Kurt Koch, *Satan's Devices*, Grand Rapids, MI: Kregel, 1978.

1329. Stephen Arroyo, *Astrology, Karma and Transformation: The Inner Dimensions of the Birth Chart*, Davis, CA: CRCS Publications, 1978.

1330. Robert A. Morey, *Horoscopes and the Christian*, Minneapolis, MN: Bethany House, 1981.

1331. Alan Oken, *Astrology: Evolution and Revolution—a Path to Higher Consciousness Through Astrology*, New York: Bantam, 1976.

1332. John Warwick Montgomery, *Principalities and Powers: The World of the Occult*, Minneapolis, MN: Bethany Fellowship, 1973.

1333. Sydney Omarr, *My World of Astrology*, Hollywood, CA: Wilshire Book Company, 1968.

1334. Bhagwan Shree Rajneesh, *The Rajneesh Bible*, vol. 1, Rajneeshpuram, OR: Rajneesh Foundation International, 1985.

1336. Wim van Dam, *Astrology and Homosexuality*, York Beach, ME: Samuel Weiser, 1985.

1337. Jess Stearn, *A Time for Astrology*, New York: Signet, 1972.

1341. Teri King, *Marriage, Divorce and Astrology*, New York: Harper & Row, 1988.

1342. Marc Edmund Jones, *The Sabian Manual: A Ritual for Living*, Boulder, CO: Sabian/Shambhala Publications, rev., 1976.

1344. Excerpted from various est publications, especially *The Graduate Review*, 1976-79 issues.

1346. Interview with Werner Erhard, "All I Can Do Is Lie," *East-West Journal*, September 1974, rpt.

1347. William Greene, *est: Four Days to Make Your Life Work*, NY: Simon and Schuster, 1976.

1348. Stewart Emery, *Actualizations: You Don't Have to Rehearse to Be Yourself*, Garden City, NY: Doubleday, 1978.

1349. James Martin, *Actualizations: Beyond est*, San Francisco: San Francisco Book Company, 1977.

1352. *The American Dowser*, May 1976, p. 90; February 1977, pp. 20-21; ref. 514:3-4.

1353. Stephan Bodian, "Editorial," "Perils of the Path" issue, *Yoga Journal*, July-August 1985.

1354. Dio Urmilla Neff, "Tumbling from the Pedestal: What Makes Spiritual Teachers Go Renegade?" *Yoga Journal*, July-August 1985.

1355. Edward Rice, *Eastern Definitions*, Garden City, NY: Doubleday, 1978.

1356. Ingrid Fischer-Schribners, et al., *The Encyclopedia of Eastern Philosophy and Religion*, Boston, MA: Shambhala, 1989.

1357. S.G.F. Brandon, ed., *Dictionary of Comparative Religion*, NY: Charles Scribner's Sons, 1970.

1358. Troy Wilson Organ, *Hinduism*, New York: Baron's Educational Series, 1974, pp. 241-42; Ninian Smart, "Indian Philosophy," in Paul Edward's ed., *The Encyclopedia of Philosophy*, vol. 4, New York: Collier Macmillan, 1973, pp. 155-56; Sarvepalli Radhakrishnan, *Indian Philosophy*, New York: Macmillan, 1951, vol. 2, p. 22; "Vedas," in James Hastings, ed., *Hastings' Encyclopedia of Religion and Ethics*, vol. 12, NY: Charles Scribner's Sons, n.d., p. 597; s.v., "India" in Samuel M. Jackson, ed., *The New Schaff-Herzog Encyclopedia of Religious Knowledge*, vol. 5, Grand Rapids, MI: Baker, 1977, p. 473; Sarvepalli Radhakrishnan and Charles A. Moore, *A Source Book in Indian Philosophy*, Princeton, NJ: Princeton University Press, 1973, p. 506.

1359. Swami Prabhavananda and Frederick Manchester, *The Spiritual Heritage of India*, New York: Doubleday & Company, 1964.

1360. S.v., "Vedas," *Encyclopaedia Britannica* 15th ed. vol. 10, Micropaedia.

1361. S.v. "Indian Philosophy," in Paul Edwards, editor-in-chief, *Encyclopedia of Philosophy*, vol. 4. New York: Collier Macmillan, 1973.

1362. E.g., s.v., "Rsi," Margaret and James Stutley, *Harper's Dictionary of Hinduism*, New York: Harper & Row, rev., 1977.

1363. Howard F. Vos, ed., *Religions in a Changing World*, Chicago, IL: Moody Press, 1969.

1364. Paramahansa Yogananda, *Autobiography of a Yogi*, Los Angeles, CA: Self Realization Fellowship, 1972.

1365. E.g., Robert A. Morey, *Battle of the Gods: The Gathering Storm in Modern Evangelicalism*, Southbridge, MA: Crown Publishers, 1989.

1366. These facts are public knowledge, conceded by knowledgeable members and/or documented in the author's individual chapters on these subjects in his *Critical Encyclopedia of New Religions and Sects in America*, passim, unpublished. Anyone familiar with Hinduism who thoroughly reads the literature of these groups cannot deny the influence of Hinduism upon them. On the Eckankar plagiarism, see *SCP Journal*, "Eckankar: A Hard Look at a New Religion," vol. 3, 1979. On Scientology, see Church of Scientology Information Service, *Scientology: A World Religion Emerges in the Space Age*, Church of Scientology of California, n.p.p., 1974, pp. 3-8. On Erhard and Muktananda, see the official biography of Erhard by W.W. Bartley III, ref 1951

1367. E.g., Da Free John, *Compulsory Dancing*, Clearlake Highlands, CA: Dawn Horse Press, 1980.

1368. A.L. Basham, "Hinduism," in R.C. Zaehner, ed., *The Concise Encyclopedia of Living Faiths*, Boston, MA: Beacon Press, 1967.

1369. S.v., "Vedanta" in *Encyclopaedia Britannica*, 15th ed., vol. 10, Micropaedia.

1370. Swami Satprakashananda, *Hinduism and Christianity*, St. Louis, MO: Vedanta Society, 1975, p. 9;

cf. Sarvepalli Radhakrishnan, *Indian Philosophy*, New York: Macmillan, 1951, vol. 2, p. 28.

1371. S.v., "Vedanta" in *Encyclopaedia Britannica* 15th ed., Micropaedia, p. 375; "Indian Philosophy," Paul Edwards, editor-in-chief, *Encyclopedia of Philosophy*, vol. 4, New York: Collier Macmillan, 1972, rpt., pp. 155-56; R. Garbe, "Vedanta" in James Hastings, ed., *Hasting's Encyclopedia of Religion and Ethics*, New York, NY: Charles Scribner's Sons, n.d., vol. 12, pp. 597-98.

1372. See Swami Nikhilananda, "A Discussion of Brahman in the Upanishads," *The Upanishads, A New Translation, Four Volumes*, New York: Bonanza/Crown Publishers, Harper & Brothers, 1949.

1373. Christopher Isherwood, "Introduction," in Christopher Isherwood, ed., *Vedanta for the Western World*, New York: Viking Press, 1968.

1374. John Yale, ed., *What Religion Is in the Words of Vivekananda*, New York: Julian Press, 1962.

1375. Paramahansa Yogananda, *Man's Eternal Quest*, Los Angeles, CA: Self Realization Fellowship, 1975.

1376. Ram Dass, "A Ten-Year Perspective," *The Journal of Transpersonal Psychology*, vol. 24, no. 2.

1377. Meher Baba, *Discourses*, vol. 3, .San Francisco, CA: Sufism Reoriented, 1973;

1378. Bubba Free John, *The Way That I Teach*, Middletown, CA: Dawn Horse Press, 1978.

1379. Bhagwan Shree Rajneesh, "Society Is an Illusion," *Sannyas*, March-April 1979.

1380. Bhagwan Shree Rajneesh, *I Am the Gate*, San Francisco, CA: Perennial Library, 1978.

1381. Robert A. McDermott, *The Essential Aurobindo*, New York: Schocken Books, 1974.

1382. Bertrand Russell, *Why I Am Not a Christian and Other Essays*, NY: Simon and Schuster/Touchstone, 1957.

1383. Moti Lal Pandit, "Yoga As Methods of Liberation," *Update: A Quarterly Journal On New Religious Movements*, Aarhus, Denmark: Dialogue Center, vol. 9, no. 4, December 1985, p. 41.

1384. John Snyder, *Reincarnation Versus Resurrection*, Chicago, IL: Moody Press, 1984, pp. 38-41; Mark Albrecht, *Reincarnation: A Christian Appraisal*, Downers Grove, IL: InterVarsity, 1982, pp. 71-78; Norman L. Geisler, J. Yutaka Amano, *The Reincarnation Sensation*, Wheaton, IL: Tyndale House Publishers, 1987, pp. 78, 82. Robert A. Morey, *Reincarnation and Christianity*, Minneapolis, MN: Bethany House, 1980, pp. 24-30, passim.

1385. Reprint of "Oh Benares" article from *National Review* in *SCP Newsletter*, 1985.

1386. Primary references are supplied in John Ankerberg, John Weldon, *Can You Trust Your Doctor? The Complete Guide to New Age Medicine and Its*

*Threat to Your Family*, Brentwood, TN: Wolgemuth & Hyatt, 1991, pp. 287-301, see *Altered States of Consciousness* herein

1387. See John Ankerberg, John Weldon, Ibid., pp. 146-47.

1388. Brooks Alexander, "Book Review: *Riders of the Cosmic Circuit*," SCP Journal, vol. 7, no. 1, 1987.

1389. Daniel Goleman, "The Buddha on Meditation and States of Consciousness" in Charles Tart, (ed.), *Transpersonal Psychologies*, New York: Harper Colophon Books, 1977.

1390. See ref. 1364:16,55-57,132,137,190, 475-79.

1391. Paramahansa Yogananda, "Where Are Our Departed Loved Ones?" *Self Realization* Magazine, Spring 1978.

1392. Sri Aurobindo and the Mother, *On Occultism*, comp. Vijay, Pondicherry, India: Sri Aurobindo Society, 1972.

1393. Sri Aurobindo, *A Practical Guide to Integral Yoga*, comp. Manishai, Pondicherry, India: Sri Aurobindo Ashram, 1973.

1394. Swami Nikhilananda, *Vivekananda, the Yogas and Other Works*, New York: Ramakrishna-Vivekananda Center, 1953.

1395. Swami Vivekananda, *Teachings of Swami Vivekananda*, Calcutta, India: Swami Budhananda, 1975, pp. 91-92.

1396. Swami Muktananda, *Mukteshwari, Part 2*, Ganeshpuri, India: Shree Gurudev Ashram, 1973.

1397. Swami Muktananda, *American Tour 1970*, Piedmont, CA: Shree Gurudev Siddha Yoga Ashram, 1974.

1398. Swami Satchidananda, *An Evening with Swami Satchidananda*, New York: Integral Yoga Institute, 1974, p. 6 (pamphlet).

1399. Sathya Sai Baba, *Sathyam-Shivam Sundaram*, Part 3, Bangalore, India: Sri Sathya Sai Publication and Education Foundation, 1973.

1400. _____, *Sathya Sai Speaks*, vol. 9, Bangalore, India: Sri Sathya Sai Publication and Education Foundation, n.d.

1401. Ian Stevenson, *Twenty Cases Suggestive of Reincarnation*, 2nd. ed., rev., Charlottesville, VA: University Press of Virginia, 1978, pp. 374-77.

1402. Swami Vishnudevananda, *The Complete Illustrated Book of Yoga*, New York: Pocket Books, 1972.

1403. Bhagwan Shree Rajneesh, *The Rajneesh Bible*, vol. 1, Rajneeshpuram, OR: Rajneesh Foundation International, 1985.

1404. Da Free John, *Scientific Proof of the Existence of God Will Soon Be Announced at the White House*, Clearlake Highlands, CA: Dawn Horse Press, 1980.

1406. John Ankerberg, John Weldon, *The Case for Jesus the Messiah*, Chattanooga, TN: Ankerberg Theological Research Institute, 1989, Rev. ed., published by Baker Books, 1996.

1407. I. M. Lewis, *Ecstatic Religion: An Anthropological Study of Spirit Possession and Shamanism*, 1975; ref. 862:17,20; ref 142; ref.583; ref561:12.

1408. Sri Aurobindo, *The Mother*, Pondicherry, India: Sri Aurobindo Ashram, 1977.

1409. Bhagwan Shree Rajneesh, "This Is Not a Democracy", "*Sannyas*," no. 4, 1978.

1410. Sathya Sai Baba, *Sathya Sai Speaks*, vol. 2, Bangalore, India, Sri Sathya Sai Publication and Education Foundation, n.d.

1411. As given by SaiBaba's principal biographer, C. B. Purdom, *The God-Man*, London: George Allen and Unwin, 1964; although a committed disciple of Sai Baba and his leading biographer, Purdom warns against excessive obedience.

1412. *Oregon Magazine*, September 1984, p. 66; *Los Angeles Times*, March 18, 1979.

1413. Bhagwan Shree Rajneesh, as cited in Vasant Joshi, *The Awakened One: The Life and Work of Bhagwan Shree Rajneesh*, San Francisco, CA: Harper & Row, 1982.

1414. Bhagwan Shree Rajneesh, as cited in Ma Satya Bharti, *Drunk on the Divine: An Account of Life in the Ashram of Bhagwan Shree Rajneesh*, New York: Grove Press, 1981.

1415. Bhagwan Shree Rajneesh, "In The Cave of the Heart Is Freedom," *Sannyas*, no. 5, 1979.

1416. Sathya Sai Baba interview in Samuel Sandweiss, *Sai Baba: The Holy Man and the Psychiatrist*, San Diego, CA: Birth Day Publishing, 1975, p. 206.

1417. Sathya Sai Baba, *Sathya Sai Speaks*, vol. 4. Bangalore, India: Sri Sathya Sai Publication and Education Foundation, n.d. (See ref. 485.)

1418. ———, *Sathya Sai Speaks*, vol. 7. Bangalore India: Sri Sathya Sai Publication and Education Foundation, n.d. (See Ref. 485.)

1419. Meher Baba, *The Path of Love*, New York: Samuel Weiser, 1976.

1421. Lakh Raj Puri, *Radha Swami Teachings*, Punjab, India: K.L. Khanna, secretary, Radha Soami Satsang Beas, 1972.

1422. Charan Singh, *Light on St. Matthew*, Punjab, India: Shri S.L. Sondhi, secretary, Radha Soami Satsang Beas, 1979.

1423. Gita Mehta, *Karma Cola: The Marketing of the Mystic East*, New York: Simon and Schuster, 1979.

1424. Bhagwan Shree Rajneesh, "Simple, Utterly Simple," *Sannyas*, no. 5, 1980.

1425. Bhagwan Shree Rajneesh, "Pulling Out Weeds," *Sannyas*, no. 5, 1980.

1426. Maharishi Mahesh Yogi, *Transcendental Meditation*, New York: New American Library, 1968.

1427. Paramahansa Yogananda, *Man's Eternal Quest*, Los Angeles, CA: Self Realization Fellowship, 1975.

1428. Bhagwan Shree Rajneesh, "Why Don't You Help Me to Become Enlightened?" *Sannyas*, no. 1, 1978.

1429. ———, "I Am the Messiah, Here and Now," *Sannyas*, no. 5, 1978.

1430. Bhagwan Shree Rajneesh as quoted in "Editorial —The Living Master," *Sannyas*, no. 4, 1980.

1431. William Rodamor, "The Secret Life of Swami Muktananda," *Co-Evolution Quarterly*, Winter 1983.

1432. Ref. 483:34; Swami Mukatananda, *Mukteshwri*, Part 2, Ganeshpuri, India: Shree Gurudev Ashram, 1973, p. 29.

1433. Romain Rolland, *The Life of Ramakrishna*, Calcutta, India: Advaita Ashrama, trans. from the original French by E.F. Malcolm-Smith, 1979.

1434. Ram Dass interview, *New Age Journal*, no. 9, p. 27; see also the interview in *The Movement*, 1976.

1435. T. George Harris, editorial, *Psychology Today*, December 1975.

1436. Sri Chinmoy, "Questions and Answers," *Aum* magazine, January 1980, p. 23.

1437. Bhagwan Shree Rajneesh, "What Can Replace the Family?" *Sannyas*, No. 1, 1978.

1438. ———, "Rajneesh International Anti-University: The No-School of School," *Sannyas*, no. 2, 1978.

1440. Swami Rama, *Life Here and Hereafter*, Glenview, IL: Himalayan National Institute, 1976.

1441. A.C. Bhaktivedanta Prabhupada, *Bhaghavad-gita As It Is*, New York: Collier Books, 1973, ch. 9, v. 30, p. 483; cf. *Back to Godhead*, no. 55, p. 25.

1442. *Bhaghavad Gita*, ch. 18, v. 17.

1443. *Kaushitaki Upanishad* 3:1-2.

1444. *Chattanooga News Free-Press*, February 24, 1991.

1445. Sandra Good, in Vincent Bugliosi, *Helter Skelter*, New York: Bantam, 1975.

1446. "Charlie Manson: Portrait in Terror," February 16, 1976, KABC TV, Los Angeles, 11:30 P.M. description by Manson prosecutor Vincent Bugliosi.

1447. R.C. Zaehner, *Our Savage God: The Perverse Use of Eastern Thought*, New York: Sheed and Ward, 1974.

1448. Bhagwan Shree Rajneesh, *Hammer on the Rock: A Darshan Diary*, New York: Grove Press, 1978.

1449. Bhagwan Shree Rajneesh, "Energy," *Sannyas*, no. 1, 1978.

1450. See e.g., Tal Brooke, *Lord of the Air*, Eugene, OR: Harvest House Publishers, 1990; Ram Dass, *Grist for the Mill*, New York: Bantam, 1979 and; Ram Dass, "Egg on My Beard," *The Yoga Journal*, November-December 1976; *The Yoga Journal*, July-August, 1985; Peter Marin, "Spiritual Obedience," *Harper's* magazine, February 1979; "The Secret Life of Swami Muktananda," *Co-Evolution Quarterly*, Winter 1983; *The (Portland) Oregonian*, December 30, 1985; and Tal Brooke, *Riders of the Cosmic*

*Circuit*, ref 249; for illustrations in the lives of many prominent gurus; see also the book by Ma Bharti, *Drunk on the Divine*, New York: Grove Press, 1980.

1451. Swami Adbhutananda, "Brahman and Maya," in Christopher Isherwood, ed., *Vedanta for the Western World*, ref. 1373.

1452. Jack Kornfield, "Sex Lives of the Gurus," *Yoga Journal*, July/August 1985.

1453. James Bjornstad, Shildes Johnson, *Stars, Signs and Salvation in the Age of Aquarius*, Minneapolis, MN: Bethany House, 1976.

1456. Alma Guinness, ed., Reader's Digest Association, *Family Guide to Natural Medicine: How to Stay Healthy the Natural Way*, Pleasantville, NY: Reader's Digest, 1993.

1467. Adelaide Bry, *est*, New York: Avon, 1976. (Her book was carefully checked by est trainers and staff for accuracy [*The Graduate Review*, June 1976, p. 9].)

1476. Kenneth Ring, "Mapping the Regions of Consciousness: A Conceptual Reformulation," *The Journal of Transpersonal Psychology*, no. 2, 1976.

1481. Robert Basil, ed., *Not Necessarily the New Age: Critical Essays*, New York: Prometheus, 1988.

1483. Inner Traditions International, Fall 1990 catalog, Rochester, VT.

1484. David and Julia Line, *Fortune Telling by Runes*, Wellingborough, Northamptonshire, England: Aquarian Press, 1985.

1485. Louis Jacolliot, *Occult Science in India and Among the Ancients*, New Hyde Park, New York: University Books, 1971.

1486. Tony Willis, *The Runic Workbook: Understanding and Using the Power of Runes*, Wellingborough, Northamptonshire, England: Aquarian Press, 1986.

1488. Ref. 1484:17-18,24,29; 1486:32,125,165,188-92; 530:74.

1490. James Legge. trans, *I Ching: Book of Changes*, New York: Bantam, 1969.

1491. E.g., John Blofeld, *I Ching*, New York: E.P. Dutton, 1968.

1492. Samuel Reifler, *I Ching*, New York: Bantam, 1981.

1493. Joseph L. Henderson, "A Commentary on the I Ching," *New Realities*, January/February 1985.

1494. David Le Mieux, *Forbidden Images: The Secrets of the Tarot*, New York: Barnes & Noble, 1985.

1495. W. Brugh Joy, *Joy's Way: A Map for the Transformational Journey*, Los Angeles: J.P. Tarcher, Inc., 1979.

1496. Alfred Douglas, *The Tarot: The Origins, Meaning and Uses of the Cards*, Baltimore, MD: Penguin, 1972.

1497. Angeles Arrien, "Tarot: An Esoteric Psychology, *New Realities*, vol. 5, no. 2.

1498. Genie Z. Laborde, "Tarot as a Hook for Fishing," *New Realities*, vol. 5, no. 2.

1499. Poem by Zen master Soen-sa, *The Graduate Review*, March 1977.

1500. Alan Vaughan, "Phantoms Stalked the Room . . ." in ref. 148.

1501. Russell Chandler, "Ouija Board Popularity Rising," *Los Angeles Times*, February 17, 1974.

1502. Carl A. Wickland, *Thirty Years Among the Dead*, Newcastle, 1974, rpt.

1503. J. Keel, "More from My Ohio Valley Notebook," *Flying Saucer Review* (British Publication), vol. 13, no. 4.

1504. *The National Observer*, June 1, 1974.

1505. Gary North in *Remnant Review*, December 5, 1980.

1506. *Moody Monthly*, January 1983.

1507. *Eternity*, December 1981.

1508. Richard Geer, *Star+Gate Keys to the Kingdom*, Orinda, CA: Stargate Enterprises, 1986.

1509. J.M. Ashmand, trans., *Ptolemy's Tetrabiblios*, Hollywood, CA: Symbols and Signs, 1976.

1510. Carl Raschke, *The Interruption of Eternity: Modern Gnosticism and the Origins of the New Religious Consciousness*, Chicago, IL: Nelson Hall, 1980.

1511. Ben Hester, "A New Look at Dowsing," ms., 1993.

1512. Gary Gygax, "The Dungeons and Dragons Magic System," *The Best of the Dragon*, Lake Geneva, WI: TSR Periodicals, 1980.

1513. ——, *Advanced Dungeons and Dragons Players' Handbook*, Lake Geneva, WI: TSR Games, 1978.

1514. ——, *Dungeons and Dragons Players' Handbook*, Lake Geneva, WI: TSR Games, 1975.

1515. Quoted in Ronald M. Enroth, "Fantasy Games: Is There an Occult Connection?" *Eternity*, December 1981.

1516. James M. Ward and Robert J. Kuntz, *Deities and Demigods: Cyclopedia of Gods and Heroes from Myth and Legend*, Lawrence Chica, ed., Lake Geneva, WI: TSR Games, 1980.

1517. *San Diego Evening Tribune*, October 13, 1980.

1518. Robert Kuntz and James Ward, *Gods, Demigods and Heroes*, Lake Geneva, WI: TSR Games, 1976.

1519. See e.g., J. Richard Greenwell, "Academia and the Occult: An Experience at Arizona," *The Skeptical Inquirer*, vol. 5, no. 1. This article discusses the course Anthropology 198W—Witchcraft and the Occult—offered at the University of Arizona.

1520. Stanley Dokupil, "Dungeons and Dragons," Berkeley, CA: Spiritual Counterfeits Project, 1982.

1521. Brian Onken and Elliot Miller, "Dungeons and Dragons," *Foreword*, vol. 4, no. 2.

**647**

1522. John Ankerberg, John Weldon, *Cult Watch: What You Need to Know About Spiritual Deception*, Eugene, OR: Harvest House Publishers, 1991.

1523. Patricia Pitmantgen, "What Would Happen to the American Psyche If, Along with Homerooms, Flag-Saluting and IQ Testing, Schools Had Daily Dream Sharing?" in ref. 1524.

1524. Gay Henricks, James Fadiman, eds., *Transpersonal Education: A Curriculum for Feeling and Being*, Englewood Cliffs, NJ: Prentice-Hall, 1976.

1525. J. Gordon Melton, Jerome Clark, and Aidan A. Kelly, *New Age Almanac*, Detroit, MI: Gale Research, 1991.

1526. Rosemary Ellen Guiley, *Harper's Encyclopedia of Mystical and Paranormal Experience*, San Francisco, CA: Harper Collins, 1991.

1527. Geoffrey Hodson, *Clairvoyant Investigations*, Wheaton, IL: Theosophical, 1984.

1528. John White, ed., *What Is Enlightenment? Exploring the Goal of the Spiritual Path*, Los Angeles, CA: J.P. Tarcher, 1984.

1531. R.C. Devon Heck and Jennifer L. Thompson, "est: Salvation or Swindle," *San Francisco Magazine*, January 1976.

1532. Walter Truett Anderson, *The Upstart Spring: Esalen and the American Awakening*, Menlo Park, CA: Addison Wesley, 1983.

1533. Donald Porter and Diane Taxon, *The est Experience*, New York: Award, 1976.

1534. Marcia Seligson, "est," *New Times*, October 18, 1974 (continuing an interview with Erhard).

1541. Robert Muller, *New Genesis: Shaping a Global Spirituality*, Garden City, NY: Doubleday/Image, 1984.

1542. W.R. Bird, *The Origin of Species Revisited: The Theories of Evolution and of Abrupt Appearance*, New York: Philosophical Library, 1989, 2 vols.

1543. Ken Wilber, *The Atman Project: A Transpersonal View of Human Development*, Wheaton, IL: Theosophical Publishing House, 1977, 1985.

1545. See ref. 238.

1546. Ken Wilber, ed., *The Holographic Paradigm and Other Paradoxes: Exploring the Leading Edge of Science*, Boulder, CO: Shambhala, 1982.

1547. See ref. 301.

1558. Fritjof Capra, *The Tao of Phisics*, Berkeley, Shambhala, 1975.

1587. Copies of the report are available from the Siddha Yoga Dham of America.

1588. Stephan Bodian, Editorial, *Yoga Journal*, July/August 1985.

1589. Bhagwan Shree Rajneesh, "God Is a Christ in a Christ," *Sannyas*, no. 3, May/June, 1978.

1590. John Ankerberg, John Weldon, *Can You Trust Your Doctor?: New Age Medicine and Its Threat to Your Family*, Brentwood, TN: Wolgemuth & Hyatt, 1990.

1591. *The New American Desk Encyclopedia*, 3rd ed., New York: Signet, 1993.

1666. J.P. Moreland, ed., *The Creation Hypothesis: Scientific Evidence for an Intelligent Designer*, Downers Grove, IL: InterVarsity, 1994; ref. 1542: passim; Norman L. Geisler, J. Kirby Anderson, *Origin Science: A Proposal for the Creation-Evolution Controversy*, Grand Rapids, MI: Baker, 1987; ref. 1667.

1667. Henry M. Morris, Gary E. Parker, *What Is Creation Science?*, San Diego, CA: Creation Life, 1982.

1707. W.W. Bartly III, *Werner Erhard: The Transformation of a Man, The Founding of est*, New York: Clarkson N. Potter, 1978.

1735. Robert A. Baker, *They Call It Hypnosis*, Buffalo, NY: Prometheus, 1990.

1736. Among the scores of critiques of modern psychology showing problems in efficacy, theoretical base, or its potential dangers are: Walter Bromberg, *From Shaman to Psychotherapist* (Regnery); Richard Stuart, *Trick or Treatment: How and When Psychotherapy Fails* (Research Press); Jeffery Moussaieff, *Against Therapy* (Athenium); Bernie Zilbergeld, *The Death of Psychiatry* (Chilton); Thomas Kiernan, *Shrinks, Etc.* (Dial); Michael and Lise Wallach, *Psychology's Sanction for Selfishness* (W.H. Freeman); Hans Strupp, et al., *Psychotherapy for Better or Worse* (Jason Aronson); and Martin and Deidre Bobgan, *The Psychological Way/The Spiritual Way* and *Psychoheresy*. These are only a few of the scores of texts critical of modern psychotherapy in addition to literally hundreds of scholarly articles.

1738. William H. Kautz and Melanie Branon, *Channeling: The Intuitive Connection*, San Francisco: Harper & Row, 1987.

1759. *The New Age Journal*, no. 7, September 1975. This issue contained two lengthy articles on est, "Werner Erhard—the Source of est," a wide-ranging interview with Erhard, and "Miracles and Realizations," comments of the *NAJ* staff, all of whom took the training.

1779. Stan Mieses, "est—Can It Make You Happy?" *Circus*, February 10, 1976.

1800. Roger Woolger, *Other Lives, Other Selves*, Garden City, NY: Doubleday, 1987.

1801. Brian L. Weiss, *Many Lives, Many Masters*, New York: Fireside, 1988.

1849. Cf. Bhagwan Shree Rajneesh, "Energy," *Sannyas*, no. 1, January/February 1978 and the kundalini issue (no. 2, 1976), Rajneesh International Foundation.

1850. This and dozens of similar reports are given in ref. 476:69-100 and passim.

1852. Willis H. Kinnear, ed., *The Creative Power of Mind*, Englewood Cliffs, NJ: Prentice-Hall, 1978.

1854. Robert Masters and Jean Houston, *Mind Games: The Guide to Inner Space*, New York: Delta, 1981.

1857. William Hornaday, Harlan Ware, "Sketches of a Philosopher," *Science of Mind* magazine, February 1979.

1882. James Dillet Freeman, *The Story of Unity*, Unity Village, MO: Unity School of Christianity, n.d.

1889. Adam Smith, *Powers of Mind*, New York: Random House, 1975.

1937. Elissa Lindsay McClain, "Should the Church Apologize to Unity?" *Christian Research Journal*, Winter/Spring 1987.

1945. John Weldon, *Christian Science*, ms.

1951. See his biographer, W. W. Bartley, *Werner Erhard: The Transformation of a Man, the Founding of est*, New York: Clarkson Potter, 1978, pp. 14, 37, 75-76, 81-82, 144-48, 158-74.

1966. Jess Stearn, *Adventures into the Psychic*, New York: Signet, 1982.

1969. See ref. 1899.

1970. John Ankerberg, John Weldon, *The Facts On Faith Movement*, Eugene, OR: Harvest House Publishers, 1993.

1984. *NSA Quarterly*, Spring 1973.

1985. Daisaku Ikeda, *Lectures on Buddhism* vol. IV, Tokyo, Japan: Seikyo Press, 1969.

2002. Ysuji Kirimura, *Fundamentals of Buddhism*, Tokyo: Nichiren Shoshu International Center, 1978.

2013. The Seikyo Times, *Lectures on the Sutra*, Tokyo, Japan: Nichiren Shoshu International Center, 1978; cf., *Seikyo Times, Lectures on the Sutra*, p.4.

2023. E.g., *Seikyo Times*, January. 1979, 14; ref. 2013:167-68; ref. 2002:93-119.

2026. C. Norman Shealy, "Perspectives on Psychic Diagnosis," in ref. 98.

2027. John Beloff, "Historical Overview," in ref. 1098.

2028. See refs. 389:239-41; 463:1-49; 500:59-64; 769:1-30.

2029. Jeanne P. Rindge, "Perspective: An Overview of Paranormal Healing," in ref. 98.

2030. J. L. Kelson, "Magician," in ref. 390.

2031. Ref. 463: ch 7, esp. pp. 87-92; see also *ARE News*, July 1977.

2032. See refs. 540:159; 463:93-94.

2033. H. L. Cayce, "The Varieties of Healing," in ref. 520.

2041. Evelyn Underhill, *Mysticism: a Study in the Nature and Development of Man's Spiritual Consciousness*, NY: E.P. Dutton, 1961.

2057. "Letters from Graduates," *The Graduate Review*, November 1976.

2064. "What Is the Purpose of the est Training?" est brochure, 1976.

2065. Werner Erhard, "The Transformation of est," *The Graduate Review*, November 1976; cf. "What's So," January 1975; *New York* magazine, September 29, 1975, p. 35.

2066. Werner Erhard, "If God Had Meant Man to Fly, He Would Have Given Him Wings," n.p., Werner Erhard, 1974.

2067. Luke Rhinehart, *The Book of est*, New York: Holt, Rinehart and Winston, 1976.

2068. Condensed by paraphrase from ref. 2067:194-96.

2069. Werner Erhard, "Life, Living and Winning the Game," *The Graduate Review*, July 1976.

2070. Rev. Stuart G. Fitch, "Making Religion Real," *The Graduate Review*, July 1977. (The Rajneesh citation is on p. 12.)

2071. See ref 1118.

2087. W. B. Crow, *A History of Magic, Witchcraft and Occultism*, North Hollywood, CA: Wilshire, 1968.

2134. See ref. 386.

2192. Stu Langer and Gary Clark, "Getting Off It with the Trainers," trainer interview, *The Graduate Review*, August 1976.

2205. Amaury de Riencourt, *The Eye of Shiva*, in ref. 823.

2206. Ken Wilber, ed., *Quantum Questions*, Boston MA: 1984.

2207. S.G. Smith, C.E. Geist, Jr., "Quantum Physics: Historical Review and Current Directions," *Creation Research Society Quarterly*, September 1986.

2208. Itzhak Bentov, *Stalking the Wild Pendulum: On the Mechanics of Consciousness*, NY: E.P. Dutton, 1977.

2209. See ref. 1546.

2210. See ref. 1558.

2211. Laura Oteri, ed., *Quantum Physics and Parapsychology*, New York: Parapsychology Foundation, 1975.

2212. Gary Zukav, *The Dancing Wu Li Masters: An Overview of the New Physics*, NY: William Morrow and Company, 1979.

2213. Michael Talbot, *Mysticism and the New Physics*, New York: Bantam, 1981.

2214. Denis Postle, *The Fabric of the Universe*, New York: Crown, 1976.

2215. P.C.W. Davies, J.R. Brown, *The Ghost in the Atom: A Discussion of the Mysteries of Quantum Physics*, NY: Cambridge University Press, 1986.

2216. Dean Halverson, "Science, Religion and the New Age," *SCP Journal*, Winter 1985.

649

2217. *New Age Journal,* July 1979.

2218. *The Christian Parapsychologist,* September 1982.

2219. "From the Hill," *American Medical Television,* CNBC, August 7, 1993, 10-10:30 A.M. EST.

2221. The False Memory Syndrome Foundation was founded in 1992 in Pennsylvania; as of 1994 it had over 8000 requests for assistance. See also Claire Safran, "Dangerous Obsession: the Truth About Repressed Memories," *McCalls,* June 1993; Lawrence Wright, "Remembering Satan," Parts 1 and 2, *New Yorker,* May 17/24, 1993; Martin Gardner, "The False Memory Syndrome," *Skeptical Inquirer,* Summer 1993; Kendrick Frazier, "The False Memory Problem: A Plea to Psychotherapists," *Skeptical Briefs,* June 1993; Leon Jaroff, "Lies of the Mind," *Time,* November 29, 1993.

2223. Keith Nichols, "An Exclusive Interview with Taisha Abelas of Carlos Castenada's 'Elusive Sorcerer's Clan,' " *Magical Blend,* October 1993.

2224. Michael Moore, *Medicinal Plants of the Pacific West,* Santa Fe, New Mexico: Red Crane, 1993.

2225. Zolar, *Zolar's Book of the Spirits,* New York: Prentice-Hall, 1987.

2226. Nathaniel Lande, *Mindstyles/Lifestyles,* Los Angeles: Price/Stern/Sloan, 1976.

2227. Source withheld.

2228. James Kettle, *The est Experience,* New York: Zebra, 1976.

2229. Robert A. Hargrove, *est: Making Life Work,* New York: Dell, 1976.

2230. Leon Jaroff, "Lies of the Mind," *Time magazine,* November 29, 1993.

2231. The Michael Digest Group, *The Michael Game,* Orinda, CA: Warwick, 1988.

2232. Anastas Harris, ed., *Mind: Evolution or Revolution? The Emergence of Holistic Education,* Del Mar, CA: Holistic Education Network, 1980.

2233. ———, ed., *Holistic Education: Education for Living,* Del Mar, CA: Holistic Education Network, 1981.

2234. *Parade Magazine,* September 20, 1992.

2235. William J. Bennett, "The Case for Religion in Schools," *Reader's Digest,* November 1992.

2236. *The Arkansas Citizen,* April 1990.

2237. Most of "A Word to the Reader" was taken from "The Facts on Your Child's Education: You Can Make a Difference," by Robert Gerow, Chattanooga, TN: Ankerberg Theological Research Institute, 1990.

2239. Rick Branch, *Watchman Expositor,* vol. 8, no. 9, 1991.

2240. *Peace, Harmony and Awareness,* part of the APPLE curriculum, copy on file, Watchman Fellowship, Birmingham, Alabama.

2241. Brooks Alexander in *Forward* magazine, Fall 1986 (current title *Christian Research Journal,* San Juan Capistrano, CA).

2242. As discussed in "Are the Public Schools Teaching Our Children New Age Religious Views?" series 1, program 2, "The John Ankerberg Show," September 1992.

2243. John Ankerberg, Craig Branch, John Weldon, *Thieves of Innocence,* Eugene, OR: Harvest House Publishers, 1993.

2244. Edward Robinson, *The Original Vision: The Study of the Religious Experience of Childhood,* New York: Seabury Press, 1983.

2245. Johanna Michaelsen, *Like Lambs to the Slaughter: Your Child and the Occult,* Eugene, OR: Harvest House Publishers, 1989.

2246. Rene Weber, "Compassion, Rootedness and Detachment: Their Role in Healing: A Conversation with Dora Kunz," in Dora Kunz, comp., *Spiritual Aspects of the Healing Arts,* Wheaton, IL: Theosophical Publishing House, 1984.

2247. Dio Neff, "Taoist Esoteric Yoga with Mantak Chia," *Yoga Journal,* March/April 1986.

2248. Thomas Armstrong, "Transpersonal Experience in Childhood," *The Journal of Transpersonal Psychology,* vol. 16, no. 2, 1984, p. 210; cf. the editors of *Psychic, Psychics: Indepth Interviews,* New York: Harper & Row, 1972, passim; and John Weldon, *Psychic Healing: An Exposé of an Occult Phenomenon,* Dallas, TX: Zola Levitt Ministries, 1991, rpt.

2251. Cf. Stanley Krippner, "Creativity and Psychic Phenomena," *Gifted Child Quarterly,* vol. 7 (1963), pp. 51-61; Stanley Krippner, R. Dreistadt, C.C. Hubbard, "The Creative Person and Non-Ordinary Reality," *Gifted Child Quarterly* (in press); cf. M.L. Anderson, "The Relations of PSI to Creativity," *Journal of Parapsychology,* vol. 26, 1962, pp. 277-92; G. Murphy, "Research and Creativeness: What It Tells Us About Extrasensory Perception," *Journal of the American Society for Psychical Research,* vol. 60, 1966.

2252. James W. Peterson, "Extrasensory Abilities of Children: An Ignored Reality?" *Learning: The Magazine for Creative Teaching,* December 1975.

2254. Annette Hollander, *How to Help Your Child Have a Spiritual Life,* New York: A & W Publishers, 1980.

2256. Gay Hendricks, Thomas B. Roberts, *The Second Centering Book: More Awareness Activities for Children,* New York: Prentice-Hall, 1977.

2257. Maureen Murdock, *Spinning Inward: Using Guided Imagery with Children for Learning, Creativity, and Relaxation,* Boston, MA: Shambhala, 1987.

2259. Barbara Clark, *Growing Up Gifted*, 3rd ed., Columbus, OH: Merrill Publishing Co., 1988.

2260. Jack Canfield, Paula Klimeck, "Education for a New Age," *New Age*, February 1978, p. 36.

2261. See ref. 1524:vii.

2262. John Dunphy, "A Religion for the New Age," *The Humanist*, January-February 1983.

2263. Thomas Sowell, "Ideological Crusaders Battle for Our Kids' Hearts and Minds," *Rocky Mountain News*, June 3, 1992.

2264. Dick Sutphen, "Infiltrating the New Age into Society," *What Is*, Summer 1986, p. 14.

2265. Stewart B. Shapiro and Louise F. Fitzgerald, "The Development of an Objective Scale to Measure a Transpersonal Orientation to Learning," *Educational and Psychological Measurement*, vol. 49, 1989.

2266. Phylis Schlafly, ed., *Child Abuse in the Classroom*, Westchester, MA: Crossway, 1988, pp. 138-41,201-02,235-36,282,423.

2267. Jack Canfield, *Self-Esteem in the Classroom*, Pasadena, CA: Christian Educator Association International, Fall 1991. See also *The Inner Classroom: Teaching with Guided Imagery*, 1981, p. 39, and Canfield's ms., "Psychosynthesis in Education: Theory and Application," 1980.

2268. Jack Canfield, *The Inner Classroom: Teaching with Guided Imagery*, Amhurst, MA: Institute for Wholistic Education, 1981.

2269. Alice A. Bailey, *The Unfinished Autobiography*, New York: Lucis Trust, 1970.

2270. All but 4, see Raymond B. Whorf, *The Tibetan's Teaching: An Analysis of the Books of the Tibetan Master Djwhal Khul as Written Down by Alice Bailey*, Ojai, CA: Meditation Groups, n.d.

2271. Stewart B. Shapiro, Louise F. Fitzgerald, "The Development of an Objective Scale to Measure a Transpersonal Orientation to Learning," *Educational and Psychological Measurement*, vol. 49, 1989.

2272. Received from Dr. Shapiro, list on file at Watchman Fellowship, Birmingham, AL.

2273. Gay Hendricks and Thomas B. Roberts, *The Second Centering Book: More Awareness Activities for Children*, New York: Prentice-Hall, 1977.

2274. Thomas B. Roberts, "States of Consciousness: A New Intellectual Direction, A New Teacher Education Direction," *Teacher Education*, March/April 1985.

2279. EEOC notice N-915, February 22, 1988, "EEOC's Policy Statement on Training Programs Conflicting with Employees' Religious Beliefs."

2280. A copy of this is available from Watchman Fellowship, Birmingham, AL, emphasis added.

2282. Martin T. Orne, A. Gorden Hammer, "Hypnosis," *Encyclopaedia Britannica, Macropaedia*, vol. 9.

2283. WWBT-TV12, "What Did Your Child Learn in School Today?" four-part video, Richmond, VA: November 7-9, 1990.

2285. Statement by Ross S. Olson, "Primary Learning Center," n.d., n.p., office phone listed as 612-887-6621.

2286. Olson statement in "Can Students Visualize Diseases Away?" (see ref. 2085).

2287. Ron F. Anderson, "Using Guided Fantasy with Children," *Elementary School Guidance and Counseling Journal*, October 1980.

2288. Robert Day and Robert Griffin, "Children's Attitudes Toward the Magic Circle," *Elementary School Guidance and Counseling Journal*, December 1980.

2289. National Research Council, *Enhancing Human Performance: Issues, Theories and Techniques*, Committee on Techniques for the Enhancement of Human Performance, Washington, D.C.: National Academy Press, 1988, pp. 16-23; cf. same text *In the Mind's Eye: Enhancing Human Performance* (Part 2), pp. 12-17.

2290. Charles Keikkinen, "Reorientation from Altered States: Please Move Carefully," *Journal of Counseling and Development*, May 1989.

2291. *TM-EX Bulletin*, a Partial Research Review, reprints available from TM-EX, P.O. Box 7565, Arlington, VA 22207 (202-728-7580).

2292. Margaret Singer and Richard Ofshe, "Thought Reform Programs and the Production of Psychiatric Casualties," *Psychiatric Annals*, April 1990.

2293. Frederick J. Heide and T.D. Borkovec, *Consulting in Clinical Psychology*, 1983, 171-82; Heide and Borkovec, *Behavioral Research Therapy Journal*, 1984.

2294. Arnold Lazarus, *Psychological Reports*, 1976, pp. 601-60

2295. Roger Walsh, Dean Shapiro, eds., *Meditation, Classic and Contemporary Perspectives*, NY: Aldine, 1984, p. 204.

2296. E.g., David Holmes, "Meditation and Somatic Arousal Reductions," *American Psychologist*, January 1984, pp. 1-10; cf. June 1985, pp. 717-31; June 1986, pp. 712-13; September 1986, pp. 1007-09; September 1987, pp. 879-81.

2311. Jean Porter, "Psychic Development," in ref. 1524.

2312. Thomas Armstrong, "Children As Healers," *Somatics*, Autumn/Winter 1984-85.

2313. Jan Ehrenwald, "The Occult," *Today's Education*, September 1991.

2314. Sylvia Z. Ramirez, "The Effects of Suggestopedia in Teaching English Vocabulary to Spanish-Dominant Chicano Third Graders," *The Elementary School Journal*, January 1986.

2315. Sheila Ostrander, Lynn Schroeder, Nancy Ostrander, "Super Learning: The Miraculous Mind-Body Approach," *New Age*, September 1979.

2316. James W. Peterson, *The Secret Life of Kids: An Exploration into Their Psychic Senses*, Wheaton, IL: Quest, 1987, foreword.

2317. Frances Vaughan Clark, "Rediscovering Transpersonal Education," *The Journal of Transpersonal Psychology*, no. 1, 1974.

2318. Hugh Redmond, "A Pioneer Program in Transpersonal Education," *The Journal of Transpersonal Psychology*, no. 1, p. 9, 1974.

2319. Joseph Chilton Pearce, "Freeing the Mind of the Magical Child," *New Age*, October 1976.

2333. Suzanne Gordon, *Lonely in America*, New York: Simon and Schuster, 1976.

2334. John Leo, "est: There Is Nothing to Get," *Time* magazine, June 7, 1976.

2335. Peter Marin, "The New Narcissism," *Harper's Magazine*, October 1975.

2336. Pat Marks, *est: The Movement and the Man*, New York: Playboy Press, 1976.

2337. Carl Frederick, *est: Playing the Game* [sic] the New Way, Delta, 1976.

2338. "Letters from Graduates," *The Graduate Review*, June 1976.

2339. Robert W. Fuller and Zara Wallace, *A Look at est in Education* (est publication), n.p.p., 1976.

2342. L. Ron Hubbard, *Scientology: A New Slant on Life* (ref. 2581), pp. 55-57,60; the last sentence is apparently from another Hubbard quote, cf. *Parents Magazine*, June 1969, p. 83.

2346. Neal Rogin, "A Trainer Is a Graduate Who Does the Training," *The Graduate Review*, May 1977.

2347. Kevin Garvey, *Christianity Today*, January 21, 1977.

2348. Michele Marill, "A New Way of Healing," *Atlanta*, May 1993.

2368. Deepak Chopra, *Ageless Body, Timeless Mind: The Quantum Alternative to Growing Old*, New York: Harmony, 1993.

2369. ———, *Perfect Health: The Complete Mind/Body Guide*, New York: Harmony, 1991.

2370. Andrew A. Skolnick, "Maharishi Ayur-Veda: Guru's Marketing Scheme Promises the World Eternal Perfect Health," *Journal of the American Medical Association*, October 2, 1991.

2373. Beth Krier, "Pulse as a Window on the State of Your Health," *Los Angeles Times*, June 3, 1986.

2379. Margaret and James Stutley, *Harper's Dictionary of Hinduism: Its Mythology, Folklore, Philosophy, Literature and History*, New York: Harper & Row, 1977.

2380. See ref. 887.

2381. George A. Mather, Larry A. Nichols, *Dictionary of Cults, Sects, Religions and the Occult*, Grand Rapids, MI: Zondervan, 1993.

2382. Richard Cavendish, *Man, Myth and Magic: An Illustrated Encyclopedia of the Supernatural*, vol. 13, New York: Marshall Cavendish Corp., 1970.

2383. S.v. "mandala," "mantra," *Encyclopaedia Britannica*, 15th ed., vol. 6, Micropaedia.

2393. Chelsea Quinn Yarbro, *Messages from Michael*, New York: Berkley, 1983.

2394. Willis Harman, Howard Rheingold, *Higher Creativity: Liberating the Unconscious for Breakthrough Insights*, Los Angeles: J.P. Tarcher, 1984.

2399. See ref. 377.

2400. Randall N. Baer, *Inside the New Age Nightmare*, Lafayette, LA: Huntington House, 1989.

2403. Erwin de Castro, B.J. Oropeza, Ron Rhodes, "Enter the Dragon?" Part 1, *Christian Research Journal*, Fall 1993.

2404. Erwin de Castro, et al., "Enter the Dragon?" Part 2, prepublication copy, *Christian Research Journal*, 1994.

2405. "Biography"—Bruce Lee, hosted by Peter Graves, January 22, 1994, A&E Network.

2406. S.v., "Mechanics, Quantum," *Encyclopaedia Britannica*, 15th ed., Macropaedia.

2407. Robert Curran, *The Haunted: One Family's Nightmare*, New York: St. Martin's Press, 1988.

2417. Anthony Campbell, *Seven States of Consciousness*, Perennial, 1974.

2418. See ref. 2379.

2419. Maharishi International University, *Inauguration of the Dawn of the Age of Enlightenment*, MIU Press, publication G186, 1975.

2424. Edmond Gruss, *The Ouija Board: A Doorway to the Occult*, Philipsburg, NJ: Presbyterian and Reformed, 1994, galley copy.

2425. Eileen J. Garrett, *Many Voices: The Autobiography of a Medium*, New York: Dell, 1969.

2426. Loyd Auerbach, *Reincarnation, Channeling and Possession: A Parapsychologist's Handbook*, New York: Warner, 1993.

2429. Robert J. Fox, "Work of the Holy Angels Recognized by Church—Given New Norms," *Fatima Family Messenger*, October-December, 1992. *The Messenger* states, "We are 100% Loyal to the Magisterium" p. 1.

2433. Raymond Moody, *Coming Back: A Psychiatrist Explores Past-Life Journeys*, New York: Bantam, 1992.

2434. John Ankerberg, John Weldon, *Protestants and Catholics—Do They Now Agree?: An Evaluation of*

*Modern Protestantism and Roman Catholicism in Light of the Bible*, Chattanooga, TN: Ankerberg Theological Research Institute, 1994. See especially the second edition (Harvest House, 1995).

2441. Nancy Gibbs, "Angels Among Us," *Time* magazine, December 27, 1993.

2446. Illustration taken from an "Ask Marilyn" column, *Parade* magazine, late July 1994.

2448. E.g., Paul C. Cooper, "Yoga for the Special Child," *Yoga Journal*, November/December 1984.

2449. Ken Wilber, "The Developmental Spectrum and Psychopathology Part II: Treatment Modalities," *The Journal of Transpersonal Psychology*, vol. 60, no. 2, 1984.

2450. Haridas Chadhuri, "The Psychophysiology of Kundalini," in ref. 236.

2451. Pat Rodegast, Judith Stanton, *Emmanuel's Book III, What Is an Angel Doing Here?* New York: Bantam, 1994.

2456. Martini, *Palmistry*, Baltimore, MD: I & M Ottenheimer, 1929.

2457. Joyce Wilson, *The Complete Book of Palmistry*, New York: Bantam, 1978.

2458. Gopi Aria, *Palmistry for the New Age*, Long Beach, CA: Morningland, 1977.

2459. Mary Anderson, *Palmistry*, Wellingborough, Northamptonshire, England: Aquarian Press, 1977.

2460. Comte C. de Saint-Germain, *The Practice of Palmistry*, New York: Samuel Weiser, 1977, rpt. of 1897 edition.

2461. Martin Steinbach, *Medical Palmistry: Health and Character in the Hands*, Secaucus, NJ: University Books, 1975.

2462. Gerie Tully, *The Secret Powers of Numerology*, New York: Pocket Books, 1977.

2463. Kevin Quinn Avery, *The Numbers of Life: The Hidden Power of Numerology*, Garden City, NJ: Doubleday, 1974, rev.

2464. Helyn Hitchcock, *Helping Yourself with Numerology*, West Nyack, NY: Parker, 1978.

2465. Vincent Lopez, *Numerology*, New York: Signet, 1969.

2466. W. Wynn Westcott, *Numbers: Their Occult Power and Mystic Virtues*, London: Theosophical Publishing House, 1974, rpt. of 1890 edition.

2467. Roberta Lee, "Numerology: A Roadmap to Life—Part 3," *Psychic Dimensions*, February 1979.

2468. Richard Cavendish, ed., *Encyclopedia of the Unexplained: Magic, Occultism and Parapsychology*, New York: McGraw Hill, 1976.

2469. Michael Alan Park, "Palmistry: Science or Hand-Jive?" *The Skeptical Inquirer*, Winter 1982-83, vol. 7, no. 2.

2470. Joseph G. Dikopolsky, "A Test of Numerology," *The Skeptical Inquirer*, Spring 1983.

2471. Victor J. Stenger, "The Spooks of Quantum Mechanics," *Skeptical Inquirer*, Fall 1990.

2472. Robert A. Johnson, *Inner Work: Using Dreams and Active Imagination for Personal Growth*, San Francisco: Harper & Row, 1986.

2473. *Shaman's Drum*, Spring 1986, p. 7, and Fall 1985, p. 23.

2474. Timothy White, "An Interview with Luisah Tesh, Daughter of Oshun," *Shaman's Drum*, Spring 1986.

2475. Alan Morvay, "An Interview with Sun Bear," *Shaman's Drum*, Winter 1985.

2476. Jim Swan, "Rolling Thunder at Work," *Shaman's Drum*, Winter 1985.

2477. Natasha Frazier, "Shamanic Survival Skills," *Shaman's Drum*, Summer 1985.

2478. *Shaman's Drum* brochure advertising a workshop with Wallace Black Elk and William S. Lyon at Rainbow Ranch, California, August 1-3, n.d.

2479. *Shaman's Drum* brochure advertising a two-day workshop on "Afro-American and West African Shamanism and Spiritualism," at the University of California, Berkeley, University YWCA, Berkeley, CA, September 6-7, n.d.

2480. Albert Villoldo, "A Journey of Initiation with Don Edwardo Calderon," *Shaman's Drum*, Fall 1985.

2481. Debra Carroll, "Dancing on the Sword's Edge," *Shaman's Drum*, Fall 1985.

2482. Natasha Frazier, "A Model of Contemporary Shamanism," *Shaman's Drum*, Fall 1985.

2483. Vicki Noble, "Female Blood Roots of Shamanism," *Shaman's Drum*, Spring 1986.

2484. Skyhawk, "Receiving the Sacred Pipe," *Shaman's Drum*, Winter 1985.

2485. *Shaman's Drum*, Winter 1985, pp. 40,49; Fall 1985, pp. 30-31,43.

2486. Richard Dobson, Natasha Frazier, "Trance, Dreams and Shamanism," *Shaman's Drum*, Spring 1986.

2487. *Shaman's Drum*, Fall 1985, pp. 11,15,29,40-41; Spring 1986, p. 42; Winter 1985, p. 22; Brooks Alexander, "Shamanism in Two Cultures: Tantric Yoga in India and Tibet," *SCP Journal*, Winter 1984.

2488. *Shaman's Drum*, Spring 1986, p. 47; Fall 1985, pp. 21,42.

2489. Doran C. McCarty, "The Making of the New Shaman," photocopy of lecture transcript given February 6, 1986.

2490. Brooks Alexander, "A Generation of Wizards: Shamanism and Contemporary Culture," *SCP Journal*, Winter 1984.

2491. John Ankerberg, John Weldon, *The Facts on Self-Esteem, Psychology and the Recovery Movement,* Eugene, OR: Harvest House Publishers, 1995.

2492. The Society for Accelerated Learning, "New Dimensions in Education—Confluent Learning," San Francisco, April 25, 1980, from ref. 2243:224.

2493. Telephone conversation between Craig Branch and Dr. Carol Schlichter, relayed to author by Craig Branch, University of Alabama, Spring 1992.

2494. Deborah Rozman, *Meditation for Children,* Boulder Creek, CA: Aslan Publishers, 1989.

2495. Deborah Rozman, *Meditating with Children: The Art of Concentration and Centering,* Boulder Creek, CA: Aslan Publishers, 1988.

2496. Brochure for Jean Houston Workshop, February 13-16, 1992, "The Hero and the Goddess," Holiday Inn, Vanderbilt University, Nashville, TN.

2497. Jean Houston, *The Possible Human,* Los Angeles, CA: J.P. Tarcher, Inc., 1982.

2498. See the articles by Jon Carlson, ed., Herbert Otto, Thomas B. Roberts, Dinkmeyer & Dinkmeyer, et al. in *Elementary School Guidance and Counseling,* vol. 14, no. 2, December 1979.

2499. Dionne Marx, "Education: N. [from Latin, *educere*] Drawing Forth That Which Is Within," *Yoga Journal,* September/October 1979.

2500. In Marilynn Carlson Webber and William D. Webber, *A Rustle of Angels: Stories About Angels in Real-Life and Scripture,* Grand Rapids: Zondervan, 1994.

2501. *Angels II: Beyond the Light,* NBC Special, October 30, 1994, 7:00 P.M., host, Stefanie Powers.

2502. Cf. M. Cameron Gray, ed., *Angels and Awakenings: Stories of the Miraculous by Great Modern Writers,* New York: Doubleday, 1994, pp. xv, xvi.

2503. Cf. John Ankerberg, John Weldon, *The Facts on Islam,* Eugene, OR: Harvest House Publishers, 1992.

2504. Billy Graham, *Angels: God's Secret Agents,* Dallas, TX: Word, 1975.

2505. Timothy Jones, *Celebration of Angels,* Nashville, TN: Nelson, 1994.

2506. David Briggs, "Heavenly Messengers Offer Comfort in Difficult Times," *Chattanooga New Free Press,* September 19, 1992, p. B5.

2507. Terry Lynn Taylor, Mary Beth Crain, *Angel Wisdom: 365 Meditations and Insights from the Heavens,* New York: HarperCollins, 1994, February 3, 13, 23; May 18; November 16 and passim.

2508. Cf. A.C. Gaebelein, *What the Bible Says About Angels,* Grand Rapids: Baker, 1987.

2509. See ref. 2508: ch. 3; C. Fred Dickason, *Angels: Elect and Evil,* Chicago: Moody Press, 1975, ch. 6; John Ankerberg, John Weldon, *The Facts on Jesus*

2510. Joan Wester Anderson, *Where Angels Walk,* New York: Valentine, 1992, pp. 26-27,34,46,94-95,121-24, 215-18, etc.

2511. Terry Lynn Taylor, *Messengers of Light: The Angel's Guide to Spiritual Growth,* Tiburon, CA: H.J. Kramer, 1990.

2512. Meredith L. Young-Sowers, *Angelic Messenger Cards: A Divination System for Spiritual Discovery,* Walpole, NH: Stillpoint, 1993.

2513. Terry Lynn Taylor, *Answers from the Angels,* Tiburon, CA: H.J. Kramer, 1993.

2514. Rosemary Ellen Guiley, *Angels of Mercy,* New York: Pocket Books, 1994.

2515. See Matthew 4:24; Mark 1:32,34; Luke 7:21; 9:1; and ref. 270.

2516. See Dickason, ref. 2509:222-25, and Ben Adam, *Astrology: The Ancient Conspiracy,* Minneapolis, MN: Bethany House, 1963, pp. 90-112.

2517. See refs. 2513:59; 2507:January 1; April 13.

2518. See ref. 2507:January 1; April 12-13, 28; September 5.

2519. See "Brief Analysis of the Book of Mormon," and "Origin of the Book of Mormon" at the beginning of the *Book of Mormon.*

2520. Cf. refs. 782/780/791:163-64,168-72; and Rudolph Steiner's lectures on necromancy, e.g., refs. 779/782.

2521. Stated to John Weldon by José Silva after taping "The John Ankerberg Show" debate in 1986.

2522. See John Weldon, Zola Levitt, *Psychic Healing,* Dallas, TX: Zola Levitt Ministries, 1991, rpt.

2523. Terry Lynn Taylor, *Creating with the Angels: An Angel-Guided Journey into Creativity,* Tiburon, CA: H.J. Kramer, 1993.

2524. See ref. 2507:June 18, 28; July 8, 22; October 20.

2525. John Randolph Price, *The Angels Within Us: A Spiritual Guide to the Twenty-two Angels that Govern Our Lives,* New York: Fawcett, 1993.

2526. E.g., Don Fearheiley, *Angels Among Us,* New York: Avon, 1993, p. 94; refs. 2525:10-17,32-33/2511:80-81,111-12.

2527. Phil Phillips, *Angels, Angels, Angels,* Lancaster, PA: Starburst, 1994.

2528. Karen Goldman, *The Angel Book,* New York: Simon and Schuster, 1992, p. 5; Karen Goldman, *Angel Voices,* New York: Simon and Schuster, 1993, p. 6.

2529. See John Ankerberg, John Weldon, *Protestants and Catholics: Do They Now Agree?* 2nd ed.: Eugene, OR: Harvest House Publishers, 1995.

2530. Redemptionist Fathers, *Handbook for Today's Catholic,* Liguori, MO: Liguori Publications, 1978.

2531. Robert C. Broderick ed., *The Catholic Encyclopedia*, New York: Nelson, 1987.

2532. Sophy Burnham, *A Book of Angels: Reflections on Angels Past and Present and True Stories of How They Touch Our Lives*, New York: Valentine, 1990, p. 48; cf. ref. 2434: ch. 11.

2533. Cf. Jay H. Lehr, ed., *Rational Readings on Environmental Concerns*, Van Nostrand Reinhold, 1992; and Michael S. Coffman, *Saviors of the Earth?* Northfield, 1991.

2534. Al Gore, *Earth in the Balance: Ecology and the Human Spirit*, Houghton Mifflin, 1992; cf. Berit Kjos, *Under the Spell of Mother Earth*, Wheaton, IL: Victor, 1992; and "Al Gore's Environmental Spirituality," *The Discerner*, January-March 1993.

2535. See ref. 2507:April 20; cf. February 18, May 14, July 29, November 1, and December 8.

2536. Cf. Paul Hawkin, *The Magic of Findhorn: An Eyewitness Account*, New York: Bantam, 1976.

2537. See ref. 2525:60,108,114,122-23.

2538. Cf. Joy Snell, *The Ministry of Angels*, New York: Citadel, 1959.

2539. See ref. 2514:221 citing English medium and angel channeler Eddie Burks.

2540. See ref. 2514:222; cf. the Hindu and Buddhist traditions of Tantrism.

2541. See ref. 2512:118; cf. pp. 46,54,58,134.

2542. Respectively, ref. 2507:November 6; October 24; November 16; Goldman, *The Angel Book*, ref. 2528, p. 50; ref. 2512:146,218.

2543. See ref. 2512:93,105,114,121,125,146.

2544. Peter L. Wison, *The Little Book of Angels*, Rockport, MA: Element, 1993.

2545. See ref. 1168:84-85.

2546. See ref. 2512:213.

2547. L. Ron Hubbard, *Dianetics Today*, Los Angeles, CA: Church of Scientology of California, 1975, p. III.

2548. ———, *Dianetics: The Evolution of a Science*, Los Angeles, CA: The American St. Hill Organization, 1971, p. 99.

2549. See ref. 2547:III and L. Ron Hubbard, LRH personal secretary office (editor), *What Is Scientology?* Los Angeles, CA: Church of Scientology of California, 1978, p. 209; cf. Christopher Evans, *Cults of Unreason*, New York: Dell, 1975, pp. 17-134, for early problems and controversies.

2550. John Warwick Montgomery, *Faith Founded on Fact*, Nashville, TN: Thomas Nelson, 1978.

2551. L. Ron Hubbard, *The Creation of Human Ability*, Los Angeles, CA: The Publications Organization Worldwide, 1968.

2552. Church of Scientology Information Service, Department of Archives, *Scientology: A World Religion Emerges in the Space Age*, Los Angeles, CA: U.S. Ministry of Public Relations, 1974.

2553. Impact or injury must be involved for an engram to register, but "The engram is the single and sole source of aberration and psychosomatic illness," L. Ron Hubbard, ref. 2547:43,47; cf. pp. 37-106, and especially pp. 38-59.

2554. E.g., ref. 2547:947-51; L. Ron Hubbard, *The Volunteer Minister's Handbook*, Los Angeles, CA: Church of Scientology of California, 1976, p. 551; cf. former 14-year member Cyril Vospers' comments in *The Mind Benders*, London, England: Neville Spearman, 1971, 164-66, and by member Peter Gillham, *Telling It Like It Is: A Course in Scientology Dissemination*, Phoenix, AZ: Institute of Applied Philosophy, 1972, p. 26.

2555. See ref. 2553, and L. Ron Hubbard, *Scientology: A History of Man*, Sussex, England: L. Ron Hubbard Communications Office, 1961, pp. 5-76, especially pp. 53-60 for a discussion of alleged evolutionary dynamics and the impact on one's current life; cf. the discussion in Christopher Evans, *Cults of Unreason*, New York: Delta, 1973, pp. 38-47; and ref. 2558:103-04.

2556. Kevin Anderson, *Report of the Board of Inquiry into Scientology*, Melbourne, Victoria, Australia: AC Brooks Government Printer, 1965, no. 9, pp. 6502-65, 68; this report is difficult to locate but contains invaluable information. ref: 2558:112n. observes God "does not figure greatly in either theory or practice"; cf. ref. 2557.

2557. See ref. 2567:200. On panentheism, see ref. 2552:21-24 with L. Ron Hubbard, *Dianetics and Scientology Technical Dictionary*, Los Angeles, CA: Church of Scientology of California, 1975, p. 429; cf. L. Ron Hubbard, *Ceremonies of the Founding of the Church of Scientology*, Los Angeles, CA: The American St. Hill Organization, 1971, p. 41; *Reality* magazine, no. 121, p. 3; ref. 2551; 227; *Advance*, no. 35, pp. 14-15; no. 36, p. 6.

2558. Roy Wallis, *The Road to Total Freedom: A Sociological Analysis of Scientology*, New York: Columbia University Press, 1977.

2559. See refs. 2555/2557/2551:9-21; Hubbard, *Technical Dictionary*, ref. 2557:432; L. Ron Hubbard *Scientology 8-8008*, Los Angeles, CA: The American St. Hill Organization, 1967, pp. 106-08.

2560. See ref. 2559, and L. Ron Hubbard, *Scientology: The Fundamentals of Thought*, Los Angeles, CA: American St. Hill Organization, 1971, pp. 91,98; Edward Lefson and Ruth Minshull, *When in Doubt, Communicate: Quotations from the Works of L. Ron Hubbard*, Ann Arbor, MI: Scientology, Ann Arbor, 1969, pp. 73,123; *Advance*, no. 19, p. 114.

2561. E.g., cf. L. Ron Hubbard, "Death," *Advance,* no. 24, pp. 9,22; and L. Ron Hubbard, *Have You Lived Before This Life?* The Church of Scientology of California, Department of Publications Worldwide, 1968, passim.

2562. See ref. 2574:113; cf. ref. 2563:255-57,307,333.

2563. Bent Corydon and L. Ron Hubbard, Jr., *L. Ron Hubbard: Messiah or Madman?* Secaucus, NJ: Lyle Stuart, 1987.

2564. Harriet Whitehead, "Reasonably Fantastic: Some Perspectives on Scientology, Science Fiction and Occultism," in Irving Zaretsky and Mark P. Leon, *Religious Movements in Contemporary America,* Princeton, NJ: Princeton University Press, 1974.

2565. See *Reader's Digest,* May 1980, September 1981; *Newsweek,* November 20, 1978; *Christianity Today,* February 20, 1975.

2566. Among the official government reports are those by Australia (1965), Britain (1971), South Africa (1972), New Zealand (1969). Popular press reports include *Today's Health,* December 1968; *Life,* November 15, 1968; *Parents* magazine, June 1969; *Christianity Today,* November 21, 1969; *The Nation,* May 22, 1972; *Reader's Digest,* May 1980; September 1981; as well as *The Washington Post, Wall Street Journal, London Sunday Times, Los Angeles Times, St. Petersburg Times,* etc. Among critical books are ref. 2563; Jon Atak, *A Piece of Blue Sky,* NY: Lyle Stuart, 1990. Cyril Vosper, *The Mind Benders;* George Malko, *Scientology: The Now Religion;* Robert Kaufman, *Inside Scientology;* Christopher Evans, *Cults of Unreason;* among television investigations are ABC News "Close-Up": *New Religions: Holiness or Heresy?* September 2, 1976, and NBC "Primetime Saturday," June 14, 1980; scholarly treatments include ref. 2558.

2567. L. Ron Hubbard, LRH personal secretary office (ed.), *What Is Scientology?* Los Angeles, CA: Church of Scientology of California, 1978.

2568. E.g., consider the tremendous extent of Hubbard's claims; see ref. 2567, and L. Ron Hubbard, *Dianetics Today,* VIII, pp. 94,108-15,618,962; *Handbook for Preclears,* Los Angeles, CA: The American St. Hill Organization, 1971, pp. 5-6; L. Ron Hubbard, *Self-Analysis,* Los Angeles, CA: The Church of Scientology of California, 1968, p. 178; Evans (ref. 2555), pp. 78-79; L. Ron Hubbard, *Scientology: The Fundamentals of Thought,* Los Angeles, CA: American St. Hill Organization, 1971, p. 119; L. Ron Hubbard, *Science of Survival,* Sussex, England: L. Ron Hubbard College of Scientology, 1951, p. 3; *Advance* magazine, no. 25, pp. 4,16; ref. 2547:115; *Advance* magazine, no. 43, back cover; no. 25, pp. 4-5,16; no. 55, p. 18; ref. 2567:199; L. Ron Hubbard,

*Scientology 8-80,* p. 7; and L. Ron Hubbard, *Scientology 8-8008,* Los Angeles, CA: The American St. Hill Organization, 1952, p. 47.

2569. See "Book Reviews," *Journal of the American Medical Association,* July 29, 1950, pp. 1220-22; *Post-Graduate Medicine,* October 1950; *Newsweek,* October 16, 1950; "Dianetics," *Consumer Reports,* August 1951; "Questions and Answers," *Today's Health,* November 1950; Ralph Lee Smith, "Scientology," *Today's Health,* December 1968; Anderson (ref. 2556), pp. 94-97.

2570. Lord Chancellor Hailsham, "The Door Wherein I Went," *The Simon Greenleaf Law Review,* vol. 4, 1984-85.

2571. E.g., John Ankerberg, John Weldon, *The Coming Darkness,* Eugene, OR: Harvest House Publishers, 1993; L. Ron Hubbard, *The Book of Case Remedies,* Clearing Series 2, exp. ed., Los Angeles, CA: American St. Hill Organization, 1971, insert A3 after p. 24; L. Ron Hubbard, *Dianetics 55!* Los Angeles, CA: The American St. Hill Organization, 1973 ed., pp. 157-59; L. Ron Hubbard, *Scientology: A History of Man* (ref. 2555), p. 50; ref. 2551:1,134,171/ref. 2547:III,466,933/ref. 2556: 98.

2572. See ref. 2556:12,83,92,126,133/ref. 2551: 241,267,149,175-76; and the following citations referenced above: L. Ron Hubbard, *Scientology 8-80,* pp. 52-53; L. Ron Hubbard, *Dianetics 55!* p. 169; L. Ron Hubbard, *Scientology: A History of Man,* p. 75; L. Ron Hubbard, *Dianetics Today,* pp. 535,623; Robert Kaufman, *Inside Scientology: How I Joined Scientology and Became Superhuman,* New York: Olympia Press, 1972, pp. 153,160,164,200-01,219-24,241; *Book of Case Remedies Second Series,* exp. ed., p. 29; *Technical Dictionary,* pp. 209-10,365; L. Ron Hubbard, *Have You Lived Before This Life?* p. 170; L. Ron Hubbard, *Dianetics Today,* pp. 281,576-77; *Reader's Digest,* May 1980, p. 89; September 1981, p. 28; cf. *Willamette Week,* Portland, OR: September 3, 1979, p. 15.

2573. E.g., Cyril Vosper, *The Mind Benders,* London, England: Neville Spearman, 1971, pp. 78-79; ref. 2556:95-97, passim.

2574. CRI files, "Penthouse Interview: L. Ron Hubbard, Jr.," *Penthouse,* June 1983 (see Atak [ref. 2566, pp. 89-104.]

2575. Christopher Evans, *Cults of Unreason,* New York: Dell, 1975.

2576. Cyril Vosper, *The Mind Benders,* London: Neville Spearman, 1971.

2577. *Source* magazine, no. 22.

2578. Richard Behar, "The Thriving Cult of Greed and Power," *Time,* May 6, 1991, pp. 50-57; Eugene H. Methrin, "Scientology: Anatomy of a Frightening

Cult," *Reader's Digest*, May 1980, pp. 86-91 (Part 2: September 1981, pp. 75-80); cf. *The Los Angeles Times*, May 17, 1978; *Reader's Digest*, May 1980; *The Skeptical Inquirer*, vol. 4, no. 3; *The Washington Post*, April 28, 1978; *New Society*, June 7, 1973; and *Time*, May 6, 1991. Ruling in the High Court in London in 1984, Justice Latey reflected the opinion of many Scientology critics when he wrote, "Scientology is both immoral and socially obnoxious . . . it is corrupt, sinister and dangerous (in Atak [ref. 2566: preface page]).

2579. For illustrations see the definitions in the Scientology *Technical Dictionary*, ref. 2557.

2580. Compare Scientology theory with L. Ron Hubbard's science-fiction works, e.g., *Ole Doc Methusala, Slaves of Sleep, Death's Deputy, The Final Blackout, The Dangerous Dimension, The Tramp, Fear, King Slayer,* and *Typewriter in the Sky.*

2581. E.g., L. Ron Hubbard, *Scientology: A New Slant on Life*, Los Angeles, CA: The American St. Hill Organization, 1971, pp. 38-39; Edward M. Lefson and Ruth Minshull, comps., ref. 2560:40.

2582. L. Ron Hubbard, *Have You Lived Before This Life?* The Church of Scientology of California, Department of Publications Worldwide, 1968.

2583. L. Ron Hubbard, "Making an O.T.—Part Two," *Advance*, no. 33.

2584. L. Ron Hubbard, "What's Wrong with This Universe?" *Advance*, no. 45.

2585. L. Ron Hubbard, *Scientology 8-8008*, Los Angeles, CA: The American St. Hill Organization, 1967.

2586. This is evident in L. Ron Hubbard's writings, e.g., in Scientology there are 58 axioms, 7 prelogics, 24 logics, and 194 axioms of Dianetics. These are held to be "self-evident" propositions or truths. The Australian Inquiry noted of the 250 "axioms" of Dianetics and Scientology that they were often "entirely unfounded assumptions" and "illogical" (ref. 2556:68). They depend on the truth of Scientology and make sense only if one understands Scientology; and even then they are difficult to comprehend, hence they are anything but "self-evident." . . . Vosper (ref. 2576:31-34) also details several serious flaws of Scientology philosophy, e.g., that Scientology prelogics contradict the axioms and that the logics contradict Scientology itself (e.g., the 7 prelogics and axiom 3; logic 6 and 17). He calls the 194 axioms of Dianetics "a mixture of established fact and convenient assumption" (Ibid., p. 35), and observes: "Although Hubbard claims his Axioms are self-evident truths, one is at a loss to put them to any direct tests for validity" (pp. 31-32).

Commenting on Hubbard's *Scientology 8-8008*, the Australian Inquiry stated, "the Board heard evidence from a highly qualified physicist, a master of science and senior lecturer in physics at the University of Melbourne, who said that much of the text of this book, if written as or claiming to be in any way scientific, was meaningless or just rubbish, and was the sort of nonsense a matriculation or first year student might 'dream up' outside his formal study periods. . . ."

The Australian Inquiry noted of Hubbard, "His writings range the gamut of medicine, and many of his theories are based on entirely erroneous ideas. . . . The Board also heard expert medical evidence that the engram as developed in scientology is unknown to medical science, and that Hubbard's engram theories are based on assumptions which are contrary to or unknown to orthodox medical knowledge and principles.

"Here, there has been an 'almost total rejection' of the assumptions of Hubbard by authoritative psychologists, psychiatrists and psychotherapists along with medical opinion . . ." (ref. 2576:17). Among others, the Australian Inquiry mentioned Hubbard's lack of knowledge of psychoanalysis: "Hubbard shows ignorance of the general literature, learning and development of psychoanalysis. He does not know or understand the meaning of many technical terms which he uses . . ." (ref. 2556:51-52).

Also (for full references see citations above):

1. Hubbard has discovered the secret of how aspirin works—it inhibits "the ability of the thetan to create and to impede the electrical conductivity of nerve channels" (Evans, *Cults of Unreason*, pp. 21-22, citing *Certainty*, vol. 18, no. 7).

2. Eyeglasses are a symptom of the decline of consciousness (Hubbard, *Scientology, A New Slant on Life*, p. 73).

3. "So far as psychosomatic illness is concerned, it is best resolved by exteriorization. One has the individual step back from his body, look at it, and patch it up, and that is about all there is to psychosomatic illness . . ." (Hubbard, *Science of Survival*, pp. 24-25).

4. Insanity is primarily a *physiological* condition, e.g., "These 'insane' [people] are most often simple cases of medically ill people—gallstones, malnutrition, deficiencies in certain vitamins, broken backs—the usual . . ." (Hubbard, *Dianetics Today*, p. 576).

5. Jesus preached Scientology, and the early Christians believed in reincarnation (Hubbard, *Scientology and the Bible*, p. 44; *Scientology: A*

657

*World Religion Emerges in the Space Age,* p. 15; *Advance,* no. 22, p. 3).

6. Jesus, Solomon, and Isaiah were Scientology "auditors" (Hubbard, *Scientology and the Bible,* p. 30). The Old Testament draws "heavily" from Hinduism, Buddhism, and Taoism (Hubbard, *The Creation of Human Ability,* p. 179).

7. Buddha was eventually canonized as a Christian saint. (Hubbard, *Science of Survival,* no. 27, p. 3).

8. Buddhism set the precedent for the "western scientific tradition" *(Advance,* no. 23, p. 5).

9. "The Christian message of love ... can be historically traced to the work of Siddhartha Buddha" *(Advance,* no. 25, p. 4).

10. The law of gravity originated from thetans in the space civilization Arslycus, who did nothing but work and work until they got the idea of mass *(Advance,* no. 17, pp. 9-10).

11. "Clears do not get colds.... When engrams about colds are lifted, no further colds appear—which is a laboratory fact—a number of germ diseases are predisposed and perpetuated by engrams. Tuberculosis is one ... " (Hubbard, *Dianetics: The Modern Science of Mental Health,* pp. 92-93).

12. "Aesthetic wavelengths" are .00000000000-000000000000002 cm. (Vosper, *The Mind Benders*).

13. "A bacteria is a physical paranoia" *(Reality,* no. 146, p. 3).

2587. L. Ron Hubbard, *The Creation of Human Ability,* 1974 ed. or earlier, p. 251.

2588. *Ability,* no. 81 [c. 1959], p. 31, from Wallis, p. 104.

2589. L. Ron Hubbard, *The Volunteer Minister's Handbook,* Los Angeles, CA: Church of Scientology of California, 1976.

2590. L. Ron Hubbard, *Dianetics: The Modern Science of Mental Health,* Sussex, England: Publications Organization Worldwide, 1968 ed.

2591. José Silva, *I Have a Hunch: The Autobiography of José Silva,* Laredo, TX: Institute of Psychorientology, 1983, vol. 1.

2592. *Mind Control Newsletter,* vol. 10, no. 9.

2593. Personal conversation with José Silva in May 1986.

2594. José Silva, *The Mystery of the Keys to the Kingdom,* Laredo, TX: Institute of Psychorientology, 1984.

2595. José Silva, *Reflections,* Laredo, TX: Institute of Psychorientology, 1982.

2596. José Silva, *I Have a Hunch: The Autobiography of José Silva,* vol. 2, Laredo, TX: Institute of Psychorientology, 1983.

2597. José Silva and Philip Miele, *The Silva Mind Control Method,* New York: Simon and Schuster, 1977.

2598. Harry McKnight, *Silva Mind Control Through Psychorientology,* Laredo, TX: Institute of Psychorientology, rev. 1975, 1976.

2599. O. Carl Simonton, et al., *Getting Well Again,* Los Angeles, CA: J.P. Tarcher, 1978.

2600. The Silva Mind Control Debate, "The John Ankerberg Show," 1986.

2601. Walter Martin, *The New Cults,* Ventura, CA: Regal, 1987, p. 259, citing V.Y. Pellegrino, *Today's Health,* vol. 53, November 1975, p. 37.

2604. Staff lecturers of Silva Mind Control International *Q & A* [Questions and Answers], Laredo, TX: Institute of Psychorientology, 1983. This book comprises reprints from selected issues of the *Mind Control Newsletter.*

2605. Ibid., vol. 11, no. 6.

2606. Ibid., vol. 11, no. 11.

2607. José Silva, *Prophesy* [sic], Laredo, TX: Institute of Psychorientology, 1984.

2608. Ecumenical Society of Psychorientology, *The Keys to the Kingdom of Heaven,* Laredo, TX: Ecumenical Society of Psychorientology, 1985.

2609. "The Silva Method: Conscious Control of the Subconscious," Mind Control Lecture Series, n.d., n.p.

2610. *Mind Control Newsletter,* vol. 12, no. 5, p. 6 (1981).

2611. Ibid., vol. 12, no. 2.

2612. Ibid., vol. 11, no. 1, pp. 1, 7.

2613. Ibid., vol. 10, no. 12, p. 4.

2614. Ibid., vol. 11, no. 7, p. 6.

2615. Ibid., vol. 11, no. 4.

2616. Ibid., vol. 10, no. 9.

2617. *The Sun Bulletin,* Binghamton, NY, March 5, 1975.

2618. Joseph H. Thayer, *Thayer's Greek-English Lexicon of the New Testament,* Grand Rapids, MI: Baker Book House, 1979.

2619. José Silva, *Mind Control Newsletter,* Special Issue, 1972.

2621. Ibid., vol. 11, no. 10.

2623. *New Times,* May 2, 1975.

2624. José Silva, *Silva Mind Control: Alpha Theta Brainwave Function,* Laredo TX, 1977, brochure.

2625. *National Observer,* August 23, 1971, SMC rpt.

2626. Asher, "Mind Control Sells Alpha, Buys Research," *American Psychological Association Monitor,* April 1973, vol. 4, no. 4, SMC rpt.

2627. C. Bigwood, "Mind Control—Something for Everyone," *Harper's Bazaar,* November 1972.

2628. Thelma Moss, *The Probability of the Impossible,* Los Angeles, CA: J.P. Tarcher, 1974.

2629. Moira Johnston, "It's Only a Game—Or Is It?" *New West,* August 25, 1980.

2631. John Rowan, "The Real Self and Mystical Experiences," *Journal of Humanistic Psychology,* Spring 1983, vol. 23, no. 2.

2634. Handwritten notes quoted from a graduate's SMC handouts.

2635. *Foreword,* vol. 4, no. 2, from Christian Research Institute, Box 500, San Juan Capistrano, CA.

2636. Academy of Parapsychology and Medicine (Palo Alto, CA), special report, Elmer and Alyce Green, "Mind Training ESP, Hypnosis and Voluntary Control of Internal States," 1972.

2637. John White, ed., *What Is Enlightenment?* Los Angeles, CA: J.P. Tarcher, 1984.

2638. Raymond Prince (ed.), *Trance and Possession States,* Montreal, R.M. Bucke Society, 1968.

2639. John Ankerberg, John Weldon, *Facts on the Mind Sciences,* Eugene, OR, Harvest House Publishers, 1994.

2640. Pearl Evans, *Hidden Danger in the Classroom,* Small Helm Press, Petaluma, CA, 1990.

2641. John Ankerberg, John Weldon, *The Facts on Creation vs. Evolution,* Eugene, OR: Harvest House Publishers, 1993.

2642. ———, *The Facts on Life After Death,* Eugene, OR: Harvest House Publishers, 1993.

2643. ———, *The Facts on UFO's and Other Supernatural Phenomena,* Eugene, OR: Harvest House Publishers, 1994

2644. Elizabeth Loftus, *The Myth of Repressed Memory: False Memories and the Allegations of Sexual Abuse,* NY: St. Martin's Press, 1994.

2645. Ruth Montgomery, *Here and Hereafter,* Fawcett Crest, 1968.

2646. ———, *A Search for Truth,* New York: Bantam, 1968.

2647. *This Week Magazine,* October 15, 1967.

2648. Jess Stearn, *The Search for a Soul: Taylor Caldwell's Past Lives,* Berkeley, CA: Berkeley Publishing, 1994.

2649. John Ankerberg, John Weldon, *The Myth of Safe Sex,* Chicago, IL: Moody Press, 1994.

2651. Karen Hoyt and J. Isamu Yamamoto, eds., and the Spiritual Counterfeits Project, *The New Age Rage,* Old Tappan, NJ: Fleming A. Revell, 1987.

2659. Elizabeth L. Hillstrom, *Testing the Spirits,* Downers Grove, IL: InterVarsity Press, 1995.

2676. J. Krishnamurti, "From Education and the Significance of Life," in ref. 1524.

2677. Charles Thomas Cayce, "Aspects of Child Rearing and Education from the Edgar Cayce Readings," *The American Theosophist,* Fall Special Issue, 1976.

2678. The Republican Platform of 1992, "The Vision Shared," Houston, TX: Charles P. Young.

2679. John W. Whitehead, *The Religious Rights of Religious Persons in Public Education,* Wheaton, IL: Crossway Books, 1991.

2680. Howard Kirschenbaum, "Democratic Procedures for School-Community Relations," *Elementary School Guidance and Counseling,* October 1982.

2682. Dean C. Halverson, "Science: Quantum Physics and Quantum Leaps," in ref. 2651.

2683. John Ankerberg, John Weldon, *The Facts on Self-Esteem, Psychology and the Recovery Movement,* Eugene, OR: Harvest House Publishers, 1995.

2684. Stoker Hunt, *Ouija: The Most Dangerous Game,* New York: Harper & Row, 1985.

2685. "French Committee Announces Results of Test of So-Called Mars Effect," *Skeptical Inquirer,* January-February 1995.

2686. Patrick Grim, ed., *Philosophy of Science and the Occult,* Albany, NY: State University of New York Press, 1982.

2687. Paul Keegan, "Into the Void," *Boston Business,* February-March 1990.

2689. "Self-Acceptance: Real and Counter," n.d.; *The Family News,* vol. 1, no. 2, July 1978, p. 7; "Questions and Answers About Lifespring," brochure, n.d.

2690. E.g., see the reviews in Geoffrey Dean, "Astrologers Strike Back—But to What Effect?" *Skeptical Inquirer,* Fall 1993, 43-49.

2691. Paula Tierney, "The est Experience," *Human Digest,* September 1976.

2693. "60 Rough Hours in an est Seminar," *San Francisco Chronicle,* December 3, 1974.

2694. "Going East," Erhard interview, *The Graduate Review,* April 1977.

2695. See refs. 2226:144-45/1347:90/2067:73,115, 159/1467:94,209.

2696. Werner Erhard, "The est Standard Training," *Biosciences Communications,* vol. 3, no. 2, 1977.

2697. Jesse Kornbluth, "The Fuhrer Over est," *New Times,* March 19, 1976.

2698. Jerry Rubin, "The est Things in Life Aren't Free," *Crawdaddy,* February 1976.

2699. Sheridan Fenwick, *Getting It: The Psychology of est,* New York: J. B. Lippincott, 1976.

2700. L.L. Glass, M.A. Kirsch, F.N. Paris, "Psychiatric Disturbances Associated with Erhard Seminars Training: A Report of Cases," *American Journal of Psychiatry,* March 1977. Part 2, absent F.N. Paris, is in the November 1977 issue. See also Jane Brody, "Reports of Psychoses after Erhard Course," *New York Times,* May 12, 1977, and *Christian Century,* November 10, 1976, for other incidents.

2701. *East-West Journal*, December 15, 1975.

2702. Personal letter from Dr. Rousas Rushdoony, 1977.

2703. Terry Schultz, "est from the Inside Looks Like 1984," *The Village Voice*, March 8, 1976.

2704. *What's So*, January 1975.

2705. Carol Giambalvo with Robert Burrows, "The Hunger Project Inside Out," *SCP Journal*, vol. 8, no. 1, 1988.

2706. Carol Giambalvo, "The Forum: est in the Heir," *SCP Journal*, vol. 8, no. 1, 1988.

2707. Robert Burrows, "Werner Erhard Revisited," *SCP Journal*, vol. 8, no. 1, 1980.

2708. Paul Keegan, "Into the Void," *Boston Business*, February/March 1990.

2710. *The Willamette Week*, Portland, OR, January 26, 1981.

2711. "Awareness Movement Goes to Japan," *Los Angeles Times*, August 30, 1978.

2712. "Response" section, *Foreword*, vol. 4, no. 2.

2713. Dean C. Halverson, *SCP Journal*, vol. 5, no. 1.

2714. *Lifespring Family News*, vol. 1, no. 1.

2715. Elliot Miller, "Lifespring: New Age Danger?" *Foreword*, vol. 4, no. 1.

2716. Ibid., vol. 4, no. 2.

2717. *Family News*, October 1978.

2718. "Lifespring" pamphlet, n.d.

2719. Lifespring, Inc., "Reasons or Results? Questions and Answers About the Lifespring Basic Training," n.p., n.d., p. 7; "Experiencing Ourselves," *Lifespring Family News*, vol. 1, no. 1, n.d., p. 2, from Dean Halverson, "Lifespring and the Sovereignty of Subjectivism," *SCP Journal*, vol. 5, no. 1, Winter 1981-82, p. 25.

2720. Alice J. Porter, "Experiencing Lifespring," *The Willamette Week*, Portland, OR, October 24, 1977.

2721. Media Transcripts, Inc., New York: Programs for "20/20" news shows, November 6, 1980/October 30, 1980; cf. ref. 2708.

2722. G.B. Sullivan, "Stop, Look, Choose...," *San Francisco Examiner*, July 26, 1976.

2723. Stewart Emery, "Why Marry?" *New Age Journal*, July 1979.

2724. Typewritten report by participant Woody Wilson at an est seminar, "Evening with the Clergy" (with Werner Erhard), November 12, 1975.

2725. Jim Fragale, "Inside est," *Blue Box*, November/December 1976.

2727. Eva Hoffman, "est: The Magic of Brutality," *Dissent*, Spring 1977.

2728. "Members of the est Advisory Board," *The Graduate Review*, June 1978.

2729. Suzanne Gordon, "Let Them East est," *Mother Jones*, December 1978.

2730. Adam Smith, "Powers of Mind—Part II: The est Experience," (interview with Werner Erhard), *New York*, September 29, 1975.

2731. Werner Erhard, "Making Relationships Work," *What's So*, January 1975.

2733. Carlos Castaneda, *The Art of Dreaming*, New York: HarperCollins, 1993.

2734. Leo Litwak, "Pay Attention, Turkeys," *New York Times*, May 2, 1976.

2735. R. Allison, *Mind in Many Pieces*, New York: Rawson Wade, 1980.

2743. Brooks Alexander, "Last Exit Before Judgment: Barbara Marks Hubbard and the 'Armageddon Alternative,'" *SCP Journal*, vol. 19, no. 2-3, 1995.

2757. Bill Rudge, *Why I Quit Karate (with Testimonies by Bob Brown, Bruce Johnson, and Michael Puckett)*, Hermitage, PA: Living Truth Publishers, 1994.

2758. Tal Brooke, "Gates of Entry for the Occult," *SCP Journal*, vol. 9., no. 1, 1989.

2763. Whether it is the individuals most responsible for forming the intellectual and experiential foundation of the New Age Movement, or the practices themselves, spiritism is characteristically the lowest common denominator involved. Consider the following list of actual or potential examples.

Occult psychologist *Carl Jung*—probably more responsible than anyone for introducing occultism into modern psychology—was heavily influenced by spiritism and had several of his own spirit guides, including "Philemon," "Ka," "Elijah," and "Salome" (*SCP Journal*, vol. 9, pp. 2,36; *ATRI News Magazine*, June 1995).

*Robert Muller* was the assistant secretary general for the United Nations for over 20 years. When he wrote his New Age text on globalism, *New Genesis: Shaping a Global Spirituality*, he was in charge of economic and social services and the coordinator of 32 specialized agencies and world programs on the United Nations. In *New Genesis*, he writes, "Global education must prepare our children for the coming of an interdependent, safe, prosperous, friendly, loving, happy planetary age as has been heralded by all great prophets. The real, the great period of human fulfillment on planet Earth is only now about to begin" (ref. 1541:8).

But Robert Muller also has a lot to say about the spirits. Not only was he the keynote speaker at the Parliament of World Religions in 1993, he strongly advocates a one-world religion and a one-world government organized through the United Nations. According to Bill Honsberger, who attended a lecture given by Muller at Evergreen High School, he spoke not only about the important work of the United Nations, but also of the numerous spirits surrounding the world ready to help those who would open themselves to them. Honsberger notes, "He had spoken about these spirits when I heard him at the Parliament also" (ref. 2798).

*Teilhard de Chardin*—perhaps the man most responsible for the spiritualization of evolution in a global and cosmic context—had mystical, occult experiences throughout his life and confessed, "Ever since my childhood an enigmatic force had been impelling me" (ref. 2792). De Chardin is one of the leading forces behind the New Age spiritual movement toward globalization.

*Marilyn Ferguson*, author of *The Aquarian Conspiracy*, a leading New Age "bible," suggests that "the spirits of the dead" helped her write her book (ref. 574:313), and has a long-time interest in channeling, especially with the entity "Lazaris," channeled through medium Jach Pursel (ref. 1481:19).

*David Spangler*, most well-known for his involvement with the Findhorn Community, has been channeling spirits since childhood. He states, "In order to accomplish it, I must enter into meditation and align with my own Higher Self, my inner spirit, for it is with that level that John [one of his spirit guides] can communicate most effectively" (ref. 2793, cited in 574:37).

According to Robert Segal in *Joseph Campbell: An Introduction*, Penguin, 1990, p. 18, Campbell, a dominant influence in the New Age, claimed he often sought the advice of his dead mentor Heinrich Zimmer and just as often received the answers, which he dutifully recorded.

*Sri Chinmoy*, an important spiritual leader associated with the United Nations, is also a spiritist (see refs. 810:53-68,87-98/811:9-20,26-33).

*Sri Aurobindo*, another pivotal Hindu guru with great influence in the West was, like most Eastern gurus, deeply involved in spiritism. Like most people we mention here, he was an intellectual source for the synthesis of East and West, and the spiritual evolutionary "enlightenment" of the planet.

*Shirley MacLaine*, of course, is well-known for her involvement with spirits, and is another leading voice in the New Age Movement.

*Barbara Marx Hubbard*, although less well-known, due to her vast financial wealth and influence among leading world politicians, industrialists, etc., is having a major impact behind the scenes. She has been influenced by spirits for almost two decades. She implicitly obeys a voice that tells her what to do: "Whenever I heard it, I was deeply relieved and joyful, and set about to follow its guidance minute by minute" (ref. 2794). She also confesses that she has united herself with this spirit, e.g., "The higher voice and my conscious mind began to weave together. It was sometimes difficult to tell which voice was speaking: Barbara's voice or the higher voice" and "then the 'voice,' which until now had seemed to be my own 'Higher Self,' became elevated and was transformed into an even Higher Voice, the Christ voice. I felt an electrifying presence of light, a field that lifted me up" (ref. 2795). Hubbard has spent many years receiving occult guidance and teachings in order to produce a Gnostic, occult commentary on the Bible—a not-infrequent characteristic of New Age leaders.

*M. Scott Peck*—few individuals have had the influence of this author of *The Road Less Traveled*, *People of the Lie*, and *A Different Drum*. His most famous book, *The Road Less Traveled*, has been on the *New York Times* bestseller list for over 500 weeks (over 10 years)—which placed him in the *Guinness Book of Records*. Despite his sincere claim to have made Christ his Lord, as stated in *People of the Lie*, his subsequent publications and associations reveal that he has become an important voice in support of New Age philosophy and practice (see e.g., his *Different Drum*, and the analysis by Warren Smith, "M. Scott Peck: Community and the Cosmic Christ" in *SCP Journal*, vol. 19, pp. 2-3, 1995). Whether or not Peck is consciously involved with spirits, we cannot say. However, he does claim he was "divinely" led to write *The Road Less Traveled* through an inner voice, and also claims divine assistance in its actual production (p. 2).

*Alice Bailey* is another key figure in the New Age Movement. She is the author of a dozen channeled texts, which continue to exert considerable influence in New Age circles.

Former renegade Catholic priest turned Episcopalian, *Matthew Fox*, Scientology founder *L. Ron Hubbard*, mediums *Ruth Montgomery* and *H.P. Blavatsky, Annie Besant, Guy Warren Ballard* (founder of the "Mighty I Am" sect), *Edgar Cayce*, scores of Eastern gurus, and scores of modern channelers all undergird the power and teachings of the New Age Movement through their direct or indirect assocations with the spirit world. Indeed, after years of study, we have yet to encounter a single leading New Age spokesperson who was not either involved in the occult or admitted having spirit guides.

What is interesting about most of these individuals is how their personal philosophies have been guided by the spirits in very anti-Christian ways— and yet they all end up with basically the same worldview. The Bible is consistently interpreted along Gnostic, occult lines, while the philosophy of the New Age itself is antibiblical. The occult philosophy of the New Age, e.g., monism, pantheism, Gnosticism, etc., insulates participants against a traditional interpretation of Scripture, while New Age Bible commentaries that interpret the Bible from an occult perspective "confirm" New Age philosophy, thereby giving it an alleged biblical justification.

Obviously, it's not just the leaders of the New Age movement who are involved in spiritism. It is the actual practices and activities of the people in the New Age Movement. It is impossible to say that every New Age technique has its origin in the spirit world, but we do know that occult practices, philosophy, and religion are in large measure dependent upon spiritistic revelations. To the extent that the New Age Movement is comprised of occult philosophy and practice, one can logically expect to find spiritistic involvement. A brief listing includes almost all of the subjects in this volume, as well as astral projection, automatic writing, consciousness research, goddess religion and creation spirituality, kundalini enlightenment, New Age Masonry, mystical energies, near-death experiences, parapsychology, poltergeists, psychic anatomies, psychic powers, Satanism and witchcraft (which have more in common with the New Age than most people suspect), transpersonal psychology, UFOs, mandalas and matras, New Age Montessori education, and anthroposophical education and medicine.

If we turn to the influential cults and new religions that have influenced the New Age Movement, we also characterstically find spiritistic and/or occult involvement. This would include the Church Universal and Triumphant, New Thought, Rosicrucianism, Science of Mind, Self-Realization Fellowship, Swdenborgianism, Transcendetnal Meditation, Zen Buddhism, and scores of others.

New Age medicine is also replete with spiritism and the occult (see pp. 494-95 for a listing). For example, Elmer Green has a spirit guide he calls "the Teacher" (ref. 46:289-90). In an interview published in *The Laughing Man*, vol. 6, no. 1, a publication sponsored by the controversial Western guru Da Free John, Dr. Green stated, "Alyce [his wife] and I hope to accomplish our task in an appropriate way for the Teacher we met back in 1939. This teacher was the kind of figure who could give one a life-long orientation. This is why I feel comfortable with the Crazy Wisdom Tradition of Enlightened Beings," (a reference to Free John's radical spiritual anarchy and nihilism).

That so many founders or leaders of New Age practices and techniques are psychics, parapsychologists, spiritists, and occultists is one reason why the New Age Movement is so permeated with occultism. We think this speaks volumes about the nature of the New Age Movement. Unfortunately, the history of occult practice is littered with human wreckage; it is, therefore, ironic to see it so thoroughly linked to concepts of human *advancement*, spiritual *enlightenment*, and *health*.

2764. Although Strieber has recently expressed confusion over the meaning and even reality of his experiences (as described in *Communion* and *Transformation*), this is hardly an unexpected phenomenon in the world of the occult. Rationalists see his "confession" and confusion as proof of Strieber's mental imbalance or as fabrication of the story. But since his demonic experiences were largely implanted into his mind to begin with, and since Strieber had a strong background in the occult, and has, apparently, been under psychiatric care (a not infrequent occurrence among those heavily involved in the occult), his own personal confusion on this issue is hardly unexpected. This does not, however, convince us that the materials relayed in these books were only fabricated by Strieber to sell books. They might have been; however they fit the pattern of genuine occult experiences so well, we doubt this.

2767. Phillip E. Johnson, *Reason in the Balance: The Case Against Naturalism in Science, Law and Education*, Downers Grove, IL: InterVarsity Press, 1995.

2772. Sri Chinmoy, *A Sri Chinmoy Primer*, Forest Hills, NY: Vishma Press, 1974.

2792. Teilhard de Chardin, *The Heart of the Matter*, New York: Harcourt Brace Jovanovich, 1979, p. 53; cf. Tal Brooke, "Preparing for the Cosmic Millennium and the Coming Global Church," and Brooks Alexander, "Last Exit Before Judgment: Barbara Marx Hubbard and the 'Armageddon Alternative,'" in *Spiritual Counterfeits Journal*, vol. 19, no. 2-3, 1995, pp. 7,42.

2793. David Spangler, *Conversations with John*, Elgin, IL: Lorian Press, 1980, p. 1, cited in 574:37.

2794. Barbara Marx Hubbard, *The Revelation: Our Crisis Is a Birth*, Sonoma, CA: The Foundation for Conscious Evolution, 1993, p. 52, from Brooks Alexander, "Last Exit Before Judgment: Barbara Marx Hubbard and the 'Armageddon Alternative,'" in *Spiritual Counterfeits Journal*, vol. 19, no. 2-3, 1995, p. 41.

2795. Hubbard, (ref. 2794), pp. 56,61 from Alexander, ref. 2794:41-42.

2798. Bill Honsberger of the Galilee Baptist Church in Denver in a letter mailed in July 1995 to supporters.

2801. Dr. Hillstrom points out the key characteristics of altered states are generally similar (see p. 25).

2809. R.C. Sproul, *Not a Chance: The Myth of Chance in Modern Science and Cosmology*, Grand Rapids, MI: Baker, 1994.

2810. Stanley L. Jaki, *God and the Cosmologists*, Regnery Gateway, 1989.

2811. Deborah Daly, "Alternative Medicine Courses Taught at U.S. Medical Schools: An Ongoing Listing," *The Journal of Alternative and Complementary Medicine*, vol. 1, no. 1, 1995. The one-third figure is from Dr. Larry Dossey with the Office of Alternative Medicine, given on a "Larry King Live" special, "Miracles and the Extraordinary," December 9, 1995.

2812. Sharon Fish, "Therapeutic Touch: Healing Science or Psychic Midwife?" *Christian Research Journal*, Summer 1995.

2813. Brooks Alexander, "Tantra: The Worship and Occult Power of Sex," *SCP Newsletter*, Summer 1985.

2814. Charles Strohmer, *The Gospel and the New Spirituality: Communicating the Truth in a World of Seekers*, Nashville, TN: Oliver-Nelson, 1996. This book shows readers how to communicate effectively to non-Christian spiritual seekers.

2815. P.M.H. Atwater, *Coming Back to Life: The After Effects of the Near-Death Experience*, NY: Dodd Mead and Company, 1988.

2816. See "Has Carl Jung's Occult Psychology Infiltrated the Church and What Are Some of the Consequences?" *Ankerberg Theological Research Institute News Magazine*, September 1995.

2817. Chris Woehr, "The Aggressive Side of Hinduism Emerges," *Christianity Today*, February 8, 1993.

# SELECT INDEX